Programming Perl

Programming Perl

Third Edition

Larry Wall, Tom Christiansen & Jon Orwant

O'REILLY®

Beijing · Cambridge · Farnham · Köln · Paris · Sebastopol · Taipei · Tokyo

Programming Perl, Third Edition

by Larry Wall, Tom Christiansen, and Jon Orwant

Copyright © 2000, 1996, 1991 O'Reilly Media, Inc. All rights reserved.
Printed in the United States of America.

Published by O'Reilly Media, Inc., 1005 Gravenstein Highway North, Sebastopol, CA 95472.

Editor, First Edition: Tim O'Reilly

Editor, Second Edition: Steve Talbott

Editor, Third Edition: Linda Mui

Technical Editor: Nathan Torkington

Production Editor: Melanie Wang

Cover Designer: Edie Freedman

Printing History:

January 1991:	First Edition.
September 1996:	Second Edition.
July 2000:	Third Edition.

Library of Congress Cataloging-in-Publication Data

Wall, Larry.
  Programming Perl/Larry Wall, Tom Christiansen & Jon Orwant.--3rd ed. p. cm.
  ISBN 0-596-00027-8
  1. Perl (Computer program language) I. Christiansen, Tom. II. Orwant, Jon. III. Title.

QA76.73.P22 W35 2000
005.13'3--dc21   00-055799

ISBN: 0-596-00027-8
ISBN13: 978-0-596-0027-1

Table of Contents

III: Perl as Technology 399

Tables

Preface

The Pursuit of Happiness

Perl is a language for getting your job done.

Of course, if your job is programming, you can get your job done with any "complete" computer language, theoretically speaking. But we know from experience that computer languages differ not so much in what they make *possible*, but in what they make *easy*. At one extreme, the so-called fourth-generation languages make it easy to do some things, but nearly impossible to do other things. At the other extreme, so-called industrial-strength languages make it equally difficult to do almost everything.

Perl is different. In a nutshell, Perl is designed to make the easy jobs easy, without making the hard jobs impossible.

And what are these "easy jobs" that ought to be easy? The ones you do every day, of course. You want a language that makes it easy to manipulate numbers and text, files and directories, computers and networks, and especially programs. It should be easy to run external programs and scan their output for interesting tidbits. It should be easy to send those same tidbits off to other programs that can do special things with them. It should be easy to develop, modify, and debug your own programs too. And, of course, it should be easy to compile and run your programs, and do it portably, on any modern operating system.

Perl does all that, and a whole lot more.

Initially designed as a glue language for Unix, Perl has long since spread to most other operating systems. Because it runs nearly everywhere, Perl is one of the most portable programming environments available today. To program C or C++

portably, you have to put in all those strange `#ifdef` markings for different operating systems. To program Java portably, you have to understand the idiosyncrasies of each new Java implementation. To program a shell script portably, you have to remember the syntax for each operating system's version of each command and somehow find the common factor that (you hope) works everywhere. And to program Visual Basic portably, you just need a more flexible definition of the word "portable". :-)

Perl happily avoids such problems while retaining many of the benefits of these other languages, with some additional magic of its own. Perl's magic comes from many sources: the utility of its feature set, the inventiveness of the Perl community, and the exuberance of the open source movement in general. But much of this magic is simply hybrid vigor; Perl has a mixed heritage and has always viewed diversity as a strength rather than a weakness. Perl is a "give me your tired, your poor" language. If you feel like a huddled mass longing to be free, Perl is for you.

Perl reaches out across cultures. Much of the explosive growth of Perl has been fueled by the hankerings of former Unix systems programmers who wanted to take along with them as much of the "old country" as they could. For them, Perl is the portable distillation of Unix culture, an oasis in the desert of "can't get there from here". On the other hand, it also works in the other direction: Windows-based web designers are often delighted to discover that they can take their Perl programs and run them unchanged on the company's Unix server.

Although Perl is especially popular with systems programmers and web developers, that's just because they discovered it first; Perl appeals to a much broader audience. From its small start as a text-processing language, Perl has grown into a sophisticated, general-purpose programming language with a rich software development environment complete with debuggers, profilers, cross-referencers, compilers, libraries, syntax-directed editors, and all the rest of the trappings of a "real" programming language—if you want them. But those are all about making hard things possible, and lots of languages can do that. Perl is unique in that it never lost its vision for keeping easy things easy.

Because Perl is both powerful and accessible, it is being used daily in every imaginable field, from aerospace engineering to molecular biology, from mathematics to linguistics, from graphics to document processing, from database manipulation to network management. Perl is used by people who are desperate to analyze or convert lots of data quickly, whether you're talking DNA sequences, web pages, or pork belly futures. Indeed, one of the jokes in the Perl community is that the next big stock market crash will probably be triggered by a bug in someone's Perl script. (On the brighter side, any unemployed stock analysts will still have a marketable skill, so to speak.)

There are many reasons for the success of Perl. Perl was a successful open source project long before the open source movement got its name. Perl is free, and will always be free. You can use Perl however you see fit, subject only to a very liberal licensing policy. If you are in business and want to use Perl, go right ahead. You can embed Perl in the commercial applications you write without fee or restriction. And if you have a problem that the Perl community can't fix, you have the ultimate backstop: the source code itself. The Perl community is not in the business of renting you their trade secrets in the guise of "upgrades". The Perl community will never "go out of business" and leave you with an orphaned product.

It certainly helps that Perl is free software. But that's not enough to explain the Perl phenomenon since many freeware packages fail to thrive. Perl is not just free; it's also fun. People feel like they can be creative in Perl because they have freedom of expression: they get to choose what to optimize for, whether that's computer speed or programmer speed, verbosity or conciseness, readability or maintainability or reusability or portability or learnability or teachability. You can even optimize for obscurity, if you're entering an Obfuscated Perl Contest.

Perl can give you all these degrees of freedom because it's a language with a split personality. It's simultaneously a very simple language and a very rich language. Perl has taken good ideas from nearly everywhere and installed them into an easy-to-use mental framework. To those who merely like it, Perl is the *Practical Extraction and Report Language*. To those who love it, Perl is the *Pathologically Eclectic Rubbish Lister*. And to the minimalists in the crowd, Perl seems like a pointless exercise in redundancy. But that's okay. The world needs a few reductionists (mainly as physicists). Reductionists like to take things apart. The rest of us are just trying to get it together.

There are many ways in which Perl is a simple language. You don't have to know many special incantations to compile a Perl program—you can just execute it like a batch file or shell script. The types and structures used by Perl are easy to use and understand. Perl doesn't impose arbitrary limitations on your data—your strings and arrays can grow as large as they like (as long as you have memory), and they're designed to scale well as they grow. Instead of forcing you to learn new syntax and semantics, Perl borrows heavily from other languages you may already be familiar with (such as C, and *awk*, and BASIC, and Python, and English, and Greek). In fact, just about any programmer can read a well-written piece of Perl code and have some idea of what it does.

Most important, you don't have to know everything there is to know about Perl before you can write useful programs. You can learn Perl "small end first". You can program in Perl Baby-Talk, and we promise not to laugh. Or more precisely, we promise not to laugh any more than we'd giggle at a child's creative way of putting things. Many of the ideas in Perl are borrowed from natural language, and one of the best ideas is that it's okay to use a subset of the language as long as you get your point across. Any level of language proficiency is acceptable in Perl culture. We won't send the language police after you. A Perl script is "correct" if it gets the job done before your boss fires you.

Though simple in many ways, Perl is also a rich language, and there is much to learn about it. That's the price of making hard things possible. Although it will take some time for you to absorb all that Perl can do, you will be glad that you have access to the extensive capabilities of Perl when the time comes that you need them.

Because of its heritage, Perl was a rich language even when it was "just" a data-reduction language, designed for navigating files, scanning large amounts of text, creating and obtaining dynamic data, and printing easily formatted reports based on that data. But somewhere along the line, Perl started to blossom. It also became a language for filesystem manipulation, process management, database administration, client-server programming, secure programming, web-based information management, and even for object-oriented and functional programming. These capabilities were not just slapped onto the side of Perl—each new capability works synergistically with the others because Perl was designed to be a glue language from the start.

But Perl can glue together more than its own features. Perl is designed to be modularly extensible. Perl allows you to rapidly design, program, debug, and deploy applications, and it also allows you to easily extend the functionality of these applications as the need arises. You can embed Perl in other languages, and you can embed other languages in Perl. Through the module importation mechanism, you can use these external definitions as if they were built-in features of Perl. Object-oriented external libraries retain their object-orientedness in Perl.

Perl helps you in other ways, too. Unlike strictly interpreted languages such as command files or shell scripts, which compile and execute a program one command at a time, Perl first compiles your whole program quickly into an intermediate format. Like any other compiler, it performs various optimizations and gives you instant feedback on everything from syntax and semantic errors to library binding mishaps. Once Perl's compiler frontend is happy with your program, it passes off the intermediate code to the interpreter to execute (or optionally to any of several modular back ends that can emit C or bytecode). This all sounds complicated, but the compiler and interpreter are quite efficient, and most of us find that the typical compile-run-fix cycle is measured in mere seconds. Together with

Perl's many fail-soft characteristics, this quick turnaround capability makes Perl a language in which you really can do rapid prototyping. Then later, as your program matures, you can tighten the screws on yourself and make yourself program with less flair but more discipline. Perl helps you with that, too, if you ask nicely.

Perl also helps you to write programs more securely. In addition to all the typical security interfaces provided by other languages, Perl also guards against accidental security errors through a unique data-tracing mechanism that automatically determines which data came from insecure sources and prevents dangerous operations before they can happen. Finally, Perl lets you set up specially protected compartments in which you can safely execute Perl code of dubious origin, disallowing dangerous operations.

But, paradoxically, the way in which Perl helps you the most has almost nothing to do with Perl and everything to do with the people who use Perl. Perl folks are, frankly, some of the most helpful folks on earth. If there's a religious quality to the Perl movement, then this is at the heart of it. Larry wanted the Perl community to function like a little bit of heaven, and by and large he seems to have gotten his wish, so far. Please do your part to keep it that way.

Whether you are learning Perl because you want to save the world, or just because you are curious, or because your boss told you to, this handbook will lead you through both the basics and the intricacies. And although we don't intend to teach you how to program, the perceptive reader will pick up some of the art, and a little of the science, of programming. We will encourage you to develop the three great virtues of a programmer: *laziness, impatience,* and *hubris.* Along the way, we hope you find the book mildly amusing in some spots (and wildly amusing in others). And if none of this is enough to keep you awake, just keep reminding yourself that learning Perl will increase the value of your resume. So keep reading.

What's New in This Edition

Well, almost everything.

Even where we kept the good bits from the previous edition (and there were quite a few good bits, we'll admit), we've heavily revised and reorganized the current edition with several goals in mind. First, we wanted to increase the accessibility of the book to people coming from backgrounds other than computer science. We've made fewer assumptions about what the reader will know in advance. At the same time, we've kept the exposition lively in the hope that people who are already familiar with some of the material will not fall asleep reading it.

Second, we wanted to present the very latest developments in Perl itself. To that end, we have not been shy about presenting the current state of the work, even where we feel that it is still experimental. While the core of Perl has been rock solid for years, the pace of development for some of the experimental extensions can be quite torrid at times. We'll tell you honestly when we think the online documentation will be more reliable than what we have written here. Perl is a blue-collar language, so we're not afraid to call a spade a shovel.

Third, we wanted you to be able to find your way around in the book more easily, so we've broken this edition up into smaller, more coherent chapters and reorganized them into meaningful parts. Here's how the new edition is laid out:

Part 1, Overview

Getting started is always the hardest part. This part presents the fundamental ideas of Perl in an informal, curl-up-in-your-favorite-chair fashion. Not a full tutorial, it merely offers a quick jump-start, which may not serve everyone's need. See the section "Offline Documentation" for books that might better suit your learning style.

Part 2, The Gory Details

This part consists of an in-depth, no-holds-barred discussion of the guts of the language at every level of abstraction, from data types, variables, and regular expressions to subroutines, modules, and objects. You'll gain a good sense of how the language works and, in the process, pick up a few hints on good software design. (And if you've never used a language with pattern matching, you're in for a special treat.)

Part 3, Perl as Technology

You can do a lot with Perl all by itself, but this part will take you to a higher level of wizardry. Here you'll learn how to make Perl jump through whatever hoops your computer sets up for it, from dealing with Unicode, interprocess communication, and multithreading, through compiling, invoking, debugging, and profiling Perl, on up to writing your own external extensions in C or C++ or interfaces to any existing API you feel like. Perl will be quite happy to talk to any interface on your computer, or for that matter, on any other computer on the Internet, weather permitting.

Part 4, Perl as Culture

Everyone understands that a culture must have a language, but the Perl community has always understood that a language must have a culture. This part is where we view Perl programming as a human activity, embedded in the real world of people. We'll cover how you can improve the way you deal with both good people and bad people. We'll also dispense a great deal of advice on how you can become a better person yourself and on how to make your programs more useful to other people.

Part 5, Reference Material

Here we've put together all the chapters in which you might want to look something up alphabetically, from special variables and functions to standard modules and pragmas. The Glossary will be particularly helpful to those who are unfamiliar with the jargon of computer science. For example, if you don't know what the meaning of "pragma" is, you could look it up right now. (If you don't know what the meaning of "is" is, we can't help you with that.)

The Standard Distribution

Most operating system vendors these days include Perl as a standard component of their systems. As of this writing, AIX, BeOS, BSDI, Debian, DG/UX, DYNIX/ptx, FreeBSD, IRIX, LynxOS, Mac OS X, OpenBSD, RedHat, SINIX, Slackware, Solaris, SuSE, and Tru64 all came with Perl as part of their standard distributions. Some companies provide Perl on separate CDs of contributed freeware or through their customer service groups. Third-party companies like ActiveState offer prebuilt Perl distributions for a variety of different operating systems, including those from Microsoft.

Even if your vendor does ship Perl as standard, you'll probably eventually want to compile and install Perl on your own. That way you'll know you have the latest version, and you'll be able to choose where to install your libraries and documentation. You'll also be able to choose whether to compile Perl with support for optional extensions such as multithreading, large files, or the many low-level debugging options available through the **-D** command-line switch. (The user-level Perl debugger is always supported.)

The easiest way to download a Perl source kit is probably to point your web browser to Perl's home page at *www.perl.com*, where you'll find download information prominently featured on the start-up page, along with links to precompiled binaries for platforms that have misplaced their C compilers.

You can also head directly to CPAN (the Comprehensive Perl Archive Network, described in Chapter 22, *CPAN*), using *http://www.perl.com/CPAN* or *http://www.cpan.org*. If those are too slow for you (and they might be because they're *very* popular), you should find a mirror close to you. The following URLs are just a few of the CPAN mirrors around the world, now numbering over one hundred:

> *http://www.funet.fi/pub/languages/perl/CPAN/*
> *ftp://ftp.funet.fi/pub/languages/perl/CPAN/*

 ftp://ftp.cs.colorado.edu/pub/perl/CPAN/
 ftp://ftp.cise.ufl.edu/pub/perl/CPAN/
 ftp://ftp.perl.org/pub/perl/CPAN/
 http://www.perl.com/CPAN-local
 http://www.cpan.org/
 http://www.perl.org/CPAN/
 http://www.cs.uu.nl/mirror/CPAN/
 http://CPAN.pacific.net.hk/

The first pair in that list, those at the *funet.fi* site, point to the master CPAN repository. The *MIRRORED.BY* file there contains a list of all other CPAN sites, so you can just get that file and then pick your favorite mirror. Some of them are available through FTP, others through HTTP (which makes a difference behind some corporate firewalls). The *http://www.perl.com/CPAN* multiplexor attempts to make this selection for you. You can change your selection if you like later.

Once you've fetched the source code and unpacked it into a directory, you should read the *README* and the *INSTALL* files to learn how to build Perl. There may also be an *INSTALL.platform* file for you to read there, where `platform` represents your operating system platform.

If your `platform` happens to be some variety of Unix, then your commands to fetch, configure, build, and install Perl might resemble what follows. First, you must choose a command to fetch the source code. You can fetch with *ftp*:

```
% ftp ftp://ftp.funet.fi/pub/languages/perl/CPAN/src/latest.tar.gz
```

(Again, feel free to substitute a nearby CPAN mirror. Of course, if you live in Finland, that *is* your nearby CPAN mirror.) If you can't use *ftp*, you can download via the Web using a browser or a command-line tool:

```
% wget http://www.funet.fi/pub/languages/perl/CPAN/src/latest.tar.gz
```

Now unpack, configure, build, and install:

```
% tar zxf latest.tar.gz          Or gunzip first, then tar xf.
% cd perl-5.6.0                   Or 5.* for whatever number.
% sh Configure -des              Assumes default answers.
% make test && make install      Install typically requires superuser.
```

This uses a conventional C development environment, so if you don't have a C compiler, you can't compile Perl. See the CPAN *ports* directory for up-to-date status on each platform to learn whether Perl comes bundled (and if so, what version), whether you can get by with the standard source kit, or whether you need a special port. Download links are given for those systems that typically require special ports or for systems from vendors who normally don't provide a C compiler (or rather, who abnormally don't provide a C compiler).

Online Documentation

Perl's extensive online documentation comes as part of the standard Perl distribution. (See the next section for offline documentation.) Additional documentation shows up whenever you install a module from CPAN.

When we refer to a "Perl manpage" in this book, we're talking about this set of online Perl manual pages, sitting on your computer. The term *manpage* is purely a convention meaning a file containing documentation—you don't need a Unix-style *man* program to read one. You may even have the Perl manpages installed as HTML pages, especially on non-Unix systems.

The online manpages for Perl have been divided into separate sections, so you can easily find what you are looking for without wading through hundreds of pages of text. Since the top-level manpage is simply called *perl*, the Unix command *man perl* should take you to it.* That page in turn directs you to more specific pages. For example, *man perlre* will display the manpage for Perl's regular expressions. The *perldoc* command often works on systems when the *man* command won't. On Macs, you need to use the *Shuck* program. Your port may also provide the Perl manpages in HTML format or your system's native help format. Check with your local sysadmin—unless you're the local sysadmin.

Navigating the Standard Manpages

In the Beginning (of Perl, that is, back in 1987), the *perl* manpage was a terse document, filling about 24 pages when typeset and printed. For example, its section on regular expressions was only two paragraphs long. (That was enough, if you knew *egrep.*) In some ways, nearly everything has changed since then. Counting the standard documentation, the various utilities, the per-platform porting information, and the scads of standard modules, we're now up over 1,500 typeset pages of documentation spread across many separate manpages. (And that's not even counting any CPAN modules you install, which is likely to be quite a few.)

But in other ways, nothing has changed: there's still a *perl* manpage kicking around. And it's still the right place to start when you don't know where to start. The difference is that once you arrive, you can't just stop there. Perl documentation is no longer a cottage industry; it's a supermall with hundreds of stores. When you walk in the door, you need to find the YOU ARE HERE to figure out which shop or department store sells what you're shopping for. Of course, once you get familiar with the mall, you'll usually know right where to go.

---

* If you still get a truly humongous page when you do that, you're probably picking up the ancient release 4 manpage. Check your MANPATH for archeological sites. (Say *perldoc perl* to find out how to configure your MANPATH based on the output of *perl -V:man.dir.*)

Here are a few of the store signs you'll see:

Manpage	Covers
perl	What Perl manpages are available
perldata	Data types
perlsyn	Syntax
perlop	Operators and precedence
perlre	Regular expressions
perlvar	Predefined variables
perlsub	Subroutines
perlfunc	Built-in functions
perlmod	How to make Perl modules work
perlref	References
perlobj	Objects
perlipc	Interprocess communication
perlrun	How to run Perl commands, plus switches
perldebug	Debugging
perldiag	Diagnostic messages

That's just a small excerpt, but it has the important parts. You can tell that if you want to learn about an operator, *perlop* is apt to have what you're looking for. And if you want to find something out about predefined variables, you'd check in *perlvar*. If you got a diagnostic message you didn't understand, you'd go to *perldiag*. And so on.

Part of the standard Perl manual is the frequently asked questions (FAQ) list. It's split up into these nine different pages:

Manpage	Covers
perlfaq1	General questions about Perl
perlfaq2	Obtaining and learning about Perl
perlfaq3	Programming tools
perlfaq4	Data manipulation
perlfaq5	Files and formats
perlfaq6	Regular expressions
perlfaq7	General Perl language issues
perlfaq8	System interaction
perlfaq9	Networking

Some manpages contain platform-specific notes:

Manpage	Covers
perlamiga	The Amiga port
perlcygwin	The Cygwin port
perldos	The MS-DOS port
perlhpux	The HP-UX port
perlmachten	The Power MachTen port
perlos2	The OS/2 port
perlos390	The OS/390 port
perlvms	The DEC VMS port
perlwin32	The MS-Windows port

(See also Chapter 25, *Portable Perl*, and the CPAN *ports* directory described earlier for porting information.)

Searching the Manpages

Nobody expects you to read through all 1,500 typeset pages just to find a needle in a haystack. There's an old saying that you can't *grep** dead trees. Besides the customary search capabilities inherent in most document-viewing programs, as of the 5.6.1 release of Perl, each main Perl manpage has its own search and display capability. You can search individual pages by using the name of the manpage as the command and passing a Perl regular expression (see Chapter 5, *Pattern Matching*) as the search pattern:

```
% perlop comma
```

```
% perlfunc split
```

```
% perlvar ARGV
```

```
% perldiag 'assigned to typeglob'
```

When you don't quite know where something is in the documentation, you can expand your search. For example, to search all the FAQs, use the *perlfaq* command (which is also a manpage):

```
% perlfaq round
```

---

* Don't forget there's a Glossary if you need it.

The *perltoc* command (which is also a manpage) searches all the manpages' collective tables of contents:

```
% perltoc typeglob
perl5005delta: Undefined value assigned to typeglob
perldata: Typeglobs and Filehandles
perldiag: Undefined value assigned to typeglob
```

Or to search the complete online Perl manual, including all headers, descriptions, and examples, for any instances of the string, use the *perlhelp* command:

```
% perlhelp CORE::GLOBAL
```

See the *perldoc* manpage for details.

Non-Perl Manpages

When we refer to non-Perl documentation, as in *getitimer*(2), this refers to the *getitimer* manpage from section 2 of the *Unix Programmer's Manual.** Manpages for syscalls such as *getitimer* may not be available on non-Unix systems, but that's probably okay, because you couldn't use the Unix syscall there anyway. If you really do need the documentation for a Unix command, syscall, or library function, many organizations have put their manpages on the web—a quick search of AltaVista for "+crypt(3) +manual" will find many copies.

Although the top-level Perl manpages are typically installed in section 1 of the standard *man* directories, we will omit appending a (1) to those manpage names in this book. You can recognize them anyway because they are all of the form "perl*mumble*".

Offline Documentation

If you'd like to learn more about Perl, here are some related publications that we recommend:

- *Perl 5 Pocket Reference*, 3d ed., by Johan Vromans (O'Reilly, 2000). This small booklet serves as a convenient quick reference for Perl.

- *Perl Cookbook*, by Tom Christiansen and Nathan Torkington (O'Reilly, 1998). This is the companion volume to the book you have in your hands right now.

---

* Section 2 is only supposed to contain direct calls into the operating system. (These are often called "system calls", but we'll consistently call them *syscalls* in this book to avoid confusion with the system function, which has nothing to do with syscalls). However, systems vary somewhat in which calls are implemented as syscalls and which are implemented as C library calls, so you could conceivably find *getitimer*(2) in section 3 instead.

- *Elements of Programming with Perl*, by Andrew L. Johnson (Manning, 1999). This book aims to teach non-programmers how to program from the ground up, and to do so using Perl.

- *Learning Perl*, 2d ed., by Randal Schwartz and Tom Christiansen (O'Reilly, 1997). This book teaches Unix sysadmins and Unix programmers the 30% of basic Perl that they'll use 70% of the time. Erik Olson retargeted a version of this book for Perl programmers on Microsoft systems; it is called *Learning Perl for Win32 Systems.*

- *Perl: The Programmer's Companion*, by Nigel Chapman (Wiley, 1997). This fine book is geared for professional computer scientists and programmers without regard to platform. It covers Perl quickly but completely.

- *Mastering Regular Expressions*, by Jeffrey Friedl (O'Reilly, 1997). Although it doesn't cover the latest additions to Perl regular expressions, this book is an invaluable reference for anyone seeking to learn how regular expressions really work.

- *Object Oriented Perl*, by Damian Conway (Manning, 1999). For beginning as well as advanced OO programmers, this astonishing book explains common and esoteric techniques for writing powerful object systems in Perl.

- *Mastering Algorithms with Perl*, by Jon Orwant, Jarkko Hietaniemi, and John Macdonald (O'Reilly, 1999). All the useful techniques from a computer science algorithms course, but without the painful proofs. This book covers fundamental and useful algorithms in the fields of graphs, text, sets, and much more.

- *Writing Apache Modules with Perl and C*, by Lincoln Stein and Doug MacEachern (O'Reilly, 1999). This guide to web programming teaches you how to extend the capabilities of the Apache web server, especially using the turbo-charged mod_perl for fast CGI scripts and via the Perl-accessible Apache API.

- *The Perl Journal*, edited by Jon Orwant. This quarterly magazine by programmers and for programmers regularly features programming insights, techniques, the latest news, and more.

There are many other Perl books and publications out there, and out of senility, we have undoubtedly forgotten to mention some good ones. (Out of mercy, we have neglected to mention some bad ones.)

In addition to the Perl-related publications listed above, we recommend the following books. They aren't about Perl directly but still come in handy for reference, consultation, and inspiration.

- *The Art of Computer Programming*, by Donald Knuth, vol. 1, *Fundamental Algorithms*; vol. 2, *Seminumerical Algorithms*; and vol. 3, *Sorting and Searching* (Addison-Wesley, 1998).

- *Introduction to Algorithms*, by Cormen, Leiserson, and Rivest (MIT Press and McGraw-Hill, 1990).

- *Algorithms in C: Fundamental Data Structures, Sorting, Searching*, 3d ed., by Robert Sedgewick (Addison-Wesley, 1997).

- *The Elements of Programming Style*, by Kernighan and Plauger (Prentice-Hall, 1988).

- *The Unix Programming Environment*, by Kernighan and Pike (Prentice-Hall, 1984).

- *POSIX Programmer's Guide*, by Donald Lewine (O'Reilly, 1991).

- *Advanced Programming in the UNIX Environment*, by W. Richard Stevens (Addison-Wesley, 1992).

- *TCP/IP Illustrated*, vols. 1–3, by W. Richard Stevens, (Addison-Wesley, 1994–1996).

- *The Lord of the Rings* by J. R. R. Tolkien (most recent printing: Houghton Mifflin, 1999).

Additional Resources

The Internet is a wonderful invention, and we're all still discovering how to use it to its full potential. (Of course, some people prefer to "discover" the Internet the way Tolkien discovered Middle Earth.)

Perl on the Web

Visit the Perl home page at *http://www.perl.com/*. It tells what's new in the Perl world and contains source code and ports, feature articles, documentation, conference schedules, and a lot more.

Also visit the Perl Mongers' web page at *http://www.perl.org* for a grassroots-level view of Perl's, er, grass roots, which grow quite thickly in every part of the world, except at the South Pole, where they have to be kept indoors. Local PM groups hold regular small meetings where you can exchange Perl lore with other Perl hackers who live in your part of the world.

Usenet Newsgroups

The Perl newsgroups are a great, if sometimes cluttered, source of information about Perl. Your first stop might be *comp.lang.perl.moderated*, a moderated, low-traffic newsgroup that includes announcements and technical discussions. Because of the moderation, the newsgroup is quite readable.

The high-traffic *comp.lang.perl.misc* group discusses everything from technical issues to Perl philosophy to Perl games and Perl poetry. Like Perl itself, *comp.lang.perl.misc* is meant to be useful, and no question is too silly to ask.*

The *comp.lang.perl.tk* group discusses how to use the popular Tk toolkit from Perl. The *comp.lang.perl.modules* group is about the development and use of Perl modules, which are the best way to get reusable code. There may be other *comp.lang.perl.whatever* newsgroups by the time you read this; look around.

If you aren't using a regular newsreader to access Usenet, but a web browser instead, prepend "`news:`" to the newsgroup name to get at one of these named newsgroups. (This only works if you have a news server.) Alternatively, if you use a Usenet searching service like Alta Vista or Deja, specify "`*perl*`" as the newsgroups to search for.

One other newsgroup you might want to check out, at least if you're doing CGI programming on the Web, is *comp.infosystems.www.authoring.cgi*. While it isn't strictly speaking a Perl group, most of the programs discussed there are written in Perl. It's the right place to go for web-related Perl issues, unless you're using `mod_perl` under Apache, in which case you might check out *comp.infosystems.www.servers.unix*.

Bug Reports

In the unlikely event that you should encounter a bug that's in Perl proper and not just in your own program, you should try to reduce it to a minimal test case and then report it with the *perlbug* program that comes with Perl. See *http://bugs.perl.org* for more info.

---

* Of course, some questions are too silly to answer. (Especially those already answered in the online manpages and FAQs. Why ask for help on a newsgroup when you could find the answer by yourself in less time than it takes to type in the question?)

Conventions Used in This Book

Some of our conventions get larger sections of their very own. Coding conventions are discussed in the section "Programming with Style" in Chapter 24, *Common Practices*. In a sense, our lexical conventions are given in the Glossary (our lexicon).

The following typographic conventions are used in this book:

Italic

is used for URLs, manpages, pathnames, and programs. New terms are also italicized when they first appear in the text. Many of these terms will have alternative definitions in the Glossary if the one in the text doesn't do it for you.

`Constant width`

is used in examples and in regular text to show any literal code. Data values are represented by `constant width` in quotes (" "), which are not part of the value.

`Constant width bold`

is used for command-line switches. This allows one to distinguish for example, between the **-w** warnings switch and the –w filetest operator. It is also used in the examples to indicate the text you type in literally.

`Constant width italic`

is used for generic code terms for which you must substitute particular values.

We give lots of examples, most of which are pieces of code that should go into a larger program. Some examples are complete programs, which you can recognize because they begin with a #! line. We start nearly all of our longer programs with:

```
#!/usr/bin/perl
```

Still other examples are things to be typed on a command line. We've used % to indicate a generic shell prompt:

```
% perl -e 'print "Hello, world.\n"'
Hello, world.
```

This style is representative of a standard Unix command line, where single quotes represent the "most quoted" form. Quoting and wildcard conventions on other systems vary. For example, many command-line interpreters under MS-DOS and VMS require double quotes instead of single quotes when you need to group arguments with spaces or wildcards in them.

Acknowledgments

Here we say nice things in public about our reviewers to make up for all the rude things we said to them in private: Todd Miller, Sharon Hopkins Rauenzahn, Rich Rauenzahn, Paul Marquess, Paul Grassie, Nathan Torkington, Johan Vromans, Jeff Haemer, Gurusamy Sarathy, Gloria Wall, Dan Sugalski, and Abigail.

We'd like to express our special gratitude to Tim O'Reilly (and his Associates) for encouraging authors to write the sort of books people might enjoy reading.

We'd Like to Hear from You

We have tested and verified all of the information in this book to the best of our ability, but you may find that features have changed (or even that we have made mistakes!). Please let us know about any errors you find, as well as your suggestions for future editions, by writing:

> O'Reilly & Associates, Inc.
> 101 Morris Street
> Sebastopol, CA 95472
> 1-800-998-9938 (in the US or Canada)
> 1-707-829-0515 (international/local)
> 1-707-829-0104 (fax)

For more information about our books, conferences, software, Resource Centers, and the O'Reilly Network, see our web site at:

> *http://www.oreilly.com*

To ask technical questions or comment on this book, send mail to *bookquestions@oreilly.com.*

We have a web site for the book, where we'll list any errata and other Camel-related information:

> *http://www.oreilly.com/catalog/pperl3*

Here you'll also find all the example code from the book available for download so you don't have to type it all in, like we did.

I

Overview

1

An Overview of Perl

Getting Started

We think that Perl is an easy language to learn and use, and we hope to convince you that we're right. One thing that's easy about Perl is that you don't have to say much before you say what you want to say. In many programming languages, you have to declare the types, variables, and subroutines you are going to use before you can write the first statement of executable code. And for complex problems demanding complex data structures, declarations are a good idea. But for many simple, everyday problems, you'd like a programming language in which you can simply say:

```
print "Howdy, world!\n";
```

and expect the program to do just that.

Perl is such a language. In fact, this example is a complete program,* and if you feed it to the Perl interpreter, it will print "`Howdy, world!`" on your screen. (The \n in the example produces a newline at the end of the output.)

And that's that. You don't have to say much *after* you say what you want to say, either. Unlike many languages, Perl thinks that falling off the end of your program is just a normal way to exit the program. You certainly *may* call the exit function explicitly if you wish, just as you *may* declare some of your variables, or even *force* yourself to declare all your variables. But it's your choice. With Perl you're free to do The Right Thing, however you care to define it.

There are many other reasons why Perl is easy to use, but it would be pointless to list them all here, because that's what the rest of the book is for. The devil may be

---

* Or script, or application, or executable, or doohickey. Whatever.

in the details, as they say, but Perl tries to help you out down there in the hot place too. At every level, Perl is about helping you get from here to there with minimum fuss and maximum enjoyment. That's why so many Perl programmers go around with a silly grin on their face.

This chapter is an overview of Perl, so we're not trying to present Perl to the rational side of your brain. Nor are we trying to be complete, or logical. That's what the following chapters are for. Vulcans, androids, and like-minded humans should skip this overview and go straight to Chapter 2, *Bits and Pieces*, for maximum information density. If, on the other hand, you're looking for a carefully paced tutorial, you should probably get Randal's nice book, *Learning Perl* (published by O'Reilly & Associates). But don't throw this book out just yet.

This chapter presents Perl to the *other* side of your brain, whether you prefer to call it associative, artistic, passionate, or merely spongy. To that end, we'll be presenting various views of Perl that will give you as clear a picture of Perl as the blind men had of the elephant. Well, okay, maybe we can do better than that. We're dealing with a camel here (see the cover). Hopefully, at least one of these views of Perl will help get you over the hump.

Natural and Artificial Languages

Languages were first invented by humans, for the benefit of humans. In the annals of computer science, this fact has occasionally been forgotten.* Since Perl was designed (loosely speaking) by an occasional linguist, it was designed to work smoothly in the same ways that natural language works smoothly. Naturally, there are many aspects to this, since natural language works well at many levels simultaneously. We could enumerate many of these linguistic principles here, but the most important principle of language design is that easy things should be easy, and hard things should be possible. (Actually, that's two principles.) They may seem obvious to you, but many computer languages fail at one or the other.

Natural languages are good at both because people are continually trying to express both easy things and hard things, so the language evolves to handle both. Perl was designed first of all to evolve, and indeed it has evolved. Many people have contributed to the evolution of Perl over the years. We often joke that a camel is a horse designed by a committee, but if you think about it, the camel is pretty well adapted for life in the desert. The camel has evolved to be relatively self-sufficient. (On the other hand, the camel has not evolved to smell good. Neither has Perl.) This is one of the many strange reasons we picked the camel to be Perl's mascot, but it doesn't have much to do with linguistics.

---

* More precisely, this fact has occasionally been remembered.

Now when someone utters the word "linguistics", many folks focus in on one of two things. Either they think of words, or they think of sentences. But words and sentences are just two handy ways to "chunk" speech. Either may be broken down into smaller units of meaning or combined into larger units of meaning. And the meaning of any unit depends heavily on the syntactic, semantic, and pragmatic context in which the unit is located. Natural language has words of various sorts: nouns and verbs and such. If someone says "dog" in isolation, you think of it as a noun, but you can also use the word in other ways. That is, a noun can function as a verb, an adjective, or an adverb when the context demands it. If you dog a dog during the dog days of summer, you'll be a dog tired dogcatcher.*

Perl also evaluates words differently in various contexts. We will see how it does that later. Just remember that Perl is trying to understand what you're saying, like any good listener does. Perl works pretty hard to try to keep up its end of the bargain. Just say what you mean, and Perl will usually "get it". (Unless you're talking nonsense, of course—the Perl parser understands Perl a lot better than either English or Swahili.)

But back to nouns. A noun can name a particular object, or it can name a class of objects generically without specifying which one is currently being referred to. Most computer languages make this distinction, only we call the particular one a value and the generic one a variable. A value just exists somewhere, who knows where, but a variable gets associated with one or more values over its lifetime. So whoever is interpreting the variable has to keep track of that association. That interpreter may be in your brain or in your computer.

Variable Syntax

A variable is just a handy place to keep something, a place with a name, so you know where to find your special something when you come back looking for it later. As in real life, there are various kinds of places to store things, some of them rather private, and some of them out in public. Some places are temporary, and other places are more permanent. Computer scientists love to talk about the "scope" of variables, but that's all they mean by it. Perl has various handy ways of dealing with scoping issues, which you'll be happy to learn later when the time is right. Which is not yet. (Look up the adjectives local, my, and our in Chapter 29, *Functions*, when you get curious, or see "Scoped Declarations" in Chapter 4, *Statements and Declarations*.)

But a more immediately useful way of classifying variables is by what sort of data they can hold. As in English, Perl's primary type distinction is between singular

---

* And you're probably dog tired of all this linguistics claptrap. But we'd like you to understand why Perl is different from the typical computer language, doggone it!

and plural data. Strings and numbers are singular pieces of data, while lists of strings or numbers are plural. (And when we get to object-oriented programming, you'll find that the typical object looks singular from the outside but plural from the inside, like a class of students.) We call a singular variable a *scalar*, and a plural variable an *array*. Since a string can be stored in a scalar variable, we might write a slightly longer (and commented) version of our first example like this:

```
$phrase = "Howdy, world!\n";        # Set a variable.
print $phrase;                      # Print the variable.
```

Note that we did not have to predefine what kind of variable $phrase is. The $ character tells Perl that phrase is a scalar variable, that is, one containing a singular value. An array variable, by contrast, would start with an @ character. (It may help you to remember that a $ is a stylized "s", for "scalar", while @ is a stylized "a", for "array".)

Perl has some other variable types, with unlikely names like "hash", "handle", and "typeglob". Like scalars and arrays, these types of variables are also preceded by funny characters. For completeness, here are all the funny characters you'll encounter:

Type	Character	Example	Is a name for:
Scalar	$	$cents	An individual value (number or string)
Array	@	@large	A list of values, keyed by number
Hash	%	%interest	A group of values, keyed by string
Subroutine	&	&how	A callable chunk of Perl code
Typeglob	*	*struck	Everything named struck

Some language purists point to these funny characters as a reason to abhor Perl. This is superficial. These characters have many benefits, not least of which is that variables can be interpolated into strings with no additional syntax. Perl scripts are also easy to read (for people who have bothered to learn Perl!) because the nouns stand out from verbs. And new verbs can be added to the language without breaking old scripts. (We told you Perl was designed to evolve.) And the noun analogy is not frivolous—there is ample precedent in English and other languages for requiring grammatical noun markers. It's how we think! (We think.)

Singularities

From our earlier example, you can see that scalars may be assigned a new value with the = operator, just as in many other computer languages. Scalar variables can be assigned any form of scalar value: integers, floating-point numbers, strings, and even esoteric things like references to other variables, or to objects. There are many ways of generating these values for assignment.

As in the Unix* shell, you can use different quoting mechanisms to make different kinds of values. Double quotation marks (double quotes) do *variable interpolation*† and *backslash interpolation* (such as turning \n into a newline) while single quotes suppress interpolation. And backquotes (the ones leaning to the left) will execute an external program and return the output of the program, so you can capture it as a single string containing all the lines of output.

```
$answer = 42;                     # an integer
$pi = 3.14159265;                 # a "real" number
$avocados = 6.02e23;              # scientific notation
$pet = "Camel";                   # string
$sign = "I love my $pet";         # string with interpolation
$cost = 'It costs $100';          # string without interpolation
$thence = $whence;                # another variable's value
$salsa = $moles * $avocados;      # a gastrochemical expression
$exit = system("vi $file");       # numeric status of a command
$cwd = `pwd`;                     # string output from a command
```

And while we haven't covered fancy values yet, we should point out that scalars may also hold references to other data structures, including subroutines and objects.

```
$ary = \@myarray;                 # reference to a named array
$hsh = \%myhash;                  # reference to a named hash
$sub = \&mysub;                   # reference to a named subroutine

$ary = [1,2,3,4,5];               # reference to an unnamed array
$hsh = {Na => 19, Cl => 35};      # reference to an unnamed hash
$sub = sub { print $state };      # reference to an unnamed subroutine

$fido = new Camel "Amelia";       # reference to an object
```

If you use a variable that has never been assigned a value, the uninitialized variable automatically springs into existence as needed. Following the principle of least surprise, the variable is created with a null value, either " " or 0. Depending on where you use them, variables will be interpreted automatically as strings, as numbers, or as "true" and "false" values (commonly called Boolean values). Remember how important context is in human languages. In Perl, various operators expect certain kinds of singular values as parameters, so we will speak of those operators as "providing" or "supplying" a scalar context to those parameters. Sometimes we'll be more specific, and say it supplies a numeric context, a string context, or a Boolean context to those parameters. (Later we'll also talk about list

---

* Here and elsewhere, when we say Unix, we mean any operating system resembling Unix, including BSD, Linux, and, of course, Unix.

† Sometimes called "substitution" by shell programmers, but we prefer to reserve that word for something else in Perl. So please call it interpolation. We're using the term in the textual sense ("this passage is a Gnostic interpolation") rather than in the mathematical sense ("this point on the graph is an interpolation between two other points").

context, which is the opposite of scalar context.) Perl will automatically convert the data into the form required by the current context, within reason. For example, suppose you said this:

```
$camels = '123';
print $camels + 1, "\n";
```

The original value of $camels is a string, but it is converted to a number to add 1 to it, and then converted back to a string to be printed out as 124. The newline, represented by "\n", is also in string context, but since it's already a string, no conversion is necessary. But notice that we had to use double quotes there—using single quotes to say '\n' would result in a two-character string consisting of a backslash followed by an "n", which is not a newline by anybody's definition.

So, in a sense, double quotes and single quotes are yet another way of specifying context. The interpretation of the innards of a quoted string depends on which quotes you use. (Later, we'll see some other operators that work like quotes syntactically but use the string in some special way, such as for pattern matching or substitution. These all work like double-quoted strings too. The *double-quote* context is the "interpolative" context of Perl, and is supplied by many operators that don't happen to resemble double quotes.)

Similarly, a reference behaves as a reference when you give it a "dereference" context, but otherwise acts like a simple scalar value. For example, we might say:

```
$fido = new Camel "Amelia";
if (not $fido) { die "dead camel"; }
$fido->saddle();
```

Here we create a reference to a Camel object and put it into the variable $fido. On the next line, we test $fido as a scalar Boolean to see if it is "true", and we throw an exception (that is, we complain) if it is not true, which in this case would mean that the new Camel constructor failed to make a proper Camel object. But on the last line, we treat $fido as a reference by asking it to look up the saddle() method for the object held in $fido, which happens to be a Camel, so Perl looks up the saddle() method for Camel objects. More about that later. For now, just remember that context is important in Perl because that's how Perl knows what you want without your having to say it explicitly, as many other computer languages force you to do.

Pluralities

Some kinds of variables hold multiple values that are logically tied together. Perl has two types of multivalued variables: arrays and hashes. In many ways, these behave like scalars—they spring into existence with nothing in them when needed, for instance. But they are different from scalars in that, when you assign to them, they supply a *list* context to the right side of the assignment rather than a scalar context.

Arrays and hashes also differ from each other. You'd use an array when you want to look something up by number. You'd use a hash when you want to look something up by name. The two concepts are complementary. You'll often see people using an array to translate month numbers into month names, and a corresponding hash to translate month names back into month numbers. (Though hashes aren't limited to holding only numbers. You could have a hash that translates month names to birthstone names, for instance.)

Arrays.   An *array* is an ordered list of scalars, accessed* by the scalar's position in the list. The list may contain numbers, or strings, or a mixture of both. (It might also contain references to subarrays or subhashes.) To assign a list value to an array, you simply group the values together (with a set of parentheses):

```
@home = ("couch", "chair", "table", "stove");
```

Conversely, if you use @home in a list context, such as on the right side of a list assignment, you get back out the same list you put in. So you could set four scalar variables from the array like this:

```
($potato, $lift, $tennis, $pipe) = @home;
```

These are called list assignments. They logically happen in parallel, so you can swap two variables by saying:

```
($alpha,$omega) = ($omega,$alpha);
```

As in C, arrays are zero-based, so while you would talk about the first through fourth elements of the array, you would get to them with subscripts 0 through 3.†
Array subscripts are enclosed in square brackets [like this], so if you want to select an individual array element, you would refer to it as $home[*n*], where *n* is the subscript (one less than the element number) you want. See the example that follows. Since the element you are dealing with is a scalar, you always precede it with a $.

---

* Or keyed, or indexed, or subscripted, or looked up. Take your pick.

† If this seems odd to you, just think of the subscript as an offset, that is, the count of how many array elements come before it. Obviously, the first element doesn't have any elements before it, and so has an offset of 0. This is how computers think. (We think.)

If you want to assign to one array element at a time, you could write the earlier assignment as:

```
$home[0] = "couch";
$home[1] = "chair";
$home[2] = "table";
$home[3] = "stove";
```

Since arrays are ordered, you can do various useful operations on them, such as the stack operations push and pop. A stack is, after all, just an ordered list, with a beginning and an end. Especially an end. Perl regards the end of your array as the top of a stack. (Although most Perl programmers think of an array as horizontal, with the top of the stack on the right.)

Hashes.   A *hash* is an unordered set of scalars, accessed* by some string value that is associated with each scalar. For this reason hashes are often called *associative arrays.* But that's too long for lazy typists to type, and we talk about them so often that we decided to name them something short and snappy. The other reason we picked the name "hash" is to emphasize the fact that they're disordered. (They are, coincidentally, implemented internally using a hash-table lookup, which is why hashes are so fast, and stay so fast no matter how many values you put into them.) You can't push or pop a hash though, because it doesn't make sense. A hash has no beginning or end. Nevertheless, hashes are extremely powerful and useful. Until you start thinking in terms of hashes, you aren't really thinking in Perl. Figure 1-1 shows the ordered elements of an array and the unordered (but named) elements of a hash.

Since the keys to a hash are not automatically implied by their position, you must supply the key as well as the value when populating a hash. You can still assign a list to it like an ordinary array, but each *pair* of items in the list will be interpreted as a key and a value. Since we're dealing with pairs of items, hashes use the funny character % to mark hash names. (If you look carefully at the % character, you can see the key and the value with a slash between them. It may help to squint.)

Suppose you wanted to translate abbreviated day names to the corresponding full names. You could write the following list assignment:

```
%longday = ("Sun", "Sunday", "Mon", "Monday", "Tue", "Tuesday",
            "Wed", "Wednesday", "Thu", "Thursday", "Fri",
            "Friday", "Sat", "Saturday");
```

But that's rather difficult to read, so Perl provides the => (equals sign, greater-than sign) sequence as an alternative separator to the comma. Using this syntactic sugar

---

* Or keyed, or indexed, or subscripted, or looked up. Take your pick.

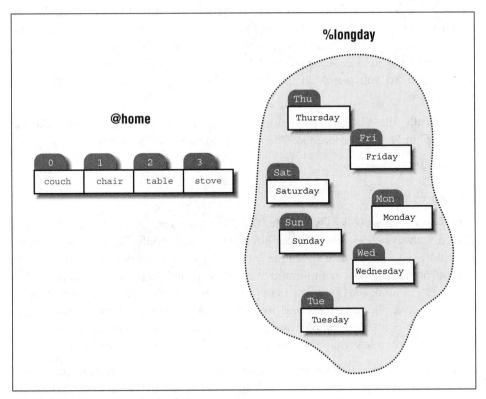

Figure 1-1. An array and a hash

(and some creative formatting), it is much easier to see which strings are the keys and which strings are the associated values.

```
%longday = (
    "Sun" => "Sunday",
    "Mon" => "Monday",
    "Tue" => "Tuesday",
    "Wed" => "Wednesday",
    "Thu" => "Thursday",
    "Fri" => "Friday",
    "Sat" => "Saturday",
);
```

Not only can you assign a list to a hash, as we did above, but if you mention a hash in list context, it'll convert the hash back to a list of key/value pairs, in a weird order. This is occasionally useful. More often people extract a list of just the keys, using the (aptly named) keys function. The key list is also unordered, but can easily be sorted if desired, using the (aptly named) sort function. Then you can use the ordered keys to pull out the corresponding values in the order you want.

Because hashes are a fancy kind of array, you select an individual hash element by enclosing the key in braces (those fancy brackets also known as "curlies"). So, for example, if you want to find out the value associated with Wed in the hash above, you would use $longday{"Wed"}. Note again that you are dealing with a scalar value, so you use $ on the front, not %, which would indicate the entire hash.

Linguistically, the relationship encoded in a hash is genitive or possessive, like the word "of" in English, or like "'s". The wife *of* Adam is Eve, so we write:

```
$wife{"Adam"} = "Eve";
```

Complexities

Arrays and hashes are lovely, simple, flat data structures. Unfortunately, the world does not always cooperate with our attempts to oversimplify. Sometimes you need to build not-so-lovely, not-so-simple, not-so-flat data structures. Perl lets you do this by pretending that complicated values are really simple ones. To put it the other way around, Perl lets you manipulate simple scalar references that happen to refer to complicated arrays and hashes. We do this all the time in natural language when we use a simple singular noun like "government" to represent an entity that is completely convoluted and inscrutable. Among other things.

To extend our previous example, suppose we want to switch from talking about Adam's wife to Jacob's wife. Now, as it happens, Jacob had four wives. (Don't try this at home.) In trying to represent this in Perl, we find ourselves in the odd situation where we'd like to pretend that Jacob's four wives were really one wife. (Don't try this at home, either.) You might think you could write it like this:

```
$wife{"Jacob"} = ("Leah", "Rachel", "Bilhah", "Zilpah");      # WRONG
```

But that wouldn't do what you want, because even parentheses and commas are not powerful enough to turn a list into a scalar in Perl. (Parentheses are used for syntactic grouping, and commas for syntactic separation.) Rather, you need to tell Perl explicitly that you want to pretend that a list is a scalar. It turns out that square brackets are powerful enough to do that:

```
$wife{"Jacob"} = ["Leah", "Rachel", "Bilhah", "Zilpah"];      # ok
```

That statement creates an unnamed array and puts a reference to it into the hash element $wife{"Jacob"}. So we have a named hash containing an unnamed array. This is how Perl deals with both multidimensional arrays and nested data structures. As with ordinary arrays and hashes, you can also assign individual elements, like this:

```
$wife{"Jacob"}[0] = "Leah";
$wife{"Jacob"}[1] = "Rachel";
$wife{"Jacob"}[2] = "Bilhah";
$wife{"Jacob"}[3] = "Zilpah";
```

You can see how that looks like a multidimensional array with one string subscript and one numeric subscript. To see something that looks more tree-structured, like a nested data structure, suppose we wanted to list not only Jacob's wives but all the sons of each of his wives. In this case we want to treat a hash as a scalar. We can use braces for that. (Inside each hash value we'll use square brackets to represent arrays, just as we did earlier. But now we have an array in a hash in a hash.)

```
$kids_of_wife{"Jacob"} = {
    "Leah"   => ["Reuben", "Simeon", "Levi", "Judah", "Issachar", "Zebulun"],
    "Rachel" => ["Joseph", "Benjamin"],
    "Bilhah" => ["Dan", "Naphtali"],
    "Zilpah" => ["Gad", "Asher"],
};
```

That would be more or less equivalent to saying:

```
$kids_of_wife{"Jacob"}{"Leah"}[0]   = "Reuben";
$kids_of_wife{"Jacob"}{"Leah"}[1]   = "Simeon";
$kids_of_wife{"Jacob"}{"Leah"}[2]   = "Levi";
$kids_of_wife{"Jacob"}{"Leah"}[3]   = "Judah";
$kids_of_wife{"Jacob"}{"Leah"}[4]   = "Issachar";
$kids_of_wife{"Jacob"}{"Leah"}[5]   = "Zebulun";
$kids_of_wife{"Jacob"}{"Rachel"}[0] = "Joseph";
$kids_of_wife{"Jacob"}{"Rachel"}[1] = "Benjamin";
$kids_of_wife{"Jacob"}{"Bilhah"}[0] = "Dan";
$kids_of_wife{"Jacob"}{"Bilhah"}[1] = "Naphtali";
$kids_of_wife{"Jacob"}{"Zilpah"}[0] = "Gad";
$kids_of_wife{"Jacob"}{"Zilpah"}[1] = "Asher";
```

You can see from this that adding a level to a nested data structure it is like adding another dimension to a multidimensional array. Perl lets you think of it either way, but the internal representation is the same.

The important point here is that Perl lets you pretend that a complex data structure is a simple scalar. On this simple kind of encapsulation, Perl's entire object-oriented structure is built. When we earlier invoked the Camel constructor like this:

```
$fido = new Camel "Amelia";
```

we created a Camel object that is represented by the scalar $fido. But the inside of the Camel is more complicated. As well-behaved object-oriented programmers, we're not supposed to care about the insides of Camels (unless we happen to be the people implementing the methods of the Camel class). But generally, an object like a Camel would consist of a hash containing the particular Camel's attributes, such as its name ("Amelia" in this case, not "fido") and the number of humps (which we didn't specify, but probably defaults to 1; check the front cover).

Simplicities

If your head isn't spinning a bit from reading that last section, then you have an unusual head. People don't generally like to deal with complex data structures, whether governmental or genealogical. So in our natural languages, we have many ways of sweeping complexity under the carpet. Many of these fall into the category of *topicalization*, which is just a fancy linguistics term for agreeing with someone about what you're going to talk about (and by exclusion, what you're probably not going to talk about). This happens on many levels in language. On a high level, we divide ourselves up into various subcultures that are interested in various subtopics and establish sublanguages that talk primarily about those subtopics. The lingo of the doctor's office ("indissoluable asphyxiant") is different from the lingo of the chocolate factory ("everlasting gobstopper"). Most of us automatically switch contexts as we go from one lingo to another.

On a conversational level, the context switch has to be more explicit, so our language gives us many ways of saying what we're about to say. We put titles on our books and headers on our sections. On our sentences, we put quaint phrases like "In regard to your recent query" or "For all X". Usually, though, we just say things like, "You know that dangley thingy that hangs down in the back of your throat?"

Perl also has several ways of topicalizing. One important topicalizer is the `package` declaration. Suppose you want to talk about `Camel`s in Perl. You'd likely start off your `Camel` module by saying:

```
package Camel;
```

This has several notable effects. One of them is that Perl will assume from this point on that any unspecified verbs or nouns are about `Camel`s. It does this by automatically prefixing any global name with the module name "`Camel::`". So if you say:

```
package Camel;
$fido = &fetch();
```

then the real name of `$fido` is `$Camel::fido` (and the real name of `&fetch` is `&Camel::fetch`, but we're not talking about verbs yet). This means that if some other module says:

```
package Dog;
$fido = &fetch();
```

Perl won't get confused, because the real name of this `$fido` is `$Dog::fido`, not `$Camel::fido`. A computer scientist would say that a package establishes a *namespace*. You can have as many namespaces as you like, but since you're only in one of them at a time, you can pretend that the other namespaces don't exist. That's how namespaces simplify reality for you. Simplification is based on pretending. (Of course, so is oversimplification, which is what we're doing in this chapter.)

Now it's important to keep your nouns straight, but it's just as important to keep your verbs straight. It's nice that `&Camel::fetch` is not confused with `&Dog::fetch` within the `Camel` and `Dog` namespaces, but the really nice thing about packages is that they classify your verbs so that *other* packages can use them. When we said:

```
$fido = new Camel "Amelia";
```

we were actually invoking the `&new` verb in the `Camel` package, which has the full name of `&Camel::new`. And when we said:

```
$fido->saddle();
```

we were invoking the `&Camel::saddle` routine, because `$fido` remembers that it is pointing to a `Camel`. This is how object-oriented programming works.

When you say `package Camel`, you're starting a new package. But sometimes you just want to borrow the nouns and verbs of an existing package. Perl lets you do that with a `use` declaration, which not only borrows verbs from another package, but also checks that the module you name is loaded in from disk. In fact, you *must* say something like:

```
use Camel;
```

before you say:

```
$fido = new Camel "Amelia";
```

because otherwise Perl wouldn't know what a `Camel` is.

The interesting thing is that you yourself don't really need to know what a `Camel` is, provided you can get someone else to write the `Camel` module for you. Even better would be if someone had *already* written the `Camel` module for you. It could be argued that the most powerful thing about Perl is not Perl itself, but CPAN (Comprehensive Perl Archive Network), which contains myriads of modules that accomplish many different tasks that you don't have to know how to do. You just have to download whatever module you like and say:

```
use Some::Cool::Module;
```

Then you can use the verbs from that module in a manner appropriate to the topic under discussion.

So, like topicalization in a natural language, topicalization in Perl "warps" the language that you'll use from there to the end of the program. In fact, some of the built-in modules don't actually introduce verbs at all, but simply warp the Perl language in various useful ways. These special modules we call *pragmas*. For instance, you'll often see people use the pragma strict, like this:

```
use strict;
```

What the strict module does is tighten up some of the rules so that you have to be more explicit about various things that Perl would otherwise guess about, such as how you want your variables to be scoped. Making things explicit is helpful when you're working on large projects. By default Perl is optimized for small projects, but with the strict pragma, Perl is also good for large projects that need to be more maintainable. Since you can add the strict pragma at any time, Perl is also good for evolving small projects into large ones, even when you didn't expect that to happen. Which is usually.

Verbs

As is typical of your typical imperative computer language, many of the verbs in Perl are commands: they tell the Perl interpreter to do something. On the other hand, as is typical of a natural language, the meanings of Perl verbs tend to mush off in various directions depending on the context. A statement starting with a verb is generally purely imperative and evaluated entirely for its side effects. (We sometimes call these verbs *procedures*, especially when they're user-defined.) A frequently seen built-in command (in fact, you've seen it already) is the print command:

```
print "Adam's wife is $wife{'Adam'}.\n";
```

This has the side effect of producing the desired output:

```
Adam's wife is Eve.
```

But there are other "moods" besides the imperative mood. Some verbs are for asking questions and are useful in conditionals such as if statements. Other verbs translate their input parameters into return values, just as a recipe tells you how to turn raw ingredients into something (hopefully) edible. We tend to call these verbs *functions*, in deference to generations of mathematicians who don't know what the word "functional" means in normal English.

An example of a built-in function would be the exponential function:

```
$e = exp(1);    # 2.718281828459 or thereabouts
```

But Perl doesn't make a hard distinction between procedures and functions. You'll find the terms used interchangeably. Verbs are also sometimes called operators (when built-in), or subroutines (when user-defined).* But call them whatever you like—they all return a value, which may or may not be a meaningful value, which you may or may not choose to ignore.

As we go on, you'll see additional examples of how Perl behaves like a natural language. But there are other ways to look at Perl too. We've already sneakily introduced some notions from mathematical language, such as subscripts, addition, and the exponential function. But Perl is also a control language, a glue language, a prototyping language, a text-processing language, a list-processing language, and an object-oriented language. Among other things.

But Perl is also just a plain old computer language. And that's how we'll look at it next.

An Average Example

Suppose you've been teaching a Perl class, and you're trying to figure out how to grade your students. You have a set of exam scores for each member of a class, in random order. You'd like a combined list of all the grades for each student, plus their average score. You have a text file (imaginatively named *grades*) that looks like this:

```
Noël 25
Ben 76
Clementine 49
Norm 66
Chris 92
Doug 42
Carol 25
Ben 12
Clementine 0
Norm 66
...
```

You can use the following script to gather all their scores together, determine each student's average, and print them all out in alphabetical order. This program assumes rather naively that you don't have two Carols in your class. That is, if there is a second entry for Carol, the program will assume it's just another score for the first Carol (not to be confused with the first Noël).

---

* Historically, Perl required you to put an ampersand character (&) on any calls to user-defined sub-routines (see `$fido = &fetch();` earlier). But with Perl version 5, the ampersand became optional, so that user-defined verbs can now be called with the same syntax as built-in verbs (`$fido = fetch();`). We still use the ampersand when talking about the *name* of the routine, such as when we take a reference to it (`$fetcher = \&fetch;`). Linguistically speaking, you can think of the ampersand form `&fetch` as an infinitive, "to fetch", or the similar form "do fetch". But we rarely say "do fetch" when we can just say "fetch". That's the real reason we dropped the mandatory ampersand in Perl 5.

By the way, the line numbers are not part of the program, any other resemblances
to BASIC notwithstanding.

```
 1  #!/usr/bin/perl
 2
 3  open(GRADES, "grades") or die "Can't open grades: $!\n";
 4  while ($line = <GRADES>) {
 5      ($student, $grade) = split(" ", $line);
 6      $grades{$student} .= $grade . " ";
 7  }
 8
 9  foreach $student (sort keys %grades) {
10      $scores = 0;
11      $total = 0;
12      @grades = split(" ", $grades{$student});
13      foreach $grade (@grades) {
14          $total += $grade;
15          $scores++;
16      }
17      $average = $total / $scores;
18      print "$student: $grades{$student}\tAverage: $average\n";
19  }
```

Now before your eyes cross permanently, we'd better point out that this example
demonstrates a lot of what we've covered so far, plus quite a bit more that we'll
explain presently. But if you let your eyes go just a little out of focus, you may
start to see some interesting patterns. Take some wild guesses now as to what's
going on, and then later on we'll tell you if you're right.

We'd tell you to try running it, but you may not know how yet.

How to Do It

Gee, right about now you're probably wondering how to run a Perl program. The
short answer is that you feed it to the Perl language interpreter program, which
coincidentally happens to be named *perl*. The long answer starts out like this:
There's More Than One Way To Do It.*

The first way to invoke *perl* (and the way most likely to work on any operating
system) is to simply call *perl* explicitly from the command line.† If you are doing

---

* That's the Perl Slogan, and you'll get tired of hearing it, unless you're the Local Expert, in which case
  you'll get tired of saying it. Sometimes it's shortened to TMTOWTDI, pronounced "tim-toady". But
  you can pronounce it however you like. After all, TMTOWTDI.

† Assuming that your operating system provides a command-line interface. If you're running an older
  Mac, you might need to upgrade to a version of BSD such as Mac OS X.

something fairly simple, you can use the **-e** switch (% in the following example represents a standard shell prompt, so don't type it). On Unix, you might type:

```
% perl -e 'print "Hello, world!\n";'
```

On other operating systems, you may have to fiddle with the quotes some. But the basic principle is the same: you're trying to cram everything Perl needs to know into 80 columns or so.*

For longer scripts, you can use your favorite text editor (or any other text editor) to put all your commands into a file and then, presuming you named the script *gradation* (not to be confused with graduation), you'd say:

```
% perl gradation
```

You're still invoking the Perl interpreter explicitly, but at least you don't have to put everything on the command line every time. And you no longer have to fiddle with quotes to keep the shell happy.

The most convenient way to invoke a script is just to name it directly (or click on it), and let the operating system find the interpreter for you. On some systems, there may be ways of associating various file extensions or directories with a particular application. On those systems, you should do whatever it is you do to associate the Perl script with the *perl* interpreter. On Unix systems that support the #! "shebang" notation (and most Unix systems do, nowadays), you can make the first line of your script be magical, so the operating system will know which program to run. Put a line resembling line 1 of our example into your program:

```
#!/usr/bin/perl
```

(If *perl* isn't in */usr/bin*, you'll have to change the #! line accordingly.) Then all you have to say is:

```
% gradation
```

Of course, this didn't work because you forgot to make sure the script was executable (see the manpage for *chmod*(1)) and in your PATH. If it isn't in your PATH, you'll have to provide a complete filename so that the operating system knows how to find your script. Something like:

```
% /home/sharon/bin/gradation
```

Finally, if you are unfortunate enough to be on an ancient Unix system that doesn't support the magic #! line, or if the path to your interpreter is longer than

---

* These types of scripts are often referred to as "one-liners". If you ever end up hanging out with other Perl programmers, you'll find that some of us are quite fond of creating intricate one-liners. Perl has occasionally been maligned as a write-only language because of these shenanigans.

32 characters (a built-in limit on many systems), you may be able to work around it like this:

```
#!/bin/sh -- # perl, to stop looping
eval 'exec /usr/bin/perl -S $0 ${1+"$@"}'
    if 0;
```

Some operating systems may require variants of this to deal with */bin/csh*, *DCL*, *COMMAND.COM*, or whatever happens to be your default command interpreter. Ask your Local Expert.

Throughout this book, we'll just use #!/usr/bin/perl to represent all these notions and notations, but you'll know what we really mean by it.

A random clue: when you write a test script, don't call your script *test*. Unix systems have a built-in *test* command, which will likely be executed instead of your script. Try *try* instead.

A not-so-random clue: while learning Perl, and even after you think you know what you're doing, we suggest using the **-w** switch, especially during development. This option will turn on all sorts of useful and interesting warning messages, not necessarily in that order. You can put the **-w** switch on the shebang line, like this:

```
#!/usr/bin/perl -w
```

Now that you know how to run your own Perl program (not to be confused with the *perl* program), let's get back to our example.

Filehandles

Unless you're using artificial intelligence to model a solipsistic philosopher, your program needs some way to communicate with the outside world. In lines 3 and 4 of our Average Example you'll see the word GRADES, which exemplifies another of Perl's data types, the *filehandle*. A filehandle is just a name you give to a file, device, socket, or pipe to help you remember which one you're talking about, and to hide some of the complexities of buffering and such. (Internally, filehandles are similar to streams from a language like C++ or I/O channels from BASIC.)

Filehandles make it easier for you to get input from and send output to many different places. Part of what makes Perl a good glue language is that it can talk to many files and processes at once. Having nice symbolic names for various external objects is just part of being a good glue language.*

---

* Some of the other things that make Perl a good glue language are: it's 8-bit clean, it's embeddable, and you can embed other things in it via extension modules. It's concise, and it "networks" easily. It's environmentally conscious, so to speak. You can invoke it in many different ways (as we saw earlier). But most of all, the language itself is not so rigidly structured that you can't get it to "flow" around your problem. It comes back to that TMTOWTDI thing again.

You create a filehandle and attach it to a file by using open. The open function takes at least two parameters: the filehandle and filename you want to associate it with. Perl also gives you some predefined (and preopened) filehandles. STDIN is your program's normal input channel, while STDOUT is your program's normal output channel. And STDERR is an additional output channel that allows your program to make snide remarks off to the side while it transforms (or attempts to transform) your input into your output.*

Since you can use the open function to create filehandles for various purposes (input, output, piping), you need to be able to specify which behavior you want. As you might do on the command line, you simply add characters to the filename.

```
open(SESAME, "filename")          # read from existing file
open(SESAME, "<filename")         #   (same thing, explicitly)
open(SESAME, ">filename")         # create file and write to it
open(SESAME, ">>filename")        # append to existing file
open(SESAME, "| output-pipe-command")  # set up an output filter
open(SESAME, "input-pipe-command |")   # set up an input filter
```

As you can see, the name you pick for the filehandle is arbitrary. Once opened, the filehandle SESAME can be used to access the file or pipe until it is explicitly closed (with, you guessed it, close(SESAME)), or until the filehandle is attached to another file by a subsequent open on the same filehandle.†

Once you've opened a filehandle for input, you can read a line using the line reading operator, <>. This is also known as the angle operator because it's made of angle brackets. The angle operator encloses the filehandle (<SESAME>) you want to read lines from. The empty angle operator, <>, will read lines from all the files specified on the command line, or STDIN, if none were specified. (This is standard behavior for many filter programs.) An example using the STDIN filehandle to read an answer supplied by the user would look something like this:

```
print STDOUT "Enter a number: ";      # ask for a number
$number = <STDIN>;                    # input the number
print STDOUT "The number is $number.\n";  # print the number
```

---

* These filehandles are typically attached to your terminal, so you can type to your program and see its output, but they may also be attached to files (and such). Perl can give you these predefined handles because your operating system already provides them, one way or another. Under Unix, processes inherit standard input, output, and error from their parent process, typically a shell. One of the duties of a shell is to set up these I/O streams so that the child process doesn't need to worry about them.

† Opening an already opened filehandle implicitly closes the first file, making it inaccessible to the filehandle, and opens a different file. You must be careful that this is what you really want to do. Sometimes it happens accidentally, like when you say open($handle,$file), and $handle happens to contain a constant string. Be sure to set $handle to something unique, or you'll just open a new file on the same filehandle. Or you can leave $handle undefined, and Perl will fill it in for you.

Did you see what we just slipped by you? What's that STDOUT doing there in those print statements? Well, that's just one of the ways you can use an output filehandle. A filehandle may be supplied as the first argument to the print statement, and if present, tells the output where to go. In this case, the filehandle is redundant, because the output would have gone to STDOUT anyway. Much as STDIN is the default for input, STDOUT is the default for output. (In line 18 of our Average Example, we left it out to avoid confusing you up till now.)

If you try the previous example, you may notice that you get an extra blank line. This happens because the line-reading operation does not automatically remove the newline from your input line (your input would be, for example, "9\n"). For those times when you do want to remove the newline, Perl provides the chop and chomp functions. chop will indiscriminately remove (and return) the last character of the string, while chomp will only remove the end of record marker (generally, "\n") and return the number of characters so removed. You'll often see this idiom for inputting a single line:

```
chop($number = <STDIN>);   # input number and remove newline
```

which means the same thing as:

```
$number = <STDIN>;         # input number
chop($number);             # remove newline
```

Operators

As we alluded to earlier, Perl is also a mathematical language. This is true at several levels, from low-level bitwise logical operations, up through number and set manipulation, on up to larger predicates and abstractions of various sorts. And as we all know from studying math in school, mathematicians love strange symbols. What's worse, computer scientists have come up with their own versions of these strange symbols. Perl has a number of these strange symbols too, but take heart, most are borrowed directly from C, FORTRAN, *sed*(1) or *awk*(1), so they'll at least be familiar to users of those languages.

The rest of you can take comfort in knowing that, by learning all these strange symbols in Perl, you've given yourself a head start on all those other strange languages.

Perl's built-in operators may be classified by number of operands into unary, binary, and trinary (or ternary) operators. They may be classified by whether they're prefix operators (which go in front of their operands) or infix operators (which go in between their operands). They may also be classified by the kinds of objects they work with, such as numbers, strings, or files. Later, we'll give you a table of all the operators, but first here are some handy ones to get you started.

Some Binary Arithmetic Operators

Arithmetic operators do what you would expect from learning them in school. They perform some sort of mathematical function on numbers. For example:

Example	Name	Result
$a + $b	Addition	Sum of $a and $b
$a * $b	Multiplication	Product of $a and $b
$a % $b	Modulus	Remainder of $a divided by $b
$a ** $b	Exponentiation	$a to the power of $b

Yes, we left out subtraction and division—we suspect you can figure out how they should work. Try them and see if you're right. (Or cheat and look in Chapter 3, *Unary and Binary Operators.*) Arithmetic operators are evaluated in the order your math teacher taught you (exponentiation before multiplication; multiplication before addition). You can always use parentheses to make it come out differently.

String Operators

There is also an "addition" operator for strings that performs concatenation (that is, joining strings end to end). Unlike some languages that confuse this with numeric addition, Perl defines a separate operator (.) for string concatenation:

```
$a = 123;
$b = 456;
print $a + $b;      # prints 579
print $a . $b;      # prints 123456
```

There's also a "multiply" operator for strings, called the *repeat* operator. Again, it's a separate operator (x) to keep it distinct from numeric multiplication:

```
$a = 123;
$b = 3;
print $a * $b;      # prints 369
print $a x $b;      # prints 123123123
```

These string operators bind as tightly as their corresponding arithmetic operators. The repeat operator is a bit unusual in taking a string for its left argument but a number for its right argument. Note also how Perl is automatically converting from numbers to strings. You could have put all the literal numbers above in quotes, and it would still have produced the same output. Internally though, it would have been converting in the opposite direction (that is, from strings to numbers).

A couple more things to think about. String concatenation is also implied by the interpolation that happens in double-quoted strings. And when you print out a list

of values, you're also effectively concatenating strings. So the following three statements produce the same output:

```
print $a . ' is equal to ' . $b . ".\n";     # dot operator
print $a, ' is equal to ', $b, ".\n";        # list
print "$a is equal to $b.\n";                # interpolation
```

Which of these you use in any particular situation is entirely up to you. (But bear
in mind that interpolation is often the most readable.)

The x operator may seem relatively worthless at first glance, but it is quite useful
at times, especially for things like this:

```
print "-" x $scrwid, "\n";
```

which draws a line across your screen, presuming $scrwid contains your screen
width, and not your screw identifier.

Assignment Operators

Although it's not exactly a mathematical operator, we've already made extensive
use of the simple assignment operator, =. Try to remember that = means "gets set
to" rather than "equals". (There is also a mathematical equality operator == that
means "equals", and if you start out thinking about the difference between them
now, you'll save yourself a lot of headache later. The == operator is like a function
that returns a Boolean value, while = is more like a procedure that is evaluated for
the side effect of modifying a variable.)

Like the operators described earlier, assignment operators are binary infix operators, which means they have an operand on either side of the operator. The right
operand can be any expression you like, but the left operand must be a valid
lvalue (which, when translated to English, means a valid storage location like a
variable, or a location in an array). The most common assignment operator is simple assignment. It determines the value of the expression on its right side, and
then sets the variable on the left side to that value:

```
$a = $b;
$a = $b + 5;
$a = $a * 3;
```

Notice the last assignment refers to the same variable twice; once for the computation, once for the assignment. There's nothing wrong with that, but it's a common
enough operation that there's a shortcut for it (borrowed from C). If you say:

```
lvalue operator= expression
```

it is evaluated as if it were:

```
lvalue = lvalue operator expression
```

except that the lvalue is not computed twice. (This only makes a difference if evaluation of the lvalue has side effects. But when it *does* make a difference, it usually does what you want. So don't sweat it.)

So, for example, you could write the previous example as:

```
$a *= 3;
```

which reads "multiply $a by 3". You can do this with almost any binary operator in Perl, even some that you can't do it with in C:

```
$line .= "\n";  # Append newline to $line.
$fill x= 80;    # Make string $fill into 80 repeats of itself.
$val ||= "2";   # Set $val to 2 if it isn't already "true".
```

Line 6 of our Average Example* contains two string concatenations, one of which is an assignment operator. And line 14 contains a +=.

Regardless of which kind of assignment operator you use, the final value of the variable on the left is returned as the value of the assignment as a whole.† This will not surprise C programmers, who will already know how to use this idiom to zero out variables:

```
$a = $b = $c = 0;
```

You'll also frequently see assignment used as the condition of a while loop, as in line 4 of our average example.

What *will* surprise C programmers is that assignment in Perl returns the actual variable as an lvalue, so that you can modify the same variable more than once in a statement. For instance, you could say:

```
($temp -= 32) *= 5/9;
```

to do an in-place conversion from Fahrenheit to Celsius. This is also why earlier in this chapter we could say:

```
chop($number = <STDIN>);
```

and have it chop the final value of $number. Generally speaking, you can use this feature whenever you want to copy something and at the same time do something else with it.

---

* Thought we'd forgotten it, didn't you?

† This is unlike, say, Pascal, in which assignment is a statement and returns no value. We said earlier that assignment is like a procedure, but remember that in Perl, even procedures return values.

Unary Arithmetic Operators

As if `$variable += 1` weren't short enough, Perl borrows from C an even shorter way to increment a variable. The autoincrement (and autodecrement) operators simply add (or subtract) one from the value of the variable. They can be placed on either side of the variable, depending on when you want them to be evaluated:

Example	Name	Result
`++$a, $a++`	Autoincrement	Add 1 to $a
`--$a, $a--`	Autodecrement	Subtract 1 from $a

If you place one of these "auto" operators before the variable, it is known as a pre-incremented (pre-decremented) variable. Its value will be changed before it is referenced. If it is placed after the variable, it is known as a post-incremented (post-decremented) variable, and its value is changed after it is used. For example:

```
$a = 5;          # $a is assigned 5
$b = ++$a;       # $b is assigned the incremented value of $a, 6
$c = $a--;       # $c is assigned 6, then $a is decremented to 5
```

Line 15 of our Average Example increments the number of scores by one, so that we'll know how many scores we're averaging. It uses a post-increment operator (`$scores++`), but in this case it doesn't matter, since the expression is in a void context, which is just a funny way of saying that the expression is being evaluated only for the side effect of incrementing the variable. The value returned is being thrown away.*

Logical Operators

Logical operators, also known as "short-circuit" operators, allow the program to make decisions based on multiple criteria without using nested `if` statements. They are known as short-circuit operators because they skip (short circuit) the evaluation of their right argument if they decide the left argument has already supplied enough information to decide the overall value. This is not just for efficiency. You are explicitly allowed to depend on this short-circuiting behavior to avoid evaluating code in the right argument that you know would blow up if the left argument were not "guarding" it. You can say "California or bust!" in Perl without busting (presuming you do get to California).

Perl actually has two sets of logical operators, a traditional set borrowed from C and a newer (but even more traditional) set of ultralow-precedence operators borrowed from BASIC. Both sets contribute to readability when used appropriately.

---

* The optimizer will notice this and optimize the post-increment into a pre-increment, because that's a bit faster to execute. (You didn't need to know that, but we hoped it would cheer you up.)

C's punctuational operators work well when you want your logical operators to bind more tightly than commas, while BASIC's word-based operators work well when you want your commas to bind more tightly than your logical operators. Often they work the same, and which set you use is a matter of personal preference. (For contrastive examples, see the section "Logical and, or, not, and xor" in Chapter 3.) Although the two sets of operators are not interchangeable due to precedence, once they're parsed, the operators themselves behave identically; precedence merely governs the extent of their arguments. Table 1-1 lists logical operators.

Table 1-1. Logical Operators

Example	Name	Result
$a && $b	And	$a if $a is false, $b otherwise
$a || $b	Or	$a if $a is true, $b otherwise
! $a	Not	True if $a is not true
$a and $b	And	$a if $a is false, $b otherwise
$a or $b	Or	$a if $a is true, $b otherwise
not $a	Not	True if $a is not true
$a xor $b	Xor	True if $a or $b is true, but not both

Since the logical operators "short-circuit" the way they do, they're often used in Perl to conditionally execute code. The following line (line 3 from our Average Example) tries to open the file *grades*:

```
open(GRADES, "grades") or die "Can't open file grades: $!\n";
```

If it opens the file, it will jump to the next line of the program. If it can't open the file, it will provide us with an error message and then stop execution.

Literally, this line means "Open *grades* or bust!" Besides being another example of natural language, the short-circuit operators preserve the visual flow. Important actions are listed down the left side of the screen, and secondary actions are hidden off to the right. (The $! variable contains the error message returned by the operating system—see Chapter 28, *Special Names*.) Of course, these logical operators can also be used within the more traditional kinds of conditional constructs, such as the if and while statements.

Some Numeric and String Comparison Operators

Comparison, or relational, operators tell us how two scalar values (numbers or strings) relate to each other. There are two sets of operators; one does numeric comparison and the other does string comparison. (In either case, the arguments will be "coerced" to have the appropriate type first.) Assuming left and right arguments of $a and $b, we have:

Comparison	Numeric	String	Return Value
Equal	==	eq	True if $a is equal to $b
Not equal	!=	ne	True if $a is not equal to $b
Less than	<	lt	True if $a is less than $b
Greater than	>	gt	True if $a is greater than $b
Less than or equal	<=	le	True if $a not greater than $b
Greater than or equal	>=	ge	True if $a not less than $b
Comparison	<=>	cmp	0 if equal, 1 if $a greater, −1 if $b greater

The last pair of operators (<=> and cmp) are entirely redundant. However, they're incredibly useful in sort subroutines (see Chapter 29).*

Some File Test Operators

The file test operators allow you to test whether certain file attributes are set before you go and blindly muck about with the files. The most basic file attribute is, of course, whether the file exists. For example, it would be very nice to know whether your mail aliases file already exists before you go and open it as a new file, wiping out everything that was in there before. Here are a few of the file test operators:

Example	Name	Result
-e $a	Exists	True if file named in $a exists
-r $a	Readable	True if file named in $a is readable
-w $a	Writable	True if file named in $a is writable
-d $a	Directory	True if file named in $a is a directory
-f $a	File	True if file named in $a is a regular file
-T $a	Text File	True if file named in $a is a text file

You might use them like this:

```
-e "/usr/bin/perl" or warn "Perl is improperly installed\n";
-f "/vmlinuz" and print "I see you are a friend of Linus\n";
```

---

* Some folks feel that such redundancy is evil because it keeps a language from being minimalistic, or orthogonal. But Perl isn't an orthogonal language; it's a diagonal language. By this we mean that Perl doesn't force you to always go at right angles. Sometimes you just want to follow the hypotenuse of the triangle to get where you're going. TMTOWTDI is about shortcuts. Shortcuts are about efficiency.

Note that a regular file is not the same thing as a text file. Binary files like */vmlinuz* are regular files, but they aren't text files. Text files are the opposite of binary files, while regular files are the opposite of "irregular" files like directories and devices.

There are a lot of file test operators, many of which we didn't list. Most of the file tests are unary Boolean operators, which is to say they take only one operand (a scalar that evaluates to a filename or a filehandle), and they return either a true or false value. A few of them return something fancier, like the file's size or age, but you can look those up when you need them in the section "Named Unary and File Test Operators" in Chapter 3.

Control Structures

So far, except for our one large example, all of our examples have been completely linear; we executed each command in order. We've seen a few examples of using the short-circuit operators to cause a single command to be (or not to be) executed. While you can write some very useful linear programs (a lot of CGI scripts fall into this category), you can write much more powerful programs if you have conditional expressions and looping mechanisms. Collectively, these are known as control structures. So you can also think of Perl as a control language.

But to have control, you have to be able to decide things, and to decide things, you have to know the difference between what's true and what's false.

What Is Truth?

We've bandied about the term truth,* and we've mentioned that certain operators return a true or a false value. Before we go any further, we really ought to explain exactly what we mean by that. Perl treats truth a little differently than most computer languages, but after you've worked with it a while, it will make a lot of sense. (Actually, we hope it'll make a lot of sense after you've read the following.)

Basically, Perl holds truths to be self-evident. That's a glib way of saying that you can evaluate almost anything for its truth value. Perl uses practical definitions of truth that depend on the type of thing you're evaluating. As it happens, there are many more kinds of truth than there are of nontruth.

---

* Strictly speaking, this is not true.

Truth in Perl is always evaluated in a scalar context. Other than that, no type coercion is done. So here are the rules for the various kinds of values a scalar can hold:

1. Any string is true except for `""` and `"0"`.

2. Any number is true except for 0.

3. Any reference is true.

4. Any undefined value is false.

Actually, the last two rules can be derived from the first two. Any reference (rule 3) would point to something with an address and would evaluate to a number or string containing that address, which is never 0 because it's always defined. And any undefined value (rule 4) would always evaluate to 0 or the null string.

And in a way, you can derive rule 2 from rule 1 if you pretend that everything is a string. Again, no string coercion is actually done to evaluate truth, but if the string coercion *were* done, then any numeric value of 0 would simply turn into the string `"0"` and be false. Any other number would not turn into the string `"0"`, and so would be true. Let's look at some examples so we can understand this better:

```
0            # would become the string "0", so false.
1            # would become the string "1", so true.
10 - 10      # 10 minus 10 is 0, would convert to string "0", so false.
0.00         # equals 0, would convert to string "0", so false.
"0"          # is the string "0", so false.
""           # is a null string, so false.
"0.00"       # is the string "0.00", neither "" nor "0", so true!
"0.00" + 0   # would become the number 0 (coerced by the +), so false.
\$a          # is a reference to $a, so true, even if $a is false.
undef()      # is a function returning the undefined value, so false.
```

Since we mumbled something earlier about truth being evaluated in a scalar context, you might be wondering what the truth value of a list is. Well, the simple fact is, none of the operations in Perl will return a list in a scalar context. They'll all notice they're in a scalar context and return a scalar value instead, and then you apply the rules of truth to that scalar. So there's no problem, as long as you can figure out what any given operator will return in a scalar context. As it happens, both arrays and hashes return scalar values that conveniently happen to be true if the array or hash contains any elements. More on that later.

The if and unless statements

We saw earlier how a logical operator could function as a conditional. A slightly more complex form of the logical operators is the `if` statement. The `if` statement evaluates a truth condition (that is, a Boolean expression) and executes a block if the condition is true:

```
if ($debug_level > 0) {
    # Something has gone wrong.  Tell the user.
    print "Debug: Danger, Will Robinson, danger!\n";
    print "Debug: Answer was '54', expected '42'.\n";
}
```

A block is one or more statements grouped together by a set of braces. Since the if statement executes a block, the braces are required by definition. If you know a language like C, you'll notice that this is different. Braces are optional in C if you have a single statement, but the braces are not optional in Perl.

Sometimes, just executing a block when a condition is met isn't enough. You may also want to execute a different block if that condition *isn't* met. While you could certainly use two if statements, one the negation of the other, Perl provides a more elegant solution. After the block, if can take an optional second condition, called else, to be executed only if the truth condition is false. (Veteran computer programmers will not be surprised at this point.)

At times you may even have more than two possible choices. In this case, you'll want to add an elsif truth condition for the other possible choices. (Veteran computer programmers may well be surprised by the spelling of "elsif", for which nobody here is going to apologize. Sorry.)

```
if ($city eq "New York") {
    print "New York is northeast of Washington, D.C.\n";
}
elsif ($city eq "Chicago") {
    print "Chicago is northwest of Washington, D.C.\n";
}
elsif ($city eq "Miami") {
    print "Miami is south of Washington, D.C.  And much warmer!\n";
}
else {
    print "I don't know where $city is, sorry.\n";
}
```

The if and elsif clauses are each computed in turn, until one is found to be true or the else condition is reached. When one of the conditions is found to be true, its block is executed and all remaining branches are skipped. Sometimes, you don't want to do anything if the condition is true, only if it is false. Using an empty if with an else may be messy, and a negated if may be illegible; it sounds weird in English to say "if not this is true, do something". In these situations, you would use the unless statement:

```
unless ($destination eq $home) {
    print "I'm not going home.\n";
}
```

There is no elsunless though. This is generally construed as a feature.

Iterative (Looping) Constructs

Perl has four main iterative statement types: while, until, for, and foreach. These statements allow a Perl program to repeatedly execute the same code.

The while and until statements

The while and until statements behave just like the if and unless statements, except that they'll execute the block repeatedly. That is, they loop. First, the conditional part of the statement is checked. If the condition is met (if it is true for a while or false for an until), the block of the statement is executed.

```
while ($tickets_sold < 10000) {
    $available = 10000 - $tickets_sold;
    print "$available tickets are available.  How many would you like: ";
    $purchase = <STDIN>;
    chomp($purchase);
    $tickets_sold += $purchase;
}
```

Note that if the original condition is never met, the loop will never be entered at all. For example, if we've already sold 10,000 tickets, we might want to have the next line of the program say something like:

```
print "This show is sold out, please come back later.\n";
```

In our Average Example earlier, line 4 reads:

```
while ($line = <GRADES>) {
```

This assigns the next line to the variable $line and, as we explained earlier, returns the value of $line so that the condition of the while statement can evaluate $line for truth. You might wonder whether Perl will get a false negative on blank lines and exit the loop prematurely. The answer is that it won't. The reason is clear if you think about everything we've said. The line input operator leaves the newline on the end of the string, so a blank line has the value "\n". And you know that "\n" is not one of the canonical false values. So the condition is true, and the loop continues even on blank lines.

On the other hand, when we finally do reach the end of the file, the line input operator returns the undefined value, which always evaluates to false. And the loop terminates, just when we wanted it to. There's no need for an explicit test of the eof function in Perl, because the input operators are designed to work smoothly in a conditional context.

In fact, almost everything is designed to work smoothly in a conditional (Boolean) context. If you mention an array in a scalar context, the length of the array is returned. So you often see command-line arguments processed like this:

```
while (@ARGV) {
    process(shift @ARGV);
}
```

The `shift` operator removes one element from the argument list each time through the loop (and returns that element). The loop automatically exits when array `@ARGV` is exhausted, that is, when its length goes to 0. And 0 is already false in Perl. In a sense, the array itself has become "false".*

The for statement

Another iterative statement is the `for` loop. The `for` loop runs exactly like the `while` loop, but looks a good deal different. (C programmers will find it very familiar though.)

```
for ($sold = 0; $sold < 10000; $sold += $purchase) {
    $available = 10000 - $sold;
    print "$available tickets are available.  How many would you like: ";
    $purchase = <STDIN>;
    chomp($purchase);
}
```

This `for` loop takes three expressions within the loop's parentheses: an expression to set the initial state of the loop variable, a condition to test the loop variable, and an expression to modify the state of the loop variable. When a `for` loop starts, the initial state is set and the truth condition is checked. If the condition is true, the block is executed. When the block finishes, the modification expression is executed, the truth condition is again checked, and if true, the block is rerun with the next value. As long as the truth condition remains true, the block and the modification expression will continue to be executed. (Note that only the middle expression is evaluated for its value. The first and third expressions are evaluated only for their side effects, and the resulting values are thrown away!)

The foreach statement

The last of Perl's iterative statements is the `foreach` statement, which is used to execute the same code for each of a known set of scalars, such as an array:

```
foreach $user (@users) {
    if (-f "$home{$user}/.nexrc") {
        print "$user is cool... they use a perl-aware vi!\n";
    }
}
```

---

* This is how Perl programmers think. So there's no need to compare 0 to 0 to see if it's false. Despite the fact that other languages force you to, don't go out of your way to write explicit comparisons like `while (@ARGV != 0)`. That's just inefficient for both you and the computer. And anyone who has to maintain your code.

Unlike the if and while statements, which provide scalar context to a conditional expression, the foreach statement provides a list context to the expression in parentheses. So the expression is evaluated to produce a list (not a scalar, even if there's only one scalar in the list). Then each element of the list is aliased to the loop variable in turn, and the block of code is executed once for each list element. Note that the loop variable refers to the element itself, rather than a copy of the element. Hence, modifying the loop variable also modifies the original array.

You'll find many more foreach loops in the typical Perl program than for loops, because it's very easy in Perl to generate the kinds of lists that foreach wants to iterate over. One idiom you'll often see is a loop to iterate over the sorted keys of a hash:

```
foreach $key (sort keys %hash) {
```

In fact, line 9 of our Average Example does precisely that.

Breaking out: next and last

The next and last operators allow you to modify the flow of your loop. It is not at all uncommon to have a special case; you may want to skip it, or you may want to quit when you encounter it. For example, if you are dealing with Unix accounts, you may want to skip the system accounts (like *root* or *lp*). The next operator would allow you to skip to the end of your current loop iteration, and start the next iteration. The last operator would allow you to skip to the end of your block, as if your loop's test condition had returned false. This might be useful if, for example, you are looking for a specific account and want to quit as soon as you find it.

```
foreach $user (@users) {
    if ($user eq "root" or $user eq "lp") {
        next;
    }
    if ($user eq "special") {
        print "Found the special account.\n";
        # do some processing
        last;
    }
}
```

It's possible to break out of multilevel loops by labeling your loops and specifying which loop you want to break out of. Together with statement modifiers (another form of conditional which we'll talk about later), this can make for extremely readable loop exits (if you happen to think English is readable):

```
LINE: while ($line = <ARTICLE>) {
    last LINE if $line eq "\n"; # stop on first blank line
    next LINE if $line =~ /^#/; # skip comment lines
```

```
    # your ad here
}
```

You may be saying, "Wait a minute, what's that funny ^# thing there inside the leaning toothpicks? That doesn't look much like English." And you're right. That's a pattern match containing a regular expression (albeit a rather simple one). And that's what the next section is about. Perl is the best text processing language in the world, and regular expressions are at the heart of Perl's text processing.

Regular Expressions

Regular expressions (a.k.a. regexes, regexps, or REs) are used by many search programs such as *grep* and *findstr*, text-munging programs like *sed* and *awk*, and editors like *vi* and *emacs*. A regular expression is a way of describing a set of strings without having to list all the strings in your set.*

Many other computer languages incorporate regular expressions (some of them even advertise "Perl5 regular expressions"!), but none of these languages integrates regular expressions into the language the way Perl does. Regular expressions are used several ways in Perl. First and foremost, they're used in conditionals to determine whether a string matches a particular pattern, because in a Boolean context they return true and false. So when you see something that looks like /foo/ in a conditional, you know you're looking at an ordinary *pattern-matching* operator:

```
if (/Windows 95/) { print "Time to upgrade?\n" }
```

Second, if you can locate patterns within a string, you can replace them with something else. So when you see something that looks like s/foo/bar/, you know it's asking Perl to substitute "bar" for "foo", if possible. We call that the *substitution* operator. It also happens to return true or false depending on whether it succeeded, but usually it's evaluated for its side effect:

```
s/Windows/Linux/;
```

Finally, patterns can specify not only where something is, but also where it *isn't*. So the split operator uses a regular expression to specify where the data isn't. That is, the regular expression defines the *separators* that delimit the fields of data. Our Average Example has a couple of trivial examples of this. Lines 5 and 12 each split strings on the space character in order to return a list of words. But you can split on any separator you can specify with a regular expression:

```
($good, $bad, $ugly) = split(/,/, "vi,emacs,teco");
```

---

* A good source of information on regular expression concepts is Jeffrey Friedl's book, *Mastering Regular Expressions* (O'Reilly & Associates).

(There are various modifiers you can use in each of these situations to do exotic things like ignore case when matching alphabetic characters, but these are the sorts of gory details that we'll cover later when we get to the gory details.)

The simplest use of regular expressions is to match a literal expression. In the case of the split above, we matched on a single comma character. But if you match on several characters in a row, they all have to match sequentially. That is, the pattern looks for a substring, much as you'd expect. Let's say we want to show all the lines of an HTML file that contain HTTP links (as opposed to FTP links). Let's imagine we're working with HTML for the first time, and we're being a little naïve. We know that these links will always have "http:" in them somewhere. We could loop through our file with this:

```
while ($line = <FILE>) {
    if ($line =~ /http:/) {
        print $line;
    }
}
```

Here, the =~ (pattern-binding operator) is telling Perl to look for a match of the regular expression "http:" in the variable $line. If it finds the expression, the operator returns a true value and the block (a print statement) is executed.*

By the way, if you don't use the =~ binding operator, Perl will search a default string instead of $line. It's like when you say, "Eek! Help me find my contact lens!" People automatically know to look around near you without your actually having to tell them that. Likewise, Perl knows that there is a default place to search for things when you don't say where to search for them. This default string is actually a special scalar variable that goes by the odd name of $_. In fact, it's not the default just for pattern matching; many operators in Perl default to using the $_ variable, so a veteran Perl programmer would likely write the last example as:

```
while (<FILE>) {
    print if /http:/;
}
```

(Hmm, another one of those statement modifiers seems to have snuck in there. Insidious little beasties.)

This stuff is pretty handy, but what if we wanted to find all of the link types, not just the HTTP links? We could give a list of link types, like "http:", "ftp:", "mailto:", and so on. But that list could get long, and what would we do when a new kind of link was added?

---

* This is very similar to what the Unix command grep 'http:' file would do. On MS-DOS you could use the *find* command, but it doesn't know how to do more complicated regular expressions. (However, the misnamed *findstr* program of Windows NT does know about regular expressions.)

```
while (<FILE>) {
    print if /http:/;
    print if /ftp:/;
    print if /mailto:/;
    # What next?
}
```

Since regular expressions are descriptive of a set of strings, we can just describe what we are looking for: a number of alphabetic characters followed by a colon. In regular expression talk (Regexese?), that would be /[a-zA-Z]+:/, where the brackets define a *character class*. The a-z and A-Z represent all alphabetic characters (the dash means the range of all characters between the starting and ending character, inclusive). And the + is a special character that says "one or more of whatever was before me". It's what we call a *quantifier*, meaning a gizmo that says how many times something is allowed to repeat. (The slashes aren't really part of the regular expression, but rather part of the pattern-match operator. The slashes are acting like quotes that just happen to contain a regular expression.)

Because certain classes like the alphabetics are so commonly used, Perl defines shortcuts for them:

Name	ASCII Definition	Code
Whitespace	[\t\n\r\f]	\s
Word character	[a-zA-Z_0-9]	\w
Digit	[0-9]	\d

Note that these match *single* characters. A \w will match any single word character, not an entire word. (Remember that + quantifier? You can say \w+ to match a word.) Perl also provides the negation of these classes by using the uppercased character, such as \D for a nondigit character.

We should note that \w is not always equivalent to [a-zA-Z_0-9] (and \d is not always [0-9]). Some locales define additional alphabetic characters outside the ASCII sequence, and \w respects them. Newer versions of Perl also know about Unicode letter and digit properties and treat Unicode characters with those properties accordingly. (Perl also considers ideographs to be \w characters.)

There is one other very special character class, written with a ".", that will match any character whatsoever.* For example, /a./ will match any string containing an "a" that is not the last character in the string. Thus it will match "at" or "am" or even "a!", but not "a", since there's nothing after the "a" for the dot to match. Since it's searching for the pattern anywhere in the string, it'll match "oasis" and "camel", but not "sheba". It matches "caravan" on the first "a". It could match on

---

* Except that it won't normally match a newline. When you think about it, a "." doesn't normally match a newline in *grep*(1) either.

the second "a", but it stops after it finds the first suitable match, searching from left to right.

Quantifiers

The characters and character classes we've talked about all match single characters. We mentioned that you could match multiple "word" characters with \w+. The + is one kind of quantifier, but there are others. All of them are placed after the item being quantified.

The most general form of quantifier specifies both the minimum and maximum number of times an item can match. You put the two numbers in braces, separated by a comma. For example, if you were trying to match North American phone numbers, the sequence \d{7,11} would match at least seven digits, but no more than eleven digits. If you put a single number in the braces, the number specifies both the minimum and the maximum; that is, the number specifies the exact number of times the item can match. (All unquantified items have an implicit {1} quantifier.)

If you put the minimum and the comma but omit the maximum, then the maximum is taken to be infinity. In other words, it will match at least the minimum number of times, plus as many as it can get after that. For example, \d{7} will match only the first seven digits (a local North American phone number, for instance, or the first seven digits of a longer number), while \d{7,} will match any phone number, even an international one (unless it happens to be shorter than seven digits). There is no special way of saying "at most" a certain number of times. Just say .{0,5}, for example, to find at most five arbitrary characters.

Certain combinations of minimum and maximum occur frequently, so Perl defines special quantifiers for them. We've already seen +, which is the same as {1,}, or "at least one of the preceding item". There is also *, which is the same as {0,}, or "zero or more of the preceding item", and ?, which is the same as {0,1}, or "zero or one of the preceding item" (that is, the preceding item is optional).

You need to be careful of a couple things about quantification. First of all, Perl quantifiers are by default *greedy*. This means that they will attempt to match as much as they can as long as the whole pattern still matches. For example, if you are matching /\d+/ against "1234567890", it will match the entire string. This is something to watch out for especially when you are using ".", any character. Often, someone will have a string like:

```
larry:JYHtPh0./NJTU:100:10:Larry Wall:/home/larry:/bin/tcsh
```

and will try to match "larry:" with /.+:/. However, since the + quantifier is greedy, this pattern will match everything up to and including "/home/larry:", because it matches as much as possible before the last colon, including all the other colons. Sometimes you can avoid this by using a negated character class, that is, by saying /[^:]+:/, which says to match one or more noncolon characters (as many as possible), up to the first colon. It's that little caret in there that negates the Boolean sense of the character class.* The other point to be careful about is that regular expressions will try to match as *early* as possible. This even takes precedence over being greedy. Since scanning happens left-to-right, this means that the pattern will match as far left as possible, even if there is some other place where it could match longer. (Regular expressions may be greedy, but they aren't into delayed gratification.) For example, suppose you're using the substitution command (s///) on the default string (variable $_, that is), and you want to remove a string of x's from the middle of the string. If you say:

```
$_ = "fred xxxxxxx barney";
s/x*//;
```

it will have absolutely no effect! This is because the x* (meaning zero or more "x" characters) will be able to match the "nothing" at the beginning of the string, since the null string happens to be zero characters wide and there's a null string just sitting there plain as day before the "f" of "fred".†

There's one other thing you need to know. By default, quantifiers apply to a single preceding character, so /bam{2}/ will match "bamm" but not "bambam". To apply a quantifier to more than one character, use parentheses. So to match "bambam", use the pattern /(bam){2}/.

Minimal Matching

If you were using an ancient version of Perl and you didn't want greedy matching, you had to use a negated character class. (And really, you were still getting greedy matching of a constrained variety.)

In modern versions of Perl, you can force nongreedy, minimal matching by placing a question mark after any quantifier. Our same username match would now be /.*?:/. That .*? will now try to match as few characters as possible, rather than as many as possible, so it stops at the first colon rather than at the last.

---

* Sorry, we didn't pick that notation, so don't blame us. That's just how negated character classes are customarily written in Unix culture.

† Don't feel bad. Even the authors get caught by this from time to time.

Nailing Things Down

Whenever you try to match a pattern, it's going to try to match in every location till it finds a match. An *anchor* allows you to restrict where the pattern can match. Essentially, an anchor is something that matches a "nothing", but a special kind of nothing that depends on its surroundings. You could also call it a rule, or a constraint, or an assertion. Whatever you care to call it, it tries to match something of zero width, and either succeeds or fails. (Failure merely means that the pattern can't match that particular way. The pattern will go on trying to match some other way, if there are any other ways left to try.)

The special symbol \b matches at a word boundary, which is defined as the "nothing" between a word character (\w) and a nonword character (\W), in either order. (The characters that don't exist off the beginning and end of your string are considered to be nonword characters.) For example,

```
/\bFred\b/
```

would match "Fred" in both "The Great Fred" and "Fred the Great", but not in "Frederick the Great" because the "d" in "Frederick" is not followed by a non-word character.

In a similar vein, there are also anchors for the beginning of the string and the end of the string. If it is the first character of a pattern, the caret (^) matches the "nothing" at the beginning of the string. Therefore, the pattern /^Fred/ would match "Fred" in "Frederick the Great" but not in "The Great Fred", whereas /Fred^/ wouldn't match either. (In fact, it doesn't even make much sense.) The dollar sign ($) works like the caret, except that it matches the "nothing" at the end of the string instead of the beginning.*

So now you can probably figure out that when we said:

```
next LINE if $line =~ /^#/;
```

we meant "Go to the next iteration of LINE loop if this line happens to begin with a # character."

Earlier we said that the sequence \d{7,11} would match a number from seven to eleven digits long. While strictly true, the statement is misleading: when you use that sequence within a real pattern match operator such as /\d{7,11}/, it does not preclude there being extra unmatched digits after the 11 matched digits! You often need to anchor quantified patterns on either or both ends to get what you expect.

---

* This is a bit oversimplified, since we're assuming here that your string contains no newlines; ^ and $ are actually anchors for the beginnings and endings of lines rather than strings. We'll try to straighten this all out in Chapter 5, *Pattern Matching* (to the extent that it can be straightened out).

Backreferences

We mentioned earlier that you can use parentheses to group things for quantifiers, but you can also use parentheses to remember bits and pieces of what you matched. A pair of parentheses around a part of a regular expression causes whatever was matched by that part to be remembered for later use. It doesn't change what the part matches, so /\d+/ and /(\d+)/ will still match as many digits as possible, but in the latter case they will be remembered in a special variable to be backreferenced later.

How you refer back to the remembered part of the string depends on where you want to do it from. Within the same regular expression, you use a backslash followed by an integer. The integer corresponding to a given pair of parentheses is determined by counting left parentheses from the beginning of the pattern, starting with one. So for example, to match something similar to an HTML tag like "<B>Bold</B>", you might use /<(.*?)>.*?<\/\1>/. This forces the two parts of the pattern to match the exact same string, such as the "B" in this example.

Outside the regular expression itself, such as in the replacement part of a substitution, you use a $ followed by an integer, that is, a normal scalar variable named by the integer. So, if you wanted to swap the first two words of a string, for example, you could use:

```
s/(\S+)\s+(\S+)/$2 $1/
```

The right side of the substitution (between the second and third slashes) is mostly just a funny kind of double-quoted string, which is why you can interpolate variables there, including backreference variables. This is a powerful concept: interpolation (under controlled circumstances) is one of the reasons Perl is a good text-processing language. The other reason is the pattern matching, of course. Regular expressions are good for picking things apart, and interpolation is good for putting things back together again. Perhaps there's hope for Humpty Dumpty after all.

List Processing

Much earlier in this chapter, we mentioned that Perl has two main contexts, scalar context (for dealing with singular things) and list context (for dealing with plural things). Many of the traditional operators we've described so far have been strictly scalar in their operation. They always take singular arguments (or pairs of singular arguments for binary operators) and always produce a singular result, even in list context. So if you write this:

```
@array = (1 + 2, 3 - 4, 5 * 6, 7 / 8);
```

you know that the list on the right side contains exactly four values, because the ordinary math operators always produce scalar values, even in the list context provided by the assignment to an array.

However, other Perl operators can produce either a scalar or a list value, depending on their context. They just "know" whether a scalar or a list is expected of them. But how will you know that? It turns out to be pretty easy to figure out, once you get your mind around a few key concepts.

First, list context has to be provided by something in the "surroundings". In the previous example, the list assignment provides it. Earlier we saw that the list of a foreach loop provides it. The print operator also provides it. But you don't have to learn these one by one.

If you look at the various syntax summaries scattered throughout the rest of the book, you'll see various operators that are defined to take a *LIST* as an argument. Those are the operators that *provide* a list context. Throughout this book, *LIST* is used as a specific technical term to mean "a syntactic construct that provides a list context". For example, if you look up sort, you'll find the syntax summary:

    sort *LIST*

That means that sort provides a list context to its arguments.

Second, at compile time (that is, while Perl is parsing your program and translating to internal opcodes), any operator that takes a *LIST* provides a list context to each syntactic element of that *LIST*. So every top-level operator or entity in the *LIST* knows at compile time that it's supposed to produce the best list it knows how to produce. This means that if you say:

    sort @dudes, @chicks, other();

then each of @dudes, @chicks, and other() knows at compile time that it's supposed to produce a list value rather than a scalar value. So the compiler generates internal opcodes that reflect this.

Later, at run time (when the internal opcodes are actually interpreted), each of those *LIST* elements produces its list in turn, and then (this is important) all the separate lists are joined together, end to end, into a single list. And that squashed-flat, one-dimensional list is what is finally handed off to the function that wanted the *LIST* in the first place. So if @dudes contains (Fred,Barney), @chicks contains (Wilma,Betty), and the other() function returns the single-element list (Dino), then the *LIST* that sort sees is:

    (Fred,Barney,Wilma,Betty,Dino)

and the *LIST* that sort returns is:

```
(Barney,Betty,Dino,Fred,Wilma)
```

Some operators produce lists (like keys), while some consume them (like print), and others transform lists into other lists (like sort). Operators in the last category can be considered filters, except that, unlike in the shell, the flow of data is from right to left, since list operators operate on arguments passed in from the right. You can stack up several list operators in a row:

```
print reverse sort map {lc} keys %hash;
```

That takes the keys of %hash and returns them to the map function, which lower-cases all the keys by applying the lc operator to each of them, and passes them to the sort function, which sorts them, and passes them to the reverse function, which reverses the order of the list elements, and passes them to the print function, which prints them.

As you can see, that's much easier to describe in Perl than in English.

There are many other ways in which list processing produces more natural code. We can't enumerate all the ways here, but for an example, let's go back to regular expressions for a moment. We talked about using a pattern in a scalar context to see whether it matched, but if instead you use a pattern in a list context, it does something else: it pulls out all the backreferences as a list. Suppose you're searching through a log file or a mailbox, and you want to parse a string containing a time of the form "12:59:59 am". You might say this:

```
($hour, $min, $sec, $ampm) = /(\d+):(\d+):(\d+) *(\w+)/;
```

That's a convenient way to set several variables simultaneously. But you could just as easily say

```
@hmsa = /(\d+):(\d+):(\d+) *(\w+)/;
```

and put all four values into one array. Oddly, by decoupling the power of regular expressions from the power of Perl expressions, list context increases the power of the language. We don't often admit it, but Perl is actually an orthogonal language in addition to being a diagonal language. Have your cake, and eat it too.

What You Don't Know Won't Hurt You (Much)

Finally, allow us to return once more to the concept of Perl as a natural language. Speakers of a natural language are allowed to have differing skill levels, to speak different subsets of the language, to learn as they go, and generally, to put the language to good use before they know the whole language. You don't know all of Perl yet, just as you don't know all of English. But that's Officially Okay in Perl culture. You can work with Perl usefully, even though we haven't even told you how to write your own subroutines yet. We've scarcely begun to explain how to view Perl as a system management language, or a rapid prototyping language, or a networking language, or an object-oriented language. We could write entire chapters about some of these things. (Come to think of it, we already did.)

But in the end, you must create your own view of Perl. It's your privilege as an artist to inflict the pain of creativity on yourself. We can teach you how *we* paint, but we can't teach you how *you* paint. There's More Than One Way To Do It.

Have the appropriate amount of fun.

II

The Gory Details

2

Bits and Pieces

We're going to start small, so this chapter is about the elements of Perl.

Since we're starting small, the progression through the next several chapters is necessarily from small to large. That is, we take a bottom-up approach, beginning with the smallest components of Perl programs and building them into more elaborate structures, much like molecules are built out of atoms. The disadvantage of this approach is that you don't necessarily get the Big Picture before getting lost in a welter of details. The advantage is that you can understand the examples as we go along. (If you're a top-down person, just turn the book over and read the chapters backward.)

Each chapter does build on the preceding chapter (or the *subsequent* chapter, if you're reading backward), so you'll need to be careful if you're the sort of person who skips around.

You're certainly welcome to peek at the reference materials toward the end of the book as we go along. (That doesn't count as skipping around.) In particular, any isolated word in `typewriter` font is likely to be found in Chapter 29, *Functions*. And although we've tried to stay operating-system neutral, if you are unfamiliar with Unix terminology and run into a word that doesn't seem to mean what you think it ought to mean, you should check whether the word is in the Glossary. If the Glossary doesn't work, the index probably will.

Atoms

Although there are various invisible things going on behind the scenes that we'll explain presently, the smallest things you generally work with in Perl are individual characters. And we do mean characters; historically, Perl freely confused bytes with characters and characters with bytes, but in this new era of global networking, we must be careful to distinguish the two.

Perl may, of course, be written entirely in the 7-bit ASCII character set. Perl also allows you to write in any 8-bit or 16-bit character set, whether it's a national character set or some other legacy character set. However, if you choose to write in one of these older, non-ASCII character sets, you may use non-ASCII characters only within string literals. You are responsible for making sure that the semantics of your program are consistent with the particular national character set you've chosen. For instance, if you're using a 16-bit encoding for an Asian national character set, keep in mind that Perl will generally think of each of your characters as two bytes, not as one character.

As described in Chapter 15, *Unicode*, we've recently added support for Unicode to Perl.* This support is pervasive throughout the language: you can use Unicode characters in identifiers (variable names and such) as well as within literal strings. When you are using Unicode, you don't need to worry about how many bits or bytes it takes to represent a character. Perl just pretends all Unicode characters are the same size (that is, size 1), even though any given character might be represented by multiple bytes internally. Perl normally represents Unicode internally as UTF-8, a variable-length encoding. (For instance, a Unicode smiley character, U-263A, would be represented internally as a three-byte sequence.)

If you'll let us drive our analogy of the physical elements a bit further, characters are atomic in the same sense as the individual atoms of the various elements. Yes, they're composed of smaller particles known as bits and bytes, but if you break a character apart (in a character accelerator, no doubt), the individual bits and bytes lose the distinguishing chemical properties of the character as a whole. Just as neutrons are an implementation detail of the U-238 atom, so too bytes are an implementation detail of the U-263A character.

So we'll be careful to say "characters" when we mean characters, and "bytes" when we mean bytes. But we don't mean to scare you—you can still do the good old-fashioned byte processing easily enough. All you have to do is tell Perl that you still want to think of bytes as characters. You can do that with a `use bytes` pragma (see Chapter 31, *Pragmatic Modules*). But even if you don't do that, Perl will still do a pretty good job of keeping small characters in 8 bits when you expect it to.

So don't sweat the small stuff. Let's move on to bigger and better things.

---

* As excited as we are about Unicode support, most of our examples will be in ASCII, since not everyone has a decent Unicode editor yet.

Molecules

Perl is a *free-form* language, but that doesn't mean that Perl is totally free of form. As computer folks usually use the term, a free-form language is one in which you can put spaces, tabs, and newlines anywhere you like—except where you can't.

One obvious place you can't put a whitespace character is in the middle of a token. A *token* is what we call a sequence of characters with a unit of meaning, much like a simple word in natural language. But unlike the typical word, a token might contain other characters besides letters, just as long as they hang together to form a unit of meaning. (In that sense, they're more like molecules, which don't have to be composed of only one particular kind of atom.) For example, numbers and mathematical operators are considered tokens. An *identifier* is a token that starts with a letter or underscore and contains only letters, digits, and underscores. A token may not contain whitespace characters because this would split the token into two tokens, just as a space in an English word turns it into two words.*

Although whitespace is allowed between any two tokens, whitespace is *required* only between tokens that would otherwise be confused as a single token. All whitespace is equivalent for this purpose. Newlines are distinguished from spaces and tabs only within quoted strings, formats, and certain line-oriented forms of quoting. Specifically, newlines do not terminate statements as they do in certain other languages (such as FORTRAN or Python). Statements in Perl are terminated with semicolons, just as they are in C and its various derivatives.

Unicode whitespace characters are allowed in a Unicode Perl program, but you need to be careful. If you use the special Unicode paragraph and line separators, be aware that Perl may count line numbers differently than your text editor does, so error messages may be more difficult to interpret. It's best to stick with good old-fashioned newlines.

Tokens are recognized greedily; if at a particular point the Perl parser has a choice between recognizing a short token or a long token, it will choose the long one. If you meant it to be two tokens, just insert some whitespace between the tokens. (We tend to put extra space around most operators anyway, just for readability.)

Comments are indicated by the # character and extend from there through the end of the line. A comment counts as whitespace for separating tokens. The Perl language attaches no special meaning to anything you might put into a comment.†

---

* The astute reader will point out that literal strings may contain whitespace characters. But strings can get away with it only because they have quotes on both ends to keep the spaces from leaking out.

† Actually, that's a small fib. The Perl parser does look for command-line switches on an initial #! line (see Chapter 19, *The Command-Line Interface*). It can also interpret the line number directives that various preprocessors produce (see the section "Generating Perl in Other Languages" in Chapter 24, *Common Practices*).

One other oddity is that if a line begins with = anywhere a statement would be legal, Perl ignores everything from that line down to the next line that begins with =cut. The ignored text is assumed to be *pod*, or "plain old documentation". The Perl distribution has programs that will extract pod commentary from Perl modules and turn it into flat text, manpages, LATEX, HTML, or (someday soon) XML documents. In a complementary fashion, the Perl parser extracts the Perl code from Perl modules and ignores the pod. So you may consider this an alternate, multiline form of commenting. You may also consider it completely nuts, but Perl modules documented this way never lose track of their documentation. See Chapter 26, *Plain Old Documentation*, for details on pod, including a description of how to effect multiline comments in Perl.

But don't look down on the normal comment character. There's something comforting about the visual effect of a nice row of # characters down the left side of a multiline comment. It immediately tells your eyes: "This is not code." You'll note that even in languages with a multiline commenting mechanisms like C, people often put a row of * characters down the left side of their comments anyway. Appearances are often more important than they appear.

In Perl, just as in chemistry and in language, you can build larger and larger structures out of the smaller ones. We already mentioned the *statement*; it's just a sequence of tokens that make up a command, that is, a sentence in the imperative mood. You can combine a sequence of statements into a *block* that is delimited by braces (also known affectionately as "curlies" by people who confuse braces with suspenders.) Blocks can in turn be combined into larger blocks. Some blocks function as *subroutines*, which can be combined into *modules*, which can be combined into *programs*. But we're getting ahead of ourselves—those are subjects for coming chapters. Let's build some more tokens out of characters.

Built-in Data Types

Before we start talking about various kinds of tokens you can build from characters, we need a few more abstractions. To be specific, we need three data types.

Computer languages vary in how many and what kinds of data types they provide. Unlike some commonly used languages that provide many confusing types for similar kinds of values, Perl provides just a few built-in data types. Consider C, in which you might run into char, short, int, long, long long, bool, wchar_t, size_t, off_t, regex_t, uid_t, u_longlong_t, pthread_key_t, fp_exception_field_type, and so on. That's just some of the integer types! Then there are floating-point numbers, and pointers, and strings.

All these complicated types correspond to just one type in Perl: the scalar. (Usually Perl's simple data types are all you need, but if not, you're free to define fancy dynamic types using Perl's object-oriented features—see Chapter 12, *Objects.*) Perl's three basic data types are: *scalars*, *arrays* of scalars, and *hashes* of scalars (also known as *associative arrays*). Some people may prefer to call these *data structures* rather than types. That's okay.

Scalars are the fundamental type from which more complicated structures are built. A scalar stores a single, simple value—typically a string or a number. Elements of this simple type may be combined into either of the two aggregate types. An *array* is an ordered list of scalars that you access with an integer subscript (or index). All indexing in Perl starts at 0. Unlike many programming languages, however, Perl treats negative subscripts as valid: instead of counting from the beginning, negative subscripts count back from the end of whatever it is you're indexing into. (This applies to various substring and sublist operations as well as to regular subscripting.) A *hash*, on the other hand, is an unordered set of *key/value* pairs that you access using strings (the *keys*) as subscripts to look up the scalars (the *values*) corresponding to a given key. Variables are always one of these three types. (Other than variables, Perl also has other abstractions that you can think of as data types, such as filehandles, directory handles, formats, subroutines, symbol tables, and symbol table entries.)

Abstractions are wonderful, and we'll collect more of them as we go along, but they're also useless in a way. You can't do anything with an abstraction directly. That's why computer languages have syntax. We need to introduce you to the various kinds of syntactic terms you can use to pull your abstract data into expressions. We like to use the technical term *term* when we want to talk in terms of these syntactic units. (Hmm, this could get terminally confusing. Just remember how your math teacher used to talk about the *terms* of an equation, and you won't go terribly wrong.)

Just like the terms in a math equation, the purpose of most terms in Perl is to produce values for operators like addition and multiplication to operate on. Unlike in a math equation, however, Perl has to *do* something with the values it calculates, not just think with a pencil in its hand about whether the two sides of the equation are equal. One of the most common things to do with a value is to store it somewhere:

```
$x = $y;
```

That's an example of the *assignment* operator (not the numeric equality operator, which is spelled == in Perl). The assignment gets the value from $y and puts it into $x. Notice that we aren't using the term $x for its value; we're using it for its location. (The old value of $x gets clobbered by the assignment.) We say that $x is an *lvalue*, meaning it's the sort of storage location we can use on the left side of an assignment. We say that $y is an *rvalue* because it's used on the right side.

There's also a third kind of value, called a *temporary* value, that you need to understand if you want to know what Perl is really doing with your lvalues and rvalues. If we do some actual math and say:

```
$x = $y + 1;
```

Perl takes the rvalue $y and adds the rvalue 1 to it, which produces a temporary value that is eventually assigned to the lvalue $x. It may help you to visualize what is going on if we tell you that Perl stores these temporary values in an internal structure called a *stack*.* The terms of an expression (the ones we're talking about in this chapter) tend to push values onto the stack, while the operators of the expression (which we'll discuss in the next chapter) tend to pop them back off the stack, perhaps leaving another temporary result on the stack for the next operator to work with. The pushes and pops all balance out—by the time the expression is done, the stack is entirely empty (or as empty as it was when we started). More about temporary values later.

Some terms can only be rvalues, such as the 1 above, while others can serve as either lvalues or rvalues. In particular, as the assignments above illustrate, a variable may function as either. And that's what our next section is about.

Variables

Not surprisingly, there are three variable types corresponding to the three abstract data types we mentioned earlier. Each of these is prefixed by what we call a *funny character*.† Scalar variables are always named with an initial $, even when referring to a scalar that is part of an array or hash. It works a bit like the English word "the". Thus, we have:

Construct	Meaning
$days	Simple scalar value $days
$days[28]	29th element of array @days
$days{'Feb'}	"Feb" value from hash %days

Note that we can use the same name for $days, @days, and %days without Perl getting confused.

---

* A stack works just like one of those spring-loaded plate dispensers you see in a buffet restaurant—you can *push* plates onto the top of the stack, or you can *pop* them off again (to use the Comp. Sci. vernacular).

† That's another technical term in computer science. (And if it wasn't before, it is now.)

There are other, fancier scalar terms, useful in specialized situations that we won't go into yet. They look like this:

Construct	Meaning
`${days}`	Same as `$days` but unambiguous before alphanumerics
`$Dog::days`	Different `$days` variable, in the `Dog` package
`$#days`	Last index of array `@days`
`$days->[28]`	29th element of array pointed to by reference `$days`
`$days[0][2]`	Multidimensional array
`$days{2000}{'Feb'}`	Multidimensional hash
`$days{2000,'Feb'}`	Multidimensional hash emulation

Entire arrays (or *slices* of arrays and hashes) are named with the funny character `@`, which works much like the words "these" or "those":

Construct	Meaning
`@days`	Array containing (`$days[0]`, `$days[1]`,... `$days[n]`)
`@days[3, 4, 5]`	Array slice containing (`$days[3]`, `$days[4]`, `$days[5]`)
`@days[3..5]`	Array slice containing (`$days[3]`, `$days[4]`, `$days[5]`)
`@days{'Jan','Feb'}`	Hash slice containing (`$days{'Jan'}`,`$days{'Feb'}`)

Entire hashes are named by `%`:

Construct	Meaning
`%days`	(`Jan => 31, Feb => $leap ? 29 : 28, ...`)

Any of these constructs may also serve as an lvalue, specifying a location you could assign a value to. With arrays, hashes, and slices of arrays or hashes, the lvalue provides multiple locations to assign to, so you can assign multiple values to them all at once:

```
@days = 1 .. 7;
```

Names

We've talked about storing values in variables, but the variables themselves (their names and their associated definitions) also need to be stored somewhere. In the abstract, these places are known as *namespaces*. Perl provides two kinds of namespaces, which are often called *symbol tables* and *lexical scopes.*[*] You may have an arbitrary number of symbol tables or lexical scopes, but every name you

---

[*] We also call them *packages* and *pads* when we're talking about Perl's specific implementations, but those longer monikers are the generic industry terms, so we're pretty much stuck with them. Sorry.

define gets stored in one or the other. We'll explain both kinds of namespaces as we go along. For now we'll just say that symbol tables are global hashes that happen to contain symbol table entries for global variables (including the hashes for other symbol tables). In contrast, lexical scopes are *unnamed* scratchpads that don't live in any symbol table, but are attached to a block of code in your program. They contain variables that can only be seen by the block. (That's what we mean by a *scope*). The *lexical* part just means, "having to do with text", which is not at all what a lexicographer would mean by it. Don't blame us.)

Within any given namespace (whether global or lexical), every variable type has its own subnamespace, determined by the funny character. You can, without fear of conflict, use the same name for a scalar variable, an array, or a hash (or, for that matter, a filehandle, a subroutine name, a label, or your pet llama). This means that $foo and @foo are two different variables. Together with the previous rules, it also means that $foo[1] is an element of @foo totally unrelated to the scalar variable $foo. This may seem a bit weird, but that's okay, because it *is* weird.

Subroutines may be named with an initial &, although the funny character is optional when calling the subroutine. Subroutines aren't generally considered lvalues, though recent versions of Perl allow you to return an lvalue from a subroutine and assign to that, so it can look as though you're assigning to the subroutine.

Sometimes you just want a name for "everything named foo" regardless of its funny character. So symbol table entries can be named with an initial *, where the asterisk stands for all the other funny characters. These are called *typeglobs*, and they have several uses. They can also function as lvalues. Assignment to *typeglobs* is how Perl implements importing of symbols from one symbol table to another. More about that later too.

Like most computer languages, Perl has a list of reserved words that it recognizes as special keywords. However, because variable names always start with a funny character, reserved words don't actually conflict with variable names. Certain other kinds of names don't have funny characters, though, such as labels and filehandles. With these, you do have to worry (a little) about conflicting with reserved words. Since most reserved words are entirely lowercase, we recommend that you pick label and filehandle names that contain uppercase letters. For example, if you say open(LOG, logfile) rather than the regrettable open(log, "logfile"), you won't confuse Perl into thinking you're talking about the built-in log operator (which does logarithms, not tree trunks). Using uppercase filehandles also improves readability* and protects you from conflict with reserved words we might add in the future. For similar reasons, user-defined modules are typically named

---

* One of the design principles of Perl is that different things should look different. Contrast this with
  languages that try to force different things to look the same, to the detriment of readability.

with initial capitals so that they'll look different from the built-in modules known as pragmas, which are named in all lowercase. And when we get to object-oriented programming, you'll notice that class names are usually capitalized for the same reason.

As you might deduce from the preceding paragraph, case is significant in identifiers—FOO, Foo, and foo are all different names in Perl. Identifiers start with a letter or underscore and may be of any length (for values of "any" ranging between 1 and 251, inclusive) and may contain letters, digits, and underscores. This includes Unicode letters and digits. Unicode ideographs also count as letters, but we don't recommend you use them unless you can read them. See Chapter 15.

Names that follow funny characters don't have to be identifiers, strictly speaking. They can start with a digit, in which case they may only contain more digits, as in $123. Names that start with anything other than a letter, digit, or underscore are (usually) limited to that one character (like $? or $$), and generally have a predefined significance to Perl. For example, just as in the Bourne shell, $$ is the current process ID and $? the exit status of your last child process.

As of version 5.6, Perl also has an extensible syntax for internal variables names. Any variable of the form ${^NAME} is a special variable reserved for use by Perl. All these non-identifier names are forced to be in the main symbol table. See Chapter 28, *Special Names*, for some examples.

It's tempting to think of identifiers and names as the same thing, but when we say *name*, we usually mean a fully qualified name, that is, a name that says which symbol table it lives in. Such names may be formed of a sequence of identifiers separated by the :: token:

```
$Santa::Helper::Reindeer::Rudolph::nose
```

That works just like the directories and filenames in a pathname:

```
/Santa/Helper/Reindeer/Rudolph/nose
```

In the Perl version of that notion, all the leading identifiers are the names of nested symbol tables, and the last identifier is the name of the variable within the most deeply nested symbol table. For instance, in the variable above, the symbol table is named Santa::Helper::Reindeer::Rudolph::, and the actual variable within that symbol table is $nose. (The value of that variable is, of course, "red".)

A symbol table in Perl is also known as a *package*, so these are often called package variables. Package variables are nominally private to the package in which they exist, but are global in the sense that the packages themselves are global. That is, anyone can name the package to get at the variable; it's just hard to do this by accident. For instance, any program that mentions $Dog::bert is asking for the $bert variable within the Dog:: package. That is an entirely separate variable from $Cat::bert. See Chapter 10, *Packages*.

Variables attached to a lexical scope are not in any package, so lexically scoped variable names may not contain the :: sequence. (Lexically scoped variables are declared with a my declaration.)

Name Lookups

So the question is, what's in a name? How does Perl figure out what you mean if you just say $bert? Glad you asked. Here are the rules the Perl parser uses while trying to understand an unqualified name in context:

1. First, Perl looks earlier in the immediately enclosing block to see whether the variable is declared in that same block with a my (or our) declaration (see those entries in Chapter 29, as well as the section "Scoped Declarations" in Chapter 4, *Statements and Declarations*). If there is a my declaration, the variable is lexically scoped and doesn't exist in any package—it exists only in that lexical scope (that is, in the block's scratchpad). Because lexical scopes are unnamed, nobody outside that chunk of program can even name your variable.*

2. If that doesn't work, Perl looks for the block enclosing that block and tries again for a lexically scoped variable in the larger block. Again, if Perl finds one, the variable belongs only to the lexical scope from the point of declaration through the end of the block in which it is declared—including any nested blocks, like the one we just came from in step 1. If Perl doesn't find a declaration, it repeats step 2 until it runs out of enclosing blocks.

3. When Perl runs out of enclosing blocks, it examines the whole compilation unit for declarations as if it were a block. (A *compilation unit* is just the entire current file, or the string currently being compiled by an eval *STRING* operator.) If the compilation unit is a file, that's the largest possible lexical scope, and Perl will look no further for lexically scoped variables, so we go to step 4. If the compilation unit is a string, however, things get fancier. A string compiled as Perl code at run time pretends that it's a block within the lexical scope from which the eval *STRING* is running, even though the actual boundaries of the lexical scope are the limits of the string containing the code rather

---

* If you use an our declaration instead of a my declaration, this only declares a lexically scoped *alias* (a nickname) for a package variable, rather than declaring a true lexically scoped variable the way my does. Outside code can still get at the real variable through its package, but in all other respects an our declaration behaves like a my declaration. This is handy when you're trying to limit your own use of globals with the use strict pragma (see the strict pragma in Chapter 31). But you should always prefer my if you don't need a global.

than any real braces. So if Perl doesn't find the variable in the lexical scope of the string, we pretend that the eval *STRING* is a block and go back to step 2, only this time starting with the lexical scope of the eval *STRING* operator instead of the lexical scope inside its string.

4. If we get here, it means Perl didn't find any declaration (either my or our) for your variable. Perl now gives up on lexically scoped variables and assumes that your variable is a package variable. If the strict pragma is in effect, you will now get an error, unless the variable is one of Perl's predefined variables or has been imported into the current package. This is because that pragma disallows the use of unqualified global names. However, we aren't done with lexical scopes just yet. Perl does the same search of lexical scopes as it did in steps 1 through 3, only this time it searches for package declarations instead of variable declarations. If it finds such a package declaration, it knows that the current code is being compiled for the package in question and prepends the declared package name to the front of the variable.

5. If there is no package declaration in any surrounding lexical scope, Perl looks for the variable name in the unnamed top-level package, which happens to have the name main when it isn't going around without a name tag. So in the absence of any declarations to the contrary, $bert means the same as $::bert, which means the same as $main::bert. (But because main is just another package in the top-level unnamed package, it's also $::main::bert, and $main::main::bert, $::main::main::bert and so on. This could be construed as a useless fact. But see "Symbol Tables" in Chapter 10.)

There are several implications to these search rules that might not be obvious, so we'll make them explicit.

• Because the file is the largest possible lexical scope, a lexically scoped variable can never be visible outside the file in which it's declared. File scopes do not nest.

• Any particular bit of Perl is compiled in at least one lexical scope and exactly one package scope. The mandatory lexical scope is, of course, the file itself. Additional lexical scopes are provided by each enclosing block. All Perl code is also compiled in the scope of exactly one package, and although the declaration of which package you're in is lexically scoped, packages themselves are not lexically constrained. That is, they're global.

• An unqualified variable name may therefore be searched for in many lexical scopes, but only one package scope, whichever one is currently in effect (which is lexically determined).

- A variable name may only attach to one scope. Although at least two different scopes (lexical and package) are active everywhere in your program, a variable can only exist in one of those scopes.

- An unqualified variable name can therefore resolve to only a single storage location, either in the first enclosing lexical scope in which it is declared, or else in the current package—but not both. The search stops as soon as that storage location is resolved, and any storage location that it would have found had the search continued is effectively hidden.

- The location of the typical variable name can be completely determined at compile time.

Now that you know all about how the Perl compiler deals with names, you sometimes have the problem that you don't *know* the name of what you want at compile time. Sometimes you want to name something indirectly; we call this the problem of *indirection*. So Perl provides a mechanism: you can always replace an alphanumeric variable name with a block containing an expression that returns a *reference* to the real data. For instance, instead of saying:

```
$bert
```

you might say:

```
${ some_expression() }
```

and if the `some_expression()` function returns a reference to variable `$bert` (or even the string, `"bert"`), it will work just as if you'd said `$bert` in the first place. On the other hand, if the function returns a reference to `$ernie`, you'll get his variable instead. The syntax shown is the most general (and least legible) form of indirection, but we'll cover several convenient variations in Chapter 8, *References*.

Scalar Values

Whether it's named directly or indirectly, and whether it's in a variable, or an array element, or is just a temporary value, a scalar always contains a single value. This value may be a number, a string, or a reference to another piece of data. Or, there might even be no value at all, in which case the scalar is said to be *undefined*. Although we might speak of a scalar as "containing" a number or a string, scalars are typeless: you are not required to declare your scalars to be of type integer or floating-point or string or whatever.*

---

* Future versions of Perl will allow you to insert `int`, `num`, and `str` type declarations, not to enforce strong typing, but only to give the optimizer hints about things that it might not figure out for itself. Generally, you'd only consider doing this in tight code that must run very fast, so we're not going to tell you how to do it yet. Optional types are also used by the pseudohash mechanism, in which case they can function as types do in a more strongly typed language. See Chapter 8 for more.

Perl stores strings as sequences of characters, with no arbitrary constraints on length or content. In human terms, you don't have to decide in advance how long your strings are going to get, and you can include any characters including null bytes within your string. Perl stores numbers as signed integers if possible, or as double-precision floating-point values in the machine's native format otherwise. Floating-point values are not infinitely precise. This is important to remember because comparisons like (10/3 == 1/3*10) tend to fail mysteriously.

Perl converts between the various subtypes as needed, so you can treat a number as a string or a string as a number, and Perl will do the Right Thing. To convert from string to number, Perl internally uses something like the C library's *atof*(3) function. To convert from number to string, it does the equivalent of an *sprintf*(3) with a format of "%.14g" on most machines. Improper conversions of a non-numeric string like foo to a number count as numeric 0; these trigger warnings if you have them enabled, but are silent otherwise. See Chapter 5, *Pattern Matching*, for examples of detecting what sort of data a string holds.

Although strings and numbers are interchangeable for nearly all intents, references are a bit different. They're strongly typed, uncastable pointers with built-in reference-counting and destructor invocation. That is, you can use them to create complex data types, including user-defined objects. But they're still scalars, for all that, because no matter how complicated a data structure gets, you often want to treat it as a single value.

By *uncastable*, we mean that you can't, for instance, convert a reference to an array into a reference to a hash. References are not castable to other pointer types. However, if you use a reference as a number or a string, you will get a numeric or string value, which is guaranteed to retain the uniqueness of the reference even though the "referenceness" of the value is lost when the value is copied from the real reference. You can compare such values or extract their type. But you can't do much else with the values, since there's no way to convert numbers or strings back into references. Usually, this is not a problem, because Perl doesn't force you to do pointer arithmetic—or even allow it. See Chapter 8 for more on references.

Numeric Literals

Numeric literals are specified in any of several customary* floating-point or integer formats:

```
$x = 12345;            # integer
$x = 12345.67;         # floating point
$x = 6.02e23;          # scientific notation
$x = 4_294_967_296;    # underline for legibility
```

---

* Customary in Unix culture, that is. If you're from a different culture, welcome to ours!

```
$x = 0377;              # octal
$x = 0xffff;            # hexadecimal
$x = 0b1100_0000;       # binary
```

Because Perl uses the comma as a list separator, you cannot use it to separate the thousands in a large number. Perl does allow you to use an underscore character instead. The underscore only works within literal numbers specified in your program, not for strings functioning as numbers or data read from somewhere else. Similarly, the leading 0x for hexadecimal, 0b for binary, and 0 for octal work only for literals. The automatic conversion of a string to a number does not recognize these prefixes—you must do an explicit conversion* with the oct function—which works for hex and binary numbers, too, as it happens, provided you supply the 0x or 0b on the front.

String Literals

String literals are usually surrounded by either single or double quotes. They work much like Unix shell quotes: double-quoted string literals are subject to backslash and variable interpolation, but single-quoted strings are not (except for \' and \\, so that you can embed single quotes and backslashes into single-quoted strings). If you want to embed any other backslash sequences such as \n (newline), you must use the double-quoted form. (Backslash sequences are also known as *escape sequences*, because you "escape" the normal interpretation of characters temporarily.)

A single-quoted string must be separated from a preceding word by a space because a single quote is a valid—though archaic—character in an identifier. Its use has been replaced by the more visually distinct :: sequence. That means that $main'var and $main::var are the same thing, but the second is generally considered easier to read for people and programs.

Double-quoted strings are subject to various forms of character interpolation, many of which will be familiar to programmers of other languages. These are listed in Table 2-1.

---

* Sometimes people think Perl should convert all incoming data for them. But there are far too many decimal numbers with leading zeros in the world to make Perl do this automatically. For example, the Zip Code for the O'Reilly & Associates office in Cambridge, MA, is 02140. The postmaster would get confused if your mailing label program turned 02140 into 1120 decimal.

Table 2-1. Backslashed Character Escapes

Code	Meaning
\n	Newline (usually LF)
\r	Carriage return (usually CR)
\t	Horizontal tab
\f	Form feed
\b	Backspace
\a	Alert (bell)
\e	ESC character
\033	ESC in octal
\x7f	DEL in hexadecimal
\cC	Control-C
\x{263a}	Unicode (smiley)
\N{*NAME*}	Named character

The \N{*NAME*} notation is usable only in conjunction with the use charnames pragma described in Chapter 31. This allows you to specify character names symbolically, as in \N{GREEK SMALL LETTER SIGMA}, \N{greek:Sigma}, or \N{sigma}—depending on how you call the pragma. See also Chapter 15.

There are also escape sequences to modify the case or "meta-ness" of subsequent characters. See Table 2-2.

Table 2-2. Translation Escapes

Code	Meaning
\u	Force next character to uppercase ("titlecase" in Unicode).
\l	Force next character to lowercase.
\U	Force all following characters to uppercase.
\L	Force all following characters to lowercase.
\Q	Backslash all following nonalphanumeric characters.
\E	End \U, \L, or \Q.

You may also embed newlines directly in your strings; that is, they can begin and end on different lines. This is often useful, but it also means that if you forget a trailing quote, the error will not be reported until Perl finds another line containing the quote character, which may be much further on in the script. Fortunately, this usually causes an immediate syntax error on the same line, and Perl is then smart enough to warn you that you might have a runaway string where it thought the string started.

Besides the backslash escapes listed above, double-quoted strings are subject to *variable interpolation* of scalar and list values. This means that you can insert the values of certain variables directly into a string literal. It's really just a handy form of string concatenation.* Variable interpolation may be done for scalar variables, entire arrays (but not hashes), single elements from an array or hash, or slices (multiple subscripts) of an array or hash. Nothing else interpolates. In other words, you may only interpolate expressions that begin with $ or @, because those are the two characters (along with backslash) that the string parser looks for. Inside strings, a literal @ that is not part of an array or slice identifier but is followed by an alphanumeric character must be escaped with a backslash (\@), or else a compilation error will result. Although a complete hash specified with a % may not be interpolated into the string, single hash values or hash slices are okay, because they begin with $ and @ respectively.

The following code segment prints out "The price is $100.":

```
$Price = '$100';                # not interpolated
print "The price is $Price.\n";  # interpolated
```

As in some shells, you can put braces around the identifier to distinguish it from following alphanumerics: `"How ${verb}able!"`. An identifier within such braces is forced to be a string, as is any single identifier within a hash subscript. For example:

```
$days{'Feb'}
```

can be written as:

```
$days{Feb}
```

and the quotes will be assumed. Anything more complicated in the subscript is interpreted as an expression, and then you'd have to put in the quotes:

```
$days{'February 29th'}    # Ok.
$days{"February 29th"}    # Also ok. "" doesn't have to interpolate.
$days{ February 29th }    # WRONG, produces parse error.
```

In particular, you should always use quotes in slices such as:

```
@days{'Jan','Feb'}    # Ok.
@days{"Jan","Feb"}    # Also ok.
@days{ Jan,  Feb }    # Kinda wrong (breaks under use strict)
```

Apart from the subscripts of interpolated array and hash variables, there are no multiple levels of interpolation. Contrary to the expectations of shell programmers,

---

* With warnings enabled, Perl may report undefined values interpolated into strings as using the concatenation or join operations, even though you don't actually use those operators there. The compiler created them for you anyway.

backticks do not interpolate within double quotes, nor do single quotes impede evaluation of variables when used within double quotes. Interpolation is extremely powerful but strictly controlled in Perl. It happens only inside double quotes, and in certain other "double-quotish" operations that we'll describe in the next section:

```
print "\n";                 # Ok, print a newline.
print \n ;                  # WRONG, no interpolative context.
```

Pick Your Own Quotes

Although we usually think of quotes as literal values, in Perl they function more like operators, providing various kinds of interpolating and pattern-matching capabilities. Perl provides the customary quote characters for these behaviors, but also provides a more general way for you to choose your quote character for any of them. In Table 2-3, any nonalphanumeric, nonwhitespace delimiter may be used in place of /. (The newline and space characters are no longer allowed as delimiters, although ancient versions of Perl once allowed this.)

Table 2-3. Quote Constructs

Customary	Generic	Meaning	Interpolates
' '	q//	Literal string	No
" "	qq//	Literal string	Yes
` `	qx//	Command execution	Yes
()	qw//	Word list	No
//	m//	Pattern match	Yes
s///	s///	Pattern substitution	Yes
y///	tr///	Character translation	No
" "	qr//	Regular expression	Yes

Some of these are simply forms of "syntactic sugar" to let you avoid putting too many backslashes into quoted strings, particularly into pattern matches where your regular slashes and backslashes tend to get all tangled.

If you choose single quotes for delimiters, no variable interpolation is done even on those forms that ordinarily interpolate. If the opening delimiter is an opening parenthesis, bracket, brace, or angle bracket, the closing delimiter will be the corresponding closing character. (Embedded occurrences of the delimiters must match in pairs.) Examples:

```
$single = q!I said, "You said, 'She said it.'"!;

$double = qq(Can't we get some "good" $variable?);
```

```
$chunk_of_code = q {
    if ($condition) {
        print "Gotcha!";
    }
};
```

The last example demonstrates that you can use whitespace between the quote specifier and its initial bracketing character. For two-element constructs like s/// and tr///, if the first pair of quotes is a bracketing pair, the second part gets its own starting quote character. In fact, the second pair needn't be the same as the first pair. So you can write things like s<foo>(bar) or tr(a-f)[A-F]. Because whitespace is also allowed between the two inner quote characters, you could even write that last one as:

```
tr (a-f)
   [A-F];
```

Whitespace is not allowed, however, when # is being used as the quoting character. q#foo# is parsed as the string 'foo', while q #foo# is parsed as the quote operator q followed by a comment. Its delimiter will be taken from the next line. Comments can also be placed in the middle of two-element constructs, which allows you to write:

```
s {foo}    # Replace foo
  {bar};   #    with bar.

tr [a-f]   # Transliterate lowercase hex
   [A-F];  #             to uppercase hex
```

Or Leave the Quotes Out Entirely

A name that has no other interpretation in the grammar will be treated as if it were a quoted string. These are known as *barewords*.* As with filehandles and labels, a bareword that consists entirely of lowercase letters risks conflict with future reserved words. If you have warnings enabled, Perl will warn you about barewords. For example:

```
@days = (Mon,Tue,Wed,Thu,Fri);
print STDOUT hello, ' ', world, "\n";
```

sets the array @days to the short form of the weekdays and prints "hello world" followed by a newline on STDOUT. If you leave the filehandle out, Perl tries to interpret hello as a filehandle, resulting in a syntax error. Because this is so error-prone, some people may wish to avoid barewords entirely. The quoting operators

---

* Variable names, filehandles, labels, and the like are not considered barewords because they have a meaning forced by a preceding token or a following token (or both). Predeclared names such as subroutines aren't barewords either. It's only a bareword when the parser has no clue.

listed earlier provide many convenient forms, including the `qw//` "quote words" construct which nicely quotes a list of space-separated words:

```
@days = qw(Mon Tue Wed Thu Fri);
print STDOUT "hello world\n";
```

You can go as far as to outlaw barewords entirely. If you say:

```
use strict 'subs';
```

then any bareword will produce a compile-time error. The restriction lasts through the end of the enclosing scope. An inner scope may countermand this by saying:

```
no strict 'subs';
```

Note that the bare identifiers in constructs like:

```
"${verb}able"
$days{Feb}
```

are not considered barewords since they're allowed by explicit rule rather than by having "no other interpretation in the grammar".

An unquoted name with a trailing double colon, such as `main::` or `Dog::`, is always treated as the package name. Perl turns the would-be bareword `Camel::` into the string "`Camel`" at compile time, so this usage is not subject to rebuke by `use strict`.

Interpolating Array Values

Array variables are interpolated into double-quoted strings by joining all elements of the array with the separator specified in the `$"` variable* (which contains a space by default). The following are equivalent:

```
$temp = join( $", @ARGV );
print $temp;

print "@ARGV";
```

Within search patterns, which also undergo double-quotish interpolation, there is an unfortunate ambiguity: is `/$foo[bar]/` to be interpreted as `/${foo}[bar]/` (where `[bar]` is a character class for the regular expression) or as `/${foo[bar]}/` (where `[bar]` is the subscript to array `@foo`? If `@foo` doesn't otherwise exist, it's obviously a character class. If `@foo` exists, Perl takes a good guess about `[bar]`, and is almost always right.† If it does guess wrong, or if you're just plain paranoid,

---

* `$LIST_SEPARATOR` if you use the English module bundled with Perl.

† The guesser is too boring to describe in full, but basically takes a weighted average of all the things that look like character classes (a-z, \w, initial ^) versus things that look like expressions (variables or reserved words).

you can force the correct interpretation with braces as shown earlier. Even if you're merely prudent, it's probably not a bad idea.

"Here" Documents

A line-oriented form of quoting is based on the Unix shell's *here-document* syntax. It's line-oriented in the sense that the delimiters are lines rather than characters. The starting delimiter is the current line, and the terminating delimiter is a line consisting of the string you specify. Following a <<, you specify the string to terminate the quoted material, and all lines following the current line down to but not including the terminating line are part of the string. The terminating string may be either an identifier (a word) or some quoted text. If quoted, the type of quote determines the treatment of the text, just as it does in regular quoting. An unquoted identifier works as though it were in double quotes. A backslashed identifier works as though it were in single quotes (for compatibility with shell syntax). There must be no space between the << and an unquoted identifier, although whitespace is permitted if you specify a quoted string instead of the bare identifier. (If you insert a space, it will be treated as a null identifier, which is valid but deprecated, and matches the first blank line—see the first Hurrah! example below.) The terminating string must appear by itself, unquoted and with no extra whitespace on either side, on the terminating line.

```
print <<EOF;    # same as earlier example
The price is $Price.
EOF

print <<"EOF";  # same as above, with explicit quotes
The price is $Price.
EOF

print <<'EOF';    # single-quoted quote
All things (e.g. a camel's journey through
A needle's eye) are possible, it's true.
But picture how the camel feels, squeezed out
In one long bloody thread, from tail to snout.
                        -- C.S. Lewis
EOF

print << x 10;    # print next line 10 times
The camels are coming!  Hurrah!  Hurrah!

print <<"" x 10;  # the preferred way to write that
The camels are coming!  Hurrah!  Hurrah!

print <<`EOC`;    # execute commands
echo hi there
echo lo there
EOC
```

```
print <<"dromedary", <<"camelid";    # you can stack them
I said bactrian.
dromedary
She said llama.
camelid

funkshun(<<"THIS", 23, <<'THAT');    # doesn't matter if they're in parens
Here's a line
or two.
THIS
And here's another.
THAT
```

Just don't forget that you have to put a semicolon on the end to finish the statement, because Perl doesn't know you're not going to try to do this:

```
print <<'odd'
2345
odd
    + 10000;    # prints 12345
```

If you want your here docs to be indented with the rest of the code, you'll need to remove leading whitespace from each line manually:

```
($quote = <<'QUOTE') =~ s/^\s+//gm;
    The Road goes ever on and on,
    down from the door where it began.
QUOTE
```

You could even populate an array with the lines of a here document as follows:

```
@sauces = <<End_Lines =~ m/(\S.*\S)/g;
    normal tomato
    spicy tomato
    green chile
    pesto
    white wine
End_Lines
```

V-String Literals

A literal that begins with a v and is followed by one or more dot-separated integers is treated as a string literal composed of characters with the specified ordinal values:

```
$crlf = v13.10;            # ASCII carriage return, line feed
```

These are called *v-strings*, short for "vector strings" or "version strings" or anything else you can think of that starts with "v" and deals with lists of integers. They provide an alternate and more legible way to construct strings when you want to specify the numeric values of each character. Thus, v1.20.300.4000 is a more winsome way to produce the same string value as any of:

```
"\x{1}\x{14}\x{12c}\x{fa0}"
pack("U*", 1, 20, 300, 4000)
chr(1) . chr(20) . chr(300) . chr(4000)
```

If such a literal has two or more dots (three or more integers), the leading v may be omitted.

```
print v9786;                # prints UTF-8 encoded SMILEY, "\x{263a}"
print v102.111.111;         # prints "foo"
print 102.111.111;          # same thing

use 5.6.0;                  # require a particular Perl version (or later)

$ipaddr = 204.148.40.9;     # the IPv4 address of oreilly.com
```

V-strings are useful for representing IP address and version numbers. In particular, since characters can have an ordinal value larger than 255 these days, v-strings provide a way to represent version numbers of any size that can be correctly compared with a simple string comparison.

Version numbers and IP addresses stored in v-strings are not human readable, since the individual integers are stored as arbitrary characters. To produce something legible, use the v flag in a printf mask, like "%vd", as described under sprintf in Chapter 29. For more on Unicode strings, see Chapter 15 and the use bytes pragma in Chapter 31; for comparing version strings using string comparison operators, see $^V in Chapter 28; and for representing IPv4 addresses, see gethostbyaddr in Chapter 29.

Other Literal Tokens

You should consider any identifier that both begins and ends with a double underscore to be reserved for special syntactic use by Perl. Two such special literals are __LINE__ and __FILE__, which represent the current line number and filename at that point in your program. They may only be used as separate tokens; they will not be interpolated into strings. Likewise, __PACKAGE__ is the name of the package the current code is being compiled into. If there is no current package (due to an empty package; directive), __PACKAGE__ is the undefined value. The token __END__ (or alternatively, a Control-D or Control-Z character) may be used to indicate the logical end of the script before the real end-of-file. Any following text is ignored, but may be read via the DATA filehandle.

The __DATA__ token functions similarly to the __END__ token, but opens the DATA filehandle within the current package's namespace, so that files you require can each have their own DATA filehandles open simultaneously. For more information, see DATA in Chapter 28.

Context

Until now we've seen several terms that can produce scalar values. Before we can discuss terms further, though, we must come to terms with the notion of *context*.

Scalar and List Context

Every operation* that you invoke in a Perl script is evaluated in a specific context, and how that operation behaves may depend on the requirements of that context. There are two major contexts: scalar and list. For example, assignment to a scalar variable, or to a scalar element of an array or hash, evaluates the righthand side in a *scalar context*:

```
$x         = funkshun();  # scalar context
$x[1]      = funkshun();  # scalar context
$x{"ray"}  = funkshun();  # scalar context
```

But assignment to an array or a hash, or to a slice of either, evaluates the right-hand side in a *list context*, even if the slice picks out only one element:

```
@x         = funkshun();  # list context
@x[1]      = funkshun();  # list context
@x{"ray"}  = funkshun();  # list context
%x         = funkshun();  # list context
```

Assignment to a list of scalars also provides a list context to the righthand side, even if there's only one element in the list:

```
($x,$y,$z) = funkshun();  # list context
($x)       = funkshun();  # list context
```

These rules do not change at all when you declare a variable by modifying the term with my or our, so we have:

```
my $x      = funkshun();  # scalar context
my @x      = funkshun();  # list context
my %x      = funkshun();  # list context
my ($x)    = funkshun();  # list context
```

You will be miserable until you learn the difference between scalar and list context, because certain operators (such as our mythical funkshun() function above) know which context they are in, and return a list in contexts wanting a list but a scalar value in contexts wanting a scalar. (If this is true of an operation, it will be mentioned in the documentation for that operation.) In computer lingo, the operations are *overloaded* on their return type. But it's a very simple kind of

---

* Here we use the term "operation" loosely to mean either an operator or a term. The two concepts fuzz into each other when you start talking about functions that parse like terms but look like unary operators.

overloading, based only on the distinction between singular and plural values, and nothing else.

If some operators respond to context, then obviously something around them has to supply the context. We've shown that assignment can supply a context to its right operand, but that's not terribly surprising, since all operators supply some kind of context to each of their operands. What you really want to know is *which* operators supply *which* context to their operands. As it happens, you can easily tell which ones supply a list context because they all have *LIST* in their syntactic descriptions. Everything else supplies a scalar context. Generally, it's quite intuitive.* If necessary, you can force a scalar context onto an argument in the middle of a *LIST* by using the `scalar` pseudofunction. Perl provides no way to force a list context in a scalar context, because anywhere you would want a list context it's already provided by the *LIST* of some controlling function.

Scalar context can be further classified into string context, numeric context, and don't-care context. Unlike the scalar versus list distinction we just made, operations never know or care which scalar context they're in. They simply return whatever kind of scalar value they want to and let Perl translate numbers to strings in string context, and strings to numbers in numeric context. Some scalar contexts don't care whether a string or a number or a reference is returned, so no conversion will happen. This happens, for example, when you are assigning the value to another variable. The new variable just takes on the same subtype as the old value.

Boolean Context

Another special don't-care scalar context is called *Boolean context*. Boolean context is simply any place where an expression is being evaluated to see whether it's true or false. When we say "true" and "false" in this book, we mean the technical definition that Perl uses: a scalar value is true if it is not the null string `""` or the number 0 (or its string equivalent, `"0"`). A reference is always true because it represents an address which is never 0. An undefined value (often called undef) is always false because it looks like either `""` or 0, depending on whether you treat it as a string or a number. (List values have no Boolean value because list values are never produced in a scalar context!)

Because Boolean context is a don't-care context, it never causes any scalar conversions to happen, though of course the scalar context itself is imposed on any operand that cares. And for many operands that care, the scalar they produce in

---

* Note, however, that the list context of a *LIST* can propagate down through subroutine calls, so it's not always obvious from inspection whether a given statement is going to be evaluated in a scalar or list context. The program can find out its context within a subroutine by using the `wantarray` function.

scalar context represents a reasonable Boolean value. That is, many operators that would produce a list in list context can be used for a true/false test in Boolean context. For instance, in list context such as that provided by the unlink operator, an array name produces the list of its values:

```
unlink @files;     # Delete all files, ignoring errors.
```

But if you use the array in a conditional (that is, in a Boolean context), the array knows it's in a scalar context and returns the number of elements in the array, which conveniently is true as long as there are any elements left. So supposing you wanted to get warnings on each file that wasn't deleted properly, you might write a loop like this:

```
while (@files) {
    my $file = shift @files;
    unlink $file or warn "Can't delete $file: $!\n";
}
```

Here @files is evaluated in the Boolean context supplied by the while statement, so Perl evaluates the array itself to see whether it's a "true array" or a "false array". It's a true array as long as there are filenames in it, but it becomes a false array as soon as the last filename is shifted out. Note that what we earlier said still holds. Despite the fact that an array contains (and can produce) a list value, we are not evaluating a list value in scalar context. We are telling the array it's a scalar and asking what it thinks of itself.

Do not be tempted to use defined @files for this. It doesn't work because the defined function is asking whether a scalar is equal to undef, but an array is not a scalar. The simple Boolean test suffices.

Void Context

Another peculiar kind of scalar context is the *void context*. This context not only doesn't care what the return value's type is, it doesn't even *want* a return value. From the standpoint of how functions work, it's no different from an ordinary scalar context. But if you have warnings enabled, the Perl compiler will warn you if you use an expression with no side effects in a place that doesn't want a value, such as in a statement that doesn't return a value. For example, if you use a string as a statement:

```
"Camel Lot";
```

you may get a warning like this:

```
Useless use of a constant in void context in myprog line 123;
```

Interpolative Context

We mentioned earlier that double-quoted literal strings do backslash interpretation and variable interpolation, but that the interpolative context (often called "double-quote context" because nobody can pronounce "interpolative") applies to more than just double-quoted strings. Some other double-quotish constructs are the generalized backtick operator qx//, the pattern match operator m//, the substitution operator s///, and the quote regex operator, qr//. The substitution operator does interpolation on its left side before doing a pattern match, and then does interpolation on its right side each time the left side matches.

The interpolative context only happens inside quotes, or things that work like quotes, so perhaps it's not fair to call it a context in the same sense as scalar and list contexts. (Then again, maybe it is.)

List Values and Arrays

Now that we've talked about context, we can talk about list literals and how they behave in context. You've already seen some list literals. List literals are denoted by separating individual values by commas (and enclosing the list in parentheses where precedence requires it). Because it (almost) never hurts to use extra parentheses, the syntax diagram of a list value is usually indicated like this:

(*LIST*)

Earlier we said that *LIST* in a syntax description indicates something that supplies list context to its arguments, but a bare list literal itself is the one partial exception to that rule, in that it supplies a list context to its arguments only when the list as a whole is in list context. The value of a list literal in list context is just the values of the arguments in the order specified. As a fancy sort of term in an expression, a list literal merely pushes a series of temporary values onto Perl's stack, to be collected off the stack later by whatever operator wants the list.

In a scalar context, however, the list literal doesn't really behave like a *LIST*, in that it doesn't supply list context to its values. Instead, it merely evaluates each of its arguments in scalar context, and returns the value of the final element. That's because it's really just the C comma operator in disguise, which is a binary operator that always throws away the value on the left and returns the value on the right. In terms of what we discussed earlier, the left side of the comma operator really provides a void context. Because the comma operator is left associative, if you have a series of comma-separated values, you always end up with the last value because the final comma throws away whatever any previous commas produced. So, to contrast the two, the list assignment:

```
@stuff = ("one", "two", "three");
```

assigns the entire list value to array @stuff, but the scalar assignment:

```
$stuff = ("one", "two", "three");
```

assigns only the value "three" to variable $stuff. Like the @files array we mentioned earlier the comma operator knows whether it is in a scalar or list context, and chooses its behavior accordingly.

It bears repeating that a list value is different from an array. A real array variable also knows its context, and in a list context, it would return its internal list of values just like a list literal. But in a scalar context it returns only the length of the array. The following assigns to $stuff the value 3:

```
@stuff = ("one", "two", "three");
$stuff = @stuff;
```

If you expected it to get the value "three", you were probably making a false generalization by assuming that Perl uses the comma operator rule to throw away all but one of the temporary values that @stuff put on the stack. But that's not how it works. The @stuff array never put all its values on the stack. It never put any of its values on the stack, in fact. It only put one value, the length of the array, because it *knew* it was in scalar context. No term or operator in scalar context will ever put a list on the stack. Instead, it will put one scalar on the stack, whatever it feels like, which is unlikely to be the last value of the list it *would* have returned in list context, because the last value is not likely to be the most useful value in scalar context. Got that? (If not, you'd better reread this paragraph, because it's important.)

Now back to true *LIST*s, the ones that do list context. Until now we've pretended that list literals were just lists of literals. But just as a string literal might interpolate other substrings, a list literal can interpolate other sublists. Any expression that returns values may be used within a list. The values so used may be either scalar values or list values, but they all become part of the new list value because *LIST*s do automatic interpolation of sublists. That is, when a *LIST* is evaluated, each element of the list is evaluated in a list context, and the resulting list value is interpolated into *LIST* just as if each individual element were a member of *LIST*. Thus arrays lose their identity in a *LIST*.* The list:

```
(@stuff,@nonsense,funkshun())
```

contains the elements of @stuff, followed by the elements of @nonsense, followed by whatever values the subroutine &funkshun decides to return when called in list

---

* Some people seem to think this is a problem, but it's not. You can always interpolate a reference to an array if you do not want it to lose its identity. See Chapter 8.

context. Note that any or all of these might have interpolated a null (empty) list, in which case it's as if no array or function call had been interpolated at that point. The null list itself is represented by the literal (). As with a null array, which interpolates as a null list and is therefore effectively ignored, interpolating the null list into another list has no effect. Thus, ((), (), ()) is equivalent to ().

A corollary to this rule is that you may place an optional comma at the end of any list value. This makes it easy to come back later and add more elements after the last one:

```
@releases = (
    "alpha",
    "beta",
    "gamma",
);
```

Or you can do away with the commas entirely: another way to specify a literal list is with the qw (quote words) syntax we mentioned earlier. This construct is equivalent to splitting a single-quoted string on whitespace. For example:

```
@froots = qw(
    apple       banana      carambola
    coconut     guava       kumquat
    mandarin    nectarine   peach
    pear        persimmon   plum
);
```

(Note that those parentheses are behaving as quote characters, not ordinary parentheses. We could just as easily have picked angle brackets or braces or slashes. But parens are pretty.)

A list value may also be subscripted like a normal array. You must put the list in parentheses (real ones) to avoid ambiguity. Though it's often used to fetch a single value out of a list, it's really a slice of the list, so the syntax is:

```
(LIST)[LIST]
```

Examples:

```
# Stat returns list value.
$modification_time = (stat($file))[9];

# SYNTAX ERROR HERE.
$modification_time = stat($file)[9];  # OOPS, FORGOT PARENS

# Find a hex digit.
$hexdigit = ('a','b','c','d','e','f')[$digit-10];

# A "reverse comma operator".
return (pop(@foo),pop(@foo))[0];
```

```
# Get multiple values as a slice.
($day, $month, $year) = (localtime)[3,4,5];
```

List Assignment

A list may be assigned to only if each element of the list is itself legal to assign to:

```
($a, $b, $c) = (1, 2, 3);
```

```
($map{red}, $map{green}, $map{blue}) = (0xff0000, 0x00ff00, 0x0000ff);
```

You may assign to undef in a list. This is useful for throwing away some of the return values of a function:

```
($dev, $ino, undef, undef, $uid, $gid) = stat($file);
```

The final list element may be an array or a hash:

```
($a, $b, @rest) = split;
my ($a, $b, %rest) = @arg_list;
```

You can actually put an array or hash anywhere in the list you assign to, but the first array or hash in the list will soak up all the remaining values, and anything after it will be set to the undefined value. This may be useful in a local or my, where you probably want the arrays initialized to be empty anyway.

You can even assign to the empty list:

```
() = funkshun();
```

That ends up calling your function in list context, but discarding the return values. If you had just called the function without an assignment, it would have instead been called in void context, which is a kind of scalar context, and might have caused the function to behave completely differently.

List assignment in scalar context returns the number of elements produced by the expression on the *right* side of the assignment:

```
$x = ( ($a, $b) = (7,7,7) );     # set $x to 3, not 2
$x = ( ($a, $b) = funk() );      # set $x to funk()'s return count
$x = ( () = funk() );            # also set $x to funk()'s return count
```

This is handy when you want to do a list assignment in a Boolean context, because most list functions return a null list when finished, which when assigned produces a 0, which is interpreted as false. Here's how you might use it in a while statement:

```
while (($login, $password) = getpwent) {
    if (crypt($login, $password) eq $password) {
        print "$login has an insecure password!\n";
    }
}
```

Array Length

You may find the number of elements in the array @days by evaluating @days in a scalar context, such as:

```
@days + 0;      # implicitly force @days into a scalar context
scalar(@days)   # explicitly force @days into a scalar context
```

Note that this only works for arrays. It does not work for list values in general. As we mentioned earlier, a comma-separated list evaluated in scalar context returns the last value, like the C comma operator. But because you almost never actually need to know the length of a list in Perl, this is not a problem.

Closely related to the scalar evaluation of @days is $#days. This will return the subscript of the last element of the array, or one less than the length, since there is (ordinarily) a 0th element. Assigning to $#days changes the length of the array. Shortening an array by this method destroys intervening values. You can gain some measure of efficiency by pre-extending an array that is going to get big. (You can also extend an array by assigning to an element beyond the end of the array.) You can truncate an array down to nothing by assigning the null list () to it. The following two statements are equivalent:

```
@whatever = ();
$#whatever = -1;
```

And the following is always true:

```
scalar(@whatever) == $#whatever + 1;
```

Truncating an array does not recover its memory. You have to undef(@whatever) to free its memory back to your process's memory pool. You probably can't free it all the way back to your system's memory pool, because few operating systems support this.

Hashes

As we said earlier, a hash is just a funny kind of array in which you look values up using key strings instead of numbers. A hash defines associations between keys and values, so hashes are often called *associative arrays* by people who are not lazy typists.

There really isn't any such thing as a hash literal in Perl, but if you assign an ordinary list to a hash, each pair of values in the list will be taken to indicate one key/value association:

```
%map = ('red',0xff0000,'green',0x00ff00,'blue',0x0000ff);
```

This has the same effect as:

```
%map = ();                # clear the hash first
$map{red}   = 0xff0000;
$map{green} = 0x00ff00;
$map{blue}  = 0x0000ff;
```

It is often more readable to use the => operator between key/value pairs. The => operator is just a synonym for a comma, but it's more visually distinctive and also quotes any bare identifiers to the left of it (just like the identifiers in braces above), which makes it convenient for several sorts of operation, including initializing hash variables:

```
%map = (
    red   => 0xff0000,
    green => 0x00ff00,
    blue  => 0x0000ff,
);
```

or initializing anonymous hash references to be used as records:

```
$rec = {
    NAME  => 'John Smith',
    RANK  => 'Captain',
    SERNO => '951413',
};
```

or using named parameters to invoke complicated functions:

```
$field = radio_group(
            NAME      => 'animals',
            VALUES    => ['camel', 'llama', 'ram', 'wolf'],
            DEFAULT   => 'camel',
            LINEBREAK => 'true',
            LABELS    => \%animal_names,
        );
```

But we're getting ahead of ourselves again. Back to hashes.

You can use a hash variable (%hash) in a list context, in which case it interpolates all its key/value pairs into the list. But just because the hash was initialized in a particular order doesn't mean that the values come back out in that order. Hashes are implemented internally using hash tables for speedy lookup, which means that the order in which entries are stored is dependent on the internal hash function used to calculate positions in the hash table, and not on anything interesting. So the entries come back in a seemingly random order. (The two elements of each key/value pair come out in the right order, of course.) For examples of how to arrange for an output ordering, see the keys function in Chapter 29.

When you evaluate a hash variable in a scalar context, it returns a true value only if the hash contains any key/value pairs whatsoever. If there are any key/value pairs at all, the value returned is a string consisting of the number of used buckets and the number of allocated buckets, separated by a slash. This is pretty much only useful to find out whether Perl's (compiled in) hashing algorithm is performing poorly on your data set. For example, you stick 10,000 things in a hash, but evaluating %HASH in scalar context reveals "1/8", which means only one out of eight buckets has been touched. Presumably that one bucket contains all 10,000 of your items. This isn't supposed to happen.

To find the number of keys in a hash, use the `keys` function in a scalar context: `scalar(keys(%HASH))`.

You can emulate a multidimensional hash by specifying more than one key within the braces, separated by commas. The listed keys are concatenated together, separated by the contents of $; ($SUBSCRIPT_SEPARATOR), which has a default value of `chr(28)`. The resulting string is used as the actual key to the hash. These two lines do the same thing:

```
$people{ $state, $county } = $census_results;
$people{ join $; => $state, $county } = $census_results;
```

This feature was originally implemented to support *a2p*, the *awk*-to-Perl translator. These days, you'd usually just use a real (well, realer) multidimensional array as described in Chapter 9, *Data Structures*. One place the old style is still useful is for hashes tied to DBM files (see DB_File in Chapter 32, *Standard Modules*), which don't support multidimensional keys.

Don't confuse multidimensional hash emulations with slices. The one represents a scalar value, and the other represents a list value:

```
$hash{ $x, $y, $z }     # a single value
@hash{ $x, $y, $z }     # a slice of three values
```

Typeglobs and Filehandles

Perl uses an special type called a *typeglob* to hold an entire symbol table entry. (The symbol table entry *foo contains the values of $foo, @foo, %foo, &foo, and several interpretations of plain old foo.) The type prefix of a typeglob is a * because it represents all types.

One use of typeglobs (or references thereto) is for passing or storing filehandles. If you want to save away a filehandle, do it this way:

```
$fh = *STDOUT;
```

or perhaps as a real reference, like this:

```
$fh = \*STDOUT;
```

This is also the way to create a local filehandle. For example:

```
sub newopen {
    my $path = shift;
    local *FH;              # not my() nor our()
    open(FH, $path) or return undef;
    return *FH;             # not \*FH!
}
$fh = newopen('/etc/passwd');
```

See the open function for other ways to generate new filehandles.

The main use of typeglobs nowadays is to alias one symbol table entry to another symbol table entry. Think of an alias as a nickname. If you say:

```
*foo = *bar;
```

it makes everything named "foo" a synonym for every corresponding thing named "bar". You can alias just one variable from a typeglob by assigning a reference instead:

```
*foo = \$bar;
```

makes $foo an alias for $bar, but doesn't make @foo an alias for @bar, or %foo an alias for %bar. All these affect global (package) variables only; lexicals cannot be accessed through symbol table entries. Aliasing global variables like this may seem like a silly thing to want to do, but it turns out that the entire module export/import mechanism is built around this feature, since there's nothing that says the symbol you're aliasing has to be in your namespace. This:

```
local *Here::blue = \$There::green;
```

temporarily makes $Here::blue an alias for $There::green, but doesn't make @Here::blue an alias for @There::green, or %Here::blue an alias for %There::green. Fortunately, all these complicated typeglob manipulations are hidden away where you don't have to look at them. See the sections "Handle References" and "Symbol Table References" in Chapter 8, the section "Symbol Tables" in Chapter 10, and Chapter 11, *Modules*, for more discussion on typeglobs and importation.

Input Operators

There are several input operators we'll discuss here because they parse as terms. Sometimes we call them pseudoliterals because they act like quoted strings in many ways. (Output operators like print parse as list operators and are discussed in Chapter 29.)

Command Input (Backtick) Operator

First of all, we have the command input operator, also known as the backtick operator, because it looks like this:

```
$info = `finger $user`;
```

A string enclosed by backticks (grave accents, technically) first undergoes variable interpolation just like a double-quoted string. The result is then interpreted as a command line by the system, and the output of that command becomes the value of the pseudoliteral. (This is modeled after a similar operator in Unix shells.) In scalar context, a single string consisting of all the output is returned. In list context, a list of values is returned, one for each line of output. (You can set $/ to use a different line terminator.)

The command is executed each time the pseudoliteral is evaluated. The numeric status value of the command is saved in $? (see Chapter 28 for the interpretation of $?, also known as $CHILD_ERROR). Unlike the *csh* version of this command, no translation is done on the return data—newlines remain newlines. Unlike in any of the shells, single quotes in Perl do not hide variable names in the command from interpretation. To pass a $ through to the shell you need to hide it with a backslash. The $user in our *finger* example above is interpolated by Perl, not by the shell. (Because the command undergoes shell processing, see Chapter 23, *Security*, for security concerns.)

The generalized form of backticks is qx// (for "quoted execution"), but the operator works exactly the same way as ordinary backticks. You just get to pick your quote characters. As with similar quoting pseudofunctions, if you happen to choose a single quote as your delimiter, the command string doesn't undergo double-quote interpolation;

```
$perl_info  = qx(ps $$);          # that's Perl's $$
$shell_info = qx'ps $$';          # that's the shell's $$
```

Line Input (Angle) Operator

The most heavily used input operator is the line input operator, also known as the angle operator or the `readline` function (since that's what it calls internally). Evaluating a filehandle in angle brackets (`STDIN`, for example) yields the next line from the associated filehandle. (The newline is included, so according to Perl's criteria for truth, a freshly input line is always true, up until end-of-file, at which point an undefined value is returned, which is conveniently false.) Ordinarily, you would assign the input value to a variable, but there is one situation where an automatic assignment happens. If and only if the line input operator is the only thing inside the conditional of a `while` loop, the value is automatically assigned to the special variable $_. The assigned value is then tested to see whether it is defined. (This may seem like an odd thing to you, but you'll use the construct frequently, so it's worth learning.) Anyway, the following lines are equivalent:

```
while (defined($_ = <STDIN>)) { print $_; }   # the longest way
while ($_ = <STDIN>) { print; }                # explicitly to $_
while (<STDIN>) { print; }                      # the short way
for (;<STDIN>;) { print; }                       # while loop in disguise
print $_ while defined($_ = <STDIN>);           # long statement modifier
print while $_ = <STDIN>;                         # explicitly to $_
print while <STDIN>;                               # short statement modifier
```

Remember that this special magic requires a while loop. If you use the input operator anywhere else, you must assign the result explicitly if you want to keep the value:

```
while (<FH1> && <FH2>) { ... }          # WRONG: discards both inputs
if (<STDIN>)       { print; }           # WRONG: prints old value of $_
if ($_ = <STDIN>) { print; }            # suboptimal: doesn't test defined
if (defined($_ = <STDIN>)) { print; }   # best
```

When you're implicitly assigning to $_ in a $_ loop, this is the global variable by that name, not one localized to the while loop. You can protect an existing value of $_ this way:

```
while (local $_ = <STDIN>) { print; }   # use local $_
```

Any previous value is restored when the loop is done. $_ is still a global variable, though, so functions called from inside that loop could still access it, intentionally or otherwise. You can avoid this, too, by declaring a lexical variable:

```
while (my $line = <STDIN>) { print $line; } # now private
```

(Both of these while loops still implicitly test for whether the result of the assignment is defined, because my and local don't change how assignment is seen by the parser.) The filehandles STDIN, STDOUT, and STDERR are predefined and pre-opened. Additional filehandles may be created with the open or sysopen functions. See those functions' documentation in Chapter 29 for details on this.

In the while loops above, we were evaluating the line input operator in a scalar context, so the operator returns each line separately. However, if you use the operator in a list context, a list consisting of all remaining input lines is returned, one line per list element. It's easy to make a *large* data space this way, so use this feature with care:

```
$one_line = <MYFILE>;    # Get first line.
@all_lines = <MYFILE>;   # Get the rest of the lines.
```

There is no while magic associated with the list form of the input operator, because the condition of a while loop always provides a scalar context (as does any conditional).

Using the null filehandle within the angle operator is special; it emulates the command-line behavior of typical Unix filter programs such as *sed* and *awk.* When you read lines from <>, it magically gives you all the lines from all the files mentioned on the command line. If no files were mentioned, it gives you standard input instead, so your program is easy to insert into the middle of a pipeline of processes.

Here's how it works: the first time <> is evaluated, the @ARGV array is checked, and if it is null, $ARGV[0] is set to "–", which when opened gives you standard input. The @ARGV array is then processed as a list of filenames. More explicitly, the loop:

```
while (<>) {
    ...                     # code for each line
}
```

is equivalent to the following Perl-like pseudocode:

```
@ARGV = ('-') unless @ARGV;      # assume STDIN iff empty
while (@ARGV) {
    $ARGV = shift @ARGV;         # shorten @ARGV each time
    if (!open(ARGV, $ARGV)) {
        warn "Can't open $ARGV: $!\n";
        next;
    }
    while (<ARGV>) {
        ...                      # code for each line
    }
}
```

except that it isn't so cumbersome to say, and will actually work. It really does shift array @ARGV and put the current filename into the global variable $ARGV. It also uses the special filehandle ARGV internally—<> is just a synonym for the more explicitly written <ARGV>, which is a magical filehandle. (The pseudocode above doesn't work because it treats <ARGV> as nonmagical.)

You can modify @ARGV before the first <> as long as the array ends up containing the list of filenames you really want. Because Perl uses its normal open function here, a filename of "–" counts as standard input wherever it is encountered, and the more esoteric features of open are automatically available to you (such as opening a "file" named "gzip -dc < file.gz|"). Line numbers ($.) continue as if the input were one big happy file. (But see the example under eof in Chapter 29 for how to reset line numbers on each file.)

If you want to set @ARGV to your own list of files, go right ahead:

```
# default to README file if no args given
@ARGV = ("README") unless @ARGV;
```

If you want to pass switches into your script, you can use one of the Getopt::* modules or put a loop on the front like this:

```
    while (@ARGV and $ARGV[0] =~ /^-/) {
        $_ = shift;
        last if /^--$/;
        if (/^-D(.*)/) { $debug = $1 }
        if (/^-v/)      { $verbose++  }
        ...               # other switches
    }
    while (<>) {
        ...               # code for each line
    }
```

The <> symbol will return false only once. If you call it again after this, it will assume you are processing another @ARGV list, and if you haven't set @ARGV, it will input from STDIN.

If the string inside the angle brackets is a scalar variable (for example, <$foo>), that variable contains an *indirect* filehandle, either the name of the filehandle to input from or a reference to such a filehandle. For example:

```
    $fh = \*STDIN;
    $line = <$fh>;
```

or:

```
    open($fh, "<data.txt");
    $line = <$fh>;
```

Filename Globbing Operator

You might wonder what happens to a line input operator if you put something fancier inside the angle brackets. What happens is that it mutates into a different operator. If the string inside the angle brackets is anything other than a filehandle name or a scalar variable (even if there are just extra spaces), it is interpreted as a filename pattern to be "globbed".* The pattern is matched against the files in the current directory (or the directory specified as part of the fileglob pattern), and the filenames so matched are returned by the operator. As with line input, names are returned one at a time in scalar context, or all at once in list context. The latter usage is more common; you often see things like:

```
    @files = <*.xml>;
```

As with other kinds of pseudoliterals, one level of variable interpolation is done first, but you can't say <$foo> because that's an indirect filehandle as explained earlier. In older versions of Perl, programmers would insert braces to force

---

* Fileglobs have nothing to do with the previously mentioned typeglobs, other than that they both use the * character in a wildcard fashion. The * character has the nickname "glob" when used like this. With typeglobs, you're globbing symbols with the same name from the symbol table. With a fileglob, you're doing wildcard matching on the filenames in a directory, just as the various shells do.

interpretation as a fileglob: <${foo}>. These days, it's considered cleaner to call the internal function directly as glob($foo), which is probably the right way to have invented it in the first place. So instead you'd write

```
@files = glob("*.xml");
```

if you despise overloading the angle operator for this. Which you're allowed to do.

Whether you use the glob function or the old angle-bracket form, the fileglob operator also does while magic like the line input operator, assigning the result to $_. (That was the rationale for overloading the angle operator in the first place.) For example, if you wanted to change the permissions on all your C code files, you might say:

```
while (glob "*.c") {
    chmod 0644, $_;
}
```

which is equivalent to:

```
while (<*.c>) {
    chmod 0644, $_;
}
```

The glob function was originally implemented as a shell command in older versions of Perl (and in even older versions of Unix), which meant it was comparatively expensive to execute and, worse still, wouldn't work exactly the same everywhere. Nowadays it's a built-in, so it's more reliable and a lot faster. See the description of the File::Glob module in Chapter 32 for how to alter the default behavior of this operator, such as whether to treat spaces in its operand (argument) as pathname separators, whether to expand tildes or braces, whether to be case insensitive, and whether to sort the return values—amongst other things.

Of course, the shortest and arguably the most readable way to do the chmod command above is to use the fileglob as a list operator:

```
chmod 0644, <*.c>;
```

A fileglob evaluates its (embedded) operand only when starting a new list. All values must be read before the operator will start over. In a list context, this isn't important because you automatically get them all anyway. In a scalar context, however, the operator returns the next value each time it is called, or a false value if you've just run out. Again, false is returned only once. So if you're expecting a single value from a fileglob, it is much better to say:

```
($file) = <blurch*>;  # list context
```

than to say:

```
$file = <blurch*>;    # scalar context
```

because the former returns all matched filenames and resets the operator, whereas
the latter alternates between returning filenames and returning false.

If you're trying to do variable interpolation, it's definitely better to use the `glob`
operator because the older notation can cause confusion with the indirect filehandle notation. This is where it becomes apparent that the borderline between terms
and operators is a bit mushy:

```
@files = <$dir/*.[ch]>;        # Works, but avoid.
@files = glob("$dir/*.[ch]");  # Call glob as function.
@files = glob $some_pattern;   # Call glob as operator.
```

We left the parentheses off of the last example to illustrate that `glob` can be used
either as a function (a term) or as a *unary* operator; that is, a prefix operator that
takes a single argument. The `glob` operator is an example of a *named unary operator*, which is just one kind of operator we'll talk about in the next chapter. Later,
we'll talk about pattern-matching operators, which also parse like terms but
behave like operators.

3

Unary and Binary Operators

In the last chapter, we talked about the various kinds of terms you might use in an expression, but to be honest, isolated terms are a bit boring. Many terms are party animals. They like to have relationships with each other. The typical young term feels strong urges to identify with and influence other terms in various ways, but there are many different kinds of social interaction and many different levels of commitment. In Perl, these relationships are expressed using operators.

Sociology has to be good for something.

From a mathematical perspective, operators are just ordinary functions with special syntax. From a linguistic perspective, operators are just irregular verbs. But as any linguist will tell you, the irregular verbs in a language tend to be the ones you use most often. And that's important from an information theory perspective because the irregular verbs tend to be shorter and more efficient in both production and recognition.

In practical terms, operators are handy.

Operators come in various flavors, depending on their *arity* (how many operands they take), their *precedence* (how hard they try to take those operands away from surrounding operators), and their *associativity* (whether they prefer to do things right to left or left to right when associated with operators of the same precedence).

Perl operators come in three arities: *unary*, *binary*, and *trinary* (or *ternary*, if your native tongue is Shibboleth). Unary operators are always prefix operators (except for the postincrement and postdecrement operators).* The others are all infix operators—unless you count the list operators, which can prefix any number of arguments. But most people just think of list operators as normal functions that you can forget to put parentheses around. Here are some examples:

```
! $x               # a unary operator
$x * $y            # a binary operator
$x ? $y : $z       # a trinary operator
print $x, $y, $z   # a list operator
```

An operator's precedence controls how tightly it binds. Operators with higher precedence grab the arguments around them before operators with lower precedence. The archetypal example is straight out of elementary math, where multiplication takes precedence over addition:

```
2 + 3 * 4          # yields 14, not 20
```

The order in which two operators of the same precedence are executed depends on their associativity. These rules also follow math conventions to some extent:

```
2 * 3 * 4          # means (2 * 3) * 4, left associative
2 ** 3 ** 4        # means 2 ** (3 ** 4), right associative
2 != 3 != 4        # illegal, nonassociative
```

Table 3-1 lists the associativity and arity of the Perl operators from highest precedence to lowest.

Table 3-1. Operator Precedence

Associativity	Arity	Precedence Class
None	0	Terms, and list operators (leftward)
Left	2	->
None	1	++ --
Right	2	**
Right	1	! ~ \ and unary + and -
Left	2	=~ !~
Left	2	* / % x
Left	2	+ - .
Left	2	<< >>
Right	0,1	Named unary operators
None	2	< > <= >= lt gt le ge
None	2	== != <=> eq ne cmp
Left	2	&

---

* Though you can think of various quotes and brackets as circumfix operators that delimit terms.

Table 3-1. Operator Precedence (continued)

Associativity	Arity	Precedence Class
Left	2	`|` `^`
Left	2	`&&`
Left	2	`||`
None	2	`..` `...`
Right	3	`?:`
Right	2	`=` `+=` `-=` `*=` and so on
Left	2	`,` `=>`
Right	0+	List operators (rightward)
Right	1	`not`
Left	2	`and`
Left	2	`or` `xor`

It may seem to you that there are too many precedence levels to remember. Well, you're right, there are. Fortunately, you've got two things going for you here. First, the precedence levels as they're defined usually follow your intuition, presuming you're not psychotic. And second, if you're merely neurotic, you can always put in extra parentheses to relieve your anxiety.

Another helpful hint is that any operators borrowed from C keep the same precedence relationship with each other, even where C's precedence is slightly screwy. (This makes learning Perl easier for C folks and C++ folks. Maybe even Java folks.)

The following sections cover these operators in precedence order. With very few exceptions, these all operate on scalar values only, not list values. We'll mention the exceptions as they come up.

Although references are scalar values, using most of these operators on references doesn't make much sense, because the numeric value of a reference is only meaningful to the internals of Perl. Nevertheless, if a reference points to an object of a class that allows overloading, you can call these operators on such objects, and if the class has defined an overloading for that particular operator, it will define how the object is to be treated under that operator. This is how complex numbers are implemented in Perl, for instance. For more on overloading, see Chapter 13, *Overloading*.

Terms and List Operators (Leftward)

Any *term* is of highest precedence in Perl. Terms include variables, quote and quotelike operators, most expressions in parentheses, or brackets or braces, and any function whose arguments are parenthesized. Actually, there aren't really any functions in this sense, just list operators and unary operators behaving as functions because you put parentheses around their arguments. Nevertheless, the name of Chapter 29 is *Functions*.

Now listen carefully. Here are a couple of rules that are very important and simplify things greatly, but may occasionally produce counterintuitive results for the unwary. If any list operator (such as print) or any named unary operator (such as chdir) is followed by a left parenthesis as the next token (ignoring whitespace), the operator and its parenthesized arguments are given highest precedence, as if it were a normal function call. The rule is this: If it *looks* like a function call, it *is* a function call. You can make it look like a nonfunction by prefixing the parentheses with a unary plus, which does absolutely nothing, semantically speaking—it doesn't even coerce the argument to be numeric.

For example, since | | has lower precedence than chdir, we get:

```
chdir $foo     || die;    # (chdir $foo) || die
chdir($foo)    || die;    # (chdir $foo) || die
chdir ($foo)   || die;    # (chdir $foo) || die
chdir +($foo)  || die;    # (chdir $foo) || die
```

but, because * has higher precedence than chdir, we get:

```
chdir $foo * 20;          # chdir ($foo * 20)
chdir($foo) * 20;         # (chdir $foo) * 20
chdir ($foo) * 20;        # (chdir $foo) * 20
chdir +($foo) * 20;       # chdir ($foo * 20)
```

Likewise for any numeric operator that happens to be a named unary operator, such as rand:

```
rand 10 * 20;             # rand (10 * 20)
rand(10) * 20;            # (rand 10) * 20
rand (10) * 20;           # (rand 10) * 20
rand +(10) * 20;          # rand (10 * 20)
```

In the absence of parentheses, the precedence of list operators such as print, sort, or chmod is either very high or very low depending on whether you look at the left side or the right side of the operator. (That's what the "Leftward" is doing in the title of this section.) For example, in:

```
@ary = (1, 3, sort 4, 2);
print @ary;        # prints 1324
```

the commas on the right of the sort are evaluated before the sort, but the commas on the left are evaluated after. In other words, a list operator tends to gobble up all the arguments that follow it, and then act like a simple term with regard to the preceding expression. You still have to be careful with parentheses:

```
# These evaluate exit before doing the print:
print($foo, exit);  # Obviously not what you want.
print $foo, exit;   # Nor this.

# These do the print before evaluating exit:
(print $foo), exit; # This is what you want.
print($foo), exit;  # Or this.
print ($foo), exit; # Or even this.
```

The easiest place to get burned is where you're using parentheses to group mathematical arguments, and you forget that parentheses are also used to group function arguments:

```
print ($foo & 255) + 1, "\n";    # prints ($foo & 255)
```

That probably doesn't do what you expect at first glance. Fortunately, mistakes of this nature generally produce warnings like "Useless use of addition in a void context" when warnings are enabled.

Also parsed as terms are the do {} and eval {} constructs, as well as subroutine and method calls, the anonymous array and hash composers [] and {}, and the anonymous subroutine composer sub {}.

The Arrow Operator

Just as in C and C++, the binary -> operator is an infix dereference operator. If the right side is a [...] array subscript, a {...} hash subscript, or a (...) subroutine argument list, the left side must be a reference (either hard or symbolic) to an array, a hash, or a subroutine, respectively. In an lvalue (assignable) context, if the left side is not a reference, it must be a location capable of holding a hard reference, in which case such a reference will be *autovivified* for you. For more on this (and some warnings about accidental autovivification) see Chapter 8, *References*.

```
$aref->[42]              # an array dereference
$href->{"corned beef"}   # a hash dereference
$sref->(1,2,3)           # a subroutine dereference
```

Otherwise, it's a method call of some kind. The right side must be a method name (or a simple scalar variable containing the method name), and the left side must evaluate to either an object (a blessed reference) or a class name (that is, a package name):

```
$yogi = Bear->new("Yogi");    # a class method call
$yogi->swipe($picnic);         # an object method call
```

The method name may be qualified with a package name to indicate in which class to start searching for the method, or with the special package name, SUPER::, to indicate that the search should start in the parent class. See Chapter 12, *Objects*.

Autoincrement and Autodecrement

The ++ and -- operators work as in C. That is, when placed before a variable, they increment or decrement the variable before returning the value, and when placed after, they increment or decrement the variable after returning the value. For example, $a++ increments the value of scalar variable $a, returning the value *before* it performs the increment. Similarly, --$b{(/(\w+)/)[0]} decrements the element of the hash %b indexed by the first "word" in the default search variable ($_) and returns the value *after* the decrement.*

The autoincrement operator has a little extra built-in magic. If you increment a variable that is numeric, or that has ever been used in a numeric context, you get a normal increment. If, however, the variable has only been used in string contexts since it was set, has a value that is not the null string, and matches the pattern /^[a-zA-Z]*[0-9]*$/, the increment is done as a string, preserving each character within its range, with carry:

```
print ++($foo = '99');      # prints '100'
print ++($foo = 'a9');      # prints 'b0'
print ++($foo = 'Az');      # prints 'Ba'
print ++($foo = 'zz');      # prints 'aaa'
```

As of this writing, magical autoincrement has not been extended to Unicode letters and digits, but it might be in the future.

The autodecrement operator, however, is not magical, and we have no plans to make it so.

---

* Okay, so that wasn't exactly fair. We just wanted to make sure you were paying attention. Here's how that expression works. First the pattern match finds the first word in $_ using the regular expression \w+. The parentheses around that cause the word to be returned as a single-element list value because the pattern match is in a list context. The list context is supplied by the list slice operator, (...)[0], which returns the first (and only) element of the list. That value is used as the key for the hash, and the hash entry (value) is decremented and returned. In general, when confronted with a complex expression, analyze it from the inside out to see what order things happen in.

Exponentiation

Binary ** is the exponentiation operator. Note that it binds even more tightly than unary minus, so -2**4 is -(2**4), not (-2)**4. The operator is implemented using C's *pow*(3) function, which works with floating-point numbers internally. It calculates using logarithms, which means that it works with fractional powers, but you sometimes get results that aren't as exact as a straight multiplication would produce.

Ideographic Unary Operators

Most unary operators just have names (see "Named Unary and File Test Operators" later in this chapter), but some operators are deemed important enough to merit their own special symbolic representation. All of these operators seem to have something to do with negation. Blame the mathematicians.

Unary ! performs logical negation, that is, "not". See not for a lower precedence version of logical negation. The value of a negated operand is true (1) if the operand is false (numeric 0, string "0", the null string, or undefined) and false ("") if the operand is true.

Unary - performs arithmetic negation if the operand is numeric. If the operand is an identifier, a string consisting of a minus sign concatenated with the identifier is returned. Otherwise, if the string starts with a plus or minus, a string starting with the opposite sign is returned. One effect of these rules is that -bareword is equivalent to "-bareword". This is most useful for Tk programmers.

Unary ~ performs bitwise negation, that is, 1's complement. By definition, this is somewhat nonportable when limited by the word size of your machine. For example, on a 32-bit machine, ~123 is 4294967172, while on a 64-bit machine, it's 18446744073709551492. But you knew that already.

What you perhaps didn't know is that if the argument to ~ happens to be a string instead of a number, a string of identical length is returned, but with all the bits of the string complemented. This is a fast way to flip a lot of bits all at once, and it's a way to flip those bits portably, since it doesn't depend on the word size of your computer. Later we'll also cover the bitwise logical operators, which have string-oriented variants as well.

Unary + has no semantic effect whatsoever, even on strings. It is syntactically useful for separating a function name from a parenthesized expression that would otherwise be interpreted as the complete list of function arguments. (See examples under the section "Terms and List Operators".) If you think about it sideways, + negates the effect that parentheses have of turning prefix operators into functions.

Unary \ creates a reference to whatever follows it. Used on a list, it creates a list of references. See the section "The Backslash Operator" in Chapter 8 for details. Do not confuse this behavior with the behavior of backslash within a string, although both forms do convey the vaguely negational notion of protecting the next thing from interpretation. This resemblance is not entirely accidental.

Binding Operators

Binary =~ binds a string expression to a pattern match, substitution, or transliteration (loosely called translation). These operations would otherwise search or modify the string contained in $_ (the default variable). The string you want to bind is put on the left, while the operator itself is put on the right. The return value indicates the success or failure of the operator on the right, since the binding operator doesn't really do anything on its own.

If the right argument is an expression rather than a pattern match, substitution, or transliteration, it will be interpreted as a search pattern at run time. That is to say, $_ =~ $pat is equivalent to $_ =~ /$pat/. This is less efficient than an explicit search, since the pattern must be checked and possibly recompiled every time the expression is evaluated. You can avoid this recompilation by precompiling the original pattern using the qr// (quote regex) operator.

Binary !~ is just like =~ except the return value is negated logically. The following expressions are functionally equivalent:

```
$string !~ /pattern/
not $string =~ /pattern/
```

We said that the return value indicates success, but there are many kinds of success. Substitutions return the number of successful matches, as do transliterations. (In fact, the transliteration operator is often used to count characters.) Since any nonzero result is true, it all works out. The most spectacular kind of true value is a list assignment of a pattern: in a list context, pattern matches can return substrings matched by the parentheses in the pattern. But again, according to the rules of list assignment, the list assignment itself will return true if anything matched and was assigned, and false otherwise. So you sometimes see things like:

```
if ( ($k,$v) = $string =~ m/(\w+)=(\w*)/ ) {
    print "KEY $k VALUE $v\n";
}
```

Let's pick that apart. The =~ has precedence over =, so =~ happens first. The =~ binds $string to the pattern match on the right, which is scanning for occurrences of things that look like *KEY=VALUE* in your string. It's in a list context because it's on the right side of a list assignment. If the pattern matches, it returns a list to be assigned to $k and $v. The list assignment itself is in a scalar context, so it returns 2, the number of values on the right side of the assignment. And 2 happens to be true, since our scalar context is also a Boolean context. When the match fails, no values are assigned, which returns 0, which is false.

For more on the politics of patterns, see Chapter 5, *Pattern Matching*.

Multiplicative Operators

Perl provides the C-like operators * (multiply), / (divide), and % (modulo). The * and / work exactly as you would expect, multiplying or dividing their two operands. Division is done in floating point, unless you've used the integer pragmatic module.

The % operator converts its operands to integers before finding the remainder according to integer division. (However, it does this integer division in floating point if necessary, so your operands can be up to 15 digits long on most 32-bit machines.) Assume that your two operands are called $a and $b. If $b is positive, then the result of $a % $b is $a minus the largest multiple of $b that is not greater than $a (which means the result will always be in the range 0 .. $b-1). If $b is negative, then the result of $a % $b is $a minus the smallest multiple of $b that is not less than $a (which means the result will be in the range $b+1 .. 0).

When use integer is in scope, % gives you direct access to the modulus operator as implemented by your C compiler. This operator is not well defined for negative operands, but will execute faster.

Binary x is the repetition operator. Actually, it's two operators. In scalar context, it returns a concatenated string consisting of the left operand repeated the number of times specified by the right operand. (For backward compatibility, it also does this in list context if the left argument is not in parentheses.)

```
print '-' x 80;                      # print row of dashes
print "\t" x ($tab/8), ' ' x ($tab%8);    # tab over
```

In list context, if the left operand is a list in parentheses, the x works as a list replicator rather than a string replicator. This is useful for initializing all the elements of an array of indeterminate length to the same value:

```
@ones = (1) x 80;        # a list of 80 1's
@ones = (5) x @ones;     # set all elements to 5
```

Similarly, you can also use x to initialize array and hash slices:

```
@keys = qw(perls before swine);
@hash{@keys} = ("") x @keys;
```

If this mystifies you, note that @keys is being used both as a list on the left side of the assignment and as a scalar value (returning the array length) on the right side of the assignment. The previous example has the same effect on %hash as:

```
$hash{perls}  = "";
$hash{before} = "";
$hash{swine}  = "";
```

Additive Operators

Strangely enough, Perl also has the customary + (addition) and − (subtraction) operators. Both operators convert their arguments from strings to numeric values if necessary and return a numeric result.

Additionally, Perl provides the . operator, which does string concatenation. For example:

```
$almost = "Fred" . "Flintstone";    # returns FredFlintstone
```

Note that Perl does not place a space between the strings being concatenated. If you want the space, or if you have more than two strings to concatenate, you can use the join operator, described in Chapter 29, *Functions*. Most often, though, people do their concatenation implicitly inside a double-quoted string:

```
$fullname = "$firstname $lastname";
```

Shift Operators

The bit-shift operators (<< and >>) return the value of the left argument shifted to the left (<<) or to the right (>>) by the number of bits specified by the right argument. The arguments should be integers. For example:

```
1 << 4;     # returns 16
32 >> 4;    # returns 2
```

Be careful, though. Results on large (or negative) numbers may vary depending on the number of bits your machine uses to represent integers.

Named Unary and File Test Operators

Some of the "functions" described in Chapter 29 are really unary operators. Table 3-2 lists all the named unary operators.

Table 3-2. Named Unary Operators

-X (file tests)	gethostbyname	localtime	return
alarm	getnetbyname	lock	rmdir
caller	getpgrp	log	scalar
chdir	getprotobyname	lstat	sin
chroot	glob	my	sleep
cos	gmtime	oct	sqrt
defined	goto	ord	srand
delete	hex	quotemeta	stat
do	int	rand	uc
eval	lc	readlink	ucfirst
exists	lcfirst	ref	umask
exit	length	require	undef

Unary operators have a higher precedence than some of the binary operators. For example:

```
sleep 4 | 3;
```

does not sleep for 7 seconds; it sleeps for 4 seconds and then takes the return value of `sleep` (typically zero) and bitwise ORs that with 3, as if the expression were parenthesized as:

```
(sleep 4) | 3;
```

Compare this with:

```
print 4 | 3;
```

which *does* take the value of 4 ORed with 3 before printing it (7 in this case), as if it were written:

```
print (4 | 3);
```

This is because `print` is a list operator, not a simple unary operator. Once you've learned which operators are list operators, you'll have no trouble telling unary operators and list operators apart. When in doubt, you can always use parentheses to turn a named unary operator into a function. Remember, if it looks like a function, it is a function.

Another funny thing about named unary operators is that many of them default to `$_` if you don't supply an argument. However, if you omit the argument but the token following the named unary operator looks like it might be the start of an argument, Perl will get confused because it's expecting a term. Whenever the Perl tokener gets to one of the characters listed in Table 3-3, the tokener returns different ent token types depending on whether it expects a term or operator.

Table 3-3. Ambiguous Characters

Character	Operator	Term
+	Addition	Unary plus
-	Subtraction	Unary minus
*	Multiplication	*typeglob
/	Division	/pattern/
<	Less than, left shift	<HANDLE>, <<END
.	Concatenation	.3333
?	?:	?pattern?
%	Modulo	%assoc
&	&, &&	&subroutine

So a typical boo-boo is:

```
next if length < 80;
```

in which the `<` looks to the parser like the beginning of the <> input symbol (a term) instead of the "less than" (an operator) you were thinking of. There's really no way to fix this and still keep Perl pathologically eclectic. If you're so incredibly lazy that you cannot bring yourself to type the two characters $_, then use one of these instead:

```
next if length() < 80;
next if (length) < 80;
next if 80 > length;
next unless length >= 80;
```

When a term is expected, a minus sign followed by a single letter will always be interpreted as a *file test* operator. A file test operator is a unary operator that takes one argument, either a filename or a filehandle, and tests the associated file to see whether something is true about it. If the argument is omitted, it tests $_, except for -t, which tests STDIN. Unless otherwise documented, it returns 1 for true and "" for false, or the undefined value if the file doesn't exist or is otherwise inaccessible. Currently implemented file test operators are listed in Table 3-4.

Table 3-4. File Test Operators

Operator	Meaning
-r	File is readable by effective UID/GID.
-w	File is writable by effective UID/GID.
-x	File is executable by effective UID/GID.
-o	File is owned by effective UID.
-R	File is readable by real UID/GID.
-W	File is writable by real UID/GID.
-X	File is executable by real UID/GID.
-O	File is owned by real UID.
-e	File exists.
-z	File has zero size.
-s	File has nonzero size (returns size).
-f	File is a plain file.
-d	File is a directory.
-l	File is a symbolic link.
-p	File is a named pipe (FIFO).
-S	File is a socket.
-b	File is a block special file.
-c	File is a character special file.
-t	Filehandle is opened to a tty.
-u	File has setuid bit set.
-g	File has setgid bit set.
-k	File has sticky bit set.
-T	File is a text file.
-B	File is a binary file (opposite of -T).
-M	Age of file (at startup) in days since modification.
-A	Age of file (at startup) in days since last access.
-C	Age of file (at startup) in days since inode change.

Note that -s/a/b/ does not do a negated substitution. Saying -exp($foo) still works as expected, however—only single letters following a minus are interpreted as file tests.

The interpretation of the file permission operators -r, -R, -w, -W, -x, and -X is based solely on the mode of the file and the user and group IDs of the user. There may be other reasons you can't actually read, write, or execute the file, such as

Andrew File System (AFS) access control lists.* Also note that for the superuser, -r, -R, -w, and -W always return 1, and -x and -X return 1 if any execute bit is set in the mode. Thus, scripts run by the superuser may need to do a stat in order to determine the actual mode of the file or temporarily set the UID to something else.

The other file test operators don't care who you are. Anybody can use the test for "regular" files:

```
while (<>) {
    chomp;
    next unless -f $_;        # ignore "special" files
    ...
}
```

The -T and -B switches work as follows. The first block or so of the file is examined for strange characters such as control codes or bytes with the high bit set (that don't look like UTF-8). If more than a third of the bytes appear to be strange, it's a binary file; otherwise, it's a text file. Also, any file containing ASCII NUL (\0) in the first block is considered a binary file. If -T or -B is used on a filehandle, the current input (standard I/O or "stdio") buffer is examined rather than the first block of the file. Both -T and -B return true on an empty file, or on a file at EOF (end-of-file) when testing a filehandle. Because Perl has to read a file to do the -T test, you don't want to use -T on special files that might hang or give you other kinds of grief. So on most occasions you'll want to test with a -f first, as in:

```
next unless -f $file && -T $file;
```

If any of the file tests (or either the stat or lstat operator) are given the special filehandle consisting of a solitary underline, then the *stat* structure of the previous file test (or stat operator) is used, thereby saving a system call. (This doesn't work with -t, and you need to remember that lstat and -l will leave values in the *stat* structure for the symbolic link, not the real file. Likewise, -l _ will always be false after a normal stat.)

Here are a couple of examples:

```
print "Can do.\n"     if -r $a || -w _ || -x _;

stat($filename);
print "Readable\n"   if -r _;
print "Writable\n"   if -w _;
print "Executable\n" if -x _;
print "Setuid\n"     if -u _;
print "Setgid\n"     if -g _;
```

---

* You may, however, override the built-in semantics with the use filetest pragma. See Chapter 31, *Pragmatic Modules.*

```
print "Sticky\n"      if -k _;
print "Text\n"        if -T _;
print "Binary\n"      if -B _;
```

File ages for –M, –A, and –C are returned in days (including fractional days) since the script started running. This time is stored in the special variable $^T ($BASE-TIME). Thus, if the file changed after the script started, you would get a negative time. Note that most time values (86,399 out of 86,400, on average) are fractional, so testing for equality with an integer without using the int function is usually futile. Examples:

```
next unless -M $file > .5;       # files are older than 12 hours
&newfile if -M $file < 0;        # file is newer than process
&mailwarning if int(-A) == 90;   # file ($_) was accessed 90 days ago today
```

To reset the script's start time to the current time, say this:

```
$^T = time;
```

Relational Operators

Perl has two classes of relational operators. One class operates on numeric values, the other on string values, as shown in Table 3-5.

Table 3-5. Relational Operators

Numeric	String	Meaning
>	gt	Greater than
>=	ge	Greater than or equal to
<	lt	Less than
<=	le	Less than or equal to

These operators return 1 for true and " " for false. Note that relational operators are nonassociating, which means that $a < $b < $c is a syntax error.

In the absence of locale declarations, string comparisons are based on the ASCII/Unicode collating sequences, and, unlike in some computer languages, trailing spaces count in the comparison. With a locale declaration, the collation order specified by the locale is used. (Locale-based collation mechanisms may or may not interact well with the Unicode collation mechanisms currently in development.)

Equality Operators

The equality operators listed in Table 3-6 are much like the relational operators.

Table 3-6. Equality Operators

Numeric	String	Meaning
==	eq	Equal to
!=	ne	Not equal to
<=>	cmp	Comparison, with signed result

The equal and not-equal operators return 1 for true and `""` for false (just as the relational operators do). The `<=>` and cmp operators return –1 if the left operand is less than the right operand, 0 if they are equal, and +1 if the left operand is greater than the right. Although the equality operators appear to be similar to the relational operators, they do have a lower precedence level, so `$a < $b <=> $c < $d` is syntactically valid.

For reasons that are apparent to anyone who has seen *Star Wars*, the `<=>` operator is known as the "spaceship" operator.

Bitwise Operators

Like C, Perl has bitwise AND, OR, and XOR (exclusive OR) operators: `&`, `|`, and `^`. You'll have noticed from your painstaking examination of the table at the start of this chapter that bitwise AND has a higher precedence than the others, but we've cheated and combined them in this discussion.

These operators work differently on numeric values than they do on strings. (This is one of the few places where Perl cares about the difference.) If either operand is a number (or has been used as a number), both operands are converted to integers, and the bitwise operation is performed between the two integers. These integers are guaranteed to be at least 32 bits long, but can be 64 bits on some machines. The point is that there's an arbitrary limit imposed by the machine's architecture.

If both operands are strings (and have not been used as numbers since they were set), the operators do bitwise operations between corresponding bits from the two strings. In this case, there's no arbitrary limit, since strings aren't arbitrarily limited in size. If one string is longer than the other, the shorter string is considered to have a sufficient number of 0 bits on the end to make up the difference.

For example, if you AND together two strings:

```
"123.45" & "234.56"
```

you get another string:

```
"020.44"
```

But if you AND together a string and a number:

```
"123.45" & 234.56
```

The string is first converted to a number, giving:

```
123.45 & 234.56
```

The numbers are then converted to integers:

```
123 & 234
```

which evaluates to 106. Note that all bit strings are true (unless they result in the string "0"). This means if you want to see whether any byte came out to nonzero, instead of writing this:

```
if ( "fred" & "\1\2\3\4" ) { ... }
```

you need to write this:

```
if ( ("fred" & "\1\2\3\4") =~ /[^\0]/ ) { ... }
```

C-Style Logical (Short-Circuit) Operators

Like C, Perl provides the && (logical AND) and || (logical OR) operators. They evaluate from left to right (with && having slightly higher precedence than ||) testing the truth of the statement. These operators are known as short-circuit operators because they determine the truth of the statement by evaluating the fewest number of operands possible. For example, if the left operand of an && operator is false, the right operand is never evaluated because the result of the operator is false regardless of the value of the right operand.

Example	Name	Result
$a && $b	And	$a if $a is false, $b otherwise
$a || $b	Or	$a if $a is true, $b otherwise

Such short circuits not only save time, but are frequently used to control the flow of evaluation. For example, an oft-appearing idiom in Perl programs is:

```
open(FILE, "somefile") || die "Can't open somefile: $!\n";
```

In this case, Perl first evaluates the open function. If the value is true (because *somefile* was successfully opened), the execution of the die function is unnecessary, and so is skipped. You can read this literally as "Open some file or die!"

The && and || operators differ from C's in that, rather than returning 0 or 1, they return the last value evaluated. In the case of ||, this has the delightful result that you can select the first of a series of scalar values that happens to be true. Thus, a reasonably portable way to find out the user's home directory might be:

```
$home = $ENV{HOME}
    || $ENV{LOGDIR}
    || (getpwuid($<))[7]
    || die "You're homeless!\n";
```

On the other hand, since the left argument is always evaluated in scalar context, you can't use || for selecting between two aggregates for assignment:

```
@a = @b || @c;          # This doesn't do the right thing
@a = scalar(@b) || @c;  # because it really means this.
@a = @b ? @b : @c;      # This works fine, though.
```

Perl also provides lower precedence and and or operators that some people find more readable and don't force you to use parentheses on list operators. They also short-circuit. See Table 1-1 for a complete list.

Range Operator

The .. range operator is really two different operators depending on the context.

In scalar context, .. returns a Boolean value. The operator is bi-stable, like an electronic flip-flop, and emulates the line-range (comma) operator of *sed, awk,* and various editors. Each scalar .. operator maintains its own Boolean state. It is false as long as its left operand is false. Once the left operand is true, the range operator stays true until the right operand is true, *after* which the range operator becomes false again. The operator doesn't become false until the next time it is evaluated. It can test the right operand and become false on the same evaluation as the one where it became true (the way *awk*'s range operator behaves), but it still returns true once. If you don't want it to test the right operand until the next evaluation (which is how *sed*'s range operator works), just use three dots (...) instead of two. With both .. and ..., the right operand is not evaluated while the operator is in the false state, and the left operand is not evaluated while the operator is in the true state.

The value returned is either the null string for false or a sequence number (beginning with 1) for true. The sequence number is reset for each range encountered. The final sequence number in a range has the string "E0" appended to it, which doesn't affect its numeric value, but gives you something to search for if you want to exclude the endpoint. You can exclude the beginning point by waiting for the sequence number to be greater than 1. If either operand of scalar .. is a numeric literal, that operand is implicitly compared to the $. variable, which contains the current line number for your input file. Examples:

```
if (101 .. 200) { print; }  # print 2nd hundred lines
next line if (1 .. /^$/);   # skip header lines of a message
s/^/> / if (/^$/ .. eof()); # quote body of a message
```

In list context, .. returns a list of values counting (by ones) from the left value to the right value. This is useful for writing for (1..10) loops and for doing slice operations on arrays:

```
for (101 .. 200) { print; }          # prints 101102...199200
@foo = @foo[0 .. $#foo];             # an expensive no-op
@foo = @foo[ -5 .. -1];              # slice last 5 items
```

If the left value is greater than the right value, a null list is returned. (To produce a list in reverse order, see the reverse operator.)

If its operands are strings, the range operator makes use of the magical autoincrement algorithm discussed earlier.* So you can say:

```
@alphabet = ('A' .. 'Z');
```

to get all the letters of the (English) alphabet, or:

```
$hexdigit = (0 .. 9, 'a' .. 'f')[$num & 15];
```

to get a hexadecimal digit, or:

```
@z2 = ('01' .. '31');  print $z2[$mday];
```

to get dates with leading zeros. You can also say:

```
@combos = ('aa' .. 'zz');
```

to get all combinations of two lowercase letters. However, be careful of something like:

```
@bigcombos = ('aaaaaa' .. 'zzzzzz');
```

since that will require lots of memory. More precisely, it'll need space to store 308,915,776 scalars. Let's hope you allocated a very large swap partition. Perhaps you should consider an iterative approach instead.

---

* If the final value specified is not in the sequence that the magical increment would produce, the sequence continues until the next value is longer than the final value specified.

Conditional Operator

As in C, ?: is the only trinary operator. It's often called the conditional operator because it works much like an if-then-else, except that, since it's an expression and not a statement, it can be safely embedded within other expressions and functions calls. As a trinary operator, its two parts separate three expressions:

> *COND* ? *THEN* : *ELSE*

If the condition *COND* is true, only the *THEN* expression is evaluated, and the value of that expression becomes the value of the entire expression. Otherwise, only the *ELSE* expression is evaluated, and its value becomes the value of the entire expression.

Scalar or list context propagates downward into the second or third argument, whichever is selected. (The first argument is always in scalar context, since it's a conditional.)

```
$a = $ok ? $b : $c;   # get a scalar
@a = $ok ? @b : @c;   # get an array
$a = $ok ? @b : @c;   # get a count of an array's elements
```

You'll often see the conditional operator embedded in lists of values to format with printf, since nobody wants to replicate the whole statement just to switch between two related values.

```
printf "I have %d camel%s.\n",
         $n,    $n == 1 ? "" : "s";
```

Conveniently, the precedence of ?: is higher than a comma but lower than most operators you'd use inside (such as == in this example), so you don't usually have to parenthesize anything. But you can add parentheses for clarity if you like. For conditional operators nested within the *THEN* parts of other conditional operators, we suggest that you put in line breaks and indent as if they were ordinary if statements:

```
$leapyear =
    $year % 4 == 0
        ? $year % 100 == 0
            ? $year % 400 == 0
                ? 1
                : 0
            : 1
        : 0;
```

For conditionals nested within the *ELSE* parts of earlier conditionals, you can do a similar thing:

```
$leapyear =
    $year % 4
        ? 0
        : $year % 100
          ? 1
          : $year % 400
          ? 0
          : 1;
```

but it's usually better to line up all the *COND* and *THEN* parts vertically:

```
$leapyear =
    $year %   4 ? 0 :
    $year % 100 ? 1 :
    $year % 400 ? 0 : 1;
```

Lining up the question marks and colons can make sense of even fairly cluttered structures:

```
printf "Yes, I like my %s book!\n",
    $i18n eq "french"   ? "chameau"          :
    $i18n eq "german"   ? "Kamel"            :
    $i18n eq "japanese" ? "\x{99F1}\x{99DD}" :
                          "camel"
```

You can assign to the conditional operator* if both the second and third arguments are legal lvalues (meaning that you can assign to them), and both are scalars or both are lists (otherwise, Perl won't know which context to supply to the right side of the assignment):

```
($a_or_b ? $a : $b) = $c;   # sets either $a or $b to have the value of $c
```

Bear in mind that the conditional operator binds more tightly than the various assignment operators. Usually this is what you want (see the $leapyear assignments above, for example), but you can't have it the other way without using parentheses. Using embedded assignments without parentheses will get you into trouble, and you might not get a parse error because the conditional operator can be parsed as an lvalue. For example, you might write this:

```
$a % 2 ? $a += 10 : $a += 2        # WRONG
```

But that would be parsed like this:

```
(($a % 2) ? ($a += 10) : $a) += 2
```

---

* This is not necessarily guaranteed to contribute to the readability of your program. But it can be used to create some cool entries in an Obfuscated Perl contest.

Assignment Operators

Perl recognizes the C assignment operators, as well as providing some of its own. There are quite a few of them:

```
=     **=     +=     *=     &=     <<=     &&=
              -=     /=     |=     >>=     ||=
              .=     %=     ^=
              x=
```

Each operator requires a target lvalue (typically a variable or array element) on the left side and an expression on the right side. For the simple assignment operator:

```
TARGET = EXPR
```

the value of the *EXPR* is stored into the variable or location designated by *TARGET*. For the other operators, Perl evaluates the expression:

```
TARGET OP= EXPR
```

as if it were written:

```
TARGET = TARGET OP EXPR
```

That's a handy mental rule, but it's misleading in two ways. First, assignment operators always parse at the precedence level of ordinary assignment, regardless of the precedence that *OP* would have by itself. Second, *TARGET* is evaluated only once. Usually that doesn't matter unless there are side effects, such as an autoincrement:

```
$var[$a++] += $value;          # $a is incremented once
$var[$a++] = $var[$a++] + $value;   # $a is incremented twice
```

Unlike in C, the assignment operator produces a valid lvalue. Modifying an assignment is equivalent to doing the assignment and then modifying the variable to which it was assigned. This is useful for modifying a copy of something, like this:

```
($tmp = $global) += $constant;
```

which is the equivalent of:

```
$tmp = $global + $constant;
```

Likewise:

```
($a += 2) *= 3;
```

is equivalent to:

```
$a += 2;
$a *= 3;
```

That's not terribly useful, but here's an idiom you see frequently:

```
($new = $old) =~ s/foo/bar/g;
```

In all cases, the value of the assignment is the new value of the variable. Since assignment operators associate right-to-left, this can be used to assign many variables the same value, as in:

```
$a = $b = $c = 0;
```

which assigns 0 to $c, and the result of that (still 0) to $b, and the result of that (*still* 0) to $a.

List assignment may be done only with the plain assignment operator, =. In list context, list assignment returns the list of new values just as scalar assignment does. In scalar context, list assignment returns the number of values that were available on the right side of the assignment, as mentioned in Chapter 2, *Bits and Pieces*. This makes it useful for testing functions that return a null list when unsuccessful (or no longer successful), as in:

```
while (($key, $value) = each %gloss) { ... }

next unless ($dev, $ino, $mode) = stat $file;
```

Comma Operators

Binary "," is the comma operator. In scalar context it evaluates its left argument in void context, throws that value away, then evaluates its right argument in scalar context and returns that value. This is just like C's comma operator. For example:

```
$a = (1, 3);
```

assigns 3 to $a. Do not confuse the scalar context use with the list context use. In list context, a comma is just the list argument separator, and inserts both its arguments into the *LIST*. It does not throw any values away.

For example, if you change the previous example to:

```
@a = (1, 3);
```

you are constructing a two-element list, while:

```
atan2(1, 3);
```

is calling the function atan2 with two arguments.

The => digraph is mostly just a synonym for the comma operator. It's useful for documenting arguments that come in pairs. It also forces any identifier to its immediate left to be interpreted as a string.

List Operators (Rightward)

The right side of a list operator governs all the list operator's arguments, which are comma separated, so the precedence of a list operator is lower than a comma if you're looking to the right. Once a list operator starts chewing up comma-separated arguments, the only things that will stop it are tokens that stop the entire expression (like semicolons or statement modifiers), or tokens that stop the current subexpression (like right parentheses or brackets), or the low precedence logical operators we'll talk about next.

Logical and, or, not, and xor

As lower precedence alternatives to &&, ||, and !, Perl provides the and, or, and not operators. The behavior of these operators is identical—in particular, and and or short-circuit like their counterparts, which makes them useful not only for logical expressions but also for control flow.

Since the precedence of these operators is much lower than the ones borrowed from C, you can safely use them after a list operator without the need for parentheses:

```
unlink "alpha", "beta", "gamma"
        or gripe(), next LINE;
```

With the C-style operators you'd have to write it like this:

```
unlink("alpha", "beta", "gamma")
        || (gripe(), next LINE);
```

But you can't just up and replace all instances of || with or. Suppose you change this:

```
$xyz = $x || $y || $z;
```

to this:

```
$xyz = $x or $y or $z;    # WRONG
```

That wouldn't do the same thing at all! The precedence of the assignment is higher than or but lower than ||, so it would always assign $x to $xyz, and then do the ors. To get the same effect as ||, you'd have to write:

```
$xyz = ( $x or $y or $z );
```

The moral of the story is that you still must learn precedence (or use parentheses) no matter which variety of logical operators you use.

There is also a logical xor operator that has no exact counterpart in C or Perl, since the only other exclusive-OR operator (^) works on bits. The xor operator can't short-circuit, since both sides must be evaluated. The best equivalent for $a xor $b is perhaps !$a != !$b. One could also write !$a ^ !$b or even $a ? !$b : !!$b, of course. The point is that both $a and $b have to evaluate to true or false in a Boolean context, and the existing bitwise operator doesn't provide a Boolean context without help.

C Operators Missing from Perl

Here is what C has that Perl doesn't:

unary &

> The address-of operator. Perl's \ operator (for taking a reference) fills the same ecological niche, however:

> ```
> $ref_to_var = \$var;
> ```

> But Perl references are much safer than C pointers.

unary *

> The dereference-address operator. Since Perl doesn't have addresses, it doesn't need to dereference addresses. It does have references though, so Perl's variable prefix characters serve as dereference operators, and indicate type as well: $, @, %, and &. Oddly enough, there actually is a * dereference operator, but since * is the funny character indicating a typeglob, you wouldn't use it the same way.

(TYPE)

> The typecasting operator. Nobody likes to be typecast anyway.

4

Statements and Declarations

A Perl program consists of a sequence of declarations and statements. A declaration may be placed anywhere a statement may be placed, but its primary effect occurs at compile time. A few declarations do double duty as ordinary statements, but most are totally transparent at run time. After compilation, the main sequence of statements is executed just once.

Unlike many programming languages, Perl doesn't require variables to be explicitly declared; they spring into existence upon their first use, whether you've declared them or not. If you try to use a value from a variable that's never had a value assigned to it, it's quietly treated as 0 when used as a number, as " " (the null string) when used as a string, or simply as false when used as a logical value. If you prefer to be warned about using undefined values as though they were real strings or numbers, or even to treat doing so as an error, the use warnings declaration will take care of that; see the section "Pragmas" at the end of this chapter.

You *may* declare your variables though, if you like, using either my or our in front of the variable name. You can even make it an error to use an undeclared variable. This kind of discipline is fine, but you have to declare that you want the discipline. Normally, Perl minds its own business about your programming habits, but under the use strict declaration, the use of undeclared variables is apprehended at compile time. Again, see the "Pragmas" section.

Simple Statements

A simple statement is an expression evaluated for its side effects. Every simple statement must end in a semicolon, unless it is the final statement in a block. In that case, the semicolon is optional—Perl knows that you must be done with the statement, since you've finished the block. But put the semicolon in anyway if it's at the end of a multiline block, because you might eventually add another line.

Even though operators like `eval {}`, `do {}`, and `sub {}` all look like compound statements, they really aren't. True, they allow multiple statements on the inside, but that doesn't count. From the outside, those operators are just terms in an expression, and thus they need an explicit semicolon if used as the last item in a statement.

Any simple statement may optionally be followed by a single modifier, just before the terminating semicolon (or block ending). The possible modifiers are:

```
if EXPR
unless EXPR
while EXPR
until EXPR
foreach LIST
```

The `if` and `unless` modifiers work pretty much as they do in English:

```
$trash->take('out') if $you_love_me;
shutup() unless $you_want_me_to_leave;
```

The `while` and `until` modifiers evaluate repeatedly. As you might expect, a `while` modifier keeps executing the expression as long as its expression remains true, and an `until` modifier keeps executing only as long as it remains false:

```
$expression++ while -e "$file$expression";
kiss('me') until $I_die;
```

The `foreach` modifier (also spelled `for`) evaluates once for each element in its *LIST*, with `$_` aliased to the current element:

```
s/java/perl/ for @resumes;
print "field: $_\n" foreach split /:/, $dataline;
```

The `while` and `until` modifiers have the usual while-loop semantics (conditional evaluated first), except when applied to a `do` *BLOCK* (or to the now-deprecated `do` *SUBROUTINE* statement), in which case the block executes once before the conditional is evaluated. This allows you to write loops like this:

```
do {
    $line = <STDIN>;
    ...
} until $line eq ".\n";
```

See the three different `do` entries in Chapter 29, *Functions*. Note also that the loop-control operators described later will not work in this construct, since modifiers don't take loop labels. You can always place an extra block around it to terminate early, or inside it to iterate early, as described later in the section "Bare Blocks". Or you could write a real loop with multiple loop controls inside. Speaking of real loops, we'll talk about compound statements next.

Compound Statements

A sequence of statements within a scope* is called a *block*. Sometimes the scope is the entire file, such as a `required` file or the file containing your main program. Sometimes the scope is a string being evaluated with `eval`. But generally, a block is surrounded by braces (`{}`). When we say scope, we mean any of these three. When we mean a block with braces, we'll use the term *BLOCK*.

Compound statements are built out of expressions and *BLOCK*s. Expressions are built out of terms and operators. In our syntax descriptions, we'll use the word *EXPR* to indicate a place where you can use any scalar expression. To indicate an expression evaluated in list context, we'll say *LIST*.

The following statements may be used to control conditional and repeated execution of *BLOCK*s. (The *LABEL* portion is optional.)

```
if (EXPR) BLOCK
if (EXPR) BLOCK else BLOCK
if (EXPR) BLOCK elsif (EXPR) BLOCK ...
if (EXPR) BLOCK elsif (EXPR) BLOCK ... else BLOCK

unless (EXPR) BLOCK
unless (EXPR) BLOCK else BLOCK
unless (EXPR) BLOCK elsif (EXPR) BLOCK ...
unless (EXPR) BLOCK elsif (EXPR) BLOCK ... else BLOCK

LABEL while (EXPR) BLOCK
LABEL while (EXPR) BLOCK continue BLOCK

LABEL until (EXPR) BLOCK
LABEL until (EXPR) BLOCK continue BLOCK

LABEL for (EXPR; EXPR; EXPR) BLOCK

LABEL foreach (LIST) BLOCK
LABEL foreach VAR (LIST) BLOCK
LABEL foreach VAR (LIST) BLOCK continue BLOCK

LABEL BLOCK
LABEL BLOCK continue BLOCK
```

Note that unlike in C and Java, these are defined in terms of *BLOCK*s, not statements. This means that the braces are required—no dangling statements allowed. If you want to write conditionals without braces there are several ways to do so.

---

* Scopes and namespaces are described in Chapter 2, *Bits and Pieces*, in the "Names" section.

The following all do the same thing:

```
unless (open(FOO, $foo))    { die "Can't open $foo: $!" }
if (!open(FOO, $foo))       { die "Can't open $foo: $!" }

die "Can't open $foo: $!"   unless open(FOO, $foo);
die "Can't open $foo: $!"   if !open(FOO, $foo);

open(FOO, $foo)             || die "Can't open $foo: $!";
open FOO, $foo             or die "Can't open $foo: $!";
```

Under most circumstances, we tend to prefer the last pair. These forms come with less eye-clutter than the others, especially the "or die" version. With the || form you need to get used to using parentheses religiously, but with the or version, it doesn't matter if you forget.

But the main reason we like the last versions better is because of how they pull the important part of the statement right up to the front of the line where you'll see it first. The error handling is shoved off to the side so that you don't have to pay attention to it unless you want to.* If you tab all your "or die" checks over to the same column on the right each time, it's even easier to read:

```
chdir $dir            or die "chdir $dir: $!";
open FOO, $file       or die "open $file: $!";
@lines = <FOO>        or die "$file is empty?";
close FOO             or die "close $file: $!";
```

if and unless Statements

The if statement is straightforward. Because BLOCKs are always bounded by braces, there is never any ambiguity regarding which particular if an else or elsif goes with. In any given sequence of if/elsif/else BLOCKs, only the first one whose condition evaluates to true is executed. If none of them is true, then the else BLOCK, if there is one, is executed. It's usually a good idea to put an else at the end of a chain of elsifs to guard against a missed case.

If you use unless in place of if, the sense of its test is reversed. That is:

```
unless ($x == 1) ...
```

is equivalent to:

```
if ($x != 1) ...
```

---

* (Like this footnote.)

or even to the unsightly:

```
if (!($x == 1)) ...
```

The scope of a variable declared in the controlling condition extends from its declaration through the rest of that conditional only, including any elsifs and the final else clause if present, but not beyond:

```
if ((my $color = <STDIN>) =~ /red/i) {
    $value = 0xff0000;
}
elsif ($color =~ /green/i) {
    $value = 0x00ff00;
}
elsif ($color =~ /blue/i) {
    $value = 0x0000ff;
}
else {
    warn "unknown RGB component '$color', using black instead\n";
    $value = 0x000000;
}
```

After the else, the $color variable is no longer in scope. If you want the scope to extend further, declare the variable beforehand.

Loop Statements

All loop statements have an optional *LABEL* in their formal syntax. (You can put a label on any statement, but it has a special meaning to a loop.) If present, the label consists of an identifier followed by a colon. It's customary to make the label uppercase to avoid potential confusion with reserved words, and so it stands out better. And although Perl won't get confused if you use a label that already has a meaning like if or open, your readers might.

while and until Statements

The while statement repeatedly executes the block as long as *EXPR* is true. If the word while is replaced by the word until, the sense of the test is reversed; that is, it executes the block only as long as *EXPR* remains false. The conditional is still tested before the first iteration, though.

The while or until statement can have an optional extra block: the continue block. This block is executed every time the block is continued, either by falling off the end of the first block or by an explicit next (a loop-control operator that goes to the next iteration). The continue block is not heavily used in practice, but it's in here so we can define the for loop rigorously in the next section.

Unlike the foreach loop we'll see in a moment, a while loop never implicitly local-izes any variables in its test condition. This can have "interesting" consequences when while loops use globals for loop variables. In particular, see the section "Line input (angle) operator" in Chapter 2 for how implicit assignment to the global $_ can occur in certain while loops, along with an example of how to deal with the problem by explicitly localizing $_. For other loop variables, however, it's best to declare them with my, as in the next example.

A variable declared in the test condition of a while or until statement is visible only in the block or blocks governed by that test. It is not part of the surrounding scope. For example:

```
while (my $line = <STDIN>) {
    $line = lc $line;
}
continue {
    print $line;    # still visible
}
# $line now out of scope here
```

Here the scope of $line extends from its declaration in the control expression throughout the rest of the loop construct, including the continue block, but not beyond. If you want the scope to extend further, declare the variable before the loop.

for Loops

The three-part for loop has three semicolon-separated expressions within its parentheses. These expressions function respectively as the initialization, the con-dition, and the re-initialization expressions of the loop. All three expressions are optional (but not the semicolons); if omitted, the condition is always true. Thus, the three-part for loop can be defined in terms of the corresponding while loop. This:

```
LABEL:
  for (my $i = 1; $i <= 10; $i++) {
    ...
  }
```

is like this:

```
{
    my $i = 1;
    LABEL:
    while ($i <= 10) {
        ...
    }
```

```
        continue {
            $i++;
        }
    }
```

except that there's not really an outer block. (We just put one there to show how the scope of the my is limited.)

If you want to iterate through two variables simultaneously, just separate the parallel expressions with commas:

```
    for ($i = 0, $bit = 0; $i < 32; $i++, $bit <<= 1) {
        print "Bit $i is set\n" if $mask & $bit;
    }
    # the values in $i and $bit persist past the loop
```

Or declare those variables to be visible only inside the for loop:

```
    for (my ($i, $bit) = (0, 1); $i < 32; $i++, $bit <<= 1) {
        print "Bit $i is set\n" if $mask & $bit;
    }
    # loop's versions of $i and $bit now out of scope
```

Besides the normal looping through array indices, for can lend itself to many other interesting applications. It doesn't even need an explicit loop variable. Here's one example that avoids the problem you get when you explicitly test for end-of-file on an interactive file descriptor, causing your program to appear to hang.

```
    $on_a_tty = -t STDIN && -t STDOUT;
    sub prompt { print "yes? " if $on_a_tty }
    for ( prompt(); <STDIN>; prompt() ) {
        # do something
    }
```

Another traditional application for the three-part for loop results from the fact that all three expressions are optional, and the default condition is true. If you leave out all three expressions, you have written an infinite loop:

```
    for (;;) {
        ...
    }
```

This is the same as writing:

```
    while (1) {
        ...
    }
```

If the notion of infinite loops bothers you, we should point out that you can always fall out of the loop at any point with an explicit loop-control operator such as last. Of course, if you're writing the code to control a cruise missile, you may not actually need an explicit loop exit. The loop will be terminated automatically at the appropriate moment.*

foreach Loops

The foreach loop iterates over a list of values by setting the control variable (*VAR*) to each successive element of the list:

```
foreach VAR (LIST) {
    ...
}
```

The foreach keyword is just a synonym for the for keyword, so you can use for and foreach interchangeably, whichever you think is more readable in a given situation. If *VAR* is omitted, the global $_ is used. (Don't worry—Perl can easily distinguish for (@ARGV) from for ($i=0; $i<$#ARGV; $i++) because the latter contains semicolons.) Here are some examples:

```
$sum = 0; foreach $value (@array) { $sum += $value }

for $count (10,9,8,7,6,5,4,3,2,1,'BOOM') {  # do a countdown
    print "$count\n"; sleep(1);
}

for (reverse 'BOOM', 1 .. 10) {             # same thing
    print "$_\n"; sleep(1);
}

for $field (split /:/, $data) {             # any LIST expression
    print "Field contains: `$field'\n";
}

foreach $key (sort keys %hash) {
    print "$key => $hash{$key}\n";
}
```

That last one is the canonical way to print out the values of a hash in sorted order. See the keys and sort entries in Chapter 29 for more elaborate examples.

There is no way with foreach to tell where you are in a list. You may compare adjacent elements by remembering the previous one in a variable, but sometimes you just have to break down and write a three-part for loop with subscripts. That's what the other kind of for loop is there for, after all.

If *LIST* consists entirely of assignable values (meaning variables, generally, not enumerated constants), you can modify each of those variables by modifying *VAR*

---

* That is, the fallout from the loop tends to occur automatically.

inside the loop. That's because the foreach loop index variable is an implicit alias for each item in the list that you're looping over. Not only can you modify a single array in place, you can also modify multiple arrays and hashes in a single list:

```
foreach $pay (@salaries) {          # grant 8% raises
    $pay *= 1.08;
}

for (@christmas, @easter) {          # change menu
    s/ham/turkey/;
}
s/ham/turkey/ for @christmas, @easter;    # same thing

for ($scalar, @array, values %hash) {
    s/^\s+//;                        # strip leading  whitespace
    s/\s+$//;                        # strip trailing whitespace
}
```

The loop variable is valid only from within the dynamic or lexical scope of the loop and will be implicitly lexical if the variable was previously declared with my. This renders it invisible to any function defined outside the lexical scope of the variable, even if called from within that loop. However, if no lexical declaration is in scope, the loop variable will be a localized (dynamically scoped) global variable; this allows functions called from within the loop to access that variable. In either case, any previous value the localized variable had before the loop will be restored automatically upon loop exit.

If you prefer, you may explicitly declare which kind of variable (lexical or global) to use. This makes it easier for maintainers of your code to know what's really going on; otherwise, they'll need to search back up through enclosing scopes for a previous declaration to figure out which kind of variable it is:

```
for my  $i    (1 .. 10) { ... }      # $i always lexical
for our $Tick (1 .. 10) { ... }      # $Tick always global
```

When a declaration accompanies the loop variable, the shorter for spelling is preferred over foreach, since it reads better in English.

Here's how a C or Java programmer might first think to code up a particular algorithm in Perl:

```
for ($i = 0; $i < @ary1; $i++) {
    for ($j = 0; $j < @ary2; $j++) {
        if ($ary1[$i] > $ary2[$j]) {
            last;          # Can't go to outer loop. :-(
        }
        $ary1[$i] += $ary2[$j];
    }
    # this is where that last takes me
}
```

But here's how a veteran Perl programmer might do it:

```
WID: foreach $this (@ary1) {
    JET: foreach $that (@ary2) {
        next WID if $this > $that;
        $this += $that;
    }
}
```

See how much easier that was in idiomatic Perl? It's cleaner, safer, and faster. It's cleaner because it's less noisy. It's safer because if code gets added between the inner and outer loops later on, the new code won't be accidentally executed, since next (explained below) explicitly iterates the outer loop rather than merely breaking out of the inner one. And it's faster because Perl executes a foreach statement more rapidly than it would the equivalent for loop, since the elements are accessed directly instead of through subscripting.

But write it however you like. TMTOWTDI.

Like the while statement, the foreach statement can also take a continue block. This lets you execute a bit of code at the bottom of each loop iteration no matter whether you got there in the normal course of events or through a next.

Speaking of which, now we can finally say it: next is next.

Loop Control

We mentioned that you can put a *LABEL* on a loop to give it a name. The loop's *LABEL* identifies the loop for the loop-control operators next, last, and redo. The *LABEL* names the loop as a whole, not just the top of the loop. Hence, a loop-control operator referring to the loop doesn't actually "go to" the loop label itself. As far as the computer is concerned, the label could just as easily have been placed at the end of the loop. But people like things labeled at the top, for some reason.

Loops are typically named for the item the loop is processing on each iteration. This interacts nicely with the loop-control operators, which are designed to read like English when used with an appropriate label and a statement modifier. The archetypal loop works on lines, so the archetypal loop label is LINE:, and the archetypal loop-control operator is something like this:

```
next LINE if /^#/;      # discard comments
```

The syntax for the loop-control operators is:

```
last LABEL
next LABEL
redo LABEL
```

The *LABEL* is optional; if omitted, the operator refers to the innermost enclosing loop. But if you want to jump past more than one level, you must use a *LABEL* to name the loop you want to affect. That *LABEL* does not have to be in your lexical scope, though it probably ought to be. But in fact, the *LABEL* can be anywhere in your dynamic scope. If this forces you to jump out of an `eval` or subroutine, Perl issues a warning (upon request).

Just as you may have as many `return` operators in a function as you like, you may have as many loop-control operators in a loop as you like. This is not to be considered wicked or even uncool. During the early days of structured programming, some people insisted that loops and subroutines have only one entry and one exit. The one-entry notion is still a good idea, but the one-exit notion has led people to write a lot of unnatural code. Much of programming consists of traversing decision trees. A decision tree naturally starts with a single trunk but ends with many leaves. Write your code with the number of loop exits (and function returns) that is natural to the problem you're trying to solve. If you've declared your variables with reasonable scopes, everything gets automatically cleaned up at the appropriate moment, no matter how you leave the block.

The `last` operator immediately exits the loop in question. The `continue` block, if any, is not executed. The following example bombs out of the loop on the first blank line:

```
LINE: while (<STDIN>) {
    last LINE if /^$/;       # exit when done with mail header
    ...
}
```

The `next` operator skips the rest of the current iteration of the loop and starts the next one. If there is a `continue` clause on the loop, it is executed just before the condition is re-evaluated, just like the third component of a three-part `for` loop. Thus it can be used to increment a loop variable, even when a particular iteration of the loop has been interrupted by a `next`:

```
LINE: while (<STDIN>) {
    next LINE if /^#/;       # skip comments
    next LINE if /^$/;       # skip blank lines
    ...
} continue {
    $count++;
}
```

The `redo` operator restarts the loop block without evaluating the conditional again. The `continue` block, if any, is not executed. This operator is often used by programs that want to fib to themselves about what was just input. Suppose you were processing a file that sometimes had a backslash at the end of a line to continue the record on the next line. Here's how you could use `redo` for that:

```
while (<>) {
    chomp;
    if (s/\\$//) {
        $_ .= <>;
        redo unless eof;      # don't read past each file's eof
    }
    # now process $_
}
```

which is the customary Perl shorthand for the more explicitly (and tediously) written version:

```
LINE: while (defined($line = <ARGV>)) {
    chomp($line);
    if ($line =~ s/\\$//) {
        $line .= <ARGV>;
        redo LINE unless eof(ARGV);
    }
    # now process $line
}
```

Here's an example from a real program that uses all three loop-control operators. Although this particular strategy of parsing command-line arguments is less common now that we have the `Getopts::*` modules bundled with Perl, it's still a nice illustration of the use of loop-control operators on named, nested loops:

```
ARG: while (@ARGV && $ARGV[0] =~ s/^-(?=.)//) {
    OPT: for (shift @ARGV) {
        m/^$/         && do {                               next ARG; };
        m/^-$/        && do {                               last ARG; };
        s/^d//        && do { $Debug_Level++;               redo OPT; };
        s/^l//        && do { $Generate_Listing++;          redo OPT; };
        s/^i(.*)//    && do { $In_Place = $1 || ".bak";     next ARG; };
        say_usage("Unknown option: $_");
    }
}
```

One more point about loop-control operators. You may have noticed that we are not calling them "statements". That's because they aren't statements—although like any expression, they can be used as statements. You can almost think of them as unary operators that just happen to cause a change in control flow. So you can use them anywhere it makes sense to use them in an expression. In fact, you can even use them where it doesn't make sense. One sometimes sees this coding error:

```
open FILE, $file
    or warn "Can't open $file: $!\n", next FILE;    # WRONG
```

The intent is fine, but the `next FILE` is being parsed as one of the arguments to `warn`, which is a list operator. So the `next` executes before the `warn` gets a chance to emit the warning. In this case, it's easily fixed by turning the `warn` list operator into the `warn` function call with some suitably situated parentheses:

```
open FILE, $file
    or warn("Can't open $file: $!\n"), next FILE;   # okay
```

However, you might find it easier to read this:

```
unless (open FILE, $file) {
    warn "Can't open $file: $!\n";
    next FILE;
}
```

Bare Blocks

A *BLOCK* by itself (labeled or not) is semantically equivalent to a loop that executes once. Thus you can use `last` to leave the block or `redo` to restart the block.* Note that this is not true of the blocks in `eval {}`, `sub {}`, or, much to everyone's surprise, `do {}`. These three are not loop blocks because they're not *BLOCK*s by themselves; the keyword in front makes them mere terms in an expression that just happen to include a code block. Since they're not loop blocks, they cannot be given a label to apply loop controls to. Loop controls may only be used on true loops, just as a `return` may only be used within a subroutine (well, or an `eval`).

Loop controls don't work in an `if` or `unless`, either, since those aren't loops. But you can always introduce an extra set of braces to give yourself a bare block, which *does* count as a loop:

```
if (/pattern/) {{
    last if /alpha/;
    last if /beta/;
    last if /gamma/;
    # do something here only if still in if()
}}
```

Here's how a block can be used to let loop-control operators work with a `do {}` construct. To `next` or `redo` a `do`, put a bare block inside:

```
do {{
    next if $x == $y;
    # do something here
}} until $x++ > $z;
```

---

* For reasons that may (or may not) become clear upon reflection, a `next` also exits the once-through block. There is a slight difference, however: a `next` will execute a `continue` block, but a `last` won't.

For `last`, you have to be more elaborate:

```
{
    do {
        last if $x = $y ** 2;
        # do something here
    } while $x++ <= $z;
}
```

And if you want both loop controls available, you'll have put a label on those blocks so you can tell them apart:

```
DO_LAST: {
            do {
DO_NEXT:        {
                    next DO_NEXT if $x == $y;
                    last DO_LAST if $x =  $y ** 2;
                    # do something here
                }
            } while $x++ <= $z;
        }
```

But certainly by that point (if not before), you'd be better off using an ordinary infinite loop with `last` at the end:

```
for (;;) {
    next if $x == $y;
    last if $x =  $y ** 2;
    # do something here
    last unless $x++ <= $z;
}
```

Case Structures

Unlike some other programming languages, Perl has no official `switch` or `case` statement. That's because Perl doesn't need one, having many ways to do the same thing. A bare block is particularly convenient for doing case structures (multiway switches). Here's one:

```
SWITCH: {
    if (/^abc/) { $abc = 1; last SWITCH; }
    if (/^def/) { $def = 1; last SWITCH; }
    if (/^xyz/) { $xyz = 1; last SWITCH; }
    $nothing = 1;
}
```

and here's another:

```
SWITCH: {
    /^abc/      && do { $abc = 1; last SWITCH; };
    /^def/      && do { $def = 1; last SWITCH; };
    /^xyz/      && do { $xyz = 1; last SWITCH; };
    $nothing = 1;
}
```

or, formatted so that each case stands out more:

```
SWITCH: {
    /^abc/      && do {
                        $abc = 1;
                        last SWITCH;
                    };
    /^def/      && do {
                        $def = 1;
                        last SWITCH;
                    };
    /^xyz/      && do {
                        $xyz = 1;
                        last SWITCH;
                    };
    $nothing = 1;
}
```

or even (horrors!):

```
if     (/^abc/) { $abc = 1 }
elsif (/^def/) { $def = 1 }
elsif (/^xyz/) { $xyz = 1 }
else           { $nothing = 1 }
```

In this next example, notice how the `last` operators ignore the `do {}` blocks, which aren't loops, and exit the `for` loop instead:

```
for ($very_nasty_long_name[$i++][$j++]->method()) {
    /this pattern/      and do { push @flags, '-e'; last; };
    /that one/          and do { push @flags, '-h'; last; };
    /something else/    and do {                    last; };
    die "unknown value: '$_'";
}
```

You might think it odd to loop over a single value, since you'll only go through the loop once. But it's convenient to use `for`/`foreach`'s aliasing capability to make a temporary, localized assignment to $_. On repeated compares against the same long value, this makes it much easier to type and therefore harder to mistype. It avoids possible side effects from evaluating the expression again. And pertinent to this section, it's also one of the most commonly seen standard idioms for implementing a switch or case structure.

Cascading use of the `?:` operator can also work for simple cases. Here we again use a `for` for its aliasing property to make repeated comparisons more legible:

```
for ($user_color_preference) {
    $value = /red/      ?   0xFF0000    :
             /green/    ?   0x00FF00    :
             /blue/     ?   0x0000FF    :
                            0x000000    ;    # black if all fail
}
```

For situations like this last one, it's sometimes better to build yourself a hash and quickly index into it to pull the answer out. Unlike the cascading conditionals we just looked at, a hash scales to an unlimited number of entries, and takes no more time to look up the first one than the last. The disadvantage is that you can only do an exact lookup, not a pattern match. If you have a hash like this:

```
%color_map = (
    azure        => 0xF0FFFF,
    chartreuse   => 0x7FFF00,
    lavender     => 0xE6E6FA,
    magenta      => 0xFF00FF,
    turquoise    => 0x40E0D0,
);
```

then exact string lookups run quickly:

```
$value = $color_map{ lc $user_color_preference } || 0x000000;
```

Even complicated multiway branching statements (with each case involving the execution of several different statements) can be turned into fast lookups. You just need to use a hash of references to functions. See the section "Hashes of Functions" in Chapter 9, *Data Structures*, for how to handle those.

goto

Although not for the faint of heart (nor for the pure of heart), Perl does support a goto operator. There are three forms: goto *LABEL*, goto *EXPR*, and goto *&NAME*.

The goto *LABEL* form finds the statement labeled with *LABEL* and resumes execution there. It cant be used to jump into any construct that requires initialization, such as a subroutine or a foreach loop. It also can't be used to jump into a construct that has been optimized away (see Chapter 18, *Compiling*). It can be used to go almost anywhere else within the current block or any block in your dynamic scope (that is, a block you were called from). You can even goto out of subroutines, but it's usually better to use some other construct. The author of Perl has never felt the need to use this form of goto (in Perl, that is—C is another matter).

The goto *EXPR* form is just a generalization of goto *LABEL*. It expects the expression to produce a label name, whose location obviously has to be resolved dynamically by the interpreter. This allows for computed gotos per FORTRAN, but isn't necessarily recommended if you're optimizing for maintainability:

```
goto(("FOO", "BAR", "GLARCH")[$i]);           # hope 0 <= i < 3

@loop_label = qw/FOO BAR GLARCH/;
goto $loop_label[rand @loop_label];           # random teleport
```

In almost all cases like this, it's usually a far, far better idea to use the structured control flow mechanisms of next, last, or redo instead of resorting to a goto. For certain applications, a hash of references to functions or the catch-and-throw pair of eval and die for exception processing can also be prudent approaches.

The goto &*NAME* form is highly magical and sufficiently removed from the ordinary goto to exempt its users from the opprobrium to which goto users are customarily subjected. It substitutes a call to the named subroutine for the currently running subroutine. This behavior is used by AUTOLOAD subroutines to load another subroutine and then pretend that the other subroutine was called in the first place. After the goto, not even caller will be able to tell that this routine was called first. The autouse, AutoLoader, and SelfLoader modules all use this strategy to define functions the first time they're called, and then to jump right to them without anyone ever knowing the functions weren't there all along.

Global Declarations

Subroutine and format declarations are global declarations. No matter where you place them, what they declare is global (it's local to a package, but packages are global to the program, so everything in a package is visible from anywhere). A global declaration can be put anywhere a statement can, but it has no effect on the execution of the primary sequence of statements—the declarations take effect at compile time.

This means you can't conditionally declare subroutines or formats by hiding them from the compiler inside a run-time conditional like an if, since only the interpreter pays attention to those conditions. Subroutine and format declarations (and use and no declarations) are seen by the compiler no matter where they occur.

Global declarations are typically put at the beginning or the end of your program, or off in some other file. However, if you're declaring any lexically scoped variables (see the next section), you'll want to make sure your format or subroutine definition falls within the scope of the variable declarations if you expect it to be able to access those private variables.

Note that we sneakily switched from talking about declarations to definitions. Sometimes it helps to split the *definition* of the subroutine from its *declaration*. The only syntactic difference between the two is that the definition supplies a *BLOCK* containing the code to be executed, while the declaration doesn't. (A subroutine definition acts as its own declaration if no declaration has been seen.) Splitting the definition from the declaration allows you to put the subroutine declaration at the front of the file and the definition at the end (with your lexically scoped variable declarations happily in the middle):

```
sub count (@);        # Compiler now knows how to call count().
my $x;                # Compiler now knows about lexical variable.
$x = count(3,2,1);    # Compiler can validate function call.
sub count (@) { @_ }  # Compiler now knows what count() means.
```

As this example shows, subroutines don't actually have to be defined before calls to them can be compiled (indeed, the definition can even by delayed until first use, if you use autoloading), but declaring subroutines helps the compiler in various ways and gives you more options in how you can call them.

Declaring a subroutine allows it to be used without parentheses, as if it were a built-in operator, from that point forward in the compilation. (We used parentheses to call count in the last example, but we didn't actually need to.) You can declare a subroutine without defining it just by saying:

```
sub myname;
$me = myname $0          or die "can't get myname";
```

A bare declaration like that declares the function to be a list operator, not a unary operator, so be careful to use or there instead of ||. The || operator binds too tightly to use after list operators, though you can always use parentheses around the list operators arguments to turn the list operator back into something that behaves more like a function call. Alternatively, you can use the prototype ($) to turn the subroutine into a unary operator:

```
sub myname ($);
$me = myname $0          || die "can't get myname";
```

That now parses as you'd expect, but you still ought to get in the habit of using or in that situation. For more on prototypes, see Chapter 6, *Subroutines*.

You *do* need to define the subroutine at some point, or you'll get an error at run time indicating that you've called an undefined subroutine. Other than defining the subroutine yourself, there are several ways to pull in definitions from elsewhere.

You can load definitions from other files with a simple require statement; this was the best way to load files in Perl 4, but there are two problems with it. First, the other file will typically insert subroutine names into a package (a symbol table) of its own choosing, not your packages. Second, a require happens at run time, so it occurs too late to serve as a declaration in the file invoking the require. There are times, however, when delayed loading is what you want.

A more useful way to pull in declarations and definitions is with the use declaration, which effectively requires the module at compile time (because use counts as a BEGIN block) and then lets you import some of the module's declarations into your own program. Thus use can be considered a kind of global declaration, in that it imports names at compile time into your own (global) package just as if you'd declared them yourself. See the section "Symbol Tables" in Chapter 10, *Packages*, for low-level mechanics on how importation works between packages; Chapter 11, *Modules*, for how to set up a module's imports and exports; and Chapter 18 for an explanation of BEGIN and its cousins, CHECK, INIT, and END, which are also global declarations of a sort because they're dealt with at compile time and can have global effects.

Scoped Declarations

Like global declarations, lexically scoped declarations have an effect at the time of compilation. Unlike global declarations, lexically scoped declarations only apply from the point of the declaration through the end of the innermost enclosing scope (block, file, or eval—whichever comes first). That's why we call them lexically scoped, though perhaps "textually scoped" would be more accurate, since lexical scoping has little to do with lexicons. But computer scientists the world over know what "lexically scoped" means, so we perpetuate the usage here.

Perl also supports dynamically scoped declarations. A *dynamic scope* also extends to the end of the innermost enclosing block, but in this case "enclosing" is defined dynamically at run time rather than textually at compile time. To put it another way, blocks nest dynamically by invoking other blocks, not by including them. This nesting of dynamic scopes may correlate somewhat to the nesting of lexical scopes, but the two are generally not identical, especially when any subroutines have been invoked.

We mentioned that some aspects of use could be considered global declarations, but other aspects of use are lexically scoped. In particular, use not only imports package symbols but also implements various magical compiler hints, known as *pragmas* (or if you're into classical forms, *pragmata*). Most pragmas are lexically scoped, including the use strict 'vars' pragma which forces you to declare your variables before you can use them. See the later section, "Pragmas".

A package declaration, oddly enough, is itself lexically scoped, despite the fact that a package is a global entity. But a package declaration merely declares the identity of the default package for the rest of the enclosing block. Undeclared, unqualified variable names* are looked up in that package. In a sense, a package is never declared at all, but springs into existence when you refer to something that belongs to that package. It's all very Perlish.

---

* Also unqualified names of subroutines, filehandles, directory handles, and formats.

Scoped Variable Declarations

Most of the rest of the chapter is about using global variables. Or rather, it's about *not* using global variables. There are various declarations that help you not use global variables—or at least, not use them foolishly.

We already mentioned the `package` declaration, which was introduced into Perl long ago to allow globals to be split up into separate packages. This works pretty well for certain kinds of variables. Packages are used by libraries, modules, and classes to store their interface data (and some of their semi-private data) to avoid conflicting with variables and functions of the same name in your main program or in other modules. If you see someone write `$Some::stuff`,* they're using the `$stuff` scalar variable from the package `Some`. See Chapter 10.

If this were all there were to the matter, Perl programs would quickly become unwieldy as they got longer. Fortunately, Perl's three scoping declarations make it easy to create completely private variables (using `my`), to give selective access to global ones (using `our`), and to provide temporary values to global variables (using `local`):

```
my $nose;
our $House;
local $TV_channel;
```

If more than one variable is listed, the list must be placed in parentheses. For `my` and `our`, the elements may only be simple scalar, array, or hash variables. For `local`, the constraints are somewhat more relaxed: you may also localize entire typeglobs and individual elements or slices of arrays and hashes:

```
my ($nose, @eyes, %teeth);
our ($House, @Autos, %Kids);
local (*Spouse, $phone{HOME});
```

Each of these modifiers offers a different sort of "confinement" to the variables they modify. To oversimplify slightly: `our` confines names to a scope, `local` confines values to a scope, and `my` confines both names and values to a scope.

Each of these constructs may be assigned to, though they differ in what they actually do with the values, since they have different mechanisms for storing values. They also differ somewhat if you *don't* (as we didn't above) assign any values to them: `my` and `local` cause the variables in question to start out with values of `undef` or `()`, as appropriate; `our`, on the other hand, leaves the current value of its associated global unchanged.

---

* Or the archaic `$Some'stuff`, which probably shouldn't be encouraged outside of Perl poetry.

Syntactically, my, our, and local are simply modifiers (like adjectives) on an lvalue expression. When you assign to a modified lvalue, the modifier doesn't change whether the lvalue is viewed as a scalar or a list. To figure how the assignment will work, just pretend that the modifier isn't there. So either of:

```
my ($foo) = <STDIN>;
my @array = <STDIN>;
```

supplies a list context to the righthand side, while:

```
my $foo = <STDIN>;
```

supplies a scalar context.

Modifiers bind more tightly (with higher precedence) than the comma does. The following example erroneously declares only one variable, not two, because the list following the modifier is not enclosed in parentheses.

```
my $foo, $bar = 1;              # WRONG
```

This has the same effect as:

```
my $foo;
$bar = 1;
```

You'll get a warning about the mistake if warnings are enabled, whether via the **-w** or **-W** command-line switches, or, preferably, through the use warnings declaration explained later in "Pragmas".

In general, it's best to declare a variable in the smallest possible scope that suits it. Since variables declared in a control-flow statement are visible only in the block governed by that statement, their visibility is reduced. It reads better in English this way, too.

```
sub check_warehouse {
    for my $widget (our @Current_Inventory) {
        print "I have a $widget in stock today.\n";
    }
}
```

The most frequently seen form of declaration is my, which declares lexically scoped variables for which both the names and values are stored in the current scope's temporary scratchpad and may not be accessed globally. Closely related is the our declaration, which enters a lexically scoped name in the current scope, just as my does, but actually refers to a global variable that anyone else could access if they wished. In other words, it's a global variable masquerading as a lexical.

The other form of scoping, dynamic scoping, applies to local variables, which despite the word "local" are really global variables and have nothing to do with the local scratchpad.

Lexically Scoped Variables: my

To help you avoid the maintenance headaches of global variables, Perl provides lexically scoped variables, often called *lexicals* for short. Unlike globals, lexicals guarantee you privacy. Assuming you don't hand out references to these private variables that would let them be fiddled with indirectly, you can be certain that every possible access to these private variables is restricted to code within one discrete and easily identifiable section of your program. That's why we picked the keyword my, after all.

A statement sequence may contain declarations of lexically scoped variables. Such declarations tend to be placed at the front of the statement sequence, but this is not a requirement. In addition to declaring variable names at compile time, the declarations act like ordinary run-time statements: each of them is elaborated within the sequence of statements as if it were an ordinary statement without the modifier:

```
my $name = "fred";
my @stuff = ("car", "house", "club");
my ($vehicle, $home, $tool) = @stuff;
```

These lexical variables are totally hidden from the world outside their immediately enclosing scope. Unlike the dynamic scoping effects of local (see the next section), lexicals are hidden from any subroutine called from their scope. This is true even if the same subroutine is called from itself or elsewhere—each instance of the subroutine gets its own "scratchpad" of lexical variables.

Unlike block scopes, file scopes don't nest; there's no "enclosing" going on, at least not textually. If you load code from a separate file with do, require, or use, the code in that file cannot access your lexicals, nor can you access lexicals from that file.

However, any scope within a file (or even the file itself) is fair game. It's often useful to have scopes larger than subroutine definitions, because this lets you share private variables among a limited set of subroutines. This is how you create variables that a C programmer would think of as "static":

```
{
    my $state = 0;

    sub on     { $state = 1 }
    sub off    { $state = 0 }
    sub toggle { $state = !$state }
}
```

The `eval` *STRING* operator also works as a nested scope, since the code in the `eval` can see its caller's lexicals (as long as the names aren't hidden by identical declarations within the `eval`'s own scope). Anonymous subroutines can likewise access any lexical variables from their enclosing scopes; if they do so, they're what are known as *closures*.[*] Combining those two notions, if a block `eval`s a string that creates an anonymous subroutine, the subroutine becomes a closure with full access to the lexicals of both the `eval` and the block, even after the `eval` and the block have exited. See the section "Closures" in Chapter 8, *References*.

The newly declared variable (or value, in the case of `local`) does not show up until the statement *after* the statement containing the declaration. Thus you could mirror a variable this way:

```
my $x = $x;
```

That initializes the new inner $x with the current value $x, whether the current meaning of $x is global or lexical. (If you don't initialize the new variable, it starts out with an undefined or empty value.)

Declaring a lexical variable of a particular name hides any previously declared lexical of the same name. It also hides any unqualified global variable of the same name, but you can always get to the global variable by explicitly qualifying it with the name of the package the global is in, for example, `$PackageName::varname`.

Lexically Scoped Global Declarations: our

A better way to access globals, especially for programs and modules running under the `use strict` declaration, is the `our` declaration. This declaration is lexically scoped in that it applies only through the end of the current scope. But unlike the lexically scoped `my` or the dynamically scoped `local`, `our` does not isolate anything to the current lexical or dynamic scope. Instead, it provides access to a global variable in the current package, hiding any lexicals of the same name that would have otherwise hidden that global from you. In this respect, `our` variables act just like `my` variables.

If you place an `our` declaration outside any brace-delimited block, it lasts through the end of the current compilation unit. Often, though, people put it just inside the top of a subroutine definition to indicate that they're accessing a global variable:

```
sub check_warehouse {
    our @Current_Inventory;
    my  $widget;
```

---

[*] As a mnemonic, note the common element between "en*clos*ing scope" and "*clos*ure". (The actual definition of closure comes from a mathematical notion concerning the completeness of sets of values and operations on those values.)

```
    foreach $widget (@Current_Inventory) {
        print "I have a $widget in stock today.\n";
    }
}
```

Since global variables are longer in life and broader in visibility than private variables, we like to use longer and flashier names for them than for temporary variable. This practice alone, if studiously followed, can do as much as use strict can toward discouraging the use of global variables, especially in less prestidigitatorial typists.

Repeated our declarations do not meaningfully nest. Every nested my produces a new variable, and every nested local a new value. But every time you use our, you're talking about *the same* global variable, irrespective of nesting. When you assign to an our variable, the effects of that assignment persist after the scope of the declaration. That's because our never creates values; it just exposes a limited form of access to the global, which lives forever:

```
our $PROGRAM_NAME = "waiter";
{
    our $PROGRAM_NAME = "server";
    # Code called here sees "server".
    ...
}
# Code executed here still sees "server".
```

Contrast this with what happens under my or local, where after the block, the outer variable or value becomes visible again:

```
my $i = 10;
{
    my $i = 99;
    ...
}
# Code compiled here sees outer variable.


local $PROGRAM_NAME = "waiter";
{
    local $PROGRAM_NAME = "server";
    # Code called here sees "server".
    ...
}
# Code executed here sees "waiter" again.
```

It usually only makes sense to assign to an our declaration once, probably at the very top of the program or module, or, more rarely, when you preface the our with a local of its own:

```
    {
        local our @Current_Inventory = qw(bananas);
        check_warehouse();   # no, we haven't no bananas :-)
    }
```

Dynamically Scoped Variables: local

Using a local operator on a global variable gives it a temporary value each time local is executed, but it does not affect that variable's global visibility. When the program reaches the end of that dynamic scope, this temporary value is discarded and the original value restored. But it's always still a global variable that just happens to hold a temporary value while that block is executing. If you call some other function while your global contains the temporary value and that function accesses that global variable, it sees the temporary value, not the original one. In other words, that other function is in your dynamic scope, even though it's presumably not in your lexical scope.*

If you have a local that looks like this:

```
    {
        local $var = $newvalue;
        some_func();
        ...
    }
```

you can think of it purely in terms of run-time assignments:

```
    {
        $oldvalue = $var;
        $var = $newvalue;
        some_func();
        ...
    }
    continue {
        $var = $oldvalue;
    }
```

The difference is that with local the value is restored no matter how you exit the block, even if you prematurely return from that scope. The variable is still the same global variable, but the value found there depends on which scope the function was called from. That's why it's called *dynamic scoping*—because it changes during run time.

As with my, you can initialize a local with a copy of the same global variable. Any changes to that variable during the execution of a subroutine (and any others called from within it, which of course can still see the dynamically scoped global)

---

* That's why lexical scopes are sometimes called *static scopes*: to contrast them with dynamic scopes and emphasize their compile-time determinability. Don't confuse this use of the term with how static is used in C or C++. The term is heavily overloaded, which is why we avoid it.

will be thrown away when the subroutine returns. You'd certainly better comment what you are doing, though:

```
# WARNING: Changes are temporary to this dynamic scope.
local $Some_Global = $Some_Global;
```

A global variable then is still completely visible throughout your whole program, no matter whether it was explicitly declared with our or just allowed to spring into existence, or whether it's holding a local value destined to be discarded when the scope exits. In tiny programs, this isn't so bad, but for large ones, you'll quickly lose track of where in the code all these global variables are being used. You can forbid accidental use of globals, if you want, through the use strict 'vars' pragma, described in the next section.

Although both my and local confer some degree of protection, by and large you should prefer my over local. Sometimes, though, you have to use local so you can temporarily change the value of an existing global variable, like those listed in Chapter 28, *Special Names*. Only alphanumeric identifiers may be lexically scoped, and many of those special variables aren't strictly alphanumeric. You also need to use local to make temporary changes to a package's symbol table as shown in the section "Symbol Tables" in Chapter 10. Finally, you can use local on a single element or a whole slice of an array or a hash. This even works if the array or hash happens to be a lexical variable, layering local's dynamic scoping behavior on top of those lexicals. We won't talk much more about the semantics of local here. See local in Chapter 29 for more information.

Pragmas

Many programming languages allow you to give hints to the compiler. In Perl, these hints are conveyed to the compiler with the use declaration. Some pragmas are:

```
use warnings;
use strict;
use integer;
use bytes;
use constant pi => ( 4 * atan2(1,1) );
```

Perl pragmas are all described in Chapter 31, *Pragmatic Modules*, but right now we'll just talk specifically about a couple that are most useful with the material covered in this chapter.

Although a few pragmas are global declarations that affect global variables or the current package, most are lexically scoped declarations whose effects are constrained to last only until the end of the enclosing block, file, or eval (whichever comes first). A lexically scoped pragma can be countermanded in an inner scope with a no declaration, which works just like use but in reverse.

Controlling Warnings

To show how this works, we'll manipulate the warnings pragma to tell Perl whether to issue warnings for questionable practices:

```
use warnings;        # Enable warnings from here till end of file.
...
{
    no warnings;     # Disable warnings through end of block.
    ...
}
# Warnings are automatically enabled again here.
```

Once warnings are enabled, Perl complains about variables used only once, variable declarations that mask other declarations in the same scope, improper conversions of strings into numbers, using undefined values as legitimate strings or numbers, trying to write to files you only opened read-only (or didn't open at all), and many other conditions documented in Chapter 33, *Diagnostic Messages*.

The use warnings pragma is the preferred way to control warnings. Old programs could only use the **-w** command-line switch or modify the global $^W variable:

```
{
    local $^W = 0;
    ...
}
```

It's much better to use the use warnings and no warnings pragmas. A pragma is better because it happens at compile time, because it's a lexical declaration and therefore cannot affect code it wasn't intended to affect, and because (although we haven't shown you in these simple examples) it affords fine-grained control over discrete classes of warnings. For more about the warnings pragma, including how to convert merely noisy warnings into fatal errors, and how to override the pragma to turn on warnings globally even if a module says not to, see use warnings in Chapter 31.

Controlling the Use of Globals

Another commonly seen declaration is the use strict pragma, which has several functions, one of which is to control the use of global variables. Normally, Perl lets you create new globals (or all too often, step on old globals) just by mentioning them. No variable declarations are necessary—by default, that is. Because unbridled use of globals can make large programs or modules painful to maintain, you may sometimes wish to discourage their accidental use. As an aid to preventing such accidents, you can say:

```
use strict 'vars';
```

This means that any variable mentioned from here to the end of the enclosing scope must refer either to a lexical variable or to an explicitly allowed global. If it's not one of those, a compilation error results. A global is explicitly allowed if one of the following is true:

- It's one of Perl's program-wide special variables (see Chapter 28).

- It's fully qualified with its package name (see Chapter 10),

- It's imported into the current package (see Chapter 11).

- It's masquerading as a lexically scoped variable via an our declaration. (This is the main reason we added our declarations to Perl.)

Of course, there's always the fifth alternative—if the pragma proves burdensome, simply countermand it within an inner block using:

```
no strict 'vars'
```

You can also turn on strict checking of symbolic dereferences and accidental use of barewords with this pragma. Normally people just say:

```
use strict;
```

to enable all three strictures. See the use strict entry in Chapter 31 for more information.

5

Pattern Matching

Perl's built-in support for pattern matching lets you search large amounts of data conveniently and efficiently. Whether you run a huge commercial portal site scanning every newsfeed in existence for interesting tidbits, or a government organization dedicated to figuring out human demographics (or the human genome), or an educational institution just trying to get some dynamic information up on your web site, Perl is the tool of choice, in part because of its database connections, but largely because of its pattern-matching capabilities. If you take "text" in the widest possible sense, perhaps 90% of what you do is 90% text processing. That's really what Perl is all about and always has been about—in fact, it's even part of Perl's name: Practical *Extraction* and Report Language. Perl's patterns provide a powerful way to scan through mountains of mere data and extract useful information from it.

You specify a pattern by creating a *regular expression* (or *regex*), and Perl's regular expression engine (the "Engine", for the rest of this chapter) then takes that expression and determines whether (and how) the pattern matches your data. While most of your data will probably be text strings, there's nothing stopping you from using regexes to search and replace any byte sequence, even what you'd normally think of as "binary" data. To Perl, bytes are just characters that happen to have an ordinal value less than 256. (More on that in Chapter 15, *Unicode.*)

If you're acquainted with regular expressions from some other venue, we should warn you that regular expressions are a bit different in Perl. First, they aren't entirely "regular" in the theoretical sense of the word, which means they can do much more than the traditional regular expressions taught in computer science classes. Second, they are used so often in Perl that they have their own special variables, operators, and quoting conventions which are tightly integrated into the language, not just loosely bolted on like any other library. Programmers new to Perl often look in vain for functions like these:

```
match( $string, $pattern );
subst( $string, $pattern, $replacement );
```

But matching and substituting are such fundamental tasks in Perl that they merit one-letter operators: m/*PATTERN*/ and s/*PATTERN*/*REPLACEMENT*/ (m// and s///, for short). Not only are they syntactically brief, but they're also parsed like double-quoted strings rather than ordinary operators; nevertheless, they operate like operators, so we'll call them that. Throughout this chapter, you'll see these operators used to match patterns against a string. If some portion of the string fits the pattern, we say that the match is successful. There are lots of cool things you can do with a successful pattern match. In particular, if you are using s///, a successful match causes the matched portion of the string to be replaced with whatever you specified as the *REPLACEMENT*.

This chapter is all about how to build and use patterns. Perl's regular expressions are potent, packing a lot of meaning into a small space. They can therefore be daunting if you try to intuit the meaning of a long pattern as a whole. But if you can break it up into its parts, and if you know how the Engine interprets those parts, you can understand any regular expression. It's not unusual to see a hundred line C or Java program expressed with a one-line regular expression in Perl. That regex may be a little harder to understand than any single line out of the longer program; on the other hand, the regex will likely be much easier to understand than the longer program taken as a whole. You just have to keep these things in perspective.

The Regular Expression Bestiary

Before we dive into the rules for interpreting regular expressions, let's see what some patterns look like. Most characters in a regular expression simply match themselves. If you string several characters in a row, they must match in order, just as you'd expect. So if you write the pattern match:

```
/Frodo/
```

you can be sure that the pattern won't match unless the string contains the substring "Frodo" somewhere. (A *substring* is just a part of a string.) The match could be anywhere in the string, just as long as those five characters occur somewhere, next to each other and in that order.

Other characters don't match themselves, but "misbehave" in some way. We call these *metacharacters*. (All metacharacters are naughty in their own right, but some are so bad that they also cause other nearby characters to misbehave as well.)

Here are the miscreants:

```
\ | ( ) [ { ^ $ * + ? .
```

Metacharacters are actually very useful and have special meanings inside patterns; we'll tell you all those meanings as we go along. But we do want to reassure you that you can always match any of these twelve characters literally by putting a backslash in front of it. For example, backslash is itself a metacharacter, so to match a literal backslash, you'd backslash the backslash: \\.

You see, backslash is one of those characters that makes other characters misbehave. It just works out that when you make a misbehaving metacharacter misbehave, it ends up behaving—a double negative, as it were. So backslashing a character to get it to be taken literally works, but only on punctuational characters; backslashing an (ordinarily well-behaved) alphanumeric character does the opposite: it turns the literal character into something special. Whenever you see such a two-character sequence:

```
\b \D \t \3 \s
```

you'll know that the sequence is a *metasymbol* that matches something strange. For instance, \b matches a word boundary, while \t matches an ordinary tab character. Notice that a tab is one character wide, while a word boundary is zero characters wide because it's the spot between two characters. So we call \b a *zero-width* assertion. Still, \t and \b are alike in that they both assert something about a particular spot in the string. Whenever you *assert* something in a regular expression, you're just claiming that that particular something has to be true in order for the pattern to match.

Most pieces of a regular expression are some sort of assertion, including the ordinary characters that simply assert that they match themselves. To be precise, they also assert that the *next* thing will match one character later in the string, which is why we talk about the tab character being "one character wide". Some assertions (like \t) eat up some of the string as they match, and others (like \b) don't. But we usually reserve the term "assertion" for the zero-width assertions. To avoid confusion, we'll call the thing with width an *atom*. (If you're a physicist, you can think of nonzero-width atoms as massive, in contrast to the zero-width assertions, which are massless like photons.)

You'll also see some metacharacters that aren't assertions; rather, they're structural (just as braces and semicolons define the structure of ordinary Perl code, but don't really do anything). These structural metacharacters are in some ways the most important ones because the crucial first step in learning to read regular expressions is to teach your eyes to pick out the structural metacharacters. Once you've learned that, reading regular expressions is a breeze.*

One such structural metacharacter is the vertical bar, which indicates *alternation*:

```
/Frodo|Pippin|Merry|Sam/
```

That means that any of those strings can trigger a match; this is covered in "Alternation" later in the chapter. And in the "Capturing and Clustering" section after that, we'll show you how to use parentheses around portions of your pattern to do *grouping*:

```
/(Frodo|Drogo|Bilbo) Baggins/
```

or even:

```
/(Frod|Drog|Bilb)o Baggins/
```

Another thing you'll see are what we call *quantifiers*, which say how many of the previous thing should match in a row. Quantifiers look like this:

```
*   +   ?   *?   {3}   {2,5}
```

You'll never see them in isolation like that, though. Quantifiers only make sense when attached to atoms—that is, to assertions that have width.† Quantifiers attach to the previous atom only, which in human terms means they normally quantify only one character. If you want to match three copies of "bar" in a row, you need to group the individual characters of "bar" into a single "molecule" with parentheses, like this:

```
/(bar){3}/
```

That will match "barbarbar". If you'd said /bar{3}/, that would match "barrr"—which might qualify you as Scottish but disqualify you as barbarbaric. (Then again, maybe not. Some of our favorite metacharacters are Scottish.) For more on quantifiers, see "Quantifiers" later.

Now that you've seen a few of the beasties that inhabit regular expressions, you're probably anxious to start taming them. However, before we discuss regular expressions in earnest, we need to backtrack a little and talk about the pattern-matching operators that make use of regular expressions. (And if you happen to spot a few more regex beasties along the way, just leave a decent tip for the tour guide.)

---

* Admittedly, a stiff breeze at times, but not something that will blow you away.

† Quantifiers are a bit like the statement modifiers in Chapter 4, *Statements and Declarations*, which can only attach to a single statement. Attaching a quantifier to a zero-width assertion would be like trying to attach a while modifier to a declaration—either of which makes about as much sense as asking your local apothecary for a pound of photons. Apothecaries only deal in atoms and such.

Pattern-Matching Operators

Zoologically speaking, Perl's pattern-matching operators function as a kind of cage for regular expressions, to keep them from getting out. This is by design; if we were to let the regex beasties wander throughout the language, Perl would be a total jungle. The world needs its jungles, of course—they're the engines of biological diversity, after all—but jungles should stay where they belong. Similarly, despite being the engines of combinatorial diversity, regular expressions should stay inside pattern match operators where they belong. It's a jungle in there.

As if regular expressions weren't powerful enough, the m// and s/// operators also provide the (likewise confined) power of double-quote interpolation. Since patterns are parsed like double-quoted strings, all the normal double-quote conventions will work, including variable interpolation (unless you use single quotes as the delimiter) and special characters indicated with backslash escapes. (See "Specific Characters" later in this chapter.) These are applied before the string is interpreted as a regular expression. (This is one of the few places in the Perl language where a string undergoes more than one pass of processing.) The first pass is not quite normal double-quote interpolation, in that it knows what it should interpolate and what it should pass on to the regular expression parser. So, for instance, any $ immediately followed by a vertical bar, closing parenthesis, or the end of the string will be treated not as a variable interpolation, but as the traditional regex assertion meaning end-of-line. So if you say:

```
$foo = "bar";
/$foo$/;
```

the double-quote interpolation pass knows that those two $ signs are functioning differently. It does the interpolation of $foo, then hands this to the regular expression parser:

```
/bar$/;
```

Another consequence of this two-pass parsing is that the ordinary Perl tokener finds the end of the regular expression first, just as if it were looking for the terminating delimiter of an ordinary string. Only after it has found the end of the string (and done any variable interpolation) is the pattern treated as a regular expression. Among other things, this means you can't "hide" the terminating delimiter of a pattern inside a regex construct (such as a character class or a regex comment, which we haven't covered yet). Perl will see the delimiter wherever it is and terminate the pattern at that point.

You should also know that interpolating variables into a pattern slows down the pattern matcher, because it feels it needs to check whether the variable has changed, in case it has to recompile the pattern (which will slow it down even further). See "Variable Interpolation" later in this chapter.

The `tr///` transliteration operator does not interpolate variables; it doesn't even use regular expressions! (In fact, it probably doesn't belong in this chapter at all, but we couldn't think of a better place to put it.) It does share one feature with `m//` and `s///`, however: it binds to variables using the `=~` and `!~` operators.

The `=~` and `!~` operators, described in Chapter 3, *Unary and Binary Operators*, bind the scalar expression on their lefthand side to one of three quote-like operators on their right: `m//` for matching a pattern, `s///` for substituting some string for a substring matched by a pattern, and `tr///` (or its synonym, `y///`) for transliterating one set of characters to another set. (You may write `m//` as `//`, without the `m`, if slashes are used for the delimiter.) If the righthand side of `=~` or `!~` is none of these three, it still counts as a `m//` matching operation, but there'll be no place to put any trailing modifiers (see "Pattern Modifiers" later), and you'll have to handle your own quoting:

```
print "matches" if $somestring =~ $somepattern;
```

Really, there's little reason not to spell it out explicitly:

```
print "matches" if $somestring =~ m/$somepattern/;
```

When used for a matching operation, `=~` and `!~` are sometimes pronounced "matches" and "doesn't match" respectively (although "contains" and "doesn't contain" might cause less confusion).

Apart from the `m//` and `s///` operators, regular expressions show up in two other places in Perl. The first argument to the `split` function is a special match operator specifying what *not* to return when breaking a string into multiple substrings. See the description and examples for `split` in Chapter 29, *Functions*. The `qr//` ("quote regex") operator also specifies a pattern via a regex, but it doesn't try to match anything (unlike `m//`, which does). Instead, the compiled form of the regex is returned for future use. See "Variable Interpolation" for more information.

You apply one of the `m//`, `s///`, or `tr///` operators to a particular string with the `=~` binding operator (which isn't a real operator, just a kind of topicalizer, linguistically speaking). Here are some examples:

```
$haystack =~ m/needle/          # match a simple pattern
$haystack =~  /needle/          # same thing

$italiano =~ s/butter/olive oil/    # a healthy substitution

$rotate13 =~ tr/a-zA-Z/n-za-mN-ZA-M/ # easy encryption (to break)
```

Without a binding operator, $_ is implicitly used as the "topic":

```
/new life/ and           # search in $_ and (if found)
    /new civilizations/  #     boldly search $_ again

s/sugar/aspartame/       # substitute a substitute into $_

tr/ATCG/TAGC/            # complement the DNA stranded in $_
```

Because s/// and tr/// change the scalar to which they're applied, you may only use them on valid lvalues:

```
"onshore" =~ s/on/off/;    # WRONG: compile-time error
```

However, m// works on the result of any scalar expression:

```
if ((lc $magic_hat->fetch_contents->as_string) =~ /rabbit/) {
    print "Nyaa, what's up doc?\n";
}
else {
    print "That trick never works!\n";
}
```

But you have to be a wee bit careful, since =~ and !~ have rather high prece-dence—in our previous example the parentheses are necessary around the left term.* The !~ binding operator works like =~, but negates the logical result of the operation:

```
if ($song !~ /words/) {
    print qq/"$song" appears to be a song without words.\n/;
}
```

Since m//, s///, and tr/// are quote operators, you may pick your own delimiters. These work in the same way as the quoting operators q//, qq//, qr//, and qw// (see the section "Pick your own quotes" in Chapter 2, *Bits and Pieces*).

```
$path =~ s#/tmp#/var/tmp/scratch#;

if ($dir =~ m[/bin]) {
    print "No binary directories please.\n";
}
```

When using paired delimiters with s/// or tr///, if the first part is one of the four customary bracketing pairs (angle, round, square, or curly), you may choose dif-ferent delimiters for the second part than you chose for the first:

```
s(egg)<larva>;
s{larva}{pupa};
s[pupa]/imago/;
```

---

* Without the parentheses, the lower-precedence lc would have applied to the whole pattern match instead of just the method call on the magic hat object.

Whitespace is allowed in front of the opening delimiters:

```
s (egg)   <larva>;
s {larva} {pupa};
s [pupa]  /imago/;
```

Each time a pattern successfully matches (including the pattern in a substitution), it sets the $', $&, and $' variables to the text left of the match, the whole match, and the text right of the match. This is useful for pulling apart strings into their components:

```
"hot cross buns" =~ /cross/;
print "Matched: <$'> $& <$'>\n";      # Matched: <hot > cross < buns>
print "Left:    <$'>\n";              # Left:    <hot >
print "Match:   <$&>\n";              # Match:   <cross>
print "Right:   <$'>\n";              # Right:   < buns>
```

For better granularity and efficiency, use parentheses to capture the particular portions that you want to keep around. Each pair of parentheses captures the substring corresponding to the *subpattern* in the parentheses. The pairs of parentheses are numbered from left to right by the positions of the left parentheses; the substrings corresponding to those subpatterns are available after the match in the numbered variables, $1, $2, $3, and so on:[*]

```
$_ = "Bilbo Baggins's birthday is September 22";
/(.*)'s birthday is (.*)/;
print "Person: $1\n";
print "Date: $2\n";
```

$', $&, $', and the numbered variables are global variables implicitly localized to the enclosing dynamic scope. They last until the next successful pattern match or the end of the current scope, whichever comes first. More on this later, in a different scope.

Once Perl sees that you need one of $', $&, or $' anywhere in the program, it provides them for every pattern match. This will slow down your program a bit. Perl uses a similar mechanism to produce $1, $2, and so on, so you also pay a price for each pattern that contains capturing parentheses. (See "Clustering" to avoid the cost of capturing while still retaining the grouping behavior.) But if you never use $' $&, or $', then patterns *without* capturing parentheses will not be penalized. So it's usually best to avoid $', $&, and $' if you can, especially in library modules. But if you must use them once (and some algorithms really appreciate their convenience), then use them at will, because you've already paid the price. $& is not so costly as the other two in recent versions of Perl.

---

[*] Not $0, though, which holds the name of your program.

Pattern Modifiers

We'll discuss the individual pattern-matching operators in a moment, but first we'd like to mention another thing they all have in common, *modifiers*.

Immediately following the final delimiter of an m//, s///, qr//, or tr/// operator, you may optionally place one or more single-letter modifiers, in any order. For clarity, modifiers are usually written as "the /o modifier" and pronounced "the slash oh modifier", even though the final delimiter might be something other than a slash. (Sometimes people say "flag" or "option" to mean "modifier"; that's okay too.)

Some modifiers change the behavior of the individual operator, so we'll describe those in detail later. Others change how the regex is interpreted, so we'll talk about them here. The m//, s///, and qr// operators* all accept the following modifiers after their final delimiter:

Modifier	Meaning
/i	Ignore alphabetic case distinctions (case insensitive).
/s	Let . match newline and ignore deprecated $* variable.
/m	Let ^ and $ match next to embedded \n.
/x	Ignore (most) whitespace and permit comments in pattern.
/o	Compile pattern once only.

The /i modifier says to match both upper- and lowercase (and title case, under Unicode). That way /perl/i would also match the strings "PROPERLY" or "Perla-ceous" (amongst other things). A use locale pragma may also have some influence on what is considered to be equivalent. (This may be a negative influence on strings containing Unicode.)

The /s and /m modifiers don't involve anything kinky. Rather, they affect how Perl treats matches against a string that contains newlines. But they aren't about whether your string actually contains newlines; they're about whether Perl should *assume* that your string contains a single line (/s) or multiple lines (/m), because certain metacharacters work differently depending on whether they're expected to behave in a line-oriented fashion or not.

Ordinarily, the metacharacter "." matches any one character *except* a newline, because its traditional meaning is to match characters within a line. With /s, how-ever, the "." metacharacter can also match a newline, because you've told Perl to ignore the fact that the string might contain multiple newlines. (The /s modifier also makes Perl ignore the deprecated $* variable, which we hope you too have

---

* The tr/// operator does not take regexes, so these modifiers do not apply.

been ignoring.) The /m modifier, on the other hand, changes the interpretation of the ^ and $ metacharacters by letting them match next to newlines within the string instead of considering only the ends of the string. See the examples in the section "Positions" later in this chapter.

The /o modifier controls pattern recompilation. Unless the delimiters chosen are single quotes (m'*PATTERN*' , s'*PATTERN*' *REPLACEMENT*' , or qr'*PATTERN*'), any variables in the pattern will be interpolated (and may cause the pattern to be recompiled) every time the pattern operator is evaluated. If you want such a pattern to be compiled once and only once, use the /o modifier. This prevents expensive run-time recompilations; it's useful when the value you are interpolating won't change during execution. However, mentioning /o constitutes a promise that you won't change the variables in the pattern. If you do change them, Perl won't even notice. For better control over recompilation, use the qr// regex quoting operator. See "Variable Interpolation" later in this chapter for details.

The /x is the *ex*pressive modifier: it allows you to *ex*ploit whitespace and *ex*planatory comments in order to *ex*pand your pattern's legibility, even *ex*tending the pattern across newline boundaries.

Er, that is to say, /x modifies the meaning of the whitespace characters (and the # character): instead of letting them do self-matching as ordinary characters do, it turns them into metacharacters that, oddly, now behave as whitespace (and comment characters) should. Hence, /x allows spaces, tabs, and newlines for formatting, just like regular Perl code. It also allows the # character, not normally special in a pattern, to introduce a comment that extends through the end of the current line within the pattern string.* If you want to match a real whitespace character (or the # character), then you'll have to put it into a character class, or escape it with a backslash, or encode it using an octal or hex escape. (But whitespace is normally matched with a \s* or \s+ sequence, so the situation doesn't arise often in practice.)

Taken together, these features go a long way toward making traditional regular expressions a readable language. In the spirit of TMTOWTDI, there's now more than one way to write a given regular expression. In fact, there's more than two ways:

```
m/\w+:(\s+\w+)\s*\d+/;       # A word, colon, space, word, space, digits.

m/\w+: (\s+ \w+) \s* \d+/x;  # A word, colon, space, word, space, digits.

m{
    \w+:                     # Match a word and a colon.
```

---

* Be careful not to include the pattern delimiter in the comment—because of its "find the end first" rule, Perl has no way of knowing you didn't intend to terminate the pattern at that point.

```
        (                       # (begin group)
            \s+                 # Match one or more spaces.
            \w+                 # Match another word.
        )                       # (end group)
        \s*                     # Match zero or more spaces.
        \d+                     # Match some digits
    }x;
```

We'll explain those new metasymbols later in the chapter. (This section was supposed to be about pattern modifiers, but we've let it get out of hand in our *excitement* about /x. Ah well.) Here's a regular expression that finds duplicate words in paragraphs, stolen right out of the *Perl Cookbook*. It uses the /x and /i modifiers, as well as the /g modifier described later.

```
# Find duplicate words in paragraphs, possibly spanning line boundaries.
#   Use /x for space and comments, /i to match both 'is'
#   in "Is is this ok?", and use /g to find all dups.
$/ = "";            # "paragrep" mode
while (<>) {
    while ( m{
                \b                  # start at a word boundary
                (\w\S+)             # find a wordish chunk
                (
                    \s+             # separated by some whitespace
                    \1              # and that chunk again
                ) +                 # repeat ad lib
                \b                  # until another word boundary
            }xig
        )
    {
        print "dup word '$1' at paragraph $.\n";
    }
}
```

When run on this chapter, it produces warnings like this:

```
dup word 'that' at paragraph 100
```

As it happens, we know that that particular instance was intentional.

The m// Operator (Matching)

```
EXPR =~ m/PATTERN/cgimosx
EXPR =~ /PATTERN/cgimosx
EXPR =~ ?PATTERN?cgimosx
m/PATTERN/cgimosx
/PATTERN/cgimosx
?PATTERN?cgimosx
```

The m// operator searches the string in the scalar *EXPR* for *PATTERN*. If / or ? is the delimiter, the initial m is optional. Both ? and ' have special meanings as delimiters: the first is a once-only match; the second suppresses variable interpolation and the six translation escapes (\U and company, described later).

If *PATTERN* evaluates to a null string, either because you specified it that way using
`//` or because an interpolated variable evaluated to the empty string, the last successfully executed regular expression not hidden within an inner block (or within
a `split`, `grep`, or `map`) is used instead.

In scalar context, the operator returns true (1) if successful, false (`""`) otherwise.
This form is usually seen in Boolean context:

```
if ($shire =~ m/Baggins/) { ... }  # search for Baggins in $shire
if ($shire =~ /Baggins/)  { ... }  # search for Baggins in $shire

if ( m#Baggins# )          { ... }  # search right here in $_
if ( /Baggins/ )           { ... }  # search right here in $_
```

Used in list context, `m//` returns a list of substrings matched by the capturing
parentheses in the pattern (that is, `$1`, `$2`, `$3`, and so on) as described later under
"Capturing and Clustering". The numbered variables are still set even when the list
is returned. If the match fails in list context, a null list is returned. If the match succeeds in list context but there were no capturing parentheses (nor `/g`), a list value
of (1) is returned. Since it returns a null list on failure, this form of `m//` can also be
used in Boolean context, but only when participating indirectly via a list assignment:

```
if (($key,$value) = /(\w+): (.*)/) { ... }
```

Valid modifiers for `m//` (in whatever guise) are shown in Table 5-1.

Table 5-1. m// Modifiers

Modifier	Meaning
/i	Ignore alphabetic case.
/m	Let ^ and $ match next to embedded \n.
/s	Let . match newline and ignore deprecated $*.
/x	Ignore (most) whitespace and permit comments in pattern.
/o	Compile pattern once only.
/g	Globally find all matches.
/cg	Allow continued search after failed /g match.

The first five modifiers apply to the regex and were described earlier. The last two
change the behavior of the match operation itself. The `/g` modifier specifies global
matching—that is, matching as many times as possible within the string. How it
behaves depends on context. In list context, `m//g` returns a list of all matches
found. Here we find all the places someone mentioned "perl", "Perl", "PERL", and
so on:

```
if (@perls = $paragraph =~ /perl/gi) {
    printf "Perl mentioned %d times.\n", scalar @perls;
}
```

If there are no capturing parentheses within the /g pattern, then the complete matches are returned. If there are capturing parentheses, then only the strings captured are returned. Imagine a string like:

```
$string = "password=xyzzy verbose=9 score=0";
```

Also imagine you want to use that to initialize a hash like this:

```
%hash = (password => "xyzzy", verbose => 9, score => 0);
```

Except, of course, you don't have a list, you have a string. To get the corresponding list, you can use the m//g operator in list context to capture all of the key/value pairs from the string:

```
%hash = $string =~ /(\w+)=(\w+)/g;
```

The (\w+) sequence captures an alphanumeric word. See the section "Capturing and Clustering".

Used in scalar context, the /g modifier indicates a *progressive match*, which makes Perl start the next match on the same variable at a position just past where the last one stopped. The \G assertion represents that position in the string; see "Positions" later in this chapter for a description of \G. If you use the /c (for "continue") modifier in addition to /g, then when the /g runs out, the failed match doesn't reset the position pointer.

If a ? is the delimiter, as in ?*PATTERN*?, this works just like a normal /*PATTERN*/ search, except that it matches only once between calls to the reset operator. This can be a convenient optimization when you want to match only the first occurrence of the pattern during the run of the program, not all occurrences. The operator runs the search every time you call it, up until it finally matches something, after which it turns itself off, returning false until you explicitly turn it back on with reset. Perl keeps track of the match state for you.

The ?? operator is most useful when an ordinary pattern match would find the last rather than the first occurrence:

```
open DICT, "/usr/dict/words" or die "Can't open words: $!\n";
while (<DICT>) {
    $first = $1 if ?(^neur.*)?;
    $last  = $1 if /(^neur.*)/;
}
print $first,"\n";          # prints "neurad"
print $last,"\n";           # prints "neurypnology"
```

The reset operator will reset only those instances of `??` compiled in the same package as the call to reset. Saying `m??` is equivalent to saying `??`.

The s/// Operator (Substitution)

```
LVALUE =~ s/PATTERN/REPLACEMENT/egimosx
s/PATTERN/REPLACEMENT/egimosx
```

This operator searches a string for *PATTERN* and, if found, replaces the matched substring with the *REPLACEMENT* text. (Modifiers are described later in this section.)

```
$lotr = $hobbit;         # Just copy The Hobbit
$lotr =~ s/Bilbo/Frodo/g;  #   and write a sequel the easy way.
```

The return value of an `s///` operation (in scalar and list contexts alike) is the number of times it succeeded (which can be more than once if used with the `/g` modifier, as described earlier). On failure, since it substituted zero times, it returns false (`""`), which is numerically equivalent to `0`.

```
if ($lotr =~ s/Bilbo/Frodo/) { print "Successfully wrote sequel." }
$change_count = $lotr =~ s/Bilbo/Frodo/g;
```

The replacement portion is treated as a double-quoted string. You may use any of the dynamically scoped pattern variables described earlier (`$``, `$&`, `$'`, `$1`, `$2`, and so on) in the replacement string, as well as any other double-quote gizmos you care to employ. For instance, here's an example that finds all the strings "revision", "version", or "release", and replaces each with its capitalized equivalent, using the `\u` escape in the replacement portion:

```
s/revision|version|release/\u$&/g;  # Use | to mean "or" in a pattern
```

All scalar variables expand in double-quote context, not just these strange ones. Suppose you had a `%Names` hash that mapped revision numbers to internal project names; for example, `$Names{"3.0"}` might be code-named "Isengard". You could use `s///` to find version numbers and replace them with their corresponding project names:

```
s/version ([0-9.]+)/the $Names{$1} release/g;
```

In the replacement string, `$1` returns what the first (and only) pair of parentheses captured. (You could use also `\1` as you would in the pattern, but that usage is deprecated in the replacement. In an ordinary double-quoted string, `\1` means a Control-A.)

If *PATTERN* is a null string, the last successfully executed regular expression is used instead. Both *PATTERN* and *REPLACEMENT* are subject to variable interpolation, but a *PATTERN* is interpolated each time the `s///` operator is evaluated as a whole, while the *REPLACEMENT* is interpolated every time the pattern matches. (The *PATTERN* can match multiple times in one evaluation if you use the `/g` modifier.)

As before, the first five modifiers in Table 5-2 alter the behavior of the regex; they're the same as in m// and qr//. The last two alter the substitution operator itself.

Table 5-2. s/// Modifiers

Modifier	Meaning
/i	Ignore alphabetic case (when matching).
/m	Let ^ and $ match next to embedded \n.
/s	Let . match newline and ignore deprecated $*.
/x	Ignore (most) whitespace and permit comments in pattern.
/o	Compile pattern once only.
/g	Replace globally, that is, all occurrences.
/e	Evaluate the right side as an expression.

The /g modifier is used with s/// to replace every match of *PATTERN* with the *REPLACEMENT* value, not just the first one found. A s///g operator acts as a global search and replace, making all the changes at once, much like list m//g, except that m//g doesn't change anything. (And s///g is not a progressive match as scalar m//g was.)

The /e modifier treats the *REPLACEMENT* as a chunk of Perl code rather than as an interpolated string. The result of executing that code is used as the replacement string. For example, s/([0-9]+)/sprintf("%#x", $1)/ge would convert all numbers into hexadecimal, changing, for example, 2581 into 0xb23. Or suppose that, in our earlier example, you weren't sure that you had names for all the versions, so you wanted to leave any others unchanged. With a little creative /x formatting, you could say:

```
s{
    version
    \s+
    (
        [0-9.]+
    )
}{
    $Names{$1}
        ? "the $Names{$1} release"
        : $&
}xge;
```

The righthand side of your s///e (or in this case, the lower side) is syntax-checked and compiled at compile time along with the rest of your program. Any syntax error is detected during compilation, and run-time exceptions are left uncaught. Each additional /e after the first one (like /ee, /eee, and so on) is equivalent to calling eval *STRING* on the result of the code, once per extra /e. This evaluates the result of the code expression and traps exceptions in the special $@ variable. See the section "Programmatic Patterns" later in the chapter for more details.

Modifying strings en passant

Sometimes you want a new, modified string without clobbering the old one upon which the new one was based. Instead of writing:

```
$lotr = $hobbit;
$lotr =~ s/Bilbo/Frodo/g;
```

you can combine these into one statement. Due to precedence, parentheses are required around the assignment, as they are with most combinations applying =~ to an expression.

```
($lotr = $hobbit) =~ s/Bilbo/Frodo/g;
```

Without the parentheses around the assignment, you'd only change $hobbit and get the number of replacements stored into $lotr, which would make a rather dull sequel.

You can't use a s/// operator directly on an array. For that, you need a loop. By a lucky coincidence, the aliasing behavior of for/foreach, combined with its use of $_ as the default loop variable, yields the standard Perl idiom to search and replace each element in an array:

```
for (@chapters) { s/Bilbo/Frodo/g }   # Do substitutions chapter by chapter.
s/Bilbo/Frodo/g for @chapters;        # Same thing.
```

As with a simple scalar variable, you can combine the substitution with an assignment if you'd like to keep the original values around, too:

```
@oldhues = ('bluebird', 'bluegrass', 'bluefish', 'the blues');
for (@newhues = @oldhues) { s/blue/red/ }
print "@newhues\n";                # prints: redbird redgrass redfish the reds
```

The idiomatic way to perform repeated substitutes on the same variable is to use a once-through loop. For example, here's how to canonicalize whitespace in a variable:

```
for ($string) {
    s/^\s+//;       # discard leading whitespace
    s/\s+$//;       # discard trailing whitespace
    s/\s+/ /g;      # collapse internal whitespace
}
```

which just happens to produce the same result as:

```
$string = join(" ", split " ", $string);
```

You can also use such a loop with an assignment, as we did in the array case:

```
for ($newshow = $oldshow) {
    s/Fred/Homer/g;
    s/Wilma/Marge/g;
    s/Pebbles/Lisa/g;
    s/Dino/Bart/g;
}
```

When a global substitution just isn't global enough

Occasionally, you can't just use a /g to get all the changes to occur, either because the substitutions have to happen right-to-left or because you need the length of $` to change between matches. You can usually do what you want by calling s/// repeatedly. However, you want the loop to stop when the s/// finally fails, so you have to put it into the conditional, which leaves nothing to do in the main part of the loop. So we just write a 1, which is a rather boring thing to do, but bored is the best you can hope for sometimes. Here are some examples that use a few more of those odd regex beasties that keep popping up:

```
# put commas in the right places in an integer
1 while s/(\d)(\d\d\d)(?!\d)/$1,$2/;

# expand tabs to 8-column spacing
1 while s/\t+/' ' x (length($&)*8 - length($`)%8)/e;

# remove (nested (even deeply nested (like this))) remarks
1 while s/\(([^()]*)\)//g;

# remove duplicate words (and triplicate (and quadruplicate...))
1 while s/\b(\w+) \1\b/$1/gi;
```

That last one needs a loop because otherwise it would turn this:

```
Paris in THE THE THE THE spring.
```

into this:

```
Paris in THE THE spring.
```

which might cause someone who knows a little French to picture Paris sitting in an artesian well emitting iced tea, since "thé" is French for "tea". A Parisian is never fooled, of course.

The tr/// Operator (Transliteration)

```
LVALUE =~ tr/SEARCHLIST/REPLACEMENTLIST/cds
tr/SEARCHLIST/REPLACEMENTLIST/cds
```

For *sed* devotees, y/// is provided as a synonym for tr///. This is why you can't call a function named y, any more than you can call a function named q or m. In all other respects, y/// is identical to tr///, and we won't mention it again.

This operator might not appear to fit into a chapter on pattern matching, since it doesn't use patterns. This operator scans a string, character by character, and replaces each occurrence of a character found in *SEARCHLIST* (which is not a regular expression) with the corresponding character from *REPLACEMENTLIST* (which is not a replacement string). It looks a bit like m// and s///, though, and you can even use the =~ or !~ binding operators on it, so we describe it here. (qr// and split are pattern-matching operators, but you don't use the binding operators on them, so they're elsewhere in the book. Go figure.)

Transliteration returns the number of characters replaced or deleted. If no string is specified via the =~ or !~ operator, the $_ string is altered. The *SEARCHLIST* and *REPLACEMENTLIST* may define ranges of sequential characters with a dash:

```
$message =~ tr/A-Za-z/N-ZA-Mn-za-m/;     # rot13 encryption.
```

Note that a range like A-Z assumes a linear character set like ASCII. But each character set has its own ideas of how characters are ordered and thus of which characters fall in a particular range. A sound principle is to use only ranges that begin from and end at either alphabets of equal case (a-e, A-E), or digits (0-4). Anything else is suspect. When in doubt, spell out the character sets in full: ABCDE.

The *SEARCHLIST* and *REPLACEMENTLIST* are not variable interpolated as double-quoted strings; you may, however, use those backslash sequences that map to a specific character, such as \n or \015.

Table 5-3 lists the modifiers applicable to the tr/// operator. They're completely different from those you apply to m//, s///, or qr//, even if some look the same.

Table 5-3. tr/// Modifiers

Modifier	Meaning
/c	Complement *SEARCHLIST*.
/d	Delete found but unreplaced characters.
/s	Squash duplicate replaced characters.

If the /c modifier is specified, the character set in *SEARCHLIST* is complemented; that is, the effective search list consists of all the characters *not* in *SEARCHLIST*. In the case of Unicode, this can represent a *lot* of characters, but since they're stored logically, not physically, you don't need to worry about running out of memory.

The /d modifier turns tr/// into what might be called the "transobliteration" operator: any characters specified by *SEARCHLIST* but not given a replacement in *REPLACEMENTLIST* are deleted. (This is slightly more flexible than the behavior of some *tr*(1) programs, which delete anything they find in *SEARCHLIST*, period.)

If the /s modifier is specified, sequences of characters converted to the same character are squashed down to a single instance of the character.

If the /d modifier is used, *REPLACEMENTLIST* is always interpreted exactly as specified. Otherwise, if *REPLACEMENTLIST* is shorter than *SEARCHLIST*, the final character is replicated until it is long enough. If *REPLACEMENTLIST* is null, the *SEARCHLIST* is replicated, which is surprisingly useful if you just want to count characters, not change them. It's also useful for squashing characters using /s.

```
tr/aeiou/!/;              # change any vowel into !
tr{/\\\r\n\b\f. }{_};     # change strange chars into an underscore

tr/A-Z/a-z/ for @ARGV;    # canonicalize to lowercase ASCII

$count = ($para =~ tr/\n//); # count the newlines in $para
$count = tr/0-9//;        # count the digits in $_

$word =~ tr/a-zA-Z//s;    # bookkeeper -> bokeper

tr/@$%*//d;               # delete any of those
tr#A-Za-z0-9+/##cd;       # remove non-base64 chars

# change en passant
($HOST = $host) =~ tr/a-z/A-Z/;

$pathname =~ tr/a-zA-Z/_/cs; # change non-(ASCII)alphas to single underbar

tr [\200-\377]
   [\000-\177];           # strip 8th bit, bytewise
```

If the same character occurs more than once in *SEARCHLIST*, only the first is used. Therefore, this:

```
tr/AAA/XYZ/
```

will change any single character A to an X (in $_).

Although variables aren't interpolated into tr///, you can still get the same effect by using eval *EXPR*:

```
$count = eval "tr/$oldlist/$newlist/";
die if $@;  # propagates exception from illegal eval contents
```

One more note: if you want to change your text to uppercase or lowercase, don't use tr///. Use the \U or \L sequences in a double-quoted string (or the equivalent uc and lc functions) since they will pay attention to locale or Unicode information and tr/a-z/A-Z/ won't. Additionally, in Unicode strings, the \u sequence and its corresponding ucfirst function understand the notion of titlecase, which for some languages may be distinct from simply converting to uppercase.

Metacharacters and Metasymbols

Now that we've admired all the fancy cages, we can go back to looking at the crit-ters in the cages, those funny-looking symbols you put inside the patterns. By now you'll have cottoned to the fact that these symbols aren't regular Perl code like function calls or arithmetic operators. Regular expressions are their own little lan-guage nestled inside of Perl. (There's a bit of the jungle in all of us.)

For all their power and expressivity, patterns in Perl recognize the same 12 tradi-tional metacharacters (the Dirty Dozen, as it were) found in many other regular expression packages:

```
\ | ( ) [ { ^ $ * + ? .
```

Some of those bend the rules, making otherwise normal characters that follow them special. We don't like to call the longer sequences "characters", so when they make longer sequences, we call them *metasymbols* (or sometimes just "symbols"). But at the top level, those twelve metacharacters are all you (and Perl) need to think about. Everything else proceeds from there.

Some simple metacharacters stand by themselves, like . and ^ and $. They don't directly affect anything around them. Some metacharacters work like prefix opera-tors, governing what follows them, like \. Others work like postfix operators, gov-erning what immediately precedes them, like *, +, and ?. One metacharacter, |, acts like an infix operator, standing between the operands it governs. There are even bracketing metacharacters that work like circumfix operators, governing something contained inside them, like (...) and [...]. Parentheses are particu-larly important, because they specify the bounds of | on the inside, and of *, +, and ? on the outside.

If you learn only one of the twelve metacharacters, choose the backslash. (Er . . . and the parentheses.) That's because backslash disables the others. When a backslash precedes a nonalphanumeric character in a Perl pattern, it always makes that next character a literal. If you need to match one of the twelve metacharacters in a pattern literally, you write them with a backslash in front. Thus, \. matches a real dot, \$ a real dollar sign, \\ a real backslash, and so on. This is known as "escaping" the metacharacter, or "quoting it", or sometimes just "backslashing" it. (Of course, you already know that backslash is used to suppress variable interpo-lation in double-quoted strings.)

Although a backslash turns a metacharacter into a literal character, its effect upon a following alphanumeric character goes the other direction. It takes something that was regular and makes it special. That is, together they make a metasymbol. An alphabetical list of these metasymbols can be found below in Table 5-7.

Metasymbol Tables

In the following tables, the Atomic column says "yes" if the given metasymbol is quantifiable (if it can match something with width, more or less). Also, we've used "..." to represent "something else". Please see the later discussion to find out what "..." means, if it is not clear from the one-line gloss in the table.)

Table 5-4 shows the basic traditional metasymbols. The first four of these are the structural metasymbols we mentioned earlier, while the last three are simple metacharacters. The . metacharacter is an example of an atom because it matches something with width (the width of a character, in this case); ^ and $ are examples of assertions, because they match something of zero width, and because they are only evaluated to see if they're true or not.

Table 5-4. General Regex Metacharacters

Symbol	Atomic	Meaning
\...	Varies	De-meta next nonalphanumeric character, meta next alphanumeric character (maybe).
...|...	No	Alternation (match one or the other).
(...)	Yes	Grouping (treat as a unit).
[...]	Yes	Character class (match one character from a set).
^	No	True at beginning of string (or after any newline, maybe).
.	Yes	Match one character (except newline, normally).
$	No	True at end of string (or before any newline, maybe).

The quantifiers, which are further described in their own section, indicate how many times the preceding atom (that is, single character or grouping) should match. These are listed in Table 5-5.

Table 5-5. Regex Quantifiers

Quantifier	Atomic	Meaning
*	No	Match 0 or more times (maximal).
+	No	Match 1 or more times (maximal).
?	No	Match 1 or 0 times (maximal).
{*COUNT*}	No	Match exactly *COUNT* times.
{*MIN*, }	No	Match at least *MIN* times (maximal).
{*MIN,MAX*}	No	Match at least *MIN* but not more than *MAX* times (maximal).
*?	No	Match 0 or more times (minimal).
+?	No	Match 1 or more times (minimal).
??	No	Match 0 or 1 time (minimal).

Table 5-5. Regex Quantifiers (continued)

Quantifier	Atomic	Meaning
{*MIN*,}?	No	Match at least *MIN* times (minimal).
{*MIN*,*MAX*}?	No	Match at least *MIN* but not more than *MAX* times (minimal).

A minimal quantifier tries to match as *few* characters as possible within its allowed range. A maximal quantifier tries to match as *many* characters as possible within its allowed range. For instance, .+ is guaranteed to match at least one character of the string, but will match all of them given the opportunity. The opportunities are discussed later in "The Little Engine That /Could(n't)?/".

You'll note that quantifiers may never be quantified.

We wanted to provide an extensible syntax for new kinds of metasymbols. Given that we only had a dozen metacharacters to work with, we chose a formerly illegal regex sequence to use for arbitrary syntactic extensions. These metasymbols are all of the form (?*KEY*...); that is, a (balanced) parenthesis followed by a question mark, followed by a *KEY* and the rest of the subpattern. The *KEY* character indicates which particular regex extension it is. See Table 5-6 for a list of these. Most of them behave structurally since they're based on parentheses, but they also have additional meanings. Again, only atoms may be quantified because they represent something that's really there (potentially).

Table 5-6. Extended Regex Sequences

Extension	Atomic	Meaning
(?#...)	No	Comment, discard.
(?:...)	Yes	Cluster-only parentheses, no capturing.
(?imsx-imsx)	No	Enable/disable pattern modifiers.
(?imsx-imsx:...)	Yes	Cluster-only parentheses plus modifiers.
(?=...)	No	True if lookahead assertion succeeds.
(?!...)	No	True if lookahead assertion fails.
(?<=...)	No	True if lookbehind assertion succeeds.
(?<!...)	No	True if lookbehind assertion fails.
(?>...)	Yes	Match nonbacktracking subpattern.
(?{...})	No	Execute embedded Perl code.
(??{...})	Yes	Match regex from embedded Perl code.
(?(...)...|...)	Yes	Match with if-then-else pattern.
(?(...)...)	Yes	Match with if-then pattern.

And finally, Table 5-7 shows all of your favorite alphanumeric metasymbols. (Symbols that are processed by the variable interpolation pass are marked with a dash in the Atomic column, since the Engine never even sees them.)

Table 5-7. Alphanumeric Regex Metasymbols

Symbol	Atomic	Meaning
\0	Yes	Match the null character (ASCII NUL).
NNN	Yes	Match the character given in octal, up to \377.
n	Yes	Match *n*th previously captured string (decimal).
\a	Yes	Match the alarm character (BEL).
\A	No	True at the beginning of a string.
\b	Yes	Match the backspace character (BS).
\b	No	True at word boundary.
\B	No	True when not at word boundary.
\c*X*	Yes	Match the control character Control-*X* (\cZ, \c[, etc.).
\C	Yes	Match one byte (C `char`) even in utf8 (dangerous).
\d	Yes	Match any digit character.
\D	Yes	Match any nondigit character.
\e	Yes	Match the escape character (ASCII ESC, not backslash).
\E	—	End case (\L, \U) or metaquote (\Q) translation.
\f	Yes	Match the form feed character (FF).
\G	No	True at end-of-match position of prior m//g.
\l	—	Lowercase the next character only.
\L	—	Lowercase till \E.
\n	Yes	Match the newline character (usually NL, but CR on Macs).
\N{*NAME*}	Yes	Match the named char (\N{`greek:Sigma`}).
\p{*PROP*}	Yes	Match any character with the named property.
\P{*PROP*}	Yes	Match any character without the named property.
\Q	—	Quote (de-meta) metacharacters till \E.
\r	Yes	Match the return character (usually CR, but NL on Macs).
\s	Yes	Match any whitespace character.
\S	Yes	Match any nonwhitespace character.
\t	Yes	Match the tab character (HT).
\u	—	Titlecase next character only.
\U	—	Uppercase (not titlecase) till \E.
\w	Yes	Match any "word" character (alphanumerics plus "_").
\W	Yes	Match any nonword character.
\x{*abcd*}	Yes	Match the character given in hexadecimal.

Table 5-7. Alphanumeric Regex Metasymbols (continued)

Symbol	Atomic	Meaning
\X	Yes	Match Unicode "combining character sequence" string.
\z	No	True at end of string only.
\Z	No	True at end of string or before optional newline.

The braces are optional on \p and \P if the property name is one character. The braces are optional on \x if the hexadecimal number is two digits or less. The braces are never optional on \N.

Only metasymbols with "Match the..." or "Match any..." descriptions may be used within character classes (square brackets). That is, character classes are limited to containing specific sets of characters, so within them you may only use metasymbols that describe other specific sets of characters, or that describe specific individual characters. Of course, these metasymbols may also be used outside character classes, along with all the other nonclassificatory metasymbols. Note however that \b is two entirely different beasties: it's a backspace character inside the character class, but a word boundary assertion outside.

There is some amount of overlap between the characters that a pattern can match and the characters an ordinary double-quoted string can interpolate. Since regexes undergo two passes, it is sometimes ambiguous which pass should process a given character. When there is ambiguity, the variable interpolation pass defers the interpretation of such characters to the regular expression parser.

But the variable interpolation pass can only defer to the regex parser when it knows it is parsing a regex. You can specify regular expressions as ordinary double-quoted strings, but then you must follow normal double-quote rules. Any of the previous metasymbols that happen to map to actual characters will still work, even though they're not being deferred to the regex parser. But you can't use any of the other metasymbols in ordinary double quotes (or in any similar constructs such as `...`, qq(...), qx(...), or the equivalent here documents). If you want your string to be parsed as a regular expression without doing any matching, you should be using the qr// (quote regex) operator.

Note that the case and metaquote translation escapes (\U and friends) must be processed during the variable interpolation pass because the purpose of those metasymbols is to influence how variables are interpolated. If you suppress variable interpolation with single quotes, you don't get the translation escapes either. Neither variables nor translation escapes (\U, etc.) are expanded in any single quoted string, nor in single-quoted m'...' or qr'...' operators. Even when you do interpolation, these translation escapes are ignored if they show up as the *result* of variable interpolation, since by then it's too late to influence variable interpolation.

Although the transliteration operator doesn't take regular expressions, any meta-symbol we've discussed that matches a single specific character also works in a tr/// operation. The rest do not (except for backslash, which continues to work in the backward way it always works.)

Specific Characters

As mentioned before, everything that's not special in a pattern matches itself. That means an /a/ matches an "a", an /=/ matches an "=", and so on. Some characters, though, aren't very easy to type in from the keyboard or, even if you manage that, don't show up on a printout; control characters are notorious for this. In a regular expression, Perl recognizes the following double-quotish character aliases:

Escape	Meaning
\0	Null character (ASCII NUL)
\a	Alarm (BEL)
\e	Escape (ESC)
\f	Form feed (FF)
\n	Newline (NL, CR on Mac)
\r	Return (CR, NL on Mac)
\t	Tab (HT)

Just as in double-quoted strings, Perl also honors the following four metasymbols in patterns:

\c*X*

A named control character, like \cC for Control-C, \cZ for Control-Z, \c[for ESC, and \c? for DEL.

NNN

A character specified using its two- or three-digit octal code. The leading 0 is optional, except for values less than 010 (8 decimal) since (unlike in double-quoted strings) the single-digit versions are always considered to be backreferences to captured strings within a pattern. Multiple digits are interpreted as the *n*th backreference if you've captured at least *n* substrings earlier in the pattern (where *n* is considered as a decimal number). Otherwise, they are interpreted as a character specified in octal.

\x{*LONGHEX*}

\x*HEX*

> A character number specified as one or two hex digits ([0-9a-fA-F]), as in
> \x1B. The one-digit form is usable only if the character following it is not a
> hex digit. If braces are used, you may use as many digits as you'd like, which
> may result in a Unicode character. For example, \x{262f} matches a Unicode
> YIN YANG.

\N{*NAME*}

> A named character, such \N{GREEK SMALL LETTER EPSILON}, \N{greek:epsilon},
> or \N{epsilon}. This requires the use charnames pragma described in
> Chapter 31, *Pragmatic Modules*, which also determines which flavors of those
> names you may use (":long", ":full", ":short" respectively, corresponding
> to the three styles just shown).

> A list of all Unicode character names can be found in your closest Unicode
> standards document, or in *PATH_TO_PERLLIB/unicode/Names.txt*.

Wildcard Metasymbols

Three special metasymbols serve as generic wildcards, each of them matching
"any" character (for certain values of "any"). These are the dot ("."), \c, and \X.
None of these may be used in a character class. You can't use the dot there
because it would match (nearly) any character in existence, so it's something of a
universal character class in its own right. If you're going to include or exclude
everything, there's not much point in having a character class. The special wildcards \c and \X have special structural meanings that don't map well to the notion
of choosing a single Unicode character, which is the level at which character
classes work.

The dot metacharacter matches any one character other than a newline. (And with
the /s modifier, it matches that, too.) Like any of the dozen special characters in a
pattern, to match a dot literally, you must escape it with a backslash. For example,
this checks whether a filename ends with a dot followed by a one-character extension:

```
if ($pathname =~ /\.(.)\z/s) {
    print "Ends in $1\n";
}
```

The first dot, the escaped one, is the literal character, and the second says "match
any character". The \z says to match only at the end of the string, and the /s modifier lets the dot match a newline as well. (Yes, using a newline as a file extension
Isn't Very Nice, but that doesn't mean it can't happen.)

The dot metacharacter is most often used with a quantifier. A `.*` matches a maximal number of characters, while a `.*?` matches a minimal number of characters. But it's also sometimes used without a quantifier for its width: `/(..):(..):(..)/` matches three colon-separated fields, each of which is two characters long.

If you use a dot in a pattern compiled under the lexically scoped `use utf8` pragma, then it will match any Unicode character. (You're not supposed to need a `use utf8` for that, but accidents will happen. The pragma may not be necessary by the time you read this.)

```
use utf8;
use charnames qw/:full/;
$BWV[887] = "G\N{MUSIC SHARP SIGN} minor";
($note, $black, $mode) = $BWV[887] =~ /^([A-G])(.)\s+(\S+)/;
print "That's lookin' sharp!\n" if $black eq chr(9839);
```

The `\X` metasymbol matches a character in a more extended sense. It really matches a string of one or more Unicode characters known as a "combining character sequence". Such a sequence consists of a base character followed by any "mark" characters (diacritical markings like cedillas or diereses) that combine with that base character to form one logical unit. `\X` is exactly equivalent to `(?:\PM\pM*)`. This allows it to match one logical character, even when that really comprises several separate characters. The length of the match in `/\X/` would exceed one character if it matched any combining characters. (And that's character length, which has little to do with byte length).

If you are using Unicode and really want to get at a single byte instead of a single character, you can use the `\C` metasymbol. This will always match one byte (specifically, one C language `char` type), even if this gets you out of sync with your Unicode character stream. See the appropriate warnings about doing this in Chapter 15.

Character Classes

In a pattern match, you may match any character that has—or that does not have—a particular property. There are four ways to specify character classes. You may specify a character class in the traditional way using square brackets and enumerating the possible characters, or you may use any of three mnemonic shortcuts: the classic Perl classes, the new Perl Unicode properties, or the standard POSIX classes. Each of these shortcuts matches only one character from its set. Quantify them to match larger expanses, such as `\d+` to match one or more digits. (An easy mistake is to think that `\w` matches a word. Use `\w+` to match a word.)

Custom Character Classes

An enumerated list of characters in square brackets is called a *character class* and matches any one of the characters in the list. For example, [aeiouy] matches a letter that can be a vowel in English. (For Welsh add a "w", for Scottish an "r".) To match a right square bracket, either backslash it or place it first in the list.

Character ranges may be indicated using a hyphen and the a-z notation. Multiple ranges may be combined; for example, [0-9a-fA-F] matches one hex "digit". You may use a backslash to protect a hyphen that would otherwise be interpreted as a range delimiter, or just put it at the beginning or end of the class (a practice which is arguably less readable but more traditional).

A caret (or circumflex, or hat, or up arrow) at the front of the character class inverts the class, causing it to match any single character *not* in the list. (To match a caret, either *don't* put it first, or better, escape it with a backslash.) For example, [^aeiouy] matches any character that isn't a vowel. Be careful with character class negation, though, because the universe of characters is expanding. For example, that character class matches consonants—and also matches spaces, newlines, and anything (including vowels) in Cyrillic, Greek, or nearly any other script, not to mention every idiograph in Chinese, Japanese, and Korean. And someday maybe even Cirth, Tengwar, and Klingon. (Linear B and Etruscan, for sure.) So it might be better to specify your consonants explicitly, such as [cbdfghjklmnpqrstvwxyz], or [b-df-hj-np-tv-z] for short. (This also solves the issue of "y" needing to be in two places at once, which a set complement would preclude.)

Normal character metasymbols are supported inside a character class, (see "Specific Characters"), such as \n, \t, \cX, \NNN, and \N{NAME}. Additionally, you may use \b within a character class to mean a backspace, just as it does in a double-quoted string. Normally, in a pattern match, it means a word boundary. But zero-width assertions don't make any sense in character classes, so here \b returns to its normal meaning in strings. You may also use any predefined character class described later in the chapter (classic, Unicode, or POSIX), but don't try to use them as endpoints of a range—that doesn't make sense, so the "-" will be interpreted literally.

All other metasymbols lose their special meaning inside square brackets. In particular, you can't use any of the three generic wildcards: ".", \X, or \C. The first often surprises people, but it doesn't make much sense to use the universal character class within a restricted one, and you often want to match a literal dot as part of a character class—when you're matching filenames, for instance. It's also meaningless to specify quantifiers, assertions, or alternation inside a character class, since the characters are interpreted individually. For example, [fee|fie|foe|foo] means the same thing as [feio|].

Classic Perl Character Class Shortcuts

Since the beginning, Perl has provided a number of character class shortcuts. These are listed in Table 5-8. All of them are backslashed alphabetic metasymbols, and in each case, the uppercase version is the negation of the lowercase version. The meanings of these are not quite as fixed as you might expect; the meanings can be influenced by locale settings. Even if you don't use locales, the meanings can change whenever a new Unicode standard comes out, adding scripts with new digits and letters. (To keep the old byte meanings, you can always use bytes. For explanations of the utf8 meanings, see "Unicode Properties" later in this chapter. In any case, the utf8 meanings are a superset of the byte meanings.)

Table 5-8. Classic Character Classes

Symbol	Meaning	As Bytes	As utf8
\d	Digit	[0-9]	\p{IsDigit}
\D	Nondigit	[^0-9]	\P{IsDigit}
\s	Whitespace	[\t\n\r\f]	\p{IsSpace}
\S	Nonwhitespace	[^ \t\n\r\f]	\P{IsSpace}
\w	Word character	[a-zA-Z0-9_]	\p{IsWord}
\W	Non-(word character)	[^a-zA-Z0-9_]	\P{IsWord}

(Yes, we know most words don't have numbers or underscores in them; \w is for matching "words" in the sense of tokens in a typical programming language. Or Perl, for that matter.)

These metasymbols may be used either outside or inside square brackets, that is, either standalone or as part of a constructed character class:

```
    if ($var =~ /\D/)        { warn "contains non-digit" }
    if ($var =~ /[^\w\s.]/)  { warn "contains non-(word, space, dot)" }
```

Unicode Properties

Unicode properties are available using \p{*PROP*} and its set complement, \P{*PROP*}. For the rare properties with one-character names, braces are optional, as in \pN to indicate a numeric character (not necessarily decimal—Roman numerals are numeric characters too). These property classes may be used by themselves or combined in a constructed character class:

```
    if ($var =~ /^\p{IsAlpha}+$/)     { print "all alphabetic" }
    if ($var =~ s/[\p{Zl}\p{Zp}]/\n/g) { print "fixed newline wannabes" }
```

Some properties are directly defined in the Unicode standard, and some properties are composites defined by Perl, based on the standard properties. Zl and Zp are standard Unicode properties representing line separators and paragraph separators, while `IsAlpha` is defined by Perl to be a property class combining the standard properties `Ll`, `Lu`, `Lt`, and `Lo`, (that is, letters that are lowercase, upper-case, titlecase, or other). As of version 5.6.0 of Perl, you need to use `utf8` for these properties to work. This restriction will be relaxed in the future.

There are a great many properties. We'll list the ones we know about, but the list is necessarily incomplete. New properties are likely to be in new versions of Unicode, and you can even define your own properties. More about that later.

The Unicode Consortium produces the online resources that turn into the various files Perl uses in its Unicode implementation. For more about these files, see Chapter 15. You can get a nice overview of Unicode in the document *PATH_TO_PERLLIB/unicode/Unicode3.html* where *PATH_TO_PERLLIB* is what is printed out by:

```
perl -MConfig -le 'print $Config{privlib}'
```

Most Unicode properties are of the form `\p{IsPROP}`. The `Is` is optional, since it's so common, but you may prefer to leave it in for readability.

Perl's Unicode properties

First, Table 5-9 lists Perl's composite properties. They're defined to be reasonably close to the standard POSIX definitions for character classes.

Table 5-9. Composite Unicode Properties

Property	Equivalent
IsASCII	`[\x00-\x7f]`
IsAlnum	`[\p{IsLl}\p{IsLu}\p{IsLt}\p{IsLo}\p{IsNd}]`
IsAlpha	`[\p{IsLl}\p{IsLu}\p{IsLt}\p{IsLo}]`
IsCntrl	`\p{IsC}`
IsDigit	`\p{Nd}`
IsGraph	`[^\pC\p{IsSpace}]`
IsLower	`\p{IsLl}`
IsPrint	`\P{IsC}`
IsPunct	`\p{IsP}`
IsSpace	`[\t\n\f\r\p{IsZ}]`
IsUpper	`[\p{IsLu}\p{IsLt}]`
IsWord	`[_\p{IsLl}\p{IsLu}\p{IsLt}\p{IsLo}\p{IsNd}]`
IsXDigit	`[0-9a-fA-F]`

Perl also provides the following composites for each of main categories of standard Unicode properties (see the next section):

Property	Meaning	Normative
IsC	Crazy control codes and such	Yes
IsL	Letters	Partly
IsM	Marks	Yes
IsN	Numbers	Yes
IsP	Punctuation	No
IsS	Symbols	No
IsZ	Separators (Zeparators?)	Yes

Standard Unicode properties

Table 5-10 lists the most basic standard Unicode properties, derived from each character's category. No character is a member of more than one category. Some properties are normative; others are merely informative. See the Unicode Standard for the standard spiel on just how normative the normative information is, and just how informative the informative information isn't.

Table 5-10. Standard Unicode Properties

Property	Meaning	Normative
IsCc	Other, Control	Yes
IsCf	Other, Format	Yes
IsCn	Other, Not assigned	Yes
IsCo	Other, Private Use	Yes
IsCs	Other, Surrogate	Yes
IsLl	Letter, Lowercase	Yes
IsLm	Letter, Modifier	No
IsLo	Letter, Other	No
IsLt	Letter, Titlecase	Yes
IsLu	Letter, Uppercase	Yes
IsMc	Mark, Combining	Yes
IsMe	Mark, Enclosing	Yes
IsMn	Mark, Nonspacing	Yes
IsNd	Number, Decimal digit	Yes
IsNl	Number, Letter	Yes
IsNo	Number, Other	Yes
IsPc	Punctuation, Connector	No
IsPd	Punctuation, Dash	No
IsPe	Punctuation, Close	No
IsPf	Punctuation, Final quote	No

Table 5-10. Standard Unicode Properties (continued)

Property	Meaning	Normative
IsPi	Punctuation, Initial quote	No
IsPo	Punctuation, Other	No
IsPs	Punctuation, Open	No
IsSc	Symbol, Currency	No
IsSk	Symbol, Modifier	No
IsSm	Symbol, Math	No
IsSo	Symbol, Other	No
IsZl	Separator, Line	Yes
IsZp	Separator, Paragraph	Yes
IsZs	Separator, Space	Yes

Another useful set of properties has to do with whether a given character can be decomposed (either canonically or compatibly) into other simpler characters. Canonical decomposition doesn't lose any formatting information. Compatibility decomposition may lose formatting information such as whether a character is a superscript.

Property	Information Lost
IsDecoCanon	Nothing
IsDecoCompat	Something (one of the following)
IsDCcircle	Circle around character
IsDCfinal	Final position preference (Arabic)
IsDCfont	Variant font preference
IsDCfraction	Vulgar fraction characteristic
IsDCinitial	Initial position preference (Arabic)
IsDCisolated	Isolated position preference (Arabic)
IsDCmedial	Medial position preference (Arabic)
IsDCnarrow	Narrow characteristic
IsDCnoBreak	Nonbreaking preference on space or hyphen
IsDCsmall	Small characteristic
IsDCsquare	Square around CJK character
IsDCsub	Subscription
IsDCsuper	Superscription
IsDCvertical	Rotation (horizontal to vertical)
IsDCwide	Wide characteristic
IsDCcompat	Identity (miscellaneous)

Here are some properties of interest to people doing bidirectional rendering:

Property	Meaning
IsBidiL	Left-to-right (Arabic, Hebrew)
IsBidiLRE	Left-to-right embedding
IsBidiLRO	Left-to-right override
IsBidiR	Right-to-left
IsBidiAL	Right-to-left Arabic
IsBidiRLE	Right-to-left embedding
IsBidiRLO	Right-to-left override
IsBidiPDF	Pop directional format
IsBidiEN	European number
IsBidiES	European number separator
IsBidiET	European number terminator
IsBidiAN	Arabic number
IsBidiCS	Common number separator
IsBidiNSM	Nonspacing mark
IsBidiBN	Boundary neutral
IsBidiB	Paragraph separator
IsBidiS	Segment separator
IsBidiWS	Whitespace
IsBidiON	Other Neutrals
IsMirrored	Reverse when used right-to-left

The following properties classify various syllabaries according to vowel sounds:

IsSylA	IsSylE	IsSylO	IsSylWAA	IsSylWII
IsSylAA	IsSylEE	IsSylOO	IsSylWC	IsSylWO
IsSylAAI	IsSylI	IsSylU	IsSylWE	IsSylWOO
IsSylAI	IsSylII	IsSylV	IsSylWEE	IsSylWU
IsSylC	IsSylN	IsSylWA	IsSylWI	IsSylWV

For example, \p{IsSylA} would match \N{KATAKANA LETTER KA} but not
\N{KATAKANA LETTER KU}.

Now that we've basically told you all these Unicode 3.0 properties, we should
point out that a few of the more esoteric ones aren't implemented in version 5.6.0
of Perl because its implementation was based in part on Unicode 2.0, and things
like the bidirectional algorithm were still being worked out. However, by the time
you read this, the missing properties may well be implemented, so we listed them
anyway.

Unicode block properties

Some Unicode properties are of the form \p{In*SCRIPT*}. (Note the distinction
between Is and In.) The In properties are for testing block ranges of a particular

SCRIPT. If you have a character, and you wonder whether it were written in Greek script, you could test with:

```
print "It's Greek to me!\n" if chr(931) =~ /\p{InGreek}/;
```

That works by checking whether a character is "in" the valid range of that script type. This may be negated with `\P{In`*SCRIPT*`}` to find out whether something *isn't* in a particular script's block, such as `\P{InDingbats}` to test whether a string contains a non-dingbat. Block properties include the following:

InArabic	InCyrillic	InHangulJamo	InMalayalam	InSyriac
InArmenian	InDevanagari	InHebrew	InMongolian	InTamil
InArrows	InDingbats	InHiragana	InMyanmar	InTelugu
InBasicLatin	InEthiopic	InKanbun	InOgham	InThaana
InBengali	InGeorgian	InKannada	InOriya	InThai
InBopomofo	InGreek	InKatakana	InRunic	InTibetan
InBoxDrawing	InGujarati	InKhmer	InSinhala	InYiRadicals
InCherokee	InGurmukhi	InLao	InSpecials	InYiSyllables

Not to mention jawbreakers like these:

InAlphabeticPresentationForms	InHalfwidthandFullwidthForms
InArabicPresentationForms-A	InHangulCompatibilityJamo
InArabicPresentationForms-B	InHangulSyllables
InBlockElements	InHighPrivateUseSurrogates
InBopomofoExtended	InHighSurrogates
InBraillePatterns	InIdeographicDescriptionCharacters
InCJKCompatibility	InIPAExtensions
InCJKCompatibilityForms	InKangxiRadicals
InCJKCompatibilityIdeographs	InLatin-1Supplement
InCJKRadicalsSupplement	InLatinExtended-A
InCJKSymbolsandPunctuation	InLatinExtended-B
InCJKUnifiedIdeographs	InLatinExtendedAdditional
InCJKUnifiedIdeographsExtensionA	InLetterlikeSymbols
InCombiningDiacriticalMarks	InLowSurrogates
InCombiningHalfMarks	InMathematicalOperators
InCombiningMarksforSymbols	InMiscellaneousSymbols
InControlPictures	InMiscellaneousTechnical
InCurrencySymbols	InNumberForms
InEnclosedAlphanumerics	InOpticalCharacterRecognition
InEnclosedCJKLettersandMonths	InPrivateUse
InGeneralPunctuation	InSuperscriptsandSubscripts
InGeometricShapes	InSmallFormVariants
InGreekExtended	InSpacingModifierLetters

And the winner is:

```
InUnifiedCanadianAboriginalSyllabics
```

See *PATH_TO_PERLLIB/unicode/In/*.pl* to get an up-to-date listing of all of these character block properties. Note that these `In` properties are only testing to see if the character is in the block of characters allocated for that script. There is no guarantee that all characters in that range are defined; you also need to test against one of the Is properties discussed earlier to see if the character is defined. There is also no guarantee that a particular language doesn't use characters outside its assigned block. In particular, many European languages mix extended Latin characters with Latin-1 characters.

But hey, if you need a particular property that isn't provided, that's not a big problem. Read on.

Defining your own character properties

To define your own property, you need to write a subroutine with the name of the property you want (see Chapter 6, *Subroutines*). The subroutine should be defined in the package that needs the property (see Chapter 10, *Packages*), which means that if you want to use it in multiple packages, you'll either have to import it from a module (see Chapter 11, *Modules*), or inherit it as a class method from the package in which it is defined (see Chapter 12, *Objects*).

Once you've got that all settled, the subroutine should return data in the same format as the files in *PATH_TO_PERLLIB/unicode/Is* directory. That is, just return a list of characters or character ranges in hexadecimal, one per line. If there is a range, the two numbers are separated by a tab. Suppose you wanted a property that would be true if your character is in the range of either of the Japanese syllabaries, known as hiragana and katakana. (Together they're known as kana). You can just put in the two ranges like this:

```
sub InKana {
    return <<'END';
3040    309F
30A0    30FF
END
}
```

Alternatively, you could define it in terms of existing property names:

```
sub InKana {
    return <<'END';
+utf8::InHiragana
+utf8::InKatakana
END
}
```

You can also do set subtraction using a "–" prefix. Suppose you only wanted the actual characters, not just the block ranges of characters. You could weed out all the undefined ones like this:

```
sub IsKana {
    return <<'END';
+utf8::InHiragana
```

```
+utf8::InKatakana
-utf8::IsCn
END
}
```

You can also start with a complemented character set using the "!" prefix:

```
sub IsNotKana {
    return <<'END';
!utf8::InHiragana
-utf8::InKatakana
+utf8::IsCn
END
}
```

Perl itself uses exactly the same tricks to define the meanings of its "classic" character classes (like \w) when you include them in your own custom character classes (like [-.\w\s]). You might think that the more complicated you get with your rules, the slower they will run, but in fact, once Perl has calculated the bit pattern for a particular 64-bit swatch of your property, it caches it so it never has to recalculate the pattern again. (It does it in 64-bit swatches so that it doesn't even have to decode your utf8 to do its lookups.) Thus, all character classes, built-in or custom, run at essentially the same speed (fast) once they get going.

POSIX-Style Character Classes

Unlike Perl's other character class shortcuts, the POSIX-style character-class syntax notation, [:*CLASS*:], is available for use *only* when constructing other character classes, that is, inside an additional pair of square brackets. For example, /[.,[:alpha:][:digit:]]/ will search for one character that is either a literal dot (because it's in a character class), a comma, an alphabetic character, or a digit.

The POSIX classes available as of revision 5.6 of Perl are shown in Table 5-11.

Table 5-11. POSIX Character Classes

Class	Meaning
alnum	Any alphanumeric, that is, an alpha or a digit.
alpha	Any letter. (That's a lot more letters than you think, unless you're thinking Unicode, in which case it's still a lot.)
ascii	Any character with an ordinal value between 0 and 127.
cntrl	Any control character. Usually characters that don't produce output as such, but instead control the terminal somehow; for example, newline, form feed, and backspace are all control characters. Characters with an ord value less than 32 are most often classified as control characters.
digit	A character representing a decimal digit, such as 0 to 9. (Includes other characters under Unicode.) Equivalent to \d.

Table 5-11. POSIX Character Classes (continued)

Class	Meaning
graph	Any alphanumeric or punctuation character.
lower	A lowercase letter.
print	Any alphanumeric or punctuation character or space.
punct	Any punctuation character.
space	Any space character. Includes tab, newline, form feed, and carriage return (and a lot more under Unicode.) Equivalent to \s.
upper	Any uppercase (or titlecase) letter.
word	Any identifier character, either an alnum or underline.
xdigit	Any hexadecimal digit. Though this may seem silly ([0-9a-fA-F] works just fine), it is included for completeness.

You can negate the POSIX character classes by prefixing the class name with a ^ following the [:. (This is a Perl extension.) For example:

POSIX	Classic
[:^digit:]	\D
[:^space:]	\S
[:^word:]	\W

If the use utf8 pragma is not requested, but the use locale pragma is, the classes correlate directly with the equivalent functions in the C library's *isalpha*(3) interface (except for word, which is a Perl extension, mirroring \w).

If the utf8 pragma is used, POSIX character classes are exactly equivalent to the corresponding Is properties listed in Table 5-9. For example [:lower:] and \p{Lower} are equivalent, except that the POSIX classes may only be used within constructed character classes, whereas Unicode properties have no such restriction and may be used in patterns wherever Perl shortcuts like \s and \w may be used.

The brackets are part of the POSIX-style [::] construct, not part of the whole character class. This leads to writing patterns like /^[[:lower:][:digit:]]+$/, to match a string consisting entirely of lowercase letters or digits (plus an optional trailing newline). In particular, this does not work:

```
42 =~ /^[:digit:]$/        # WRONG
```

That's because it's not inside a character class. Rather, it *is* a character class, the one representing the characters ":", "i", "t", "g", and "d". Perl doesn't care that you specified ":" twice.

Here's what you need instead:

```
42 =~ /^[[:digit:]]+$/
```

The POSIX character classes [.cc.] and [=cc=] are recognized but produce an error indicating they are not supported. Trying to use *any* POSIX character class in older verions of Perl is likely to fail miserably, and perhaps even silently. If you're going to use POSIX character classes, it's best to require a new version of Perl by saying:

```
use 5.6.0;
```

Quantifiers

Unless you say otherwise, each item in a regular expression matches just once. With a pattern like /nop/, each of those characters must match, each right after the other. Words like "panoply" or "xenophobia" are fine, because *where* the match occurs doesn't matter.

If you wanted to match both "xenophobia" and "Snoopy", you couldn't use the /nop/ pattern, since that requires just one "o" between the "n" and the "p", and Snoopy has two. This is where *quantifiers* come in handy: they say how many times something may match, instead of the default of matching just once. Quantifiers in a regular expression are like loops in a program; in fact, if you think of a regex as a program, then they *are* loops. Some loops are exact, like "repeat this match five times only" ({5}). Others give both lower and upper bounds on the match count, like "repeat this match at least twice but no more than four times" ({2,4}). Others have no closed upper bound at all, like "match this at least twice, but as many times as you'd like" ({2,}).

Table 5-12 shows the quantifiers that Perl recognizes in a pattern.

Table 5-12. Regex Quantifiers Compared

Maximal	Minimal	Allowed Range
{*MIN,MAX*}	{*MIN,MAX*}?	Must occur at least *MIN* times but no more than *MAX* times
{*MIN,*}	{*MIN,*}?	Must occur at least *MIN* times
{*COUNT*}	{*COUNT*}?	Must match exactly *COUNT* times
*	*?	0 or more times (same as {0,})
+	+?	1 or more times (same as {1,})
?	??	0 or 1 time (same as {0,1})

Something with a * or a ? doesn't actually have to match. That's because they can match 0 times and still be considered a success. A + may often be a better fit, since it has to be there at least once.

Don't be confused by the use of "exactly" in the previous table. It refers only to the repeat count, not the overall string. For example, $n =~ /\d{3}/ doesn't say "is this string exactly three digits long?" It asks whether there's any point within $n at which three digits occur in a row. Strings like "101 Morris Street" test true, but so do strings like "95472" or "1-800-555-1212". All *contain* three digits at one or more points, which is all you asked about. See the section "Positions" for how to use positional assertions (as in /^\d{3}$/) to nail this down.

Given the opportunity to match something a variable number of times, maximal quantifiers will elect to maximize the repeat count. So when we say "as many times as you'd like", the greedy quantifier interprets this to mean "as many times as you can possibly get away with", constrained only by the requirement that this not cause specifications later in the match to fail. If a pattern contains two open-ended quantifiers, then obviously both cannot consume the entire string: characters used by one part of the match are no longer available to a later part. Each quantifier is greedy at the expense of those that follow it, reading the pattern left to right.

That's the traditional behavior of quantifiers in regular expressions. However, Perl permits you to reform the behavior of its quantifiers: by placing a ? after that quantifier, you change it from maximal to minimal. That doesn't mean that a minimal quantifier will always match the smallest number of repetitions allowed by its range, any more than a maximal quantifier must always match the greatest number allowed in its range. The overall match must still succeed, and the minimal match will take as much as it needs to succeed, and no more. (Minimal quantifiers value contentment over greed.)

For example, in the match:

```
"exasperate" =~ /e(.*)e/    # $1 now "xasperat"
```

the .* matches "xasperat", the longest possible string for it to match. (It also stores that value in $1, as described in the section "Capturing and Clustering" later in the chapter.) Although a shorter match was available, a greedy match doesn't care. Given two choices at the same starting point, it always returns the *longer* of the two.

Contrast this with this:

```
"exasperate" =~ /e(.*?)e/   # $1 now "xasp"
```

Here, the minimal matching version, .*?, is used. Adding the ? to * makes *? take on the opposite behavior: now given two choices at the same starting point, it always returns the *shorter* of the two.

Although you could read *? as saying to match zero or more of something but preferring zero, that doesn't mean it will always match zero characters. If it did so here, for example, and left $1 set to `""`, then the second "e" wouldn't be found, since it doesn't immediately follow the first one.

You might also wonder why, in minimally matching `/e(.*?)e/`, Perl didn't stick "rat" into $1. After all, "rat" also falls between two e's, and is shorter than "xasp". In Perl, the minimal/maximal choice applies only when selecting the shortest or longest from among several matches that all have the same starting point. If two possible matches exist, but these start at different offsets in the string, then their lengths don't matter—nor does it matter whether you've used a minimal quantifier or a maximal one. The earliest of several valid matches always wins out over all latecomers. It's only when multiple possible matches start at the same point that you use minimal or maximal matching to break the tie. If the starting points differ, there's no tie to break. Perl's matching is normally *leftmost longest*; with minimal matching, it becomes *leftmost shortest*. But the "leftmost" part never varies and is the dominant criterion.*

There are two ways to defeat the leftward leanings of the pattern matcher. First, you can use an earlier greedy quantifier (typically `.*`) to try to slurp earlier parts of the string. In searching for a match for a greedy quantifier, it tries for the longest match first, which effectively searches the rest of the string right-to-left:

```
"exasperate" =~ /.*e(.*?)e/   # $1 now "rat"
```

But be careful with that, since the overall match now includes the entire string up to that point.

The second way to defeat leftmostness to use positional assertions, discussed in the next section.

Positions

Some regex constructs represent *positions* in the string to be matched, which is a location just to the left or right of a real character. These metasymbols are examples of *zero-width* assertions because they do not correspond to actual characters in the string. We often just call them "assertions". (They're also known as "anchors" because they tie some part of the pattern to a particular position.)

You can always manipulate positions in a string without using patterns. The built-in `substr` function lets you extract and assign to substrings, measured from the beginning of the string, the end of the string, or from a particular numeric offset. This might be all you need if you were working with fixed-length records, for

---

* Not all regex engines work this way. Some believe in overall greed, in which the longest match always wins, even if it shows up later. Perl isn't that way. You might say that eagerness holds priority over greed (or thrift). For a more formal discussion of this principle and many others, see the section "The Little Engine That /Could(n't)?/".

instance. Patterns are only necessary when a numeric offset isn't sufficient. But most of the time, offsets aren't sufficient—at least, not sufficiently convenient, compared to patterns.

Beginnings: The \A and ^ Assertions

The \A assertion matches only at the beginning of the string, no matter what. However, the ^ assertion is the traditional beginning-of-line assertion as well as a beginning-of-string assertion. Therefore, if the pattern uses the /m modifier* and the string has embedded newlines, ^ also matches anywhere inside the string immediately following a newline character:

```
/\Abar/      # Matches "bar" and "barstool"
/^bar/       # Matches "bar" and "barstool"
/^bar/m      # Matches "bar" and "barstool" and "sand\nbar"
```

Used in conjunction with /g, the /m modifier lets ^ match many times in the same string:

```
s/^\s+//gm;              # Trim leading whitespace on each line
$total++ while /^./mg;   # Count nonblank lines
```

Endings: The \z, \Z, and $ Assertions

The \z metasymbol matches at the end of the string, no matter what's inside. \z matches right before the newline at the end of the string if there is a newline, or at the end if there isn't. The $ metacharacter usually means the same as \z. However, if the /m modifier was specified and the string has embedded newlines, then $ can also match anywhere inside the string right in front of a newline:

```
/bot\z/      # Matches "robot"
/bot\Z/      # Matches "robot" and "abbot\n"
/bot$/       # Matches "robot" and "abbot\n"
/bot$/m      # Matches "robot" and "abbot\n" and "robot\nrules"

/^robot$/    # Matches "robot" and "robot\n"
/^robot$/m   # Matches "robot" and "robot\n" and "this\nrobot\n"
/\Arobot\Z/  # Matches "robot" and "robot\n"
/\Arobot\z/  # Matches only "robot" -- but why didn't you use eq?
```

As with ^, the /m modifier lets $ match many times in the same string when used with /g. (These examples assume that you've read a multiline record into $_, perhaps by setting $/ to "" before reading.)

---

* Or you've set the deprecated $* variable to 1 and you're not overriding $* with the /s modifier.

```
s/\s*$//gm;    # Trim trailing whitespace on each line in paragraph

while (/^([^:]+):\s*(.*)/gm ) {   # get mail header
    $headers{$1} = $2;
}
```

In "Variable Interpolation" later in this chapter, we'll discuss how you can interpolate variables into patterns: if $foo is "bc", then /a$foo/ is equivalent to /abc/. Here, the $ does not match the end of the string. For a $ to match the end of the string, it must be at the end of the pattern or immediately be followed by a vertical bar or closing parenthesis.

Boundaries: The \b and \B Assertions

The \b assertion matches at any word boundary, defined as the position between a \w character and a \W character, in either order. If the order is \W\w, it's a beginning-of-word boundary, and if the order is \w\W, it's an end-of-word boundary. (The ends of the string count as \W characters here.) The \B assertion matches any position that is *not* a word boundary, that is, the middle of either \w\w or \W\W.

```
/\bis\b/    # matches "what it is" and "that is it"
/\Bis\B/    # matches "thistle" and "artist"
/\bis\B/    # matches "istanbul" and "so--isn't that butter?"
/\Bis\b/    # matches "confutatis" and "metropolis near you"
```

Because \W includes all punctuation characters (except the underscore), there are \b boundaries in the middle of strings like "isn't", "booktech@oreilly.com", "M.I.T.", and "key/value".

Inside a character class ([\b]), a \b represents a backspace rather than a word boundary.

Progressive Matching

When used with the /g modifier, the pos function allows you to read or set the offset where the next progressive match will start:

```
$burglar = "Bilbo Baggins";
while ($burglar =~ /b/gi) {
    printf "Found a B at %d\n", pos($burglar)-1;
}
```

(We subtract one from the position because that was the length of the string we were looking for, and pos is always the position just past the match.)

The code above prints:

```
Found a B at 0
Found a B at 3
Found a B at 6
```

After a failure, the match position normally resets back to the start. If you also apply the /c (for "continue") modifier, then when the /g runs out, the failed match doesn't reset the position pointer. This lets you continue your search past that point without starting over at the very beginning.

```
$burglar = "Bilbo Baggins";
while ($burglar =~ /b/gci) {          # ADD /c
    printf "Found a B at %d\n", pos($burglar)-1;
}
while ($burglar =~ /i/gi) {
    printf "Found an I at %d\n", pos($burglar)-1;
}
```

Besides the three B's it found earlier, Perl now reports finding an i at position 10. Without the /c, the second loop's match would have restarted from the beginning and found another i at position 1 first.

Where You Left Off: The \G Assertion

Whenever you start thinking in terms of the pos function, it's tempting to start carving your string up with substr, but this is rarely the right thing to do. More often, if you started with pattern matching, you should continue with pattern matching. However, if you're looking for a positional assertion, you're probably looking for \G.

The \G assertion represents within the pattern the same point that pos represents outside of it. When you're progressively matching a string with the /g modifier (or you've used the pos function to directly select the starting point), you can use \G to specify the position just after the previous match. That is, it matches the location immediately before whatever character would be identified by pos. This allows you to remember where you left off:

```
($recipe = <<'DISH') =~ s/^\s+//gm;
    Preheat oven to 451 deg. fahrenheit.
    Mix 1 ml. dilithium with 3 oz. NaCl and
    stir in 4 anchovies.  Glaze with 1 g.
    mercury.  Heat for 4 hours and let cool
    for 3 seconds.  Serves 10 aliens.
DISH

$recipe =~ /\d+ /g;
$recipe =~ /\G(\w+)/;              # $1 is now "deg"
$recipe =~ /\d+ /g;
$recipe =~ /\G(\w+)/;              # $1 is now "ml"
$recipe =~ /\d+ /g;
$recipe =~ /\G(\w+)/;              # $1 is now "oz"
```

The \G metasymbol is often used in a loop, as we demonstrate in our next example. We "pause" after every digit sequence, and at that position, we test whether there's an abbreviation. If so, we grab the next two words. Otherwise, we just grab the next word:

```
pos($recipe) = 0;                        # Just to be safe, reset \G to 0
while ( $recipe =~ /(\d+) /g ) {
    my $amount = $1;
    if ($recipe =~ / \G (\w{0,3}) \. \s+ (\w+) /x) {  # abbrev. + word
        print "$amount $1 of $2\n";
    } else {
        $recipe =~ / \G (\w+) /x;                  # just a word
        print "$amount $1\n";
    }
}
```

That produces:

```
451 deg of fahrenheit
1 ml of dilithium
3 oz of NaCl
4 anchovies
1 g of mercury
4 hours
3 seconds
10 aliens
```

Capturing and Clustering

Patterns allow you to group portions of your pattern together into subpatterns and to remember the strings matched by those subpatterns. We call the first behavior *clustering* and the second one *capturing*.

Capturing

To capture a substring for later use, put parentheses around the subpattern that matches it. The first pair of parentheses stores its substring in $1, the second pair in $2, and so on. You may use as many parentheses as you like; Perl just keeps defining more numbered variables for you to represent these captured strings.

Some examples:

```
/(\d)(\d)/  # Match two digits, capturing them into $1 and $2
/(\d+)/     # Match one or more digits, capturing them all into $1
/(\d)+/     # Match a digit one or more times, capturing the last into $1
```

Note the difference between the second and third patterns. The second form is usually what you want. The third form does *not* create multiple variables for multiple digits. Parentheses are numbered when the pattern is compiled, not when it is matched.

Captured strings are often called *backreferences* because they refer back to parts of the captured text. There are actually two ways to get at these backreferences. The numbered variables you've seen are how you get at backreferences outside of a pattern, but inside the pattern, that doesn't work. You have to use \1, \2, etc.* So to find doubled words like "the the" or "had had", you might use this pattern:

```
/\b(\w+) \1\b/i
```

But most often, you'll be using the $1 form, because you'll usually apply a pattern and then do something with the substrings. Suppose you have some text (a mail header) that looks like this:

```
From: gnat@perl.com
To: camelot@oreilly.com
Date: Mon, 17 Jul 2000 09:00:00 -1000
Subject: Eye of the needle
```

and you want to construct a hash that maps the text before each colon to the text afterward. If you were looping through this text line by line (say, because you were reading it from a file) you could do that as follows:

```
while (<>) {
    /^(.*?): (.*)$/;     # Pre-colon text into $1, post-colon into $2
    $fields{$1} = $2;
}
```

Like $`, $&, and $', these numbered variables are dynamically scoped through the end of the enclosing block or `eval` string, or to the next successful pattern match, whichever comes first. You can use them in the righthand side (the replacement part) of a substitute, too:

```
s/^(\S+) (\S+)/$2 $1/; # Swap first two words
```

Groupings can nest, and when they do, the groupings are counted by the location of the left parenthesis. So given the string "Primula Brandybuck", the pattern:

```
/^((\w+) (\w+))$/
```

would capture "Primula Brandybuck" into $1, "Primula" into $2, and "Brandybuck" into $3. This is depicted in Figure 5-1.

---

* You can't use $1 for a backreference within the pattern because that would already have been interpolated as an ordinary variable back when the regex was compiled. So we use the traditional \1 backreference notation inside patterns. For two- and three-digit backreference numbers, there is some ambiguity with octal character notation, but that is neatly solved by considering how many captured patterns are available. For instance, if Perl sees a \11 metasymbol, it's equivalent to $11 only if there are at least 11 substrings captured earlier in the pattern. Otherwise, it's equivalent to \011, that is, a tab character.

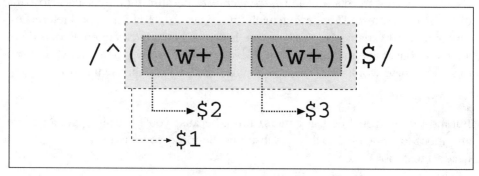

Figure 5-1. Creating backreferences with parentheses

Patterns with captures are often used in list context to populate a list of values, since the pattern is smart enough to return the captured substrings as a list:

```
($first, $last)        = /^(\w+) (\w+)$/;
($full, $first, $last) = /^((\w+) (\w+))$/;
```

With the /g modifier, a pattern can return multiple substrings from multiple matches, all in one list. Suppose you had the mail header we saw earlier all in one string (in $_, say). You could do the same thing as our line-by-line loop, but with one statement:

```
%fields = /^(.*?): (.*)$/gm;
```

The pattern matches four times, and each time it matches, it finds two substrings. The /gm match returns all of these as a flat list of eight strings, which the list assignment to %fields will conveniently interpret as four key/value pairs, thus restoring harmony to the universe.

Several other special variables deal with text captured in pattern matches. $& contains the entire matched string, $` everything to the left of the match, $' everything to the right. $+ contains the contents of the last backreference.

```
$_ = "Speak, <EM>friend</EM>, and enter.";
m[ (<.*?>) (.*?) (</.*?>) ]x;        # A tag, then chars, then an end tag
print "prematch: $`\n";              # Speak,
print "match: $&\n";                 # <EM>friend</EM>
print "postmatch: $'\n";             # , and enter.
print "lastmatch: $+\n";             # </EM>
```

For more explanation of these magical Elvish variables (and for a way to write them in English), see Chapter 28, *Special Names*.

The @- (@LAST_MATCH_START) array holds the offsets of the beginnings of any submatches, and @+ (@LAST_MATCH_END) holds the offsets of the ends:

```
#!/usr/bin/perl
$alphabet = "abcdefghijklmnopqrstuvwxyz";
$alphabet =~ /(hi).*(stu)/;

print "The entire match began at $-[0] and ended at $+[0]\n";
print "The first  match began at $-[1] and ended at $+[1]\n";
print "The second match began at $-[2] and ended at $+[2]\n";
```

If you really want to match a literal parenthesis character instead of having it interpreted as a metacharacter, backslash it:

```
/\(e.g., .*?\)/
```

This matches a parenthesized example (e.g., this statement). But since dot is a wildcard, this also matches any parenthetical statement with the first letter e and third letter g (ergo, this statement too).

Clustering

Bare parentheses both cluster and capture. But sometimes you don't want that. Sometimes you just want to group portions of the pattern without creating a backreference. You can use an extended form of parentheses to suppress capturing: the (?:*PATTERN*) notation will *cluster* without capturing.

There are at least three reasons you might want to cluster without capturing:

1. To quantify something.

2. To limit the scope of interior alternation; for example, /^cat|cow|dog$/ needs to be /^(?:cat|cow|dog)$/ so that the cat doesn't run away with the ^.

3. To limit the scope of an embedded pattern modifier to a particular subpattern, such as in /foo(?-i:Case_Matters)bar/i. (See the next section, "Cloistered Pattern Modifiers.")

In addition, it's more efficient to suppress the capture of something you're not going to use. On the minus side, the notation is a little noisier, visually speaking.

In a pattern, a left parenthesis immediately followed by a question mark denotes a regex *extension*. The current regular expression bestiary is relatively fixed—we don't dare create a new metacharacter, for fear of breaking old Perl programs. Instead, the extension syntax is used to add new features to the bestiary.

In the remainder of the chapter, we'll see many more regex extensions, all of which cluster without capturing, as well as doing something else. The (?:*PATTERN*) extension is just special in that it does nothing else. So if you say:

```
@fields = split(/\b(?:a|b|c)\b/)
```

it's like:

```
@fields = split(/\b(a|b|c)\b/)
```

but doesn't spit out extra fields. (The `split` operator is a bit like `m//g` in that it will emit extra fields for all the captured substrings within the pattern. Ordinarily, `split` only returns what it *didn't* match. For more on `split` see Chapter 29.)

Cloistered Pattern Modifiers

You may *cloister* the `/i`, `/m`, `/s`, and `/x` modifiers within a portion of your pattern by inserting them (without the slash) between the `?` and `:` of the clustering notation. If you say:

```
/Harry (?i:s) Truman/
```

it matches both "`Harry S Truman`" and "`Harry s Truman`", whereas:

```
/Harry (?x: [A-Z] \.? \s )?Truman/
```

matches both "`Harry S Truman`" and "`Harry S. Truman`", as well as "`Harry Truman`", and:

```
/Harry (?ix: [A-Z] \.? \s )?Truman/
```

matches all five, by combining the `/i` and `/x` modifiers within the cloister.

You can also subtract modifiers from a cloister with a minus sign:

```
/Harry (?x-i: [A-Z] \.? \s )?Truman/i
```

This matches any capitalization of the name—but if the middle initial is provided, it must be capitalized, since the `/i` applied to the overall pattern is suspended inside the cloister.

By omitting the colon and *PATTERN*, you can export modifier settings to an outer cluster, turning it into a cloister. That is, you can selectively turn modifiers on and off for the cluster one level outside the modifiers' parentheses, like so:

```
/(?i)foo/             # Equivalent to /foo/i
/foo((?-i)bar)/i      # "bar" must be lower case
/foo((?x-i) bar)/     # Enables /x and disables /i for "bar"
```

Note that the second and third examples create backreferences. If that wasn't what you wanted, then you should have been using `(?-i:bar)` and `(?x-i: bar)`, respectively.

Setting modifiers on a portion of your pattern is particularly useful when you want "`.`" to match newlines in part of your pattern but not in the rest of it. Setting `/s` on the whole pattern doesn't help you there.

Alternation

Inside a pattern or subpattern, use the | metacharacter to specify a set of possibilities, any one of which could match. For instance:

```
/Gandalf|Saruman|Radagast/
```

matches Gandalf or Saruman or Radagast. The alternation extends only as far as the innermost enclosing parentheses (whether capturing or not):

```
/prob|n|r|l|ate/     # Match prob, n, r, l, or ate
/pro(b|n|r|l)ate/    # Match probate, pronate, prorate, or prolate
/pro(?:b|n|r|l)ate/ # Match probate, pronate, prorate, or prolate
```

The second and third forms match the same strings, but the second form captures the variant character in $1 and the third form does not.

At any given position, the Engine tries to match the first alternative, and then the second, and so on. The relative length of the alternatives does not matter, which means that in this pattern:

```
/(Sam|Samwise)/
```

$1 will never be set to Samwise no matter what string it's matched against, because Sam will always match first. When you have overlapping matches like this, put the longer ones at the beginning.

But the ordering of the alternatives only matters at a given position. The outer loop of the Engine does left-to-right matching, so the following always matches the first Sam:

```
"'Sam I am,' said Samwise" =~ /(Samwise|Sam)/;   # $1 eq "Sam"
```

But you can force right-to-left scanning by making use of greedy quantifiers, as discussed earlier in "Quantifiers":

```
"'Sam I am,' said Samwise" =~ /.*(Samwise|Sam)/; # $1 eq "Samwise"
```

You can defeat any left-to-right (or right-to-left) matching by including any of the various positional assertions we saw earlier, such as \G, ^, and $. Here we anchor the pattern to the end of the string:

```
"'Sam I am,' said Samwise" =~ /(Samwise|Sam)$/;  # $1 eq "Samwise"
```

That example factors the $ out of the alternation (since we already had a handy pair of parentheses to put it after), but in the absence of parentheses you can also distribute the assertions to any or all of the individual alternatives, depending on how you want them to match. This little program displays lines that begin with either a __DATA__ or __END__ token:

```
#!/usr/bin/perl
while (<>) {
    print if /^__DATA__|^__END__/;
}
```

But be careful with that. Remember that the first and last alternatives (before the first | and after the last one) tend to gobble up the other elements of the regular expression on either side, out to the ends of the expression, unless there are enclosing parentheses. A common mistake is to ask for:

```
/^cat|dog|cow$/
```

when you really mean:

```
/^(cat|dog|cow)$/
```

The first matches "cat" at the beginning of the string, or "dog" anywhere, or "cow" at the end of the string. The second matches any string consisting solely of "cat" or "dog" or "cow". It also captures $1, which you may not want. You can also say:

```
/^cat$|^dog$|^cow$/
```

We'll show you another solution later.

An alternative can be empty, in which case it always matches.

```
/com(pound|)/;       # Matches "compound" or "com"
/com(pound(s|)|)/;   # Matches "compounds", "compound", or "com"
```

This is much like using the ? quantifier, which matches 0 times or 1 time:

```
/com(pound)?/;       # Matches "compound" or "com"
/com(pound(s?))?/;   # Matches "compounds", "compound", or "com"
/com(pounds?)?/;     # Same, but doesn't use $2
```

There is one difference, though. When you apply the ? to a subpattern that captures into a numbered variable, that variable will be undefined if there's no string to go there. If you used an empty alternative, it would still be false, but would be a defined null string instead.

Staying in Control

As any good manager knows, you shouldn't micromanage your employees. Just tell them what you want, and let them figure out the best way of doing it. Similarly, it's often best to think of a regular expression as a kind of specification: "Here's what I want; go find a string that fits the bill."

On the other hand, the best managers also understand the job their employees are trying to do. The same is true of pattern matching in Perl. The more thoroughly you understand of how Perl goes about the task of matching any particular pattern, the more wisely you'll be able to make use of Perl's pattern matching capabilities.

One of the most important things to understand about Perl's pattern-matching is when *not* to use it.

Letting Perl Do the Work

When people of a certain temperament first learn regular expressions, they're often tempted to see everything as a problem in pattern matching. And while that may even be true in the larger sense, pattern matching is about more than just evaluating regular expressions. It's partly about looking for your car keys where you dropped them, not just under the streetlamp where you can see better. In real life, we all know that it's a lot more efficient to look in the right places than the wrong ones.

Similarly, you should use Perl's control flow to decide which patterns to execute, and which ones to skip. A regular expression is pretty smart, but it's smart like a horse. It can get distracted if it sees too much at once. So sometimes you have to put blinders onto it. For example, you'll recall our earlier example of alternation:

```
/Gandalf|Saruman|Radagast/
```

That works as advertised, but not as well as it might, because it searches every position in the string for every name before it moves on to the next position. Astute readers of *The Lord of the Rings* will recall that, of the three wizards named above, Gandalf is mentioned much more frequently than Saruman, and Saruman is mentioned much more frequently than Radagast. So it's generally more efficient to use Perl's logical operators to do the alternation:

```
/Gandalf/ || /Saruman/ || /Radagast/
```

This is yet another way of defeating the "leftmost" policy of the Engine. It only searches for Saruman if Gandalf was nowhere to be seen. And it only searches for Radagast if Saruman is also absent.

Not only does this change the order in which things are searched, but it sometimes allows the regular expression optimizer to work better. It's generally easier to optimize searching for a single string than for several strings simultaneously. Similarly, anchored searches can often be optimized if they're not too complicated.

You don't have to limit your control of the control flow to the || operator. Often you can control things at the statement level. You should always think about weeding out the common cases first. Suppose you're writing a loop to process a configuration file. Many configuration files are mostly comments. It's often best to discard comments and blank lines early before doing any heavy-duty processing, even if the heavy duty processing would throw out the comments and blank lines in the course of things:

```
while (<CONF>) {
    next if /^#/;
    next if /^\s*(#|$)/;
    chomp;
    munchabunch($_);
}
```

Even if you're not trying to be efficient, you often need to alternate ordinary Perl expressions with regular expressions simply because you want to take some action that is not possible (or very difficult) from within the regular expression, such as printing things out. Here's a useful number classifier:

```
warn "has nondigits"        if      /\D/;
warn "not a natural number" unless /^\d+$/;              # rejects -3
warn "not an integer"       unless /^-?\d+$/;            # rejects +3
warn "not an integer"       unless /^[+-]?\d+$/;
warn "not a decimal number" unless /^-?\d+\.?\d*$/;      # rejects .2
warn "not a decimal number" unless /^-?(?:\d+(?:\.\d*)?|\.\d+)$/;
warn "not a C float"
        unless /^([+-]?)(?=\d|\.\d)\d*(\.\d*)?([Ee]([+-]?\d+))?$/;
```

We could stretch this section out a lot longer, but really, that sort of thing is what this whole book is about. You'll see many more examples of the interplay of Perl code and pattern matching as we go along. In particular, see the later section "Programmatic Patterns". (It's okay to read the intervening material first, of course.)

Variable Interpolation

Using Perl's control flow mechanisms to control regular expression matching has its limits. The main difficulty is that it's an "all or nothing" approach; either you run the pattern, or you don't. Sometimes you know the general outlines of the pattern you want, but you'd like to have the capability of parameterizing it. Variable interpolation provides that capability, much like parameterizing a subroutine lets you have more influence over its behavior than just deciding whether to call it or not. (More about subroutines in the next chapter).

One nice use of interpolation is to provide a little abstraction, along with a little readability. With regular expressions you may certainly write things concisely:

```
if ($num =~ /^[-+]?\d+\.?\d*$/) { ... }
```

But what you mean is more apparent when you write:

```
$sign = '[-+]?';
$digits = '\d+';
$decimal = '\.?';
$more_digits = '\d*';
$number = "$sign$digits$decimal$more_digits";
...
if ($num =~ /^$number$/o) { ... }
```

We'll cover this use of interpolation more under "Generated patterns" later in this chapter. We'll just point out that we used the /o modifier to suppress recompilation because we don't expect $number to change its value over the course of the program.

Another cute trick is to turn your tests inside out and use the variable string to pattern-match against a set of known strings:

```
chomp($answer = <STDIN>);
if    ("SEND" =~ /^\Q$answer/i) { print "Action is send\n" }
elsif ("STOP" =~ /^\Q$answer/i) { print "Action is stop\n" }
elsif ("ABORT" =~ /^\Q$answer/i) { print "Action is abort\n" }
elsif ("LIST" =~ /^\Q$answer/i) { print "Action is list\n" }
elsif ("EDIT" =~ /^\Q$answer/i) { print "Action is edit\n" }
```

This lets your user perform the "send" action by typing any of S, SE, SEN, or SEND (in any mixture of upper- and lowercase). To "stop", they'd have to type at least ST (or St, or sT, or st).

When backslashes happen

When you think of double-quote interpolation, you usually think of both variable and backslash interpolation. But as we mentioned earlier, for regular expressions there are two passes, and the interpolation pass defers most of the backslash interpretation to the regular expression parser (which we discuss later). Ordinarily, you don't notice the difference, because Perl takes pains to hide the difference. (One sequence that's obviously different is the \b metasymbol, which turns into a word boundary assertion—outside of character classes, anyway. Inside a character class where assertions make no sense, it reverts to being a backspace, as it is normally.)

It's actually fairly important that the regex parser handle the backslashes. Suppose you're searching for tab characters in a pattern with a /x modifier:

```
($col1, $col2) = /(.*?) \t+ (.*?)/x;
```

If Perl didn't defer the interpretation of \t to the regex parser, the \t would have turned into whitespace, which the regex parser would have ignorantly ignored because of the /x. But Perl is not so ignoble, or tricky.

You can trick yourself though. Suppose you abstracted out the column separator, like this:

```
$colsep = "\t+";                    # (double quotes)
($col1, $col2) = /(.*?) $colsep (.*?)/x;
```

Now you've just blown it, because the \t turns into a real tab before it gets to the regex parser, which will think you said /(.*?)+(.*?)/ after it discards the white-space. Oops. To fix, avoid /x, or use single quotes. Or better, use qr//. (See the next section.)

The only double-quote escapes that are processed as such are the six translation escapes: \U, \u, \L, \l, \Q, and \E. If you ever look into the inner workings of the Perl regular expression compiler, you'll find code for handling escapes like \t for tab, \n for newline, and so on. But you won't find code for those six translation escapes. (We only listed them in Table 5-7 because people expect to find them there.) If you somehow manage to sneak any of them into the pattern without going through double-quotish evaluation, they won't be recognized.

How could they find their way in? Well, you can defeat interpolation by using single quotes as your pattern delimiter. In m'...', qr'...', and s'...'...', the single quotes suppress variable interpolation and the processing of translation escapes, just as they would in a single-quoted string. Saying m'\ufrodo' won't find a capitalized version of poor frodo. However, since the "normal" backslash characters aren't really processed on that level anyway, m'\t\d' still matches a real tab followed by any digit.

Another way to defeat interpolation is through interpolation itself. If you say:

```
$var = '\U';
/${var}frodo/;
```

poor frodo remains uncapitalized. Perl won't redo the interpolation pass for you just because you interpolated something that looks like it might want to be reinter-polated. You can't expect that to work any more than you'd expect this double interpolation to work:

```
$hobbit = 'Frodo';
$var = '$hobbit';           # (single quotes)
/$var/;                     # means m'$hobbit', not m'Frodo'.
```

Here's another example that shows how most backslashes are interpreted by the regex parser, not by variable interpolation. Imagine you have a simple little *grep*-style program written in Perl:[*]

---

[*] If you didn't know what a *grep* program was before, you will now. No system should be without *grep*—we believe *grep* is the most useful small program ever invented. (It logically follows that we don't believe Perl is a small program.)

```
#!/usr/bin/perl
$pattern = shift;
while (<>) {
    print if /$pattern/o;
}
```

If you name that program *pgrep* and call it this way:

```
% pgrep '\t\d' *.c
```

then you'll find that it prints out all lines of all your C source files in which a digit follows a tab. You didn't have to do anything special to get Perl to realize that \t was a tab. If Perl's patterns *were* just double-quote interpolated, you would have; fortunately, they aren't. They're recognized directly by the regex parser.

The real *grep* program has a **-i** switch that turns off case-sensitive matching. You don't have to add such a switch to your *pgrep* program; it can already handle that without modification. You just pass it a slightly fancier pattern, with an embedded /i modifier:

```
% pgrep '(?i)ring' LotR*.pod
```

That now searches for any of "Ring", "ring", "RING", and so on. You don't see this feature too much in literal patterns, since you can always just write /ring/i. But for patterns passed in on the command line, in web search forms, or embedded in configuration files, it can be a lifesaver. (Speaking of rings.)

The qr// quote regex operator

Variables that interpolate into patterns necessarily do so at run time, not compile time. This slows down execution because Perl has to check whether you've changed the contents of the variable; if so, it would have to recompile the regular expression. As mentioned in "Pattern-Matching Operators", if you promise never to change the pattern, you can use the /o option to interpolate and compile only once:

```
print if /$pattern/o;
```

Although that works fine in our *pgrep* program, in the general case, it doesn't. Imagine you have a slew of patterns, and you want to match each of them in a loop, perhaps like this:

```
foreach $item (@data) {
    foreach $pat (@patterns) {
        if ($item =~ /$pat/) { ... }
    }
}
```

You couldn't write /$pat/o because the meaning of $pat varies each time through the inner loop.

The solution to this is the qr/*PATTERN*/imosx operator. This operator quotes—and compiles—its *PATTERN* as a regular expression. *PATTERN* is interpolated the same way as in m/*PATTERN*/. If ' is used as the delimiter, no interpolation of variables (or the six translation escapes) is done. The operator returns a Perl value that may be used instead of the equivalent literal in a corresponding pattern match or substitute. For example:

```
$regex = qr/my.STRING/is;
s/$regex/something else/;
```

is equivalent to:

```
s/my.STRING/something else/is;
```

So for our nested loop problem above, preprocess your pattern first using a separate loop:

```
@regexes = ();
foreach $pat (@patterns) {
    push @regexes, qr/$pat/;
}
```

Or all at once using Perl's map operator:

```
@regexes = map { qr/$_/ } @patterns;
```

And then change the loop to use those precompiled regexes:

```
foreach $item (@data) {
    foreach $re (@regexes) {
        if ($item =~ /$re/) { ... }
    }
}
```

Now when you run the match, Perl doesn't have to create a compiled regular expression on each if test, because it sees that it already has one.

The result of a qr// may even be interpolated into a larger match, as though it were a simple string:

```
$regex = qr/$pattern/;
$string =~ /foo${regex}bar/;    # interpolate into larger patterns
```

This time, Perl does recompile the pattern, but you could always chain several qr// operators together into one.

The reason this works is because the qr// operator returns a special kind of object that has a stringification overload as described in Chapter 13, *Overloading*. If you print out the return value, you'll see the equivalent string:

```
$re = qr/my.STRING/is;
print $re;                      # prints (?si-xm:my.STRING)
```

The /s and /i modifiers were enabled in the pattern because they were supplied to qr//. The /x and /m, however, are disabled because they were not.

Any time you interpolate strings of unknown provenance into a pattern, you should be prepared to handle any exceptions thrown by the regex compiler, in case someone fed you a string containing untamable beasties:

```
$re = qr/$pat/is;                   # might escape and eat you
$re = eval { qr/$pat/is } || warn ...  # caught it in an outer cage
```

For more on the eval operator, see Chapter 29.

The Regex Compiler

After the variable interpolation pass has had its way with the string, the regex parser finally gets a shot at trying to understand your regular expression. There's not actually a great deal that can go wrong at this point, apart from messing up the parentheses, or using a sequence of metacharacters that doesn't mean anything. The parser does a recursive-descent analysis of your regular expression and, if it parses, turns it into a form suitable for interpretation by the Engine (see the next section). Most of the interesting stuff that goes on in the parser involves optimizing your regular expression to run as fast as possible. We're not going to explain that part. It's a trade secret. (Rumors that looking at the regular expression code will drive you insane are greatly exaggerated. We hope.)

But you might like to know what the parser actually thought of your regular expression, and if you ask it politely, it will tell you. By saying use re "debug", you can examine how the regex parser processes your pattern. (You can also see the same information by using the **–Dr** command-line switch, which is available to you if your Perl was compiled with the **–DDEBUGGING** flag during installation.)

```
#!/usr/bin/perl
use re "debug";
"Smeagol" =~ /^Sm(.*)g[aeiou]l$/;
```

The output is below. You can see that prior to execution Perl compiles the regex and assigns meaning to the components of the pattern: BOL for the beginning of line (^), REG_ANY for the dot, and so on:

```
Compiling REx '^Sm(.*)g[aeiou]l$'
size 24 first at 2
rarest char l at 0
rarest char S at 0
   1: BOL(2)
   2: EXACT <Sm>(4)
   4: OPEN1(6)
```

```
 6:    STAR(8)
 7:      REG_ANY(0)
 8:  CLOSE1(10)
10:  EXACT <g>(12)
12:  ANYOF[aeiou](21)
21:  EXACT <l>(23)
23:  EOL(24)
24:  END(0)
anchored 'Sm' at 0 floating 'l'$ at 4..2147483647
     (checking anchored) anchored(BOL) minlen 5
Omitting $' $& $' support.
```

Some of the lines summarize the conclusions of the regex optimizer. It knows that the string must start with "Sm", and that therefore there's no reason to do the ordinary left-to-right scan. It knows that the string must end with an "l", so it can reject out of hand any string that doesn't. It knows that the string must be at least five characters long, so it can ignore any string shorter than that right off the bat. It also knows what the rarest character in each constant string is, which can help in searching "studied" strings. (See study in Chapter 29.)

It then goes on to trace how it executes the pattern:

```
EXECUTING...

Guessing start of match, REx '^Sm(.*)g[aeiou]l$' against 'Smeagol'...
Guessed: match at offset 0
Matching REx '^Sm(.*)g[aeiou]l$' against 'Smeagol'
  Setting an EVAL scope, savestack=3
    0 <> <Smeagol>           |  1:  BOL
    0 <> <Smeagol>           |  2:  EXACT <Sm>
    2 <Sm> <eagol>           |  4:  OPEN1
    2 <Sm> <eagol>           |  6:  STAR
                        REG_ANY can match 5 times out of 32767...
  Setting an EVAL scope, savestack=3
    7 <Smeagol> <>           |  8:  CLOSE1
    7 <Smeagol> <>           | 10:  EXACT <g>
                    failed...
    6 <Smeago> <l>           |  8:  CLOSE1
    6 <Smeago> <l>           | 10:  EXACT <g>
                    failed...
    5 <Smeag> <ol>           |  8:  CLOSE1
    5 <Smeag> <ol>           | 10:  EXACT <g>
                    failed...
    4 <Smea> <gol>           |  8:  CLOSE1
    4 <Smea> <gol>           | 10:  EXACT <g>
    5 <Smeag> <ol>           | 12:  ANYOF[aeiou]
    6 <Smeago> <l>           | 21:  EXACT <l>
    7 <Smeagol> <>           | 23:  EOL
    7 <Smeagol> <>           | 24:  END
Match successful!
Freeing REx: '^Sm(.*)g[aeiou]l$'
```

If you follow the stream of whitespace down the middle of Smeagol, you can actually see how the Engine overshoots to let the .* be as greedy as possible, then backtracks on that until it finds a way for the rest of the pattern to match. But that's what the next section is about.

The Little Engine That /Could(n't)?/

And now we'd like to tell you the story of the Little Regex Engine that says, "I think I can. I think I can. I think I can."

In this section, we lay out the rules used by Perl's regular expression engine to match your pattern against a string. The Engine is extremely persistent and hardworking. It's quite capable of working even after you think it should quit. The Engine doesn't give up until it's certain there's no way to match the pattern against the string. The Rules below explain how the Engine "thinks it can" for as long as possible, until it *knows* it can or can't. The problem for our Engine is that its task is not merely to pull a train over a hill. It has to search a (potentially) very complicated space of possibilities, keeping track of where it has been and where it hasn't.

The Engine uses a nondeterministic finite-state automaton (NFA, not to be confused with NFL, a nondeterministic football league) to find a match. That just means that it keeps track of what it has tried and what it hasn't, and when something doesn't pan out, it backs up and tries something else. This is known as *backtracking*. (Er, sorry, we didn't invent these terms. Really.) The Engine is capable of trying a million subpatterns at one spot, then giving up on all those, backing up to within one choice of the beginning, and trying the million subpatterns again at a different spot. The Engine is not terribly intelligent; just persistent, and thorough. If you're cagey, you can give the Engine an efficient pattern that doesn't let it do a lot of silly backtracking.

When someone trots out a phrase like "Regexes choose the leftmost, longest match", that means that Perl generally prefers the leftmost match over longest match. But the Engine doesn't realize it's "preferring" anything, and it's not really thinking at all, just gutting it out. The overall preferences are an emergent behavior resulting from many individual and unrelated choices. Here are those choices:*

Rule 1

> The Engine tries to match as far left in the string as it can, such that the entire regular expression matches under Rule 2.

---

* Some of these choices may be skipped if the regex optimizer has any say, which is equivalent to the Little Engine simply jumping through the hill via quantum tunneling. But for this discussion we're pretending the optimizer doesn't exist.

The Engine starts just before the first character and tries to match the entire pattern starting there. The entire pattern matches if and only if the Engine reaches the end of the pattern before it runs off the end of the string. If it matches, it quits immediately—it doesn't keep looking for a "better" match, even though the pattern might match in many different ways.

If it is unable to match the pattern at the first position in the string, it admits temporary defeat and moves to the next position in the string, between the first and second characters, and tries all the possibilities again. If it succeeds, it stops. If it fails, it continues on down the string. The pattern match as a whole doesn't fail until it has tried to match the entire regular expression at every position in the string, including after the last character.

A string of n characters actually provides $n + 1$ positions to match at. That's because the beginnings and the ends of matches are *between* the characters of the string. This rule sometimes surprises people when they write a pattern like /x*/ that can match zero or more "x" characters. If you try that pattern on a string like "fox", it won't find the "x". Instead, it will immediately match the null string before the "f" and never look further. If you want it to match one or more x characters, you need to use /x+/ instead. See the quantifiers under Rule 5.

A corollary to this rule is that any pattern matching the null string is guaranteed to match at the leftmost position in the string (in the absence of any zero-width assertions to the contrary).

Rule 2

When the Engine encounters a set of alternatives (separated by | symbols), either at the top level or at the current "cluster" level, it tries them left-to-right, stopping on the first successful match that allows successful completion of the entire pattern.

A set of alternatives matches a string if any of the alternatives match under Rule 3. If none of the alternatives matches, it backtracks to the Rule that invoked this Rule, which is usually Rule 1, but could be Rule 4 or 6, if we're within a cluster. That rule will then look for a new position at which to apply Rule 2.

If there's only one alternative, then either it matches or it doesn't, and Rule 2 still applies. (There's no such thing as zero alternatives, because a null string always matches.)

Rule 3

Any particular alternative matches if every *item* listed in the alternative matches sequentially according to Rules 4 and 5 (such that the entire regular expression can be satisfied).

An item consists of either an *assertion,* which is covered in Rule 4, or a *quantified atom,* covered by Rule 5. Items that have choices on how to match are given a "pecking order" from left to right. If the items cannot be matched in order, the Engine backtracks to the next alternative under Rule 2.

Items that must be matched sequentially aren't separated in the regular expression by anything syntactic—they're merely juxtaposed in the order they must match. When you ask to match /^foo/, you're actually asking for four items to be matched one after the other. The first is a zero-width assertion, matched under Rule 4, and the other three are ordinary characters that must match themselves, one after the other, under Rule 5.

The left-to-right pecking order means that in a pattern like:

```
/x*y*/
```

x* gets to pick one way to match, and then y* tries all its ways. If that fails, then x* gets to pick its second choice, and make y* try all of its ways again. And so on. The items to the right "vary faster", to borrow a phrase from multi-dimensional arrays.

Rule 4

If an assertion does not match at the current position, the Engine backtracks to Rule 3 and retries higher-pecking-order items with different choices.

Some assertions are fancier than others. Perl supports many regex extensions, some of which are zero-width assertions. For example, the positive lookahead (?=...) and the negative lookahead (?!...) don't actually match any characters, but merely assert that the regular expression represented by ... would (or would not) match at this point, were we to attempt it, hypothetically speaking.*

Rule 5

A quantified atom matches only if the atom itself matches some number of times that is allowed by the quantifier. (The atom itself is matched according to Rule 6.)

---

* In actual fact, the Engine *does* attempt it. The Engine goes back to Rule 2 to test the subpattern, and then wipes out any record of how much string was eaten, returning only the success or failure of the subpattern as the value of the assertion. (It does, however, remember any captured substrings.)

Different quantifiers require different numbers of matches, and most of them allow a range of numbers of matches. Multiple matches must all match in a row; that is, they must be adjacent within the string. An unquantified atom is assumed to have a quantifier requiring exactly one match (that is, /x/ is the same as /x{1}/). If no match can be found at the current position for any allowed quantity of the atom in question, the Engine backtracks to Rule 3 and retries higher-pecking-order items with different choices.

The quantifiers are *, +, ?, *?, +?, ??, and the various brace forms. If you use the {*COUNT*} form, then there is no choice, and the atom must match exactly that number of times or not at all. Otherwise, the atom can match over a range of quantities, and the Engine keeps track of all the choices so that it can backtrack if necessary. But then the question arises as to which of these choices to try first. One could start with the maximal number of matches and work down, or the minimal number of matches and work up.

The traditional quantifiers (without a trailing question mark) specify *greedy* matching; that is, they attempt to match as many characters as possible. To find the greediest match, the Engine has to be a little bit careful. Bad guesses are potentially rather expensive, so the Engine doesn't actually count down from the maximum value, which after all could be Very Large and cause millions of bad guesses. What the Engine actually does is a little bit smarter: it first counts *up* to find out how many matching atoms (in a row) are really there in the string, and then it uses *that* actual maximum as its first choice. (It also remembers all the shorter choices in case the longest one doesn't pan out.) It then (at long last) tries to match the rest of the pattern, assuming the longest choice to be the best. If the longest choice fails to produce a match for the rest of the pattern, it backtracks and tries the next longest.

If you say /.*foo/, for example, it will try to match the maximal number of "any" characters (represented by the dot) clear out to the end of the line before it ever tries looking for "foo"; and then when the "foo" doesn't match there (and it can't, because there's not enough room for it at the end of the string), the Engine will back off one character at a time until it finds a "foo". If there is more than one "foo" in the line, it'll stop on the last one, since that will really be the *first* one it encounters as it backtracks. When the entire pattern succeeds using some particular length of .*, the Engine knows it can throw away all the other shorter choices for .* (the ones it would have used had the current "foo" not panned out).

By placing a question mark after any greedy quantifier, you turn it into a frugal quantifier that chooses the smallest quantity for the first try. So if you say /.*?foo/, the .*? first tries to match 0 characters, then 1 character, then 2, and

so on until it can match the "foo". Instead of backtracking backward, it backtracks forward, so to speak, and ends up finding the first "foo" on the line
instead of the last.

Rule 6

Each atom matches according to the designated semantics of its type. If the
atom doesn't match (or does match, but doesn't allow a match of the rest of
the pattern), the Engine backtracks to Rule 5 and tries the next choice for the
atom's quantity.

Atoms match according to the following types:

- A regular expression in parentheses, (...), matches whatever the regular
  expression (represented by ...) matches according to Rule 2. Parentheses
  therefore serve as a clustering operator for quantification. Bare parentheses also have the side effect of capturing the matched substring for later
  use in a *backreference*. This side effect can be suppressed by using
  (?:...) instead, which has only the clustering semantics—it doesn't store
  anything in $1, $2, and so on. Other forms of parenthetical atoms (and
  assertions) are possible—see the rest of this chapter.

- A dot matches any character, except maybe newline.

- A list of characters in square brackets (a *character class*) matches any one
  of the characters specified by the list.

- A backslashed letter matches either a particular character or a character
  from a set of characters, as listed in Table 5-7.

- Any other backslashed character matches that character.

- Any character not mentioned above matches itself.

That all sounds rather complicated, but the upshot of it is that, for each set of
choices given by a quantifier or alternation, the Engine has a knob it can twiddle.
It will twiddle those knobs until the entire pattern matches. The Rules just say in
which order the Engine is allowed to twiddle those knobs. Saying the Engine
prefers the leftmost match merely means it twiddles the start position knob the
slowest. And backtracking is just the process of untwiddling the knob you just
twiddled in order to try twiddling a knob higher in the pecking order, that is, one
that varies slower.

Here's a more concrete example, a program that detects when two consecutive
words share a common ending and beginning:

```
$a = 'nobody';
$b = 'bodysnatcher';
if ("$a $b" =~ /^(\w+)(\w+) \2(\w+)$/) {
    print "$2 overlaps in $1-$2-$3\n";
}
```

This prints:

```
body overlaps in no-body-snatcher
```

You might think that $1 would first grab up all of "nobody" due to greediness. And in fact, it does—at first. But once it's done so, there aren't any further characters to put in $2, which needs characters put into it because of the + quantifier. So the Engine backs up and $1 begrudgingly gives up one character to $2. This time the space character matches successfully, but then it sees \2, which represents a measly "y". The next character in the string is not a "y", but a "b". This makes the Engine back up all the way and try several more times, eventually forcing $1 to surrender the body to $2. Habeas corpus, as it were.

Actually, that won't quite work out if the overlap is itself the product of a doubling, as in the two words "rococo" and "cocoon". The algorithm above would have decided that the overlapping string, $2, must be just "co" rather than "coco". But we don't want a "rocococoon"; we want a "rococoon". Here's one of those places you can outsmart the Engine. Adding a minimal matching quantifier to the $1 part gives the much better pattern /^(\w+?)(\w+) \2(\w+)$/, which does exactly what we want.

For a much more detailed discussion of the pros and cons of various kinds of regular expression engines, see Jeffrey Friedl's book, *Mastering Regular Expressions*. Perl's regular expression Engine works very well for many of the everyday problems you want to solve with Perl, and it even works okay for those not-so-everyday problems, if you give it a little respect and understanding.

Fancy Patterns

Lookaround Assertions

Sometimes you just need to sneak a peek. There are four regex extensions that help you do just that, and we call them *lookaround* assertions because they let you scout around in a hypothetical sort of way, without committing to matching any characters. What these assertions assert is that some pattern would (or would not) match if we were to try it. The Engine works it all out for us by actually trying to match the hypothetical pattern, and then pretending that it didn't match (if it did).

When the Engine peeks ahead from its current position in the string, we call it a *lookahead* assertion. If it peeks backward, we call it a *lookbehind* assertion. The lookahead patterns can be any regular expression, but the lookbehind patterns may only be fixed width, since they have to know where to start the hypothetical match from.

While these four extensions are all zero-width assertions, and hence do not consume characters (at least, not officially), you can in fact capture substrings within them if you supply extra levels of capturing parentheses.

(?=*PATTERN*) (positive lookahead)

When the Engine encounters (?=*PATTERN*), it looks ahead in the string to ensure that *PATTERN* occurs. If you'll recall, in our earlier duplicate word remover, we had to write a loop because the pattern ate too much each time through:

```
$_ = "Paris in THE THE THE THE spring.";

# remove duplicate words (and triplicate (and quadruplicate...))
1 while s/\b(\w+) \1\b/$1/gi;
```

Whenever you hear the phrase "ate too much", you should always think "lookahead assertion". (Well, almost always.) By peeking ahead instead of gobbling up the second word, you can write a one-pass duplicate word remover like this:

```
s/ \b(\w+) \s (?= \1\b ) //gxi;
```

Of course, this isn't quite right, since it will mess up valid phrases like "The clothes you DON DON't fit."

(?!*PATTERN*) (negative lookahead)

When the Engine encounters (?!*PATTERN*), it looks ahead in the string to ensure that *PATTERN* does *not* occur. To fix our previous example, we can add a negative lookahead assertion after the positive assertion to weed out the case of contractions:

```
s/ \b(\w+) \s (?= \1\b (?! '\w))//xgi;
```

That final \w is necessary to avoid confusing contractions with words at the ends of single-quoted strings. We can take this one step further, since earlier in this chapter we intentionally used "that that particular", and we'd like our program to not "fix" that for us. So we can add an alternative to the negative lookahead in order to pre-unfix that "that", (thereby demonstrating that any pair of parentheses can be used to cluster alternatives):

```
s/ \b(\w+) \s (?= \1\b (?! '\w | \s particular))//gix;
```

Now we know that that particular phrase is safe. Unfortunately, the Gettysburg Address is still broken. So we add another exception:

```
s/ \b(\w+) \s (?= \1\b (?! '\w | \s particular | \s nation))//igx;
```

This is just starting to get out of hand. So let's do an Official List of Exceptions, using a cute interpolation trick with the $" variable to separate the alternatives with the | character:

```
@thatthat = qw(particular nation);
local $" = '|';
s/ \b(\w+) \s (?= \1\b (?! '\w | \s (?: @thatthat )))//xig;
```

`(?<=PATTERN)` (positive lookbehind)

When the Engine encounters `(?<=PATTERN)`, it looks backward in the string to ensure that *PATTERN* already occurred.

Our example still has a problem. Although it now lets Honest Abe say things like "that that nation", it also allows "Paris, in the the nation of France". We can add a positive lookbehind assertion in front of our exception list to make sure that we apply our `@thatthat` exceptions only to a real "that that".

```
s/ \b(\w+) \s (?= \1\b (?! '\w | (?<= that) \s (?: @thatthat )))//ixg;
```

Yes, it's getting terribly complicated, but that's why this section is called "Fancy Patterns", after all. If you need to complicate the pattern any more than we've done so far, judicious use of comments and `qr//` will help keep you sane. Or at least saner.

`(?<!PATTERN)` (negative lookbehind)

When the Engine encounters `(?<!PATTERN)`, it looks backward in the string to ensure that *PATTERN* did not occur.

Let's go for a really simple example this time. How about the easy version of that old spelling rule, "I before E except after C"? In Perl, you spell it:

```
s/(?<!c)ei/ie/g
```

You'll have to weigh for yourself whether you want to handle any of the exceptions. (For example, "weird" is spelled weird, especially when you spell it "wierd".)

Nonbacktracking Subpatterns

As described in "The Little Engine That /Could(n't)?/", the Engine often backtracks as it proceeds through the pattern. You can block the Engine from backtracking back through a particular set of choices by creating a *nonbacktracking subpattern*. A nonbacktracking subpattern looks like `(?>PATTERN)`, and it works exactly like a simple `(?:PATTERN)`, except that once *PATTERN* has found a match, it suppresses backtracking on any of the quantifiers or alternatives inside the subpattern. (Hence, it is meaningless to use this on a *PATTERN* that doesn't contain quantifiers or alternatives.) The only way to get it to change its mind is to backtrack to something before the subpattern and reenter the subpattern from the left.

It's like going into a car dealership. After a certain amount of haggling over the price, you deliver an ultimatum: "Here's my best offer; take it or leave it." If they don't take it, you don't go back to haggling again. Instead, you backtrack clear out the door. Maybe you go to another dealership, and start haggling again. You're allowed to haggle again, but only because you reentered the nonbacktracking pattern again in a different context.

For devotees of Prolog or SNOBOL, you can think of this as a scoped cut or fence operator.

Consider how in `"aaab" =~ /(?:a*)ab/`, the `a*` first matches three a's, but then gives up one of them because the last `a` is needed later. The subgroup sacrifices some of what it wants in order for the whole match to succeed. (Which is like letting the car salesman talk you into giving him more of your money because you're afraid to walk away from the deal.) In contrast, the subpattern in `"aaab" =~ /(?>a*)ab/` will never give up what it grabs, even though this behavior causes the whole match to fail. (As the song says, you have to know when to hold 'em, when to fold 'em, and when to walk away.)

Although `(?>PATTERN)` is useful for changing the behavior of a pattern, it's mostly used for speeding up the failure of certain matches that you know will fail anyway (unless they succeed outright). The Engine can take a spectacularly long time to fail, particular with nested quantifiers. The following pattern will succeed almost instantly:

```
$_ = "aaaaaaaaaaaaaaaaaaaaaaaaaaaaaaaaaaaaaaaaaaaaaaaaaaaaaaaaaaaaaaaab";
/a*a*a*a*a*a*a*a*a*a*a*a*a*a*a*a*a*a*a*a*a*a*a*a*a*a*a*a*[b]/;
```

But success is not the problem. Failure is. If you remove that final "b" from the string, the pattern will probably run for many, many years before failing. Many, many millennia. Actually, billions and billions of years.* You can see by inspection that the pattern can't succeed if there's no "b" on the end of the string, but the regex optimizer is not smart enough (as of this writing) to figure out that `/[b]/` is equivalent to `/b/`. But if you give it a hint, you can get it to fail quickly while still letting it succeed where it can:

```
/(?>a*a*a*a*a*a*a*a*a*a*a*a*a*a*a*a*a*a*a*a*a*a*a*a*a*a*a*a*)[b]/;
```

For a (hopefully) more realistic example, imagine a program that's supposed to read in a paragraph at a time and show just the lines that are continued, where

---

* Actually, it's more on the order of septillions and septillions. We don't know exactly how long it would take. We didn't care to wait around watching it not fail. In any event, your computer is likely to crash before the heat death of the universe, and this regular expression takes longer than either of those.

contination lines are specified with trailing backslashes. Here's a sample from Perl's *Makefile* that uses this line-continuation convention:

```
# Files to be built with variable substitution before miniperl
# is available.
sh = Makefile.SH cflags.SH config_h.SH makeaperl.SH makedepend.SH \
        makedir.SH myconfig.SH writemain.SH
```

You could write your simple program this way:

```
#!/usr/bin/perl -00p
while ( /( (.+) ( (?<=\\) \n .* )+ ) /gx) {
    print "GOT $.: $1\n\n";
}
```

That works, but it's really quite slow. That's because the Engine backtracks a character at a time from the end of the line, shrinking what's in $1. This is pointless. And writing it without the extraneous captures doesn't help much. Using:

```
(.+(?:(?<=\\)\n.*)+)
```

for a pattern is somewhat faster, but not much. This is where a nonbacktracking subpattern helps a lot. The pattern:

```
((?>.+)(?:(?<=\\)\n.*)+)
```

does the same thing, but more than an order of magnitude faster because it doesn't waste time backtracking in search of something that isn't there.

You'll never get a success with (?>...) that you wouldn't get with (?:...) or even a simple (...). But if you're going to fail, it's best to fail quickly and get on with your life.

Programmatic Patterns

Most Perl programs tend to follow an imperative (also called procedural) programming style, like a series of discrete commands laid out in a readily observable order: "Preheat oven, mix, glaze, heat, cool, serve to aliens." Sometimes into this mix you toss a few dollops of functional programming ("Use a little more glaze than you think you need, even after taking this into account, recursively"), or sprinkle it with bits of object-oriented techniques ("but please hold the anchovy objects"). Often it's a combination of all of these.

But the regular expression Engine takes a completely different approach to problem solving, more of a declarative approach. You describe goals in the language of regular expressions, and the Engine implements whatever logic is needed to solve your goals. Logic programming languages (such as Prolog) don't always get as much exposure as the other three styles, but they're more common than you'd think. Perl couldn't even be built without *make*(1) or *yacc*(1), both of which could be considered, if not purely declarative languages, at least hybrids that blend imperative and logic programming together.

You can do this sort of thing in Perl, too, by blending goal declarations and imperative code together more miscibly than we've done so far, drawing upon the strengths of both. You can programmatically build up the string you'll eventually present to the regex Engine, in a sense creating a program that writes a new program on the fly.

You can also supply ordinary Perl expressions as the replacement part of s/// via the /e modifier. This allows you to dynamically generate the replacement string by executing a bit of code every time the pattern matches.

Even more elaborately, you can interject bits of code wherever you'd like in a middle of a pattern using the (?{ *CODE* }) extension, and that code will be executed every time the Engine encounters that code as it advances and recedes in its intricate backtracking dance.

Finally, you can use s///ee or (??{ *CODE* }) to add another level of indirection: the *results* of executing those code snippets will themselves be re-evaluated for further use, creating bits of program and pattern on the fly, just in time.

Generated patterns

It has been said* that programs that write programs are the happiest programs in the world. In Jeffrey Friedl's book, *Mastering Regular Expressions*, the final tour de force demonstrates how to write a program that produces a regular expression to determine whether a string conforms to the RFC 822 standard; that is, whether it contains a standards-compliant, valid mail header. The pattern produced is several thousand characters long, and about as easy to read as a crash dump in pure binary. But Perl's pattern matcher doesn't care about that; it just compiles up the pattern without a hitch and, even more interestingly, executes the match very quickly—much more quickly, in fact, than many short patterns with complex backtracking requirements.

That's a very complicated example. Earlier we showed you a very simple example of the same technique when we built up a $number pattern out of its components (see the section "Variable Interpolation"). But to show you the power of this programmatic approach to producing a pattern, let's work out a problem of medium complexity.

Suppose you wanted to pull out all the words with a certain vowel-consonant sequence; for example, "audio" and "eerie" both follow a VVCVV pattern.

---

* By Andrew Hume, the famous Unix philosopher.

Although describing what counts as a consonant or a vowel is easy, you wouldn't ever want to type that in more than once. Even for our simple VVCVV case, you'd need to type in a pattern that looked something like this:

```
^[aeiouy][aeiouy][cbdfghjklmnpqrstvwxzy][aeiouy][aeiouy]$
```

A more general-purpose program would accept a string like "VVCVV" and programmatically generate that pattern for you. For even more flexibility, it could accept a word like "audio" as input and use that as a template to infer "VVCVV", and from that, the long pattern above. It sounds complicated, but really isn't, because we'll let the program generate the pattern for us. Here's a simple *cvmap* program that does all of that:

```perl
#!/usr/bin/perl
$vowels = 'aeiouy';
$cons   = 'cbdfghjklmnpqrstvwxzy';
%map = (C => $cons, V => $vowels);   # init map for C and V

for $class ($vowels, $cons) {        # now for each type
    for (split //, $class) {         # get each letter of that type
        $map{$_} .= $class;          # and map the letter back to the type
    }
}

for $char (split //, shift) {        # for each letter in template word
    $pat .= "[$map{$char}]";         # add appropriate character class
}

$re = qr/^${pat}$/i;                 # compile the pattern
print "REGEX is $re\n";              # debugging output
@ARGV = ('/usr/dict/words')          # pick a default dictionary
    if -t && !@ARGV;

while (<>) {                         # and now blaze through the input
    print if /$re/;                  # printing any line that matches
}
```

The %map variable holds all the interesting bits. Its keys are each letter of the alphabet, and the corresponding value is all the letters of its type. We throw in C and V, too, so you can specify either "VVCVV" or "audio", and still get out "eerie". Each character in the argument supplied to the program is used to pull out the right character class to add to the pattern. Once the pattern is created and compiled up with qr//, the match (even a very long one) will run quickly. Here's what you might get if you run this program on "fortuitously":

```
% cvmap fortuitously /usr/dict/words
REGEX is (?i-xsm:^[cbdfghjklmnpqrstvwxzy][aeiouy][cbdfghjklmnpqrstvwxzy][cbd
fghjklmnpqrstvwxzy][aeiouy][aeiouy][cbdfghjklmnpqrstvwxzy][aeiouy][aeiouy][c
bdfghjklmnpqrstvwxzy][cbdfghjklmnpqrstvwxzy][aeiouycbdfghjklmnpqrstvwxzy]$)
carriageable
circuitously
```

```
fortuitously
languorously
marriageable
milquetoasts
sesquiquarta
sesquiquinta
villainously
```

Looking at that REGEX, you can see just how much villainous typing you saved by programming languorously, albeit circuitously.

Substitution evaluations

When the /e modifier ("e" is for expression evaluation) is used on an s/*PATTERN*/*CODE*/e expression, the replacement portion is interpreted as a Perl expression, not just as a double-quoted string. It's like an embedded do { *CODE* }. Even though it looks like a string, it's really just a code block that gets compiled up at the same time as rest of your program, long before the substitution actually happens.

You can use the /e modifier to build replacement strings with fancier logic than double-quote interpolation allows. This shows the difference:

```
s/(\d+)/$1 * 2/;     # Replaces "42" with "42 * 2"
s/(\d+)/$1 * 2/e;    # Replaces "42" with "84"
```

And this converts Celsius temperatures into Fahrenheit:

```
$_ = "Preheat oven to 233C.\n";
s/\b(\d+\.?\d*)C\b/int($1 * 1.8 + 32) . "F"/e;   # convert to 451F
```

Applications of this technique are limitless. Here's a filter that modifies its files in place (like an editor) by adding 100 to every number that starts a line (and that is followed by a colon, which we only peek at, but don't actually match, or replace):

```
% perl -pi -e 's/^(\d+)(?=:)/100 + $1/e' filename
```

Now and then, you want to do more than just use the string you matched in another computation. Sometimes you want that string to *be* a computation, whose own evaluation you'll use for the replacement value. Each additional /e modifier after the first wraps an eval around the code to execute. The following two lines do the same thing, but the first one is easier to read:

```
s/PATTERN/CODE/ee
s/PATTERN/eval(CODE)/e
```

You could use this technique to replace mentions of simple scalar variables with their values:

```
s/(\$\w+)/$1/eeg;       # Interpolate most scalars' values
```

Because it's really an `eval`, the `/ee` even finds lexical variables. A slightly more elaborate example calculates a replacement for simple arithmetical expressions on (nonnegative) integers:

```
$_ = "I have 4 + 19 dollars and 8/2 cents.\n";
s{ (
        \d+ \s*          # find an integer
        [+*/-]           # and an arithmetical operator
        \s* \d+          # and another integer
   )
}{ $1 }eegx;            # then expand $1 and run that code
print;                  # "I have 23 dollars and 4 cents."
```

Like any other `eval` *STRING*, compile-time errors (like syntax problems) and run-time exceptions (like dividing by zero) are trapped. If so, the `$@` (`$EVAL_ERROR`) variable says what went wrong.

Match-time code evaluation

In most programs that use regular expressions, the surrounding program's run-time control structure drives the logical execution flow. You write `if` or `while` loops, or make function or method calls, that wind up calling a pattern-matching operation now and then. Even with `s///e`, it's the substitution operator that is in control, executing the replacement code only after a successful match.

With *code subpatterns*, the normal relationship between regular expression and program code is inverted. As the Engine is applying its Rules to your pattern at match time, it may come across a regex extension of the form `(?{ CODE })`. When triggered, this subpattern doesn't do any matching or any looking about. It's a zero-width assertion that always "succeeds", evaluated only for its side effects. Whenever the Engine needs to progress over the code subpattern as it executes the pattern, it runs that code.

```
"glyph" =~ /.+ (?{ print "hi" }) ./x;  # Prints "hi" twice.
```

As the Engine tries to match `glyph` against this pattern, it first lets the `.+` eat up all five letters. Then it prints "hi". When it finds that final dot, all five letters have been eaten, so it needs to backtrack back to the `.+` and make it give up one of the letters. Then it moves forward through the pattern again, stopping to print "hi" again before assigning `h` to the final dot and completing the match successfully.

The braces around the *CODE* fragment are intended to remind you that it is a block of Perl code, and it certainly behaves like a block in the lexical sense. That is, if you use `my` to declare a lexically scoped variable in it, it is private to the block. But if you use `local` to localize a dynamically scoped variable, it may not do what you expect. A (?{ *CODE* }) subpattern creates an implicit dynamic scope that is valid throughout the rest of the pattern, until it either succeeds or backtracks through the code subpattern. One way to think of it is that the block doesn't actually return when it gets to the end. Instead, it makes an invisible recursive call to the Engine to try to match the rest of the pattern. Only when that recursive call is finished does it return from the block, delocalizing the localized variables.*

In the next example, we initialize $i to 0 by including a code subpattern at the beginning of the pattern. Then we match any number of characters with .*—but we place another code subpattern in between the . and the * so we can count how many times . matches.

```
$_ = 'lothlorien';
m/ (?{ $i = 0 })              # Set $i to 0
   (.     (?{ $i++ })    )*   # Update $i, even after backtracking
   lori                       # Forces a backtrack
 /x;
```

The Engine merrily goes along, setting $i to 0 and letting the .* gobble up all 10 characters in the string. When it encounters the literal lori in the pattern, it backtracks and gives up those four characters from the .*. After the match, $i will still be 10.

If you wanted $i to reflect how many characters the .* actually ended up with, you could make use of the dynamic scope within the pattern:

```
$_ = 'lothlorien';
m/ (?{ $i = 0 })
   (. (?{ local $i = $i + 1; }) )*  # Update $i, backtracking-safe.
   lori
   (?{ $result = $i })              # Copy to non-localized location.
 /x;
```

Here, we use local to ensure that $i contains the number of characters matched by .*, regardless of backtracking. $i will be forgotten after the regular expression ends, so the code subpattern, (?{ $result = $i }), ensures that the count will live on in $result.

The special variable $^R (described in Chapter 28) holds the result of the last (?{ *CODE* }) that was executed as part of a successful match.

---

* People who are familiar with recursive descent parsers may find this behavior confusing because such compilers return from a recursive function call whenever they figure something out. The Engine doesn't do that—when it figures something out, it goes *deeper* into recursion (even when exiting a parenthetical group!). A recursive descent parser is at a minimum of recursion when it succeeds at the end, but the Engine is at a local *maximum* of recursion when it succeeds at the end of the pattern. You might find it helpful to dangle the pattern from its left end and think of it as a skinny representation of a call graph tree. If you can get that picture into your head, the dynamic scoping of local variables will make more sense. (And if you can't, you're no worse off than before.)

You can use a `(?{ CODE })` extension as the *COND* of a `(?(COND)IFTRUE|IFFALSE)`. If you do this, `$^R` will not be set, and you may omit the parentheses around the conditional:

```
"glyph" =~ /.+(?(?{ $foo{bar} gt "symbol" }).|signet)./;
```

Here, we test whether `$foo{bar}` is greater than `symbol`. If so, we include . in the pattern, and if not, we include `signet` in the pattern. Stretched out a bit, it might be construed as more readable:

```
"glyph" =~ m{
    .+                              # some anythings
    (?(?{                           # if
            $foo{bar} gt "symbol"   # this is true
        })
        .                           # match another anything
        |                           # else
            signet                  # match signet
    )
    .                               # and one more anything
}x;
```

When `use re 'eval'` is in effect, a regex is allowed to contain `(?{ CODE })` subpatterns even if the regular expression interpolates variables:

```
/(.*?) (?{length($1) < 3 && warn}) $suffix/;  # Error without use re 'eval'
```

This is normally disallowed since it is a potential security risk. Even though the pattern above may be innocuous because `$suffix` is innocuous, the regex parser can't tell which parts of the string were interpolated and which ones weren't, so it just disallows code subpatterns entirely if there were any interpolations.

If the pattern is obtained from tainted data, even `use re 'eval'` won't allow the pattern match to proceed.

When `use re 'taint'` is in effect and a tainted string is the target of a regex, the captured subpatterns (either in the numbered variables or in the list of values returned by `m//` in list context) are tainted. This is useful when regex operations on tainted data are meant not to extract safe substrings, but merely to perform other transformations. See Chapter 23, *Security*, for more on tainting. For the purpose of this pragma, precompiled regular expressions (usually obtained from `qr//`) are not considered to be interpolated:

```
/foo${pat}bar/
```

This is allowed if `$pat` is a precompiled regular expression, even if `$pat` contains `(?{ CODE })` subpatterns.

Earlier we showed you a bit of what use re 'debug' prints out. A more primitive debugging solution is to use (?{ *CODE* }) subpatterns to print out what's been matched so far during the match:

```
"abcdef" =~ / .+ (?{print "Matched so far: $&\n"}) bcdef $/x;
```

This prints:

```
Matched so far: abcdef
Matched so far: abcde
Matched so far: abcd
Matched so far: abc
Matched so far: ab
Matched so far: a
```

showing the .+ grabbing all the letters and giving them up one by one as the Engine backtracks.

Match-time pattern interpolation

You can build parts of your pattern from within the pattern itself. The (??{ *CODE* }) extension allows you to insert code that evaluates to a valid pattern. It's like saying /$pattern/, except that you can generate $pattern at run time—more specifically, at match time. For instance:

```
/\w (??{ if ($threshold > 1) { "red" } else { "blue" } }) \d/x;
```

This is equivalent to /\wred\d/ if $threshold is greater than 1, and /\wblue\d/ otherwise.

You can include backreferences inside the evaluated code to derive patterns from just-matched substrings (even if they will later become unmatched through back-tracking). For instance, this matches all strings that read the same backward as forward (known as palindromedaries, phrases with a hump in the middle):

```
/^ (.+) .? (??{quotemeta reverse $1}) $/xi;
```

You can balance parentheses like so:

```
$text =~ /( \(+ ) (.*?) (??{ '\)' x length $1 })/x;
```

This matches strings of the form (shazam!) and (((shazam!))), sticking shazam! into $2. Unfortunately, it doesn't notice whether the parentheses in the middle are balanced. For that we need recursion.

Fortunately, you can do recursive patterns too. You can have a compiled pattern that uses (??{ *CODE* }) to refer to itself. Recursive matching is pretty irregular, as regular expressions go. Any text on regular expressions will tell you that a standard regex can't match nested parentheses correctly. And that's correct. It's also correct that Perl's regexes aren't standard. The following pattern* matches a set of nested parentheses, however deep they go:

```
$np = qr{
            \(
            (?:
                (?> [^()]+ )     # Non-parens without backtracking
            |
                (??{ $np })      # Group with matching parens
            )*
            \)
        }x;
```

You could use it like this to match a function call:

```
$funpat = qr/\w+$np/;
'myfunfun(1,(2*(3+4)),5)' =~ /^$funpat$/;    # Matches!
```

Conditional interpolation

The (?(*COND*)*IFTRUE*|*IFFALSE*) regex extension is similar to Perl's ?: operator. If *COND* is true, the *IFTRUE* pattern is used; otherwise, the *IFFALSE* pattern is used. The *COND* can be a backreference (expressed as a bare integer, without the \ or $), a lookaround assertion, or a code subpattern. (See the sections "Lookaround Assertions" and "Match-time code evaluation" earlier in this chapter.)

If the *COND* is an integer, it is treated as a backreference. For instance, consider:

```
#!/usr/bin/perl
$x = 'Perl is free.';
$y = 'ManagerWare costs $99.95.';

foreach ($x, $y) {
    /^(\w+) (?:is|(costs)) (?(2)(\$\d+)|\w+)/;  # Either (\$\d+) or \w+
    if ($3) {
        print "$1 costs money.\n";         # ManagerWare costs money.
    } else {
        print "$1 doesn't cost money.\n";  # Perl doesn't cost money.
    }
}
```

Here, the *COND* is (2), which is true if a second backreference exists. If that's the case, (\$\d+) is included in the pattern at that point (creating the $3 backreference); otherwise, \w+ is used.

---

* Note that you can't declare the variable in the same statement in which you're going to use it. You can always declare it earlier, of course.

If the *COND* is a lookaround or code subpattern, the truth of the assertion is used to determine whether to include *IFTRUE* or *IFFALSE*:

```
/[ATGC]+(?(?<=AA)G|C)$/;
```

This uses a lookbehind assertion as the *COND* to match a DNA sequence that ends in either AAG, or some other base combination and C.

You can omit the |*IFFALSE* alternative. If you do, the *IFTRUE* pattern will be included in the pattern as usual if the *COND* is true, but if the condition isn't true, the Engine will move on to the next portion of the pattern.

Defining Your Own Assertions

You can't change how Perl's Engine works, but if you're sufficiently warped, you can change how it sees your pattern. Since Perl interprets your pattern similarly to double-quoted strings, you can use the wonder of overloaded string constants to see to it that text sequences of your choosing are automatically translated into other text sequences.

In the example below, we specify two transformations to occur when Perl encounters a pattern. First, we define \tag so that when it appears in a pattern, it's automatically translated to (?:<.*?>), which matches most HTML and XML tags. Second, we "redefine" the \w metasymbol so that it handles only English letters.

We'll define a package called Tagger that hides the overloading from our main program. Once we do that, we'll be able to say:

```
use Tagger;
$_ = '<I>camel</I>';
print "Tagged camel found" if /\tag\w+\tag/;
```

Here's *Tagger.pm*, couched in the form of a Perl module (see Chapter 11):

```
package Tagger;
use overload;

sub import { overload::constant 'qr' => \&convert }

sub convert {
    my $re = shift;
    $re =~ s/ \\tag   /<.*?>/xg;
    $re =~ s/ \\w     /[A-Za-z]/xg;
    return $re;
}

1;
```

The `Tagger` module is handed the pattern immediately before interpolation, so you can bypass the overloading by bypassing interpolation, as follows:

```
$re = '\tag\w+\tag';    # This string begins with \t, a tab
print if /$re/;          # Matches a tab, followed by an "a"...
```

If you wanted the interpolated variable to be customized, call the `convert` function directly:

```
$re = '\tag\w+\tag';           # This string begins with \t, a tab
$re = Tagger::convert $re;     # expand \tag and \w
print if /$re/;                # $re becomes <.*?>[A-Za-z]+<.*?>
```

Now if you're still wondering what those `sub` thingies are there in the `Tagger` module, you'll find out soon enough because that's what our next chapter is all about.

6

Subroutines

Like many languages, Perl provides for user-defined subroutines.* These subroutines may be defined anywhere in the main program, loaded in from other files via the do, require, or use keywords, or generated at run time using eval. You can even load them at run time with the mechanism described in the section "Autoloading" in Chapter 10, *Packages*. You can call a subroutine indirectly, using a variable containing either its name or a reference to the routine, or through an object, letting the object determine which subroutine should really be called. You can generate anonymous subroutines, accessible only through references, and if you want, use these to clone new, nearly identical functions via *closures*, which are covered in the section by that name in Chapter 8, *References*.

Syntax

To declare a named subroutine without defining it, use one of these forms:

```
sub NAME
sub NAME PROTO
sub NAME       ATTRS
sub NAME PROTO ATTRS
```

To declare and define a named subroutine, add a *BLOCK*:

```
sub NAME                   BLOCK
sub NAME PROTO             BLOCK
sub NAME       ATTRS BLOCK
sub NAME PROTO ATTRS BLOCK
```

---

* We'll also call them *functions*, but functions are the same thing as subroutines in Perl. Sometimes we'll even call them *methods*, which are defined the same way, but called differently.

To create an anonymous subroutine or closure, leave out the *NAME*:

```
sub                    BLOCK
sub       PROTO        BLOCK
sub              ATTRS BLOCK
sub       PROTO ATTRS BLOCK
```

PROTO and *ATTRS* stand for the prototype and attributes, each of which is discussed in its own section later in the chapter. They're not so important—the *NAME* and the *BLOCK* are the essential parts, even when they're missing.

For the forms without a *NAME*, you still have to provide some way of calling the subroutine. So be sure to save the return value since this form of sub declaration is not only compiled at compile time as you would expect, but also produces a run-time return value:

```
$subref = sub BLOCK;
```

To import subroutines defined in another module, say:

```
use MODULE qw(NAME1 NAME2 NAME3...);
```

To call subroutines directly, say:

```
NAME(LIST)          # & is optional with parentheses.
NAME LIST           # Parens optional if sub predeclared/imported.
&NAME               # Exposes current @_ to that subroutine,
                    # (and circumvents prototypes).
```

To call subroutines indirectly (by name or by reference), use any of these:

```
&$subref(LIST)      # The & is not optional on indirect call
$subref->(LIST)     # (unless using infix notation).
&$subref            # Exposes current @_ to that subroutine.
```

The official name of a subroutine includes the & prefix. A subroutine may be called using the prefix, but the & is usually optional, and so are the parentheses if the subroutine has been predeclared. However, the & is not optional when you're just naming the subroutine, such as when it's used as an argument to defined or undef or when you want to generate a reference to a named subroutine by saying $subref = \&name. Nor is the & optional when you want to make an indirect subroutine call using the &$subref() or &{$subref}() constructs. However, the more convenient $subref->() notation does not require it. See Chapter 8 for more about references to subroutines.

Perl doesn't force a particular capitalization style on your subroutine names. However, one loosely held convention is that functions called indirectly by Perl's runtime system (BEGIN, CHECK, INIT, END, AUTOLOAD, DESTROY, and all the functions mentioned in Chapter 14, *Tied Variables*) are in all capitals, so you might want to avoid using that style. (But subroutines used for constant values are customarily named with all caps too. That's okay. We hope . . .)

Semantics

Before you get too worked up over all that syntax, just remember that the normal way to define a simple subroutine ends up looking like this:

```
sub razzle {
    print "Ok, you've been razzled.\n";
}
```

and the normal way to call it is simply:

```
razzle();
```

In this case, we ignored inputs (arguments) and outputs (return values). But the Perl model for passing data into and out of a subroutine is really quite simple: all function parameters are passed as one single, flat list of scalars, and multiple return values are likewise returned to the caller as one single, flat list of scalars. As with any *LIST*, any arrays or hashes passed in these lists will interpolate their values into the flattened list, losing their identities—but there are several ways to get around this, and the automatic list interpolation is frequently quite useful. Both parameter lists and return lists may contain as many or as few scalar elements as you'd like (though you may put constraints on the parameter list by using prototypes). Indeed, Perl is designed around this notion of *variadic* functions (those taking any number of arguments), unlike C, where they're sort of grudgingly kludged in so that you can call *printf*(3).

Now, if you're going to design a language around the notion of passing varying numbers of arbitrary arguments, you'd better make it easy to process those arbitrary lists of arguments. Any arguments passed to a Perl routine come in as the array @_. If you call a function with two arguments, they are accessible inside the function as the first two elements of that array: $_[0] and $_[1]. Since @_ is a just a regular array with an irregular name, you can do anything to it you'd normally do to an array.* The array @_ is a local array, but its values are aliases to the actual scalar parameters. (This is known as pass-by-reference semantics.) Thus you can modify the actual parameters if you modify the corresponding element of @_. (This is rarely done, however, since it's so easy to return interesting values in Perl.)

The return value of the subroutine (or of any other block, for that matter) is the value of the last expression evaluated. Or you may use an explicit return statement to specify the return value and exit the subroutine from any point in the subroutine. Either way, as the subroutine is called in a scalar or list context, so also is the final expression of the routine evaluated in that same scalar or list context.

---

* This is an area where Perl is *more* orthogonal than the typical programming language.

Tricks with Parameter Lists

Perl does not yet have named formal parameters, but in practice all you do is copy
the values of @_ to a my list, which serves nicely for a list of formal parameters.
(Not coincidentally, copying the values changes the pass-by-reference semantics
into pass-by-value, which is how people usually expect parameters to work anyway, even if they don't know the fancy computer science terms for it.) Here's a
typical example:

```
sub maysetenv {
    my ($key, $value) = @_;
    $ENV{$key} = $value unless $ENV{$key};
}
```

But you aren't required to name your parameters, which is the whole point of the
@_ array. For example, to calculate a maximum, you can just iterate over @_
directly:

```
sub max {
    my $max = shift(@_);
    for my $item (@_) {
        $max = $item if $max < $item;
    }
    return $max;
}

$bestday = max($mon,$tue,$wed,$thu,$fri);
```

Or you can fill an entire hash at once:

```
sub configuration {
    my %options = @_;
    print "Maximum verbosity.\n" if $options{VERBOSE} == 9;
}

configuration(PASSWORD => "xyzzy", VERBOSE => 9, SCORE => 0);
```

Here's an example of not naming your formal arguments so that you can modify
your actual arguments:

```
upcase_in($v1, $v2);  # this changes $v1 and $v2
sub upcase_in {
    for (@_) { tr/a-z/A-Z/ }
}
```

You aren't allowed to modify constants in this way, of course. If an argument were
actually a scalar literal like "hobbit" or read-only scalar variable like $1, and you
tried to change it, Perl would raise an exception (presumably fatal, possibly career-
threatening). For example, this won't work:

```
upcase_in("frederick");
```

It would be much safer if the upcase_in function were written to return a copy of its parameters instead of changing them in place:

```
($v3, $v4) = upcase($v1, $v2);
sub upcase {
    my @parms = @_;
    for (@parms) { tr/a-z/A-Z/ }
    # Check whether we were called in list context.
    return wantarray ? @parms : $parms[0];
}
```

Notice how this (unprototyped) function doesn't care whether it was passed real scalars or arrays. Perl will smash everything into one big, long, flat @_ parameter list. This is one of the places where Perl's simple argument-passing style shines. The upcase function will work perfectly well without changing the upcase definition even if we feed it things like this:

```
@newlist = upcase(@list1, @list2);
@newlist = upcase( split /:/, $var );
```

Do not, however, be tempted to do this:

```
(@a, @b) = upcase(@list1, @list2);   # WRONG
```

Why not? Because, like the flat incoming parameter list in @_, the return list is also flat. So this stores everything in @a and empties out @b by storing the null list there. See the later section "Passing References" for alternatives.

Error Indications

If you want your function to return in such a way that the caller will realize there's been an error, the most natural way to do this in Perl is to use a bare return statement without an argument. That way when the function is used in scalar context, the caller gets undef, and when used in list context, the caller gets a null list.

Under extraordinary circumstances, you might choose to raise an exception to indicate an error. Use this measure sparingly, though; otherwise, your whole program will be littered with exception handlers. For example, failing to open a file in a generic file-opening function is hardly an exceptional event. However, ignoring that failure might well be. The wantarray built-in returns undef if your function was called in void context, so you can tell if you're being ignored:

```
if ($something_went_awry) {
    return if defined wantarray;  # good, not void context.
    die "Pay attention to my error, you danglesocket!!!\n";
}
```

Scoping Issues

Subroutines may be called recursively because each call gets its own argument array, even when the routine calls itself. If a subroutine is called using the & form, the argument list is optional. If the & is used but the argument list is omitted, something special happens: the @_ array of the calling routine is supplied implicitly. This is an efficiency mechanism that new users may wish to avoid.

```
&foo(1,2,3);     # pass three arguments
foo(1,2,3);      # the same

foo();           # pass a null list
&foo();          # the same

&foo;            # foo() gets current args, like foo(@_), but faster!
foo;             # like foo() if sub foo predeclared, else bareword "foo"
```

Not only does the & form make the argument list optional, but it also disables any prototype checking on the arguments you do provide. This is partly for historical reasons and partly to provide a convenient way to cheat if you know what you're doing. See the section "Prototypes" later in this chapter.

Variables you access from inside a function that haven't been declared private to that function are not necessarily global variables; they still follow the normal block-scoping rules of Perl. As explained in the "Names" section of Chapter 2, *Bits and Pieces*, this means they look first in the surrounding lexical scope (or scopes) for resolution, then on to the single package scope. From the viewpoint of a subroutine, then, any my variables from an enclosing lexical scope are still perfectly visible.

For example, the bumpx function below has access to the file-scoped $x lexical variable because the scope where the my was declared—the file itself—hasn't been closed off before the subroutine is defined:

```
# top of file
my $x = 10;      # declare and initialize variable
sub bumpx { $x++ }  # function can see outer lexical variable
```

C and C++ programmers would probably think of $x as a "file static" variable. It's private as far as functions in other files are concerned, but global from the perspective of functions declared after the my. C programmers who come to Perl looking for what they would call "static variables" for files or functions find no such keyword in Perl. Perl programmers generally avoid the word "static", because static systems are dead and boring, and because the word is so muddled in historical usage.

Although Perl doesn't include the word "static" in its lexicon, Perl programmers have no problem creating variables that are private to a function and persist across function calls. There's just no special word for these. Perl's richer scoping primitives combine with automatic memory management in ways that someone looking for a "static" keyword might never think of trying.

Lexical variables don't get automatically garbage collected just because their scope has exited; they wait to get recycled until they're no longer *used*, which is much more important. To create private variables that aren't automatically reset across function calls, enclose the whole function in an extra block and put both the my declaration and the function definition within that block. You can even put more than one function there for shared access to an otherwise private variable:

```
{
    my $counter = 0;
    sub next_counter { return ++$counter }
    sub prev_counter { return --$counter }
}
```

As always, access to the lexical variable is limited to code within the same lexical scope. The names of the two functions, on the other hand, are globally accessible (within the package), and, since they were defined inside $counter's scope, they can still access that variable even though no one else can.

If this function is loaded via require or use, then this is probably just fine. If it's all in the main program, you'll need to make sure any run-time assignment to my is executed early enough, either by putting the whole block before your main program, or alternatively, by placing a BEGIN or INIT block around it to make sure it gets executed before your program starts:

```
BEGIN {
    my @scale = ('A' .. 'G');
    my $note  = -1;
    sub next_pitch { return $scale[ ($note += 1) %= @scale ] };
}
```

The BEGIN doesn't affect the subroutine definition, nor does it affect the persistence of any lexicals used by the subroutine. It's just there to ensure the variables get initialized before the subroutine is ever called. For more on declaring private and global variables, see my and our respectively in Chapter 29, *Functions*. The BEGIN and INIT constructs are explained in Chapter 18, *Compiling*.

Passing References

If you want to pass more than one array or hash into or out of a function, and you want them to maintain their integrity, then you'll need to use an explicit pass-by-reference mechanism. Before you do that, you need to understand references as detailed in Chapter 8. This section may not make much sense to you otherwise. But hey, you can always look at the pictures...

Here are a few simple examples. First, let's define a function that expects a reference to an array. When the array is large, it's much faster to pass it in as a single reference than a long list of values:

```
$total = sum ( \@a );

sub sum {
    my ($aref)  = @_;
    my ($total) = 0;
    foreach (@$aref) { $total += $_ }
    return $total;
}
```

Let's pass in several arrays to a function and have it pop each of them, returning a new list of all their former last elements:

```
@tailings = popmany ( \@a, \@b, \@c, \@d );

sub popmany {
    my @retlist = ();
    for my $aref (@_) {
        push @retlist, pop @$aref;
    }
    return @retlist;
}
```

Here's how you might write a function that does a kind of set intersection by returning a list of keys occurring in all the hashes passed to it:

```
@common = inter( \%foo, \%bar, \%joe );
sub inter {
    my %seen;
    for my $href (@_) {
        while (my $k = each %$href ) {
            $seen{$k}++;
        }
    }
    return grep { $seen{$_} == @_ } keys %seen;
}
```

So far, we're just using the normal list return mechanism. What happens if you want to pass or return a hash? Well, if you're only using one of them, or you don't mind them concatenating, then the normal calling convention is okay, although a little expensive.

As we explained earlier, where people get into trouble is here:

```
(@a, @b) = func(@c, @d);
```

or here:

```
(%a, %b) = func(%c, %d);
```

That syntax simply won't work. It just sets @a or %a and clears @b or %b. Plus the function doesn't get two separate arrays or hashes as arguments: it gets one long list in @_, as always.

You may want to arrange for your functions to use references for both input and output. Here's a function that takes two array references as arguments and returns the two array references ordered by the number of elements they have in them:

```
($aref, $bref) = func(\@c, \@d);
print "@$aref has more than @$bref\n";
sub func {
    my ($cref, $dref) = @_;
    if (@$cref > @$dref) {
        return ($cref, $dref);
    } else {
        return ($dref, $cref);
    }
}
```

For passing filehandles or directory handles into or out of functions, see the sections "Filehandle References" and "Symbol Table References" in Chapter 8.

Prototypes

Perl lets you define your own functions to be called like Perl's built-in functions. Consider push(@array, $item), which must tacitly receive a reference to @array, not just the list values held in @array, so that the array can be modified. *Prototypes* let you declare subroutines to take arguments just like many of the built-ins, that is, with certain constraints on the number and types of arguments. We call them "prototypes", but they work more like automatic templates for the calling context than like what C or Java programmers would think of as prototypes. With these templates, Perl will automatically add implicit backslashes, or calls to scalar, or whatever else it takes to get things to show up in a way that matches the template. For instance, if you declare:

```
sub mypush (\@@);
```

then mypush takes arguments exactly like push does. For this to work, the declaration of the function to be called must be visible at compile time. The prototype only affects the interpretation of function calls when the & character is omitted. In other words, if you call it like a built-in function, it behaves like a built-in function. If you call it like an old-fashioned subroutine, then it behaves like an old-fashioned subroutine. The & suppresses prototype checks and associated contextual effects.

Since prototypes are taken into consideration only at compile time, it naturally falls out that they have no influence on subroutine references like \&foo or on indirect subroutine calls like &{$subref} or $subref->(). Method calls are not influenced by prototypes, either. That's because the actual function to be called is indeterminate at compile time, depending as it does on inheritance, which is dynamically determined in Perl.

Since the intent is primarily to let you define subroutines that work like built-in functions, here are some prototypes you might use to emulate the corresponding built-ins:

Declared as	Called as
sub mylink ($$)	mylink $old, $new
sub myreverse (@)	myreverse $a,$b,$c
sub myjoin ($@)	myjoin ":",$a,$b,$c
sub mypop (\@)	mypop @array
sub mysplice (\@$$@)	mysplice @array,@array,0,@pushme
sub mykeys (\%)	mykeys %{$hashref}
sub mypipe (**)	mypipe READHANDLE, WRITEHANDLE
sub myindex ($$;$)	myindex &getstring, "substr"
	myindex &getstring, "substr", $start
sub mysyswrite (*$;$$)	mysyswrite OUTF, $buf
	mysyswrite OUTF, $buf, length($buf)-$off, $off
sub myopen (*;$@)	myopen HANDLE
	myopen HANDLE, $name
	myopen HANDLE, "-|", @cmd
sub mygrep (&@)	mygrep { /foo/ } $a,$b,$c
sub myrand ($)	myrand 42
sub mytime ()	mytime

Any backslashed prototype character (shown between parentheses in the left column above) represents an actual argument (exemplified in the right column), which absolutely must start with that character. Just as the first argument to keys must start with %, so too must the first argument to mykeys.

A semicolon separates mandatory arguments from optional arguments. (It would be redundant before @ or %, since lists can be null.) Unbackslashed prototype characters have special meanings. Any unbackslashed @ or % eats all the rest of the actual arguments and forces list context. (It's equivalent to *LIST* in a syntax description.) An argument represented by $ has scalar context forced on it. An & requires a reference to a named or anonymous subroutine.

A * allows the subroutine to accept anything in that slot that would be accepted by a built-in as a filehandle: a bare name, a constant, a scalar expression, a type-glob, or a reference to a typeglob. The value will be available to the subroutine either as a simple scalar or (in the latter two cases) as a reference to the typeglob. If you wish to always convert such arguments to a typeglob reference, use Symbol::qualify_to_ref as follows:

```
use Symbol 'qualify_to_ref';

sub foo (*) {
    my $fh = qualify_to_ref(shift, caller);
    ...
}
```

Note how the last three examples in the table are treated specially by the parser. mygrep is parsed as a true list operator, myrand is parsed as a true unary operator with unary precedence the same as rand, and mytime is truly argumentless, just like time.

That is, if you say:

```
mytime +2;
```

you'll get mytime() + 2, not mytime(2), which is how it would be parsed without the prototype, or with a unary prototype.

The mygrep example also illustrates how & is treated specially when it is the first argument. Ordinarily, an & prototype would demand an argument like \&foo or sub{}. When it is the first argument, however, you can leave off the sub of your anonymous subroutine, and just pass a bare block in the "indirect object" slot (with no comma after it). So one nifty thing about the & prototype is that you can generate new syntax with it, provided the & is in the initial position:

```
sub try (&$) {
    my ($try, $catch) = @_;
    eval { &$try };
    if ($@) {
        local $_ = $@;
        &$catch;
    }
}
sub catch (&) { $_[0] }
```

```
try {
    die "phooey";
}                          # not the end of the function call!
catch {
    /phooey/ and print "unphooey\n";
};
```

This prints "unphooey". What happens is that `try` is called with two arguments, the anonymous function {die "phooey";} and the return value of the `catch` function, which in this case is nothing but its own argument, the entire block of yet another anonymous function. Within `try`, the first function argument is called while protected within an `eval` block to trap anything that blows up. If something does blow up, the second function is called with a local version of the global `$_` variable set to the raised exception.* If this all sounds like pure gobbledygook, you'll have to read about `die` and `eval` in Chapter 29, and then go check out anonymous functions and closures in Chapter 8. On the other hand, if it intrigues you, you might check out the `Error` module on CPAN, which uses this to implement elaborately structured exception handling with `try`, `catch`, `except`, `otherwise`, and `finally` clauses.

Here's a reimplementation of the `grep` operator (the built-in one is more efficient, of course):

```
sub mygrep (&@) {
    my $coderef = shift;
    my @result;
    foreach $_ (@_) {
        push(@result, $_) if &$coderef;
    }
    return @result;
}
```

Some folks would prefer to see full alphanumeric prototypes. Alphanumerics have been intentionally left out of prototypes for the express purpose of someday adding named, formal parameters. (Maybe.) The current mechanism's main goal is to let module writers enforce a certain amount of compile-time checking on module users.

Inlining Constant Functions

Functions prototyped with (), meaning that they take no arguments at all, are parsed like the `time` built-in. More interestingly, the compiler treats such functions as potential candidates for inlining. If the result of that function, after Perl's optimization and constant-folding pass, is either a constant or a lexically scoped scalar

---

* Yes, there are still unresolved issues having to do with the visibility of @_. We're ignoring that question for the moment. But if we make @_ lexically scoped someday, as already occurs in the experimental threaded versions of Perl, those anonymous subroutines can act like closures.

with no other references, then that value will be used in place of calls to that function. Calls made using &*NAME* are never inlined, however, just as they are not subject to any other prototype effects. (See the use constant pragma in Chapter 31, *Pragmatic Modules*, for an easy way to declare such constants.)

Both versions of these functions to compute π will be inlined by the compiler:

```
sub pi ()           { 3.14159 }           # Not exact, but close
sub PI ()           { 4 * atan2(1, 1) }   # As good as it gets
```

In fact, all of the following functions are inlined because Perl can determine everything at compile time:

```
sub FLAG_FOO ()     { 1 << 8 }
sub FLAG_BAR ()     { 1 << 9 }
sub FLAG_MASK ()    { FLAG_FOO | FLAG_BAR }

sub OPT_GLARCH ()   { (0x1B58 & FLAG_MASK) == 0 }
sub GLARCH_VAL ()   {
    if (OPT_GLARCH) { return 23 }
    else            { return 42 }
}

sub N () { int(GLARCH_VAL) / 3 }
BEGIN {                     # compiler runs this block at compile time
    my $prod = 1;           # persistent, private variable
    for (1 .. N) { $prod *= $_ }
    sub NFACT () { $prod }
}
```

In the last example, the NFACT function is inlined because it has a void prototype and the variable it returns is not changed by that function—and furthermore can't be changed by anyone else, since it's in a lexical scope. So the compiler replaces uses of NFACT with that value, which was precomputed at compile time because of the surrounding BEGIN.

If you redefine a subroutine that was eligible for inlining, you'll get a mandatory warning. (You can use this warning to tell whether the compiler inlined a particular subroutine.) The warning is considered severe enough not to be optional, because previously compiled invocations of the function will still use the old value of the function. If you need to redefine the subroutine, ensure that it isn't inlined either by dropping the () prototype (which changes calling semantics, so beware) or by thwarting the inlining mechanism in some other way, such as:

```
sub not_inlined () {
    return 23 if $$;
}
```

See Chapter 18 for more about what happens during the compilation and execution phases of your program's life.

Care with Prototypes

It's probably best to put prototypes on new functions, not retrofit prototypes onto older ones. These are context templates, not ANSI C prototypes, so you must be especially careful about silently imposing a different context. Suppose, for example, you decide that a function should take just one parameter, like this:

```
sub func ($) {
    my $n = shift;
    print "you gave me $n\n";
}
```

That makes it a unary operator (like the `rand` built-in) and changes how the compiler determines the function's arguments. With the new prototype, the function consumes just one, scalar-context argument instead of many arguments in list context. If someone has been calling it with an array or list expression, even if that array or list contained just a single element, where before it worked, now you've got something completely different:

```
func @foo;              # counts @foo elements
func split /:/;         # counts number of fields returned
func "a", "b", "c";     # passes "a" only, discards "b" and "c"
func("a", "b", "c");    # suddenly, a compiler error!
```

You've just supplied an implicit `scalar` in front of the argument list, which can be more than a bit surprising. The old `@foo` that used to hold one thing doesn't get passed in. Instead, 1 (the number of elements in `@foo`) is now passed to `func`. And the `split`, being called in scalar context, scribbles all over your `@_` parameter list. In the third example, because `func` has been prototyped as a unary operator, only "a" is passed in; then the return value from `func` is discarded as the comma operator goes on to evaluate the next two items and return "c." In the final example, the user now gets a syntax error at compile time on code that used to compile and run just fine.

If you're writing new code and would like a unary operator that takes only a scalar variable, not any old scalar expression, you could prototype it to take a scalar *reference*:

```
sub func (\$) {
    my $nref = shift;
    print "you gave me $$nref\n";
}
```

Now the compiler won't let anything by that doesn't start with a dollar sign:

```
func @foo;              # compiler error, saw @, want $
func split/:/;          # compiler error, saw function, want $
func $s;                # this one is ok -- got real $ symbol
func $a[3];             # and this one
```

```
func $h{stuff}[-1];      # or even this
func 2+5;                # scalar expr still a compiler error
func ${ \(2+5) };        # ok, but is the cure worse than the disease?
```

If you aren't careful, you can get yourself into trouble with prototypes. But if you are careful, you can do a lot of neat things with them. This is all very powerful, of course, and should only be used in moderation to make the world a better place.

Subroutine Attributes

A subroutine declaration or definition may have a list of attributes associated with it. If such an attribute list is present, it is broken up at whitespace or colon boundaries and treated as though a use attributes had been seen. See the use attributes pragma in Chapter 31 for internal details. There are three standard attributes for subroutines: locked, method, and lvalue.

The locked and method Attributes

```
# Only one thread is allowed into this function.
sub afunc : locked { ... }

# Only one thread is allowed into this function on a given object.
sub afunc : locked method { ... }
```

Setting the locked attribute is meaningful only when the subroutine or method is intended to be called by multiple threads simultaneously. When set on a non-method subroutine, Perl ensures that a lock is acquired on the subroutine itself before that subroutine is entered. When set on a method subroutine (that is, one also marked with the method attribute), Perl ensures that any invocation of it implicitly locks its first argument (the object) before execution.

Semantics of this lock are the same as using the lock operator on the subroutine as the first statement in that routine. See Chapter 17, *Threads*, for more on locking.

The method attribute can be used by itself:

```
sub afunc : method { ... }
```

Currently this has only the effect of marking the subroutine so as not to trigger the "Ambiguous call resolved as CORE::%s" warning. (We may make it mean more someday.)

The attribute system is user-extensible, letting you create your own attribute names. These new attributes must be valid as simple identifier names (without any punctuation other than the "_" character). They may have a parameter list appended, which is currently only checked for whether its parentheses nest properly.

Here are examples of valid syntax (even though the attributes are unknown):

```
sub fnord (&\%) : switch(10,foo(7,3))  :  expensive;
sub plugh () : Ugly('\(") :Bad;
sub xyzzy : _5x5 { ... }
```

Here are examples of invalid syntax:

```
sub fnord : switch(10,foo();  # ()-string not balanced
sub snoid : Ugly('(');        # ()-string not balanced
sub xyzzy : 5x5;              # "5x5" not a valid identifier
sub plugh : Y2::north;        # "Y2::north" not a simple identifier
sub snurt : foo + bar;        # "+" not a colon or space
```

The attribute list is passed as a list of constant strings to the code that associates them with the subroutine. Exactly how this works (or doesn't) is highly experimental. Check *attributes*(3) for current details on attribute lists and their manipulation.

The lvalue Attribute

It is possible to return a modifiable scalar value from a subroutine, but only if you declare the subroutine to return an lvalue:

```
my $val;
sub canmod : lvalue {
    $val;
}
sub nomod {
    $val;
}

canmod() = 5;   # Assigns to $val.
nomod()  = 5;   # ERROR
```

If you're passing parameters to an lvalued subroutine, you'll usually want parentheses to disambiguate what's being assigned:

```
canmod $x  = 5;   # assigns 5 to $x first!
canmod 42  = 5;   # can't change a constant; compile-time error
canmod($x) = 5;   # this is ok
canmod(42) = 5;   # and so is this
```

If you want to be sneaky, you can get around this in the particular case of a subroutine that takes one argument. Declaring the function with a prototype of ($) causes the function to be parsed with the precedence of a named unary operator. Since named unaries have higher precedence than assignment, you no longer need the parentheses. (Whether this is desirable or not is left up to the style police.)

You don't have to be sneaky in the particular case of a subroutine that allows zero arguments (that is, with a () prototype). You can without ambiguity say this:

```
canmod = 5;
```

That works because no valid term begins with =. Similarly, lvalued method calls can omit the parentheses when you don't pass any arguments:

```
$obj->canmod = 5;
```

We promise not to break those two constructs in future versions of Perl. They're handy when you want to wrap object attributes in method calls (so that they can be inherited like method calls but accessed like variables).

The scalar or list context of both the lvalue subroutine and the righthand side of an assignment to that subroutine is determined as if the subroutine call were replaced by a scalar. For example, consider:

```
data(2,3) = get_data(3,4);
```

Both subroutines here are called in scalar context, while in:

```
(data(2,3)) = get_data(3,4);
```

and in:

```
(data(2),data(3)) = get_data(3,4);
```

all the subroutines are called in list context.

The current implementation does not allow arrays and hashes to be returned from lvalue subroutines directly. You can always return a reference instead.

7

Formats

Perl has a mechanism to help you generate simple reports and charts. To facilitate this, Perl helps you code up your output page close to how it will look when it's printed. It can keep track of things like how many lines are on a page, the current page number, when to print page headers, and so on. Keywords are borrowed from FORTRAN: format to declare and write to execute; see the relevant entries in Chapter 29, *Functions*. Fortunately, the layout is much more legible, more like the PRINT USING statement of BASIC. Think of it as a poor man's *nroff*(1). (If you know *nroff*, that may not sound like a recommendation.)

Formats, like packages and subroutines, are declared rather than executed, so they may occur at any point in your program. (Usually it's best to keep them all together.) They have their own namespace apart from all the other types in Perl. This means that if you have a function named "Foo", it is not the same thing as a format named "Foo". However, the default name for the format associated with a given filehandle is the same as the name of that filehandle. Thus, the default format for STDOUT is named "STDOUT", and the default format for filehandle TEMP is named "TEMP". They just look the same. They aren't.

Output record formats are declared as follows:

```
format NAME =
FORMLIST
.
```

If *NAME* is omitted, format STDOUT is defined. *FORMLIST* consists of a sequence of lines, each of which may be of one of three types:

- A comment, indicated by putting a # in the first column.

- A "picture" line giving the format for one output line.

- An argument line supplying values to plug into the previous picture line.

Picture lines are printed exactly as they look, except for certain fields that substitute values into the line.* Each substitution field in a picture line starts with either @ (at) or ^ (caret). These lines do not undergo any kind of variable interpolation. The @ field (not to be confused with the array marker @) is the normal kind of field; the other kind, the ^ field, is used to do rudimentary multiline text-block filling. The length of the field is supplied by padding out the field with multiple <, >, or | characters to specify, respectively, left justification, right justification, or centering. If the variable exceeds the width specified, it is truncated.

As an alternate form of right justification, you may also use # characters (after an initial @ or ^) to specify a numeric field. You can insert a . in place of one of the # characters to line up the decimal points. If any value supplied for these fields contains a newline, only the text up to the newline is printed. Finally, the special field @* can be used for printing multiline, nontruncated values; it should generally appear on a picture line by itself.

The values are specified on the following line in the same order as the picture fields. The expressions providing the values should be separated by commas. The expressions are all evaluated in a list context before the line is processed, so a single list expression could produce multiple list elements. The expressions may be spread out to more than one line if enclosed in braces. (If so, the opening brace must be the first token on the first line). This lets you line up the values under their respective format fields for easier reading.

If an expression evaluates to a number with a decimal part, and if the corresponding picture specifies that the decimal part should appear in the output (that is, any picture except multiple # characters without an embedded .), the character used for the decimal point is always determined by the current LC_NUMERIC locale. This means that if, for example, the run-time environment happens to specify a German locale, a comma will be used instead of a period. See the *perllocale* manpage for more information.

Inside an expression, the whitespace characters \n, \t, and \f are all considered equivalent to a single space. Thus, you could think of this filter as being applied to each value in the format:

---

* Even those fields maintain the integrity of the columns you put them in, however. There is nothing in a picture line that can cause fields to grow or shrink or shift back and forth. The columns you see are sacred in a WYSIWYG sense—assuming you're using a fixed-width font. Even control characters are assumed to have a width of one.

```
$value =~ tr/\n\t\f/ /;
```

The remaining whitespace character, \r, forces the printing of a new line if the picture line allows it.

Picture fields that begin with ^ rather than @ are treated specially. With a # field, the field is blanked out if the value is undefined. For other field types, the caret enables a kind of fill mode. Instead of an arbitrary expression, the value supplied must be a scalar variable name that contains a text string. Perl puts as much text as it can into the field, and then chops off the front of the string so that the next time the variable is referenced, more of the text can be printed. (Yes, this means that the variable itself is altered during execution of the write call and is not preserved. Use a scratch variable if you want to preserve the original value.) Normally you would use a sequence of fields lined up vertically to print out a block of text. You might wish to end the final field with the text "...", which will appear in the output if the text was too long to appear in its entirety. You can change which characters are legal to "break" on (or after) by changing the variable $: (that's $FORMAT_LINE_BREAK_CHARACTERS if you're using the English module) to a list of the desired characters.

Using ^ fields can produce variable-length records. If the text to be formatted is short, just repeat the format line with the ^ field in it a few times. If you just do this for short data you'd end up getting a few blank lines. To suppress lines that would end up blank, put a ~ (tilde) character anywhere in the line. (The tilde itself will be translated to a space upon output.) If you put a second tilde next to the first, the line will be repeated until all the text in the fields on that line are exhausted. (This works because the ^ fields chew up the strings they print. But if you use a field of the @ variety in conjunction with two tildes, the expression you supply had better not give the same value every time forever! Use a shift, or some other operator with a side effect that exhausts the set of values.)

Top-of-form processing is by default handled by a format with the same name as the current filehandle with _TOP concatenated to it. It's triggered at the top of each page. See write in Chapter 29.

Here are some examples:

```
# a report on the /etc/passwd file
format STDOUT_TOP =
                    Passwd File
Name               Login    Office   Uid   Gid Home
---------------------------------------------------------------------
.
format STDOUT =
@<<<<<<<<<<<<<<<<<< @|||||||| @<<<<<<@>>>> @>>>> @<<<<<<<<<<<<<<<<<<
$name,             $login,   $office,$uid,$gid, $home
.
```

```
# a report from a bug report form
format STDOUT_TOP =
                         Bug Reports
@<<<<<<<<<<<<<<<<<<<<<<<    @|||        @>>>>>>>>>>>>>>>>>>>>>>>>>
$system,                   $%,         $date
------------------------------------------------------------------
.
format STDOUT =
Subject: @<<<<<<<<<<<<<<<<<<<<<<<<<<<<<<<<<<<<<<<<<<<<<<<<<<<<<<<<
         $subject
Index: @<<<<<<<<<<<<<<<<<<<<<<<<<   ^<<<<<<<<<<<<<<<<<<<<<<<<<<<<<
          $index,                  $description
Priority: @<<<<<<<<<< Date: @<<<<<<< ^<<<<<<<<<<<<<<<<<<<<<<<<<<<<<
            $priority,      $date,   $description
From: @<<<<<<<<<<<<<<<<<<<<<<<<<<<<   ^<<<<<<<<<<<<<<<<<<<<<<<<<<<<<
        $from,                       $description
Assigned to: @<<<<<<<<<<<<<<<<<<<<   ^<<<<<<<<<<<<<<<<<<<<<<<<<<<<<
               $programmer,          $description
~                                    ^<<<<<<<<<<<<<<<<<<<<<<<<<<<<<
                                     $description
~                                    ^<<<<<<<<<<<<<<<<<<<<<<<<<<<<<
                                     $description
~                                    ^<<<<<<<<<<<<<<<<<<<<<<<<<<<<<
                                     $description
~                                    ^<<<<<<<<<<<<<<<<<<<<<<<<<<<<<
                                     $description
~                                    ^<<<<<<<<<<<<<<<<<<<<<<<<<<<...
                                     $description
.
```

Lexical variables are not visible within a format unless the format is declared within the scope of the lexical variable.

It is possible to intermix prints with writes on the same output channel, but you'll have to handle the $- special variable ($FORMAT_LINES_LEFT if you're using the English module) yourself.

Format Variables

The current format name is stored in the variable $~ ($FORMAT_NAME), and the current top-of-form format name is in $^ ($FORMAT_TOP_NAME). The current output page number is stored in $% ($FORMAT_PAGE_NUMBER), and the number of lines on the page is in $= ($FORMAT_LINES_PER_PAGE). Whether to flush the output buffer on this handle automatically is stored in $| ($OUTPUT_AUTOFLUSH). The string to be output before each top of page (except the first) is stored in $^L ($FORMAT_FORMFEED). These variables are set on a per-filehandle basis, so you'll need to select the filehandle associated with a format in order to affect its format variables:

```
select((select(OUTF),
        $~ = "My_Other_Format",
        $^ = "My_Top_Format"
       )[0]);
```

Pretty ugly, eh? It's a common idiom though, so don't be too surprised when you see it. You can at least use a temporary variable to hold the previous filehandle:

```
$ofh = select(OUTF);
$~ = "My_Other_Format";
$^ = "My_Top_Format";
select($ofh);
```

This is a much better approach in general because not only does legibility improve, but you now have an intermediary statement in the code to stop on when you're single-stepping in the debugger. If you use the English module, you can even read the variable names:

```
use English;
$ofh = select(OUTF);
$FORMAT_NAME     = "My_Other_Format";
$FORMAT_TOP_NAME = "My_Top_Format";
select($ofh);
```

But you still have those funny calls to select. If you want to avoid them, use the FileHandle module bundled with Perl. Now you can access these special variables using lowercase method names instead:

```
use FileHandle;
OUTF->format_name("My_Other_Format");
OUTF->format_top_name("My_Top_Format");
```

Much better!

Since the values line following your picture line may contain arbitrary expressions (for @ fields, not ^ fields), you can farm out more sophisticated processing to other functions, like sprintf or one of your own. For example, to insert commas into a number:

```
format Ident =
    @<<<<<<<<<<<<<<
    commify($n)
.
```

To get a real @, ~, or ^ into the field, do this:

```
format Ident =
I have an @ here.
        "@"
.
```

To center a whole line of text, do something like this:

```
format Ident =
@|||||||||||||||||||||||||||||||||||||||||||||||||||||||||||||||
                        "Some text line"
.
```

The > field-length indicator ensures that the text will be right-justified within the field, but the field as a whole occurs exactly where you show it occurring. There is no built-in way to say "float this field to the right-hand side of the page, however wide it is." You have to specify where it goes relative to the left margin. The truly desperate can generate their own format on the fly, based on the current number of columns (not supplied), and then eval it:

```
$format  = "format STDOUT = \n"
         . '^' . '<' x $cols . "\n"
         . '$entry' . "\n"
         . "\t^" . "<" x ($cols-8) . "~~\n"
         . '$entry' . "\n"
         . ".\n";
print $format if $Debugging;
eval $format;
die $@ if $@;
```

The most important line there is probably the print. What the print would print out looks something like this:

```
format STDOUT =
^<<<<<<<<<<<<<<<<<<<<<<<<<<<<<<<<<<<<<<<<<<<<<<<<<<<<
$entry
     ^<<<<<<<<<<<<<<<<<<<<<<<<<<<<<<<<<<<<<<<<<<<<~~
$entry
.
```

Here's a little program that behaves like the *fmt*(1) Unix utility:

```
format =
^<<<<<<<<<<<<<<<<<<<<<<<<<<<<<<<<<<<<<<<<<<<<< ~~
$_


.

$/ = "";
while (<>) {
    s/\s*\n\s*/ /g;
    write;
}
```

Footers

While $^ ($FORMAT_TOP_NAME) contains the name of the current header format, there is no corresponding mechanism to do the same thing automatically for a footer. Not knowing how big a format is going to be until you evaluate it is one of the major problems. It's on the TODO list.*

Here's one strategy: if you have a fixed-size footer, you can get footers by checking $- ($FORMAT_LINES_LEFT) before each write and then print the footer yourself if necessary.

Here's another strategy; open a pipe to yourself, using open(MESELF, "|-") (see the open entry in Chapter 29) and always write to MESELF instead of STDOUT. Have your child process postprocess its STDIN to rearrange headers and footers however you like. Not very convenient, but doable.

Accessing Formatting Internals

For low-level access to the internal formatting mechanism, you may use the built-in formline operator and access $^A (the $ACCUMULATOR variable) directly. (Formats essentially compile into a sequence of calls to formline.) For example:

```
$str = formline <<'END', 1,2,3;
@<<<  @|||  @>>>
END

print "Wow, I just stored '$^A' in the accumulator!\n";
```

Or to create an swrite subroutine that is to write as sprintf is to printf, do this:

```
use Carp;
sub swrite {
    croak "usage: swrite PICTURE ARGS" unless @_;
    my $format = shift;
    $^A = "";
    formline($format, @_);
    return $^A;
}

$string = swrite(<<'END', 1, 2, 3);
Check me out
@<<<  @|||  @>>>
END
print $string;
```

---

* That doesn't guarantee we'll ever do it, of course. Formats are somewhat passé in this age of WWW, Unicode, XML, XSLT, and whatever the next few things after that are.

If you were using the `FileHandle` module, you could use `formline` as follows to wrap a block of text at column 72:

```
use FileHandle;
STDOUT->formline("^" . ("<" x 72) . "~~\n", $long_text);
```

8

References

For both practical and philosophical reasons, Perl has always been biased in favor of flat, linear data structures. And for many problems, this is just what you want.

Suppose you wanted to build a simple table (two-dimensional array) showing vital statistics—age, eye color, and weight—for a group of people. You could do this by first creating an array for each individual:

```
@john = (47, "brown", 186);
@mary = (23, "hazel", 128);
@bill = (35, "blue",  157);
```

You could then construct a single, additional array consisting of the names of the other arrays:

```
@vitals = ('john', 'mary', 'bill');
```

To change John's eyes to "red" after a night on the town, we want a way to change the contents of the @john array given only the simple string "john". This is the basic problem of *indirection*, which various languages solve in various ways. In C, the most common form of indirection is the pointer, which lets one variable hold the memory address of another variable. In Perl, the most common form of indirection is the *reference*.

What Is a Reference?

In our example, $vitals[0] has the value "john". That is, it contains a string that happens to be the name of another (global) variable. We say that the first variable *refers* to the second, and this sort of reference is called a *symbolic* reference, since

Perl has to look up @john in a symbol table to find it. (You might think of symbolic references as analogous to symbolic links in the filesystem.) We'll talk about symbolic references later in this chapter.

The other kind of reference is a *hard* reference, and this is what most Perl programmers use to accomplish their indirections (if not their indiscretions). We call them hard references not because they're difficult, but because they're real and solid. If you like, think of hard references as real references and symbolic references as fake references. It's like the difference between true friendship and mere name-dropping. When we don't specify which type of reference we mean, it's a hard reference. Figure 8-1 depicts a variable named $bar referring to the contents of a scalar named $foo which has the value "bot".

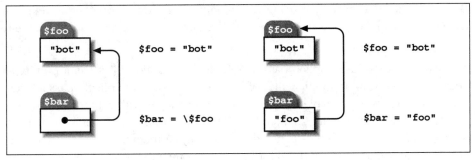

Figure 8-1. A hard reference and a symbolic reference

Unlike a symbolic reference, a real reference refers not to the name of another variable (which is just a container for a value) but to an actual value itself, some internal glob of data. There's no good word for that thing, but when we have to, we'll call it a *referent*. Suppose, for example, that you create a hard reference to a lexically scoped array named @array. This hard reference, and the referent it refers to, will continue to exist even after @array goes out of scope. A referent is only destroyed when all the references to it are eliminated.

A referent doesn't really have a name of its own, apart from the references to it. To put it another way, every Perl variable name lives in some kind of symbol table, holding one hard reference to its underlying (otherwise nameless) referent. That referent might be simple, like a number or string, or complex, like an array or hash. Either way, there's still exactly one reference from the variable to its value. You might create additional hard references to the same referent, but if so, the variable doesn't know (or care) about them.*

---

* If you're curious, you can determine the underlying refcount with the Devel::Peek module, bundled with Perl.

A symbolic reference is just a string that happens to name something in a package symbol table. It's not so much a distinct type as it is something you do with a string. But a hard reference is a different beast entirely. It is the third of the three kinds of fundamental scalar data types, the other two being strings and numbers. A hard reference doesn't know something's name just to refer to it, and it's actually completely normal for there to *be* no name to use in the first place. Such totally nameless referents are called *anonymous*; we discuss them in "Anonymous Data" below.

To *reference* a value, in the terminology of this chapter, is to create a hard reference to it. (There's a special operator for this creative act.) The reference so created is simply a scalar, which behaves in all familiar contexts just like any other scalar. To *dereference* this scalar means to use the reference to get at the referent. Both referencing and dereferencing occur only when you invoke certain explicit mechanisms; implicit referencing or dereferencing never occurs in Perl. Well, almost never.

A function call *can* use implicit pass-by-reference semantics—if it has a prototype declaring it that way. If so, the caller of the function doesn't explicitly pass a reference, although you still have to dereference it explicitly within the function. See the section "Prototypes" in Chapter 6, *Subroutines*. And to be perfectly honest, there's also some behind-the-scenes dereferencing happening when you use certain kinds of filehandles, but that's for backward compatibility and is transparent to the casual user. Finally, two built-in functions, `bless` and `lock`, each take a reference for their argument but implicitly dereference it to work their magic on what lies behind. But those confessions aside, the basic principle still holds that Perl isn't interested in muddling your levels of indirection.

A reference can point to any data structure. Since references are scalars, you can store them in arrays and hashes, and thus build arrays of arrays, arrays of hashes, hashes of arrays, arrays of hashes and functions, and so on. There are examples of these in Chapter 9, *Data Structures*.

Keep in mind, though, that Perl arrays and hashes are internally one-dimensional. That is, their elements can hold only scalar values (strings, numbers, and references). When we use a phrase like "array of arrays", we really mean "array of references to arrays", just as when we say "hash of functions" we really mean "hash of references to subroutines". But since references are the only way to implement such structures in Perl, it follows that the shorter, less accurate phrase is not so inaccurate as to be false, and therefore should not be totally despised, unless you're into that sort of thing.

Creating References

There are several ways to create references, most of which we will describe before explaining how to use (dereference) the resulting references.

The Backslash Operator

You can create a reference to any named variable or subroutine with a backslash. (You may also use it on an anonymous scalar value like 7 or "camel", although you won't often need to.) This operator works like the & (address-of) operator in C—at least at first glance.

Here are some examples:

```
$scalarref = \$foo;
$constref  = \186_282.42;
$arrayref  = \@ARGV;
$hashref   = \%ENV;
$coderef   = \&handler;
$globref   = \*STDOUT;
```

The backslash operator can do more than produce a single reference. It will generate a whole list of references if applied to a list. See the section "Other Tricks You Can Do with Hard References" for details.

Anonymous Data

In the examples just shown, the backslash operator merely makes a duplicate of a reference that is already held in a variable name—with one exception. The 186_282.42 isn't referenced by a named variable—it's just a value. It's one of those *anonymous* referents we mentioned earlier. Anonymous referents are accessed only through references. This one happens to be a number, but you can create anonymous arrays, hashes, and subroutines as well.

The anonymous array composer

You can create a reference to an anonymous array with square brackets:

```
$arrayref = [1, 2, ['a', 'b', 'c', 'd']];
```

Here we've composed an anonymous array of three elements, whose final element is a reference to an anonymous array of four elements (depicted in Figure 8-2). (The multidimensional syntax described later can be used to access this. For example, $arrayref->[2][1] would have the value "b".)

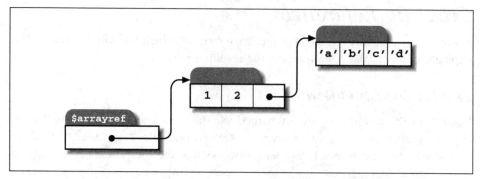

Figure 8-2. A reference to an array, whose third element is itself an array reference

We now have one way to represent the table at the beginning of the chapter:

```
$table = [ [ "john", 47, "brown", 186],
           [ "mary", 23, "hazel", 128],
           [ "bill", 35, "blue",  157] ];
```

Square brackets work like this only where the Perl parser is expecting a term in an expression. They should not be confused with the brackets in an expression like $array[6]—although the mnemonic association with arrays is intentional. Inside a quoted string, square brackets don't compose anonymous arrays; instead, they become literal characters in the string. (Square brackets do still work for subscripting in strings, or you wouldn't be able to print string values like "VAL=$array[6]\n". And to be totally honest, you can in fact sneak anonymous array composers into strings, but only when embedded in a larger expression that is being interpolated. We'll talk about this cool feature later in the chapter because it involves dereferencing as well as referencing.)

The anonymous hash composer

You can create a reference to an anonymous hash with braces:

```
$hashref = {
    'Adam'   => 'Eve',
    'Clyde'  => $bonnie,
    'Antony' => 'Cleo' . 'patra',
};
```

For the values (but not the keys) of the hash, you can freely mix other anonymous array, hash, and subroutine composers to produce as complicated a structure as you like.

We now have another way to represent the table at the beginning of the chapter:

```
$table = {
            "john" => [ 47, "brown", 186 ],
            "mary" => [ 23, "hazel", 128 ],
            "bill" => [ 35, "blue",  157 ],
};
```

That's a hash of arrays. Choosing the best data structure is a tricky business, and the next chapter is devoted to it. But as a teaser, we could even use a hash of hashes for our table:

```
$table = {
            "john" => { age    => 47,
                        eyes   => "brown",
                        weight => 186,
                      },
            "mary" => { age    => 23,
                        eyes   => "hazel",
                        weight => 128,
                      },
            "bill" => { age    => 35,
                        eyes   => "blue",
                        weight => 157,
                      },
};
```

As with square brackets, braces work like this only where the Perl parser is expecting a term in an expression. They should not be confused with the braces in an expression like $hash{key}—although the mnemonic association with hashes is (again) intentional. The same caveats apply to the use of braces within strings.

There is one additional caveat which didn't apply to square brackets. Since braces are also used for several other things (including blocks), you may occasionally have to disambiguate braces at the beginning of a statement by putting a + or a return in front, so that Perl realizes the opening brace isn't starting a block. For example, if you want a function to make a new hash and return a reference to it, you have these options:

```
sub hashem {        { @_ } }   # Silently WRONG -- returns @_.
sub hashem {       +{ @_ } }   # Ok.
sub hashem { return { @_ } }   # Ok.
```

The anonymous subroutine composer

You can create a reference to an anonymous subroutine by using sub without a subroutine name:

```
$coderef = sub { print "Boink!\n" };   # Now &$coderef prints "Boink!"
```

Note the presence of the semicolon, required here to terminate the expression. (It isn't required after the more common usage of sub *NAME* {} that declares and defines a named subroutine.) A nameless sub {} is not so much a declaration as it is an operator—like do {} or eval {}—except that the code inside isn't executed immediately. Instead, it just generates a reference to the code, which in our example is stored in $coderef. However, no matter how many times you execute the line shown above, $coderef will still refer to the same anonymous subroutine.*

Object Constructors

Subroutines can also return references. That may sound trite, but sometimes you are *supposed* to use a subroutine to create a reference rather than creating the reference yourself. In particular, special subroutines called *constructors* create and return references to objects. An object is simply a special kind of reference that happens to know which class it's associated with, and constructors know how to create that association. They do so by taking an ordinary referent and turning it into an object with the bless operator, so we can speak of an object as a blessed reference. There's nothing religious going on here; since a class acts as a user-defined type, blessing a referent simply makes it a user-defined type in addition to a built-in one. Constructors are often named new—especially by C++ programmers—but they can be named anything in Perl.

Constructors can be called in any of these ways:

```
$objref = Doggie::->new(Tail => 'short', Ears => 'long');   #1
$objref = new Doggie:: Tail => 'short', Ears => 'long';     #2
$objref = Doggie->new(Tail => 'short', Ears => 'long');     #3
$objref = new Doggie Tail => 'short', Ears => 'long';       #4
```

The first and second invocations are the same. They both call a function named new that is supplied by the Doggie module. The third and fourth invocations are the same as the first two, but are slightly more ambiguous: the parser will get confused if you define your own subroutine named Doggie. (Which is why people typically stick with lowercase names for subroutines and uppercase for modules.) The fourth invocation can also get confused if you've defined your own new subroutine and don't happen to have done either a require or a use of the Doggie module, either of which has the effect of declaring the module. Always declare your modules if you want to use #4. (And watch out for stray Doggie subroutines.)

See Chapter 12, *Objects* for a discussion of Perl objects.

---

* But even though there's only one anonymous subroutine, there may be several copies of the lexical variables in use by the subroutine, depending on when the subroutine reference was generated. These are discussed later in the section "Closures".

Handle References

References to filehandles or directory handles can be created by referencing the typeglob of the same name:

```
splutter(\*STDOUT);

sub splutter {
    my $fh = shift;
    print $fh "her um well a hmmm\n";
}

$rec = get_rec(\*STDIN);
sub get_rec {
    my $fh = shift;
    return scalar <$fh>;
}
```

If you're passing around filehandles, you can also use the bare typeglob to do so: in the example above, you could have used *STDOUT or *STDIN instead of *STDOUT and *STDIN.

Although you can usually use typeglob and references to typeglobs interchangeably, there are a few places where you can't. Simple typeglobs can't be blessed into objectdom, and typeglob references can't be passed back out of the scope of a localized typeglob.

When generating new filehandles, older code would often do something like this to open a list of files:

```
for $file (@names) {
    local *FH;
    open(*FH, $file) || next;
    $handle{$file} = *FH;
}
```

That still works, but now it's just as easy to let an undefined variable autovivify an anonymous typeglob:

```
for $file (@names) {
    my $fh;
    open($fh, $file) || next;
    $handle{$file} = $fh;
}
```

With indirect filehandles, it doesn't matter whether you use use typeglobs, references to typeglobs, or one of the more exotic I/O objects. You just use a scalar that—one way or another—gets interpreted as a filehandle. For most purposes, you can use either a typeglob or a typeglob reference almost indiscriminately. As we admitted earlier, there is some implicit dereferencing magic going on here.

Symbol Table References

In unusual circumstances, you might not know what type of reference you need when your program is written. A reference can be created by using a special syntax, affectionately known as the *foo{THING} syntax. *foo{THING} returns a reference to the *THING* slot in *foo, which is the symbol table entry holding the values of $foo, @foo, %foo, and friends.

```
$scalarref = *foo{SCALAR};     # Same as \$foo
$arrayref  = *ARGV{ARRAY};     # Same as \@ARGV
$hashref   = *ENV{HASH};       # Same as \%ENV
$coderef   = *handler{CODE};   # Same as \&handler
$globref   = *foo{GLOB};       # Same as \*foo
$ioref     = *STDIN{IO};       # Er...
```

All of these are self-explanatory except for *STDIN{IO}. It yields the actual internal IO::Handle object that the typeglob contains, that is, the part of the typeglob that the various I/O functions are actually interested in. For compatibility with previous versions of Perl, *foo{FILEHANDLE} is a synonym for the hipper *foo{IO} notation.

In theory, you can use a *HANDLE{IO} anywhere you'd use a *HANDLE or a *HANDLE, such as for passing handles into or out of subroutines, or storing them in larger data structures. (In practice, there are still some wrinkles to be ironed out.) The advantage of them is that they access only the real I/O object you want, not the whole typeglob, so you run no risk of clobbering more than you want to through a typeglob assignment (although if you always assign to a scalar variable instead of to a typeglob, you'll be okay). One disadvantage is that there's no way to autovivify one as of yet.*

```
splutter(*STDOUT);
splutter(*STDOUT{IO});

sub splutter {
    my $fh = shift;
    print $fh "her um well a hmmm\n";
}
```

Both invocations of splutter() print "her um well a hmmm".

The *foo{THING} thing returns undef if that particular *THING* hasn't been seen by the compiler yet, except when *THING* is SCALAR. It so happens that *foo{SCALAR} returns a reference to an anonymous scalar even if $foo hasn't been seen yet. (Perl always adds a scalar to any typeglob as an optimization to save a bit of code elsewhere. But don't depend on it to stay that way in future releases.)

---

* Currently, open my $fh autovivifies a typeglob instead of an IO::Handle object, but someday we may fix that, so you shouldn't rely on the typeglobbedess of what open currently autovivifies.

Implicit Creation of References

A final method for creating references is not really a method at all. References of an appropriate type simply spring into existence if you dereference them in an lvalue context that assumes they exist. This is extremely useful, and is also What You Expect. This topic is covered later in this chapter, where we'll discuss how to dereference all of the references we've created so far.

Using Hard References

Just as there are numerous ways to create references, there are also several ways to use, or *dereference*, a reference. There is just one overriding principle: Perl does no implicit referencing or dereferencing.* When a scalar is holding a reference, it always behaves like a simple scalar. It doesn't magically start being an array or hash or subroutine; you have to tell it explicitly to do so, by dereferencing it.

Using a Variable as a Variable Name

When you encounter a scalar like $foo, you should be thinking "the scalar value of foo." That is, there's a foo entry in the symbol table, and the $ funny character is a way of looking at whatever scalar value might be inside. If what's inside is a reference, you can look inside *that* (dereferencing $foo) by prepending another funny character. Or looking at it the other way around, you can replace the literal foo in $foo with a scalar variable that points to the actual referent. This is true of any variable type, so not only is $$foo the scalar value of whatever $foo refers to, but @$bar is the array value of whatever $bar refers to, %$glarch is the hash value of whatever $glarch refers to, and so on. The upshot is that you can put an extra funny character on the front of any simple scalar variable to dereference it:

```
$foo         = "three humps";
$scalarref   = \$foo;          # $scalarref is now a reference to $foo
$camel_model = $$scalarref;    # $camel_model is now "three humps"
```

Here are some other dereferences:

```
$bar = $$scalarref;

push(@$arrayref, $filename);
$$arrayref[0] = "January";               # Set the first element of @$arrayref
@$arrayref[4..6] = qw/May June July/;    # Set several elements of @$arrayref

%$hashref = (KEY => "RING", BIRD => "SING");  # Initialize whole hash
$$hashref{KEY} = "VALUE";                     # Set one key/value pair
@$hashref{"KEY1","KEY2"} = ("VAL1","VAL2");   # Set two more pairs
```

---

* We already confessed that this was a small fib. We're not about to do so again.

```
&$coderef(1,2,3);
```

```
print $handleref "output\n";
```

This form of dereferencing can only make use of a simple scalar variable (one without a subscript). That is, dereferencing happens *before* (or binds tighter than) any array or hash lookups. Let's use some braces to clarify what we mean: an expression like $$arrayref[0] is equivalent to ${$arrayref}[0] and means the first element of the array referred to by $arrayref. That is not at all the same as ${$arrayref[0]}, which is dereferencing the first element of the (probably non-existent) array named @arrayref. Likewise, $$hashref{KEY} is the same as ${$hashref}{KEY}, and has nothing to do with ${$hashref{KEY}}, which would be dereferencing an entry in the (probably nonexistent) hash named %hashref. You will be miserable until you understand this.

You can achieve multiple levels of referencing and dereferencing by concatenating the appropriate funny characters. The following prints "howdy":

```
$refrefref = \\\"howdy";
print $$$$refrefref;
```

You can think of the dollar signs as operating right to left. But the beginning of the chain must still be a simple, unsubscripted scalar variable. There is, however, a way to get fancier, which we already sneakily used earlier, and which we'll explain in the next section.

Using a BLOCK as a Variable Name

Not only can you dereference a simple variable name, you can also dereference the contents of a *BLOCK*. Anywhere you'd put an alphanumeric identifier as part of a variable or subroutine name, you can replace the identifier with a *BLOCK* returning a reference of the correct type. In other words, the earlier examples could all be disambiguated like this:

```
$bar = ${$scalarref};
push(@{$arrayref}, $filename);
${$arrayref}[0] = "January";
@{$arrayref}[4..6] = qw/May June July/;
${$hashref}{"KEY"} = "VALUE";
@{$hashref}{"KEY1","KEY2"} = ("VAL1","VAL2");
&{$coderef}(1,2,3);
```

not to mention:

```
$refrefref = \\\"howdy";
print ${${${$refrefref}}};
```

Admittedly, it's silly to use the braces in these simple cases, but the *BLOCK* can contain any arbitrary expression. In particular, it can contain subscripted expressions.

In the following example, `$dispatch{$index}` is assumed to contain a reference to a subroutine (sometimes called a "coderef"). The example invokes the subroutine with three arguments.

```
&{ $dispatch{$index} }(1, 2, 3);
```

Here, the *BLOCK* is necessary. Without that outer pair of braces, Perl would have treated `$dispatch` as the coderef instead of `$dispatch{$index}`.

Using the Arrow Operator

For references to arrays, hashes, or subroutines, a third method of dereferencing involves the use of the -> infix operator. This form of syntactic sugar makes it easier to get at individual array or hash elements, or to call a subroutine indirectly.

The type of the dereference is determined by the right operand, that is, by what follows directly after the arrow. If the next thing after the arrow is a bracket or brace, the left operand is treated as a reference to an array or a hash, respectively, to be subscripted by the expression on the right. If the next thing is a left parenthesis, the left operand is treated as a reference to a subroutine, to be called with whatever parameters you supply in the parentheses on the right.

Each of these next trios is equivalent, corresponding to the three notations we've introduced. (We've inserted some spaces to line up equivalent elements.)

```
$  $arrayref  [2] = "Dorian";       #1
${ $arrayref }[2] = "Dorian";       #2
   $arrayref->[2] = "Dorian";       #3

$  $hashref  {KEY} = "F#major";     #1
${ $hashref }{KEY} = "F#major";     #2
   $hashref->{KEY} = "F#major";     #3

&  $coderef  (Presto => 192);       #1
&{ $coderef }(Presto => 192);       #2
   $coderef->(Presto => 192);       #3
```

You can see that the initial funny character is missing from the third notation in each trio. The funny character is guessed at by Perl, which is why it can't be used to dereference complete arrays, complete hashes, or slices of either. As long as you stick with scalar values, though, you can use any expression to the left of the ->, including another dereference, because multiple arrow operators associate left to right:

```
print $array[3]->{"English"}->[0];
```

You can deduce from this expression that the fourth element of `@array` is intended to be a hash reference, and the value of the "English" entry in that hash is intended to be an array reference.

Note that $array[3] and $array->[3] are not the same. The first is talking about the fourth element of @array, while the second one is talking about the fourth element of the (possibly anonymous) array whose reference is contained in $array.

Suppose now that $array[3] is undefined. The following statement is still legal:

```
$array[3]->{"English"}->[0] = "January";
```

This is one of those cases mentioned earlier in which references spring into existence (or "autovivify") when used as an lvalue (that is, when a value is being assigned to it). If $array[3] was undefined, it's automatically defined as a hash reference so that we can set a value for $array[3]->{"English"} in it. Once that's done, $array[3]->{"English"} is automatically defined as an array reference so that we can assign something to the first element in that array. Note that rvalues are a little different: print $array[3]->{"English"}->[0] only defines $array[3] and $array[3]->{"English"}, not $array[3]->{"English"}->[0], since the final element is not an lvalue. (The fact that it defines the first two at all in an rvalue context could be considered a bug. We may fix that someday.)

The arrow is optional between brackets or braces, or between a closing bracket or brace and a parenthesis for an indirect function call. So you can shrink the previous code down to:

```
$dispatch{$index}(1, 2, 3);
$array[3]{"English"}[0] = "January";
```

In the case of ordinary arrays, this gives you multidimensional arrays that are just like C's array:

```
$answer[$x][$y][$z] += 42;
```

Well, okay, not *entirely* like C's arrays. For one thing, C doesn't know how to grow its arrays on demand, while Perl does. Also, some constructs that are similar in the two languages parse differently. In Perl, the following two statements do the same thing:

```
$listref->[2][2] = "hello";    # Pretty clear
$$listref[2][2]  = "hello";    # A bit confusing
```

This second of these statements may disconcert the C programmer, who is accustomed to using *a[i] to mean "what's pointed to by the *i*th element of a". But in Perl, the five characters ($ @ * % &) effectively bind more tightly than braces or brackets.* Therefore, it is $$listref and not $listref[2] that is taken to be a

---

* But not because of operator precedence. The funny characters in Perl are not operators in that sense. Perl's grammar simply prohibits anything more complicated than a simple variable or block from following the initial funny character, for various funny reasons.

reference to an array. If you want the C behavior, either you have to write
${$listref[2]} to force the $listref[2] to get evaluated before the leading $
dereferencer, or you have to use the -> notation:

```
$listref[2]->[$greeting] = "hello";
```

Using Object Methods

If a reference happens to be a reference to an object, then the class that defines
that object probably provides methods to access the innards of the object, and you
should generally stick to those methods if you're merely using the class (as
opposed to implementing it). In other words, be nice, and don't treat an object
like a regular reference, even though Perl lets you when you really need to. Perl
does not enforce encapsulation. We are not totalitarians here. We do expect some
basic civility, however.

In return for this civility, you get complete orthogonality between objects and data
structures. Any data structure can behave as an object when you want it to. Or
not, when you don't.

Pseudohashes

A *pseudohash* is any reference to an array whose first element is a reference to a
hash. You can treat the pseudohash reference as either an array reference (as you
would expect) or a hash reference (as you might not expect). Here's an example
of a pseudohash:

```
$john = [ {age => 1, eyes => 2, weight => 3}, 47, "brown", 186 ];
```

The underlying hash in $john->[0] defines the names ("age", "eyes", "weight") of
the array elements that follow (47, "brown", 186). Now you can access an element
with both hash and array notations:

```
$john->{weight}          # Treats $john as a hashref
$john->[3]               # Treats $john as an arrayref
```

Pseudohash magic is not deep; it only knows one "trick": how to turn a hash
dereference into an array dereference. When adding another element to a pseudohash, you have to explicitly tell the underlying mapping hash where the element
will reside before you can use the hash notation:

```
$john->[0]{height} = 4;     # height is to be element 4
$john->{height} = "tall";   # Or $john->[4] = "tall"
```

Perl raises an exception if you try to delete a key from a pseudohash, although
you can always delete keys from the mapping hash. Perl also raises an exception

if you try to access a nonexistent key, where "existence" means presence in the mapping hash:

```
delete $john->[0]{height};  # Deletes from the underlying hash only
$john->{height};            # This now raises an exception
$john->[4];                 # Still prints "tall"
```

Don't try to splice the array unless you know what you're doing. If the array elements move around, the mapping hash values will still refer to the *old* element positions, unless you change those explicitly, too. Pseudohash magic is not deep.

To avoid inconsistencies, you can use the `fields::phash` function provided by the use `fields` pragma to create a pseudohash:

```
use fields;
$ph = fields::phash(age => 47, eyes => "brown", weight => 186);
print $ph->{age};
```

There are two ways to check for the existence of a key in a pseudohash. The first is to use `exists`, which checks whether the given field has ever been set. It acts this way to match the behavior of a real hash. For instance:

```
use fields;
$ph= fields::phash([qw(age eyes brown)], [47]);
$ph->{eyes} = undef;

print exists $ph->{age};     # True, 'age' was set in declaration.
print exists $ph->{weight};  # False, 'weight' has not been used.
print exists $ph->{eyes};    # True, your 'eyes' have been touched.
```

The second way is to use `exists` on the mapping hash sitting in the first array element. This checks whether the given key is a valid field for that pseudohash:

```
print exists $ph->[0]{age};   # True, 'age' is a valid field
print exists $ph->[0]{name};  # False, 'name' can't be used
```

Unlike what happens in a real hash, calling `delete` on a pseudohash element deletes only the array value corresponding to the key, not the real key in the mapping hash. To delete the key, you have to explicitly delete it from the mapping hash. Once you do that, you may no longer use that key name as a pseudohash subscript:

```
print delete $ph->{age};      # Removes and returns $ph->[1], 47
print exists $ph->{age};      # Now false
print exists $ph->[0]{age};   # True, 'age' key still usable
print delete $ph->[0]{age};   # Now 'age' key is gone
print $ph->{age};             # Run-time exception
```

You've probably begun to wonder what could possibly have motivated this masquerade of arrays prancing about in hashes' clothing. Arrays provide faster lookups and more efficient storage, while hashes offer the convenience of naming (instead of numbering) your data; pseudohashes provide the best of both worlds. But it's not until you consider Perl's compilation phase that the greatest benefit becomes apparent. With the help of a pragma or two, the compiler can verify proper access to valid fields, so you can find out about nonexistent subscripts (or spelling errors) before your program starts to run.

Pseudohashes' properties of speed, efficiency, and compile-time access checking (you might even think of it as type safety) are especially handy for creating efficient and robust class modules. See the discussion of the `use fields` pragma in Chapter 12 and Chapter 31, *Pragmatic Modules*.

Pseudohashes are a new and relatively experimental feature; as such, the underlying implementation may well change in the future. To protect yourself from such changes, always go through the `fields` module's documented interface via its `phash` and `new` functions.

Other Tricks You Can Do with Hard References

As mentioned earlier, the backslash operator is usually used on a single referent to generate a single reference, but it doesn't have to be. When used on a list of referents, it produces a list of corresponding references. The second line of the following example does the same thing as the first line, since the backslash is automatically distributed throughout the whole list.

```
@reflist = (\$s, \@a, \%h, \&f);    # List of four references
@reflist = \($s,  @a   %h,  &f);    # Same thing
```

If a parenthesized list contains exactly one array or hash, then all of its values are interpolated and references to each returned:

```
@reflist = \(@x);                   # Interpolate array, then get refs
@reflist = map { \$_ } @x;          # Same thing
```

This also occurs when there are internal parentheses:

```
@reflist = \(@x, (@y));             # But only single aggregates expand
@reflist = (\@x, map { \$_ } @y);   # Same thing
```

If you try this with a hash, the result will contain references to the values (as you'd expect), but references to *copies* of the keys (as you might not expect).

Since array and hash slices are really just lists, you can backslash a slice of either of these to get a list of references. Each of the next three lines does exactly the same thing:

```
@envrefs = \@ENV{'HOME', 'TERM'};        # Backslashing a slice
@envrefs = \( $ENV{HOME},  $ENV{TERM} ); # Backslashing a list
@envrefs = ( \$ENV{HOME}, \$ENV{TERM} ); # A list of two references
```

Since functions can return lists, you can apply a backslash to them. If you have more than one function to call, first interpolate each function's return values into a larger list and then backslash the whole thing:

```
@reflist = \fx();
@reflist = map { \$_ } fx();                    # Same thing

@reflist = \( fx(), fy(), fz() );
@reflist = ( \fx(), \fy(), \fz() );             # Same thing
@reflist = map { \$_ } fx(), fy(), fz();        # Same thing
```

The backslash operator always supplies a list context to its operand, so those functions are all called in list context. If the backslash is itself in scalar context, you'll end up with a reference to the last value of the list returned by the function:

```
@reflist = \localtime();     # Ref to each of nine time elements
$lastref = \localtime();     # Ref to whether it's daylight savings time
```

In this regard, the backslash behaves like the named Perl list operators, such as print, reverse, and sort, which always supply a list context on their right no matter what might be happening on their left. As with named list operators, use an explicit scalar to force what follows into scalar context:

```
$dateref = \scalar localtime();     # \"Sat Jul 16 11:42:18 2000"
```

You can use the ref operator to determine what a reference is pointing to. Think of ref as a "typeof" operator that returns true if its argument is a reference and false otherwise. The value returned depends on the type of thing referenced. Built-in types include SCALAR, ARRAY, HASH, CODE, GLOB, REF, LVALUE, IO, IO::Handle, and Regexp. Here, we use it to check subroutine arguments:

```
sub sum {
    my $arrayref = shift;
    warn "Not an array reference" if ref($arrayref) ne "ARRAY";
    return eval join("+", @$arrayref);
}
```

If you use a hard reference in a string context, it'll be converted to a string containing both the type and the address: SCALAR(0x1fc0e). (The reverse conversion cannot be done, since reference count information is lost during stringification—and also because it would be dangerous to let programs access a memory address named by an arbitrary string.)

You can use the bless operator to associate a referent with a package functioning as an object class. When you do this, ref returns the class name instead of the internal type. An object reference used in a string context returns a string with the external and internal types, and the address in memory: MyType=HASH(0x20d10) or IO::Handle=IO(0x186904). See Chapter 12 for more details about objects.

Since the way in which you dereference something always indicates what sort of referent you're looking for, a typeglob can be used the same way a reference can, despite the fact that a typeglob contains multiple referents of various types. So `${*main::foo}` and `${\$main::foo}` both access the same scalar variable, although the latter is more efficient.

Here's a trick for interpolating the return value of a subroutine call into a string:

```
print "My sub returned @{[ mysub(1,2,3) ]} that time.\n";
```

It works like this. At compile time, when the `@{...}` is seen within the double-quoted string, it's parsed as a block that returns a reference. Within the block, there are square brackets that create a reference to an anonymous array from whatever is in the brackets. So at run time, `mysub(1,2,3)` is called in list context, and the results are loaded into an anonymous array, a reference to which is then returned within the block. That array reference is then immediately dereferenced by the surrounding `@{...}`, and the array value is interpolated into the double-quoted string just as an ordinary array would be. This chicanery is also useful for arbitrary expressions, such as:

```
print "We need @{ [$n + 5] } widgets!\n";
```

Be careful though: square brackets supply a list context to their expression. In this case it doesn't matter, although the earlier call to `mysub` might care. When it does matter, use an explicit `scalar` to force the context:

```
print "mysub returns @{ [scalar mysub(1,2,3)] } now.\n";
```

Closures

Earlier we talked about creating anonymous subroutines with a nameless `sub {}`. You can think of those subroutines as defined at run time, which means that they have a time of generation as well as a location of definition. Some variables might be in scope when the subroutine is created, and different variables might be in scope when the subroutine is called.

Forgetting about subroutines for a moment, consider a reference that refers to a lexical variable:

```
{
    my $critter = "camel";
    $critterref = \$critter;
}
```

The value of `$$critterref` will remain "camel" even though `$critter` disappears after the closing curly brace. But `$critterref` could just as well have referred to a subroutine that refers to `$critter`:

```
{
    my $critter = "camel";
    $critterref = sub { return $critter };
}
```

This is a *closure*, which is a notion out of the functional programming world of LISP and Scheme.* It means that when you define an anonymous function in a particular lexical scope at a particular moment, it pretends to run in that scope even when later called from outside that scope. (A purist would say it doesn't have to pretend—it actually *does* run in that scope.)

In other words, you are guaranteed to get the same copy of a lexical variable each time, even if other instances of that lexical variable have been created before or since for other instances of that closure. This gives you a way to set values used in a subroutine when you define it, not just when you call it.

You can also think of closures as a way to write a subroutine template without using eval. The lexical variables act as parameters for filling in the template, which is useful for setting up little bits of code to run later. These are commonly called *callbacks* in event-based programming, where you associate a bit of code with a keypress, mouse click, window exposure, and so on. When used as callbacks, closures do exactly what you expect, even if you don't know the first thing about functional programming. (Note that this closure business only applies to my variables. Global variables work as they've always worked, since they're neither created nor destroyed the way lexical variables are.)

Another use for closures is within *function generators*; that is, functions that create and return brand new functions. Here's an example of a function generator implemented with closures:

```
sub make_saying {
    my $salute = shift;
    my $newfunc = sub {
        my $target = shift;
        print "$salute, $target!\n";
    };
    return $newfunc;              # Return a closure
}

$f = make_saying("Howdy");        # Create a closure
$g = make_saying("Greetings");    # Create another closure

# Time passes...

$f->("world");
$g->("earthlings");
```

---

* In this context, the word "functional" should not be construed as an antonym of "dysfunctional".

This prints:

```
Howdy, world!
Greetings, earthlings!
```

Note in particular how $salute continues to refer to the actual value passed into make_saying, despite the fact that the my $salute has gone out of scope by the time the anonymous subroutine runs. That's what closures are all about. Since $f and $g hold references to functions that, when called, still need access to the distinct versions of $salute, those versions automatically stick around. If you now overwrite $f, *its* version of $salute would automatically disappear. (Perl only cleans up when you're not looking.)

Perl doesn't provide references to object methods (described in Chapter 12) but you can get a similar effect using a closure. Suppose you want a reference not just to the subroutine the method represents, but one which, when invoked, would call that method on a particular object. You can conveniently remember both the object and the method as lexical variables bound up inside a closure:

```
sub get_method_ref {
    my ($self, $methodname) = @_;
    my $methref = sub {
        # the @_ below is not the same as the one above!
        return $self->$methodname(@_);
    };
    return $methref;
}

my $dog = new Doggie::
            Name => "Lucky",
            Legs => 3,
            Tail => "clipped";

our $wagger = get_method_ref($dog, 'wag');
$wagger->("tail");        # Calls $dog->wag('tail').
```

Not only can you get Lucky to wag what's left of his tail now, even once the lexical $dog variable has gone out of scope and Lucky is nowhere to be seen, the global $wagger variable can still get him to wag his tail, wherever he is.

Closures as function templates

Using a closure as a function template allows you to generate many functions that act similarly. Suppose you want a suite of functions that generate HTML font changes for various colors:

```
print "Be ", red("careful"), "with that ", green("light"), "!!!";
```

The red and green functions would be very similar. We'd like to name our functions, but closures don't have names since they're just anonymous subroutines with an attitude. To get around that, we'll perform the cute trick of naming our anonymous subroutines. You can bind a coderef to an existing name by assigning it to a typeglob of the name of the function you want. (See the section "Symbol Tables" in Chapter 10, *Packages*. In this case, we'll bind it to two different names, one uppercase and one lowercase:

```
@colors = qw(red blue green yellow orange purple violet);
for my $name (@colors) {
    no strict 'refs';       # Allow symbolic references
    *$name = *{uc $name} = sub { "<FONT COLOR='$name'>;@_</FONT>" };
}
```

Now you can call functions named red, RED, blue, BLUE, and so on, and the appropriate closure will be invoked. This technique reduces compile time and conserves memory, and is less error-prone as well, since syntax checks happen during compilation. It's critical that any variables in the anonymous subroutine be lexicals in order to create a closure. That's the reason for the my above.

This is one of the few places where giving a prototype to a closure makes sense. If you wanted to impose scalar context on the arguments of these functions (probably not a wise idea for this example), you could have written it this way instead:

```
*$name = sub ($) { "<FONT COLOR='$name'>$_[0]</FONT>" };
```

That's almost good enough. However, since prototype checking happens during compile time, the run-time assignment above happens too late to be of much use. You could fix this by putting the whole loop of assignments within a BEGIN block, forcing it to occur during compilation. (More likely, you'd put it out in a module that you use at compile time.) Then the prototypes will be visible during the rest of the compilation.

Nested subroutines

If you are accustomed (from other programming languages) to using subroutines nested within other subroutines, each with their own private variables, you'll have to work at it a bit in Perl. Named subroutines do not nest properly, although anonymous ones do.* Anyway, we can emulate nested, lexically scoped subroutines using closures. Here's an example:

```
sub outer {
    my $x = $_[0] + 35;
    local *inner = sub { return $x * 19 };
    return $x + inner();
}
```

---

* To be more precise, globally named subroutines don't nest. Unfortunately, that's the only kind of named subroutine declaration we have. We haven't yet implemented lexically scoped, named subroutines (known as my subs), but when we do, they should nest correctly.

Now `inner` can only be called from within `outer`, because of the temporary assignments of the closure. But when it is, it has normal access to the lexical variable `$x` from the scope of `outer`.

This has the interesting effect of creating a function local to another function, something not normally supported in Perl. Because `local` is dynamically scoped, and because function names are global to their package, any other function that `outer` called could also call the temporary version of `inner`. To prevent that, you'd need an extra level of indirection:

```
sub outer {
    my $x = $_[0] + 35;
    my $inner = sub { return $x * 19 };
    return $x + $inner->();
}
```

Symbolic References

What happens if you try to dereference a value that is not a hard reference? The value is then treated as a *symbolic reference*. That is, the reference is interpreted as a string representing the *name* of a global variable.

Here is how this works:

```
$name = "bam";
$$name = 1;               # Sets $bam
$name->[0] = 4;           # Sets the first element of @bam
$name->{X} = "Y";         # Sets the X element of %bam to Y
@$name = ();              # Clears @bam
keys %$name;              # Yields the keys of %bam
&$name;                   # Calls &bam
```

This is very powerful, and slightly dangerous, in that it's possible to intend (with the utmost sincerity) to use a hard reference, but to accidentally use a symbolic reference instead. To protect against that, you can say:

```
use strict 'refs';
```

and then only hard references will be allowed for the rest of the enclosing block. An inner block may countermand the decree with:

```
no strict 'refs';
```

It is also important to understand the difference between the following two lines of code:

```
${identifier};     # Same as $identifier.
${"identifier"};   # Also $identifier, but a symbolic reference.
```

Because the second form is quoted, it is treated as a symbolic reference and will generate an error if use strict 'refs' is in effect. Even if strict 'refs' is not in effect, it can only refer to a package variable. But the first form is identical to the unbracketed form, and will refer to even a lexically scoped variable if one is declared. The next example shows this (and the next section discusses it).

Only package variables are accessible through symbolic references, because symbolic references always go through the package symbol table. Since lexical variables aren't in a package symbol table, they are therefore invisible to this mechanism. For example:

```
our $value  = "global";
{
    my $value = "private";
    print "Inside, mine is ${value}, ";
    print "but ours is ${'value'}.\n";
}
print "Outside, ${value} is again ${'value'}.\n";
```

which prints:

```
Inside, mine is private, but ours is global.
Outside, global is again global.
```

Braces, Brackets, and Quoting

In the previous section, we pointed out that ${identifier} is not treated as a symbolic reference. You might wonder how this interacts with reserved words, and the short answer is that it doesn't. Despite the fact that push is a reserved word, these two statements print "pop on over":

```
$push = "pop on ";
print "${push}over";
```

The reason is that, historically, this use of braces is how Unix shells have isolated a variable name from subsequent alphanumeric text that would otherwise be interpreted as part of the name. It's how many people expect variable interpolation to work, so we made it work the same way in Perl. But with Perl, the notion extends further and applies to any braces used in generating references, whether or not they're inside quotes. This means that:

```
print ${push} . 'over';
```

or even (since spaces never matter):

```
print ${ push } . 'over';
```

both print "pop on over", even though the braces are outside of double quotes. The same rule applies to any identifier used for subscripting a hash. So, instead of writing:

```
$hash{ "aaa" }{ "bbb" }{ "ccc" }
```

you can just write:

```
$hash{ aaa }{ bbb }{ ccc }
```

or:

```
$hash{aaa}{bbb}{ccc}
```

and not worry about whether the subscripts are reserved words. So this:

```
$hash{ shift }
```

is interpreted as `$hash{"shift"}`. You can force interpretation as a reserved word by adding anything that makes it more than a mere identifier:

```
$hash{ shift() }
$hash{ +shift   }
$hash{ shift @_ }
```

References Don't Work as Hash Keys

Hash keys are stored internally as strings.* If you try to store a reference as a key in a hash, the key value will be converted into a string:

```
$x{ \$a } = $a;
($key, $value) = each %x;
print $$key;                    # WRONG
```

We mentioned earlier that you can't convert a string back to a hard reference. So if you try to dereference `$key`, which contains a mere string, it won't return a hard dereference, but rather a symbolic dereference—and since you probably don't have a variable named `SCALAR(0x1fc0e)`, you won't accomplish what you're attempting. You might want to do something more like:

```
$r = \@a;
$x{ $r } = $r;
```

Then at least you can use the hash *value*, which will be a hard reference, instead of the key, which won't.

Although you can't store a reference as a key, if (as in the earlier example) you use a hard reference in a string context, it *is* guaranteed to produce a unique

---

* They're also stored *externally* as strings, such as when you put them into a DBM file. In fact, DBM files *require* that their keys (and values) be strings.

string, since the address of the reference is included as part of the resulting string. So you can in fact use a reference as a unique hash key. You just can't dereference it later.

There is one special kind of hash in which you *are* able to use references as keys. Through the magic* of the `Tie::RefHash` module bundled with Perl, the thing we just said you couldn't do, you can do:

```
use Tie::RefHash;
tie my %h, 'Tie::RefHash';
%h = (
    ["this", "here"]   => "at home",
    ["that", "there"]  => "elsewhere",
);
while ( my($keyref, $value) = each %h ) {
    print "@$keyref is $value\n";
}
```

In fact, by tying different implementations to the built-in types, you can make scalars, hashes, and arrays behave in many of the ways we've said you can't. That'll show us! Stupid authors . . .

For more about tying, see Chapter 14, *Tied Variables*.

Garbage Collection, Circular References, and Weak References

High-level languages typically allow programmers not to worry about deallocating memory when they're done using it. This automatic reclamation process is known as *garbage collection*. For most purposes, Perl uses a fast and simple reference-based garbage collector.

When a block is exited, its locally scoped variables are normally freed up, but it is possible to hide your garbage so that Perl's garbage collector can't find it. One serious concern is that unreachable memory with a nonzero reference count will normally not get freed. Therefore, circular references are a bad idea:

```
{                         # make $a and $b point to each other
    my ($a, $b);
    $a = \$b;
    $b = \$a;
}
```

---

* Yes, that *is* a technical term, as you'll notice if you muddle through the *mg.c* file in the Perl source distribution.

or more simply:

```
{                    # make $a point to itself
    my $a;
    $a = \$a;
}
```

Even though `$a` should be deallocated at the end of the block, it isn't. When building recursive data structures, you'll have to break (or weaken; see below) the self-
reference yourself if you want to reclaim the memory before your program (or
thread) exits. (Upon exit, the memory will be reclaimed for you automatically via a
costly but complete mark-and-sweep garbage collection.) If the data structure is an
object, you can use a DESTROY method to break the reference automatically; see
"Garbage Collection with DESTROY Methods" in Chapter 12.

A similar situation can occur with *caches*—repositories of data designed for faster-
than-normal retrieval. Outside the cache, there are references to data inside the
cache. The problem occurs when all of those references are deleted, but the cache
data with its internal reference remains. The existence of any reference prevents
the referent from being reclaimed by Perl, even though we want cache data to disappear as soon as it's no longer needed. As with circular references, we want a
reference that doesn't affect the reference count, and therefore doesn't delay
garbage collection.

Weak references solve the problems caused by circular references and cache data
by allowing you to "weaken" any reference; that is, make it not affect the reference count. When the last nonweak reference to an object is deleted, the object is
destroyed and all the weak references to the object are automatically freed.

To use this feature, you need the WeakRef package from CPAN, which contains
additional documentation. Weak references are an experimental feature. But hey,
somebody's gotta be the guinea pig.

9

Data Structures

Perl provides for free many of the data structures that you have to build yourself in other programming languages. The stacks and queues that budding computer scientists learn about are both just arrays in Perl. When you push and pop (or shift and unshift) an array, it's a stack; when you push and shift (or unshift and pop) an array, it's a queue. And many of the tree structures in the world are built only to provide fast, dynamic access to a conceptually flat lookup table. Hashes, of course, are built into Perl, and provide fast, dynamic access to a conceptually flat lookup table, only without the mind-numbingly recursive data structures that are claimed to be beautiful by people whose minds have been suitably numbed already.

But sometimes you want nested data structures because they most naturally model the problem you're trying to solve. So Perl lets you combine and nest arrays and hashes to create arbitrarily complex data structures. Properly applied, they can be used to create linked lists, binary trees, heaps, B-trees, sets, graphs, and anything else you can devise. See *Mastering Algorithms with Perl* (O'Reilly, 1999), the *Perl Cookbook* (O'Reilly, 1998), or CPAN, the central repository for all such modules. But simple combinations of arrays and hashes may be all you ever need, so they're what we'll talk about in this chapter.

Arrays of Arrays

There are many kinds of nested data structures. The simplest kind to build is an array of arrays, also called a two-dimensional array or a matrix. (The obvious generalization applies: an array of arrays of arrays is a three-dimensional array, and so on for higher dimensions.) It's reasonably easy to understand, and nearly everything that applies here will also be applicable to the fancier data structures that we'll explore in subsequent sections.

Creating and Accessing a Two-Dimensional Array

Here's how to put together a two-dimensional array:

```
# Assign a list of array references to an array.
@AoA = (
        [ "fred", "barney" ],
        [ "george", "jane", "elroy" ],
        [ "homer", "marge", "bart" ],
);

print $AoA[2][1];    # prints "marge"
```

The overall list is enclosed by parentheses, not brackets, because you're assigning a list and not a reference. If you wanted a reference to an array instead, you'd use brackets:

```
# Create an reference to an array of array references.
$ref_to_AoA = [
    [ "fred", "barney", "pebbles", "bamm bamm", "dino", ],
    [ "homer", "bart", "marge", "maggie", ],
    [ "george", "jane", "elroy", "judy", ],
];

print $ref_to_AoA->[2][3];    # prints "judy"
```

Remember that there is an implied -> between every pair of adjacent braces or brackets. Therefore these two lines:

```
$AoA[2][3]
$ref_to_AoA->[2][3]
```

are equivalent to these two lines:

```
$AoA[2]->[3]
$ref_to_AoA->[2]->[3]
```

There is, however, no implied -> before the first pair of brackets, which is why the dereference of $ref_to_AoA requires the initial ->. Also remember that you can count backward from the end of an array with a negative index, so:

```
$AoA[0][-2]
```

is the next-to-last element of the first row.

Growing Your Own

Those big list assignments are well and good for creating a fixed data structure, but what if you want to calculate each element on the fly, or otherwise build the structure piecemeal?

Let's read in a data structure from a file. We'll assume that it's a plain text file, where each line is a row of the structure, and each line consists of elements delimited by whitespace. Here's how to proceed:*

```
while (<>) {
    @tmp = split;              # Split elements into an array.
    push @AoA, [ @tmp ];       # Add an anonymous array reference to @AoA.
}
```

Of course, you don't need to name the temporary array, so you could also say:

```
while (<>) {
    push @AoA, [ split ];
}
```

If you want a reference to an array of arrays, you can do this:

```
while (<>) {
    push @$ref_to_AoA, [ split ];
}
```

Both of those examples add new rows to the array of arrays. What about adding new columns? If you're just dealing with two-dimensional arrays, it's often easiest to use simple assignment:†

```
for $x (0 .. 9) {                    # For each row...
    for $y (0 .. 9) {                # For each column...
        $AoA[$x][$y] = func($x, $y); # ...set that cell
    }
}

for $x ( 0..9 ) {                    # For each row...
    $ref_to_AoA->[$x][3] = func2($x); # ...set the fourth column
}
```

It doesn't matter in what order you assign the elements, nor does it matter whether the subscripted elements of @AoA are already there or not; Perl will gladly create them for you, setting intervening elements to the undefined value as need be. (Perl will even create the original reference in $ref_to_AoA for you if it needs to.) If you just want to append to a row, you have to do something a bit funnier:

```
# Append new columns to an existing row.
push @{ $AoA[0] }, "wilma", "betty";
```

---

* Here as in other chapters, we omit (for clarity) the my declarations that you would ordinarily put in. In this example, you'd normally write my @tmp = split.

† As with the temp assignment earlier, we've simplified; the loops in this chapter would likely be written for my $x in real code.

Notice that this wouldn't work:

```
push $AoA[0], "wilma", "betty";   # WRONG!
```

That won't even compile, because the argument to push must be a real array, not just a reference to an array. Therefore, the first argument absolutely must begin with an @ character. What comes after the @ is somewhat negotiable.

Access and Printing

Now let's print the data structure. If you only want one element, this is sufficient:

```
print $AoA[3][2];
```

But if you want to print the whole thing, you can't just say:

```
print @AoA;            # WRONG
```

It's wrong because you'll see stringified references instead of your data. Perl never automatically dereferences for you. Instead, you have to roll yourself a loop or two. The following code prints the whole structure, looping through the elements of @AoA and dereferencing each inside the print statement:

```
for $row ( @AoA ) {
    print "@$row\n";
}
```

If you want to keep track of subscripts, you might do this:

```
for $i ( 0 .. $#AoA ) {
    print "row $i is: @{$AoA[$i]}\n";
}
```

or maybe even this (notice the inner loop):

```
for $i ( 0 .. $#AoA ) {
    for $j ( 0 .. $#{$AoA[$i]} ) {
        print "element $i $j is $AoA[$i][$j]\n";
    }
}
```

As you can see, things are getting a bit complicated. That's why sometimes it's easier to use a temporary variable on your way through:

```
for $i ( 0 .. $#AoA ) {
    $row = $AoA[$i];
    for $j ( 0 .. $#{$row} ) {
        print "element $i $j is $row->[$j]\n";
    }
}
```

Slices

If you want to access a slice (part of a row) of a multidimensional array, you're going to have to do some fancy subscripting. The pointer arrows give us a nice way to access a single element, but no such convenience exists for slices. You can always extract the elements of your slice one-by-one with a loop:

```
@part = ();
for ($y = 7; $y < 13; $y++) {
    push @part, $AoA[4][$y];
}
```

This particular loop could be replaced with an array slice:

```
@part = @{ $AoA[4] } [ 7..12 ];
```

If you want a *two-dimensional slice*, say, with $x running from 4..8 and $y from 7..12, here's one way to do it:

```
@newAoA = ();
for ($startx = $x = 4; $x <= 8; $x++) {
    for ($starty = $y = 7; $y <= 12; $y++) {
        $newAoA[$x - $startx][$y - $starty] = $AoA[$x][$y];
    }
}
```

In this example, the individual values within our destination two-dimensional array, @newAoA, are assigned one by one, taken from a two-dimensional subarray of @AoA. An alternative is to create anonymous arrays, each consisting of a desired slice of an @AoA subarray, and then put references to these anonymous arrays into @newAoA. We would then be writing references into @newAoA (subscripted once, so to speak) instead of subarray values into a twice-subscripted @newAoA. This method eliminates the innermost loop:

```
for ($x = 4; $x <= 8; $x++) {
    push @newAoA, [ @{ $AoA[$x] } [ 7..12 ] ];
}
```

Of course, if you do this often, you should probably write a subroutine called something like extract_rectangle. And if you do it very often with large collections of multidimensional data, you should probably use the PDL (Perl Data Language) module, available from CPAN.

Common Mistakes

As mentioned earlier, Perl arrays and hashes are one-dimensional. In Perl, even "multidimensional" arrays are actually one-dimensional, but the values along that dimension are references to other arrays, which collapse many elements into one.

If you print these values out without dereferencing them, you will get the stringified references rather than the data you want. For example, these two lines:

```
@AoA = ( [2, 3], [4, 5, 7], [0] );
print "@AoA";
```

result in something like:

```
ARRAY(0x83c38) ARRAY(0x8b194) ARRAY(0x8b1d0)
```

On the other hand, this line displays 7:

```
print $AoA[1][2];
```

When constructing an array of arrays, remember to compose new references for
the subarrays. Otherwise, you will just create an array containing the element
counts of the subarrays, like this:

```
for $i (1..10) {
    @array = somefunc($i);
    $AoA[$i] = @array;        # WRONG!
}
```

Here @array is being accessed in a scalar context, and therefore yields the count of
its elements, which is dutifully assigned to $AoA[$i]. The proper way to assign the
reference will be shown in a moment.

After making the previous mistake, people realize they need to assign a reference,
so the next mistake people naturally make involves taking a reference to the same
memory location over and over again:

```
for $i (1..10) {
    @array = somefunc($i);
    $AoA[$i] = \@array;       # WRONG AGAIN!
}
```

Every reference generated by the second line of the for loop is the same, namely,
a reference to the single array @array. Yes, this array changes on each pass
through the loop, but when everything is said and done, $AoA contains 10 refer-
ences to the same array, which now holds the last set of values assigned to it.
print @{$AoA[1]} will reveal the same values as print @{$AoA[2]}.

Here's a more successful approach:

```
for $i (1..10) {
    @array = somefunc($i);
    $AoA[$i] = [ @array ];    # RIGHT!
}
```

The brackets around @array create a new anonymous array, into which the elements of @array are copied. We then store a reference to that new array.

A similar result—though more difficult to read—would be produced by:

```
for $i (1..10) {
    @array = somefunc($i);
    @{$AoA[$i]} = @array;
}
```

Since `$AoA[$i]` needs to be a new reference, the reference springs into existence. Then, the preceding @ dereferences this new reference, with the result that the values of `@array` are assigned (in list context) to the array referenced by `$AoA[$i]`. You might wish to avoid this construct for clarity's sake.

But there *is* a situation in which you might use it. Suppose `@AoA` is already an array of references to arrays. That is, you've made assignments like:

```
$AoA[3] = \@original_array;
```

And now suppose that you want to change `@original_array` (that is, you want to change the fourth row of `$AoA`) so that it refers to the elements of `@array`. This code will work:

```
@{$AoA[3]} = @array;
```

In this case, the reference itself does not change, but the elements of the referenced array do. This overwrites the values of `@original_array`.

Finally, the following dangerous-looking code actually works fine:

```
for $i (1..10) {
    my @array = somefunc($i);
    $AoA[$i] = \@array;
}
```

That's because the lexically scoped `my @array` variable is created afresh on each pass through the loop. So even though it looks as though you've stored the same variable reference each time, you haven't. This is a subtle distinction, but the technique can produce more efficient code, at the risk of misleading less-enlightened programmers. (It's more efficient because there's no copy in the final assignment.) On the other hand, if you have to copy the values anyway (which the first assignment in the loop is doing), then you might as well use the copy implied by the brackets and avoid the temporary variable:

```
for $i (1..10) {
    $AoA[$i] = [ somefunc($i) ];
}
```

In summary:

```
$AoA[$i] = [ @array ];   # Safest, sometimes fastest
$AoA[$i] = \@array;      # Fast but risky, depends on my-ness of array
@{ $AoA[$i] } = @array;  # A bit tricky
```

Once you've mastered arrays of arrays, you'll want to tackle more complex data structures. If you're looking for C structures or Pascal records, you won't find any special reserved words in Perl to set these up for you. What you get instead is a more flexible system. If your idea of a record structure is less flexible than this, or if you'd like to provide your users with something more opaque and rigid, then you can use the object-oriented features detailed in Chapter 12, *Objects*.

Perl has just two ways of organizing data: as ordered lists stored in arrays and accessed by position, or as unordered key/value pairs stored in hashes and accessed by name. The best way to represent a record in Perl is with a hash reference, but how you choose to organize such records will vary. You might want to keep an ordered list of these records that you can look up by number, in which case you'd use an array of hash references to store the records. Or, you might wish to look the records up by name, in which case you'd maintain a hash of hash references. You could even do both at once, with pseudohashes.

In the following sections, you will find code examples detailing how to compose (from scratch), generate (from other sources), access, and display several different data structures. We first demonstrate three straightforward combinations of arrays and hashes, followed by a hash of functions and more irregular data structures. We end with a demonstration of how these data structures can be saved. These examples assume that you have already familiarized yourself with the explanations set forth earlier in this chapter.

Hashes of Arrays

Use a hash of arrays when you want to look up each array by a particular string rather than merely by an index number. In our example of television characters, instead of looking up the list of names by the zeroth show, the first show, and so on, we'll set it up so we can look up the cast list given the name of the show.

Because our outer data structure is a hash, we can't order the contents, but we can use the sort function to specify a particular output order.

Composition of a Hash of Arrays

You can create a hash of anonymous arrays as follows:

```
# We customarily omit quotes when the keys are identifiers.
%HoA = (
    flintstones        => [ "fred", "barney" ],
    jetsons            => [ "george", "jane", "elroy" ],
    simpsons           => [ "homer", "marge", "bart" ],
);
```

To add another array to the hash, you can simply say:

```
$HoA{teletubbies} = [ "tinky winky", "dipsy", "laa-laa", "po" ];
```

Generation of a Hash of Arrays

Here are some techniques for populating a hash of arrays. To read from a file with the following format:

```
flintstones: fred barney wilma dino
jetsons:     george jane elroy
simpsons:    homer marge bart
```

you could use either of the following two loops:

```
while ( <> ) {
    next unless s/^(.*?):\s*//;
    $HoA{$1} = [ split ];
}

while ( $line = <> ) {
    ($who, $rest) = split /:\s*/, $line, 2;
    @fields = split ' ', $rest;
    $HoA{$who} = [ @fields ];
}
```

If you have a subroutine `get_family` that returns an array, you can use it to stuff `%HoA` with either of these two loops:

```
for $group ( "simpsons", "jetsons", "flintstones" ) {
    $HoA{$group} = [ get_family($group) ];
}

for $group ( "simpsons", "jetsons", "flintstones" ) {
    @members = get_family($group);
    $HoA{$group} = [ @members ];
}
```

You can append new members to an existing array like so:

```
push @{ $HoA{flintstones} }, "wilma", "pebbles";
```

Access and Printing of a Hash of Arrays

You can set the first element of a particular array as follows:

```
$HoA{flintstones}[0] = "Fred";
```

To capitalize the second Simpson, apply a substitution to the appropriate array element:

```
$HoA{simpsons}[1] =~ s/(\w)/\u$1/;
```

You can print all of the families by looping through the keys of the hash:

```
for $family ( keys %HoA ) {
    print "$family: @{ $HoA{$family} }\n";
}
```

With a little extra effort, you can add array indices as well:

```
for $family ( keys %HoA ) {
    print "$family: ";
    for $i ( 0 .. $#{ $HoA{$family} } ) {
        print " $i = $HoA{$family}[$i]";
    }
    print "\n";
}
```

Or sort the arrays by how many elements they have:

```
for $family ( sort { @{$HoA{$b}} <=> @{$HoA{$a}} } keys %HoA ) {
    print "$family: @{ $HoA{$family} }\n"
}
```

Or even sort the arrays by the number of elements and then order the elements ASCIIbetically (or to be precise, utf8ically):

```
# Print the whole thing sorted by number of members and name.
for $family ( sort { @{$HoA{$b}} <=> @{$HoA{$a}} } keys %HoA ) {
    print "$family: ", join(", ", sort @{ $HoA{$family} }), "\n";
}
```

Arrays of Hashes

An array of hashes is useful when you have a bunch of records that you'd like to access sequentially, and each record itself contains key/value pairs. Arrays of hashes are used less frequently than the other structures in this chapter.

Composition of an Array of Hashes

You can create an array of anonymous hashes as follows:

```
@AoH = (
    {
        husband  => "barney",
        wife     => "betty",
        son      => "bamm bamm",
    },
    {
        husband => "george",
        wife    => "jane",
        son     => "elroy",
    },
```

```
    {
        husband => "homer",
        wife    => "marge",
        son     => "bart",
    },
);
```

To add another hash to the array, you can simply say:

```
push @AoH, { husband => "fred", wife => "wilma", daughter => "pebbles" };
```

Generation of an Array of Hashes

Here are some techniques for populating an array of hashes. To read from a file
with the following format:

```
husband=fred friend=barney
```

you could use either of the following two loops:

```
while ( <> ) {
    $rec = {};
    for $field ( split ) {
        ($key, $value) = split /=/, $field;
        $rec->{$key} = $value;
    }
    push @AoH, $rec;
}

while ( <> ) {
    push @AoH, { split /[\s=]+/ };
}
```

If you have a subroutine get_next_pair that returns key/value pairs, you can use it
to stuff @AoH with either of these two loops:

```
while ( @fields = get_next_pair() ) {
    push @AoH, { @fields };
}

while (<>) {
    push @AoH, { get_next_pair($_) };
}
```

You can append new members to an existing hash like so:

```
$AoH[0]{pet} = "dino";
$AoH[2]{pet} = "santa's little helper";
```

Access and Printing *of an Array of Hashes*

You can set a key/value pair of a particular hash as follows:

```
$AoH[0]{husband} = "fred";
```

To capitalize the husband of the second array, apply a substitution:

```
$AoH[1]{husband} =~ s/(\w)/\u$1/;
```

You can print all of the data as follows:

```
for $href ( @AoH ) {
    print "{ ";
    for $role ( keys %$href ) {
        print "$role=$href->{$role} ";
    }
    print "}\n";
}
```

and with indices:

```
for $i ( 0 .. $#AoH ) {
    print "$i is { ";
    for $role ( keys %{ $AoH[$i] } ) {
        print "$role=$AoH[$i]{$role} ";
    }
    print "}\n";
}
```

Hashes of Hashes

A multidimensional hash is the most flexible of Perl's nested structures. It's like building up a record that itself contains other records. At each level, you index into the hash with a string (quoted when necessary). Remember, however, that the key/value pairs in the hash won't come out in any particular order; you can use the sort function to retrieve the pairs in whatever order you like.

Composition *of a Hash of Hashes*

You can create a hash of anonymous hashes as follows:

```
%HoH = (
    flintstones => {
        husband   => "fred",
        pal       => "barney",
    },
    jetsons => {
        husband   => "george",
        wife      => "jane",
        "his boy" => "elroy",   # Key quotes needed.
    },
```

```
    simpsons => {
        husband   => "homer",
        wife      => "marge",
        kid       => "bart",
    },
);
```

To add another anonymous hash to %HoH, you can simply say:

```
$HoH{ mash } = {
    captain  => "pierce",
    major    => "burns",
    corporal => "radar",
};
```

Generation of a Hash of Hashes

Here are some techniques for populating a hash of hashes. To read from a file with the following format:

```
flintstones: husband=fred pal=barney wife=wilma pet=dino
```

you could use either of the following two loops:

```
while ( <> ) {
    next unless s/^(.*?):\s*//;
    $who = $1;
    for $field ( split ) {
        ($key, $value) = split /=/, $field;
        $HoH{$who}{$key} = $value;
    }
}

while ( <> ) {
    next unless s/^(.*?):\s*//;
    $who = $1;
    $rec = {};
    $HoH{$who} = $rec;
    for $field ( split ) {
        ($key, $value) = split /=/, $field;
        $rec->{$key} = $value;
    }
}
```

If you have a subroutine get_family that returns a list of key/value pairs, you can use it to stuff %HoH with either of these three snippets:

```
for $group ( "simpsons", "jetsons", "flintstones" ) {
    $HoH{$group} = { get_family($group) };
}

for $group ( "simpsons", "jetsons", "flintstones" ) {
    @members = get_family($group);
    $HoH{$group} = { @members };
}
```

```
sub hash_families {
    my @ret;
    for $group ( @_ ) {
        push @ret, $group, { get_family($group) };
    }
    return @ret;
}
%HoH = hash_families( "simpsons", "jetsons", "flintstones" );
```

You can append new members to an existing hash like so:

```
%new_folks = (
    wife => "wilma",
    pet  => "dino";
);
for $what (keys %new_folks) {
    $HoH{flintstones}{$what} = $new_folks{$what};
}
```

Access and Printing of a Hash of Hashes

You can set a key/value pair of a particular hash as follows:

```
$HoH{flintstones}{wife} = "wilma";
```

To capitalize a particular key/value pair, apply a substitution to an element:

```
$HoH{jetsons}{'his boy'} =~ s/(\w)/\u$1/;
```

You can print all the families by looping through the keys of the outer hash and then looping through the keys of the inner hash:

```
for $family ( keys %HoH ) {
    print "$family: ";
    for $role ( keys %{ $HoH{$family} } ) {
        print "$role=$HoH{$family}{$role} ";
    }
    print "\n";
}
```

In very large hashes, it may be slightly faster to retrieve both keys and values at the same time using each (which precludes sorting):

```
while ( ($family, $roles) = each %HoH ) {
    print "$family: ";
    while ( ($role, $person) = each %$roles ) {
        print "$role=$person ";
    }
    print "\n";
}
```

(Unfortunately, it's the large hashes that really need to be sorted, or you'll never find what you're looking for in the printout.) You can sort the families and then the roles as follows:

```
for $family ( sort keys %HoH ) {
    print "$family: ";
    for $role ( sort keys %{ $HoH{$family} } ) {
        print "$role=$HoH{$family}{$role} ";
    }
    print "\n";
}
```

To sort the families by the number of members (instead of ASCIIbetically (or utf8ically)), you can use keys in a scalar context:

```
for $family ( sort { keys %{$HoH{$a}} <=> keys %{$HoH{$b}} } keys %HoH ) {
    print "$family: ";
    for $role ( sort keys %{ $HoH{$family} } ) {
        print "$role=$HoH{$family}{$role} ";
    }
    print "\n";
}
```

To sort the members of a family in some fixed order, you can assign ranks to each:

```
$i = 0;
for ( qw(husband wife son daughter pal pet) ) { $rank{$_} = ++$i }

for $family ( sort { keys %{$HoH{$a}} <=> keys %{$HoH{$b}} } keys %HoH ) {
    print "$family: ";
    for $role ( sort { $rank{$a} <=> $rank{$b} } keys %{ $HoH{$family} } ) {
        print "$role=$HoH{$family}{$role} ";
    }
    print "\n";
}
```

Hashes of Functions

When writing a complex application or network service in Perl, you might want to make a large number of commands available to your users. Such a program might have code like this to examine the user's selection and take appropriate action:

```
if     ($cmd =~ /^exit$/i)     { exit }
elsif ($cmd =~ /^help$/i)     { show_help() }
elsif ($cmd =~ /^watch$/i)    { $watch = 1 }
elsif ($cmd =~ /^mail$/i)     { mail_msg($msg) }
elsif ($cmd =~ /^edit$/i)     { $edited++; editmsg($msg); }
elsif ($cmd =~ /^delete$/i)   { confirm_kill() }
else {
    warn "Unknown command: '$cmd'; Try 'help' next time\n";
}
```

You can also store references to functions in your data structures, just as you can store references to arrays or hashes:

```
%HoF = (                              # Compose a hash of functions
    exit    => sub { exit },
    help    => \&show_help,
    watch   => sub { $watch = 1 },
    mail    => sub { mail_msg($msg) },
    edit    => sub { $edited++; editmsg($msg); },
    delete  => \&confirm_kill,
);

if   ($HoF{lc $cmd}) { $HoF{lc $cmd}->() }   # Call function
else { warn "Unknown command: '$cmd'; Try 'help' next time\n" }
```

In the second to last line, we check whether the specified command name (in lowercase) exists in our "dispatch table", %HoF. If so, we invoke the appropriate command by dereferencing the hash value as a function and pass that function an empty argument list. We could also have dereferenced it as &{ $HoF{lc $cmd} }(), or, as of the 5.6 release of Perl, simply $HoF{lc $cmd}().

More Elaborate Records

So far, what we've seen in this chapter are simple, two-level, homogeneous data structures: each element contains the same kind of referent as all the other elements at that level. It certainly doesn't have to be that way. Any element can hold any kind of scalar, which means that it could be a string, a number, or a reference to anything at all. The reference could be an array or hash reference, or a pseudo-hash, or a reference to a named or anonymous function, or an object. The only thing you can't do is to stuff multiple referents into one scalar. If you find yourself trying to do that, it's a sign that you need an array or hash reference to collapse multiple values into one.

In the sections that follow, you will find code examples designed to illustrate many of the possible types of data you might want to store in a record, which we'll implement using a hash reference. The keys are uppercase strings, a convention sometimes employed (and occasionally unemployed, but only briefly) when the hash is being used as a specific record type.

Composition, Access, and Printing of More Elaborate Records

Here is a record with six disparate fields:

```
$rec = {
    TEXT      => $string,
    SEQUENCE  => [ @old_values ],
```

```
    LOOKUP     => { %some_table },
    THATCODE   => \&some_function,
    THISCODE   => sub { $_[0] ** $_[1] },
    HANDLE     => \*STDOUT,
};
```

The TEXT field is a simple string, so you can just print it:

```
print $rec->{TEXT};
```

SEQUENCE and LOOKUP are regular array and hash references:

```
print $rec->{SEQUENCE}[0];
$last = pop @{ $rec->{SEQUENCE} };

print $rec->{LOOKUP}{"key"};
($first_k, $first_v) = each %{ $rec->{LOOKUP} };
```

THATCODE is a named subroutine and THISCODE is an anonymous subroutine, but they're invoked identically:

```
$that_answer = $rec->{THATCODE}->($arg1, $arg2);
$this_answer = $rec->{THISCODE}->($arg1, $arg2);
```

With an extra pair of braces, you can treat $rec->{HANDLE} as an indirect object:

```
print { $rec->{HANDLE} } "a string\n";
```

If you're using the FileHandle module, you can even treat the handle as a regular object:

```
use FileHandle;
$rec->{HANDLE}->autoflush(1);
$rec->{HANDLE}->print("a string\n");
```

Composition, Access, and Printing of Even More Elaborate Records

Naturally, the fields of your data structures can themselves be arbitrarily complex data structures in their own right:

```
%TV = (
    flintstones => {
        series    => "flintstones",
        nights    => [ "monday", "thursday", "friday" ],
        members   => [
            { name => "fred",    role => "husband", age  => 36, },
            { name => "wilma",   role => "wife",    age  => 31, },
            { name => "pebbles", role => "kid",     age  =>  4, },
        ],
    },
```

```
    jetsons    => {
        series  => "jetsons",
        nights  => [ "wednesday", "saturday" ],
        members => [
            { name => "george", role => "husband", age  => 41, },
            { name => "jane",    role => "wife",    age  => 39, },
            { name => "elroy",   role => "kid",     age  => 9, },
        ],
    },

    simpsons   => {
        series  => "simpsons",
        nights  => [ "monday" ],
        members => [
            { name => "homer", role => "husband", age => 34, },
            { name => "marge", role => "wife",    age => 37, },
            { name => "bart",  role => "kid",     age => 11, },
        ],
    },
);
```

Generation of a Hash of Complex Records

Because Perl is quite good at parsing complex data structures, you might just put your data declarations in a separate file as regular Perl code, and then load them in with the do or require built-in functions. Another popular approach is to use a CPAN module (such as XML::Parser) to load in arbitrary data structures expressed in some other language (such as XML).

You can build data structures piecemeal:

```
$rec = {};
$rec->{series} = "flintstones";
$rec->{nights} = [ find_days() ];
```

Or read them in from a file (here, assumed to be in field=value syntax):

```
@members = ();
while (<>) {
    %fields = split /[\s=]+/;
    push @members, { %fields };
}
$rec->{members} = [ @members ];
```

And fold them into larger data structures keyed by one of the subfields:

```
$TV{ $rec->{series} } = $rec;
```

You can use extra pointer fields to avoid duplicate data. For example, you might want a "kids" field included in a person's record, which might be a reference to an array containing references to the kids' own records. By having parts of your data structure refer to other parts, you avoid the data skew that would result from updating the data in one place but not in another:

```
for $family (keys %TV) {
    my $rec = $TV{$family};    # temporary pointer
    @kids = ();
    for $person ( @{$rec->{members}} ) {
        if ($person->{role} =~ /kid|son|daughter/) {
            push @kids, $person;
        }
    }
    # $rec and $TV{$family} point to same data!
    $rec->{kids} = [ @kids ];
}
```

The `$rec->{kids} = [ @kids ]` assignment copies the array contents—but they are merely references to uncopied data. This means that if you age Bart as follows:

```
$TV{simpsons}{kids}[0]{age}++;            # increments to 12
```

then you'll see the following result, because `$TV{simpsons}{kids}[0]` and `$TV{simpsons}{members}[2]` both point to the same underlying anonymous hash table:

```
print $TV{simpsons}{members}[2]{age};     # also prints 12
```

Now, to print the entire `%TV` structure:

```
for $family ( keys %TV ) {
    print "the $family";
    print " is on ", join (" and ", @{ $TV{$family}{nights} }), "\n";
    print "its members are:\n";
    for $who ( @{ $TV{$family}{members} } ) {
        print " $who->{name} ($who->{role}), age $who->{age}\n";
    }
    print "children: ";
    print join (", ", map { $_->{name} } @{ $TV{$family}{kids} } );
    print "\n\n";
}
```

Saving Data Structures

If you want to save your data structures for use by another program later, there are many ways to do it. The easiest way is to use Perl's `Data::Dumper` module, which turns a (possibly self-referential) data structure into a string that can be saved externally and later reconstituted with `eval` or `do`.

```
use Data::Dumper;
$Data::Dumper::Purity = 1;         # since %TV is self-referential
open (FILE, "> tvinfo.perldata") or die "can't open tvinfo: $!";
print FILE Data::Dumper->Dump([\%TV], ['*TV']);
close FILE                         or die "can't close tvinfo: $!";
```

A separate program (or the same program) can then read in the file later:

```
open (FILE, "< tvinfo.perldata") or die "can't open tvinfo: $!";
undef $/;                        # read in file all at once
eval <FILE>;                     # recreate %TV
die "can't recreate tv data from tvinfo.perldata: $@" if $@;
close FILE                       or die "can't close tvinfo: $!";
print $TV{simpsons}{members}[2]{age};
```

or simply:

```
do "tvinfo.perldata"             or die "can't recreate tvinfo: $! $@";
print $TV{simpsons}{members}[2]{age};
```

Many other solutions are available, with storage formats ranging from packed binary (very fast) to XML (very interoperable). Check out a CPAN mirror near you today!

10

Packages

In this chapter, we get to start having fun, because we get to start talking about software design. If we're going to talk about good software design, we have to talk about Laziness, Impatience, and Hubris, the basis of good software design.

We've all fallen into the trap of using cut-and-paste when we should have defined a higher-level abstraction, if only just a loop or subroutine.* To be sure, some folks have gone to the opposite extreme of defining ever-growing mounds of higher-level abstractions when they should have used cut-and-paste.† Generally, though, most of us need to think about using more abstraction rather than less.

Caught somewhere in the middle are the people who have a balanced view of how much abstraction is good, but who jump the gun on writing their own abstractions when they should be reusing existing code.‡

Whenever you're tempted to do any of these things, you need to sit back and think about what will do the most good for you and your neighbor over the long haul. If you're going to pour your creative energies into a lump of code, why not make the world a better place while you're at it? (Even if you're only aiming for the program to *succeed*, you need to make sure it fits the right ecological niche.)

The first step toward ecologically sustainable programming is simply this: don't litter in the park. When you write a chunk of code, think about giving the code its own namespace, so that your variables and functions don't clobber anyone else's, or vice versa. A namespace is a bit like your home, where you're allowed to be as

---

* This is a form of False Laziness.

† This is a form of False Hubris.

‡ You guessed it—this is False Impatience. But if you're determined to reinvent the wheel, at least try to invent a better one.

messy as you like, as long as you keep your external interface to other citizens moderately civil. In Perl, a namespace is called a *package*. Packages provide the fundamental building block upon which the higher-level concepts of modules and classes are constructed.

Like the notion of "home", the notion of "package" is a bit nebulous. Packages are independent of files. You can have many packages in a single file, or a single package that spans several files, just as your home could be one small garret in a larger building (if you're a starving artist), or it could comprise several buildings (if your name happens to be Queen Elizabeth). But the usual size of a home is one building, and the usual size of a package is one file. Perl provides some special help for people who want to put one package in one file, as long as you're willing to give the file the same name as the package and use an extension of *.pm*, which is short for "perl module". The *module* is the fundamental unit of reusability in Perl. Indeed, the way you use a module is with the use command, which is a compiler directive that controls the importation of subroutines and variables from a module. Every example of use you've seen until now has been an example of module reuse.

The Comprehensive Perl Archive Network, or CPAN, is where you should put your modules if other people might find them useful. Perl has thrived because of the willingness of programmers to share the fruits of their labor with the community. Naturally, CPAN is also where you can find modules that others have thoughtfully uploaded for everyone to use. See Chapter 22, *CPAN*, and *www.cpan.org* for details.

The trend over the last 25 years or so has been to design computer languages that enforce a state of paranoia. You're expected to program every module as if it were in a state of siege. Certainly there are some feudal cultures where this is appropriate, but not all cultures are like this. In Perl culture, for instance, you're expected to stay out of someone's home because you weren't invited in, not because there are bars on the windows.[*]

This is not a book about object-oriented methodology, and we're not here to convert you into a raving object-oriented zealot, even if you want to be converted. There are already plenty of books out there for that. Perl's philosophy of object-oriented design fits right in with Perl's philosophy of everything else: use object-oriented design where it makes sense, and avoid it where it doesn't. Your call.

In OO-speak, every object belongs to a grouping called a *class*. In Perl, classes and packages and modules are all so closely related that novices can often think

---

[*] But Perl provides some bars if you want them, too. See "Handling Insecure Code" in Chapter 23, *Security*.

of them as being interchangeable. The typical class is implemented by a module that defines a package with the same name as the class. We'll explain all of this in the next few chapters.

When you use a module, you benefit from direct software reuse. With classes, you benefit from indirect software reuse when one class uses another through inheritance. And with classes, you get something more: a clean interface to another namespace. Everything in a class is accessed indirectly, insulating the class from the outside world.

As we mentioned in Chapter 8, *References*, object-oriented programming in Perl is accomplished through references whose referents know which class they belong to. In fact, now that you know about references, you know almost everything difficult about objects. The rest of it just "lays under the fingers", as a pianist would say. You will need to practice a little, though.

One of your basic finger exercises consists of learning how to protect different chunks of code from inadvertently tampering with each other's variables. Every chunk of code belongs to a particular *package*, which determines what variables and subroutines are available to it. As Perl encounters a chunk of code, it is compiled into what we call the *current package*. The initial current package is called "main", but you can switch the current package to another one at any time with the package declaration. The current package determines which symbol table is used to find your variables, subroutines, I/O handles, and formats.

Any variable not declared with my is associated with a package—even seemingly omnipresent variables like $_ and %SIG. In fact, there's really no such thing as a global variable in Perl, just package variables. (Special identifiers like _ and SIG merely seem global because they default to the main package instead of the current one.)

The scope of a package declaration is from the declaration itself through the end of the enclosing scope (block, file, or eval—whichever comes first) or until another package declaration at the same level, which supersedes the earlier one. (This is a common practice).

All subsequent identifiers (including those declared with our, but not including those declared with my or those qualified with a different package name) will be placed in the symbol table belonging to the current package. (Variables declared with my are independent of packages; they are always visible within, and only within, their enclosing scope, regardless of any package declarations.)

Typically, a package declaration will be the first statement of a file meant to be included by require or use. But again, that's by convention. You can put a package declaration anywhere you can put a statement. You could even put it at the end of a block, in which case it would have no effect whatsoever. You can switch into a package in more than one place; a package declaration merely selects the symbol table to be used by the compiler for the rest of that block. (This is how a given package can span more than one file.)

You can refer to identifiers* in other packages by prefixing ("qualifying") the identifier with the package name and a double colon: `$Package::Variable`. If the package name is null, the `main` package is assumed. That is, `$::sail` is equivalent to `$main::sail`.†

The old package delimiter was a single quote, so in old Perl programs you'll see variables like `$main'sail` and `$somepack'horse`. But the double colon is now the preferred delimiter, in part because it's more readable to humans, and in part because it's more readable to *emacs* macros. It also makes C++ programmers feel like they know what's going on—as opposed to using the single quote as the separator, which was there to make Ada programmers feel like they knew what's going on. Because the old-fashioned syntax is still supported for backward compatibility, if you try to use a string like `"This is $owner's house"`, you'll be accessing `$owner::s`; that is, the `$s` variable in package `owner`, which is probably not what you meant. Use braces to disambiguate, as in `"This is ${owner}'s house"`.

The double colon can be used to chain together identifiers in a package name: `$Red::Blue::var`. This means the `$var` belonging to the `Red::Blue` package. The `Red::Blue` package has nothing to do with any `Red` or `Blue` packages that might happen to exist. That is, a relationship between `Red::Blue` and `Red` or `Blue` may have meaning to the person writing or using the program, but it means nothing to Perl. (Well, other than the fact that, in the current implementation, the symbol table `Red::Blue` happens to be stored in the symbol table `Red`. But the Perl language makes no use of that directly.)

For this reason, every `package` declaration must declare a complete package name. No package name ever assumes any kind of implied "prefix", even if (seemingly) declared within the scope of some other package declaration.

---

* By identifiers, we mean the names used as symbol table keys for accessing scalar variables, array variables, hash variables, subroutines, file or directory handles, and formats. Syntactically speaking, labels are also identifiers, but they aren't put into a particular symbol table; rather, they are attached directly to the statements in your program. Labels cannot be package qualified.

† To clear up another bit of potential confusion, in a variable name like `$main::sail`, we use the term "identifier" to talk about `main` and `sail`, but not `main::sail`. We call that a variable name instead, because identifiers cannot contain colons.

Only identifiers (names starting with letters or an underscore) are stored in a package's symbol table. All other symbols are kept in the main package, including all the nonalphabetic variables, like $!, $?, and $_. In addition, when unqualified, the identifiers STDIN, STDOUT, STDERR, ARGV, ARGVOUT, ENV, INC, and SIG are forced to be in package main, even when used for other purposes than their built-in ones. Don't name your package m, s, y, tr, q, qq, qr, qw, or qx unless you're looking for a lot of trouble. For instance, you won't be able to use the qualified form of an identifier as a filehandle because it will be interpreted instead as a pattern match, a substitution, or a transliteration.

Long ago, variables beginning with an underscore were forced into the main package, but we decided it was more useful for package writers to be able to use a leading underscore to indicate semi-private identifiers meant for internal use by that package only. (Truly private variables can be declared as file-scoped lexicals, but that works best when the package and module have a one-to-one relationship, which is common but not required.)

The %SIG hash (which is for trapping signals; see Chapter 16, *Interprocess Communication*) is also special. If you define a signal handler as a string, it's assumed to refer to a subroutine in the main package unless another package name is explicitly used. Use a fully qualified signal handler name if you want to specify a particular package, or avoid strings entirely by assigning a typeglob or a function reference instead:

```
$SIG{QUIT} = "Pkg::quit_catcher"; # fully qualified handler name
$SIG{QUIT} = "quit_catcher";      # implies "main::quit_catcher"
$SIG{QUIT} = *quit_catcher;       # forces current package's sub
$SIG{QUIT} = \&quit_catcher;      # forces current package's sub
$SIG{QUIT} = sub { print "Caught SIGQUIT\n" };   # anonymous sub
```

The notion of "current package" is both a compile-time and run-time concept. Most variable name lookups happen at compile time, but run-time lookups happen when symbolic references are dereferenced, and also when new bits of code are parsed under eval. In particular, when you eval a string, Perl knows which package the eval was invoked in and propagates that package inward when evaluating the string. (You can always switch to a different package inside the eval string, of course, since an eval string counts as a block, just like a file loaded in with do, require, or use.)

Alternatively, if an eval wants to find out what package it's in, the special symbol __PACKAGE__ contains the current package name. Since you can treat it as a string, you could use it in a symbolic reference to access a package variable. But if you were doing that, chances are you should have declared the variable with our instead so it could be accessed as if it were a lexical.

Symbol Tables

The contents of a package are collectively called a *symbol table*. Symbol tables are stored in a hash whose name is the same as the package, but with two colons appended. The `main` symbol table's name is thus `%main::`. Since `main` also happens to be the default package, Perl provides `%::` as an abbreviation for `%main::`.

Likewise, the symbol table for the `Red::Blue` package is named `%Red::Blue::`. As it happens, the `main` symbol table contains all other top-level symbol tables, including itself, so `%Red::Blue::` is also `%main::Red::Blue::`.

When we say that a symbol table "contains" another symbol table, we mean that it contains a reference to the other symbol table. Since `main` is the top-level package, it contains a reference to itself, with the result that `%main::` is the same as `%main::main::`, and `%main::main::main::`, and so on, ad infinitum. It's important to check for this special case if you write code that traverses all symbol tables.

Inside a symbol table's hash, each key/value pair matches a variable name to its value. The keys are the symbol identifiers, and the values are the corresponding typeglobs. So when you use the `*NAME` typeglob notation, you're really just accessing a value in the hash that holds the current package's symbol table. In fact, the following have (nearly) the same effect:

```
*sym = *main::variable;
*sym = $main::{"variable"};
```

The first is more efficient because the `main` symbol table is accessed at compile time. It will also create a new typeglob by that name if none previously exists, whereas the second form will not.

Since a package is a hash, you can look up the keys of the package and get to all the variables of the package. Since the values of the hash are typeglobs, you can dereference them in several ways. Try this:

```
foreach $symname (sort keys %main::) {
    local *sym = $main::{$symname};
    print "\$$symname is defined\n" if defined $sym;
    print "\@$symname is nonnull\n" if          @sym;
    print "\%$symname is nonnull\n" if          %sym;
}
```

Since all packages are accessible (directly or indirectly) through the `main` package, you can write Perl code to visit every package variable in your program. The Perl debugger does precisely that when you ask it to dump all your variables with the `V` command. Note that if you do this, you won't see variables declared with `my` since those are independent of packages, although you will see variables declared with `our`. See Chapter 20, *The Perl Debugger*.

Earlier we said that only identifiers are stored in packages other than `main`. That was a bit of a fib: you can use any string you want as the key in a symbol table hash—it's just that it wouldn't be valid Perl if you tried to use a non-identifier directly:

```
$!@#$%           = 0;        # WRONG, syntax error.
${'!@#$%'}       = 1;        # Ok, though unqualified.

${'main::!@#$%'} = 2;        # Can qualify within the string.
print ${ $main::{'!@#$%'} }  # Ok, prints 2!
```

Assignment to a typeglob performs an aliasing operation; that is,

```
*dick = *richard;
```

causes variables, subroutines, formats, and file and directory handles accessible via the identifier `richard` to also be accessible via the symbol `dick`. If you want to alias only a particular variable or subroutine, assign a reference instead:

```
*dick = \$richard;
```

That makes `$richard` and `$dick` the same variable, but leaves `@richard` and `@dick` as separate arrays. Tricky, eh?

This is how the `Exporter` works when importing symbols from one package to another. For example:

```
*SomePack::dick = \&OtherPack::richard;
```

imports the `&richard` function from package `OtherPack` into `SomePack`, making it available as the `&dick` function. (The `Exporter` module is described in the next chapter.) If you precede the assignment with a `local`, the aliasing will only last as long as the current dynamic scope.

This mechanism may be used to retrieve a reference from a subroutine, making the referent available as the appropriate data type:

```
*units = populate() ;        # Assign \%newhash to the typeglob
print $units{kg};            # Prints 70; no dereferencing needed!

sub populate {
    my %newhash = (km => 10, kg => 70);
    return \%newhash;
}
```

Likewise, you can pass a reference into a subroutine and use it without dereferencing:

```
%units = (miles => 6, stones => 11);
fillerup( \%units );         # Pass in a reference
print $units{quarts};        # Prints 4
```

```
sub fillerup {
    local *hashsym = shift;    # Assign \%units to the typeglob
    $hashsym{quarts} = 4;      # Affects %units; no dereferencing needed!
}
```

These are tricky ways to pass around references cheaply when you don't want to have to explicitly dereference them. Note that both techniques only work with package variables; they would not have worked had we declared %units with my.

Another use of symbol tables is for making "constant" scalars:

```
*PI = \3.14159265358979;
```

Now you cannot alter $PI, which is probably a good thing, all in all. This isn't the same as a constant subroutine, which is optimized at compile time. A constant subroutine is one prototyped to take no arguments and to return a constant expression; see the section "Inlining Constant Functions" in Chapter 6, *Subroutines*, for details. The use constant pragma (see Chapter 31, *Pragmatic Modules*) is a convenient shorthand:

```
use constant PI => 3.14159;
```

Under the hood, this uses the subroutine slot of *PI, instead of the scalar slot used earlier. It's equivalent to the more compact (but less readable):

```
*PI = sub () { 3.14159 };
```

That's a handy idiom to know anyway—assigning a sub {} to a typeglob is the way to give a name to an anonymous subroutine at run time.

Assigning a typeglob reference to another typeglob (*sym = *oldvar) is the same as assigning the entire typeglob, because Perl automatically dereferences the typeglob reference for you. And when you set a typeglob to a simple string, you get the entire typeglob named by that string, because Perl looks up the string in the current symbol table. The following are all equivalent to one another, though the first two compute the symbol table entry at compile time, while the last two do so at run time:

```
*sym =    *oldvar;
*sym = \*oldvar;         # autodereference
*sym = *{"oldvar"};      # explicit symbol table lookup
*sym =    "oldvar";      # implicit symbol table lookup
```

When you perform any of the following assignments, you're replacing just one of the references within the typeglob:

```
*sym = \$frodo;
*sym = \@sam;
*sym = \%merry;
*sym = \&pippin;
```

If you think about it sideways, the typeglob itself can be viewed as a kind of hash, with entries for the different variable types in it. In this case, the keys are fixed, since a typeglob can contain exactly one scalar, one array, one hash, and so on. But you can pull out the individual references, like this:

```
*pkg::sym{SCALAR}      # same as \$pkg::sym
*pkg::sym{ARRAY}       # same as \@pkg::sym
*pkg::sym{HASH}        # same as \%pkg::sym
*pkg::sym{CODE}        # same as \&pkg::sym
*pkg::sym{GLOB}        # same as \*pkg::sym
*pkg::sym{IO}          # internal file/dir handle, no direct equivalent
*pkg::sym{NAME}        # "sym" (not a reference)
*pkg::sym{PACKAGE}     # "pkg" (not a reference)
```

You can say *foo{PACKAGE} and *foo{NAME} to find out what name and package the *foo symbol table entry comes from. This may be useful in a subroutine that is passed typeglobs as arguments:

```
sub identify_typeglob {
    my $glob = shift;
    print 'You gave me ', *{$glob}{PACKAGE}, '::', *{$glob}{NAME}, "\n";
}

identify_typeglob(*foo);
identify_typeglob(*bar::glarch);
```

This prints:

```
You gave me main::foo
You gave me bar::glarch
```

The *foo{*THING*} notation can be used to obtain references to individual elements of *foo. See the section "Symbol Table References" in Chapter 8 for details.

This syntax is primarily used to get at the internal filehandle or directory handle reference, because the other internal references are already accessible in other ways. (The old *foo{FILEHANDLE} is still supported to mean *foo{IO}, but don't let its name fool you into thinking it can distinguish filehandles from directory handles.) But we thought we'd generalize it because it looks kind of pretty. Sort of. You probably don't need to remember all this unless you're planning to write another Perl debugger.

Autoloading

Normally, you can't call a subroutine that isn't defined. However, if there is a subroutine named AUTOLOAD in the undefined subroutine's package (or in the case of an object method, in the package of any of the object's base classes), then the

AUTOLOAD subroutine is called with the same arguments that would have been passed to the original subroutine. You can define the AUTOLOAD subroutine to return values just like a regular subroutine, or you can make it define the routine that didn't exist and then call that as if it'd been there all along.

The fully qualified name of the original subroutine magically appears in the package-global $AUTOLOAD variable, in the same package as the AUTOLOAD routine. Here's a simple example that gently warns you about undefined subroutine invocations instead of exiting:

```
sub AUTOLOAD {
    our $AUTOLOAD;
    warn "Attempt to call $AUTOLOAD failed.\n";
}

blarg(10);                # our $AUTOLOAD will be set to main::blarg
print "Still alive!\n";
```

Or you can return a value on behalf of the undefined subroutine:

```
sub AUTOLOAD {
    our $AUTOLOAD;
    return "I see $AUTOLOAD(@_)\n";
}

print blarg(20);          # prints: I see main::blarg(20)
```

Your AUTOLOAD subroutine might load a definition for the undefined subroutine using eval or require, or use the glob assignment trick discussed earlier, and then execute that subroutine using the special form of goto that can erase the stack frame of the AUTOLOAD routine without a trace. Here we define the subroutine by assigning a closure to the glob:

```
sub AUTOLOAD {
    my $name = our $AUTOLOAD;
    *$AUTOLOAD = sub { print "I see $name(@_)\n" };
    goto &$AUTOLOAD;      # Restart the new routine.
}

blarg(30);                # prints: I see main::blarg(30)
glarb(40);                # prints: I see main::glarb(40)
blarg(50);                # prints: I see main::blarg(50)
```

The standard AutoSplit module is used by module writers to split their modules into separate files (with filenames ending in *.al*), each holding one routine. The files are placed in the *auto/* directory of your system's Perl library, after which the files can be autoloaded on demand by the standard AutoLoader module.

A similar approach is taken by the SelfLoader module, except that it autoloads functions from the file's own DATA area, which is less efficient in some ways and more efficient in others. Autoloading of Perl functions by AutoLoader and Self-Loader is analogous to dynamic loading of compiled C functions by DynaLoader, except that autoloading is done at the granularity of the function call, whereas dynamic loading is done at the granularity of the complete module, and will usually link in many C or C++ functions all at once. (Note that many Perl programmers get along just fine without the AutoSplit, AutoLoader, SelfLoader, or DynaLoader modules. You just need to know that they're there, in case you *can't* get along just fine without them.)

One can have great fun with AUTOLOAD routines that serve as wrappers to other interfaces. For example, let's pretend that any function that isn't defined should just call system with its arguments. All you'd do is this:

```perl
sub AUTOLOAD {
    my $program = our $AUTOLOAD;
    $program =~ s/.*:://;  # trim package name
    system($program, @_);
}
```

(Congratulations, you've now implemented a rudimentary form of the Shell module that comes standard with Perl.) You can call your autoloader (on Unix) like this:

```perl
date();
who('am', 'i');
ls('-l');
echo("Abadugabudabuda...");
```

In fact, if you predeclare the functions you want to call that way, you can pretend they're built-ins and omit the parentheses on the call:

```perl
sub date (;$$);        # Allow zero to two arguments.
sub who (;$$$$);       # Allow zero to four args.
sub ls;                # Allow any number of args.
sub echo ($@);         # Allow at least one arg.

date;
who "am", "i";
ls "-l";
echo "That's all, folks!";
```

11

Modules

The module is the fundamental unit of code reuse in Perl. Under the hood, it's just a package defined in a file of the same name (with *.pm* on the end). In this chapter, we'll explore how you can use other people's modules and create your own.

Perl comes bundled with a large number of modules, which you can find in the *lib* directory of your Perl distribution. Many of those modules are described in Chapter 32, *Standard Modules*, and Chapter 31, *Pragmatic Modules*. All the standard modules also have extensive online documentation, which (horrors) may be more up-to-date than this book. Try the *perldoc* command if your *man* command doesn't work.

The Comprehensive Perl Archive Network (CPAN) contains a worldwide repository of modules contributed by the Perl community, and is discussed in Chapter 22, *CPAN*. See also *http://www.cpan.org*.

Using Modules

Modules come in two flavors: traditional and object-oriented. Traditional modules define subroutines and variables for the caller to import and use. Object-oriented modules function as class definitions and are accessed through method calls, described in Chapter 12, *Objects*. Some modules do both.

Perl modules are typically included in your program by saying:

    use MODULE LIST;

or just:

    use MODULE;

MODULE must be an identifier naming the module's package and file. (The syntax descriptions here are meant to be suggestive; the full syntax of the use statement is given in Chapter 29, *Functions*.)

The use statement does a preload of *MODULE* at compile time and then an import of the symbols you've requested so that they'll be available for the rest of the compilation. If you do not supply a *LIST* of symbols that you want, the symbols named in the module's internal @EXPORT array are used—assuming you're using the Exporter module, described in "Module Privacy and the Exporter" later in this chapter. (If you do supply a *LIST*, all your symbols must be mentioned in the module's @EXPORT or @EXPORT_OK arrays, or an error will result.)

Since modules use the Exporter to import symbols into the current package, you can use symbols from the module without providing a package qualifier:

```
use Fred;      # If Fred.pm has @EXPORT = qw(flintstone)
flintstone();  # ...this calls Fred::flintstone().
```

All Perl module files have the extension *.pm*. Both use and require assume this (as well as the quotes) so that you don't have to spell out "*MODULE*.pm". Using the bare identifier helps to differentiate new modules from *.pl* and *.ph* libraries used in old versions of Perl. It also introduces *MODULE* as an official module name, which helps the parser in certain ambiguous situations. Any double colons in the module name are translated into your system's directory separator, so if your module is named Red::Blue::Green, Perl might look for it as *Red/Blue/Green.pm*.

Perl will search for modules in each of the directories listed in the @INC array. Since use loads modules at compile time, any modifications to @INC need to occur at compile time as well. You can do this with the lib pragma described in Chapter 31 or with a BEGIN block. Once a module is included, a key/value pair will be added to the %INC hash. The key will be the module filename (Red/Blue/Green.pm in our example) and the value will be the full pathname, which might be something like C:/perl/site/lib/Red/Blue/Green.pm for a properly installed module on a Windows system.

Module names should be capitalized unless they're functioning as pragmas. Pragmas are in effect compiler directives (hints for the compiler), so we reserve the lowercase pragma names for future use.

When you use a module, any code inside the module is executed, just as it would be for an ordinary require. If you really don't care whether the module is pulled in at compile time or run time, you can just say:

```
require MODULE;
```

In general, however, use is preferred over require because it looks for modules during compilation, so you learn about any mistakes sooner.

These two statements do almost the same thing:

```
require MODULE;
require "MODULE.pm";
```

They differ in two ways, however. In the first statement, require translates any double colons in the module name into your system's directory separator, just as use does. The second case does no translation, forcing you to specify the pathname of your module literally, which is less portable. The other difference is that the first require tells the compiler that the expressions with indirect object notation involving "*MODULE*" (such as $ob = purge *MODULE*) are method calls, not function calls. (Yes, this really can make a difference, if there's a conflicting definition of purge in your own module.)

Because the use declaration and the related no declaration imply a BEGIN block, the compiler loads the module (and runs any executable initialization code in it) as soon as it encounters that declaration, *before* it compiles the rest of the file. This is how pragmas can change the compiler's behavior, and also how modules are able to declare subroutines that are then visible as list operators for the remainder of compilation. This will not work if you use require instead of use. Just about the only reason to use require is if you have two modules that each need a function from the other. (And we're not sure that's a good reason.)

Perl modules always load a *.pm* file, but that file may in turn load associated files, such as dynamically linked C or C++ libraries or autoloaded Perl subroutine definitions. If so, the additional shenanigans will be entirely transparent to the module user. It is the responsibility of the *.pm* file to load (or arrange to autoload) any additional functionality. The POSIX module happens to perform both dynamic loading and autoloading, but the user can say just:

```
use POSIX;
```

to get all the exported functions and variables.

Creating Modules

Earlier, we said that there are two ways for a module to make its interface available to your program: by exporting symbols or by allowing method calls. We'll show you an example of the first style here; the second style is for object-oriented modules and is described in the next chapter. (Object-oriented modules should export nothing, since the whole idea of methods is that Perl finds them for you automatically, based on the type of the object.)

To construct a module called `Bestiary`, create a file called *Bestiary.pm* that looks like this:

```
package     Bestiary;
require     Exporter;

our @ISA       = qw(Exporter);
our @EXPORT    = qw(camel);       # Symbols to be exported by default
our @EXPORT_OK = qw($weight);     # Symbols to be exported on request
our $VERSION   = 1.00;            # Version number

### Include your variables and functions here

sub camel { print "One-hump dromedary" }

$weight = 1024;

1;
```

A program can now say `use Bestiary` to be able to access the `camel` function (but not the `$weight` variable), and `use Bestiary qw(camel $weight)` to access both the function and the variable.

You can also create modules that dynamically load code written in C. See Chapter 21, *Internals and Externals*, for details.

Module Privacy and the Exporter

Perl does not automatically patrol private/public borders within its modules— unlike languages such as C++, Java, and Ada, Perl isn't obsessed with enforced privacy. A Perl module would prefer that you stay out of its living room because you weren't invited, not because it has a shotgun.

The module and its user have a contract, part of which is common law and part of which is written. Part of the common law contract is that a module refrain from changing any namespace it wasn't asked to change. The written contract for the module (that is, the documentation) may make other provisions. But then, having read the contract, you presumably know that when you say `use RedefineTheWorld` you're redefining the world, and you're willing to risk the consequences. The most common way to redefine worlds is to use the `Exporter` module. As we'll see later in the chapter, you can even redefine built-ins with this module.

When you use a module, the module typically makes some variables or functions available to your program, or more specifically, to your program's current package. This act of exporting symbols from the module (and thus importing them into your program) is sometimes called *polluting* your namespace. Most modules use `Exporter` to do this; that's why most modules say something like this near the top:

```
require Exporter;
our @ISA = ("Exporter");
```

These two lines make the module inherit from the Exporter class. Inheritance is described in the next chapter, but all you need to know is our Bestiary module can now export symbols into other packages with lines like these:

```
our @EXPORT    = qw($camel %wolf ram);        # Export by default
our @EXPORT_OK = qw(leopard @llama $emu);      # Export by request
our %EXPORT_TAGS = (                            # Export as group
                camelids => [qw($camel @llama)],
                critters => [qw(ram $camel %wolf)],
            );
```

From the viewpoint of the exporting module, the @EXPORT array contains the names of variables and functions to be exported by default: what your program gets when it says use Bestiary. Variables and functions in @EXPORT_OK are exported only when the program specifically requests them in the use statement. Finally, the key/value pairs in %EXPORT_TAGS allow the program to include particular groups of the symbols listed in @EXPORT and @EXPORT_OK.

From the viewpoint of the importing package, the use statement specifies a list of symbols to import, a group named in %EXPORT_TAGS, a pattern of symbols, or nothing at all, in which case the symbols in @EXPORT would be imported from the module into your program.

You can include any of these statements to import symbols from the Bestiary module:

```
use Bestiary;                  # Import @EXPORT symbols
use Bestiary ();               # Import nothing
use Bestiary qw(ram @llama);   # Import the ram function and @llama array
use Bestiary qw(:camelids);    # Import $camel and @llama
use Bestiary qw(:DEFAULT);     # Import @EXPORT symbols
use Bestiary qw(/am/);         # Import $camel, @llama, and ram
use Bestiary qw(/^\$/);        # Import all scalars
use Bestiary qw(:critters !ram); # Import the critters, but exclude ram
use Bestiary qw(:critters !:camelids);
                               # Import critters, but no camelids
```

Leaving a symbol off the export lists (or removing it explicitly from the import list with the exclamation point) does not render it inaccessible to the program using the module. The program will always be able to access the contents of the module's package by fully qualifying the package name, like %Bestiary::gecko. (Since lexical variables do not belong to packages, privacy is still possible: see "Private Methods" in the next chapter.)

You can say BEGIN { $Exporter::Verbose=1 } to see how the specifications are being processed and what is actually being imported into your package.

The Exporter is itself a Perl module, and if you're curious you can see the type-glob trickery it uses to export symbols from one package into another. Inside the Exporter module, the key function is named import, which performs the necessary aliasing to make a symbol in one package appear to be in another. In fact, a use Bestiary *LIST* statement is exactly equivalent to:

```
BEGIN {
    require Bestiary;
    import Bestiary LIST;
}
```

This means that your modules don't have to use the Exporter. A module can do anything it jolly well pleases when it's used, since use just calls the ordinary import method for the module, and you can define that method to do anything you like.

Exporting without using Exporter's import method

The Exporter defines a method called export_to_level, used for situations where (for some reason) you can't directly call Exporter's import method. The export_to_level method is invoked like this:

```
MODULE->export_to_level($where_to_export, @what_to_export);
```

where $where_to_export is an integer indicating how far up the calling stack to export your symbols, and @what_to_export is an array listing the symbols to export (usually @_).

For example, suppose our Bestiary had an import function of its own:

```
package Bestiary;
@ISA = qw(Exporter);
@EXPORT_OK = qw ($zoo);

sub import {
    $Bestiary::zoo = "menagerie";
}
```

The presence of this import function prevents Exporter's import function from being inherited. If you want Bestiary's import function to behave just like Exporter's import function once it sets $Bestiary::zoo, you'd define it as follows:

```
sub import {
    $Bestiary::zoo = "menagerie";
    Bestiary->export_to_level(1, @_);
}
```

This exports symbols to the package one level "above" the current package. That is, to whatever program or module is using the Bestiary.

Version checking

If your module defines a $VERSION variable, a program using your module can ensure that the module is sufficiently recent. For example:

```
use Bestiary 3.14;   # The Bestiary must be version 3.14 or later
use Bestiary v1.0.4; # The Bestiary must be version 1.0.4 or later
```

These are converted into calls to `Bestiary->require_version`, which your module then inherits.

Managing unknown symbols

In some situations, you may want to *prevent* certain symbols from being exported. Typically, this applies to modules that have functions or constants that might not make sense on some systems. You can prevent the `Exporter` from exporting those symbols by placing them in the `@EXPORT_FAIL` array.

If a program attempts to import any of these symbols, the `Exporter` gives the module an opportunity to handle the situation before generating an error. It does this by calling an `export_fail` method with a list of the failed symbols, which you might define as follows (assuming your module uses the `Carp` module):

```
sub export_fail {
    my $class = shift;
    carp "Sorry, these symbols are unavailable: @_";
    return @_;
}
```

The `Exporter` provides a default `export_fail` method, which simply returns the list unchanged and makes the `use` fail with an exception raised for each symbol. If `export_fail` returns an empty list, no error is recorded and all the requested symbols are exported.

Tag-handling utility functions

Since the symbols listed within `%EXPORT_TAGS` must also appear in either `@EXPORT` or `@EXPORT_OK`, the `Exporter` provides two functions to let you add those tagged sets of symbols:

```
%EXPORT_TAGS = (foo => [qw(aa bb cc)], bar => [qw(aa cc dd)]);

Exporter::export_tags('foo');      # add aa, bb and cc to @EXPORT
Exporter::export_ok_tags('bar');   # add aa, cc and dd to @EXPORT_OK
```

Specifying names that are not tags is erroneous.

Overriding Built-in Functions

Many built-in functions may be *overridden*, although (like knocking holes in your walls) you should do this only occasionally and for good reason. Typically, this might be done by a package attempting to emulate missing built-in functionality on a non-Unix system. (Do not confuse overriding with *overloading*, which adds additional object-oriented meanings to built-in operators, but doesn't override much of anything. See the discussion of the overload module in Chapter 13, *Overloading* for more on that.)

Overriding may be done only by importing the name from a module—ordinary predeclaration isn't good enough. To be perfectly forthcoming, it's the assignment of a code reference to a typeglob that triggers the override, as in *open = \&myopen. Furthermore, the assignment must occur in some other package; this makes accidental overriding through typeglob aliasing intentionally difficult. However, if you really want to do your own overriding, don't despair, because the subs pragma lets you predeclare subroutines via the import syntax, so those names then override the built-in ones:

```
use subs qw(chdir chroot chmod chown);
chdir $somewhere;
sub chdir { ... }
```

In general, modules should not export built-in names like open or chdir as part of their default @EXPORT list, since these names may sneak into someone else's namespace and change the semantics unexpectedly. If the module includes the name in the @EXPORT_OK list instead, importers will be forced to explicitly request that the built-in name be overridden, thus keeping everyone honest.

The original versions of the built-in functions are always accessible via the CORE pseudopackage. Therefore, CORE::chdir will always be the version originally compiled into Perl, even if the chdir keyword has been overridden.

Well, almost always. The foregoing mechanism for overriding built-in functions is restricted, quite deliberately, to the package that requests the import. But there is a more sweeping mechanism you can use when you wish to override a built-in function everywhere, without regard to namespace boundaries. This is achieved by defining the function in the CORE::GLOBAL pseudopackage. Below is an example that replaces the glob operator with something that understands regular expressions. (Note that this example does not implement everything needed to cleanly override Perl's built-in glob, which behaves differently depending on whether it appears in a scalar or list context. Indeed, many Perl built-ins have such context-sensitive behaviors, and any properly written override should adequately support these. For a fully functional example of glob overriding, study the File::Glob module bundled with Perl.) Anyway, here's the antisocial version:

```
*CORE::GLOBAL::glob = sub {
    my $pat = shift;
    my @got;
    local *D;
    if (opendir D, '.') {
        @got = grep /$pat/, readdir D;
        closedir D;
    }
    return @got;
}

package Whatever;

print <^[a-z_]+\.pm\$>;          # show all pragmas in the current directory
```

By overriding glob globally, this preemptively forces a new (and subversive) behavior for the glob operator in *every* namespace, without the cognizance or cooperation of modules that own those namespaces. Naturally, this must be done with extreme caution—if it must be done at all. And it probably mustn't.

Our overriding philosophy is: it's nice to be important, but it's more important to be nice.

12

Objects

First of all, you need to understand packages and modules; see Chapter 10, *Packages*, and Chapter 11, *Modules*. You also need to know about references and data structures; see Chapter 8, *References* and Chapter 9, *Data Structures*. It's also helpful to understand a little about object-oriented programming (OOP), so in the next section we'll give you a little course on OOL (object-oriented lingo).

Brief Refresher on Object-Oriented Lingo

An *object* is a data structure with a collection of behaviors. We generally speak of the behaviors as acted out by the object directly, sometimes to the point of anthropomorphizing the object. For example, we might say that a rectangle "knows" how to display itself on the screen, or that it "knows" how to compute its own area.

Every object gets its behaviors by virtue of being an *instance* of a *class*. The class defines *methods*: behaviors that apply to the class and its instances. When the distinction matters, we refer to methods that apply only to a particular object as *instance methods* and those that apply to the entire class as *class methods*. But this is only a convention—to Perl, a method is just a method, distinguished only by the type of its first argument.

You can think of an instance method as some action performed by a particular object, such as printing itself out, copying itself, or altering one or more of its properties ("set this sword's name to Anduril"). Class methods might perform operations on many objects collectively ("display all swords") or provide other operations that aren't dependent on any particular object ("from now on, whenever a new sword is forged, register its owner in this database"). Methods that generate instances (objects) of a class are called *constructor methods* ("create a sword with a gem-studded hilt and a secret inscription"). These are usually class methods ("make me a new sword") but can also be instance methods ("make a copy just like this sword here").

A class may *inherit* methods from *parent classes*, also known as *base classes* or *superclasses*. If it does, it's known as a *derived class* or a *subclass*. (Confusing the issue further, some literature uses "base class" to mean a "most super" superclass. That's not what we mean by it.) Inheritance makes a new class that behaves just like an existing one but also allows for altered or added behaviors not found in its parents. When you invoke a method whose definition is not found in the class, Perl automatically consults the parent classes for a definition. For example, a sword class might inherit its `attack` method from a generic blade class. Parents can themselves have parents, and Perl will search those classes as well when it needs to. The blade class might in turn inherit its `attack` method from an even more generic weapon class.

When the `attack` method is invoked on an object, the resulting behavior may depend on whether that object is a sword or an arrow. Perhaps there wouldn't be any difference at all, which would be the case if both swords and arrows inherited their attacking behavior from the generic weapon class. But if there were a difference in behaviors, the method dispatch mechanism would always select the `attack` method suitable for the object in question. The useful property of always selecting the most appropriate behavior for a particular type of object is known as *polymorphism*. It's an important form of not caring.

You have to care about the innards of your objects when you're implementing a class, but when you *use* a class, you should be thinking of its objects as black boxes. You can't see what's inside, you shouldn't need to know how it works, and you interact with the box only on its terms: via the methods provided by the class. Even if you know what those methods do to the object, you should resist the urge to fiddle around yourself. It's like the remote control for your television set: even if you know what's going on inside it, you shouldn't monkey with its innards without good reason.

Perl lets you peer inside the object from outside the class when you need to. But doing so breaks its *encapsulation*, the principle that all access to an object should be through methods alone. Encapsulation decouples the published interface (how an object should be used) from the implementation (how it actually works). Perl does not have an explicit interface facility apart from this unwritten contract between designer and user. Both parties are expected to exercise common sense and common decency: the user by relying only upon the documented interface, the designer by not breaking that interface.

Perl doesn't force a particular style of programming on you, and it doesn't have the obsession with privacy that some other object-oriented languages do. Perl does have an obsession with freedom, however, and one of the freedoms you have as a Perl programmer is the right to select as much or as little privacy as you like. In fact, Perl can have stronger privacy in its classes and objects than C++. That is, Perl does not restrict you from anything, and in particular it doesn't restrict you from restricting yourself, if you're into that kind of thing. The sections "Private Methods" and "Closures as Objects" later in this chapter demonstrate how you can increase your dosage of discipline.

Admittedly, there's a lot more to objects than this, and a lot of ways to find out more about object-oriented design. But that's not our purpose here. So, on we go.

Perl's Object System

Perl doesn't provide any special syntax for defining objects, classes, or methods. Instead, it reuses existing constructs to implement these three concepts.*

Here are some simple definitions that you may find reassuring:

An *object* is simply a reference . . . er, a referent.
> Since references let individual scalars represent larger collections of data, it shouldn't be a surprise that references are used for all objects. Technically, an object isn't the reference proper—it's really the referent that the reference points at. This distinction is frequently blurred by Perl programmers, however, and since we feel it's a lovely metonymy, we will perpetuate the usage here when it suits us.†

A *class* is simply a package.
> A package serves as a class by using the package's subroutines to execute the class's methods, and by using the package's variables to hold the class's global data. Often, a module is used to hold one or more classes.

A *method* is simply a subroutine.
> You just declare subroutines in the package you're using as the class; these will then be used as the class's methods. Method invocation, a new way to call subroutines, passes an extra argument: the object or package used for invoking the method.

---

* Now *there's* an example of software reuse for you!

† We prefer linguistic vigor over mathematical rigor. Either you will agree or you won't.

Method Invocation

If you were to boil down all of object-oriented programming into one quintessential notion, it would be *abstraction*. It's the single underlying theme you'll find running through all those 10-dollar words that OO enthusiasts like to bandy about, like polymorphism and inheritance and encapsulation. We believe in those fancy words, but we'll address them from the practical viewpoint of what it means to invoke methods. Methods lie at the heart of the object system because they provide the abstraction layer needed to implement all these fancy terms. Instead of directly accessing a piece of data sitting in an object, you invoke an instance method. Instead of directly calling a subroutine in some package, you invoke a class method. By interposing this level of indirection between class use and class implementation, the program designer remains free to tinker with the internal workings of the class, with little risk of breaking programs that use it.

Perl supports two different syntactic forms for invoking methods. One uses a familiar style you've already seen elsewhere in Perl, and the second is a form you may recognize from other programming languages. No matter which form of method invocation is used, the subroutine constituting the method is always passed an extra initial argument. If a class is used to invoke the method, that argument will be the name of the class. If an object is used to invoke the method, that argument will be the reference to the object. Whichever it is, we'll call it the method's *invocant*. For a class method, the invocant is the name of a package. For an instance method, the invocant is a reference that specifies an object.

In other words, the invocant is whatever the method was invoked *with*. Some OO literature calls this the method's *agent* or its *actor*. Grammatically, the invocant is neither the subject of the action nor the receiver of that action. It's more like an indirect object, the beneficiary on whose behalf the action is performed—just like the word "me" in the command, "Forge me a sword!" Semantically, you can think of the invocant as either an invoker or an invokee, whichever fits better into your mental apparatus. We're not going to tell you how to think. (Well, not about that.)

Most methods are invoked explicitly, but methods may also be invoked implicitly when triggered by object destructors, overloaded operators, or tied variables. Properly speaking, these are not regular subroutine calls, but rather method invocations automatically triggered by Perl on behalf of an object. Destructors are described later in this chapter, overloading is described in Chapter 13, *Overloading*, and ties are described in Chapter 14, *Tied Variables*.

One difference between methods and regular subroutines is when their packages are resolved—that is, how early (or late) Perl decides which code should be executed for the method or subroutine. A subroutine's package is resolved during compilation, before your program begins to run.* In contrast, a method's package isn't resolved until it is actually invoked. (Prototypes are checked at compile time, which is why regular subroutines can use them but methods can't.)

The reason a method's package can't be resolved earlier is relatively straightforward: the package is determined by the class of the invocant, and the invocant isn't known until the method is actually invoked. At the heart of OO is this simple chain of logic: once the invocant is known, the invocant's class is known, and once the class is known, the class's inheritance is known, and once the class's inheritance is known, the actual subroutine to call is known.

The logic of abstraction comes at a price. Because of the late resolution of methods, an object-oriented solution in Perl is likely to run slower than the corresponding non-OO solution. For some of the fancier techniques described later, it could be a *lot* slower. However, many common problems are solved not by working faster, but by working smarter. That's where OO shines.

Method Invocation Using the Arrow Operator

We mentioned that there are two styles of method invocation. The first style for invoking a method looks like this:

```
INVOCANT->METHOD(LIST)
INVOCANT->METHOD
```

For obvious reasons, this style is usually called the arrow form of invocation. (Do not confuse -> with =>, the "double-barreled" arrow used as a fancy comma.) Parentheses are required if there are any arguments. When executed, the invocation first locates the subroutine determined jointly by the class of the *INVOCANT* and the *METHOD* name, and then calls that subroutine, passing *INVOCANT* as its first argument.

When *INVOCANT* is a reference, we say that *METHOD* is invoked as an instance method, and when *INVOCANT* is a package name, we say that *METHOD* is invoked as a class method. There really is no difference between the two, other than that the package name is more obviously associated with the class itself than with the objects of the class. You'll have to take our word for it that the objects also know

---

* More precisely, the subroutine call is resolved down to a particular typeglob, a reference to which is stuffed into the compiled opcode tree. The meaning of that typeglob is negotiable even at run time—this is how AUTOLOAD can autoload a subroutine for you. Normally, however, the meaning of the typeglob is also resolved at compile time by the definition of an appropriately named subroutine.

their class. We'll tell you in a bit how to associate an object with a class name, but you can use objects without knowing that.

For example, to construct an object using the class method summon and then invoke the instance method speak on the resulting object, you might say this:

```
$mage = Wizard->summon("Gandalf");    # class method
$mage->speak("friend");               # instance method
```

The summon and speak methods are defined by the Wizard class—or one of the classes from which it inherits. But you shouldn't worry about that. Do not meddle in the affairs of Wizards.

Since the arrow operator is left associative (see Chapter 3, *Unary and Binary Operators*), you can even combine the two statements into one:

```
Wizard->summon("Gandalf")->speak("friend");
```

Sometimes you want to invoke a method without knowing its name ahead of time. You can use the arrow form of method invocation and replace the method name with a simple scalar variable:

```
$method = "summon";
$mage = Wizard->$method("Gandalf");  # Invoke Wizard->summon

$travel = $companion eq "Shadowfax" ? "ride" : "walk";
$mage->$travel("seven leagues");     # Invoke $mage->ride or $mage->walk
```

Although you're using the name of the method to invoke it indirectly, this usage is not forbidden by use strict 'refs', since *all* method calls are in fact looked up symbolically at the time they're resolved.

In our example, we stored the name of a subroutine in $travel, but you could also store a subroutine reference. This bypasses the method lookup algorithm, but sometimes that's exactly what you want to do. See both the section "Private Methods" and the discussion of the can method in the section "UNIVERSAL: The Ultimate Ancestor Class". To create a reference to a particular method being called on a particular instance, see the section "Closures" in Chapter 8.

Method Invocation Using Indirect Objects

The second style of method invocation looks like this:

```
METHOD INVOCANT (LIST)
METHOD INVOCANT LIST
METHOD INVOCANT
```

The parentheses around *LIST* are optional; if omitted, the method acts as a list operator. So you can have statements like the following, all of which use this style of method call:

```
$mage = summon Wizard "Gandalf";
$nemesis = summon Balrog home => "Moria", weapon => "whip";
move $nemesis "bridge";
speak $mage "You cannot pass";
break $staff;                 # safer to use: break $staff ();
```

The list operator syntax should be familiar to you; it's the same style used for passing filehandles to print or printf:

```
print STDERR "help!!!\n";
```

It's also similar to English sentences like "Give Gollum the Preciousss", so we call it the *indirect object* form. The invocant is expected in the *indirect object slot*. When you read about passing a built-in function like system or exec something in its "indirect object slot", this means that you're supplying this extra, comma-less argument in the same place you would when you invoke a method using the indirect object syntax.

The indirect object form even permits you to specify the *INVOCANT* as a *BLOCK* that evaluates to an object (reference) or class (package). This lets you combine those two invocations into one statement this way:

```
speak { summon Wizard "Gandalf" } "friend";
```

Syntactic Snafus with Indirect Objects

One syntax will often be more readable than the other. The indirect object syntax is less cluttered, but suffers from several forms of syntactic ambiguity. The first is that the *LIST* part of an indirect object invocation is parsed the same as any other list operator. Thus, the parentheses of:

```
enchant $sword ($pips + 2) * $cost;
```

are assumed to surround all the arguments, regardless of what comes afterward. It would therefore be.be equivalent to this:

```
($sword->enchant($pips + 2)) * $cost;
```

That's unlikely to do what you want: enchant is only being called with $pips + 2, and the method's return value is then multiplied by $cost. As with other list operators, you must also be careful of the precedence of && and || versus and and or.

For example, this:

```
name $sword $oldname || "Glamdring";    # can't use "or" here!
```

becomes the intended:

```
$sword->name($oldname || "Glamdring");
```

but this:

```
speak $mage "friend" && enter();         # should've been "and" here!
```

becomes the dubious:

```
$mage->speak("friend" && enter());
```

which could be fixed by rewriting into one of these equivalent forms:

```
enter() if $mage->speak("friend");
$mage->speak("friend") && enter();
speak $mage "friend" and enter();
```

The second syntactic infelicity of the indirect object form is that its *INVOCANT* is limited to a name, an unsubscripted scalar variable, or a block.* As soon as the parser sees one of these, it has its *INVOCANT*, so it starts looking for its *LIST*. So these invocations:

```
move $party->{LEADER};          # probably wrong!
move $riders[$i];               # probably wrong!
```

actually parse as these:

```
$party->move->{LEADER};
$riders->move([$i]);
```

rather than what you probably wanted:

```
$party->{LEADER}->move;
$riders[$i]->move;
```

The parser only looks a little ways ahead to find the invocant for an indirect object, not even as far as it would look for a unary operator. This oddity does not arise with the first notation, so you might wish to stick with the arrow as your weapon of choice.

Even English has a similar issue here. Think about the command, "Throw your cat out the window a toy mouse to play with." If you parse that sentence too quickly, you'll end up throwing the cat, not the mouse (unless you notice that the cat is already out the window). Like Perl, English has two different syntaxes for

---

* Attentive readers will recall that this is precisely the same list of syntactic items that are allowed after a funny character to indicate a variable dereference—for example, @ary, @$aryref, or @{$aryref}.

expressing the agent: "Throw your cat the mouse" and "Throw the mouse to your cat." Sometimes the longer form is clearer and more natural, and sometimes the shorter one is. At least in Perl, you're required to use braces around any complicated indirect object.

Package-Quoted Classes

The final syntactic ambiguity with the indirect object style of method invocation is that it may not be parsed as a method call at all, because the current package may have a subroutine of the same name as the method. When using a class method with a literal package name as the invocant, there is a way to resolve this ambiguity while still keeping the indirect object syntax: package-quote the classname by appending a double colon to it.

```
$obj = method CLASS::;   # forced to be "CLASS"->method
```

This is important because the commonly seen notation:

```
$obj = new CLASS;        # might not parse as method
```

will not always behave properly if the current package has a subroutine named new or CLASS. Even if you studiously use the arrow form instead of the indirect object form to invoke methods, this can, on rare occasion, still be a problem. At the cost of extra punctuation noise, the CLASS:: notation guarantees how Perl will parse your method invocation. The first two examples below do not always parse the same way, but the second two do:

```
$obj = new ElvenRing;            # could be new("ElvenRing")
                                 # or even new(ElvenRing())
$obj = ElvenRing->new;           # could be ElvenRing()->new()

$obj = new ElvenRing::;          # always "ElvenRing"->new()
$obj = ElvenRing::->new;         # always "ElvenRing"->new()
```

This package-quoting notation can be made prettier with some creative alignment:

```
$obj = new ElvenRing::
            name    => "Narya",
            owner   => "Gandalf",
            domain  => "fire",
            stone   => "ruby";
```

Still, you may say, "Oh, ugh!" at that double colon, so we'll tell you that you can almost always get away with a bare class name, provided two things are true. First, there is no subroutine of the same name as the class. (If you follow the convention that subroutine names like new start lowercase and class names like ElvenRing start uppercase, this is never a problem.) Second, the class has been loaded with one of:

```
    use ElvenRing;
    require ElvenRing;
```

Either of these declarations ensures that Perl knows `ElvenRing` is a module name, which forces any bare name like `new` before the class name `ElvenRing` to be interpreted as a method call, even if you happen to have declared a `new` subroutine of your own in the current package. People don't generally get into trouble with indirect objects unless they start cramming multiple classes into the same file, in which case Perl might not know that a particular package name was supposed to be a class name. People who name subroutines with names that look like `ModuleNames` also come to grief eventually.

Object Construction

All objects are references, but not all references are objects. A reference won't work as an object unless its referent is specially marked to tell Perl what package it belongs to. The act of marking a referent with a package name—and therefore, its class, since a class is just a package—is known as *blessing*. You can think of the blessing as turning a reference into an object, although it's more accurate to say that it turns the reference into an object reference.

The `bless` function takes either one or two arguments. The first argument is a reference and the second is the package to bless the referent into. If the second argument is omitted, the current package is used.

```
    $obj = { };                 # Get reference to anonymous hash.
    bless($obj);                # Bless hash into current package.
    bless($obj, "Critter");     # Bless hash into class Critter.
```

Here we've used a reference to an anonymous hash, which is what people usually use as the data structure for their objects. Hashes are extremely flexible, after all. But allow us to emphasize that you can bless a reference to anything you can make a reference to in Perl, including scalars, arrays, subroutines, and typeglobs. You can even bless a reference to a package's symbol table hash if you can think of a good reason to. (Or even if you can't.) Object orientation in Perl is completely orthogonal to data structure.

Once the referent has been blessed, calling the built-in `ref` function on its reference returns the name of the blessed class instead of the built-in type, such as `HASH`. If you want the built-in type, use the `reftype` function from the `attributes` module. See `use attributes` in Chapter 31, *Pragmatic Modules*.

And that's how to make an object. Just take a reference to something, give it a class by blessing it into a package, and you're done. That's all there is to it if you're designing a minimal class. If you're using a class, there's even less to it, because the author of a class will have hidden the `bless` inside a method called a *constructor*, which creates and returns instances of the class. Because `bless` returns its first argument, a typical constructor can be as simple as this:

```
package Critter;
sub spawn { bless {}; }
```

Or, spelled out slightly more explicitly:

```
package Critter;
sub spawn {
    my    $self = {};         # Reference to an empty anonymous hash
    bless $self, "Critter";   # Make that hash a Critter object
    return $self;             # Return the freshly generated Critter
}
```

With that definition in hand, here's how one might create a `Critter` object:

```
$pet = Critter->spawn;
```

Inheritable Constructors

Like all methods, a constructor is just a subroutine, but we don't call it as a subroutine. We always invoke it as a method—a class method, in this particular case, because the invocant is a package name. Method invocations differ from regular subroutine calls in two ways. First, they get the extra argument we discussed earlier. Second, they obey inheritance, allowing one class to use another's methods.

We'll describe the underlying mechanics of inheritance more rigorously in the next section, but for now, some simple examples of its effects should help you design your constructors. For instance, suppose we have a `Spider` class that inherits methods from the `Critter` class. In particular, suppose the `Spider` class doesn't have its own `spawn` method. The following correspondences apply:

Method Call	Resulting Subroutine Call
`Critter->spawn()`	`Critter::spawn("Critter")`
`Spider->spawn()`	`Critter::spawn("Spider")`

The subroutine called is the same in both cases, but the argument differs. Note that our `spawn` constructor above completely ignored its argument, which means our `Spider` object was incorrectly blessed into class `Critter`. A better constructor would provide the package name (passed in as the first argument) to `bless`:

```
sub spawn {
    my $class =  shift;       # Store the package name
    my $self  =  { };
    bless($self, $class);     # Bless the reference into that package
    return $self;
}
```

Now you could use the same subroutine for both these cases:

```
$vermin = Critter->spawn;
$shelob = Spider->spawn;
```

And each object would be of the proper class. This even works indirectly, as in:

```
$type  = "Spider";
$shelob = $type->spawn;           # same as "Spider"->spawn
```

That's still a class method, not an instance method, because its invocant holds a string and not a reference.

If $type were an object instead of a class name, the previous constructor definition wouldn't have worked, because bless needs a class name. But for many classes, it makes sense to use an existing object as the template from which to create another. In these cases, you can design your constructors so that they work with either objects or class names:

```
sub spawn {
    my $invocant = shift;
    my $class    = ref($invocant) || $invocant;  # Object or class name
    my $self     = { };
    bless($self, $class);
    return $self;
}
```

Initializers

Most objects maintain internal information that is indirectly manipulated by the object's methods. All our constructors so far have created empty hashes, but there's no reason to leave them empty. For instance, we could have the constructor accept extra arguments to store into the hash as key/value pairs. The OO literature often refers to such data as *properties*, *attributes*, *accessors*, *member data*, *instance data*, or *instance variables*. The section "Instance Variables" later in this chapter discusses attributes in more detail.

Imagine a Horse class with instance attributes like "name" and "color":

```
$steed = Horse->new(name => "Shadowfax", color => "white");
```

If the object is implemented as a hash reference, the key/value pairs can be interpolated directly into the hash once the invocant is removed from the argument list:

```
sub new {
    my $invocant = shift;
    my $class = ref($invocant) || $invocant;
    my $self = { @_ };             # Remaining args become attributes
    bless($self, $class);          # Bestow objecthood
    return $self;
}
```

This time we used a method named new for the class's constructor, which just might lull C++ programmers into thinking they know what's going on. But Perl doesn't consider "new" to be anything special; you may name your constructors whatever you like. Any method that happens to create and return an object is a de facto constructor. In general, we recommend that you name your constructors whatever makes sense in the context of the problem you're solving. For example, constructors in the Tk module are named after the widgets they create. In the DBI module, a constructor named connect returns a database handle object, and another constructor named prepare is invoked as an instance method and returns a statement handle object. But if there is no suitable context-specific constructor name, new is perhaps not a terrible choice. Then again, maybe it's not such a bad thing to pick a random name to force people to read the interface contract (meaning the class documentation) before they use its constructors.

Elaborating further, you can set up your constructor with default key/value pairs, which the user could later override by supplying them as arguments:

```
sub new {
    my $invocant = shift;
    my $class    = ref($invocant) || $invocant;
    my $self = {
        color   => "bay",
        legs    => 4,
        owner   => undef,
        @_,                    # Override previous attributes
    };
    return bless $self, $class;
}


$ed       = Horse->new;                       # A 4-legged bay horse
$stallion = Horse->new(color => "black");     # A 4-legged black horse
```

This Horse constructor ignores its invocant's existing attributes when used as an instance method. You could create a second constructor designed to be called as an instance method, and if designed properly, you could use the values from the invoking object as defaults for the new one:

```
$steed  = Horse->new(color => "dun");
$foal   = $steed->clone(owner => "EquuGen Guild, Ltd.");

sub clone {
    my $model = shift;
    my $self  = $model->new(%$model, @_);
    return $self;     # Previously blessed by ->new
}
```

(You could also have rolled this functionality directly into new, but then the name wouldn't quite fit the function.)

Notice how even in the clone constructor, we don't hardcode the name of the Horse class. We have the original object invoke its own new method, whatever that may be. If we had written that as Horse->new instead of $model->new, then the class wouldn't have facilitated inheritance by a Zebra or Unicorn class. You wouldn't want to clone Pegasus and suddenly find yourself with a horse of a different color.

Sometimes, however, you have the opposite problem: rather than trying to share one constructor among several classes, you're trying to have several constructors share one class's object. This happens whenever a constructor wants to call a base class's constructor to do part of the construction work. Perl doesn't do hierarchical construction for you. That is, Perl does not automatically call the constructors (or the destructors) for any base classes of the class requested, so your constructor will have to do that itself and then add any additional attributes the derived class needs. So the situation is not unlike the clone routine, except that instead of copying an existing object into the new object, you want to call your base class's constructor and then transmogrify the new base object into your new derived object.

Class Inheritance

As with the rest of Perl's object system, inheritance of one class by another requires no special syntax to be added to the language. When you invoke a method for which Perl finds no subroutine in the invocant's package, that package's @ISA array* is examined. This is how Perl implements inheritance: each element of a given package's @ISA array holds the name of another package, which is searched when methods are missing. For example, the following makes the Horse class a subclass of the Critter class. (We declare @ISA with our because it has to be a package variable, not a lexical declared with my.)

```
package Horse;
our @ISA = "Critter";
```

You should now be able to use a Horse class or object everywhere that a Critter was previously used. If your new class passes this *empty subclass test*, you know that Critter is a proper base class, fit for inheritance.

Suppose you have a Horse object in $steed and invoke a move method on it:

```
$steed->move(10);
```

Because $steed is a Horse, Perl's first choice for that method is the Horse::move subroutine. If there isn't one, instead of raising a run-time exception, Perl consults the first element of @Horse::ISA, which directs it to look in the Critter package for Critter::move. If this subroutine isn't found either, and Critter has *its* own

---

* Pronounced "is a", as in "A horse is a critter."

@Critter::ISA array, then that too will be consulted for the name of an ancestral package that might supply a move method, and so on back up the inheritance hierarchy until we come to a package without an @ISA.

The situation we just described is *single inheritance*, where each class has only one parent. Such inheritance is like a linked list of related packages. Perl also supports *multiple inheritance*; just add more packages to the class's @ISA. This kind of inheritance works more like a tree data structure, because every package can have more than one immediate parent. Some people find this to be sexier.

When you invoke a method *methname* on an invocant of type *classname*, Perl tries six different ways to find a subroutine to use:

1. First, Perl looks in the invocant's own package for a subroutine named *class-name*::*methname*. If that fails, inheritance kicks in, and we go to step 2.

2. Next, Perl checks for methods inherited from base classes by looking in all *parent* packages listed in @*classname*::ISA for a *parent*::*methname* subroutine. The search is left-to-right, recursive, and depth-first. The recursion assures that grandparent classes, great-grandparent classes, great-great-grandparent classes, and so on, are all searched.

3. If that fails, Perl looks for a subroutine named UNIVERSAL::*methname*.

4. At this point, Perl gives up on *methname* and starts looking for an AUTOLOAD. First, it looks for a subroutine named *classname*::AUTOLOAD.

5. Failing that, Perl searches all *parent* packages listed in @*classname*::ISA, for any *parent*::AUTOLOAD subroutine. The search is again left-to-right, recursive, and depth-first.

6. Finally, Perl looks for a subroutine named UNIVERSAL::AUTOLOAD.

Perl stops after the first successful attempt and invokes that subroutine. If no subroutine is found, an exception is raised, one that you'll see frequently:

```
Can't locate object method "methname" via package "classname"
```

If you've built a debugging version of Perl using the **–DDEBUGGING** option to your C compiler, by using Perl's **–Do** switch, you can watch it go through each of these steps when it resolves method invocation.

We will discuss the inheritance mechanism in more detail as we go along.

Inheritance Through @ISA

If @ISA contains more than one package name, the packages are all searched in left-to-right order. The search is depth-first, so if you have a Mule class set up for inheritance this way:

```
package Mule;
our @ISA = ("Horse", "Donkey");
```

Perl looks for any methods missing from `Mule` first in `Horse` (and any of its ancestors, like `Critter`) before going on to search through `Donkey` and its ancestors.

If a missing method is found in a base class, Perl internally caches that location in the current class for efficiency, so the next time it has to find the method, it doesn't have to look as far. Changing `@ISA` or defining new methods invalidates the cache and causes Perl to perform the lookup again.

When Perl searches for a method, it makes sure that you haven't created a circular inheritance hierarchy. This could happen if two classes inherit from one another, even indirectly through other classes. Trying to be your own great-grandfather is too paradoxical even for Perl, so the attempt raises an exception. However, Perl does not consider it an error to inherit from more than one class sharing a common ancestry, which is rather like cousins marrying. Your inheritance hierarchy just stops looking like a tree and starts to look like a directed acyclic graph. This doesn't bother Perl—so long as the graph really is acyclic.

When you set `@ISA`, the assignment normally happens at run time, so unless you take precautions, code in `BEGIN`, `CHECK`, or `INIT` blocks won't be able to use the inheritance hierarchy. One precaution (or convenience) is the use `base` pragma, which lets you `require` classes and add them to `@ISA` at compile time. Here's how you might use it:

```
package Mule;
use base ("Horse", "Donkey");   # declare superclasses
```

This is a shorthand for:

```
package Mule;
BEGIN {
    our @ISA = ("Horse", "Donkey");
    require Horse;
    require Donkey;
}
```

except that use `base` also takes into account any use `fields` declarations.

Sometimes folks are surprised that including a class in `@ISA` doesn't `require` the appropriate module for you. That's because Perl's class system is largely orthogonal to its module system. One file can hold many classes (since they're just packages), and one package may be mentioned in many files. But in the most common situation, where one package and one class and one module and one file all end up being pretty interchangeable if you squint enough, the use `base` pragma offers a declarative syntax that establishes inheritance, loads in module files, and accommodates any declared base class fields. It's one of those convenient diagonals we keep mentioning.

See the descriptions of use base and use fields in Chapter 31 for further details.

Accessing Overridden Methods

When a class defines a method, that subroutine overrides methods of the same name in any base classes. Imagine that you've a Mule object (which is derived from class Horse and class Donkey), and you decide to invoke your object's breed method. Although the parent classes have their own breed methods, the designer of the Mule class overrode those by supplying the Mule class with its own breed method. That means the following cross is unlikely to be productive:

```
$stallion = Horse->new(gender => "male");
$molly = Mule->new(gender => "female");
$colt = $molly->breed($stallion);
```

Now suppose that through the miracle of genetic engineering, you find some way around a mule's notorious sterility problem, so you want to skip over the nonviable Mule::breed method. You *could* call your method as an ordinary subroutine, being sure to pass the invocant explicitly:

```
$colt = Horse::breed($molly, $stallion);
```

However, this sidesteps inheritance, which is nearly always the wrong thing to do. It's perfectly imaginable that no Horse::breed subroutine exists because both Horses and Donkeys derive that behavior from a common parent class called Equine. If, on the other hand, you want to specify that Perl should *start* searching for a method in a particular class, just use ordinary method invocation but qualify the method name with the class:

```
$colt = $molly->Horse::breed($stallion);
```

Occasionally, you'll want a method in a derived class to act as a wrapper around some method in a base class. The method in the derived class can itself invoke the method in the base class, adding its own actions before or after that invocation. You *could* use the notation just demonstrated to specify at which class to start the search. But in most cases of overridden methods, you don't want to have to know or specify which parent class's overridden method to execute.

That's where the SUPER pseudoclass comes in handy. It lets you invoke an overridden base class method without having to specify which class defined that method.* The following subroutine looks in the current package's @ISA without making you specify particular classes:

---

* This is not to be confused with the mechanism mentioned in Chapter 11 for overriding Perl's built-in functions, which aren't object methods and so aren't overridden by inheritance. You call overridden built-ins via the CORE pseudopackage, not the SUPER pseudopackage.

```
package Mule;
our @ISA = qw(Horse Donkey);
sub kick {
    my $self = shift;
    print "The mule kicks!\n";
    $self->SUPER::kick(@_);
}
```

The SUPER pseudopackage is meaningful only when used *inside* a method. Although the implementer of a class can employ SUPER in their own code, someone who merely uses a class's objects cannot.

SUPER does not always work as you might like when multiple inheritance is involved. As you'd expect, it follows @ISA just as the regular inheritance mechanism does: in left-to-right, recursive, depth-first order. If both Horse and Donkey had a speak method, and you preferred the Donkey method, you'd have to name that parent class explicitly:

```
sub speak {
    my $self = shift;
    print "The mule speaks!\n";
    $self->Donkey::speak(@_);
}
```

More elaborate approaches to multiple inheritance situations can be crafted using the UNIVERSAL::can method described in the next section. Or you can grab the Class::Multimethods module from CPAN, which provides many elaborate solutions, including finding the closest match instead of leftmost one.

Every bit of code in Perl knows what its current package is, as determined by the last package statement. A SUPER method consults the @ISA only of the package into which the call to SUPER was compiled. It does not care about the class of the invocant, nor about the package of the subroutine that was called. This can cause problems if you try to define methods in another class by merely playing tricks with the method name:

```
package Bird;
use Dragonfly;
sub Dragonfly::divebomb { shift->SUPER::divebomb(@_) }
```

Unfortunately, this invokes Bird's superclass, not Dragonfly's. To do what you're trying to do, you need to explicitly switch into the appropriate package for the compilation of SUPER as well:

```
package Bird;
use Dragonfly;
{
    package Dragonfly;
    sub divebomb { shift->SUPER::divebomb(@_) }
}
```

As this example illustrates, you never need to edit a module file just to add methods to an existing class. Since a class is just a package, and a method just a subroutine, all you have to do is define a function in that package as we've done here, and the class suddenly has a new method. No inheritance required. Only the package matters, and since packages are global, any package can be accessed from anywhere in the program. (Did we mention we're going to install a jacuzzi in your living room next week?)

UNIVERSAL: The Ultimate Ancestor Class

If no method definition with the right name is found after searching the invocant's class and all its ancestor classes recursively, one more check for a method of that name is made in the special predefined class called UNIVERSAL. This package never appears in an @ISA, but is always consulted when an @ISA check fails. You can think of UNIVERSAL as the ultimate ancestor from which all classes implicitly derive.

The following predefined methods are available in class UNIVERSAL, and thus in all classes. These all work regardless of whether they are invoked as class methods or object methods.

INVOCANT->isa(*CLASS*)

> The isa method returns true if *INVOCANT*'s class is *CLASS* or any class inheriting from *CLASS*. Instead of a package name, *CLASS* may also be one of the built-in types, such as "HASH" or "ARRAY". (Checking for an exact type does not bode well for encapsulation or polymorphism, though. You should be relying on method dispatch to give you the right method.)

```
use FileHandle;
if (FileHandle->isa("Exporter")) {
    print "FileHandle is an Exporter.\n";
}

$fh = FileHandle->new();
if ($fh->isa("IO::Handle")) {
    print "\$fh is some sort of IOish object.\n";
}
if ($fh->isa("GLOB")) {
    print "\$fh is really a GLOB reference.\n";
}
```

INVOCANT->can(*METHOD*)

> The can method returns a reference to the subroutine that would be called if *METHOD* were applied to *INVOCANT*. If no such subroutine is found, can returns undef.

```
if ($invocant->can("copy")) {
    print "Our invocant can copy.\n";
}
```

This could be used to conditionally invoke a method only if one exists:

```
$obj->snarl if $obj->can("snarl");
```

Under multiple inheritance, this allows a method to invoke all overridden base class methods, not just the leftmost one:

```
sub snarl {
    my $self = shift;
    print "Snarling: @_\n";
    my %seen;
    for my $parent (@ISA) {
        if (my $code = $parent->can("snarl")) {
            $self->$code(@_) unless $seen{$code}++;
        }
    }
}
```

We use the %seen hash to keep track of which subroutines we've already called, so we can avoid calling the same subroutine more than once. This could happen if several parent classes shared a common ancestor.

Methods that would trigger an AUTOLOAD (described in the next section) will not be accurately reported unless the package has declared (but not defined) the subroutines it wishes to have autoloaded.

INVOCANT->VERSION(*NEED*)

The VERSION method returns the version number of *INVOCANT*'s class, as stored in the package's $VERSION variable. If the *NEED* argument is provided, it verifies that the current version isn't less than *NEED* and raises an exception if it is. This is the method that use invokes to determine whether a module is sufficiently recent.

```
use Thread 1.0;   # calls Thread->VERSION(1.0)
print "Running version ", Thread->VERSION, " of Thread.\n";
```

You may supply your own VERSION method to override the method in UNIVERSAL. However, this will cause any classes derived from your class to use the overridden method, too. If you don't want that to happen, you should design your method to delegate other classes' version requests back up to UNIVERSAL.

The methods in UNIVERSAL are built-in Perl subroutines, which you may call if you fully qualify them and pass two arguments, as in UNIVERSAL::isa($formobj, "HASH"). (This is not recommended, though, because can usually has the answer you're really looking for.)

You're free to add your own methods to class UNIVERSAL. (You should be careful, of course; you could really mess someone up who is expecting *not* to find the method name you're defining, perhaps so that they can autoload it from somewhere else.) Here we create a copy method that objects of all classes can use if they've not defined their own. (We fail spectacularly if invoked on a class instead of an object.)

```
use Data::Dumper;
use Carp;
sub UNIVERSAL::copy {
    my $self = shift;
    if (ref $self) {
        return eval Dumper($self);  # no CODE refs
    } else {
        confess "UNIVERSAL::copy can't copy class $self";
    }
}
```

This `Data::Dumper` strategy doesn't work if the object contains any references to subroutines, because they cannot be properly reproduced. Even if the source were available, the lexical bindings would be lost.

Method Autoloading

Normally, when you call an undefined subroutine in a package that defines an AUTOLOAD subroutine, the AUTOLOAD subroutine is called in lieu of raising an exception (see the section "Autoloading" in Chapter 10). With methods, this works a little differently. If the regular method search (through the class, its ancestors, and finally UNIVERSAL) fails to find a match, the same sequence is run again, this time looking for an AUTOLOAD subroutine. If found, this subroutine is called as a method, with the package's $AUTOLOAD variable set to the fully qualified name of the subroutine on whose behalf AUTOLOAD was called.

You need to be a bit cautious when autoloading methods. First, the AUTOLOAD subroutine should return immediately if it's being called on behalf of a method named DESTROY, unless your goal was to simulate DESTROY, which has a special meaning to Perl described in the section "Instance Destructors" later in this chapter.

```
sub AUTOLOAD {
    return if our $AUTOLOAD =~ /::DESTROY$/;
    ...
}
```

Second, if the class is providing an AUTOLOAD safety net, you won't be able to use UNIVERSAL::can on a method name to check whether it's safe to invoke. You have to check for AUTOLOAD separately:

```
if ($obj->can("methname") || $obj->can("AUTOLOAD")) {
    $obj->methname();
}
```

Finally, under multiple inheritance, if a class inherits from two or more classes each of which has an AUTOLOAD, only the leftmost will ever be triggered, since Perl stops as soon as it finds the first AUTOLOAD.

The last two quirks are easily circumvented by declaring the subroutines in the package whose AUTOLOAD is supposed to manage those methods. You can do this either with individual declarations:

```
package Goblin;
sub kick;
sub bite;
sub scratch;
```

or with the use subs pragma, which is more convenient if you have many methods to declare:

```
package Goblin;
use subs qw(kick bite scratch);
```

Even though you've only declared these subroutines and not defined them, this is enough for the system to think they're real. They show up in a UNIVERSAL::can check, and, more importantly, they show up in step 2 of the search for a method, which will never progress to step 3, let alone step 4.

"But, but," you exclaim, "they invoke AUTOLOAD, don't they?" Well, yes, they do eventually, but the mechanism is different. Having found the method stub via step 2, Perl tries to call it. When it is discovered that the method isn't all it was cracked up to be, the AUTOLOAD method search kicks in again, but this time, it starts its search in the class containing the stub, which restricts the method search to that class and its ancestors (and UNIVERSAL). That's how Perl finds the correct AUTOLOAD to run and knows to ignore AUTOLOADs from the wrong part of the original inheritance tree.

Private Methods

There is one way to invoke a method so that Perl ignores inheritance altogether. If instead of a literal method name, you specify a simple scalar variable containing a reference to a subroutine, then the subroutine is called immediately. In the description of UNIVERSAL->can in the previous section, the last example invokes all overridden methods using the subroutine's reference, not its name.

An intriguing aspect of this behavior is that it can be used to implement private method calls. If you put your class in a module, you can make use of the file's lexical scope for privacy. First, store an anonymous subroutine in a file-scoped lexical:

```
# declare private method
my $secret_door = sub {
    my $self = shift;
    ...
};
```

Later on in the file, you can use that variable as though it held a method name. The closure will be called directly, without regard to inheritance. As with any other method, the invocant is passed as an extra argument.

```
sub knock {
    my $self = shift;
    if ($self->{knocked}++ > 5) {
        $self->$secret_door();
    }
}
```

This enables the file's own subroutines (the class methods) to invoke a method that code outside that lexical scope cannot access.

Instance Destructors

As with any other referent in Perl, when the last reference to an object goes away, its memory is implicitly recycled. With an object, you have the opportunity to capture control just as this is about to happen by defining a DESTROY subroutine in the class's package. This method is triggered automatically at the appropriate moment, with the about-to-be-recycled object as its only argument.

Destructors are rarely needed in Perl, because memory management is handled automatically for you. Some objects, though, may have state outside the memory system that you'd like to attend to, such as filehandles or database connections.

```
package MailNotify;
sub DESTROY {
    my $self = shift;
    my $fh   = $self->{mailhandle};
    my $id   = $self->{name};
    print $fh "\n$id is signing off at " . localtime() . "\n";
    close $fh;  # close pipe to mailer
}
```

Just as Perl uses only a single method to construct an object even when the constructor's class inherits from one or more other classes, Perl also uses only one DESTROY method per object destroyed regardless of inheritance. In other words, Perl does not do hierarchical destruction for you. If your class overrides a superclass's destructor, then your DESTROY method may need to invoke the DESTROY method for any applicable base classes:

```
sub DESTROY {
    my $self = shift;
    # check for an overridden destructor...
    $self->SUPER::DESTROY if $self->can("SUPER::DESTROY");
    # now do your own thing before or after
}
```

This applies only to inherited classes; an object that is simply *contained* within the current object—as, for example, one value in a larger hash—will be freed and destroyed automatically. This is one reason why containership via mere aggregation (sometimes called a "has-a" relationship) is often cleaner and clearer than inheritance (an "is-a" relationship). In other words, often you really only need to store one object inside another directly instead of through inheritance, which can add unnecessary complexity. Sometimes when users reach for multiple inheritance, single inheritance will suffice.

Explicitly calling DESTROY is possible but seldom needed. It might even be harmful since running the destructor more than once on the same object could prove unpleasant.

Garbage Collection with DESTROY Methods

As described in the section "Garbage Collection, Circular References, and Weak References" in Chapter 8, a variable that refers to itself (or multiple variables that refer to one another indirectly) will not be freed until the program (or embedded interpreter) is about to exit. If you want to reclaim the memory any earlier, you usually have to explicitly break the reference or weaken it using the WeakRef module on CPAN.

With objects, an alternative solution is to create a container class that holds a pointer to the self-referential data structure. Define a DESTROY method for the containing object's class that manually breaks the circularities in the self-referential structure. You can find an example of this in Chapter 13 of the *Perl Cookbook* in the recipe 13.13, "Coping with Circular Data Structures".

When an interpreter shuts down, all its objects are destroyed, which is important for multithreaded or embedded Perl applications. Objects are always destroyed in a separate pass before ordinary references. This is to prevent DESTROY methods from using references that have themselves been destroyed. (And also because plain references are only garbage-collected in embedded interpreters, since exiting a process is a very *fast* way of reclaiming references. But exiting won't run the object destructors, so Perl does that first.)

Managing Instance Data

Most classes create objects that are essentially just data structures with several internal data fields (instance variables) plus methods to manipulate them.

Perl classes inherit methods, not data, but as long as all access to the object is through method calls anyway, this works out fine. If you want data inheritance, you have to effect it through method inheritance. By and large, this is not a necessity in Perl, because most classes store the attributes of their object in an anonymous hash. The object's instance data is contained within this hash, which serves as its own little namespace to be carved up by whatever classes do something with the object. For example, if you want an object called $city to have a data field named elevation, you can simply access $city->{elevation}. No declarations are necessary. But method wrappers have their uses.

Suppose you want to implement a Person object. You decide to have a data field called "name", which by a strange coincidence you'll store under the key name in the anonymous hash that will serve as the object. But you don't want users touching the data directly. To reap the rewards of encapsulation, users need methods to access that instance variable without lifting the veil of abstraction.

For example, you might make a pair of accessor methods:

```
sub get_name {
    my $self = shift;
    return $self->{name};
}

sub set_name {
    my $self     = shift;
    $self->{name} = shift;
}
```

which leads to code like this:

```
$him = Person->new();
$him->set_name("Frodo");
$him->set_name( ucfirst($him->get_name) );
```

You could even combine both methods into one:

```
sub name {
    my $self = shift;
    if (@_) { $self->{name} = shift }
    return $self->{name};
}
```

This would then lead to code like this:

```
$him = Person->new();
$him->name("Frodo");
$him->name( ucfirst($him->name) );
```

The advantage of writing a separate function for each instance variable (which for our Person class might be name, age, height, and so on) is that it is direct, obvious, and flexible. The drawback is that every time you want a new class, you end up defining one or two nearly identical methods per instance variable. This isn't too bad for the first few, and you're certainly welcome to do it that way if you'd like. But when convenience is preferred over flexibility, you might prefer one of the techniques described in the following sections.

Note that we will be varying the implementation, not the interface. If users of your class respect the encapsulation, you'll be able to transparently swap one implementation for another without the users noticing. (Family members in your inheritance tree using your class for a subclass or superclass might not be so forgiving, since they know you far better than strangers do.) If your users have been peeking and poking into the private affairs of your class, the inevitable disaster is their own fault and none of your concern. All you can do is live up to your end of the contract by maintaining the interface. Trying to stop everyone else in the world from ever doing something slightly wicked will take up all your time and energy—and in the end, fail anyway.

Dealing with family members is more challenging. If a subclass overrides a superclass's attribute accessor, should it access the same field in the hash, or not? An argument can be made either way, depending on the nature of the attribute. For the sake of safety in the general case, each accessor can prefix the name of the hash field with its own classname, so that subclass and superclass can both have their own version. Several of the examples below, including the standard `Struct::Class` module, use this subclass-safe strategy. You'll see accessors resembling this:

```
sub name {
    my $self = shift;
    my $field = __PACKAGE__ . "::name";
    if (@_) { $self->{$field} = shift }
    return $self->{$field};
}
```

In each of the following examples, we create a simple `Person` class with fields `name`, `race`, and `aliases`, each with an identical interface but a completely different implementation. We're not going to tell you which one we like the best, because we like them all the best, depending on the occasion. And tastes differ. Some folks prefer stewed conies; others prefer fissssh.

Field Declarations with use fields

Objects don't have to be implemented as anonymous hashes. Any reference will do. For example, if you used an anonymous array, you could set up a constructor like this:

```
sub new {
    my $invocant = shift;
    my $class = ref($invocant) || $invocant;
    return bless [], $class;
}
```

and have accessors like these:

```
sub name {
    my $self = shift;
    if (@_) { $self->[0] = shift }
    return $self->[0];
}

sub race {
    my $self = shift;
    if (@_) { $self->[1] = shift }
    return $self->[1];
}

sub aliases {
    my $self = shift;
    if (@_) { $self->[2] = shift }
    return $self->[2];
}
```

Arrays are somewhat faster to access than hashes and don't take up quite as much memory, but they're not at all convenient to use. You have to keep track of the index numbers (not just in your class, but in your superclass, too), which must somehow indicate which pieces of the array your class is using. Otherwise, you might reuse a slot.

The use fields pragma addresses all of these points:

```
package Person;
use fields qw(name race aliases);
```

This pragma does not create accessor methods for you, but it does rely on some built-in magic (called *pseudohashes*) to do something similar. (You may wish to wrap accessors around the fields anyway, as we do in the following example.) Pseudohashes are array references that you can use like hashes because they have an associated key map table. The use fields pragma sets this key map up for you, effectively declaring which fields are valid for the Person object; this makes the Perl compiler aware of them. If you declare the type of your object variable (as in my Person $self, in the next example), the compiler is smart enough to optimize access to the fields into straight array accesses. Perhaps more importantly, it validates field names for type safety (well, typo safety, really) at compile time. (See the section "Pseudohashes" in Chapter 8.)

A constructor and sample accessors would look like this:

```
package Person;
use fields qw(name race aliases);
sub new {
    my $type = shift;
    my Person $self = fields::new(ref $type || $type);
```

```
        $self->{name} = "unnamed";
        $self->{race}  = "unknown";
        $self->{aliases} = [];
        return $self;
    }
    sub name {
        my Person $self = shift;
        $self->{name} = shift if @_;
        return $self->{name};
    }
    sub race {
        my Person $self = shift;
        $self->{race} = shift if @_;
        return $self->{race};
    }
    sub aliases {
        my Person $self = shift;
        $self->{aliases} = shift if @_;
        return $self->{aliases};
    }
    1;
```

If you misspell one of the literal keys used to access the pseudohash, you won't have to wait until run time to learn about this. The compiler knows what type of object $self is supposed to refer to (because you told it), so it can check that the code accesses only those fields that Person objects actually have. If you have horses on the brain and try to access a nonexistent field (such as $self->{mane}), the compiler can flag this error right away and will never turn the erroneous program over to the interpreter to run.

There's still a bit of repetition in declaring methods to get at instance variables, so you still might like to automate the creation of simple accessor methods using one of the techniques below. However, because all these techniques use some sort of indirection, if you use them, you will lose the compile-time benefits of typo-checking lexically typed hash accesses. You'll still keep the (small) time and space advantages, though.

If you do elect to use a pseudohash to implement your class, any class that inherits from this one must be aware of that underlying pseudohash implementation. If an object is implemented as a pseudohash, all participants in the inheritance hierarchy should employ the use base and use fields declarations. For example,

```
    package Wizard;
    use base "Person";
    use fields qw(staff color sphere);
```

This makes the Wizard module a subclass of class Person, and loads the *Person.pm* file. It also registers three new fields in this class to go along with those from Person. That way when you write:

```
my Wizard $mage = fields::new("Wizard");
```

you'll get a pseudohash object with access to both classes' fields:

```
$mage->name("Gandalf");
$mage->color("Grey");
```

Since all subclasses must know that they are using a pseudohash implementation, they should use the direct pseudohash notation for both efficiency and type safety:

```
$mage->{name} = "Gandalf";
$mage->{color} = "Grey";
```

If you want to keep your implementations interchangeable, however, outside users of your class must use the accessor methods.

Although use base supports only single inheritance, this is seldom a severe restriction. See the descriptions of use base and use fields in Chapter 31.

Generating Classes with Class::Struct

The standard Class::Struct module exports a function named struct. This creates all the trapping you'll need to get started on an entire class. It generates a constructor named new, plus accessor methods for each of the data fields (instance variables) named in that structure.

For example, if you put the class in a *Person.pm* file:

```
package Person;
use Class::Struct;
struct Person => {        # create a definition for a "Person"
    name    => '$',  #     name field is a scalar
    race    => '$',  #     race field is also a scalar
    aliases => '@',  #     but aliases field is an array ref
};
1;
```

Then you could use that module this way:

```
use Person;
my $mage = Person->new();
$mage->name("Gandalf");
$mage->race("Istar");
$mage->aliases( ["Mithrandir", "Olorin", "Incanus"] );
```

The Class::Struct module created all four of those methods. Because it follows the subclass-safe policy of always prefixing the field name with the class name, it also permits an inherited class to have its own separate field of the same name as a base class field without conflict. That means in this case that "Person::name" rather than just "name" is used for the hash key for that particular instance variable.

Fields in a `struct` declaration don't have to be basic Perl types. They can also specify other classes, but classes created with `struct` work best because the function makes assumptions about how the classes behave that aren't generally true of all classes. For example, the `new` method for the appropriate class is invoked to initialize the field, but many classes have constructors with other names.

See the description of `Class::Struct` in Chapter 32, *Standard Modules*, and its online documentation for more information. Many standard modules use `Class::Struct` to implement their classes, including `User::pwent` and `Net::hostent`. Reading their code can prove instructive.

Generating Accessors with Autoloading

As we mentioned earlier, when you invoke a nonexistent method, Perl has two different ways to look for an `AUTOLOAD` method, depending on whether you declared a stub method. You can use this property to provide access to the object's instance data without writing a separate function for each instance. Inside the `AUTOLOAD` routine, the name of the method actually invoked can be retrieved from the `$AUTOLOAD` variable. Consider the following code:

```
use Person;
$him = Person->new;
$him->name("Aragorn");
$him->race("Man");
$him->aliases( ["Strider", "Estel", "Elessar"] );
printf "%s is of the race of %s.\n", $him->name, $him->race;
print "His aliases are: ", join(", ", @{$him->aliases}), ".\n";
```

As before, this version of the `Person` class implements a data structure with three fields: `name`, `race`, and `aliases`:

```
package Person;
use Carp;

my %Fields = (
    "Person::name"    => "unnamed",
    "Person::race"    => "unknown",
    "Person::aliases" => [],
);

# The next declaration guarantees we get our own autoloader.
use subs qw(name race aliases);

sub new {
    my $invocant = shift;
    my $class = ref($invocant) || $invocant;
    my $self  = { %Fields, @_ };    # clone like Class::Struct
    bless $self, $class;
    return $self;
}
```

```
sub AUTOLOAD {
    my $self = shift;
    # only handle instance methods, not class methods
    croak "$self not an object" unless ref($invocant);
    my $name = our $AUTOLOAD;
    return if $name =~ /::DESTROY$/;
    unless (exists $self->{$name}) {
        croak "Can't access `$name' field in $self";
    }
    if (@_) { return $self->{$name} = shift }
    else    { return $self->{$name} }
}
```

As you see, there are no methods named name, race, or aliases anywhere to be
found. The AUTOLOAD routine takes care of all that. When someone uses
$him->name("Aragorn"), the AUTOLOAD subroutine is called with $AUTOLOAD set to
"Person::name". Conveniently, by leaving it fully qualified, it's in exactly the right
form for accessing fields of the object hash. That way if you use this class as part
of a larger class hierarchy, you don't conflict with uses of the same name in other
classes.

Generating Accessors with Closures

Most accessor methods do essentially the same thing: they simply fetch or store a
value from that instance variable. In Perl, the most natural way to create a family
of near-duplicate functions is looping around a closure. But closures are anonymous functions lacking names, and methods need to be named subroutines in the
class's package symbol table so that they can be called by name. This is no problem—just assign the closure reference to a typeglob of the appropriate name.

```
package Person;

sub new {
    my $invocant = shift;
    my $self = bless({}, ref $invocant || $invocant);
    $self->init();
    return $self;
}

sub init {
    my $self = shift;
    $self->name("unnamed");
    $self->race("unknown");
    $self->aliases([]);
}

for my $field (qw(name race aliases)) {
    my $slot = __PACKAGE__ . "::$field";
    no strict "refs";          # So symbolic ref to typeglob works.
```

```
    *$slot = sub {
        my $self = shift;
        $self->{$field} = shift if @_;
        return $self->{$field};
    };
}
```

Closures are the cleanest hand-rolled way to create a multitude of accessor methods for your instance data. It's efficient for both the computer and you. Not only do all the accessors share the same bit of code (they only need their own lexical pads), but later if you decide to add another attribute, the changes required are minimal: just add one more word to the `for` loop's list, and perhaps something to the `init` method.

Using Closures for Private Objects

So far, these techniques for managing instance data have offered no mechanism for "protection" from external access. Anyone outside the class can open up the object's black box and poke about inside—if they don't mind voiding the warranty. Enforced privacy tends to get in the way of people trying to get their jobs done. Perl's philosophy is that it's better to encapsulate one's data with a sign that says:

```
IN CASE OF FIRE
    BREAK GLASS
```

You should respect such encapsulation when possible, but still have easy access to the contents in an emergency situation, like for debugging.

But if you do want to enforce privacy, Perl isn't about to get in your way. Perl offers low-level building blocks that you can use to surround your class and its objects with an impenetrable privacy shield—one stronger, in fact, than that found in many popular object-oriented languages. Lexical scopes and the lexical variables inside them are the key components here, and closures play a pivotal role.

In the section "Private Methods," we saw how a class can use closures to implement methods that are invisible outside the module file. Later we'll look at accessor methods that regulate class data so private that not even the rest of the class has unrestricted access. Those are still fairly traditional uses of closures. The truly interesting approach is to use a closure as the very object itself. The object's instance variables are locked up inside a scope to which the object alone—that is, the closure—has free access. This is a very strong form of encapsulation; not only is it proof against external tampering, even other methods in the same class must use the proper access methods to get at the object's instance data.

Here's an example of how this might work. We'll use closures both for the objects themselves and for the generated accessors:

```
package Person;
sub new {
    my $invocant = shift;
    my $class = ref($invocant) || $invocant;
    my $data = {
        NAME    => "unnamed",
        RACE    => "unknown",
        ALIASES => [],
    };
    my $self = sub {
        my $field = shift;
        #############################
        ### ACCESS CHECKS GO HERE ###
        #############################
        if (@_) { $data->{$field} = shift }
        return    $data->{$field};
    };
    bless($self, $class);
    return $self;
}
# generate method names
for my $field (qw(name race aliases)) {
    no strict "refs";  # for access to the symbol table
    *$field = sub {
        my $self = shift;
        return $self->(uc $field, @_);
    };
}
```

The object created and returned by the new method is no longer a hash, as it was in other constructors we've looked at. It's a closure with unique access to the attribute data stored in the hash referred to by $data. Once the constructor call is finished, the only access to $data (and hence to the attributes) is via the closure.

In a call like $him->name("Bombadil"), the invoking object stored in $self is the closure that was blessed and returned by the constructor. There's not a lot one can do with a closure beyond calling it, so we do just that with $self->(uc $field, @_). Don't be fooled by the arrow; this is just a regular indirect function call, not a method invocation. The initial argument is the string "name", and any remaining arguments are whatever else was passed in.* Once we're executing inside the closure, the hash reference inside $data is again accessible. The closure is then free to permit or deny access to whatever it pleases.

---

* Sure, the double-function call is slow, but if you wanted fast, would you really be using objects in the first place?

No one outside the closure object has unmediated access to this very private instance data, not even other methods in the class. They could try to call the closure the way the methods generated by the for loop do, perhaps setting an instance variable the class never heard of. But this approach is easily blocked by inserting various bits of code in the constructor where you see the comment about access checks. First, we need a common preamble:

```
use Carp;
local $Carp::CarpLevel = 1;  # Keeps croak messages short
my ($cpack, $cfile) = caller();
```

Now for each of the checks. The first one makes sure the specified attribute name exists:

```
croak "No valid field '$field' in object"
    unless exists $data->{$field};
```

This one allows access only by callers from the same file:

```
carp "Unmediated access denied to foreign file"
    unless $cfile eq __FILE__;
```

This one allows access only by callers from the same package:

```
carp "Unmediated access denied to foreign package ${cpack}::"
    unless $cpack eq __PACKAGE__;
```

And this one allows access only by callers whose classes inherit ours:

```
carp "Unmediated access denied to unfriendly class ${cpack}::"
    unless $cpack->isa(__PACKAGE__);
```

All these checks block unmediated access only. Users of the class who politely use the class's designated methods are under no such restriction. Perl gives you the tools to be just as persnickety as you want to be. Fortunately, not many people want to be.

But some people ought to be. Persnickety is good when you're writing flight control software. If you either want or ought to be one of those people, and you prefer using working code over reinventing everything on your own, check out Damian Conway's Tie::SecureHash module on CPAN. It implements restricted hashes with support for public, protected, and private persnicketations. It also copes with the inheritance issues that we've ignored in the previous example. Damian has also written an even more ambitious module, Class::Contract, that imposes a formal software engineering regimen over Perl's flexible object system. This module's feature list reads like a checklist from a computer science professor's software engineering textbook,* including enforced encapsulation, static inheritance, and design-by-contract condition checking for object-oriented Perl, along with a declarative syntax for attribute, method, constructor, and destructor definitions at both the object and class level, and preconditions, post-conditions, and class invariants. Whew!

New Tricks

As of release 5.6 of Perl, you can also declare a method to indicate that it returns an lvalue. This is done with the lvalue subroutine attribute (not to be confused with object attributes). This experimental feature allows you to treat the method as something that would appear on the lefthand side of an equal sign:

```
package Critter;

sub new {
    my $class = shift;
    my $self = { pups => 0, @_ };     # Override default.
    bless $self, $class;
}

sub pups : lvalue {                   # We'll assign to pups() later.
    my $self = shift;
    $self->{pups};
}

package main;
$varmint = Critter->new(pups => 4);
$varmint->pups *= 2;                  # Assign to $varmint->pups!
$varmint->pups =~ s/(.)/$1$1/;        # Modify $varmint->pups in place!
print $varmint->pups;                 # Now we have 88 pups.
```

This lets you pretend $varmint->pups is a variable while still obeying encapsulation. See the section "The lvalue Attribute" in Chapter 6, *Subroutines*.

If you're running a threaded version of Perl and want to ensure that only one thread can call a particular method on an object, you can use the locked and method attributes to do that:

```
sub pups : locked method {
    ...
}
```

When any thread invokes the pups method on an object, Perl locks the object before execution, preventing other threads from doing the same. See the section "The locked and method Attributes" in Chapter 6.

---

* Can you guess what Damian's job is? By the way, we highly recommend his book, *Object Oriented Perl* (Manning Publications, 1999).

Managing Class Data

We've looked at several approaches to accessing per-object data values. Sometimes, though, you want some common state shared by all objects of a class. Instead of being an attribute of just one instance of the class, these variables are global to the entire class, no matter which class instance (object) you use to access them through. (C++ programmers would think of these as static member data.) Here are some situations where class variables might come in handy:

- To keep a count of all objects ever created, or how many are still kicking around.

- To keep a list of all objects over which you can iterate.

- To store the name or file descriptor of a log file used by a class-wide debugging method.

- To keep collective data, like the total amount of cash dispensed by all ATMs in a network in a given day.

- To track the last object created by a class, or the most accessed object.

- To keep a cache of in-memory objects that have already been reconstituted from persistent memory.

- To provide an inverted lookup table so you can find an object based on the value one of its attributes.

The question comes down to deciding where to store the state for those shared attributes. Perl has no particular syntactic mechanism to declare class attributes, any more than it has for instance attributes. Perl provides the developer with a broad set of powerful but flexible features that can be uniquely crafted to the particular demands of the situation. You can then select the mechanism that makes the most sense for the given situation instead of having to live with someone else's design decisions. Alternatively, you can live with the design decisions someone else has packaged up and put onto CPAN. Again, TMTOWTDI.

Like anything else pertaining to a class, class data shouldn't be accessed directly, especially from outside the implementation of the class itself. It doesn't say much for encapsulation to set up carefully controlled accessor methods for instance variables but then invite the public in to diddle your class variables directly, such as by setting `$SomeClass::Debug = 1`. To establish a clear firewall between interface and implementation, you can create accessor methods to manipulate class data similar to those you use for instance data.

Imagine we want to keep track of the total world population of Critter objects. We'll store that number in a package variable, but provide a method called population so that users of the class don't have to know about the implementation.

```
Critter->population()        # Access via class name
$gollum->population()        # Access via instance
```

Since a class in Perl is just a package, the most natural place to store class data is in a package variable. Here's a simple implementation of such a class. The population method ignores its invocant and just returns the current value of the package variable, $Population. (Some programmers like to capitalize their globals.)

```
package Critter;
our $Population = 0;
sub population { return $Population; }
sub DESTROY { $Population-- }
sub spawn {
    my $invocant = shift;
    my $class = ref($invocant) || $invocant;
    $Population++;
    return bless { name => shift || "anon" }, $class;
}
sub name {
    my $self = shift;
    $self->{name} = shift if @_;
    return $self->{name};
}
```

If you want to make class data methods that work like accessors for instance data, do this:

```
our $Debugging = 0;      # class datum
sub debug {
    shift;                   # intentionally ignore invocant
    $Debugging = shift if @_;
    return $Debugging;
}
```

Now you can set the overall debug level through the class or through any of its instances.

Because it's a package variable, $Debugging is globally accessible. But if you change the our variable to my, then only code later in that same file can see it. You can go still further—you can restrict unfettered access to class attributes even from the rest of class itself. Wrap the variable declaration in a block scope:

```
{
    my $Debugging = 0;             # lexically scoped class datum
    sub debug {
        shift;                        # intentionally ignore invocant
        $Debugging = shift if @_;
```

```
            return $Debugging;
        }
    }
```

Now no one is allowed to read or write the class attributes without using the accessor method, since only that subroutine is in the same scope as the variable and has access to it.

If a derived class inherits these class accessors, then these still access the original data, no matter whether the variables were declared with our or my. The data isn't package-relative. You might look at it as methods executing in the class in which they were originally defined, not in the class that invoked them.

For some kinds of class data, this approach works fine, but for others, it doesn't. Suppose we create a Warg subclass of Critter. If we want to keep our populations separate, Warg can't inherit Critter's population method, because that method as written always returns the value of $Critter::Population.

You'll have to decide on a case-by-case basis whether it makes any sense for class attributes to be package relative. If you want package-relative attributes, use the invocant's class to locate the package holding the class data:

```
sub debug {
    my $invocant = shift;
    my $class    = ref($invocant) || $invocant;
    my $varname = $class . "::Debugging";
    no strict "refs";         # to access package data symbolically
    $$varname = shift if @_;
    return $$varname;
}
```

We temporarily rescind strict references because otherwise we couldn't use the fully qualified symbolic name for the package global. This is perfectly reasonable: since all package variables by definition live in a package, there's nothing wrong with accessing them via that package's symbol table.

Another approach is to make everything an object needs—even its global class data—available via that object (or passed in as parameters). To do this, you'll often have to make a dedicated constructor for each class, or at least have a dedicated initialization routine to be called by the constructor. In the constructor or initializer, you store references to any class data directly in the object itself, so nothing ever has to go looking for it. The accessor methods use the object to find a reference to the data.

Rather than put the complexity of locating the class data in each method, just let the object tell the method where the data is located. This approach works well only when the class data accessor methods are invoked as instance methods, because the class data could be in unreachable lexicals you couldn't get at using a package name.

No matter how you roll it, package-relative class data is always a bit awkward. It's really a lot cleaner if, when you inherit a class data accessor method, you effectively inherit the state data that it's accessing as well. See the *perltootc* manpage for numerous, more elaborate approaches to management of class data.

Summary

That's about all there is to it, except for everything else. Now you just need to go off and buy a book about object-oriented design methodology and bang your forehead with it for the next six months or so.

13

Overloading

Objects are cool, but sometimes they're just a little *too* cool. Sometimes you would rather they behaved a little less like objects and a little more like regular data types. But there's a problem: objects are referents represented by references, and references aren't terribly useful except as references. You can't add references, or print them, or (usefully) apply many of Perl's built-in operators. The only thing you can do is dereference them. So you find yourself writing many explicit method invocations, like this:

```
print $object->as_string;
$new_object = $subject->add($object);
```

Such explicit dereferencing is in general a good thing; you should never confuse your references with your referents, except when you want to confuse them. Now would be one of those times. If you design your class with *overloading*, you can pretend the references aren't there and simply say:

```
print $object;
$new_object = $subject + $object;
```

When you overload one of Perl's built-in operators, you define how it behaves when it's applied to objects of a particular class. A number of standard Perl modules use overloading, such as `Math::BigInt`, which lets you create `Math::BigInt` objects that behave just like regular integers but have no size limits. You can add them with +, divide them with /, compare them with <=>, and print them with `print`.

Note that overloading is not the same as autoloading, which is loading a missing function or method on demand. Neither is it the same as overriding, which is one function or method masking another. Overloading hides nothing; it adds meaning to an operation that would have been nonsense on a mere reference.

The overload Pragma

The use overload pragma implements operator overloading. You provide it with a key/value list of operators and their associated behaviors:

```
package MyClass;

use overload    '+' => \&myadd,              # coderef
                '<' => "less_than",          # named method
              'abs' => sub { return @_ };    # anonymous subroutine
```

Now when you try to add two MyClass objects, the myadd subroutine will be called to create the result.

When you try to compare two MyClass objects with the < operator, Perl notices that the behavior is specified as a string and interprets the string as a method name and not simply as a subroutine name. In the example above, the less_than method might be supplied by the MyClass package itself or inherited from a base class of MyClass, but the myadd subroutine must be supplied by the current package. The anonymous subroutine for abs supplies itself even more directly. However these routines are supplied, we'll call them *handlers*.

For unary operators (those taking only one operand, like abs), the handler specified for the class is invoked whenever the operator is applied to an object of that class.

For binary operators like + or <, the handler is invoked whenever the first operand is an object of the class *or* when the second operand is an object of the class and the first operand has no overloading behavior. That's so you can say either:

```
$object + 6
```

or:

```
6 + $object
```

without having to worry about the order of operands. (In the second case, the operands will be *swapped* when passed to the handler). If our expression was:

```
$animal + $vegetable
```

and $animal and $vegetable were objects of different classes, both of which used overloading, then the overloading behavior of $animal would be triggered. (We'll hope the animal likes vegetables.)

There is only one trinary (ternary) operator in Perl, ?:, and you can't overload it. Fortunately.

Overload Handlers

When an overloaded operator is, er, operated, the corresponding handler is invoked with three arguments. The first two arguments are the two operands. If the operator only uses one operand, the second argument is undef.

The third argument indicates whether the first two arguments were swapped. Even under the rules of normal arithmetic, some operations, like addition or multiplication, don't usually care about the order of their arguments, but others, like subtraction and division, do.* Consider the difference between:

```
$object - 6
```

and:

```
6 - $object
```

If the first two arguments to a handler have been swapped, the third argument will be true. Otherwise, the third argument will be false, in which case there is a finer distinction as well: if the handler has been triggered by another handler involving assignment (as in += using + to figure out how to add), then the third argument is not merely false, but undef. This distinction enables some optimizations.

As an example, here is a class that lets you manipulate a bounded range of numbers. It overloads both + and – so that the result of adding or subtracting objects constrains the values within the range 0 and 255:

```perl
package ClipByte;

use overload '+' => \&clip_add,
             '-' => \&clip_sub;

sub new {
    my $class = shift;
    my $value = shift;
    return bless \$value => $class;
}

sub clip_add {
    my ($x, $y) = @_;
    my ($value) = ref($x) ? $$x : $x;
    $value      += ref($y) ? $$y : $y;
    $value = 255 if $value > 255;
    $value =   0 if $value < 0;
    return bless \$value => ref($x);
}
```

---

* Your overloaded objects are not required to respect the rules of normal arithmetic, of course, but it's usually best not to surprise people. Oddly, many languages make the mistake of overloading + with string concatenation, which is not commutative and only vaguely additive. For a different approach, see Perl.

```
sub clip_sub {
    my ($x, $y, $swap) = @_;
    my ($value) = (ref $x) ? $$x : $x;
    $value    -= (ref $y) ? $$y : $y;
    if ($swap) { $value = -$value }
    $value = 255 if $value > 255;
    $value =   0 if $value < 0;
    return bless \$value => ref($x);
}

package main;

$byte1 = ClipByte->new(200);
$byte2 = ClipByte->new(100);

$byte3 = $byte1 + $byte2;     # 255
$byte4 = $byte1 - $byte2;     # 100
$byte5 = 150 - $byte2;        # 50
```

You'll note that every function here is by necessity a constructor, so each one takes care to bless its new object back into the current class, whatever that is; we assume our class might be inherited. We also assume that if $y is a reference, it's a reference to an object of our own type. Instead of testing ref($y), we could have called $y->isa("ClipByte") if we wanted to be more thorough (and run slower).

Overloadable Operators

You can only overload certain operators, which are shown in Table 13-1. The operators are also listed in the %overload::ops hash made available when you use overload, though the categorization is a little different there.

Table 13-1. Overloadable Operators

Category	Operators
Conversion	`"" 0+ bool`
Arithmetic	`+ - * / % ** x . neg`
Logical	`!`
Bitwise	`& | ~ ^ ! << >>`
Assignment	`+= -= *= /= %= **= x= .= <<= >>= ++ --`
Comparison	`== < <= > >= != <=> lt le gt ge eq ne cmp`
Mathematical	`atan2 cos sin exp abs log sqrt`
Iterative	`<>`
Dereference	`${} @{} %{} &{} *{}`
Pseudo	`nomethod fallback =>`

Note that neg, bool, nomethod, and fallback are not actual Perl operators. The five dereferencers, "", and 0+ probably don't *seem* like operators either. Nevertheless, they are all valid keys for the parameter list you provide to use overload. This is not really a problem. We'll let you in on a little secret: it's a bit of a fib to say that the overload pragma overloads operators. It overloads the underlying operations, whether invoked explicitly via their "official" operators, or implicitly via some related operator. (The pseudo-operators we mentioned can only be invoked implicitly.) In other words, overloading happens not at the syntactic level, but at the semantic level. The point is not to look good. The point is to do the right thing. Feel free to generalize.

Note also that = does *not* overload Perl's assignment operator, as you might expect. That would not do the right thing. More on that later.

We'll start by discussing the conversion operators, not because they're the most obvious (they aren't), but because they're the most useful. Many classes overload nothing but stringification, specified by the " " key. (Yes, that really is two double-quotes in a row.)

Conversion operators: " ", 0+, bool
> These three keys let you provide behaviors for Perl's automatic conversions to strings, numbers, and Boolean values, respectively.
>
> We say that *stringification* occurs when any nonstring variable is used as a string. It's what happens when you convert a variable into a string via printing, interpolation, concatenation, or even by using it as a hash key. Stringification is also why you see something like SCALAR(0xba5fe0) when you try to print an object.
>
> We say that *numification* occurs when a nonnumeric variable is converted into a number in any numeric context, such as any mathematical expression, array index, or even as an operand of the .. range operator.
>
> Finally, while nobody here quite has the nerve to call it *boolification,* you can define how an object should be interpreted in a Boolean context (such as if, unless, while, for, and, or, &&, ||, ?:, or the block of a grep expression) by creating a bool handler.
>
> Any of the three conversion operators can be *autogenerated* if you have any one of them (we'll explain autogeneration later). Your handlers can return any value you like. Note that if the operation that triggered the conversion is also overloaded, *that* overloading will occur immediately afterward.
>
> Here's a demonstration of " " that invokes an object's as_string handler upon stringification. Don't forget to quote the quotes:
>
> ```
> package Person;
>
> use overload q("") => \&as_string;
> ```

```
sub new {
    my $class = shift;
    return bless { @_ } => $class;
}

sub as_string {
    my $self = shift;
    my ($key, $value, $result);
    while (($key, $value) = each %$self) {
        $result .= "$key => $value\n";
    }
    return $result;
}

$obj = Person->new(height => 72, weight => 165, eyes => "brown");

print $obj;
```

Instead of something like `Person=HASH(0xba1350)`, this prints (in hash order):

```
weight => 165
height => 72
eyes => brown
```

(We sincerely hope this person was not measured in kg and cm.)

Arithmetic operators: +, -, *, /, %, **, x, ., neg

These should all be familiar except for `neg`, which is a special overloading key for the unary minus: the - in -123. The distinction between the `neg` and - keys allows you to specify different behaviors for unary minus and binary minus, more commonly known as subtraction.

If you overload - but not `neg`, and then try to use a unary minus, Perl will emulate a `neg` handler for you. This is known as *autogeneration*, where certain operators can be reasonably deduced from other operators (on the assumption that the overloaded operators will have the same relationships as the regular operators). Since unary minus can be expressed as a function of binary minus (that is, -123 is equivalent to 0 - 123), Perl doesn't force you to overload `neg` when - will do. (Of course, if you've arbitrarily defined binary minus to divide the second argument by the first, unary minus will be a fine way to throw a divide-by-0 exception.)

Concatenation via the . operator can be autogenerated via the stringification handler (see `""` above).

Logical operator: !

If a handler for ! is not specified, it can be autogenerated using the `bool`, `""`, or `0+` handler. If you overload the ! operator, the `not` operator will also trigger whatever behavior you requested. (Remember our little secret?)

You may be surprised at the absence of the other logical operators, but most logical operators can't be overloaded because they short-circuit. They're really control-flow operators that need to be able to delay evaluation of some of their arguments. That's also the reason the ?: operator isn't overloaded.

Bitwise operators: &, |, ~, ^, <<, >>

The ~ operator is a unary operator; all the others are binary. Here's how we could overload >> to do something like chop:

```
package ShiftString;

use overload
    '>>' => \&right_shift,
    '""' => sub { ${ $_[0] } };

sub new {
    my $class = shift;
    my $value = shift;
    return bless \$value => $class;
}

sub right_shift {
    my ($x, $y) = @_;
    my $value = $$x;
    substr($value, -$y) = "";
    return bless \$value => ref($x);
}

$camel = ShiftString->new("Camel");
$ram = $camel >> 2;
print $ram;              # Cam
```

Assignment operators: +=, -=, *=, /=, %=, **=, x=, .=, <<=, >>=, ++, --

These assignment operators might change the value of their arguments or leave them as is. The result is assigned to the lefthand operand only if the new value differs from the old one. This allows the same handler to be used to overload both += and +. Although this is permitted, it is seldom recommended, since by the semantics described later under "When an Overload Handler Is Missing (nomethod and fallback)", Perl will invoke the handler for + anyway, assuming += hasn't been overloaded directly.

Concatenation (.=) can be autogenerated using stringification followed by ordinary string concatenation. The ++ and -- operators can be autogenerated from + and - (or += and -=).

Handlers implementing ++ and -- are expected to *mutate* (alter) their arguments. If you wanted autodecrement to work on letters as well as numbers, you could do that with a handler as follows:

```perl
package MagicDec;

use overload
    q(--) => \&decrement,
    q("") => sub { ${ $_[0] } };

sub new {
    my $class = shift;
    my $value = shift;
    bless \$value => $class;
}

sub decrement {
    my @string = reverse split(//, ${ $_[0] } );
    my $i;
    for ($i = 0; $i < @string; $i++ ) {
        last unless $string[$i] =~ /a/i;
        $string[$i] = chr( ord($string[$i]) + 25 );
    }
    $string[$i] = chr( ord($string[$i]) - 1 );
    my $result = join('', reverse @string);
    $_[0] = bless \$result => ref($_[0]);
}

package main;

for $normal (qw/perl NZ Pa/) {
    $magic = MagicDec->new($normal);
    $magic--;
    print "$normal goes to $magic\n";
}
```

That prints out:

```
perl goes to perk
NZ goes to NY
Pa goes to Oz
```

exactly reversing Perl's magical string autoincrement operator.

The ++$a operation can be autogenerated using $a += 1 or $a = $a + 1, and $a-- using $a -= 1 or $a = $a - 1. However, this does not trigger the copying behavior that a real ++ operator would. See "The Copy Constructor" later in this chapter.

Comparison operators: ==, <, <=, >, >=, !=, <=>, lt, le, gt, ge, eq, ne, cmp

If <=> is overloaded, it can be used to autogenerate behaviors for <, <=, >, >=, ==, and !=. Similarly, if cmp is overloaded, it can be used to autogenerate behaviors for lt, le, gt, ge, eq, and ne.

Note that overloading cmp won't let you sort objects as easily as you'd like, because what will be compared are the stringified versions of the objects instead of the objects themselves. If that was your goal, you'd want to overload "" as well.

Mathematical functions: atan2, cos, sin, exp, abs, log, sqrt

If abs is unavailable, it can be autogenerated from < or <=> combined with either unary minus or subtraction.

An overloaded - can be used to autogenerate missing handlers for unary minus or for the abs function, which may also be separately overloaded. (Yes, we know that abs looks like a function, whereas unary minus looks like an operator, but they aren't all that different as far as Perl's concerned.)

Iterative operator: <>

The <> handler can be triggered by using either readline (when it reads from a filehandle, as in while (<FH>)) or glob (when it is used for fileglobbing, as in @files = <*.*>).

```perl
package LuckyDraw;

use overload
    '<>' => sub {
        my $self = shift;
        return splice @$self, rand @$self, 1;
    };


sub new {
    my $class = shift;
    return bless [@_] => $class;
}

package main;

$lotto = new LuckyDraw 1 .. 51;

for (qw(1st 2nd 3rd 4th 5th 6th)) {
    $lucky_number = <$lotto>;
    print "The $_ lucky number is: $lucky_number.\n";
}

$lucky_number = <$lotto>;
print "\nAnd the bonus number is: $lucky_number.\n";
```

In California, this prints:

```
The 1st lucky number is: 18
The 2nd lucky number is: 11
The 3rd lucky number is: 40
```

```
The 4th lucky number is: 7
The 5th lucky number is: 51
The 6th lucky number is: 33

And the bonus number is: 5
```

Dereference operators: ${}, @{}, %{}, &{}, *{}

Attempts to dereference scalar, array, hash, subroutine, and glob references can be intercepted by overloading these five symbols.

The online Perl documentation for overload demonstrates how you can use this operator to simulate your own pseudohashes. Here's a simpler example that implements an object as an anonymous array but permits hash referencing. Don't try to treat it as a real hash; you won't be able to delete key/value pairs from the object. If you want to combine array and hash notations, use a real pseudohash (as it were).

```
package PsychoHash;

use overload '%{}' => \&as_hash;

sub as_hash {
    my ($x) = shift;
    return { @$x };
}

sub new {
    my $class = shift;
    return bless [ @_ ] => $class;
}

$critter = new PsychoHash( height => 72, weight => 365, type => "camel" );

print $critter->{weight};    # prints 365
```

Also see Chapter 14, *Tied Variables*, for a mechanism to let you redefine basic operations on hashes, arrays, and scalars.

When overloading an operator, try not to create objects with references to themselves. For instance,

```
use overload '+' => sub { bless [ \$_[0], \$_[1] ] };
```

This is asking for trouble, since if you say $animal += $vegetable, the result will make $animal a reference to a blessed array reference whose first element is $animal. This is a *circular reference*, which means that even if you destroy $animal, its memory won't be freed until your process (or interpreter) terminates. See "Garbage Collection, Circular References, and Weak References" in Chapter 8, *References*.

The Copy Constructor (=)

Although it looks like a regular operator, = has a special and slightly subintuitive meaning as an overload key. It does *not* overload the Perl assignment operator. It can't, because that operator has to be reserved for assigning references, or everything breaks.

The handler for = is used in situations where a mutator (such as ++, --, or any of the assignment operators) is applied to a reference that shares its object with another reference. The = handler lets you intercept the mutator and copy the object yourself so that the copy alone is mutated. Otherwise, you'd clobber the original.

```
$copy = $original;    # copies only the reference
++$copy;              # changes underlying shared object
```

Now, bear with us. Suppose that $original is a reference to an object. To make ++$copy modify only $copy and not $original, a copy of $copy is first made, and $copy is assigned a reference to this new object. This operation is not performed until ++$copy is executed, so $copy coincides with $original before the increment—but not afterward. In other words, it's the ++ that recognizes the need for the copy and calls out to your copy constructor.

The need for copying is recognized only by mutators such as ++ or +=, or by nomethod, which is described later. If the operation is autogenerated via +, as in:

```
$copy = $original;
$copy = $copy + 1;
```

then no copying occurs, because + doesn't know it's being used as a mutator.

If the copy constructor is required during the execution of some mutator, but a handler for = was not specified, it can be autogenerated as a string copy provided the object is a plain scalar and not something fancier.

For example, the code actually executed for the sequence:

```
$copy = $original;
...
++$copy;
```

might end up as something like this:

```
$copy = $original;
...
$copy = $copy->clone(undef, "");
$copy->incr(undef, "");
```

This assumes $original points to an overloaded object, ++ was overloaded with \&incr, and = was overloaded with \&clone.

Similar behavior is triggered by $copy = $original++, which is interpreted as $copy = $original; ++$original.

When an Overload Handler Is Missing (nomethod and fallback)

If you apply an unoverloaded operator to an object, Perl first tries to autogenerate a behavior from other overloaded operators using the rules described earlier. If that fails, Perl looks for an overloading behavior for nomethod and uses that if available. That handler is to operators what an AUTOLOAD subroutine is to subroutines: it's what you do when you can't think of what else to do.

If used, the nomethod key should be followed by a reference to a handler that accepts four arguments, (not three as all the other handlers expect). The first three arguments are no different than in any other handler; the fourth is a string corresponding to the operator whose handler is missing. This serves the same purpose as the $AUTOLOAD variable does in AUTOLOAD subroutines.

If Perl has to look for a nomethod handler but can't find one, an exception is raised.

If you want to prevent autogeneration from occurring, or you want a failed autogeneration attempt to result in no overloading at all, you can define the special fallback overloading key. It has three useful states:

undef

> If fallback is not set, or is explicitly set to undef, the sequence of overloading events is unaffected: handlers are sought, autogeneration is attempted, and finally the nomethod handler is invoked. If that fails, an exception is raised.

false

> If fallback is set to a defined but false value (like 0), autogeneration is never attempted. Perl will call the nomethod handler if one exists, but raise an exception otherwise.

true

> This is nearly the same behavior as for undef, but no exception is raised if an appropriate handler cannot be synthesized via autogeneration. Instead, Perl reverts to following the unoverloaded behavior for that operator, as though there were no use overload pragma in the class at all.

Overloading Constants

You can change how constants are interpreted by Perl with `overload::constant`, which is most usefully placed in a package's `import` method. (If you do this, you should properly invoke `overload::remove_constant` in the package's `unimport` method so that the package can clean up after itself when you ask it to.)

Both `overload::constant` and `overload::remove_constant` expect a list of key/value pairs. The keys should be any of `integer`, `float`, `binary`, `q`, and `qr`, and each value should be the name of a subroutine, an anonymous subroutine, or a code reference that will handle the constants.

```
sub import { overload::constant ( integer => \&integer_handler,
                                  float   => \&float_handler,
                                  binary  => \&base_handler,
                                  q       => \&string_handler,
                                  qr      => \&regex_handler ) }
```

Any handlers you provide for `integer` and `float` will be invoked whenever the Perl tokener encounters a constant number. This is independent of the `use constant` pragma; simple statements such as

```
$year = cube(12) + 1;        # integer
$pi   = 3.14159265358979;    # float
```

will trigger whatever handler you requested.

The `binary` key lets you intercept binary, octal, and hexadecimal constants. `q` handles single-quoted strings (including strings introduced with `q`) and constant substrings within `qq`- and `qx`-quoted strings and here documents. Finally, `qr` handles constant pieces within regular expressions, as described at the end of Chapter 5, *Pattern Matching*.

The handler will be passed three arguments. The first argument is the original constant, in whatever form it was provided to Perl. The second argument is how Perl actually interpreted the constant; for instance, `123_456` will appear as `123456`.

The third argument is defined only for strings handled by the `q` and `qr` handlers, and will be one of `qq`, `q`, `s`, or `tr` depending on how the string is to be used. `qq` means that the string is from an interpolated context, such as double quotes, backticks, an `m//` match, or the pattern of an `s///` substitution. `q` means that the string is from an uninterpolated context, `s` means that the constant is a replacement string in an `s///` substitution, and `tr` means that it's a component of a `tr///` or `y///` expression.

The handler should return a scalar, which will be used in place of the constant. Often, that scalar will be a reference to an overloaded object, but there's nothing preventing you from doing something more dastardly:

```
package DigitDoubler;    # A module to be placed in DigitDoubler.pm
use overload;

sub import { overload::constant ( integer => \&handler,
                                  float   => \&handler ) }

sub handler {
    my ($orig, $interp, $context) = @_;
    return $interp * 2;              # double all constants
}

1;
```

Note that `handler` is shared by both keys, which works okay in this case. Now when you say:

```
use DigitDoubler;

$trouble = 123;      # trouble is now 246
$jeopardy = 3.21;    # jeopardy is now 6.42
```

you redefine the world.

If you intercept string constants, it is recommended that you provide a concatenation operator (".") as well, since an interpolated expression like `"ab$cd!!"` is merely a shortcut for the longer `'ab' . $cd . '!!'`. Similarly, negative numbers are considered negations of positive constants, so you should provide a handler for `neg` when you intercept integers or floats. (We didn't need to do that earlier, because we're returning actual numbers, not overloaded object references.)

Note that `overload::constant` does not propagate into run-time compilation inside `eval`, which can be either a bug or a feature depending on how you look at it.

Public Overload Functions

As of the 5.6 release of Perl, the `use overload` pragma provides the following functions for public consumption.

`overload::StrVal(OBJ)`

This function returns the string value that *OBJ* would have in absence of stringification overloading (`""`).

```
overload::Overloaded(OBJ)
```
This function returns a true value if *OBJ* is subject to any operator overloading at all, and false otherwise.

```
overload::Method(OBJ, OPERATOR)
```
This function returns a reference to whatever code implements the overloading for *OPERATOR* when it operates on *OBJ*, or undef if no such overloading exists.

Inheritance and Overloading

Inheritance interacts with overloading in two ways. The first occurs when a handler is named as a string rather than provided as a code reference or anonymous subroutine. When named as a string, the handler is interpreted as a method, and can therefore be inherited from superclasses.

The second interaction between inheritance and overloading is that any class derived from a overloaded class is itself subject to that overloading. In other words, overloading is itself inherited. The set of handlers in a class is the union of handlers of all that class's ancestors, recursively. If a handler can be found in several different ancestors, the handler actually used is governed by the usual rules for method inheritance. For example, if class Alpha inherits from classes Beta and Gamma in that order, and class Beta overloads + with \&Beta::plus_sub, but class Gamma overloads + with the string "plus_meth", then Beta::plus_sub will be called when you try to apply + to an Alpha object.

Since the value of the fallback key is not a handler, its inheritance is not governed by the rules given above. In the current implementation, the fallback value from the first overloaded ancestor is used, but this is accidental and subject to change without notice (well, without much notice).

Run-Time Overloading

Since use statements are executed at compile time, the only way to change overloading during run time is:

```
eval " use overload '+' => \&my_add ";
```
You can also say:

```
eval " no overload '+', '--', '<=' ";
```
although the use of these constructs during run time is questionable.

Overloading Diagnostics

If your Perl was compiled with -DDEBUGGING, you can view diagnostic messages for overloading when you run a program with the **-Do** switch or its equivalent. You can also deduce which operations are overloaded using the m command of Perl's built-in debugger.

If you're feeling overloaded now, maybe the next chapter will tie things back together for you.

14

Tied Variables

Some human endeavors require a disguise. Sometimes the intent is to deceive, but more often, the intent is to communicate something true at a deeper level. For instance, many job interviewers expect you to dress up in a tie to indicate that you're seriously interested in fitting in, even though both of you know you'll never wear a tie on the job. It's odd when you think about it: tying a piece of cloth around your neck can magically get you a job. In Perl culture, the *tie* operator plays a similar role: it lets you create a seemingly normal variable that, behind the disguise, is actually a full-fledged Perl object that is expected to have an interesting personality of its own. It's just an odd bit of magic, like pulling Bugs Bunny out of a hat.

Put another way, the funny characters $, @, %, or * in front of a variable name tell Perl and its programmers a great deal—they each imply a particular set of archetypal behaviors. You can warp those behaviors in various useful ways with tie, by associating the variable with a class that implements a new set of behaviors. For instance, you can create a regular Perl hash, and then tie it to a class that makes the hash into a database, so that when you read values from the hash, Perl magically fetches data from an external database file, and when you set values in the hash, Perl magically stores data in the external database file. In this case, "magically" means "transparently doing something very complicated". You know the old saying: any technology sufficiently advanced is indistinguishable from a Perl script. (Seriously, people who play with the guts of Perl use *magic* as a technical term referring to any extra semantics attached to variables such as %ENV or %SIG. Tied variables are just an extension of that.)

Perl already has built-in dbmopen and dbmclose functions that magically tie hash variables to databases, but those functions date back to the days when Perl had no tie. Now tie provides a more general mechanism. In fact, Perl itself implements dbmopen and dbmclose in terms of tie.

You can tie a scalar, array, hash, or filehandle (via its typeglob) to any class that provides appropriately named methods to intercept and emulate normal accesses to those variables. The first of those methods is invoked at the point of the tie itself: tying a variable always invokes a constructor, which, if successful, returns an object that Perl squirrels away where you don't see it, down inside the "normal" variable. You can always retrieve that object later using the tied function on the normal variable:

```
tie VARIABLE, CLASSNAME, LIST;  # binds VARIABLE to CLASSNAME
$object = tied VARIABLE;
```

Those two lines are equivalent to:

```
$object = tie VARIABLE, CLASSNAME, LIST;
```

Once it's tied, you treat the normal variable normally, but each access automatically invokes methods on the underlying object; all the complexity of the class is hidden behind those method invocations. If later you want to break the association between the variable and the class, you can untie the variable:

```
untie VARIABLE;
```

You can almost think of tie as a funny kind of bless, except that it blesses a bare variable instead of an object reference. It also can take extra parameters, just as a constructor can—which is not terribly surprising, since it actually does invoke a constructor internally, whose name depends on which type of variable you're tying: either TIESCALAR, TIEARRAY, TIEHASH, or TIEHANDLE.* These constructors are invoked as class methods with the specified CLASSNAME as their invocant, plus any additional arguments you supplied in LIST. (The VARIABLE is not passed to the constructor.)

These four constructors each return an object in the customary fashion. They don't really care whether they were invoked from tie, nor do any of the other methods in the class, since you can always invoke them directly if you'd like. In one sense, all the magic is in the tie, not in the class implementing the tie. It's just an ordinary class with funny method names, as far as the class is concerned. (Indeed, some tied modules provide extra methods that aren't visible through the tied variable; these methods must be called explicitly as you would any other object

---

* Since the constructors have separate names, you could even provide a single class that implements all of them. That would allow you to tie scalars, arrays, hashes, and filehandles all to the same class, although this is not generally done, since it would make the other magical methods tricky to write.

method. Such extra methods might provide services like file locking, transaction protection, or anything else an instance method might do.)

So these constructors `bless` and return an object reference just as any other constructor would. That reference need not refer to the same type of variable as the one being tied; it just has to be blessed, so that the tied variable can find its way back to your class for succor. For instance, our long TIEARRAY example will use a hash-based object, so it can conveniently hold additional information about the array it's emulating.

The `tie` function will not `use` or `require` a module for you—you must do that yourself explicitly, if necessary, before calling the `tie`. (On the other hand, the dbmopen function will, for backward compatibility, attempt to `use` one or another DBM implementation. But you can preempt its selection with an explicit `use`, provided the module you `use` is one of the modules in dbmopen's list of modules to try. See the online docs for the AnyDBM_File module for a fuller explanation.)

The methods called by a tied variable have predetermined names like FETCH and STORE, since they're invoked implicitly (that is, triggered by particular events) from within the innards of Perl. These names are in ALLCAPS, a convention we often follow for such implicitly called routines. (Other special names that follow this convention include BEGIN, CHECK, INIT, END, DESTROY, and AUTOLOAD, not to mention UNIVERSAL->VERSION. In fact, nearly all of Perl's predefined variables and filehandles are in uppercase: STDIN, SUPER, CORE, CORE::GLOBAL, DATA, @EXPORT, @INC, @ISA, @ARGV, and %ENV. Of course, built-in operators and pragmas go to the opposite extreme and have no capitals at all.)

The first thing we'll cover is extremely simple: how to tie a scalar variable.

Tying Scalars

To implement a tied scalar, a class must define the following methods: TIESCALAR, FETCH, and STORE (and possibly DESTROY). When you `tie` a scalar variable, Perl calls TIESCALAR. When you read the tied variable, it calls FETCH, and when you assign a value to the variable, it calls STORE. If you've kept the object returned by the initial `tie` (or if you retrieve it later using `tied`), you can access the underlying object yourself—this does not trigger its FETCH or STORE methods. As an object, it's not magical at all, but rather quite objective.

If a DESTROY method exists, Perl invokes it when the last reference to the tied object disappears, just as for any other object. That happens when your program ends or when you call `untie`, which eliminates the reference used by the tie. However, `untie` doesn't eliminate any outstanding references you might have stored elsewhere; DESTROY is deferred until those references are gone, too.

The `Tie::Scalar` and `Tie::StdScalar` packages, both found in the standard
`Tie::Scalar` module, provide some simple base class definitions if you don't want
to define all of these methods yourself. `Tie::Scalar` provides elemental methods
that do very little, and `Tie::StdScalar` provides methods that make a tied scalar
behave like a regular Perl scalar. (Which seems singularly useless, but sometimes
you just want a bit of a wrapper around the ordinary scalar semantics, for example, to count the number of times a particular variable is set.)

Before we show you our elaborate example and complete description of all the
mechanics, here's a taste just to whet your appetite—and to show you how easy it
really is. Here's a complete program:

```perl
#!/usr/bin/perl
package Centsible;
sub TIESCALAR { bless \my $self, shift }
sub STORE { ${ $_[0] } = $_[1] }   # do the default thing
sub FETCH { sprintf "%.02f", ${ my $self = shift } } # round value

package main;
tie $bucks, "Centsible";
$bucks = 45.00;
$bucks *= 1.0715; # tax
$bucks *= 1.0715; # and double tax!
print "That will be $bucks, please.\n";
```

When run, that program produces:

```
That will be 51.67, please.
```

To see the difference it makes, comment out the call to `tie`; then you'll get:

```
That will be 51.66505125, please.
```

Admittedly, that's more work than you'd normally go through to round numbers.

Scalar-Tying Methods

Now that you've seen a sample of what's to come, let's develop a more elaborate
scalar-tying class. Instead of using any canned package for the base class (especially since scalars are so simple), we'll look at each of the four methods in turn,
building an example class named `ScalarFile`. Scalars tied to this class contain regular strings, and each such variable is implicitly associated with a file where that
string is stored. (You might name your variables to remind you which file you're
referring to.) Variables are tied to the class this way:

```perl
use ScalarFile;       # load ScalarFile.pm
tie $camel, "ScalarFile", "/tmp/camel.lot";
```

Once the variable has been tied, its previous contents are clobbered, and the internal connection between the variable and its object overrides the variable's normal

semantics. When you ask for the value of $camel, it now reads the contents of *tmp/camel.lot*, and when you assign a value to $camel, it writes the new contents out to */tmp/camel.lot*, obliterating any previous occupants.

The tie is on the variable, not the value, so the tied nature of a variable does not propagate across assignment. For example, let's say you copy a variable that's been tied:

```
$dromedary = $camel;
```

Instead of reading the value in the ordinary fashion from the $camel scalar variable, Perl invokes the FETCH method on the associated underlying object. It's as though you'd written this:

```
$dromedary = (tied $camel)->FETCH():
```

Or if you remember the object returned by tie, you could use that reference directly, as in the following sample code:

```
$clot = tie $camel, "ScalarFile", "/tmp/camel.lot";
$dromedary = $camel;          # through the implicit interface
$dromedary = $clot->FETCH();  # same thing, but explicitly
```

If the class provides methods besides TIESCALAR, FETCH, STORE, and DESTROY, you could use $clot to invoke them manually. However, one normally minds one's own business and leaves the underlying object alone, which is why you often see the return value from tie ignored. You can still get at the object via tied if you need it later (for example, if the class happens to document any extra methods you need). Ignoring the returned object also eliminates certain kinds of errors, which we'll cover later.

Here's the preamble of our class, which we will put into *ScalarFile.pm*:

```
package ScalarFile;
use Carp;                  # Propagate error messages nicely.
use strict;                # Enforce some discipline on ourselves.
use warnings;              # Turn on lexically scoped warnings.
use warnings::register;    # Allow user to say "use warnings 'ScalarFile'".
my $count = 0;             # Internal count of tied ScalarFiles.
```

The standard Carp module exports the carp, croak, and confess subroutines, which we'll use in the code later in this section. As usual, see Chapter 32, *Standard Modules*, or the online docs for more about Carp.

The following methods are defined by the class.

CLASSNAME->TIESCALAR(*LIST*)

The TIESCALAR method of the class is triggered whenever you tie a scalar variable. The optional *LIST* contains any parameters needed to initialize the object properly. (In our example, there is only one parameter: the name of the file.)

The method should return an object, but this doesn't have to be a reference to a scalar. In our example, though, it is.

```
sub TIESCALAR {               # in ScalarFile.pm
    my $class    = shift;
    my $filename = shift;
    $count++;                 # A file-scoped lexical, private to class.
    return bless \$filename, $class;
}
```

Since there's no scalar equivalent to the anonymous array and hash composers, [] and {}, we merely bless a lexical variable's referent, which effectively becomes anonymous as soon as the name goes out of scope. This works fine (you could do the same thing with arrays and hashes) as long as the variable really is lexical. If you try this trick on a global, you might think you're getting away with it, until you try to create another *camel.lot*. Don't be tempted to write something like this:

```
sub TIESCALAR { bless \$_[1], $_[0] }    # WRONG, could refer to global.
```

A more robustly written constructor might check that the filename is accessible. We check first to see if the file is readable, since we don't want to clobber the existing value. (In other words, we shouldn't assume the user is going to write first. They might be treasuring their old Camel Lot file from a previous run of the program.) If we can't open or create the filename specified, we'll indicate the error gently by returning undef and optionally printing a warning via carp. (We could just croak instead—it's a matter of taste whether you prefer fish or frogs.) We'll use the warnings pragma to determine whether the user is interested in our warning:

```
sub TIESCALAR {               # in ScalarFile.pm
    my $class    = shift;
    my $filename = shift;
    my $fh;
    if (open $fh, "<", $filename or
        open $fh, ">", $filename)
    {
        close $fh;
        $count++;
        return bless \$filename, $class;
    }
    carp "Can't tie $filename: $!" if warnings::enabled();
    return;
}
```

Given such a constructor, we can now associate the scalar $string with the file *camel.lot*:

```
tie ($string, "ScalarFile", "camel.lot") or die;
```

(We're still assuming some things we shouldn't. In a production version of this, we'd probably open the filehandle once and remember the filehandle as well as the filename for the duration of the tie, keeping the handle exclusively locked with `flock` the whole time. Otherwise we're open to race conditions—see "Timing Glitches" in Chapter 23, *Security*.)

SELF->FETCH

This method is invoked whenever you access the tied variable (that is, read its value). It takes no arguments beyond the object tied to the variable. In our example, that object contains the filename.

```
sub FETCH {
    my $self  = shift;
    confess "I am not a class method" unless ref $self;
    return unless open my $fh, $$self;
    read($fh, my $value, -s $fh);  # NB: don't use -s on pipes!
    return $value;
}
```

This time we've decided to blow up (raise an exception) if FETCH gets something other than a reference. (Either it was invoked as a class method, or someone miscalled it as a subroutine.) There's no other way for us to return an error, so it's probably the right thing to do. In fact, Perl would have raised an exception in any event as soon as we tried to dereference $self; we're just being polite and using `confess` to spew a complete stack backtrace onto the user's screen. (If that can be considered polite.)

We can now see the contents of *camel.lot* when we say this:

```
tie($string, "ScalarFile", "camel.lot");
print $string;
```

SELF->STORE(*VALUE*)

This method is run when the tied variable is set (assigned). The first argument, *SELF*, is as always the object associated with the variable; *VALUE* is whatever was assigned to the variable. (We use the term "assigned" loosely—any operation that modifies the variable can call STORE.)

```
sub STORE {
    my($self,$value) = @_;
    ref $self                   or confess "not a class method";
    open my $fh, ">", $$self    or croak "can't clobber $$self: $!";
    syswrite($fh, $value) == length $value
                                or croak "can't write to $$self: $!";
    close $fh                   or croak "can't close $$self: $!";
    return $value;
}
```

After "assigning" it, we return the new value—because that's what assignment does. If the assignment wasn't successful, we croak out the error. Possible causes might be that we didn't have permission to write to the associated file, or the disk filled up, or gremlins infested the disk controller. Sometimes you control the magic, and sometimes the magic controls you.

We can now write to *camel.lot* when we say this:

```
tie($string, "ScalarFile", "camel.lot");
$string = "Here is the first line of camel.lot\n";
$string .= "And here is another line, automatically appended.\n";
```

SELF->DESTROY

This method is triggered when the object associated with the tied variable is about to be garbage collected, in case it needs to do something special to clean up after itself. As with other classes, such a method is seldom necessary, since Perl deallocates the moribund object's memory for you automatically. Here, we'll define a DESTROY method that decrements our count of tied files:

```
sub DESTROY {
    my $self = shift;
    confess "wrong type" unless ref $self;
    $count--;
}
```

We might then also supply an extra class method to retrieve the current count. Actually, it doesn't care whether it's called as a class method or an object method, but you don't have an object anymore after the DESTROY, now do you?

```
sub count {
    # my $invocant = shift;
    $count;
}
```

You can call this as a class method at any time like this:

```
if (ScalarFile->count) {
    warn "Still some tied ScalarFiles sitting around somewhere...\n";
}
```

That's about all there is to it. Actually, it's more than all there is to it, since we've done a few nice things here for the sake of completeness, robustness, and general aesthetics (or lack thereof). Simpler TIESCALAR classes are certainly possible.

Magical Counter Variables

Here's a simple Tie::Counter class, inspired by the CPAN module of the same name. Variables tied to this class increment themselves by 1 every time they're used. For example:

```
tie my $counter, "Tie::Counter", 100;
@array = qw /Red Green Blue/;
for my $color (@array) {              # Prints:
    print " $counter $color\n";       #    100   Red
}                                     #    101   Green
                                      #    102   Blue
```

The constructor takes as an optional extra argument the first value of the counter,
which defaults to 0. Assigning to the counter will set a new value. Here's the class:

```
package Tie::Counter;
sub FETCH     { ++ ${ $_[0] } }
sub STORE     { ${ $_[0] } = $_[1] }
sub TIESCALAR {
    my ($class, $value) = @_;
    $value = 0 unless defined $value;
    bless \$value => $class;
}
1;  # if in module
```

See how small that is? It doesn't take much code to put together a class like this.

Magically Banishing $_

This curiously exotic tie class is used to outlaw unlocalized uses of $_. Instead of
pulling in the module with use, which invokes the class's import method, this
module should be loaded with no to call the seldom-used unimport method. The
user says:

```
no Underscore;
```

And then all uses of $_ as an unlocalized global raise an exception.

Here's a little test suite for the module:

```
#!/usr/bin/perl
no Underscore;
@tests = (
    "Assignment"  => sub { $_ = "Bad" },
    "Reading"     => sub { print },
    "Matching"    => sub { $x = /badness/ },
    "Chop"        => sub { chop },
    "Filetest"    => sub { -x },
    "Nesting"     => sub { for (1..3) { print } },
);

while ( ($name, $code) = splice(@tests, 0, 2) ) {
    print "Testing $name: ";
    eval { &$code };
    print $@ ? "detected" : " missed!";
    print "\n";
}
```

which prints out the following:

```
Testing Assignment: detected
Testing Reading: detected
Testing Matching: detected
Testing Chop: detected
Testing Filetest: detected
Testing Nesting: 123 missed!
```

The last one was "missed" because it was properly localized by the for loop and thus safe to access.

Here's the curiously exotic Underscore module itself. (Did we mention that it's curiously exotic?) It works because tied magic is effectively hidden by a local. The module does the tie in its own initialization code so that a require also works.

```
package Underscore;
use Carp;
sub TIESCALAR { bless \my $dummy => shift }
sub FETCH { croak 'Read access to $_ forbidden'  }
sub STORE { croak 'Write access to $_ forbidden' }
sub unimport { tie($_, __PACKAGE__) }
sub import    { untie $_ }
tie($_, __PACKAGE__) unless tied $_;
1;
```

It's hard to usefully mix calls to use and no for this class in your program, because they all happen at compile time, not run time. You could call Underscore->import and Underscore->unimport directly, just as use and no do. Normally, though, to renege and let yourself freely use $_ again, you'd just use local on it, which is the whole point.

Tying Arrays

A class implementing a tied array must define at least the methods TIEARRAY, FETCH, and STORE. There are many optional methods: the ubiquitous DESTROY method, of course, but also the STORESIZE and FETCHSIZE methods used to provide $#array and scalar(@array) access. In addition, CLEAR is triggered when Perl needs to empty the array, and EXTEND when Perl would have pre-extended allocation in a real array.

You may also define the POP, PUSH, SHIFT, UNSHIFT, SPLICE, DELETE, and EXISTS methods if you want the corresponding Perl functions to work on the tied array. The Tie::Array class can serve as a base class to implement the first five of those functions in terms of FETCH and STORE. (Tie::Array's default implementation of DELETE and EXISTS simply calls croak.) As long as you define FETCH and STORE, it doesn't matter what kind of data structure your object contains.

On the other hand, the `Tie::StdArray` class (defined in the standard `Tie::Array` module) provides a base class with default methods that assume the object contains a regular array. Here's a simple array-tying class that makes use of this. Because it uses `Tie::StdArray` as its base class, it only needs to define the methods that should be treated in a nonstandard way.

```perl
#!/usr/bin/perl
package ClockArray;
use Tie::Array;
our @ISA = 'Tie::StdArray';
sub FETCH {
    my($self,$place) = @_;
    $self->[ $place % 12 ];
}
sub STORE {
    my($self,$place,$value) = @_;
    $self->[ $place % 12 ] = $value;
}

package main;
tie my @array, 'ClockArray';
@array = ( "a" ... "z" );
print "@array\n";
```

When run, the program prints out "y z o p q r s t u v w x". This class provides an array with only a dozen slots, like hours of a clock, numbered 0 through 11. If you ask for the 15th array index, you really get the 3rd one. Think of it as a travel aid for people who haven't learned how to read 24-hour clocks.

Array-Tying Methods

That's the simple way. Now for some nitty-gritty details. To demonstrate, we'll implement an array whose bounds are fixed at its creation. If you try to access anything beyond those bounds, an exception is raised. For example:

```perl
use BoundedArray;
tie @array, "BoundedArray", 2;

$array[0] = "fine";
$array[1] = "good";
$array[2] = "great";
$array[3] = "whoa";    # Prohibited; displays an error message.
```

The preamble code for the class is as follows:

```perl
package BoundedArray;
use Carp;
use strict;
```

To avoid having to define SPLICE later, we'll inherit from the Tie::Array class:

```
use Tie::Array;
our @ISA = ("Tie::Array");
```

CLASSNAME->TIEARRAY(*LIST*)

As the constructor for the class, TIEARRAY should return a blessed reference through which the tied array will be emulated.

In this next example, just to show you that you don't *really* have to return an array reference, we'll choose a hash reference to represent our object. A hash works out well as a generic record type: the value in the hash's "BOUND" key will store the maximum bound allowed, and its "DATA" value will hold the actual data. If someone outside the class tries to dereference the object returned (doubtless thinking it an array reference), an exception is raised.

```
sub TIEARRAY {
    my $class = shift;
    my $bound = shift;
    confess "usage: tie(\@ary, 'BoundedArray', max_subscript)"
        if @_ || $bound =~ /\D/;
    return bless { BOUND => $bound, DATA => [] }, $class;
}
```

We can now say:

```
tie(@array, "BoundedArray", 3);  # maximum allowable index is 3
```

to ensure that the array will never have more than four elements. Whenever an individual element of the array is accessed or stored, FETCH and STORE will be called just as they were for scalars, but with an extra index argument.

SELF->FETCH(*INDEX*)

This method is run whenever an individual element in the tied array is accessed. It receives one argument after the object: the index of the value we're trying to fetch.

```
sub FETCH {
    my ($self, $index) = @_;
    if ($index > $self->{BOUND}) {
        confess "Array OOB: $index > $self->{BOUND}";
    }
    return $self->{DATA}[$index];
}
```

SELF->STORE(*INDEX*, *VALUE*)

This method is invoked whenever an element in the tied array is set. It takes two arguments after the object: the index at which we're trying to store something and the value we're trying to put there. For example:

```
sub STORE {
    my($self, $index, $value) = @_;
    if ($index > $self->{BOUND} ) {
        confess "Array OOB: $index > $self->{BOUND}";
    }
    return $self->{DATA}[$index] = $value;
}
```

SELF->DESTROY

Perl calls this method when the tied variable needs to be destroyed and its memory reclaimed. This is almost never needed in a language with garbage collection, so for this example we'll just leave it out.

SELF->FETCHSIZE

The FETCHSIZE method should return the total number of items in the tied array associated with *SELF*. It's equivalent to scalar(@array), which is usually equal to $#array + 1.

```
sub FETCHSIZE {
    my $self = shift;
    return scalar @{$self->{DATA}};
}
```

SELF->STORESIZE(*COUNT*)

This method sets the total number of items in the tied array associated with *SELF* to be *COUNT*. If the array shrinks, you should remove entries beyond *COUNT*. If the array grows, you should make sure the new positions are undefined. For our BoundedArray class, we also ensure that the array doesn't grow beyond the limit initially set.

```
sub STORESIZE {
    my ($self, $count) = @_;
    if ($count > $self->{BOUND}) {
        confess "Array OOB: $count > $self->{BOUND}";
    }
    $#{$self->{DATA}} = $count;
}
```

SELF->EXTEND(*COUNT*)

Perl uses the EXTEND method to indicate that the array is likely to expand to hold *COUNT* entries. That way you can can allocate memory in one big chunk instead of in many successive calls later on. Since our BoundedArrays have fixed upper bounds, we won't define this method.

SELF->EXISTS(*INDEX*)

This method verifies that the element at *INDEX* exists in the tied array. For our BoundedArray, we just employ Perl's built-in exists after verifying that it's not an attempt to look past the fixed upper bound.

```
sub EXISTS  {
    my ($self, $index) = @_;
    if ($index > $self->{BOUND}) {
        confess "Array OOB: $index > $self->{BOUND}";
    }
    exists $self->{DATA}[$index];
}
```

SELF->DELETE(*INDEX*)

The DELETE method removes the element at *INDEX* from the tied array *SELF*. For our BoundedArray class, the method looks nearly identical to EXISTS, but this is not the norm.

```
sub DELETE {
    my ($self, $index) = @_;
    print STDERR "deleting!\n";
    if ($index > $self->{BOUND}) {
        confess "Array OOB: $index > $self->{BOUND}";
    }
    delete $self->{DATA}[$index];
}
```

SELF->CLEAR

This method is called whenever the array has to be emptied. That happens when the array is set to a list of new values (or an empty list), but not when it's provided to the undef function. Since a cleared BoundedArray always satisfies the upper bound, we don't need check anything here:

```
sub CLEAR {
    my $self = shift;
    $self->{DATA} = [];
}
```

If you set the array to a list, CLEAR will trigger but won't see the list values. So if you violate the upper bound like so:

```
tie(@array, "BoundedArray", 2);
@array = (1, 2, 3, 4);
```

the CLEAR method will still return successfully. The exception will only be raised on the subsequent STORE. The assignment triggers one CLEAR and four STOREs.

SELF->PUSH(*LIST*)

This method appends the elements of *LIST* to the array. Here's how it might look for our BoundedArray class:

```
sub PUSH    {
    my $self = shift;
    if (@_ + $#{$self->{DATA}} > $self->{BOUND}) {
        confess "Attempt to push too many elements";
    }
```

```
            push @{$self->{DATA}}, @_;
    }
```

SELF->UNSHIFT(LIST)

This method prepends the elements of *LIST* to the array. For our `BoundedArray` class, the subroutine would be similar to `PUSH`.

SELF->POP

The `POP` method removes the last element of the array and returns it. For `BoundedArray`, it's a one-liner:

```
    sub POP { my $self = shift; pop @{$self->{DATA}} }
```

SELF->SHIFT

The `SHIFT` method removes the first element of the array and returns it. For `BoundedArray`, it's similar to `POP`.

SELF->SPLICE(OFFSET, LENGTH, LIST)

This method lets you splice the *SELF* array. To mimic Perl's built-in `splice`, *OFFSET* should be optional and default to zero, with negative values counting back from the end of the array. *LENGTH* should also be optional, defaulting to rest of the array. *LIST* can be empty. If it's properly mimicking the built-in, the method will return a list of the original *LENGTH* elements at *OFFSET* (that is, the list of elements to be replaced by *LIST*).

Since splicing is a somewhat complicated operation, we won't define it at all; we'll just use the `SPLICE` subroutine from the `Tie::Array` module that we got for free when we inherited from `Tie::Array`. This way we define `SPLICE` in terms of other `BoundedArray` methods, so the bounds checking will still occur.

That completes our `BoundedArray` class. It warps the semantics of arrays just a little. But we can do better, and in very much less space.

Notational Convenience

One of the nice things about variables is that they interpolate. One of the not-so-nice things about functions is that they don't. You can use a tied array to make a function that can be interpolated. Suppose you want to interpolate random integers in a string. You can just say:

```
#!/usr/bin/perl
package RandInterp;
sub TIEARRAY { bless \my $self };
sub FETCH { int rand $_[1] };

package main;
tie @rand, "RandInterp";
```

```
for (1,10,100,1000) {
    print "A random integer less than $_ would be $rand[$_]\n";
}
$rand[32] = 5;     # Will this reformat our system disk?
```

When run, this prints:

```
A random integer less than 1 would be 0
A random integer less than 10 would be 3
A random integer less than 100 would be 46
A random integer less than 1000 would be 755
Can't locate object method "STORE" via package "RandInterp" at foo line 10.
```

As you can see, it's no big deal that we didn't even implement STORE. It just blows up like normal.

Tying Hashes

A class implementing a tied hash should define eight methods. TIEHASH constructs new objects. FETCH and STORE access the key/value pairs. EXISTS reports whether a key is present in the hash, and DELETE removes a key along with its associated value.* CLEAR empties the hash by deleting all key/value pairs. FIRSTKEY and NEXTKEY iterate over the key/value pairs when you call keys, values, or each. And as usual, if you want to perform particular actions when the object is deallocated, you may define a DESTROY method. (If this seems like a lot of methods, you didn't read the last section on arrays attentively. In any event, feel free to inherit the default methods from the standard Tie::Hash module, redefining only the interesting ones. Again, Tie::StdHash assumes the implementation is also a hash.)

For example, suppose you want to create a hash where every time you assign a value to a key, instead of overwriting the previous contents, the new value is appended to an array of values. That way when you say:

```
$h{$k} = "one";
$h{$k} = "two";
```

It really does:

```
push @{ $h{$k} }, "one";
push @{ $h{$k} }, "two";
```

That's not a very complicated idea, so you should be able to use a pretty simple module. Using Tie::StdHash as a base class, it is. Here's a Tie::AppendHash that does just that:

---

* Remember that Perl distinguishes between a key not existing in the hash and a key existing in the hash but having a corresponding value of undef. The two possibilities can be tested with exists and defined, respectively.

```
package Tie::AppendHash;
use Tie::Hash;
our @ISA = ("Tie::StdHash");
sub STORE {
    my ($self, $key, $value) = @_;
    push @{$self->{key}}, $value;
}
1;
```

Hash-Tying Methods

Here's an example of an interesting tied-hash class: it gives you a hash represent-ing a particular user's dot files (that is, files whose names begin with a period, which is a naming convention for initialization files under Unix). You index into the hash with the name of the file (minus the period) and get back that dot file's contents. For example:

```
use DotFiles;
tie %dot, "DotFiles";
if ( $dot{profile} =~ /MANPATH/ or
     $dot{login}   =~ /MANPATH/ or
     $dot{cshrc}   =~ /MANPATH/   ) {
    print "you seem to set your MANPATH\n";
}
```

Here's another way to use our tied class:

```
# Third argument is the name of a user whose dot files we will tie to.
tie %him, "DotFiles", "daemon";
foreach $f (keys %him) {
    printf "daemon dot file %s is size %d\n", $f, length $him{$f};
}
```

In our `DotFiles` example we implement the object as a regular hash containing several important fields, of which only the {CONTENTS} field will contain what the user thinks of as the hash. Here are the object's actual fields:

Field	Contents
USER	Whose dot files this object represents.
HOME	Where those dot files live.
CLOBBER	Whether we are allowed to change or remove those dot files.
CONTENTS	The hash of dot file names and content mappings.

Here's the start of *DotFiles.pm*:

```
package DotFiles;
use Carp;
sub whowasi { (caller(1))[3] . "()" }
my $DEBUG = 0;
sub debug { $DEBUG = @_ ? shift : 1 }
```

For our example, we want to be able to turn on debugging output to help in tracing during development, so we set up $DEBUG for that. We also keep one convenience function around internally to help print out warnings: whowasi returns the name of the function that called the current function (whowasi's "grandparent" function).

Here are the methods for the DotFiles tied hash:

CLASSNAME->TIEHASH(LIST)

Here's the DotFiles constructor:

```
sub TIEHASH {
    my $self  = shift;
    my $user  = shift || $>;
    my $dotdir = shift || "";

    croak "usage: @{[ &whowasi ]} [USER [DOTDIR]]" if @_;

    $user = getpwuid($user) if $user =~ /^\d+$/;
    my $dir = (getpwnam($user))[7]
            or croak "@{ [&whowasi] }: no user $user";
    $dir .= "/$dotdir" if $dotdir;

    my $node = {
        USER      => $user,
        HOME      => $dir,
        CONTENTS  => {},
        CLOBBER   => 0,
    };

    opendir DIR, $dir
            or croak "@{[&whowasi]}: can't opendir $dir: $!";
    for my $dot ( grep /^\./ && -f "$dir/$_", readdir(DIR)) {
        $dot =~ s/^\.//;
        $node->{CONTENTS}{$dot} = undef;
    }
    closedir DIR;

    return bless $node, $self;
}
```

It's probably worth mentioning that if you're going to apply file tests to the values returned by the above readdir, you'd better prepend the directory in question (as we do). Otherwise, since no chdir was done, you'd likely be testing the wrong file.

SELF->FETCH(KEY)

This method implements reading an element from the tied hash. It takes one argument after the object: the key whose value we're trying to fetch. The key is a string, and you can do anything you like with it (consistent with its being a string).

Here's the fetch for our `DotFiles` example:

```
sub FETCH {
    carp &whowasi if $DEBUG;
    my $self = shift;
    my $dot = shift;
    my $dir = $self->{HOME};
    my $file = "$dir/.$dot";

    unless (exists $self->{CONTENTS}->{$dot} || -f $file) {
        carp "@{[&whowasi]}: no $dot file" if $DEBUG;
        return undef;
    }

    # Implement a cache.
    if (defined $self->{CONTENTS}->{$dot}) {
        return $self->{CONTENTS}->{$dot};
    } else {
        return $self->{CONTENTS}->{$dot} = `cat $dir/.$dot`;
    }
}
```

We cheated a little by running the Unix *cat*(1) command, but it would be more portable (and more efficient) to open the file ourselves. On the other hand, since dotfiles are a Unixy concept, we're not that concerned. Or shouldn't be. Or something...

SELF->STORE(*KEY*, *VALUE*)

This method does the dirty work whenever an element in the tied hash is set (written). It takes two arguments after the object: the key under which we're storing the new value, and the value itself.

For our `DotFiles` example, we won't let users overwrite a file without first invoking the `clobber` method on the original object returned by `tie`:

```
sub STORE {
    carp &whowasi if $DEBUG;
    my $self  = shift;
    my $dot   = shift;
    my $value = shift;
    my $file  = $self->{HOME} . "/.$dot";

    croak "@{[&whowasi]}: $file not clobberable"
        unless $self->{CLOBBER};

    open(F, "> $file") or croak "can't open $file: $!";
    print F $value;
    close(F);
}
```

If someone wants to clobber something, they can say:

```
$ob = tie %daemon_dots, "daemon";
$ob->clobber(1);
$daemon_dots{signature} = "A true daemon\n";
```

But they could alternatively set {CLOBBER} with tied:

```
tie %daemon_dots, "DotFiles", "daemon";
tied(%daemon_dots)->clobber(1);
```

or as one statement:

```
(tie %daemon_dots, "DotFiles", "daemon")->clobber(1);
```

The clobber method is simply:

```
sub clobber {
    my $self = shift;
    $self->{CLOBBER} = @_ ? shift : 1;
}
```

SELF->DELETE(*KEY*)

This method handles requests to remove an element from the hash. If your emulated hash uses a real hash somewhere, you can just call the real delete. Again, we'll be careful to check whether the user really wants to clobber files:

```
sub DELETE    {
    carp &whowasi if $DEBUG;
    my $self = shift;
    my $dot = shift;
    my $file = $self->{HOME} . "/.$dot";
    croak "@{[&whowasi]}: won't remove file $file"
        unless $self->{CLOBBER};
    delete $self->{CONTENTS}->{$dot};
    unlink $file or carp "@{[&whowasi]}: can't unlink $file: $!";
}
```

SELF->CLEAR

This method is run when the whole hash needs to be cleared, usually by assigning the empty list to it. In our example, that would remove all the user's dot files! It's such a dangerous thing that we'll require CLOBBER to be set higher than 1 before this can happen:

```
sub CLEAR {
    carp &whowasi if $DEBUG;
    my $self = shift;
    croak "@{[&whowasi]}: won't remove all dotfiles for $self->{USER}"
        unless $self->{CLOBBER} > 1;
    for my $dot ( keys %{$self->{CONTENTS}}) {
        $self->DELETE($dot);
    }
}
```

SELF->EXISTS (*KEY*)

This method runs when the user invokes the exists function on a particular hash. In our example, we'll look at the {CONTENTS} hash element to find the answer:

```
sub EXISTS   {
    carp &whowasi if $DEBUG;
    my $self = shift;
    my $dot  = shift;
    return exists $self->{CONTENTS}->{$dot};
}
```

SELF->FIRSTKEY

This method is called when the user begins to iterate through the hash, such as with a keys, values, or each call. By calling keys in a scalar context, we reset its internal state to ensure that the next each used in the return statement will get the first key.

```
sub FIRSTKEY {
    carp &whowasi if $DEBUG;
    my $self = shift;
    my $temp = keys %{$self->{CONTENTS}};
    return scalar each %{$self->{CONTENTS}};
}
```

SELF->NEXTKEY (*PREVKEY*)

This method is the iterator for a keys, values, or each function. *PREVKEY* is the last key accessed, which Perl knows to supply. This is useful if the NEXTKEY method needs to know its previous state to calculate the next state.

For our example, we are using a real hash to represent the tied hash's data, except that this hash is stored in the hash's CONTENTS field instead of in the hash itself. So we can just rely on Perl's each iterator:

```
sub NEXTKEY   {
    carp &whowasi if $DEBUG;
    my $self = shift;
    return scalar each %{ $self->{CONTENTS} }
}
```

SELF->DESTROY

This method is triggered when a tied hash's object is about to be deallocated. You don't really need it except for debugging and extra cleanup. Here's a very simple version:

```
sub DESTROY   {
    carp &whowasi if $DEBUG;
}
```

Now that we've given you all those methods, your homework is to go back and find the places we interpolated @{[&whowasi]} and replace them with a simple tied scalar named $whowasi that does the same thing.

Tying Filehandles

A class implementing a tied filehandle should define the following methods: TIEHANDLE and at least one of PRINT, PRINTF, WRITE, READLINE, GETC, and READ. The class can also provide a DESTROY method, and BINMODE, OPEN, CLOSE, EOF, FILENO, SEEK, TELL, READ, and WRITE methods to enable the corresponding Perl built-ins for the tied filehandle. (Well, that isn't quite true: WRITE corresponds to syswrite and has nothing to do with Perl's built-in write function for printing with format declarations.)

Tied filehandles are especially useful when Perl is embedded in another program (such as Apache or *vi*) and output to STDOUT or STDERR needs to be redirected in some special way.

But filehandles don't actually have to be tied to a file at all. You can use output statements to build up an in-memory data structure and input statements to read them back in. Here's an easy way to reverse a sequence of print and printf statements without reversing the individual lines:

```perl
package ReversePrint;
use strict;
sub TIEHANDLE {
    my $class = shift;
    bless [], $class;
}
sub PRINT {
    my $self = shift;
    push @$self, join '', @_;
}
sub PRINTF {
    my $self = shift;
    my $fmt = shift;
    push @$self, sprintf $fmt, @_;
}
sub READLINE {
    my $self = shift;
    pop @$self;
}

package main;
my $m = "--MORE--\n";
tie *REV, "ReversePrint";

# Do some prints and printfs.
print REV "The fox is now dead.$m";
```

```
printf REV <<"END", int rand 10000000;
The quick brown fox jumps over
over the lazy dog %d times!
END

print REV <<"END";
The quick brown fox jumps
over the lazy dog.
END

# Now read back from the same handle.
print while <REV>;
```

This prints:

```
The quick brown fox jumps
over the lazy dog.
The quick brown fox jumps over
over the lazy dog 3179357 times!
The fox is now dead.--MORE--
```

Filehandle-Tying Methods

For our extended example, we'll create a filehandle that uppercases strings printed to it. Just for kicks, we'll begin the file with <SHOUT> when it's opened and end with </SHOUT> when it's closed. That way we can rant in well-formed XML.

Here's the top of our *Shout.pm* file that will implement the class:

```
package Shout;
use Carp;                    # So we can croak our errors
```

We'll now list the method definitions in *Shout.pm*.

CLASSNAME->TIEHANDLE(LIST)

This is the constructor for the class, which as usual should return a blessed reference.

```
sub TIEHANDLE {
    my $class = shift;
    my $form = shift;
    open my $self, $form, @_   or croak "can't open $form@_: $!";
    if ($form =~ />/) {
        print $self   "<SHOUT>\n";
        $$self->{WRITING} = 1;      # Remember to do end tag
    }
    return bless $self, $class;   # $self is a glob ref
}
```

Here, we open a new filehandle according to the mode and filename passed to the tie operator, write <SHOUT> to the file, and return a blessed reference to it. There's a lot of stuff going on in that open statement, but we'll just point out that, in addition to the usual "open or die" idiom, the my $self furnishes an undefined scalar to open, which knows to autovivify it into a typeglob. The fact that it's a typeglob is also significant, because not only does the typeglob contain the real I/O object of the file, but it also contains various other handy data structures that come along for free, like a scalar ($$$self), an array (@$$self), and a hash (%$$self). (We won't mention the subroutine, &$$self.)

The $form is the filename-or-mode argument. If it's a filename, @_ is empty, so it behaves as a two-argument open. Otherwise, $form is the mode for the rest of the arguments.

After the open, we test to see whether we should write the beginning tag. If so, we do. And right away, we use one of those glob data structures we mentioned. That $$self->{WRITING} is an example of using the glob to store interesting information. In this case, we remember whether we did the beginning tag so we know whether to do the corresponding end tag. We're using the %$$self hash, so we can give the field a decent name. We could have used the scalar as $$$self, but that wouldn't be self-documenting. (Or it would *only* be self-documenting, depending on how you look at it.)

SELF->PRINT(*LIST*)

This method implements a print to the tied handle. The *LIST* is whatever was passed to print. Our method below uppercases each element of *LIST*:

```
sub PRINT {
    my $self = shift;
    print $self map {uc} @_;
}
```

SELF->READLINE

This method supplies the data when the filehandle is read from via the angle operator (<FH>) or readline. The method should return undef when there is no more data.

```
sub READLINE {
    my $self = shift;
    return <$self>;
}
```

Here, we simply return <$self> so that the method will behave appropriately depending on whether it was called in scalar or list context.

SELF->GETC

This method runs whenever getc is used on the tied filehandle.

```
sub GETC {
    my $self = shift;
    return getc($self);
}
```

Like several of the methods in our Shout class, the GETC method simply calls its corresponding Perl built-in and returns the result.

SELF->OPEN(*LIST*)

Our TIEHANDLE method itself opens a file, but a program using the Shout class that calls open afterward triggers this method.

```
sub OPEN {
    my $self = shift;
    my $form = shift;
    my $name = "$form@_";
    $self->CLOSE;
    open($self, $form, @_)       or croak "can't reopen $name: $!";
    if ($form =~ />/) {
        print $self "<SHOUT>\n" or croak "can't start print: $!";
        $$self->{WRITING} = 1;     # Remember to do end tag
    }
    else {
        $$self->{WRITING} = 0;     # Remember not to do end tag
    }
    return 1;
}
```

We invoke our own CLOSE method to explicitly close the file in case the user didn't bother to. Then we open a new file with whatever filename was specified in the open and shout at it.

SELF->CLOSE

This method deals with the request to close the handle. Here, we seek to the end of the file and, if that was successful, print </SHOUT> before using Perl's built-in close.

```
sub CLOSE {
    my $self = shift;
    if ($$self->{WRITING}) {
        $self->SEEK(0, 2)             or return;
        $self->PRINT("</SHOUT>\n")    or return;
    }
    return close $self;
}
```

SELF->SEEK(*LIST*)

When you seek on a tied filehandle, the SEEK method gets called.

```
sub SEEK {
    my $self = shift;
    my ($offset, $whence) = @_;
    return seek($self, $offset, $whence);
}
```

SELF->TELL

This method is invoked when `tell` is used on the tied handle.

```
sub TELL {
    my $self = shift;
    return tell $self;
}
```

SELF->PRINTF(*LIST*)

This method is run whenever `printf` is used on the tied handle. The *LIST* will contain the format and the items to be printed.

```
sub PRINTF {
    my $self = shift;
    my $template = shift;
    return $self->PRINT(sprintf $template, @_);
}
```

Here, we use `sprintf` to generate the formatted string and pass it to PRINT for uppercasing. There's nothing that requires you to use the built-in `sprintf` function though. You could interpret the percent escapes to suit your own purpose.

SELF->READ(*LIST*)

This method responds when the handle is read using `read` or `sysread`. Note that we modify the first argument of *LIST* "in-place", mimicking `read`'s ability to fill in the scalar passed in as its second argument.

```
sub READ {
    my ($self, undef, $length, $offset) = @_;
    my $bufref = \$_[1];
    return read($self, $$bufref, $length, $offset);
}
```

SELF->WRITE(*LIST*)

This method gets invoked when the handle is written to with `syswrite`. Here, we uppercase the string to be written.

```
sub WRITE {
    my $self = shift;
    my $string = uc(shift);
    my $length = shift || length $string;
    my $offset = shift || 0;
    return syswrite $self, $string, $length, $offset;
}
```

SELF->EOF

This method returns a Boolean value when a filehandle tied to the Shout class is tested for its end-of-file status using `eof`.

```
sub EOF {
    my $self = shift;
    return eof $self;
}
```

***SELF*->BINMODE(*DISC*)**

This method specifies the I/O discipline to be used on the filehandle. If none is specified, it puts the tied filehandle into binary mode (the :raw discipline), for filesystems that distinguish between text and binary files.

```
sub BINMODE {
    my $self = shift;
    my $disc = shift || ":raw";
    return binmode $self, $disc;
}
```

That's how you'd write it, but it's actually useless in our case because the open already wrote on the handle. So in our case we should probably make it say:

```
sub BINMODE { croak("Too late to use binmode") }
```

***SELF*->FILENO**

This method should return the file descriptor (fileno) associated with the tied filehandle by the operating system.

```
sub FILENO {
    my $self = shift;
    return fileno $self;
}
```

***SELF*->DESTROY**

As with the other types of ties, this method is triggered when the tied object is about to be destroyed. This is useful for letting the object clean up after itself. Here, we make sure that the file is closed, in case the program forgot to call close. We could just say close $self, but it's better to invoke the CLOSE method of the class. That way if the designer of the class decides to change how files are closed, this DESTROY method won't have to be modified.

```
sub DESTROY {
    my $self = shift;
    $self->CLOSE;       # Close the file using Shout's CLOSE method.
}
```

Here's a demonstration of our Shout class:

```
#!/usr/bin/perl
use Shout;
tie(*FOO, Shout::, ">filename");
print FOO "hello\n";        # Prints HELLO.
seek FOO, 0, 0;             # Rewind to beginning.
@lines = <FOO>;            # Calls the READLINE method.
close FOO;                 # Close file explicitly.
```

```
open(FOO, "+<", "filename");      # Reopen FOO, calling OPEN.
seek(FOO, 8, 0);                  # Skip the "<SHOUT>\n".
sysread(FOO, $inbuf, 5);          # Read 5 bytes from FOO into $inbuf.
print "found $inbuf\n";           # Should print "hello".
seek(FOO, -5, 1);                 # Back up over the "hello".
syswrite(FOO, "ciao!\n", 6);      # Write 6 bytes into FOO.
untie(*FOO);                      # Calls the CLOSE method implicitly.
```

After running this, the file contains:

```
<SHOUT>
CIAO!
</SHOUT>
```

Here are some more strange and wonderful things to do with that internal glob. We use the same hash as before, but with new keys PATHNAME and DEBUG. First we install a stringify overloading so that printing one of our objects reveals the pathname (see Chapter 13, *Overloading*):

```
# This is just so totally cool!
use overload q("") => sub { $_[0]->pathname };

# This is the stub to put in each function you want to trace.
sub trace {
    my $self = shift;
    local $Carp::CarpLevel = 1;
    Carp::cluck("\ntrace magical method") if $self->debug;
}

# Overload handler to print out our path.
sub pathname {
    my $self = shift;
    confess "i am not a class method" unless ref $self;
    $$self->{PATHNAME} = shift if @_;
    return $$self->{PATHNAME};
}
# Dual moded.
sub debug {
    my $self = shift;
    my $var = ref $self ? \$$self->{DEBUG} : \our $Debug;
    $$var = shift if @_;
    return ref $self ? $$self->{DEBUG} || $Debug : $Debug;
}
```

And then call trace on entry to all your ordinary methods like this:

```
sub GETC { $_[0]->trace;            # NEW
    my($self) = @_;
    getc($self);
}
```

And also set the pathname in TIEHANDLE and OPEN:

```
sub TIEHANDLE {
    my $class    = shift;
    my $form = shift;
    my $name = "$form@_";           # NEW
    open my $self, $form, @_  or croak "can't open $name: $!";
    if ($form =~ />/) {
        print $self  "<SHOUT>\n";
        $$self->{WRITING} = 1;      # Remember to do end tag
    }
    bless $self, $class;            # $fh is a glob ref
    $self->pathname($name);         # NEW
    return $self;
}

sub OPEN { $_[0]->trace;           # NEW
    my $self = shift;
    my $form = shift;
    my $name = "$form@_";
    $self->CLOSE;
    open($self, $form, @_)      or croak "can't reopen $name: $!";
    $self->pathname($name);         # NEW
    if ($form =~ />/) {
        print $self "<SHOUT>\n" or croak "can't start print: $!";
        $$self->{WRITING} = 1;      # Remember to do end tag
    }
    else {
        $$self->{WRITING} = 0;      # Remember not to do end tag
    }
    return 1;
}
```

Somewhere you also have to call $self->debug(1) to turn debugging on. When you do that, all your Carp::cluck calls will produce meaningful messages. Here's one that we get while doing the reopen above. It shows us three deep in method calls, as we're closing down the old file in preparation for opening the new one:

```
trace magical method at foo line 87
    Shout::SEEK('>filename', '>filename', 0, 2) called at foo line 81
    Shout::CLOSE('>filename') called at foo line 65
    Shout::OPEN('>filename', '+<', 'filename') called at foo line 141
```

Creative Filehandles

You can tie the same filehandle to both the input and the output of a two-ended pipe. Suppose you wanted to run the *bc*(1) (arbitrary precision calculator) program this way:

```
use Tie::Open2;

tie *CALC, 'Tie::Open2', "bc -l";
$sum = 2;
```

```
for (1 .. 7) {
    print CALC "$sum * $sum\n";
    $sum = <CALC>;
    print "$_: $sum";
    chomp $sum;
}
close CALC;
```

One would expect it to print this:

```
1: 4
2: 16
3: 256
4: 65536
5: 4294967296
6: 18446744073709551616
7: 340282366920938463463374607431768211456
```

One's expectations would be correct if one had the *bc*(1) program on one's computer, and one also had Tie::Open2 defined as follows. This time we'll use a blessed array for our internal object. It contains our two actual filehandles for reading and writing. (The dirty work of opening a double-ended pipe is done by IPC::Open2; we're just doing the fun part.)

```
package Tie::Open2;
use strict;
use Carp;
use Tie::Handle;  # do not inherit from this!
use IPC::Open2;

sub TIEHANDLE {
    my ($class, @cmd) = @_;
    no warnings 'once';
    my @fhpair = \do { local(*RDR, *WTR) };
    bless $_, 'Tie::StdHandle' for @fhpair;
    bless(\@fhpair => $class)->OPEN(@cmd) || die;
    return \@fhpair;
}

sub OPEN {
    my ($self, @cmd) = @_;
    $self->CLOSE if grep {defined} @{ $self->FILENO };
    open2(@$self, @cmd);
}

sub FILENO {
    my $self = shift;
    [ map { fileno $self->[$_] } 0,1 ];
}

for my $outmeth ( qw(PRINT PRINTF WRITE) ) {
    no strict 'refs';
    *$outmeth = sub {
```

```
          my $self = shift;
          $self->[1]->$outmeth(@_);
      };
  }
  for my $inmeth ( qw(READ READLINE GETC) ) {
      no strict 'refs';
      *$inmeth = sub {
          my $self = shift;
          $self->[0]->$inmeth(@_);
      };
  }
  for my $doppelmeth ( qw(BINMODE CLOSE EOF)) {
      no strict 'refs';
      *$doppelmeth = sub {
          my $self = shift;
          $self->[0]->$doppelmeth(@_) && $self->[1]->$doppelmeth(@_);
      };
  }
  for my $deadmeth ( qw(SEEK TELL)) {
      no strict 'refs';
      *$deadmeth = sub {
          croak("can't $deadmeth a pipe");
      };
  }
  1;
```

The final four loops are just incredibly snazzy, in our opinion. For an explanation of what's going on, look back at the section entitled "Closures as Function Templates" in Chapter 8, *References.*

Here's an even wackier set of classes. The package names should give you a clue as to what they do.

```
use strict;
package Tie::DevNull;

    sub TIEHANDLE {
        my $class = shift;
        my $fh = local *FH;
        bless \$fh, $class;
    }
    for (qw(READ READLINE GETC PRINT PRINTF WRITE)) {
        no strict 'refs';
        *$_  = sub { return };
    }

package Tie::DevRandom;

    sub READLINE { rand() . "\n"; }
    sub TIEHANDLE {
        my $class = shift;
        my $fh = local *FH;
        bless \$fh, $class;
    }
```

```perl
    sub FETCH { rand() }
    sub TIESCALAR {
        my $class = shift;
        bless \my $self, $class;
    }

package Tie::Tee;

    sub TIEHANDLE {
        my $class = shift;
        my @handles;
        for my $path (@_) {
            open(my $fh, ">$path") || die "can't write $path";
            push @handles, $fh;
        }
        bless \@handles, $class;
    }

    sub PRINT {
        my $self = shift;
        my $ok = 0;
        for my $fh (@$self) {
            $ok += print $fh @_;
        }
        return $ok == @$self;
    }
```

The `Tie::Tee` class emulates the standard Unix *tee*(1) program, which sends one stream of output to multiple different destinations. The `Tie::DevNull` class emulates the null device, */dev/null* on Unix systems. And the `Tie::DevRandom` class produces random numbers either as a handle or as a scalar, depending on whether you call TIEHANDLE or TIESCALAR! Here's how you call them:

```perl
package main;

tie *SCATTER,    "Tie::Tee", qw(tmp1 - tmp2 >tmp3 tmp4);
tie *RANDOM,     "Tie::DevRandom";
tie *NULL,       "Tie::DevNull";
tie my $randy,   "Tie::DevRandom";

for my $i (1..10) {
    my $line = <RANDOM>;
    chomp $line;
    for my $fh (*NULL, *SCATTER) {
        print $fh "$i: $line $randy\n";
    }
}
```

This produces something like the following on your screen:

```
1: 0.124115571686165 0.20872819474074
2: 0.156618299751194 0.678171662366353
3: 0.799749050426126 0.300184963960792
4: 0.599474551447884 0.213935286029916
```

```
 5: 0.700232143543861 0.800773751296671
 6: 0.201203608274334 0.0654303290639575
 7: 0.605381294683365 0.718162304090487
 8: 0.452976481105495 0.574026269121667
 9: 0.736819876983848 0.391737610662044
10: 0.518606540417331 0.381805078272308
```

But that's not all! It wrote to your screen because of the – in the *SCATTER tie
above. But that line also told it to create files *tmp1*, *tmp2*, and *tmp4*, as well as to
append to file *tmp3*. (We also wrote to the *NULL filehandle in the loop, though of
course that didn't show up anywhere interesting, unless you're interested in black
holes.)

A Subtle Untying Trap

If you intend to make use of the object returned from tie or tied, and the class
defines a destructor, there is a subtle trap you must guard against. Consider this
(admittedly contrived) example of a class that uses a file to log all values assigned
to a scalar:

```perl
package Remember;

sub TIESCALAR {
    my $class = shift;
    my $filename = shift;
    open(my $handle, ">", $filename)
        or die "Cannot open $filename: $!\n";
    print $handle "The Start\n";
    bless {FH => $handle, VALUE => 0}, $class;
}

sub FETCH {
    my $self = shift;
    return $self->{VALUE};
}

sub STORE {
    my $self = shift;
    my $value = shift;
    my $handle = $self->{FH};
    print $handle "$value\n";
    $self->{VALUE} = $value;
}

sub DESTROY {
    my $self = shift;
    my $handle = $self->{FH};
    print $handle "The End\n";
    close $handle;
}

1;
```

Here is an example that makes use of our Remember class:

```
use strict;
use Remember;

my $fred;
$x = tie $fred, "Remember", "camel.log";
$fred = 1;
$fred = 4;
$fred = 5;
untie $fred;
system "cat camel.log";
```

This is the output when it is executed:

```
The Start
1
4
5
The End
```

So far, so good. Let's add an extra method to the Remember class that allows comments in the file—say, something like this:

```
sub comment {
    my $self = shift;
    my $message = shift;
    print { $self->{FH} } $handle $message, "\n";
}
```

And here is the previous example, modified to use the comment method:

```
use strict;
use Remember;

my ($fred, $x);
$x = tie $fred, "Remember", "camel.log";
$fred = 1;
$fred = 4;
comment $x "changing...";
$fred = 5;
untie $fred;
system "cat camel.log";
```

Now the file will be empty, which probably wasn't what you intended. Here's why. Tying a variable associates it with the object returned by the constructor. This object normally has only one reference: the one hidden behind the tied variable itself. Calling "untie" breaks the association and eliminates that reference. Since there are no remaining references to the object, the DESTROY method is triggered.

However, in the example above we stored a second reference to the object tied to $x. That means that after the untie there will still be a valid reference to the object. DESTROY won't get triggered, and the file won't get flushed and closed. That's why there was no output: the filehandle's buffer was still in memory. It won't hit the disk until the program exits.

To detect this, you could use the **-w** command-line flag, or include the use warnings "untie" pragma in the current lexical scope. Either technique would identify a call to untie while there were still references to the tied object remaining. If so, Perl prints this warning:

```
untie attempted while 1 inner references still exist
```

To get the program to work properly and silence the warning, eliminate any extra references to the tied object *before* calling untie. You can do that explicitly:

```
undef $x;
untie $fred;
```

Often though you can solve the problem simply by making sure your variables go out of scope at the appropriate time.

Tie Modules on CPAN

Before you get all inspired to write your own tie module, you should check to see if someone's already done it. There are lots of tie modules on CPAN, with more every day. (Well, every month, anyway.) Table 14-1 lists some of them.

Table 14-1. Tie Modules on CPAN

Module	Description
GnuPG::Tie::Encrypt	Ties a filehandle interface to encryption with the GNU Privacy Guard.
IO::WrapTie	Wraps tied objects in an IO::Handle interface.
MLDBM	Transparently stores complex data values, not just flat strings, in a DBM file.
Net::NISplusTied	Ties hashes to NIS+ tables.
Tie::Cache::LRU	Implements a least-recently used cache.
Tie::Const	Provides constant scalars and hashes.
Tie::Counter	Enchants a scalar variable to increment upon each access.
Tie::CPHash	Implements a case-preserving but case-insensitive hash.
Tie::DB_FileLock	Provides locking access to Berkeley DB 1.x.
Tie::DBI	Ties hashes to DBI relational databases.
Tie::DB_Lock	Ties hashes to databases using shared and exclusive locks.

Table 14-1. Tie Modules on CPAN (continued)

Module	Description
`Tie::Dict`	Ties a hash to an RPC dict server.
`Tie::Dir`	Ties a hash for reading directories.
`Tie::DirHandle`	Ties directory handles.
`Tie::FileLRUCache`	Implements a lightweight, filesystem-based, persistent LRU cache.
`Tie::FlipFlop`	Implements a tie that alternates between two values.
`Tie::HashDefaults`	Lets a hash have default values.
`Tie::HashHistory`	Tracks history of all changes to a hash.
`Tie::IxHash`	Provides ordered associative arrays for Perl.
`Tie::LDAP`	Implements an interface to an LDAP database.
`Tie::Persistent`	Provides persistent data structures via `tie`.
`Tie::Pick`	Randomly picks (and removes) an element from a set.
`Tie::RDBM`	Ties hashes to relational databases.
`Tie::SecureHash`	Supports namespace-based encapsulation.
`Tie::STDERR`	Sends output of your `STDERR` to another process such as a mailer.
`Tie::Syslog`	Ties a filehandle to automatically syslog its output.
`Tie::TextDir`	Ties a directory of files.
`Tie::TransactHash`	Edits a hash in transactions without changing the order during the transaction.
`Tie::VecArray`	Provides an array interface to a bit vector.
`Tie::Watch`	Places watch points on Perl variables.
`Win32::TieRegistry`	Provides powerful and easy ways to manipulate a Microsoft Windows registry.

III

Perl as Technology

15

Unicode

If you do not yet know what Unicode is, you will soon—even if you skip reading this chapter—because working with Unicode is becoming a necessity. (Some people think of it as a necessary evil, but it's really more of a necessary good. In either case, it's a necessary pain.)

Historically, people made up character sets to reflect what they needed to do in the context of their own culture. Since people of all cultures are naturally lazy, they've tended to include only the symbols they needed, excluding the ones they didn't need. That worked fine as long as we were only communicating with other people of our own culture, but now that we're starting to use the Internet for cross-cultural communication, we're running into problems with the exclusive approach. It's hard enough to figure out how to type accented characters on an American keyboard. How in the world (literally) can one write a multilingual web page?

Unicode is the answer, or at least part of the answer (see also XML). Unicode is an inclusive rather than an exclusive character set. While people can and do haggle over the various details of Unicode (and there are plenty of details to haggle over), the overall intent is to make everyone sufficiently happy* with Unicode so that they'll willingly use Unicode as the international medium of exchange for textual data. Nobody is forcing you to use Unicode, just as nobody is forcing you to read this chapter (we hope). People will always be allowed to use their old exclusive character sets within their own culture. But in that case (as we say), portability suffers.

---

* Or in some cases, insufficiently unhappy.

The Law of Conservation of Suffering says that if we reduce the suffering in one place, suffering must increase elsewhere. In the case of Unicode, we must suffer the migration from byte semantics to character semantics. Since, through an accident of history, Perl was invented by an American, Perl has historically confused the notions of bytes and characters. In migrating to Unicode, Perl must somehow unconfuse them.

Paradoxically, by getting Perl itself to unconfuse bytes and characters, we can allow the Perl programmer to confuse them, relying on Perl to keep them straight, just as we allow programmers to confuse numbers and strings and rely on Perl to convert back and forth as necessary. To the extent possible, Perl's approach to Unicode is the same as its approach to everything else: Just Do The Right Thing. Ideally, we'd like to achieve these four Goals:

Goal #1:

> Old byte-oriented programs should not spontaneously break on the old byte-oriented data they used to work on.

Goal #2:

> Old byte-oriented programs should magically start working on the new character-oriented data when appropriate.

Goal #3:

> Programs should run just as fast in the new character-oriented mode as in the old byte-oriented mode.

Goal #4:

> Perl should remain one language, rather than forking into a byte-oriented Perl and a character-oriented Perl.

Taken together, these Goals are practically impossible to reach. But we've come remarkably close. Or rather, we're still in the process of coming remarkably close, since this is a work in progress. As Unicode continues to evolve, so will Perl. But our overarching plan is to provide a safe migration path that gets us where we want to go with minimal casualties along the way. How we do that is the subject of the next section.

Building Character

In releases of Perl prior to 5.6, all strings were viewed as sequences of bytes.* In versions 5.6 and later, however, a string may contain characters wider than a byte. We now view strings not as sequences of bytes, but as sequences of numbers in the range 0 .. 2**32-1 (or in the case of 64-bit computers, 0 .. 2**64-1). These

---

* You may prefer to call them "octets"; that's okay, but we think the two words are pretty much synonymous these days, so we'll stick with the blue-collar word.

numbers represent abstract characters, and the larger the number, the "wider" the character, in some sense; but unlike many languages, Perl is not tied to any particular width of character representation. Perl uses a variable-length encoding (based on UTF-8), so these abstract character numbers may, or may not, be packed one number per byte. Obviously, character number 18,446,744,073,709,551,615 (that is, "\x{ffff_ffff_ffff_ffff}") is never going to fit into a byte (in fact, it takes 13 bytes), but if all the characters in your string are in the range 0..127 decimal, then they are certainly packed one per byte, since UTF-8 is the same as ASCII in the lowest seven bits.

Perl uses UTF-8 only when it thinks it is beneficial, so if all the characters in your string are in the range 0..255, there's a good chance the characters are all packed in bytes—but in the absence of other knowledge, you can't be sure because internally Perl converts between fixed 8-bit characters and variable-length UTF-8 characters as necessary. The point is, you shouldn't have to worry about it most of the time, because the character semantics are preserved at an abstract level regardless of representation.

In any event, if your string contains any character numbers larger than 255 decimal, the string is certainly stored in UTF-8. More accurately, it is stored in Perl's extended version of UTF-8, which we call *utf8*, in honor of a pragma by that name, but mostly because it's easier to type. (And because "real" UTF-8 is only allowed to contain character numbers blessed by the Unicode Consortium. Perl's utf8 is allowed to contain any character numbers you need to get your job done. Perl doesn't give a rip whether your character numbers are officially correct or just correct.)

We said you shouldn't worry about it most of the time, but people like to worry anyway. Suppose you use a v-string to represent an IPv4 address:

```
$locaddr = v127.0.0.1;     # Certainly stored as bytes.
$oreilly = v204.148.40.9;  # Might be stored as bytes or utf8.
$badaddr = v2004.148.40.9; # Certainly stored as utf8.
```

Everyone can figure out that $badaddr will not work as an IP address. So it's easy to think that if O'Reilly's network address gets forced into a UTF-8 representation, it will no longer work. But the characters in the string are abstract numbers, not bytes. Anything that uses an IPv4 address, such as the gethostbyaddr function, should automatically coerce the abstract character numbers back into a byte representation (and fail on $badaddr).

The interfaces between Perl and the real world have to deal with the details of the representation. To the extent possible, existing interfaces try to do the right thing without your having to tell them what to do. But you do occasionally have to give instructions to some interfaces (such as the open function), and if you write your own interface to the real world, it will need to be either smart enough to figure things out for itself or at least smart enough to follow instructions when you want it to behave differently than it would by default.*

Since Perl worries about maintaining transparent character semantics within the language itself, the only place you need to worry about byte versus character semantics is in your interfaces. By default, all your old Perl interfaces to the outside world are byte-oriented, so they produce and consume byte-oriented data. That is to say, on the abstract level, all your strings are sequences of numbers in the range 0..255, so if nothing in the program forces them into utf8 representations, your old program continues to work on byte-oriented data just as it did before. So put a check mark by Goal #1 above.

If you want your old program to work on new character-oriented data, you must mark your character-oriented interfaces such that Perl knows to expect character-oriented data from those interfaces. Once you've done this, Perl should automatically do any conversions necessary to preserve the character abstraction. The only difference is that you've introduced some strings into your program that are marked as potentially containing characters higher than 255, so if you perform an operation between a byte string and utf8 string, Perl will internally coerce the byte string into a utf8 string before performing the operation. Typically, utf8 strings are coerced back to byte strings only when you send them to a byte interface, at which point, if the string contains characters larger than 255, you have a problem that can be handled in various ways depending on the interface in question. So you can put a check mark by Goal #2.

Sometimes you want to mix code that understands character semantics with code that has to run with byte semantics, such as I/O code that reads or writes fixed-size blocks. In this case, you may put a use bytes declaration around the byte-oriented code to force it to use byte semantics even on strings marked as utf8 strings. You are then responsible for any necessary conversions. But it's a way of enforcing a stricter local reading of Goal #1, at the expense of a looser global reading of Goal #2.

---

* On some systems, there may be ways of switching all your interfaces at once. If the **-C** command-line switch is used, (or the global ${^WIDE_SYSTEM_CALLS} variable is set to 1), all system calls will use the corresponding wide character APIs. (This is currently only implemented on Microsoft Windows.) The current plan of the Linux community is that all interfaces will switch to UTF-8 mode if $ENV{LC_CTYPE} is set to "UTF-8". Other communities may take other approaches. Our mileage may vary.

Goal #3 has largely been achieved, partly by doing lazy conversions between byte and utf8 representations and partly by being sneaky in how we implement potentially slow features of Unicode, such as character property lookups in huge tables.

Goal #4 has been achieved by sacrificing a small amount of interface compatibility in pursuit of the other Goals. By one way of looking at it, we didn't fork into two different Perls; but by another way of looking at it, revision 5.6 of Perl *is* a forked version of Perl with regard to earlier versions, and we don't expect people to switch from earlier versions until they're sure the new version will do what they want. But that's always the case with new versions, so we'll allow ourselves to put a check mark by Goal #4 as well.

Effects of Character Semantics

The upshot of all this is that a typical built-in operator will operate on characters unless it is in the scope of a use bytes pragma. However, even outside the scope of use bytes, if all of the operands of the operator are stored as 8-bit characters (that is, none of the operands are stored in utf8), then character semantics are indistinguishable from byte semantics, and the result of the operator will be stored in 8-bit form internally. This preserves backward compatibility as long as you don't feed your program any characters wider than Latin-1.

The utf8 pragma is primarily a compatibility device that enables recognition of UTF-8 in literals and identifiers encountered by the parser. It may also be used for enabling some of the more experimental Unicode support features. Our long-term goal is to turn the utf8 pragma into a no-op.

The use bytes pragma will never turn into a no-op. Not only is it necessary for byte-oriented code, but it also has the side effect of defining byte-oriented wrappers around certain functions for use outside the scope of use bytes. As of this writing, the only defined wrapper is for length, but there are likely to be more as time goes by. To use such a wrapper, say:

```
use bytes ();   # Load wrappers without importing byte semantics.
...
$charlen =          length("\x{ffff_ffff}");   # Returns 1.
$bytelen = bytes::length("\x{ffff_ffff}");   # Returns 7.
```

Outside the scope of a use bytes declaration, Perl version 5.6 works (or at least, is intended to work) like this:

* Strings and patterns may now contain characters that have an ordinal value larger than 255:

  ```
  use utf8;
  $convergence = "⌫ ☜";
  ```

Presuming you have a Unicode-capable editor to edit your program, such characters will typically occur directly within the literal strings as UTF-8 characters. For now, you have to declare a use utf8 at the top of your program to enable the use of UTF-8 in literals.

If you don't have a Unicode editor, you can always specify a particular character in ASCII with an extension of the \x notation. A character in the Latin-1 range may be written either as \x{ab} or as \xab, but if the number exceeds two hexidecimal digits, you must use braces. Unicode characters are specified by putting the hexadecimal code within braces after the \x. For instance, a Unicode smiley face is \x{263A}. There is no syntactic construct in Perl that assumes Unicode characters are exactly 16 bits, so you may not use \u263A as you can in other languages; \x{263A} is the closest equivalent.

For inserting named characters via \N{*CHARNAME*}, see the use charnames pragma in Chapter 31, *Pragmatic Modules*.

- Identifiers within the Perl script may contain Unicode alphanumeric characters, including ideographs:

```
use utf8;
$人++;        # A child is born.
```

Again, use utf8 is needed (for now) to recognize UTF-8 in your script. You are currently on your own when it comes to using the canonical forms of characters—Perl doesn't (yet) attempt to canonicalize variable names for you. We recommend that you canonicalize your programs to Normalization Form C, since that's what Perl will someday canonicalize to by default. See *www.unicode.org* for the latest technical report on canonicalization.

- Regular expressions match characters instead of bytes. For instance, dot matches a character instead of a byte. If the Unicode Consortium ever gets around to approving the Tengwar script, then (despite the fact that such characters are represented in four bytes of UTF-8), this matches:

```
"\N{TENGWAR LETTER SILME NUQUERNA}" =~ /^.$/
```

The \C pattern is provided to force a match on a single byte ("char" in C, hence \C). Use \C with care, since it can put you out of sync with the character boundaries in your string, and you may get "Malformed UTF-8 character" errors. You may not use \C in square brackets, since it doesn't represent any particular character or set of characters.

- Character classes in regular expressions match characters instead of bytes and match against the character properties specified in the Unicode properties database. So \w can be used to match an ideograph:

  ```
  "人" =~ /\w/
  ```

- Named Unicode properties and block ranges can be used as character classes via the new \p (matches property) and \P (doesn't match property) constructs. For instance, \p{Lu} matches any character with the Unicode uppercase property, while \p{M} matches any mark character. Single-letter properties may omit the brackets, so mark characters can be matched by \pM also. Many predefined character classes are available, such as \p{IsMirrored} and \p{InTibetan}:

  ```
  "\N{greek:Iota}" =~ /\p{Lu}/
  ```

  You may also use \p and \P within square bracket character classes. (In version 5.6.0 of Perl, you need to use utf8 for character properties to work right. This restriction will be lifted in the future.) See Chapter 5, *Pattern Matching*, for details of matching on Unicode properties.

- The special pattern \X matches any extended Unicode sequence (a "combining character sequence" in Standardese), where the first character is a base character and subsequent characters are mark characters that apply to the base character. It is equivalent to (?:\PM\pM*):

  ```
  "o\N{COMBINING TILDE BELOW}" =~ /\X/
  ```

  You may not use \X in square brackets, because it might match multiple characters and it doesn't match any particular character or set of characters.

- The tr/// operator transliterates characters instead of bytes. To turn all characters outside the Latin-1 range into a question mark, you could say:

  ```
  tr/\0-\x{10ffff}/\0-\xff?/;        # utf8 to latin1 char
  ```

- Case translation operators use the Unicode case translation tables when provided character input. Note that uc translates to uppercase, while ucfirst translates to titlecase (for languages that make the distinction). Naturally the corresponding backslash sequences have the same semantics:

  ```
  $x = "\u$word";        # titlecase first letter of $word
  $x = "\U$word";        # uppercase $word
  $x = "\l$word";        # lowercase first letter of $word
  $x = "\L$word";        # lowercase $word
  ```

Be careful, because the Unicode case translation tables don't attempt to provide round-trip mappings in every instance, particularly for languages that use different numbers of characters for titlecase or uppercase than they do for the equivalent lowercase letter. As they say in the standard, while the case properties themselves are normative, the case mappings are only informational.

- Most operators that deal with positions or lengths in the string will automatically switch to using character positions, including chop, substr, pos, index, rindex, sprintf, write, and length. Operators that deliberately don't switch include vec, pack, and unpack. Operators that really don't care include chomp, as well as any other operator that treats a string as a bucket of bits, such as the default sort and the operators dealing with filenames.

```
use bytes;
$bytelen = length("I do 合氣道.");    # 15 bytes
no bytes;
$charlen = length("I do 合氣道.");    # but 9 characters
```

- The pack/unpack letters "c" and "C" do *not* change, since they're often used for byte-oriented formats. (Again, think "char" in the C language.) However, there is a new "U" specifier that will convert between UTF-8 characters and integers:

```
pack("U*", 1, 20, 300, 4000) eq v1.20.300.4000
```

- The chr and ord functions work on characters:

```
chr(1).chr(20).chr(300).chr(4000) eq v1.20.300.4000
```

In other words, chr and ord are like pack("U") and unpack("U"), not like pack("C") and unpack("C"). In fact, the latter two are how you now emulate byte-oriented chr and ord if you're too lazy to use bytes.

- And finally, scalar reverse reverses by character rather than by byte:

```
"☞ ☜" eq reverse "☜ ☞"
```

If you look in directory *PATH_TO_PERLLIB/unicode*, you'll find a number of files that have to do with defining the semantics above. The Unicode properties database from the Unicode Consortium is in a file called *Unicode.300* (for Unicode 3.0). This file has already been processed by *mktables.PL* into lots of little *.pl* files in the same directory (and in subdirectories *Is/*, *In/*, and *To/*), some of which are automatically slurped in by Perl to implement things like \p (see the *Is/* and *In/* directories) and uc (see the *To/* directory). Other files are slurped in by modules like the use charnames pragma (see *Name.pl*). But as of this writing, there are still a number of files that are just sitting there waiting for you to write an access module for them:

ArabLink.pl
ArabLnkGrp.pl
Bidirectional.pl
Block.pl
Category.pl
CombiningClass.pl
Decomposition.pl
JamoShort.pl
Number.pl
To/Digit.pl

A much more readable summary of Unicode, with many hyperlinks, is in *PATH_TO_PERLLIB/unicode/Unicode3.html*.

Note that when the Unicode consortium comes out with a new version, some of these filenames are likely to change, so you'll have to poke around. You can find *PATH_TO_PERLLIB* with the following incantation:

```
% perl -MConfig -le 'print $Config{privlib}'
```

To find out just about everything there is to find out about Unicode, you should check out *The Unicode Standard, Version 3.0* (ISBN 0-201-61633-5).

Caution, 人 Working

As of this writing (that is, with respect to version 5.6.0 of Perl), there are still some caveats on use of Unicode. (Check your online docs for updates.)

- The existing regular expression compiler does not produce polymorphic opcodes. This means that the determination of whether a particular pattern will match Unicode characters is made when the pattern is compiled (based on whether the pattern contains Unicode characters) and not when the matching happens at run time. This needs to be changed to adaptively match Unicode if the string to be matched is Unicode.

- There is currently no easy way to mark data read from a file or other external source as being utf8. This will be a major area of focus in the near future and is probably already fixed as you read this.

- There is no method for automatically coercing input and output to some encoding other than UTF-8. This is planned in the near future, however, so check your online docs.

- Use of locales with utf8 may lead to odd results. Currently, there is some attempt to apply 8-bit locale information to characters in the range 0..255, but this is demonstrably incorrect for locales that use characters above that range (when mapped into Unicode). It will also tend to run slower. Avoidance of locales is strongly encouraged.

Unicode is fun—you just have to define fun correctly.

16

Interprocess Communication

Computer processes have almost as many ways of communicating as people do. The difficulties of interprocess communication should not be underestimated. It doesn't do you any good to listen for verbal cues when your friend is using only body language. Likewise, two processes can communicate only when they agree on the means of communication, and on the conventions built on top of that. As with any kind of communication, the conventions to be agreed upon range from lexical to pragmatic: everything from which lingo you'll use, up to whose turn it is to talk. These conventions are necessary because it's very difficult to communicate bare semantics in the absence of context.

In our lingo, interprocess communication is usually pronounced IPC. The IPC facilities of Perl range from the very simple to the very complex. Which facility you should use depends on the complexity of the information to be communicated. The simplest kind of information is almost no information at all: just the awareness that a particular event has happened at a particular point in time. In Perl, these events are communicated via a signal mechanism modeled on the Unix signal system.

At the other extreme, the socket facilities of Perl allow you to communicate with any other process on the Internet using any mutually supported protocol you like. Naturally, this freedom comes at a price: you have to go through a number of steps to set up the connections and make sure you're talking the same language as the process on the other end. This may in turn require you to adhere to any number of other strange customs, depending on local conventions. To be protocoligorically correct, you might even be required to speak a language like XML, or Java, or Perl. Horrors.

Sandwiched in between are some facilities intended primarily for communicating with processes on the same machine. These include good old-fashioned files, pipes, FIFOs, and the various System V IPC syscalls. Support for these facilities varies across platforms; modern Unix systems (including Apple's Mac OS X) should support all of them, and, except for signals and SysV IPC, most of the rest are supported on any recent Microsoft operating systems, including pipes, forking, file locking, and sockets.*

More information about porting in general can be found in the standard Perl documentation set (in whatever format your system displays it) under *perlport*. Microsoft-specific information can be found under *perlwin32* and *perlfork*, which are installed even on non-Microsoft systems. For textbooks, we suggest the following:

- The *Perl Cookbook*, by Tom Christiansen and Nathan Torkington (O'Reilly and Associates, 1998), chapters 16 through 18.

- *Advanced Programming in the UNIX Environment*, by W. Richard Stevens (Addison-Wesley, 1992).

- *TCP/IP Illustrated*, by W. Richard Stevens, Volumes I–III (Addison-Wesley, 1992–1996).

Signals

Perl uses a simple signal-handling model: the `%SIG` hash contains references (either symbolic or hard) to user-defined signal handlers. Certain events cause the operating system to deliver a signal to the affected process. The handler corresponding to that event is called with one argument containing the name of the signal that triggered it. To send a signal to another process, you use the `kill` function. Think of it as sending a one-bit piece of information to the other process.† If that process has installed a signal handler for that signal, it can execute code when it receives the signal. But there's no way for the sending process to get any sort of return value, other than knowing that the signal was legally sent. The sender receives no feedback saying what, if anything, the receiving process did with the signal.

We've classified this facility as a form of IPC, but in fact, signals can come from various sources, not just other processes. A signal might also come from your own process, or it might be generated when the user at the keyboard types a particular sequence like Control-C or Control-Z, or it might be manufactured by the kernel when a special event transpires, such as when a child process exits, or when your

---

* Well, except for `AF_UNIX` sockets.

† Actually, it's more like five or six bits, depending on how many signals your OS defines and on whether the other process makes use of the fact that you *didn't* send a different signal.

process runs out of stack space or hits a file size or memory limit. But your own process can't easily distinguish among these cases. A signal is like a package that arrives mysteriously on your doorstep with no return address. You'd best open it carefully.

Since entries in the %SIG array can be hard references, it's common practice to use anonymous functions for simple signal handlers:

```
$SIG{INT}  = sub { die "\nOutta here!\n" };
$SIG{ALRM} = sub { die "Your alarm clock went off" };
```

Or you could create a named function and assign its name or reference to the appropriate slot in the hash. For example, to intercept interrupt and quit signals (often bound to Control-C and Control-\ on your keyboard), set up a handler like this:

```
sub catch_zap {
    my $signame = shift;
    our $shucks++;
    die "Somebody sent me a SIG$signame!";
}
$shucks = 0;
$SIG{INT}  = 'catch_zap';   # always means &main::catch_zap
$SIG{INT}  = \&catch_zap;   # best strategy
$SIG{QUIT} = \&catch_zap;   # catch another, too
```

Notice how all we do in the signal handler is set a global variable and then raise an exception with die. Whenever possible, try to avoid anything more complicated than that, because on most systems the C library is not re-entrant. Signals are delivered asynchronously,* so calling any print functions (or even anything that needs to *malloc*(3) more memory) could in theory trigger a memory fault and subsequent core dump if you were already in a related C library routine when the signal was delivered. (Even the die routine is a bit unsafe unless the process is executing within an eval, which suppresses the I/O from die, which keeps it from calling the C library. Probably.)

An even easier way to trap signals is to use the sigtrap pragma to install simple, default signal handlers:

```
use sigtrap qw(die INT QUIT);
use sigtrap qw(die untrapped normal-signals
    stack-trace any error-signals);
```

The pragma is useful when you don't want to bother writing your own handler, but you still want to catch dangerous signals and perform an orderly shutdown. By default, some of these signals are so fatal to your process that your program

---

* Synchronizing signal delivery with Perl-level opcodes is scheduled for a future release of Perl, which should solve the matter of signals and core dumps.

will just stop in its tracks when it receives one. Unfortunately, that means that any END functions for at-exit handling and DESTROY methods for object finalization are not called. But they *are* called on ordinary Perl exceptions (such as when you call die), so you can use this pragma to painlessly convert the signals into exceptions. Even though you aren't dealing with the signals yourself, your program still behaves correctly. See the description of use sigtrap in Chapter 31, *Pragmatic Modules*, for many more features of this pragma.

You may also set the %SIG handler to either of the strings "IGNORE" or "DEFAULT", in which case Perl will try to discard the signal or allow the default action for that signal to occur (though some signals can be neither trapped nor ignored, such as the KILL and STOP signals; see *signal*(3), if you have it, for a list of signals available on your system and their default behaviors).

The operating system thinks of signals as numbers rather than names, but Perl, like most people, prefers symbolic names to magic numbers. To find the names of the signals, list out the keys of the %SIG hash, or use the *kill -l* command if you have one on your system. You can also use Perl's standard Config module to determine your operating system's mapping between signal names and signal numbers. See *Config*(3) for an example of this.

Because %SIG is a global hash, assignments to it affect your entire program. It's often more considerate to the rest of your program to confine your signal catching to a restricted scope. Do this with a local signal handler assignment, which goes out of effect once the enclosing block is exited. (But remember that local values are visible in functions called from within that block.)

```
    {
        local $SIG{INT} = 'IGNORE';
        ...        # Do whatever you want here, ignoring all SIGINTs.
        fn();      # SIGINTs ignored inside fn() too!
        ...        # And here.
    }              # Block exit restores previous $SIG{INT} value.

    fn();          # SIGINTs not ignored inside fn() (presumably).
```

Signaling Process Groups

Processes (under Unix, at least) are organized into process groups, generally corresponding to an entire job. For example, when you fire off a single shell command that consists of a series of filter commands that pipe data from one to the other, those processes (and their child processes) all belong to the same process group. That process group has a number corresponding to the process number of the process group leader. If you send a signal to a positive process number, it just sends the signal to the process, but if you send a signal to a negative number, it sends that signal to every process whose process group number is the corresponding positive number, that is, the process number of the process group leader. (Conveniently for the process group leader, the process group ID is just $$.)

Suppose your program wants to send a hang-up signal to all child processes it started directly, plus any grandchildren started by those children, plus any great-grandchildren started by those grandchildren, and so on. To do this, your program first calls setpgrp(0,0) to become the leader of a new process group, and any processes it creates will be part of the new group. It doesn't matter whether these processes were started manually via fork, automaticaly via piped opens, or as backgrounded jobs with system("cmd &"). Even if those processes had children of their own, sending a hang-up signal to your entire process group will find them all (except for processes that have set their own process group or changed their UID to give themselves diplomatic immunity to your signals).

```
{
    local $SIG{HUP} = 'IGNORE';    # exempt myself
    kill(HUP, -$$);                # signal my own process group
}
```

Another interesting signal is signal number 0. This doesn't actually affect the target process, but instead checks that it's alive and hasn't changed its UID. That is, it checks whether it's legal to send a signal, without actually sending one.

```
unless (kill 0 => $kid_pid) {
    warn "something wicked happened to $kid_pid";
}
```

Signal number 0 is the only signal that works the same under Microsoft ports of Perl as it does in Unix. On Microsoft systems, kill does not actually deliver a signal. Instead, it forces the target process to exit with the status indicated by the signal number. This may be fixed someday. The magic 0 signal, however, still behaves in the standard, nondestructive fashion.

Reaping Zombies

When a process exits, its parent is sent a CHLD signal by the kernel and the process becomes a zombie* until the parent calls wait or waitpid. If you start another process in Perl using anything except fork, Perl takes care of reaping your zombied children, but if you use a raw fork, you're expected to clean up after yourself. On many but not all kernels, a simple hack for autoreaping zombies is to set $SIG{CHLD} to 'IGNORE'. A more flexible (but tedious) approach is to reap them

---

* Yes, that really is the technical term.

yourself. Because more than one child may have died before you get around to
dealing with them, you must gather your zombies in a loop until there aren't any
more:

```
use POSIX ":sys_wait_h";
sub REAPER { 1 until waitpid(-1, WNOHANG) == -1) }
```

To run this code as needed, you can either set a CHLD signal handler for it:

```
$SIG{CHLD} = \&REAPER;
```

or, if you're running in a loop, just arrange to call the reaper every so often. This is
the best approach because it isn't subject to the occasional core dump that signals
can sometimes trigger in the C library. However, it's expensive if called in a tight
loop, so a reasonable compromise is to use a hybrid strategy where you minimize
the risk within the handler by doing as little as possible and waiting until outside
to reap zombies:

```
our $zombies = 0;
$SIG{CHLD} = sub { $zombies++ };
sub reaper {
    my $zombie;
    our %Kid_Status;  # store each exit status
    $zombies = 0;
    while (($zombie = waitpid(-1, WNOHANG)) != -1) {
        $Kid_Status{$zombie} = $?;
    }
}
while (1) {
    reaper() if $zombies;
    ...
}
```

This code assumes your kernel supports reliable signals. Old SysV traditionally
didn't, which made it impossible to write correct signal handlers there. Ever since
way back in the 5.003 release, Perl has used the *sigaction*(2) syscall where available, which is a lot more dependable. This means that unless you're running on an
ancient operating system or with an ancient Perl, you won't have to reinstall your
handlers and risk missing signals. Fortunately, all BSD-flavored systems (including
Linux, Solaris, and Mac OS X) plus all POSIX-compliant systems provide reliable
signals, so the old broken SysV behavior is more a matter of historical note than of
current concern.

With these newer kernels, many other things will work better, too. For example,
"slow" syscalls (those that can block, like read, wait, and accept) will restart automatically if interrupted by a signal. In the bad old days, user code had to remember to check explicitly whether each slow syscall failed with $! ($ERRNO) set to

EINTR and, if so, restart. This wouldn't happen just from INT signals; even innocuous signals like TSTP (from a Control-Z) or CONT (from foregrounding the job) would abort the syscall. Perl now restarts the syscall for you automatically if the operating system allows it to. This is generally construed to be a feature.

You can check whether you have the more rigorous POSIX-style signal behavior by loading the Config module and checking whether $Config{d_sigaction} has a true value. To find out whether slow syscalls are restartable, check your system documentation on *sigaction*(2) or *sigvec*(3), or scrounge around your C *sys/signal.h* file for SV_INTERRUPT or SA_RESTART. If one or both symbols are found, you probably have restartable syscalls.

Timing Out Slow Operations

A common use for signals is to impose time limits on long-running operations. If you're on a Unix system (or any other POSIX-conforming system that supports the ALRM signal), you can ask the kernel to send your process an ALRM at some point in the future:

```
use Fcntl ':flock';
eval {
    local $SIG{ALRM} = sub { die "alarm clock restart" };
    alarm 10;                  # schedule alarm in 10 seconds
    eval {
        flock(FH, LOCK_EX)  # a blocking, exclusive lock
            or die "can't flock: $!";
    };
    alarm 0;                   # cancel the alarm
};
alarm 0;                   # race condition protection
die if $@ && $@ !~ /alarm clock restart/; # reraise
```

If the alarm hits while you're waiting for the lock, and you simply catch the signal and return, you'll go right back into the flock because Perl automatically restarts syscalls where it can. The only way out is to raise an exception through die and then let eval catch it. (This works because the exception winds up calling the C library's *longjmp*(3) function, which is what really gets you out of the restarting syscall.)

The nested exception trap is included because calling flock would raise an exception if flock is not implemented on your platform, and you need to make sure to clear the alarm anyway. The second alarm 0 is provided in case the signal comes in after running the flock but before getting to the first alarm 0. Without the second alarm, you would risk a tiny race condition—but size doesn't matter in race conditions; they either exist or they don't. And we prefer that they don't.

Blocking Signals

Now and then, you'd like to delay receipt of a signal during some critical section of code. You don't want to blindly ignore the signal, but what you're doing is too important to interrupt. Perl's %SIG hash doesn't implement signal blocking, but the POSIX module does, through its interface to the *sigprocmask*(2) syscall:

```
use POSIX qw(:signal_h);
$sigset   = POSIX::SigSet->new;
$blockset = POSIX::SigSet->new(SIGINT, SIGQUIT, SIGCHLD);
sigprocmask(SIG_BLOCK, $blockset, $sigset)
    or die "Could not block INT,QUIT,CHLD signals: $!\n";
```

Once the three signals are all blocked, you can do whatever you want without fear of being bothered. When you're done with your critical section, unblock the signals by restoring the old signal mask:

```
sigprocmask(SIG_SETMASK, $sigset)
    or die "Could not restore INT,QUIT,CHLD signals: $!\n";
```

If any of the three signals came in while blocked, they are delivered immediately. If two or more different signals are pending, the order of delivery is not defined. Additionally, no distinction is made between having received a particular signal once while blocked and having received it many times.* For example, if nine child processes exited while you were blocking CHLD signals, your handler (if you had one) would still be called only once after you unblocked. That's why, when you reap zombies, you should always loop until they're all gone.

Files

Perhaps you've never thought about files as an IPC mechanism before, but they shoulder the lion's share of interprocess communication—far more than all other means combined. When one process deposits its precious data in a file and another process later retrieves that data, those processes have communicated. Files offer something unique among all forms of IPC covered here: like a papyrus scroll unearthed after millennia buried in the desert, a file can be unearthed and read long after its writer's personal end.† Factoring in persistence with comparative ease of use, it's no wonder that files remain popular.

Using files to transmit information from the dead past to some unknown future poses few surprises. You write the file to some permanent medium like a disk, and that's about it. (You might tell a web server where to find it, if it contains HTML.)

---

* Traditionally, that is. Countable signals may be implemented on some real-time systems according to the latest specs, but we haven't seen these yet.

† Presuming that a process can have a personal end.

The interesting challenge is when all parties are still alive and trying to communicate with one another. Without some agreement about whose turn it is to have their say, reliable communication is impossible; agreement may be achieved through file locking, which is covered in the next section. In the section after that, we discuss the special relationship that exists between a parent process and its children, which allows related parties to exchange information through inherited access to the same files.

Files certainly have their limitations when it comes to things like remote access, synchronization, reliability, and session management. Other sections of the chapter cover various IPC mechanisms invented to address such limitations.

File Locking

In a multitasking environment, you need to be careful not to collide with other processes that are trying to use the same file you're using. As long as all processes are just reading, there's no problem, but as soon as even one process needs to write to the file, complete chaos ensues unless some sort of locking mechanism acts as traffic cop.

Never use the mere existence of a filename (that is, -e $file) as a locking indication, because a race condition exists between the test for existence of that filename and whatever you plan to do with it (like create it, open it, or unlink it). See the section "Handling Race Conditions" in Chapter 23, *Security*, for more about this.

Perl's portable locking interface is the flock(*HANDLE,FLAGS*) function, described in Chapter 29, *Functions*. Perl maximizes portability by using only the simplest and most widespread locking features found on the broadest range of platforms. These semantics are simple enough that they can be emulated on most systems, including those that don't support the traditional syscall of that name, such as System V or Windows NT. (If you're running a Microsoft system earlier than NT, though, you're probably out of luck, as you would be if you're running a system from Apple before Mac OS X.)

Locks come in two varieties: shared (the LOCK_SH flag) and exclusive (the LOCK_EX flag). Despite the suggestive sound of "exclusive", processes aren't required to obey locks on files. That is, flock only implements *advisory locking*, which means that locking a file does not stop another process from reading or even writing the file. Requesting an exclusive lock is just a way for a process to let the operating system suspend it until all current lockers, whether shared or exclusive, are finished with it. Similarly, when a process asks for a shared lock, it is just suspending itself until there is no exclusive locker. Only when all parties use the file-locking mechanism can a contended file be accessed safely.

Therefore, `flock` is a blocking operation by default. That is, if you can't get the lock you want immediately, the operating system suspends your process till you can. Here's how to get a blocking, shared lock, typically used for reading a file:

```
use Fcntl qw(:DEFAULT :flock);
open(FH, "< filename")  or die "can't open filename: $!";
flock(FH, LOCK_SH)      or die "can't lock filename: $!";
# now read from FH
```

You can try to acquire a lock in a nonblocking fashion by including the LOCK_NB flag in the `flock` request. If you can't be given the lock right away, the function fails and immediately returns false. Here's an example:

```
flock(FH, LOCK_SH | LOCK_NB)
    or die "can't lock filename: $!";
```

You may wish to do something besides raising an exception as we did here, but you certainly don't dare do any I/O on the file. If you are refused a lock, you shouldn't access the file until you can get the lock. Who knows what scrambled state you might find the file in? The main purpose of the nonblocking mode is to let you go off and do something else while you wait. But it can also be useful for producing friendlier interactions by warning users that it might take a while to get the lock, so they don't feel abandoned:

```
use Fcntl qw(:DEFAULT :flock);
open(FH, "< filename")  or die "can't open filename: $!";
unless (flock(FH, LOCK_SH | LOCK_NB)) {
    local $| = 1;
    print "Waiting for lock on filename...";
    flock(FH, LOCK_SH)  or die "can't lock filename: $!";
    print "got it.\n"
}
# now read from FH
```

Some people will be tempted to put that nonblocking lock into a loop. The main problem with nonblocking mode is that, by the time you get back to checking again, someone else may have grabbed the lock because you abandoned your place in line. Sometimes you just have to get in line and wait. If you're lucky there will be some magazines to read.

Locks are on filehandles, not on filenames.* When you close the file, the lock dissolves automatically, whether you close the file explicitly by calling `close` or implicitly by reopening the handle or by exiting your process.

---

* Actually, locks aren't on filehandles—they're on the file descriptors associated with the filehandles since the operating system doesn't know about filehandles. That means that all our `die` messages about failing to get a lock on filenames are technically inaccurate. But error messages of the form "I can't get a lock on the file represented by the file descriptor associated with the filehandle originally opened to the path *filename*, although by now *filename* may represent a different file entirely than our handle does" would just confuse the user (not to mention the reader).

To get an exclusive lock, typically used for writing, you have to be more careful. You cannot use a regular open for this; if you use an open mode of <, it will fail on files that don't exist yet, and if you use >, it will clobber any files that do. Instead, use sysopen on the file so it can be locked before getting overwritten. Once you've safely opened the file for writing but haven't yet touched it, successfully acquire the exclusive lock and only *then* truncate the file. Now you may overwrite it with the new data.

```
use Fcntl qw(:DEFAULT :flock);
sysopen(FH, "filename", O_WRONLY | O_CREAT)
    or die "can't open filename: $!";
flock(FH, LOCK_EX)
    or die "can't lock filename: $!";
truncate(FH, 0)
    or die "can't truncate filename: $!";
# now write to FH
```

If you want to modify the contents of a file in place, use sysopen again. This time you ask for both read and write access, creating the file if needed. Once the file is opened, but before you've done any reading or writing, get the exclusive lock and keep it around your entire transaction. It's often best to release the lock by closing the file because that guarantees all buffers are written before the lock is released.

An update involves reading in old values and writing out new ones. You must do both operations under a single exclusive lock, lest another process read the (imminently incorrect) value after (or even before) you do, but before you write. (We'll revisit this situation when we cover shared memory later in this chapter.)

```
use Fcntl qw(:DEFAULT :flock);

sysopen(FH, "counterfile", O_RDWR | O_CREAT)
    or die "can't open counterfile: $!";
flock(FH, LOCK_EX)
    or die "can't write-lock counterfile: $!";
$counter = <FH> || 0;  # first time would be undef
seek(FH, 0, 0)
    or die "can't rewind counterfile : $!";
print FH $counter+1, "\n"
    or die "can't write counterfile: $!";

# next line technically superfluous in this program, but
# a good idea in the general case
truncate(FH, tell(FH))
    or die "can't truncate counterfile: $!";
close(FH)
    or die "can't close counterfile: $!";
```

You can't lock a file you haven't opened yet, and you can't have a single lock that applies to more than one file. What you can do, though, is use a completely separate file to act as a sort of semaphore, like a traffic light, to provide controlled access to something else through regular shared and exclusive locks on the semaphore file. This approach has several advantages. You can have one lockfile that controls access to multiple files, avoiding the kind of deadlock that occurs when one process tries to lock those files in one order while another process is trying to lock them in a different order. You can use a semaphore file to lock an entire directory of files. You can even control access to something that's not even in the filesystem, like a shared memory object or the socket upon which several preforked servers would like to call accept.

If you have a DBM file that doesn't provide its own explicit locking mechanism, an auxiliary lockfile is the best way to control concurrent access by multiple agents. Otherwise, your DBM library's internal caching can get out of sync with the file on disk. Before calling dbmopen or tie, open and lock the semaphore file. If you open the database with O_RDONLY, you'll want to use LOCK_SH for the lock. Otherwise, use LOCK_EX for exclusive access to updating the database. (Again, this only works if all participants agree to pay attention to the semaphore.)

```perl
use Fcntl qw(:DEFAULT :flock);
use DB_File;  # demo purposes only; any db is fine

$DBNAME  = "/path/to/database";
$LCK     = $DBNAME . ".lockfile";

# use O_RDWR if you expect to put data in the lockfile
sysopen(DBLOCK, $LCK, O_RDONLY | O_CREAT)
    or die "can't open $LCK: $!";

# must get lock before opening database
flock(DBLOCK, LOCK_SH)
    or die "can't LOCK_SH $LCK: $!";

tie(%hash, "DB_File", $DBNAME, O_RDWR | O_CREAT)
    or die "can't tie $DBNAME: $!";
```

Now you can safely do whatever you'd like with the tied %hash. When you're done with your database, make sure you explicitly release those resources, and in the opposite order that you acquired them:

```perl
untie %hash;    # must close database before lockfile
close DBLOCK;   # safe to let go of lock now
```

If you have the GNU DBM library installed, you can use the standard GDBM_File module's implicit locking. Unless the initial tie contains the GDBM_NOLOCK flag, the library makes sure that only one writer may open a GDBM file at a time, and that readers and writers do not have the database open at the same time.

Passing Filehandles

Whenever you create a child process using fork, that new process inherits all its parent's open filehandles. Using filehandles for interprocess communication is easiest to illustrate by using plain files first. Understanding how this works is essential for mastering the fancier mechanisms of pipes and sockets described later in this chapter.

The simplest example opens a file and starts up a child process. The child then uses the filehandle already opened for it:

```
open(INPUT, "< /etc/motd")       or die "/etc/motd: $!";
if ($pid = fork) { waitpid($pid,0) }
else {
    defined($pid)            or die "fork: $!";
    while (<INPUT>) { print "$.: $_" }
    exit;  # don't let child fall back into main code
}
# INPUT handle now at EOF in parent
```

Once access to a file has been granted by open, it stays granted until the filehandle is closed; changes to the file's permissions or to the owner's access privileges have no effect on accessibility. Even if the process later alters its user or group IDs, or the file has its ownership changed to a different user or group, that doesn't affect filehandles that are already open. Programs running under increased permissions (like set-id programs or systems daemons) often open a file under their increased rights and then hand off the filehandle to a child process that could not have opened the file on its own.

Although this feature is of great convenience when used intentionally, it can also create security issues if filehandles accidentally leak from one program to the next. To avoid granting implicit access to all possible filehandles, Perl automatically closes any filehandles it has opened (including pipes and sockets) whenever you explicitly exec a new program or implicitly execute one through a call to a piped open, system, or qx// (backticks). The system filehandles STDIN, STDOUT, and STDERR are exempt from this because their main purpose is to provide communications linkage between programs. So one way of passing a filehandle to a new program is to copy the filehandle to one of the standard filehandles:

```
open(INPUT, "< /etc/motd")       or die "/etc/motd: $!";
if ($pid = fork) { wait }
else {
    defined($pid)            or die "fork: $!";
    open(STDIN, "<&INPUT")   or die "dup: $!";
    exec("cat", "-n")        or die "exec cat: $!";
}
```

If you really want the new program to gain access to a filehandle other than these three, you can, but you have to do one of two things. When Perl opens a new file (or pipe or socket), it checks the current setting of the $^F ($SYSTEM_FD_MAX) variable. If the numeric file descriptor used by that new filehandle is greater than $^F, the descriptor is marked as one to close. Otherwise, Perl leaves it alone, and new programs you exec will inherit access.

It's not always easy to predict what file descriptor your newly opened filehandle will have, but you can temporarily set your maximum system file descriptor to some outrageously high number for the duration of the open:

```
# open file and mark INPUT to be left open across execs
{
    local $^F = 10_000;
    open(INPUT, "< /etc/motd")    or die "/etc/motd: $!";
} # old value of $^F restored on scope exit
```

Now all you have to do is get the new program to pay attention to the descriptor number of the filehandle you just opened. The cleanest solution (on systems that support this) is to pass a special filename that equates to a file descriptor. If your system has a directory called */dev/fd* or */proc/$$/fd* containing files numbered from 0 through the maximum number of supported descriptors, you can probably use this strategy. (Many Linux operating systems have both, but only the */proc* version tends to be correctly populated. BSD and Solaris prefer */dev/fd*. You'll have to poke around at your system to see which looks better for you.) First, open and mark your filehandle as one to be left open across execs as shown in the previous code, then fork like this:

```
if ($pid = fork) { wait }
else {
    defined($pid)                 or die "fork: $!";
    $fdfile = "/dev/fd/" . fileno(INPUT);
    exec("cat", "-n", $fdfile)    or die "exec cat: $!";
}
```

If your system supports the fcntl syscall, you may diddle the filehandle's close-on-exec flag manually. This is convenient for those times when you didn't realize back when you created the filehandle that you would want to share it with your children.

```
use Fcntl qw/F_SETFD/;

fcntl(INPUT, F_SETFD, 0)
    or die "Can't clear close-on-exec flag on INPUT: $!\n";
```

You can also force a filehandle to close:

```
fcntl(INPUT, F_SETFD, 1)
    or die "Can't set close-on-exec flag on INPUT: $!\n";
```

You can also query the current status:

```
use Fcntl qw/F_SETFD F_GETFD/;

printf("INPUT will be %s across execs\n",
    fcntl(INPUT, F_GETFD, 1) ? "closed" : "left open");
```

If your system doesn't support file descriptors named in the filesystem, and you want to pass a filehandle other than STDIN, STDOUT, or STDERR, you can still do so, but you'll have to make special arrangements with that program. Common strategies for this are to pass the descriptor number through an environment variable or a command-line option.

If the executed program is in Perl, you can use open to convert a file descriptor into a filehandle. Instead of specifying a filename, use "&=" followed by the descriptor number.

```
if (defined($ENV{input_fdno}) && $ENV{input_fdno}) =~ /^\d$/) {
    open(INPUT, "<&=$ENV{input_fdno}")
        or die "can't fdopen $ENV{input_fdno} for input: $!";
}
```

It gets even easier than that if you're going to be running a Perl subroutine or program that expects a filename argument. You can use the descriptor-opening feature of Perl's regular open function (but not sysopen or three-argument open) to make this happen automatically. Imagine you have a simple Perl program like this:

```
#!/usr/bin/perl -p
# nl - number input lines
printf "%6d  ", $.;
```

Presuming you've arranged for the INPUT handle to stay open across execs, you can call that program this way:

```
$fdspec = '<&=' . fileno(INPUT);
system("nl", $fdspec);
```

or to catch the output:

```
@lines = `nl '$fdspec'`;  # single quotes protect spec from shell
```

Whether or not you exec another program, if you use file descriptors inherited across fork, there's one small gotcha. Unlike variables copied across a fork, which actually get duplicate but independent copies, file descriptors really *are* the same in both processes. If one process reads data from the handle, the seek pointer (file position) advances in the other process, too, and that data is no longer available to either process. If they take turns reading, they'll leapfrog over each other in the file. This makes intuitive sense for handles attached to serial devices, pipes, or sockets, since those tend to be read-only devices with ephemeral data. But this behavior may surprise you with disk files. If this is a problem, reopen any files that need separate tracking after the fork.

The fork operator is a concept derived from Unix, which means it might not be implemented correctly on all non-Unix/non-POSIX platforms. Notably, fork works on Microsoft systems only if you're running Perl 5.6 (or better) on Windows 98 (or later). Although fork is implemented via multiple concurrent execution streams within the same program on these systems, these aren't the sort of threads where all data is shared by default; here, only file descriptors are. See also Chapter 17, *Threads*.

Pipes

A *pipe* is a unidirectional I/O channel that can transfer a stream of bytes from one process to another. Pipes come in both named and nameless varieties. You may be more familiar with nameless pipes, so we'll talk about those first.

Anonymous Pipes

Perl's open function opens a pipe instead of a file when you append or prepend a pipe symbol to the second argument to open. This turns the rest of the arguments into a command, which will be interpreted as a process (or set of processes) that you want to pipe a stream of data either into or out of. Here's how to start up a child process that you intend to write to:

```
open SPOOLER, "| cat -v | lpr -h 2>/dev/null"
    or die "can't fork: $!";
local $SIG{PIPE} = sub { die "spooler pipe broke" };
print SPOOLER "stuff\n";
close SPOOLER or die "bad spool: $! $?";
```

This example actually starts up two processes, the first of which (running *cat*) we print to directly. The second process (running *lpr*) then receives the output of the first process. In shell programming, this is often called a *pipeline*. A pipeline can have as many processes in a row as you like, as long as the ones in the middle know how to behave like *filters*; that is, they read standard input and write standard output.

Perl uses your default system shell (*/bin/sh* on Unix) whenever a pipe command contains special characters that the shell cares about. If you're only starting one command, and you don't need—or don't want—to use the shell, you can use the multi-argument form of a piped open instead:

```
open SPOOLER, "|-", "lpr", "-h"    # requires 5.6.1
    or die "can't run lpr: $!";
```

If you reopen your program's standard output as a pipe to another program, anything you subsequently print to STDOUT will be standard input for the new program. So to page your program's output,* you'd use:

```
if (-t STDOUT) {             # only if stdout is a terminal
    my $pager = $ENV{PAGER} || 'more';
    open(STDOUT, "| $pager")    or die "can't fork a pager: $!";
}
END {
    close(STDOUT)               or die "can't close STDOUT: $!"
}
```

When you're writing to a filehandle connected to a pipe, always explicitly close that handle when you're done with it. That way your main program doesn't exit before its offspring.

Here's how to start up a child process that you intend to read from:

```
open STATUS, "netstat -an 2>/dev/null |"
    or die "can't fork: $!";
while (<STATUS>) {
    next if /^(tcp|udp)/;
    print;
}
close STATUS or die "bad netstat: $! $?";
```

You can open a multistage pipeline for input just as you can for output. And as before, you can avoid the shell by using an alternate form of open:

```
open STATUS, "-|", "netstat", "-an"    # requires 5.6.1
    or die "can't run netstat: $!";
```

But then you don't get I/O redirection, wildcard expansion, or multistage pipes, since Perl relies on your shell to do those.

You might have noticed that you can use backticks to accomplish the same effect as opening a pipe for reading:

```
print grep { !/^(tcp|udp)/ } `netstat -an 2>&1`;
die "bad netstat" if $?;
```

---

* That is, let them view it one screenful at a time, not set off random bird calls.

While backticks are extremely handy, they have to read the whole thing into memory at once, so it's often more efficient to open your own piped filehandle and process the file one line or record at a time. This gives you finer control over the whole operation, letting you kill off the child process early if you like. You can also be more efficient by processing the input as it's coming in, since computers can interleave various operations when two or more processes are running at the same time. (Even on a single-CPU machine, input and output operations can happen while the CPU is doing something else.)

Because you're running two or more processes concurrently, disaster can strike the child process any time between the open and the close. This means that the parent must check the return values of both open and close. Checking the open isn't good enough, since that will only tell you whether the fork was successful, and possibly whether the subsequent command was successfully launched. (It can tell you this only in recent versions of Perl, and only if the command is executed directly by the forked child, not via the shell.) Any disaster that happens after that is reported from the child to the parent as a nonzero exit status. When the close function sees that, it knows to return a false value, indicating that the actual status value should be read from the $? ($CHILD_ERROR) variable. So checking the return value of close is just as important as checking open. If you're writing to a pipe, you should also be prepared to handle the PIPE signal, which is sent to you if the process on the other end dies before you're done sending to it.

Talking to Yourself

Another approach to IPC is to make your program talk to itself, in a manner of speaking. Actually, your process talks over pipes to a forked copy of itself. It works much like the piped open we talked about in the last section, except that the child process continues executing your script instead of some other command.

To represent this to the open function, you use a pseudocommand consisting of a minus. So the second argument to open looks like either "-|" or "|-", depending on whether you want to pipe from yourself or to yourself. As with an ordinary fork command, the open function returns the child's process ID in the parent process but 0 in the child process. Another asymmetry is that the filehandle named by the open is used only in the parent process. The child's end of the pipe is hooked to either STDIN or STDOUT as appropriate. That is, if you open a pipe *to* minus with |-, you can write to the filehandle you opened, and your kid will find this in STDIN:

```
if (open(TO, "|-")) {
    print TO $fromparent;
}
else {
    $tochild = <STDIN>;
```

```
        exit;
    }
```

If you open a pipe *from* minus with -|, you can read from the filehandle you
opened, which will return whatever your kid writes to STDOUT:

```
if (open(FROM, "-|")) {
    $toparent = <FROM>;
}
else {
    print STDOUT $fromchild;
    exit;
}
```

One common application of this construct is to bypass the shell when you want to
open a pipe from a command. You might want to do this because you don't want
the shell to interpret any possible metacharacters in the filenames you're trying to
pass to the command. If you're running release 5.6.1 or greater of Perl, you can
use the multi-argument form of open to get the same result.

Another use of a forking open is to safely open a file or command even while
you're running under an assumed UID or GID. The child you fork drops any special access rights, then safely opens the file or command and acts as an intermediary, passing data between its more powerful parent and the file or command it
opened. Examples can be found in the section "Accessing Commands and Files
Under Reduced Privileges", in Chapter 23.

One creative use of a forking open is to filter your own output. Some algorithms
are much easier to implement in two separate passes than they are in just one
pass. Here's a simple example in which we emulate the Unix *tee*(1) program by
sending our normal output down a pipe. The agent on the other end of the pipe
(one of our own subroutines) distributes our output to all the files specified:

```
tee("/tmp/foo", "/tmp/bar", "/tmp/glarch");

while (<>) {
    print "$ARGV at line $. => $_";
}
close(STDOUT)  or die "can't close STDOUT: $!";

sub tee {
    my @output = @_;
    my @handles = ();
    for my $path (@output) {
        my $fh;  # open will fill this in
        unless (open ($fh, ">", $path)) {
            warn "cannot write to $path: $!";
            next;
        }
        push @handles, $fh;
    }
```

```
        # reopen STDOUT in parent and return
        return if my $pid = open(STDOUT, "|-");
        die "cannot fork: $!" unless defined $pid;

        # process STDIN in child
        while (<STDIN>) {
            for my $fh (@handles) {
                print $fh $_ or die "tee output failed: $!";
            }
        }
        for my $fh (@handles) {
            close($fh) or die "tee closing failed: $!";
        }
        exit;   # don't let the child return to main!
    }
```

This technique can be applied repeatedly to push as many filters on your output stream as you wish. Just keep calling functions that fork-open STDOUT, and have the child read from its parent (which it sees as STDIN) and pass the massaged output along to the next function in the stream.

Another interesting application of talking to yourself with fork-open is to capture the output from an ill-mannered function that always splats its results to STDOUT. Imagine if Perl only had `printf` and no `sprintf`. What you'd need would be something that worked like backticks, but with Perl functions instead of external commands:

```
    badfunc("arg");                            # drat, escaped!
    $string = forksub(\&badfunc, "arg");       # caught it as string
    @lines  = forksub(\&badfunc, "arg");       # as separate lines

    sub forksub {
        my $kidpid = open my $self, "-|";
        defined $kidpid           or die "cannot fork: $!";
        shift->(@_), exit         unless $kidpid;
        local $/                  unless wantarray;
        return <$self>;           # closes on scope exit
    }
```

We're not claiming this is efficient; a tied filehandle would probably be a good bit faster. But it's a lot easier to code up if you're in more of a hurry than your computer is.

Bidirectional Communication

Although using `open` to connect to another command over a pipe works reasonably well for unidirectional communication, what about bidirectional communication? The obvious approach doesn't actually work:

```
open(PROG_TO_READ_AND_WRITE, "| some program |")   # WRONG!
```

and if you forget to enable warnings, then you'll miss out entirely on the diagnostic message:

```
Can't do bidirectional pipe at myprog line 3.
```

The open function doesn't allow this because it's rather prone to deadlock unless you're quite careful. But if you're determined, you can use the standard IPC::Open2 library module to attach two pipes to a subprocess's STDIN and STDOUT. There's also an IPC::Open3 module for tridirectional I/O (allowing you to also catch your child's STDERR), but this requires either an awkward select loop or the somewhat more convenient IO::Select module. But then you'll have to avoid Perl's buffered input operations like <> (readline).

Here's an example using open2:

```
use IPC::Open2;
local (*Reader, *Writer);
$pid = open2(\*Reader, \*Writer, "bc -l");
$sum = 2;
for (1 .. 5) {
    print Writer "$sum * $sum\n";
    chomp($sum = <Reader>);
}
close Writer;
close Reader;
waitpid($pid, 0);
print "sum is $sum\n";
```

You can also autovivify lexical filehandles:

```
my ($fhread, $fhwrite);
$pid = open2($fhread, $fhwrite, "cat -u -n");
```

The problem with this in general is that standard I/O buffering is really going to ruin your day. Even though your output filehandle is autoflushed (the library does this for you) so that the process on the other end will get your data in a timely manner, you can't usually do anything to force it to return the favor. In this particular case, we were lucky: bc expects to operate over a pipe and knows to flush each output line. But few commands are so designed, so this seldom works out unless you yourself wrote the program on the other end of the double-ended pipe. Even simple, apparently interactive programs like *ftp* fail here because they won't do line buffering on a pipe. They'll only do it on a tty device.

The IO::Pty and Expect modules from CPAN can help with this because they provide a real tty (actually, a real pseudo-tty, but it acts like a real one). This gets you line buffering in the other process without modifying its program.

If you split your program into several processes and want these to all have a conversation that goes both ways, you can't use Perl's high-level pipe interfaces, because these are all unidirectional. You'll need to use two low-level `pipe` function calls, each handling one direction of the conversation:

```
pipe(FROM_PARENT, TO_CHILD)      or die "pipe: $!";
pipe(FROM_CHILD,  TO_PARENT)     or die "pipe: $!";
select((select(TO_CHILD), $| = 1))[0]);   # autoflush
select((select(TO_PARENT), $| = 1))[0]);  # autoflush

if ($pid = fork) {
    close FROM_PARENT; close TO_PARENT;
    print TO_CHILD "Parent Pid $$ is sending this\n";
    chomp($line = <FROM_CHILD>);
    print "Parent Pid $$ just read this: '$line'\n";
    close FROM_CHILD; close TO_CHILD;
    waitpid($pid,0);
} else {
    die "cannot fork: $!" unless defined $pid;
    close FROM_CHILD; close TO_CHILD;
    chomp($line = <FROM_PARENT>);
    print "Child Pid $$ just read this: '$line'\n";
    print TO_PARENT "Child Pid $$ is sending this\n";
    close FROM_PARENT; close TO_PARENT;
    exit;
}
```

On many Unix systems, you don't actually have to make two separate `pipe` calls to achieve full duplex communication between parent and child. The `socketpair` syscall provides bidirectional connections between related processes on the same machine. So instead of two `pipe`s, you only need one `socketpair`.

```
use Socket;
socketpair(Child, Parent, AF_UNIX, SOCK_STREAM, PF_UNSPEC)
    or die "socketpair: $!";

# or letting perl pick filehandles for you
my ($kidfh, $dadfh);
socketpair($kidfh, $dadfh, AF_UNIX, SOCK_STREAM, PF_UNSPEC)
    or die "socketpair: $!";
```

After the `fork`, the parent closes the `Parent` handle, then reads and writes via the `Child` handle. Meanwhile, the child closes the `Child` handle, then reads and writes via the `Parent` handle.

If you're looking into bidirectional communications because the process you'd like to talk to implements a standard Internet service, you should usually just skip the middleman and use a CPAN module designed for that exact purpose. (See the "Sockets" section later for a list of a some of these.)

Named Pipes

A named pipe (often called a FIFO) is a mechanism for setting up a conversation between unrelated processes on the same machine. The names in a "named" pipe exist in the filesystem, which is just a funny way to say that you can put a special file in the filesystem namespace that has another process behind it instead of a disk.*

A FIFO is convenient when you want to connect a process to an unrelated one. When you open a FIFO, your process will block until there's a process on the other end. So if a reader opens the FIFO first, it blocks until the writer shows up—and vice versa.

To create a named pipe, use the POSIX `mkfifo` function—if you're on a POSIX system, that is. On Microsoft systems, you'll instead want to look into the `Win32::Pipe` module, which, despite its possible appearance to the contrary, creates named pipes. (Win32 users create anonymous pipes using `pipe` just like the rest of us.)

For example, let's say you'd like to have your *.signature* file produce a different answer each time it's read. Just make it a named pipe with a Perl program on the other end that spits out random quips. Now every time any program (like a mailer, newsreader, finger program, and so on) tries to read from that file, that program will connect to your program and read in a dynamic signature.

In the following example, we use the rarely seen -p file test operator to determine whether anyone (or anything) has accidentally removed our FIFO.† If they have, there's no reason to try to open it, so we treat this as a request to exit. If we'd used a simple `open` function with a mode of "> $fpath", there would have been a tiny race condition that would have risked accidentally creating the signature as a plain file if it disappeared between the -p test and the open. We couldn't use a "+< $fpath" mode, either, because opening a FIFO for read-write is a nonblocking open (this is only true of FIFOs). By using `sysopen` and omitting the O_CREAT flag, we avoid this problem by never creating a file by accident.

```
use Fcntl;              # for sysopen
chdir;                  # go home
$fpath = '.signature';
$ENV{PATH} .= ":/usr/games";

unless (-p $fpath) {    # not a pipe
    if (-e _) {         # but a something else
        die "$0: won't overwrite .signature\n";
```

---

* You can do the same thing with Unix-domain sockets, but you can't use open on those.

† Another use is to see if a filehandle is connected to a pipe, named or anonymous, as in -p STDIN.

```
        } else {
            require POSIX;
            POSIX::mkfifo($fpath, 0666) or die "can't mknod $fpath: $!";
            warn "$0: created $fpath as a named pipe\n";
        }
    }

    while (1) {
        # exit if signature file manually removed
        die "Pipe file disappeared" unless -p $fpath;
        # next line blocks until there's a reader
        sysopen(FIFO, $fpath, O_WRONLY)
            or die "can't write $fpath: $!";
        print FIFO "John Smith (smith\@host.org)\n", `fortune -s`;
        close FIFO;
        select(undef, undef, undef, 0.2);  # sleep 1/5th second
    }
```

The short sleep after the close is needed to give the reader a chance to read what
was written. If we just immediately loop back up around and open the FIFO again
before our reader has finished reading the data we just sent, then no end-of-file is
seen because there's once again a writer. We'll both go round and round until during one iteration, the writer falls a little behind and the reader finally sees that elu-
sive end-of-file. (And we were worried about race conditions?)

System V IPC

Everyone hates System V IPC. It's slower than paper tape, carves out insidious
little namespaces completely unrelated to the filesystem, uses human-hostile numbers to name its objects, and is constantly losing track of its own mind. Every so
often, your sysadmin has to go on a search-and-destroy mission to hunt down
these lost SysV IPC objects with *ipcs*(1) and kill them with *ipcrm*(1), hopefully
before the system runs out of memory.

Despite all this pain, ancient SysV IPC still has a few valid uses. The three kinds of
IPC objects are shared memory, semaphores, and messages. For message passing,
sockets are the preferred mechanisms these days, and they're a lot more portable,
too. For simple uses of semaphores, the filesystem tends to get used. As for shared
memory—well, now there's a problem for you. If you have it, the more modern
mmap(2) syscall fits the bill,* but the quality of the implementation varies from
system to system. It also requires a bit of care to avoid letting Perl reallocate your
strings from where *mmap*(2) put them. But when programmers look into using
mmap(2), they hear these incoherent mumbles from the resident wizards about
how it suffers from dodgy cache coherency issues on systems without something
called a "unified buffer cache"—or maybe it was a "flycatcher unibus"—and,

---

* There's even an Mmap module on CPAN.

figuring the devil they know is better than the one they don't, run quickly back to the SysV IPC they know and hate for all their shared memory needs.

Here's a little program that demonstrates controlled access to a shared memory buffer by a brood of sibling processes. SysV IPC objects can also be shared among *unrelated* processes on the same computer, but then you have to figure out how they're going to find each other. To mediate safe access, we'll create a semaphore per piece.*

Every time you want to get or put a new value into the shared memory, you have to go through the semaphore first. This can get pretty tedious, so we'll wrap access in an object class. IPC::Shareable goes one step further, wrapping its object class in a tie interface.

This program runs until you interrupt it with a Control-C or equivalent:

```
#!/usr/bin/perl -w
use v5.6.0;    # or better
use strict;
use sigtrap qw(die INT TERM HUP QUIT);
my $PROGENY = shift(@ARGV) || 3;
eval { main() };    # see DESTROY below for why
die if $@ && $@ !~ /^Caught a SIG/;
print "\nDone.\n";
exit;

sub main {
    my $mem = ShMem->alloc("Original Creation at " . localtime);
    my(@kids, $child);
    $SIG{CHLD} = 'IGNORE';
    for (my $unborn = $PROGENY; $unborn > 0; $unborn--) {
        if ($child = fork) {
            print "$$ begat $child\n";
            next;
        }
        die "cannot fork: $!" unless defined $child;
        eval {
            while (1) {
                $mem->lock();
                $mem->poke("$$ " . localtime)
                    unless $mem->peek =~ /^$$\b/o;
                $mem->unlock();
            }
        };
```

---

* It would be more realistic to create a pair of semaphores for each bit of shared memory, one for reading and the other for writing, and in fact, that's what the IPC::Shareable module on CPAN does. But we're trying to keep things simple here. It's worth admitting, though, that with a couple of semaphores, you could then make use of pretty much the only redeeming feature of SysV IPC: you could perform atomic operations on entire sets of semaphores as one unit, which is occasionally useful.

```
            die if $@ && $@ !~ /^Caught a SIG/;
            exit;  # child death

    }
    while (1) {
            print "Buffer is ", $mem->get, "\n";
            sleep 1;
    }
}
```

And here's the `ShMem` package, which that program uses. You can just tack it on to the end of the program, or put it in its own file (with a "1;" at the end) and `require` it from the main program. (The two IPC modules it uses in turn are found in the standard Perl distribution.)

```
package ShMem;
use IPC::SysV qw(IPC_PRIVATE IPC_RMID IPC_CREAT S_IRWXU);
use IPC::Semaphore;
sub MAXBUF() { 2000 }

sub alloc {     # constructor method
    my $class = shift;
    my $value = @_ ? shift : '';

    my $key = shmget(IPC_PRIVATE, MAXBUF, S_IRWXU) or die "shmget: $!";
    my $sem = IPC::Semaphore->new(IPC_PRIVATE, 1, S_IRWXU | IPC_CREAT)
                        or die "IPC::Semaphore->new: $!";
    $sem->setval(0,1)      or die "sem setval: $!";

    my $self = bless {
        OWNER    => $$,
        SHMKEY   => $key,
        SEMA     => $sem,
    } => $class;

    $self->put($value);
    return $self;
}
```

Now for the fetch and store methods. The `get` and `put` methods lock the buffer, but `peek` and `poke` don't, so the latter two should be used only while the object is manually locked—which you have to do when you want to retrieve an old value and store back a modified version, all under the same lock. The demo program does this in its `while (1)` loop. The entire transaction must occur under the same lock, or the testing and setting wouldn't be atomic and might bomb.

```
sub get {
    my $self = shift;
    $self->lock;
    my $value = $self->peek(@_);
    $self->unlock;
    return $value;
}
```

```
sub peek {
    my $self = shift;
    shmread($self->{SHMKEY}, my $buff='', 0, MAXBUF) or die "shmread: $!";
    substr($buff, index($buff, "\0")) = '';
    return $buff;
}
sub put {
    my $self = shift;
    $self->lock;
    $self->poke(@_);
    $self->unlock;
}
sub poke {
    my($self,$msg) = @_;
    shmwrite($self->{SHMKEY}, $msg, 0, MAXBUF) or die "shmwrite: $!";
}
sub lock {
    my $self = shift;
    $self->{SEMA}->op(0,-1,0) or die "semop: $!";
}
sub unlock {
    my $self = shift;
    $self->{SEMA}->op(0,1,0) or die "semop: $!";
}
```

Finally, the class needs a destructor so that when the object goes away, we can manually deallocate the shared memory and the semaphore stored inside the object. Otherwise, they'll outlive their creator, and you'll have to resort to *ipcs* and *ipcrm* (or a sysadmin) to get rid of them. That's why we went through the elaborate wrappers in the main program to convert signals into exceptions: it that all destructors get run, SysV IPC objects get deallocated, and sysadmins get off our case.

```
sub DESTROY {
    my $self = shift;
    return unless $self->{OWNER} == $$;   # avoid dup dealloc
    shmctl($self->{SHMKEY}, IPC_RMID, 0)    or warn "shmctl RMID: $!";
    $self->{SEMA}->remove()                 or warn "sema->remove: $!";
}
```

Sockets

The IPC mechanisms discussed earlier all have one severe restriction: they're designed for communication between processes running on the same computer. (Even though files can sometimes be shared across machines through mechanisms like NFS, locking fails miserably on many NFS implementations, which takes away most of the fun of concurrent access.) For general-purpose networking, sockets are the way to go. Although sockets were invented under BSD, they quickly spread to other forms of Unix, and nowadays you can find a socket interface on nearly every viable operating system out there. If you don't have sockets on your machine, you're going to have tremendous difficulty using the Internet.

With sockets, you can do both virtual circuits (as TCP streams) and datagrams (as UDP packets). You may be able to do even more, depending on your system. But the most common sort of socket programming uses TCP over Internet-domain sockets, so that's the kind we cover here. Such sockets provide reliable connections that work a little bit like bidirectional pipes that aren't restricted to the local machine. The two killer apps of the Internet, email and web browsing, both rely almost exclusively on TCP sockets.

You also use UDP heavily without knowing it. Every time your machine tries to find a site on the Internet, it sends UDP packets to your DNS server asking it for the actual IP address. You might use UDP yourself when you want to send and receive datagrams. Datagrams are cheaper than TCP connections precisely because they aren't connection oriented; that is, they're less like making a telephone call and more like dropping a letter in the mailbox. But UDP also lacks the reliability that TCP provides, making it more suitable for situations where you don't care whether a packet or two gets folded, spindled, or mutilated. Or for when you know that a higher-level protocol will enforce some degree of redundancy or fail-softness (which is what DNS does.)

Other choices are available but far less common. You can use Unix-domain sockets, but they only work for local communication. Various systems support various other non-IP-based protocols. Doubtless these are somewhat interesting to someone somewhere, but we'll restrain ourselves from talking about them somehow.

The Perl functions that deal with sockets have the same names as the corresponding syscalls in C, but their arguments tend to differ for two reasons: first, Perl filehandles work differently from C file descriptors; and second, Perl already knows the length of its strings, so you don't need to pass that information. See Chapter 29 for details on each socket-related syscall.

One problem with ancient socket code in Perl was that people would use hard-coded values for constants passed into socket functions, which destroys portability. Like most syscalls, the socket-related ones quietly but politely return undef when they fail, instead of raising an exception. It is therefore essential to check these functions' return values, since if you pass them garbage, they aren't going to be very noisy about it. If you ever see code that does anything like explicitly setting $AF_INET = 2, you know you're in for big trouble. An immeasurably superior approach is to use the Socket module or the even friendlier IO::Socket module, both of which are standard. These modules provide various constants and helper functions you'll need for setting up clients and servers. For optimal success, your socket programs should always start out like this (and don't forget to add the **-T** taint-checking switch to the shebang line for servers):

```
#!/usr/bin/perl -w
use strict;
use sigtrap;
use Socket;  # or IO::Socket
```

As noted elsewhere, Perl is at the mercy of your C libraries for much of its system behavior, and not all systems support all sorts of sockets. It's probably safest to stick with normal TCP and UDP socket operations. For example, if you want your code to stand a chance of being portable to systems you haven't thought of, don't expect there to be support for a reliable sequenced-packet protocol. Nor should you expect to pass open file descriptors between unrelated processes over a local Unix-domain socket. (Yes, you can really do that on many Unix machines—see your local *recvmsg*(2) manpage.)

If you just want to use a standard Internet service like mail, news, domain name service, FTP, Telnet, the Web, and so on, then instead of starting from scratch, try using existing CPAN modules for these. Prepackaged modules designed for these include Net::SMTP (or Mail::Mailer), Net::NNTP, Net::DNS, Net::FTP, Net::Telnet, and the various HTTP-related modules. The libnet and libwww module suites both comprise many individual networking modules. Module areas on CPAN you'll want to look at are section 5 on Networking and IPC, section 15 on WWW-related modules, and section 16 on Server and Daemon Utilities.

In the sections that follow, we present several sample clients and servers without a great deal of explanation of each function used, as that would mostly duplicate the descriptions we've already provided in Chapter 29.

Networking Clients

Use Internet-domain sockets when you want reliable client-server communication between potentially different machines.

To create a TCP client that connects to a server somewhere, it's usually easiest to use the standard IO::Socket::INET module:

```
use IO::Socket::INET;

$socket = IO::Socket::INET->new(PeerAddr => $remote_host,
                                PeerPort => $remote_port,
                                Proto    => "tcp",
                                Type     => SOCK_STREAM)
      or die "Couldn't connect to $remote_host:$remote_port : $!\n";
```

```
# send something over the socket,
print $socket "Why don't you call me anymore?\n";

# read the remote answer,
$answer = <$socket>;

# and terminate the connection when we're done.
close($socket);
```

A shorthand form of the call is good enough when you just have a host and port combination to connect to, and are willing to use defaults for all other fields:

```
$socket = IO::Socket::INET->new("www.yahoo.com:80")
    or die "Couldn't connect to port 80 of yahoo: $!";
```

To connect using the basic Socket module:

```
use Socket;

# create a socket
socket(Server, PF_INET, SOCK_STREAM, getprotobyname('tcp'));

# build the address of the remote machine
$internet_addr = inet_aton($remote_host)
    or die "Couldn't convert $remote_host into an Internet address: $!\n";
$paddr = sockaddr_in($remote_port, $internet_addr);

# connect
connect(Server, $paddr)
    or die "Couldn't connect to $remote_host:$remote_port: $!\n";

select((select(Server), $| = 1)[0]);  # enable command buffering

# send something over the socket
print Server "Why don't you call me anymore?\n";

# read the remote answer
$answer = <Server>;

# terminate the connection when done
close(Server);
```

If you want to close only your side of the connection, so that the remote end gets an end-of-file, but you can still read data coming from the server, use the shutdown syscall for a half-close:

```
# no more writing to server
shutdown(Server, 1);     # Socket::SHUT_WR constant in v5.6
```

Networking Servers

Here's a corresponding server to go along with it. It's pretty easy with the standard IO::Socket::INET class:

```
use IO::Socket::INET;

$server = IO::Socket::INET->new(LocalPort => $server_port,
                                Type      => SOCK_STREAM,
                                Reuse     => 1,
                                Listen    => 10 )    # or SOMAXCONN
    or die "Couldn't be a tcp server on port $server_port: $!\n";

while ($client = $server->accept()) {
    # $client is the new connection
}

close($server);
```

You can also write that using the lower-level Socket module:

```
use Socket;

# make the socket
socket(Server, PF_INET, SOCK_STREAM, getprotobyname('tcp'));

# so we can restart our server quickly
setsockopt(Server, SOL_SOCKET, SO_REUSEADDR, 1);

# build up my socket address
$my_addr = sockaddr_in($server_port, INADDR_ANY);
bind(Server, $my_addr)
    or die "Couldn't bind to port $server_port: $!\n";

# establish a queue for incoming connections
listen(Server, SOMAXCONN)
    or die "Couldn't listen on port $server_port: $!\n";

# accept and process connections
while (accept(Client, Server)) {
    # do something with new Client connection
}

close(Server);
```

The client doesn't need to bind to any address, but the server does. We've specified its address as INADDR_ANY, which means that clients can connect from any available network interface. If you want to sit on a particular interface (like the external side of a gateway or firewall machine), use that interface's real address instead. (Clients can do this, too, but rarely need to.)

If you want to know which machine connected to you, call getpeername on the client connection. This returns an IP address, which you'll have to translate into a name on your own (if you can):

```
use Socket;
$other_end = getpeername(Client)
    or die "Couldn't identify other end: $!\n";
($port, $iaddr) = unpack_sockaddr_in($other_end);
$actual_ip = inet_ntoa($iaddr);
$claimed_hostname = gethostbyaddr($iaddr, AF_INET);
```

This is trivially spoofable because the owner of that IP address can set up their reverse tables to say anything they want. For a small measure of additional confidence, translate back the other way again:

```
@name_lookup = gethostbyname($claimed_hostname)
    or die "Could not reverse $claimed_hostname: $!\n";
@resolved_ips = map { inet_ntoa($_) } @name_lookup[ 4 .. $#name_lookup ];
$might_spoof = !grep { $actual_ip eq $_ } @resolved_ips;
```

Once a client connects to your server, your server can do I/O both to and from that client handle. But while the server is so engaged, it can't service any further incoming requests from other clients. To avoid getting locked down to just one client at a time, many servers immediately fork a clone of themselves to handle each incoming connection. (Others fork in advance, or multiplex I/O between several clients using the select syscall.)

```
REQUEST:
while (accept(Client, Server)) {
    if ($kidpid = fork) {
        close Client;          # parent closes unused handle
        next REQUEST;
    }
    defined($kidpid)   or die "cannot fork: $!" ;

    close Server;              # child closes unused handle

    select(Client);            # new default for prints
    $| = 1;                    # autoflush

    # per-connection child code does I/O with Client handle
    $input = <Client>;
    print Client "output\n";   # or STDOUT, same thing

    open(STDIN,  "<<&Client")   or die "can't dup client: $!";
    open(STDOUT, ">&Client")    or die "can't dup client: $!";
    open(STDERR, ">&Client")    or die "can't dup client: $!";

    # run the calculator, just as an example
    system("bc -l");     # or whatever you'd like, so long as
                         # it doesn't have shell escapes!
    print "done\n";      # still to client
```

```
        close Client;
        exit;  # don't let the child back to accept!
    }
```

This server clones off a child with `fork` for each incoming request. That way it can handle many requests at once, as long as you can create more processes. (You might want to limit this.) Even if you don't `fork`, the `listen` will allow up to SOMAXCONN (usually five or more) pending connections. Each connection uses up some resources, although not as much as a process. Forking servers have to be careful about cleaning up after their expired children (called "zombies" in Unix-speak) because otherwise they'd quickly fill up your process table. The REAPER code discussed in the section "Signals" will take care of that for you, or you may be able to assign `$SIG{CHLD} = 'IGNORE'`.

Before running another command, we connect the standard input and output (and error) up to the client connection. This way any command that reads from STDIN and writes to STDOUT can also talk to the remote machine. Without the reassignment, the command couldn't find the client handle—which by default gets closed across the `exec` boundary, anyway.

When you write a networking server, we strongly suggest that you use the **-T** switch to enable taint checking even if you aren't running setuid or setgid. This is always a good idea for servers and any other program that runs on behalf of someone else (like all CGI scripts), because it lessens the chances that people from the outside will be able to compromise your system. See the section "Handling Insecure Data" in Chapter 23 for much more about all this.

One additional consideration when writing Internet programs: many protocols specify that the line terminator should be CRLF, which can be specified various ways: `"\015\12"`, or `"\xd\xa"`, or even `chr(13).chr(10)`. As of version 5.6 of Perl, saying `v13.10` also produces the same string. (On many machines, you can also use `"\r\n"` to mean CRLF, but don't use `"\r\n"` if you want to be portable to Macs, where the meanings of `\r` and `\n` are reversed!) Many Internet programs will in fact accept a bare `"\012"` as a line terminator, but that's because Internet programs usually try to be liberal in what they accept and strict in what they emit. (Now if only we could get people to do the same . . .)

Message Passing

As we mentioned earlier, UDP communication involves much lower overhead but provides no reliability, since there are no promises that messages will arrive in a proper order—or even that they will arrive at all. UDP is often said to stand for Unreliable Datagram Protocol.

Still, UDP offers some advantages over TCP, including the ability to broadcast or multicast to a whole bunch of destination hosts at once (usually on your local subnet). If you find yourself getting overly concerned about reliability and starting to build checks into your message system, then you probably should just use TCP to start with. True, it costs more to set up and tear down a TCP connection, but if you can amortize that over many messages (or one long message), it doesn't much matter.

Anyway, here's an example of a UDP program. It contacts the UDP time port of the machines given on the command line, or everybody it can find using the universal broadcast address if no arguments were supplied.* Not all machines have a time server enabled, especially across firewall boundaries, but those that do will send you back a 4-byte integer packed in network byte order that represents what time that machine thinks it is. The time returned, however, is in the number of seconds since 1900. You have to subtract the number of seconds between 1900 and 1970 to feed that time to the `localtime` or `gmtime` conversion functions.

```perl
#!/usr/bin/perl
# clockdrift - compare other systems' clocks with this one
#              without arguments, broadcast to anyone listening.
#              wait one-half second for an answer.

use v5.6.0;  # or better
use warnings;
use strict;
use Socket;

unshift(@ARGV, inet_ntoa(INADDR_BROADCAST))
    unless @ARGV;

socket(my $msgsock, PF_INET, SOCK_DGRAM, getprotobyname("udp"))
    or die "socket: $!";

# Some borked machines need this.  Shouldn't hurt anyone else.
setsockopt($msgsock, SOL_SOCKET, SO_BROADCAST, 1)
    or die "setsockopt: $!";

my $portno = getservbyname("time", "udp")
    or die "no udp time port";

for my $target (@ARGV) {
    print "Sending to $target:$portno\n";
    my $destpaddr = sockaddr_in($portno, inet_aton($target));
    send($msgsock, "x", 0, $destpaddr)
        or die "send: $!";
}
```

---

* If that doesn't work, run *ifconfig* –*a* to find the proper local broadcast address.

```perl
# daytime service returns 32-bit time in seconds since 1900
my $FROM_1900_TO_EPOCH = 2_208_988_800;
my $time_fmt = "N";    # and it does so in this binary format
my $time_len = length(pack($time_fmt, 1));   # any number's fine

my $inmask = '';   # string to store the fileno bits for select
vec($inmask, fileno($msgsock), 1) = 1;

# wait only half a second for input to show up
while (select(my $outmask = $inmask, undef, undef, 0.5)) {
    defined(my $srcpaddr = recv($msgsock, my $bintime, $time_len, 0))
        or die "recv: $!";
    my($port, $ipaddr) = sockaddr_in($srcpaddr);
    my $sendhost = sprintf "%s [%s]",
                    gethostbyaddr($ipaddr, AF_INET) || 'UNKNOWN',
                    inet_ntoa($ipaddr);
    my $delta = unpack($time_fmt, $bintime) -
                    $FROM_1900_TO_EPOCH - time();
    print "Clock on $sendhost is $delta seconds ahead of this one.\n";
}
```

17

Threads

Parallel programming is much harder than it looks. Imagine taking a recipe from a cookbook and converting it into something that several dozen chefs can work on all at the same time. You can take two approaches.

One approach is to give each chef a private kitchen, complete with its own supply of raw materials and utensils. For recipes that can be divided up into parts easily, and for foods that can be transported from kitchen to kitchen easily, this approach works well because it keeps the chefs out of each other's kitchens.

Alternatively, you can just put all the chefs into one kitchen, and let them work things out, like who gets to use the mixer when. This can get messy, especially when the meat cleavers start to fly.

These two approaches correspond to two models of parallel programming on computers. The first is the multiprocessing model typical of traditional Unix systems, in which each thread of control has its own set of resources, which taken together we call a process. The second model is the multithreading model, in which each thread of control shares resources with all other threads of control. Or doesn't share, as the case may be (and upon occasion must be).

We all know that chefs like to be in control; that's okay, because chefs *need* to be in control in order to accomplish what we want them to accomplish. But chefs need to be organized, one way or another.

Perl supports both models of organization. In this chapter we'll call them the *process model* and the *thread model*.

The Process Model

We'll not discuss the process model in great detail here, simply because it's pervasive throughout the rest of this book. Perl originated on Unix systems, so it is steeped in the notion that each process does its own thing. If a process wants to start some parallel processing, then logically it has to start a parallel process; that is, it must fork a new heavyweight process, which by default shares little with the parent process except some file descriptors. (It may seem like parent and child are sharing a lot more, but most of the state of the parent process is merely duplicated in the child process and not really shared in a logical sense. The operating system may of course exhibit laziness in enforcing that logical separation, in which case we call it copy-on-write semantics, but we wouldn't be doing the copy at all unless there were a logical separation first.)

Historically, this industrial-strength view of multiprocessing has posed a bit of a problem on Microsoft systems, because Windows has not had a well-developed multiprocessing model (and what it does have in that regard, it doesn't often rely on for parallel programming). It has typically taken a multithreading approach instead.

However, through heroic efforts, version 5.6 of Perl now implements the `fork` operation on Windows by cloning a new interpreter object within the same process. That means that most examples using `fork` in the rest of the book will now work on Windows. The cloned interpreter shares immutable code with other interpreters but gets its own copy of data to play with. (There can still be problems with C libraries that don't understand threads, of course.)

This approach to multiprocessing has been christened *ithreads*, short for "interpreter threads". The initial impetus for implementing ithreads was to emulate `fork` for Microsoft systems. However, we quickly realized that, although the other interpreters are running as distinct threads, they're running in the same process, so it would be easy to make these separate interpreters share data, even though they don't share by default.

This is the opposite of the typical threading model, in which everything is shared by default, and you have to take pains *not* to share something. But you should not view these two models as totally distinct from each other, because they are both trying to bridge the same river; they're just building from opposite shores. The actual solution to any parallel processing problem is going to involve some degree of sharing, together with some degree of selfishness.

So over the long run, the intent is to extend the ithreads model to allow as much sharing as you need or want. However, as of this writing, the only user-visible interface for ithreads is the `fork` call under Microsoft ports of Perl. We think that, eventually, this approach will produce cleaner programs than the standard threading approach. Basically, it's easier to run an economy where you assume everyone owns what they own, rather than assuming that everyone owns everything. Not that people aren't expected to share in a capitalist economy, or peculate* in a communist economy. These things tend toward the middle. Socialism happens. But with large groups of people, sharing everything by default only works when you have a "head chef" with a big meat cleaver who thinks he owns everything.

Of course, the actual government of any computer is run by that fascist dictator known as the operating system. But a wise dictator knows when to let the people think they're capitalists—and when to let them think they're communists.

The Thread Model

The thread model of multiprocessing was first introduced to Perl as an experimental feature in version 5.005. (By "thread model", we mean threads that share data resources by default, not the new ithreads of version 5.6.) In some senses, this thread model is still an experimental feature even in 5.6, because Perl is a rich language and multithreading can make a muddle of even the simplest language. There are still various nooks and crannies of Perl semantics that don't interact very well with the notion of everything being shared. The new ithreads model is an attempt to bypass these problems, and at some future point, the current thread model may be subsumed under the ithread model (when we get an interface to ithreads that says "share everything you can by default"). But despite its warts, the current "experimental" thread model continues to be useful in many real-world situations where the only alternative to being a guinea pig is even less desirable. Reasonably robust applications can be written in threaded Perl, but you have to be very careful. You should at least consider using `fork` instead, if you can think of a way to solve your problem with pipes instead of shared data structures.

But some algorithms are easier to express if multiple tasks have easy and efficient access to the same pool of data.† This makes for code that can be smaller and simpler. And because the kernel does not have to copy page tables for data (even if doing copy-on-write) at thread creation time, it should be faster to start a task this way. Likewise, context switches can be faster if the kernel doesn't need to swap page tables. (In fact, for user-level threads, the kernel doesn't get involved at all—though of course user-level threads have issues that kernel threads don't.)

---

* peculate: *v.i.*, to swipe the People's Property from the commons in the middle of the night; to embezzle from the public something that is not necessarily money (˘L. *peculiar*, "not common"), cf *embrace, extend, GPL*.

† The System V shared memory model discussed in the last chapter does not exactly qualify as "easy and efficient".

That's the good news. Now for some more disclaimers. We already mentioned that threading is somewhat experimental in Perl, but even if it weren't, programming with threads is treacherous. The ability of one execution stream to poke holes willy-nilly into the data space of another exposes more opportunity for disaster than you can possibly imagine. You might say to yourself, "That's easy to fix, I'll just put locks on any shared data." Okay, locking of shared data is indispensable, but getting the locking protocols correct is notoriously difficult, with errors producing deadlock or nondeterministic results. If you have timing problems in your program, using threads will not only exacerbate them, but it will make them harder to locate.

Not only are you responsible for keeping your own shared data straight, but you are required to keep the data straight of all the Perl modules and C libraries you call into. Your Perl code can be 100% threadsafe, and if you call into a nonthread-safe module or C subroutine without providing your own semaphore protection, you're toast. You should assume any module is not threadsafe until proven otherwise. That even includes some of the standard modules. Maybe even most of them.

Have we discouraged you yet? No? Then we'll point out that you're pretty much at the mercy of your operating system's threading library when it comes to scheduling and preemption policies. Some thread libraries only do thread switching on blocking system calls. Some libraries block the whole process if a single thread makes a blocking system call. Some libraries only switch threads on quantum expiration (either thread or process). Some libraries only switch threads explicitly.

Oh, and by the way, if your process receives a signal, which thread the signal is delivered to is completely system dependent.

To do thread programming in Perl, you must build a special version of Perl following the directions given in the *README.threads* file in the Perl source directory. This special Perl is pretty much guaranteed to run a bit slower than your standard Perl executable.

Do not assume that just because you know how threads are programmed in other models (POSIX, DEC, Microsoft, etc.) you know how threads work with Perl. As with other things in Perl, Perl is Perl, not C++ or Java or whatnot. For example, there are no real-time thread priorities (and no way to work around their absence). There are also no mutexes. Just use regular locking or perhaps the `Thread::Semaphore` module or the `cond_wait` facilities.

Still not discouraged? Good, because threads are really cool. You're scheduled to have some fun.

The Thread Module

The current interface for Perl threads is defined by the Thread module. Additionally, one new Perl keyword was added, the lock operator. We'll talk about lock later in this chapter. Other standard thread modules build on this basic interface.

The Thread module provides these class methods:

Method	Use
new	Construct a new Thread.
self	Return my current Thread object.
list	Return list of Thread objects.

And, for Thread objects, it provides these object methods:

Method	Use
join	Harvest a thread (propagate errors).
eval	Harvest a thread (trap errors).
equal	Compare two threads for identity.
tid	Return the internal thread ID.

In addition, the Thread module provides these importable functions:

Function	Use
yield	Tell the scheduler to run a different thread.
async	Construct a Thread via closure.
cond_signal	Wake up exactly one thread that is cond_wait()ing on a variable.
cond_broadcast	Wake up all threads that may be cond_wait()ing on a variable.
cond_wait	Wait on a variable until awakened by a cond_signal() or cond_broadcast() on that variable.

Thread creation

You can spawn a thread in one of two ways, either by using the Thread->new class method or by using the async function. In either case, the returned value is a Thread object. Thread->new takes a code reference indicating a function to run and arguments to pass to that function:

```
use Thread;
...
$t = Thread->new( \&func, $arg1, $arg2);
```

Often you'll find yourself wanting to pass a closure as the first argument without supplying any additional arguments:

```
my $something;
$t = Thread->new( sub { say($something) } );
```

For this special case, the `async` function provides some notational relief (that is, syntactic sugar):

```
use Thread qw(async);
...
my $something;
$t = async {
    say($something);
};
```

You'll note that we explicitly import the `async` function. You may, of course, use the fully qualified name `Thread::async` instead, but then your syntactic sugar isn't so sweet. Since `async` takes only a closure, anything you want to pass to it must be a lexical variable in scope at the time.

Thread destruction

Once begun—and subject to the whims of your threading library—the thread will keep running on its own until its top-level function (the function you passed to the constructor) returns. If you want to terminate a thread early, just `return` from within that top-level function.*

Now it's all very well for your top-level subroutine to return, but who does it return *to*? The thread that spawned this thread has presumably gone on to do other things and is no longer waiting at a method call for a response. The answer is simple enough: the thread waits until someone issues a method call that *does* wait for a return value. That method call is called `join`, because it conceptually joins two threads back into one:

```
$retval = $t->join();     # harvest thread $t
```

The operation of `join` is reminiscent of `waitpid` on a child process. If the thread has already shut down, the `join` method returns immediately with the return value of the thread's top-level subroutine. If the thread is not done, `join` acts as a blocking call that suspends the calling thread indefinitely. (There is no time-out facility.) When the thread eventually completes, the `join` returns.

Unlike `waitpid`, however, which can only harvest the process's own children, any thread can `join` any other thread within the process. That is, it is not a necessity for the joining thread be the main thread or the parent thread. The only restrictions are that a thread can't `join` itself (which would be like officiating at your

---

* Don't call `exit`! That would try to take down your entire process, and possibly succeed. But the process won't actually exit until all threads exit, and some of them may refuse to exit on an `exit`. More on that later.

own funeral), and a thread can't join a thread that has already been joined (which would be like two funeral directors fighting each other over the body). If you try to do either of those things, an exception will be raised.

The return value of join doesn't have to be a scalar value—it can also be a list:

```
use Thread 'async';

$t1 = async {
    my @stuff = getpwuid($>);
    return @stuff;
};

$t2 = async {
    my $motd = `cat /etc/motd`;
    return $motd;
};

@retlist = $t1->join();
$retval  = $t2->join();

print "1st kid returned @retlist\n";
print "2nd kid returned $retval\n";
```

In fact, the return expression of a thread is always evaluated in list context, even if join is called in a scalar context, in which case the last value of the list is returned.

Catching exceptions from join

If a thread terminates with an uncaught exception, this does not immediately kill the whole program. That would be naughty. Instead, when a join is run on that thread, the join itself raises the exception. Using join on a thread indicates a willingness to propagate any exceptions raised by that thread. If you'd rather trap the exception right then and there, use the eval method, which, like its built-in counterpart, causes the exception to be put into $@:

```
$retval = $t->eval();   # catch join errors
if ($@) {
    warn "thread failed: $@";
}
else {
    print "thread returned $retval\n";
}
```

Although there's no rule to this effect, you might want to adopt a practice of joining a thread only from within the thread that created the one you're joining. That is, you harvest a child thread only from the parent thread that spawned it. This makes it a little easier to keep track of which exceptions you might need to handle where.

The detach method

As another alternative method of shutting down threads, if you don't plan to join a thread later to get its return value, you can call the detach method on it so that Perl will clean it up for you. It can no longer be joined. It's a little bit like when a process is inherited by the *init* program under Unix, except that the only way to do that under Unix is for the parent process to die.

The detach method does not "background" the thread; if you try to exit the main program and a detached thread is still running, the exit will hang until the thread exits on its own. Rather, detach just spares you from clean up. It merely tells Perl not to keep the return value and exit status of the thread after it finishes. In a sense, detach tells Perl to do an implicit join when the thread finishes and then throw away the results. That can be important: if you neither join nor detach a thread that returns some very large list, that storage will be lost until the end, because Perl would have to hang onto it on the off chance (very off, in this case) that someone would want to join that thread sometime in the future.

An exception raised in a detached child thread also no longer propagates up through a join, since there will never be one. Use eval {} wisely in the top-level function, and find some other way to report errors.

Identifying threads

Every Perl thread has a distinguishing thread identification number, which the tid object method returns:

```
$his_tidno = $t1->tid();
```

A thread can access its own thread object through the Thread->self call. Don't confuse that with the thread ID: to figure out its own thread ID, a thread does this:

```
$mytid = Thread->self->tid();   # $$ for threads, as it were.
```

To compare one thread object with another, do any of these:

```
Thread::equal($t1, $t2)
$t1->equal($t2)
$t1->tid() == $td->tid()
```

Listing current threads

You can get a list of current thread objects in the current process using the Thread->list class method call. The list includes both running threads and threads that are done but haven't been joined yet. You can do this from any thread.

```
for my $t (Thread->list()) {
    printf "$t has tid = %d\n", $t->tid();
}
```

Yielding the processor

The `Thread` module supports an importable function named `yield`. Its job is to cause the calling thread to surrender the processor. Unfortunately, details of what this really does are completely dependent on which flavor of thread implementation you have. Nevertheless, it's considered a nice gesture to relinquish control of the CPU occasionally:

```
use Thread 'yield';
yield();
```

You don't have to use parentheses. This is even safer, syntactically speaking, because it catches the seemingly inevitable "yeild" typo:

```
use strict;
use Thread 'yield';
yeild;          # Compiler wails, then bails.
yield;          # Ok.
```

Data Access

What we've gone over so far isn't really too hard, but we're about to fix that. Nothing we've done has actually exercised the parallel nature of threads. Accessing shared data changes all that.

Threaded code in Perl has the same constraints regarding data visibility as any other bit of Perl code. Globals are still accessed via global symbol tables, and lexicals are still accessed via some containing lexical scope (scratchpad).

However, the fact that multiple threads of control exist in the program throws a clinker into the works. Two threads can't be allowed to access the same global variable simultaneously, or they may tromp on each other. (The result of the tromping depends on the nature of the access.) Similarly, two threads can't be allowed to access the same lexical variable simultaneously, because lexical variables also behave like globals if they are declared outside the scope of closures being used by threads. Starting threads via subroutine references (using `Thread->new`) rather than via closures (using `async`) can help limit access to lexicals, if that's what you want. (Sometimes it isn't, though.)

Perl solves the problem for certain built-in special variables, like `$!` and `$_` and `@_` and the like, by making them thread-specific data. The bad news is that all your basic, everyday package variables are unprotected from tromping.

The good news is that you don't generally have to worry about your lexical variables at all, presuming they were declared inside the current thread, since each thread will instantiate its own lexical scope upon entry, separate from any other thread. You only have to worry about lexicals if they're shared between threads, by passing references around, for example, or by referring to lexicals from within closures running under multiple threads.

Synchronizing access with lock

When more than one agent can access the same item at the same time, collisions happen, just like at an intersection. Careful locking is your only defense.

The built-in `lock` function is Perl's red-light/green-light mechanism for access control. Although `lock` is a keyword of sorts, it's a shy one, in that the built-in function is *not* used if the compiler has already seen a `sub lock {}` definition in user code. This is for backward compatibility. `CORE::lock` is always the built-in, though. (In a *perl* not built for threading, calling `lock` is not an error; it's a harmless no-op, at least in recent versions.)

Just as the `flock` operator only blocks other instances of `flock`, not the actual I/O, so too the `lock` operator only blocks other instances of `lock`, not regular data access. They are, in effect, *advisory* locks. Just like traffic lights.*

You can `lock` individual scalar variables and entire arrays and hashes as well.

```
lock $var;
lock @values;
lock %table;
```

However, using `lock` on an aggregate does not implicitly lock all that aggregate's scalar components:

```
lock @values;       # in thread 1
...
lock $values[23];   # in thread 2 -- won't block!
```

If you lock a reference, this automatically locks access to the referent. That is, you get one dereference for free. This is handy because objects are always hidden behind a reference, and you often want to lock objects. (And you almost never want to lock references.)

The problem with traffic lights, of course, is that they're red half the time, and then you have to wait. Likewise, `lock` is a blocking call—your thread will hang there until the lock is granted. There is no time-out facility. There is no unlock facility, either, because locks are dynamically scoped. They persist until their block, file, or `eval` has finished. When they go out of scope, they are freed automatically.

---

* Some railroad crossing signals are mandatory (the ones with gates), and some folks think locks should be mandatory too. But just picture a world in which every intersection has arms that go up and down whenever the lights change.

Locks are also recursive. That means that if you lock a variable in one function, and that function recurses while holding the lock, the same thread can successfully lock the same variable again. The lock is finally dropped when all frames owning the locks have exited.

Here's a simple demo of what can happen if you don't have locking. We'll force a context switch using `yield` to show the kind of problem that can also happen accidentally under preemptive scheduling:

```
use Thread qw/async yield/;
my $var = 0;
sub abump {
    if ($var == 0) {
        yield;
        $var++;
    }
}

my $t1 = new Thread \&abump;
my $t2 = new Thread \&abump;

for my $t ($t1, $t2) { $t->join }
print "var is $var\n";
```

That code always prints 2 (for some definition of always) because we decided to do the bump after seeing its value was 0, but before we could do so, another thread decided the same thing.

We can fix that collision by the trivial addition of a lock before we examine $var. Now this code always prints 1:

```
sub abump {
    lock $var;
    if ($var == 0) {
        yield;
        $var++;
    }
}
```

Remember that there's no explicit `unlock` function. To control unlocking, just add another, nested scoping level so the lock is released when that scope terminates:

```
sub abump {
    {
        lock $var;
        if ($var == 0) {
            yield;
            $var++;
        }
    } # lock released here!
    # other code with unlocked $var
}
```

Deadlock

Deadlock is the bane of thread programmers because it's easy to do by accident and hard to avoid even when you try to. Here's a simple example of deadlock:

```
my $t1 = async {
    lock $a; yield; lock $b;
    $a++; $b++
};
my $t2 = async {
    lock $b; yield; lock $a;
    $b++; $a++
};
```

The solution here is for all parties who need a particular set of locks to grab them in the same order.

It's also good to minimize the duration of time you hold locks. (At least, it's good to do so for performance reasons. But if you do it to reduce the risk of deadlock, all you're doing is making it harder to reproduce and diagnose the problem.)

Locking subroutines

You can also put a lock on a subroutine:

```
lock &func;
```

Unlike locks on data, which are advisory only, subroutine locks are *mandatory*. No one else but the thread with the lock may enter the subroutine.

Consider the following code, which contains race conditions involving the $done variable. (The yields are for demonstration purposes only).

```
use Thread qw/async yield/;
my $done = 0;
sub frob {
    my $arg = shift;
    my $tid = Thread->self->tid;
    print "thread $tid: frob $arg\n";
    yield;
    unless ($done) {
        yield;
        $done++;
        frob($arg + 10);
    }
}
```

If you run it this way:

```
my @t;
for my $i (1..3) {
    push @t, Thread->new(\&frob, $i);
}
```

```
for (@t) { $_->join }
print "done is $done\n";
```

here's the output (well, sometimes—it's not deterministic):

```
thread 1: frob 1
thread 2: frob 2
thread 3: frob 3
thread 1: frob 11
thread 2: frob 12
thread 3: frob 13
done is 3
```

However, if you run it this way:

```
for my $i (1..3) {
    push @t, async {
        lock &frob;
        frob($i);
    };
}
for (@t) { $_->join }
print "done is $done\n";
```

here's the output:

```
thread 1: frob 1
thread 1: frob 11
thread 2: frob 2
thread 3: frob 3
done is 1
```

The locked attribute

Although obeying a subroutine lock is mandatory, nothing forces anyone to lock them in the first place. You could say that the placement of the lock is advisory. But some subroutines would really like to be able to require that they be locked before being called.

The `locked` subroutine attribute addresses this. It's faster than calling `lock &sub` because it's known at compile time, not just at run time. But the behavior is the same as when we locked it explicitly earlier. The syntax is as follows:

```
sub frob : locked {
    # as before
}
```

If you have a function prototype, it comes between the name and any attributes:

```
sub frob ($) : locked {
    # as before
}
```

Locking methods

Automatic locking on a subroutine is really cool, but sometimes it's overkill. When you're invoking an object method, it doesn't generally matter if multiple methods are running simultaneously as long as they're all running on behalf of different objects. So you'd really like to lock the object that the method is being called on instead. Adding a `method` attribute to the subroutine definition does this:

```
sub frob : locked method {
    # as before
}
```

If called as a method, the invoking object is locked, providing serial access to that object, but allowing the method to be called on other objects. If the method isn't called on an object, the attribute still tries to do the right thing: if you call a locked method as a class method (`Package->new` rather than `$obj->new`) the package's symbol table is locked. If you call a locked method as a normal subroutine, Perl will raise an exception.

Condition variables

A condition variable allows a thread to give up the processor until some criterion is satisfied. Condition variables are meant as points of coordination between threads when you need more control than a mere lock provides. On the other hand, you don't really need more *overhead* than the lock provides, and condition variables are designed with this in mind. You just use ordinary locks plus ordinary conditionals. If the condition fails, then you'll have to take extraordinary measures via the `cond_wait` function; but we optimize for success, since in a well-designed application, we shouldn't be bottlenecking on the current condition anyway.

Besides locking and testing, the basic operations on condition variables consist of either sending or receiving a "signal" event (not a real signal in the `%SIG` sense). Either you suspend your own execution to wait for an event to be received, or you send an event to wake up other threads waiting for the particular condition. The `Thread` module provides three importable functions to do this: `cond_wait`, `cond_signal`, and `cond_broadcast`. These are the primitive mechanisms upon which more abstract modules like `Thread::Queue` and `Thread::Semaphore` are based. It's often more convenient to use those abstractions, when possible.

The `cond_wait` function takes a variable already locked by the current thread, unlocks that variable, and then blocks until another thread does a `cond_signal` or `cond_broadcast` for that same locked variable.

The variable blocked by cond_wait is relocked after cond_wait returns. If multiple threads are cond_waiting the same variable, all but one reblock because they can't regain the lock on the variable. Therefore, if you're only using cond_wait for synchronization, give up the lock as soon as possible.

The cond_signal function takes a variable already locked by the current thread and unblocks one thread that's currently in a cond_wait on that variable. If more than one thread is blocked in a cond_wait on that variable, only one is unblocked, and you can't predict which one. If no threads are blocked in a cond_wait on that variable, the event is discarded.

The cond_broadcast function works like cond_signal, but unblocks all threads blocked in a cond_wait on the locked variable, not just one. (Of course, it's still the case that only one thread can have the variable locked at a time.)

The cond_wait function is intended to be a last-resort kind of thing that a thread does only if the condition it wants isn't met. The cond_signal and cond_broadcast indicate that the condition is changing. The scheme is supposed to be this: lock, then check to see whether the condition you want is met; if it is, fine, and if it isn't, cond_wait until it *is* fine. The emphasis should be on avoiding blocking if at all possible. (Generally a good piece of advice when dealing with threads.)

Here's an example of passing control back and forth between two threads. Don't be fooled by the fact that the actual conditions are over on the right in statement modifiers; cond_wait is never called unless the condition we're waiting for is false.

```
use Thread qw(async cond_wait cond_signal);
my $wait_var = 0;
async {
    lock $wait_var;
    $wait_var = 1;
    cond_wait $wait_var  until $wait_var == 2;
    cond_signal($wait_var);
    $wait_var = 1;
    cond_wait $wait_var  until $wait_var == 2;
    $wait_var = 1;
    cond_signal($wait_var);
};

async {
    lock $wait_var;
    cond_wait $wait_var  until $wait_var == 1;
    $wait_var = 2;
    cond_signal($wait_var);
    cond_wait $wait_var  until $wait_var == 1;
    $wait_var = 2;
    cond_signal($wait_var);
    cond_wait $wait_var  until $wait_var == 1;
};
```

Other Thread Modules

Several modules are built on top of the `cond_wait` primitive.

Queues

The standard `Thread::Queue` module provides a way to pass objects between threads without worrying about locks or synchronization. This interface is much easier:

Method	Use
new	Construct a new `Thread::Queue`.
enqueue	Push one or more scalars on to the end of the queue.
dequeue	Shift the first scalar off the front of the queue. The `dequeue` method blocks if there are no items present.

Notice how similar a queue is to a regular pipe, except that instead of sending bytes, you get to pass around full scalars, including references and blessed objects!

Here's an example derived from the *perlthrtut* manpage:

```
use Thread qw/async/;
use Thread::Queue;

my $Q = Thread::Queue->new();
async {
    while (defined($datum = $Q->dequeue)) {
        print "Pulled $datum from queue\n";
    }
};

$Q->enqueue(12);
$Q->enqueue("A", "B", "C");
$Q->enqueue($thr);
sleep 3;
$Q->enqueue(\%ENV);
$Q->enqueue(undef);
```

Here's what you get for output:

```
Pulled 12 from queue
Pulled A from queue
Pulled B from queue
Pulled C from queue
Pulled Thread=SCALAR(0x8117200) from queue
Pulled HASH(0x80dfd8c) from queue
```

Notice how $Q was in scope when the asynchronous thread was launched via an async closure. Threads are under the same scoping rules as anything else in Perl. The example above would not have worked had $Q been declared after the call to async.

Semaphores

Thread::Semaphore provides you with threadsafe, counting semaphore objects to implement your favorite p() and v() operations. Because most of us don't associate these operations with the Dutch words *passeer* ("pass") and *verlaat* ("leave"), the module calls these operations "down" and "up" respectively. (In some of the literature, they're called "wait" and "signal".) The following methods are supported:

Method	Use
new	Construct a new Thread::Semaphore.
down	Allocate one or more items.
up	Deallocate one or more items.

The new method creates a new semaphore and initializes its count to the specified number. If no number is specified, the semaphore's count is set to 1. (The number represents some pool of items that can "run out" if they're all allocated.)

```
use Thread::Semaphore;
$mutex = Thread::Semaphore->new($MAX);
```

The down method decreases the semaphore's count by the specified number, or by 1 if no number is given. It can be interpreted as an attempt to allocate some or all of a resource. If the semaphore's count drops below zero, this method blocks until the semaphore's count is equal to or larger than the amount you're requesting. Call it like this:

```
$mutex->down();
```

The up method increases the semaphore's count by the specified number, or 1 if no number is given. It can be interpreted as freeing up some quantity of a previously allocated resource. This unblocks at least one thread that was blocked trying to down the semaphore, provided that the up raises the semaphore count above what the down is trying to decrement it by. Call it like this:

```
$mutex->up();
```

Other standard threading modules

Thread::Signal allows you to start up a thread that is designated to receive your process's %SIG signals. This addresses the still-vexing problem that signals are unreliable as currently implemented in Perl and their imprudent use can cause occasional core dumps.

These modules are still in development and may not produce the desired results on your system. Then again, they may. If they don't, it's because someone like you hasn't fixed them yet. Perhaps someone like you should pitch in and help.

18

Compiling

If you came here looking for a Perl compiler, you may be surprised to discover that you already have one—your *perl* program (typically */usr/bin/perl*) already contains a Perl compiler. That might not be what you were thinking, and if it wasn't, you may be pleased to know that we do also provide *code generators* (which some well-meaning folks call "compilers"), and we'll discuss those toward the end of this chapter. But first we want to talk about what we think of as The Compiler. Inevitably there's going to be a certain amount of low-level detail in this chapter that some people will be interested in, and some people will not. If you find that you're not, think of it as an opportunity to practice your speed-reading skills.

Imagine that you're a conductor who's ordered the score for a large orchestral work. When the box of music arrives, you find several dozen booklets, one for each member of the orchestra with just their part in it. But curiously, your master copy with all the parts is missing. Even more curiously, the parts you *do* have are written out using plain English instead of musical notation. Before you can put together a program for performance, or even give the music to your orchestra to play, you'll first have to translate the prose descriptions into the normal system of notes and bars. Then you'll need to compile the individual parts into one giant score so that you can get an idea of the overall program.

Similarly, when you hand the source code of your Perl script over to *perl* to execute, it is no more useful to the computer than the English description of the symphony was to the musicians. Before your program can run, Perl needs to compile* these English-looking directions into a special symbolic representation. Your program still isn't running, though, because the compiler only compiles. Like the

---

* Or translate, or transform, or transfigure, or transmute, or transmogrify.

conductor's score, even after your program has been converted to an instruction format suitable for interpretation, it still needs an active agent to interpret those instructions.

The Life Cycle of a Perl Program

You can break up the life cycle of a Perl program into four distinct phases, each with separate stages of its own. The first and the last are the most interesting ones, and the middle two are optional. The stages are depicted in Figure 18-1.

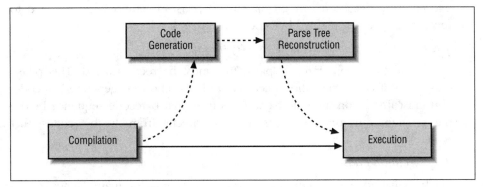

Figure 18-1. The life cycle of a Perl program

1. *The Compilation Phase*

    During phase 1, the *compile phase*, the Perl compiler converts your program into a data structure called a *parse tree*. Along with the standard parsing techniques, Perl employs a much more powerful one: it uses BEGIN blocks to guide further compilation. BEGIN blocks are handed off to the interpreter to be run as as soon as they are parsed, which effectively runs them in FIFO order (first in, first out). This includes any use and no declarations; these are really just BEGIN blocks in disguise. Any CHECK, INIT, and END blocks are scheduled by the compiler for delayed execution.

    Lexical declarations are noted, but assignments to them are not executed. All eval BLOCKs, s///e constructs, and noninterpolated regular expressions are compiled here, and constant expressions are pre-evaluated. The compiler is now done, unless it gets called back into service later. At the end of this phase, the interpreter is again called up to execute any scheduled CHECK blocks in LIFO order (last in, first out). The presence or absence of a CHECK block determines whether we next go to phase 2 or skip over to phase 4.

2. *The Code Generation Phase (optional)*

    CHECK blocks are installed by code generators, so this optional phase occurs when you explicitly use one of the code generators (described later in "Code Generators"). These convert the compiled (but not yet run) program into either C source code or serialized Perl bytecodes—a sequence of values expressing internal Perl instructions. If you choose to generate C source code, it can eventually produce a file called an *executable image* in native machine language.*

    At this point, your program goes into suspended animation. If you made an executable image, you can go directly to phase 4; otherwise, you need to reconstitute the freeze-dried bytecodes in phase 3.

3. *The Parse Tree Reconstruction Phase (optional)*

    To reanimate the program, its parse tree must be reconstructed. This phase exists only if code generation occurred and you chose to generate bytecode. Perl must first reconstitute its parse trees from that bytecode sequence before the program can run. Perl does not run directly from the bytecodes; that would be slow.

4. *The Execution Phase*

    Finally, what you've all been waiting for: running your program. Hence, this is also called the *run phase*. The interpreter takes the parse tree (which it got either directly from the compiler or indirectly from code generation and subsequent parse tree reconstruction) and executes it. (Or, if you generated an executable image file, it can be run as a standalone program since it contains an embedded Perl interpreter.)

    At the start of this phase, before your main program gets to run, all scheduled INIT blocks are executed in FIFO order. Then your main program is run. The interpreter can call back into the compiler as needed upon encountering an eval *STRING*, a do *FILE* or require statement, an s///ee construct, or a pattern match with an interpolated variable that is found to contain a legal code assertion.

---

* Your original script is an executable file too, but it's not machine language, so we don't call it an image. An image file is called that because it's a verbatim copy of the machine codes your CPU knows how to execute directly.

When your main program finishes, any delayed END blocks are finally executed, this time in LIFO order. The very first one seen will execute last, and then you're done. (END blocks are skipped only if you exec or your process is blown away by an uncaught catastrophic error. Ordinary exceptions are not considered catastrophic.)

Now we'll discuss these phases in greater detail, and in a different order.

Compiling Your Code

Perl is always in one of two modes of operation: either it is compiling your program, or it is executing it—never both at the same time. Throughout this book, we refer to certain events as happening at compile time, or we say that "the Perl compiler does this and that". At other points, we mention that something else occurs at run time, or that "the Perl interpreter does this and that". Although you can get by with thinking of both the compiler and interpreter as simply "Perl", understanding which of these two roles Perl is playing at any given point is essential to understanding why many things happen as they do. The *perl* executable implements both roles: first the compiler, then the interpreter. (Other roles are possible, too; *perl* is also an optimizer and a code generator. Occasionally, it's even a trickster—but all in good fun.)

It's also important to understand the distinction between compile phase and compile time, and between run phase and run time. A typical Perl program gets one compile phase, and then one run phase. A "phase" is a large-scale concept. But compile time and run time are small-scale concepts. A given compile phase does mostly compile-time stuff, but it also does some run-time stuff via BEGIN blocks. A given run phase does mostly run-time stuff, but it can do compile-time stuff through operators like eval *STRING*.

In the typical course of events, the Perl compiler reads through your entire program source before execution starts. This is when Perl parses the declarations, statements, and expressions to make sure they're syntactically legal.* If it finds a syntax error, the compiler attempts to recover from the error so it can report any other errors later in the source. Sometimes this works, and sometimes it doesn't; syntax errors have a noisy tendency to trigger a cascade of false alarms. Perl bails out in frustration after about 10 errors.

---

* No, there's no formal syntax diagram like a BNF, but you're welcome to peruse the *perly.y* file in the Perl source tree, which contains the *yacc*(1) grammar Perl uses. We recommend that you stay out of the lexer, which has been known to induce eating disorders in lab rats.

In addition to the interpreter that processes the BEGIN blocks, the compiler processes your program with the connivance of three notional agents. The *lexer* scans for each minimal unit of meaning in your program. These are sometimes called "lexemes", but you'll more often hear them referred to as *tokens* in texts about programming languages. The lexer is sometimes called a tokener or a scanner, and what it does is sometimes called lexing or tokenizing. The *parser* then tries to make sense out of groups of these tokens by assembling them into larger constructs, such as expressions and statements, based on the grammar of the Perl language. The *optimizer* rearranges and reduces these larger groupings into more efficient sequences. It picks its optimizations carefully, not wasting time on marginal optimizations, because the Perl compiler has to be blazing fast when used as a load-and-go compiler.

This doesn't happen in independent stages, but all at once with a lot of cross talk between the agents. The lexer occasionally needs hints from the parser to know which of several possible token types it's looking at. (Oddly, lexical scope is one of the things the lexical analyzer *doesn't* understand, because that's the other meaning of "lexical".) The optimizer also needs to keep track of what the parser is doing, because some optimizations can't happen until the parse has reached a certain point, like finishing an expression, statement, block, or subroutine.

You may think it odd that the Perl compiler does all these things at once instead of one after another, but it's really just the same messy process you go through to understand natural language on the fly, while you're listening to it or reading it. You don't wait till the end of a chapter to figure out what the first sentence meant. You could think of the following correspondences:

Computer Language	Natural Language
Character	Letter
Token	Morpheme
Term	Word
Expression	Phrase
Statement	Sentence
Block	Paragraph
File	Chapter
Program	Story

Assuming the parse goes well, the compiler deems your input a valid story, er, program. If you use the **-c** switch when running your program, it prints out a "syntax OK" message and exits. Otherwise, the compiler passes the fruits of its efforts on to other agents. These "fruits" come in the form of a *parse tree*. Each fruit on the tree—or *node*, as it's called—represents one of Perl's internal *opcodes*, and the branches on the tree represent that tree's historical growth pattern. Eventually, the nodes will be strung together linearly, one after another, to indicate the execution order in which the run-time system will visit those nodes.

Each opcode is the smallest unit of executable instruction that Perl can think about. You might see an expression like $a = -($b + $c) as one statement, but Perl thinks of it as six separate opcodes. Laid out in a simplified format, the parse tree for that expression would look like Figure 18-2. The numbers represent the visitation order that the Perl run-time system will eventually follow.

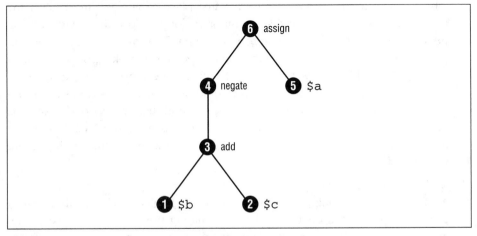

Figure 18-2. Opcode visitation order of $a = -($b + $c)

Perl isn't a one-pass compiler as some might imagine. (One-pass compilers are great at making things easy for the computer and hard for the programmer.) It's really a multipass, optimizing compiler consisting of at least three different logical passes that are interleaved in practice. Passes 1 and 2 run alternately as the compiler repeatedly scurries up and down the parse tree during its construction; pass 3 happens whenever a subroutine or file is completely parsed. Here are those passes:

Pass 1: Bottom-Up Parsing

During this pass, the parse tree is built up by the *yacc*(1) parser using the tokens it's fed from the underlying lexer (which could be considered another logical pass in its own right). Bottom-up just means that the parser knows about the leaves of the tree before it knows about its branches and root. It really does figure things out from bottom to top in Figure 18-2, since we drew the root at the top, in the idiosyncratic fashion of computer scientists. (And linguists.)

As each opcode node is constructed, per-opcode sanity checks verify correct semantics, such as the correct number and types of arguments used to call built-in functions. As each subsection of the tree takes shape, the optimizer considers what transformations it can apply to the entire subtree now beneath it. For instance, once it knows that a list of values is being fed to a function that takes a specific number of arguments, it can throw away the opcode that records the number of arguments for functions that take a varying number of arguments. A more important optimization, known as *constant folding*, is described later in this section.

This pass also constructs the node visitation order used later for execution, which is a really neat trick because the first place to visit is almost never the top node. The compiler makes a temporary loop of opcodes, with the top node pointing to the first opcode to visit. When the top-level opcode is incorporated into something bigger, that loop of opcodes is broken, only to make a bigger loop with the new top node. Eventually the loop is broken for good when the start opcode gets poked into some other structure such as a subroutine descriptor. The subroutine caller can still find that first opcode despite its being way down at the bottom of the tree, as it is in Figure 18-2. There's no need for the interpreter to recurse back down the parse tree to figure out where to start.

Pass 2: Top-Down Optimizer

A person reading a snippet of Perl code (or of English code, for that matter) cannot determine the context without examining the surrounding lexical elements. Sometimes you can't decide what's really going on until you have more information. Don't feel bad, though, because you're not alone: neither can the compiler. In this pass, the compiler descends back down the subtree it's just built to apply local optimizations, the most notable of which is *context propagation*. The compiler marks subjacent nodes with the appropriate contexts (void, scalar, list, reference, or lvalue) imposed by the current node. Unwanted opcodes are nulled out but not deleted, because it's now too late to reconstruct the execution order. We'll rely on the third pass to remove them from the provisional execution order determined by the first pass.

Pass 3: Peephole Optimizer

Certain units of code have their own storage space in which they keep lexically scoped variables. (Such a space is called a *scratchpad* in Perl lingo.) These units include `eval` *STRING*s, subroutines, and entire files. More importantly from the standpoint of the optimizer, they each have their own entry point, which means that while we know the execution order from here on, we can't know what happened before, because the construct could have been called from anywhere. So when one of these units is done being parsed, Perl runs a peephole optimizer on that code. Unlike the previous two passes, which walked the branch structure of the parse tree, this pass traverses the code in linear execution order, since this is basically the last opportunity to do so before we cut the opcode list off from the parser. Most optimizations were already performed in the first two passes, but some can't be.

Assorted late-term optimizations happen here, including stitching together the final execution order by skipping over nulled out opcodes, and recognizing when various opcode juxtapositions can be reduced to something simpler. The recognition of chained string concatenations is one important optimization, since you'd really like to avoid copying a string back and forth each time you add a little bit to the end. This pass doesn't just optimize; it also does a great deal of "real" work: trapping barewords, generating warnings on questionable constructs, checking for code unlikely to be reached, resolving pseudohash keys, and looking for subroutines called before their prototypes had been compiled.

Pass 4: Code Generation

This pass is optional; it isn't used in the normal scheme of things. But if any of the three code generators—B::Bytecode, B::C, and B::CC—are invoked, the parse tree is accessed one final time. The code generators emit either serialized Perl bytecodes used to reconstruct the parse tree later or literal C code representing the state of the compile-time parse tree.

Generation of C code comes in two different flavors. B::C simply reconstructs the parse tree and runs it using the usual runops() loop that Perl itself uses during execution. B::CC produces a linearized and optimized C equivalent of the run-time code path (which resembles a giant jump table) and executes that instead.

During compilation, Perl optimizes your code in many, many ways. It rearranges code to make it more efficient at execution time. It deletes code that can never be reached during execution, like an if (0) block, or the elsifs and the else in an if (1) block. If you use lexically typed variables declared with my ClassName $var or our ClassName $var, and the ClassName package was set up with the use fields pragma, accesses to constant fields from the underlying pseudohash are typochecked at compile time and converted into array accesses instead. If you supply the sort operator with a simple enough comparison routine, such as {$a <=> $b} or {$b cmp $a}, this is replaced by a call to compiled C code.

Perl's most dramatic optimization is probably the way it resolves constant expressions as soon as possible. For example, consider the parse tree shown in Figure 18-2. If nodes 1 and 2 had both been literals or constant functions, nodes 1 through 4 would have been replaced by the result of that computation, something like Figure 18-3.

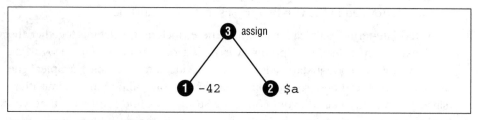

Figure 18-3. Constant folding

This is called *constant folding*. Constant folding isn't limited to simple cases such as turning 2**10 into 1024 at compile time. It also resolves function calls—both built-ins and user-declared subroutines that meet the criteria from the section "Inlining Constant Functions" in Chapter 6, *Subroutines*. Reminiscent of FORTRAN compilers' notorious knowledge of their own intrinsic functions, Perl also knows which of its own built-ins to call during compilation. That's why if you try to take the log of 0.0 or the sqrt of a negative constant, you'll incur a compilation error, not a run-time error, and the interpreter is never run at all.*

Even arbitrarily complicated expressions are resolved early, sometimes triggering the deletion of complete blocks such as the one here:

```
if (2 * sin(1)/cos(1) < 3 && somefn()) { whatever() }
```

No code is generated for what can never be evaluated. Because the first part is always false, neither somefn nor whatever can ever be called. (So don't expect to goto labels inside that block, because it won't even exist at run time.) If somefn were an inlinable constant function, then even switching the evaluation order like this:

```
if (somefn() && 2 * sin(1)/cos(1) < 3)) { whatever() }
```

wouldn't change the outcome, since the entire expression still resolves at compile time. If whatever were inlinable, it wouldn't be called at run time, nor even during compilation; its value would just be inserted as though it were a literal constant.

---

* Actually, we're oversimplifying here. The interpreter does get run, because that's how the constant folder is implemented. But it is run immediately at compile time, similar to how BEGIN blocks are executed.

You would then incur a warning about a "Useless use of a constant in void context". This might surprise you if you didn't realize it was a constant. However, if whatever were the last statement evaluated in a function called in a nonvoid context (as determined by the optimizer), you wouldn't see the warning.

You can see the final result of the constructed parse tree after all optimization stages with *perl -Dx*. (The **-D** switch requires a special, debugging-enabled build of Perl). Also see the section on B::Deparse described below.

All in all, the Perl compiler works hard (but not *too* hard) to optimize code so that, come run time, overall execution is sped up. It's about time to get your program running, so let's do that now.

Executing Your Code

To the first approximation, Sparc programs only run on Sparc machines, Intel programs only run on Intel machines, and Perl programs only run on Perl machines. A Perl machine possesses those attributes that a Perl program would find ideal in a computer: memory that is automatically allocated and deallocated, fundamental data types that are dynamic strings, arrays, and hashes, and have no size limits, and systems that all behave pretty much the same way. The job of the Perl interpreter is to make whatever computer it happens to be running on appear to be one of these idealistic Perl machines.

This fictitious machine presents the illusion of a computer specially designed to do nothing but run Perl programs. Each opcode produced by the compiler is a fundamental command in this emulated instruction set. Instead of a hardware program counter, the interpreter just keeps track of the current opcode to execute. Instead of a hardware stack pointer, the interpreter has its own virtual stack. This stack is very important because the Perl virtual machine (which we refuse to call a PVM) is a stack-based machine. Perl opcodes are internally called *PP codes* (short for "push-pop codes") because they manipulate the interpreter's virtual stack to find all operands, process temporary values, and store all results.

If you've ever programmed in Forth or PostScript, or used an HP scientific calculator with RPN ("Reverse Polish Notation") entry, you know how a stack machine works. Even if you haven't, the concept is simple: to add 3 and 4, you do things in the order 3 4 + instead of the more conventional 3 + 4. What this means in terms of the stack is that you push 3 and then 4 onto the stack, and + then pops both arguments off the stack, adds them, and pushes 7 back onto the stack, where it will sit until you do something else with it.

Compared with the Perl compiler, the Perl interpreter is a straightforward, almost boring, program. All it does is step through the compiled opcodes, one at a time, and dispatch them to the Perl run-time environment, that is, the Perl virtual machine. It's just a wad of C code, right?

Actually, it's not boring at all. A Perl virtual machine keeps track of a great deal of dynamic context on your behalf so that you don't have to. Perl maintains quite a few stacks, which you don't have to understand, but which we'll list here anyway just to impress you:

operand stack
> That's the stack we already talked about.

save stack
> Where localized values are saved pending restoration. Many internal routines also localize values without your knowing it.

scope stack
> The lightweight dynamic context that controls when the save stack should be "popped".

context stack
> The heavyweight dynamic context; who called whom to get where you are now. The `caller` function traverses this stack. Loop-control functions scan this stack to find out which loop to control. When you peel back the context stack, the scope stack gets peeled back appropriately, which restores all your local variables from the save stack, even if you left the earlier context by nefarious methods such as raising an exception and *longjmp*(3)ing out.

jumpenv stack
> The stack of *longjmp*(3) contexts that allows us to raise exceptions or exit expeditiously.

return stack
> Where we came from when we entered this subroutine.

mark stack
> Where the current variadic argument list on the operand stack starts.

recursive lexical pad stacks
> Where the lexical variables and other "scratch register" storage is kept when subroutines are called recursively.

And of course, there's the C stack on which all the C variables are stored. Perl actually tries to avoid relying on C's stack for the storage of saved values, since *longjmp*(3) bypasses the proper restoration of such values.

All this is to say that the usual view of an interpreter, a program that interprets another program, is really woefully inadequate to describe what's going on here. Yes, there's some C code implementing some opcodes, but when we say "interpreter", we mean something more than that, in the same way that when we say "musician", we mean something more than a set of DNA instructions for turning notes into sounds. Musicians are real, live organisms and have "state". So do interpreters.

Specifically, all this dynamic and lexical context, along with the global symbol tables, plus the parse trees, plus a thread of execution, is what we call an interpreter. As a context for execution, an interpreter really starts its existence even before the compiler starts, and can run 'in rudimentary form even as the compiler is building up the interpreter's context. In fact, that's precisely what's happening when the compiler calls into the interpreter to execute BEGIN blocks and such. And the interpreter can turn around and use the compiler to build itself up further. Every time you define another subroutine or load another module, the particular virtual Perl machine we call an interpreter is redefining itself. You can't really say that either the compiler or the interpreter is in control, because they're cooperating to control the bootstrap process we commonly call "running a Perl script". It's like bootstrapping a child's brain. Is it the DNA doing it or is it the neurons? A little of both, we think, with some input from external programmers.

It's possible to run multiple interpreters in the same process; they may or may not share parse trees, depending on whether they were started by cloning an existing interpreter or by building a new interpreter from scratch. It's also possible to run multiple threads in a single interpreter, in which case they share not only parse trees but also global symbols—see Chapter 17, *Threads*.

But most Perl programs use only a single Perl interpreter to execute their compiled code. And while you can run multiple, independent Perl interpreters within one process, the current API for this is only accessible from C.* Each individual Perl interpreter serves the role of a completely separate process, but doesn't cost as much to create as a whole new process does. That's how Apache's mod_perl extension gets such great performance: when you launch a CGI script under mod_perl, that script has already been compiled into Perl opcodes, eliminating the need for recompilation—but more importantly, eliminating the need to start a new process, which is the real bottleneck. Apache initializes a new Perl interpreter in an existing process and hands that interpreter the previously compiled code to execute. Of course, there's much more to it than that—there always is. For more about mod_perl, see *Writing Apache Modules with Perl and C* (O'Reilly, 1999).

---

* With one exception, so far: revision 5.6.0 of Perl can do cloned interpreters in support of fork emulation on Microsoft Windows. There may well be a Perl API to "ithreads", as they're called, by the time you read this.

Many other applications such as *nvi*, *vim*, and *innd* can embed Perl interpreters; we can't hope to list them all here. There are a number of commercial products that don't even advertise that they have embedded Perl engines. They just use it internally because it gets their job done in style.

Compiler Backends

So, if Apache can compile a Perl program now and execute it later, why can't you? Apache and other programs that contain embedded Perl interpreters have it easy—they never store the parse tree to an external file. If you're content with that approach, and don't mind using the C API to get at it, you can do the same thing. See the section "Embedding Perl" in Chapter 21, *Internals and Externals*, to learn how to access Perl from an enclosing C framework.

If you don't want to go that route, or have other needs, then there are a few options available. Instead of feeding the opcode output from the Perl compiler immediately into a Perl interpreter, you can invoke any of several alternative backends instead. These backends can serialize and store the compiled opcodes to an external file or even convert them into a couple different flavors of C code.

Please be aware that the code generators are all extremely experimental utilities that shouldn't be expected to work in a production environment. In fact, they shouldn't even be expected to work in a nonproduction environment except maybe once in a blue moon. Now that we've set your expectations low enough that any success at all will necessarily surpass them, it's safe to tell you how the backends work.

Some of the backend modules are code generators, like `B::Bytecode`, `B::C`, and `B::CC`. Others are really code-analysis and debugging tools, like `B::Deparse`, `B::Lint`, and `B::Xref`. Beyond those backends, the standard release includes several other low-level modules of potential interest to would-be authors of Perl code-development tools. Other backend modules can be found on CPAN, including (as of this writing) `B::Fathom`, `B::Graph`, `B::JVM::Jasmin`, and `B::Size`.

When you're using the Perl compiler for anything other than feeding the interpreter, the O module (that is, using the *O.pm* file) stands between the compiler and assorted backend modules. You don't call the backends directly; instead, you call the middle end, which in turn calls the designated backend. So, if you had a module called `B::Backend`, you would invoke it on a given script this way:

```
% perl -MO=Backend SCRIPTNAME
```

Some backends take options, specified as:

```
% perl -MO=Backend,OPTS SCRIPTNAME
```

Some backends already have their own frontends to invoke their middle ends for you so you don't have to remember their M.O. In particular, *perlcc*(1) invokes that code generator, which can be cumbersome to fire up.

Code Generators

The three current backends that convert Perl opcodes into some other format are all emphatically experimental. (Yes, we said this before, but we don't want you to forget.) Even when they happen to produce output that runs correctly, the resulting programs may take more disk space, more memory, and more CPU time than than they would ordinarily. This is an area of ongoing research and development. Things will get better.

The Bytecode Generator

The B::Bytecode module writes the parse tree's opcodes out in a platform-independent encoding. You can take a Perl script compiled down to bytecodes and copy that to any other machine with Perl installed on it.

The standard but currently experimental *perlcc*(1) command knows how to convert Perl source code into a byte-compiled Perl program. All you have to do is:

```
% perlcc -b -o pbyscript srcscript
```

And now you should be able to directly "execute" the resulting *pbyscript*. The start of that file looks somewhat like this:

```
#!/usr/bin/perl
use ByteLoader 0.03;
^C^@^E^A^C^@^@^@^A^F^@^C^@^@^@^B^F^@^C^@^@^@^C^F^@^C^@^@^@
B^@^@^@^H9^A8M-^?M-^?M-^?M-^?7M-^?M-^?M-^?M-^?6^@^@^@^A6^@
^G^D^D^@^@^@^KR^@^@^@^HS^@^@^@^HV^@M-2W<^FU^@^@^@^@X^Y@Z^@
...
```

There you find a small script header followed by purely binary data. This may seem like deep magic, but its dweomer, er, dwimmer is at most a minor one. The ByteLoader module uses a technique called a *source filter* to alter the source code before Perl gets a chance to see it. A source filter is a kind of preprocessor that applies to everything below it in the current file. Instead of being limited to simplistic transformations the way macro processors like *cpp*(1) and *m4*(1) are, here there are no constraints. Source filters have been used to augment Perl's syntax, to compress or encrypt source code, even to write Perl programs in Latin. E perlibus unicode; cogito, ergo substr; carp dbm, et al. Er, caveat scriptor.

The ByteLoader module is a source filter that knows how to disassemble the serialized opcodes produced by B::Bytecode to reconstruct the original parse tree. The reconstituted Perl code is spliced into the current parse tree without using the compiler. When the interpreter hits those opcodes, it just executes them as though they'd been there waiting for it all along.

The C Code Generators

The remaining code generators, B::C and B::CC, both produce C code instead of serialized Perl opcodes. The code they generate is far from readable, and if you try to read it you'll just go blind. It's not something you can use to plug little translated Perl-to-C bits into a larger C program. For that, see Chapter 21.

The B::C module just writes out the C data structures needed to recreate the entire Perl run-time environment. You get a dedicated interpreter with all the compiler-built data structures pre-initialized. In some senses, the code generated is like what B::Bytecode produces. Both are a straight translation of the opcode trees that the compiler built, but where B::Bytecode lays them out in symbolic form to be recreated later and plugged into a running Perl interpreter, B::C lays those opcodes down in C. When you compile this C code with your C compiler and link in the Perl library, the resulting program won't need a Perl interpreter installed on the target system. (It might need some shared libraries, though, if you didn't link everything statically.) However, this program isn't really any different than the regular Perl interpreter that runs your script. It's just precompiled into a standalone executable image.

The B::CC module, however, tries to do more than that. The beginning of the C source file it generates looks pretty much like what B::C produced,* but eventually, any similarity ends. In the B::C code, you have a big opcode table in C that's manipulated just as the interpreter would do on its own, whereas in the C code generated by B::CC is laid out in the order corresponding to the run-time flow of your program. It even has a C function corresponding to each function in your program. Some amount of optimization based on variable types is done; a few benchmarks can run twice as fast as in the standard interpreter. This is the most ambitious of the current code generators, the one that holds the greatest promise for the future. By no coincidence, it is also the least stable of the three.

Computer science students looking for graduate thesis projects need look no further. There are plenty of diamonds in the rough waiting to be polished off here.

---

* But then, so does everything once you've gone blind. Didn't we warn you not to peek?

Code Development Tools

The O module has many interesting Modi Operandi beyond feeding the exasperatingly experimental code generators. By providing relatively painless access to the Perl compiler's output, this module makes it easy to build other tools that need to know everything about a Perl program.

The B::Lint module is named after *lint*(1), the C program verifier. It inspects programs for questionable constructs that often trip up beginners but don't normally trigger warnings. Call the module directly:

```
% perl -MO=Lint,all myprog
```

Only a few checks are currently defined, such as using an array in an implicit scalar context, relying on default variables, and accessing another package's (nominally private) identifiers that start with _. See *B::Lint*(3) for details.

The B::Xref module generates cross-reference listings of the declaration and use of all variables (both global and lexically scoped), subroutines, and formats in a program, broken down by file and subroutine. Call the module this way:

```
% perl -MO=Xref myprog > myprof.pxref
```

For instance, here's a partial report:

```
Subroutine parse_argv
  Package (lexical)
    $on                 i113, 114
    $opt                i113, 114
    %getopt_cfg         i107, 113
    @cfg_args           i112, 114, 116, 116
  Package Getopt::Long
    $ignorecase         101
    &GetOptions         &124
  Package main
    $Options            123, 124, 141, 150, 165, 169
    %$Options           141, 150, 165, 169
    &check_read         &167
    @ARGV               121, 157, 157, 162, 166, 166
```

This shows that the parse_argv subroutine had four lexical variables of its own; it also accessed global identifiers from both the main package and from Getopt::Long. The numbers are the lines where that item was used: a leading i indicates that the item was first introduced at the following line number, and a leading & means a subroutine was called there. Dereferences are listed separately, which is why both $Options and %$Options are shown.

The `B::Deparse` is a pretty printer that can demystify Perl code and help you understand what transformations the optimizer has taken with your code. For example, this shows what defaults Perl uses for various constructs:

```
% perl -MO=Deparse -ne 'for (1 .. 10) { print if -t }'
LINE: while (defined($_ = <ARGV>)) {
    foreach $_ (1 .. 10) {
        print $_ if -t STDIN;
    }
}
```

The **-p** switch adds parentheses so you can see Perl's idea of precedence:

```
% perl -MO=Deparse,-p -e 'print $a ** 3 + sqrt(2) / 10 ** -2 ** $c'
print((($a ** 3) + (1.4142135623731 / (10 ** (-(2 ** $c))))));
```

You can use **-q** to see what primitives interpolated strings are compiled into:

```
% perl -MO=Deparse,-q -e '"A $name and some @ARGV\n"'
'A ' . $name . ' and some ' . join($", @ARGV) . "\n";
```

And this shows how Perl really compiles a three-part for loop into a while loop:

```
% perl -MO=Deparse -e 'for ($i=0;$i<10;$i++) { $x++ }'
$i = 0;
while ($i < 10) {
    ++$x;
}
continue {
    ++$i
}
```

You could even call `B::Deparse` on a Perl bytecode file produced by *perlcc -b*, and have it decompile that binary file for you. Serialized Perl opcodes may be a tad tough to read, but strong encryption they are not.

Avant-Garde Compiler, Retro Interpreter

There's a right time to think about everything; sometimes that time is beforehand, and sometimes it's after. Sometimes it's somewhere in the middle. Perl doesn't presume to know when it's the right time to think, so it gives the programmer a number of options for telling it when to think. Other times it knows that some sort of thinking is necessary but doesn't have any idea what it ought to think, so it needs ways of asking your program. Your program answers these kinds of questions by defining subroutines with names appropriate to what Perl is trying to find out.

Not only can the compiler call into the interpreter when it wants to be forward thinking, but the interpreter can also call back to the compiler when it wants to revise history. Your program can use several operators to call back into the compiler. Like the compiler, the interpreter can also call into named subroutines when it wants to find things out. Because of all this give and take between the compiler, the interpreter, and your program, you need to be aware of what things happen when. First we'll talk about when these named subroutines are triggered.

In Chapter 10, *Packages*, we saw how a package's AUTOLOAD subroutine is triggered when an undefined function in that package is called. In Chapter 12, *Objects*, we met the DESTROY method which is invoked when an object's memory is about to be automatically reclaimed by Perl. And in Chapter 14, *Tied Variables*, we encountered the many functions implicitly called when a tied variable is accessed.

These subroutines all follow the convention that, if a subroutine is triggered automatically by either the compiler or the interpreter, we write its name in uppercase. Associated with the different stages of your program's lifetime are four other such subroutines, named BEGIN, CHECK, INIT, and END. The sub keyword is optional before their declarations. Perhaps they are better called "blocks", because they're in some ways more like named blocks than real subroutines.

For instance, unlike regular subroutines, there's no harm in declaring these blocks multiple times, since Perl keeps track of when to call them, so you never have to call them by name. (They are also unlike regular subroutines in that shift and pop act as though you were in the main program, and so they act on @ARGV by default, not @_.)

These four block types run in this order:

BEGIN

> Runs ASAP (as soon as parsed) whenever encountered during compilation, before compiling the rest of the file.

CHECK

> Runs when compilation is complete, but before the program starts. (CHECK can mean "checkpoint" or "double-check" or even just "stop".)

INIT

> Runs at the beginning of execution right before the main flow of your program starts.

END

> Runs at the end of execution right after the program finishes.

If you declare more than one of these by the same name, even in separate modules, the BEGINs all run before any CHECKs, which all run before any INITs, which all run before any ENDs—which all run dead last, after your main program has finished. Multiple BEGINs and INITs run in declaration order (FIFO), and the CHECKs and ENDs run in inverse declaration order (LIFO).

This is probably easiest to see in a demo:

```
#!/usr/bin/perl -l
print       "start main running here";
die         "main now dying here\n";
die         "XXX: not reached\n";
END         { print "1st END: done running"    }
CHECK       { print "1st CHECK: done compiling" }
INIT        { print "1st INIT: started running" }
END         { print "2nd END: done running"    }
BEGIN       { print "1st BEGIN: still compiling" }
INIT        { print "2nd INIT: started running" }
BEGIN       { print "2nd BEGIN: still compiling" }
CHECK       { print "2nd CHECK: done compiling" }
END         { print "3rd END: done running"    }
```

When run, that demo program produces this output:

```
1st BEGIN: still compiling
2nd BEGIN: still compiling
2nd CHECK: done compiling
1st CHECK: done compiling
1st INIT: started running
2nd INIT: started running
start main running here
main now dying here
3rd END: done running
2nd END: done running
1st END: done running
```

Because a BEGIN block executes immediately, it can pull in subroutine declarations, definitions, and importations before the rest of the file is even compiled. These can alter how the compiler parses the rest of the current file, particularly if you import subroutine definitions. At the very least, declaring a subroutine lets it be used as a list operator, making parentheses optional. If the imported subroutine is declared with a prototype, calls to it can be parsed like built-ins and can even override built-ins of the same name in order to give them different semantics. The use declaration is just a BEGIN block with an attitude.

END blocks, by contrast, are executed as *late* as possible: when your program exits the Perl interpreter, even if as a result of an untrapped die or other fatal exception. There are two situations in which an END block (or a DESTROY method) is skipped. It isn't run if, instead of exiting, the current process just morphs itself from one program to another via exec. A process blown out of the water by an uncaught signal also skips its END routines. (See the use sigtrap pragma described in Chapter 31, *Pragmatic Modules*, for an easy way to convert catchable signals into exceptions. For general information on signal handling, see "Signals" in Chapter 16, *Interprocess Communication*.) To avoid all END processing, you can

call POSIX::_exit, say kill -9, $$, or just exec any innocuous program, such as
/bin/true on Unix systems.

Inside an END block, $? contains the status the program is going to exit with. You
can modify $? from within the END block to change the exit value of the program.
Beware of changing $? accidentally by running another program with system or
backticks.

If you have several END blocks within a file, they execute in *reverse* order of their
definition. That is, the last END block defined is the first one executed when your
program finishes. This reversal enables related BEGIN and END blocks to nest the
way you'd expect, if you pair them up. For example, if the main program and a
module it loads both have their own paired BEGIN and END subroutines, like so:

```
BEGIN { print "main begun" }
END   { print "main ended" }
use Module;
```

and in that module, these declarations:

```
BEGIN { print "module begun" }
END   { print "module ended" }
```

then the main program knows that its BEGIN will always happen first, and its END
will always happen last. (Yes, BEGIN is really a compile-time block, but similar
arguments apply to paired INIT and END blocks at run time.) This principle is
recursively true for any file that includes another when both have declarations like
these. This nesting property makes these blocks work well as package construc-
tors and destructors. Each module can have its own set-up and tear-down func-
tions that Perl will call automatically. This way the programmer doesn't have to
remember that if a particular library is used, what special initialization or clean-up
code ought to be invoked, and when. The module's declarations assure these
events.

If you think of an eval *STRING* as a call *back* from the interpreter to the compiler,
then you might think of a BEGIN as a call *forward* from the compiler into the inter-
preter. Both temporarily put the current activity on hold and switch modes of
operation. When we say that a BEGIN block is executed as early as possible, we
mean it's executed just as soon as it is completely defined, even before the rest of
the containing file is parsed. BEGIN blocks are therefore executed during compile
time, never during run time. Once a BEGIN block has run, it is immediately unde-
fined and any code it used is returned to Perl's memory pool. You couldn't call a
BEGIN block as a subroutine even if you tried, because by the time it's there, it's
already gone.

Similar to BEGIN blocks, INIT blocks are run just before the Perl run time begins execution, in "first in, first out" (FIFO) order. For example, the code generators documented in *perlcc* make use of INIT blocks to initialize and resolve pointers to XSUBs. INIT blocks are really just like BEGIN blocks, except they let the programmer distinguish construction that must happen at compile phase from construction that must happen at run phase. When you're running a script directly, that's not terribly important because the compiler gets invoked every time anyway; but when compilation is separate from execution, the distinction can be crucial. The compiler may only be invoked once, and the resulting executable may be invoked many times.

Similar to END blocks, CHECK blocks are run just after the Perl compile phase ends but before run phase begins, in LIFO order. CHECK blocks are useful for "winding down" the compiler just as END blocks are useful for winding down your program. In particular, the backends all use CHECK blocks as the hook from which to invoke their respective code generators. All they need to do is put a CHECK block into their own module, and it will run at the right time, so you don't have to install a CHECK into your program. For this reason, you'll rarely write a CHECK block yourself, unless you're writing such a module.

Putting it all together, Table 18-1 lists various constructs with details on when they compile and when they run the code represented by "...".

Table 18-1. What Happens When

Block or Expression	Compiles During Phase	Traps Compile Errors	Runs During Phase	Traps Run Errors	Call Trigger Policy
use ...	C	No	C	No	Now
no ...	C	No	C	No	Now
BEGIN {...}	C	No	C	No	Now
CHECK {...}	C	No	C	No	Late
INIT {...}	C	No	R	No	Early
END {...}	C	No	R	No	Late
eval {...}	C	No	R	Yes	Inline
eval "..."	R	Yes	R	Yes	Inline
foo(...)	C	No	R	No	Inline
sub foo {...}	C	No	R	No	Call anytime
eval "sub {...}"	R	Yes	R	No	Call later
s/pat/.../e	C	No	R	No	Inline
s/pat/"..."/ee	R	Yes	R	Yes	Inline

Now that you know the score, we hope you'll be able to compose and perform your Perl pieces with greater confidence.

19

The Command-Line Interface

This chapter is about aiming Perl in the right direction before you fire it off. There are various ways to aim Perl, but the two primary ways are through switches on the command line and through environment variables. Switches are the more immediate and precise way to aim a particular command. Environment variables are more often used to set general policy.

Command Processing

It is fortunate that Perl grew up in the Unix world, because that means its invocation syntax works pretty well under the command interpreters of other operating systems, too. Most command interpreters know how to deal with a list of words as arguments and don't care if an argument starts with a minus sign. There are, of course, some sticky spots where you'll get fouled up if you move from one system to another. You can't use single quotes under MS-DOS as you do under Unix, for instance. And on systems like VMS, some wrapper code has to jump through hoops to emulate Unix I/O redirection. Wildcard interpretation is a wildcard. Once you get past those issues, however, Perl treats its switches and arguments much the same on any operating system.

Even when you don't have a command interpreter per se, it's easy to execute a Perl program from another program written in any language. Not only can the calling program pass arguments in the ordinary way, it can also pass information via environment variables and, if your operating system supports them, inherited file descriptors (see "Passing Filehandles" in Chapter 16, *Interprocess Communication*. Even exotic argument-passing mechanisms can easily be encapsulated in a module, then brought into your Perl program via a simple use directive.

Perl parses command-line switches in the standard fashion.* That is, it expects any switches (words beginning with a minus) to come first on the command line. After that usually comes the name of the script, followed by any additional arguments to be passed into the script. Some of these additional arguments may themselves look like switches, but if so, they must be processed by the script, because Perl quits parsing switches as soon as it sees a nonswitch, or the special "--" switch that says, "I am the last switch."

Perl gives you some flexibility in where you place the source code for your program. For small, quick-and-dirty jobs, you can program Perl entirely from the command line. For larger, more permanent jobs, you can supply a Perl script as a separate file. Perl looks for a script to compile and run in any one of these three ways:

1. Specified line by line via **-e** switches on the command line. For example:

    ```
    % perl -e "print 'Hello, World.'"
    Hello, World.
    ```

2. Contained in the file specified by the first filename on the command line. Systems supporting the #! notation on the first line of an executable script invoke interpreters this way on your behalf.

3. Passed in implicitly via standard input. This method works only when there are no filename arguments; to pass arguments to a standard-input script you must use method 2, explicitly specifying a "-" for the script name. For example:

    ```
    % echo "print qq(Hello, @ARGV.)" | perl - World
    Hello, World.
    ```

With methods 2 and 3, Perl starts parsing the input file from the beginning—unless you've specified a **-x** switch, in which case it scans for the first line starting with #! and containing the word "perl", and starts there instead. This is useful for running a script embedded in a larger message. If so, you might indicate the end of the script using the __END__ token.

Whether or not you use **-x**, the #! line is always examined for switches when the line is parsed. That way, if you're on a platform that allows only one argument with the #! line, or worse, doesn't even recognize the #! line as special, you can still get consistent switch behavior regardless of how Perl was invoked, even if **-x** was used to find the beginning of the script.

Warning: because older versions of Unix silently chop off kernel interpretation of the #! line after 32 characters, some switches may end up getting to your program

---

* Presuming you agree that Unix is both standard and fashionable.

intact, and others not; you could even get a "–" without its letter, if you're not careful. You probably want to make sure that all your switches fall either before or after that 32-character boundary. Most switches don't care whether they're processed redundantly, but getting a "–" instead of a complete switch would cause Perl to try to read its source code from the standard input instead of from your script. And a partial **-I** switch could also cause odd results. However, some switches do care if they are processed twice, like combinations of **-1** and **-0**. Either put all the switches after the 32-character boundary (if applicable), or replace the use of **-0***DIGITS* with BEGIN{ $/ = "\0*DIGITS*"; }. Of course, if you're not on a Unix system, you're guaranteed not to have this particular problem.

Parsing of #! switches starts from where "perl" is first mentioned in the line. The sequences "–*" and "– " are specifically ignored for the benefit of *emacs* users, so that, if you're so inclined, you can say:

```
#!/bin/sh -- # -*- perl -*- -p
eval 'exec perl -S $0 ${1+"$@"}'
    if 0;
```

and Perl will see only the **-p** switch. The fancy "-*- perl -*-" gizmo tells *emacs* to start up in Perl mode; you don't need it if you don't use *emacs*. The **-S** mess is explained later under the description of that switch.

A similar trick involves the *env*(1) program, if you have it:

```
#!/usr/bin/env perl
```

The previous examples use a relative path to the Perl interpreter, getting whatever version is first in the user's path. If you want a specific version of Perl, say, *perl5.6.1*, place it directly in the #! line's path, whether with the *env* program, with the **-S** mess, or with a regular #! processing.

If the #! line does *not* contain the word "perl", the program named after the #! is executed instead of the Perl interpreter. For example, suppose you have an ordinary Bourne shell script out there that says:

```
#!/bin/sh
echo "I am a shell script"
```

If you feed that file to Perl, then Perl will run */bin/sh* for you. This is slightly bizarre, but it helps people on machines that don't recognize #!, because—by setting their SHELL environment variable—they can tell a program (such as a mailer) that their shell is */usr/bin/perl*, and Perl will then dispatch the program to the correct interpreter for them, even though their kernel is too stupid to do so.

But back to Perl scripts that are really Perl scripts. After locating your script, Perl compiles the entire program into an internal form (see Chapter 18, *Compiling*). If any compilation errors arise, execution does not even begin. (This is unlike the typical shell script or command file, which might run part-way through before finding a syntax error.) If the script is syntactically correct, it is executed. If the script runs off the end without hitting an exit or die operator, an implicit exit(0) is supplied by Perl to indicate successful completion to your caller. (This is unlike the typical C program, where you're likely to get a random exit status if your program just terminates in the normal way.)

#! *and Quoting on Non-Unix Systems*

Unix's #! technique can be simulated on other systems:

Macintosh

A Perl program on a Macintosh will have the appropriate Creator and Type, so that double-clicking them will invoke the Perl application.

MS-DOS

Create a batch file to run your program, and codify it in ALTERNATIVE_SHEBANG. See the *dosish.h* file in the top level of the Perl source distribution for more information about this.

OS/2

Put this line:

```
extproc perl -S -your_switches
```

as the first line in **.cmd* file (**-s** works around a bug in *cmd.exe*'s "extproc" handling).

VMS

Put these lines:

```
% perl -mysw 'f$env("procedure")' 'p1' 'p2' 'p3' 'p4' 'p5' 'p6' 'p7' 'p8' !
$ exit++ + ++$status != 0 and $exit = $status = undef;
```

at the top of your program, where *-mysw* are any command-line switches you want to pass to Perl. You can now invoke the program directly by typing perl program, as a DCL procedure by saying @program, or implicitly via DCL$PATH by using just the name of the program. This incantation is a bit much to remember, but Perl will display it for you if you type in perl "-V:startperl". If you can't remember that—well, that's why you bought this book.

Win??

When using the ActiveState distribution of Perl under some variant of Microsoft's Windows suite of operating systems (that is, Win95, Win98, Win00,* WinNT, but not Win3.1), the installation procedure for Perl modifies the Windows Registry to associate the *.pl* extension with the Perl interpreter.

If you install another port of Perl, including the one in the Win32 directory of the Perl distribution, then you'll have to modify the Windows Registry yourself.

Note that using a *.pl* extension means you can no longer tell the difference between an executable Perl program and a "perl library" file. You could use *.plx* for a Perl program instead to avoid this. This is much less of an issue these days, since most Perl modules are now in *.pm* files.

Command interpreters on non-Unix systems often have extraordinarily different ideas about quoting than Unix shells have. You'll need to learn the special characters in your command interpreter (*, \, and " are common) and how to protect whitespace and these special characters to run one-liners via the **-e** switch. You might also have to change a single **%** to a **%%**, or otherwise escape it, if that's a special character for your shell.

On some systems, you may have to change single quotes to double quotes. But don't do that on Unix or Plan9 systems, or anything running a Unix-style shell, such as systems from the MKS Toolkit or from the Cygwin package produced by the Cygnus folks, now at Redhat. Microsoft's new Unix emulator called Interix is also starting to look, ahem, interixing.

For example, on Unix and Mac OS X, use:

```
% perl -e 'print "Hello world\n"'
```

On Macintosh (pre Mac OS X), use:

```
print "Hello world\n"
```

then run "Myscript" or Shift-Command-R.

On VMS, use:

```
$ perl -e "print ""Hello world\n"""
```

or again with qq//:

```
$ perl -e "print qq(Hello world\n)"
```

---

* Er, pardon the technical difficulties . . .

And on MS-DOS et al., use:

```
A:> perl -e "print \"Hello world\n\""
```

or use qq// to pick your own quotes:

```
A:> perl -e "print qq(Hello world\n)"
```

The problem is that neither of those is reliable: it depends on the command interpreter you're using there. If *4DOS* were the command shell, this would probably work better:

```
perl -e "print <Ctrl-x>"Hello world\n<Ctrl-x>""
```

The *CMD.EXE* program seen on Windows NT seems to have slipped a lot of standard Unix shell functionality in when nobody was looking, but just try to find documentation for its quoting rules.

On the Macintosh,* all this depends on which environment you are using. MPW, which can be used as a shell for MacPerl, is much like Unix shells in its support for several quoting variants, except that it makes free use of the Macintosh's non-ASCII characters as control characters.

There is no general solution to all of this. It's just a mess. If you aren't on a Unix system but want to do command-line things, your best bet is to acquire a better command interpreter than the one your vendor supplied you, which shouldn't be too hard.

Or just write it all in Perl, and forget the one-liners.

Location of Perl

Although this may seem obvious, Perl is useful only when users can easily find it. When possible, it's good for both */usr/bin/perl* and */usr/local/bin/perl* to be symlinks to the actual binary. If that can't be done, system administrators are strongly encouraged to put Perl and its accompanying utilities into a directory typically found along a user's standard PATH, or in some other obvious and convenient place.

In this book, we use the standard #!/usr/bin/perl notation on the first line of the program to mean whatever particular mechanism works on your system. If you care about running a specific version of Perl, use a specific path:

```
#!/usr/local/bin/perl5.6.0
```

---

* At least, prior to release of Mac OS X, which, happily enough, is a BSD-derived system.

If you just want to be running *at least* some version number, but don't mind higher ones, place a statement like this near the top of your program:

```
use v5.6.0;
```

(Note: earlier versions of Perl use numbers like 5.005 or 5.004_05. Nowadays we would think of those as 5.5.0 and 5.4.5, but versions of Perl older than 5.6.0 won't understand that notation.)

Switches

A single-character command-line *switch* without its own argument may always be combined (bundled) with a switch following it.

```
#!/usr/bin/perl -spi.bak     # same as -s -p -i.bak
```

Switches are also known as options or flags. Whatever you call them, here are the ones Perl recognizes:

-- Terminates switch processing, even if the next argument starts with a minus. It has no other effect.

-0OCTNUM

-0 Specifies the record separator ($/) as an octal number. If OCTNUM is not present, the NUL character (that's ASCII character 0, Perl's "\0") is the separator. Other switches may precede or follow the octal number. For example, if you have a version of *find*(1) that can print filenames terminated by the null character, you can say this:

```
% find . -name '*.bak' -print0 | perl -n0e unlink
```

The special value 00 makes Perl read files in paragraph mode, equivalent to setting the $/ variable to "". The value 0777 makes Perl slurp in whole files at once. This is equivalent to undefining the $/ variable. We use 0777 since there is no ASCII character with that value. (Unfortunately, there *is* a Unicode character with that value, \N{LATIN SMALL LETTER O WITH STROKE AND ACUTE}, but something tells us you won't be delimiting your records with that.)

-a Turns on autosplit mode, but only when used with **-n** or **-p**. An implicit split command to the @F array is done as the first thing inside the implicit while loop produced by the **-n** and **-p** switches. So:

```
% perl -ane 'print pop(@F), "\n";'
```

is equivalent to:

```
LINE: while (<>) {
    @F = split(' ');
    print pop(@F), "\n";
}
```

A different field separator may be specified by passing a regular expression for split to the **-F** switch. For example, these two calls are equivalent:

```
% awk -F: '$7 && $7 !~ /^\/bin/' /etc/passwd
% perl -F: -lane 'print if $F[6] && $F[6] !~ m(^/bin)' /etc/passwd
```

-c Causes Perl to check the syntax of the script and then exit without executing what it's just compiled. Technically, it does a bit more than that: it will execute any BEGIN or CHECK blocks and any use directives, since these are considered to occur before the execution of your program. It no longer executes any INIT or END blocks, however. The older but rarely useful behavior may still be obtained by putting:

```
BEGIN { $^C = 0; exit; }
```

at the end of your main script.

-C Enables Perl to use the native wide-character APIs on the target system, if supported (as of version 5.6.0 it works on Microsoft platforms only). The special variable ${^WIDE_SYSTEM_CALLS} reflects the state of this switch.

-d Runs the script under the Perl debugger. See Chapter 20, *The Perl Debugger.*

-d:*MODULE*

Runs the script under the control of a debugging or tracing module installed in the Perl library as Devel::*MODULE*. For example, **-d:DProf** executes the script using the Devel::DProf profiler. See also the debugging section in Chapter 20.

-D*LETTERS*

-D*NUMBER*

Sets debugging flags. (This only works if debugging is compiled into your version of Perl as described below.) You may specify either a *NUMBER* that is the sum of the bits you want, or a list of *LETTERS*. To see how it executes your script, for instance, use **-D14** or **-Dslt**. Another useful value is **-D1024** or **-Dx**, which lists your compiled syntax tree. And **-D512** or **-Dr** displays compiled regular expressions. The numeric value is available internally as the special variable $^D. Table 19-1 lists the assigned bit values.

Table 19-1. -D Options

Bit	Letter	Meaning
1	p	Tokenizing and parsing
2	s	Stack snapshots
4	l	Label stack processing
8	t	Trace execution
16	o	Method and overloading resolution
32	c	String/numeric conversions

Table 19-1. -D Options (continued)

Bit	Letter	Meaning
64	P	Print preprocessor command for **-P**
128	m	Memory allocation
256	f	Format processing
512	r	Regex parsing and execution
1024	x	Syntax tree dump
2048	u	Tainting checks
4096	L	Memory leaks (needs **-DLEAKTEST** when compiling Perl)
8192	H	Hash dump—usurps `values()`
16384	X	Scratchpad allocation
32768	D	Cleaning up
65536	S	Thread synchronization

All these flags require a Perl executable that was specially built for debugging. However, because this is not the default, you won't be able to use the **-D** switch at all unless you or your sysadmin built this special debugging version of Perl. See the *INSTALL* file in the Perl source directory for details, but the short story is that you need to pass **-DDEBUGGING** to your C compiler when compiling Perl itself. This flag is automatically set if you include the **-g** option when *Configure* asks you about optimizer and debugger flags.

If you're just trying to get a printout of each line of Perl code as it executes (the way that *sh -x* provides for shell scripts), you can't use Perl's **-D** switch. Instead do this:

```
# Bourne shell syntax
$ PERLDB_OPTS="NonStop=1 AutoTrace=1 frame=2" perl -dS program

# csh syntax
% (setenv PERLDB_OPTS "NonStop=1 AutoTrace=1 frame=2"; perl -dS program)
```

See Chapter 20 for details and variations.

-e *PERLCODE*

May be used to enter one or more lines of script. If **-e** is used, Perl will not look for the program's filename in the argument list. The *PERLCODE* argument is treated as if it ended with a newline, so multiple **-e** commands may be given to build up a multiline program. (Make sure to use semicolons where you would in a normal program stored in a file.) Just because **-e** supplies a newline on each argument doesn't imply that you must use multiple **-e** switches; if your shell supports multiline quoting like *sh*, *ksh*, or *bash*, you may pass a multiline script as one **-e** argument:

```
$ perl -e 'print "Howdy, ";
           print "@ARGV!\n";' world
Howdy, world!
```

With *csh* it's probably better to use multiple **-e** switches:

```
% perl -e 'print "Howdy, ";' \
       -e 'print "@ARGV!\n";' world
Howdy, world!
```

Both implicit and explicit newlines count in the line numbering, so the second print is on line 2 of the **-e** script in either case.

-F*PATTERN*

Specifies the pattern to split on when autosplitting via the **-a** switch (has no effect otherwise). The pattern may be surrounded by slashes (//), double quotes (""), or single quotes (''). Otherwise, it will be automatically put in single quotes. Remember that to pass quotes through a shell, you'll have to quote your quotes, and how you can do that depends on the shell.

-h Prints a summary of Perl's command-line options.

-i*EXTENSION*

-i Specifies that files processed by the <> construct are to be edited in place. It does this by renaming the input file, opening the output file by the original name, and selecting that output file as the default for calls to print, printf, and write.*

The *EXTENSION* is used to modify the name of the old file to make a backup copy. If no *EXTENSION* is supplied, no backup is made and the current file is overwritten. If the *EXTENSION* doesn't contain a *, then that string is appended to the end of the current filename. If the *EXTENSION* does contain one or more * characters, then each * is replaced by the filename currently being processed. In Perl terms, you could think of this as:

```
($backup = $extension) =~ s/\*/$file_name/g;
```

This allows you to use a prefix for the backup file, instead of—or even in addition to—a suffix:

```
% perl -pi'orig_*' -e 's/foo/bar/' xyx     # backup to 'orig_xyx'
```

You can even put backup copies of the original files into another directory (provided that the directory already exists):

```
% perl -pi'old/*.orig' -e 's/foo/bar/' xyx # backup to 'old/xyx.orig'
```

---

* Technically, this isn't really "in place". It's the same filename, but a different physical file.

These pairs of one-liners are equivalent:

```
% perl -pi -e 's/foo/bar/' xyx          # overwrite current file
% perl -pi'*' -e 's/foo/bar/' xyx       # overwrite current file

% perl -pi'.orig' -e 's/foo/bar/' xyx   # backup to 'xyx.orig'
% perl -pi'*.orig' -e 's/foo/bar/' xyx  # backup to 'xyx.orig'
```

From the shell, saying:

```
% perl -p -i.orig -e "s/foo/bar/;"
```

is the same as using the program:

```
#!/usr/bin/perl -pi.orig
s/foo/bar/;
```

which is convenient shorthand for the remarkably longer:

```
#!/usr/bin/perl
$extension = '.orig';
LINE: while (<>) {
    if ($ARGV ne $oldargv) {
        if ($extension !~ /\*/) {
            $backup = $ARGV . $extension;
        }
        else {
            ($backup = $extension) =~ s/\*/$ARGV/g;
        }
        unless (rename($ARGV, $backup)) {
            warn "cannot rename $ARGV to $backup: $!\n";
            close ARGV;
            next;
        }
        open(ARGVOUT, ">$ARGV");
        select(ARGVOUT);
        $oldargv = $ARGV;
    }
    s/foo/bar/;
}
continue {
    print;  # this prints to original filename
}
select(STDOUT);
```

This long code is virtually identical to the simple one-liner with the **-i** switch, except that the **-i** form doesn't need to compare $ARGV to $oldargv to know when the filename has changed. It does, however, use ARGVOUT for the selected filehandle and restore the old STDOUT as the default output filehandle after the loop. Like the code above, Perl creates the backup file irrespective of whether any output has truly changed. See the description of the eof function for examples of how to use use eof without parentheses to locate the end of each input file, in case you want to append to each file or to reset line numbering.

If, for a given file, Perl is unable to create the backup file as specified in the *EXTENSION*, it will issue a warning to that effect and continue processing any other remaining files listed.

You cannot use **-i** to create directories or to strip extensions from files. Nor can you use it with a ~ to indicate a home directory—which is just as well, since some folks like to use that character for their backup files:

```
% perl -pi~ -e 's/foo/bar/' file1 file2 file3...
```

Finally, the **-i** switch does not stop Perl from running if no filenames are given on the command line. When this happens, no backup is made since the original file cannot be determined, and processing proceeds from STDIN to STDOUT as might be expected.

-I*DIRECTORY*

Directories specified by **-I** are prepended to @INC, which holds the search path for modules. **-I** also tells the C preprocessor where to search for include files. The C preprocessor is invoked with **-P**; by default it searches */usr/include* and */usr/lib/perl*. Unless you're going to be using the C preprocessor (and almost no one does any more), you're better off using the use lib directive within your script. Like use lib, however, the **-I** switch implicitly adds platform-specific directories. See use lib in Chapter 31, *Pragmatic Modules*, for details.

-l*OCTNUM*

-l Enables automatic line-end processing. It has two effects: first, it automatically chomps the line terminator when used with **-n** or **-p**, and second, it sets $\ to the value of *OCTNUM* so that any print statements will have a line terminator of ASCII value *OCTNUM* added back on. If *OCTNUM* is omitted, **-l** sets $\ to the current value of $/, typically newline. So, to trim lines to 80 columns, say this:

```
% perl -lpe 'substr($_, 80) = ""'
```

Note that the assignment $\ = $/ is done when the switch is processed, so the input record separator can be different from the output record separator if the **-l** switch is followed by a **-0** switch:

```
% gnufind / -print0 | perl -ln0e 'print "found $_" if -p'
```

This sets $\ to newline and later sets $/ to the null character. (Note that 0 would have been interpreted as part of the **-l** switch had it followed the **-l** directly. That's why we bundled the **-n** switch between them.)

-m and **-M**

These switches load a *MODULE* as if you'd executed a use, unless you specify -*MODULE* instead of *MODULE*, in which case they invoke no. For example, **-Mstrict** is like use strict, while **-M-strict** is like no strict.

-m*MODULE*

Executes use *MODULE* () before executing your script.

-M*MODULE*

-M'*MODULE* **...'**

Executes use *MODULE* before executing your script. The command is formed by mere interpolation of the rest of the argument after the **-M**, so you can use quotes to add extra code after the module name, for example, **-M'MODULE qw(foo bar)'**.

-M*MODULE=arg1,arg2...*

A little built-in syntactic sugar means you can also say **-Mmodule=foo,bar** as a shortcut for **-M'module qw(foo bar)'**. This avoids the need to use quotes when importing symbols. The actual code generated by **-Mmodule=foo,bar** is:

```
use module split(/,/, q{foo,bar})
```

Note that the = form removes the distinction between **-m** and **-M**, but it's better to use the uppercase form to avoid confusion.

You may only use the **-M** and **-m** switches from a real command-line invocation of Perl, not as options picked up on the #! line. (Hey, if you're gonna put it in the file, why not just write the equivalent use or no instead?)

-n Causes Perl to assume the following loop around your script, which makes it iterate over filename arguments much as *sed -n* or *awk* do:

```
LINE:
while (<>) {
    ...                        # your script goes here
}
```

You may use LINE as a loop label from within you script, even though you can't see the actual label in your file.

Note that the lines are not printed by default. See **-p** to have lines printed. Here is an efficient way to delete all files older than a week:

```
find . -mtime +7 -print | perl -nle unlink
```

This is faster than using the *-exec* switch of *find*(1) because you don't have to start a process on every filename found. By an amazing coincidence, BEGIN and END blocks may be used to capture control before or after the implicit loop, just as in *awk*.

-p   Causes Perl to assume the following loop around your script, which makes it iterate over filename arguments much as *sed* does:

```
LINE:
while (<>) {
    ...              # your script goes here
}
continue {
    print or die "-p destination: $!\n";
}
```

You may use LINE as a loop label from within you script, even though you can't see the actual label in your file.

If a file named by an argument cannot be opened for some reason, Perl warns you about it, and moves on to the next file. Note that the lines are printed automatically. An error occurring during printing is treated as fatal. By yet another amazing coincidence, BEGIN and END blocks may be used to capture control before or after the implicit loop, just as in *awk*.

-P   Causes your script to be run through the C preprocessor before compilation by Perl. (Since both comments and *cpp*(1) directives begin with the # character, you should avoid starting comments with any words recognized by the C preprocessor such as "if", "else" or "define".) Whether you use **-P** switch or not, Perl still pays attention to #line directives to control the line number and filename, so any preprocessor can apprise Perl of these things. See the section "Generating Perl in Other Languages" in Chapter 24, *Common Practices*.

-s   Enables rudimentary switch-parsing for switches on the command line after the script name but before any filename arguments or a "--" switch-processing terminator. Any switch found is removed from @ARGV, and a variable by the same name as the switch is set in Perl. Switch bundling is not allowed because multicharacter switches are permitted.

The following script prints "true" only when the script is invoked with a -foo switch.

```
#!/usr/bin/perl -s
if ($foo) { print "true\n" }
```

If the switch is of the form **-xxx=yyy**, the $xxx variable is set to whatever follows the equals sign in that argument ("yyy" in this case). The following script prints "true" if and only if the script is invoked with a -foo=bar switch.

```
#!/usr/bin/perl -s
if ($foo eq 'bar') { print "true\n" }
```

-S Makes Perl use the PATH environment variable to search for the script (unless the name of the script contains directory separators).

Typically, this switch is used to help emulate #! startup on platforms that don't support #!. On many platforms that have a shell compatible with Bourne or C shell, you can use this:

```
#!/usr/bin/perl
eval "exec /usr/bin/perl -S $0 $*"
        if $running_under_some_shell;
```

The system ignores the first line and feeds the script to */bin/sh*, which proceeds to try to execute the Perl script as a shell script. The shell executes the second line as a normal shell command, and thus starts up the Perl interpreter. On some systems, $0 doesn't always contain the full pathname, so **-S** tells Perl to search for the script if necessary. After Perl locates the script, it parses the lines and ignores them because the variable $running_under_some_shell is never true. A better construct than $* would be ${1+"$@"}, which handles embedded spaces and such in the filenames but doesn't work if the script is being interpreted by *csh*. In order to start up *sh* instead of *csh*, some systems have to replace the #! line with a line containing just a colon, which Perl will politely ignore. Other systems can't control that and need a totally devious construct that will work under any of *csh*, *sh*, or *perl*, such as the following:

```
eval '(exit $?0)' && eval 'exec /usr/bin/perl -S $0 ${1+"$@"}'
    & eval 'exec /usr/bin/perl -S $0 $argv:q'
                if 0;
```

Yes, it's ugly, but so are the systems that work* this way.

On some platforms, the **-S** switch also makes Perl append suffixes to the filename while searching for it. For example, on Win32 platforms, the *.bat* and *.cmd* suffixes are appended if a lookup for the original name fails and the name does not already end in one of those suffixes. If your Perl was built with debugging enabled, you can use Perl's **-Dp** switch to watch how the search progresses.

If the filename supplied contains directory separators (even as just a relative pathname, not an absolute one), and if the file is not found, those platforms that implicitly append file extensions (not Unix) will do so and look for the file with those extensions added, one by one.

On DOS-like platforms, if the script does not contain directory separators, it will first be searched for in the current directory before being searched for in the PATH. On Unix platforms, the script will be searched for strictly on the

---

* We use the term advisedly.

PATH, due to security concerns about accidentally executing something in the current working directory without explicitly requesting this.

-T Forces "taint" checks to be turned on so you can test them. Ordinarily these checks are done only when running setuid or setgid. It's a good idea to turn them on explicitly for programs run on another's behalf, such as CGI programs. See Chapter 23, *Security*.

Note that, for security reasons, Perl must see this option quite early; usually this means it must appear early on the command line or in the #! line. If it's not early enough, Perl complains.

-u Causes Perl to dump core after compiling your script. You can then in theory take this core dump and turn it into an executable file by using the *undump* program (not supplied). This speeds startup at the expense of some disk space (which you can minimize by stripping the executable). If you want to execute a portion of your script before dumping, use Perl's dump operator instead. Note: availability of *undump* is platform specific; it may not be available for a specific port of Perl. It has been superseded by the new Perl-to-C code generator, which is much more portable (but still experimental).

-U Allows Perl to do unsafe operations. Currently the only "unsafe" operations are unlinking directories while running as superuser, and running setuid programs with fatal taint checks turned into warnings. Note that warnings must be enabled to actually produce the taint-check warnings.

-v Prints the version and patch level of your Perl executable, along with a bit of extra information.

-V Prints a summary of the major Perl configuration values and the current value of @INC.

-V:*NAME*

Prints to STDOUT the value of the named configuration variable. The *NAME* may contain regex characters, like "." to match any character, or ".*" to match any optional sequence of characters.

```
% perl -V:man.dir
man1dir='/usr/local/man/man1'
man3dir='/usr/local/man/man3'

% perl -V:'.*threads'
d_oldpthreads='undef'
use5005threads='define'
useithreads='undef'
usethreads='define'
```

If you ask for a configuration variable that doesn't exist, its value will be reported as "UNKNOWN". Configuration information is available from within a program using the Config module, although patterns are not supported for the hash subscripts:

```
% perl -MConfig -le 'print $Config{man1dir}'
/usr/local/man/man1
```

See the Config module in Chapter 32, *Standard Modules*.

-w Prints warnings about variables that are mentioned only once and scalar values that are used before being set. Also warns about redefined subroutines, and references to undefined filehandles or filehandles opened read-only that you are attempting to write on. Also warns you if you use values as numbers that don't look like numbers, if you use an array as though it were a scalar, if your subroutines recurse more than 100 deep, and innumerable other things. See every entry labelled "(W)" in Chapter 33, *Diagnostic Messages*.

This switch just sets the global $^W variable. It has no effect on lexical warnings—see the **-W** and **-X** switches for that. You can enable or disable specific warnings via the use warnings pragma, described in Chapter 31.

-W Unconditionally and permanently enables all warnings throughout the program, even if warnings were disabled locally using no warnings or $^W = 0. This includes all files loaded via use, require, or do. Think of it as the Perl equivalent of the *lint*(1) command.

-x*DIRECTORY*

-x Tells Perl to extract a script that is embedded in a message. Leading garbage will be discarded until the first line that starts with #! and contains the string "perl". Any meaningful switches on that line after the word "perl" will be applied. If a directory name is specified, Perl will switch to that directory before running the script. The **-x** switch controls the disposal of leading garbage only, not trailing garbage. The script must be terminated with __END__ or __DATA__ if there is trailing garbage to be ignored. (The script can process any or all of the trailing garbage via the DATA filehandle if desired. It could even in theory seek to the beginning of the file and process the leading garbage.)

-X Unconditionally and permanently disables all warnings, the exact opposite of what the **-w** flag does.

Environment Variables

In addition to the various switches that explicitly modify Perl's behavior, you can set various environment variables to influence various underlying behaviors. How you set up these environment variables is system dependent, but one trick you should know if you use *sh*, *ksh*, or *bash* is that you can temporarily set an environment variable for a single command, as if it were a funny kind of switch. It has to be set in front of the command:

```
$ PATH='/bin:/usr/bin' perl myproggie
```

You can do something similar with a subshell in *csh* and *tcsh*:

```
% (setenv PATH "/bin:/usr/bin"; perl myproggie)
```

Otherwise, you'd typically set environment variables in some file with a name resembling *.cshrc* or *.profile* in your home directory. Under *csh* and *tcsh* you'd say:

```
% setenv PATH '/bin:/usr/bin'
```

And under *sh*, *ksh*, and *bash* you'd say:

```
$ PATH='/bin:/usr/bin'; export PATH
```

Other systems will have other ways of setting these on a semi-permanent basis. Here are the environment variables Perl pays attention to:

HOME

  Used if chdir is called without an argument.

LC_ALL, LC_CTYPE, LC_COLLATE, LC_NUMERIC, PERL_BADLANG

  Environment variables that control how Perl handles data specific to particular natural languages. See the online docs for *perllocale*.

LOGDIR

  Used if chdir has no argument, but HOME is not set.

PATH

  Used in executing subprocesses, and for finding the program if the **-s** switch is used.

PERL5LIB

  A colon-separated list of directories in which to look for Perl library files before looking in the standard library and the current directory. Any architecture-specific directories under the specified locations are automatically included if they exist. If PERL5LIB is not defined, PERLLIB is consulted for backward compatibility with older releases.

When running taint checks (either because the program was running setuid or setgid, or the **-T** switch was used), neither of these library variables is used. Such programs must employ the use lib pragma for that purpose.

PERL5OPT

Default command-line switches. Switches in this variable are taken as if they were on every Perl command line. Only the **-[DIMUdmw]** switches are allowed. When running taint checks (because the program was running setuid or setgid, or the **-T** switch was used), this variable is ignored. If PERL5OPT begins with **-T**, tainting will be enabled, causing any subsequent options to be ignored.

PERL5DB

The command used to load the debugger code. The default is:

```
BEGIN { require 'perl5db.pl' }
```

See Chapter 20 for more uses of this variable.

PERL5SHELL (Microsoft ports only)

May be set to an alternative shell that Perl must use internally for executing commands via backticks or system. Default is cmd.exe /x/c on WinNT and command.com /c on Win95. The value is considered to be space separated. Precede any character that needs to be protected (like a space or backslash) with a backslash.

Note that Perl doesn't use COMSPEC for this purpose because COMSPEC has a high degree of variability among users, leading to portability concerns. Besides, Perl can use a shell that may not be fit for interactive use, and setting COMSPEC to such a shell may interfere with the proper functioning of other programs (which usually look in COMSPEC to find a shell fit for interactive use).

PERLLIB

A colon-separated list of directories in which to look for Perl library files before looking in the standard library and the current directory. If PERL5LIB is defined, PERLLIB is not used.

PERL_DEBUG_MSTATS

Relevant only if Perl is compiled with the malloc function included with the Perl distribution (that is, if perl -V:d_mymalloc yields "define"). If set, this causes memory statistics to be displayed after execution. If set to an integer greater than one, also causes memory statistics to be displayed after compilation.

PERL_DESTRUCT_LEVEL

   Relevant only if your Perl executable was built with debugging enabled, this
   controls the behavior of global destruction of objects and other references.

Apart from these, Perl itself uses no other environment variables, except to make
them available to the program being executed and to any child processes that program launches. Some modules, standard or otherwise, may care about other environment variables. For example, the use re pragma uses PERL_RE_TC and
PERL_RE_COLORS, the Cwd module uses PWD, and the CGI module uses the many environment variables set by your HTTP daemon (that is, your web server) to pass
information to the CGI script.

Programs running setuid would do well to execute the following lines before
doing anything else, just to keep people honest:

```
$ENV{PATH}  = '/bin:/usr/bin';    # or whatever you need
$ENV{SHELL} = '/bin/sh' if exists $ENV{SHELL};
delete @ENV{qw(IFS CDPATH ENV BASH_ENV)};
```

See Chapter 23 for details.

20

The Perl Debugger

First of all, have you tried the use warnings pragma?

If you invoke Perl with the **–d** switch, your program will be run inside the Perl debugger. This works like an interactive Perl environment, prompting for debugger commands that let you examine source code, set breakpoints, dump out your function-call stack, change the values of variables, and so on. Any command not recognized by the debugger is directly executed (using eval) as Perl code in the package of the code currently being debugged. (The debugger uses the DB package for its own state information, to avoid trampling yours.) This is so wonderfully convenient that people often fire up the debugger just to test out Perl constructs interactively. In that case, it doesn't matter what program you tell Perl to debug, so we'll choose one without much meaning:

```
% perl -de 42
```

In Perl, the debugger is not a program completely separate from the one being debugged, the way it usually is in a typical programming environment. Instead, the **–d** flag tells the compiler to insert source information into the parse trees it's about to hand off to the interpreter. That means your code must first compile correctly for the debugger to work on it. If that is successful, the interpreter preloads a special Perl library file containing the debugger itself.

```
% perl -d /path/to/program
```

The program will halt immediately before the first run-time executable statement (but see the section "Using the Debugger" regarding compile-time statements) and ask you to enter a debugger command. Whenever the debugger halts and shows you a line of code, it displays the line that it's *about* to execute, not the one just executed.

As the debugger encounters a line, it first checks for a breakpoint, prints it (if the debugger is in trace mode), performs any actions (created with the a command described later in "Debugger Commands"), and finally prompts the user if a breakpoint is present or if the debugger is in single-step mode. If not, it evaluates the line normally and continues to the next line.

Using the Debugger

The debugger prompt is something like:

```
DB<8>
```

or even:

```
DB<<17>>
```

where the number shows how many commands you've executed. A *csh*-like history mechanism allows you to access previous commands by number. For example, !17 would repeat command number 17. The number of angle brackets indicates the depth of the debugger. For example, you get more than one set of brackets if you're already at a breakpoint and then print out the result of a function call that itself also has a breakpoint.

If you want to enter a multiline command, such as a subroutine definition with several statements, you may escape the newline that would normally end the debugger command with a backslash. Here's an example:

```
DB<1> for (1..3) {          \
cont:      print "ok\n";   \
cont: }
ok
ok
ok
```

Let's say you want to fire up the debugger on a little program of yours (let's call it *camel_flea*) and stop it as soon as it gets down to a function named infested. Here's how you'd do that:

```
% perl -d camel_flea

Loading DB routines from perl5db.pl version 1.07
Editor support available.

Enter h or `h h' for help, or `man perldebug' for more help.

main::(camel_flea:2):    pests('bactrian', 4);
  DB<1>
```

The debugger halts your program right before the first run-time executable statement (but see below about compile-time statements) and asks you to enter a command. Again, whenever the debugger stops to show you a line of code, it displays the line it's *about* to execute, not the one it just executed. The line displayed may not look exactly like it did in your source file, particularly if you've run it through any kind of preprocessor.

Now, you'd like to stop as soon as your program gets to the `infested` function, so you establish a breakpoint there like so:

```
DB<1> b infested
DB<2> c
```

The debugger now continues until it hits that function, at which point it says this:

```
main::infested(camel_flea:8):        my $bugs = int rand(3);
```

To look at a "window" of source code around the breakpoint, use the w command:

```
DB<2> w
5        }
6
7        sub infested {
8==>b        my $bugs = int rand(3);
9:           our $Master;
10:          contaminate($Master);
11:          warn "needs wash"
12               if $Master && $Master->isa("Human");
13
14:          print "got $bugs\n";

DB<2>
```

As you see by the `==>` marker, your current line is line 8, and by the `b` there, you know it has a breakpoint on it. If you'" had set an action, there also would also have been an `a` there. The line numbers with colons are breakable; the rest are not.

To see who called whom, ask for a stack backtrace using the **T** command:

```
DB<2> T
$ = main::infested called from file 'Ambulation.pm' line 4
@ = Ambulation::legs(1, 2, 3, 4) called from file 'camel_flea' line 5
. = main::pests('bactrian', 4) called from file 'camel_flea' line 2
```

The initial character (`$`, `@`, or `.`) tells whether the function was called in a scalar, list, or void context, respectively. There are three lines because you were three functions deep when you ran the stack backtrace. Here's what each line means:

- The first line says you were in the function `main::infested` when you ran the stack trace. It tells you the function was called in a scalar context from line 4 of the file *Ambulation.pm*. It also shows that it was called without any arguments whatsoever, meaning it was called as `&infested` instead of the normal way, as `infested()`.

- The second line shows that the function `Ambulation::legs` was called in list context from line number 5 of the *camel_flea* file, with those four arguments.

- The third line shows that `main::pests` was called in void context from line 2 of *camel_flea*.

If you have compile-phase executable statements such as code from `BEGIN` and `CHECK` blocks or use statements, these will *not* ordinarily be stopped by the debugger, although `requires` and `INIT` blocks will, since they happen after the transition to run phase (see Chapter 18, *Compiling*). Compile-phase statements can be traced with the `AutoTrace` option set in `PERLDB_OPTS`.

You can exert a little control over the Perl debugger from within your Perl program itself. You might do this, for example, to set an automatic breakpoint at a certain subroutine whenever a particular program is run under the debugger. From your own Perl code, however, you can transfer control back to the debugger using the following statement, which is harmless if the debugger is not running:

```
$DB::single = 1;
```

If you set `$DB::single` to 2, it's equivalent to the n command, whereas a value of 1 emulates the s command. The `$DB::trace` variable should be set to 1 to simulate the t command.

Another way to debug a module is to set breakpoint on *load*ing:

```
DB<7> b load c:/perl/lib/Carp.pm
Will stop on load of 'c:/perl/lib/Carp.pm'.
```

and then restart the debugger using the R command. For finer control, you can use the `b compile subname` to stop as soon as possible after a particular subroutine is compiled.

Debugger Commands

When you type commands into the debugger, you don't need to terminate them with a semicolon. Use a backslash to continue lines (but only in the debugger).

Since the debugger uses `eval` to execute commands, `my`, `our`, and `local` settings will disappear once the command returns. If a debugger command coincides with some function in your own program, simply precede the function call with anything that doesn't look like a debugger command, such as a leading `;` or a `+`.

If the output of a debugger built-in command scrolls past your screen, just precede the command with a leading pipe symbol so it's run through your pager:

```
DB<1> |h
```

The debugger has plenty of commands, and we divide them (somewhat arbitrarily) into stepping and running, breakpoints, tracing, display, locating code, automatic command execution, and, of course, miscellaneous.

Perhaps the most important command is h, which provides help. If you type h h at the debugger prompt, you'll get a compact help listing designed to fit on one screen. If you type h *COMMAND*, you'll get help on that debugger command.

Stepping and Running

The debugger operates by *stepping* through your program line by line. The following commands let you control what you skip over and where you stop.

s
s *EXPR*

> The s debugger command single-steps through the program. That is, the debugger will execute the next line of your program until another statement is reached, descending into subroutine calls as necessary. If the next line to execute involves a function call, then the debugger stops at the first line inside that function. If an *EXPR* is supplied that includes function calls, these will be single-stepped, too.

n
n *EXPR*

> The n command executes subroutine calls, without stepping through them, until the beginning of the next statement at this same level (or higher). If an *EXPR* is supplied that includes function calls, those functions will be executed with stops before each statement.

<ENTER>

> If you just hit enter at the debugger prompt, the previous n or s command is repeated.

.   The . command returns the internal debugger pointer to the line last executed and prints out that line.

r   This command continues until the currently executing subroutine returns. It displays the return value if the PrintRet option is set, which it is by default.

Breakpoints

```
b
b LINE
b CONDITION
b LINE CONDITION
b SUBNAME
b SUBNAME CONDITION
b postpone SUBNAME
b postpone SUBNAME CONDITION
b compile SUBNAME
b load FILENAME
```

The b debugger command sets a *breakpoint* before LINE, telling the debugger to stop the program at that point so that you can poke around. If LINE is omitted, sets a breakpoint on the line that's about to execute. If CONDITION is specified, it's evaluated each time the statement is reached: a breakpoint is triggered only if CONDITION is true. Breakpoints may only be set on lines that begin an executable statement. Note that conditions don't use if:

```
b 237 $x > 30
b 237 ++$count237 < 11
b 33 /pattern/i
```

The b SUBNAME form sets a (possibly conditional) breakpoint before the first line of the named subroutine. SUBNAME may be a variable containing a code reference; if so, CONDITION is not supported.

There are several ways to set a breakpoint on code that hasn't even been compiled yet. The b postpone form sets a (possibly conditional) breakpoint at the first line of SUBNAME after it is compiled.

The b compile form sets a breakpoint on the first statement to be executed after SUBNAME is compiled. Note that unlike the postpone form, this statement is outside the subroutine in question because the subroutine hasn't been called yet, only compiled.

The b load form sets a breakpoint on the first executed line of the file. The FILENAME should be a full pathname as found in the %INC values.

```
d
d LINE
```

This command deletes the breakpoint at LINE; if omitted, it deletes the breakpoint on the line about to execute.

D   This command deletes all breakpoints.

L   This command lists all the breakpoints and actions.

c
c *LINE*

This command continues execution, optionally inserting a one-time-only
breakpoint at the specified *LINE*.

Tracing

T   This command produces a stack backtrace.

t
t *EXPR*

This command toggles trace mode, which prints out every line in your program as it is evaluated. See also the `AutoTrace` option discussed later in this
chapter. If an *EXPR* is provided, the debugger will trace through its execution.
See also the later section "Unattended Execution".

W
W *EXPR*

This command adds *EXPR* as a global watch expression. (A watch expression is
an expression that will cause a breakpoint when its value changes.) If no
EXPR is provided, all watch expressions are deleted.

Display

Perl's debugger has several commands for examining data structures while your
program is stopped at a breakpoint.

p
p *EXPR*

This command is the same as `print DB::OUT` *EXPR* in the current package. In
particular, since this is just Perl's own `print` function, nested data structures
and objects are not shown—use the x command for that. The `DB::OUT` handle
prints to your terminal (or perhaps an editor window) no matter where standard output may have been redirected.

x
x *EXPR*

The x command evaluates its expression in list context and displays the result,
pretty-printed. That is, nested data structures are printed out recursively and
with unviewable characters suitably encoded.

V
V *PKG*
V *PKG VARS*

This command displays all (or when you specify *VARS*, some) variables in the specified *PKG* (defaulting to the main package) using a pretty printer. Hashes show their keys and values, control characters are rendered legibly, nested data structures print out in a legible fashion, and so on. This is similar to calling the x command on each applicable variable, except that x works with lexical variables, too. Also, here you type the identifiers *without* a type specifier such as $ or @, like this:

```
V Pet::Camel SPOT FIDO
```

In place of a variable name in *VARS*, you can use ~*PATTERN* or !*PATTERN* to print existing variables whose names either match or don't match the specified pattern.

X
X *VARS*

This command is the same as V *CURRENTPACKAGE*, where *CURRENTPACKAGE* is the package that the current line was compiled into.

H
H -*NUMBER*

This command displays the last *NUMBER* commands. Only commands longer than one character are stored in the history. (Most of them would be s or n, otherwise.) If *NUMBER* is omitted, all commands are listed.

Locating Code

Inside the debugger, you can extract and display parts of your program with these commands.

l
l *LINE*
l *SUBNAME*
l *MIN+INCR*
l *MIN-MAX*

The l command lists the next few lines of your program, or the specified *LINE* if provided, or the first few lines of the *SUBNAME* subroutine or code reference.

The l *MIN+INCR* form lists *INCR*+1 lines, starting at *MIN*. The l *MIN-MAX* form lists lines *MIN* through *MAX*.

-     This command lists the previous few lines of your program.

w

w *LINE*

Lists a window (a few lines) around the given source *LINE*, or the current line if no *LINE* is supplied.

f *FILENAME*

This command lets you view a different program or `eval` statement. If the *FILENAME* is not a full pathname as found in the values of `%INC`, it is interpreted as a regular expression to find the filename you mean.

/ *PATTERN* **/**

This command searches forward in the program for *PATTERN*; the final / is optional. The entire *PATTERN* is optional, too, and if omitted, repeats the previous search.

? *PATTERN* **?**

This command searches backward for *PATTERN*; the final ? is optional. It repeats the previous search if *PATTERN* is omitted.

S

S *PATTERN*

S ! *PATTERN*

The S command lists those subroutine names matching (or, with !, those not matching) *PATTERN*. If no *PATTERN* is provided, all subroutines are listed.

Actions and Command Execution

From inside the debugger, you can specify actions to be taken at particular times. You can also launch external programs.

a

a *COMMAND*

a *LINE*

a *LINE COMMAND*

This command sets an action to take before *LINE* executes, or the current line if *LINE* is omitted. For example, this prints out `$foo` every time line 53 is reached:

```
a 53 print "DB FOUND $foo\n"
```

If no *COMMAND* is specified, the action on the specified *LINE* is deleted. With neither *LINE* nor *COMMAND*, the action on the current line is deleted.

A   The A debugger command deletes all actions.

<

< ?

< *EXPR*

<< *EXPR*

The < *EXPR* form specifies a Perl expression to be evaluated before every debugger prompt. You can add another expression with the << *EXPR* form, list them with < ?, and delete them all with a plain <.

>

> ?

> *EXPR*

>> *EXPR*

The > commands behave just like their < cousins but are executed after the debugger prompt instead of before.

{

{ ?

{ *COMMAND*

{{ *COMMAND*

The { debugger commands behave just like < but specify a debugger command to be executed before the debugger prompt instead of a Perl expression. A warning is issued if you appear to have accidentally entered a block of code instead. If that's what you really mean to do, write it with ;{ ... } or even do { ... }.

!

! *NUMBER*

! *-NUMBER*

! *PATTERN*

A lone ! repeats the previous command. The *NUMBER* specifies which command from the history to execute; for instance, ! 3 executes the third command typed into the debugger. If a minus sign precedes the *NUMBER*, the commands are counted backward: ! -3 executes the third-to-last command. If a *PATTERN* (no slashes) is provided instead of a *NUMBER*, the last command that began with *PATTERN* is executed. See also the recallCommand debugger option.)

!! *CMD*

This debugger command runs the external command *CMD* in a subprocess, which will read from DB::IN and write to DB::OUT. See also the shellBang debugger option. This command uses whatever shell is named in $ENV{SHELL}, which can sometimes interfere with proper interpretation of status, signal, and core dump information. If you want a consistent exit value from the command, set $ENV{SHELL} to /bin/sh.

|
|*DBCMD*
||*PERLCMD*

> The |*DBCMD* command runs the debugger command *DBCMD*, piping DB::OUT to $ENV{PAGER}. This is often used with commands that would otherwise produce long output, such as:
>
>   DB<1> |V main
>
> Note that this is for debugger commands, not commands you'd type from your shell. If you wanted to pipe the external command *who* through your pager, you could do something like this:
>
>   DB<1> !!who | more
>
> The ||*PERLCMD* command is like |*DBCMD*, but DB::OUT is temporarily selected as well, so any commands that call print, printf, or write without a filehandle will also be sent down the pipe. For example, if you had a function that generated loads of output by calling print, you'd use this command instead of the previous one to page through that output:
>
>   DB<1> sub saywho { print "Users: ", `who` }
>   DB<2> ||saywho()

Miscellaneous Commands

q *and* ^D

> These commands quit the debugger. This is the recommended way to exit, although typing exit twice sometimes works. Set the inhibit_exit option to 0 if you want to be able to step off the end of the program and remain in the debugger anyway. You may also need to set $DB::finished to 0 if you want to step through global destruction.

R   Restart the debugger by execing a new session. The debugger tries to maintain your history across sessions, but some internal settings and command-line options may be lost. The following settings are currently preserved: history, breakpoints, actions, debugger options, and the Perl command-line options **-w**, **-I**, and **-e**.

=
= *ALIAS*
= *ALIAS VALUE*

> This command prints out the current value of *ALIAS* if no *VALUE* is given. With a *VALUE*, it defines a new debugger command with the name *ALIAS*. If both *ALIAS* and *VALUE* are omitted, all current aliases are listed. For example:
>
>   = quit q

An *ALIAS* should be a simple identifier, and should translate to a simple identifier as well. You can do more sophisticated aliasing by adding your own entries to %DB::aliases directly. See "Debugger Customization" later in this chapter.

man

man *MANPAGE*

This command calls your system's default documentation viewer on the given page or on the viewer itself if *MANPAGE* is omitted. If that viewer is *man*, the current %Config information is used to invoke it. The "perl" prefix will be automatically supplied for you when necessary; this lets you type man debug and man op from the debugger.

On systems that do not normally have the *man* utility, the debugger invokes *perldoc*; if you want to change that behavior, set $DB::doccmd to whatever viewer you like. This may be set in an *rc* file or through direct assignment.

O

O *OPTION* ...

O *OPTION?* ...

O *OPTION=VALUE*...

The O command lets you manipulate debugger options, which are listed in "Debugger Options" later in this chapter. The O *OPTION* form sets each of the listed debugger options to 1. If a question mark follows an *OPTION*, its current value is displayed.

The O *OPTION=VALUE* form sets the values; if *VALUE* has internal whitespace, it should be quoted. For example, you could set O pager="less -MQeicsNfr" to use *less* with those specific flags. You may use either single or double quotes, but if you do, you must escape embedded instances of the same sort of quote that you began with. You must also escape any backslash that immediately precedes the quote but is not meant to escape the quote itself. In other words, just follow single-quoting rules irrespective of the quote actually used. The debugger responds by showing you the value of the option just set, always using single-quoted notation for its output:

```
DB<1> O OPTION='this isn\'t bad'
          OPTION = 'this isn\'t bad'

DB<2> O OPTION="She said, \"Isn't it?\""
          OPTION = 'She said, "Isn\'t it?"'
```

For historical reasons, the =*VALUE* is optional, but defaults to 1 only where safe to do so—that is, mostly for Boolean options. It is better to assign a specific *VALUE* using =. The *OPTION* can be abbreviated, but unless you're trying to be intentionally cryptic, it probably should not be. Several options can be set together. See the section "Debugger Options" for a list of these.

Debugger Customization

The debugger probably contains enough configuration hooks that you'll never have to modify it yourself. You may change debugger behavior from within the debugger using its O command, from the command line via the PERLDB_OPTS environment variable, and by running any preset commands stored in *rc* files.

Editor Support for Debugging

The debugger's command-line history mechanism doesn't provide command-line editing like many shells do: you can't retrieve previous lines with ^p, or move to the beginning of the line with ^a, although you can execute previous lines with the exclamation point syntax familiar to shell users. However, if you install the Term::ReadKey and Term::ReadLine modules from CPAN, you will have full editing capabilities similar to what GNU *readline*(3) provides.

If you have *emacs* installed on your system, it can interact with the Perl debugger to provide an integrated software development environment reminiscent of its interactions with C debuggers. Perl comes with a start file for making *emacs* act like a syntax-directed editor that understands (some of) Perl's syntax. Look in the *emacs* directory of the Perl source distribution. Users of *vi* should also look into *vim* (and *gvim*, the mousey and windy version) for coloring of Perl keywords.

A similar setup by one of us (Tom) for interacting with any vendor-shipped *vi* and the X11 window system is also available. This works similarly to the integrated multiwindow support that *emacs* provides, where the debugger drives the editor. However, at the time of this writing, its eventual location in the Perl distribution is uncertain. But we thought you should know of the possibility.

Customizing with Init Files

You can do some customization by setting up either a *.perldb* or *perldb.ini* file (depending on your operating system), which contains initialization code. This init file holds Perl code, not debugger commands, and is processed before the PERLDB_OPTS environment variable is looked at. For instance, you could make aliases by adding entries to the %DB::alias hash this way:

```
$alias{len}  = 's/^len(.*)/p length($1)/';
$alias{stop} = 's/^stop (at|in)/b/';
$alias{ps}   = 's/^ps\b/p scalar /';
$alias{quit} = 's/^quit(\s*)/exit/';
$alias{help} = 's/^help\s*$/|h/';
```

You can change options from within your init file using function calls into the debugger's internal API:

```
parse_options("NonStop=1 LineInfo=db.out AutoTrace=1 frame=2");
```

If your init file defines the subroutine `afterinit`, that function is called after debugger initialization ends. The init file may be located in the current directory or in the home directory. Because this file contains arbitrary Perl commands, for security reasons, it must be owned by the superuser or the current user, and writable by no one but its owner.

If you want to modify the debugger, copy *perl5db.pl* from the Perl library to another name and hack it to your heart's content. You'll then want to set your `PERL5DB` environment variable to say something like this:

```
BEGIN { require "myperl5db.pl" }
```

As a last resort, you could also use `PERL5DB` to customize the debugger by directly setting internal variables or calling internal debugger functions. Be aware, though, that any variables and functions not documented either here or else in the online *perldebug*, *perldebguts*, or *DB* manpages are considered to be for internal use only and are subject to change without notice.

Debugger Options

The debugger has numerous options that you can set with the `o` command, either interactively or from the environment or from an init file.

`recallCommand, ShellBang`
> The characters used to recall a command or spawn a shell. By default, both are set to `!`.

`pager`
> Program to use for output of pager-piped commands (those beginning with a `|` character.) By default, `$ENV{PAGER}` will be used. Because the debugger uses your current terminal characteristics for bold and underlining, if the chosen pager does not pass escape sequences through unchanged, the output of some debugger commands will not be readable when sent through the pager.

`tkRunning`
> Run under the `Tk` module while prompting (with `ReadLine`).

`signalLevel, warnLevel, dieLevel`
> Set the level of verbosity. By default, the debugger leaves your exceptions and warnings alone because altering them can break correctly running programs.

> To disable this default safe mode, set these values to something higher than 0. At a level of 1, you get backtraces upon receiving any kind of warning (this is often annoying) or exception (this is often valuable). Unfortunately, the

debugger cannot distinguish fatal exceptions from nonfatal ones. If dieLevel is 1, then your nonfatal exceptions are also traced and unceremoniously altered if they came from evaled strings or from any kind of eval within modules you're attempting to load. If dieLevel is 2, the debugger doesn't care where they came from: it usurps your exception handler and prints out a trace, and then modifies all exceptions with its own embellishments. This may perhaps be useful for some tracing purposes, but it tends to hopelessly confuse any program that takes its exception handling seriously.

The debugger will attempt to print a message when any uncaught INT, BUS, or SEGV signal arrives. If you're in a slow syscall (like a wait or an accept, or a read from your keyboard or a socket) and haven't set up your own $SIG{INT} handler, then you won't be able to Control-C your way back to the debugger, because the debugger's own $SIG{INT} handler doesn't understand that it needs to raise an exception to *longjmp*(3) out of slow syscalls.

AutoTrace

Set the trace mode (similar to t command, but can be put into PERLDB_OPTS).

LineInfo

Assign the file or pipe to print line number info to. If it is a pipe (say, |visual_perl_db), then a short message is used. This is the mechanism used to interact with a slave editor or visual debugger, such as the special *vi* or *emacs* hooks, or the *ddd* graphical debugger.

inhibit_exit

If 0, allows stepping off the end of the program.

PrintRet

Print return value after r command if set (default).

ornaments

Affects screen appearance of the command line (see the online docs for Term::ReadLine). There is currently no way to disable ornaments, which can render some output illegible on some displays or with some pagers. This is considered a bug.

frame

Affects printing of messages on entry and exit from subroutines. If frame & 2 is false, messages are printed on entry only. (Printing on exit might be useful if interspersed with other messages.)

If frame & 4, arguments to functions are printed, plus context and caller info. If frame & 8, overloaded stringify and tied FETCH are enabled on the printed arguments. If frame & 16, the return value from the subroutine is printed.

The length at which the argument list is truncated is governed by the next option.

`maxTraceLen`

> Length to truncate the argument list when the `frame` option's bit 4 is set.

The following options affect what happens with the V, X, and x commands:

`arrayDepth, hashDepth`

> Print only the first n elements. If n is omitted, all of the elements will be printed.

`compactDump, veryCompact`

> Change the style of array and hash output. If `compactDump` is enabled, short arrays may be printed on one line.

`globPrint`

> Print contents of typeglobs.

`DumpDBFiles`

> Display arrays holding debugged files.

`DumpPackages`

> Display symbol tables of packages.

`DumpReused`

> Display contents of "reused" addresses.

`quote, HighBit, undefPrint`

> Change the style of string display. The default value for `quote` is auto; you can enable double-quotish or single-quotish format by setting it to " or ', respectively. By default, characters with their high bit set are printed verbatim.

`UsageOnly`

> Instead of showing the contents of a package's variables, with this option enabled, you get a rudimentary per-package memory usage dump based on the total size of the strings found in package variables. Because the package symbol table is used, lexical variables are ignored.

Unattended Execution

During startup, options are initialized from $ENV{PERLDB_OPTS}. You may place the initialization options TTY, noTTY, ReadLine, and NonStop there.

If your init file contains:

```
parse_options("NonStop=1 LineInfo=tperl.out AutoTrace");
```

then your program will run without human intervention, putting trace information into the file *db.out*. (If you interrupt it, you'd better reset LineInfo to */dev/tty* if you expect to see anything.)

The following options can be specified only at startup. To set them in your init file, call `parse_options("OPT=VAL")`.

TTY

The terminal to use for debugging I/O.

noTTY

If set, the debugger goes into NonStop mode and will not connect to a terminal. If interrupted (or if control goes to the debugger via explicit setting of `$DB::signal` or `$DB::single` from the Perl program), it connects to a terminal specified in the TTY option at startup, or to a terminal found at run time using the Term::Rendezvous module of your choice.

This module should implement a method named new that returns an object with two methods: IN and OUT. These should return filehandles for the debugger to use as input and output. The new method should inspect an argument containing the value of `$ENV{PERLDB_NOTTY}` at startup, or `"/tmp/perldbtty$$"` otherwise. This file is not inspected for proper ownership or wide-open write access, so security hazards are theoretically possible.

ReadLine

If false, ReadLine support in the debugger is disabled in order to debug applications that themselves use a ReadLine module.

NonStop

If set, the debugger goes into noninteractive mode until interrupted, or your program sets `$DB::signal` or `$DB::single`.

Options can sometimes be uniquely abbreviated by the first letter, but we recommend that you always spell them out in full, for legibility and future compatibility.

Here's an example of using the PERLDB_OPTS environment variable to set options automatically.[*] It runs your program noninteractively, printing information on each entry into a subroutine and for each line executed. Output from the debugger's trace are placed into the *tperl.out* file. This lets your program still use its regular standard input and output, without the trace information getting in the way.

```
$ PERLDB_OPTS="NonStop frame=1 AutoTrace LineInfo=tperl.out" perl -d myprog
```

If you interrupt the program, you'll need to quickly reset to O Line-Info=/dev/tty or whatever makes sense on your platform. Otherwise, you won't see the debugger's prompting.

---

[*] We're using *sh* shell syntax to show environment variable settings. Users of other shells should adjust accordingly.

Debugger Support

Perl provides special debugging hooks at both compile time and run time for creating debugging environments such as the standard debugger. These hooks are not to be confused with the *perl -D* options, which are usable only if your Perl was built with **-DDEBUGGING** support.

For example, whenever you call Perl's built-in `caller` function from the package `DB`, the arguments that the corresponding stack frame was called with are copied to the the `@DB::args` array. When you invoke Perl with the **-d** switch, the following additional features are enabled:

- Perl inserts the contents of `$ENV{PERL5DB}` (or `BEGIN {require 'perl5db.pl'}` if not present) before the first line of your program.

- The array `@{"_<$filename"}` holds the lines of `$filename` for all files compiled by Perl. The same for `evaled` strings that contain subroutines or are currently being executed. The `$filename` for `evaled` strings looks like `(eval 34)`. Code assertions in regular expressions look like `(re_eval 19)`.

- The hash `%{"_<$filename"}` contains breakpoints and actions keyed by line number. You can set individual entries as opposed to the whole hash. Perl only cares about Boolean truth here, although the values used by *perl5db.pl* have the form `"$break_condition\0$action"`. Values in this hash are magical in numeric context: they are zeros if the line is not breakable.

  The same holds for evaluated strings that contain subroutines or are currently being executed. The `$filename` for `evaled` strings looks like `(eval 34)` or `(re_eval 19)`.

- The scalar `${"_<$filename"}` contains `"_<$filename"`. This is also the case for evaluated strings that contain subroutines or are currently being executed. The `$filename` for `evaled` strings looks like `(eval 34)` or `(re_eval 19)`.

- After each `required` file is compiled, but before it is executed, `DB::postponed(*{"_<$filename"})` is called if the subroutine `DB::postponed` exists. Here, the `$filename` is the expanded name of the `required` file, as found in the values of `%INC`.

- After each subroutine *subname* is compiled, the existence of `$DB::postponed{`*subname*`}` is checked. If this key exists, `DB::postponed(`*subname*`)` is called if the `DB::postponed` subroutine also exists.

- A hash `%DB::sub` is maintained, whose keys are subroutine names and whose values have the form *filename:startline-endline*. *filename* has the form `(eval 34)` for subroutines defined inside `evals`, or `(re_eval 19)` for those within regular expression code assertions.

- When the execution of your program reaches a point that might hold a breakpoint, the DB::DB() subroutine is called if any of the variables $DB::trace, $DB::single, or $DB::signal is true. These variables are not localizable. This feature is disabled when executing inside DB::DB(), including functions called from it unless $^D & (1<<30) holds true.

- When execution of the program reaches a subroutine call, a call to &DB::sub(*args*) is made instead, with $DB::sub holding the name of the called subroutine. This doesn't happen if the subroutine was compiled in the DB package.

Note that if &DB::sub needs external data for it to work, no subroutine call is possible until this is done. For the standard debugger, the $DB::deep variable (how many levels of recursion deep into the debugger you can go before a mandatory break) gives an example of such a dependency.

Writing Your Own Debugger

The minimal working debugger consists of one line:

```
sub DB::DB {}
```

which, since it does nothing whatsoever, can easily be defined via the PERL5DB environment variable:

```
% PERL5DB="sub DB::DB {}" perl -d your-program
```

Another tiny debugger, slightly more useful, could be created like this:

```
sub DB::DB {print ++$i; scalar <STDIN>}
```

This little debugger would print the sequential number of each encountered statement and would wait for you to hit a newline before continuing.

The following debugger, small though it may appear, is really quite functional:

```
{
    package DB;
    sub DB  {}
    sub sub {print ++$i, " $sub\n"; &$sub}
}
```

It prints the sequential number of the subroutine call and the name of the called subroutine. Note that &DB::sub must be compiled from the package DB, as we've done here.

If you base your new debugger on the current debugger, there are some hooks that can help you customize it. At startup, the debugger reads your init file from the current directory or your home directory. After the file is read, the debugger reads the PERLDB_OPTS environment variable and parses this as the remainder of an o ... line such as you might enter at the debugger prompt.

The debugger also maintains magical internal variables, such as @DB::dbline, %DB::dbline, which are aliases for @{"::_<current_file"} %{"::_<current_file"}. Here *current_file* is the currently selected file, either explicitly chosen with the debugger's f command or implicitly by flow of execution.

Some functions can help with customization. DB::parse_options(*STRING*) parses a line like the o option. DB::dump_trace(*SKIP*[, *COUNT*]) skips the specified number of frames and returns a list containing information about the calling frames (all of them, if *COUNT* is missing). Each entry is a reference to a hash with keys "context" (either ., $, or @), "sub" (subroutine name, or info about eval), "args" (undef or a reference to an array), "file", and "line". DB::print_trace(*FH*, *SKIP*[, *COUNT*[, *SHORT*]]) prints formatted info about caller frames to the supplied filehandle. The last two functions may be convenient as arguments to the debugger's < and << commands.

You don't need to learn all that—most of us haven't. In fact, when we need to debug a program, we usually just insert a few print statements here and there and rerun the program.

On our better days, we'll even remember to turn on warnings first. That often spotlights the problem right away, thus saving a great deal of wear and tear on our hair (what's left of it). But when that doesn't work, it's nice to know that, waiting for you patiently behind that **-d** switch, there is a lovely debugger that can do darn near anything *except* find your bug for you.

But if you're going to remember one thing about customizing the debugger, perhaps it is this: don't limit your notion of bugs to things that make Perl unhappy. It's also a bug if your program makes *you* unhappy. Earlier, we showed you a couple of really simple custom debuggers. In the next section, we'll show you an example of a different sort of custom debugger, one that may (or may not) help you debug the bug known as "Is this thing ever gonna finish?"

The Perl Profiler

Do you want to make your program faster? Well, of course you do. But first you should stop and ask yourself, "Do I really need to spend time making this program faster?" Recreational optimization can be fun,* but normally there are better uses for your time. Sometimes you just need to plan ahead and start the program when

---

* Or so says Nathan Torkington, who contributed this section of the book.

you're going on a coffee break. (Or use it as an excuse for one.) But if your program absolutely must run faster, you should begin by profiling it. A profiler can tell you which parts of your program take the most time to execute, so you won't waste time optimizing a subroutine that has an insignificant effect on the overall execution time.

Perl comes with a profiler, the `Devel::DProf` module. You can use it to profile the Perl program in *mycode.pl* by typing:

```
perl -d:DProf mycode.pl
```

Even though we've called it a profiler—since that's what it does—the mechanism DProf employs is the very same one we discussed earlier in this chapter. DProf is just a debugger that records the time Perl entered and left each subroutine.

When your profiled script terminates, DProf will dump the timing information to a file called *tmon.out*. The *dprofpp* program that came with Perl knows how to analyze *tmon.out* and produce a report. You may also use *dprofpp* as a frontend for the whole process with the **-p** switch (see described later).

Given this program:

```
outer();

sub outer {
    for (my $i=0; $i < 100; $i++) { inner() }
}

sub inner {
    my $total = 0;
    for (my $i=0; $i < 1000; $i++) { $total += $i }
}

inner();
```

the output of *dprofpp* is:

```
Total Elapsed Time = 0.537654 Seconds
  User+System Time = 0.317552 Seconds
Exclusive Times
%Time ExclSec CumulS #Calls sec/call Csec/c  Name
 85.0   0.270  0.269    101   0.0027 0.0027  main::inner
 2.83   0.009  0.279      1   0.0094 0.2788  main::outer
```

Note that the percentage numbers don't add up to 100. In fact, in this case, they're pretty far off, which should tip you off that you need to run the program longer. As a general rule, the more profiling data you can collect, the better your statistical sample. If we increase the outer loop to run 1000 times instead of 100 times, we'll get more accurate results:

```
Total Elapsed Time = 2.875946 Seconds
  User+System Time = 2.855946 Seconds
Exclusive Times
%Time ExclSec CumulS #Calls sec/call Csec/c  Name
 99.3   2.838  2.834   1001   0.0028 0.0028  main::inner
 0.14   0.004  2.828      1   0.0040 2.8280  main::outer
```

The first line reports how long the program took to run, from start to finish. The second line displays the total of two different numbers: the time spent executing your code ("user") and the time spent in the operating system executing system calls made by your code ("system"). (We'll have to forgive a bit of false precision in these numbers—the computer's clock almost certainly does not tick every millionth of a second. It might tick every hundredth of a second if you're lucky.)

The "user+system" times can be changed with command-line options to *dprofpp*. **-r** displays elapsed time, **-s** displays system time only, and **-u** displays user time only.

The rest of the report is a breakdown of the time spent in each subroutine. The "Exclusive Times" line indicates that when subroutine outer called subroutine inner, the time spent in inner didn't count towards outer's time. To change this, causing inner's time to be counted towards outer's, give the **-I** option to *dprofpp*.

For each subroutine, the following is reported: %Time, the percentage of time spent in this subroutine call; ExclSec, the time in seconds spent in this subroutine not including those subroutines called from it; CumulS, the time in seconds spent in this subroutine and those called from it; #Calls, the number of calls to the subroutine; sec/call, the average time in seconds of each call to the subroutine not including those called from it; Csec/c, the average time in seconds of each call to the subroutine and those called from it.

Of those, the most useful figure is %Time, which will tell you where your time goes. In our case, the inner subroutine takes the most time, so we should try to optimize that subroutine, or find an algorithm that will call it less. :-)

Options to *dprofpp* provide access to other information or vary the way the times are calculated. You can also make *dprofpp* run the script for you in the first place, so you don't have to remember the **-d:DProf** switch:

-p *SCRIPT*
> Tells *dprofpp* that it should profile the given *SCRIPT* and then interpret its profile data. See also **-Q**.

-Q Used with **-p** to tell *dprofpp* to quit after profiling the script, without interpreting the data.

-a Sort output alphabetically by subroutine name rather than by decreasing percentage of time.

-R Count anonymous subroutines defined in the same package separately. The default behavior is to count all anonymous subroutines as one, named `main::__ANON__`.

-I Display all subroutine times inclusive of child subroutine times.

-l Sort by number of calls to the subroutines. This may help identify candidates for inlining.

-O *COUNT*
    Show only the top *COUNT* subroutines. The default is 15.

-q Do not display column headers.

-T Display the subroutine call tree to standard output. Subroutine statistics are not displayed.

-t Display the subroutine call tree to standard output. Subroutine statistics are not displayed. A function called multiple (consecutive) times at the same calling level is displayed once, with a repeat count.

-S Produce output structured by the way your subroutines call one another:

```
    main::inner x 1        0.008s
    main::outer x 1        0.467s = (0.000 + 0.468)s
       main::inner x 100   0.468s
```

Read this as follows: the top level of your program called `inner` once, and it ran for 0.008s elapsed time, and the top level called `outer` once and it ran for 0.467s inclusively (0s in `outer` itself, 0.468s in the subroutines called from `outer`) calling `inner` 100 times (which ran for 0.468s). Whew, got that?

Branches at the same level (for example, `inner` called once and `outer` called once) are sorted by inclusive time.

-U Do not sort. Display in the order found in the raw profile.

-v Sort by average time spent in subroutines during each call. This may help identify candidates for hand optimization by inlining subroutine bodies.

-g *subroutine*
    Ignore subroutines except *subroutine* and whatever is called from it.

Other options are described in *dprofpp*(1), its standard manpage.

DProf is not your only choice of profiler. CPAN also holds `Devel::SmallProf`, which reports the time spent in each line of your program. That can help you figure out if you're using some particular Perl construct that is being surprisingly expensive. Most of the built-in functions are pretty efficient, but it's easy to accidentally write a regular expression whose overhead increases exponentially with the size of the input. See also the "Efficiency" section in Chapter 24, *Common Practices*, for other helpful hints.

Now go take that coffee break. You'll need it for the next chapter.

21

Internals and Externals

As we discussed in Chapter 18, *Compiling*, *perl* (the program) contains both a compiler and an interpreter for programs written in Perl (the language). The Perl compiler/interpreter is itself written in C. In this chapter, we'll sketch how that C program works from the perspective of someone who wants either to extend or to embed Perl. When you *extend* Perl, you're putting a chunk of C code (called the *extension*) under the control of Perl, and when you *embed* Perl you're putting a Perl interpreter* under the control of a larger C program.

The brief coverage we provide here is no substitute for the online documentation of Perl's innards: see the documentation for *perlguts*, *perlxs*, *perlxstut*, *perlcall*, *perlapi*, and *h2xs*, all bundled with Perl. Again, unless you're extending or embedding Perl, you will never need to know any of this stuff.

Presuming you need to know, what you need to know first is a bit about Perl's guts. You'll also need to know C for most of what follows. You'll need a C compiler to run the examples. If your end goal is to create a module for other people to use, they'll need a C compiler too. Many of these examples will only run on Unix-like systems. Oh, and this material is subject to change in future releases of Perl.

In other words, here be dragons.

---

* While we are careful to distinguish the compiler from the interpreter when that distinction is important, it gets a bit wearisome to keep saying "compiler/interpreter", so we often just shorten that to "interpreter" to mean the whole glob of C code and data that functions like one instance of *perl* (the program); when you're embedding Perl, you can have multiple instances of the interpreter, but each behaves like its own little *perl*.

How Perl Works

When the Perl compiler is fed a Perl program, the first task it performs is *lexical analysis*: breaking down the program into its basic syntactic elements (often called *tokens*). If the program is:

```
print "Hello, world!\n";
```

the lexical analyzer breaks it down into three tokens: print, "Hello, world!\n", and the final semicolon. The token sequence is then *parsed*, fixing the relationship between the tokens. In Perl, the boundary between lexical analysis and parsing is blurred more than in other languages. (Other computer languages, that is. If you think about all the different meanings new Critter might have depending on whether there's a Critter package or a subroutine named new, you'll understand why. On the other hand, we disambiguate these kinds of things all the time in English.)

Once a program has been parsed and (presumably) understood, it is compiled into a tree of *opcodes* representing low-level operations, and finally that tree of operations is executed—unless you invoked Perl with the **-c** ("check syntax") switch, which exits upon completing the compilation phase. It is during compilation, not execution, that BEGIN blocks, CHECK blocks, and use statements are executed.

Internal Data Types

As the tree of opcodes constituting a compiled Perl program is executed, Perl values are created, manipulated, and destroyed. The data types you're familiar with in Perl all have corresponding data types in the C under Perl's hood, and you'll need to know about those types when you pass data between the two languages.

Three C typedefs correspond to Perl's three basic data types: the SV (scalar value), AV (array value), and HV (hash value). In addition, an IV is a simple signed integer type guaranteed to be large enough to hold either a pointer or an integer; and I32 and I16 are types guaranteed to be large enough to hold 32 bits and 16 bits, respectively. For storing unsigned versions of these last three typedefs, there exist UV, U32, and U16 typedefs as well. All of these typedefs can be manipulated with the C functions described in the *perlguts* documentation. We sketch the behaviors of some of those functions below:

- There are four types of values that can be copied into an SV: an integer value (IV), a double (NV), a string (PV), and another scalar (SV). There are dozens of functions for SVs to let you create, modify, grow, and check for the truth or definedness of the Perl scalars they represent. Perl references are implemented as an RV, a special type of SV.

- When an AV is created, it can be created empty or populated with SVs, which makes sense since an array is a collection of scalars.

- The HV has associated C functions for storing, fetching, deleting, and checking for the existence of key/value pairs in the hash the HV represents.

- There is also a GV (glob value), which can hold references to any of the values associated with a variable identifier: a scalar value, an array value, a hash value, a subroutine, an I/O handle, or a format.

When you extend Perl, you will sometimes need to know about these values when you create bindings to C functions. When you embed Perl, you'll need to know about these values when you exchange data with the Perl interpreter included in your C program.

Extending Perl (Using C from Perl)

If you want to use C source code (or a C library) from Perl, you need to create a library that can be either dynamically loaded or statically linked into your *perl* executable. (Dynamic loading is usually preferred, to minimize the number of different *perl* executables sitting around being different.) You create that library by creating an *XS* file (ending in *.xs*) containing a series of wrapper subroutines. The wrapper subroutines are not Perl subroutines, however; they are in the XS language, and we call such a subroutine an *XSUB*, for "eXternal SUBroutine". An XSUB can wrap a C function from an external library, a C function elsewhere in the XS file, or naked C code in the XSUB itself. You then use the *xsubpp* utility bundled with Perl to take the XS file and translate it into C code that can be compiled into a library that Perl will understand.

Assuming your operating system supports dynamic linking, the end result will be a Perl module that behaves like any other module written in 100% pure Perl, but runs compiled C code under the hood. It does this by pulling arguments from Perl's argument stack, converting the Perl values to the formats expected by a particular C function (specified through an XSUB declaration), calling the C function, and finally transferring the return values of the C function back to Perl. These return values may be passed back to Perl either by putting them on the Perl stack or by modifying the arguments supplied from the Perl side. (If your system doesn't support dynamic linking, you have another hoop to jump through, and we'll discuss that in the next section.)

The previous description is a somewhat simplified view of what really happens. Since Perl allows more flexible calling conventions than C, XSUBs can do much more in practice, such as checking input parameters for validity, throwing exceptions, returning undef or an empty list, calling different C functions based on numbers and types of the arguments, or providing an object-oriented interface. Again, see the *perlxs* and *perlxstut* manpages.

XS and XSUBs

XS is a convenience: there's nothing stopping you from writing glue code directly in C and linking it into your Perl executable. However, this would be tedious, especially if you need to write glue for multiple C functions, or if you're not familiar with the Perl stack discipline and other arcana. XS lets you write a concise description of what should be done by the glue, and the XS compiler *xsubpp* handles the rest.

For people who don't find XS convenient enough, the SWIG system automatically generates simple XSUBs. See *http://www.swig.org* for more information.

The XS language allows you to describe the mapping between a C function and a Perl function. It also allows you to create a Perl function that is a wrapper around pure C code that you write yourself. When XS is used merely to map between C and Perl, the XSUB declaration is almost identical to a declaration of a C function. In such circumstances, a tool called *h2xs* (bundled with Perl) is able to translate an entire C header file into a corresponding XS file that provides glue to the C functions and macros.

The *xsubpp* tool creates the constructs necessary to let an XSUB manipulate Perl values and the glue necessary to let Perl call the XSUB.

An XS file begins with any C code you want to include, which will often be nothing more than a set of #include directives. After a MODULE keyword, the remainder of the file should be in the XS "language", a combination of XS directives and XSUB definitions. We'll see an example of an entire XS file soon, but in the meantime here is a simple XSUB definition that allows a Perl program to access a C library function called *sin*(3). The XSUB specifies the return type (a double length floating-point number), the function name and argument list (with one argument dubbed x), and the type of the argument (another double):

```
double
sin(x)
    double x
```

More complicated XSUBs will often contain other bits of XS code. Each section of an XSUB starts with a keyword followed by a colon, such as INIT: or CLEANUP:. However, the first two lines of an XSUB always contain the same data: a description of the return type and the name of the function and its parameters. Whatever immediately follows these is considered to be an INPUT: section unless explicitly marked with another keyword. The various keywords are all explained in the *perlxs* manpage, which you should read to learn about everything you can do with XSUBs.

If your system does not have the capability to dynamically load shared libraries, you can still use XSUBs, but you must statically link the XSUBs with the rest of Perl, creating a new Perl executable (to sit around and be different). The XSUB build mechanism will check the system and build a shared library if possible, or else a static library. Optionally, it can build a new statically linked executable with that static library linked in. (But you might want to delay that to bundle all your new extensions into a single executable sitting around being the same, as it were.)

If your system can link libraries dynamically but you still want to build a statically linked executable, you can run `make perl` instead of `make` in the following examples. You should then run `make test_static` instead of `make test` to test your extension.

The *xsubpp* program also needs to know how to convert from Perl's data types to C's data types. Often it can guess, but with user-defined types you may need to help it out by specifying the conversion in a *typemap* file. The default conversions are stored in *PATH-TO-PERLLIB/ExtUtils/typemap*.

The typemap is split into three sections. The first section, labeled `TYPEMAP`, tells the compiler which of the code fragments in the following two sections should be used to map between C types and Perl values. The second section, `INPUT`, contains C code specifying how Perl values should be converted to C types. The third section, `OUTPUT`, contains C code specifying how to translate C types into Perl values.

Creating Extensions

A proper extension consists of several files: one containing the XS code, plus other supporting files that help Perl figure out what to do with the XS code. You can create all of these files by hand, but it's easier to use the *h2xs* tool, which creates a skeletal extension that you can then flesh out:

```
h2xs -A -n Mytest
```

This creates a directory named *Mytest*, possibly under *ext/* if that directory exists in the current directory. Six files will be created in the *Mytest* directory: *MANIFEST*, *Makefile.PL*, *Mytest.pm*, *Mytest.xs*, *test.pl*, and *Changes*. We describe the first four below.

MANIFEST

> The *MANIFEST* file contains the names of all the files just created in the *Mytest* directory. If you add more files to your extension and intend to distribute it to the wide world, add the filenames here. This is tested by some systems to ensure that your distribution is complete.

Makefile.PL

This is a Perl program that generates a *Makefile* (which is then passed to *make* or an equivalent). *Makefile.PL* is described further in "Creating CPAN Modules" in Chapter 22, *CPAN*.

Mytest.pm

Users will use this module when they want to load your extension. You're expected to fill in the blanks in the skeletal module created for you by *h2xs*:

```
package Mytest;

use strict;
use warnings;

require Exporter;
require DynaLoader;

our @ISA = qw(Exporter DynaLoader);
# Items to export into callers namespace by default. Note: do not export
# names by default without a very good reason. Use EXPORT_OK instead.
# Do not simply export all your public functions/methods/constants.
our @EXPORT = qw(

);
our $VERSION = '0.01';

bootstrap Mytest $VERSION;

# Preloaded methods go here.

# Autoload methods go after __END__, and are processed by the autosplit program.

1;
__END__
# Below is the stub of documentation for your module. You better edit it!
```

Most extension modules will require the Exporter and DynaLoader extensions. After setting @ISA (for inheritance) and @EXPORT (to make functions available to the package using the module), the initialization code tells Perl to bootstrap the XS code. Perl then dynamically links the shared library into the *perl* process at run time.

Mytest.xs

The *Mytest.xs* file contains the XSUBs that tell Perl how to pass data to the compiled C routines. Initially, *Mytest.xs* will look something like this:

```
#include "EXTERN.h"
#include "perl.h"
#include "XSUB.h"


MODULE = Mytest          PACKAGE = Mytest
```

Let's edit the XS file by adding this to the end of the file:

```
void
hello()
    CODE:
        printf("Hello, world!\n");
```

When you run `perl Makefile.PL`, the *Makefile* that *make* needs will be created:

```
% perl Makefile.PL
Checking if your kit is complete...
Looks good
Writing Makefile for Mytest
```

Running *make* will now produce output that looks something like this (some long lines have been shortened for clarity and some extraneous lines have been deleted):

```
% make
umask 0 && cp Mytest.pm ./blib/Mytest.pm
perl xsubpp -typemap typemap Mytest.xs >Mytest.tc && mv Mytest.tc Mytest.c
cc -c Mytest.c
Running Mkbootstrap for Mytest ()
chmod 644 Mytest.bs
LD_RUN_PATH="" ld -o ./blib/PA-RISC1.1/auto/Mytest/Mytest.sl -b Mytest.o
chmod 755 ./blib/PA-RISC1.1/auto/Mytest/Mytest.sl
cp Mytest.bs ./blib/PA-RISC1.1/auto/Mytest/Mytest.bs
chmod 644 ./blib/PA-RISC1.1/auto/Mytest/Mytest.bs
Manifying ./blib/man3/Mytest.3
```

We assume that the *make* program that Perl uses to build programs is called *make*. Instead of running *make* in these examples, you may have to substitute whatever *make* program Perl has been configured to use. You can find out what that program is with:

```
% perl -V:make
```

Running *make* created a directory called *blib* (for "build library") in the current working directory. This directory will contain the shared library that we will build. Once we're sure we know what we're doing, we can install it from that directory into its final resting place. Until then, we'll have to explicitly add the *blib* directory to Perl's @INC array by using the ExtUtils::testlib module. If we now create a file called *hello* that looks like this:

```
use ExtUtils::testlib;    # adds blib/* directories to @INC
use Mytest;
Mytest::hello();
```

we can burrow down from Perl into C:

```
% perl hello
Hello, world!
```

Once your extension is complete and passes all its tests, you can install it with `make install`.

You will need write permission for your Perl library. (If you don't have permission, you can specify another directory as shown in "Installing CPAN modules" in Chapter 22.)

XSUB Input and Output

Continuing with the previous example, we'll add a second XSUB, which takes a single numeric argument as input and returns 1 if the number is even, or 0 if the number is odd:

```
int
is_even(x)
        int x
    CODE:
        RETVAL = (x % 2 == 0);
    OUTPUT:
        RETVAL
```

The list of output parameters occurs at the very end of the function, just after the `OUTPUT:` directive. The use of `RETVAL` tells Perl that you wish to send this value back as the return value of the XSUB. Had we wanted the function to modify its input parameter, we would have used `x` in place of `RETVAL`.

We can rebuild our new shared library with the same steps as before, generating a *Makefile* from the *Makefile.PL* file and running *make*.

In order to verify that our extension works, we'll create a test suite in *test.pl*. This file is set up by *h2xs* to mimic the test script that Perl itself has. Within the script, you may run tests to confirm that the extension behaves properly, printing `ok` when it does and `not ok` when it doesn't. Change the print statement in the `BEGIN` block of *test.pl* to `print "1..4\n";`, and add the following code to the end of the file:

```
print Mytest::is_even(0) == 1 ? "ok 2" : "not ok 2", "\n";
print Mytest::is_even(1) == 0 ? "ok 3" : "not ok 3", "\n";
print Mytest::is_even(2) == 1 ? "ok 4" : "not ok 4", "\n";
```

The test script will be executed when you type `make test`.

Using Functions from an External C Library

So far, our two examples haven't relied on any C code outside of the XS file. Now we'll use some functions from the C math library:

```
void
round(arg)
        double  arg
    CODE:
        if (arg > 0.0) {
                arg = floor(arg + 0.5);
        } else if (arg < 0.0) {
                arg = ceil(arg - 0.5);
        } else {
                arg = 0.0;
        }
    OUTPUT:
        arg
```

Note that the round we define above does not return a value, but instead changes the value of its argument in place.

The *floor*(3) and *ceil*(3) functions are part of the C math library. If you were compiling a C program and needed to link in the math library, you'd append **-lm** to the command line, so that's what you put into the LIBS line in *Makefile.PL*:

```
'LIBS'  => ['-lm'],   # Link in the 'm' math library
```

Generate the *Makefile* and run *make*. Change the BEGIN block to run nine tests and add the following to *test.pl*:

```
$i = -1.5; Mytest::round($i); print $i == -2.0 ? "ok 5" : "not ok 5", "\n";
$i = -1.1; Mytest::round($i); print $i == -1.0 ? "ok 6" : "not ok 6", "\n";
$i = 0.0; Mytest::round($i); print $i == 0.0 ? "ok 7" : "not ok 7", "\n";
$i = 0.5; Mytest::round($i); print $i == 1.0 ? "ok 8" : "not ok 8", "\n";
$i = 1.2; Mytest::round($i); print $i == 1.0 ? "ok 9" : "not ok 9", "\n";
```

Running make test should now print out that all nine tests are okay.

The *perlxstut* documentation bundled with Perl has several more examples of Perl extensions, including an example that uses *h2xs* to automatically make an entire C library available to Perl.

Embedding Perl (Using Perl from C)

You can access a Perl interpreter from C by *embedding* Perl inside your C program. Since Perl is itself a C program, embedding consists of taking the important chunks of Perl and integrating them into yours.

Note that embedding isn't necessary if your only goal is to use a standalone Perl program and you don't mind launching a separate process to do so. You can use a function like C's *popen*(3) to exchange data between your C program and any external Perl program, just like you can use Perl's open(PIPE, "| program") or the IPC::Open2 and IPC::Open3 modules to exchange data between your Perl program and any other program. But if you want to avoid the overhead of launching a separate process, you can embed an interpreter into your C program.

When developing long-running applications (say, for embedding in a web server), it's a good idea to maintain a single persistent interpreter rather than creating and destroying interpreters over and over again. The major reason is speed, since Perl will only be loaded into memory once. By using a persistent Perl interpreter, Apache's mod_perl module avoids loading Perl into memory anew every time someone hits an Apache web page. The *perlembed* manpage provides an example of a persistent interpreter, as well as an example of how a Perl program can manage multiple simultaneous interpreters (another big plus for web servers).

Compiling Embedded Programs

When you embed Perl in C, your C program will usually allocate, "run", and deallocate a PerlInterpreter object, which is a C struct defined in the *libperl* library that was built in the process of configuring Perl for your system. The *libperl* library (along with *EXTERN.h* and *perl.h*, which you'll also need) resides in a directory that will vary from system to system. You should be able to find out the name of that directory with:

```
% perl -MConfig -e "print $Config{archlib}"
```

You should compile your program in exactly the same way that your *perl* executable was compiled. First, you'll need to know what C compiler was used to build Perl on your machine. You can learn that from:

```
% perl -MConfig -e "print $Config{cc}"
```

You can figure out what to put on the rest of the command line with the standard ExtUtils::Embed module. If you had a C program named *interp.c* and your C compiler was *cc*, you could compile it for embedding as follows:

```
% cc -o interp interp.c `perl -MExtUtils::Embed -e ccopts -e ldopts`
```

Adding a Perl Interpreter to Your C Program

As it turns out, *perl* (the C program) is a good example of embedding Perl (the language), so a simple demonstration of embedding can be found in the file *miniperlmain.c*, included with the Perl source code. Here's a nonportable version of *miniperlmain.c* containing the essentials of embedding:

```
#include <EXTERN.h>              /* from the Perl distribution    */
#include <perl.h>                /* from the Perl distribution    */

static PerlInterpreter *my_perl; /***    The Perl interpreter    ***/

int main(int argc, char **argv, char **env)
{
    my_perl = perl_alloc();
    perl_construct(my_perl);
    perl_parse(my_perl, NULL, argc, argv, (char **)NULL);
    perl_run(my_perl);
    perl_destruct(my_perl);
    perl_free(my_perl);
}
```

When this is compiled with the command line above, you'll be able to use *interp* just like a regular Perl interpreter:

```
% interp -e "printf('%x', 3735928559)"
deadbeef
```

You can also execute Perl statements stored in a file by placing the filename in `argv[1]` before calling `perl_run`.

Calling a Perl Subroutine from C

If a Perl program contains a subroutine that you want to call from a C program, you can create a Perl interpreter and then use one of the functions beginning with `call_` documented in the *perlcall* manpage to invoke the subroutine. Let's assume this is our Perl program, called *showtime.pl*:

```
print "I shan't be printed.";

sub showtime {
    print time;
}
```

In this example, we'll use `call_argv` to invoke the `showtime` subroutine from this C program, called *showtime.c*:

```
#include <EXTERN.h>
#include <perl.h>

static PerlInterpreter *my_perl;

int main(int argc, char **argv, char **env)
{
    char *args[] = { NULL };
    my_perl = perl_alloc();
    perl_construct(my_perl);
```

```
        perl_parse(my_perl, NULL, argc, argv, NULL);

        /*** skipping perl_run() ***/

        call_argv("showtime", G_DISCARD | G_NOARGS, args);

        perl_destruct(my_perl);
        perl_free(my_perl);
    }
```

Here, we assume showtime is a Perl subroutine that takes no arguments (that's the G_NOARGS) and for which we can ignore the return value (that's the G_DISCARD). Those flags, and others, are discussed in *perlcall*. We compile and run *showtime* as follows:

```
% cc -o showtime showtime.c `perl -MExtUtils::Embed -e ccopts -e ldopts`
% showtime showtime.pl
963852741
```

In this particular case, we don't call perl_run, but in general it's considered good form so that DESTROY methods and END blocks are executed at the right time.

If you want to pass arguments to the Perl subroutine, you can add strings to the NULL-terminated args list passed to call_argv. For other data types, or to examine return values, you'll need to manipulate the Perl stack. That's touched on lightly later; for the down and dirty, read the *perlcall* manpage bundled with Perl.

Evaluating a Perl Statement from C

Perl provides two functions for evaluating snippets of Perl code: eval_sv and eval_pv, described in the *perlapi* manpage. Arguably, these are the only routines you'll ever need to execute Perl code from within your C program. The code executed can be as long as you wish, contain multiple statements, and employ use, require, or do to include other Perl files.

eval_pv lets you evaluate individual Perl strings and then extract variables for coercion into C types. The following program, *string.c*, executes three Perl strings, extracting an int from the first, a float from the second, and a char * from the third:

```
#include <EXTERN.h>
#include <perl.h>

static PerlInterpreter *my_perl;

main (int argc, char **argv, char **env)
{
    STRLEN n_a;
    char *embedding[] = { "", "-e", "0" };
```

```
        my_perl = perl_alloc();
        perl_construct( my_perl );

        perl_parse(my_perl, NULL, 3, embedding, NULL);
        perl_run(my_perl);

        /** Treat $a as an integer **/
        eval_pv("$a = 3; $a **= 2", TRUE);
        printf("a = %d\n", SvIV(get_sv("a", FALSE)));

        /** Treat $a as a float **/
        eval_pv("$a = 3.14; $a **= 2", TRUE);
        printf("a = %f\n", SvNV(get_sv("a", FALSE)));

        /** Treat $a as a string **/
        eval_pv("$a = 'relreP kcaH rehtonA tsuJ'; $a = reverse($a);", TRUE);
        printf("a = %s\n", SvPV(get_sv("a", FALSE), n_a));

        perl_destruct(my_perl);
        perl_free(my_perl);
    }
```

All of the functions with Sv in their names convert Perl scalars to C types. They're
described in the *perlguts* and *perlapi* manpages. If you compile and run this program, you'll see the results of using SvIV to create an int, SvNV to create a float,
and SvPV to create a C string:

```
a = 9
a = 9.859600
a = Just Another Hack Perler
```

In the previous example, we've created a global variable to temporarily store the
computed value of our evaluated expression. It is also possible (and in most cases
better form) to use the return value of eval_pv instead of throwing it away:

```
SV *val = eval_pv("reverse 'relreP kcaH rehtonA tsuJ'", TRUE);
printf("%s\n", SvPV(val,n_a));
```

The *perlembed* manpage bundled with Perl includes a demonstration of eval_sv
that lets you make use of Perl's regular expression capabilities from your C
program.

Fiddling with the Perl Stack from C

When trying to explain stacks, most computer science textbooks* mumble something about spring-loaded columns of cafeteria plates: the last thing you pushed
on the stack is the first thing you pop off. That'll do for our purposes: your C pro-

---

* Plus the occasional Perl book.

gram will push some arguments onto "the Perl stack", shut its eyes while some magic happens, and then pop the results—the return value of your Perl subroutine—off the stack.

We'll present an example here without much explanation. To really understand what's going on, you'll need to know how to convert between C types and Perl types, with newSViv and sv_setnv and newAV and all their friends described in the *perlguts* and *perlapi* manpages. Then you'll need to read *perlcall* to learn how to manipulate the Perl stack.

Because C has no built-in function for integer exponentiation, let's make Perl's ** operator available to it. (This is less useful than it sounds, since Perl implements ** with C's *pow*(3) function.) First we'll create an exponentiation function in a library file called *power.pl*:

```
sub expo {
    my ($a, $b) = @_;
    return $a ** $b;
}
```

Now we'll create a C program, *power.c*, with a function called PerlPower that pushes the two arguments onto the stack, invokes expo, and pops the return value out:

```
#include <EXTERN.h>
#include <perl.h>

static PerlInterpreter *my_perl;

/* "Real programmers can write assembly code in any language." */

static void
PerlPower(int a, int b)
{
    dSP;                                /* initialize stack pointer      */
    ENTER;                              /* everything created after here */
    SAVETMPS;                           /* ...is a temporary variable.   */
    PUSHMARK(SP);                       /* remember the stack pointer    */
    XPUSHs(sv_2mortal(newSViv(a)));     /* push the base onto the stack  */
    XPUSHs(sv_2mortal(newSViv(b)));     /* push the exponent onto stack  */
    PUTBACK;                            /* make local stack pointer global */
    call_pv("expo", G_SCALAR);          /* call the function             */
    SPAGAIN;                            /* refresh stack pointer         */
                                        /* pop the return value from stack */
    printf ("%d to the %dth power is %d.\n", a, b, POPi);
    PUTBACK;
    FREETMPS;                           /* free that return value        */
    LEAVE;                              /* ...and the XPUSHed "mortal" args */
}
```

```
int main (int argc, char **argv, char **env)
{
  char *my_argv[] = { "", "power.pl" };

  my_perl = perl_alloc();
  perl_construct( my_perl );

  perl_parse(my_perl, NULL, 2, my_argv, (char **)NULL);
  perl_run(my_perl);

  PerlPower(3, 4);                        /*** Compute 3 ** 4 ***/

  perl_destruct(my_perl);
  perl_free(my_perl);
}
```

You can compile *power.c* into *power* like so:

```
% cc -o power power.c `perl -MExtUtils::Embed -e ccopts -e ldopts`
% power
3 to the 4th power is 81.
```

Now your *power* program can sit around being different too.

The Moral of the Story

You can sometimes write faster code in C, but you can always write code faster in Perl. Since you can use each from the other, just combine their strengths as you see fit. (And tell the dragons we said "Hi.")

IV

Perl as Culture

22

CPAN

CPAN (the Comprehensive Perl Archive Network) is the central repository for everything Perl. It contains the collected wisdom of the entire Perl community: hundreds of Perl modules and scripts, several books' worth of documentation, and the entire Perl distribution. If it's written in Perl, and it's helpful and free, it's probably on CPAN. CPAN is mirrored worldwide, and you can find a nearby mirror with the CPAN multiplexer at *http://www.perl.com/CPAN*. The multiplexer will remember which mirror you choose so that when you visit *http://www.perl.com/CPAN/* (note the trailing slash) you'll be automatically redirected to that mirror. Alternatively, you can start at *www.cpan.org*. The interface is different, but the data is the same.

Once you get to the main CPAN directory, you'll see some subdirectories:

authors

> This directory contains numerous subdirectories, one for each contributor of software. For example, if you wanted to find Lincoln Stein's great CGI module[*] and you happened to know for a fact that he wrote it, you could look in *authors/Lincoln_Stein*. If you didn't know he wrote it, you could look in the *modules* directory described below.

doc

> This directory holds all manner of Perl documentation, including all of Perl's official manpages in several different arrangements and formats, such as text, HTML, PostScript, and Perl's native pod format, documented in Chapter 26, *Plain Old Documentation*.

---

[*] Now part of the standard Perl distribution.

modules

> This directory contains modules written either in Perl or in a combination of both Perl and C. See the discussion of the *modules* directory below.

ports

> This directory contains the source code and sometimes also precompiled executable images of Perl ports to operating systems that are not directly supported in the standard distribution, or for which compilers are notoriously hard to come by. These ports are the individual efforts of their respective authors and may not all function precisely as described in this book. These days few systems should require special ports. The index document of this directory is interesting to look through anyway because it also includes information detailing when each system vendor began shipping Perl.

scripts

> This directory contains a small collection of diverse Perl programs from all over the world. These are useful as standalone programs and perhaps as examples (although the code isn't subject to quality control checks). Right now, there aren't many programs listed, but we hope this area will become richer in time. The Perl Power Tools project (PPT) is also to be found here. PPT aims to recreate all the standard Unix utilities in Perl. Most of the standard ones are done already, plus some that aren't standard.

src Within this directory, you will find the source code for the standard Perl distribution. Actually, for two standard Perl distributions. One is marked *stable*, and the other *devel*. (The index page for this directory explains the details.) These are really just links to the appropriate versions. As of this writing, *stable.tar.gz* is a symbolic link to *perl-5.6.0.tar.gz*,[*] but it will likely point to a higher version number by the time you read this. This giant file contains the full source code and documentation for Perl. Configuration and installation should be relatively straightforward on most platforms. If not, see *ports* described earlier.

The CPAN modules Directory

Although CPAN contains the complete source code for Perl, plus a few binary distributions for systems bereft of C compilers, as well as a smattering of programs, CPAN is best known for its collection of modules.

---

[*] The general scheme is that if the second number in the version is even, it's a maintenance release; if it's odd, it's a development release. The trailing *.tar.gz* extension, which is sometimes written *.tgz*, indicates that it's in the standard Internet format of a GNU-zipped *tar* archive, commonly known as a "tarball".

When we say "modules", we mean three things: 100% pure Perl modules (described in Chapter 11, *Modules*, and Chapter 12, *Objects*), extensions (modules depending on C code, described in Chapter 21, *Internals and Externals*), and pragmas (modules containing special instructions for the Perl compiler, described in Chapter 31, *Pragmatic Modules*). There are also module *bundles* on CPAN. Bundles are collections of modules that interoperate somehow and are typically the result of a module developer wanting to provide a turnkey solution to a set of problems. If one module depends on another module (and possibly a particular version), developers will often bundle the modules together. See `Bundle-XML`, for instance.

One way to browse the CPAN modules is to visit *http://search.cpan.org*, which provides a search engine frontend to CPAN. Another way is to visit your local CPAN mirror and enter the *modules* directory, where you'll see three subdirectories: *by-authors*, *by-category*, and *by-module*. The *by-module* directory may be the most useful if your browser has search capabilities—although (lamentably) some modules are only available in the author directories. If you search by category, you'll have the following choices:

Perl core modules, language extensions, and documentation tools
> This includes pragmas and other standard modules, modules that help you write Perl differently, modules related to the Perl compiler, source filters, and modules related to Perl's pod documentation format. This category also includes modules for generating Java bytecode.

Development support
> This category includes modules for creating modules and examining how Perl runs programs.

Operating system interfaces and hardware drivers
> Here you'll find modules for interacting with strange entities like operating systems, PalmPilots, and serial ports.

Networking, device control, and interprocess communication
> This includes modules that implement network protocols, manipulate network data, operate modems, and control the appliances in your house.

Data types and data type utilities
> This category has modules for math, statistics, algorithms, data structures (and their persistent storage), dates and times, object-oriented programming, PDL (the Perl Data Language, for serious number crunching), and POE (the Perl Object Environment, an object-oriented, event-driven scheduler).

Database interfaces

Here you'll find modules that let you operate several dozen database systems from Perl, most of them with Perl's DBI system. This includes the database-specific DBD modules.

User interfaces (character and graphical)

This includes modules for manipulating user terminals (command-line editing and *curses*(3)-style character graphics), as well as Perl/Tk and bindings to Gtk, Gnome, Sx, and Qt for writing your own GUIs in Perl.

Interfaces to or emulations of other programming languages

This category has modules for using other programming languages from Perl or letting you pretend that Perl is something it isn't. If you're interested in using Perl from C or C from Perl, see Chapter 21.

Filenames, filesystems, and file locking

This includes modules for inspecting, creating, locking, and otherwise manipulating files and directories.

String processing, language text processing, parsing, and searching

This category contains modules for manipulating text: hyphenating, wrapping, parsing, stemming, and searching. This includes modules for manipulating PostScript, fonts, XML, and RTF.

Option, argument, parameter, and configuration file processing

This category contains modules for processing command-line arguments (the **-x** in *myperlprog -x*) and for managing configuration files (like dot files).

Internationalization and locale

This includes modules for tailoring your Perl program for a particular country and language.

Authentication, security, and encryption

Here you'll find modules for managing user passwords, computing message digests, encrypting data, and authenticating users.

World Wide Web, HTML, HTTP, CGI, MIME

This category has modules that let you create CGI-based web pages, web robots, and web-based content management systems. Other modules let you manage cookies, parse HTML and MIME messages, and manipulate web caches. There is also a special section just for Perl modules that you can embed into the Apache web server.

Server and daemon utilities
> This includes modules for creating network and event servers.

Archiving, compression, and conversion
> Here you'll find modules for zipping and tarring files, and converting between file formats (even the Apple II file format).

Images, pixmap, and bitmap manipulation, drawing, and graphing
> This category contains modules for creating graphs, GIFs, VRML, and for working with the Gimp.

Mail and Usenet news
> In this category, you'll find modules for sending, receiving, and filtering mail and netnews.

Control flow utilities
> This category contains modules for executing Perl code at odd times.

Filehandle, directory handle, and input/output stream utilities
> Here are modules for input from and output to files, including log files. Includes all `IO::` modules and an `Expect` module for automating conversations with network services or other interactive programs.

Microsoft Windows modules
> This includes modules for manipulating the Windows registry, ASP, ODBC, OLE, and other technologies specific to Windows.

Miscellaneous modules
> Here you'll find modules for astronomy, biology, chemistry, validating credit cards (or invalidating credit cards), mortgage amortizations, audio, video, MIDI, weather, and games.

Using CPAN Modules

Most modules that you'll find on CPAN are in "tarball" form. That is, they have a file extension ending in *.tar.gz*, and expand into a directory with the module code and any auxiliary files, usually including a *README* and a *Makefile.PL* file.

There are four steps for making CPAN modules available to your programs: decompression, unpacking, building, and installation. How each of those steps work depend on your operating system and the module being installed, so we can't give you a foolproof recipe that will work all the time. When in doubt, read the *README* and *INSTALL* files that were hopefully distributed with the module. Also read the *perlmodinstall* manpage.

But you may never have to think about the installation procedure if you use the
CPAN module (bundled with the Perl distribution) or PPM (the Perl Package Manager, bundled with the ActiveState distribution of Perl). To use the CPAN module
(not to be confused with CPAN itself), type:

```
% perl -MCPAN -e "shell"
```

at your command line to begin the configuration process. After you've answered a
variety of questions about how you'd like to retrieve files, you can install a module
by typing:

```
install Some::Module
```

in the CPAN module's shell, or by typing:

```
% perl -MCPAN -e "install 'Some::Module'"
```

from your normal command line.

If you don't have the convenience of either the CPAN module or PPM, you'll need
to go through the steps in the following sections by hand. Instructions are provided for Unix, Windows, and Macintosh; for other operating systems, consult the
perlmodinstall manpage.

Decompressing and Unpacking CPAN Modules

Most of the thousands of utilities on CPAN are compressed so that they take up
less space. Once you've retrieved a module tarball, you first need to turn it into a
directory tree on your system by decompressing ("unzipping") and unpacking the
tarball. On Unix, you can use *gzip* and *tar* to do this. (On many systems, *tar* will
do both.) On Windows, *WinZip* will both decompress and unpack tarballs. On a
Macintosh, you can either use *StuffIt* and *DropStuff*, *MacGzip*, or *suntar*.

Building CPAN Modules

A minority of CPAN modules come with C code that you'll need to compile for
your system, which is naturally a problem for systems that lack a C compiler. The
standard procedure for building a CPAN module (with or without C code) is the
following three commands, executed from the command line. (If you don't have a
command line, or a *make*-equivalent, you'll need to resort to more drastic, system-
dependent measures. Windows users have a command line but might need to use
the *nmake* utility instead of *make*.)

```
% perl Makefile.PL
```

```
% make
```

```
% make test
```

The *perl Makefile.PL* command will try to create a *Makefile*, which the subsequent *make* command uses to determine what utilities need to be built and in what order. The final command, *make test*, runs the test suite that the module author hopefully included.

Installing CPAN Modules into the Perl Library

Presuming you've followed the previous steps, you now have a module that has been built and tested, but not yet installed into Perl's library. When Perl was installed on your system, a *lib* directory was created to hold modules, pragmas, and related files. That's the Perl library, which is usually something like */usr/local/lib/perl5* on Unix systems and *C:\PERL\LIB* by default on Windows systems. Modules installed after Perl was built are stored in the *site_perl* subdirectory of the Perl library. You can see the names of all your library directories (and a bunch of other stuff) by saying:

```
% perl -V
```

To install the module, type:

```
% make install
```

Superuser access is normally required, even for installing modules into your site-specific Perl library directories.

With a little work, you can install the module in a directory outside your Perl library (such as your home directory). If you would normally have typed *perl Makefile.PL* to create a *Makefile*, you could instead use this incantation:

```
% perl Makefile.PL LIB=/my/dir/perllib  \
       INSTALLMAN1DIR=/my/dir/man/man1  \
       INSTALLMAN3DIR=/my/dir/man/man3  \
          INSTALLBIN=/my/dir/bin        \
       INSTALLSCRIPT=/my/dir/scripts
```

This will install the modules somewhere in the */my/dir/perllib* directory and any remaining files where they need to go. (If you find yourself typing this a lot, you could even write a little Perl program to do it for you. Perl is good for things like that.)

Then you can have Perl search your special directory for modules by adding:

```
use lib "/my/dir/perllib";
```

before your program attempts to load in the module. You may also set the PERL5LIB environment variable to that directory, or use Perl's **-I** switch. See the use lib pragma in Chapter 31 for examples of doing this.

Creating CPAN Modules

If you have a module that you think others might find useful, consider making the world a better place by uploading it to CPAN. The server that handles new module submissions is called PAUSE (the Perl Authors Upload Server) and can be found at *https://pause.kbx.de/pause/*. Before you can upload your module, you'll have to get a PAUSE account. This is about as close as you can get to being a "registered Perl developer".

If you call yourself a registered Perl developer, you should know enough to document your modules. Perl has a convention of embedding documentation inside your source code. (That way, you never lose it.) This embedded documentation is in a format called "pod" (for Plain Old Documentation) and is described in Chapter 26.

You should consider making your module thread safe. See Chapter 17, *Threads*.

You should also worry a little bit about whether your cute little module does things that could break the security of people who use it, because other folks may have some Really Good Reasons to be more concerned about security than you are (yet). See Chapter 23, *Security*, for all about how to avoid being responsible for the outbreak of World War III and other such nuisances.

Modules meant to be distributed on CPAN should include a Perl program named *Makefile.PL* that, when run, generates a *Makefile*, and a *README* file briefly explaining what the module is and how to install it. The *Makefile* will expect your module to include a test suite as well. You can create all these files at once with the *h2xs* utility:

```
h2xs -X -n Foo::Bar
```

(Substitute **-A** for **-X** if you're building a module that has an XS component. XS is described in Chapter 21.) The *h2xs* program creates a single directory with skeletal files for you to flesh out. When you've finished, you can upload the tarballed directory to PAUSE.

The *Makefile.PL* generated by *h2xs* will look something like this:

```
use ExtUtils::MakeMaker;
# See lib/ExtUtils/MakeMaker.pm for details of how to influence
# the contents of the Makefile that is written.
WriteMakefile(
    NAME         => 'Mytest',
    VERSION_FROM => 'Mytest.pm', # finds $VERSION
    LIBS         => [''],   # e.g., '-lm'
    DEFINE       => '',     # e.g., '-DHAVE_SOMETHING'
    INC          => '',     # e.g., '-I/usr/include/other'
);
```

The first thing *Makefile.PL* does is to pull in the ExtUtils::MakeMaker module. MakeMaker's WriteMakefile function has oodles of options (where oodles is defined as approximately 88) to help you customize what happens after the user downloads your module from CPAN and types *perl MakeFile.PL* to begin building it. The nice thing about all this is that, since the user is presumably running the *perl* that will be used later, you have a wealth of configuration information available (via the Config module or the $^O special variable) to help you decide how to drive MakeMaker. On the other hand, MakeMaker is really good at finding decent defaults for almost everything, so the skeletal file written *h2xs* may well be all you need, with perhaps a tweak or two. For more on this, see the extensive online docs for ExtUtils::MakeMaker.

When writing a Perl module for general consumption, you should allow for the possibility that the user's version of Perl may differ from yours. You should always put an English description of any dependencies (particular versions of Perl, or system requirements, or other modules) into the *README* file. However, even that may not be sufficient, since someone using the slick CPAN module to automatically download and install your module might never see the warning. So you should check those dependencies in *Makefile.PL*. Here's how you might ensure that the person who downloaded your module is running Perl 5.6 or greater:

```
eval { require 5.6.0 }
    or die <<'EOD';
############
### This module requires lvaluable subroutines, which are not available
### in versions of Perl earlier than 5.6.  Please upgrade!
############
EOD
```

Internal Testing

The standard instructions for installing a module tell the user to run *make test* after building the module with *make*. So please include a decent test script with any module that you upload to CPAN. You should emulate the ok/not ok style that Perl uses in its own test suite, so that it's easy for the user to determine the outcome of each test case. The *test.pl* file generated by *h2xs* will help get you started. Chapter 21 has some examples of tests that you can add to the end of *test.pl*.

If you have many test cases, you might want to mimic Perl's test suite by creating a subdirectory named *t/* in the module's directory and appending *.t* to the names of your different test scripts. When you run *make test*, all test files will be executed automatically.

External Testing

Modules uploaded to CPAN are tested by a variety of volunteers on different platforms. These CPAN testers are notified by mail of each new upload, and reply to the list with PASS, FAIL, NA (not applicable to this platform), or UNKNOWN (unknown), along with any relevant notations. You can find the mailing list for CPAN testers at *cpan-testers@perl.org*; test results are posted at *http://testers.cpan.org/*.

That's all just the preliminary testing, of course. The real testing begins when someone plugs your little module into a web server that's cranking out a million pages a day. Or uses your module to help design the airplane you'll be riding in someday soon.

So go ahead, skip writing those pesky little tests. See if we care . . .

23

Security

Whether you're dealing with a user sitting at the keyboard typing commands or someone sending information across the network, you need to be careful about the data coming into your programs, since the other person may, either maliciously or accidentally, send you data that will do more harm than good. Perl provides a special security-checking mechanism called *taint mode*, whose purpose is to isolate tainted data so that you won't use it to do something you didn't intend to do. For instance, if you mistakenly trust a tainted filename, you might end up appending an entry to your password file when you thought you were appending to a log file. The mechanism of tainting is covered in the section "Handling Insecure Data".

In multitasking environments, offstage actions by unseen actors can affect the security of your own program. If you presume exclusive ownership of external objects (especially files) as though yours were the only process on the system, you expose yourself to errors substantially subtler than those that come from directly handling data or code of dubious provenance. Perl helps you out a little here by detecting some situations that are beyond your control, but for those that you can control, the key is understanding which approaches are proof against unseen meddlers. The section "Handling Timing Glitches" discusses these matters.

If the data you get from a stranger happens to be a bit of source code to execute, you need to be even more careful than you would with their data. Perl provides checks to intercept stealthy code masquerading as data so you don't execute it unintentionally. If you do want to execute foreign code, though, the Safe module lets you quarantine suspect code where it can't do any harm and might possibly do some good. These are the topics of the section "Handling Insecure Code".

Handling Insecure Data

Perl makes it easy to program securely even when your program is being used by someone less trustworthy than the program itself. That is, some programs need to grant limited privileges to their users, without giving away other privileges. Setuid and setgid programs fall into this category on Unix, as do programs running in various privileged modes on other operating systems that support such notions. Even on systems that don't, the same principle applies to network servers and to any programs run by those servers (such as CGI scripts, mailing list processors, and daemons listed in */etc/inetd.conf*). All such programs require a higher level of scrutiny than normal.

Even programs run from the command line are sometimes good candidates for taint mode, especially if they're meant to be run by a privileged user. Programs that act upon untrusted data, like those that generate statistics from log files or use LWP::* or Net::* to fetch remote data, should probably run with tainting explicitly turned on; programs that are not prudent risk being turned into "Trojan horses". Since programs don't get any kind of thrill out of risk taking, there's no particular reason for them not to be careful.

Compared with Unix command-line shells, which are really just frameworks for calling other programs, Perl is easy to program securely because it's straightforward and self-contained. Unlike most shell programming languages, which are based on multiple, mysterious substitution passes on each line of the script, Perl uses a more conventional evaluation scheme with fewer hidden snags. Additionally, because the language has more built-in functionality, it can rely less upon external (and possibly untrustworthy) programs to accomplish its purposes.

Under Unix, Perl's home town, the preferred way to compromise system security was to cajole a privileged program into doing something it wasn't supposed to do. To stave off such attacks, Perl developed a unique approach for coping with hostile environments. Perl automatically enables taint mode whenever it detects its program running with differing real and effective user or group IDs.* Even if the file containing your Perl script doesn't have the setuid or setgid bits turned on, that script can still find itself executing in taint mode. This happens if your script was invoked by another program that was *itself* running under differing IDs. Perl programs that weren't designed to operate under taint mode tend to expire prema-

---

* The setuid bit in Unix permissions is mode 04000, and the setgid bit is 02000; either or both may be set to grant the user of the program some of the privileges of the owner (or owners) of the program. (These are collectively known as set-id programs.) Other operating systems may confer special privileges on programs in other ways, but the principle is the same.

turely when caught violating safe tainting policy. This is just as well, since these are the sorts of shenanigans that were historically perpetrated on shell scripts to compromise system security. Perl isn't that gullible.

You can also enable taint mode explicitly with the **-T** command-line switch. You should do this for daemons, servers, and any programs that run on behalf of someone else, such as CGI scripts. Programs that can be run remotely and anonymously by anyone on the Net are executing in the most hostile of environments. You should not be afraid to say "No!" occasionally. Contrary to popular belief, you can exercise a great deal of prudence without dehydrating into a wrinkled prude.

On the more security-conscious sites, running all CGI scripts under the **-T** flag isn't just a good a idea: it's the law. We're not claiming that running in taint mode is sufficient to make your script secure. It's not, and it would take a whole book just to mention everything that would. But if you aren't executing your CGI scripts under taint mode, you've needlessly abandoned the strongest protection Perl can give you.

While in taint mode, Perl takes special precautions called *taint checks* to prevent traps both obvious and subtle. Some of these checks are reasonably simple, such as verifying that dangerous environment variables aren't set and that directories in your path aren't writable by others; careful programmers have always used checks like these. Other checks, however, are best supported by the language itself, and it is these checks especially that contribute to making a privileged Perl program more secure than the corresponding C program, or a Perl CGI script more secure than one written in any language without taint checks. (Which, as far as we know, is any language other than Perl.)

The principle is simple: you may not use data derived from outside your program to affect something else outside your program—at least, not by accident. Anything that comes from outside your program is marked as tainted, including all command-line arguments, environment variables, and file input. Tainted data may not be used directly or indirectly in any operation that invokes a subshell, nor in any operation that modifies files, directories, or processes. Any variable set within an expression that has previously referenced a tainted value becomes tainted itself, even if it is logically impossible for the tainted value to influence the variable. Because taintedness is associated with each scalar, some individual values in an array or hash might be tainted and others might not. (Only the values in a hash can be tainted, though, not the keys.)

The following code illustrates how tainting would work if you executed all these statements in order. Statements marked "Insecure" will trigger an exception, whereas those that are "OK" will not.

```
$arg = shift(@ARGV);          # $arg is now tainted (due to @ARGV).
$hid = "$arg, 'bar'";         # $hid also tainted (due to $arg).
$line = <>;                   # Tainted (reading from external file).
$path = $ENV{PATH};           # Tainted due to %ENV, but see below.
$mine = 'abc';                # Not tainted.

system "echo $mine";          # Insecure until PATH set.
system "echo $arg";           # Insecure: uses sh with tainted $arg.
system "echo", $arg;          # OK once PATH set (doesn't use sh).
system "echo $hid";           # Insecure two ways: taint, PATH.

$oldpath = $ENV{PATH};        # $oldpath is tainted (due to %ENV).
$ENV{PATH} = '/bin:/usr/bin'; # (Makes it OK to execute other programs.)
$newpath = $ENV{PATH};        # $newpath is NOT tainted.

delete @ENV{qw{IFS
               CDPATH
               ENV
               BASH_ENV}};    # Makes %ENV safer.

system "echo $mine";          # OK, is secure once path is reset.
system "echo $hid";           # Insecure via tainted $hid.

open(OOF, "< $arg");          # OK (read-only opens not checked).
open(OOF, "> $arg");          # Insecure (trying to write to tainted arg).

open(OOF, "echo $arg|")       # Insecure due to tainted $arg, but...
    or die "can't pipe from echo: $!";

open(OOF,"-|")                # Considered OK: see below for taint
    or exec "echo", $arg      #   exemption on exec'ing a list.
    or die "can't exec echo: $!";

open(OOF,"-|", "echo", $arg)  # Same as previous, likewise OKish.
    or die "can't pipe from echo: $!";

$shout = `echo $arg`;         # Insecure via tainted $arg.
$shout = `echo abc`;          # $shout is tainted due to backticks.
$shout2 = `echo $shout`;      # Insecure via tainted $shout.

unlink $mine, $arg;           # Insecure via tainted $arg.
umask $arg;                   # Insecure via tainted $arg.

exec "echo $arg";             # Insecure via tainted $arg passed to shell.
exec "echo", $arg;            # Considered OK! (But see below.)
exec "sh", '-c', $arg;        # Considered OK, but isn't really!
```

If you try to do something insecure, you get an exception (which unless trapped,
becomes a fatal error) such as "Insecure dependency" or "Insecure $ENV{PATH}".
See the section "Cleaning Up Your Environment" later.

If you pass a *LIST* to a system, exec, or pipe open, the arguments are not inspected for taintedness, because with a *LIST* of arguments, Perl doesn't need to invoke the potentially dangerous shell to run the command. You can still easily write an insecure system, exec, or pipe open using the *LIST* form, as demonstrated in the final example above. These forms are exempt from checking because you are presumed to know what you're doing when you use them.

Sometimes, though, you can't tell how many arguments you're passing. If you supply these functions with an array* that contains just one element, then it's just as though you passed one string in the first place, so the shell might be used. The solution is to pass an explicit path in the indirect-object slot:

```
system @args;               # Won't call the shell unless @args == 1.
system { $args[0] } @args;  # Bypasses shell even with one-argument list.
```

Detecting and Laundering Tainted Data

To test whether a scalar variable contains tainted data, you can use the following is_tainted function. It makes use of the fact that eval *STRING* raises an exception if you try to compile tainted data. It doesn't matter that the $nada variable used in the expression to compile will always be empty; it will still be tainted if $arg is tainted. The outer eval *BLOCK* isn't doing any compilation. It's just there to catch the exception raised if the inner eval is given tainted data. Since the $@ variable is guaranteed to be nonempty after each eval if an exception was raised and empty otherwise, we return the result of testing whether its length was zero:

```
sub is_tainted {
    my $arg = shift;
    my $nada = substr($arg, 0, 0);  # zero-length
    local $@;  # preserve caller's version
    eval { eval "# $nada" };
    return length($@) != 0;
}
```

But testing for taintedness only gets you so far. Usually you know perfectly well which variables contain tainted data—you just have to clear the data's taintedness. The only official way to bypass the tainting mechanism is by referencing submatches returned by an earlier regular expression match.† When you write a pattern that contains capturing parentheses, you can access the captured substrings through match variables like $1, $2, and $+, or by evaluating the pattern in list context. Either way, the presumption is that you knew what you were doing when

---

* Or a function that produces a list.

† An unofficial way is by storing the tainted string as the key to a hash and fetching back that key. Because keys aren't really full SVs (internal name scalar values), they don't carry the taint property. This behavior may be changed someday, so don't rely on it. Be careful when handling keys, lest you unintentionally untaint your data and do something unsafe with them.

you wrote the pattern and wrote it to weed out anything dangerous. So you need to give it some real thought—never blindly untaint, or else you defeat the entire mechanism.

It's better to verify that the variable contains only good characters than to check whether it contains any bad characters. That's because it's far too easy to miss bad characters that you never thought of. For example, here's a test to make sure $string contains nothing but "word" characters (alphabetics, numerics, and underscores), hyphens, at signs, and dots:

```
if ($string =~ /^([-\@\w.]+)$/) {
    $string = $1;                    # $string now untainted.
}
else {
    die "Bad data in $string";       # Log this somewhere.
}
```

This renders $string fairly secure to use later in an external command, since /\w+/ doesn't normally match shell metacharacters, nor are those other characters going to mean anything special to the shell.* Had we used /(.+)/s instead, it would have been unsafe because that pattern lets everything through. But Perl doesn't check for that. When untainting, be exceedingly careful with your patterns. Laundering data by using regular expressions is the *only* approved internal mechanism for untainting dirty data. And sometimes it's the wrong approach entirely. If you're in taint mode because you're running set-id and not because you intentionally turned on **-T**, you can reduce your risk by forking a child of lesser privilege; see the section "Cleaning Up Your Environment".

The use re 'taint' pragma disables the implicit untainting of any pattern matches through the end of the current lexical scope. You might use this pragma if you just want to extract a few substrings from some potentially tainted data, but since you aren't being mindful of security, you'd prefer to leave the substrings tainted to guard against unfortunate accidents later.

Imagine you're matching something like this, where $fullpath is tainted:

```
($dir, $file) = $fullpath =~ m!(.*/)(.*)!s;
```

By default, $dir and $file would now be untainted. But you probably didn't want to do that so cavalierly, because you never really thought about the security issues. For example, you might not be terribly happy if $file contained the string "; rm -rf * ;", just to name one rather egregious example. The following code leaves the two result variables tainted if $fullpath was tainted:

---

* Unless you were using an intentionally broken locale. Perl assumes that your system's locale definitions are potentially compromised. Hence, when running under the use locale pragma, patterns with a symbolic character class in them, such as \w or [[:alpha:]], produce tainted results.

```
{
    use re 'taint';
    ($dir, $file) = $fullpath =~ m!(.*/)(.*)!s;
}
```

A good strategy is to leave submatches tainted by default over the whole source file and only selectively permit untainting in nested scopes as needed:

```
use re 'taint';
# remainder of file now leaves $1 etc tainted
{
    no re 'taint';
    # this block now untaints re matches
    if ($num =~ /^(\d+)$/) {
        $num = $1;
    }
}
```

Input from a filehandle or a directory handle is automatically tainted, except when it comes from the special filehandle, DATA. If you want to, you can mark other handles as trusted sources via the IO::Handle module's untaint function:

```
use IO::Handle;

IO::Handle::untaint(*SOME_FH);          # Either procedurally
SOME_FH->untaint();                     # or using the OO style.
```

Turning off tainting on an entire filehandle is a risky move. How do you *really* know it's safe? If you're going to do this, you should at least verify that nobody but the owner can write to the file.* If you're on a Unix filesystem (and one that prudently restricts *chown*(2) to the superuser), the following code works:

```
use File::stat;
use Symbol 'qualify_to_ref';
sub handle_looks_safe(*) {
    my $fh = qualify_to_ref(shift, caller);
    my $info = stat($fh);
    return unless $info;

    # owner neither superuser nor "me", whose
    # real uid is in the $< variable
    if ($info->uid != 0 && $info->uid != $<) {
        return 0;
    }

    # check whether group or other can write file.
    # use 066 to detect for readability also
    if ($info->mode & 022) {
        return 0;
```

---

* Although you can untaint a directory handle, too, this function only works on a filehandle. That's because given a directory handle, there's no portable way to extract its file descriptor to stat.

```
    }
    return 1;
}

use IO::Handle;
SOME_FH->untaint() if handle_looks_safe(*SOME_FH);
```

We called stat on the filehandle, not the filename, to avoid a dangerous race condition. See the section "Handling Race Conditions" later in this chapter.

Note that this routine is only a good start. A slightly more paranoid version would check all parent directories as well, even though you can't reliably stat a directory handle. But if any parent directory is world-writable, you know you're in trouble whether or not there are race conditions.

Perl has its own notion of which operations are dangerous, but it's still possible to get into trouble with other operations that don't care whether they use tainted values. It's not always enough to be careful of input. Perl output functions don't test whether their arguments are tainted, but in some environments, this matters. If you aren't careful of what you output, you might just end up spitting out strings that have unexpected meanings to whoever is processing the output. If you're running on a terminal, special escape and control codes could cause the viewer's terminal to act strangely. If you're in a web environment and you blindly spit back out data that was given to you, you could unknowingly produce HTML tags that would drastically alter the page's appearance. Worse still, some markup tags can even execute code back on the browser.

Imagine the common case of a guest book where visitors enter their own messages to be displayed when others come calling. A malicious guest could supply unsightly HTML tags or put in <SCRIPT>...</SCRIPT> sequences that execute code (like JavaScript) back in the browsers of subsequent guests.

Just as you should carefully check for only good characters when inspecting tainted data that accesses resources on your own system, you should apply the same care in a web environment when presenting data supplied by a user. For example, to strip the data of any character not in the specified list of good characters, try something like this:

```
$new_guestbook_entry =~ tr[_a-zA-Z0-9 ,./!?()@+*-][]dc;
```

You certainly wouldn't use that to clean up a filename, since you probably don't want filenames with spaces or slashes, just for starters. But it's enough to keep your guest book free of sneaky HTML tags and entities. Each data-laundering case is a little bit different, so always spend time deciding what is and what is not permitted. The tainting mechanism is intended to catch stupid mistakes, not to remove the need for thought.

Cleaning Up Your Environment

When you execute another program from within your Perl script, no matter how, Perl checks to make sure your PATH environment variable is secure. Since it came from your environment, your PATH starts out tainted, so if you try to run another program, Perl raises an "Insecure $ENV{PATH}" exception. When you set it to a known, untainted value, Perl makes sure that each directory in that path is non-writable by anyone other than the directory's owner and group; otherwise, it raises an "Insecure directory" exception.

You may be surprised to find that Perl cares about your PATH even when you specify the full pathname of the command you want to execute. It's true that with an absolute filename, the PATH isn't used to find the executable to run. But there's no reason to trust the program you're running not to turn right around and execute some *other* program and get into trouble because of the insecure PATH. So Perl forces you to set a secure PATH before you call any program, no matter how you say to call it.

The PATH isn't the only environment variable that can bring grief. Because some shells use the variables IFS, CDPATH, ENV, and BASH_ENV, Perl makes sure that those are all either empty or untainted before it will run another command. Either set these variables to something known to be safe, or else delete them from the environment altogether:

```
delete @ENV{qw(IFS CDPATH ENV BASH_ENV)};    # Make %ENV safer
```

Features convenient in a normal environment can become security concerns in a hostile one. Even if you remember to disallow filenames containing newlines, it's important to understand that open accesses more than just named files. Given appropriate ornamentation on the filename argument, one- or two-argument calls to open can also run arbitrary external commands via pipes, fork extra copies of the current process, duplicate file descriptors, and interpret the special filename "-" as an alias for standard input or output. It can also ignore leading and trailing whitespace that might disguise such fancy arguments from your check patterns. While it's true that Perl's taint checking will catch tainted arguments used for pipe opens (unless you use a separated argument list) and any file opens that aren't read-only, the exception this raises is still likely to make your program misbehave.

If you intend to use any externally derived data as part of a filename to open, at least include an explicit mode separated by a space. It's probably safest, though, to use either the low-level sysopen or the three-argument form of open:

```
# Magic open--could be anything
open(FH, $file)            or die "can't magic open $file: $!";
```

```
# Guaranteed to be a read-only file open and not a pipe
# or fork, but still groks file descriptors and "-",
# and ignores whitespace at either end of name.
open(FH, "< $file")          or die "can't open $file: $!";

# WYSIWYG open: disables all convenience features.
open(FH, "<", $file)         or die "can't open $file: $!";

# Same properties as WYSIWYG 3-arg version.
require Fcntl;
sysopen(FH, $file, O_RDONLY)     or die "can't sysopen $file: $!";
```

Even these steps aren't quite good enough. Perl doesn't prevent you from opening tainted filenames for reading, so you need to be careful of what you show people. A program that opens an arbitrary, user-supplied filename for reading and then reveals that file's contents is still a security problem. What if it's a private letter? What if it's your system password file? What if it's salary information or your stock portfolio?

Look closely at filenames provided by a potentially hostile user* before opening them. For example, you might want to verify that there are no sneaky directory components in the path. Names like "../../../../../../../etc/passwd" are notorious tricks of this sort. You can protect yourself by making sure there are no slashes in the pathname (assuming that's your system's directory separator). Another common trick is to put newlines or semicolons into filenames that will later be interpreted by some poor, witless command-line interpreter that can be fooled into starting a new command in the middle of the filename. This is why taint mode discourages uninspected external commands.

Accessing Commands and Files Under Reduced Privileges

The following discussion pertains to some nifty security facilities of Unix-like systems. Users of other systems may safely (or rather, unsafely) skip this section.

If you're running set-id, try to arrange that, whenever possible, you do dangerous operations with the privileges of the user, not the privileges of the program. That is, whenever you're going to call open, sysopen, system, backticks, and any other file or process operations, you can protect yourself by setting your effective UID or GID back to the real UID or GID. In Perl, you can do this for setuid scripts by saying $> = $< (or $EUID = $UID if you use English) and for setgid scripts by saying $) = $(($EGID = $GID). If both IDs are set, you should reset both. However,

---

* And on the Net, the only users you can trust not to be potentially hostile are the ones who are being *actively* hostile instead.

sometimes this isn't feasible, because you might still need those increased privileges later in your program.

For those cases, Perl provides a reasonably safe way to open a file or pipe from within a set-id program. First, fork a child using the special open syntax that connects the parent and child by a pipe. In the child, reset the user and group IDs back to their original or known safe values. You also get to modify any of the child's per-process attributes without affecting the parent, letting you change the working directory, set the file creation mask, or fiddle with environment variables. No longer executing under extra privileges, the child process at last calls open and passes whatever data it manages to access on behalf of the mundane but demented user back up to its powerful but justly paranoid parent.

Even though system and exec don't use the shell when you supply them with more than one argument, the backtick operator admits no such alternative calling convention. Using the forking technique, we easily emulate backticks without fear of shell escapes, and with reduced (and therefore safer) privileges:

```perl
use English;    # to use $UID, etc
die "Can't fork open: $!"   unless defined($pid = open(FROMKID, "-|"));
if ($pid) {             # parent
    while (<FROMKID>) {
        # do something
    }
    close FROMKID;
}
else {
    $EUID = $UID;   # setuid(getuid())
    $EGID = $GID;   # setgid(getgid()), and initgroups(2) on getgroups(2)
    chdir("/")      or die "can't chdir to /: $!";
    umask(077);
    $ENV{PATH} = "/bin:/usr/bin";
    exec 'myprog', 'arg1', 'arg2';
    die "can't exec myprog: $!";
}
```

This is by far the best way to call other programs from a set-id script. You make sure never to use the shell to execute anything, and you drop your privileges before you yourself exec the program. (But because the list forms of system, exec, and pipe open are specifically exempted from taint checks on their arguments, you must still be careful of what you pass in.)

If you don't need to drop privileges, and just want to implement backticks or a pipe open without risking the shell intercepting your arguments, you could use this:

```perl
open(FROMKID, "-|") or exec("myprog", "arg1", "arg2")
    or die "can't run myprog: $!";
```

and then just read from FROMKID in the parent. As of the 5.6.1 release of Perl, you can write that as:

```
open(FROMKID, "-|", "myprog", "arg1", "arg2");
```

The forking technique is useful for more than just running commands from a set-id program. It's also good for opening files under the ID of whoever ran the program. Suppose you had a setuid program that needed to open a file for writing. You don't want to run the open under your extra privileges, but you can't permanently drop them, either. So arrange for a forked copy that's dropped its privileges to do the open for you. When you want to write to the file, write to the child, and it will then write to the file for you.

```perl
use English;

defined ($pid = open(SAFE_WRITER, "|-"))
    or die "Can't fork: $!";

if ($pid) {
    # you're the parent. write data to SAFE_WRITER child
    print SAFE_WRITER "@output_data\n";
    close SAFE_WRITER
        or die $! ? "Syserr closing SAFE_WRITER writer: $!"
                  : "Wait status $? from SAFE_WRITER writer";
}
else {
    # you're the child, so drop extra privileges
    ($EUID, $EGID) = ($UID, $GID);

    # open the file under original user's rights
    open(FH, "> /some/file/path")
        or die "can't open /some/file/path for writing: $!";

    # copy from parent (now stdin) into the file
    while (<STDIN>) {
        print FH $_;
    }
    close(FH)   or die "close failed: $!";
    exit;       # Don't forget to make the SAFE_WRITER disappear.
}
```

Upon failing to open the file, the child prints an error message and exits. When the parent writes to the now-defunct child's filehandle, it triggers a broken pipe signal (SIGPIPE), which is fatal unless trapped or ignored. See the section "Signals" in Chapter 16, *Interprocess Communication*.

Handling Timing Glitches

Sometimes your program's behavior is exquisitely sensitive to the timing of external events beyond your control. This is always a concern when other programs, particularly inimical ones, might be vying with your program for the same resources (such as files or devices). In a multitasking environment, you cannot predict the order in which processes waiting to run will be granted access to the processor. Instruction streams among all eligible processes are interleaved, so first one process gets some CPU, and then another process, and so on. Whose turn it is to run, and how long they're allowed to run, appears to be random. With just one program that's not a problem, but with several programs sharing common resources, it can be.

Thread programmers are especially sensitive to these issues. They quickly learn not to say:

```
$var++ if $var == 0;
```

when they should say:

```
{
    lock($var);
    $var++ if $var == 0;
}
```

The former produces unpredictable results when multiple execution threads attempt to run this code at the same time. (See Chapter 17, *Threads*.) If you think of files as shared objects, and processes as threads contending for access to those shared objects, you can see how the same issues arise. A process, after all, is really just a thread with an attitude. Or vice versa.

Timing unpredictabilities affect both privileged and nonprivileged situations. We'll first describe how to cope with a long-standing bug in old Unix kernels that affects any set-id program. Then we'll move on to discuss race conditions in general, how they can turn into security holes, and steps you can take to avoid falling into these holes.

Unix Kernel Security Bugs

Beyond the obvious problems that stem from giving special privileges to interpreters as flexible and inscrutable as shells, older versions of Unix have a kernel bug that makes any set-id script insecure before it ever gets to the interpreter. The problem is not the script itself, but a race condition in what the kernel does when it finds a set-id executable script. (The bug doesn't exist on machines that don't recognize #! in the kernel.) When a kernel opens such a file to see which interpreter to run, there's a delay before the (now set-id) interpreter starts up and reopens the file. That delay gives malicious entities a chance to change the file, especially if your system supports symbolic links.

Fortunately, sometimes this kernel "feature" can be disabled. Unfortunately, there are a couple of different ways to disable it. The system can outlaw scripts with the set-id bits set, which doesn't help much. Alternatively, it can ignore the set-id bits on scripts. In the latter case, Perl can emulate the setuid and setgid mechanism when it notices the (otherwise useless) set-id bits on Perl scripts. It does this via a special executable called *suidperl*, which is automatically invoked for you if it's needed.*

However, if the kernel set-id script feature *isn't* disabled, Perl will complain loudly that your setuid script is insecure. You'll either need to disable the kernel set-id script "feature", or else put a C wrapper around the script. A C wrapper is just a compiled program that does nothing except call your Perl program. Compiled programs are not subject to the kernel bug that plagues set-id scripts.

Here's a simple wrapper, written in C:

```
#define REAL_FILE "/path/to/script"
main(ac, av)
    char **av;
{
    execv(REAL_FILE, av);
}
```

Compile this wrapper into an executable image and then make *it* rather than your script set-id. Be sure to use an absolute filename, since C isn't smart enough to do taint checking on your PATH.

(Another possible approach is to use the experimental C code generator for the Perl compiler. A compiled image of your script will not have the race condition. See Chapter 18, *Compiling*.)

Vendors in recent years have finally started to provide systems free of the set-id bug. On such systems, when the kernel gives the name of the set-id script to the interpreter, it no longer uses a filename subject to meddling, but instead passes a special file representing the file descriptor, like */dev/fd/3*. This special file is already opened on the script so that there can be no race condition for evil scripts

---

* Needed *and* permitted—if Perl detects that the filesystem on which the script resides was mounted with the nosuid option, that option will still be honored. You can't use Perl to sneak around your sysadmin's security policy this way.

to exploit.* Most modern versions of Unix use this approach to avoid the race condition inherent in opening the same filename twice.

Handling Race Conditions

Which runs us right into the topic of race conditions. What are they really? Race conditions turn up frequently in security discussions. (Although less often than they turn up in insecure programs. Unfortunately.) That's because they're a fertile source of subtle programming errors, and such errors can often be turned into security *exploits* (the polite term for screwing up someone's security). A race condition exists when the result of several interrelated events depends on the ordering of those events, but that order cannot be guaranteed due to nondeterministic timing effects. Each event races to be the first one done, and the final state of the system is anybody's guess.

Imagine you have one process overwriting an existing file, and another process reading that same file. You can't predict whether you read in old data, new data, or a haphazard mixture of the two. You can't even know whether you've read all the data. The reader could have won the race to the end of the file and quit. Meanwhile, if the writer kept going after the reader hit end-of-file, the file would grow past where the reader stopped reading, and the reader would never know it.

Here the solution is simple: just have both parties `flock` the file. The reader typically requests a shared lock, and the writer typically requests an exclusive one. So long as all parties request and respect these advisory locks, reads and writes cannot be interleaved, and there's no chance of mutilated data. See the section "File Locking" in Chapter 16.

You risk a far less obvious form of race condition every time you let operations on a filename govern subsequent operations on that file. When used on filenames rather than filehandles, the file test operators represent something of a garden path leading straight into a race condition. Consider this code:

```
if (-e $file) {
    open(FH, "< $file")
        or die "can't open $file for reading: $!";
}
else {
    open(FH, "> $file")
        or die "can't open $file for writing: $!";
}
```

---

* On these systems, Perl should be compiled with **-DSETUID_SCRIPTS_ARE_SECURE_NOW**. The *Configure* program that builds Perl tries to figure this out for itself, so you should never have to specify this explicitly.

The code looks just about as straightforward as it gets, but it's still subject to races. There's no guarantee that the answer returned by the -e test will still be valid by the time either open is called. In the if block, another process could have removed the file before it could be opened, and you wouldn't find the file you thought was going to be there. In the else block, another process could have created the file before the second open could get its turn to create the file, so the file that you thought would not be there, would be. The simple open function creates new files but overwrites existing ones. You may think you want to overwrite any existing file, but consider that the existing file might be a newly created alias or symbolic link to a file elsewhere on the system that you very much don't want to overwrite. You may think you know what a filename means at any particular instant, but you can never really be sure, as long as any other processes with access to the file's directory are running on the same system.

To fix this problem of overwriting, you'll need to use sysopen, which provides individual controls over whether to create a new file or to clobber an existing one. And we'll ditch that -e file existence test since it serves no useful purpose here and only increases our exposure to race conditions.

```
use Fcntl qw/O_WRONLY O_CREAT O_EXCL/;
open(FH, "<", $file)
    or sysopen(FH, $file, O_WRONLY | O_CREAT | O_EXCL)
    or die "can't create new file $file: $!";
```

Now even if the file somehow springs into existence between when open fails and when sysopen tries to open a new file for writing, no harm is done, because with the flags provided, sysopen will refuse to open a file that already exists.

If someone is trying to trick your program into misbehaving, there's a good chance they'll go about it by having files appear and disappear when you're not expecting. One way to reduce the risk of deception is by promising yourself you'll never operate on a filename more than once. As soon as you have the file opened, forget about the filename (except maybe for error messages), and operate only on the handle representing the file. This is much safer because, even though someone could play with your filenames, they can't play with your filehandles. (Or if they can, it's because you let them—see "Passing Filehandles" in Chapter 16.)

Earlier in this chapter, we showed a handle_looks_safe function which called Perl's stat function on a filehandle (not a filename) to check its ownership and permissions. Using the filehandle is critical to correctness—if we had used the name of the file, there would have been no guarantee that the file whose attributes we were inspecting was the same one we just opened (or were about to open). Some pesky evil doer could have deleted our file and quickly replaced it with a file of nefarious design, sometime between the stat and the open. It wouldn't matter which was called first; there'd still be the opportunity for foul play between the two. You may think that the risk is very small because the window is very short, but there are many cracking scripts out in the world that will be perfectly happy to run your program thousands of times to catch it the one time it wasn't careful enough. A smart cracking script can even lower the priority of your program so it gets interrupted more often than usual, just to speed things up a little. People work hard on these things—that's why they're called *exploits*.

By calling stat on a filehandle that's already open, we only access the filename once and so avoid the race condition. A good strategy for avoiding races between two events is to somehow combine both into one, making the operation atomic.* Since we access the file by name only once, there can't be any race condition between multiple accesses, so it doesn't matter whether the name changes. Even if our cracker deletes the file we opened (yes, that can happen) and puts a different one there to trick us with, we still have a handle to the real, original file.

Temporary Files

Apart from allowing buffer overruns (which Perl scripts are virtually immune to) and trusting untrustworthy input data (which taint mode guards against), creating temporary files improperly is one of the most frequently exploited security holes. Fortunately, temp file attacks usually require crackers to have a valid user account on the system they're trying to crack, which drastically reduces the number of potential bad guys.

Careless or casual programs use temporary files in all kinds of unsafe ways, like placing them in world-writable directories, using predictable filenames, and not making sure the file doesn't already exist. Whenever you find a program with code like this:

```
open(TMP, ">/tmp/foo.$$")
    or die "can't open /tmp/foo.$$: $!";
```

you've just found all three of those errors at once. That program is an accident waiting to happen.

The way the exploit plays out is that the cracker first plants a file with the same name as the one you'll use. Appending the PID isn't enough for uniqueness; sur-

---

* Yes, you may still perform atomic operations in a nuclear-free zone. When Democritus gave the word "atom" to the indivisible bits of matter, he meant literally something that could not be cut: *a-* (not) + *tomos* (cuttable). An atomic operation is an action that can't be interrupted. (Just you try interrupting an atomic bomb sometime.)

prising though it may sound, guessing PIDs really isn't difficult.* Now along comes the program with the careless open call, and instead of creating a new temporary file for its own purposes, it overwrites the cracker's file instead.

So what harm can that do? A lot. The cracker's file isn't really a plain file, you see. It's a symbolic link (or sometimes a hard link), probably pointing to some critical file that crackers couldn't normally write to on their own, such as */etc/passwd*. The program thought it opened a brand new file in */tmp*, but it clobbered an existing file somewhere else instead.

Perl provides two functions that address this issue, if properly used. The first is POSIX::tmpnam, which just returns a filename that you're expected to open for yourself:

```
# Keep trying names until we get one that's brand new.
use POSIX;
do {
    $name = tmpnam();
} until sysopen(TMP, $name, O_RDWR | O_CREAT | O_EXCL, 0600);
# Now do I/O using TMP handle.
```

The second is IO::File::new_tmpfile, which gives you back an already opened handle:

```
# Or else let the module do that for us.
use IO::File;
my $fh = IO::File::new_tmpfile();  # this is POSIX's tmpfile(3)
# Now do I/O using $fh handle.
```

Neither approach is perfect, but of the two, the first is the better approach. The major problem with the second one is that Perl is subject to the foibles of whatever implementation of *tmpfile*(3) happens to be in your system's C library, and you have no guarantee that this function doesn't do something just as dangerous as the open we're trying to fix. (And some, sadly enough, do.) A minor problem is that it doesn't give you the name of the file at all. Although it's better if you can handle a temp file without a name—because that way you'll never provoke a race condition by trying to open it again—often you can't.

The major problem with the first approach is that you have no control over the location of the pathname, as you do with the C library's *mkstemp*(3) function. For one thing, you never want to put the file on an NFS-mounted filesystem. The O_EXCL flag is not guaranteed to work correctly under NFS, so multiple processes that request an exclusive create at nearly the same time might all succeed. For another, because the path returned is probably in a directory others can write to, someone could plant a symbolic link pointing to a nonexistent file, forcing you to

---

* Unless you're on a system like OpenBSD, which randomizes new PID assignments.

create your file in a location they prefer.* If you have any say in it, don't put temp files in a directory that anyone else can write to. If you must, make sure to use the O_EXCL flag to sysopen, and try to use directories with the owner-delete-only flag (the sticky bit) set on them.

As of version 5.6.1 of Perl, there is a third way. The standard File::Temp module takes into account all the difficulties we've mentioned. You might use the default options like this:

```
use File::Temp "tempfile";
$handle = tempfile();
```

Or you might specify some of the options like this:

```
use File::Temp "tempfile";
($handle, $filename) = tempfile("plughXXXXXX",
                                DIR => "/var/spool/adventure",
                                SUFFIX = '.dat');
```

The File::Temp module also provides security-conscious emulations of the other functions we've mentioned (though the native interface is better because it gives you an opened filehandle, not just a filename, which is subject to race conditions). See Chapter 32, *Standard Modules*, for a longer description of the options and semantics of this module.

Once you have your filehandle, you can do whatever you want with it. It's open for both reading and writing, so you can write to the handle, seek back to the beginning, and then if you want, overwrite what you'd just put there or read it back again. The thing you really, *really* want to avoid doing is ever opening that filename again, because you can't know for sure that it's really the same file you opened the first time around.†

When you launch another program from within your script, Perl normally closes all filehandles for you to avoid another vulnerability. If you use fcntl to clear your close-on-exec flag (as demonstrated at the end of the entry on open in Chapter 29, *Functions*), other programs you call will inherit this new, open file descriptor. On systems that support the */dev/fd/* directory, you could provide another program with a filename that really means the file descriptor by constructing it this way:

```
$virtname = "/dev/fd/" . fileno(TMP);
```

---

* A solution to this, which works only under some operating systems, is to call sysopen and OR in the O_NOFOLLOW flag. This makes the function fail if the final component of the path is a symbolic link.

† Except afterwards by doing a stat on both filehandles and comparing the first two return values of each (the device/inode pair). But it's too late by then because the damage is already done. All you can do is detect the damage and abort (and maybe sneakily send email to the system administrator).

If you only needed to call a Perl subroutine or program that's expecting a filename as an argument, and you knew that subroutine or program used regular open for it, you could pass the handle using Perl's notation for indicating a filehandle:

```
$virtname = "=&" . fileno(TMP);
```

When that file "name" is passed with a regular Perl open of one or two arguments (not three, which would dispel this useful magic), you gain access to the duplicated descriptor. In some ways, this is more portable than passing a file from */dev/fd/*, because it works everywhere that Perl works; not all systems have a */dev/fd/* directory. On the other hand, the special Perl open syntax for accessing file descriptors by number works only with Perl programs, not with programs written in other languages.

Handling Insecure Code

Taint checking is just the sort of security blanket you need if you want to catch bogus data you ought to have caught yourself, but didn't think to catch before passing off to the system. It's a bit like the optional warnings Perl can give you—they may not indicate a real problem, but on average the pain of dealing with the false positives is less than the pain of not dealing with the false negatives. With tainting, the latter pain is even more insistent, because using bogus data doesn't just give the wrong answers; it can blow your system right out of the water, along with your last two years of work. (And maybe your next two, if you didn't make good backups.) Taint mode is useful when you trust yourself to write honest code but don't necessarily trust whoever is feeding you data not to try to trick you into doing something regrettable.

Data is one thing. It's quite another matter when you don't even trust the code you're running. What if you fetch an applet off the Net and it contains a virus, or a time bomb, or a Trojan horse? Taint checking is useless here because the data you're feeding the program may be fine—it's the code that's untrustworthy. You're placing yourself in the position of someone who receives a mysterious device from a stranger, with a note that says, "Just hold this to your head and pull the trigger." Maybe you think it will dry your hair, but you might not think so for very long.

In this realm, prudence is synonymous with paranoia. What you want is a system that lets you impose a quarantine on suspicious code. The code can continue to exist, and even perform certain functions, but you don't let it wander around doing just anything it feels like. In Perl, you can impose a kind of quarantine using the Safe module.

Safe Compartments

The `Safe` module lets you set up a *sandbox*, a special compartment in which all system operations are trapped, and namespace access is carefully controlled. The low-level, technical details of this module are in a state of flux, so here we'll take a more philosophical approach.

Restricting namespace access

At the most basic level, a `Safe` object is like a safe, except the idea is to keep the bad people in, not out. In the Unix world, there is a syscall known as *chroot*(2) that can permanently consign a process to running only in a subdirectory of the directory structure—in its own private little hell, if you will. Once the process is put there, there is no way for it to reach files outside, because there's no way for it to *name* files outside.* A `Safe` object is a little like that, except that instead of being restricted to a subset of the filesystem's directory structure, it's restricted to a subset of Perl's package structure, which is hierarchical just as the filesystem is.

Another way to look at it is that the `Safe` object is like one of those observation rooms with one-way mirrors that the police put suspicious characters into. People on the outside can look into the room, but those inside can't see out.

When you create a `Safe` object, you may give it a package name if you want. If you don't, a new one will be chosen for you:

```
use Safe;
my $sandbox = Safe->new("Dungeon");
$Dungeon::foo = 1;   # Direct access is discouraged, though.
```

If you fully qualify variables and functions using the package name supplied to the new method, you can access them in that package from the outside, at least in the current implementation. This may change however, since the current plan is to clone the symbol table into a new interpreter. Slightly more upward compatible might be to set things up first before creating the `Safe`, as shown below. This is likely to continue working and is a handy way to set up a `Safe` that has to start off with a lot of "state". (Admittedly, $Dungeon::foo isn't a lot of state.)

```
use Safe;
$Dungeon::foo = 1;   # Still direct access, still discouraged.
my $sandbox = Safe->new("Dungeon");
```

---

* Some sites do this for executing all CGI scripts, using loopback, read-only mounts. It's something of a pain to set up, but if someone ever escapes, they'll find there's nowhere to go.

But Safe also provides a way to access the compartment's globals even if you don't know the name of the compartment's package. So for maximal upward compatibility (though less than maximal speed), we suggest you use the reval method:

```
use Safe;
my $sandbox = Safe->new();
$sandbox->reval('$foo = 1');
```

(In fact, that's the same method you'll use to run suspicious code.) When you pass code into the compartment to compile and run, that code thinks that it's really living in the main package. What the outside world calls $Dungeon::foo, the code inside thinks of as $main::foo, or $::foo, or just $foo if you aren't running under use strict. It won't work to say $Dungeon::foo inside the compartment, because that would really access $Dungeon::Dungeon::foo. By giving the Safe object its own notion of main, variables and subroutines in the rest of your program are protected.

To compile and run code inside the compartment, use the reval ("restricted eval") method, passing the code string as its argument. Just as with any other eval *STRING* construct, compilation errors and run-time exceptions in reval don't kill your program. They just abort the reval and leave the exception in $@, so make sure to check it after every reval call.

Using the initializations given earlier, this code will print out that "foo is now 2":

```
$sandbox->reval('$foo++; print "foo is now $main::foo\n"');
if ($@) {
    die "Couldn't compile code in box: $@";
}
```

If you just want to compile code and not run it, wrap your string in a subroutine declaration:

```
$sandbox->reval(q{
    our $foo;
    sub say_foo {
        print "foo is now $main::foo\n";
    }
}, 1);
die if $@;        # check compilation
```

This time we passed reval a second argument which, since it's true, tells reval to compile the code under the strict pragma. From within the code string, you can't disable strictness, either, because importing and unimporting are just two of the things you can't normally do in a Safe compartment. There are a lot of things you can't do normally in a Safe compartment—see the next section.

Once you've created the `say_foo` function in the compartment, these are pretty much the same:

```
$sandbox->reval('say_foo()');        # Best way.
die if $@;

$sandbox->varglob('say_foo')->();    # Call through anonymous glob.

Dungeon::say_foo();                  # Direct call, strongly discouraged.
```

Restricting operator access

The other important thing about a `Safe` object is that Perl limits the available operations within the sandbox. (You might well let your kid take a bucket and shovel into the sandbox, but you'd probably draw the line at a bazooka.) It's not enough to protect just the rest of your program; you need to protect the rest of your computer, too.

When you compile Perl code in a `Safe` object, either with `reval` or `rdo` (the restricted version of the `do FILE` operator), the compiler consults a special, per-compartment access-control list to decide whether each individual operation is deemed safe to compile. This way you don't have to stress out (much) worrying about unforeseen shell escapes, opening files when you didn't mean to, strange code assertions in regular expressions, or most of the external access problems folks normally fret about. (Or ought to.)

The interface for specifying which operators should be permitted or restricted is currently under redesign, so we only show how to use the default set of them here. For details, consult the online documentation for the `Safe` module.

The `Safe` module doesn't offer complete protection against *denial-of-service attacks*, especially when used in its more permissive modes. Denial-of-service attacks consume all available system resources of some type, denying other processes access to essential system facilities. Examples of such attacks include filling up the kernel process table, dominating the CPU by running forever in a tight loop, exhausting available memory, and filling up a filesystem. These problems are very difficult to solve, especially portably. See the end of the section "Code Masquerading as Data" for more discussion of denial-of-service attacks.

Safe examples

Imagine you've got a CGI program that manages a form into which the user may enter an arbitrary Perl expression and get back the evaluated result.* Like all external input, the string comes in tainted, so Perl won't let you `eval` it yet—you'll first

---

* Please don't laugh. We really have seen web pages that do this. Without a `Safe`!

have to untaint it with a pattern match. The problem is that you'll never be able to devise a pattern that can detect all possible threats. And you don't dare just untaint whatever you get and send it through the built-in `eval`. (If you do that, *we* will be tempted to break into your system and delete the script.)

That's where `reval` comes in. Here's a CGI script that processes a form with a single form field, evaluates (in scalar context) whatever string it finds there, and prints out the formatted result:

```
#!/usr/bin/perl -lTw
use strict;
use CGI::Carp 'fatalsToBrowser';
use CGI qw/:standard escapeHTML/;
use Safe;

print header(-type => "text/html;charset=UTF-8"),
      start_html("Perl Expression Results");
my $expr = param("EXPR") =~ /^([^;]+)/
              ? $1 # return the now-taintless portion
              : croak("no valid EXPR field in form");
my $answer = Safe->new->reval($expr);
die if $@;

print p("Result of", tt(escapeHTML($expr)),
             "is", tt(escapeHTML($answer)));
```

Imagine some evil user feeding you "`print `cat /etc/passwd`" (or worse) as the input string. Thanks to the restricted environment that disallows backticks, Perl catches the problem during compilation and returns immediately. The string in `$@` is "quoted execution (``, qx) trapped by operation mask", plus the customary trailing information identifying where the problem happened.

Because we didn't say otherwise, the compartments we've been creating all used the default set of allowable operations. How you go about declaring specific operations permitted or forbidden isn't important here. What is important is that this is completely under the control of your program. And since you can create multiple `Safe` objects in your program, you can confer various degrees of trust upon various chunks of code, depending on where you got them from.

If you'd like to play around with `Safe`, here's a little interactive Perl calculator. It's a calculator in that you can feed it numeric expressions and immediately see their results. But it's not limited to numbers alone. It's more like the looping example under `eval` in Chapter 29, where you can take whatever they give you, evaluate it, and give them back the result. The difference is that the `Safe` version doesn't execute just anything you feel like. You can run this calculator interactively at your terminal, typing in little bits of Perl code and checking the answers, to get a feel for what sorts of protection `Safe` provides.

```
#!/usr/bin/perl -w
# safecalc - demo program for playing with Safe
use strict;
use Safe;
my $sandbox = Safe->new();
while (1) {
    print "Input: ";
    my $expr = <STDIN>;
    exit unless defined $expr;
    chomp($expr);
    print "$expr produces ";
    local $SIG{__WARN__} = sub { die @_ };
    my $result = $sandbox->reval($expr, 1);
    if ($@ =~ s/at \(eval \d+\).*//) {
        printf "[%s]: %s", $@ =~ /trapped by operation mask/
            ? "Security Violation" : "Exception", $@;
    }
    else {
        print "[Normal Result] $result\n";
    }
}
```

Warning: the Safe module is currently being redesigned to run each compartment within a completely independent Perl interpreter inside the same process. (This is the strategy that Apache's mod_perl employs when running precompiled Perl scripts.) Details are still hazy at this time, but our crystal ball suggests that blindly poking at things inside the compartment using a named package won't get you very far after the impending rewrite. If you're running a version of Perl later than 5.6, check the release notes in *perldelta*(1) to see what's changed, or consult the documentation for the Safe module itself. (Of course, you always do that anyway, right?)

Code Masquerading as Data

Safe compartments are available for when the really scary stuff is going down, but that doesn't mean you should let down your guard totally when you're doing the everyday stuff around home. You need to cultivate an awareness of your surroundings and look at things from the point of view of someone wanting to break in. You need to take proactive steps like keeping things well lit and trimming the bushes that can hide various lurking problems.

Perl tries to help you in this area, too. Perl's conventional parsing and execution scheme avoids the pitfalls that shell programming languages often fall prey to. There are many extremely powerful features in the language, but by design, they're syntactically and semantically bounded in ways that keep things under the control of the programmer. With few exceptions, Perl evaluates each token only once. Something that looks like it's being used as a simple data variable won't suddenly go rooting around in your filesystem.

Unfortunately, that sort of thing can happen if you call out to the shell to run other programs for you, because then you're running under the shell's rules instead of Perl's. The shell is easy to avoid, though—just use the list argument forms of the system, exec, or piped open functions. Although backticks don't have a list-argument form that is proof against the shell, you can always emulate them as described in the section "Accessing Commands and Files Under Reduced Privileges". (While there's no syntactic way to make backticks take an argument list, a multi-argument form of the underlying readpipe operator is in development; but as of this writing, it isn't quite ready for prime time.)

When you use a variable in an expression (including when you interpolate it into a double-quoted string), there's No Chance that the variable will contain Perl code that does something you aren't intending.* Unlike the shell, Perl never needs defensive quotes around variables, no matter what might be in them.

```
$new = $old;                # No quoting needed.
print "$new items\n";       # $new can't hurt you.

$phrase = "$new items\n";   # Nor here, neither.
print $phrase;              # Still perfectly ok.
```

Perl takes a "what you see is what you get" approach. If you don't see an extra level of interpolation, then it doesn't happen. It *is* possible to interpolate arbitrary Perl expressions into strings, but only if you specifically ask Perl to do that. (Even so, the contents are still subject to taint checking if you're in taint mode.)

```
$phrase = "You lost @{[ 1 + int rand(6) ]} hit points\n";
```

Interpolation is not recursive, however. You can't just hide an arbitrary expression in a string:

```
$count = '1 + int rand(6)';        # Some random code.
$saying = "$count hit points";     # Merely a literal.
$saying = "@{[$count]} hit points"; # Also a literal.
```

Both assignments to $saying would produce "1 + int rand(6) hit points", without evaluating the interpolated contents of $count as code. To get Perl to do that, you have to call eval *STRING* explicitly:

```
$code = '1 + int rand(6)';
$die_roll = eval $code;
die if $@;
```

If $code were tainted, that eval *STRING* would raise its own exception. Of course, you almost never want to evaluate random user code—but if you did, you should look into using the Safe module. You may have heard of it.

---

* Although if you're generating a web page, it's possible to emit HTML tags, including JavaScript code, that might do something that the remote browser isn't expecting.

There is one place where Perl can sometimes treat data as code; namely, when the pattern in a qr//, m//, or s/// operator contains either of the new regular expression assertions, (?{ *CODE* }) or (??{ *CODE* }). These pose no security issues when used as literals in pattern matches:

```
$cnt = $n = 0;
while ($data =~ /( \d+ (?{ $n++ }) | \w+ )/gx) {
    $cnt++;
}
print "Got $cnt words, $n of which were digits.\n";
```

But existing code that interpolates variables into matches was written with the assumption that the data is data, not code. The new constructs might have introduced a security hole into previously secure programs. Therefore, Perl refuses to evaluate a pattern if an interpolated string contains a code assertion, and raises an exception instead. If you really need that functionality, you can always enable it with the lexically scoped use re 'eval' pragma. (You still can't use tainted data for an interpolated code assertion, though.)

A completely different sort of security concern that can come up with regular expressions is denial-of-service problems. These can make your program quit too early, or run too long, or exhaust all available memory—and sometimes even dump core, depending on the phase of the moon.

When you process user-supplied patterns, you don't have to worry about interpreting random Perl code. However, the regular expression engine has its own little compiler and interpreter, and the user-supplied pattern is capable of giving the regular expression compiler heartburn. If an interpolated pattern is not a valid pattern, a run-time exception is raised, which is fatal unless trapped. If you do try to trap it, make sure to use only eval *BLOCK*, not eval *STRING*, because the extra evaluation level of the latter would in fact allow the execution of random Perl code. Instead, do something like this:

```
if (not eval { "" =~ /$match/; 1 }) {
    # (Now do whatever you want for a bad pattern.)
}
else {
    # We know pattern is at least safe to compile.
    if ($data =~ /$match/) { ... }
}
```

A more troubling denial-of-service problem is that given the right data and the right search pattern, your program can appear to hang forever. That's because some pattern matches require exponential time to compute, and this can easily exceed the MTBF rating on our solar system. If you're especially lucky, these computationally intensive patterns will also require exponential storage. If so, your program will exhaust all available virtual memory, bog down the rest of the system, annoy your users, and either die with an orderly "Out of memory!" error or else leave behind a really big core dump file, though perhaps not as large as the solar system.

Like most denial-of-service attacks, this one is not easy to solve. If your platform supports the alarm function, you could time out the pattern match. Unfortunately, Perl cannot (currently) guarantee that the mere act of handling a signal won't ever trigger a core dump. (This is scheduled to be fixed in a future release.) You can always try it, though, and even if it the signal isn't handled gracefully, at least the program won't run forever.

If your system supports per-process resource limits, you could set these in your shell before calling the Perl program, or use the BSD::Resource module from CPAN to do so directly from Perl. The Apache web server allows you to set time, memory, and file size limits on CGI scripts that it launches.

Finally, we hope we've left you with some unresolved feelings of insecurity. Remember, just because you're paranoid doesn't mean they're not out to get you. So you might as well enjoy it.

24

Common Practices

Ask almost any Perl programmer, and they'll be glad to give you reams of advice on how to program. We're no different (in case you hadn't noticed). In this chapter, rather than trying to tell you about specific features of Perl, we'll go at it from the other direction and use a more scattergun approach to describe idiomatic Perl. Our hope is that, by putting together various bits of things that seemingly aren't related, you can soak up some of the feeling of what it's like to actually "think Perl". After all, when you're programming, you don't write a bunch of expressions, then a bunch of subroutines, then a bunch of objects. You have to go at everything all at once, more or less. So this chapter is a bit like that.

There is, however, a rudimentary organization to the chapter, in that we'll start with the negative advice and work our way towards the positive advice. We don't know if that will make you feel any better, but it makes us feel better.

Common Goofs for Novices

The biggest goof of all is forgetting to use warnings, which identifies many errors. The second biggest goof is forgetting to use strict when it's appropriate. These two pragmas can save you hours of head-banging when your program starts getting bigger. (And it will.) Yet another faux pas is to forget to consult the online FAQ. Suppose you want to find out if Perl has a round function. You might try searching the FAQ first:

```
% perlfaq round
```

Apart from those "metagoofs", there are several kinds of programming traps. Some traps almost everyone falls into, and other traps you'll fall into only if you come from a particular culture that does things differently. We've separated these out in the following sections.

Universal Blunders

- Putting a comma after the filehandle in a `print` statement. Although it looks extremely regular and pretty to say:

  ```
  print STDOUT, "goodbye", $adj, "world!\n";    # WRONG
  ```

  this is nonetheless incorrect, because of that first comma. What you want instead is the indirect object syntax:

  ```
  print STDOUT "goodbye", $adj, "world!\n";     # ok
  ```

  The syntax works this way so that you can say:

  ```
  print $filehandle "goodbye", $adj, "world!\n";
  ```

  where `$filehandle` is a scalar holding the name of a filehandle at run time. This is distinct from:

  ```
  print $notafilehandle, "goodbye", $adj, "world!\n";
  ```

  where `$notafilehandle` is simply a string that is part of the list of things to be printed. See "indirect object" in the Glossary.

- Using `==` instead of `eq` and `!=` instead of `ne`. The `==` and `!=` operators are *numeric* tests. The other two are *string* tests. The strings `"123"` and `"123.00"` are equal as numbers, but not equal as strings. Also, any nonnumeric string is numerically equal to zero. Unless you are dealing with numbers, you almost always want the string comparison operators instead.

- Forgetting the trailing semicolon. Every statement in Perl is terminated by a semicolon or the end of a block. Newlines aren't statement terminators as they are in *awk*, Python, or FORTRAN. Remember that Perl is like C.

  A statement containing a here document is particularly prone to losing its semicolon. It ought to look like this:

  ```
  print <<'FINIS';
  A foolish consistency is the hobgoblin of little minds,
  adored by little statesmen and philosophers and divines.
                        --Ralph Waldo Emerson
  FINIS
  ```

- Forgetting that a *BLOCK* requires braces. Naked statements are not *BLOCK*s. If you are creating a control structure such as a `while` or an `if` that requires one or more *BLOCK*s, you *must* use braces around each *BLOCK*. Remember that Perl is *not* like C.

- Not saving $1, $2, and so on, across regular expressions. Remember that every new m/atch/ or s/ubsti/tution/ will set (or clear, or mangle) your $1, $2...variables, as well as $`, $&, $', and friends. One way to save them right away is to evaluate the match within a list context, as in:

    ```
    my ($one, $two) = /(\w+) (\w+)/;
    ```

- Not realizing that a local also changes the variable's value as seen by other subroutines called within the scope of the local. It's easy to forget that local is a run-time statement that does dynamic scoping, because there's no equivalent in languages like C. See the section "Scoped Declarations" in Chapter 4, *Statements and Declarations*. Usually you want a my anyway.

- Losing track of brace pairings. A good text editor will help you find the pairs. Get one. (Or two.)

- Using loop control statements in do {} while. Although the braces in this control structure look suspiciously like part of a loop *BLOCK*, they aren't.

- Using $foo[1] when you mean $foo[0]. Perl arrays begin at zero by default.

- Saying @foo[0] when you mean $foo[0]. The @foo[0] reference is an array *slice*, meaning an array consisting of the single element $foo[0]. Sometimes this doesn't make any difference, as in:

    ```
    print "the answer is @foo[0]\n";
    ```

    but it makes a big difference for things like:

    ```
    @foo[0] = <STDIN>;
    ```

    which will slurp up all the rest of STDIN, assign the *first* line to $foo[1], and discard everything else. This is probably not what you intended. Get into the habit of thinking that $ means a single value, while @ means a list of values, and you'll do okay.

- Forgetting the parentheses of a list operator like my:

    ```
    my $x, $y = (4, 8);      # WRONG
    my ($x, $y) = (4, 8);    # ok
    ```

- Forgetting to select the right filehandle before setting $^, $~, or $|. These variables depend on the currently selected filehandle, as determined by select(FILEHANDLE). The initial filehandle so selected is STDOUT. You should really be using the filehandle methods from the FileHandle module instead. See Chapter 28, *Special Names*.

Frequently Ignored Advice

Practicing Perl Programmers should take note of the following:

- Remember that many operations behave differently in a list context than they do in a scalar one. For instance:

  ```
  ($x) = (4, 5, 6);        # List context; $x is set to 4
  $x  = (4, 5, 6);        # Scalar context; $x is set to 6

  @a  = (4, 5, 6);
  $x  = @a;               # Scalar context; $x is set to 3 (the array length)
  ```

- Avoid barewords if you can, especially all lowercase ones. You can't tell just by looking at it whether a word is a function or a bareword string. By using quotes on strings and parentheses around function call arguments, you won't ever get them confused. In fact, the pragma use strict at the beginning of your program makes barewords a compile-time error—probably a good thing.

- You can't tell just by looking which built-in functions are unary operators (like chop and chdir), which are list operators (like print and unlink), and which are argumentless (like time). You'll want to learn them by reading Chapter 29, *Functions*. As always, use parentheses if you aren't sure—or even if you aren't sure you're sure. Note also that user-defined subroutines are by default list operators, but they can be declared as unary operators with a prototype of ($) or argumentless with a prototype of ().

- People have a hard time remembering that some functions default to $_, or @ARGV, or whatever, while others do not. Take the time to learn which are which, or avoid default arguments.

- <FH> is not the name of a filehandle, but an angle operator that does a line-input operation on the handle. This confusion usually manifests itself when people try to print to the angle operator:

  ```
  print <FH> "hi";     # WRONG, omit angles
  ```

- Remember also that data read by the angle operator is assigned to $_ only when the file read is the sole condition in a while loop:

  ```
  while (<FH>) { }   # Data assigned to $_.
  <FH>;              # Data read and discarded!
  ```

- Don't use = when you need =~; the two constructs are quite different:

  ```
  $x =  /foo/;  # Searches $_ for "foo", puts result in $x
  $x =~ /foo/;  # Searches $x for "foo", discards result
  ```

- Use my for local variables whenever you can get away with it. Using local merely gives a temporary value to a global variable, which leaves you open to unforeseen side effects of dynamic scoping.

- Don't use `local` on a module's exported variables. If you localize an exported variable, its exported value will not change. The local name becomes an alias to a new value but the external name is still an alias for the original.

C Traps

Cerebral C programmers should take note of the following:

- Curlies are required for `if` and `while` blocks.

- You must use `elsif` rather than "else if" or "elif". Syntax like this:

```
if (expression) {
    block;
}
else if (another_expression) {        # WRONG
    another_block;
}
```

is illegal. The `else` part is always a block, and a naked `if` is not a block. You mustn't expect Perl to be exactly the same as C. What you want instead is:

```
if (expression) {
    block;
}
elsif (another_expression) {
    another_block;
}
```

Note also that "elif" is "file" spelled backward. Only Algol-ers would want a keyword that was the same as another word spelled backward.

- The `break` and `continue` keywords from C become in Perl `last` and `next`, respectively. Unlike in C, these do *not* work within a `do {} while` construct.

- There's no switch statement. (But it's easy to build one on the fly; see "Bare Blocks" and "Case Structures" in Chapter 4.)

- Variables begin with $, @, or % in Perl.

- Comments begin with #, not /*.

- You can't take the address of anything, although a similar operator in Perl is the backslash, which creates a reference.

- `ARGV` must be capitalized. `$ARGV[0]` is C's `argv[1]`, and C's `argv[0]` ends up in `$0`.

- Syscalls such as `link`, `unlink`, and `rename` return true for success, not 0.

- The signal handlers in `%SIG` deal with signal names, not numbers.

Shell Traps

Sharp shell programmers should take note of the following:

- Variables are prefixed with $, @, or % on the left side of the assignment as well as the right. A shellish assignment like:

```
camel='dromedary';      # WRONG
```

won't be parsed the way you expect. You need:

```
$camel='dromedary';      # ok
```

- The loop variable of a `foreach` also requires a $. Although *csh* likes:

```
foreach hump (one two)
    stuff_it $hump
end
```

in Perl, this is written as:

```
foreach $hump ("one", "two") {
    stuff_it($hump);
}
```

- The backtick operator does variable interpolation without regard to the presence of single quotes in the command.

- The backtick operator does no translation of the return value. In Perl, you have to trim the newline explicitly, like this:

```
chomp($thishost = `hostname`);
```

- Shells (especially *csh*) do several levels of substitution on each command line. Perl does interpolation only within certain constructs such as double quotes, backticks, angle brackets, and search patterns.

- Shells tend to interpret scripts a little bit at a time. Perl compiles the entire program before executing it (except for `BEGIN` blocks, which execute before the compilation is done).

- Program arguments are available via `@ARGV`, not $1, $2, and so on.

- The environment is not automatically made available as individual scalar variables. Use the standard `Env` module if you want that to happen.

Previous Perl Traps

Penitent Perl 4 (and Prior) Programmers should take note of the following changes between release 4 and release 5 that might affect old scripts:

- @ now always interpolates an array in double-quotish strings. Some programs may now need to use backslashes to protect any @ that shouldn't interpolate.

- Barewords that used to look like strings to Perl will now look like subroutine calls if a subroutine by that name is defined before the compiler sees them. For example:

```
sub SeeYa { die "Hasta la vista, baby!" }
$SIG{'QUIT'} = SeeYa;
```

In prior versions of Perl, that code would set the signal handler. Now, it actually calls the function! You may use the **-w** switch to find such risky usage or use strict to outlaw it.

- Identifiers starting with "_" are no longer forced into package main, except for the bare underscore itself (as in $_, @_, and so on).

- A double colon is now a valid package separator in an identifier. Thus, the statement:

```
print "$a::$b::$c\n";
```

now parses $a:: as the variable reference, where in prior versions only the $a was considered to be the variable reference. Similarly:

```
print "$var::abc::xyz\n";
```

is now interpreted as a single variable $var::abc::xyz, whereas in prior versions, the variable $var would have been followed by the constant text ::abc::xyz.

- s'$pattern'replacement' now performs no interpolation on $pattern. (The $ would be interpreted as an end-of-line assertion.) This behavior occurs only when using single quotes as the substitution delimiter; in other substitutions, $pattern is always interpolated.

- The second and third arguments of splice are now evaluated in scalar context rather than in list context.

- These are now semantic errors because of precedence:

```
shift @list + 20;    # Now parses like shift(@list + 20), illegal!
$n = keys %map + 20; # Now parses like keys(%map + 20), illegal!
```

Because if those were to work, then this couldn't:

```
sleep $dormancy + 20;
```

- The precedence of assignment operators is now the same as the precedence of assignment. Previous versions of Perl mistakenly gave them the precedence of the associated operator. So you now must parenthesize them in expressions like:

```
/foo/ ? ($a += 2) : ($a -= 2);
```

  Otherwise:

```
/foo/ ? $a += 2 : $a -= 2;
```

  would be erroneously parsed as:

```
(/foo/ ? $a += 2 : $a) -= 2;
```

  On the other hand:

```
$a += /foo/ ? 1 : 2;
```

  now works as a C programmer would expect.

- `open FOO || die` is incorrect. You need parentheses around the filehandle, because `open` has the precedence of a list operator.

- The elements of argument lists for formats are now evaluated in list context. This means you can interpolate list values now.

- You can't do a `goto` into a block that is optimized away. Darn.

- It is no longer legal to use whitespace as the name of a variable or as a delimiter for any kind of quote construct. Double darn.

- The `caller` function now returns a false value in scalar context if there is no caller. This lets modules determine whether they're being required or run directly.

- `m//g` now attaches its state to the searched string rather than the regular expression. See Chapter 5, *Pattern Matching*, for further details.

- `reverse` is no longer allowed as the name of a `sort` subroutine.

- *taintperl* is no longer a separate executable. There is now a **-T** switch to turn on tainting when it isn't turned on automatically.

- Double-quoted strings may no longer end with an unescaped $ or @.

- The archaic `if` *BLOCK* *BLOCK* syntax is no longer supported.

- Negative array subscripts now count from the end of the array.

- The comma operator in a scalar context is now guaranteed to give a scalar context to its arguments.

- The ** operator now binds more tightly than unary minus.

- Setting $#array lower now discards array elements immediately.

- delete is not guaranteed to return the deleted value for tied arrays, since this capability may be onerous for some modules to implement.

- The construct "this is $$x", which used to interpolate the process ID at that point, now tries to dereference $x. $$ by itself still works fine, however.

- The behavior of foreach when it iterates over a list that is not an array has changed slightly. It used to assign the list to a temporary array but now, for efficiency, no longer does so. This means that you'll now be iterating over the actual values, not copies of the values. Modifications to the loop variable can change the original values, even after the grep! For instance:

```
% perl4 -e '@a = (1,2,3); for (grep(/./, @a)) { $_++ }; print "@a\n"'
1 2 3
% perl5 -e '@a = (1,2,3); for (grep(/./, @a)) { $_++ }; print "@a\n"'
2 3 4
```

To retain prior Perl semantics, you'd need to explicitly assign your list to a temporary array and then iterate over that. For example, you might need to change:

```
foreach $var (grep /x/, @list) { ... }
```

to:

```
foreach $var (my @tmp = grep /x/, @list) { ... }
```

Otherwise changing $var will clobber the values of @list. (This most often happens when you use $_ for the loop variable and call subroutines in the loop that don't properly localize $_.)

- Some error messages and warnings will be different.

- Some bugs may have been inadvertently removed.

Efficiency

While most of the work of programming may be simply getting your program working properly, you may find yourself wanting more bang for the buck out of your Perl program. Perl's rich set of operators, data types, and control constructs are not necessarily intuitive when it comes to speed and space optimization. Many trade-offs were made during Perl's design, and such decisions are buried in the guts of the code. In general, the shorter and simpler your code is, the faster it runs, but there are exceptions. This section attempts to help you make it work just a wee bit better.

If you want it to work a lot better, you can play with the Perl compiler backend described in Chapter 18, *Compiling*, or rewrite your inner loop as a C extension as illustrated in Chapter 21, *Internals and Externals*.

Note that optimizing for time may sometimes cost you in space or programmer efficiency (indicated by conflicting hints below). Them's the breaks. If programming was easy, they wouldn't need something as complicated as a human being to do it, now would they?

Time Efficiency

- Use hashes instead of linear searches. For example, instead of searching through @keywords to see if $_ is a keyword, construct a hash with:

    ```
    my %keywords;
    for (@keywords) {
        $keywords{$_}++;
    }
    ```

    Then you can quickly tell if $_ contains a keyword by testing $keyword{$_} for a nonzero value.

- Avoid subscripting when a foreach or list operator will do. Not only is subscripting an extra operation, but if your subscript variable happens to be in floating point because you did arithmetic, an extra conversion from floating point back to integer is necessary. There's often a better way to do it. Consider using foreach, shift, and splice operations. Consider saying use integer.

- Avoid goto. It scans outward from your current location for the indicated label.

- Avoid printf when print will do.

- Avoid $& and its two buddies, $` and $'. Any occurrence in your program causes all matches to save the searched string for possible future reference. (However, once you've blown it, it doesn't hurt to have more of them.)

- Avoid using eval on a string. An eval of a string (although not of a BLOCK) forces recompilation every time through. The Perl parser is pretty fast for a parser, but that's not saying much. Nowadays there's almost always a better way to do what you want anyway. In particular, any code that uses eval merely to construct variable names is obsolete since you can now do the same directly using symbolic references:

    ```
    no strict 'refs';
    $name = "variable";
    $$name = 7;              # Sets $variable to 7
    ```

- Avoid eval STRING inside a loop. Put the loop into the eval instead, to avoid redundant recompilations of the code. See the study operator in Chapter 29 for an example of this.

- Avoid run-time-compiled patterns. Use the */pattern/o* (once only) pattern modifier to avoid pattern recompilation when the pattern doesn't change over the life of the process. For patterns that change occasionally, you can use the fact that a null pattern refers back to the previous pattern, like this:

```
"foundstring" =~ /$currentpattern/;        # Dummy match (must succeed).
while (<>) {
    print if //;
}
```

  Alternatively, you can precompile your regular expression using the qr quote construct. You can also use eval to recompile a subroutine that does the match (if you only recompile occasionally). That works even better if you compile a bunch of matches into a single subroutine, thus amortizing the subroutine call overhead.

- Short-circuit alternation is often faster than the corresponding regex. So:

```
print if /one-hump/ || /two/;
```

  is likely to be faster than:

```
print if /one-hump|two/;
```

  at least for certain values of one-hump and two. This is because the optimizer likes to hoist certain simple matching operations up into higher parts of the syntax tree and do very fast matching with a Boyer-Moore algorithm. A complicated pattern tends to defeat this.

- Reject common cases early with next if. As with simple regular expressions, the optimizer likes this. And it just makes sense to avoid unnecessary work. You can typically discard comment lines and blank lines even before you do a split or chop:

```
while (<>) {
    next if /^#/;
    next if /^$/;
    chop;
    @piggies = split(/,/);
    ...
}
```

- Avoid regular expressions with many quantifiers or with big {*MIN*,*MAX*} numbers on parenthesized expressions. Such patterns can result in exponentially slow backtracking behavior unless the quantified subpatterns match on their first "pass". You can also use the (?>...) construct to force a subpattern to either match completely or fail without backtracking.

- Try to maximize the length of any nonoptional literal strings in regular expressions. This is counterintuitive, but longer patterns often match faster than shorter patterns. That's because the optimizer looks for constant strings and hands them off to a Boyer-Moore search, which benefits from longer strings. Compile your pattern with Perl's **-Dr** debugging switch to see what Dr. Perl thinks the longest literal string is.

- Avoid expensive subroutine calls in tight loops. There is overhead associated with calling subroutines, especially when you pass lengthy parameter lists or return lengthy values. In order of increasing desperation, try passing values by reference, passing values as dynamically scoped globals, inlining the subroutine, or rewriting the whole loop in C. (Better than all of those solutions is if you can define the subroutine out of existence by using a smarter algorithm.)

- Avoid getc for anything but single-character terminal I/O. In fact, don't use it for that either. Use sysread.

- Avoid frequent substrs on long strings, especially if the string contains UTF-8. It's okay to use substr at the front of a string, and for some tasks you can keep the substr at the front by "chewing up" the string as you go with a four-argument substr, replacing the part you grabbed with "":

```
while ($buffer) {
    process(substr($buffer, 0, 10, ""));
}
```

- Use pack and unpack instead of multiple substr invocations.

- Use substr as an lvalue rather than concatenating substrings. For example, to replace the fourth through seventh characters of $foo with the contents of the variable $bar, don't do this:

```
$foo = substr($foo,0,3) . $bar . substr($foo,7);
```

Instead, simply identify the part of the string to be replaced and assign into it, as in:

```
substr($foo, 3, 4) = $bar;
```

But be aware that if $foo is a huge string and $bar isn't exactly the length of the "hole", this can do a lot of copying too. Perl tries to minimize that by copying from either the front or the back, but there's only so much it can do if the substr is in the middle.

- Use s/// rather than concatenating substrings. This is especially true if you can replace one constant with another of the same size. This results in an in-place substitution.

- Use statement modifiers and equivalent and and or operators instead of full-blown conditionals. Statement modifiers (like $ring = 0 unless $engaged) and logical operators avoid the overhead of entering and leaving a block. They can often be more readable too.

- Use $foo = $a || $b || $c. This is much faster (and shorter to say) than:

```
if ($a) {
    $foo = $a;
}
elsif ($b) {
    $foo = $b;
}
elsif ($c) {
    $foo = $c;
}
```

Similarly, set default values with:

```
$pi ||= 3;
```

- Group together any tests that want the same initial string. When testing a string for various prefixes in anything resembling a switch structure, put together all the /^a/ patterns, all the /^b/ patterns, and so on.

- Don't test things you know won't match. Use last or elsif to avoid falling through to the next case in your switch statement.

- Use special operators like study, logical string operations, pack 'u', and unpack '%' formats.

- Beware of the tail wagging the dog. Misstatements resembling (<STDIN>)[0] can cause Perl much unnecessary work. In accordance with Unix philosophy, Perl gives you enough rope to hang yourself.

- Factor operations out of loops. The Perl optimizer does not attempt to remove invariant code from loops. It expects you to exercise some sense.

- Strings can be faster than arrays.

- Arrays can be faster than strings. It all depends on whether you're going to reuse the strings or arrays and which operations you're going to perform. Heavy modification of each element implies that arrays will be better, and occasional modification of some elements implies that strings will be better. But you just have to try it and see.

- my variables are faster than local variables.

- Sorting on a manufactured key array may be faster than using a fancy sort subroutine. A given array value will usually be compared multiple times, so if the sort subroutine has to do much recalculation, it's better to factor out that calculation to a separate pass before the actual sort.

- If you're deleting characters, tr/abc//d is faster than s/[abc]//g.

- print with a comma separator may be faster than concatenating strings. For example:

```
print $fullname{$name} . " has a new home directory " .
    $home{$name} . "\n";
```

  has to glue together the two hashes and the two fixed strings before passing them to the low-level print routines, whereas:

```
print $fullname{$name}, " has a new home directory ",
    $home{$name}, "\n";
```

  doesn't. On the other hand, depending on the values and the architecture, the concatenation may be faster. Try it.

- Prefer join("", ...) to a series of concatenated strings. Multiple concatenations may cause strings to be copied back and forth multiple times. The join operator avoids this.

- split on a fixed string is generally faster than split on a pattern. That is, use split(/ /, ...) rather than split(/ +/, ...) if you know there will only be one space. However, the patterns /\s+/, /^/, and / / are specially optimized, as is the special split on whitespace.

- Pre-extending an array or string can save some time. As strings and arrays grow, Perl extends them by allocating a new copy with some room for growth and copying in the old value. Pre-extending a string with the x operator or an array by setting $#array can prevent this occasional overhead and reduce memory fragmentation.

- Don't undef long strings and arrays if they'll be reused for the same purpose. This helps prevent reallocation when the string or array must be re-extended.

- Prefer "\0" x 8192 over unpack("x8192",()).

- system("mkdir ...") may be faster on multiple directories if the *mkdir* syscall isn't available.

- Avoid using eof if return values will already indicate it.

- Cache entries from files (like *passwd* and *group* files) that are apt to be reused. It's particularly important to cache entries from the network. For example, to cache the return value from gethostbyaddr when you are converting numeric addresses (like 204.148.40.9) to names (like "www.oreilly.com"), you can use something like:

```
sub numtoname {
    local ($_) = @_;
    unless (defined $numtoname{$_}) {
        my (@a) = gethostbyaddr(pack('C4', split(/\./)),2);
        $numtoname{$_} = @a > 0 ? $a[0] : $_;
    }
    return $numtoname{$_};
}
```

- Avoid unnecessary syscalls. Operating system calls tend to be rather expensive. So for example, don't call the time operator when a cached value of $now would do. Use the special _ filehandle to avoid unnecessary *stat*(2) calls. On some systems, even a minimal syscall may execute a thousand instructions.

- Avoid unnecessary system calls. The system function has to fork a subprocess in order to execute the program you specify—or worse, execute a shell to execute the program. This can easily execute a million instructions.

- Worry about starting subprocesses, but only if they're frequent. Starting a single *pwd*, *hostname*, or *find* process isn't going to hurt you much—after all, a shell starts subprocesses all day long. We do occasionally encourage the toolbox approach, believe it or not.

- Keep track of your working directory yourself rather than calling *pwd* repeatedly. (A standard module is provided for this. See Cwd in Chapter 30, *The Standard Perl Library*.)

- Avoid shell metacharacters in commands—pass lists to system and exec where appropriate.

- Set the sticky bit on the Perl interpreter on machines without demand paging:

```
chmod +t /usr/bin/perl
```

- To cache function results, use the Memoize module on CPAN.

Space Efficiency

- You can use vec for compact integer array storage if the integers are of fixed width. (Integers of variable width can be stored in a UTF-8 string.)

- Prefer numeric values over equivalent string values—they require less memory.

- Use `substr` to store constant-length strings in a longer string.

- Use the `Tie::SubstrHash` module for very compact storage of a hash array, if the key and value lengths are fixed.

- Use `__END__` and the `DATA` filehandle to avoid storing program data as both a string and an array.

- Prefer `each` to `keys` where order doesn't matter.

- Delete or `undef` globals that are no longer in use.

- Use some kind of DBM to store hashes.

- Use temp files to store arrays.

- Use pipes to offload processing to other tools.

- Avoid list operations and entire file slurps.

- Avoid using `tr///`. Each `tr///` expression must store a sizable translation table.

- Don't unroll your loops or inline your subroutines.

Programmer Efficiency

- Use defaults.

- Use funky shortcut command-line switches like **-a**, **-n**, **-p**, **-s**, and **-i**.

- Use `for` to mean `foreach`.

- Run system commands with backticks.

- Use `<*>` and such.

- Use patterns created at run time.

- Use *, +, and {} liberally in your patterns.

- Process whole arrays and slurp entire files.

- Use `getc`.

- Use `$``, `$&`, and `$'`.

- Don't check error values on `open`, since `<HANDLE>` and `print HANDLE` will simply behave as no-ops when given an invalid handle.

- Don't `close` your files—they'll be closed on the next `open`.

- Don't pass subroutine arguments. Use globals.

- Don't name your subroutine parameters. You can access them directly as $_[*EXPR*].

- Use whatever you think of first.

Maintainer Efficiency

- Don't use defaults.

- Use foreach to mean foreach.

- Use meaningful loop labels with next and last.

- Use meaningful variable names.

- Use meaningful subroutine names.

- Put the important thing first on the line using and, or, and statement modifiers (like exit if $done).

- Close your files as soon as you're done with them.

- Use packages, modules, and classes to hide your implementation details.

- Pass arguments as subroutine parameters.

- Name your subroutine parameters using my.

- Parenthesize for clarity.

- Put in lots of (useful) comments.

- Include embedded pod documentation.

- use warnings.

- use strict.

Porter Efficiency

- Wave a handsome tip under his nose.

- Avoid functions that aren't implemented everywhere. You can use eval tests to see what's available.

- Use the Config module or the $^O variable to find out what kind of machine you're running on.

- Don't expect native float and double to pack and unpack on foreign machines.

- Use network byte order (the "n" and "N" formats for pack) when sending binary data over the network.

- Don't send binary data over the network. Send ASCII. Better, send UTF-8. Better yet, send money.

- Check $] or $^V to see if the current version supports all the features you use.

- Don't use $] or $^V. Use `require` or `use` with a version number.

- Put in the `eval exec` hack even if you don't use it, so your program will run on those few systems that have Unix-like shells but don't recognize the #! notation.

- Put the `#!/usr/bin/perl` line in even if you don't use it.

- Test for variants of Unix commands. Some *find* programs can't handle the -*xdev* switch, for example.

- Avoid variant Unix commands if you can do it internally. Unix commands don't work too well on MS-DOS or VMS.

- Put all your scripts and manpages into a single network filesystem that's mounted on all your machines.

- Publish your module on CPAN. You'll get lots of feedback if it's not portable.

User Efficiency

- Instead of making users enter data line by line, pop users into their favorite editor.

- Better yet, use a GUI like the Perl/Tk extension, where users can control the order of events. (Perl/Tk is available on CPAN.)

- Put up something for users to read while you continue doing work.

- Use autoloading so that the program *appears* to run faster.

- Give the option of helpful messages at every prompt.

- Give a helpful usage message if users don't give correct input.

- Display the default action at every prompt, and maybe a few alternatives.

- Choose defaults for beginners. Allow experts to change the defaults.

- Use single character input where it makes sense.

- Pattern the interaction after other things the user is familiar with.

- Make error messages clear about what needs fixing. Include all pertinent information such as filename and error code, like this:

      open(FILE, $file) or die "$0: Can't open $file for reading: $!\n";

- Use `fork && exit` to detach from the terminal when the rest of the script is just batch processing.

- Allow arguments to come from either the command line or standard input.

- Don't put arbitrary limitations into your program.

- Prefer variable-length fields over fixed-length fields.

- Use text-oriented network protocols.

- Tell everyone else to use text-oriented network protocols!

- Tell everyone else to tell everyone else to use text-oriented network protocols!!!

- Be vicariously lazy.

- Be nice.

Programming with Style

You'll certainly have your own preferences in regard to formatting, but there are some general guidelines that will make your programs easier to read, understand, and maintain.

The most important thing is to run your programs under the use warnings pragma. (You can turn off unwanted warnings with no warnings.) You should also always run under use strict or have a good reason not to. The use sigtrap and even the use diagnostics pragmas may also prove of benefit.

Regarding aesthetics of code layout, about the only thing Larry cares strongly about is that the closing brace of a multiline *BLOCK* should be "outdented" to line up with the keyword that started the construct. Beyond that, he has other preferences that aren't so strong. Examples in this book (should) all follow these coding conventions:

- Use four-column indents.

- An opening brace should be put on the same line as its preceding keyword, if possible; otherwise, line them up vertically.

```
while ($condition) {        # for short ones, align with keywords
    # do something
}

# if the condition wraps, line up the braces with each other
while ($this_condition and $that_condition
        and $this_other_long_condition)
{
    # do something
}
```

- Put space before the opening brace of a multiline *BLOCK*.

- A short *BLOCK* may be put on one line, including braces.

- Omit the semicolon in a short, one-line *BLOCK*.

- Surround most operators with space.

- Surround a "complex" subscript (inside brackets) with space.

- Put blank lines between chunks of code that do different things.

- Put a newline between a closing brace and `else`.

- Do not put space between a function name and its opening parenthesis.

- Do not put space before a semicolon.

- Put space after each comma.

- Break long lines after an operator (but before `and` and `or`, even when spelled `&&` and `||`).

- Line up corresponding items vertically.

- Omit redundant punctuation as long as clarity doesn't suffer.

Larry has his reasons for each of these things, but he doesn't claim that everyone else's mind works the same as his does (or doesn't).

Here are some other, more substantive style issues to think about:

- Just because you *can* do something a particular way doesn't mean you *should* do it that way. Perl is designed to give you several ways to do anything, so consider picking the most readable one. For instance:

  ```
  open(FOO,$foo)  or die "Can't open $foo: $!";
  ```

  is better than:

  ```
  die "Can't open $foo: $!"   unless open(FOO,$foo);
  ```

  because the second way hides the main point of the statement in a modifier. On the other hand:

  ```
  print "Starting analysis\n" if $verbose;
  ```

  is better than:

  ```
  $verbose and print "Starting analysis\n";
  ```

  since the main point isn't whether the user typed **-v** or not.

- Similarly, just because an operator lets you assume default arguments doesn't mean that you have to make use of the defaults. The defaults are there for lazy programmers writing one-shot programs. If you want your program to be readable, consider supplying the argument.

- Along the same lines, just because you *can* omit parentheses in many places doesn't mean that you ought to:

```
return print reverse sort num values %array;
return print(reverse(sort num (values(%array))));
```

  When in doubt, parenthesize. At the very least it will let some poor schmuck bounce on the % key in *vi*.

  Even if *you* aren't in doubt, consider the mental welfare of the person who has to maintain the code after you, and who will probably put parentheses in the wrong place.

- Don't go through silly contortions to exit a loop at the top or the bottom. Perl provides the `last` operator so you can exit in the middle. You can optionally "outdent" it to make it more visible:

```
LINE:
    for (;;) {
        statements;
      last LINE if $foo;
        next LINE if /^#/;
        statements;
    }
```

- Don't be afraid to use loop labels—they're there to enhance readability as well as to allow multilevel loop breaks. See the example just given.

- Avoid using `grep`, `map`, or backticks in a void context, that is, when you just throw away their return values. Those functions all have return values, so use them. Otherwise, use a `foreach` loop or the `system` function.

- For portability, when using features that may not be implemented on every machine, test the construct in an `eval` to see whether it fails. If you know the version or patch level of a particular feature, you can test $] (`$PERL_VERSION` in the English module) to see whether the feature is there. The `Config` module will also let you interrogate values determined by the *Configure* program when Perl was installed.

- Choose mnemonic identifiers. If you can't remember what mnemonic means, you've got a problem.

- Although short identifiers like `$gotit` are probably okay, use underscores to separate words. It is generally much easier to read `$var_names_like_this` than `$VarNamesLikeThis`, especially for non-native speakers of English. Besides, the same rule works for `$VAR_NAMES_LIKE_THIS`.

  Package names are sometimes an exception to this rule. Perl informally reserves lowercase module names for pragmatic modules like `integer` and strict. Other modules should begin with a capital letter and use mixed case, but should probably omit underscores due to name-length limitations on certain primitive filesystems.

- You may find it helpful to use letter case to indicate the scope or nature of a variable. For example:

```
$ALL_CAPS_HERE    # constants only (beware clashes with Perl vars!)
$Some_Caps_Here   # package-wide global/static
$no_caps_here     # function scope my() or local() variables
```

For various vague reasons, function and method names seem to work best as all lowercase. For example, $obj->as_string().

You can use a leading underscore to indicate that a variable or function should not be used outside the package that defined it. (Perl does not enforce this; it's just a form of documentation.)

- If you have a really hairy regular expression, use the /x modifier and put in some whitespace to make it look a little less like line noise.

- Don't use slash as a delimiter when your regular expression already has too many slashes or backslashes.

- Don't use quotes as delimiters when your string contains the same kind of quote. Use the q//, qq//, or qx// pseudofunctions instead.

- Use the and and or operators to avoid having to parenthesize list operators so much and to reduce the incidence of punctuational operators like && and ||. Call your subroutines as if they were functions or list operators to avoid excessive ampersands and parentheses.

- Use here documents instead of repeated print statements.

- Line up corresponding things vertically, especially if they're too long to fit on one line anyway:

```
$IDX = $ST_MTIME;
$IDX = $ST_ATIME        if $opt_u;
$IDX = $ST_CTIME        if $opt_c;
$IDX = $ST_SIZE         if $opt_s;

mkdir $tmpdir, 0700 or die "can't mkdir $tmpdir: $!";
chdir($tmpdir)      or die "can't chdir $tmpdir: $!";
mkdir 'tmp',   0777 or die "can't mkdir $tmpdir/tmp: $!";
```

- That which we tell you three times is true:

Always check the return codes of system calls.
Always check the return codes of system calls.
ALWAYS CHECK THE RETURN CODES OF SYSTEM CALLS!

Error messages should go to STDERR and should say which program caused the problem and what the failed call and its arguments were. Most importantly, for failed syscalls, messages should contain the standard system error message for what went wrong. Here's a simple but sufficient example:

```
opendir(D, $dir)  or die "Can't opendir $dir: $!";
```

- Line up your transliterations when it makes sense:

```
tr [abc]
   [xyz];
```

- Think about reusability. Why waste brainpower on a one-shot script when you might want to do something like it again? Consider generalizing your code. Consider writing a module or object class. Consider making your code run cleanly with use strict and **-w** in effect. Consider giving away your code. Consider changing your whole world view. Consider ... oh, never mind.

- Be consistent.

- Be nice.

Fluent Perl

We've touched on a few idioms in the preceding sections (not to mention the preceding chapters), but there are many other idioms you'll commonly see if you read programs by accomplished Perl programmers. When we speak of idiomatic Perl in this context, we don't just mean a set of arbitrary Perl expressions with fossilized meanings. Rather, we mean Perl code that shows an understanding of the flow of the language, what you can get away with when, and what that buys you. And when to buy it.

We can't hope to list all the idioms you might see—that would take a book as big as this one. Maybe two. (See the *Perl Cookbook*, for instance.) But here are some of the important idioms, where "important" might be defined as "that which induces hissy fits in people who think they already know just how computer languages ought to work".

- Use => in place of a comma anywhere you think it improves readability:

```
return bless $mess => $class;
```

This reads, "Bless this mess into the specified class." Just be careful not to use it after a word that you don't want autoquoted:

```
sub foo () { "FOO" }
sub bar () { "BAR" }
print foo => bar;   # prints fooBAR, not FOOBAR;
```

Another good place to use => is near a literal comma that might get confused visually:

```
join(", " => @array);
```

Perl provides you with more than one way to do things so that you can exercise your ability to be creative. Exercise it!

- Use the singular pronoun to increase readability:

```
for (@lines) {
    $_ .= "\n";
}
```

The $_ variable is Perl's version of a pronoun, and it essentially means "it". So the code above means "for each line, append a newline to *it*." Nowadays you might even spell that:

```
$_ .= "\n" for @lines;
```

The $_ pronoun is so important to Perl that its use is mandatory in grep and map. Here is one way to set up a cache of common results of an expensive function:

```
%cache = map { $_ => expensive($_) } @common_args;
$xval = $cache{$x} || expensive($x);
```

- Omit the pronoun to increase readability even further.*
- Use loop controls with statement modifiers.

```
while (<>) {
    next if /^=for\s+(index|later)/;
    $chars += length;
    $words += split;
    $lines += y/\n//;
}
```

This is a fragment of code we used to do page counts for this book. When you're going to be doing a lot of work with the same variable, it's often more readable to leave out the pronouns entirely, contrary to common belief.

The fragment also demonstrates the idiomatic use of next with a statement modifier to short-circuit a loop.

The $_ variable is always the loop control variable in grep and map, but the program's reference to it is often implicit:

```
@haslen = grep { length } @random;
```

---

* In this section, multiple bullet items in a row all refer to the subsequent example, since some of our examples illustrate more than one idiom.

Here we take a list of random scalars and only pick the ones that have a length greater than 0.

- Use for to set the antecedent for a pronoun:

```
for ($episode) {
    s/fred/barney/g;
    s/wilma/betty/g;
    s/pebbles/bambam/g;
}
```

So what if there's only one element in the loop? It's a convenient way to set up "it", that is, $_. Linguistically, this is known as topicalization. It's not cheating, it's communicating.

- Implicitly reference the plural pronoun, @_.

- Use control flow operators to set defaults:

```
sub bark {
    my Dog $spot = shift;
    my $quality  = shift || "yapping";
    my $quantity = shift || "nonstop";
    ...
}
```

Here we're implicitly using the other Perl pronoun, @_, which means "them". The arguments to a function always come in as "them". The shift operator knows to operate on @_ if you omit it, just as the ride operator at Disneyland might call out "Next!" without specifying which queue is supposed to shift. (There's no point in specifying, because there's only one queue that matters.)

The || can be used to set defaults despite its origins as a Boolean operator, since Perl returns the first true value. Perl programmers often manifest a cavalier attitude toward the truth; the line above would break if, for instance, you tried to specify a quantity of 0. But as long as you never want to set either $quality or $quantity to a false value, the idiom works great. There's no point in getting all superstitious and throwing in calls to defined and exists all over the place. You just have to understand what it's doing. As long as it won't accidentally be false, you're fine.

- Use assignment forms of operators, including control flow operators:

```
$xval = $cache{$x} ||= expensive($x);
```

Here we don't initialize our cache at all. We just rely on the ||= operator to call expensive($x) and assign it to $cache{$x} only if $cache{$x} is false. The result of that is whatever the new value of $cache{$x} is. Again, we take the cavalier approach towards truth, in that if we cache a false value, expensive($x) will get called again. Maybe the programmer knows that's okay, because expensive($x) isn't expensive when it returns false. Or maybe the programmer knows that expensive($x) never returns a false value at all. Or maybe the programmer is just being sloppy. Sloppiness can be construed as a form of creativity.

- Use loop controls as operators, not just as statements. And . . .

- Use commas like small semicolons:

```
while (<>) {
    $comments++, next if /^#/;
    $blank++, next    if /^\s*$/;
    last              if /^__END__/;
    $code++;
}
print "comment = $comments\nblank = $blank\ncode = $code\n";
```

This shows an understanding that statement modifiers modify statements, while next is a mere operator. It also shows the comma being idiomatically used to separate expressions much like you'd ordinarily use a semicolon. (The difference being that the comma keeps the two expressions as part of the same statement, under the control of the single statement modifier.)

- Use flow control to your advantage:

```
while (<>) {
    /^#/      and $comments++, next;
    /^\s*$/   and $blank++, next;
    /^__END__/ and last;
    $code++;
}
print "comment = $comments\nblank = $blank\ncode = $code\n";
```

Here's the exact same loop again, only this time with the patterns out in front. The perspicacious Perl programmer understands that it compiles down to exactly the same internal codes as the previous example. The if modifier is just a backward and (or &&) conjunction, and the unless modifier is just a backward or (or ||) conjunction.

- Use the implicit loops provided by the **-n** and **-p** switches.

- Don't put semicolon at the end of a one-line block:

```
#!/usr/bin/perl -n
$comments++, next LINE if /#/;
$blank++, next LINE    if /^\s*$/;
last LINE              if /^__END__/;
$code++;

END { print "comment = $comments\nblank = $blank\ncode = $code\n" }
```

This is essentially the same program as before. We put an explicit LINE label on the loop control operators because we felt like it, but we didn't really need to, since the implicit LINE loop supplied by **-n** is the innermost enclosing loop.

We used an END to get the final print statement outside the implicit main loop, just as in *awk*.

- Use here docs when the printing gets ferocious.

- Use a meaningful delimiter on the here doc:

```
END { print <<"COUNTS" }
comment = $comments
blank = $blank
code = $code
COUNTS
```

Rather than using multiple prints, the fluent Perl programmer uses a multiline string with interpolation. And despite our calling it a Common Goof earlier, we've brazenly left off the trailing semicolon because it's not necessary at the end of the END block. (If we ever turn it into a multiline block, we'll put the semicolon back in.)

- Do substitutions and translations en passant on a scalar:

```
($new = $old) =~ s/bad/good/g;
```

Since lvalues are lvaluable, so to speak, you'll often see people changing a value "in passing" while it's being assigned. This could actually save a string copy internally (if we ever get around to implementing the optimization):

```
chomp($answer = <STDIN>);
```

Any function that modifies an argument in place can do the en passant trick. But wait, there's more!

- Don't limit yourself to changing scalars en passant:

```
for (@new = @old) { s/bad/good/g }
```

Here we copy @old into @new, changing everything in passing (not all at once, of course—the block is executed repeatedly, one "it" at a time).

- Pass named parameters using the fancy => comma operator.

- Rely on assignment to a hash to do even/odd argument processing:

```
sub bark {
    my DOG $spot = shift;
    my %parm = @_;
    my $quality  = $parm{QUALITY}  || "yapping";
    my $quantity = $parm{QUANTITY} || "nonstop";
    ...
}

$fido->bark( QUANTITY => "once",
             QUALITY => "woof" );
```

Named parameters are often an affordable luxury. And with Perl, you get them for free, if you don't count the cost of the hash assignment.

- Repeat Boolean expressions until false.

- Use minimal matching when appropriate.

- Use the /e modifier to evaluate a replacement expression:

```
#!/usr/bin/perl -p
1 while s/^(.*?)(\t+)/$1 . ' ' x (length($2) * 4 - length($1) % 4)/e;
```

This program fixes any file you receive from someone who mistakenly thinks they can redefine hardware tabs to occupy 4 spaces instead of 8. It makes use of several important idioms. First, the 1 while idiom is handy when all the work you want to do in the loop is actually done by the conditional. (Perl is smart enough not to warn you that you're using 1 in a void context.) We have to repeat this substitution because each time we substitute some number of spaces in for tabs, we have to recalculate the column position of the next tab from the beginning.

The (.*?) matches the smallest string it can up until the first tab, using the minimal matching modifier (the question mark). In this case, we could have used an ordinary greedy * like this: ([^\t]*). But that only works because a tab is a single character, so we can use a negated character class to avoid running past the first tab. In general, the minimal matcher is much more elegant, and doesn't break if the next thing that must match happens to be longer than one character.

The /e modifier does a substitution using an expression rather than a mere string. This lets us do the calculations we need right when we need them.

- Use creative formatting and comments on complex substitutions:

```
#!/usr/bin/perl -p
1 while s{
        ^                       # anchor to beginning
        (                       # start first subgroup
            .*?                 # match minimal number of characters
        )                       # end first subgroup
        (                       # start second subgroup
            \t+                 # match one or more tabs
        )                       # end second subgroup
    }
    {
        my $spacelen = length($2) * 4;  # account for full tabs
        $spacelen -= length($1) % 4;    # account for the uneven tab
        $1 . ' ' x $spacelen;           # make correct number of spaces
    }ex;
```

This is probably overkill, but some people find it more impressive than the previous one-liner. Go figure.

- Go ahead and use $` if you feel like it:

```
1 while s/(\t+)/' ' x (length($1) * 4 - length($`) % 4)/e;
```

Here's the shorter version, which uses $`, which is known to impact performance. Except that we're only using the length of it, so it doesn't really count as bad.

- Use the offsets directly from the @- (@LAST_MATCH_START) and @+ (@LAST_MATCH_END) arrays:

```
1 while s/\t+/' ' x (($+[0] - $-[0]) * 4 - $-[0] % 4)/e;
```

This one's even shorter. (If you don't see any arrays there, try looking for array elements instead.) See @- and @+ in Chapter 28.

- Use eval with a constant return value:

```
sub is_valid_pattern {
    my $pat = shift;
    return eval { "" =~ /$pat/; 1 } || 0;
}
```

You don't have to use the eval {} operator to return a real value. Here we always return 1 if it gets to the end. However, if the pattern contained in $pat blows up, the eval catches it and returns undef to the Boolean conditional of the || operator, which turns it into a defined 0 (just to be polite, since undef is also false but might lead someone to believe that the is_valid_pattern subroutine is misbehaving, and we wouldn't want that, now would we?).

- Use modules to do all the dirty work.

- Use object factories.

- Use callbacks.

- Use stacks to keep track of context.

- Use negative subscripts to access the end of an array or string:

```
use XML::Parser;

$p = new XML::Parser Style => 'subs';
setHandlers $p Char => sub { $out[-1] .= $_[1] };

push @out, "";

sub literal {
    $out[-1] .= "C<";
    push @out, "";
}
```

```
sub literal_ {
    my $text = pop @out;
    $out[-1] .= $text . ">";
}
...
```

This is a snippet from the 250-line program we used to translate the XML version of the old Camel book back into pod format so we could edit it for this edition with a Real Text Editor.

The first thing you'll notice is that we rely on the XML::Parser module (from CPAN) to parse our XML correctly, so we don't have to figure out how. That cuts a few thousand lines out of our program right there (presuming we're reimplementing in Perl everything XML::Parser does for us,* including translation from almost any character set into UTF-8).

XML::Parser uses a high-level idiom called an *object factory*. In this case, it's a parser factory. When we create an XML::Parser object, we tell it which style of parser interface we want, and it creates one for us. This is an excellent way to build a testbed application when you're not sure which kind of interface will turn out to be the best in the long run. The subs style is just one of XML::Parser's interfaces. In fact, it's one of the oldest interfaces, and probably not even the most popular one these days.

The setHandlers line shows a method call on the parser, not in arrow notation, but in "indirect object" notation, which lets you omit the parens on the arguments, among other things. The line also uses the named parameter idiom we saw earlier.

The line also shows another powerful concept, the notion of a callback. Instead of us calling the parser to get the next item, we tell it to call us. For named XML tags like <literal>, this interface style will automatically call a subroutine of that name (or the name with an underline on the end for the corresponding end tag). But the data between tags doesn't have a name, so we set up a Char callback with the setHandlers method.

Next we initialize the @out array, which is a stack of outputs. We put a null string into it to represent that we haven't collected any text at the current tag embedding level (0 initially).

Now is when that callback comes back in. Whenever we see text, it automatically gets appended to the final element of the array, via the $out[-1] idiom in the callback. At the outer tag level, $out[-1] is the same as $out[0], so $out[0] ends up with our whole output. (Eventually. But first we have to deal with tags.)

---

* Actually, XML::Parser is just a fancy wrapper around James Clark's *expat* XML parser.

Suppose we see a `<literal>` tag. Then the `literal` subroutine gets called, appends some text to the current output, then pushes a new context onto the @out stack. Now any text up until the closing tag gets appended to that new end of the stack. When we hit the closing tag, we pop the $text we've collected back off the @out stack, and append the rest of the transmogrified data to the new (that is, the old) end of stack, the result of which is to translate the XML string, `<literal>text</literal>`, into the corresponding pod string, C<*text*>.

The subroutines for the other tags are just the same, only different.

- Use `my` without assignment to create an empty array or hash.

- Split the default string on whitespace.

- Assign to lists of variables to collect however many you want.

- Use autovivification of undefined references to create them.

- Autoincrement undefined array and hash elements to create them.

- Use autoincrement of a `%seen` hash to determine uniqueness.

- Assign to a handy `my` temporary in the conditional.

- Use the autoquoting behavior of braces.

- Use an alternate quoting mechanism to interpolate double quotes.

- Use the `?:` operator to switch between two arguments to a `printf`.

- Line up `printf` args with their `%` field:

```
my %seen;
while (<>) {
    my ($a, $b, $c, $d) = split;
    print unless $seen{$a}{$b}{$c}{$d}++;
}
if (my $tmp = $seen{fee}{fie}{foe}{foo}) {
    printf qq(Saw "fee fie foe foo" [sic] %d time%s.\n"),
                                $tmp, $tmp == 1 ? "" : "s";
}
```

These nine lines are just chock full of idioms. The first line makes an empty hash because we don't assign anything to it. We iterate over input lines setting "it", that is, $_, implicitly, then using an argumentless `split` which splits "it" on whitespace. Then we pick off the four first words with a list assignment, throwing any subsequent words away. Then we remember the first four words in a four-dimensional hash, which automatically creates (if necessary) the first three reference elements and final count element for the autoincrement to increment. (Under `use warnings`, the autoincrement will never warn that you're using undefined values, because autoincrement is an accepted way to define undefined values.) We then print out the line if we've never seen a line starting with these four words before, because the autoincrement is a postin-crement, which, in addition to incrementing the hash value, will return the old true value if there was one.

After the loop, we test `%seen` again to see if a particular combination of four words was seen. We make use of the fact that we can put a literal identifier into braces and it will be autoquoted. Otherwise, we'd have to say `$seen{"fee"}{"fie"}{"foe"}{"foo"}`, which is a drag even when you're not running from a giant.

We assign the result of `$seen{fee}{fie}{foe}{foo}` to a temporary variable even before testing it in the Boolean context provided by the `if`. Because assignment returns its left value, we can still test the value to see if it was true. The `my` tells your eye that it's a new variable, and we're not testing for equality but doing an assignment. It would also work fine without the `my`, and an expert Perl programmer would still immediately notice that we used one `=` instead of two `==`. (A semiskilled Perl programmer might be fooled, however. Pascal programmers of any skill level will foam at the mouth.)

Moving on to the `printf` statement, you can see the `qq()` form of double quotes we used so that we could interpolate ordinary double quotes as well as a newline. We could've directly interpolated `$tmp` there as well, since it's effec-tively a double-quoted string, but we chose to do further interpolation via `printf`. Our temporary `$tmp` variable is now quite handy, particularly since we don't just want to interpolate it, but also test it in the conditional of a `?:` oper-ator to see whether we should pluralize the word "time". Finally, note that we lined up the two fields with their corresponding `%` markers in the `printf` for-mat. If an argument is too long to fit, you can always go to the next line for the next argument, though we didn't have to in this case.

Whew! Had enough? There are many more idioms we could discuss, but this book is already sufficiently heavy. But we'd like to talk about one more idiomatic use of Perl, the writing of program generators.

Program Generation

Almost from the time people first figured out that they could write programs, they started writing programs that write other programs. We often call these *program generators*. (If you're a history buff, you might know that RPG stood for Report Program Generator long before it stood for Role Playing Game.) Nowadays they'd probably be called "program factories", but the generator people got there first, so they got to name it.

Now, anyone who has written a program generator knows that it can make your eyes go crossed even when you're wide awake. The problem is simply that much of your program's data looks like real code, but isn't (at least not yet). The same text file contains both stuff that does something and similar looking stuff that doesn't. Perl has various features that make it easy to mix Perl together with other languages, textually speaking.

(Of course, these features also make it easier to write Perl in Perl, but that's rather to be expected by now, we should think.)

Generating Other Languages in Perl

Perl is (among other things) a text-processing language, and most computer languages are textual. Beyond that, Perl's lack of arbitrary limits together with the various quoting and interpolation mechanisms make it easy to visually isolate the code of the other language you're spitting out. For example, here is a small chunk of *s2p*, the *sed*-to-*perl* translator:

```
print &q(<<"EOT");
:       #!$bin/perl
:       eval 'exec $bin/perl -S \$0 \${1+"\$@"}'
:            if \$running_under_some_shell;
:
EOT
```

Here the enclosed text happens to be legal in two languages, both Perl and *sh*. We've used an idiom right off the bat that will preserve your sanity in the writing of a program generator: the trick of putting a "noise" character and a tab on the front of every quoted line, which visually isolates the enclosed code, so you can tell at a glance that it's not the code that is actually being executed. One variable, $bin, is interpolated in the multiline quote in two places, and then the string is passed through a function to strip the colon and tab.

Of course, you aren't required to use multiline quotes. One often sees CGI scripts containing millions of print statements, one per line. It seems a bit like driving to church in an F-16, but hey, if it gets you there... (We will admit that a column of print statements has its own form of visual distinctiveness.)

When you are embedding a large, multiline quote containing some other language (such as HTML), it's often helpful to pretend you're programming inside-out, enclosing Perl into the other language instead, much as you might do with overtly everted languages such as PHP:

```
print <<"XML";
    <stuff>
    <nonsense>
    blah blah blah @{[ scalar EXPR ]} blah blah blah
```

```
        blah blah blah @{[ LIST ]} blah blah blah
        </nonsense>
        </stuff>
XML
```

You can use either of those two tricks to interpolate the values of arbitrarily complicated expressions into the long string.

Some program generators don't look much like program generators, depending on how much of their work they hide from you. In Chapter 22, *CPAN*, we saw how a small *Makefile.PL* program could be used to write a *Makefile*. The *Makefile* can easily be 100 times bigger than the *Makefile.PL* that produced it. Think how much wear and tear that saves your fingers. Or don't think about it—that's the point, after all.

Generating Perl in Other Languages

It's easy to generate other languages in Perl, but the converse is also true. Perl can easily be generated in other languages because it's both concise and malleable. You can pick your quotes not to interfere with the other language's quoting mechanisms. You don't have to worry about indentation, or where you put your line breaks, or whether to backslash your backslashes Yet Again. You aren't forced to define a package as a single string in advance, since you can slide into your package's namespace repeatedly, whenever you want to evaluate more code in that package.

Another thing that makes it easy to write Perl in other languages (including Perl) is the `#line` directive. Perl knows how to process these as special directives that reconfigure its idea of the current filename and line number. This can be useful in error or warning messages, especially for strings processed with `eval` (which, when you think about it, is just Perl writing Perl). The syntax for this mechanism is the one used by the C preprocessor: when Perl encounters a # symbol and the word `line`, followed by a number and a filename, it sets `__LINE__` to the number and `__FILE__` to the filename.*

Here are some examples that you can test by typing into *perl* directly. We've used a Control-D to indicate end-of-file, which is typical on Unix. DOS/Windows and VMS users can type Control-Z. If your shell uses something else, you'll have to use that to tell *perl* you're done. Alternatively, you can always type in `__END__` to tell the compiler there's nothing left to parse.

---

* Technically, it matches the pattern `/^#\s*line\s+(\d+)\s*(?:\s"([^"]+)")?\s*$/`, with $1 providing the line number for the next line, and $2 providing the optional filename specified within quotes. (A null filename leaves `__FILE__` unchanged.)

Here, Perl's built-in warn function prints out the new filename and line number:

```
% perl
# line 2000 "Odyssey"
# the "#" on the previous line must be the first char on line
warn "pod bay doors";  # or die
^D
pod bay doors at Odyssey line 2001.
```

And here, the exception raised by die within the eval found its way into the $@ ($EVAL_ERROR) variable, along with the temporary new filename and line:

```
# line 1996 "Odyssey"
eval qq{
#line 2025 "Hal"
    die "pod bay doors";
};
print "Problem with $@";
warn "I'm afraid I can't do that";
^D
Problem with pod bay doors at Hal line 2025.
I'm afraid I can't do that at Odyssey line 2001.
```

This shows how a #line directive affects only the current compilation unit (file or eval *STRING*), and that when that unit is done being compiled, the previous settings are automatically restored. This way you can set up your own messages inside an eval *STRING* or do *FILE* without affecting the rest of your program.

Perl has a **-P** switch that invokes the C preprocessor, which emits #line directives. The C preprocessor was the original impetus for implementing #line, but it is seldom used these days, since there are usually better ways to do what we used to rely on it for. Perl has a number of other preprocessors, however, including the AutoSplit module. The JPL (Java Perl Lingo) preprocessor turns *.jpl* files into *.java*, *.pl*, *.h*, and *.c* files. It makes use of #line to keep the error messages accurate.

One of the very first Perl preprocessors was the *sed*-to-*perl* translator, *s2p*. In fact, Larry delayed the initial release of Perl in order to complete *s2p* and *awk*-to-*perl* (*a2p*), because he thought they'd improve the acceptance of Perl. Hmm, maybe they did.

See the online docs for more on these, as well as the *find2perl* translator.

Source Filters

If you can write a program to translate random stuff into Perl, then why not have a way of invoking that translator from within Perl?

The notion of a source filter started with the idea that a script or module should be able to decrypt itself on the fly, like this:

```
#!/usr/bin/perl
use MyDecryptFilter;
@*x$]'0uN&k^Zx02jZ^X{.?s!(f;9Q/^A^@~~8H]|,%@^P:q-=
    ...
```

But the idea grew from there, and now a source filter can be defined to do any transformation on the input text you like. Put that together with the notion of the **-x** switch mentioned in Chapter 19, *The Command-Line Interface*, and you have a general mechanism for pulling any chunk of program out of a message and executing it, regardless of whether it's written in Perl or not.

Using the `Filter` module from CPAN, one can now even do things like programming Perl in *awk*:

```
#!/usr/bin/perl
use Filter::exec "a2p";            # the awk-to-perl translator
1,30 { print $1 }
```

Now that's definitely what you might call idiomatic. But we won't pretend for a moment that it's common practice.

25

Portable Perl

A world with only one operating system makes portability easy, and life boring. We prefer a larger genetic pool of operating systems, as long as the ecosystem doesn't divide too cleanly into predators and prey. Perl runs on dozens of operating systems, and because Perl programs aren't platform dependent, the same program can run on all of those systems without modification.

Well, almost. Perl tries to give the programmer as many features as possible, but if you make use of features particular to a certain operating system, you'll necessarily reduce the portability of your program to other systems. In this section, we'll provide some guidelines for writing portable Perl code. Once you make a decision about how portable you want to be, you'll know where the lines are drawn, and you can stay within them.

Looking at it another way, writing portable code is usually about willfully limiting your available choices. Naturally, it takes discipline and sacrifice to do that, two traits that Perl programmers might be unaccustomed to.

Be aware that not all Perl programs have to be portable. There is no reason not to use Perl to glue Unix tools together, or to prototype a Macintosh application, or to manage the Windows registry. If it makes sense to sacrifice portability, go ahead.*

In general, note that the notions of a user ID, a "home" directory, and even the state of being logged in will exist only on multi-user platforms.

The special $^O variable tells you what operating system your Perl was built on. This is provided to speed up code that would otherwise have to use Config to get

---

* Not every conversation has to be cross-culturally correct. Perl tries to give you at least one way to do the Right Thing but doesn't try to force it on you rigidly. In this respect, Perl more closely resembles your mother tongue than a nanny's tongue.

the same information via $Config{osname}. (Even if you've pulled in Config for other reasons, it still saves you the price of a tied-hash lookup.)

To get more detailed information about the platform, you can look at the rest of the information in the %Config hash, which is made available by the standard Config module. For example, to check whether the platform has the lstat call, you can check $Config{d_lstat}. See Config's online documentation for a full description of available variables, and the *perlport* manpage for a listing of the behavior of Perl built-in functions on different platforms. Here are the Perl functions whose behavior varies the most across platforms:

-X (file tests), accept, alarm, bind, binmode, chmod, chown, chroot, connect, crypt, dbmclose, dbmopen, dump, endgrent, endhostent, endnetent, endprotoent, endpwent, endservent, exec, fcntl, fileno, flock, fork, getgrent, getgrgid, getgrnam, gethostbyaddr, gethostbyname, gethostent, getlogin, getnetbyaddr, getnetbyname, getnetent, getpeername, getpgrp, getppid, getpriority, getprotobyname, getprotobynumber, getprotoent, getpwent, getpwnam, getpwuid, getservbyport, getservent, getservbyname, getsockname, getsockopt, glob, ioctl, kill, link, listen, lstat, msgctl, msgget, msgrcv, msgsnd, open, pipe, qx, readlink, readpipe, recv, select, semctl, semget, semop, send, sethostent, setgrent, setnetent, setpgrp, setpriority, setprotoent, setpwent, setservent, setsockopt, shmctl, shmget, shmread, shmwrite, shutdown, socket, socketpair, stat, symlink, syscall, sysopen, system, times, truncate, umask, utime, wait, waitpid

Newlines

On most operating systems, lines in files are terminated by one or two characters that signal the end of the line. The characters vary from system to system. Unix traditionally uses \012 (that is, the octal 12 character in ASCII), one type of DOSish I/O uses \015\012, and Macs uses \015. Perl uses \n to represent a "logical" newline, regardless of platform. In MacPerl, \n always means \015. In DOSish Perls, \n usually means \012, but when accessing a file in "text mode", it is translated to (or from) \015\012, depending on whether you're reading or writing. Unix does the same thing on terminals in canonical mode. \015\012 is commonly referred to as CRLF.

Because DOS distinguishes between text files and binary files, DOSish Perls have limitations when using seek and tell on a file in "text mode". For best results, only seek to locations obtained from tell. If you use Perl's built-in binmode function on the filehandle, however, you can usually seek and tell with impunity.

A common misconception in socket programming is that \n will be \012 everywhere. In many common Internet protocols, \012 and \015 are specified, and the values of Perl's \n and \r are not reliable since they vary from system to system:

```
print SOCKET "Hi there, client!\015\012";   # right
print SOCKET "Hi there, client!\r\n";       # wrong
```

However, using \015\012 (or \cM\cJ, or \x0D\x0A, or even v13.10) can be tedious and unsightly, as well as confusing to those maintaining the code. The Socket module supplies some Right Things for those who want them:

```
use Socket qw(:DEFAULT :crlf);
print SOCKET "Hi there, client!$CRLF"       # right
```

When reading from a socket, remember that the default input record separator $/ is \n, which means you have to do some extra work if you're not sure what you'll be seeing across the socket. Robust socket code should recognize either \012 or \015\012 as end of line:

```
use Socket qw(:DEFAULT :crlf);
local ($/) = LF;        # not needed if $/ is already \012

while (<SOCKET>) {
    s/$CR?$LF/\n/;      # replace LF or CRLF with logical newline
}
```

Similarly, code that returns text data—such as a subroutine that fetches a web page—should often translate newlines. A single line of code will often suffice:

```
$data =~ s/\015?\012/\n/g;
return $data;
```

Endianness and Number Width

Computers store integers and floating-point numbers in different orders (*big-endian* or *little-endian*) and different widths (32-bit and 64-bit being the most common today). Normally, you won't have to think about this. But if your program sends binary data across a network connection, or onto disk to be read by a different computer, you may need to take precautions.

Conflicting orders can make an utter mess out of numbers. If a little-endian host (such as an Intel CPU) stores 0x12345678 (305,419,896 in decimal), a big-endian host (such as a Motorola CPU) will read it as 0x78563412 (2,018,915,346 in decimal). To avoid this problem in network (socket) connections, use the pack and unpack formats n and N, which write unsigned short and long numbers in big-endian order (also called "network" order) regardless of the platform.

You can explore the endianness of your platform by unpacking a data structure packed in native format such as:

```
print unpack("h*", pack("s2", 1, 2)), "\n";
# '10002000' on e.g. Intel x86 or Alpha 21064 in little-endian mode
# '00100020' on e.g. Motorola 68040
```

To determine your endianness, you could use either of these statements:

```
$is_big_endian    = unpack("h*", pack("s", 1)) =~ /01/;
$is_little_endian = unpack("h*", pack("s", 1)) =~ /^1/;
```

Even if two systems have the same endianness, there can still be problems when transferring data between 32-bit and 64-bit platforms. There is no good solution other than to avoid transferring or storing raw binary numbers. Either transfer and store numbers as text instead of binary, or use modules like `Data::Dumper` or `Storable` to do this for you. You really want to be using text-oriented protocols in any event—they're more robust, more maintainable, and more extensible than binary protocols.

Of course, with the advent of XML and Unicode, our definition of text is getting more flexible. For instance, between two systems running Perl 5.6.0 (or newer), you can transport a sequence of integers encoded as characters in `utf8` (Perl's version of UTF-8). If both ends are running on an architecture with 64-bit integers, you can exchange 64-bit integers. Otherwise, you're limited to 32-bit integers. Use `pack` with a `U*` template to send, and `unpack` with a `U*` template to receive.

Files and Filesystems

File path components are separated with / on Unix, with \ on Windows, and with : on Macs. Some systems support neither hard links (`link`) nor symbolic links (`symlink`, `readlink`, `lstat`). Some systems pay attention to capitalization of filenames, some don't, and some pay attention when creating files but not when reading them.

There are modules that can help. The standard `File::Spec` modules provide some functions of the Right Thing persuasion:

```
use File::Spec::Functions;
chdir( updir() );        # go up one directory
$file = catfile( curdir(), 'temp', 'file.txt' );
```

That last line reads in *./temp/file.txt* on Unix and Windows, or *:temp:file.txt* on Macs, or *[.temp]file.txt* on VMS, and stores the file's contents in `$file`.

The `File::Basename` module, another platform-tolerant module bundled with Perl, splits a pathname into its components: the base filename, the full path to the directory, and the file suffix.

Here are some tips for writing portable file-manipulating Perl programs:

• Don't use two files of the same name with different case, like *test.pl* and *Test.pl*, since some platforms ignore capitalization.

- Constrain filenames to the 8.3 convention (eight-letter names and three-letter extensions) where possible. You can often get away with longer filenames as long as you make sure the filenames will remain unique when shoved through an 8.3-sized hole in the wall. (Hey, it's gotta be easier than shoving a camel through the eye of a needle.)

- Minimize nonalphanumeric characters in filenames. Using underscores is often okay, but it wastes a character that could better be used for uniqueness on 8.3 systems. (Remember, that's why we don't usually put underscores into module names.)

- Likewise, when using the `AutoSplit` module, try to constrain your subroutine names to eight characters or less, and don't give two subroutines the same name with different case. If you need longer subroutine names, make the first eight characters of each unique.

- Always use < explicitly to open a file for reading; otherwise, on systems that allow punctuation in filenames, a file prefixed with a > character could result in a file being wiped out, and a file prefixed with a | character could result in a pipe open. That's because the two-argument form of `open` is magical and will interpret characters like >, <, and |, which may be the wrong thing to do. (Except when it's right.)

```
open(FILE,       $existing_file) or die $!;  # wrongish
open(FILE,     "<$existing_file") or die $!;  # righter
open(FILE, "<", $existing_file)   or die $!;  # righterer
```

- Don't assume text files will end with a newline. They should, but sometimes people forget, especially when their text editor helps them forget.

System Interaction

Platforms that rely on a graphical user interface sometimes lack command lines, so programs requiring a command-line interface might not work everywhere. You can't do much about this, except upgrade.

Some other tips:

- Some platforms can't delete or rename files that are in use, so remember to close files when you are done with them. Don't `unlink` or `rename` an open file. Don't `tie` or `open` a file already tied or opened; `untie` or `close` it first.

- Don't open the same file more than once at a time for writing, since some operating systems put mandatory locks on such files.

- Don't depend on a specific environment variable existing in `%ENV`, and don't assume that anything in `%ENV` will be case sensitive or case preserving. Don't assume Unix inheritance semantics for environment variables; on some systems, they may be visible to all other processes.

- Don't use signals or %SIG.

- Try to avoid filename globbing. Use opendir, readdir, and closedir instead. (As of release 5.6.0 of Perl, basic filename globbing is much more portable than it was, but some systems may still chafe under the Unixisms of the default interface if you try to get fancy.)

- Don't assume specific values of the error numbers or strings stored in $!.

Interprocess Communication (IPC)

To maximize portability, don't try to launch new processes. That means you should avoid system, exec, fork, pipe, ` `, qx//, or open with a |.

The main problem is not the operators themselves; commands that launch external processes are generally supported on most platforms (though some do not support any type of forking). Problems are more likely to arise when you invoke external programs that have names, locations, output, or argument semantics that vary across platforms.

One especially popular bit of Perl code is opening a pipe to *sendmail* so that your programs can send mail:

```
open(MAIL, '|/usr/lib/sendmail -t') or die "cannot fork sendmail: $!";
```

This won't work on platforms without *sendmail*. For a portable solution, use one of the CPAN modules to send your mail, such as Mail::Mailer and Mail::Send in the MailTools distribution, or Mail::Sendmail.

The Unix System V IPC functions (msg*(), sem*(), shm*()) are not always available, even on some Unix platforms.

External Subroutines (XS)

XS code can usually be made to work with any platform, but libraries and header files might not be readily available, or the XS code itself might be platform specific. If the libraries and headers are portable, then it's a reasonable guess that the XS code can be made portable as well.

A different type of portability issue arises when writing XS code: the availability of a C compiler on the end user's platform. C brings with it its own portability issues, and writing XS code will expose you to some of those. Writing in pure Perl is an easier way to achieve portability because Perl's configuration process goes through extreme agonies to hide C's portability blemishes from you.*

Standard Modules

In general, the standard modules (modules bundled with Perl) work on all platforms. Notable exceptions are the CPAN.pm module (which currently makes connections to external programs that may not be available), platform-specific modules (such as ExtUtils::MM_VMS), and DBM modules.

There is no single DBM module available on all platforms. SDBM_File and the others are generally available on all Unix and DOSish ports, but not in MacPerl, where only NBDM_File and DB_File are available.

The good news is that at least one DBM module should be available, and Any-DBM_File will use whichever module it can find. With such uncertainty, you should use only the features common to all DBM implementations. For instance, keep your records to no more than 1K bytes. See the AnyDBM_File module documentation for more details.

Dates and Times

Where possible, use the ISO-8601 standard ("*YYYY-MM-DD*") to represent dates. Strings like "1987-12-18" can be easily converted into a system-specific value with a module like Date::Parse. A list of time and date values (such as that returned by the built-in localtime function) can be converted to a system-specific representation using Time::Local.

The built-in time function will always return the number of seconds since the beginning of the "epoch", but operating systems differ in their opinions of when that was. On many systems, the epoch began on January 1, 1970, at 00:00:00 UTC, but it began 66 years earlier on Macs, and on VMS it began on November 17, 1858, at 00:00:00. So for portable times you may want to calculate an offset for the epoch:

```
require Time::Local;
$offset = Time::Local::timegm(0, 0, 0, 1, 0, 70);
```

The value for $offset in Unix and Windows will always be 0, but on Macs and VMS it may be some large number. $offset can then be added to a Unix time value to get what should be the same value on any system.

---

* Some people on the margins of society run Perl's *Configure* script as a cheap form of entertainment. People have even been known to stage "Configure races", between competing systems and wager large sums on them. This practice is now outlawed in most of the civilized world.

A system's representation of the time of day and the calendar date can be controlled in widely different ways. Don't assume the time zone is stored in $ENV{TZ}. Even if it is, don't assume that you can control the time zone through that variable.

Internationalization

Use Unicode inside your program. Do any translation to and from other character sets at your interfaces to the outside world. See Chapter 15, *Unicode*.

Outside the world of Unicode, you should assume little about character sets and nothing about the ord values of characters. Do not assume that the alphabetic characters have sequential ord values. The lowercase letters may come before or after the uppercase letters; the lowercase and uppercase may be interlaced so that both a and A come before b; the accented and other international characters may be interlaced so that ä comes before b.

If your program is to operate on a POSIX system (a rather large assumption), consult the *perllocale* manpage for more information about POSIX locales. Locales affect character sets and encodings, and date and time formatting, among other things. Proper use of locales will make your program a little bit more portable, or at least more convenient and native-friendly for non-English users. But be aware that locales and Unicode don't mix well yet.

Style

When it is necessary to have platform-specific code, consider keeping it in one place to ease porting to other platforms. Use the Config module and the special variable $^O to differentiate between platforms.

Be careful in the tests you supply with your module or programs. A module's code may be fully portable, but its tests may well not be. This often happens when tests spawn other processes or call external programs to aid in the testing, or when (as noted above) the tests assume certain things about the filesystem and paths. Be careful not to depend on a specific output style for errors, even when checking $! for "standard" errors after a syscall. Use the Errno module instead.

Remember that good style transcends both time and culture, so for maximum portability, you must seek to understand the universal amidst the exigencies of your existence. The coolest people are not prisoners of the latest cool fad; they don't have to be, because they are not worried about being "in" with respect to their own culture, programmatically or otherwise. Fashion is a variable, but style is a constant.

26

Plain Old Documentation

One of the principles underlying Perl's design is that simple things should be simple, and hard things should be possible. Documentation should be simple.

Perl supports a simple text markup format called *pod* that can stand on its own or be freely intermixed with your source code to create embedded documentation. Pod can be converted to many other formats for printing or viewing, or you can just read it directly, because it's plain.

Pod is not as expressive as languages like XML, LATEX, *troff*(1), or even HTML. This is intentional: we sacrificed that expressiveness for simplicity and convenience. Some text markup languages make authors write more markup than text, which makes writing harder than it has to be, and reading next to impossible. A good format, like a good movie score, stays in the background without causing distraction.

Getting programmers to write documentation is almost as hard as getting them to wear ties. Pod was designed to be so easy to write that even a programmer could do it—and would. We don't claim that pod is sufficient for writing a book, although it was sufficient for writing this one.

Pod in a Nutshell

Most document formats require the entire document to be in that format. Pod is more forgiving: you can embed pod in any sort of file, relying on *pod translators* to extract the pod. Some files consist entirely of 100% pure pod. But other files, notably Perl programs and modules, may contain dollops of pod sprinkled about wherever the author feels like it. Perl simply skips over the pod text when parsing the file for execution.

The Perl lexer knows to begin skipping when, at a spot where it would ordinarily find a statement, it instead encounters a line beginning with an equal sign and an identifier, like this:

```
=head1 Here There Be Pods!
```

That text, along with all remaining text up through and including a line beginning with =cut, will be ignored. This allows you to intermix your source code and your documentation freely, as in:

```
=item snazzle

The snazzle() function will behave in the most spectacular
form that you can possibly imagine, not even excepting
cybernetic pyrotechnics.

=cut

sub snazzle {
    my $arg = shift;
    ....
}

=item razzle

The razzle() function enables autodidactic epistemology generation.

=cut

sub razzle {
    print "Epistemology generation unimplemented on this platform.\n";
}
```

For more examples, look at any standard or CPAN Perl module. They're all supposed to come with pod, and nearly all do, except for the ones that don't.

Since pod is recognized by the Perl lexer and thrown out, you may also use an appropriate pod directive to quickly comment out an arbitrarily large section of code. Use a =for pod block to comment out one paragraph, or a =begin/=end pair for a larger section. We'll cover the syntax of those pod directives later. Remember, though, that in both cases, you're still in pod mode afterwards, so you need to =cut back to the compiler.

```
print "got 1\n";

=for commentary
This paragraph alone is ignored by anyone except the
mythical "commentary" translator. When it's over, you're
still in pod mode, not program mode.
print "got 2\n";
```

```
=cut

# ok, real program again
print "got 3\n";

=begin comment

print "got 4\n";

all of this stuff
here will be ignored
by everyone

print "got 5\n";

=end comment

=cut

print "got 6\n";
```

This will print out that it got 1, 3, and 6. Remember that these pod directives can't go just anywhere. You have to put them only where the parser is expecting to see a new statement, not just in the middle of an expression or at other arbitrary locations.

From the viewpoint of Perl, all pod markup is thrown out, but from the viewpoint of pod translators, it's the code that is thrown out. Pod translators view the remaining text as a sequence of paragraphs separated by blank lines. All modern pod translators parse pod the same way, using the standard `Pod::Parser` module. They differ only in their output, since each translator specializes in one output format.

There are three kinds of paragraphs: verbatim paragraphs, command paragraphs, and prose paragraphs.

Verbatim Paragraphs

Verbatim paragraphs are used for literal text that you want to appear as is, such as snippets of code. A verbatim paragraph must be indented; that is, it must begin with a space or tab character. The translator should reproduce it exactly, typically in a constant width font, with tabs assumed to be on eight-column boundaries. There are no special formatting escapes, so you can't play font games to italicize or embolden. A < character means a literal <, and nothing else.

Pod Directives

All pod directives start with = followed by an identifier. This may be followed by any amount of arbitrary text that the directive can use however it pleases. The only syntactic requirement is that the text must all be one paragraph. Currently recognized directives (sometimes called *pod commands*) are:

=head1
=head2

. . .

> The =head1, =head2, . . . directives produce headings at the level specified. The rest of the text in the paragraph is treated as the heading description. These are similar to the .SH and .SS section and subsection headers in *man*(7), or to <H1> . . . </H1> and <H2> . . . </H2> tags in HTML. In fact, that's exactly what those translators convert these directives into.

=cut

> The =cut directive indicates the end of a stretch of pod. (There might be more pod later in the document, but if so it will be introduced with another pod directive.)

=pod

> The =pod directive does nothing beyond telling the compiler to lay off parsing code through the next =cut. It's useful for adding another paragraph to the document if you're mixing up code and pod a lot.

=over *NUMBER*
=item *SYMBOL*
=back

> The =over directive starts a section specifically for the generation of a list using the =item directive. At the end of your list, use =back to end it. The *NUMBER*, if provided, hints to the formatter how many spaces to indent. Some formatters aren't rich enough to respect the hint, while others are *too* rich to respect it, insofar as it's difficult when working with proportional fonts to make anything line up merely by counting spaces. (However, four spaces is generally construed as enough room for bullets or numbers.)
>
> The actual type of the list is indicated by the *SYMBOL* on the individual items. Here is a bulleted list:
>
> ```
> =over 4
>
> =item *
>
> Mithril armor
>
> =item *
> ```

```
    Elven cloak

    =back
```

And a numbered list:

```
    =over 4

    =item 1.

    First, speak "friend".

    =item 2.

    Second, enter Moria.

    =back
```

And a named list:

```
    =over 4

    =item armor()

    Description of the armor() function

    =item chant()

    Description of the chant() function

    =back
```

You may nest lists of the same or different types, but some basic rules apply: don't use =item outside an =over/=back block; use at least one =item inside an =over/=back block; and perhaps most importantly, keep the type of the items consistent within a given list. Either use =item * for each item to produce a bulleted list, or =item 1., =item 2., and so on to produce numbered list, or use =item foo, =item bar, and so on to produce a named list. If you start with bullets or numbers, stick with them, since formatters are allowed to use the first =item type to decide how to format the list.

As with everything in pod, the result is only as good as the translator. Some translators pay attention to the particular numbers (or letters, or Roman numerals) following the =item, and others don't. The current *pod2html* translator, for instance, is quite cavalier: it strips out the sequence indicators entirely without looking at them to infer what sequence you're using, then wraps the entire list inside <OL> and </OL> tags so that the browser can display it as an ordered list in HTML. This is not to be construed a feature; it may eventually be fixed.

```
=for TRANSLATOR
=begin TRANSLATOR
=end TRANSLATOR
```

=for, =begin, and =end let you include special sections to be passed through unaltered, but only to particular formatters. Formatters that recognize their own names, or aliases for their names, in *TRANSLATOR* pay attention to that directive; any others completely ignore them. The directive =for specifies that just the rest of this paragraph is destined *for* a particular translator.

```
=for html
<p> This is a <flash>raw</flash> <small>HTML</small> paragraph </p>
```

The paired =begin and =end directives work similarly to =for, but instead of accepting a single paragraph only, they treat all text between matched =begin and =end as destined for a particular translator. Some examples:

```
=begin html

<br>Figure 1.<IMG SRC="figure1.png"><br>

=end html

=begin text


    ---------------
    |  foo        |
    |        bar  |
    ---------------


^^^^ Figure 1. ^^^^

=end text
```

Values of *TRANSLATOR* commonly accepted by formatters include roff, man, troff, nroff, tbl, eqn, latex, tex, html, and text. Some formatters will accept some of these as synonyms. No translator accepts comment—that's just the customary word for something to be ignored by everybody. Any unrecognized word would serve the same purpose. While writing this book, we often left notes for ourselves under the directive =for later.

Note that =begin and =end do nest, but only in the sense that the outermost matched set causes everything in the middle to be treated as nonpod, even if it happens to contain other =*word* directives. That is, as soon as any translator sees =begin foo, it will either ignore or process *everything* down to the corresponding =end foo.

Pod Sequences

The third type of paragraph is simply "flowed" text. That is, if a paragraph doesn't start with either whitespace or an equals sign, it's taken as a plain paragraph: regular text that's typed in with as few frills as possible. Newlines are treated as equivalent to spaces. It's largely up to the translator to make it look nice, because programmers have more important things to do. It is assumed that translators will apply certain common heuristics—see the section "Pod Translators and Modules" later in this chapter.

You can do some things explicitly, however. Inside either ordinary paragraphs or heading/item directives (but not in verbatim paragraphs), you may use special sequences to adjust the formatting. These sequences always start with a single capital letter followed by a left angle bracket, and extend through the matching (not necessarily the next) right angle bracket. Sequences may contain other sequences.

Here are the sequences defined by pod:

I<*text*>

Italicized text, used for emphasis, book titles, names of ships, and manpage references such as "*perlpod*(1)".

B<*text*>

Emboldened text, used almost exclusively for command-line switches and sometimes for names of programs.

C<*text*>

Literal code, probably in a fixed-width font like Courier. Not needed on simple items that the translator should be able to infer as code, but you should put it anyway.

S<*text*>

Text with nonbreaking spaces. Often surrounds other sequences.

L<*name*>

A cross reference (link) to a name:

L<*name*>

Manual page

L<*name/ident*>

Item in manual page

L<*name/"sec"*>

Section in other manual page

L<"sec">

Section in this manual page (the quotes are optional)

L</"sec">
Ditto

The next five sequences are the same as those above, but the output will be only *text*, with the link information hidden as in HTML:

L<text|name>
L<text|name/ident>
L<text|name/"sec">
L<text|"sec">
L<text|/"sec">

The *text* cannot contain the characters / and |, and should contain < or > only in matched pairs.

F<pathname>

Used for filenames. This is traditionally rendered the same as I.

X<entry>

An index entry of some sort. As always, it's up to the translator to decide what to do. The pod specification doesn't dictate that.

E<escape>

A named character, similar to HTML escapes:

E<lt>

A literal < (optional except in other interior sequences and when preceded by a capital letter)

E<gt>

A literal > (optional except in other interior sequences)

E<sol>

A literal / (needed in L<> only)

E<verbar>

A literal | (needed in L<> only)

E<NNN>

Character number *NNN*, probably in ISO-8859-1, but maybe Unicode. Shouldn't really matter, in the abstract . . .

E<entity>

Some nonnumeric HTML entity, such as E<Agrave>.

Z<>

A zero-width character. This is nice for putting in front of sequences that might confuse something. For example, if you had a line in regular prose that had to start with an equals sign, you could write that as:

```
Z<>=can you see
```

or for something with a "From" in it, so the mailer doesn't put a > in front:

```
Z<>From here on out...
```

Most of the time, you'll need only a single set of angle brackets to delimit one of these pod sequences. Sometimes, however, you will want to put a < or > inside a sequence. (This is particularly common when using a C<> sequence to provide a constant-width font for a snippet of code.) As with all things in Perl, there is more than one way to do it. One way is to simply represent the closing bracket with an E sequence:

```
C<$a E<lt>=E<gt> $b>
```

This produces "$a <=> $b".

A more readable, and perhaps more "plain" way, is to use an alternate set of delimiters that doesn't require the angle brackets to be escaped. Doubled angle brackets (C<< *stuff* >>) may be used, provided there is whitespace immediately following the opening delimiter and immediately preceding the closing one. For example, the following will work:

```
C<< $a <=> $b >>
```

You may use as many repeated angle-brackets as you like so long as you have the same number of them on both sides, and you make sure that whitespace immediately follows the last < of the left side and immediately precedes the first > of the right side. So the following will also work:

```
C<<< $a <=> $b >>>
C<<<< $a <=> $b >>>>
```

All these end up spitting out $a <=> $b in a constant-width font.

The extra whitespace inside on either end goes away, so you should leave whitespace on the outside if you want it. Also, the two inside chunks of extra whitespace don't overlap, so if the first thing being quoted is >>, it isn't taken as the closing delimiter:

```
The C<< >> >> right shift operator.
```

This produces "The >> right shift operator."

Note that pod sequences *do* nest. That means you can write "The I<Santa MarE<iacute>a> left port already" to produce "The *Santa María* left port already", or "B<touch> S<B<-t> I<time>> I<file>" to produce "**touch -t** *time file*", and expect this to work properly.

Pod Translators and Modules

Perl is bundled with several pod translators that convert pod documents (or the embedded pod in other types of documents) into various formats. All should be 8-bit clean.

pod2text

> Converts pod into text. Normally, this text will be 7-bit ASCII, but it will be 8-bit if it had 8-bit input, or specifically ISO-8859-1 (or Unicode) if you use sequences like LE<uacute>thien for *Lúthien* or EE<auml>rendil for *Eärendil.*
>
> If you have a file with pod in it, the easiest (although perhaps not the prettiest) way to view just the formatted pod would be:
>
> ```
> % pod2text File.pm | more
> ```
>
> Then again, pod is supposed to be human readable without formatting.

pod2man

> Converts pod into Unix manpage format suitable for viewing through *nroff*(1) or creating typeset copies via *troff*(1). For example:
>
> ```
> % pod2man File.pm | nroff -man | more
> ```
>
> or
>
> ```
> % pod2man File.pm | troff -man -Tps -t > tmppage.ps
> % ghostview tmppage.ps
> ```
>
> and to print:
>
> ```
> % lpr -Ppostscript tmppage.ps
> ```

pod2html

> Converts pod into HTML for use with your favorite viewer:
>
> ```
> % pod2html File.pm > tmppage.html
> % lynx tmppage.html
> % netscape -remote "openURL(file:`pwd`/tmppage.html)"
> ```
>
> That last one is a *netscape* hack that works if you already have *netscape* running somewhere to tell that incarnation to load the page. Otherwise, just call it as you did *lynx.*

pod2latex

> Converts pod into LaTeX.

Additional translators are available on CPAN for other formats.

Translators exhibit different default behaviors depending on the output format. For instance, if your pod has a prose paragraph saying:

```
This is a $variable right here
```

then *pod2html* will turn that into:

```
This is a <STRONG>$variable</STRONG> right here
```

but *pod2text* will leave it unadorned, since the dollar should be enough to let it be read.

You should write your pod as close to plain text as you possibly can, with as few explicit markups as you can get away with. It is up to the individual translator to decide how things in your text should be represented. That means letting the translator figure out how to create paired quotes, how to fill and adjust text, how to find a smaller font for words in all capitals, etc. Since these were written to process Perl documentation, most translators* should also recognize unadorned items like these and render them appropriately:

- `FILEHANDLE`

- `$scalar`

- `@array`

- `function()`

- `manpage(3r)`

- `somebody@someplace.com`

- `http://foo.com/`

Perl also comes with several standard modules for parsing and converting pod, including `Pod::Checker` (and the associated *podchecker* utility) for checking the syntax of pod documents, `Pod::Find` for finding pod documents in directory trees, and `Pod::Parser` for creating your own pod utilities.

Note that pod translators should only look at paragraphs beginning with a pod directive (this makes parsing easier), whereas the compiler actually knows to look for pod escapes even in the middle of a paragraph. This means that the following secret stuff will be ignored by both the compiler and the translators.

```
$a=3;
=secret stuff
warn "Neither POD nor CODE!?"
=cut back
print "got $a\n";
```

You probably shouldn't rely upon the `warn` being podded out forever. Not all pod translators are well-behaved in this regard, and the compiler may someday become pickier.

---

* If you're designing a general-purpose pod translator, not one for Perl code, your criteria may vary.

Writing Your Own Pod Tools

Pod was designed first and foremost to be easy to write. As an added benefit, pod's simplicity also lends itself to writing simple tools for processing pod. If you're looking for pod directives, just set your input record separator to paragraph mode (perhaps with the **-00** switch), and only pay attention to paragraphs that look poddish.

For example, here's a simple *olpod* program to produce a pod outline:

```
#!/usr/bin/perl -100n
# olpod - outline pod
next unless /^=head/;
s/^=head(\d)\s+/ ' ' x ($1 * 4 - 4)/e;
print $_, "\n";
```

If you run that on the current chapter of this book, you'll get something like this:

```
Plain Old Documentation
    Pod in a Nutshell
        Verbatim Paragraphs
        Pod Directives
        Pod Sequences
    Pod Translators and Modules
    Writing Your Own Pod Tools
    Pod Pitfalls
    Documenting Your Perl Programs
```

That pod outliner didn't really pay attention to whether it was in a valid pod block or not. Since pod and nonpod can intermingle in the same file, running general-purpose tools to search or analyze the whole file doesn't always make sense. But that's no problem, given how easy it is to write tools for pod. Here's a tool that *is* aware of the difference between pod and nonpod, and produces only the pod:

```
#!/usr/bin/perl -00
# catpod - cat out just the pods
while (<>) {
    if (! $inpod) { $inpod = /^=/;                }
    if ($inpod)   { $inpod = !/^=cut/; print; }
} continue {
    if (eof)      {  close ARGV; $inpod = ''; }
}
```

You could use that program on another Perl program or module, then pipe the output along to another tool. For example, if you have the *wc*(1) program* to count lines, words, and characters, you could feed it *catpod* output to consider only pod in its counting:

---

* And if you don't, get the Perl Power Tools version from the CPAN *scripts* directory.

```
% catpod MyModule.pm | wc
```

There are plenty of places where pod allows you to write primitive tools trivially using plain, straightforward Perl. Now that you have *catpod* to use as a component, here's another tool to show just the indented code:

```
#!/usr/bin/perl -n00
# podlit - print the indented literal blocks from pod input
print if /^\s/;
```

What would you do with that? Well, you might want to do *perl -wc* checks on the code in the document, for one thing. Or maybe you want a flavor of *grep*(1)* that only looks at the code examples:

```
% catpod MyModule.pm | podlit | grep funcname
```

This tool-and-filter philosophy of interchangeable (and separately testable) parts is a sublimely simple and powerful approach to designing reusable software components. It's a form of laziness to just put together a minimal solution that gets the job done today—for certain kinds of jobs, at least.

For other tasks, though, this can even be counterproductive. Sometimes it's more work to write a tool from scratch, sometimes less. For those we showed you earlier, Perl's native text-processing prowess makes it expedient to use brute force. But not everything works that way. As you play with pod, you might notice that although its directives are simple to parse, its sequences can get a little dicey. Although some, um, subcorrect translators don't accommodate this, sequences can nest within other sequences and can have variable-length delimiters.

Instead of coding up all that parsing code on your own, laziness looks for another solution. The standard `Pod::Parser` module fits that bill. It's especially useful for complicated tasks, like those that require real parsing of the internal bits of the paragraphs, conversion into alternative output formats, and so on. It's easier to use the module for complicated cases, because the amount of code you end up writing is smaller. It's also better because the tricky parsing is already worked out for you. It's really the same principle as using *catpod* in a pipeline.

The `Pod::Parser` module takes an interesting approach to its job. It's an object-oriented module of a different flavor than most you've seen in this book. Its primary goal isn't so much to provide objects for direct manipulation as it is to provide a base class upon which other classes can be built.

You create your own class and inherit from `Pod::Parser`. Then you declare subroutines to serve as callback methods for your parent class's parser to invoke. It's a very different way of programming than the procedural programs given earlier. In

---

* And if you don't have *grep*, see previous footnote.

a sense, it's more of a declarative programming style, because to get the job done, you simply register functions and let other entities invoke them for you. The program's tiresome logic is handled elsewhere. You just give some plug-and-play pieces.

Here's a rewrite of the original *catpod* program given earlier, but this time it uses the `Pod::Parser` module to create our own subclass:

```perl
#!/usr/bin/perl
# catpod2, class and program

package catpod_parser;
use Pod::Parser;
@ISA = qw(Pod::Parser);
sub command {
    my ($parser, $command, $paragraph, $line_num) = @_;
    my $out_fh = $parser->output_handle();
    $paragraph .= "\n" unless substr($paragraph, -1) eq "\n";
    $paragraph .= "\n" unless substr($paragraph, -2) eq "\n\n";
    print $out_fh "=$command $paragraph";
}

sub verbatim {
    my ($parser, $paragraph, $line_num) = @_;
    my $out_fh = $parser->output_handle();
    print $out_fh $paragraph;
}

sub textblock {
    my ($parser, $paragraph, $line_num) = @_;
    my $out_fh = $parser->output_handle();
    print $out_fh $paragraph;
}
sub interior_sequence {
    my ($parser, $seq_command, $seq_argument) = @_;
    return "$seq_command<$seq_argument>";
}

if (!caller) {
    package main;
    my $parser = catpod_parser::->new();
    unshift @ARGV, '-' unless @ARGV;
    for (@ARGV) { $parser->parse_from_file($_); }
}
1;
__END__

=head1 NAME
docs describing the new catpod program here
```

As you see, it's a good bit longer and more complicated. It's also more extensible because all you have to do is plug in your own methods when you want your subclass to act differently than its base class.

The last bit at the end there, where it says !caller, checks whether the file is being used as a module or as a program. If it's being used as a program, then there is no caller. So it fires up its own parser (using the new method it inherited) and runs that parser on the command-line arguments. If no filenames were supplied, it assumes standard input, just as the previous version did.

Following the module code is an __END__ marker, a blank line without whitespace on it, and then the program/module's own pod documentation. This is an example of one file that's a program *and* a module *and* its own documentation. It's probably several other things as well.

Pod Pitfalls

Pod is fairly straightforward, but it's still possible to flub a few things:

- It's really easy to leave out the trailing angle bracket.

- It's really easy to leave out the trailing =back directive.

- It's easy to accidentally put a blank line into the middle of a long =for comment directive. Consider using =begin/=end instead.

- If you mistype one of the tags on a =begin/=end pair, it'll eat the rest of your file (podwise). Consider using =for instead.

- Pod translators require paragraphs to be separated by completely empty lines; that is, by two or more consecutive newline (\n) characters. If you have a line with spaces or tabs on it, it will not be treated as a blank line. This can cause two or more paragraphs to be treated as one.

- The meaning of a "link" is not defined by pod, and it's up to each translator to decide what to do with it. (If you're starting to get the idea that most decisions have been deferred to the translators, not pod, you're right.) Translators will often add wording around a L<> link, so that "L<foo(1)>" becomes "the *foo*(1) manpage", for example. So you shouldn't write things like "the L<foo> manpage" if you want the translated document to read sensibly: that would end up saying "the the *foo*(1) manpage manpage".

  If you need total control of the text used for a link, use the form L<show this text|foo> instead.

The standard *podchecker* program checks pod syntax for errors and warnings. For example, it checks for unknown pod sequences and for seemingly blank lines containing whitespace. It is still advisable to pass your document through two or more different pod translators and proofread the results. Some of the problems you find may be idiosyncrasies of the particular translators, which you may or may not wish to work around.

And, as always, Everything is Subject To Change at the Whim of the Random Hacker.

Documenting Your Perl Programs

We hope you document your code, whether or not you're a Random Hacker. If you do, you may wish to include the following sections in your pod:

=head1 NAME

> The name of your program or module.

=head1 SYNOPSIS

> A one-line description of what your program or module does (purportedly).

=head1 DESCRIPTION

> The bulk of your documentation. (Bulk is good in this context.)

=head1 AUTHOR

> Who you are. (Or an alias, if you are ashamed of your program.)

=head1 BUGS

> What you did wrong (and why it wasn't really your fault).

=head1 SEE ALSO

> Where people can find related information (so they can work around your bugs).

=head1 COPYRIGHT

> The copyright statement. If you wish to assert an explicit copyright, you should say something like:

```
Copyright 2013, Randy Waterhouse.  All Rights Reserved.
```

> Many modules also add:

```
This program is free software.  You may copy or
redistribute it under the same terms as Perl itself.
```

One caveat: if you're going to put your pod at the end of the file, and you're using an __END__ or __DATA__ token, make sure to put an empty line before the first pod directive:

```
__END__

=head1 NAME

Modern - I am the very model of a modern major module
```

Without the empty line before the =head1, the pod translators will ignore the start of your (extensive, accurate, cultured) documentation.

27

Perl Culture

This book is a part of Perl culture, so we can't hope to put everything we know about Perl culture in here. We can only whet your appetite with a little history, and a little art—some would say "very little art". For a much larger dose of Perl culture, see *www.perl.org* and *www.perl.com*. (Larry keeps copies of all his (official) ravings at *www.wall.org/~larry*.) Or just get acquainted with some other Perl programmers. We can't tell you what sort of people they'll be—about the only personality trait Perl programmers have in common is that they're all pathologically helpful.

History Made Practical

In order to understand why Perl is defined the way it is (or isn't), one must first understand why Perl even exists. So, let's drag out the old dusty history book . . . .

Way back in 1986, Larry was a systems programmer on a project developing multi-level-secure wide-area networks. He was in charge of an installation consisting of three VAXen and three Suns on the West Coast, connected over an encrypted, 1200-baud serial line to a similar configuration on the East Coast. Since Larry's primary job was support (he wasn't a programmer on the project, just the system guru), he was able to exploit his three virtues (laziness, impatience, and hubris) to develop and enhance all sorts of useful tools—such as *rn, patch,* and *warp.**

---

* It was at about this time that Larry latched onto the phrase "feeping creaturism" in a desperate attempt to justify on the basis of biological necessity his overwhelming urge to add "just one more feature". After all, if Life Is Simply Too Complicated, why not programs too? Especially programs like *rn* that really ought to be treated as advanced Artificial Intelligence projects so that they can read your news for you. Of course, some people say that the *patch* program is already *too* smart.

One day, after Larry had just finished ripping *rn* to shreds, leaving it in pieces on the floor of his directory, the great Manager came to him and said, "Larry, we need a configuration management and control system for all six VAXen and all six Suns. We need it in a month. Go to it!"

So, Larry, never being one to shirk work, asked himself what was the best way to have a bicoastal CM system, without writing it from scratch, that would allow viewing of problem reports on both coasts, with approvals and control. The answer came to him in one word: B-news.*

Larry went off and installed news on these machines and added two control commands: an "append" command to append to an existing article, and a "synchronize" command to keep the article numbers the same on both coasts. CM would be done using RCS (Revision Control System), and approvals and submissions would be done using news and *rn*. Fine so far.

Then the great Manager asked him to produce reports. News was maintained in separate files on a master machine, with lots of cross-references between files. Larry's first thought was "Let's use *awk*." Unfortunately, the *awk* of that day couldn't handle opening and closing of multiple files based on information in the files. Larry didn't want to have to code a special-purpose tool. As a result, a new language was born.

This new tool wasn't originally called Perl. Larry bandied about a number of names with his officemates and cohorts (Dan Faigin, who wrote this history, and Mark Biggar, his brother-in-law, who also helped greatly with the initial design). Larry actually considered and rejected every three- or four-letter word in the dictionary. One of the earliest names was "Gloria", after his sweetheart (and wife). He soon decided that this would cause too much domestic confusion.

The name then became "Pearl", which mutated into our present-day "Perl", partly because Larry saw a reference to another language called PEARL, but mostly because he's too lazy to type five letters all the time. And, of course, so that Perl could be used as a four-letter word. (You'll note, however, the vestiges of the former spelling in the acronym's gloss: "Practical Extraction *And* Report Language".)

This early Perl lacked many of the features of today's Perl. Pattern matching and filehandles were there, scalars were there, and formats were there, but there were very few functions, no associative arrays, and only a crippled implementation of regular expressions, borrowed from *rn*. The manpage was only 15 pages long. But Perl was faster than *sed* and *awk* and began to be used on other applications on the project.

---

* That is, the second implementation of Usenet transport software.

But Larry was needed elsewhere. Another great Manager came over one day and said, "Larry, support R&D." And Larry said, okay. He took Perl with him and discovered that it was turning into a good tool for system administration. He borrowed Henry Spencer's beautiful regular expression package and butchered it into something Henry would prefer not to think about during dinner. Then Larry added most of the goodies he wanted, and a few goodies other people wanted. He released it on the network.* The rest, as they say, is history.†

Which goes something like this: Perl 1.0 was released on December 18, 1987; some people still take Perl's Birthday seriously. Perl 2.0 follows in June 1988, and Randal Schwartz creates the legendary "Just Another Perl Hacker" signature. In 1989, Tom Christiansen presents the first public Perl tutorial at the Baltimore Usenix. With Perl 3.0 in October 1989, the language is released and distributed for the first time under the terms of the GNU Public License.

In March of 1990, Larry writes the first Perl Poem (see the following section). Then he and Randal write the first edition of this book, The Pink Camel; it is published in early 1991. Perl 4.0 is released simultaneously; it includes an Artistic License as well as the GPL.

The unveiling of the much anticipated Perl 5 occurs in October 1994. A complete rewrite of Perl, it includes objects and modules. The advent of Perl 5 even merits coverage by *The Economist*. In 1995, CPAN is officially introduced to the Perl community. Jon Orwant begins publishing *The Perl Journal* in 1996. After a long gestation, the second edition of this book, The Blue Camel, appears that fall. The first O'Reilly Perl Conference (TPC) is held in San Jose, California, in the summer of 1997. Notable events are now occurring almost daily, so for the rest of history, check out the Perl Timeline on CPAST, the Comprehensive Perl Arcana Society Tapestry (*history.perl.org*).

Perl Poetry

The forgery in the attendant sidebar appeared on Usenet on April Fool's Day, 1990. It is presented here without comment, merely to show how disgusting the metaphors of a typical programming language really are. So much for anything resembling literary value. Larry is particularly relieved that "Black Perl", originally written for Perl 3, no longer parses under Perl 5.

---

* More astonishingly, he kept on releasing it as he went to work at Jet Propulsion Lab, then at NetLabs and Seagate. Nowadays, other people do most of the real work, and Larry pretends to work for O'Reilly & Associates (a small company that publishes pamphlets about computers and stuff).

† And this, so to speak, is a footnote to history. When Perl was started, *rn* had just been ripped to pieces in anticipation of a major rewrite. Since he started work on Perl, Larry hasn't touched *rn*. It is still in pieces. Occasionally, Larry threatens to rewrite *rn* in Perl, but never seriously.

Larry's, er, corpus has fortunately been overshadowed by that of the reigning Perl
Poet, Sharon Hopkins. She has written quite a few Perl poems, as well as a paper
on Perl poetry that she presented at the Usenix Winter 1992 Technical Conference,
entitled "Camels and Needles: Computer Poetry Meets the Perl Programming Language". (The paper is available as *misc/poetry.ps* on CPAN.) Besides being the
most prolific Perl poet, Sharon is also the most widely published, having had the
following poem published in both the *Economist* and the *Guardian*:

```
#!/usr/bin/perl

APPEAL:

listen (please, please);

open yourself, wide;
    join (you, me),
connect (us,together),

tell me.

do something if distressed;

    @dawn, dance;
    @evening, sing;
    read (books,$poems,stories) until peaceful;
    study if able;

    write me if-you-please;

sort your feelings, reset goals, seek (friends, family, anyone);

        do*not*die (like this)
        if sin abounds;

keys (hidden), open (locks, doors), tell secrets;
do not, I-beg-you, close them, yet.

                        accept (yourself, changes),
                        bind (grief, despair);

require truth, goodness if-you-will, each moment;

select (always), length(of-days)

# listen (a perl poem)
# Sharon Hopkins
# rev. June 19, 1995
```

Perl Poetry

Article 970 of comp.lang.perl:
Path: jpl-devvax!pl-dexxav!lwall
From: lwall@jpl-dexxav.JPL.NASA.GOV (Larry Wall)
Newsgroups: news.groups,rec.arts.poems,comp.lang.perl
Subject: CALL FOR DISCUSSION: comp.lang.perl.poems
Message-ID: <0401@jpl-devvax.JPL.NASA.GOV>
Date: 1 Apr 90 00:00:00 GMT
Reply-To: lwall@jpl-devvax.JPL.NSAS.GOV (Larry Wall)
Organization: Jet Prepulsion Laboratory, Pasadena, CA
Lines: 61

It has come to my attention that there is a crying need for a place for people to express both their emotional and technical natures simultaneously. Several people have sent me some items which don't fit into any newsgroup. Perhaps it's because I recently posted to both comp.lang.perl and to rec.arts.poems, but people seem to be writing poems in Perl, and they're asking me where they should post them. Here is a sampling:

From a graduate student (in finals week), the following haiku:

```
study, write, study,
do review (each word) if time.
close book. sleep? what's that?
```

And someone writing from Fort Lauderdale writes:

```
sleep, close together,
sort of sin each spring & wait;
50% die
```

A person who wishes to remain anonymous wrote the following example of "Black Perl". (The Pearl poet would have been shocked, no doubt.)

```
BEFOREHAND: close door, each window & exit;  wait until time.
    open spellbook, study, read (scan, select, tell us);
write it, print the hex while each watches,
    reverse its length, write again;
    kill spiders, pop them, chop, split, kill them.
        unlink arms, shift, wait & listen (listening, wait),
sort the flock (then, warn the "goats" & kill the "sheep");
    kill them, dump qualms, shift moralities,
    values aside, each one;
        die sheep! die to reverse the system
        you accept (reject, respect);
next step,
    kill the next sacrifice, each sacrifice,
    wait, redo ritual until "all the spirits are pleased";
    do it ("as they say").
do it(*everyone***must***participate***in***forbidden**s*e*x*).
return last victim; package body;
    exit crypt (time, times & "half a time") & close it,
    select (quickly) & warn your next victim;
AFTERWORDS: tell nobody.
    wait, wait until time;
    wait until next year, next decade;
        sleep, sleep, die yourself,
        die at last
```

I tried that, and it actually parses in Perl. It doesn't appear to do anything useful, however. I think I'm glad, actually... I hereby propose the creation of comp.lang.perl.poems as a place for such items, so we don't clutter the perl or poems newsgroups with things that may be of interest to neither. Or, alternately, we should create rec.arts.poems.perl for items such as those above which merely parse, and don't do anything useful. (There is precedent in rec.arts.poems, after all.) Then also create comp.lang.perl.poems for poems that actually do something, such as this haiku of my own:

```
print STDOUT q
Just another Perl hacker,
unless $spring
```

Larry Wall   lwall@jpl-devvax.jpl.nasa.gov

V

Reference Material

28

Special Names

This chapter is about variables that have special meanings to Perl. Most of the punctuational names have reasonable mnemonics, or analogs in one of the shells (or both). But if you want to use long variable names as synonyms, just say:

    use English;

at the top of your program. This aliases all the short names to long names in the current package. Some of these variables even have medium names, generally borrowed from *awk*. Most people eventually settle on using the short names, at least for the more commonly used variables. Throughout this book, we consistently refer to the short names, but also often mention the long names (in parentheses) so that you can look them up easily in this chapter.

The semantics of these variables can be quite magical. (To create your own magic, see Chapter 14, *Tied Variables*.) A few of these variables are read-only. If you try to assign values to them, an exception will be raised.

In what follows, we'll first provide a concise listing of the variables and functions for which Perl assigns a special meaning, grouped by type, so you can look up variables when you're not sure of the proper name. Then we'll explain all of the variables alphabetically under their proper name (or their least improper name).

Special Names Grouped by Type

We used the word "type" loosely—the sections here actually group variables more by their scope, that is, where they're visible from.

Regular Expression Special Variables

The following special variables related to pattern matching are visible throughout the dynamic scope in which the pattern match occurred (except for $*, which is deprecated). In other words, they behave as though they were declared with `local`, so you needn't declare them that way yourself. See Chapter 5, *Pattern Matching*.

```
$*
$digits
@+ (@LAST_MATCH_END)
@- (@LAST_MATCH_START)
$+ ($LAST_PAREN_MATCH)
$^R ($LAST_REGEXP_CODE_RESULT)
$& ($MATCH)
$' ($POSTMATCH)
$` ($PREMATCH)
```

Per-Filehandle Variables

These special variables never need to be mentioned in a `local` because they always refer to some value pertaining to the currently selected output filehandle— each filehandle keeps its own set of values. When you `select` another filehandle, the old filehandle remembers the values it had for these variables, and the variables now reflect the values of the new filehandle. See also the `FileHandle` module in Chapter 32, *Standard Modules*.

```
$| ($AUTOFLUSH, $OUTPUT_AUTOFLUSH)
$- ($FORMAT_LINES_LEFT)
$= ($FORMAT_LINES_PER_PAGE)
$~ ($FORMAT_NAME)
$% ($FORMAT_PAGE_NUMBER)
$^ ($FORMAT_TOP_NAME)
```

Per-Package Special Variables

These special variables exist separately in each package. There should be no need to localize them, since `sort` automatically does so on $a and $b, and the rest are probably best left alone (though you will need to declare them with `our` if you use `strict`).

```
$a
$b
@EXPORT
@EXPORT_OK
%EXPORT_TAGS
%FIELDS
@ISA
```

```
%OVERLOAD
$VERSION
```

Program-wide Special Variables

These variables are truly global in the fullest sense—they mean the same thing in every package, because they're all forced into package main when unqualified (except for @F, which is special in main, but not forced). If you want a temporary copy of one of these, you must localize it in the current dynamic scope.

```
%ENV                                     $< ($UID, $REAL_USER_ID)
%INC                                     $> ($EUID, $EFFECTIVE_USER_ID)
%SIG                                     $? ($CHILD_ERROR)
%!                                       $@ ($EVAL_ERROR)
%^H                                      $[
                                         $\ ($ORS, $OUTPUT_RECORD_SEPARATOR)
@_                                       $] ($OLD_PERL_VERSION)
@ARGV                                    $^A ($ACCUMULATOR)
@F                                       $^C ($COMPILING)
@INC                                     $^D ($DEBUGGING)
                                         $^E ($EXTENDED_OS_ERROR)
$_ ($ARG)                                $^F ($SYSTEM_FD_MAX)
$0 ($PROGRAM_NAME)                       $^H
$ARGV                                    $^I ($INPLACE_EDIT)
                                         $^L ($FORMAT_FORMFEED)
$! ($ERRNO, $OS_ERROR)                   $^M
$" ($LIST_SEPARATOR)                     $^O ($OSNAME)
$#                                       $^P ($PERLDB)
$$ ($PID, $PROCESS_ID)                   $^R ($LAST_REGEXP_CODE_RESULT)
$( ($GID, $REAL_GROUP_ID)                $^S (EXCEPTIONS_BEING_CAUGHT)
$) ($EGID, $EFFECTIVE_GROUP_ID)          $^T ($BASETIME)
$, ($OFS, $OUTPUT_FIELD_SEPARATOR)       $^V ($PERL_VERSION)
$. ($NR, $INPUT_LINE_NUMBER)             $^W ($WARNING)
$/ ($RS, $INPUT_RECORD_SEPARATOR)        ${^WARNING_BITS}
$: ($FORMAT_LINE_BREAK_CHARACTERS)       ${^WIDE_SYSTEM_CALLS}
$; ($SUBSEP, $SUBSCRIPT_SEPARATOR)       $^X ($EXECUTABLE_NAME)
```

Per-Package Special Filehandles

Except for DATA, which is always per-package, the following filehandles are always assumed to be in main when not fully qualified with another package name:

```
_ (underline)
ARGV
ARGVOUT
DATA
STDIN
STDOUT
STDERR
```

Per-Package Special Functions

The following subroutine names have a special meaning to Perl. They're always called implicitly because of some event, such as accessing a tied variable or trying to call an undefined function. We don't describe them in this chapter since they all receive heavy-duty coverage elsewhere in the book.

Undefined function call interceptor (see Chapter 10, *Packages*):

    AUTOLOAD

Moribund objects' finalization (see Chapter 12, *Objects*):

    DESTROY

Exception objects (see die in the next chapter):

    PROPAGATE

Auto-init and auto-cleanup functions (see Chapter 18, *Compiling*):

    BEGIN, CHECK, INIT, END

Tie methods (see Chapter 14):

    BINMODE, CLEAR, CLOSE, DELETE, EOF, EXISTS, EXTEND, FETCH, FETCHSIZE,
    FILENO, FIRSTKEY, GETC, NEXTKEY, OPEN, POP, PRINT, PRINTF, PUSH, READ,
    READLINE, SEEK, SHIFT, SPLICE, STORE, STORESIZE, TELL, TIEARRAY,
    TIEHANDLE, TIEHASH, TIESCALAR, UNSHIFT, WRITE

Special Variables in Alphabetical Order

We've alphabetized these entries according to the long variable name. If you don't know the long name of a variable, you can find it in the previous section. (Variables without alphabetical names are sorted to the front.)

So that we don't have to keep repeating ourselves, each variable description starts with one or more of these annotations:

Annotation	Meaning
XXX	Deprecated, *do not use* in anything new.
NOT	Not Officially There (internal use only).
ALL	Truly global, shared by all packages.
PKG	Package global; each package can have its own.
FHA	Filehandle attribute; one per I/O object.
DYN	Dynamically scoped automatically (implies ALL).
LEX	Lexically scoped at compile time.
RO	Read only; raises an exception if you modify.

When more than one variable name or symbol is listed, only the short one is available by default. Using the English module makes the longer synonyms available to the current package, and only to the current package, even if the variable is marked [ALL].

Entries of the form *method HANDLE EXPR* show object-oriented interfaces to the perfilehandle variables provided by the FileHandle and various IO:: modules. (You may also use the *HANDLE->method(EXPR)* notation if you prefer.) These let you avoid having to call select to change the default output handle before examining or changing that variable. Each such method returns the old value of the FileHandle attribute; a new value is set if the *EXPR* argument is supplied. If not supplied, most of the methods do nothing to the current value, except for autoflush, which assumes an argument of 1, just to be different.

_ *(underline)*

> [ALL] This is the special filehandle used to cache the information from the last successful stat, lstat, or file test operator (like -w $file or -d $file).

$*digits*

> [DYN,RO] The numbered variables $1, $2, and so on (up just as high as you want)* contain the text that is matched by the corresponding set of parentheses in the last matched pattern within the currently active dynamic scope. (Mnemonic: like *digits*.)

$[

> [XXX,LEX] The index of the first element in an array and of the first character in a substring. Default is 0, but we used to set it to 1 to make Perl behave more like *awk* (or FORTRAN) when subscripting and when evaluating the index and substr functions. Because it was found to be so dangerous, assignment to $[is now treated as a lexically scoped compiler directive and cannot influence the behavior of any other file. (Mnemonic: [begins subscripts.)

$#

> [XXX,ALL] Don't use this; use printf instead. $# contains the output format for printed numbers, in a half-hearted attempt to emulate *awk*'s OFMT variable. (Mnemonic: # is the number sign, but if you're sharp, you'll just forget it so you don't make a hash of your program and get pounded for it.)

$*

> [XXX,ALL] Wow, three deprecated variables in a row! This one can (but shouldn't) be set to true to get Perl to assume /m on every pattern match that doesn't have an explicit /s. (Mnemonic: * matches multiple things.)

> * Although many regular expression engines only support up to nine backreferences, Perl has no such limit, so if you go around writing $768, Perl won't mind, although maintainers of your code might if you actually use that many parentheses in your regular expressions.

Names

$a   [PKG] This variable is used by the sort function to hold the first of each pair of values to be compared ($b is the second of each pair). The package for $a is the same one that the sort operator was compiled in, which is not necessarily the same as the one its comparison function was compiled into. This variable is implicitly localized within the sort comparison block. Because it is a global, it is exempt from use strict complaints. Because it is an alias for the actual array value, you might think you can modify it, but you shouldn't. See the sort function.

$ACCUMULATOR
$^A

[ALL] The current value of the write accumulator for format lines. A format contains formline commands that put their result into $^A. After calling its format, write prints out the contents of $^A and empties it. So you never actually see the contents of $^A unless you call formline yourself and then look at it. See the formline function.

$ARG
$_   [ALL] The default input and pattern-search space. These pairs are equivalent:

```
while (<>) {...}     # equivalent only in unadorned while test
while (defined($_ = <>)) {...}

chomp
chomp($_)

/^Subject:/
$_ =~ /^Subject:/

tr/a-z/A-Z/
$_ =~ tr/a-z/A-Z/
```

Here are the places where Perl will assume $_ if you don't specify something to operate on:

- List functions like print and unlink, and unary functions like ord, pos, and int, as well as the all file tests (except for -t, which defaults to STDIN). All functions that default to $_ are so marked in Chapter 29, *Functions*.

- The pattern-matching operations m// and s/// and the transliteration operations y/// and tr///, when used without an =~ operator.

- The iterator variable in a foreach loop (even when spelled for or when used as a statement modifier) if no other variable is supplied.

- The implicit iterator variable in the `grep` and `map` functions. (There is no way to specify a different variable for these.)

- The default place to put an input record when a `<FH>`, `readline`, or `glob` operation's result is tested by itself as the sole criterion of a `while` test. This assignment does not occur outside of a `while` test or if any additional elements are included in the `while` expression.

(Mnemonic: underline is the underlying operand in certain operations.)

@ARG

`@_` [ALL] Within a subroutine, this array holds the argument list passed to that subroutine. See Chapter 6, *Subroutines*. A `split` in scalar context splits to this array, but this usage is deprecated.

ARGV

[ALL] The special filehandle that iterates over command-line filenames in `@ARGV`. Usually written as the null filehandle in the angle operator: `<>`.

$ARGV

[ALL] Contains the name of the current file when reading from the `ARGV` handle using the `<>` or `readline` operators.

@ARGV

[ALL] The array containing the command-line arguments intended for the script. Note that `$#ARGV` is generally the number of arguments minus one, since `$ARGV[0]` is the first argument, not the command name; use `scalar @ARGV` for the number of program arguments. See `$0` for the program name.

ARGVOUT

[ALL] The special filehandle is used while processing the `ARGV` handle under the **-i** switch or the `$^I` variable. See the **-i** switch in Chapter 19, *The Command-Line Interface*.

`$b` [PKG] The variable, companion to `$a`, used in `sort` comparisons. See `$a` and the `sort` function for details.

$BASETIME

$^T

[ALL] The time at which the script began running, in seconds since the epoch (the beginning of 1970, for Unix systems). The values returned by the **-M**, **-A**, and **-C** file tests are relative to this moment.

$CHILD_ERROR

`$?` [ALL] The status returned by the last pipe close, backtick (`` ` ``) command, or `wait`, `waitpid`, or `system` functions. Note that this is not just the simple exit code, but the entire 16-bit status word returned by the underlying *wait*(2) or *waitpid*(2) syscall (or equivalent). Thus, the exit value of the subprocess is in the high byte, that is, $? >> 8; in the low byte, $? & 127 says which signal (if any) the process died from, while $? & 128 reports whether its demise produced a core dump. (Mnemonic: similar to $? in the *sh* and its offspring.)

Inside an END block, $? contains the value that is going to be given to exit. You can modify $? in an END to change the exit status of the script.

Under VMS, the pragma use vmsish 'status' makes $? reflect the true VMS exit status, instead of the default emulation of POSIX status.

If the h_errno variable is supported in C, its numeric value is returned via $? if any of the gethost*() functions fail.

$COMPILING
$^C

[ALL] The current value of the internal flag associated with the **-c** switch, mainly of use with **-MO** and the *perlcc*(1) tool to let code alter its behavior when being compiled for code generation. For example, you might want to AUTOLOAD at compile time instead of using the normal, deferred loading so that code can be generated right away. See Chapter 18.

DATA

[PKG] This special filehandle refers to anything following either the __END__ token or the __DATA__ token in the current file. The __END__ token always opens the main::DATA filehandle, and so is used in the main program. The __DATA__ token opens the DATA handle in whichever package is in effect at the time, so different modules can each have their own DATA filehandle, since they (presumably) have different package names.

$DEBUGGING
$^D

[ALL] The current value of the internal debugging flags, set from the **-D** switch on the command line; see Chapter 19 for the bit values. (Mnemonic: value of the **-D** switch.)

$EFFECTIVE_GROUP_ID
$EGID

$) [ALL] The effective GID (group ID) of this process. If you are on a machine that supports membership in multiple groups simultaneously, $) gives a space-separated list of groups you are in. The first number is the one returned by *getegid*(2), and the subsequent ones by *getgroups*(2), one of which may be the same as the first number.

Similarly, a value assigned to $) must also be a space-separated list of numbers. The first number is used to set the effective GID, and the rest (if any) are passed to the *setgroups*(2) syscall. To get the effect of an empty list for setgroups, just repeat the new effective GID; for example, to force an effective GID of 5 and an effectively empty setgroups list, say:

```
$) = "5 5";
```

(Mnemonic: parentheses are used to *group* things. The effective GID is the group that's *right* for you, if you're running setgid.) Note: $<, $>, $(, and $) can only be set on machines that support the corresponding system set-id routine. $(and $) can be swapped only on machines supporting *setregid*(2).

$EFFECTIVE_USER_ID
$EUID
$> [ALL] The effective UID of this process as returned by the *geteuid*(2) syscall. Example:

```
$< = $>;              # set real to effective uid
($<,$>) = ($>,$<);    # swap real and effective uid
```

(Mnemonic: it's the UID you went *to*, if you're running setuid.) Note: $< and $> can only be swapped on machines supporting *setreuid*(2). And sometimes not even then.

%ENV
[ALL] The hash containing your current environment variables. Setting a value in %ENV changes the environment for both your process and child processes launched after the assignment. (It cannot change a parent process's environment on any system resembling Unix.)

```
$ENV{PATH}  = "/bin:/usr/bin";
$ENV{PAGER} = "less";
$ENV{LESS}  = "MQeicsnf";  # our favorite switches to less(1)
system "man perl";         # picks up new settings
```

To remove something from your environment, make sure to use the delete function instead of undef on the hash value.

Note that processes running as *crontab*(5) entries inherit a particularly impoverished set of environment variables. (If your program runs fine from the command line but not under *cron*, this is probably why.) Also note that you should set $ENV{PATH}, $ENV{SHELL}, $ENV{BASH_ENV}, and $ENV{IFS} if you are running as a setuid script. See Chapter 23, *Security*.

$EVAL_ERROR
$@ [ALL] The currently raised exception or the Perl syntax error message from the last eval operation. (Mnemonic: where was the syntax error "at"?) Unlike $! ($OS_ERROR), which is set on failure but not cleared on success, $@ is guaranteed to be set (to a true value) if the last eval had a compilation error or runtime exception, and guaranteed to be cleared (to a false value) if no such problem occurred.

Warning messages are not collected in this variable. You can, however, set up a routine to process warnings by setting $SIG{__WARN__} as described later in this section.

Note that the value of $@ may be an exception object rather than a string. If so, you can still probably treat it as a string if the exception object has stringification overloading defined for its class. If you propagate an exception by saying:

```
die if $@;
```

then an exception object will call $@->PROPAGATE to see what to do. (A string exception merely adds a "propagated at" line to the string.)

$EXCEPTIONS_BEING_CAUGHT
$^S

> [ALL] This variable reflects the current state of the interpreter, returning true if inside an eval, false otherwise. It's undefined if parsing of the current compilation unit hasn't finished yet, which may be the case in $SIG{__DIE__} and $SIG{__WARN__} handlers. (Mnemonic: state of eval.)

$EXECUTABLE_NAME
$^X

> [ALL] The name that the *perl* binary itself was executed as, from C's argv[0].

@EXPORT

> [PKG] This array variable is consulted by the Exporter module's import method to find the list of other package variables and subroutines to be exported by default when the module is used, or when the :DEFAULT import tag is used. It is not exempt from use strict complaints, so it must be declared with our or fully qualified by package name if you've enabled that pragma. However, all variables whose names begin with the string "EXPORT" are exempt from warnings about being used only once. See Chapter 11, *Modules*.

@EXPORT_OK

> [PKG] This array variable is consulted by the Exporter module's import method to determine whether a requested import is legal. It is not exempt from use strict. See Chapter 11.

%EXPORT_TAGS

> [PKG] This hash variable is consulted by the Exporter module's import method when an import symbol with a leading colon is requested, as in use POSIX ":sys_wait_h". The keys are the colon tags, but without the leading colon. The values should be references to arrays containing symbols to import when the colon tag is requested, all of which must also appear in either @EXPORT or @EXPORT_OK. It is not exempt from use strict. See Chapter 11.

$EXTENDED_OS_ERROR

$^E

> [ALL] Error information specific to the current operating system. Under Unix, `$^E` is identical to `$!` (`$OS_ERROR`), but it differs under OS/2, VMS, and Microsoft systems, and on MacPerl. See your port's information for specifics. Caveats mentioned in the description of `$!` generally apply to `$^E` as well. (Mnemonic: extra error explanation.)

@F [PKG] The array into which the input line's fields are split when the **-a** command-line switch is given. If the **-a** option is not used, this array has no special meaning. (This array is actually only `@main::F`, and not in all packages at once.)

%FIELDS

> [NOT,PKG] This hash is for internal use by the `use fields` pragma to determine the current legal fields in an object hash. See `use fields`, `use base`, and "Field Declarations with use fields" in Chapter 12.

format_formfeed *HANDLE EXPR*

$FORMAT_FORMFEED

$^L

> [ALL] What a `write` function implicitly outputs to perform a form feed before it emits a top of form header. Default is `"\f"`.

format_lines_left *HANDLE EXPR*

$FORMAT_LINES_LEFT

$- [FHA] The number of lines left on the page of the currently selected output handle, for use with the `format` declaration and the `write` function. (Mnemonic: `lines_on_page` - `lines_printed`.)

format_lines_per_page *HANDLE EXPR*

$FORMAT_LINES_PER_PAGE

$= [FHA] The current page length (printable lines) of the currently selected output handle, for use with `format` and `write`. Default is 60. (Mnemonic: = has horizontal lines.)

format_line_break_characters *HANDLE EXPR*

$FORMAT_LINE_BREAK_CHARACTERS

$: [ALL] The current set of characters after which a string may be broken to fill continuation fields (starting with ^) in a format. Default is `" \n-"`, to break on whitespace or hyphens. (Mnemonic: a colon is a technical word meaning part of a line in poetry. Now you just have to remember the mnemonic...)

format_name *HANDLE EXPR*

$FORMAT_NAME

$~   [FHA] The name of the current report format for the currently selected output
     handle. Default is the filehandle's name. (Mnemonic: takes a turn after $^.)

format_page_number *HANDLE EXPR*

$FORMAT_PAGE_NUMBER

$%   [FHA] The current page number of the currently selected output handle, for
     use with format and write. (Mnemonic: % is the page number register in
     troff(1). What, you don't know what *troff* is?)

format_top_name *HANDLE EXPR*

$FORMAT_TOP_NAME

$^   [FHA] The name of the current top-of-page format for the currently selected
     output handle. Default is name of the filehandle with _TOP appended.
     (Mnemonic: points to top of page.)

$^H

     [NOT,LEX] This variable contains lexically scoped status bits (a.k.a. hints) for
     the Perl parser. This variable is strictly for internal use only. Its availability,
     behavior, and contents are subject to change without notice. If you touch it,
     you will undoubtedly die a horrible death of some loathsome tropical disease
     unknown to science. (Mnemonic: we won't give you a hint.)

%^H

     [NOT,LEX] The %^H hash provides the same lexical scoping semantics as $^H,
     making it useful for implementation of lexically scoped pragmas. Read the dire
     warnings listed under $^H, and then add to them the fact that this variable is
     still experimental.

%INC

     [ALL] The hash containing entries for the filename of each Perl file loaded via
     do *FILE*, require, or use. The key is the filename you specified, and the value
     is the location of the file actually found. The require operator uses this array
     to determine whether a given file has already been loaded. For example:

```
% perl -MLWP::Simple -le 'print $INC{"LWP/Simple.pm"}'
/opt/perl/5.6.0/lib/site_perl/LWP/Simple.pm
```

@INC

     [ALL] The array containing the list of directories where Perl modules may be
     found by do *FILE*, require, or use. It initially consists of the arguments to any
     -I command-line switches and directories in the PERL5LIB environment vari-
     able, followed by the default Perl libraries, such as:

```
/usr/local/lib/perl5/5.6.0/sun4-solaris
/usr/local/lib/perl5/5.6.0
/usr/local/lib/perl5/site_perl/5.6.0/sun4-solaris
/usr/local/lib/perl5/site_perl/5.6.0
/usr/local/lib/perl5/site_perl/5.00552/sun4-solaris
/usr/local/lib/perl5/site_perl/5.00552
/usr/local/lib/perl5/site_perl/5.005/sun4-solaris
/usr/local/lib/perl5/site_perl/5.005
/usr/local/lib/perl5/site_perl
```

followed by ".", to represent the current directory. If you need to modify this list from within your program, try the use lib pragma, which not only modifies the variable at compile time, but also adds in any related architecture-dependent directories (such as those that contain the shared libraries used by XS modules):

```
use lib "/mypath/libdir/";
use SomeMod;
```

$INPLACE_EDIT
$^I

[ALL] The current value of the inplace-edit extension. Use undef to disable inplace editing. You can use this from within your program to get the same behavior as the **-i** switch provides. For example, to do the equivalent of this command:

```
% perl -i.orig -pe 's/foo/bar/g' *.c
```

you can use the following equivalent code in your program:

```
local $^I   = '.orig';
local @ARGV = glob("*.c");
while (<>) {
    s/foo/bar/g;
    print;
}
```

(Mnemonic: value of the **-i** switch.)

$INPUT_LINE_NUMBER
$NR
$.

[ALL] The current record number (usually line number) for the last filehandle you read from (or called seek or tell on). The value may be different from the actual physical line number in the file, depending on what notion of "line" is in effect—see $/ ($INPUT_RECORD_SEPARATOR) on how to affect that. An explicit close on a filehandle resets the line number. Because <> never does an explicit close, line numbers increase across ARGV files (but see examples under eof). Localizing $. also localizes Perl's notion of "the last read filehandle". (Mnemonic: many programs use "." to mean the current line number.)

`$INPUT_RECORD_SEPARATOR`

`$RS`

`$/`   [ALL] The input record separator, newline by default, which is consulted by
the `readline` function, the `<FH>` operator, and the `chomp` function. It works
like *awk*'s RS variable, and, if set to the null string, treats one or more blank
lines as a record terminator. (But a blank line must contain no hidden spaces
or tabs.) You may set it to a multicharacter string to match a multicharacter
terminator, but you may not set it to a pattern—*awk* has to be better at something.

Note that setting `$/` to `"\n\n"` means something slightly different than setting
it to `""`, if the file contains consecutive blank lines. Setting it to `""` will treat
two or *more* consecutive blank lines as a single blank line. Setting it to `"\n\n"`
means Perl will blindly assume that a third newline belongs to the next paragraph.

Entirely undefining `$/` makes the next line input operation slurp in the
remainder of the file as one scalar value:

```
undef $/;            # enable whole-file mode
$_ = <FH>;           # whole file now here
s/\n[ \t]+/ /g;      # fold indented lines
```

If you're using the `while (<>)` construct to access the ARGV handle while `$/`
is undefined, each read gets the next file:

```
undef $/;
while (<>) {         # $_ has the whole next file in it
    ...
}
```

Although we used `undef` above, it's safer to undefine `$/` using `local`:

```
{
    local $/;
    $_ = <FH>;
}
```

Setting `$/` to a reference to either an integer, a scalar containing an integer, or
a scalar that's convertible to an integer will make `readline` and `<FH>` operations read in fixed-length records (with the maximum record size being the
referenced integer) instead of variable-length records terminated by a particular string. So this:

```
$/ = \32768; # or \"32768" or \$scalar_var_containing_32768
open(FILE, $myfile);
$record = <FILE>;
```

will read a record of no more than 32,768 bytes from the FILE handle. If
you're not reading from a record-oriented file (or your operating system

doesn't have record-oriented files), then you'll likely get a full chunk of data with every read. If a record is larger than the record size you've set, you'll get the record back in pieces. Record mode mixes well with line mode only on systems where standard I/O supplies a *read*(3) function; VMS is a notable exception.

Calling `chomp` when `$/` is set to enable record mode—or when it is undefined—has no effect. See also the **-0** (the digit) and the **-1** (the letter) command-line switches in Chapter 19. (Mnemonic: / is used to separate lines when quoting poetry.)

@ISA

[PKG] This array contains names of other packages to look through when a method call cannot be found in the current package. That is, it contains the base classes of the package. The `use base` pragma sets this implicitly. It is not exempt from `use strict`. See Chapter 12.

@LAST_MATCH_END

@+ [DYN,RO] This array holds the offsets of the ends of the last successful submatches in the currently active dynamic scope. `$+[0]` is the offset of the end of the entire match. This is the same value the `pos` function returns when called on the variable that was matched against. (When we say "offset of the end", we really mean the offset to the first character *following* the end of whatever matched, so that we can subtract beginning offsets from end offsets and arrive at the length.) The *n*th element of this array holds the offset of the *n*th submatch, so `$+[1]` is the offset where `$1` ends, `$+[2]` the offset where `$2` ends, and so on. You can use `$#+` to determine how many subgroups were in the last successful match. See also `@-` (`@LAST_MATCH_START`).

After a successful match against some variable `$var`:

- `$‘` is the same as `substr($var, 0, $-[0])`
- `$&` is the same as `substr($var, $-[0], $+[0] - $-[0])`
- `$’` is the same as `substr($var, $+[0])`
- `$1` is the same as `substr($var, $-[1], $+[1] - $-[1])`
- `$2` is the same as `substr($var, $-[2], $+[2] - $-[2])`
- `$3` is the same as `substr($var, $-[3], $+[3] - $-[3])`, and so on.

@LAST_MATCH_START

@- [DYN,RO] This array holds the offsets of the beginnings of the last successful submatches in the currently active dynamic scope. `$-[0]` is the offset of the beginning of the entire match. The *n*th element of this array holds the offset of the *n*th submatch, so $-[1] is the offset where $1 begins, $-[2] the offset where $2 begins, and so on. You can use $#- to determine how many subgroups were in the last successful match. See also @+ (@LAST_MATCH_END).

$LAST_PAREN_MATCH

$+   [DYN,RO] This returns the last parenthesized submatch from the last successful pattern in the currently active dynamic scope. This is useful when you don't know (or care) which of a set of alternative patterns matched. (Mnemonic: be positive and forward looking.) Example:

```
$rev = $+   if /Version: (.*)|Revision: (.*)/;
```

$LAST_REGEXP_CODE_RESULT

$^R

[DYN] This contains the result of the last snippet of code executed inside a successful pattern with the (?{ *CODE* }) construct. $^R gives you a way to execute code and remember the result for use later in the pattern, or even afterward.

As the Perl regular expression engine moves through the pattern, it may encounter multiple (?{ *CODE* }) expressions. As it does, it remembers each value of $^R so that if it later has to backtrack past an expression, it restores the previous value of $^R. In other words, $^R has a dynamic scope within the pattern, much like $1 and friends.

So $^R is not simply the result of the last snippet of code executed inside a pattern. It's the result of the last snippet of code *leading to a successful match*. A corollary is that if the match was not successful, $^R will be restored to whatever value it had before the match occurred.

If the (?{ *CODE* }) pattern is functioning directly as the conditional of a (?(*COND*)*IFTRUE*|*IFFALSE*) subpattern, $^R is not set.

$LIST_SEPARATOR

$"   [ALL] When an array or slice is interpolated into a double-quoted string (or the like), this variable specifies the string to put between individual elements. Default is a space. (Mnemonic: obvious, one hopes.)

$^M

[ALL] By default, running out of memory is not trappable. However, if your *perl* was compiled to take advantage of $^M, you may use it as an emergency memory pool. If your Perl is compiled with **-DPERL_EMERGENCY_SBRK** and uses Perl's `malloc`, then:

```
$^M = 'a' x (1 << 16);
```

would allocate a 64K buffer for emergency use. See the *INSTALL* file in the Perl source distribution directory for information on how to enable this option.

As a disincentive to casual use of this advanced feature, there is no use English long name for this variable (and we won't tell you what the mnemonic is).

$MATCH

$& [DYN,RO] The string matched by the last successful pattern match in the currently active dynamic scope. (Mnemonic: like & in some editors.)

$OLD_PERL_VERSION

$] [ALL] Returns the version + patchlevel/1000. It can be used to determine at the beginning of a script whether the Perl interpreter executing the script is in the right range of versions. (Mnemonic: is this version of Perl in the right bracket?) Example:

```
warn "No checksumming!\n" if $] < 3.019;
die "Must have prototyping available\n" if $] < 5.003;
```

See also the documentation of use *VERSION* and require *VERSION* for a convenient way to fail if the Perl interpreter is too old. See $^V for a more flexible UTF-8 representation of the Perl version.

$OSNAME

$^O

[ALL] This variable contains the name of the platform (usually the operating system) the current *perl* binary was compiled for. It's a cheap alternative to pulling it out of the Config module.

$OS_ERROR

$ERRNO

$! [ALL] If used in a numeric context, yields the current value of the last syscall error, with all the usual caveats. (This means that you shouldn't depend on the value of $! to be anything in particular unless you've gotten a specific error return indicating a system error.) If used in a string context, $! yields the corresponding system error string. You can assign an error number to $! if, for instance, you want $! to return the string for that particular error, or you want to set the exit value for die. See also the Errno module in Chapter 32. (Mnemonic: what just went bang?)

%OS_ERROR

%ERRNO

%! [ALL] This hash is defined only if you've loaded the standard Errno module described in Chapter 32. Once you've done this, you can subscript into %! using a particular error string, and its value is true only if that's the current error. For example, $!{ENOENT} is true only if the C errno variable is currently set to the C #define value, ENOENT. This is convenient for accessing vendor-specific symbols.

autoflush *HANDLE EXPR*
$OUTPUT_AUTOFLUSH
$AUTOFLUSH

$| [FHA] If set to true, forces a buffer flush after every print, printf, and write on the currently selected output handle. (We call this *command buffering*. Contrary to popular belief, setting this variable does not turn off buffering.) The default is false, which on many systems means that STDOUT will be line buffered if output is to the terminal, and block buffered otherwise, even on pipes and sockets. Setting this variable is useful when you are outputting to a pipe, such as when you are running a Perl script under *rsh*(1) and want to see the output as it's happening. If you have pending, unflushed data in the currently selected filehandle's output buffer when this variable is set to true, that buffer will be immediately flushed as a side-effect of assignment. See the one-argument form of select for examples of controlling buffering on filehandles other than STDOUT. (Mnemonic: when you want your pipes to be piping hot.)

This variable has no effect on input buffering; for that, see getc in Chapter 29 or the example in the POSIX module in Chapter 32.

$OUTPUT_FIELD_SEPARATOR
$OFS

$, [ALL] The output field separator (terminator, actually) for print. Ordinarily, print simply prints out the list elements you specify without anything between them. Set this variable as you would set *awk*'s OFS variable to specify what is printed between fields. (Mnemonic: what is printed when there is a ",", in your print statement.)

$OUTPUT_RECORD_SEPARATOR
$ORS

$\ [ALL] The output record separator (terminator, actually) for print. Ordinarily, print simply prints out the comma-separated fields you specify, with no trailing newline or record separator assumed. Set this variable as you would set *awk*'s ORS variable to specify what is printed at the end of the print. (Mnemonic: you set $\ instead of adding "\n" at the end of the print. Also, it's just like /, but it's what you get "back" from Perl.) See also the **-l** (for "line") command-line switch in Chapter 19.

%OVERLOAD

[NOT,PKG] This hash's entries are set internally by the use overload pragma to implement operator overloading for objects of the current package's class. See Chapter 13, *Overloading*.

$PERLDB

$^P

[NOT,ALL] The internal variable for enabling the Perl debugger (*perl -d*).

$PERL_VERSION

$^V

[ALL] The revision, version, and subversion of the Perl interpreter, represented as a binary "version string". V-strings don't generally have a a numeric value, but this variable is dual-valued, and has a numeric value equivalent to the old $] variable; that is, a floating-point number that amounts to revision + version/1000 + subversion/1,000,000. The string value is made of UTF-8 characters: chr($revision) . chr($version) . chr($subversion). This means that $^V is *not* printable. To print it, you have to say:

```
printf "%vd", $^V;
```

On the plus side, it also means that ordinary string comparison can be used to determine whether the Perl interpreter executing your script is in the right range of versions. (This applies to any version numbers represented with v-strings, not just Perl's.) Example:

```
warn "No 'our' declarations!\n" if $^V lt v5.6;
```

See the documentation of use *VERSION* and require *VERSION* for a convenient way to fail if the running Perl interpreter is older than you were hoping. See also $] for the original representation of the Perl version.

$POSTMATCH

$' [DYN,RO] The string following whatever was matched by the last successful pattern in the currently active dynamic scope. (Mnemonic: ' often follows a quoted string.) Example:

```
$_ = 'abcdefghi';
/def/;
print "$`:$&:$'\n";          # prints abc:def:ghi
```

Thanks to dynamic scope, Perl can't know which patterns will need their results saved away into these variables, so mentioning $` or $' anywhere in a program incurs a performance penalty on all pattern matches throughout the program. This isn't much of an issue in small programs, but you probably should avoid this pair when you're writing reusable module code. The example above can be equivalently recoded like this, but without the global performance hit:

```
$_ = 'abcdefghi';
/(.*?)(def)(.*)/s;           # /s in case $1 contains newlines
print "$1:$2:$3\n";          # prints abc:def:ghi
```

$PREMATCH

$` [DYN,RO] The string preceding whatever was matched by the last successful pattern in the currently active dynamic scope. (Mnemonic: ` often precedes a quoted string.) See the performance note under $' previously.

$PROCESS_ID
$PID

$$ [ALL] The process number (PID) of the Perl running this script. This variable is automatically updated upon a fork. In fact, you can even set $$ yourself; this will not, however, change your PID. That would be a neat trick. (Mnemonic: same as in the various shells.)

You need to be careful not to use $$ anywhere it might be misinterpreted as a dereference: $$alphanum. In this situation, write ${$}alphanum to distinguish it from ${$alphanum}.

$PROGRAM_NAME

$0 [ALL] Contains the name of the file containing the Perl script being executed. Assignment to $0 is magical: it attempts to modify the argument area that the *ps*(1) program normally reports on. This is more useful as a way of indicating the current program state than it is for hiding the program you're running. But it doesn't work on all systems. (Mnemonic: same as *sh, ksh, bash*, etc.)

$REAL_GROUP_ID
$GID

$([ALL] The real group ID (GID) of this process. If you are on a platform that supports simultaneous membership in multiple groups, $(gives a space-separated list of groups you are in. The first number is the one returned by *getgid*(2), and the subsequent ones by *getgroups*(2), one of which may be the same as the first number.

However, a value assigned to $(must be a single number used to set the real GID. So the value given by $(should *not* be assigned back to $(without being forced to be numeric, such as by adding zero. This is because you can have only one real group. See $) ($EFFECTIVE_GROUP_ID) instead, which allows you to set multiple effective groups.

(Mnemonic: parentheses are used to *group* things. The real GID is the group you *left*, if you're running setgid.)

$REAL_USER_ID
$UID

$< [ALL] The real user ID (UID) of this process as returned by the *getuid*(2) syscall. Whether and how you can modify this is subject to the vagaries of your system's implementation—see examples under $> ($EFFECTIVE_USER_ID). (Mnemonic: it's the UID you came *from*, if you're running setuid.)

%SIG

[ALL] The hash used to set signal handlers for various signals. (See the section "Signals" in Chapter 16, *Interprocess Communication*.) For example:

```
sub handler {
    my $sig = shift;    # 1st argument is signal name
    syswrite STDERR, "Caught a SIG$sig--shutting down\n";
                        # Avoid standard I/O in async handlers to suppress
                        # core dumpage.  (Even that string concat is risky.)
    close LOG;          # This calls standard I/O, so may dump core anyway!
    exit 1;             # But since we're exiting, no harm in trying.
}

$SIG{INT}  = \&handler;
$SIG{QUIT} = \&handler;
...
$SIG{INT}  = 'DEFAULT';    # restore default action
$SIG{QUIT} = 'IGNORE';     # ignore SIGQUIT
```

The %SIG hash contains undefined values corresponding to those signals for which no handler has been set. A handler may be specified as a subroutine reference or as a string. A string value that is not one of the two special actions "DEFAULT" or "IGNORE" is the name of a function, which, if unqualified by package, is interpreted to be the main package. Here are some other examples:

```
$SIG{PIPE} = "Plumber";    # okay, assumes main::Plumber
$SIG{PIPE} = \&Plumber;    # fine, use Plumber from current package
```

Certain internal hooks can also be set using the %SIG hash. The routine indicated by $SIG{__WARN__} is called when a warning message is about to be printed. The warning message is passed as the first argument. The presence of a __WARN__ hook causes the ordinary printing of warnings to STDERR to be suppressed. You can use this to save warnings in a variable or to turn warnings into fatal errors, like this:

```
local $SIG{__WARN__} = sub { die $_[0] };
eval $proggie;
```

This is similar to saying:

```
use warnings qw/FATAL all/;
eval $proggie;
```

except that the first has dynamic scope, whereas the second has lexical scope.

The routine indicated by $SIG{__DIE__} provides a way to turn a frog exception into a prince exception with a magical kiss, which often doesn't work.

The best use is for a moribund program that's about to die of an untrapped exception to do some last-moment processing on its way out. You can't save yourself this way, but you can give one last hurrah.

The exception message is passed as the first argument. When a __DIE__ hook routine returns, exception processing continues as it would have in the absence of the hook, unless the hook routine itself exits via a goto, a loop exit, or a die. The __DIE__ handler is explicitly disabled during the call, so that you yourself can then call the real die from a __DIE__ handler. (If it weren't disabled, the handler would call itself recursively forever.) The handler for $SIG{__WARN__} works similarly.

Only the main program should set $SIG{__DIE__}, not modules. That's because currently, even exceptions that are being trapped still trigger a $SIG{__DIE__} handler. This is strongly discouraged because of its potential for breaking innocent modules who aren't expecting their predicted exceptions to be mysteriously altered. Use this feature only as a last resort, and if you must, always put a local on the front to limit the period of danger.

Do not attempt to build an exception-handling mechanism on this feature. Use eval {} to trap exceptions instead.

STDERR

[ALL] The special filehandle for standard error in any package.

STDIN

[ALL] The special filehandle for standard input in any package.

STDOUT

[ALL] The special filehandle for standard output in any package.

$SUBSCRIPT_SEPARATOR

$SUBSEP

$; [ALL] The subscript separator for multidimensional hash emulation. If you refer to a hash element as:

```
$foo{$a,$b,$c}
```

it really means:

```
$foo{join($;, $a, $b, $c)}
```

But don't put:

```
@foo{$a,$b,$c}        # a slice--note the @
```

which means:

```
($foo{$a},$foo{$b},$foo{$c})
```

The default is `"\034"`, the same as SUBSEP in *awk*. Note that if your keys contain binary data, there might not be any safe value for `$;`. (Mnemonic: comma—the syntactic subscript separator—is a semi-semicolon. Yeah, we know, it's pretty lame, but `$,` is already taken for something more important.)

Although we haven't deprecated this feature, you should instead consider using "real" multidimensional hashes now, such as `$foo{$a}{$b}{$c}` instead of `$foo{$a,$b,$c}`. The fake ones may be easier to sort, however, and are much more amenable to use as DBM files.

`$SYSTEM_FD_MAX`
`$^F`

[ALL] The maximum "system" file descriptor, ordinarily 2. System file descriptors are passed to new programs during an `exec`, while higher file descriptors are not. Also, during an `open`, system file descriptors are preserved even if the `open` fails. (Ordinary file descriptors are closed before the `open` is attempted and stay closed if the `open` fails.) Note that the close-on-exec status of a file descriptor will be decided according to the value of `$^F` at the time of the `open`, not the time of the `exec`. Avoid this by temporarily jacking `$^F` through the roof first:

```
{
    local $^F = 10_000;
    pipe(HITHER,THITHER) or die "can't pipe: $!";
}
```

`$VERSION`

[PKG] This variable is accessed whenever a minimum acceptable version of a module is specified, as in `use SomeMod 2.5`. If `$SomeMod::VERSION` is less than that, an exception is raised. Technically, it's the `UNIVERSAL->VERSION` method that looks at this variable, so you could define your own `VERSION` function in the current package if you want something other than the default behavior. See Chapter 12.

`$WARNING`
`$^W`

[ALL] The current Boolean value of the global warning switch (not to be confused with the global warming switch, about which we hear many global warnings). See also the `use warnings` pragma in Chapter 31, *Pragmatic Modules*, and the **-W** and **-X** command-line switches for lexically scoped warnings, which are unaffected by this variable. (Mnemonic: the value is related to the **-w** switch.)

${^WARNING_BITS}

   [NOT,ALL] The current set of warning checks enabled by the use warnings
   pragma. See use warnings in Chapter 31 for more details.

${^WIDE_SYSTEM_CALLS}

   [ALL] Global flag that enables all syscalls made by Perl to use wide-character
   APIs native to the system, if available. This can also be enabled from the
   command line using the **-C** command-line switch. The initial value is typically
   0 for compatibility with Perl versions earlier than 5.6, but may be automatically
   set to 1 by Perl if the system provides a user-settable default (such as via
   $ENV{LC_CTYPE}). The use bytes pragma always overrides the effect of this flag
   in the current lexical scope.

Now brace yourself for a *big* chapter . . .

29

Functions

This chapter describes the built-in Perl functions in alphabetical order* for convenient reference. Each function description begins with a brief summary of the syntax for that function. Parameter names like *THIS* represent placeholders for actual
expressions, and the text following the syntax summary will describe the semantics of supplying (or omitting) the actual arguments.

You can think of functions as terms in an expression, along with literals and variables. Or you can think of them as prefix operators that process the arguments
after them. We call them operators half the time anyway.

Some of these operators, er, functions take a *LIST* as an argument. Elements of the
LIST should be separated by commas (or by =>, which is just a funny kind of
comma). The elements of the *LIST* are evaluated in a list context, so each element
will return either a scalar or a list value, depending on its sensitivity to list context.
Each returned value, whether scalar or list, will be interpolated as part of the overall sequence of scalar values. That is, all the lists get flattened into one list. From
the viewpoint of the function receiving the arguments, the overall argument *LIST* is
always a single-dimensional list value. (To interpolate an array as a single element,
you must explicitly create and interpolate a reference to the array instead.)

Predefined Perl functions may be used either with or without parentheses around
their arguments; the syntax summaries in this chapter omit the parentheses. If you
do use parentheses, the simple but occasionally surprising rule is this: if it looks
like a function, then it *is* a function, so precedence doesn't matter. Otherwise, it's a
list operator or unary operator, and precedence does matter. Be careful, because

---

* Sometimes tightly related functions are grouped together in the system manpages, so we respect that
grouping here. To find the description of endpwent, for instance, you'll have to look under getpwent.

even if you put whitespace between the keyword and its left parenthesis, that doesn't keep it from being a function:

```
print 1+2*4;        # Prints 9.
print(1+2) * 4;     # Prints 3!
print (1+2)*4;      # Also prints 3!
print +(1+2)*4;     # Prints 12.
print ((1+2)*4);    # Prints 12.
```

If you run Perl with the **-w** switch, it will warn you about this. For example, the second and third lines above produce messages like this:

```
print (...) interpreted as function at - line 2.
Useless use of integer multiplication in void context at - line 2.
```

Given the simple definition of some functions, you have considerable latitude in how you pass arguments. For instance, the most common way to use chmod is to pass the file permissions (the mode) as an initial argument:

```
chmod 0644, @array;
```

but the definition of chmod just says:

```
chmod LIST
```

so you could just as well say:

```
unshift @array, 0644;
chmod @array;
```

If the first argument of the list is not a valid mode, chmod will fail, but that's a run-time semantic problem unrelated to the syntax of the call. If the semantics require any special arguments to be passed first, the text will describe these restrictions.

In contrast to the simple *LIST* functions, other functions impose additional syntactic constraints. For instance, push has a syntax summary that looks like this:

```
push ARRAY, LIST
```

This means that push requires a proper array as its first argument, but doesn't care about its subsequent arguments. That's what the *LIST* at the end means. (*LIST*s always come at the end, since they gobble up all remaining values.) Whenever a syntax summary contains any arguments before the *LIST*, those arguments are syntactically distinguished by the compiler, not just semantically distinguished by the interpreter when it runs later. Such arguments are never evaluated in list context. They may be evaluated in scalar context, or they may be special referential arguments such as the array in push. (The description will tell you which is which.)

For those operations that are based directly on the C library's functions, we do not attempt to duplicate your system's documentation. When a `function` description says to see *function*(2), that means that you should look up the corresponding C version of that function to learn more about its semantics. The number in parentheses indicates the section of the system programmer's manual in which you will find the manpage, if you have the manpages installed. (And in which you won't, if you don't.)

These manpages may document system-dependent behavior like shadow password files, access control lists, and so forth. Many Perl functions that derive from C library functions in Unix are emulated even on non-Unix platforms. For example, although your operating system might not support the *flock*(2) or *fork*(2) syscalls, Perl will do its best to emulate them anyway by using whatever native facilities your platform provides.

Occasionally, you'll find that the documented C function has more arguments than the corresponding Perl function. Generally, the missing arguments are things that Perl knows already, such as the length of the previous argument, so you needn't supply them in Perl. Any remaining disparities are caused by the different ways Perl and C specify filehandles and success/failure values.

In general, functions in Perl that serve as wrappers for syscalls of the same name (like *chown*(2), *fork*(2), *closedir*(2), etc.) all return true when they succeed and `undef` otherwise, as mentioned in the descriptions that follow. This is different from the C library's interfaces to these operations, which all return –1 on failure. Exceptions to this rule are `wait`, `waitpid`, and `syscall`. Syscalls also set the special `$!` (`$OS_ERROR`) variable on failure. Other functions do not, except accidentally.

For functions that can be used in either scalar or list context, failure is generally indicated in scalar context by returning a false value (usually `undef`) and in list context by returning the null list. Successful execution is generally indicated by returning a value that will evaluate to true (in context).

Remember the following rule: there is *no* rule that relates the behavior of a function in list context to its behavior in scalar context, or vice versa. It might do two totally different things.

Each function knows the context in which it was called. The same function that returns a list when called in list context will, when called in scalar context, return whichever kind of value would be most appropriate. Some functions return the length of the list that would have been returned in list context. Some operators return the first value in the list. Some functions return the last value in the list. Some functions return the "other" value, when something can be looked up either by number or by name. Some functions return a count of successful operations. In general, Perl functions do exactly what you want, unless you want consistency.

One final note: we've tried to be very consistent in our use of the terms "byte" and "character". Historically, these terms have been confused with each other (and with themselves). But when we say "byte" we always mean an octet, 8 bits. When we say "character", we mean an abstract character, usually a Unicode character, which may be represented by one or more bytes within your strings.

But notice that we said "usually". Perl purposefully confuses bytes with characters in the scope of a use bytes declaration, so whenever we say "character", you should take it to mean a byte in a use bytes context, and a Unicode character otherwise. In other words, use bytes just warps the definition of character back to what it was in older versions of Perl. So, for instance, when we say that a scalar reverse reverses a string character by character, don't ask us whether that *really* means characters or bytes, because the answer is, "Yes, it does."

Perl Functions by Category

Here are Perl's functions and function-like keywords, arranged by category. Some functions appear under more than one heading.

Scalar manipulation

> chomp, chop, chr, crypt, hex, index, lc, lcfirst, length, oct, ord, pack, q//, qq//, reverse, rindex, sprintf, substr, tr///, uc, ucfirst, y///

Regular expressions and pattern matching

> m//, pos, qr//, quotemeta, s///, split, study

Numeric functions

> abs, atan2, cos, exp, hex, int, log, oct, rand, sin, sqrt, srand

Array processing

> pop, push, shift, splice, unshift

List processing

> grep, join, map, qw//, reverse, sort, unpack

Hash processing

> delete, each, exists, keys, values

Input and output

> binmode, close, closedir, dbmclose, dbmopen, die, eof, fileno, flock, format, getc, print, printf, read, readdir, readpipe, rewinddir, seek, seekdir, select (ready file descriptors), syscall, sysread, sysseek, syswrite, tell, telldir, truncate, warn, write

Fixed-length data and records

> pack, read, syscall, sysread, sysseek, syswrite, unpack, vec

Filehandles, files, and directories

> chdir, chmod, chown, chroot, fcntl, glob, ioctl, link, lstat, mkdir, open, opendir, readlink, rename, rmdir, select (ready file descriptors), select (output filehandle), stat, symlink, sysopen, umask, unlink, utime

Flow of program control

> caller, continue, die, do, dump, eval, exit, goto, last, next, redo, return, sub, wantarray

Scoping

> caller, import, local, my, no, our, package, use

Miscellaneous

> defined, dump, eval, formline, lock, prototype, reset, scalar, undef, wantarray

Processes and process groups

> alarm, exec, fork, getpgrp, getppid, getpriority, kill, pipe, qx//, setpgrp, setpriority, sleep, system, times, wait, waitpid

Library modules

> do, import, no, package, require, use

Classes and objects

> bless, dbmclose, dbmopen, package, ref, tie, tied, untie, use

Low-level socket access

> accept, bind, connect, getpeername, getsockname, getsockopt, listen, recv, send, setsockopt, shutdown, socket, socketpair

System V interprocess communication

> msgctl, msgget, msgrcv, msgsnd, semctl, semget, semop, shmctl, shmget, shmread, shmwrite

Fetching user and group information

> endgrent, endhostent, endnetent, endpwent, getgrent, getgrgid, getgrnam, getlogin, getpwent, getpwnam, getpwuid, setgrent, setpwent

Fetching network information

> endprotoent, endservent, gethostbyaddr, gethostbyname, gethostent, getnetbyaddr, getnetbyname, getnetent, getprotobyname, getprotobynumber, getprotoent, getservbyname, getservbyport, getservent, sethostent, setnetent, setprotoent, setservent

Time

> gmtime, localtime, time, times

Functions

Perl Functions in Alphabetical Order

Many of the following function names are annotated with, um, annotations. Here are their meanings:

$_   Uses $_ ($ARG) as a default variable.

$!   Sets $! ($OS_ERROR) on syscall errors.

$@   Raises exceptions; use eval to trap $@ ($EVAL_ERROR).

$?   Sets $? ($CHILD_ERROR) when child process exits.

T   Taints returned data.

T   Taints returned data under some system, locale, or handle settings.

X
ARG   Raises an exception if given an argument of inappropriate type.

X
RO   Raises an exception if modifying a read-only target.

X
T   Raises an exception if fed tainted data.

X
U   Raises an exception if unimplemented on current platform.

Functions that return tainted data when fed tainted data are not marked, since that's most of them. In particular, if you use any function on %ENV or @ARGV, you'll get tainted data.

Functions marked with **X**/**ARG** raise an exception when they require, but do not receive, an argument of a particular type (such as filehandles for I/O operations, references for blessing, etc.).

Functions marked with **X**/**RO** sometimes need to alter their arguments. If they can't modify the argument because it's marked read-only, they'll raise an exception. Examples of read-only variables are the special variables containing data captured during a pattern match and variables that are really aliases to constants.

Functions marked with **X**/**U** may not be implemented on all platforms. Although many of these are named after functions in the Unix C library, don't assume that just because you aren't running Unix, you can't call any of them. Many are emulated, even those you might never expect to see—such as fork on Win32 systems, which works as of the 5.6 release of Perl. For more information about the portability and behavior of system-specific functions, see the *perlport* manpage, plus any platform-specific documentation that came with your Perl port.

Functions that raise other miscellaneous exceptions are marked with **$@**, including math functions that throw range errors, such as sqrt(-1).

abs

$\boxed{\text{S\_}}$

```
abs VALUE
abs
```

This function returns the absolute value of its argument.

```
$diff = abs($first - $second);
```

Note: here and in subsequent examples, good style (and the use strict pragma) would dictate that you add a my modifier to declare a new lexically scoped variable, like this:

```
my $diff = abs($first - $second);
```

However, we've omitted my from most of our examples for clarity. Just assume that any such variable was declared earlier, if that cranks your rotor.

accept

$\boxed{\text{S!}}$ $\boxed{\substack{\text{X}\\\text{ARG}}}$ $\boxed{\substack{\text{X}\\\text{U}}}$

```
accept SOCKET, PROTOSOCKET
```

This function is used by server processes that wish to listen for socket connections from clients. *PROTOSOCKET* must be a filehandle already opened via the socket operator and bound to one of the server's network addresses or to INADDR_ANY. Execution is suspended until a connection is made, at which point the *SOCKET* filehandle is opened and attached to the newly made connection. The original *PROTO-SOCKET* remains unchanged; its only purpose is to be cloned into a real socket. The function returns the connected address if the call succeeds, false otherwise. For example:

```
unless ($peer = accept(SOCK, PROTOSOCK)) {
    die "Can't accept a connection: $!\n";
}
```

On systems that support it, the close-on-exec flag will be set for the newly opened file descriptor, as determined by the value of $^F ($SYSTEM_FD_MAX).

See *accept*(2). See also the example in the section "Sockets" in Chapter 16, *Interprocess Communication*.

alarm

$\boxed{\text{S\_}}$ $\boxed{\substack{\text{X}\\\text{U}}}$

```
alarm EXPR
alarm
```

This function sends a SIGALRM signal to the current process after *EXPR* seconds.

Only one timer may be active at once. Each call disables the previous timer, and an *EXPR* of 0 may be supplied to cancel the previous timer without starting a new one. The return value is the amount of time remaining on the previous timer.

```
print "Answer me within one minute, or die: ";
alarm(60);                # kill program in one minute
$answer = <STDIN>;
$timeleft = alarm(0);  # clear alarm
print "You had $timeleft seconds remaining\n";
```

It is usually a mistake to intermix `alarm` and `sleep` calls, because many systems use the *alarm*(2) syscall mechanism to implement *sleep*(3). On older machines, the elapsed time may be up to one second less than you specified because of how seconds are counted. Additionally, a busy system may not get around to running your process immediately. See Chapter 16 for information on signal handling.

For alarms of finer granularity than one second, you might be able to use the `syscall` function to access *setitimer*(2) if your system supports it. The CPAN module, `Time::HiRes`, also provides functions for this purpose.

atan2

```
atan2 Y, X
```

This function returns the principal value of the arc tangent of Y/X in the range $-\pi$ to π. A quick way to get an approximate value of π is to say:

```
$pi = atan2(1,1) * 4;
```

For the tangent operation, you may use the `tan` function from either the `Math::Trig` or the `POSIX` modules, or just use the familiar relation:

```
sub tan { sin($_[0]) / cos($_[0]) }
```

bind   [S!] [X ARG] [X U] [X T]

```
bind SOCKET, NAME
```

This function attaches an address (a name) to an already opened socket specified by the *SOCKET* filehandle. The function returns true if it succeeded, false otherwise. *NAME* should be a packed address of the proper type for the socket.

```
use Socket;
$port_number = 80;       # pretend we want to be a web server
$sockaddr = sockaddr_in($port_number, INADDR_ANY);
bind SOCK, $sockaddr or die "Can't bind $port_number: $!\n";
```

See *bind*(2). See also the examples in the section "Sockets" in Chapter 16.

binmode

```
binmode FILEHANDLE, DISCIPLINES
binmode FILEHANDLE
```

This function arranges for the *FILEHANDLE* to have the semantics specified by the *DISCIPLINES* argument. If *DISCIPLINES* is omitted, binary (or "raw") semantics are applied to the filehandle. If *FILEHANDLE* is an expression, the value is taken as the name of the filehandle or a reference to a filehandle, as appropriate.

The binmode function should be called after the open but before any I/O is done on the filehandle. The only way to reset the mode on a filehandle is to reopen the file, since the various disciplines may have treasured up various bits and pieces of data in various buffers. This restriction may be relaxed in the future.

In the olden days, binmode was used primarily on operating systems whose run-time libraries distinguished text from binary files. On those systems, the purpose of binmode was to turn off the default text semantics. However, with the advent of Unicode, all programs on all systems must take some cognizance of the distinction, even on Unix and Mac systems. These days there is only one kind of binary file (as far as Perl is concerned), but there are many kinds of text files, which Perl would also like to treat in a single way. So Perl has a single internal format for Unicode text, UTF-8. Since there are many kinds of text files, text files often need to be translated upon input into UTF-8, and upon output back into some legacy character set, or some other representation of Unicode. You can use disciplines to tell Perl how exactly (or inexactly) to do these translations.*

For example, a discipline of ":text" will tell Perl to do generic text processing without telling Perl which kind of text processing to do. But disciplines like ":utf8" and ":latin1" tell Perl which text format to read and write. On the other hand, the ":raw" discipline tells Perl to keep its cotton-pickin' hands off the data. For more on how disciplines work (or will work), see the open function. The rest of this discussion describes what binmode does without the *DISCIPLINES* argument, that is, the historical meaning of binmode, which is equivalent to:

```
binmode FILEHANDLE, ":raw";
```

Unless instructed otherwise, Perl will assume your freshly opened file should be read or written in text mode. Text mode means that \n (newline) will be your internal line terminator. All systems use \n as the internal line terminator, but what that really represents varies from system to system, device to device, and even file to file, depending on how you access the file. In such legacy systems (including MS-DOS and VMS), what your program sees as a \n may not be what's physically

---

* More precisely, you *will* be able to use disciplines for this, but we're still implementing them as of this writing.

stored on disk. The operating system might, for example, store text files with
\cM\cJ sequences that are translated on input to appear as \n to your program,
and have \n from your program translated back to \cM\cJ on output to a file. The
binmode function disables this automatic translation on such systems.

In the absence of a *DISCIPLINES* argument, binmode has no effect under Unix or
Mac OS, both of which use \n to end each line and represent that as a single character. (It may, however, be a different character: Unix uses \cJ and older Macs use
\cM. Doesn't matter.)

The following example shows how a Perl script might read a GIF image from a
file and print it to the standard output. On systems that would otherwise alter the
literal data into something other than its exact physical representation, you must
prepare both handles. While you could use a ":raw" discipline directly in the GIF
open, you can't do that so easily with pre-opened filehandles like STDOUT:

```
binmode STDOUT;
open(GIF, "vim-power.gif") or die "Can't open vim-power.gif: $!\n";
binmode GIF;
while (read(GIF, $buf, 1024)) {
    print STDOUT $buf;
}
```

bless   [X / ARG]

```
bless REF, CLASSNAME
bless REF
```

This function tells the referent pointed to by reference *REF* that it is now an object
in the *CLASSNAME* package—or the current package if no *CLASSNAME* is specified. If
REF is not a valid reference, an exception is raised. For convenience, bless returns
the reference, since it's often the last function in a constructor subroutine. For
example:

```
$pet = Beast->new(TYPE => "cougar", NAME => "Clyde");

# then in Beast.pm:
sub new {
    my $class  = shift;
    my %attrs = @_;
    my $self  = { %attrs };
    return bless($self, $class);
}
```

You should generally bless objects into *CLASSNAME*s that are mixed case. Namespaces with all lowercase names are reserved for internal use as Perl pragmata
(compiler directives). Built-in types (such as "SCALAR", "ARRAY", "HASH", etc., not to
mention the base class of all classes, "UNIVERSAL") all have uppercase names, so
you may wish to avoid such package names as well.

Make sure that CLASSNAME is not false; blessing into false packages is not supported and may result in unpredictable behavior.

It is not a bug that there is no corresponding curse operator. (But there is a sin operator.) See also Chapter 12, *Objects*, for more about the blessing (and blessings) of objects.

caller

```
caller EXPR
caller
```

This function returns information about the stack of current subroutine calls and such. Without an argument, it returns the package name, filename, and line number that the currently executing subroutine was called from:

```
($package, $filename, $line) = caller;
```

Here's an example of an exceedingly picky function, making use of the special tokens __PACKAGE__ and __FILE__ described in Chapter 2, *Bits and Pieces*:

```
sub careful {
    my ($package, $filename) = caller;
    unless ($package eq __PACKAGE__ && $filename eq __FILE__) {
        die "You weren't supposed to call me, $package!\n";
    }
    print "called me safely\n";
}

sub safecall {
    careful();
}
```

When called with an argument, caller evaluates EXPR as the number of stack frames to go back before the current one. For example, an argument of 0 means the current stack frame, 1 means the caller, 2 means the caller's caller, and so on. The function also reports additional information as shown here:

```
$i = 0;
while (($package, $filename, $line, $subroutine,
        $hasargs, $wantarray, $evaltext, $is_require,
        $hints, $bitmask) = caller($i++) )
{
    ...
}
```

If the frame is a subroutine call, $hasargs is true if it has its own @_ array (not one borrowed from its caller). Otherwise, $subroutine may be "(eval)" if the frame is not a subroutine call, but an eval. If so, additional elements $evaltext and $is_require are set: $is_require is true if the frame is created by a require or use statement, and $evaltext contains the text of the eval EXPR statement. In particular, for a eval *BLOCK* statement, $filename is "(eval)", but $evaltext is undefined. (Note also that each use statement creates a require frame inside an eval *EXPR* frame.) The $hints and $bitmask are internal values; please ignore them unless you're a member of the thaumatocracy.

In a fit of even deeper magic, caller also sets the array @DB::args to the arguments passed in the given stack frame—but only when called from within the DB package. See Chapter 20, *The Perl Debugger*.

chdir   [S!] [X̲T̲]

```
chdir EXPR
chdir
```

This function changes the current process's working directory to *EXPR*, if possible. If *EXPR* is omitted, the caller's home directory is used. The function returns true upon success, false otherwise.

```
chdir "$prefix/lib" or die "Can't cd to $prefix/lib: $!\n";
```

See also the Cwd module, described in Chapter 32, *Standard Modules*, which lets you keep track of your current directory automatically.

chmod   [S!] [X̲T̲]

```
chmod LIST
```

This function changes the permissions of a list of files. The first element of the list must be the numerical mode, as in the *chmod*(2) syscall. The function returns the number of files successfully changed. For example:

```
$cnt = chmod 0755, 'file1', 'file2';
```

will set $cnt to 0, 1, or 2, depending on how many files were changed. Success is measured by lack of error, not by an actual change, because a file may have had the same mode before the operation. An error probably means you lacked sufficient privileges to change its mode because you were neither the file's owner nor the superuser. Check $! to find the actual reason for failure.

Here's a more typical usage:

```
chmod(0755, @executables) == @executables
        or die "couldn't chmod some of @executables: $!";
```

If you need to know which files didn't allow the change, use something like this:

```
@cannot = grep {not chmod 0755, $_} 'file1', 'file2', 'file3';
die "$0: could not chmod @cannot\n" if @cannot;
```

This idiom makes use of the grep function to select only those elements of the list for which the chmod function failed.

When using nonliteral mode data, you may need to convert an octal string to a number using the oct function. That's because Perl doesn't automatically assume a string contains an octal number just because it happens to have a leading "0".

```
$DEF_MODE = 0644;    # Can't use quotes here!
PROMPT: {
    print "New mode? ";
    $strmode = <STDIN>;
        exit unless defined $strmode;    # test for eof
    if ($strmode =~ /^\s*$/) {           # test for blank line
        $mode = $DEF_MODE;
    }
    elsif ($strmode !~ /^\d+$/) {
        print "Want numeric mode, not $strmode\n";
        redo PROMPT;
    }
    else {
        $mode = oct($strmode);           # converts "755" to 0755
    }
    chmod $mode, @files;
}
```

This function works with numeric modes much like the Unix *chmod*(2) syscall. If you want a symbolic interface like the one the *chmod*(1) command provides, see the File::chmod module on CPAN.

You can also import the symbolic S_I* constants from the Fcntl module:

```
use Fcntl ':mode';
chmod S_IRWXU|S_IRGRP|S_IXGRP|S_IROTH|S_IXOTH, @executables;
```

Some people consider that more readable than 0755. Go figure.

chomp

```
chomp VARIABLE
chomp LIST
chomp
```

This function (normally) deletes a trailing newline from the end of a string contained in a variable. This is a slightly safer version of chop (described next) in that it has no effect upon a string that doesn't end in a newline. More specifically, it deletes the terminating string corresponding to the current value of $/, and not just any last character.

Unlike chop, chomp returns the number of characters deleted. If $/ is "" (in paragraph mode), chomp removes all trailing newlines from the selected string (or strings, if chomping a *LIST*). You cannot chomp a literal, only a variable.

For example:

```
while (<PASSWD>) {
    chomp;   # avoid \n on last field
    @array = split /:/;
    ...
}
```

With version 5.6, the meaning of chomp changes slightly in that input disciplines are allowed to override the value of the $/ variable and mark strings as to how they should be chomped. This has the advantage that an input discipline can recognize more than one variety of line terminator (such as Unicode paragraph and line separators), but still safely chomp whatever terminates the current line.

chop $_ X RO

```
chop VARIABLE
chop LIST
chop
```

This function chops off the last character of a string variable and returns the character chopped. The chop operator is used primarily to remove the newline from the end of an input record, and is more efficient than using a substitution. If that's all you're doing, then it would be safer to use chomp, since chop always shortens the string no matter what's there, and chomp is more selective.

You cannot chop a literal, only a variable.

If you chop a *LIST* of variables, each string in the list is chopped:

```
@lines = `cat myfile`;
chop @lines;
```

You can chop anything that is an lvalue, including an assignment:

```
chop($cwd = `pwd`);
chop($answer = <STDIN>);
```

This is different from:

```
$answer = chop($tmp = <STDIN>);   # WRONG
```

which puts a newline into $answer because chop returns the character chopped, not the remaining string (which is in $tmp). One way to get the result intended here is with substr:

```
$answer = substr <STDIN>, 0, -1;
```

But this is more commonly written as:

```
chop($answer = <STDIN>);
```

In the most general case, chop can be expressed in terms of substr:

```
$last_char = chop($var);
$last_char = substr($var, -1, 1, "");    # same thing
```

Once you understand this equivalence, you can use it to do bigger chops. To chop more than one character, use substr as an lvalue, assigning a null string. The following removes the last five characters of $caravan:

```
substr($caravan, -5) = "";
```

The negative subscript causes substr to count from the end of the string instead of the beginning. If you wanted to save the characters so removed, you could use the four-argument form of substr, creating something of a quintuple chop:

```
$tail = substr($caravan, -5, 5, "");
```

chown

$! X U X T

```
chown LIST
```

This function changes the owner and group of a list of files. The first two elements of the list must be the *numeric* UID and GID, in that order. A value of –1 in either position is interpreted by most systems to leave that value unchanged. The function returns the number of files successfully changed. For example:

```
chown($uidnum, $gidnum, 'file1', 'file2') == 2
        or die "can't chown file1 or file2: $!";
```

will set $cnt to 0, 1, or 2, depending on how many files got changed (in the sense that the operation succeeded, not in the sense that the owner was different afterward). Here's a more typical usage:

```
chown($uidnum, $gidnum, @filenames) == @filenames
        or die "can't chown @filenames: $!";
```

Here's a subroutine that accepts a username, looks up the user and group IDs for you, and does the chown:

```
sub chown_by_name {
    my($user, @files) = @_;
    chown((getpwnam($user))[2,3], @files) == @files
            or die "can't chown @files: $!";
}

chown_by_name("fred", glob("*.c"));
```

However, you may not want the group changed as the previous function does, because the */etc/passwd* file associates each user with a single group even though that user may be a member of many secondary groups according to */etc/group*. An alternative is to pass a -1 for the GID, which leaves the group of the file unchanged. If you pass a -1 as the UID and a valid GID, you can set the group without altering the owner.

On most systems, you are not allowed to change the ownership of the file unless you're the superuser, although you should be able to change the group to any of your secondary groups. On insecure systems, these restrictions may be relaxed, but this is not a portable assumption. On POSIX systems, you can detect which rule applies like this:

```
use POSIX qw(sysconf _PC_CHOWN_RESTRICTED);
# only try if we're the superuser or on a permissive system
if ($> == 0 || !sysconf(_PC_CHOWN_RESTRICTED) ) {
    chown($uidnum, -1, $filename)
        or die "can't chown $filename to $uidnum: $!";
}
```

chr   `$_`

```
chr NUMBER
chr
```

This function returns the character represented by that *NUMBER* in the character set. For example, chr(65) is "A" in either ASCII or Unicode, and chr(0x263a) is a Unicode smiley face. For the reverse of chr, use ord.

If you'd rather specify your characters by name than by number (for example, "\N{WHITE SMILING FACE}" for a Unicode smiley), see charnames in Chapter 31, *Pragmatic Modules*.

chroot   `$_` `$!` `X U` `X T`

```
chroot FILENAME
chroot
```

If successful, *FILENAME* becomes the new root directory for the current process— the starting point for pathnames beginning with "/". This directory is inherited across exec calls and by all subprocesses forked after the chroot call. There is no way to undo a chroot. For security reasons, only the superuser can use this function. Here's some code that approximates what many FTP servers do:

```
chroot((getpwnam('ftp'))[7])
    or die "Can't do anonymous ftp: $!\n";
```

This function is unlikely to work on non-Unix systems. See *chroot*(2).

close

```
close FILEHANDLE
close
```

This function closes the file, socket, or pipe associated with *FILEHANDLE*. (It closes the currently selected filehandle if the argument is omitted.) It returns true if the close is successful, false otherwise. You don't have to close *FILEHANDLE* if you are immediately going to do another open on it, since the next open will close it for you. (See open.) However, an explicit close on an input file resets the line counter ($.), while the implicit close done by open does not.

FILEHANDLE may be an expression whose value can be used as an indirect filehandle (either the real filehandle name or a reference to anything that can be interpreted as a filehandle object).

If the filehandle came from a piped open, close will return false if any underlying syscall fails or if the program at the other end of the pipe exited with nonzero status. In the latter case, the close forces $! ($OS_ERROR) to zero. So if a close on a pipe returns a nonzero status, check $! to determine whether the problem was with the pipe itself (nonzero value) or with the program at the other end (zero value). In either event, $? ($CHILD_ERROR) contains the wait status value (see its interpretation under system) of the command associated with the other end of the pipe. For example:

```
open(OUTPUT, '| sort -rn | lpr -p')  # pipe to sort and lpr
    or die "Can't start sortlpr pipe: $!";
print OUTPUT @lines;                  # print stuff to output
close OUTPUT                          # wait for sort to finish
    or warn $! ? "Syserr closing sortlpr pipe: $!"
               : "Wait status $? from sortlpr pipe";
```

A filehandle produced by *dup*(2)ing a pipe is treated as an ordinary filehandle, so close will not wait for the child on that filehandle. You have to wait for the child by closing the original filehandle. For example:

```
open(NETSTAT, "netstat -rn |")
    or die "can't run netstat: $!";
open(STDIN, "<&NETSTAT")
    or die "can't dup to stdin: $!";
```

If you close STDIN above, there is no wait, but if you close NETSTAT, there is.

If you somehow manage to reap an exited pipe child on your own, the close will fail. This could happen if you had a $SIG{CHLD} handler of your own that got triggered when the pipe child exited, or if you intentionally called waitpid on the process ID returned from the open call.

closedir   `S!` `X ARG` `X U`

```
closedir DIRHANDLE
```

This function closes a directory opened by `opendir` and returns the success of that operation. See the examples under `readdir`. *DIRHANDLE* may be an expression whose value can be used as an indirect dirhandle, usually the real dirhandle name.

connect   `S!` `X ARG` `X T` `X U`

```
connect SOCKET, NAME
```

This function initiates a connection with another process that is waiting at an `accept`. The function returns true if it succeeded, false otherwise. *NAME* should be a packed network address of the proper type for the socket. For example, assuming `SOCK` is a previously created socket:

```
use Socket;

my ($remote, $port) = ("www.perl.com", 80);
my $destaddr = sockaddr_in($port, inet_aton($remote));
connect SOCK, $destaddr
    or die "Can't connect to $remote at port $port: $!";
```

To disconnect a socket, use either `close` or `shutdown`. See also the examples in the section "Sockets" in Chapter 16. See *connect*(2).

cos   `S_`

```
cos EXPR
cos
```

This function returns the cosine of *EXPR* (expressed in radians). For example, the following script will print a cosine table of angles measured in degrees:

```
# Here's the lazy way of getting degrees-to-radians.

$pi = atan2(1,1) * 4;
$piover180 = $pi/180;

# Print table.
for ($deg = 0; $deg <= 90; $deg++) {
    printf "%3d %7.5f\n", $deg, cos($deg * $piover180);
}
```

For the inverse cosine operation, you may use the `acos()` function from the `Math::Trig` or `POSIX` modules, or use this relation:

```
sub acos { atan2( sqrt(1 - $_[0] * $_[0]), $_[0] ) }
```

crypt

```
crypt PLAINTEXT, SALT
```

This function computes a one-way hash of a string exactly in the manner of *crypt*(3). This is somewhat useful for checking the password file for lousy passwords,* although what you really want to do is prevent people from adding the bad passwords in the first place.

crypt is intended to be a one-way function, much like breaking eggs to make an omelette. There is no (known) way to decrypt an encrypted password apart from exhaustive, brute-force guessing.

When verifying an existing encrypted string, you should use the encrypted text as the *SALT* (like crypt($plain, $crypted) eq $crypted). This allows your code to work with the standard crypt, and with more exotic implementations, too.

When choosing a new *SALT*, you minimally need to create a random two character string whose characters come from the set [./0-9A-Za-z] (like join '', ('.', '/', 0..9, 'A'..'Z', 'a'..'z')[rand 64, rand 64]). Older implementations of crypt only needed the first two characters of the *SALT*, but code that only gives the first two characters is now considered nonportable. See your local *crypt*(3) man-page for interesting details.

Here's an example that makes sure that whoever runs this program knows their own password:

```
$pwd = (getpwuid ($<))[1];    # Assumes we're on Unix.

system "stty -echo";   # or look into Term::ReadKey on CPAN
print "Password: ";
chomp($word = <STDIN>);
print "\n";
system "stty echo";

if (crypt($word, $pwd) ne $pwd) {
    die "Sorry...\n";
} else {
    print "ok\n";
}
```

Of course, typing in your own password to whoever asks for it is unwise.

Shadow password files are slightly more secure than traditional password files, and you might have to be a superuser to access them. Because few programs should run under such powerful privileges, you might have the program maintain its own

---

* Only people with honorable intentions are allowed to do this.

independent authentication system by storing the crypt strings in a different file than */etc/passwd* or */etc/shadow.*

The crypt function is unsuitable for encrypting large quantities of data, not least of all because you can't get the information back. Look at the *by-module/Crypt* and *by-module/PGP* directories on your favorite CPAN mirror for a slew of potentially useful modules.

dbmclose   [S!] [X U]

> dbmclose *HASH*

This function breaks the binding between a DBM (database management) file and a hash. dbmclose is really just a call to untie with the proper arguments, but is provided for backward compatibility with ancient versions of Perl.

dbmopen   [S!] [X U]

> dbmopen *HASH, DBNAME, MODE*

This binds a DBM file to a hash (that is, an associative array). (DBM stands for database management, and consists of a set of C library routines that allow random access to records via a hashing algorithm.) *HASH* is the name of the hash (including the %). *DBNAME* is the name of the database (without any *.dir* or *.pag* extension). If the database does not exist and a valid *MODE* is specified, the database is created with the protection specified by *MODE*, as modified by the umask. To prevent creation of the database if it doesn't exist, you may specify a *MODE* of undef, and the function will return false if it can't find an existing database. Values assigned to the hash prior to the dbmopen are not accessible.

The dbmopen function is really just a call to tie with the proper arguments, but is provided for backward compatibility with ancient versions of Perl. You can control which DBM library you use by using the tie interface directly or by loading the appropriate module before you call dbmopen. Here's an example that works on some systems for versions of DB_File similar to the version in your Netscape browser:

```
use DB_File;
dbmopen(%NS_Hist, "$ENV{HOME}/.netscape/history.dat", undef)
    or die "Can't open netscape history file: $!";

while (($url, $when) = each %NS_Hist) {
    next unless defined($when);
    chop ($url, $when);           # kill trailing null bytes
    printf "Visited %s at %s.\n", $url,
        scalar(localtime(unpack("V",$when)));
}
```

If you don't have write access to the DBM file, you can only read the hash variables, not set them. If you want to test whether you can write, either use a file test like `-w $file`, or try setting a dummy hash entry inside an `eval {}`, which will trap the exception.

Functions such as `keys` and `values` may return huge list values when used on large DBM files. You may prefer to use the `each` function to iterate over large DBM files so that you don't load the whole thing in memory at once.

Hashes bound to DBM files have the same limitations as the type of DBM package you're using, including restrictions on how much data you can put into a bucket. If you stick to short keys and values, it's rarely a problem. See also the `DB_File` module in Chapter 32.

Another thing you should bear in mind is that many existing DBM databases contain null-terminated keys and values because they were set up with C programs in mind. The Netscape history file and the old *sendmail* aliases file are examples. Just use `"$key\0"` when pulling out a value, and remove the null from the value.

```
$alias = $aliases{"postmaster\0"};
chop $alias;   # kill the null
```

There is currently no built-in way to lock a generic DBM file. Some would consider this a bug. The `GDBM_File` module does attempt to provide locking at the granularity of the entire file. When in doubt, your best bet is to use a separate lock file.

defined

```
defined EXPR
defined
```

This function returns a Boolean value saying whether *EXPR* has a defined value or not. Most of the data you deal with is defined, but a scalar that contains no valid string, numeric, or reference value is said to contain the undefined value, or `undef` for short. Initializing a scalar variable to a particular value will define it, and it will stay defined until you assign an undefined value to it or explicitly call the `undef` function on that variable.

Many operations return `undef` under exceptional conditions, such as at end-of-file, when using an uninitialized variable's value, an operating system error, etc. Since `undef` is just one kind of false value, a simple Boolean test does not distinguish between `undef`, numeric zero, the null string, and the one-character string, "0"—all of which are equally false. The `defined` function allows you to distinguish between an undefined null string and a defined null string when you're using operators that might return a real null string.

Here is a fragment that tests a scalar value from a hash:

```
print if defined $switch{D};
```

When used on a hash element like this, `defined` only tells you whether the value is defined, not whether the key has an entry in the hash. It's possible to have a key whose value is undefined; the key itself however still exists. Use `exists` to determine whether the hash key exists.

In the next example we exploit the convention that some operations return the undefined value when you run out of data:

```
print "$val\n" while defined($val = pop(@ary));
```

And in this one, we do the same thing with the `getpwent` function for retrieving information about the system's users.

```
setpwent();
while (defined($name = getpwent())) {
    print "<<$name>>\n";
}
endpwent();
```

The same thing goes for error returns from syscalls that could validly return a false value:

```
die "Can't readlink $sym: $!"
    unless defined($value = readlink $sym);
```

You may also use `defined` to see whether a subroutine has been defined yet. This makes it possible to avoid blowing up on nonexistent subroutines (or subroutines that have been declared but never given a definition):

```
indir("funcname", @arglist);
sub indir {
    my $subname = shift;
    no strict 'refs';  # so we can use subname indirectly
    if (defined &$subname) {
        &$subname(@_);    # or $subname->(@_);
    }
    else {
        warn "Ignoring call to invalid function $subname";
    }
}
```

Use of `defined` on aggregates (hashes and arrays) is deprecated. (It used to report whether memory for that aggregate had ever been allocated.) Instead, use a simple Boolean test to see whether the array or hash has any elements:

```
if (@an_array) { print "has array elements\n" }
if (%a_hash)   { print "has hash members\n"   }
```

See also `undef` and `exists`.

delete

```
delete EXPR
```

This function deletes an element (or a slice of elements) from the specified hash or array. (See unlink if you want to delete a file.) The deleted elements are returned in the order specified, though this behavior is not guaranteed for tied variables such as DBM files. After the delete operation, the exists function will return false on any deleted key or index. (In contrast, after the undef function, the exists function continues to return true, because the undef function only undefines the value of the element, but doesn't delete the element itself.)

Deleting from the %ENV hash modifies the environment. Deleting from a hash that is bound to a (writable) DBM file deletes the entry from that DBM file.

Historically, you could only delete from a hash, but with Perl version 5.6 you may also delete from an array. Deleting from an array causes the element at the specified position to revert to a completely uninitialized state, but it doesn't close up the gap, since that would change the positions of all the subsequent entries. Use a splice for that. (However, if you delete the final element in an array, the array size will shrink by one (or more, depending on the position of the next largest existing element (if any))).

EXPR can be arbitrarily complicated, provided that the final operation is a hash or array lookup:

```
# set up array of array of hash
$dungeon[$x][$y] = \%properties;

# delete one property from hash
delete $dungeon[$x][$y]{"OCCUPIED"};

# delete three properties all at once from hash
delete @{ $dungeon[$x][$y] }{ "OCCUPIED", "DAMP", "LIGHTED" };

# delete reference to %properties from array
delete $dungeon[$x][$y];
```

The following naïve example inefficiently deletes all the values of a %hash:

```
foreach $key (keys %hash) {
    delete $hash{$key};
}
```

And so does this:

```
delete @hash{keys %hash};
```

Functions

But both of these are slower than just assigning the empty list or undefining it:

```
%hash = ();         # completely empty %hash
undef %hash;        # forget %hash ever existed
```

Likewise for arrays:

```
foreach $index (0 .. $#array) {
    delete $array[$index];
}
```

and:

```
delete @array[0 .. $#array];
```

are less efficient than either of:

```
@array = ();        # completely empty @array
undef @array;       # forget @array ever existed
```

die $@

```
die LIST
die
```

Outside an `eval`, this function prints the concatenated value of *LIST* to STDERR and exits with the current value of `$!` (the C-library `errno` variable). If `$!` is 0, it exits with the value of `$? >> 8` (which is the status of the last reaped child from a system, wait, close on a pipe, or `command`). If `$? >> 8` is 0, it exits with 255.

Within an `eval`, the function sets the `$@` variable to the error message that would have otherwise been produced, then aborts the `eval`, which returns `undef`. The `die` function can thus be used to raise named exceptions that can be caught at a higher level in the program. See `eval` later in this chapter.

If *LIST* is a single object reference, that object is assumed to be an exception object and is returned unmodified as the exception in `$@`.

If *LIST* is empty and `$@` already contains a string value (typically from a previous `eval`) that value is reused after appending `"\t...propagated"`. This is useful for propagating (reraising) exceptions:

```
eval { ... };
die unless $@ =~ /Expected exception/;
```

If *LIST* is empty and `$@` already contains an exception object, the `$@->PROPAGATE` method is called to determine how the exception should be propagated.

If *LIST* is empty and `$@` is empty, then the string `"Died"` is used.

If the final value of *LIST* does not end in a newline (and you're not passing an exception object), the current script filename, line number, and input line number (if any) are appended to the message, as well as a newline. Hint: sometimes appending ", stopped" to your message will cause it to make better sense when the string "at scriptname line 123" is appended. Suppose you are running script *canasta*; consider the difference between the following two ways of dying:

```
die "/usr/games is no good";
die "/usr/games is no good, stopped";
```

which produce, respectively:

```
/usr/games is no good at canasta line 123.
/usr/games is no good, stopped at canasta line 123.
```

If you want your own error messages reporting the filename and line number, use the __FILE__ and __LINE__ special tokens:

```
die '"', __FILE__, '", line ', __LINE__, ", phooey on you!\n";
```

This produces output like:

```
"canasta", line 38, phooey on you!
```

One other style issue—consider the following equivalent examples:

```
die "Can't cd to spool: $!\n"    unless chdir '/usr/spool/news';

chdir '/usr/spool/news'          or die "Can't cd to spool: $!\n"
```

Because the important part is the chdir, the second form is generally preferred.

See also exit, warn, %SIG, and the Carp module.

do (block)

```
do BLOCK
```

The do *BLOCK* form executes the sequence of statements in the *BLOCK* and returns the value of the last expression evaluated in the block. When modified by a while or until statement modifier, Perl executes the *BLOCK* once before testing the loop condition. (On other statements the loop modifiers test the conditional first.) The do *BLOCK* itself does *not* count as a loop, so the loop control statements next, last, or redo cannot be used to leave or restart the block. See the section "Bare Blocks" in Chapter 4, *Statements and Declarations*, for workarounds.

do (file)   [S!] [T] [X/T]

```
do FILE
```

The do *FILE* form uses the value of *FILE* as a filename and executes the contents of the file as a Perl script. Its primary use is (or rather was) to include subroutines from a Perl subroutine library, so that:

```
do 'stat.pl';
```

is rather like:

```
scalar eval `cat stat.pl`;   # `type stat.pl` on Windows
```

except that do is more efficient, more concise, keeps track of the current filename for error messages, searches all the directories listed in the @INC array, and updates %INC if the file is found. (See Chapter 28, *Special Names.*) It also differs in that code evaluated with do *FILE* cannot see lexicals in the enclosing scope, whereas code in eval *FILE* does. It's the same, however, in that it reparses the file every time you call it—so you might not want to do this inside a loop unless the filename itself changes at each loop iteration.

If do can't read the file, it returns undef and sets $! to the error. If do can read the file but can't compile it, it returns undef and sets an error message in $@. If the file is successfully compiled, do returns the value of the last expression evaluated.

Inclusion of library modules (which have a mandatory *.pm* suffix) is better done with the use and require operators, which also do error checking and raise an exception if there's a problem. They also offer other benefits: they avoid duplicate loading, help with object-oriented programming, and provide hints to the compiler on function prototypes.

But do *FILE* is still useful for such things as reading program configuration files. Manual error checking can be done this way:

```
# read in config files: system first, then user
for $file ("/usr/share/proggie/defaults.rc",
          "$ENV{HOME}/.someprogrc")
{
    unless ($return = do $file) {
        warn "couldn't parse $file: $@" if $@;
        warn "couldn't do $file: $!"    unless defined $return;
        warn "couldn't run $file"       unless $return;
    }
}
```

A long-running daemon could periodically examine the timestamp on its configuration file, and if the file has changed since it was last read in, the daemon could use do to reload that file. This is more tidily accomplished with do than with require or use.

do (subroutine) $s@$

```
do SUBROUTINE(LIST)
```

The do *SUBROUTINE(LIST)* is a deprecated form of a subroutine call. An exception is raised if the *SUBROUTINE* is undefined. See Chapter 6, *Subroutines*.

dump

```
dump LABEL
dump
```

This function causes an immediate core dump. Primarily this is so that you can use the *undump* program (not supplied) to turn your core dump into an executable binary after having initialized all your variables at the beginning of the program. When the new binary is executed it will begin by executing a goto LABEL (with all the restrictions that goto suffers). Think of it as a goto with an intervening core dump and reincarnation. If *LABEL* is omitted, the program is restarted from the top. Warning: any files opened at the time of the dump will *not* be open any more when the program is reincarnated, with possible resulting confusion on the part of Perl. See also the **-u** command-line option in Chapter 19, *The Command-Line Interface*.

This function is now largely obsolete, partly because it's difficult in the extreme to convert a core file into an executable in the general case, and because various compiler backends for generating portable bytecode and compilable C code have superseded it.

If you're looking to use dump to speed up your program, check out the discussion of efficiency matters in Chapter 24, *Common Practices*, as well the Perl native-code generator in Chapter 18, *Compiling*. You might also consider autoloading or self-loading, which at least make your program *appear* to run faster.

each

```
each HASH
```

This function steps through a hash one key/value pair at a time. When called in list context, each returns a two-element list consisting of the key and value for the next element of a hash, so that you can iterate over it. When called in scalar context, each returns just the key for the next element in the hash. When the hash is entirely read, the empty list is returned, which when assigned produces a false value in scalar context, such as a loop test. The next call to each after that will start iterating again. The typical use is as follows, using predefined %ENV hash:

```
while (($key,$value) = each %ENV) {
    print "$key=$value\n";
}
```

Internally, a hash maintains its own entries in an apparently random order. The each function iterates through this sequence because every hash remembers which entry was last returned. The actual ordering of this sequence is subject to change in future versions of Perl, but is guaranteed to be in the same order as the keys (or values) function would produce on the same (unmodified) hash.

There is a single iterator for each hash, shared by all each, keys, and values function calls in the program; it can be reset by reading all the elements from the hash, or by evaluating keys %hash or values %hash. If you add or delete elements of a hash while you're iterating over it, the resulting behavior is not well-defined: entries might get skipped or duplicated.

See also keys, values, and sort.

eof

```
eof FILEHANDLE
eof()
eof
```

This function returns true if the next read on *FILEHANDLE* would return end-of-file, or if *FILEHANDLE* is not open. *FILEHANDLE* may be an expression whose value gives the real filehandle, or a reference to a filehandle object of some sort. An eof without an argument returns the end-of-file status for the last file read. An eof() with empty parentheses () tests the ARGV filehandle (most commonly seen as the null filehandle in <>). Therefore, inside a while (<>) loop, an eof() with parentheses will detect the end of only the last of a group of files. Use eof (without the parentheses) to test *each* file in a while (<>) loop. For example, the following code inserts dashes just before the last line of the *last* file:

```
while (<>) {
    if (eof()) {
        print "-" x 30, "\n";
    }
    print;
}
```

On the other hand, this script resets line numbering on *each* input file:

```
# reset line numbering on each input file
while (<>) {
    next if /^\s*#/;        # skip comments
    print "$.\t$_";
} continue {
    close ARGV if eof;      # Not eof()!
}
```

Like "$" in a *sed* program, eof tends to show up in line number ranges. Here's a script that prints lines from /pattern/ to end of each input file:

```
while (<>) {
    print if /pattern/ .. eof;
}
```

Here, the flip-flop operator (..) evaluates the pattern match for each line. Until the pattern matches, the operator returns false. When it finally matches, the operator starts returning true, causing the lines to be printed. When the eof operator finally returns true (at the end of the file being examined), the flip-flop operator resets, and starts returning false again for the next file in @ARGV.

Warning: The eof function reads a byte and then pushes it back on the input stream with *ungetc*(3), so it is not useful in an interactive context. In fact, experienced Perl programmers rarely use eof, since the various input operators already behave politely in while-loop conditionals. See the example in the description of foreach in Chapter 4.

eval

```
eval BLOCK
eval EXPR
eval
```

The eval keyword serves two distinct but related purposes in Perl. These purposes are represented by two forms of syntax, eval *BLOCK* and eval *EXPR*. The first form traps run-time exceptions (errors) that would otherwise prove fatal, similar to the "try block" construct in C++ or Java. The second form compiles and executes little bits of code on the fly at run time, and also (conveniently) traps any exceptions just like the first form. But the second form runs much slower than the first form, since it must parse the string every time. On the other hand, it is also more general. Whichever form you use, eval is the preferred way to do all exception handling in Perl.

For either form of eval, the value returned from an eval is the value of the last expression evaluated, just as with subroutines. Similarly, you may use the return operator to return a value from the middle of the eval. The expression providing the return value is evaluated in void, scalar, or list context, depending on the context of the eval itself. See wantarray for more on how the evaluation context can be determined.

If there is a trappable error (including any produced by the die operator), eval returns undef and puts the error message (or object) in $@. If there is no error, $@ is guaranteed to be set to the null string, so you can test it reliably afterward for errors. A simple Boolean test suffices:

```
eval { ... };    # trap run-time errors
if ($@) { ... }    # handle error
```

The eval *BLOCK* form is syntax-checked at compile time, so it is quite efficient. (People familiar with the slow eval *EXPR* form are occasionally confused on this issue.) Since the code in the *BLOCK* is compiled at the same time as the surrounding code, this form of eval cannot trap syntax errors.

The eval *EXPR* form can trap syntax errors because it parses the code at run time. (If the parse is unsuccessful, it places the parse error in $@, as usual.) Otherwise, it executes the value of *EXPR* as though it were a little Perl program. The code is executed in the context of the current Perl program, which means that it can see any enclosing lexicals from a surrounding scope, and that any non-local variable settings remain in effect after the eval is complete, as do any subroutine or format definitions. The code of the eval is treated as a block, so any locally scoped variables declared within the eval last only until the eval is done. (See my and local.) As with any code in a block, a final semicolon is not required.

Here is a simple Perl shell. It prompts the user to enter a string of arbitrary Perl code, compiles and executes that string, and prints whatever error occurred:

```
print "\nEnter some Perl code: ";

while (<STDIN>) {
    eval;
    print $@;
    print "\nEnter some more Perl code: ";
}
```

Here is a *rename* program to do a mass renaming of files using a Perl expression:

```
#!/usr/bin/perl
# rename - change filenames
$op = shift;
for (@ARGV) {
    $was = $_;
    eval $op;
    die if $@;
    # next line calls the built-in function, not the script by the same name
    rename($was,$_) unless $was eq $_;
}
```

You'd use that program like this:

```
$ rename 's/\.orig$//'           *.orig
$ rename 'y/A-Z/a-z/ unless /^Make/'    *
$ rename '$_ .= ".bad"'          *.f
```

Since eval traps errors that would otherwise prove fatal, it is useful for determining whether particular features (such as fork or symlink) are implemented.

Because `eval` *BLOCK* is syntax-checked at compile time, any syntax error is reported earlier. Therefore, if your code is invariant and both `eval` *EXPR* and `eval` *BLOCK* will suit your purposes equally well, the *BLOCK* form is preferred. For example:

```
# make divide-by-zero nonfatal
eval { $answer = $a / $b; };     warn $@ if $@;

# same thing, but less efficient if run multiple times
eval '$answer = $a / $b';        warn $@ if $@;

# a compile-time syntax error (not trapped)
eval { $answer = };              # WRONG

# a run-time syntax error
eval '$answer =';                # sets $@
```

Here, the code in the *BLOCK* has to be valid Perl code to make it past the compile phase. The code in the *EXPR* doesn't get examined until run time, so it doesn't cause an error until run time.

The block of `eval` *BLOCK* does *not* count as a loop, so the loop control statements `next`, `last`, or `redo` cannot be used to leave or restart the block.

exec

```
exec PATHNAME LIST
exec LIST
```

The `exec` function terminates the current program and executes an external command *and never returns!!!* Use `system` instead of `exec` if you want to recover control after the commands exits. The `exec` function fails and returns false only if the command does not exist *and* if it is executed directly instead of via your system's command shell (discussed below).

If there is only one scalar argument, the argument is checked for shell metacharacters. If metacharacters are found, the entire argument is passed to the system's standard command interpreter (*/bin/sh* under Unix). If there are no metacharacters, the argument is split into words and executed directly, since in the interests of efficiency this bypasses all the overhead of shell processing. It also gives you more control of error recovery should the program not exist.

If there is more than one argument in *LIST*, or if *LIST* is an array with more than one value, the system shell will never be used. This also bypasses any shell processing of the command. The presence or absence of metacharacters in the arguments doesn't affect this list-triggered behavior, which makes it the preferred form in security-conscious programs that do not wish to expose themselves to potential shell escapes.

This example causes the currently running Perl program to replace itself with the
echo program, which then prints out the current argument list:

```
exec 'echo', 'Your arguments are: ', @ARGV;
```

This example shows that you can exec a pipeline, not just a single program.

```
exec "sort $outfile | uniq"
    or die "Can't do sort/uniq: $!\n";
```

Ordinarily, exec never returns—if it does return, it always returns false, and you
should check $! to find out what went wrong. Be aware that in older releases of
Perl, exec (and system) did not flush your output buffer, so you needed to enable
command buffering by setting $| on one or more filehandles to avoid lost output
in the case of exec, or misordered output in the case of system. This situation was
largely remedied in the 5.6 release of Perl.

When you ask the operating system to execute a new program within an existing
process (as Perl's exec function does), you tell the system the location of the program to execute, but you also tell the new program (through its first argument) the
name under which the program was invoked. Customarily, the name you tell it is
just a copy of the location of the program, but it doesn't necessarily have to be,
since there are two separate arguments at the level of the C language. When it is
not a copy, you have the odd result that the new program thinks it's running
under a name that may be totally different from the actual pathname where the
program resides. Often this doesn't matter to the program in question, but some
programs do care and adopt a different persona depending on what they think
their name is. For example, the *vi* editor looks to see whether it was called as "vi"
or as "view". If invoked as "view", it automatically enables read-only mode, just as
though it was called with the **-R** command-line option.

This is where exec's optional *PATHNAME* parameter comes into play. Syntactically, it
goes in the indirect-object slot like the filehandle for print or printf. Therefore, it
doesn't take a comma after it, because it's not exactly part of the argument list. (In
a sense, Perl takes the opposite approach from the operating system in that it
assumes the first argument is the important one, and lets you modify the pathname
if it differs.) For example:

```
$editor = "/usr/bin/vi";
exec $editor "view", @files      # trigger read-only mode
    or die "Couldn't execute $editor: $!\n";
```

As with any other indirect object, you can also replace the simple scalar holding
the program name with a block containing arbitrary code, which simplifies the
previous example to:

```
exec { "/usr/bin/vi" } "view", @files      # trigger read-only mode
    or die "Couldn't execute /usr/bin/vi: $!\n";
```

As we mentioned earlier, **exec** treats a discrete list of arguments as an indication that it should bypass shell processing. However, there is one place where you might still get tripped up. The **exec** call (and **system**, too) will not distinguish between a single scalar argument and an array containing only one element.

```
@args = ("echo surprise");   # just one element in list
exec @args                   # still subject to shell escapes
    or die "exec: $!";       #   because @args == 1
```

To avoid this, you can use the *PATHNAME* syntax, explicitly duplicating the first argument as the pathname, which forces the rest of the arguments to be interpreted as a list, even if there is only one of them:

```
exec { $args[0] } @args   # safe even with one-argument list
    or die "can't exec @args: $!";
```

The first version, the one without the curlies, runs the *echo* program, passing it "**surprise**" as an argument. The second version doesn't—it tries to run a program literally called *echo surprise*, doesn't find it (we hope), and sets $! to a nonzero value indicating failure.

Because the **exec** function is most often used shortly after a **fork**, it is assumed that anything that normally happens when a Perl process terminates should be skipped. Upon an **exec**, Perl will not call your **END** blocks, nor will it call any **DESTROY** methods associated with any objects. Otherwise, your child process would end up doing the cleanup you expected the parent process to do. (We wish that were the case in real life.)

Because it's such a common mistake to use **exec** instead of **system**, Perl warns you if there is a following statement that isn't **die**, **warn**, or **exit** when run with the popular **-w** command-line option, or if you've used the **use warnings qw(exec syntax)** pragma. If you really want to follow an **exec** with some other statement, you can use either of these styles to avoid the warning:

```
exec ('foo')   or print STDERR "couldn't exec foo: $!";
{ exec ('foo') }; print STDERR "couldn't exec foo: $!";
```

As the second line above shows, a call to **exec** that is the last statement in a block is exempt from this warning.

See also **system**.

exists

> exists *EXPR*

This function returns true if the specified hash key or array index exists in its hash
or array. It doesn't matter whether the corresponding value is true or false, or
whether the value is even defined.

```
print "True\n"      if          $hash{$key};
print "Defined\n"   if defined $hash{$key};
print "Exists\n"    if exists  $hash{$key};

print "True\n"      if          $array[$index];
print "Defined\n"   if defined $array[$index];
print "Exists\n"    if exists  $array[$index];
```

An element can be true only if it's defined, and can be defined only if it exists, but
the reverse doesn't necessarily hold.

EXPR can be arbitrarily complicated, provided that the final operation is a hash key
or array index lookup:

```
if (exists $hash{A}{B}{$key}) { ... }
```

Although the last element will not spring into existence just because its existence
was tested, intervening ones will. Thus $$hash{"A"} and $hash{"A"}->{"B"} will
both spring into existence. This is not a function of exists, *per se*; it happens any-
where the arrow operator is used (explicitly or implicitly):

```
undef $ref;
if (exists $ref->{"Some key"}) { }
print $ref;    # prints HASH(0x80d3d5c)
```

Even though the "Some key" element didn't spring into existence, the previously
undefined $ref variable did suddenly come to hold an anonymous hash. This is a
surprising instance of *autovivification* in what does not at first—or even second—
glance appear to be an lvalue context. This behavior is likely to be fixed in a
future release. As a workaround, you can nest your calls:

```
if ($ref                             and
    exists $ref->[$x]                and
    exists $ref->[$x][$y]            and
    exists $ref->[$x][$y]{$key} and
    exists $ref->[$x][$y]{$key}[2] ) { ... }
```

If *EXPR* is the name of a subroutine, the exists function will return true if that sub-
routine has been declared, even if it has not yet been defined. The following will
just print "Exists":

```
sub flub;
print "Exists\n"      if exists &flub;
print "Defined\n"     if defined &flub;
```

Using exists on a subroutine name can be useful for an AUTOLOAD subroutine that needs to know whether a particular package wants a particular subroutine to be defined. The package can indicate this by declaring a stub sub like flub.

exit

```
exit EXPR
exit
```

This function evaluates EXPR as an integer and exits immediately with that value as the final error status of the program. If EXPR is omitted, the function exits with 0 status (meaning "no error"). Here's a fragment that lets a user exit the program by typing x or X:

```
$ans = <STDIN>;
exit if $ans =~ /^[Xx]/;
```

You shouldn't use exit to abort a subroutine if there's any chance that someone might want to trap whatever error happened. Use die instead, which can be trapped by an eval. Or use one of die's wrappers from the Carp module, like croak or confess.

We said that the exit function exits immediately, but that was a bald-faced lie. It exits as soon as possible, but first it calls any defined END routines for at-exit handling. These routines cannot abort the exit, although they can change the eventual exit value by setting the $? variable. Likewise, any class that defines a DESTROY method will invoke that method on behalf of all its objects before the real program exits. If you really need to bypass exit processing, you can call the POSIX module's _exit function to avoid all END and destructor processing. And if POSIX isn't available, you can exec "/bin/false" or some such.

exp

```
exp EXPR
exp
```

This function returns *e* to the power of EXPR. To get the value of *e*, just use exp(1). For general exponentiation of different bases, use the ** operator we stole from FORTRAN:

```
use Math::Complex;
print -exp(1) ** (i * pi);    # prints 1
```

fcntl

> fcntl *FILEHANDLE, FUNCTION, SCALAR*

This function calls your operating system's file control functions, as documented in the *fcntl*(2) manpage. Before you call fcntl, you'll probably first have to say:

```
use Fcntl;
```

to load the correct constant definitions.

SCALAR will be read or written (or both) depending on the *FUNCTION*. A pointer to the string value of *SCALAR* will be passed as the third argument of the actual *fcntl* call. (If *SCALAR* has no string value but does have a numeric value, that value will be passed directly rather than passing a pointer to the string value.) See the Fcntl module for a description of the more common permissible values for *FUNCTION*.

The fcntl function will raise an exception if used on a system that doesn't implement *fcntl*(2). On systems that do implement it, you can do such things as modify the close-on-exec flags (if you don't want to play with the $^F ($SYSTEM_FD_MAX) variable), modify the nonblocking I/O flags, emulate the *lockf*(3) function, and arrange to receive the SIGIO signal when I/O is pending.

Here's an example of setting a filehandle named REMOTE to be nonblocking at the system level. This makes any input operation return immediately if nothing is available when reading from a pipe, socket, or serial line that would otherwise block. It also works to cause output operations that normally would block to return a failure status instead. (For those, you'll likely have to negotiate $| as well.)

```
use Fcntl qw(F_GETFL F_SETFL O_NONBLOCK);

$flags = fcntl(REMOTE, F_GETFL, 0)
            or die "Can't get flags for the socket: $!\n";

$flags = fcntl(REMOTE, F_SETFL, $flags | O_NONBLOCK)
            or die "Can't set flags for the socket: $!\n";
```

The return value of fcntl (and ioctl) is as follows:

Syscall Returns	Perl Returns
-1	undef
0	String "0 but true"
anything else	That number

Thus Perl returns true on success and false on failure, yet you can still easily determine the actual value returned by the operating system:

```
$retval = fcntl(...) || -1;
printf "fcntl actually returned %d\n", $retval;
```

Here, even the string "0 but true" prints as 0, thanks to the %d format. This string is true in Boolean context and 0 in numeric context. (It is also happily exempt from the normal warnings on improper numeric conversions.)

fileno X ARG

```
fileno FILEHANDLE
```

This function returns the file descriptor underlying a filehandle. If the filehandle is not open, fileno returns undef. A *file descriptor* is a small, non-negative integer like 0 or 1, in contrast to filehandles like STDIN and STDOUT, which are symbols. Unfortunately, the operating system doesn't know about your cool symbols. It only thinks of open files in terms of these small file numbers, and although Perl will usually do the translations for you automatically, occasionally you have to know the actual file descriptor.

So, for example, the fileno function is useful for constructing bitmaps for select and for passing to certain obscure system calls if *syscall*(2) is implemented. It's also useful for double-checking that the open function gave you the file descriptor you wanted and for determining whether two filehandles use the same system file descriptor.

```
if (fileno(THIS) == fileno(THAT)) {
    print "THIS and THAT are dups\n";
}
```

If FILEHANDLE is an expression, the value is taken as an indirect filehandle, generally its name or a reference to something resembling a filehandle object.

One caution: don't count on the association of a Perl filehandle and a numeric file descriptor throughout the life of the program. If a file has been closed and reopened, the file descriptor may change. Perl takes a bit of trouble to try to ensure that certain file descriptors won't be lost if an open on them fails, but it only does this for file descriptors that don't exceed the current value of the special $^F ($SYSTEM_FD_MAX) variable (by default, 2). Although filehandles STDIN, STDOUT, and STDERR start out with file descriptors of 0, 1, and 2 (the Unix standard convention), even they can change if you start closing and opening them with wild abandon. You can't get into trouble with 0, 1, and 2 as long as you always reopen immediately after closing. The basic rule on Unix systems is to pick the lowest available descriptor, and that'll be the one you just closed.

Functions

flock

```
flock FILEHANDLE, OPERATION
```

The flock function is Perl's portable file-locking interface, although it locks only entire files, not records. The function manages locks on the file associated with *FILEHANDLE*, returning true for success and false otherwise. To avoid the possibility of lost data, Perl flushes your *FILEHANDLE* before locking or unlocking it. Perl might implement its flock in terms of *flock*(2), *fcntl*(2), *lockf*(3), or some other platform-specific lock mechanism, but if none of these is available, calling flock raises an exception. See the section "File Locking" in Chapter 16.

OPERATION is one of LOCK_SH, LOCK_EX, or LOCK_UN, possibly ORed with LOCK_NB. These constants are traditionally valued 1, 2, 8, and 4, but you can use the symbolic names if you import them from the Fcntl module, either individually or as a group using the :flock tag.

LOCK_SH requests a shared lock, so it's typically used for reading. LOCK_EX requests an exclusive lock, so it's typically used for writing. LOCK_UN releases a previously requested lock; closing the file also releases any locks. If the LOCK_NB bit is used with LOCK_SH or LOCK_EX, flock returns immediately rather than waiting for an unavailable lock. Check the return status to see whether you got the lock you asked for. If you don't use LOCK_NB, you might wait indefinitely for the lock to be granted.

Another nonobvious but traditional aspect of flock is that its locks are *merely advisory*. Discretionary locks are more flexible but offer fewer guarantees than mandatory ones. This means that files locked with flock may be modified by programs that do not also use flock. Cars that stop for red lights get on well with each other, but not with cars that don't stop for red lights. Drive defensively.

Some implementations of flock cannot lock things over the network. While you could in theory use the more system-specific fcntl for that, the jury (having sequestered itself on the case for a decade or so) is still out on whether this is (or even can be) reliable.

Here's a mailbox appender for Unix systems that use *flock*(2) to lock mailboxes:

```perl
use Fcntl qw/:flock/;        # import LOCK_* constants
sub mylock {
    flock(MBOX, LOCK_EX)
        or die "can't lock mailbox: $!";
    # in case someone appended while we were waiting
    # and our stdio buffer is out of sync
    seek(MBOX, 0, 2)
        or die "can't seek to the end of mailbox: $!";
}
```

```
open(MBOX, ">>/usr/spool/mail/$ENV{'USER'}")
    or die "can't open mailbox: $!";

mylock();
print MBOX $msg, "\n\n";
close MBOX
    or die "can't close mailbox: $!";
```

On systems that support a real *flock*(2) syscall, locks are inherited across `fork` calls. Other implementations are not so lucky, and are likely to lose the locks across forks. See also the section on "File Locking" in Chapter 16 for other `flock` examples.

fork

```
fork
```

This function creates two processes out of one by invoking the *fork*(2) syscall. If it succeeds, the function returns the new child process's ID to the parent process and 0 to the child process. If the system doesn't have sufficient resources to allocate a new process, the call fails and returns `undef`. File descriptors (and sometimes locks on those descriptors) are shared, while everything else is copied—or at least made to look that way.

In versions of Perl prior to 5.6, unflushed buffers remain unflushed in both processes, which means you may need to set $| on one or more filehandles earlier in the program to avoid duplicate output.

A nearly bulletproof way to launch a child process while checking for "cannot fork" errors would be:

```
use Errno qw(EAGAIN);
FORK: {
    if ($pid = fork) {
        # parent here
        # child process pid is available in $pid
    }
    elsif (defined $pid) { # $pid is zero here if defined
        # child here
        # parent process pid is available with getppid
    }
    elsif ($! == EAGAIN) {
        # EAGAIN is the supposedly recoverable fork error
        sleep 5;
        redo FORK;
    }
    else {
        # weird fork error
        die "Can't fork: $!\n";
    }
}
```

These precautions are not necessary on operations that do an implicit *fork*(2), such as system, backticks, or opening a process as a filehandle, because Perl automatically retries a fork on a temporary failure when it's doing the fork for you. Be careful to end the child code with an exit, or else your child will inadvertently leave the conditional block and start executing code intended only for the parent process.

If you fork without ever waiting on your children, you will accumulate zombies (exited processes whose parents haven't waited on them yet). On some systems, you can avoid this by setting $SIG{CHLD} to "IGNORE"; on most, you must wait for your moribund children. See the wait function for examples of doing this, or see the "Signals" section of Chapter 16 for more on SIGCHLD.

If a forked child inherits system file descriptors like STDIN and STDOUT that are connected to a remote pipe or socket, you may have to reopen these in the child to */dev/null*. That's because even when the parent process exits, the child will live on with its copies of those filehandles. The remote server (such as, say, a CGI script or a background job launched from a remote shell) will appear to hang because it's still waiting for all copies to be closed. Reopening the system filehandles to something else fixes this.

On most systems supporting *fork*(2), great care has gone into making it extremely efficient (for example, using copy-on-write technology on data pages), making it the dominant paradigm for multitasking over the last few decades. The fork function is unlikely to be implemented efficiently, or perhaps at all, on systems that don't resemble Unix. For example, Perl 5.6 emulates a proper fork even on Microsoft systems, but no assurances can be made on performance at this point. You might have more luck there with the Win32::Process module.

format

```
format NAME =
    picture line
    value list
    ...
    .
```

This function declares a named sequence of picture lines (with associated values) for use by the write function. If NAME is omitted, the name defaults to STDOUT, which happens to be the default format name for the STDOUT filehandle. Since, like a sub declaration, this is a package-global declaration that happens at compile time, any variables used in the value list need to be visible at the point of the format's declaration. That is, lexically scoped variables must be declared earlier in the file, while dynamically scoped variables merely need to be set at the time write is called. Here's an example (which assumes we've already calculated $cost and $quantity):

```
my $str = "widget";                # Lexically scoped variable.

format Nice_Output =
Test: @<<<<<<<< @|||||| @>>>>>
      $str,      $%,     '$' . int($num)
.


local $~ = "Nice_Output";          # Select our format.
local $num = $cost * $quantity;    # Dynamically scoped variable.

write;
```

Like filehandles, format names are identifiers that exist in a symbol table (package) and may be fully qualified by package name. Within the typeglobs of a symbol table's entries, formats reside in their own namespace, which is distinct from filehandles, directory handles, scalars, arrays, hashes, and subroutines. Like those other six types, however, a format named Whatever would also be affected by a local on the *Whatever typeglob. In other words, a format is just another gadget contained in a typeglob, independent of the other gadgets.

The "Format Variables" section in Chapter 7, *Formats* contains numerous details and examples of their use. Chapter 28 describes the internal format-specific variables, and the English and IO::Handle modules provide easier access to them.

formline

```
formline PICTURE, LIST
```

This is an internal function used by formats, although you may also call it yourself. It always returns true. It formats a list of values according to the contents of *PICTURE*, placing the output into the format output accumulator, $^A (or $ACCUMULATOR if you use the English module). Eventually, when a write is done, the contents of $^A are written to some filehandle, but you could also read $^A yourself and then set $^A back to "". A format typically does one formline per line of form, but the formline function itself doesn't care how many newlines are embedded in the *PICTURE*. This means that the ~ and ~~ tokens will treat the entire *PICTURE* as a single line. You may therefore need to use multiple formlines to implement a single record-format, just as the format compiler does internally.

Be careful if you put double quotes around the picture, since an @ character may be taken to mean the beginning of an array name. See "Formats" in Chapter 6 for example uses.

getc

```
getc FILEHANDLE
getc
```

This function returns the next byte from the input file attached to *FILEHANDLE*. It returns undef at end-of-file, or if an I/O error was encountered. If *FILEHANDLE* is omitted, the function reads from STDIN.

This function is somewhat slow, but occasionally useful for single-character (byte, really) input from the keyboard—provided you manage to get your keyboard input unbuffered. This function requests unbuffered input from the standard I/O library. Unfortunately, the standard I/O library is not so standard as to provide a portable way to tell the underlying operating system to supply unbuffered keyboard input to the standard I/O system. To do that, you have to be slightly more clever, and in an operating-system-dependent fashion. Under Unix you might say this:

```
if ($BSD_STYLE) {
  system "stty cbreak </dev/tty >/dev/tty 2>&1";
} else {
  system "stty", "-icanon", "eol", " ......";
}

$key = getc;

if ($BSD_STYLE) {
  system "stty -cbreak </dev/tty >/dev/tty 2>&1";
} else {
  system "stty", "icanon", "eol", "^@"; # ASCII NUL
}
print "\n";
```

This code puts the next character (byte) typed on the terminal in the string $key. If your *stty* program has options like cbreak, you'll need to use the code where $BSD_STYLE is true. Otherwise, you'll need to use the code where it is false. Determining the options for *stty*(1) is left as an exercise to the reader.

The POSIX module provides a more portable version of this using the POSIX::getattr function. See also the Term::ReadKey module from your nearest CPAN site for a more portable and flexible approach.

getgrent

[X U]

```
getgrent
setgrent
endgrent
```

These routines iterate through your */etc/group* file (or maybe someone else's */etc/group* file, if it's coming from a server somewhere). The return value from getgrent in list context is:

```
($name, $passwd, $gid, $members)
```

where $members contains a space-separated list of the login names of the members of the group. To set up a hash for translating group names to GIDs, say this:

```
while (($name, $passwd, $gid) = getgrent) {
    $gid{$name} = $gid;
}
```

In scalar context, getgrent returns only the group name. The standard User::grent module supports a by-name interface to this function. See *getgrent*(3).

getgrgid

[X U]

```
getgrgid GID
```

This function looks up a group file entry by group number. The return value in list context is:

```
($name, $passwd, $gid, $members)
```

where $members contains a space-separated list of the login names of the members of the group. If you want to do this repeatedly, consider caching the data in a hash using getgrent.

In scalar context, getgrgid returns only the group name. The User::grent module supports a by-name interface to this function. See *getgrgid*(3).

getgrnam

[X U]

```
getgrnam NAME
```

This function looks up a group file entry by group name. The return value in list context is:

```
($name, $passwd, $gid, $members)
```

where $members contains a space-separated list of the login names of the members of the group. If you want to do this repeatedly, consider caching the data in a hash using getgrent.

In scalar context, getgrnam returns only the numeric group ID. The User::grent module supports a by-name interface to this function. See *getgrnam*(3).

gethostbyaddr   ⌈X⌉
                                                                          ⌊U⌋

> gethostbyaddr ADDR, ADDRTYPE

This function translates addresses into names (and alternate addresses). *ADDR* should be a packed binary network address, and *ADDRTYPE* should in practice usually be AF_INET (from the Socket module). The return value in list context is:

```
($name, $aliases, $addrtype, $length, @addrs) =
    gethostbyaddr($packed_binary_address, $addrtype);
```

where @addrs is a list of packed binary addresses. In the Internet domain, each address is (historically) four bytes long, and can be unpacked by saying something like:

```
($a, $b, $c, $d) = unpack('C4', $addrs[0]);
```

Alternatively, you can convert directly to dot vector notation with the v modifier to sprintf:

```
$dots = sprintf "%vd", $addrs[0];
```

The inet_ntoa function from the Socket module is useful for producing a printable version. This approach will become important if and when we all ever manage to switch over to IPv6.

```
use Socket;
$printable_address = inet_ntoa($addrs[0]);
```

In scalar context, gethostbyaddr returns only the host name.

To produce an *ADDR* from a dot vector, say this:

```
use Socket;
$ipaddr = inet_aton("127.0.0.1");        # localhost
$claimed_hostname = gethostbyaddr($ipaddr, AF_INET);
```

Interestingly, with version 5.6 of Perl you can skip the inet_aton() and use the new v-string notation that was invented for version numbers but happens to work for IP addresses as well:

```
$ipaddr = v127.0.0.1;
```

See the section "Sockets" in Chapter 16 for more examples. The Net::hostent module supports a by-name interface to this function. See *gethostbyaddr*(3).

gethostbyname

```
gethostbyname NAME
```

This function translates a network hostname to its corresponding addresses (and other names). The return value in list context is:

```
($name, $aliases, $addrtype, $length, @addrs) =
    gethostbyname($remote_hostname);
```

where @addrs is a list of raw addresses. In the Internet domain, each address is (historically) four bytes long, and can be unpacked by saying something like:

```
($a, $b, $c, $d) = unpack('C4', $addrs[0]);
```

You can convert directly to vector notation with the v modifier to sprintf:

```
$dots = sprintf "%vd", $addrs[0];
```

In scalar context, gethostbyname returns only the host address:

```
use Socket;
$ipaddr = gethostbyname($remote_host);
printf "%s has address %s\n",
    $remote_host, inet_ntoa($ipaddr);
```

See "Sockets" in Chapter 16 for another approach. The Net::hostent module supports a by-name interface to this function. See also *gethostbyname*(3).

gethostent

```
gethostent
sethostent STAYOPEN
endhostent
```

These functions iterate through your */etc/hosts* file and return each entry one at a time. The return value from gethostent is:

```
($name, $aliases, $addrtype, $length, @addrs)
```

where @addrs is a list of raw addresses. In the Internet domain, each address is four bytes long, and can be unpacked by saying something like:

```
($a, $b, $c, $d) = unpack('C4', $addrs[0]);
```

Scripts that use gethostent should not be considered portable. If a machine uses a name server, it would have to interrogate most of the Internet to try to satisfy a request for all the addresses of every machine on the planet. So gethostent is unimplemented on such machines. See *gethostent*(3) for other details.

The Net::hostent module supports a by-name interface to this function.

getlogin   ⊠̲ᵤ̲

```
getlogin
```

This function returns the current login name if found. On Unix systems, this is read from the *utmp*(5) file. If it returns false, use getpwuid instead. For example:

```
$login = getlogin() || (getpwuid($<))[0] || "Intruder!!";
```

getnetbyaddr   ⊠̲ᵤ̲

```
getnetbyaddr ADDR, ADDRTYPE
```

This function translates a network address to the corresponding network name or names. The return value in list context is:

```
use Socket;
($name, $aliases, $addrtype, $net) = getnetbyaddr(127, AF_INET);
```

In scalar context, getnetbyaddr returns only the network name. The Net::netent module supports a by-name interface to this function. See *getnetbyaddr*(3).

getnetbyname   ⊠̲ᵤ̲

```
getnetbyname NAME
```

This function translates a network name to its corresponding network address. The return value in list context is:

```
($name, $aliases, $addrtype, $net) = getnetbyname("loopback");
```

In scalar context, getnetbyname returns only the network address. The Net::netent module supports a by-name interface to this function. See *getnetbyname*(3).

getnetent   ⊠̲ᵤ̲

```
getnetent
setnetent STAYOPEN
endnetent
```

These functions iterate through your */etc/networks* file. The return value in list context is:

```
($name, $aliases, $addrtype, $net) = getnetent();
```

In scalar context, getnetent returns only the network name. The Net::netent module supports a by-name interface to this function. See *getnetent*(3).

The concept of network names seems rather quaint these days; most IP addresses are on unnamed (and unnameable) subnets.

getpeername

getpeername SOCKET

This function returns the packed socket address of the other end of the SOCKET connection. For example:

```
use Socket;
$hersockaddr      = getpeername SOCK;
($port, $heraddr) = sockaddr_in($hersockaddr);
$herhostname      = gethostbyaddr($heraddr, AF_INET);
$herstraddr       = inet_ntoa($heraddr);
```

getpgrp

getpgrp PID

This function returns the current process group for the specified PID (use a PID of 0 for the current process). Invoking getpgrp will raise an exception if used on a machine that doesn't implement *getpgrp*(2). If PID is omitted, the function returns the process group of the current process (the same as using a PID of 0). On systems implementing this operator with the POSIX *getpgrp*(2) syscall, PID must be omitted or, if supplied, must be 0.

getppid

getppid

This function returns the process ID of the parent process. On the typical Unix system, if your parent process ID changes to 1, it means your parent process has died and you've been adopted by the *init*(8) program.

getpriority

getpriority WHICH, WHO

This function returns the current priority for a process, a process group, or a user. See *getpriority*(2). Invoking getpriority will raise an exception if used on a machine that doesn't implement *getpriority*(2).

The BSD::Resource module from CPAN provides a more convenient interface, including the PRIO_PROCESS, PRIO_PGRP, and PRIO_USER symbolic constants to supply for the WHICH argument. Although these are traditionally set to 0, 1, and 2 respectively, you really never know what may happen within the dark confines of C's #include files.

A value of 0 for *WHO* means the current process, process group, or user, so to get the priority of the current process, use:

```
$curprio = getpriority(0, 0);
```

getprotobyname

```
getprotobyname NAME
```

This function translates a protocol name to its corresponding number. The return value in list context is:

```
($name, $aliases, $protocol_number) = getprotobyname("tcp");
```

When called in scalar context, getprotobyname returns only the protocol number. The Net::proto module supports a by-name interface to this function. See *getprotobyname*(3).

getprotobynumber

```
getprotobynumber NUMBER
```

This function translates a protocol number to its corresponding name. The return value in list context is:

```
($name, $aliases, $protocol_number) = getprotobynumber(6);
```

When called in scalar context, getprotobynumber returns only the protocol name. The Net::proto module supports a by-name interface to this function. See *getprotobynumber*(3).

getprotoent

```
getprotoent
setprotoent STAYOPEN
endprotoent
```

These functions iterate through the */etc/protocols* file. In list context, the return value from getprotoent is:

```
($name, $aliases, $protocol_number) = getprotoent();
```

When called in scalar context, getprotoent returns only the protocol name. The Net::proto module supports a by-name interface to this function. See *getprotent*(3).

getpwent

```
getpwent
setpwent
endpwent
```

These functions conceptually iterate through your */etc/passwd* file, though this may involve the */etc/shadow* file if you're the superuser and are using shadow passwords, or NIS (née YP) or NIS+ if you're using either of those. The return value in list context is:

```
($name,$passwd,$uid,$gid,$quota,$comment,$gcos,$dir,$shell) = getpwent();
```

Some machines may use the quota and comment fields for other than their named purposes, but the remaining fields will always be the same. To set up a hash for translating login names to UIDs, say this:

```
while (($name, $passwd, $uid) = getpwent()) {
    $uid{$name} = $uid;
}
```

In scalar context, getpwent returns only the username. The User::pwent module supports a by-name interface to this function. See *getpwent*(3).

getpwnam

```
getpwnam NAME
```

This function translates a username to the corresponding */etc/passwd* file entry. The return value in list context is:

```
($name,$passwd,$uid,$gid,$quota,$comment,$gcos,$dir,$shell) = getpwnam("daemon");
```

On systems that support shadow passwords, you will have to be the superuser to retrieve the actual password. Your C library should notice that you're suitably empowered and open the */etc/shadow* file (or wherever it keeps the *shadow* file). At least, that's how it's supposed to work. Perl will try to do this if your C library is too stupid to notice.

For repeated lookups, consider caching the data in a hash using getpwent.

In scalar context, getpwnam returns only the numeric user ID. The User::pwent module supports a by-name interface to this function. See *getpwnam*(3) and *passwd*(5).

Functions

getpwuid   ⊤ X̲U̲

> getpwuid *UID*

This function translates a numeric user ID to the corresponding */etc/passwd* file entry. The return value in list context is:

>   ($name,$passwd,$uid,$gid,$quota,$comment,$gcos,$dir,$shell) = getpwuid(2);

For repeated lookups, consider caching the data in a hash using getpwent.

In scalar context, getpwuid returns the username. The User::pwent module supports a by-name interface to this function. See *getpwnam*(3) and *passwd*(5).

getservbyname   X̲U̲

> getservbyname *NAME*, *PROTO*

This function translates a service (port) name to its corresponding port number. *PROTO* is a protocol name such as "tcp". The return value in list context is:

>   ($name, $aliases, $port_number, $protocol_name) = getservbyname("www", "tcp");

In scalar context, getservbyname returns only the service port number. The Net::servent module supports a by-name interface to this function. See *getservbyname*(3).

getservbyport   X̲U̲

> getservbyport *PORT*, *PROTO*

This function translates a service (port) number to its corresponding names. *PROTO* is a protocol name such as "tcp". The return value in list context is:

>   ($name, $aliases, $port_number, $protocol_name) = getservbyport(80, "tcp");

In scalar context, getservbyport returns only the service name. The Net::servent module supports a by-name interface to this function. See *getservbyport*(3).

getservent   X̲U̲

> getservent
> setservent *STAYOPEN*
> endservent

This function iterates through the */etc/services* file or its equivalent. The return value in list context is:

>   ($name, $aliases, $port_number, $protocol_name) = getservent();

In scalar context, getservent returns only the service port name. The Net::servent module supports a by-name interface to this function. See *getservent*(3).

getsockname

        getsockname *SOCKET*

This function returns the packed socket address of this end of the *SOCKET* connection. (And why wouldn't you know your own address already? Maybe because you bound an address containing wildcards to the server socket before doing an `accept` and now you need to know what interface someone used to connect to you. Or you were passed a socket by your parent process—*inetd*, for example.)

```
use Socket;
$mysockaddr = getsockname(SOCK);
($port, $myaddr) = sockaddr_in($mysockaddr);
$myname = gethostbyaddr($myaddr,AF_INET);
printf "I am %s [%vd]\n", $myname, $myaddr;
```

getsockopt

        getsockopt *SOCKET*, *LEVEL*, *OPTNAME*

This function returns the socket option requested, or **undef** if there is an error. See `setsockopt` for more information.

glob

        glob *EXPR*
        glob

This function returns the value of *EXPR* with filename expansions such as a shell would do. This is the internal function implementing the `<*>` operator.

For historical reasons, the algorithm matches the *csh*(1)'s style of expansion, not the Bourne shell's. Versions of Perl before the 5.6 release used an external process, but 5.6 and later perform globs internally. Files whose first character is a dot (".") are ignored unless this character is explicitly matched. An asterisk ("*") matches any sequence of any character (including none). A question mark ("?") matches any one character. A square bracket sequence ("[...]") specifies a simple character class, like "[chy0-9]". Character classes may be negated with a circumflex, as in "*.[^oa]", which matches any non-dot files whose names contain a period followed by one character which is neither an "a" nor an "o" at the end of the name. A tilde ("~") expands to a home directory, as in "~/.*rc" for all the current user's "rc" files, or "~jane/Mail/*" for all of Jane's mail files. Braces may be used for alternation, as in "~/.{mail,ex,csh,twm,}rc" to get those particular rc files.

If you want to glob filenames that might contain whitespace, you'll want to use the **File::Glob** module directly, since **glob** grandfathers the use of whitespace to separate multiple patterns such as `<*.c *.h>`. For details, see `File::Glob` in Chapter 32. Calling `glob` (or the `<*>` operator) automatically uses that module, so if the module mysteriously vaporizes from your library, an exception is raised.

When you call `open`, Perl does not expand wildcards, including tildes. You need to `glob` the result first.

```
open(MAILRC, "~/.mailrc")                  # WRONG: tilde is a shell thing
    or die "can't open ~/.mailrc: $!";

open(MAILRC, (glob("~/.mailrc"))[0])       # expand tilde first
    or die "can't open ~/.mailrc: $!";
```

The `glob` function is not related to the Perl notion of typeglobs, other than that they both use a `*` to represent multiple items.

See also the "Filename globbing operator" section of Chapter 2.

gmtime

```
gmtime EXPR
gmtime
```

This function converts a time as returned by the `time` function to a nine-element list with the time correct for the Greenwich time zone (a.k.a. GMT, or UTC, or even Zulu in certain cultures, not including the Zulu culture, oddly enough). It's typically used as follows:

```
# 0    1     2     3     4     5     6     7     8
($sec,$min,$hour,$mday,$mon,$year,$wday,$yday,$isdst) = gmtime;
```

If, as in this case, the *EXPR* is omitted, it does `gmtime(time())`. The Perl library module `Time::Local` contains a subroutine, `timegm`, that can convert the list back into a time value.

All list elements are numeric and come straight out of a `struct tm` (that's a C programming structure—don't sweat it). In particular this means that `$mon` has the range `0..11` with January as month 0, and `$wday` has the range `0..6` with Sunday as day 0. You can remember which ones are zero-based because those are the ones you're always using as subscripts into zero-based arrays containing month and day names.

For example, to get the current month in London, you might say:

```
$london_month = (qw(Jan Feb Mar Apr May Jun
                    Jul Aug Sep Oct Nov Dec))[(gmtime)[4]];
```

`$year` is the number of years since 1900; that is, in year 2023, `$year` is 123, *not* simply 23. To get the 4-digit year, just say `$year + 1900`. To get the 2-digit year (for example "01" in 2001), use `sprintf("%02d", $year % 100)`.

In scalar context, `gmtime` returns a *ctime*(3)-like string based on the GMT time value. The `Time::gmtime` module supports a by-name interface to this function. See also `POSIX::strftime()` for a more fine-grained approach to formatting times.

This scalar value is *not* locale dependent but is instead a Perl built-in. Also see the `Time::Local` module and the *strftime*(3) and *mktime*(3) functions available via the `POSIX` module. To get somewhat similar but locale-dependent date strings, set up your locale environment variables appropriately (please see the *perllocale* manpage), and try:

```
use POSIX qw(strftime);
$now_string = strftime "%a %b %e %H:%M:%S %Y", gmtime;
```

The `%a` and `%b` escapes, which represent the short forms of the day of the week and the month of the year, may not necessarily be three characters wide in all locales.

goto   `$@`

```
goto LABEL
goto EXPR
goto &NAME
```

`goto` *LABEL* finds the statement labeled with *LABEL* and resumes execution there. If the *LABEL* cannot be found, an exception is raised. It cannot be used to go into any construct that requires initialization, such as a subroutine or a `foreach` loop. It also can't be used to go into a construct that is optimized away. It can be used to go almost anywhere else within the dynamic scope,* including out of subroutines, but for that purpose it's usually better to use some other construct such as `last` or `die`. The author of Perl has never felt the need to use this form of `goto` (in Perl, that is—C is another matter).

Going to even greater heights of orthogonality (and depths of idiocy), Perl allows `goto` *EXPR*, which expects *EXPR* to evaluate to a label name, whose location is *guaranteed* to be unresolvable until run time since the label is unknown when the statement is compiled. This allows for computed `goto`s per FORTRAN, but isn't necessarily recommended† if you're optimizing for maintainability:

```
goto +("FOO", "BAR", "GLARCH")[$i];
```

The unrelated `goto` *&NAME* is highly magical, substituting a call to the named subroutine for the currently running subroutine. This construct may be used without

---

* This means that if it doesn't find the label in the current routine, it looks back through the routines that called the current routine for the label, thus making it nearly impossible to maintain your program.

† Understatement is reputed to be funny, so we thought we'd try one here.

shame by AUTOLOAD subroutines that wish to load another subroutine and then pretend that this new subroutine—and not the original one—had been called in the first place (except that any modifications to @_ in the original subroutine are propagated to the replacement subroutine). After the goto, not even caller will be able to tell that the original AUTOLOAD routine was called first.

grep

```
grep EXPR, LIST
grep BLOCK LIST
```

This function evaluates *EXPR* or *BLOCK* in Boolean context for each element of *LIST*, temporarily setting $_ to each element in turn, much like the foreach construct. In list context, it returns a list of those elements for which the expression is true. (The operator is named after a beloved Unix program that extracts lines out of a file that match a particular pattern. In Perl, the expression is often a pattern, but doesn't have to be.) In scalar context, grep returns the number of times the expression was true.

If @all_lines contains lines of code, this example weeds out comment lines:

```
@code_lines = grep !/^\s*#/, @all_lines;
```

Because $_ is an implicit alias to each list value, altering $_ will modify the elements of the original list. While this is useful and supported, it can occasionally cause bizarre results if you aren't expecting it. For example:

```
@list = qw(barney fred dino wilma);
@greplist = grep { s/^[bfd]// } @list;
```

@greplist is now "arney", "red", "ino", but @list is now "arney", "red", "ino", "wilma"! Ergo, Caveat Programmor.

See also map. The following two statements are functionally equivalent:

```
@out = grep { EXPR } @in;
@out = map { EXPR ? $_ : () } @in
```

hex $_

```
hex EXPR
hex
```

This function interprets *EXPR* as a hexadecimal string and returns the equivalent decimal value. A leading "0x" is ignored, if present. To interpret strings that might start with any of 0, 0b, or 0x, see oct. The following code sets $number to 4,294,906,560:

```
$number = hex("ffff12c0");
```

To do the inverse function, use `sprintf`:

```
sprintf "%lx", $number;        # (That's an ell, not a one.)
```

Hex strings may only represent integers. Strings that would cause integer overflow trigger a warning.

import

```
import CLASSNAME LIST
import CLASSNAME
```

There is no built-in `import` function. It is merely an ordinary class method defined (or inherited) by modules that wish to export names to another module through the `use` operator. See `use` for details.

index

```
index STR, SUBSTR, OFFSET
index STR, SUBSTR
```

This function searches for one string within another. It returns the position of the first occurrence of *SUBSTR* in *STR*. The *OFFSET*, if specified, says how many characters from the start to skip before beginning to look. Positions are based at 0 (or whatever you've set the subscript base $[variable to—but don't do that). If the substring is not found, the function returns one less than the base, ordinarily -1. To work your way through a string, you might say:

```
$pos = -1;
while (($pos = index($string, $lookfor, $pos)) > -1) {
    print "Found at $pos\n";
    $pos++;
}
```

int

```
int EXPR
int
```

This function returns the integer portion of *EXPR*. If you're a C programmer, you're apt to forget to use `int` in conjunction with division, which is a floating-point operation in Perl:

```
$average_age = 939/16;       # yields 58.6875 (58 in C)
$average_age = int 939/16;   # yields 58
```

You should not use this function for generic rounding, because it truncates towards 0 and because machine representations of floating-point numbers can

sometimes produce counterintuitive results. For example, int(-6.725/0.025) produces –268 rather than the correct –269; that's because the value is really more like
–268.999999999999994315658. Usually, the sprintf, printf, or the POSIX::floor and
POSIX::ceil functions will serve you better than will int.

```
$n = sprintf("%.0f", $f);   # round (not trunc) to nearest integer
```

ioctl   S! [X ARG] [X RO] [X T] [X U]

```
ioctl FILEHANDLE, FUNCTION, SCALAR
```

This function implements the *ioctl*(2) syscall which controls I/O. To get the correct
function definitions, first you'll probably have to say:

```
require "sys/ioctl.ph";      # perhaps /usr/local/lib/perl/sys/ioctl.ph
```

If *sys/ioctl.ph* doesn't exist or doesn't have the correct definitions, you'll have to
roll your own based on your C header files such as *sys/ioctl.h*. (The Perl distribution includes a script called *h2ph* to help you do this, but running it is nontrivial.)
SCALAR will be read or written (or both) depending on the *FUNCTION*—a pointer to
the string value of *SCALAR* will be passed as the third argument of the actual
ioctl(2) call. (If *SCALAR* has no string value but does have a numeric value, that
value will be passed directly rather than a pointer to the string value.) The pack
and unpack functions are useful for manipulating the values of structures used by
ioctl. The following example determines how many bytes are available for reading using the FIONREAD ioctl:

```
require 'sys/ioctl.ph';

$size = pack("L", 0);
ioctl(FH, FIONREAD(), $size)
    or die "Couldn't call ioctl: $!\n";
$size = unpack("L", $size);
```

If *h2ph* wasn't installed or doesn't work for you, you can *grep* the include files by
hand or write a small C program to print out the value.

The return value of ioctl (and fcntl) is as follows:

Syscall Returns	Perl Returns
–1	undef
0	String "0 but true"
Anything else	That number

Thus Perl returns true on success and false on failure, yet you can still easily
determine the actual value returned by the operating system:

```
$retval = ioctl(...) || -1;
printf "ioctl actually returned %d\n", $retval;
```

The special string "0 but true" is exempt from **-w** complaints about improper numeric conversions.

Calls to `ioctl` should not be considered portable. If, say, you're merely turning off echo once for the whole script, it's more portable to say:

```
system "stty -echo";   # Works on most Unix boxen.
```

Just because you *can* do something in Perl doesn't mean you *ought* to. To quote the Apostle Paul, "Everything is permissible—but not everything is beneficial."

For still better portability, you might look at the `Term::ReadKey` module from CPAN.

join

```
join EXPR, LIST
```

This function joins the separate strings of *LIST* into a single string with fields separated by the value of *EXPR*, and returns the string. For example:

```
$rec = join ':', $login,$passwd,$uid,$gid,$gcos,$home,$shell;
```

To do the opposite, see `split`. To join things together into fixed-position fields, see `pack`. The most efficient way to concatenate many strings together is to `join` them with a null string:

```
$string = join "", @array;
```

Unlike `split`, `join` doesn't take a pattern as its first argument, and will produce a warning if you try.

keys

```
keys HASH
```

This function returns a list consisting of all the keys of the indicated *HASH*. The keys are returned in an apparently random order, but it is the same order produced by either the `values` or `each` function (assuming the hash has not been modified between calls). As a side effect, it resets *HASH*'s iterator. Here is a (rather cork-brained) way to print your environment:

```
@keys   = keys   %ENV;    # keys are in the same order as
@values = values %ENV;    # values, as this demonstrates
while (@keys) {
    print pop(@keys), '=', pop(@values), "\n";
}
```

You're more likely to want to see the environment sorted by keys:

```
foreach $key (sort keys %ENV) {
    print $key, '=', $ENV{$key}, "\n";
}
```

You can sort the values of a hash directly, but that's somewhat useless in the absence of any way to map the values back to the keys. To sort a hash by value, you generally need to sort the keys by providing a comparison function that accesses the values based on the keys. Here's a descending numeric sort of a hash by its values:

```
foreach $key (sort { $hash{$b} <=> $hash{$a} } keys %hash) {
    printf "%4d %s\n", $hash{$key}, $key;
}
```

Using keys on a hash bound to a largish DBM file will produce a largish list, causing you to have a largish process. You might prefer to use the each function here, which will iterate over the hash entries one by one without slurping them all into a single gargantuan list.

In scalar context, keys returns the number of elements of the hash (and resets the each iterator). However, to get this information for tied hashes, including DBM files, Perl must walk the entire hash, so it's not efficient then. Calling keys in a void context helps with that.

Used as an lvalue, keys increases the number of hash buckets allocated for the given hash. (This is similar to pre-extending an array by assigning a larger number to $#array.) Pre-extending your hash can gain a measure of efficiency if you happen to know the hash is going to get big, and how big it's going to get. If you say:

```
keys %hash = 1000;
```

then %hash will have at least 1000 buckets allocated for it (you get 1024 buckets, in fact, since it rounds up to the next power of two). You can't shrink the number of buckets allocated for the hash using keys in this way (but you needn't worry about doing this by accident, as trying has no effect). The buckets will be retained even if you do %hash = (). Use undef %hash if you want to free the storage while %hash is still in scope.

See also each, values, and sort.

kill $! [X/ARG] [X/U] [X/T]

```
kill SIGNAL, LIST
```

This function sends a signal to a list of processes. For *SIGNAL*, you may use either an integer or a quoted signal name (without a "SIG" on the front). Trying to use an unrecognized *SIGNAL* name raises an exception. The function returns the number of processes successfully signalled. If *SIGNAL* is negative, the function kills process groups instead of processes. (On SysV, a negative process number will also kill process groups, but that's not portable.) A PID of zero sends the signal to all processes of the same group ID as the sender. For example:

```
$cnt = kill 1, $child1, $child2;
kill 9, @goners;
kill 'STOP', getppid        # Can *so* suspend my login shell...
        unless getppid == 1;    # (But don't taunt init(8).)
```

A *SIGNAL* of 0 tests whether a process is still alive and that you still have permission to signal it. No signal is sent. This way you can check whether the process is still alive and hasn't changed its UID.

```
use Errno qw(ESRCH EPERM);
if (kill 0 => $minion) {
    print "$minion is alive!\n";
} elsif ($! == EPERM) {            # changed UID
    print "$minion has escaped my control!\n";
} elsif ($! == ESRCH) {
    print "$minion is deceased.\n";  # or zombied
} else {
    warn "Odd; I couldn't check on the status of $minion: $!\n";
}
```

See the section "Signals" in Chapter 16.

last   `$@`

```
last LABEL
last
```

The `last` operator immediately exits the loop in question, just like the break statement in C or Java (as used in loops). If the *LABEL* is omitted, the operator refers to the innermost enclosing loop. The `continue` block, if any, is not executed.

```
LINE: while (<MAILMSG>) {
    last LINE if /^$/; # exit when done with header
    # rest of loop here
}
```

`last` cannot be used to exit a block which returns a value, such as eval {}, sub {}, or do {}, and should not be used to exit a grep or map operation. With warnings enabled, Perl will warn you if you `last` out of a loop that's not in your current lexical scope, such as a loop in a calling subroutine.

A block by itself is semantically identical to a loop that executes once. Thus `last` can be used to effect an early exit out of such a block.

See also Chapter 4 for illustrations of how `last`, `next`, `redo`, and `continue` work.

Functions

lc $\boxed{\text{s\_}}$ $\boxed{\text{T}}$

```
lc EXPR
lc
```

This function returns a lowercased version of *EXPR*. This is the internal function implementing the \L escape in double-quoted strings. Your current LC_CTYPE locale is respected if use locale is in effect, though how locales interact with Unicode is still a topic of ongoing research, as they say. See the *perllocale* manpage for the most recent results.

lcfirst $\boxed{\text{s\_}}$ $\boxed{\text{T}}$

```
lcfirst EXPR
lcfirst
```

This function returns a version of *EXPR* with the first character lowercased. This is the internal function implementing the \l escape in double-quoted strings. Your current LC_CTYPE locale is respected if you use locale and if we figure out how that relates to Unicode.

length $\boxed{\text{s\_}}$

```
length EXPR
length
```

This function returns the length in characters of the scalar value *EXPR*. If *EXPR* is omitted, it returns the length of $_. (But be careful that the next thing doesn't look like the start of an *EXPR*, or Perl's lexer will get confused. For example, length < 10 won't compile. When in doubt, use parentheses.)

Do not try to use length to find the size of an array or hash. Use scalar @array for the size of an array, and scalar keys %hash for the number of key/value pairs in a hash. (The scalar is typically omitted when redundant.)

To find the length of a string in bytes rather than characters, say:

```
$blen = do { use bytes; length $string; };
```

or:

```
$blen = bytes::length($string);    # must use bytes first
```

link $\boxed{\text{s!}}$ $\boxed{\text{X}_\text{U}}$ $\boxed{\text{X}_\text{T}}$

```
link OLDFILE, NEWFILE
```

This function creates a new filename linked to the old filename. The function returns true for success, false otherwise. See also symlink later in this chapter. This function is unlikely to be implemented on non-Unix-style filesystems.

listen

$! ARG U

```
listen SOCKET, QUEUESIZE
```

This function tells the system that you're going to be accepting connections on this *SOCKET* and that the system can queue the number of waiting connections specified by *QUEUESIZE*. Imagine having call-waiting on your phone, with up to 17 callers queued. (Gives me the willies!) The function returns true if it succeeded, false otherwise.

```
use Socket;
listen(PROTOSOCK, SOMAXCONN)
    or die "cannot set listen queue on PROTOSOCK: $!";
```

See accept. See also the section "Sockets" in Chapter 16. See *listen*(2).

local

```
local EXPR
```

This operator does not create a local variable; use my for that. Instead, it localizes existing variables; that is, it causes one or more global variables to have locally scoped values within the innermost enclosing block, eval, or file. If more than one variable is listed, the list must be placed in parentheses because the operator binds more tightly than commas. All listed variables must be legal lvalues, that is, something you could assign to; this can include individual elements of arrays or hashes.

This operator works by saving the current values of the specified variables on a hidden stack and restoring them upon exiting the block, subroutine, eval, or file. After the local is executed, but before the scope is exited, any subroutines and executed formats will see the local, inner value, instead of the previous, outer value because the variable is still a global variable, despite having a localized value. The technical term for this is "dynamic scoping". See the section "Scoped Declarations" in Chapter 4.

The *EXPR* may be assigned to if desired, which allows you to initialize your variables as you localize them. If no initializer is given, all scalars are initialized to undef, and all arrays and hashes to (). As with ordinary assignment, if you use parentheses around the variables on the left (or if the variable is an array or hash), the expression on the right is evaluated in list context. Otherwise, the expression on the right is evaluated in scalar context.

In any event, the expression on the right is evaluated before the localization, but the initialization happens after localization, so you can initialize a localized variable with its nonlocalized value. For instance, this code demonstrates how to make a temporary modification to a global array:

```
if ($sw eq '-v') {
    # init local array with global array
    local @ARGV = @ARGV;
    unshift @ARGV, 'echo';
    system @ARGV;
}
# @ARGV restored
```

You can also temporarily modify global hashes:

```
# temporarily add a couple of entries to the %digits hash
if ($base12) {
    # (NOTE: We're not claiming this is efficient!)
    local(%digits) = (%digits, T => 10, E => 11);
    parse_num();
}
```

You can use local to give temporary values to individual elements of arrays and hashes, even lexically scoped ones:

```
if ($protected) {
    local $SIG{INT} = 'IGNORE';
    precious();      # no interrupts during this function
}                    # previous handler (if any) restored
```

You can also use local on typeglobs to create local filehandles without loading any bulky object modules:

```
local *MOTD;              # protect any global MOTD handle
my $fh = do { local *FH };  # create new indirect filehandle
```

(As of the 5.6 release of Perl, a plain my $fh; is good enough, because if you give an undefined variable where a real filehandle is expected, like the first argument to open or socket, Perl now autovivifies a brand new filehandle for you.)

But in general, you usually want to use my instead of local, because local isn't really what most people think of as "local", or even "lo-cal". See my.

localtime

```
localtime EXPR
localtime
```

This function converts the value returned by time to a nine-element list with the time corrected for the local time zone. It's typically used as follows:

```
# 0    1    2    3    4    5    6    7    8
($sec,$min,$hour,$mday,$mon,$year,$wday,$yday,$isdst) = localtime;
```

If, as in this case, EXPR is omitted, it does localtime(time()).

All list elements are numeric and come straight out of a struct tm. (That's a bit of C programming lingo—don't worry about it.) In particular, this means that $mon has the range `0..11` with January as month 0, and `$wday` has the range `0..6` with Sunday as day 0. You can remember which ones are zero-based because those are the ones you're always using as subscripts into zero-based arrays containing month and day names.

For example, to get the name of the current day of the week:

```
$thisday = (Sun,Mon,Tue,Wed,Thu,Fri,Sat)[(localtime)[6]];
```

`$year` is the number of years since 1900, that is, in year 2023, `$year` is 123, *not* simply 23. To get the 4-digit year, just say `$year + 1900`. To get the 2-digit year (for example "01" in 2001), use `sprintf("%02d", $year % 100)`.

The Perl library module `Time::Local` contains a subroutine, `timelocal`, that can convert in the opposite direction.

In scalar context, `localtime` returns a *ctime*(3)-like string. For example, the *date*(1) command can be (almost)* emulated with:

```
perl -le 'print scalar localtime'
```

See also the standard `POSIX` module's `strftime` function for a more fine-grained approach to formatting times. The `Time::localtime` module supports a by-name interface to this function.

lock

```
lock THING
```

The `lock` function places a lock on a variable, subroutine, or object referenced by *THING* until the lock goes out of scope. For backward compatibility, this function is a built-in only if your version of Perl was compiled with threading enabled, and if you've said `use Threads`. Otherwise, Perl will assume this is a user-defined function. See Chapter 17, *Threads*.

log

```
log EXPR
log
```

This function returns the natural logarithm (that is, base *e*) of *EXPR*. If *EXPR* is negative, it raises an exception. To get the log of another base, use basic algebra: the base-*N* log of a number is equal to the natural log of that number divided by the natural log of *N*. For example:

---

* *date*(1) prints the timezone, whereas scalar `localtime` does not.

```
sub log10 {
    my $n = shift;
    return log($n)/log(10);
}
```

For the inverse of log, see exp.

lstat   ⬚S_ ⬚S! ⬚X̲U

```
lstat EXPR
lstat
```

This function does the same thing as Perl's stat function (including setting the special _ filehandle), but if the last component of the filename is a symbolic link, it stats the symbolic link itself instead of the file that the symbolic link points to. (If symbolic links are unimplemented on your system, a normal stat is done instead.)

m//   ⬚T ⬚X̲T

```
/PATTERN/
m/PATTERN/
```

This is the match operator, which interprets *PATTERN* as a regular expression. The operator is parsed as a double-quoted string rather than as a function. See Chapter 5, *Pattern Matching*.

map

```
map BLOCK LIST
map EXPR, LIST
```

This function evaluates the *BLOCK* or *EXPR* for each element of *LIST* (locally setting $_ to each element) and returns the list comprising the results of each such evaluation. It evaluates *BLOCK* or *EXPR* in list context, so each element of *LIST* may map to zero, one, or more elements in the returned value. These are all flattened into one list. For instance:

```
@words = map { split ' ' } @lines;
```

splits a list of lines into a list of words. But often there is a one-to-one mapping between input values and output values:

```
@chars = map chr, @nums;
```

translates a list of numbers to the corresponding characters. And here's an example of a one-to-two mapping:

```
%hash = map { genkey($_) => $_ } @array;
```

which is just a funny functional way to write this:

```
%hash = ();
foreach $_ (@array) {
    $hash{genkey($_)} = $_;
}
```

Because $_ is an alias (implicit reference) into the list's values, this variable can be used to modify the elements of the array. This is useful and supported, although it can cause bizarre results if the *LIST* is not a named array. Using a regular foreach loop for this purpose may be clearer. See also grep; map differs from grep in that map returns a list consisting of the results of each successive evaluation of *EXPR*, whereas grep returns a list consisting of each value of *LIST* for which *EXPR* evaluates to true.

mkdir

```
mkdir FILENAME, MASK
mkdir FILENAME
```

This function creates the directory specified by *FILENAME*, giving it permissions specified by the numeric *MASK* as modified by the current umask. If the operation succeeds, it returns true; otherwise, it returns false.

If *MASK* is omitted, a mask of 0777 is assumed, which is almost always what you want anyway. In general, creating directories with permissive *MASK*s (like 0777) and letting the user modify that with their umask is better than supplying a restrictive *MASK* and giving the user no way to be more permissive. The exception to this rule is when the file or directory should be kept private (mail files, for instance). See umask.

If the *mkdir*(2) syscall is not built into your C library, Perl emulates it by calling the *mkdir*(1) program for each directory. If you are creating a long list of directories on such a system, it'll be more efficient to call the *mkdir* program yourself with the list of directories than it is to start zillions of subprocesses.

msgctl

```
msgctl ID, CMD, ARG
```

This function calls the System V IPC *msgctl*(2) syscall; see *msgctl*(2) for more details. You may have to use IPC::SysV first to get the correct constant definitions. If *CMD* is IPC_STAT, then *ARG* must be a variable that will hold the returned msqid_ds C structure. Return values are like ioctl and fcntl: undef for error, "0 but true" for zero, or the actual return value otherwise.

This function is available only on machines supporting System V IPC, which turns out to be far fewer than those supporting sockets.

msgget $!   X/U

```
msgget KEY, FLAGS
```

This function calls the System V IPC *msgget*(2) syscall. See *msgget*(2) for details. The function returns the message queue ID, or undef if there is an error. Before calling, you should use IPC::SysV.

This function is available only on machines supporting System V IPC.

msgrcv $!   X/U

```
msgrcv ID, VAR, SIZE, TYPE, FLAGS
```

This function calls the *msgrcv*(2) syscall to receive a message from message queue *ID* into variable *VAR* with a maximum message size of *SIZE*. See *msgrcv*(2) for details. When a message is received, the message type will be the first thing in *VAR*, and the maximum length of *VAR* is *SIZE* plus the size of the message type. The function returns true if successful, or false if there is an error. Before calling, you should use IPC::SysV.

This function is available only on machines supporting System V IPC.

msgsnd $!   X/U

```
msgsnd ID, MSG, FLAGS
```

This function calls the *msgsnd*(2) syscall to send the message *MSG* to the message queue *ID*. See *msgsnd*(2) for details. *MSG* must begin with the long integer message type. You can create a message like this:

```
$msg = pack "L a*", $type, $text_of_message;
```

The function returns true if successful, or false if there is an error. Before calling, use IPC::SysV.

This function is available only on machines supporting System V IPC.

my

```
my TYPE EXPR : ATTRIBUTES
my EXPR : ATTRIBUTES
my TYPE EXPR
my EXPR
```

This operator declares one or more private variables to exist only within the innermost enclosing block, subroutine, eval, or file. If more than one variable is listed, the list must be placed in parentheses because the operator binds more tightly than commas. Only simple scalars or complete arrays and hashes may be declared this way.

The variable name cannot be package qualified, because package variables are all globally accessible through their corresponding symbol table, and lexical variables are unrelated to any symbol table. Unlike `local`, then, this operator has nothing to do with global variables, other than hiding any other variable of the same name from view within its scope (that is, where the private variable exists). A global variable can always be accessed through its package-qualified form, however, or through a symbolic reference.

A private variable's scope does not start until the statement *after* its declaration. The variable's scope extends into any enclosed blocks thereafter, up to the end of the scope of the variable itself.

However, this means that any subroutines you call from within the scope of a private variable cannot see the private variable unless the block that defines the subroutine itself is also textually enclosed within the scope of that variable. That sounds complicated, but it's not once you get the hang of it. The technical term for this is *lexical scoping*, so we often call these *lexical variables*. In C culture, they're sometimes called "auto" variables, since they're automatically allocated and deallocated at scope entry and exit.

The *EXPR* may be assigned to if desired, which allows you to initialize your lexical variables. (If no initializer is given, all scalars are initialized to the undefined value and all arrays and hashes to the empty list.) As with ordinary assignment, if you use parentheses around the variables on the left (or if the variable is an array or hash), the expression on the right is evaluated in list context. Otherwise, the expression on the right is evaluated in scalar context. For example, you can name your formal subroutine parameters with a list assignment, like this:

```
my ($friends, $romans, $countrymen) = @_;
```

But be careful not to omit the parentheses indicating list assignment, like this:

```
my $country = @_;   # right or wrong?
```

This assigns the length of the array (that is, the number of the subroutine's arguments) to the variable, since the array is being evaluated in scalar context. You can profitably use scalar assignment for a formal parameter though, as long as you use the `shift` operator. In fact, since object methods are passed the object as the first argument, many method subroutines start off by "stealing" the first argument:

```
sub simple_as {
    my $self = shift;   # scalar assignment
    my ($a,$b,$c) = @_; # list assignment
    ...
}
```

Functions

If you attempt to declare a lexically scoped subroutine with `my sub`, Perl will die with the message that this feature has not been implemented yet. (Unless, of course, this feature *has* been implemented yet.)

The *TYPE* and *ATTRIBUTES* are optional, which is just as well, since they're both considered experimental. Here's what a declaration that uses them might look like:

```
my Dog $spot :ears(short) :tail(long);
```

The *TYPE*, if specified, indicates what kind of scalar or scalars are declared in *EXPR*, either directly as one or more scalar variables, or indirectly through an array or hash. If *TYPE* is the name of the class, the scalars will be assumed to contain references to objects of that type, or to objects compatible with that type. In particular, derived classes are considered compatible. That is, assuming `Collie` is derived from `Dog`, you might declare:

```
my Dog $lassie = new Collie;
```

Your declaration claims that you will use the `$lassie` object consistently with its being a `Dog` object. The fact that it's actually a `Collie` object shouldn't matter as long as you only try to do `Dog` things. Through the magic of virtual methods, the implementation of those `Dog` methods might well be in the `Collie` class, but the declaration above is only talking about the interface, not the implementation. In theory.

Interestingly, up through version 5.6.0, the only time Perl pays attention to the *TYPE* declaration is when the corresponding class has declared fields with the `use fields` pragma. Together, these declarations allow the pseudohash implementation of a class to "show through" to code outside the class, so that hash lookups can be optimized by the compiler into array lookups. In a sense, the pseudohash *is* the interface to such a class, so our theory remains intact, if a bit battered. For more on pseudohashes, see the section "Pseudohashes" in Chapter 8, *References*.

In the future, other types of classes may interpret the *TYPE* differently. The *TYPE* declaration should be considered a generic type interface that might someday be instantiated in various ways depending on the class. In fact, the *TYPE* might not even be an official class name. We're reserving the lowercase type names for Perl, because one of the ways we'd like to extend the type interface is to allow optional low-level type declarations such as `int`, `num`, `str`, and `ref`. These declarations will not be for the purpose of strong typing; rather, they'll be hints to the compiler telling it to optimize the storage of the variable with the assumption that the variable will be used mostly as declared. The semantics of scalars will stay pretty much the same—you'll still be able to add two `str` scalars, or print an `int` scalar, just as though they were the ordinary polymorphic scalars you're familiar with. But with an `int` declaration Perl might decide to store only the integer value and forget about caching the resulting string as it currently does. Loops with `int` loop variables might run faster, particularly in code compiled down to C. In particular, arrays of numbers could be stored much more compactly. As a limiting case, the built-in vec function might even become obsolete when we can write declarations such as:

```
my bit @bitstring;
```

The *ATTRIBUTES* declaration is even more experimental. We haven't done much more than reserve the syntax and prototype the internal interface; see the use attributes pragma in Chapter 31 for more on that. The first attribute we'll implement is likely to be constant:

```
my num $PI : constant = atan2(1,1) * 4;
```

But there are many other possibilities, such as establishing default values for arrays and hashes, or letting variables be shared among cooperating interpreters. Like the type interface, the attribute interface should be considered a generic interface, a kind of workbench for inventing new syntax and semantics. We do not know how Perl will evolve in the next 10 years. We only know that we can make it easier on ourselves by planning for that in advance.

See also local, our, and the section "Scoped Declarations" in Chapter 4.

new

```
new CLASSNAME LIST
new CLASSNAME
```

There is no built-in new function. It is merely an ordinary constructor method (that is, a user-defined subroutine) that is defined or inherited by the *CLASSNAME* class (that is, package) to let you construct objects of type *CLASSNAME*. Many constructors are named "new", but only by convention, just to trick C++ programmers into thinking they know what's going on. Always read the documentation of the class in question so you know how to call its constructors; for example, the constructor that creates a list box in the Tk widget set is just called Listbox(). See Chapter 12.

next

```
next LABEL
next
```

The next operator is like the continue statement in C: it starts the next iteration of the loop designated by *LABEL*:

```
LINE: while (<STDIN>) {
    next LINE if /^#/;      # discard comments
    ...
}
```

If there were a continue block in this example, it would be executed immediately following the invocation of next. When *LABEL* is omitted, the operator refers to the innermost enclosing loop.

A block by itself is semantically identical to a loop that executes once. Thus, next will exit such a block early (via the continue block, if there is one).

next cannot be used to exit a block that returns a value, such as eval {}, sub {}, or do {}, and should not be used to exit a grep or map operation. With warnings enabled, Perl will warn you if you next out of a loop not in your current lexical scope, such as a loop in a calling subroutine. See the section "Loop Statements" in Chapter 4.

no   `$@`

> no *MODULE LIST*

See the use operator, which is the opposite of no, kind of. Most standard modules do not unimport anything, making no a no-op, as it were. The pragmatic modules tend to be more obliging here. If the *MODULE* cannot be found, an exception is raised.

oct   `$_`

> oct *EXPR*
> oct

This function interprets *EXPR* as an octal string and returns the equivalent decimal value. If *EXPR* happens to start with "0x", it is interpreted as a hexadecimal string instead. If *EXPR* starts off with "0b", it is interpreted as a string of binary digits. The following will properly convert to numbers any input strings in decimal, binary, octal, and hex bases written in standard C or C++ notation:

```
$val = oct $val if $val =~ /^0/;
```

To perform the inverse function, use sprintf with an appropriate format:

```
$perms = (stat("filename"))[2] & 07777;
$oct_perms = sprintf "%lo", $perms;
```

The oct function is commonly used when a data string such as "644" needs to be converted into a file mode, for example. Although Perl will automatically convert strings into numbers as needed, this automatic conversion assumes base 10.

open

```
open FILEHANDLE, MODE, LIST
open FILEHANDLE, EXPR
open FILEHANDLE
```

The open function associates an internal *FILEHANDLE* with an external file specification given by *EXPR* or *LIST*. It may be called with one, two, or three arguments (or more if the third argument is a command, and you're running at least version 5.6.1 of Perl). If three or more arguments are present, the second argument specifies the access *MODE* in which the file should be opened, and the third argument (*LIST*) supplies the actual filename or the command to execute, depending on the mode. In the case of a command, additional arguments may be supplied if you wish to invoke the command directly without involving a shell, much like system or exec. Or the command may be supplied as a single argument (the third one), in which case the decision to invoke the shell depends on whether the command contains shell metacharacters. (Don't use more than three arguments if the arguments are ordinary filenames; it won't work.) If the *MODE* is not recognized, open raises an exception.

If only two arguments are present, the mode and filename/command are assumed to be combined in the second argument. (And if you don't specify a mode in the second argument, just a filename, then the file is opened read-only to be on the safe side.)

With only one argument, the package scalar variable of the same name as the *FILEHANDLE* must contain the filename and optional mode:

```
$LOG = ">logfile";        # $LOG must not be declared my!
    open LOG or die "Can't open logfile: $!";
```

But don't do that. It's not stylin'. Forget we mentioned it.

The open function returns true when it succeeds and undef otherwise. If the open starts up a pipe to a child process, the return value will be the process ID of that new process. As with any syscall, always check the return value of open to make sure it worked. But this isn't C or Java, so don't use an if statement when the or operator will do. You can also use ||, but if you do, use parentheses on the open. If you choose to omit parentheses on the function call to turn it into a list operator, be careful to use "or die" after the list rather than "|| die", because the precedence of || is higher than list operators like open, and the || will bind to your last argument, not the whole open:

```
open LOG, ">logfile" || die "Can't create logfile: $!";   # WRONG
open LOG, ">logfile" or die "Can't create logfile: $!";   # ok
```

That looks rather intense, but typically you'd introduce some whitespace to tell your eye where the list operator ends:

```
open LOG, ">logfile"
        or die "Can't create logfile: $!";
```

As that example shows, the *FILEHANDLE* argument is often just a simple identifier (normally uppercase), but it may also be an expression whose value provides a reference to the actual filehandle. (The reference may be either a symbolic reference to the filehandle name or a hard reference to any object that can be interpreted as a filehandle.) This is called an *indirect filehandle*, and any function that takes a *FILEHANDLE* as its first argument can handle indirect filehandles as well as direct ones. But open is special in that if you supply it with an undefined variable for the indirect filehandle, Perl will automatically define that variable for you, that is, autovivifying it to contain a proper filehandle reference. One advantage of this is that the filehandle will be closed automatically when there are no further references to it, typically when the variable goes out of scope:

```
{
        my $fh;                    # (uninitialized)
        open($fh, ">logfile")      # $fh is autovivified
            or die "Can't create logfile: $!";
        ...                        # do stuff with $fh
}                                  # $fh closed here
```

The my $fh declaration can be readably incorporated into the open:

```
open my $fh, ">logfile" or die ...
```

The > symbol you've been seeing in front of the filename is an example of a mode. Historically, the two-argument form of open came first. The recent addition of the three-argument form lets you separate the mode from the filename, which has the advantage of avoiding any possible confusion between the two. In the following example, we know that the user is not trying to open a filename that happens to start with ">". We can be sure that they're specifying a *MODE* of ">", which opens the file named in *EXPR* for writing, creating the file if it doesn't exist and truncating the file down to nothing if it already exists:

```
open(LOG, ">", "logfile")  or die "Can't create logfile: $!";
```

In the shorter forms, the filename and mode are in the same string. The string is parsed much as the typical shell processes file and pipe redirections. First, any leading and trailing whitespace is removed from the string. Then the string is examined, on either end if need be, for characters specifying how the file is to be opened. Whitespace is allowed between the mode and the filename.

The modes that indicate how to open a file are shell-like redirection symbols. A list of these symbols is provided in Table 29-1. (To access a file with combinations of open modes not covered by this table, see the low-level sysopen function.)

Table 29-1. *Modes for open*

Mode	Read Access	Write Access	Append Only	Create Nonexisting	Clobber Existing
< *PATH*	Y	N	N	N	N
> *PATH*	N	Y	N	Y	Y
>> *PATH*	N	Y	Y	Y	N
+< *PATH*	Y	Y	N	N	N
+> *PATH*	Y	Y	N	Y	Y
+>> *PATH*	Y	Y	Y	Y	N
| *COMMAND*	N	Y	n/a	n/a	n/a
COMMAND |	Y	N	n/a	n/a	n/a

If the mode is "<" or nothing, an existing file is opened for input. If the mode is ">", the file is opened for output, which truncates existing files and creates nonexistent ones. If the mode is ">>", the file is created if needed and opened for appending, and all output is automatically placed at the end of the file. If a new file is created because you used a mode of ">" or ">>" and the file did not previously exist, access permissions will depend on the process's current umask under the rules described for that function.

Here are common examples:

```
open(INFO,      "datafile")  || die("can't open datafile: $!");
open(INFO,    "< datafile")  || die("can't open datafile: $!");
open(RESULTS, "> runstats")  || die("can't open runstats: $!");
open(LOG,     ">> logfile ") || die("can't open logfile:  $!");
```

If you prefer the low-punctuation version, you can write:

```
open INFO,      "datafile"  or die "can't open datafile: $!";
open INFO,    "< datafile"  or die "can't open datafile: $!";
open RESULTS, "> runstats"  or die "can't open runstats: $!";
open LOG,     ">> logfile " or die "can't open logfile:  $!";
```

When opened for reading, the special filename "-" refers to STDIN. When opened for writing, the same special filename refers to STDOUT. Normally, these are specified as "<-" and ">-", respectively.

```
open(INPUT,  "-" ) or die;   # re-open standard input for reading
open(INPUT,  "<-") or die;   # same thing, but explicit
open(OUTPUT, ">-") or die;   # re-open standard output for writing
```

This way the user can supply a program with a filename that will use the standard input or the standard output, but the author of the program doesn't have to write special code to know about this.

You may also place a "+" in front of any of these three modes to request simultaneous read and write. However, whether the file is clobbered or created and whether it must already exist is still governed by your choice of less-than or greater-than signs. This means that "+<" is almost always preferred for read/write updates, as the dubious "+>" mode would first clobber the file before you could ever read anything from it. (Use that mode only if you want to reread only what you just wrote.)

```
open(DBASE, "+< database")
    or die "can't open existing database in update mode: $!";
```

You can treat a file opened for update as a random-access database and use `seek` to move to a particular byte number, but the variable-length records of regular text files usually make it impractical to use read-write mode to update such files. See the **-i** command-line option in Chapter 19 for a different approach to updating.

If the leading character in *EXPR* is a pipe symbol, `open` fires up a new process and connects a write-only filehandle to the command. This way you can write into that handle and what you write will show up on that command's standard input. For example:

```
open(PRINTER, "| lpr -Plp1")    or die "can't fork: $!";
print PRINTER "stuff\n";
close(PRINTER)                   or die "lpr/close failed: $?/$!";
```

If the trailing character in *EXPR* is a pipe symbol, `open` again launches a new process, but this time with a read-only filehandle connected to it. This allows whatever the command writes to its standard output to show up on your handle for reading. For example:

```
open(NET, "netstat -i -n |")    or die "can't fork: $!";
while (<NET>) { ... }
close(NET)                       or die "can't close netstat: $!/$?";
```

Explicitly closing any piped filehandle causes the parent process to wait for the child to finish and returns the status code in $? ($CHILD_ERROR). It's also possible for `close` to set $! ($OS_ERROR). See the examples under `close` and `system` for how to interpret these error codes.

Any pipe command containing shell metacharacters such as wildcards or I/O redirections is passed to your system's canonical shell (*/bin/sh* on Unix), so those shell-specific constructs can be processed first. If no metacharacters are found, Perl launches the new process itself without calling the shell.

You may also use the three-argument form to start up pipes. Using that style, the equivalent of the previous pipe opens would be:

```
open(PRINTER, "|-", "lpr -Plp1")    or die "can't fork: $!";
open(NET, "-|", "netstat -i -n")    or die "can't fork: $!";
```

Here the minus in the second argument represents the command in the third argument. These commands don't happen to invoke the shell, but if you want to guarantee no shell processing occurs, new versions of Perl let you say:

```
open(PRINTER, "|-", "lpr", "-Plp1")    or die "can't fork: $!";
open(NET, "-|", "netstat", "-i", "-n") or die "can't fork: $!";
```

If you use the two-argument form to open a pipe to or from the special command "-",* an implicit fork is done first. (On systems that can't fork, this raises an exception. Microsoft systems did not support fork prior to the 5.6 release of Perl.) In this case, the minus represents your new child process, which is a copy of the parent. The return value from this forking open is the process ID of the child when examined from the parent process, 0 when examined from the child process, and the undefined value undef if the fork fails—in which case, there is no child. For example:

```
defined($pid = open(FROM_CHILD, "-|"))
        or die "can't fork: $!";

if ($pid) {
        @parent_lines = <FROM_CHILD>;  # parent code
}
else {
        print STDOUT @child_lines;     # child code
}
```

The filehandle behaves normally for the parent, but for the child process, the parent's input (or output) is piped from (or to) the child's STDOUT (or STDIN). The child process does not see the parent's filehandle opened. (This is conveniently indicated by the 0 PID.) Typically you'd use this construct instead of the normal piped open when you want to exercise more control over just how the pipe command gets executed (such as when you are running setuid) and don't want to have to scan shell commands for metacharacters. The following piped opens are roughly equivalent:

```
open FH,              "| tr  'a-z'  'A-Z'";   # pipe to shell command
open FH, "|-",        'tr', 'a-z', 'A-Z';     # pipe to bare command
open FH, "|-" or exec 'tr', 'a-z', 'A-Z' or die; # pipe to child
```

as are these:

```
open FH,              "cat   -n 'file' |";    # pipe from shell command
open FH, "-|",        'cat', '-n', 'file';    # pipe from bare command
open FH, "-|" or exec 'cat', '-n', 'file' or die; # pipe from child
```

---

* Or you can think of it as leaving the command off of the three-argument forms above.

For more elaborate uses of fork open, see the sections "Talking to Yourself" in Chapter 16 and "Cleaning Up Your Environment" in Chapter 23, *Security*.

When starting a command with open, you must choose either input or output: "cmd|" for reading or "|cmd" for writing. You may not use open to start a command that pipes both in and out, as the (currently) illegal notation, "|cmd|", might appear to indicate. However, the standard IPC::Open2 and IPC::Open3 library routines give you a close equivalent. For details on double-ended pipes, see the section "Bidirectional Communication" in Chapter 16.

You may also, in the Bourne shell tradition, specify an *EXPR* beginning with >&, in which case the rest of the string is interpreted as the name of a filehandle (or file descriptor, if numeric) to be duplicated using the *dup2*(2) syscall.* You may use & after >, >>, <, +>, +>>, and +<. (The specified mode should match the mode of the original filehandle.)

One reason you might want to do this would be if you already had a filehandle open and wanted to make another handle that's really a duplicate of the first one.

```
open(SAVEOUT, ">&SAVEERR") or die "couldn't dup SAVEERR: $!";
open(MHCONTEXT, "<&4")     or die "couldn't dup fd4: $!";
```

That means that if a function is expecting a filename, but you don't want to give it a filename because you already have the file open, you can just pass the filehandle with a leading ampersand. It's best to use a fully qualified handle though, just in case the function happens to be in a different package:

```
somefunction("&main::LOGFILE");
```

Another reason to "dup" filehandles is to temporarily redirect an existing filehandle without losing track of the original destination. Here is a script that saves, redirects, and restores STDOUT and STDERR:

```
#!/usr/bin/perl
open SAVEOUT, ">&STDOUT";
open SAVEERR, ">&STDERR";

open STDOUT, ">foo.out" or die "Can't redirect stdout";
open STDERR, ">&STDOUT" or die "Can't dup stdout";

select STDERR; $| = 1;        # enable autoflush
select STDOUT; $| = 1;        # enable autoflush

print STDOUT "stdout 1\n";    # these I/O streams propagate to
print STDERR "stderr 1\n";    # subprocesses too
```

---

* This doesn't (currently) work with I/O objects on typeglob references by filehandle autovivification, but you can always use fileno to fetch the file descriptor and dup that.

```
system("some command");        # uses new stdout/stderr

close STDOUT;
close STDERR;

open STDOUT, ">&SAVEOUT";
open STDERR, ">&SAVEERR";

print STDOUT "stdout 2\n";
print STDERR "stderr 2\n";
```

If the filehandle or descriptor number is preceded by a &= combination instead of a simple &, then instead of creating a completely new file descriptor, Perl makes the *FILEHANDLE* an alias for the existing descriptor using the *fdopen*(3) C library call. This is slightly more parsimonious of systems resources, although that's less of a concern these days.

```
$fd = $ENV{"MHCONTEXTFD"};
open(MHCONTEXT, "<&=$fdnum")
        or die "couldn't fdopen descriptor $fdnum: $!";
```

Filehandles STDIN, STDOUT, and STDERR always remain open across an exec. Other filehandles, by default, do not. On systems supporting the fcntl function, you may modify the close-on-exec flag for a filehandle.

```
use Fcntl qw(F_GETFD F_SETFD);
$flags = fcntl(FH, F_SETFD, 0)
        or die "Can't clear close-on-exec flag on FH: $!\n";
```

See also the special $^F ($SYSTEM_FD_MAX) variable in Chapter 28.

With the one- or two-argument form of open, you have to be careful when you use a string variable as a filename, since the variable may contain arbitrarily weird characters (particularly when the filename has been supplied by arbitrarily weird characters on the Internet). If you're not careful, parts of the filename might get interpreted as a *MODE* string, ignorable whitespace, a dup specification, or a minus. Here's one historically interesting way to insulate yourself:

```
$path =~ s#^(\s)#./$1#;
open (FH, "< $path\0") or die "can't open $path: $!";
```

But that's still broken in several ways. Instead, just use the three-argument form of open to open any arbitrary filename cleanly and without any (extra) security risks:

```
open(FH, "<", $path) or die "can't open $path: $!";
```

On the other hand, if what you're looking for is a true, C-style *open*(2) syscall with all its attendant belfries and whistle-stops, then check out sysopen:

```
use Fcntl;
sysopen(FH, $path, O_RDONLY) or die "can't open $path: $!";
```

If you're running on a system that distinguishes between text and binary files, you may need to put your filehandle into binary mode—or forgo doing so, as the case may be—to avoid mutilating your files. On such systems, if you use text mode on a binary file, or binary mode on a text file, you probably won't like the results.

Systems that need the binmode function are distinguished from those that don't by the format used for text files. Those that don't need it terminate each line with a single character that corresponds to what C thinks is a newline, \n. Unix and Mac OS fall into this category. VMS, MVS, MS-whatever, and S&M operating systems of other varieties treat I/O on text files and binary files differently, so they need binmode.

Or its equivalent. As of the 5.6 release of Perl, you can specify binary mode in the open function without a separate call to binmode. As part of the *MODE* argument (but only in the three-argument form), you may specify various input and output disciplines. To do the equivalent of a binmode, use the three argument form of open and stuff a discipline of :raw in after the other *MODE* characters:

```
open(FH, "<:raw", $path) or die "can't open $path: $!";
```

Since this is a very new feature, there will certainly be more disciplines by the time you read this than there were when we wrote it. However, we can reasonably predict that there will in all likelihood be disciplines resembling some or all of the ones in Table 29-2.

Table 29-2. I/O Disciplines

Discipline	Meaning
:raw	Binary mode; do no processing
:text	Default text processing
:def	Default declared by "use open"
:latin1	File should be ISO-8859-1
:ctype	File should be LC_CTYPE
:utf8	File should be UTF-8
:utf16	File should be UTF-16
:utf32	File should be UTF-32
:uni	Intuit Unicode (UTF-*)
:any	Intuit Unicode/Latin1/LC_CTYPE
:xml	Use encoding specified in file
:crlf	Intuit newlines
:para	Paragraph mode
:slurp	Slurp mode

You'll be able to stack disciplines that make sense to stack, so, for instance, you could say:

```
open(FH, "<:para:crlf:uni", $path) or die "can't open $path: $!";
while ($para = <FH>) { ... }
```

That would set up disciplines to:

- read in some form of Unicode and translate to Perl's internal UTF-8 format if the file isn't already in UTF-8,
- look for variants of line-ending sequences, translating them all to \n, and
- process the file into paragraph-sized chunks, much as $/ = "" does.

If you want to set the default open mode (:def) to something other than :text, you can declare that at the top of your file with the open pragma:

```
use open IN => ":any", OUT => ":utf8";
```

In fact, it would be really nice if that were the default :text discipline someday. It perfectly captures the spirit of "Be liberal in what you accept, and strict in what you produce."

opendir

```
opendir DIRHANDLE, EXPR
```

This function opens a directory named *EXPR* for processing by readdir, telldir, seekdir, rewinddir, and closedir. The function returns true if successful. Directory handles have their own namespace separate from filehandles.

ord

```
ord EXPR
ord
```

This function returns the numeric value (ASCII, Latin-1, or Unicode) of the first character of *EXPR*. The return value is always unsigned. If you want a signed value, use unpack('c', *EXPR*). If you want all the characters of the string converted to a list of numbers, use unpack('U*', *EXPR*) instead.

our

```
our TYPE EXPR : ATTRIBUTES
our EXPR : ATTRIBUTES
our TYPE EXPR
our EXPR
```

An our declares one or more variables to be valid globals within the enclosing block, file, or eval. That is, our has the same rules as a my declaration for determination of visibility, but does not create a new private variable; it merely allows unfettered access to the existing package global. If more than one value is listed, the list must be placed in parentheses.

The primary use of an `our` declaration is to hide the variable from the effects of a `use strict "vars"` declaration; since the variable is masquerading as a `my` variable, you are permitted to use the declared global variable without qualifying it with its package. However, just like the `my` variable, this only works within the lexical scope of the `our` declaration. In this respect, it differs from `use vars`, which affects the entire package and is not lexically scoped.

`our` is also like `my` in that you are allowed to declare variables with a *TYPE* and with *ATTRIBUTES*. Here is the syntax:

```
our Dog $spot :ears(short) :tail(long);
```

As of this writing, it's not entirely clear what that will mean. Attributes could affect either the global or the local interpretation of `$spot`. On the one hand, it would be most like `my` variables for attributes to warp the current local view of `$spot` without interfering with other views of the global in other places. On the other hand, if one module declares `$spot` to be a `Dog`, and another declares `$spot` to be a `Cat`, you could end up with meowing dogs or barking cats. This is a subject of ongoing research, which is a fancy way to say we don't know what we're talking about yet. (Except that we do know what to do with the *TYPE* declaration when the variable refers to a pseudohash—see "Managing Instance Data" in Chapter 12.)

Another way in which `our` is like `my` is in its visibility. An `our` declaration declares a global variable that will be visible across its entire lexical scope, even across package boundaries. The package in which the variable is located is determined at the point of the declaration, not at the point of use. This means the following behavior holds and is deemed to be a feature:

```
package Foo;
our $bar;       # $bar is $Foo::bar for rest of lexical scope
$bar = 582;

package Bar;
print $bar;     # prints 582, just as if "our" had been "my"
```

However, the distinction between `my` creating a new, private variable and `our` exposing an existing, global variable is important, especially in assignments. If you combine a run-time assignment with an `our` declaration, the value of the global variable does not disappear once the `our` goes out of scope. For that, you need `local`:

```
($x, $y) = ("one", "two");
print "before block, x is $x, y is $y\n";
{
    our $x = 10;
    local our $y = 20;
    print "in block, x is $x, y is $y\n";
}
print "past block, x is $x, y is $y\n";
```

That prints out:

```
before block, x is one, y is two
in block, x is 10, y is 20
past block, x is 10, y is two
```

Multiple our declarations in the same lexical scope are allowed if they are in different packages. If they happen to be in the same package, Perl will emit warnings if you ask it to.

```
use warnings;
package Foo;
our $bar;          # declares $Foo::bar for rest of lexical scope
$bar = 20;

package Bar;
our $bar = 30;     # declares $Bar::bar for rest of lexical scope
print $bar;        # prints 30

our $bar;          # emits warning
```

See also local, my, and the section "Scoped Declarations" in Chapter 4.

pack

`$@`

```
pack TEMPLATE, LIST
```

This function takes a *LIST* of ordinary Perl values and converts them into a string of bytes according to the *TEMPLATE* and returns this string. The argument list will be padded or truncated as necessary. That is, if you provide fewer arguments than the *TEMPLATE* requires, pack assumes additional null arguments. If you provide more arguments than the *TEMPLATE* requires, the extra arguments are ignored. Unrecognized format elements in *TEMPLATE* will raise an exception.

The template describes the structure of the string as a sequence of fields. Each field is represented by a single character that describes the type of the value and its encoding. For instance, a format character of N specifies an unsigned four-byte integer in big-endian byte order.

Fields are packed in the order given in the template. For example, to pack an unsigned one-byte integer and a single-precision floating-point value into a string, you'd say:

```
$string = pack("Cf", 244, 3.14);
```

The first byte of the returned string has the value 244. The remaining bytes are the encoding of 3.14 as a single-precision float. The particular encoding of the floating point number depends on your computer's hardware.

Some important things to consider when packing are:

- the type of data (such as integer or float or string),
- the range of values (such as whether your integers will fit into one, two, four, or maybe even eight bytes; or whether you're packing 8-bit or Unicode characters),
- whether your integers are signed or unsigned, and
- the encoding to use (such as native, little-endian, or big-endian packing of bits and bytes).

Table 29-3 lists the format characters and their meanings. (Other characters can occur in formats as well; these are described later.)

Table 29-3. Template Characters for pack/unpack

Character	Meaning
a	A null-padded string of bytes
A	A space-padded string of bytes
b	A bit string, in ascending bit order inside each byte (like vec)
B	A bit string, in descending bit order inside each byte
c	A signed char (8-bit integer) value
C	An unsigned char (8-bit integer) value; see U for Unicode
d	A double-precision floating-point number in native format
f	A single-precision floating-point number in native format
h	A hexadecimal string, low nybble first
H	A hexadecimal string, high nybble first
i	A signed integer value, native format
I	An unsigned integer value, native format
l	A signed long value, always 32 bits
L	An unsigned long value, always 32 bits
n	A 16-bit short in "network" (big-endian) order
N	A 32-bit long in "network" (big-endian) order

Table 29-3. Template Characters for pack/unpack (continued)

Character	Meaning
p	A pointer to a null-terminated string
P	A pointer to a fixed-length string
q	A signed quad (64-bit integer) value
Q	An unsigned quad (64-bit integer) value
s	A signed short value, always 16 bits
S	An unsigned short value, always 16 bits
u	A uuencoded string
U	A Unicode character number
v	A 16-bit short in "VAX" (little-endian) order
V	A 32-bit long in "VAX" (little-endian) order
w	A BER compressed integer
x	A null byte (skip forward a byte)
X	Back up a byte
z	A null-terminated (and null-padded) string of bytes
@	Null-fill to absolute position

You may freely place whitespace and comments in your TEMPLATEs. Comments start with the customary # symbol and extend up through the first newline (if any) in the TEMPLATE.

Each letter may be followed by a number indicating the *count*, interpreted as a repeat count or length of some sort, depending on the format. With all formats except a, A, b, B, h, H, P, and Z, *count* is a repeat count, so pack gobbles up that many values from the LIST. A * for the *count* means however many items are left.

The a, A, and z formats gobble just one value, but pack it as a byte string of length *count*, padding with nulls or spaces as necessary. When unpacking, A strips trailing spaces and nulls, z strips everything after the first null, and a returns the literal data unmolested. When packing, a and z are equivalent.

Similarly, the b and B formats pack a string *count* bits long. Each byte of the input field generates 1 bit of the result based on the least-significant bit of each input byte (that is, on ord($byte) % 2). Conveniently, that means bytes 0 and 1 generate bits 0 and 1. Starting from the beginning of the input string, each 8-tuple of bytes is converted to a single byte of output. If the length of the input string is not divisible by 8, the remainder is packed as if padded by 0's. Similarly, during unpacking any extra bits are ignored. If the input string is longer than needed, extra bytes are ignored. A * for the *count* means to use all bytes from the input field. On unpacking, the bits are converted to a string of 0s and 1s.

The h and H formats pack a string of *count* nybbles (4-bit groups often represented as hexadecimal digits).

The p format packs a pointer to a null-terminated string. You are responsible for ensuring the string is not a temporary value (which can potentially get deallocated before you get around to using the packed result). The P format packs a pointer to a structure of the size indicated by *count*. A null pointer is created if the corresponding value for p or P is undef.

The / character allows packing and unpacking of strings where the packed structure contains a byte count followed by the string itself. You write *length-item/string-item*. The *length-item* can be any pack template letter, and describes how the length value is packed. The ones likely to be of most use are integer-packing ones like n (for Java strings), w (for ASN.1 or SNMP) and N (for Sun XDR). The *string-item* must, at present, be A*, a*, or Z*. For unpack, the length of the string is obtained from the *length-item*, but if you put in the *, it will be ignored.

```
unpack 'C/a', "\04Gurusamy";       # gives 'Guru'
unpack 'a3/A* A*', '007 Bond J ';  # gives (' Bond','J')
pack 'n/a* w/a*','hello,','world'; # gives "hello,world"
```

The *length-item* is not returned explicitly from unpack. Adding a *count* to the *length-item* letter is unlikely to do anything useful, unless that letter is A, a, or Z. Packing with a *length-item* of a or Z may introduce null (\0) characters, which Perl does not regard as legal in numeric strings.

The integer formats s, S, l, and L may be immediately followed by a ! to signify native shorts or longs instead of exactly 16 or 32 bits respectively. Today, this is an issue mainly in 64-bit platforms, where the native shorts and longs as seen by the local C compiler can be different than these values. (i! and I! also work but only because of completeness; they are identical to i and I.)

The actual sizes (in bytes) of native shorts, ints, longs, and long longs on the platform where Perl was built are also available via the Config module:

```
use Config;
print $Config{shortsize},    "\n";
print $Config{intsize},      "\n";
print $Config{longsize},     "\n";
print $Config{longlongsize}, "\n";
```

Just because *Configure* knows the size of a long long, doesn't necessarily imply that you have q or Q formats available to you. (Some systems do, but you're probably not running one. Yet.)

Integer formats of greater than one byte in length (s, S, i, I, l, and L) are inherently nonportable between processors because they obey the native byte order and endianness. If you want portable packed integers, use the formats n, N, v, and V; their byte endianness and size are known.

Floating-point numbers are in the native machine format only. Because of the variety of floating formats and lack of a standard "network" representation, no facility for interchange has been made. This means that packed floating-point data written on one machine may not be readable on another. This is a problem even when both machines use IEEE floating-point arithmetic, because the endian-ness of the memory representation is not part of the IEEE spec.

Perl uses doubles internally for all floating-point calculation, so converting from double into float, then back again to double will lose precision. This means that unpack("f", pack("f", $foo)) will not generally equal $foo.

You are responsible for any alignment or padding considerations expected by other programs, particularly those programs that were created by a C compiler with its own idiosyncratic notions of how to lay out a C struct on the particular architecture in question. You'll have to add enough x's while packing to make up for this. For example, a C declaration of:

```
struct foo {
        unsigned char c;
        float f;
};
```

might be written out in a "C x f" format, a "C x3 f" format, or even a "f C" format—just to name a few. The pack and unpack functions handle their input and output as flat sequences of bytes because there is no way for them to know where the bytes are going to or coming from.

Let's look at some examples. This first pair packs numeric values into bytes:

```
$out = pack "CCCC", 65, 66, 67, 68;      # $out eq "ABCD"
$out = pack "C4", 65, 66, 67, 68;        # same thing
```

This one does the same thing with Unicode circled letters:

```
$foo = pack("U4",0x24b6,0x24b7,0x24b8,0x24b9);
```

This does a similar thing, with a couple of nulls thrown in:

```
$out = pack "CCxxCC", 65, 66, 67, 68;    # $out eq "AB\0\0CD"
```

Packing your shorts doesn't imply that you're portable:

```
$out = pack "s2", 1, 2;     # "\1\0\2\0" on little-endian
                            # "\0\1\0\2" on big-endian
```

On binary and hex packs, the *count* refers to the number of bits or nybbles, not the number of bytes produced:

```
$out = pack "B32", "01010000011001010111001001101100";
$out = pack "H8", "5065726c";     # both produce "Perl"
```

The length on an a field applies only to one string:

```
$out = pack "a4", "abcd", "x", "y", "z";     # "abcd"
```

To get around that limitation, use multiple specifiers:

```
$out = pack "aaaa",  "abcd", "x", "y", "z";   # "axyz"
$out = pack "a" x 4, "abcd", "x", "y", "z";   # "axyz"
```

The a format does null filling:

```
$out = pack "a14", "abcdefg";    # "abcdefg\0\0\0\0\0\0\0"
```

This template packs a C struct tm record (at least on some systems):

```
$out = pack "i9pl", gmtime(), $tz, $toff;
```

Generally, the same template may also be used in the unpack function, although some formats act differently, notably a, A, and Z.

If you want to join fixed-width text fields together, use pack with a *TEMPLATE* of several A or a formats:

```
$string = pack("A10" x 10, @data);
```

If you want to join variable-width text fields with a separator, use the join function instead:

```
$string = join(" and ", @data);
$string = join("", @data);                # null separator
```

Although all of our examples used literal strings as templates, there is no reason you couldn't pull in your templates from a disk file. You could build an entire relational database system around this function. (What that would prove about you we won't get into.)

package

```
package NAMESPACE
package
```

This is not really a function, but a declaration that says that the rest of the inner-most enclosing scope belongs to the indicated symbol table or namespace. (The scope of a package declaration is thus the same as the scope of a my or our declaration.) Within its scope, the declaration causes the compiler to resolve all unqualified global identifiers by looking them up in the declared package's symbol table.

A package declaration affects only global variables—including those on which you've used local—not lexical variables created with my. It only affects unqualified global variables; global variables that are qualified with a package name of their own ignore the current declared package. Global variables declared with our are unqualified and therefore respect the current package, but only at the point of declaration, after which they behave like my variables. That is, for the rest of their lexical scope, our variables are "nailed" to the package in use at the point of declaration, even if a subsequent package declaration intervenes.

Typically, you would put a package declaration as the first thing in a file that is to be included by the require or use operator, but you can put one anywhere a statement would be legal. When creating a traditional or objected-oriented module file, it is customary to name the package the same name as the file to avoid confusion. (It's also customary to name such packages beginning with a capital letter because lowercase modules are by convention interpreted as pragmatic modules.)

You can switch into a given package in more than one place; it merely influences which symbol table is used by the compiler for the rest of that block. (If the compiler sees another package declaration at the same level, the new declaration overrides the previous one.) Your main program is assumed to start with an invisible package main declaration.

You can refer to variables, subroutines, handles, and formats in other packages by qualifying the identifier with the package name and a double colon: $Package::Variable. If the package name is null, the main package is assumed. That is, $::sail is equivalent to $main::sail, as well as to $main'sail, which is still occasionally seen in older code.

Here's an example:

```
package main;       $sail = "hale and hearty";
package Mizzen;     $sail = "tattered";
package Whatever;
print "My main sail is $main::sail.\n";
print "My mizzen sail is $Mizzen::sail.\n";
```

This prints:

```
My main sail is hale and hearty.
My mizzen sail is tattered.
```

The symbol table for a package is stored in a hash with a name ending in a double colon. The main package's symbol table is named %main:: for example. So the existing package symbol *main::sail can also be accessed as $main::{"sail"}.

If *NAMESPACE* is omitted, then there is no current package, and all identifiers must be fully qualified or declared as lexicals. This is stricter than use strict since it also extends to function names.

Functions

See Chapter 10, *Packages*, for more information about packages. See my earlier in this chapter for other scoping issues.

pipe $! X ARG X U

```
pipe READHANDLE, WRITEHANDLE
```

Like the corresponding syscall, this function opens a pair of connected pipes—see *pipe*(2). This call is usually used right before a fork, after which the pipe's reader should close WRITEHANDLE, and the writer close READHANDLE. (Otherwise the pipe won't indicate EOF to the reader when the writer closes it.) If you set up a loop of piped processes, deadlock can occur unless you are remarkably careful. In addition, note that Perl's pipes use standard I/O buffering, so you may need to set $| ($OUTPUT_AUTOFLUSH) on your WRITEHANDLE to flush after each output operation, depending on the application—see select (output filehandle).

(As with open, if either filehandle is undefined, it will be autovivfied.)

Here's a small example:

```
pipe(README, WRITEME);
unless ($pid = fork) {  #                     child
    defined $pid or die "can't fork: $!";
    close(README);
    for $i (1..5) { print WRITEME "line $i\n" }
    exit;
}
$SIG{CHLD} = sub { waitpid($pid, 0) };
close(WRITEME);
@strings = <README>;
close(README);
print "Got:\n", @strings;
```

Notice how the writer closes the read end and the reader closes the write end. You can't use one pipe for two-way communication. Either use two different pipes or the socketpair syscall for that. See the section "Pipes" in Chapter 16.

pop

```
pop ARRAY
pop
```

This function treats an array like a stack—it pops (removes) and returns the last value of the array, shortening the array by one element. If ARRAY is omitted, the function pops @_ within the lexical scope of subroutines and formats; it pops @ARGV at file scopes (typically the main program) or within the lexical scopes established by the eval STRING, BEGIN {}, CHECK {}, INIT {}, and END {} constructs. It has the same effect as:

```
$tmp = $ARRAY[$#ARRAY--];
```

or:

```
$tmp = splice @ARRAY, -1;
```

If there are no elements in the array, pop returns undef. (But don't depend on that to tell you when the array is empty if your array contains undef values!) See also push and shift. If you want to pop more than one element, use splice.

The pop requires its first argument to be an array, not a list. If you just want the last element of a list, use this:

```
( LIST ) [-1]
```

pos

```
pos SCALAR
pos
```

This function returns the location in *SCALAR* where the last m//g search over *SCALAR* left off. It returns the offset of the character *after* the last one matched. (That is, it's equivalent to length($`) + length($&).) This is the offset where the next m//g search on that string will start. Remember that the offset of the beginning of the string is 0. For example:

```
$graffito = "fee fie foe foo";
while ($graffito =~ m/e/g) {
    print pos $graffito, "\n";
}
```

prints 2, 3, 7, and 11, the offsets of each of the characters following an "e". The pos function may be assigned a value to tell the next m//g where to start:

```
$graffito = "fee fie foe foo";
pos $graffito = 4;  # Skip the fee, start at fie
while ($graffito =~ m/e/g) {
        print pos $graffito, "\n";
}
```

This prints only 7 and 11. The regular expression assertion \G matches only at the location currently specified by pos for the string being searched. See the section "Positions" in Chapter 5.

print

```
print FILEHANDLE LIST
print LIST
print
```

This function prints a string or a comma-separated list of strings. If set, the contents of the $\ ($OUTPUT_RECORD_SEPARATOR) variable will be implicitly printed at the end of the list. The function returns true if successful, false otherwise. *FILEHANDLE* may be a scalar variable name (unsubscripted), in which case the variable contains either the name of the actual filehandle or a reference to a filehandle object of some sort. As with any other indirect object, *FILEHANDLE* may also be a block that returns such a value:

```
print { $OK ? "STDOUT" : "STDERR" } "stuff\n";
print { $iohandle[$i] } "stuff\n";
```

If *FILEHANDLE* is a variable and the next token is a term, it may be misinterpreted as an operator unless you interpose a + or put parentheses around the arguments. For example:

```
print $a - 2;    # prints $a - 2 to default filehandle (usually STDOUT)
print $a (- 2);  # prints -2 to filehandle specified in $a
print $a -2;     # also prints -2 (weird parsing rules :-)
```

If *FILEHANDLE* is omitted, the function prints to the currently selected output filehandle, initially STDOUT. To set the default output filehandle to something other than STDOUT, use the select *FILEHANDLE* operation.* If *LIST* is also omitted, the function prints $_. Because print takes a *LIST*, anything in the *LIST* is evaluated in list context. Thus, when you say:

```
print OUT <STDIN>;
```

it is not going to print the next line from standard input, but all the rest of the lines from standard input up to end-of-file, since that's what <STDIN> returns in list context. If you want the other thing, say:

```
print OUT scalar <STDIN>;
```

Also, remembering the if-it-looks-like-a-function-it-is-a-function rule, be careful not to follow the print keyword with a left parenthesis unless you want the corresponding right parenthesis to terminate the arguments to the print—interpose a + or put parens around all the arguments:

```
print (1+2)*3, "\n";      # WRONG
print +(1+2)*3, "\n";     # ok
print ((1+2)*3, "\n");    # ok
```

printf

```
printf FILEHANDLE FORMAT, LIST
printf FORMAT, LIST
```

This function prints a formatted string to *FILEHANDLE* or, if omitted, the currently selected output filehandle, initially STDOUT. The first item in the *LIST* must be a

---

* Thus, STDOUT isn't really the default filehandle for print. It's merely the *default* default filehandle.

string that says how to format the rest of the items. This is similar to the C library's *printf*(3) and *fprintf*(3) functions. The function is equivalent to:

```
print FILEHANDLE sprintf FORMAT, LIST
```

except that $\ ($OUTPUT_RECORD_SEPARATOR) is not appended. If use locale is in effect, the character used for the decimal point in formatted floating-point numbers is affected by the LC_NUMERIC locale.

An exception is raised only if an invalid reference type is used as the *FILEHANDLE* argument. Unrecognized formats are passed through intact. Both situations trigger warnings if they're enabled.

See the print and sprintf functions elsewhere in this chapter. The description of sprintf includes the list of format specifications. We'd duplicate them here, but this book is already an ecological disaster.

If you omit both the *FORMAT* and the *LIST*, $_ is used—but in that case, you should have been using print. Don't fall into the trap of using a printf when a simple print would do. The print function is more efficient and less error prone.

prototype

```
prototype FUNCTION
```

Returns the prototype of a function as a string (or undef if the function has no prototype). *FUNCTION* is a reference to, or the name of, the function whose prototype you want to retrieve.

If *FUNCTION* is a string starting with CORE::, the rest is taken as a name for Perl built-in, and an exception is raised if there is no such built-in. If the built-in is not *overridable* (such as qw//) or its arguments cannot be expressed by a prototype (such as system), the function returns undef because the built-in does not really behave like a Perl function. Otherwise, the string describing the equivalent prototype is returned.

push

```
push ARRAY, LIST
```

This function treats *ARRAY* as a stack and pushes the values of *LIST* onto the end of *ARRAY*. The length of *ARRAY* increases by the length of *LIST*. The function returns this new length. The push function has the same effect as:

```
foreach $value (listfunc()) {
    $array[++$#array] = $value;
}
```

or:

```
splice @array, @array, 0, listfunc();
```

but it is more efficient (for both you and your computer). You can use `push` in combination with `shift` to make a fairly time-efficient shift register or queue:

```
for (;;) {
    push @array, shift @array;
    ...
}
```

See also `pop` and `unshift`.

q/STRING/

```
q/STRING/
qq/STRING/
qr/STRING/
qw/STRING/
qx/STRING/
```

Generalized quotes. See the "Pick your own quotes" section Chapter 2. For status annotations on `qx//`, see `readpipe`. For status annotations on `qr//`, see `m//`. See also "Staying in Control" in Chapter 5.

quotemeta   `$_`

```
quotemeta EXPR
quotemeta
```

This function returns the value of *EXPR* with all nonalphanumeric characters back-slashed. (That is, all characters not matching `/[A-Za-z_0-9]/` will be preceded by a backslash in the returned string, regardless of locale settings.) This is the internal function implementing the `\Q` escape in interpolative contexts (including double-quoted strings, backticks, and patterns).

rand

```
rand EXPR
rand
```

This function returns a pseudorandom floating-point number greater than or equal to 0 and less than the value of *EXPR*. (*EXPR* should be positive.) If *EXPR* is omitted, the function returns a floating-point number between 0 and 1 (including 0, but excluding 1). `rand` automatically calls `srand` unless `srand` has already been called. See also `srand`.

To get an integral value, such as for a die roll, combine this with int, as in:

```
$roll = int(rand 6) + 1;       # $roll now a number between 1 and 6
```

Because Perl uses your own C library's pseudorandom number function, like *random*(3) or *drand48*(3), the quality of the distribution is not guaranteed. If you need stronger randomness, such as for cryptographic purposes, you might consult instead the documentation on *random*(4) (if your system has a */dev/random* or */dev/urandom* device), the CPAN module Math::TrulyRandom, or a good textbook on computational generation of pseudorandom numbers, such as the second volume of Knuth.*

read

```
read FILEHANDLE, SCALAR, LENGTH, OFFSET
read FILEHANDLE, SCALAR, LENGTH
```

This function attempts to read *LENGTH* bytes of data into variable *SCALAR* from the specified *FILEHANDLE*. The function returns the number of bytes read or 0 at end-of-file. It returns undef on error. *SCALAR* will grow or shrink to the length actually read. The *OFFSET*, if specified, determines where in the variable to start putting bytes, so that you can read into the middle of a string.

To copy data from filehandle FROM into filehandle TO, you could say:

```
while (read(FROM, $buf, 16384)) {
    print TO $buf;
}
```

The opposite of a read is simply a print, which already knows the length of the string you want to write and can write a string of any length. Don't make the mistake of using write, which is solely used with formats.

Perl's read function is implemented in terms of standard I/O's *fread*(3) function, so the actual *read*(2) syscall may read more than *LENGTH* bytes to fill the input buffer, and *fread*(3) may do more than one *read*(2) syscall in order to fill the buffer. To gain greater control, specify the real syscall using sysread. Calls to read and sysread should not be intermixed unless you are into heavy wizardry (or pain). Whichever one you use, be aware that when reading from a file containing Unicode or any other multibyte encoding, the buffer boundary may fall in the middle of a character.

---

* Knuth, D.E. *The Art of Computer Programming, Seminumerical Algorithms*, vol. 2, 3d ed. (Reading, Mass.: Addison-Wesley, 1997). ISBN 0-201-89684-2.

Functions

readdir $\boxed{\text{S!}}$ $\boxed{\text{T}}$ $\boxed{\text{X}\atop\text{ARG}}$ $\boxed{\text{X}\atop\text{U}}$

```
readdir DIRHANDLE
```

This function reads directory entries (which are simple filenames) from a directory
handle opened by opendir. In scalar context, this function returns the next directory entry, if any; otherwise, it returns undef. In list context, it returns all the rest of
the entries in the directory, which will be a null list if there are no entries. For
example:

```
opendir(THISDIR, ".") or die "serious dainbramage: $!";
@allfiles = readdir THISDIR;
closedir THISDIR;
print "@allfiles\n";
```

That prints all the files in the current directory on one line. If you want to avoid
the "." and ".." entries, incant one of these (whichever you think is least unread-
able):

```
@allfiles = grep { $_ ne '.' and $_ ne '..' } readdir THISDIR;
@allfiles = grep { not /^[.][.]?\z/ } readdir THISDIR;
@allfiles = grep { not /^\.{1,2}\z/ } readdir THISDIR;
@allfiles = grep !/^\.\.?\z/, readdir THISDIR;
```

And to avoid all .* files (like the *ls* program):

```
@allfiles = grep !/^\./, readdir THISDIR;
```

To get just text files, say this:

```
@textfiles = grep -T, readdir THISDIR;
```

But watch out on that last one because the result of readdir needs to have the
directory part glued back on if it's not the current directory—like this:

```
opendir(THATDIR, $path) or die "can't opendir $path: $!";
@dotfiles = grep { /^\./ && -f } map { "$path/$_" } readdir(THATDIR);
closedir THATDIR;
```

readline $\boxed{\text{S!}}$ $\boxed{\text{T}}$ $\boxed{\text{X}\atop\text{ARG}}$

```
readline FILEHANDLE
```

This is the internal function implementing the <FILEHANDLE> operator, but you can
use it directly. The function reads the next record from *FILEHANDLE*, which may be
a filehandle name or an indirect filehandle expression that returns either the name
of the actual filehandle or a reference to anything resembling a filehandle object,
such as a typeglob. (Versions of Perl prior to 5.6 accept only a typeglob.) In scalar
context, each call reads and returns the next record until end-of-file is reached,

whereupon the subsequent call returns `undef`. In list context, `readline` reads records until end-of-file is reached and then returns a list of records. By "record", we normally mean a line of text, but changing the value of $/ (`$INPUT_RECORD_SEPARATOR`) from its default value causes this operator to "chunk" the text differently. Likewise, some input disciplines such as `:para` (paragraph mode) will return records in chunks other than lines. Setting the `:slurp` discipline (or undefining $/) makes the chunk size entire files.

When slurping files in scalar context, if you happen to slurp an empty file, `readline` returns `""` the first time, and `undef` each subsequent time. When slurping from magical `ARGV` filehandle, each file returns one chunk (again, null files return as `""`), followed by a single `undef` when the files are exhausted.

The `<FILEHANDLE>` operator is discussed in more detail in the section "Input Operators" in Chapter 2.

```
$line = <STDIN>;
$line = readline(STDIN);        # same thing
$line = readline(*STDIN);       # same thing
$line = readline(\*STDIN);      # same thing

open my $fh, "<&=STDIN" or die;
bless $fh => 'AnyOldClass';
$line = readline($fh);          # same thing
```

readline

[S_] [S!] [T] [X̲U]

```
readlink EXPR
readlink
```

This function returns the filename pointed to by a symbolic link. *EXPR* should evaluate to a filename, the last component of which is a symbolic link. If it is not a symbolic link, or if symbolic links are not implemented on the filesystem, or if some system error occurs, `undef` is returned, and you should check the error code in $!.

Be aware that the returned symlink may be relative to the location you specified. For instance, you may say:

```
readlink "/usr/local/src/express/yourself.h"
```

and `readlink` might return:

```
../express.1.23/includes/yourself.h
```

which is not directly usable as a filename unless your current directory happens to be /usr/local/src/express.

Functions

readpipe $! $? T X̲T X̲U

```
readpipe scalar EXPR
readpipe LIST (proposed)
```

This is the internal function implementing the qx// quote construct (also known as the backticks operator). It is occasionally handy when you need to specify your *EXPR* in a way that wouldn't be handy using the quoted form. Be aware that we may change this interface in the future to support a *LIST* argument in order to make it more like the exec function, so don't assume that it will continue to provide scalar context for *EXPR*. Supply the scalar yourself, or try the *LIST* form. Who knows, it might work by the time you read this.

recv $! T X̲ARG X̲RO X̲U

```
recv SOCKET, SCALAR, LEN, FLAGS
```

This function receives a message on a socket. It attempts to receive *LENGTH* bytes of data into variable *SCALAR* from the specified *SOCKET* filehandle. The function returns the address of the sender, or undef if there's an error. *SCALAR* will grow or shrink to the length actually read. The function takes the same flags as *recv*(2). See the section "Sockets" in Chapter 16.

redo $@

```
redo LABEL
redo
```

The redo operator restarts a loop block without reevaluating the conditional. The continue block, if any, is not executed. If the *LABEL* is omitted, the operator refers to the innermost enclosing loop. This operator is normally used by programs that wish to deceive themselves about what was just input:

```
# A loop that joins lines continued with a backslash.
while (<STDIN>) {
    if (s/\\\n$// && defined($nextline = <STDIN>)) {
        $_ .= $nextline;
        redo;
    }
    print;  # or whatever...
}
```

redo cannot be used to exit a block that returns a value such as eval {}, sub {}, or do {}, and should not be used to exit a grep or map operation. With warnings enabled, Perl will warn you if you redo a loop not in your current lexical scope.

A block by itself is semantically identical to a loop that executes once. Thus redo inside such a block will effectively turn it into a looping construct. See the section "Loop Control" in Chapter 4.

ref

$_

```
ref EXPR
ref
```

The `ref` operator returns a true value if *EXPR* is a reference, false otherwise. The value returned depends on the type of thing the reference refers to. Built-in types include:

```
SCALAR
ARRAY
HASH
CODE
GLOB
REF
LVALUE
IO::Handle
```

If the referenced object has been blessed into a package, then that package name is returned instead. You can think of `ref` as a "typeof" operator.

```
if (ref($r) eq "HASH") {
    print "r is a reference to a hash.\n";
}
elsif (ref($r) eq "Hump") {    # Naughty--see below.
    print "r is a reference to a Hump object.\n";
}
elsif (not ref $r) {
    print "r is not a reference at all.\n";
}
```

It's considered bad OO style to test your object's class for equality to any particular class name, since a derived class will have a different name, but should be allowed access to the base class's methods. It's better to use the UNIVERSAL method `isa` as follows:

```
if ($r->isa("Hump") }
    print "r is a reference to a Hump object, or subclass.\n";
}
```

It's usually best not to test at all, since the OO mechanism won't send the object to your method unless it thinks it's appropriate in the first place. See Chapter 8 and Chapter 12 for more details. See also the `reftype` function under the `use attributes` pragma in Chapter 31.

rename

S! X
T

```
rename OLDNAME, NEWNAME
```

This function changes the name of a file. It returns true for success, false otherwise. It will not (usually) work across filesystem boundaries, although on a Unix system the *mv* command can sometimes be used to compensate for this. If a file named *NEWNAME* already exists, it will be destroyed. Non-Unix systems might have additional restrictions.

See the standard `File::Copy` module for cross-filesystem renames.

require   `$_` `$!` `$@` `$|`

```
require VERSION
require EXPR
require
```

This function asserts a dependency of some kind on its argument.

If the argument is a string, `require` loads and executes the Perl code found in the separate file whose name is given by the string. This is similar to performing a `do` on a file, except that `require` checks to see whether the library file has been loaded already and raises an exception if any difficulties are encountered. (It can thus be used to express file dependencies without worrying about duplicate compilation.) Like its cousins `do` and `use`, `require` knows how to search the include path stored in the `@INC` array and to update `%INC` upon success. See Chapter 28.

The file must return true as the last value to indicate successful execution of any initialization code, so it's customary to end such a file with `1;` unless you're sure it'll return true otherwise.

If `require`'s argument is a version number of the form 5.6.2, `require` demands that the currently executing version of Perl be at least that version. (Perl also accepts a floating point number such as 5.005_03 for compatibility with older versions of Perl, but that form is now discouraged because folks from other cultures don't understand it.) Thus, a script that requires Perl version 5.6 can put as its first line:

```
require 5.6.0;          # or require v5.6.0
```

and earlier versions of Perl will abort. Like all `require`s, however, this is done at run-time. You might prefer to say `use 5.6.0` for a compile-time check. See also `$PERL_VERSION` in Chapter 28.

If `require`'s argument is a bare package name (see `package`), `require` assumes an automatic *.pm* suffix, making it easy to load standard modules. This behavior is like `use`, except that it happens at run time rather than compile time, and the `import` method is not called. For example, to pull in *Socket.pm* without introducing any symbols into the current package, say this:

```
require Socket;         # instead of "use Socket;"
```

However, you can get the same effect with the following, which has the advantage of giving a compile-time warning if *Socket.pm* can't be located:

```
use Socket ();
```

Using `require` on a bare name also replaces any `::` in the package name with your system's directory separator, traditionally `/`. In other words, if you try this:

```
require Foo::Bar;          # a splendid bare name
```

The require function looks for the *Foo/Bar.pm* file in the directories specified in the @INC array. But if you try this:

```
$class = 'Foo::Bar';
require $class;            # $class is not a bare name
```

or this:

```
require "Foo::Bar";        # quoted literal not a bare name
```

the require function will look for the *Foo::Bar* file in the @INC array and will complain about not finding *Foo::Bar* there. If so, you can do this:

```
eval "require $class";
```

See also do *FILE*, the use command, the use `lib` pragma, and the standard FindBin module.

reset

```
reset EXPR
reset
```

This function is generally used (or abused) at the top of a loop or in a continue block at the end of a loop, to clear global variables or reset ?? searches so that they work again. The expression is interpreted as a list of single characters (hyphens are allowed for ranges). All scalar variables, arrays, and hashes beginning with one of those letters are reset to their pristine state. If the expression is omitted, one-match searches (?*PATTERN*?) are reset to match again. The function resets variables or searches for the current package only. It always returns true.

To reset all "x" variables, say this:

```
reset 'X';
```

To reset all lowercase variables, say this:

```
reset 'a-z';
```

Lastly, to just reset ?? searches, say:

```
reset;
```

Resetting "A-Z" in package main is not recommended since you'll wipe out your global ARGV, INC, ENV, and SIG arrays and hashes.

Lexical variables (created by `my`) are not affected. Use of `reset` is vaguely deprecated because it easily clears out entire namespaces and because the `??` operator is itself vaguely deprecated.

See also the `delete_package()` function from the standard `Symbol` module, and the whole issue of Safe compartments documented in the section "Safe Compartments" in Chapter 23.

return   `$@`

```
return EXPR
return
```

This operator causes the current subroutine (or `eval` or `do FILE`) to return immediately with the specified value. Attempting to use `return` outside these three places raises an exception. Note also that an `eval` cannot do a `return` on behalf of the subroutine that called the `eval`.

EXPR may be evaluated in list, scalar, or void context, depending on how the return value will be used, which may vary from one execution to the next. That is, the supplied expression will be evaluated in the context of the subroutine invocation. If the subroutine was called in a scalar context, *EXPR* is also evaluated in scalar context. If the subroutine was invoked in list context, then *EXPR* is also evaluated in list context and can return a list value. A `return` with no argument returns the scalar value `undef` in scalar context, an empty list `()` in list context, and (naturally) nothing at all in void context. The context of the subroutine call can be determined from within the subroutine by using the (misnamed) `wantarray` function.

reverse

```
reverse LIST
```

In list context, this function returns a list value consisting of the elements of *LIST* in the opposite order. The function can be used to create descending sequences:

```
for (reverse 1 .. 10) { ... }
```

Because of the way hashes flatten into lists when passed as a *LIST*, `reverse` can also be used to invert a hash, presuming the values are unique:

```
%barfoo = reverse %foobar;
```

In scalar context, the function concatenates all the elements of *LIST* and then returns the reverse of that resulting string, character by character.

A small hint: reversing a list sorted earlier by a user-defined function can often be achieved more easily by sorting the list in the opposite direction in the first place.

rewinddir

$\boxed{\text{S!}}$ $\boxed{\substack{\text{X} \\ \text{ARG}}}$ $\boxed{\substack{\text{X} \\ \text{U}}}$

> `rewinddir` *DIRHANDLE*

This function sets the current position to the beginning of the directory for the `readdir` routine on *DIRHANDLE*. The function may not be available on all machines that support `readdir`—`rewinddir` dies if unimplemented. It returns true on success, false otherwise.

rindex

> `rindex` *STR, SUBSTR, POSITION*
> `rindex` *STR, SUBSTR*

This function works just like `index` except that it returns the position of the *last* occurrence of *SUBSTR* in *STR* (a reverse `index`). The function returns $-1 if not *SUBSTR* is found. Since $[is virtually always 0 nowadays, the function virtually always returns -1. *POSITION*, if specified, is the rightmost position that may be returned. To work your way through a string backward, say:

```
$pos = length $string;
while (($pos = rindex $string, $lookfor, $pos) >= 0) {
    print "Found at $pos\n";
    $pos--;
}
```

rmdir

$\boxed{\text{S\_}}$ $\boxed{\text{S!}}$ $\boxed{\substack{\text{X} \\ \text{T}}}$

> `rmdir` *FILENAME*
> `rmdir`

This function deletes the directory specified by *FILENAME* if the directory is empty. If the function succeeds, it returns true; otherwise, it returns false. See also the `File::Path` module if you want to remove the contents of the directory first and don't care to shell out to call `rm -r` for some reason. (Such as not having a shell, or an *rm* command, because you haven't got PPT yet.)

s///

$\boxed{\text{T}}$ $\boxed{\substack{\text{X} \\ \text{RO}}}$ $\boxed{\substack{\text{X} \\ \text{T}}}$

> `s///`

The substitution operator. See the section "Pattern-Matching Operators" in Chapter 5.

scalar

```
scalar EXPR
```

This pseudofunction may be used within a *LIST* to force *EXPR* to be evaluated in scalar context when evaluation in the list context would produce a different result. For example:

```
my ($nextvar) = scalar <STDIN>;
```

prevents <STDIN> from reading all the lines from standard input before doing the assignment, since assignment to a list (even a my list) provides a list context. (Without the scalar in this example, the first line from <STDIN> would still be assigned to $nextvar, but the subsequent lines would be read and thrown away, since the list we're assigning to is only able to receive a single scalar value.)

Of course, a simpler, less-cluttered way would be to just leave the parentheses off, thereby changing the list context to a scalar one:

```
my $nextvar = <STDIN>;
```

Since a print function is a *LIST* operator, you have to say:

```
print "Length is ", scalar(@ARRAY), "\n";
```

if you want the length of @ARRAY to be printed out.

There's no "list" function corresponding to scalar since, in practice, one never needs to force evaluation in a list context. That's because any operation that wants *LIST* already provides a list context to its list arguments for free.

Because scalar is a unary operator, if you accidentally use a parenthesized list for the *EXPR*, this behaves as a scalar comma expression, evaluating all but the last element in void context and returning the final element evaluated in scalar context. This is seldom what you want. The following single statement:

```
print uc(scalar(&foo,$bar)),$baz;
```

is the (im)moral equivalent of these two:

```
&foo;
print(uc($bar),$baz);
```

See Chapter 2 for more details on the comma operator. See "Prototypes" in Chapter 6 for more on unary operators.

seek

```
seek FILEHANDLE, OFFSET, WHENCE
```

This function positions the file pointer for *FILEHANDLE*, just like the *fseek*(3) call of standard I/O. The first position in a file is at offset 0, not offset 1. Also, offsets refer to byte positions, not line numbers. In general, since line lengths vary, it's not possible to access a particular line number without examining the whole file up to that point, unless all your lines are known to be of a particular length, or you've built an index that translates line numbers into byte offsets. (The same restrictions apply to character positions in files with variable-length character encodings: the operating system doesn't know what characters are, only bytes.)

FILEHANDLE can be an expression whose value gives either the name of the actual filehandle or a reference to anything resembling a filehandle object. The function returns true upon success, false otherwise. For handiness, the function can calculate offsets from various file positions for you. The value of *WHENCE* specifies which file position your *OFFSET* uses for its starting point: 0, the beginning of the file; 1, the current position in the file; or 2, the end of the file. The *OFFSET* can be negative for a *WHENCE* of 1 or 2. If you'd like to use symbolic values for *WHENCE*, you may use SEEK_SET, SEEK_CUR, and SEEK_END from either the IO::Seekable or the POSIX module, or as of the 5.6 release of Perl, the Fcntl module.

If you want to position the file for sysread or syswrite, don't use seek; standard I/O buffering makes its effect on the file's system position unpredictable and nonportable. Use sysseek instead.

Due to the rules and rigors of ANSI C, on some systems you have to do a seek whenever you switch between reading and writing. Amongst other things, this may have the effect of calling the standard I/O library's *clearerr*(3) function. A *WHENCE* of 1 (SEEK_CUR) with an *OFFSET* 0 is useful for not moving the file position:

```
seek(TEST,0,1);
```

One interesting use for this function is to allow you to follow growing files, like this:

```
for (;;) {
    while (<LOG>) {
        grok($_);            # Process current line.
    }
    sleep 15;
    seek LOG,0,1;            # Reset end-of-file error.
}
```

Functions

The final seek clears the end-of-file error without moving the pointer. Depending on how standard your C library's standard I/O implementation happens to be, you may need something more like this:

```
for (;;) {
    for ($curpos = tell FILE; <FILE>; $curpos = tell FILE) {
        grok($_);               # Process current line.
    }
    sleep $for_a_while;
    seek FILE, $curpos, 0; # Reset end-of-file error.
}
```

Similar strategies can be used to remember the seek addresses of each line in an array.

seekdir   S! ᵪARG ᵪU

```
seekdir DIRHANDLE, POS
```

This function sets the current position for the next call to readdir on *DIRHANDLE*. *POS* must be a value returned by telldir. This function has the same caveats about possible directory compaction as the corresponding system library routine. The function may not be implemented everywhere that readdir is. It's certainly not implemented where readdir isn't.

select (output filehandle)   ᵪARG

```
select FILEHANDLE
select
```

For historical reasons, there are two select operators that are totally unrelated to each other. See the next section for the other one. This version of the select operator returns the currently selected output filehandle and, if *FILEHANDLE* is supplied, sets the current default filehandle for output. This has two effects: first, a write or a print without a filehandle will default to this *FILEHANDLE*. Second, special variables related to output will refer to this output filehandle. For example, if you have to set the same top-of-form format for more than one output filehandle, you might do the following:

```
select REPORT1;
$^ = 'MyTop';
select REPORT2;
$^ = 'MyTop';
```

But note that this leaves REPORT2 as the currently selected filehandle. This could be construed as antisocial, since it could really foul up some other routine's print or write statements. Properly written library routines leave the currently selected filehandle the same on exit as it was upon entry. To support this, *FILEHANDLE* may be an expression whose value gives the name of the actual filehandle. Thus, you can save and restore the currently selected filehandle like this:

```
my $oldfh = select STDERR; $| = 1; select $oldfh;
```

or idiomatically but somewhat obscurely like this:

```
select((select(STDERR), $| = 1)[0])
```

This example works by building a list consisting of the returned value from `select(STDERR)` (which selects `STDERR` as a side effect) and `$| = 1` (which is always 1), but sets autoflushing on the now-selected `STDERR` as a side effect. The first element of that list (the previously selected filehandle) is now used as an argument to the outer `select`. Bizarre, right? That's what you get for knowing just enough Lisp to be dangerous.

You can also use the standard `SelectSaver` module to automatically restore the previous `select` upon scope exit.

However, now that we've explained all that, we should point out that you rarely need to use this form of `select` nowadays, because most of the special variables you would want to set have object-oriented wrapper methods to do it for you. So instead of setting `$|` directly, you might say:

```
use IO::Handle;            # Unfortunately, this is *not* a small module.
STDOUT->autoflush(1);
```

And the earlier format example might be coded as:

```
use IO::Handle;
REPORT1->format_top_name("MyTop");
REPORT2->format_top_name("MyTop");
```

select (ready file descriptors) `S!` `X U`

```
select RBITS, WBITS, EBITS, TIMEOUT
```

The four-argument `select` operator is totally unrelated to the previously described `select` operator. This operator is used to discover which (if any) of your file descriptors are ready to do input or output, or to report an exceptional condition. (This helps you avoid having to do polling.) It calls the *select*(2) syscall with the bit masks you've specified, which you can construct using `fileno` and `vec`, like this:

```
$rin = $win = $ein = "";
vec($rin, fileno(STDIN), 1)  = 1;
vec($win, fileno(STDOUT), 1) = 1;
$ein = $rin | $win;
```

If you want to `select` on many filehandles, you might wish to write a subroutine:

```
sub fhbits {
    my @fhlist = @_;
    my $bits;
    for (@fhlist) {
        vec($bits, fileno($_), 1) = 1;
    }
    return $bits;
}
$rin = fhbits(qw(STDIN TTY MYSOCK));
```

If you wish to use the same bit masks repeatedly (and it's more efficient if you do), the usual idiom is:

```
($nfound, $timeleft) =
    select($rout=$rin, $wout=$win, $eout=$ein, $timeout);
```

Or to block until any file descriptor becomes ready:

```
$nfound = select($rout=$rin, $wout=$win, $eout=$ein, undef);
```

As you can see, calling `select` in scalar context just returns `$nfound`, the number of ready descriptors found.

The `$wout=$win` trick works because the value of an assignment is its left side, so `$wout` gets clobbered first by the assignment and then by the `select`, while `$win` remains unchanged.

Any of the arguments can also be `undef`, in which case they're ignored. The *TIME-OUT*, if not `undef`, is in seconds, which may be fractional. (A timeout of 0 effects a poll.) Not many implementations are capable of returning `$timeleft`. If not, they always return `$timeleft` equal to the supplied `$timeout`.

The standard `IO::Select` module provides a more user-friendly interface to `select`, mostly because it does all the bit mask work for you.

One use for `select` is to sleep with a finer resolution than `sleep` allows. To do this, specify `undef` for all the bitmasks. So, to sleep for (at least) 4.75 seconds, use:

```
select undef, undef, undef, 4.75;
```

(On some non-Unix systems the triple `undef` may not work, and you may need to fake up at least one bitmask for a valid descriptor that won't ever be ready.)

One should probably not attempt to mix buffered I/O (like `read` or `<HANDLE>`) with `select`, except as permitted by POSIX, and even then only on truly POSIX systems. Use `sysread` instead.

semctl   `S!` `X U`

```
semctl ID, SEMNUM, CMD, ARG
```

This function calls the System V IPC function *semctl*(2). You'll probably have to say use IPC::SysV first to get the correct constant definitions. If CMD is IPC_STAT or GETALL, then ARG must be a variable that will hold the returned semid_ds structure or semaphore value array. As with ioctl and fcntl, return values are undef for error, "0 but true" for zero, and the actual return value otherwise.

See also the IPC::Semaphore module. This function is available only on machines supporting System V IPC.

semget   `S!` `X U`

```
semget KEY, NSEMS, SIZE, FLAGS
```

This function calls the System V IPC syscall *semget*(2). Before calling, you should use IPC::SysV to get the correct constant definitions. The function returns the semaphore ID, or undef if there is an error.

See also the IPC::Semaphore module. This function is available only on machines supporting System V IPC.

semop   `S!` `X U`

```
semop KEY, OPSTRING
```

This function calls the System V IPC syscall *semop*(2) to perform semaphore operations such as signalling and waiting. Before calling, you should use IPC::SysV to get the correct constant definitions.

OPSTRING must be a packed array of semop structures. You can make each semop structure by saying pack("s*", $semnum, $semop, $semflag). The number of semaphore operations is implied by the length of OPSTRING. The function returns true if successful, or false if there is an error.

The following code waits on semaphore $semnum of semaphore id $semid:

```
$semop = pack "s*", $semnum, -1, 0;
semop $semid, $semop or die "Semaphore trouble: $!\n";
```

To signal the semaphore, simply replace –1 with 1.

See the section "System V IPC" in Chapter 16. See also the IPC::Semaphore module. This function is available only on machines supporting System V IPC.

Functions

send

```
send SOCKET, MSG, FLAGS, TO
send SOCKET, MSG, FLAGS
```

This function sends a message on a socket. It takes the same flags as the syscall of the same name—see *send*(2). On unconnected sockets, you must specify a destination to send *TO*, which then makes Perl's send work like *sendto*(2). The C syscall *sendmsg*(2) is currently unimplemented in standard Perl. The send function returns the number of bytes sent, or undef if there is an error.

(Some non-Unix systems improperly treat sockets as different from ordinary file descriptors, with the result that you must always use send and recv on sockets rather than the handier standard I/O operators.)

One error that at least one of us makes frequently is to confuse Perl's send with C's send and write:

```
send SOCK, $buffer, length $buffer      # WRONG
```

This will mysteriously fail depending on the relationship of the string length to the *FLAGS* bits expected by the system. See the section "Message Passing" in Chapter 16 for examples.

setpgrp

```
setpgrp PID, PGRP
```

This function sets the current process group (*PGRP*) for the specified *PID* (use a *PID* of 0 for the current process). Invoking setpgrp will raise an exception if used on a machine that doesn't implement *setpgrp*(2). Beware: some systems will ignore the arguments you provide and always do setpgrp(0, $$). Fortunately, those are the arguments one usually wants to provide. If the arguments are omitted, they default to 0,0. The BSD 4.2 version of setpgrp did not accept any arguments, but in BSD 4.4, it is a synonym for the setpgid function. For better portability (by some definition), use the setpgid function in the POSIX module directly. If what you're really trying to do is daemonize your script, consider the POSIX::setsid() function as well. Note that the POSIX version of setpgrp does not accept arguments, so only setpgrp(0,0) is truly portable.

setpriority

```
setpriority WHICH, WHO, PRIORITY
```

This function sets the current *PRIORITY* for a process, a process group, or a user, as specified by the *WHICH* and *WHO*. See *setpriority*(2). Invoking setpriority will raise an exception if used on a machine that doesn't implement *setpriority*(2). To "nice" your process down by four units (the same as executing your program with *nice*(1)), try:

```
setpriority 0, 0, getpriority(0, 0) + 4;
```

The interpretation of a given priority may vary from one operating system to the next. Some priorities may be unavailable to nonprivileged users.

See also the `BSD::Resource` module from CPAN.

setsockopt

S! X ARG X U

```
setsockopt SOCKET, LEVEL, OPTNAME, OPTVAL
```

This function sets the socket option requested. The function returns undef on error. *LEVEL* specifies which protocol layer you're aiming the call at, or SOL_SOCKET for the socket itself at the top of all the layers. *OPTVAL* may be specified as undef if you don't want to pass an argument. A common option to set on a socket is SO_REUSEADDR, to get around the problem of not being able to bind to a particular address while the previous TCP connection on that port is still making up its mind to shut down. That would look like this:

```
use Socket;
socket(SOCK, ...) or die "Can't make socket: $!\n";
setsockopt(SOCK, SOL_SOCKET, SO_REUSEADDR, 1)
        or warn "Can't do setsockopt: $!\n";
```

See *setsockopt*(2) for other possible values.

shift

```
shift ARRAY
shift
```

This function shifts the first value of the array off and returns it, shortening the array by one and moving everything down. (Or up, or left, depending on how you visualize the array list. We like left.) If there are no elements in the array, the function returns undef.

If *ARRAY* is omitted, the function shifts @_ within the lexical scope of subroutines and formats; it shifts @ARGV at file scopes (typically the main program) or within the lexical scopes established by the eval *STRING*, BEGIN {}, CHECK {}, INIT {}, and END {} constructs.

Subroutines often start by copying their arguments into lexical variables, and shift can be used for this:

```
sub marine {
        my $fathoms = shift;   # depth
        my $fishies = shift;   # number of fish
        my $o2      = shift;   # oxygen concentration
        # ...
}
```

shift is also used to process arguments at the front of your program:

```
while (defined($_ = shift)) {
        /^[^-]/    && do { unshift @ARGV, $_; last };
        /^-w/      && do { $WARN = 1;          next };
        /^-r/      && do { $RECURSE = 1;       next };
        die "Unknown argument $_\n";
}
```

You might also consider the Getopt::Std and Getopt::Long modules for processing program arguments.

See also unshift, push, pop, and splice. The shift and unshift functions do the same thing to the left end of an array that pop and push do to the right end.

shmctl   [S!] [X̱ʊ]

>   shmctl *ID*, *CMD*, *ARG*

This function calls the System V IPC syscall, *shmctl*(2). Before calling, you should use IPC::SysV to get the correct constant definitions.

If *CMD* is IPC_STAT, then *ARG* must be a variable that will hold the returned shmid_ds structure. Like ioctl and fcntl, the function returns undef for error, "0 but true" for zero, and the actual return value otherwise.

This function is available only on machines supporting System V IPC.

shmget   [S!] [X̱ʊ]

>   shmget *KEY*, *SIZE*, *FLAGS*

This function calls the System V IPC syscall, *shmget*(2). The function returns the shared memory segment ID, or undef if there is an error. Before calling, use SysV::IPC.

This function is available only on machines supporting System V IPC.

shmread   [S!] [X̱ʊ]

>   shmread *ID*, *VAR*, *POS*, *SIZE*

This function reads from the shared memory segment *ID* starting at position *POS* for size *SIZE* (by attaching to it, copying out, and detaching from it). *VAR* must be a variable that will hold the data read. The function returns true if successful, or false if there is an error.

This function is available only on machines supporting System V IPC.

shmwrite

```
shmwrite ID, STRING, POS, SIZE
```

This function writes to the shared memory segment *ID* starting at position *POS* for size *SIZE* (by attaching to it, copying in, and detaching from it). If *STRING* is too long, only *SIZE* bytes are used; if *STRING* is too short, nulls are written to fill out *SIZE* bytes. The function returns true if successful, or false if there is an error.

This function is available only on machines supporting System V IPC. (You're probably tired of reading that—we're getting tired of saying it.)

shutdown

```
shutdown SOCKET, HOW
```

This function shuts down a socket connection in the manner indicated by *HOW*. If *HOW* is 0, further receives are disallowed. If *HOW* is 1, further sends are disallowed. If *HOW* is 2, everything is disallowed.

```
shutdown(SOCK, 0);      # no more reading
shutdown(SOCK, 1);      # no more writing
shutdown(SOCK, 2);      # no more I/O at all
```

This is useful with sockets when you want to tell the other side you're done writing but not done reading, or vice versa. It's also a more insistent form of close because it also disables any copies of those file descriptors held in forked processes.

Imagine a server that wants to read its client's request until end of file, then send an answer. If the client calls close, that socket is now invalid for I/O, so no answer would ever come back. Instead, the client should use shutdown to half-close the connection:

```
print SERVER "my request\n";    # send some data
shutdown(SERVER, 1);            # send eof; no more writing
$answer = <SERVER>;            # but you can still read
```

(If you came here trying to figure out how to shut down your system, you'll have to execute an external program to do that. See system.)

sin $[s_]$

```
sin EXPR
sin
```

Sorry, there's nothing wicked about this operator. It merely returns the sine of *EXPR* (expressed in radians).

For the inverse sine operation, you may use `Math::Trig` or the `POSIX` module's `asin` function, or use this relation:

```
sub asin { atan2($_[0], sqrt(1 - $_[0] * $_[0])) }
```

sleep

```
sleep EXPR
sleep
```

This function causes the script to sleep for *EXPR* seconds, or forever if no *EXPR*, and returns the number of seconds slept. It may be interrupted by sending the process a `SIGALRM`. On some older systems, it may sleep up to a full second less than what you requested, depending on how it counts seconds. Most modern systems always sleep the full amount. They may appear to sleep longer than that, however, because your process might not be scheduled right away in a busy multitasking system. If available, the `select` (ready file descriptors) call can give you better resolution. You may also be able to use `syscall` to call the *getitimer*(2) and *setitimer*(2) routines that some Unix systems support. You probably cannot mix `alarm` and `sleep` calls, because `sleep` is often implemented using `alarm`.

See also the `POSIX` module's `sigpause` function.

socket $[S!]$ $[\frac{X}{ARG}]$ $[\frac{X}{T}]$ $[\frac{X}{U}]$

```
socket SOCKET, DOMAIN, TYPE, PROTOCOL
```

This function opens a socket of the specified kind and attaches it to filehandle *SOCKET*. *DOMAIN*, *TYPE*, and *PROTOCOL* are specified the same as for *socket*(2). If undefined, *SOCKET* will be autovivified. Before using this function, your program should contain the line:

```
use Socket;
```

This gives you the proper constants. The function returns true if successful. See the examples in the section "Sockets" in Chapter 16.

On systems that support a close-on-exec flag on files, the flag will be set for the newly opened file descriptor, as determined by the value of `$^F`. See the `$^F` (`$SYSTEM_FD_MAX`) variable in Chapter 28.

socketpair

```
socketpair SOCKET1, SOCKET2, DOMAIN, TYPE, PROTOCOL
```

This function creates an unnamed pair of sockets in the specified domain, of the specified type. *DOMAIN*, *TYPE*, and *PROTOCOL* are specified the same as for *socketpair*(2). If either socket argument is undefined, it will be autovivified. The function returns true if successful, false otherwise. On a system where *socketpair*(2) is unimplemented, calling this function raises an exception.

This function is typically used just before a fork. One of the resulting processes should close *SOCKET1*, and the other should close *SOCKET2*. You can use these sockets bidirectionally, unlike the filehandles created by the pipe function. Some systems define pipe in terms of socketpair, in which a call to pipe(Rdr, Wtr) is essentially:

```
use Socket;
socketpair(Rdr, Wtr, AF_UNIX, SOCK_STREAM, PF_UNSPEC);
shutdown(Rdr, 1);        # no more writing for reader
shutdown(Wtr, 0);        # no more reading for writer
```

On systems that support a close-on-exec flag on files, the flag will be set for the newly opened file descriptors, as determined by the value of $^F. See the $^F ($SYSTEM_FD_MAX) variable in Chapter 28. See also the example at the end of the section "Bidirectional Communication" in Chapter 16.

sort

```
sort USERSUB LIST
sort BLOCK LIST
sort LIST
```

This function sorts the *LIST* and returns the sorted list value. By default, it sorts in standard string comparison order (undefined values sort before defined null strings, which sort before everything else). When the use locale pragma is in effect, sort *LIST* sorts *LIST* according to the current collation locale.

USERSUB, if given, is the name of a subroutine that returns an integer less than, equal to, or greater than 0, depending on how the elements of the list are to be ordered. (The handy <=> and cmp operators can be used to perform three-way numeric and string comparisons.) If a *USERSUB* is given but that function is undefined, sort raises an exception.

In the interests of efficiency, the normal calling code for subroutines is bypassed, with the following effects: the subroutine may not be a recursive subroutine (nor may you exit the block or routine with a loop control operator), and the two elements to be compared are not passed into the subroutine via @_, but rather by temporarily setting the global variables $a and $b in the package in which the sort was compiled (see the examples that follow). The variables $a and $b are aliases to the real values, so don't modify them in the subroutine.

The comparison subroutine is required to behave. If it returns inconsistent results (sometimes saying $x[1] is less than $x[2] and sometimes saying the opposite, for example), the results are not well defined. (That's another reason you shouldn't modify $a and $b.)

USERSUB may be a scalar variable name (unsubscripted), in which case the value provides either a symbolic or a hard reference to the actual subroutine to use. (A symbolic name rather than a hard reference is allowed even when the use strict 'refs' pragma is in effect.) In place of a *USERSUB*, you can provide a *BLOCK* as an anonymous, inline sort subroutine.

To do an ordinary numeric sort, say this:

```
sub numerically { $a <=> $b }
@sortedbynumber = sort numerically 53,29,11,32,7;
```

To sort in descending order, you could simply apply reverse after the sort, or you could reverse the order of $a and $b in the sort routine:

```
@descending = reverse sort numerically 53,29,11,32,7;

sub reverse_numerically { $b <=> $a }
@descending = sort reverse_numerically 53,29,11,32,7;
```

To sort strings without regard to case, run $a and $b through lc before comparing:

```
@unsorted = qw/sparrow Ostrich LARK catbird blueJAY/;
@sorted = sort { lc($a) cmp lc($b) } @unsorted;
```

(Under Unicode, the use of lc for case canonicalization is vaguely preferred to the use of uc, since some languages differentiate titlecase from uppercase. But that doesn't matter for basic ASCII sorting, and if you're going to do Unicode sorting right, your canonicalization routines are going to be a lot fancier than lc.)

Sorting hashes by value is a common use of the sort function. For example, if a %sales_amount hash records department sales, doing a hash lookup in the sort routine allows the hash keys to be sorted according to their corresponding values:

```
# sort from highest to lowest department sales
sub bysales { $sales_amount{$b} <=> $sales_amount{$a} }

for $dept (sort bysales keys %sale_amount) {
    print "$dept => $sales_amount{$dept}\n";
}
```

You can perform additional levels of sorting by cascading multiple comparisons using the || or or operators. This works nicely because the comparison operators conveniently return 0 for equivalence, causing them to fall through to the next comparison. Here, the hash keys are sorted first by their associated sales amounts and then by the keys themselves (in case two or more departments have the same sales amount):

```
sub by_sales_then_dept {
    $sales_amount{$b} <=> $sales_amount{$a}
        ||
    $a cmp $b
}

for $dept (sort by_sales_then_dept keys %sale_amount) {
    print "$dept => $sales_amount{$dept}\n";
}
```

Functions

Assume that @recs is an array of hash references, where each hash contains fields such as FIRSTNAME, LASTNAME, AGE, HEIGHT, and SALARY. The following routine sorts to the front of the list those records for people who are first richer, then taller, then younger, then less alphabetically challenged:

```
sub prospects {
    $b->{SALARY}      <=>  $a->{SALARY}
        ||
    $b->{HEIGHT}      <=>  $a->{HEIGHT}
        ||
    $a->{AGE}         <=>  $b->{AGE}
        ||
    $a->{LASTNAME}    cmp  $b->{LASTNAME}
        ||
    $a->{FIRSTNAME}   cmp  $b->{FIRSTNAME}
}

@sorted = sort prospects @recs;
```

Any useful information that can be derived from $a and $b can serve as the basis of a comparison in a sort routine. For example, if lines of text are to be sorted according to specific fields, split could be used within the sort routine to derive the fields.

```
@sorted_lines = sort {
    @a_fields = split /:/, $a;       # colon-separated fields
    @b_fields = split /:/, $b;

    $a_fields[3] <=> $b_fields[3]    # numeric sort on 4th field, then
        ||
    $a_fields[0] cmp $b_fields[0]    # string sort on 1st field, then
        ||
    $b_fields[2] <=> $a_fields[2]    # reverse numeric sort on 3rd field
        ||
```

```
        ...                             # etc.

    } @lines;
```

However, because sort performs the sort routine many times using different pairings of values for $a and $b, the previous example will resplit each line more often
than needed.

To avoid the expense of repeated derivations such as the splitting of lines in order
to compare their fields, perform the derivation once per value prior to the sort and
save the derived information. Here, anonymous arrays are created to encapsulate
each line along with the results of splitting the line:

```
    @temp = map { [$_, split /:/] } @lines;
```

Next, the array references are sorted:

```
    @temp = sort {
        @a_fields = @$a[1..$#$a];
        @b_fields = @$b[1..$#$b];

        $a_fields[3] <=> $b_fields[3]   # numeric sort on 4th field, then
            ||
        $a_fields[0] cmp $b_fields[0]   # string sort on 1st field, then
            ||
        $b_fields[2] <=> $a_fields[2]   # reverse numeric sort on 3rd field
            ||
        ...                             # etc.

    } @temp;
```

Now that the array references are sorted, the original lines can be retrieved from
the anonymous arrays:

```
    @sorted_lines = map { $_->[0] } @temp;
```

Putting it all together, this map-sort-map technique, often referred to as the
Schwartzian Transform, can be performed in one statement:

```
    @sorted_lines = map { $_->[0] }
                    sort {
                        @a_fields = @$a[1..$#$a];
                        @b_fields = @$b[1..$#$b];

                        $a_fields[3] <=> $b_fields[3]
                            ||
                        $a_fields[0] cmp $b_fields[0]
                            ||
                        $b_fields[2] <=> $a_fields[2]
                            ||
                        ...
                    }
                    map { [$_, split /:/] } @lines;
```

Do not declare $a and $b as lexical variables (with my). They are package globals (though they're exempt from the usual restrictions on globals when you're using use strict). You do need to make sure your sort routine is in the same package though, or else qualify $a and $b with the package name of the caller.

That being said, in version 5.6 you *can* write sort subroutines with the standard argument passing method (and, not coincidentally, use XS subroutines as sort subroutines), provided that you declare the sort subroutine with a prototype of ($$). And if you do that, then you can in fact declare $a and $b as lexicals:

```
sub numerically ($$) {
        my ($a, $b) = @_;
        $a <=> $b;
}
```

And someday, when full prototypes are implemented, you'll just say:

```
sub numerically ($a, $b) { $a <=> $b }
```

and then we'll be back where we started, more or less.

splice

```
splice ARRAY, OFFSET, LENGTH, LIST
splice ARRAY, OFFSET, LENGTH
splice ARRAY, OFFSET
splice ARRAY
```

This function removes the elements designated by *OFFSET* and *LENGTH* from an *ARRAY*, and replaces them with the elements of *LIST*, if any. If *OFFSET* is negative, the function counts backward from the end of the array, but if that would land before the beginning of the array, an exception is raised. In list context, splice returns the elements removed from the array. In scalar context, it returns the last element removed, or undef if there was none. If the number of new elements doesn't equal the number of old elements, the array grows or shrinks as necessary, and elements after the splice change their position correspondingly. If *LENGTH* is omitted, the function removes everything from *OFFSET* onward. If *OFFSET* is omitted, the array is cleared as it is read. The following equivalences hold (assuming $[is 0):

Direct Method	Splice Equivalent
push(@a, $x, $y)	splice(@a, @a, 0, $x, $y)
pop(@a)	splice(@a, -1)
shift(@a)	splice(@a, 0, 1)
unshift(@a, $x, $y)	splice(@a, 0, 0, $x, $y)
$a[$x] = $y	splice(@a, $x, 1, $y)
(@a, @a = ())	splice(@a)

The `splice` function is also handy for carving up the argument list passed to a sub-routine. For example, assuming list lengths are passed before lists:

```
sub list_eq {         # compare two list values
    my @a = splice(@_, 0, shift);
    my @b = splice(@_, 0, shift);
    return 0 unless @a == @b;        # same length?
    while (@a) {
        return 0 if pop(@a) ne pop(@b);
    }
    return 1;
}
if (list_eq($len, @foo[1..$len], scalar(@bar), @bar)) { ... }
```

It would be cleaner to use array references for this, however.

split $_ T

```
split /PATTERN/, EXPR, LIMIT
split /PATTERN/, EXPR
split /PATTERN/
split
```

This function scans a string given by *EXPR* for separators, and splits the string into a list of substrings, returning the resulting list value in list context or the count of substrings in scalar context.* The separators are determined by repeated pattern matching, using the regular expression given in *PATTERN*, so the separators may be of any size and need not be the same string on every match. (The separators are not ordinarily returned; exceptions are discussed later in this section.) If the *PATTERN* doesn't match the string at all, `split` returns the original string as a single substring. If it matches once, you get two substrings, and so on. You may supply regular expression modifiers to the *PATTERN*, like */PATTERN/*i, */PATTERN/*x, etc. The //m modifier is assumed when you split on the pattern /^/.

If *LIMIT* is specified and positive, the function splits into no more than that many fields (though it may split into fewer if it runs out of separators). If *LIMIT* is negative, it is treated as if an arbitrarily large *LIMIT* has been specified. If *LIMIT* is omitted or zero, trailing null fields are stripped from the result (which potential users of `pop` would do well to remember). If *EXPR* is omitted, the function splits the $_ string. If *PATTERN* is also omitted or is the literal space, " ", the function splits on whitespace, /\s+/, after skipping any leading whitespace.

---

* Scalar context also causes `split` to write its result to @_, but this usage is deprecated.

Strings of any length can be split:

```
@chars  = split //,   $word;
@fields = split /:/,   $line;
@words  = split " ",   $paragraph;
@lines  = split /^/,   $buffer;
```

A pattern capable of matching either the null string or something longer than the null string (for instance, a pattern consisting of any single character modified by a * or ?) will split the value of *EXPR* into separate characters wherever it matches the null string between characters; non-null matches will skip over the matched separator characters in the usual fashion. (In other words, a pattern won't match in one spot more than once, even if it matched with a zero width.) For example:

```
print join ':', split / */, 'hi there';
```

produces the output "h:i:t:h:e:r:e". The space disappears because it matches as part of the separator. As a trivial case, the null pattern // simply splits into separate characters, and spaces do not disappear. (For normal pattern matches, a // pattern would repeat the last successfully matched pattern, but split's pattern is exempt from that wrinkle.)

The *LIMIT* parameter splits only part of a string:

```
($login, $passwd, $remainder) = split /:/, $_, 3;
```

We encourage you to split to lists of names like this in order to make your code self-documenting. (For purposes of error checking, note that $remainder would be undefined if there were fewer than three fields.) When assigning to a list, if *LIMIT* is omitted, Perl supplies a *LIMIT* one larger than the number of variables in the list, to avoid unnecessary work. For the split above, *LIMIT* would have been 4 by default, and $remainder would have received only the third field, not all the rest of the fields. In time-critical applications, it behooves you not to split into more fields than you really need. (The trouble with powerful languages is that they let you be powerfully stupid at times.)

We said earlier that the separators are not returned, but if the *PATTERN* contains parentheses, then the substring matched by each pair of parentheses is included in the resulting list, interspersed with the fields that are ordinarily returned. Here's a simple example:

```
split /([-,])/, "1-10,20";
```

produces the list value:

```
(1, '-', 10, ',', 20)
```

Functions

With more parentheses, a field is returned for each pair, even if some pairs don't match, in which case undefined values are returned in those positions. So if you say:

```
split /(-)|(,)/, "1-10,20";
```

you get the value:

```
(1, '-', undef, 10, undef, ',', 20)
```

The */PATTERN/* argument may be replaced with an expression to specify patterns that vary at run time. As with ordinary patterns, to do run-time compilation only once, use /$variable/o.

As a special case, if the expression is a single space (" "), the function splits on whitespace just as split with no arguments does. Thus, split(" ") can be used to emulate *awk*'s default behavior. In contrast, split(/ /) will give you as many null initial fields as there are leading spaces. (Other than this special case, if you supply a string instead of a regular expression, it'll be interpreted as a regular expression anyway.) You can use this property to remove leading and trailing whitespace from a string and to collapse intervening stretches of whitespace into a single space:

```
$string = join(' ', split(' ', $string));
```

The following example splits an RFC 822 message header into a hash containing $head{Date}, $head{Subject}, and so on. It uses the trick of assigning a list of pairs to a hash, based on the fact that separators alternate with separated fields. It makes use of parentheses to return part of each separator as part of the returned list value. Since the split pattern is guaranteed to return things in pairs by virtue of containing one set of parentheses, the hash assignment is guaranteed to receive a list consisting of key/value pairs, where each key is the name of a header field. (Unfortunately, this technique loses information for multiple lines with the same key field, such as Received-By lines. Ah, well. . . .)

```
$header =~ s/\n\s+/ /g;       # Merge continuation lines.
%head = ('FRONTSTUFF', split /^(\S*?):\s*/m, $header);
```

The following example processes the entries in a Unix *passwd*(5) file. You could leave out the chomp, in which case $shell would have a newline on the end of it.

```
open PASSWD, '/etc/passwd';
while (<PASSWD>) {
    chomp;          # remove trailing newline
    ($login, $passwd, $uid, $gid, $gcos, $home, $shell) =
          split /:/;
    ...
}
```

Here's how to process each word of each line of each file of input to create a word-frequency hash.

```
while (<>) {
    foreach $word (split) {
        $count{$word}++;
    }
}
```

The inverse of split is performed by join (except that join can only join with the same separator between all fields). To break apart a string with fixed-position fields, use unpack.

sprintf

```
sprintf FORMAT, LIST
```

This function returns a string formatted by the usual printf conventions of the C library function *sprintf*. See *sprintf*(3) or *printf*(3) on your system for an explanation of the general principles. The FORMAT string contains text with embedded field specifiers into which the elements of LIST are substituted, one per field.

Perl does its own sprintf formatting—it emulates the C function *sprintf*, but it doesn't use it.* As a result, any nonstandard extensions in your local *sprintf*(3) function are not available from Perl.

Perl's sprintf permits the universally known conversions shown in Table 29-4.

Table 29-4. Formats for sprintf

Field	Meaning
%%	A percent sign
%c	A character with the given number
%s	A string
%d	A signed integer, in decimal
%u	An unsigned integer, in decimal
%o	An unsigned integer, in octal
%x	An unsigned integer, in hexadecimal
%e	A floating-point number, in scientific notation
%f	A floating-point number, in fixed decimal notation
%g	A floating-point number, in %e or %f notation

---

* Except for floating-point numbers, and even then only the standard modifiers are allowed.

In addition, Perl permits the following widely supported conversions:

Field	Meaning
%X	Like %x, but using uppercase letters
%E	Like %e, but using an uppercase "E"
%G	Like %g, but with an uppercase "E" (if applicable)
%b	An unsigned integer, in binary
%p	A pointer (outputs the Perl value's address in hexadecimal)
%n	Special: *stores* the number of characters output so far into the next variable in the argument list

Finally, for backward (and we do mean "backward") compatibility, Perl permits these unnecessary but widely supported conversions:

Field	Meaning
%i	A synonym for %d
%D	A synonym for %ld
%U	A synonym for %lu
%O	A synonym for %lo
%F	A synonym for %f

Perl permits the following universally known flags between the % and the conversion character:

Flag	Meaning
space	Prefix positive number with a space
+	Prefix positive number with a plus sign
–	Left-justify within the field
0	Use zeros, not spaces, to right-justify
#	Prefix nonzero octal with "0", nonzero hex with "0x"
number	Minimum field width
.number	"Precision": digits after decimal point for floating-point numbers, maximum length for string, minimum length for integer
l	Interpret integer as C type long or unsigned long
h	Interpret integer as C type short or unsigned short (if no flags are supplied, interpret integer as C type int or unsigned)

There are also two Perl-specific flags:

Flag	Meaning
V	Interpret integer as Perl's standard integer type
v	Interpret string as a vector of integers, output as numbers separated either by dots, or by an arbitrary string received from the argument list when the flag is preceded by *

If your Perl understands "quads" (64-bit integers) either because the platform natively supports them or because Perl has been specifically compiled with that ability, then the characters d u o x X b i D U O print quads, and they may optionally be preceded by 11, L, or q. For example, %11d %16LX %qo.

If Perl understands "long doubles" (this requires that the platform support long doubles), the flags e f g E F G may optionally be preceded by 11 or L. For example, %11f %Lg.

Where a number would appear in the flags, an asterisk ("*") may be used instead, in which case Perl uses the next item in the argument list as the given number (that is, as the field width or precision). If a field width obtained through "*" is negative, it has the same effect as the "-" flag: left-justification.

The v flag is useful for displaying ordinal values of characters in arbitrary strings:

```
sprintf "version is v%vd\n", $^V;          # Perl's version
sprintf "address is %vd\n", $addr;         # IPv4 address
sprintf "address is %*vX\n", ":", $addr;   # IPv6 address
sprintf "bits are %*vb\n", " ", $bits;     # random bit strings
```

sqrt $\boxed{\$\_}$ $\boxed{\$@}$

```
sqrt EXPR
sqrt
```

This function returns the square root of *EXPR*. For other roots such as cube roots, you can use the ** operator to raise something to a fractional power. Don't try either of these approaches with negative numbers, as that poses a slightly more complex problem (and raises an exception). But there's a standard module to take care of even that:

```
use Math::Complex;
print sqrt(-2);    # prints 1.4142135623731i
```

srand

```
srand EXPR
srand
```

This function sets the random number seed for the rand operator. If *EXPR* is omitted, it uses a semirandom value supplied by the kernel (if it supports the */dev/urandom* device) or based on the current time and process ID, among other things. It's usually not necessary to call srand at all, because if it is not called explicitly, it is called implicitly at the first use of the rand operator. However, this was not true in versions of Perl prior to 5.004, so if your script needs to run under older Perl versions, it should call srand.

Frequently called programs (like CGI scripts) that simply use time ^ $$ for a seed can fall prey to the mathematical property that a^b == (a+1)^(b+1) one-third of the time. So don't do that. Use this instead:

```
srand( time() ^ ($$ + ($$ << 15)) );
```

You'll need something much more random than the default seed for cryptographic purposes. On some systems the */dev/random* device is suitable. Otherwise, check-summing the compressed output of one or more rapidly changing operating system status programs is the usual method. For example:

```
srand (time ^ $$ ^ unpack "%32L*", `ps wwaxl | gzip`);
```

If you're particularly concerned with this, see the Math::TrulyRandom module in CPAN.

Do *not* call srand multiple times in your program unless you know exactly what you're doing and why you're doing it. The point of the function is to "seed" the rand function so that rand can produce a different sequence each time you run your program. Just do it once at the top of your program, or you *won't* get random numbers out of rand!

stat

[S_] [S!] [X ARG]

```
stat FILEHANDLE
stat EXPR
stat
```

In scalar context, this function returns a Boolean value that indicates whether the call succeeded. In list context, it returns a 13-element list giving the statistics for a file, either the file opened via *FILEHANDLE*, or named by *EXPR*. It's typically used as follows:

```
($dev,$ino,$mode,$nlink,$uid,$gid,$rdev,$size,
    $atime,$mtime,$ctime,$blksize,$blocks)
        = stat $filename;
```

Not all fields are supported on all filesystem types; unsupported fields return 0. Table 29-5 lists the meanings of the fields.

Table 29-5. Fields Returned by stat

Index	Field	Meaning
0	$dev	Device number of filesystem
1	$ino	Inode number
2	$mode	File mode (type and permissions)
3	$nlink	Number of (hard) links to the file
4	$uid	Numeric user ID of file's owner
5	$gid	Numeric group ID of file's designated group
6	$rdev	The device identifier (special files only)
7	$size	Total size of file, in bytes
8	$atime	Last access time in seconds since the epoch
9	$mtime	Last modify time in seconds since the epoch
10	$ctime	Inode change time (*not* creation time!) in seconds since the epoch
11	$blksize	Preferred blocksize for file system I/O
12	$blocks	Actual number of blocks allocated

$dev and $ino, taken together, uniquely identify a file on the same system. The $blksize and $blocks are likely defined only on BSD-derived filesystems. The $blocks field (if defined) is reported in 512-byte blocks. The value of $blocks*512 can differ greatly from $size for files containing unallocated blocks, or "holes", which aren't counted in $blocks.

If stat is passed the special filehandle consisting of an underline, no actual *stat*(2) is done, but the current contents of the stat structure from the last stat, lstat, or stat-based file test operator (such as -r, -w, and -x) are returned.

Because the mode contains both the file type and its permissions, you should mask off the file type portion and printf or sprintf using a "%o" if you want to see the real permissions:

```
$mode = (stat($filename))[2];
printf "Permissions are %04o\n", $mode & 07777;
```

The File::stat module provides a convenient, by-name access mechanism:

```
use File::stat;
$sb = stat($filename);
printf "File is %s, size is %s, perm %04o, mtime %s\n",
    $filename, $sb->size, $sb->mode & 07777,
    scalar localtime $sb->mtime;
```

You can also import symbolic definitions of the various mode bits from the Fcntl module. See the online documentation for more details.

Hint: if you need only the size of the file, check out the -s file test operator, which returns the size in bytes directly. There are also file tests that return the ages of files in days.

study $_

```
study SCALAR
study
```

This function takes extra time in order to study *SCALAR* in anticipation of doing many pattern matches on the string before it is next modified. This may or may not save time, depending on the nature and number of patterns you are searching on, and on the distribution of character frequencies in the string to be searched—you probably want to compare run times with and without it to see which runs faster. Those loops that scan for many short constant strings (including the constant parts of more complex patterns) will benefit most from study. If all your pattern matches are constant strings anchored at the front, study won't help at all, because no scanning is done. You may have only one study active at a time—if you study a different scalar the first is "unstudied".

The way study works is this: a linked list of every character in the string to be searched is made, so we know, for example, where all the "k" characters are. From each search string, the rarest character is selected, based on some static frequency tables constructed from some C programs and English text. Only those places that contain this rarest character are examined.

For example, here is a loop that inserts index-producing entries before any line containing a certain pattern:

```
while (<>) {
    study;
    print ".IX foo\n"      if /\bfoo\b/;
    print ".IX bar\n"      if /\bbar\b/;
    print ".IX blurfl\n"   if /\bblurfl\b/;
    ...
    print;
}
```

In searching for /\bfoo\b/, only those locations in $_ that contain "f" will be looked at, because "f" is rarer than "o". This is a big win except in pathological cases. The only question is whether it saves you more time than it took to build the linked list in the first place.

If you have to look for strings that you don't know until run time, you can build an entire loop as a string and eval that to avoid recompiling all your patterns all the time. Together with setting $/ to input entire files as one record, this can be very fast, often faster than specialized programs like *fgrep*(1). The following scans a list of files (@files) for a list of words (@words), and prints out the names of those files that contain a case-insensitive match:

```
$search = 'while (<>) { study;';
foreach $word (@words) {
    $search .= "++\$seen{\$ARGV} if /\\b$word\\b/i;\n";
}
$search .= "}";
@ARGV = @files;
undef $/;                   # slurp each entire file
eval $search;               # this screams
die $@ if $@;               # in case eval failed
$/ = "\n";                  # restore normal input terminator
foreach $file (sort keys(%seen)) {
    print "$file\n";
}
```

Now that we have the qr// operator, complicated run-time evals as seen above are less necessary. This does the same thing:

```
@pats = ();
foreach $word (@words) {
    push @pats, qr/\b${word}\b/i;
}
@ARGV = @files;
undef $/;                   # slurp each entire file
while (<>) {
    for $pat (@pats) {
        $seen{$ARGV}++ if /$pat/;
    }
}
$/ = "\n";                  # restore normal input terminator
foreach $file (sort keys(%seen)) {
    print "$file\n";
}
```

sub

Named declarations:

```
sub NAME PROTO ATTRS
sub NAME ATTRS
sub NAME PROTO
sub NAME
```

Named definitions:

```
sub NAME PROTO ATTRS BLOCK
sub NAME ATTRS BLOCK
sub NAME PROTO BLOCK
sub NAME BLOCK
```

Unnamed definitions:

```
sub PROTO ATTRS BLOCK
sub ATTRS BLOCK
sub PROTO BLOCK
sub BLOCK
```

The syntax of subroutine declarations and definitions looks complicated, but is actually pretty simple in practice. Everything is based on the syntax:

```
sub NAME PROTO ATTRS BLOCK
```

All four fields are optional; the only restrictions are that the fields that do occur must occur in that order, and that you must use at least one of *NAME* or *BLOCK*. For the moment, we'll ignore the *PROTO* and *ATTRS*; they're just modifiers on the basic syntax. The *NAME* and the *BLOCK* are the important parts to get straight:

- If you just have a *NAME* and no *BLOCK*, it's a declaration of that name (and if you ever want to call the subroutine, you'll have to supply a definition with both a *NAME* and a *BLOCK* later). Named declarations are useful because the parser treats a name specially if it knows it's a user-defined subroutine. You can call such a subroutine either as a function or as an operator, just like built-in functions. These are sometimes called *forward* declarations.

- If you have both a *NAME* and a *BLOCK*, it's a standard named subroutine definition (and a declaration too, if you didn't declare the name previously). Named definitions are useful because the *BLOCK* associates an actual meaning (the body of the subroutine) with the declaration. That's all we mean when we say it defines the subroutine rather than just declaring it. The definition is like the declaration, however, in that the surrounding code doesn't see it, and it returns no inline value by which you could reference the subroutine.

- If you have just have a *BLOCK* without a *NAME*, it's a nameless definition, that is, an anonymous subroutine. Since it doesn't have a name, it's not a declaration at all, but a real operator that returns a reference to the anonymous subroutine body at run time. This is extremely useful for treating code as data. It allows you to pass odd chunks of code around to be used as callbacks, and maybe even as closures if the sub definition operator refers to any lexical variables outside of itself. That means that different calls to the same sub operator will do the bookkeeping necessary to keep the correct "version" of each such lexical variable in sight for the life of the closure, even if the original scope of the lexical variable has been destroyed.

In any of these three cases, either one or both of the *PROTO* and *ATTRS* may occur after the *NAME* and/or before the *BLOCK*. A prototype is a list of characters in parentheses that tell the parser how to treat arguments to the function. Attributes are introduced by a colon and supply additional information to the parser about the function. Here's a typical definition that includes all four fields:

```
sub numstrcmp ($$) : locked {
    my ($a, $b) = @_;
    return $a <=> $b || $a cmp $b;
}
```

For details on attribute lists and their manipulation, see the `attributes` pragma in Chapter 31. See also Chapter 6 and "Anonymous Subroutines" in Chapter 8.

substr

```
substr EXPR, OFFSET, LENGTH, REPLACEMENT
substr EXPR, OFFSET, LENGTH
substr EXPR, OFFSET
```

This function extracts a substring out of the string given by *EXPR* and returns it. The substring is extracted starting at *OFFSET* characters from the front of the string. (Note: if you've messed with $[, the beginning of the string isn't at 0, but since you haven't messed with it (have you?), it is.) If *OFFSET* is negative, the substring starts that far from the end of the string instead. If *LENGTH* is omitted, everything to the end of the string is returned. If *LENGTH* is negative, the length is calculated to leave that many characters off the end of the string. Otherwise, *LENGTH* indicates the length of the substring to extract, which is sort of what you'd expect.

You may use `substr` as an lvalue (something to assign to), in which case *EXPR* must also be a legal lvalue. If you assign something shorter than the length of your substring, the string will shrink, and if you assign something longer than the length, the string will grow to accommodate it. To keep the string the same length, you may need to pad or chop your value using `sprintf` or the `x` operator. If you attempt to assign to an unallocated area past the end of the string, `substr` raises an exception.

To prepend the string `"Larry"` to the current value of $_, use:

```
substr($var, 0, 0) = "Larry";
```

To instead replace the first character of $_ with `"Moe"`, use:

```
substr($var, 0, 1) = "Moe";
```

And finally, to replace the last character of $var with `"Curly"`, use:

```
substr($var, -1) = "Curly";
```

An alternative to using `substr` as an lvalue is to specify the *REPLACEMENT* string as the fourth argument. This allows you to replace parts of the *EXPR* and return what was there before in one operation, just as you can with `splice`. The next example

also replaces the last character of $var with "Curly" and puts that replaced charac-
ter into $oldstr:

```
$oldstr = substr($var, -1, 1, "Curly");
```

You don't have to use lvalue substr only with assignment. This replaces any
spaces with dots, but only in the last 10 characters in the string:

```
substr($var, -10) =~ s/ /./g;
```

symlink   S! X T X U

```
symlink OLDNAME, NEWNAME
```

This function creates a new filename symbolically linked to the old filename. The
function returns true for success, false otherwise. On systems that don't support
symbolic links, it raises an exception at run time. To check for that, use eval to
trap the potential error:

```
$can_symlink = eval { symlink("",""); 1 };
```

Or use the Config module. Be careful if you supply a relative symbolic link, since
it'll be interpreted relative to the location of the symbolic link itself, not to your
current working directory.

See also link and readlink earlier in this chapter.

syscall   S! X RO X T X U

```
syscall LIST
```

This function calls the system call (meaning a syscall, not a shell command) specified as the first element of the list passes the remaining elements as arguments to
the system call. (Many of these calls are now more readily available through modules like POSIX.) The function raises an exception if *syscall*(2) is unimplemented.

The arguments are interpreted as follows: if a given argument is numeric, the argument is passed as a C integer. If not, a pointer to the string value is passed. You
are responsible for making sure the string is long enough to receive any result that
might be written into it; otherwise, you're looking at a core dump. You can't use a
string literal (or other read-only string) as an argument to syscall because Perl has
to assume that any string pointer might be written through. If your integer arguments are not literals and have never been interpreted in a numeric context, you
may need to add 0 to them to force them to look like numbers.

`syscall` returns whatever value was returned by the system call invoked. By C coding conventions, if that system call fails, `syscall` returns –1 and sets $! (errno). Some system calls legitimately return –1 if successful. The proper way to handle such calls is to assign $!=0; before the call and check the value of $! if `syscall` returns –1.

Not all system calls can be accessed this way. For example, Perl supports passing up to 14 arguments to your system call, which in practice should usually suffice. However, there's a problem with syscalls that return multiple values. Consider `syscall(&SYS_pipe)`: it returns the file number of the read end of the pipe it creates. There is no way to retrieve the file number of the other end. You can avoid this instance of the problem by using `pipe` instead. To solve the generic problem, write XSUBs (external subroutine modules, a dialect of C) to access the system calls directly. Then put your new module onto CPAN, and become wildly popular.

The following subroutine returns the current time as a floating-point number rather than as integer seconds as `time` returns. (It will only work on machines that support the *gettimeofday*(2) syscall.)

```
sub finetime() {
    package main;    # for next require
    require 'syscall.ph';
    # presize buffer to two 32-bit longs...
    my $tv = pack("LL", ());
    syscall(&SYS_gettimeofday, $tv, undef) >= 0
        or die "gettimeofday: $!";
    my($seconds, $microseconds) = unpack("LL", $tv);
    return $seconds + ($microseconds / 1_000_000);
}
```

Suppose Perl didn't support the *setgroups*(2) syscall,* but your kernel did. You could still get at it this way:

```
require 'syscall.ph';
syscall(&SYS_setgroups, scalar @newgids, pack("i*", @newgids))
        or die "setgroups: $!";
```

You may have to run *h2ph* as indicated in the Perl installation instructions for *syscall.ph* to exist. Some systems may require a `pack` template of "II" instead. Even more disturbing, `syscall` assumes the size equivalence of the C types `int`, `long`, and `char*`. Try not to think of `syscall` as the epitome of portability.

See the `Time::HiRes` module from CPAN for a more rigorous approach to fine-grained timing issues.

---

* Although through $(, it does.

sysopen $\boxed{\text{S!}}$ $\boxed{\substack{\text{X}\\\text{ARG}}}$

```
sysopen FILEHANDLE, FILENAME, MODE, MASK
sysopen FILEHANDLE, FILENAME, MODE
```

The sysopen function opens the file whose filename is given by *FILENAME* and associates it with *FILEHANDLE*. If *FILEHANDLE* is an expression, its value is used as the name of, or reference to, the filehandle. If *FILEHANDLE* is a variable whose value is undefined, a value will be created for you. The return value is true if the call succeeds, false otherwise.

This function is a direct interface to your operating system's *open*(2) syscall followed by an *fdopen*(3) library call. As such, you'll need to pretend you're a C programmer for a bit here. The possible values and flag bits of the *MODE* parameter are available through the Fcntl module. Because different systems support different flags, don't count on all of them being available on your system. Consult your *open*(2) manpage or its local equivalent for details. Nevertheless, the following flags should be present on any system with a reasonably standard C library:

Flag	Meaning
O_RDONLY	Read only.
O_WRONLY	Write only.
O_RDWR	Read and write.
O_CREAT	Create the file if it doesn't exist.
O_EXCL	Fail if the file already exists.
O_APPEND	Append to the file.
O_TRUNC	Truncate the file.
O_NONBLOCK	Nonblocking access.

Many other options are possible, however. Here are some less common flags:

Flag	Meaning
O_NDELAY	Old synonym for O_NONBLOCK.
O_SYNC	Writes block until data is physically written to the underlying hardware. O_ASYNC, O_DSYNC, and O_RSYNC may also be seen.
O_EXLOCK	flock with LOCK_EX (advisory only).
O_SHLOCK	flock with LOCK_SH (advisory only).
O_DIRECTORY	Fail if the file is *not* a directory.
O_NOFOLLOW	Fail if the last path component is a symbolic link.
O_BINARY	binmode the handle for Microsoft systems. An O_TEXT may also sometimes exist to get the opposite behavior.
O_LARGEFILE	Some systems need this for files over 2 GB.
O_NOCTTY	Opening a terminal file won't make that terminal become the process's controlling terminal if you don't have one yet. Usually no longer needed.

The O_EXCL flag is *not* for locking: here, exclusiveness means that if the file already exists, sysopen fails.

If the file named by *FILENAME* does not exist and the *MODE* includes the O_CREAT flag, then sysopen creates the file with initial permissions determined by the *MASK* argument (or 0666 if omitted) as modified by your process's current umask. This default is reasonable: see the entry on umask for an explanation.

Filehandles opened with open and sysopen may be used interchangeably. You do not need to use sysread and friends just because you happened to open the file with sysopen, nor are you precluded from doing so if you opened it with open. Both can do things that the other can't. Regular open can open pipes, fork processes, set disciplines, duplicate file handles, and convert a file descriptor number into a filehandle. It also ignores leading and trailing whitespace in filenames and respects "-" as a special filename. But when it comes to opening actual files, sysopen can do anything that open can.

The following examples show equivalent calls to both functions. We omit the or die $! checks for clarity, but make sure to always check return values in your programs. We'll restrict ourselves to using only flags available on virtually all operating systems. It's just a matter of controlling the values that you OR together using the bitwise | operator to pass in *MODE* argument.

- Open a file for reading:

    ```
    open(FH, "<", $path);
    sysopen(FH, $path, O_RDONLY);
    ```

- Open a file for writing, creating a new file if needed, or truncating an old file:

    ```
    open(FH, ">", $path);
    sysopen(FH, $path, O_WRONLY | O_TRUNC | O_CREAT);
    ```

- Open a file for appending, creating one if necessary:

    ```
    open(FH, ">>", $path);
    sysopen(FH, $path, O_WRONLY | O_APPEND | O_CREAT);
    ```

- Open a file for update, where the file must already exist:

    ```
    open(FH, "+<", $path);
    sysopen(FH, $path, O_RDWR);
    ```

And here are things you can do with sysopen but *not* with regular open:

- Open and create a file for writing, which must not previously exist:

    ```
    sysopen(FH, $path, O_WRONLY | O_EXCL | O_CREAT);
    ```

Functions

- Open a file for appending, which must already exist:

      sysopen(FH, $path, O_WRONLY | O_APPEND);

- Open a file for update, creating a new file if necessary:

      sysopen(FH, $path, O_RDWR | O_CREAT);

- Open a file for update, which must not already exist:

      sysopen(FH, $path, O_RDWR | O_EXCL | O_CREAT);

- Open a write-only file without blocking, but not creating it if it doesn't exist:

      sysopen(FH, $path, O_WRONLY | O_NONBLOCK);

The `FileHandle` module described in Chapter 32 provides a set of object-oriented synonyms (plus a small bit of new functionality) for opening files. You are welcome to call the appropriate `FileHandle` methods* on any handle created with `open`, `sysopen`, `pipe`, `socket`, or `accept`, even if you didn't use the module to initialize those handles.

sysread

      sysread FILEHANDLE, SCALAR, LENGTH, OFFSET
      sysread FILEHANDLE, SCALAR, LENGTH

This function attempts to read *LENGTH* bytes of data into variable *SCALAR* from the specified *FILEHANDLE* using a low-level syscall, *read*(2). The function returns the number of bytes read, or 0 at EOF.† The `sysread` function returns `undef` on error. *SCALAR* will grow or shrink to the length actually read. The *OFFSET*, if specified, says where in the string to start putting the bytes, so that you can read into the middle of a string that's being used as a buffer. For an example of using *OFFSET*, see `syswrite`. An exception is raised if *LENGTH* is negative or if *OFFSET* points outside the string.

You should be prepared to handle the problems (like interrupted syscalls) that standard I/O normally handles for you. Because it bypasses standard I/O, do not mix `sysread` with other kinds of reads, `print`, `printf`, `write`, `seek`, `tell`, or `eof` on the same filehandle unless you are into heavy wizardry (and/or pain). Also, please be aware that, when reading from a file containing Unicode or any other multibyte encoding, the buffer boundary may fall in the middle of a character.

---

* Really `IO::File` or `IO::Handle` methods.

† There is no `syseof` function, which is okay, since `eof` doesn't work well on device files (like terminals) anyway. Use `sysread` and check for a return value for 0 to decide whether you're done.

sysseek

$\boxed{\text{S!}}$ $\boxed{\substack{\text{X}\\\text{ARG}}}$

> sysseek FILEHANDLE, POSITION, WHENCE

This function sets *FILEHANDLE*'s system position using the syscall *lseek*(2). It bypasses standard I/O, so mixing this with reads (other than sysread), print, write, seek, tell, or eof may cause confusion. *FILEHANDLE* may be an expression whose value gives the name of the filehandle. The values for *WHENCE* are 0 to set the new position to *POSITION*, 1 to set the it to the current position plus *POSITION*, and 2 to set it to EOF plus *POSITION* (typically negative). For *WHENCE*, you may use the constants SEEK_SET, SEEK_CUR, and SEEK_END from the standard IO::Seekable and POSIX modules—or, as of the 5.6 release, from Fcntl, which is more portable and convenient.

Returns the new position, or undef on failure. A position of zero is returned as the special string "0 but true", which can be used numerically without producing warnings.

system

$\boxed{\text{S!}}$ $\boxed{\text{S?}}$ $\boxed{\substack{\text{X}\\\text{T}}}$

> system PATHNAME LIST
> system LIST

This function executes any program on the system for you and returns that program's exit status—not its output. To capture the output from a command, use backticks or qx// instead. The system function works exactly like exec, except that system does a fork first and then, after the exec, waits for the executed program to complete. That is, it runs the program for you and returns when it's done, whereas exec *replaces* your running program with the new one, so it never returns if the replacement succeeds.

Argument processing varies depending on the number of arguments, as described under exec, including determining whether the shell will be called and whether you've lied to the program about its name by specifying a separate *PATHNAME*.

Because system and backticks block SIGINT and SIGQUIT, sending one of those signals (such as from a Control-C) to the program being run doesn't interrupt your main program. But the other program you're running *does* get the signal. Check the return value from system to see whether the program you were running exited properly or not.

```
@args = ("command", "arg1", "arg2");
system(@args) == 0
    or die "system @args failed: $?"
```

The return value is the exit status of the program as returned through the *wait*(2) syscall. Under traditional semantics, to get the real exit value, divide by 256 or shift right by 8 bits. That's because the lower byte has something else in it. (Two somethings, really.) The lowest seven bits indicate the signal number that killed the process (if any), and the eighth bit indicates whether the process dumped core. You can check all possible failure possibilities, including signals and core dumps, by inspecting $? ($CHILD_ERROR):

```
$exit_value  = $? >> 8;
$signal_num  = $? & 127;    # or 0x7f, or 0177, or 0b0111_1111
$dumped_core = $? & 128;    # or 0x80, or 0200, or 0b1000_0000
```

When the program has been run through the system shell* because you had only one argument and that argument had shell metacharacters in it, normal return codes are subject to that shell's additional quirks and capabilities. In other words, under those circumstances, you may be unable to recover the detailed information described earlier.

syswrite   `$!` `$@` `X ARG`

```
syswrite FILEHANDLE, SCALAR, LENGTH, OFFSET
syswrite FILEHANDLE, SCALAR, LENGTH
syswrite FILEHANDLE, SCALAR
```

This function attempts to write *LENGTH* bytes of data from variable *SCALAR* to the specified *FILEHANDLE* using the *write*(2) syscall. The function returns the number of bytes written, or undef on error. The *OFFSET*, if specified, says where in the string to start writing from. (You might do this if you were using the string as a buffer, for instance, or if you needed to recover from a partial write.) A negative *OFFSET* specifies that writing should start that many bytes backward from the end of the string. If *SCALAR* is empty, the only *OFFSET* permitted is 0. An exception is raised if *LENGTH* is negative or if *OFFSET* points outside the string.

To copy data from filehandle FROM into filehandle TO, you can use something like:

```
use Errno qw/EINTR/;
$blksize = (stat FROM)[11] || 16384;   # preferred block size?
while ($len = sysread FROM, $buf, $blksize) {
    if (!defined $len) {
        next if $! == EINTR;
        die "System read error: $!\n";
    }
    $offset = 0;
    while ($len) {              # Handle partial writes.
        $written = syswrite TO, $buf, $len, $offset;
        die "System write error: $!\n" unless defined $written;
        $offset += $written;
        $len    -= $written;
    }
}
```

---

* That's */bin/sh* by definition, or whatever makes sense on your platform, but not whatever shell the user just happens to be using at the time.

You must be prepared to handle the problems that standard I/O normally handles for you, such as partial writes. Because `syswrite` bypasses the C standard I/O library, do not mix calls to it with reads (other than `sysread`), writes (like `print`, `printf`, or `write`), or other stdio functions like `seek`, `tell`, or `eof` unless you are into heavy wizardry.*

tell

```
tell FILEHANDLE
tell
```

This function returns the current file position (in bytes, zero-based) for *FILEHANDLE*. This value typically will be fed to the `seek` function at some future time to get back to the current position. *FILEHANDLE* may be an expression giving the name of the actual filehandle, or a reference to a filehandle object. If *FILEHANDLE* is omitted, the function returns the position of the file last read. File positions are only meaningful on regular files. Devices, pipes, and sockets have no file position.

There is no `systell` function. Use `sysseek(FH, 0, 1)` for that. Seek `seek` for an example telling how to use `tell`.

telldir

```
telldir DIRHANDLE
```

This function returns the current position of the `readdir` routines on *DIRHANDLE*. This value may be given to `seekdir` to access a particular location in a directory. The function has the same caveats about possible directory compaction as the corresponding system library routine. This function might not be implemented everywhere that `readdir` is. Even if it is, no calculation may be done with the return value. It's just an opaque value, meaningful only to `seekdir`.

tie

```
tie VARIABLE, CLASSNAME, LIST
```

This function binds a variable to a package class that will provide the implementation for the variable. *VARIABLE* is the variable (scalar, array, or hash) or typeglob (representing a filehandle) to be tied. *CLASSNAME* is the name of a class implementing objects of an appropriate type.

Any additional arguments are passed to the appropriate constructor method of the class, meaning one of `TIESCALAR`, `TIEARRAY`, `TIEHASH`, or `TIEHANDLE`. (If the appropriate method is not found, an exception is raised.) Typically, these are arguments

---

* Or pain.

such as might be passed to the *dbm_open*(3) function of C, but their meaning is package dependent. The object returned by the constructor is in turn returned by the `tie` function, which can be useful if you want to access other methods in *CLASSNAME*. (The object can also be accessed through the `tied` function.) So, a class for tying a hash to an ISAM implementation might provide an extra method to traverse a set of keys sequentially (the "S" of ISAM), since your typical DBM implementation can't do that.

Functions such as `keys` and `values` may return huge list values when used on large objects like DBM files. You may prefer to use the `each` function to iterate over such. For example:

```
use NDBM_File;
tie %ALIASES, "NDBM_File", "/etc/aliases", 1, 0
    or die "Can't open aliases: $!\n";
while (($key,$val) = each %ALIASES) {
    print $key, ' = ', $val, "\n";
}
untie %ALIASES;
```

A class implementing a hash should provide the following methods:

```
TIEHASH CLASS, LIST
FETCH SELF, KEY
STORE SELF, KEY, VALUE
DELETE SELF, KEY
CLEAR SELF
EXISTS SELF, KEY
FIRSTKEY SELF
NEXTKEY SELF, LASTKEY
DESTROY SELF
```

A class implementing an ordinary array should provide the following methods:

```
TIEARRAY CLASS, LIST
FETCH SELF, SUBSCRIPT
STORE SELF, SUBSCRIPT, VALUE
FETCHSIZE SELF
STORESIZE SELF, COUNT
CLEAR SELF
PUSH SELF, LIST
POP SELF
SHIFT SELF
UNSHIFT SELF, LIST
SPLICE SELF, OFFSET, LENGTH, LIST
EXTEND SELF, COUNT
DESTROY SELF
```

A class implementing a scalar should provide the following methods:

```
TIESCALAR CLASS, LIST
FETCH SELF,
STORE SELF, VALUE
DESTROY SELF
```

A class implementing a filehandle should have the following methods:

```
TIEHANDLE CLASS, LIST
READ SELF, SCALAR, LENGTH, OFFSET
READLINE SELF
GETC SELF
WRITE SELF, SCALAR, LENGTH, OFFSET
PRINT SELF, LIST
PRINTF SELF, FORMAT, LIST
CLOSE SELF
DESTROY SELF
```

Not all methods indicated above need be implemented: the `Tie::Hash`, `Tie::Array`, `Tie::Scalar`, and `Tie::Handle` modules provide base classes that have reasonable defaults. See Chapter 14, *Tied Variables*, for a detailed discussion of all these methods. Unlike dbmopen, the tie function will not use or require a module for you—you need to do that explicitly yourself. See the `DB_File` and `Config` modules for interesting tie implementations.

tied

```
tied VARIABLE
```

This function returns a reference to the object underlying the scalar, array, hash, or typeglob contained in *VARIABLE* (the same value that was originally returned by the tie call that bound the variable to a package). It returns the undefined value if *VARIABLE* isn't tied to a package. So, for example, you can use:

```
ref tied %hash
```

to find out which package your hash is tied to. (Presuming you've forgotten.)

time

```
time
```

This function returns the number of nonleap seconds since "the epoch", traditionally 00:00:00 on January 1st, 1970, UTC.* The returned value is suitable for feeding to gmtime and localtime, for comparison with file modification and access times returned by stat, and for feeding to utime.

---

* Not to be confused with the "epic", which is about the making of Unix. (Other operating systems may have a different epoch, not to mention a different epic.)

```
$start = time();
system("some slow command");
$end   = time();
if ($end - $start > 1) {
    print "Program started: ", scalar localtime($start), "\n";
    print "Program ended:   ", scalar localtime($end), "\n";
}
```

times

```
times
```

In list context, this function returns a four-element list giving the user and system CPU times, in seconds (probably fractional), for this process and terminated children of this process.

```
($user, $system, $cuser, $csystem) = times();
printf "This pid and its kids have consumed %.3f seconds\n",
        $user + $system + $cuser + $csystem;
```

In scalar context, returns just the user time. For example, to time the execution speed of a section of Perl code:

```
$start = times();
...
$end = times();
printf "that took %.2f CPU seconds of user time\n",
        $end - $start;
```

tr///

```
tr///
y///
```

This is the transliteration (also called translation) operator, which is like the y/// operator in the Unix *sed* program, only better, in everybody's humble opinion. See Chapter 5.

truncate

```
truncate FILEHANDLE, LENGTH
truncate EXPR, LENGTH
```

This function truncates the file opened on *FILEHANDLE*, or named by *EXPR*, to the specified length. The function raises an exception if *ftruncate*(2) or an equivalent isn't implemented on your system. (You can always truncate a file by copying the front of it, if you have the disk space.) The function returns true on success, undef otherwise.

uc

```
uc EXPR
uc
```

This function returns an uppercased version of *EXPR*. This is the internal function implementing the \U escape in double-quoted strings. Perl will try to do the right thing with respect to your current locale settings, but we're still working out how that interacts with Unicode. See the *perllocalle* manpage for the latest guess. In any event, when Perl uses the Unicode tables, uc translates to uppercase rather than to titlecase. See ucfirst for titlecase translation.

ucfirst

```
ucfirst EXPR
ucfirst
```

This function returns a version of *EXPR* with the first character capitalized (title-cased in "Unicodese"), and other characters left alone. This is the internal function implementing the \u escape in double-quoted strings. Your current LC_CTYPE locale may be respected if you use locale and your data doesn't look like Unicode, but we make no guarantees at this time.

To force the initial character to titlecase and everything else to lowercase, use:

```
ucfirst lc $word
```

which is equivalent to "\u\L$word".

umask

```
umask EXPR
umask
```

This function sets the umask for the process and returns the old one using the *umask*(2) syscall. Your umask tells the operating system which permission bits to *disallow* when creating a new file, including files that happen to be directories. If *EXPR* is omitted, the function merely returns the current umask. For example, to ensure that the "user" bits are allowed, and the "other" bits disallowed, try something like:

```
umask((umask() & 077) | 7);   # don't change the group bits
```

Remember that a umask is a number, usually given in octal; it is *not* a string of octal digits. See also oct, if all you have is a string. Remember also that the umask's bits are complemented compared to ordinary permissions.

The Unix permission rwxr-x--- is represented as three sets of three bits, or three octal digits: 0750 (the leading 0 indicates octal and doesn't count as one of the digits). Since the umask's bits are flipped, it represents disabled permissions bits. The permission (or "mode") values you supply to mkdir or sysopen are modified by your umask, so even if you tell sysopen to create a file with permissions 0777, if your umask is 0022, the file is created with permissions 0755. If your umask were 0027 (group can't write; others can't read, write, or execute), then passing sysopen a *MASK* of 0666 would create a file with mode 0640 (since 0666 & ~0027 is 0640).

Here's some advice: supply a creation mode of 0666 for regular files (in sysopen) and one of 0777 both for directories (in mkdir) and for executable files. This gives users the freedom of choice: if they want protected files, they choose process umasks of 022, 027, or even the particularly antisocial mask of 077. Programs should rarely if ever make policy decisions better left to the user. The exception to this rule is programs that write files that should be kept private: mail files, web browser cookies, .rhosts files, and so on.

If *umask*(2) is not implemented on your system and you are trying to restrict your *own* access (that is, if *EXPR* & 0700) > 0), you'll trigger a run-time exception. If *umask*(2) is not implemented and you are not trying to restrict your own access, the function simply returns undef.

undef

```
undef EXPR
undef
```

undef is the name by which we refer to the abstraction known as "the undefined value". It also conveniently happens to be the name of a function that always returns the undefined value. We happily confuse the two.

Coincidentally, the undef function can also explicitly undefine an entity if you supply its name as an argument. The *EXPR* argument, if specified, must be an lvalue. Hence you may only use this on a scalar value, an entire array or hash, a subroutine name (using the & prefix), or a typeglob. Any storage associated with the object will be recovered for reuse (though not returned to the system, for most operating systems). The undef function will probably not do what you expect on most special variables. Using it on a read-only variable like $1 raises an exception.

The undef function is a unary operator, not a list operator, so you can only undefine one thing at a time. Here are some uses of undef as a unary operator:

```
undef $foo;
undef $bar{'blurfl'};     # Different from delete $bar{'blurfl'};
undef @ary;
undef %hash;
undef &mysub;
undef *xyz;               # destroys $xyz, @xyz, %xyz, &xyz, etc.
```

Without an argument, `undef` is just used for its value:

```
select(undef, undef, undef, $naptime);

return (wantarray ? () : undef) if $they_blew_it;
return if $they_blew_it;  # same thing
```

You may use `undef` as a placeholder on the left side of a list assignment, in which case the corresponding value from the right side is simply discarded. Apart from that, you may not use `undef` as an lvalue.

```
($a, $b, undef, $c) = &foo;        # Ignore third value returned
```

Also, do not try to compare anything to `undef`—it doesn't do what you think. All it does is compare against 0 or the null string. Use the `defined` function to determine if a value is defined.

unlink

⟨S_⟩ ⟨S!⟩ ⟨X↑⟩

```
unlink LIST
unlink
```

This function deletes a list of files.* The function returns the number of filenames successfully deleted. Some sample examples:

```
$count = unlink 'a', 'b', 'c';
unlink @goners;
unlink glob("*.orig");
```

The `unlink` function will not delete directories unless you are superuser and the supply **-U** command-line option to Perl. Even if these conditions are met, be warned that unlinking a directory can inflict Serious Damage on your filesystem. Use `rmdir` instead.

Here's a simple *rm* command with very simple error checking:

```
#!/usr/bin/perl
@cannot = grep {not unlink} @ARGV;
die "$0: could not unlink @cannot\n" if @cannot;
```

unpack

⟨S@⟩

```
unpack TEMPLATE, EXPR
```

This function does the reverse of `pack`: it expands a string (*EXPR*) representing a data structure into a list of values according to the *TEMPLATE* and returns those values. In scalar context, it can be used to unpack a single value. The *TEMPLATE* here

---

* Actually, under a POSIX filesystem, it removes the directory entries (filenames) that refer to the real files. Since a file may be referenced (linked) from more than one directory, the file isn't removed until the last reference to it is removed.

has much the same format as it has in the pack function—it specifies the order and type of the values to be unpacked. See pack for a detailed description of *TEM-PLATE*. An invalid element in the *TEMPLATE*, or an attempt to move outside the string with the x, X, or @ formats, raises an exception.

The string is broken into chunks described by the *TEMPLATE*. Each chunk is converted separately to a value. Typically, the bytes of the string either are the result of a pack, or represent a C structure of some kind.

If the repeat count of a field is larger than the remainder of the input string allows, the repeat count is silently decreased. (Normally, you'd use a repeat count of * here, anyway.) If the input string is longer than what *TEMPLATE* describes, the rest of the string is ignored.

The unpack function is also useful for plain text data, too, not just binary data. Imagine that you had a data file that contained records that looked like this:

```
1986 Ender's Game          Orson Scott Card
1985 Neuromancer           William Gibson
1984 Startide Rising       David Brin
1983 Foundation's Edge     Isaac Asimov
1982 Downbelow Station     C. J. Cherryh
1981 The Snow Queen        Joan D. Vinge
```

you can't use split to parse out the fields because they have no distinct separator. Instead, fields are determined by their byte-offset into the record. So even though this is a regular text record, because it's in a fixed format, you want to use unpack to pull it apart:

```perl
while (<>) {
        ($year, $title, $author) = unpack("A4 x A23 A*", $_);
        print "$author won ${year}'s Hugo for $title.\n";
}
```

(The reason we wrote ${year}'s there is because Perl would have treated $year's as meaning $year::s.)

Here's a complete *uudecode* program:

```perl
#!/usr/bin/perl
$_ = <> until ($mode,$file) = /^begin\s*(\d*)\s*(\S*)/;
open(OUT,"> $file") if $file ne "";
while (<>) {
    last if /^end/;
    next if /[a-z]/;
    next unless int((((ord() - 32) & 077) + 2) / 3) ==
                int(length() / 4);
    print OUT unpack "u", $_;
}
chmod oct($mode), $file;
```

In addition to fields allowed in pack, you may prefix a field with *&number* to produce a simple *number*-bit additive checksum of the items instead of the items themselves. Default is a 16-bit checksum. The checksum is calculated by summing numeric values of expanded values (for string fields, the sum of ord($char) is taken, and for bit fields, the sum of zeros and ones). For example, the following computes the same number as the SysV *sum*(1) program:

```
undef $/;
$checksum = unpack ("%32C*", <>) % 65535;
```

The following efficiently counts the number of set bits in a bitstring:

```
$setbits = unpack "%32b*", $selectmask;
```

Here's a simple BASE64 decoder:

```
while (<>) {
    tr#A-Za-z0-9+/##cd;              # remove non-base64 chars
    tr#A-Za-z0-9+/# -_#;            # convert to uuencoded format
    $len = pack("c", 32 + 0.75*length);  # compute length byte
    print unpack("u", $len . $_);   # uudecode and print
}
```

unshift

    unshift ARRAY, LIST

This function does the opposite of shift. (Or the opposite of push, depending on how you look at it.) It prepends *LIST* to the front of the array, and returns the new number of elements in the array:

    unshift @ARGV, '-e', $cmd unless $ARGV[0] =~ /^-/;

Note the *LIST* is prepended whole, not one element at a time, so the prepended elements stay in the same order. Use reverse to do the reverse.

untie

    untie VARIABLE

Breaks the binding between the variable or typeglob contained in *VARIABLE* and the package that it's tied to. See tie, and all of Chapter 14, but especially the section "A Subtle Untying Trap".

Functions

use $! $@

```
use MODULE VERSION LIST
use MODULE VERSION ()
use MODULE VERSION
use MODULE LIST
use MODULE ()
use MODULE
use VERSION
```

The use declaration loads in a module, if it hasn't been loaded before, and imports subroutines and variables into the current package from the named module. (Technically speaking, it imports some semantics into the current package from the named module, generally by aliasing certain subroutine or variable names into your package.) Most use declarations looks like this:

```
use MODULE LIST;
```

That is exactly equivalent to saying:

```
BEGIN { require MODULE; import MODULE LIST; }
```

The BEGIN forces the require and import to happen at compile time. The require makes sure the module is loaded into memory if it hasn't been yet. The import is not a built-in—it's just an ordinary class method call into the package named by MODULE to tell that module to pull the list of features back into the current package. The module can implement its import method any way it likes, though most modules just choose to derive their import method via inheritance from the Exporter class that is defined in the Exporter module. See Chapter 11, *Modules*, and the Exporter module for more information. If no import method can be found, then the call is skipped without murmur.

If you don't want your namespace altered, explicitly supply an empty list:

```
use MODULE ();
```

That is exactly equivalent to the following:

```
BEGIN { require MODULE; }
```

If the first argument to use is a version number like 5.6.2, the currently executing version of Perl must be at least as modern as the version specified. If the current version of Perl is less than VERSION, an error message is printed and Perl exits immediately. This is useful for checking the current Perl version before loading library modules that depend on newer versions, since occasionally we have to "break" the misfeatures of older versions of Perl. (We try not to break things any more than we have to. In fact, we often try to break things less than we have to.)

Speaking of not breaking things, Perl still accepts old version numbers of the form:

```
use 5.005_03;
```

However, in order to align better with industry standards, Perl 5.6 now accepts, (and we prefer to see) the three-tuple form:

```
use 5.6.0;    # That's version 5, subversion 6, patchlevel 0.
```

If the *VERSION* argument is present after *MODULE*, then the use will call the VERSION method in class *MODULE* with the given *VERSION* as an argument. Note that there is no comma after *VERSION*! The default VERSION method, which is inherited from the UNIVERSAL class, croaks if the given version is larger than the value of the variable $Module::VERSION.

See Chapter 32 for a list of standard modules.

Because use provides a wide-open interface, pragmas (compiler directives) are also implemented via modules. Examples of currently implemented pragmas include:

```
use autouse 'Carp' => qw(carp croak);
use bytes;
use constant PI => 4 * atan2(1,1);
use diagnostics;
use integer;
use lib '/opt/projects/spectre/lib';
use locale;
use sigtrap qw(die INT QUIT);
use strict   qw(subs vars refs);
use warnings "deprecated";
```

Many of these pragmatic modules import semantics into the current lexical scope. (This is unlike ordinary modules, which only import symbols into the current package, which has little relation to the current lexical scope other than that the lexical scope is being compiled with that package in mind. That is to say ... oh, never mind, see Chapter 11.)

There's a corresponding declaration, no, that "unimports" any meanings originally imported by use that have since become, er, unimportant:

```
no integer;
no strict 'refs';
no utf8;
no warnings "unsafe";
```

See Chapter 31 for a list of standard pragmas.

Functions

utime

[S!] [X/T] [X/U]

```
utime LIST
```

This function changes the access and modification times on each file of a list of files. The first two elements of the list must be the *numerical* access and modification times, in that order. The function returns the number of files successfully changed. The inode change time of each file is set to the current time. Here's an example of a *touch* command that sets the modification date of the file (assuming you're the owner) to about a month in the future:

```
#!/usr/bin/perl
# montouch - post-date files now + 1 month
$day = 24 * 60 * 60;              # 24 hours of seconds
$later = time() + 30 * $day;     # 30 days is about a month
utime $later, $later, @ARGV;
```

and here's a more sophisticated *touch*-like command with a smattering of error checking:

```
#!/usr/bin/perl
# montouch - post-date files now + 1 month
$later = time() + 30 * 24 * 60 * 60;
@cannot = grep {not utime $later, $later, $_} @ARGV;
die "$0: Could not touch @cannot.\n" if @cannot;
```

To read the times from existing files, use `stat` and then pass the appropriate fields through `localtime` or `gmtime` for printing.

values

```
values HASH
```

This function returns a list consisting of all the values in the indicated *HASH*. The values are returned in an apparently random order, but it is the same order as either the `keys` or `each` function would produce on the same hash. Oddly, to sort a hash by its values, you usually need to use the `keys` function, so see the example under `keys` for that.

You can modify the values of a hash using this function because the returned list contains aliases of the values, not just copies. (In earlier versions, you needed to use a hash slice for that.)

```
for (@hash{keys %hash}) { s/foo/bar/g }    # old way
for (values %hash)      { s/foo/bar/g }    # now changes values
```

Using `values` on a hash that is bound to a humongous DBM file is bound to produce a humongous list, causing you to have a humongous process. You might prefer to use the `each` function, which will iterate over the hash entries one by one without slurping them all into a single gargantuan, er, humongous list.

vec

```
vec EXPR, OFFSET, BITS
```

The vec function provides compact storage of lists of unsigned integers. These integers are packed as tightly as possible within an ordinary Perl string. The string in *EXPR* is treated as a bit string made up of some arbitrary number of elements depending on the length of the string.

OFFSET specifies the index of the particular element you're interested in. The syntaxes for reading and writing the element are the same, since vec stores or returns the value of the element depending on whether you use it in an lvalue or an rvalue context.

BITS specifies how wide each element is in bits, which must be a power of two: 1, 2, 4, 8, 16, or 32 (and also 64 on some platforms). (An exception is raised if any other value is used.) Each element can therefore contain an integer in the range $0..(2**BITS)-1$. For the smaller sizes, as many elements as possible are packed into each byte. When *BITS* is 1, there are eight elements per byte. When *BITS* is 2, there are four elements per byte. When *BITS* is 4, there are two elements (traditionally called nybbles) per byte. And so on. Integers larger than a byte are stored in big-endian order.

A list of unsigned integers can be stored in a single scalar variable by assigning them individually to the vec function. (If *EXPR* is not a valid lvalue, an exception is raised.) In the following example, the elements are each 4 bits wide:

```
$bitstring = "";
$offset = 0;

foreach $num (0, 5, 5, 6, 2, 7, 12, 6) {
    vec($bitstring, $offset++, 4) = $num;
}
```

If an element off the end of the string is written to, Perl will first extend the string with sufficiently many zero bytes.

The vectors stored in the scalar variable can be subsequently retrieved by specifying the correct *OFFSET*.

```
$num_elements = length($bitstring)*2;  # 2 elements per byte

foreach $offset (0 .. $num_elements-1) {
    print vec($bitstring, $offset, 4), "\n";
}
```

If the selected element is off the end of the string, a value of 0 is returned.

Strings created with vec can also be manipulated with the logical operators |, &, ^, and ~. These operators will assume that a bit string operation is desired when both operands are strings. See the examples of this in Chapter 3, *Unary and Binary Operators*, in the section "Bitwise Operators".

If *BITS* == 1, a bitstring can be created to store a series of bits all in one scalar. The ordering is such that vec($bitstring,0,1) is guaranteed to go into the lowest bit of the first byte of the string.

```
@bits = (0,0,1,0, 1,0,1,0, 1,1,0,0, 0,0,1,0);

$bitstring = "";
$offset = 0;

foreach $bit (@bits) {
    vec($bitstring, $offset++, 1) = $bit;
}

print "$bitstring\n";          # "TC", ie. '0x54', '0x43'
```

A bit string can be translated to or from a string of 1's and 0's by supplying a "b*" template to pack or unpack. Alternatively, pack can be used with a "b*" template to create the bit string from a string of 1's and 0's. The ordering is compatible with that expected by vec.

```
$bitstring = pack "b*", join('', @bits);
print "$bitstring\n";   # "TC", same as before
```

unpack can be used to extract the list of 0's and 1's from the bit string.

```
@bits = split(//, unpack("b*", $bitstring));
print "@bits\n";           # 0 0 1 0 1 0 1 0 1 1 0 0 0 0 1 0
```

If you know the exact length in bits, it can be used in place of the "*".

See select for additional examples of using bitmaps generated with vec. See pack and unpack for higher-level manipulation of binary data.

wait   S! S? X̲U̲

```
wait
```

This function waits for a child process to terminate and returns the PID of the deceased process, or -1 if there are no child processes (or on some systems, if child processes are being automatically reaped). The status is returned in $? as described under system. If you get zombie child processes, you should be calling this function, or waitpid.

If you expected a child and didn't find it with wait, you probably had a call to system, a close on a pipe, or backticks between the fork and the wait. These constructs also do a *wait*(2) and may have harvested your child process. Use waitpid to avoid this problem.

waitpid

[S!] [S?] [X/U]

```
waitpid PID, FLAGS
```

This function waits for a particular child process to terminate and returns the PID when the process is dead, −1 if there are no child processes, or 0 if the *FLAGS* specify nonblocking and the process isn't dead yet. The status of the dead process is returned in $? as described under system. To get valid flag values, you'll need to import the ":sys_wait_h" import tag group from the POSIX module. Here's an example that does a nonblocking wait for all pending zombie processes.

```
use POSIX ":sys_wait_h";
do {
    $kid = waitpid(-1,&WNOHANG);
} until $kid == -1;
```

On systems that implement neither the *waitpid*(2) nor *wait4*(2) syscall, *FLAGS* may be specified only as 0. In other words, you can wait for a specific *PID* there, but you can't do so in nonblocking mode.

On some systems, a return value of −1 could mean that child processes are being automatically reaped because you set $SIG{CHLD} = 'IGNORE'.

wantarray

```
wantarray
```

This function returns true if the context of the currently executing subroutine is looking for a list value, and false otherwise. The function returns a defined false value ("") if the calling context is looking for a scalar, and the undefined false value (undef) if the calling context isn't looking for anything; that is, if it's in void context.

Here's are examples of typical usage:

```
return unless defined wantarray;    # don't bother doing more
my @a = complex_calculation();
return wantarray ? @a : \@a;
```

See also caller. This function should really have been named "wantlist", but we named it back when list contexts were still called array contexts.

warn

[S!]

```
warn LIST
warn
```

This function produces an error message, printing *LIST* to STDERR just like die, but doesn't try to exit or throw an exception. For example:

```
warn "Debug enabled" if $debug;
```

If *LIST* is empty and $@ already contains a value (typically from a previous eval), the string "\t...caught" is appended following $@ on STDERR. (This is similar to the way die propagates errors, except that warn doesn't propagate (reraise) the exception.) If the message string supplied is empty, the message "Warning: Something's wrong" is used.

As with die, if the strings supplied don't end in a newline, file and line number information is automatically appended. The warn function is unrelated to Perl's -w command-line option, but can be used in conjunction with it, such as when you wish to emulate built-ins:

```
warn "Something wicked\n" if $^W;
```

No message is printed if there is a $SIG{__WARN__} handler installed. It is the handler's responsibility to deal with the message as it sees fit. One thing you might want to do is promote a mere warning into an exception:

```
local $SIG{__WARN__} = sub {
    my $msg = shift;
    die $msg if $msg =~ /isn't numeric/;
};
```

Most handlers must therefore make arrangements to display the warnings that they are not prepared to deal with, by calling warn again in the handler. This is perfectly safe; it won't produce an endless loop because __WARN__ hooks are not called from inside __WARN__ hooks. This behavior differs slightly from that of $SIG{__DIE__} handlers (which don't suppress the error text, but can instead call die again to change it).

Using a __WARN__ handler provides a powerful way to silence all warnings, even the so-called mandatory ones. Sometimes you need to wrap this in a BEGIN{} block so that it can happen at compile time:

```
# wipe out *all* compile-time warnings
BEGIN { $SIG{__WARN__} = sub { warn $_[0] if $DOWARN } }
my $foo = 10;
my $foo = 20;            # no warning about duplicate my $foo,
                         # but hey, you asked for it!

# no compile-time or run-time warnings before here
$DOWARN = 1;             # *not* a built-in variable

# run-time warnings enabled after here
warn "\$foo is alive and $foo!";    # does show up
```

See the use warnings pragma for lexically scoped control of warnings. See the Carp module's carp and cluck functions for other ways to produce warning messages.

write

```
write FILEHANDLE
write
```

This function writes a formatted record (possibly multiline) to the specified file-handle, using the format associated with that filehandle—see the section "Format Variables" in Chapter 7. By default the format associated with a filehandle is the one having the same name as the filehandle. However, the format for a filehandle may be changed by altering the $~ variable after you select that handle:

```
$old_fh = select(HANDLE);
$~ = "NEWNAME";
select($old_fh);
```

or by saying:

```
use IO::Handle;
HANDLE->format_name("NEWNAME");
```

Since formats are put into a package namespace, you may have to fully qualify the format name if the format was declared in a different package:

```
$~ = "OtherPack::NEWNAME";
```

Top-of-form processing is handled automatically: if there is insufficient room on the current page for the formatted record, the page is advanced by writing a form feed, a special top-of-page format is used for the new page header, and then the record is written. The number of lines remaining on the current page is in the variable $-, which can be set to 0 to force a new page on the next write. (You may need to select the filehandle first.) By default, the name of the top-of-page format is the name of the filehandle with "_TOP" appended, but the format for a filehandle may be changed altering the $^ variable after selecting that handle, or by saying:

```
use IO::Handle;
HANDLE->format_top_name("NEWNAME_TOP");
```

If *FILEHANDLE* is unspecified, output goes to the current default output filehandle, which starts out as STDOUT, but may be changed by the single-argument form of the select operator. If the *FILEHANDLE* is an expression, then the expression is evaluated to determine the actual *FILEHANDLE* at run time.

If a specified format or the current top-of-page format does not exist, an exception is raised.

The write function is *not* the opposite of read. Unfortunately. Use print for simple string output. If you looked up this entry because you wanted to bypass standard I/O, see syswrite.

y//

```
y///
```

The transliteration (historically, also called translation) operator, also known as tr///. See Chapter 5.

## 30

The Standard Perl Library

The standard Perl distribution contains much more than just the *perl* executable that executes your scripts. It also includes hundreds of modules filled with reusable code. Because the standard modules are available everywhere, if you use one of them in your program, you can run your program anywhere Perl is installed, without any extra installation steps.

Library Science

Before we enumerate these modules in the following chapters, let's review a bit of the terminology we've been splattering about.

namespace

A *namespace* is a place to keep names so they won't be confused with names in other namespaces. This leaves you with the simpler problem of not confusing the namespaces themselves. There are two ways to avoid confusing namespaces with each other: give them unique names, or give them unique locations. Perl lets you do both: named namespaces are called packages and unnamed namespaces are called lexical scopes. Since lexical scopes can be no larger than a file, and since the standard modules are file-sized (at minimum), it follows that all module interfaces must make use of named namespaces (packages) if they're to be used by anyone outside the file.

package

A *package* is Perl's standard mechanism for declaring a named namespace. It's a simple mechanism for grouping together related functions and variables. Just as two directories can both contain a (different) file named *fred*, two different

Library

parts of a Perl program can each have its own $fred variable or &fred function. Even though these variables or functions seem to have the same name as one another, those names reside in distinct namespaces managed by the package declaration. Package names are used to identify both modules and classes, as described in Chapter 11, *Modules*, and in Chapter 12, *Objects*.

library

The term *library* is unfortunately rather overloaded in Perl culture. These days we normally use the term to mean the entire set of Perl modules installed on your system.

Historically, a Perl library was also a single file containing a collection of subroutines sharing some common purpose. Such a file often has the file extension *.pl*, short for "perl library". We still use that extension for random bits of Perl code that you pull in with do *FILE* or with require. Although it's not a full-fledged module, a library file typically declares itself to be in a distinct package so related variables and subroutines can be kept together and don't accidentally interfere with other variables in your program. There is no mandatory extension; others besides *.pl* sometimes occur as explained later in this chapter. These simple, unstructured library files have been largely superseded by the module.

module

A Perl *module* is a library file that conforms to certain specific conventions that allow one or more files implementing that module to be brought in with a single use declaration at compile time. Module filenames must always end in *.pm*, because the use declaration assumes it. The use declaration will also translate the package separator :: to whatever your directory separator is, so that the directory structure in your Perl library can match your package structure. Chapter 11 describes how to create your own Perl modules.

class

A *class* is just a module that implements methods for objects associated with the module's package name. If you're interested in object-oriented modules, see Chapter 12.

pragma

A *pragma* is just a special module that twiddles Perl's internal knobs. See Chapter 31, *Pragmatic Modules*.

extension

An *extension* is a Perl module that, in addition to loading a *.pm* file, also loads a shared library implementing the module's semantics in C or C++.

program

A Perl *program* is code designed to be run as an independent entity; also known as a *script* when you don't want anyone to expect much from it, an *application* when it's big and complicated, an *executable* when its caller doesn't care what language it was written in, or an *enterprise solution* when it costs a fortune. Perl programs might exist as source code, bytecode, or native machine code. If it's something you might run from the command line, we'll call it a program.

A Tour of the Perl Library

You'll save an enormous amount of time if you make the effort to familiarize yourself with the standard Perl library, because there's no reason to reinvent those particular wheels. You should be aware, however, that this collection contains a wide range of material. Although some libraries may be extremely helpful, others might be completely irrelevant to your needs. For example, if you're only writing in 100% pure Perl, those modules that support the dynamic loading of C and C++ extensions aren't going to help you much.

Perl expects to find library modules somewhere in its library "include" path, @INC. This array specifies the ordered list of directories Perl searches when you load in some library code using the keywords do, require, or use. You can easily list out those directories by calling Perl with the **–V** switch for Very Verbose Version information, or with this simple code:

```
% perl -le "print foreach @INC"
/usr/libdata/perl5/sparc-openbsd/5.00503
/usr/local/libdata/perl5/sparc-openbsd/5.00503
/usr/libdata/perl5
/usr/local/libdata/perl5
/usr/local/libdata/perl5/site_perl/sparc-openbsd
/usr/libdata/perl5/site_perl/sparc-openbsd
/usr/local/libdata/perl5/site_perl
/usr/libdata/perl5/site_perl
.
```

That's only one sample of possible output. Every installation of Perl uses its own paths. The important thing is that, although contents will vary depending upon your vendor's and your site's installation policy, you can rely upon all standard libraries being installed with Perl. If you want to find out where a file was actually loaded from, consult the %INC variable. For a module file, you can find exactly where Perl is getting it from with this command:

```
% perldoc -l MODULE
```

If you look through the directories in @INC and their subdirectories, you'll find several different kinds of files installed. Most have names ending in *.pm*, but some end in *.pl*, *.ph*, *.al*, or *.so*. The ones that most interest you are the first set, because a suffix of *.pm* indicates that the file is a proper Perl module. More on those in a minute.

The few files you see there ending in *.pl* are those old Perl libraries we mentioned earlier. They are included for compatibility with ancient releases of Perl from the 80s and early 90s. Because of this, Perl code that worked back in, say, 1990, should continue to behave properly without any fuss even if you have a modern version of Perl installed. When writing new code that makes use of the standard Perl library, you should always elect to use the *.pm* version over any *.pl*, where possible. That's because modules don't pollute your namespace the way many of the old *.pl* files do.

One note on the use of the *.pl* extension: it means Perl library, not Perl program. Although *.pl* is sometimes used to identify Perl programs on web servers that need to distinguish executable programs from static content in the same directory, we suggest that you use a suffix of *.plx* instead to indicate an executable Perl program. (Similar advice holds for operating systems that choose interpreters based on filename extensions.)

Files with extensions of *.al* are small pieces of larger modules that will be automatically loaded when you use their parent *.pm* file. If you build your module layout using the standard *h2xs* tool that comes with Perl (and if you haven't used Perl's **-A** flag), the make install procedure will use the AutoLoader module to create these little *.al* files for you.

The *.ph* files were made by the standard *h2ph* program, a somewhat aging but still occasionally necessary tool that does its best to translate C preprocessor directives into Perl. The resulting *.ph* files contain constants sometimes needed by low-level functions like ioctl, fcntl, or syscall. (Nowadays most of these values are more conveniently and portably available in standard modules such as the POSIX, Errno, Fcntl, or Socket modules.) See *perlinstall* for how to install these optional but sometimes important components.

One last file extension you might encounter while poking around is *.so* (or whatever your system uses for shared libraries). These *.so* files are platform-dependent portions of extension modules. Originally written in C or C++, these modules have been compiled into dynamically relocatable object code. The end user doesn't need to be aware of their existence, however, because the module interface hides them. When the user code says require Module or use Module, Perl loads *Module.pm* and executes it, which lets the module pull in any other necessary pieces, such as *Module.so* or any autoloaded *.al* components. In fact, the module could load anything it jolly well pleases, including 582 other modules. It could download all of CPAN if it felt like it, and maybe the last two years of *freshmeat.net* archives.

A module is not just a static chunk of code in Perl. It's an active agent that figures out how to implement an interface on your behalf. It may follow all the standard conventions, or it may not. It's allowed to do anything to warp the meaning of the rest of your program, up to and including translating the rest of your program into SPITBOL. This sort of chicanery is considered perfectly fair as long as it's well documented. When you use such a Perl module, you're agreeing to *its* contract, not a standard contract written by Perl.

So you'd best read the fine print.

31

Pragmatic Modules

A *pragma* is a special kind of module that affects the compilation phase of your program. Some pragmatic modules (or *pragmata*, for short (or *pragmas*, for shorter)) may also affect the execution phase of your program. Think of these as hints to the compiler. Because they need to be seen at compile time, they'll only work when invoked by a use or a no, because by the time a require or a do is run, compilation is long since over.

By convention, pragma names are written in all lowercase because lowercase module names are reserved for the Perl distribution itself. When writing your own modules, use at least one capital letter in the module name to avoid conflict with pragma names.

Unlike regular modules, most pragmas limit their effects to the rest of the inner-most enclosing block from which they were invoked. In other words, they're lexically scoped, just like my variables. Ordinarily, the lexical scope of an outer block covers any inner block embedded within it, but an inner block may countermand a lexically scoped pragma from an outer block by using the no statement:

```
use strict;
use integer;
{
    no strict 'refs';       # allow symbolic references
    no integer;             # resume floating-point arithmetic
    # ....
}
```

More so than the other modules Perl ships with, the pragmas form an integral and essential part of the Perl compilation environment. It's hard to use the compiler well if you don't know how to pass hints to it, so we'll put some extra effort into describing pragmas.

Another thing to be aware of is that we often use pragmas to prototype features that later get encoded into "real" syntax. So in some programs you'll see deprecated pragmas like use attrs whose functionality is now supported directly by subroutine declaration syntax. Similarly, use vars is in the process of being replaced by our declarations. And use subs may someday be replaced by an override attribute on ordinary subroutine declarations. We're not in a terrible hurry to break the old ways of doing things, but we do think the new ways are prettier.

use attributes

```
sub afunc : method;
my $closure = sub : method { ... };

use attributes;
@attrlist = attributes::get(\&afunc);
```

The attributes pragma has two purposes. The first is to provide an internal mechanism for declaring *attribute lists*, which are optional properties associated with subroutine declarations and (someday soon) variable declarations. (Since it's an internal mechanism, you don't generally use this pragma directly.) The second purpose is to provide a way to retrieve those attribute lists at run time using the attributes::get function call. In this capacity, attributes is just a standard module, not a pragma.

Only a few built-in attributes are currently handled by Perl. Package-specific attributes are allowed by an experimental extension mechanism described in the section "Package-specific Attribute Handling" of the *attributes*(3) manpage.

Attribute setting occurs at compile time; attempting to set an unrecognized attribute is a compilation error. (The error is trappable by eval, but it still stops the compilation within that eval block.)

Only three built-in attributes for subroutines are currently implemented: locked, method, and lvalue. See Chapter 6, *Subroutines*, and Chapter 17, *Threads*, for further discussion of these. There are currently no built-in attributes for variables as there are for subroutines, but we can think of several we might like, such as constant.

The attributes pragma provides two subroutines for general use. They may be imported if you ask for them.

get This function returns a (possibly empty) list of attributes given a single input parameter that's a reference to a subroutine or variable. The function raises an exception by invoking Carp::croak if passed invalid arguments.

Pragmata

reftype

This function acts somewhat like the built-in `ref` function, but it always returns the underlying, built-in Perl data type of the referenced value, ignoring any package into which it might have been blessed.

Precise details of attribute handling remain in flux, so you'd best check out the online documentation included with your Perl release to see what state it's all in.

use autouse

```
use autouse 'Carp' => qw(carp croak);
carp "this carp was predeclared and autoused";
```

This pragma provides a mechanism for run-time demand loading of a particular module only when a function from that module really gets called. It does this by providing a stub function that replaces itself with the real call once triggered. This is similar in spirit to the way the standard `AutoLoader` and `SelfLoader` modules behave. In short, it's a performance hack to help make your Perl program start up faster (on average) by avoiding compilation of modules that might never ever be called during a given execution run.

How `autouse` behaves depends on whether the module is already loaded. For example, if the module `Module` is already loaded, then the declaration:

```
use autouse 'Module' => qw(func1 func2($;$) Module::func3);
```

is equivalent to the simple import of two functions:

```
use Module qw(func1 func2);
```

This assumes that `Module` defines `func2()` with prototype `($;$)`, and that `func1()` and `func3()` have no prototypes. (More generally, this also assumes that `Module` uses `Exporter`'s standard `import` method; otherwise, a fatal error is raised.) In any event, it completely ignores `Module::func3` since that is presumably already declared.

If, on the other hand, `Module` has not yet been loaded when the `autouse` pragma is parsed, the pragma declares functions `func1` and `func2` to be in the current package. It also declares a function `Module::func3` (which could be construed as mildly antisocial, were it not for the fact that the nonexistence of the `Module` module has even more antisocial consequences). When these functions are called, they make sure the `Module` in question is loaded and then replace themselves with calls to the real functions just loaded.

Because the autouse pragma moves portions of your program's execution from compile time to run time, this can have unpleasant ramifications. For example, if the module you autouse has some initialization that is expected to be done early, this may not happen early enough. Autousing can also hide bugs in your code when important checks are moved from compile time to run time.

In particular, if the prototype you've specified on autouse line is wrong, you will not find out about it until the corresponding function is executed (which may be months or years later, for a rarely called function). To partially alleviate this problem, you could write your code like this during code development:

```
use Chase;
use autouse Chase => qw(hue($) cry(&$));
cry "this cry was predeclared and autoused";
```

The first line ensures that errors in your argument specification will be found early. When your program graduates from development into production mode, you can comment out the regular loading of the Chase module and leave just the autousing call in place. That way you get safety during development and performance during production.

use base

```
use base qw(Mother Father);
```

This pragma lets a programmer conveniently declare a derived class based upon the listed parent classes. The declaration above is roughly equivalent to:

```
BEGIN {
    require Mother;
    require Father;
    push @ISA, qw(Mother Father);
}
```

The use base pragma takes care of any require needed. When the strict 'vars' pragma is in scope, use base lets you (in effect) assign to @ISA without first having to declare our @ISA. (Since the use base pragma happens at compile time, it's best to avoid diddling @ISA on your own at run time.)

But beyond this, use base has another property. If any named base class makes use of the fields facility described under use fields later in this chapter, then the pragma initializes the package's special field attributes from the base class. (Multiple inheritance of field classes is *not* supported. The use base pragma raises an exception if more than one named base class has fields.)

Any base class not yet loaded will be loaded automatically via `require`. However, whether to `require` a base class package is determined not by the customary inspection of `%INC`, but by the absence of a global `$VERSION` in the base package. This hack keeps Perl from repeatedly trying (and failing) to load a base class that isn't in its own requirable file (because, for example, it's loaded as part of some other module's file). If `$VERSION` is not detected after successfully loading a file, `use base` will define `$VERSION` in the base package, setting it to the string "-1, defined by base.pm".

use blib

From the command line:

```
% perl -Mblib program [args...]
% perl -Mblib=DIR program [args...]
```

From your Perl program:

```
use blib;
use blib 'DIR';
```

This pragma is intended primarily as a way of testing arbitrary Perl programs against an uninstalled version of a package through Perl's `-M` command-line switch. It assumes your directory structure was produced by the standard `ExtUtils::MakeMaker` module.

The pragma looks for a *blib* directory structure starting in the directory named *DIR* (or current directory if none was specified), and if it doesn't find a *blib* directory there, works its way back up through your ".." directories, scanning up to five levels of parent directory.

use bytes

```
use bytes;
no bytes;
```

The `use bytes` pragma disables character semantics for the rest of the lexical scope in which it appears. The `no bytes` pragma can be used to reverse the effect of `use bytes` within the current lexical scope.

Perl normally assumes character semantics in the presence of character data (that is, data from a source marked as being of a particular character encoding).

To understand the implications and differences between character semantics and byte semantics, see Chapter 15, *Unicode*. A visit to Tokyo might also help.

use charnames

```
use charnames HOW;
print "\N{CHARSPEC} is a funny character";
```

This lexically scoped pragma enables named characters to be interpolated into strings using the \N{*CHARSPEC*} notation:

```
use charnames ':full';
print "\N{GREEK SMALL LETTER SIGMA} is called sigma.\n";
```

```
use charnames ':short';
print "\N{greek:Sigma} is an upper-case sigma.\n";
```

```
use charnames qw(cyrillic greek);
print "\N{sigma} is Greek sigma, and \N{be} is Cyrillic b.\n";
```

The pragma supports *HOW* arguments :full and :short, as well as specific script names.* The *HOW* argument determines how the character specified by the *CHARSPEC* in \N{*CHARSPEC*}} is to be searched for. If :full is present, the *CHARSPEC* is first looked for in the Unicode character tables as a complete Unicode character name. If :short is present and *CHARSPEC* has the form *SCRIPTNAME*:*CHARNAME*, *CHARNAME* is looked for as a letter in script *SCRIPTNAME*. If *HOW* contains specific script names, *CHARSPEC* is looked for as an individual *CHARNAME* in each of the given scripts, in the specified order.

For lookup of *CHARNAME* inside a given script *SCRIPTNAME*, the pragma looks in the table of standard Unicode names for patterns of the form:

```
SCRIPTNAME CAPITAL LETTER CHARNAME
SCRIPTNAME SMALL LETTER CHARNAME
SCRIPTNAME LETTER CHARNAME
```

If *CHARNAME* is entirely lowercase (as in \N{sigma}), the CAPITAL variant is ignored. Otherwise, the SMALL variant is ignored.

You can write your own module that works like the charnames pragma but defines character names differently. However, the interface to that is still experimental, so see the manpage for the latest.

---

* By which we don't mean Perl scripts. We mean "script" as in some particular style of written letters, like Roman or Greek or Cyrillic. Unfortunately, "script" is the technical term for that, and we're not likely to persuade the Unicode Consortium to use a different term.

use constant

```
use constant BUFFER_SIZE    => 4096;
use constant ONE_YEAR       => 365.2425 * 24 * 60 * 60;
use constant PI             => 4 * atan2 1, 1;
use constant DEBUGGING      => 0;
use constant ORACLE         => 'oracle@cs.indiana.edu';
use constant USERNAME       => scalar getpwuid($<);
use constant USERINFO       => getpwuid($<);

sub deg2rad { PI * $_[0] / 180 }

print "This line does nothing"     unless DEBUGGING;

# references can be declared constant
use constant CHASH          => { foo => 42 };
use constant CARRAY         => [ 1,2,3,4 ];
use constant CPSEUDOHASH    => [ { foo => 1}, 42 ];
use constant CCODE          => sub { "bite $_[0]\n" };

print CHASH->{foo};
print CARRAY->[$i];
print CPSEUDOHASH->{foo};
print CCODE->("me");
print CHASH->[10];                          # compile-time error
```

This pragma declares the named symbol to be an immutable constant* with the given scalar or list value. You must make a separate declaration for each symbol. Values are evaluated in list context. You may override this with scalar as we did above.

Since these constants don't have a $ on the front, you can't interpolate them directly into double-quotish strings, although you may do so indirectly:

```
print "The value of PI is @{[ PI ]}.\n";
```

Because list constants are returned as lists, not as arrays, you must subscript a list-valued constant using extra parentheses as you would any other list expression:

```
$homedir = USERINFO[7];         # WRONG
$homedir = (USERINFO)[7];       # ok
```

Although using all capital letters for constants is recommended to help them stand out and to help avoid potential collisions with other keywords and subroutine names, this is merely a convention. Constant names must begin with a letter, but it need not be a capital one.

---

* Implemented as a subroutine taking no arguments and returning the same constant each time.

Constants are not private to the lexical scope in which they occur. Instead, they are simply argumentless subroutines in the symbol table of the package issuing the declaration. You may refer to a constant *CONST* from package Other as Other::*CONST*. Read more about compile-time inlining of such subroutines in the section "Inlining Constant Functions" in Chapter 6.

As with all use directives, use constant happens at compile time. It's therefore misleading at best to place a constant declaration inside a conditional statement, such as if ($foo) { use constant ... }.

Omitting the value for a symbol gives it the value of undef in scalar context or the empty list, (), in a list context. But it is probably best to declare these explicitly:

```
use constant CAMELIDS      => ();
use constant CAMEL_HOME    => undef;
```

Restrictions on use constant

List constants are not currently inlined the way scalar constants are. And it is not possible to have a subroutine or keyword with the same name as a constant. This is probably a Good Thing.

You cannot declare more than one named constant at a time:

```
use constant FOO => 4, BAR => 5;     # WRONG
```

That defines a constant named FOO whose return list is (4, "BAR", 5). You need this instead:

```
use constant FOO => 4
use constant BAR => 5;
```

You can get yourself into trouble if you use a constant in a context that automatically quotes bare names. (This is true for any subroutine call, not just constants.) For example, you can't say $hash{*CONSTANT*} because *CONSTANT* will be interpreted as a string. Use $hash{*CONSTANT*()} or $hash{+*CONSTANT*} to prevent the quoting mechanism from kicking in. Similarly, since the => operator quotes its left operand if that operand is a bare name, you must say *CONSTANT*() => 'value' instead of *CONSTANT* => 'value'.

At some point, you'll be able to use a constant attribute on variable declarations:

```
my $PI : constant = 4 * atan2(1,1);
```

This has all the advantages of being a variable rather than a subroutine. It has all the disadvantages of not being implemented yet.

use diagnostics

```
use diagnostics;              # compile-time enable
use diagnostics -verbose;

enable  diagnostics;          # run-time enable
disable diagnostics;          # run-time disable
```

This pragma expands the normal, terse diagnostics and suppresses duplicate warnings. It augments the short versions with the more explicative and endearing descriptions found in Chapter 33, *Diagnostic Messages*. Like other pragmas, it also affects the compilation phase of your program, not just the run phase.

When you use diagnostics at the start of your program, this automatically enables Perl's **-w** command-line switch by setting $^W to 1. The remainder of your whole compilation will then be subject to enhanced diagnostics. These still go out on STDERR.

Because of the interaction between run-time and compile-time issues, and because it's probably not a good idea anyway, you may not use no diagnostics to turn them off at compile time. However, you may control their behavior at run time using the disable and enable methods. (Make sure you do the use first, or else you won't be able to get at the methods.)

The -verbose flag first prints out the *perldiag* manpage's introduction before any other diagnostics are issued. The $diagnostics::PRETTY variable can be set (before the use) to generate nicer escape sequences for pagers like *less*(1) or *more*(1):

```
BEGIN { $diagnostics::PRETTY = 1 }
use diagnostics;
```

Warnings dispatched from Perl and detected by this pragma are each displayed only once. This is useful when you're caught in a loop that's generating the same warning (like uninitialized value) over and over again. Manually generated warnings, such as those stemming from calls to warn or carp, are unaffected by this duplicate detection mechanism.

Here are some examples of using the diagnostics pragma. The following file is certain to trigger a few errors at both run time and compile time:

```
use diagnostics;
print NOWHERE "nothing\n";
print STDERR "\n\tThis message should be unadorned.\n";
warn "\tThis is a user warning";
print "\nDIAGNOSTIC TESTER: Please enter a <CR> here: ";
my $a, $b = scalar <STDIN>;
print "\n";
print $x/$y;
```

Here's the output:

```
Parentheses missing around "my" list at diagtest line 6 (#1)

    (W parenthesis) You said something like

        my $foo, $bar = @_;

    when you meant

        my ($foo, $bar) = @_;

Remember that "my", "our", and "local" bind tighter than comma.

Name "main::NOWHERE" used only once: possible typo at diagtest line 2 (#2)

    (W once) Typographical errors often show up as unique variable
        names.  If you had a good reason for having a unique name,
        then just mention it again somehow to suppress the message.
        The our declaration is provided for this purpose.

Name "main::b" used only once: possible typo at diagtest line 6 (#2)
Name "main::x" used only once: possible typo at diagtest line 8 (#2)
Name "main::y" used only once: possible typo at diagtest line 8 (#2)

Filehandle main::NOWHERE never opened at diagtest line 2 (#3)

    (W unopened) An I/O operation was attempted on a filehandle that
        was never initialized.  You need to do an open() or a socket()
        call, or call a constructor from the FileHandle package.

        This message should be unadorned.
        This is a user warning at diagtest line 4.

DIAGNOSTIC TESTER: Please enter a <CR> here:
Use of uninitialized value in division (/) at diagtest line 8 (#4)

    (W uninitialized) An undefined value was used as if it were
        already defined.  It was interpreted as a "" or a 0, but maybe
        it was a mistake.  To suppress this warning assign a defined
        value to your variables.

Illegal division by zero at diagtest line 8 (#5)

    (F) You tried to divide a number by 0.  Either something was
        wrong in your logic, or you need to put a conditional in to
        guard against meaningless input.

Uncaught exception from user code:
        Illegal division by zero at diagtest line 8.
```

Diagnostic messages derive from the *perldiag.pod* file. If an extant $SIG{__WARN__} handler is discovered, this will still be honored, but only after the diagnostics::splainthis function (the pragma's $SIG{__WARN__} interceptor) has had its way with your warnings. Perl does not currently support stacked handlers, so this is the best we can do for now. There is a $diagnostics::DEBUG variable you may set if you're desperately curious about what sorts of things are being intercepted:

```
BEGIN { $diagnostics::DEBUG = 1 }
use diagnostics;
```

use fields

In the Pet module:

```
package Pet;
use strict;
use fields qw(name weight _Pet_pid);
my $PID = 0;
sub new {
    my Pet $self = shift;
    unless (ref $self) {
        $self = fields::new($self);
        $self->{_Pet_pid} = "this is Pet's secret ID";
    }
    $self->{name} = "Hey, you!";
    $self->{weight} = 20;
    return $self;
}
1;
```

In a separate program, *demopet*:

```
use Pet;
my Pet $rock = new Pet;             # typed lexical

$rock->{name}     = "quartz";
$rock->{weight}   = "2kg";
$rock->{_Pet_pid} = 1233;           # private attribute

$rock->{color}    = "blue";         # generates compile-time error
```

In the Dog module:

```
package Dog;
use strict;
use base 'Pet';                     # inherit fields and methods from Pet
use fields qw(name pedigree);       # override Pet name attribute,
                                    # add new pedigree attribute
use fields qw(wag _Dog_private);    # not shared with Pet
sub new {
    my $class = shift;
    my $self = fields::new($class);
    $self->SUPER::new();            # init base fields
    $self->{pedigree} = "none";     # init own fields
    return $self;
}
```

In a separate program, *demodog*:

```
use Dog;

my Dog $spot = new Dog;            # typed lexical

$spot->{name}     = "Theloneus";   # not inherited
$spot->{weight}   = "30lbs";       # inherited
$spot->{pedigree} = "mutt";        # not inherited

$spot->{color}    = "brown";       # generates compile-time error
$spot->{_Pet_pid} = 3324;          # generates compile-time error
```

The `fields` pragma provides a method of declaring class fields that can be type checked at compile time. This relies on a feature known as pseudohashes: if a typed lexical variable (`my Pet $rock`) is holding a reference (the `Pet` object) and is used to access a hash element (`$rock->{name}`), and if there exists a package with the same name as the declared type that has set up class fields using the `fields` pragma, then the operation is turned into an array access at compile time, provided the field specified is valid.

The related `base` pragma will combine fields from base classes and any fields declared using the `fields` pragma. This enables field inheritance to work properly.

Field names that start with an underscore character are made private to the class and are not visible to subclasses. Inherited fields can be overridden but will generate a warning if warnings are enabled.

The effect of all this is that you can have objects with named fields which are as compact as arrays and as fast to access. This only works as long as the objects are accessed through properly typed lexical variables, though. If the variables are not typed, access is only checked at run time, so your program runs slower because it has to do both a hash access and an array access. In addition to field declarations, the following functions are supported:

new

The `fields::new` function creates and blesses a pseudohash into the specified class (which may also be specified by passing an object of that class). The object is created with the fields declared earlier for that class using the `fields` pragma. This makes it possible to write a constructor like this:

```
package Critter::Sounds;
use fields qw(cat dog bird);

sub new {
    my Critter::Sounds $self = shift;
    $self = fields::new($self) unless ref $self;
    $self->{cat} = 'meow';                        # scalar element
    @$self{'dog','bird'} = ('bark','tweet');      # slice
    return $self;
}
```

phash

The `fields::phash` function creates and initializes a plain (unblessed) pseudo-hash. You should always use this function to create pseudohashes instead of creating them directly, in case we decide to change the implementation.

If the first argument to `phash` is a reference to an array, the pseudohash will be created with keys from that array. If a second argument is supplied, it must also be a reference to an array whose elements will be used as the values. If the second array contains less elements than the first, the trailing elements of the pseudohash will not be initialized. This makes it particularly useful for creating a pseudohash from subroutine arguments:

```
sub dogtag {
    my $tag = fields::phash([qw(name rank ser_num)], [@_]);
}
```

Alternatively, you can pass a list key/value pairs that will be used to construct the pseudohash:

```
my $tag = fields::phash(name => "Joe",
                        rank => "captain",
                        ser_num => 42);

my $pseudohash = fields::phash(%args);
```

For more on pseudohashes, see the section "Pseudohashes" in Chapter 8, *References.*

The current implementation keeps the declared fields in the `%FIELDS` hash of the calling package, but this may change in future versions, so it's best to rely on this pragma's interface to manage your fields.

use filetest

```
$can_perhaps_read = -r "file";       # use the mode bits
{
    use filetest 'access';           # intuit harder
    $can_really_read = -r "file";
}
$can_perhaps_read = -r "file";       # use the mode bits again
```

This lexically scoped pragma tells the compiler to change the behavior of the unary file test operators -r, -w, -x, -R, -W, and -X, documented in Chapter 3, *Unary and Binary Operators*. The default behavior for these file tests is to use the mode bits returned by the `stat` family of calls. However, this may not always be the right thing to do, such as when a filesystem understands ACLs (access control lists). In environments such as AFS where this matters, the `use filetest` pragma may help the permission operators to return results more consistent with other tools.

There may be a slight performance decrease in the affected file test operators under use filetest, since on some systems the extended functionality needs to be emulated.

Warning: any notion of using file tests for security purposes is a lost cause from the start. There is a window open for race conditions, because there's no way to guarantee that the permissions will not change between the test and the real operation. If you are the least bit serious about security, you won't use file test operators to decide whether something *will* work. Instead, just go ahead try the real operation, then test for whether that operation succeeded. (You should be doing that anyway.) See the section "Handling Timing Glitches" in Chapter 23, *Security.*

use filetest 'access'

Currently only one import, access, is implemented. Calling use filetest 'access' enables the use of *access*(2) or similar syscalls when performing file tests, and no filetest 'access' similarly disables it. This extended file test functionality is used only when the operator's operand (or, if you prefer, the unary function's argument) is a real filename, not when it is a filehandle.

use integer

```
use integer;
$x = 10/3;
# $x is now 3, not 3.33333333333333333
```

This lexically scoped pragma tells the compiler to use integer operations from here through the end of the enclosing block. On many machines, this doesn't matter a great deal for most computations, but on those few remaining architectures without floating-point hardware, it can amount to a dramatic performance difference.

Note that this pragma affects certain numeric operations, not the numbers themselves. For example, if you run this code:

```
use integer;
$x = 1.8;
$y = $x + 1;
$z = -1.8;
```

you'll be left with $x == 1.8, $y == 2 and $z == -1. The $z case happens because unary - counts as an operation, so the value 1.8 is truncated to 1 before its sign bit is flipped. Likewise, functions that expect floating-point numbers, such as sqrt or the trig functions, still receive and return floats even under use integer. So sqrt(1.44) is 1.2, but 0 + sqrt(1.44) is now just 1.

Native integer arithmetic as provided by your C compiler is used. This means that Perl's own semantics for arithmetic operations might not be preserved. One common source of trouble is the modulus of negative numbers. Perl may do it one way, but your hardware may do it another:

```
% perl -le 'print (4 % -3)'
-2
% perl -Minteger -le 'print (4 % -3)'
1
```

use less

```
use less;                # These are all UNIMPLEMENTED!

use less 'CPU';
use less 'memory';
use less 'time';
use less 'disk';
use less 'fat';          # great with "use locale";
```

Currently unimplemented, this pragma is intended to someday give hints to the compiler, code-generator, or interpreter to enable certain trade-offs.

It is not an error to ask to use less of something that Perl doesn't know how to make less of right now.

use lib

```
use lib "$ENV{HOME}/libperl";    # add ~/libperl
no lib ".";                      # remove cwd
```

This pragma simplifies the manipulation of @INC at compile time. It is typically used to add extra directories to Perl's search path so that later do, require, and use statements will find library files that aren't located in Perl's default search path. It's especially important with use, since that happens at compile time too, and setting @INC normally (that is, at run time) would be too late.

Parameters to use lib are prepended to the beginning of Perl's search path. Saying use lib *LIST* is *almost* the same as saying BEGIN { unshift(@INC, *LIST*) }, but use lib *LIST* includes support for platform-specific directories. For each given directory $dir in its argument list, the lib pragma also checks to see whether a directory named *$dir/$archname/auto* exists. If so, the *$dir/$archname* directory is assumed to be a corresponding platform-specific directory, so is added to @INC (in front of $dir).

To avoid redundant additions that slow access time and waste a small amount of memory, trailing duplicate entries in @INC are removed when entries are added.

Normally, you should only *add* directories to @INC. If you do need to delete directories from @INC, take care to delete only those that you yourself added, or those that you're somehow certain aren't needed by other modules in your program. Other modules may have added directories to your @INC that they need for correct operation.

The no lib pragma deletes all instances of each named directory from @INC. It also deletes any corresponding platform-specific directory as described earlier.

When the lib pragma is loaded, it saves the current value of @INC to the array @lib::ORIG_INC, so to restore the original, just copy that array to the real @INC.

Even though @INC typically includes dot ("."), the current directory, this really isn't as useful as you'd think. For one thing, the dot entry comes at the end, not the start, so that modules installed in the current directory don't suddenly override system versions. You could say use lib "." if that's what you really want. More annoyingly, it's the current directory of the Perl process, not the directory that the script was installed into, which makes it completely unreliable. If you create a program plus some modules for that program to use, it will work while you're developing, but it won't work when you aren't running in the directory the files live in.

One solution for this is to use the standard FindBin module:

```
use FindBin;                # where was script installed?
use lib $FindBin::Bin;      # use that dir for libs, too
```

The FindBin module tries to guess the full path to the directory in which the running process's program was installed. Don't use this for security purposes, because malicious programs can usually deceive it if they try hard enough. But unless you're intentionally trying to break the module, it should work as intended. The module provides a $FindBin::Bin variable (which you may import) that contains the module's guess of where the program was installed. You can then use the lib pragma to add that directory to your @INC, thus producing an executable-relative path.

Some programs expect to be installed in a *bin* directory and then find their library modules in "cousin" files installed in a *lib* directory at the same level as *bin*. For example, programs might go in */usr/local/apache/bin* or */opt/perl/bin*, and libraries go in */usr/local/apache/lib* and */opt/perl/lib*. This code takes care of that neatly:

```
use FindBin qw($Bin);
use lib "$Bin/../lib";
```

If you find yourself specifying the same use lib in several unrelated programs, you might consider setting the PERL5LIB environment variable instead. See the description of the PERL5LIB environment variable in Chapter 19, *The Command-Line Interface*.

```
# syntax for sh, bash, ksh, or zsh
$ PERL5LIB=$HOME/perllib; export PERL5LIB

# syntax for csh or tcsh
% setenv PERL5LIB ~/perllib
```

If you want to use optional directories on just this program without changing its source, look into the **-I** command-line switch:

```
% perl -I ~/perllib program-path args
```

See the Chapter 19 for more about using **-I** from the command line.

use locale

```
@x = sort @y;        # ASCII sorting order
{
    use locale;
    @x = sort @y;    # Locale-defined sorting order
}
@x = sort @y;        # ASCII sorting order again
```

This lexically scoped pragma tells the compiler to enable (or disable, under no locale) the use of POSIX locales for built-in operations. Enabling locales tells Perl's case-conversion functions and pattern-matching engine to be respectful of your language environment, allowing for characters with diacritical markings, etc. If this pragma is in effect and your C library knows about POSIX locales, Perl looks to your LC_CTYPE setting for regular expressions and to your LC_COLLATE setting for string comparisons like those in sort.

Since locales are more a form of nationalization than of internationalization, the use of locales may interact oddly with Unicode. See Chapter 15 for more on internationalization.

use open

```
use open IN => ":crlf", OUT => ":raw";
```

The open pragma declares one or more default disciplines for I/O operations. Any open and readpipe (that is, qx// or backticks) operators found within the lexical scope of this pragma that do not specify their own disciplines will use the declared defaults. Neither open with an explicit set of disciplines, nor sysopen under any cirumstances, is influenced by this pragma.

Only the two disciplines :raw and :crlf are currently available (though as of this writing we expect a :utf8 discipline to be along shortly). On legacy systems that distinguish between those two translation modes when opening files, the :raw discipline corresponds to "binary mode", and `:crlf` to "text mode". (These two disciplines are currently no-ops on platforms where `binmode` is a no-op, but only for now; see the `open` function in Chapter 29, *Functions*, for a longer description of the semantics we expect of various disciplines.)

Full-fledged support for I/O disciplines is currently unimplemented. When they are eventually supported, this pragma will serve as one of the interfaces to declare default disciplines for all I/O. At that time, any default disciplines declared by this pragma will be available by the special discipline name ":DEFAULT" and usable within handle constructors that allow disciplines to be specified. This will make it possible to stack new disciplines over the default ones.

```
open (FH, "<:para :DEFAULT", $file) or die "can't open $file: $!";
```

Once complete, full support for I/O disciplines will enable all supported disciplines to work on all platforms.

use overload

In the `Number` module:

```
package Number;
use overload "+" => \&myadd,
             "-" => \&mysub,
             "*=" => "multiply_by";
```

In your program:

```
use Number;
$a = new Number 57;
$b = $a + 5;
```

The built-in operators work well on strings and numbers, but make little sense when applied to object references (since, unlike C or C++, Perl doesn't allow pointer arithmetic). The `overload` pragma lets you redefine the meanings of these built-in operations when applied to objects of your own design. In the previous example, the call to the pragma redefines three operations on `Number` objects: addition will call the `Number::myadd` function, subtraction will call the `Number::mysub` function, and the multiplicative assignment operator will call the `multiply_by` method in class `Number` (or one of its base classes). We say of these operators that they are now *overloaded* because they have additional meanings overlaid on them (and not because they have too many meanings—though that may also be the case).

For much more on overloading, see Chapter 13, *Overloading*.

Pragmata

use re

This pragma controls the use of regular expressions. It has four possible invocations: "taint" and "eval", which are lexically scoped, plus "debug" and "debugcolor", which aren't.

```
use re 'taint';
# Contents of $match are tainted if $dirty was also tainted.
($match) = ($dirty =~ /^(.*)$/s);

# Allow code interpolation:
use re 'eval';
$pat = '(?{ $var = 1 })';        # embedded code execution
/alpha${pat}omega/;              # won't fail unless under -T
                                 # and $pat is tainted

use re 'debug';                  # like "perl -Dr"
/^(.*)$/s;                       # output debugging info during
                                 #    compile time and run time

use re 'debugcolor';             # same as 'debug',
                                 #    but with colored output
```

When use re 'taint' is in effect and a tainted string is the target of a regex, the numbered regex variables and values returned by the m// operator in list context are all tainted. This is useful when regex operations on tainted data aren't meant to extract safe substrings, but to perform other transformations. See the discussion on tainting in Chapter 23.

When use re 'eval' is in effect, a regex is allowed to contain assertions that execute Perl code, which are of the form (?{ ... }), even when the regex contains interpolated variables. Execution of code segments resulting from variable interpolation into a regex is normally disallowed for security reasons: you don't want programs that read patterns from config files, command-line arguments, or CGI form fields to suddenly start executing arbitrary code if they weren't designed to expect this possibility. This use of the pragma allows only untainted strings to be interpolated; tainted data will still cause an exception to be raised (if you're running with taint checks enabled). See also Chapter 5, *Pattern Matching*, and Chapter 23.

For the purposes of this pragma, interpolation of precompiled regular expressions (produced by the qr// operator) is not considered variable interpolation. Nevertheless, when you build the qr// pattern it needs to have use re 'eval' in effect if any of its interpolated strings contain code assertions. For example:

```
$code = '(?{ $n++ })';     # code assertion
$str  = '\b\w+\b' . $code; # build string to interpolate
```

```
$line =~ /$str/;      # this needs use re 'eval'

$pat = qr/$str/;      # this also needs use re 'eval'
$line =~ /$pat/;      # but this doesn't need use re 'eval'
```

Under use re 'debug', Perl emits debugging messages when compiling and when executing regular expressions. The output is the same as that obtained by running a "debugging Perl" (one compiled with **-DDEBUGGING** passed to the C compiler) and then executing your Perl program under Perl's **-Dr** command-line switch. Depending on how complicated your pattern is, the resulting output can be overwhelming. Calling use re 'debugcolor' enables more colorful output that can be useful, provided your terminal understands color sequences. Set your PERL_RE_TC environment variable to a comma-separated list of relevant *termcap*(5) properties for highlighting. For more details, see Chapter 20, *The Perl Debugger*.

use sigtrap

```
use sigtrap;
use sigtrap qw(stack-trace old-interface-signals);  # same thing

use sigtrap qw(BUS SEGV PIPE ABRT);
use sigtrap qw(die INT QUIT);
use sigtrap qw(die normal-signals);
use sigtrap qw(die untrapped normal-signals);
use sigtrap qw(die untrapped normal-signals
               stack-trace any error-signals);

use sigtrap 'handler' => \&my_handler, 'normal-signals';
use sigtrap qw(handler my_handler normal-signals stack-trace error-signals);
```

The sigtrap pragma installs some simple signal handlers on your behalf so that you don't have to worry about them. This is useful in situations where an untrapped signal would cause your program to misbehave, like when you have END {} blocks, object destructors, or other at-exit processing that needs to be run no matter how your program happens to terminate.

The sigtrap pragma provides two simple signal handlers for your use. One provides a Perl stack trace, and the other throws an ordinary exception via die. Alternately, you can supply your own handler for the pragma to install. You may specify predefined sets of signals to trap; you can also supply your own explicit list of signals. The pragma can optionally install handlers for only those signals that have not otherwise been handled.

Arguments passed to use sigtrap are processed in order. When a user-supplied signal name or the name of one of sigtrap's predefined signal lists is encountered, a handler is immediately installed. When an option is encountered, this affects only those handlers installed later in processing the argument list.

Signal Handlers

These options affect which handler will be used for signals installed later:

stack-trace
> This pragma-supplied handler outputs a Perl stack trace to STDERR and then tries to dump core. This is the default signal handler.

die
> This pragma-supplied handler calls die via Carp::croak with a message indicating the signal caught.

handler *YOURHANDLER*
> *YOURHANDLER* will be used as the handler for signals installed later. *YOURHANDLER* can be any value valid for assignment into %SIG. Remember that the proper functioning of many C library calls (particularly standard I/O calls) cannot be guaranteed within a signal handler. Worse, it's hard to guess which bits of C library code are called from which bits of Perl code. (On the other hand, many of the signals that sigtrap traps are pretty vile—they're gonna take you down anyway, so there's not much harm in *trying* to do something, now is there?)

Predefined Signal Lists

The sigtrap pragma has a few built-in lists of signals to trap:

normal-signals
> These are the signals a program might normally expect to encounter, and which, by default, cause it to terminate. They are the HUP, INT, PIPE, and TERM signals.

error-signals
> These are the signals that usually indicate a serious problem with the Perl interpreter or with your program. They are the ABRT, BUS, EMT, FPE, ILL, QUIT, SEGV, SYS, and TRAP signals.

old-interface-signals
> These are the signals that were trapped by default under an older version of sigtrap's interface. They are ABRT, BUS, EMT, FPE, ILL, PIPE, QUIT, SEGV, SYS, TERM, and TRAP. If no signals or signals lists are passed to use sigtrap, this list is used.

If your platform does not implement a particular signal named in the predefined lists, that signal name will be silently ignored. (The signal itself can't be ignored, because it doesn't exist.)

Other Arguments to sigtrap

untrapped

> This token suppresses the installation of handlers for subsequently listed signals if they're already been trapped or ignored.

any

> This token installs handlers for all subsequently listed signals. This is the default behavior.

signal

> Any argument that looks like a signal name (that is, one matching the pattern /^[A-Z][A-Z0-9]*$/) requests sigtrap to handle that signal.

number

> A numeric argument requires the version number of the sigtrap pragma to be at least *number*. This works is just like most regular modules that have a $VERSION package variable:

```
% perl -Msigtrap -le 'print $sigtrap::VERSION'
1.02
```

Examples of sigtrap

Provide a stack trace for the old interface signals:

```
use sigtrap;
```

Same thing, but more explicitly:

```
use sigtrap qw(stack-trace old-interface-signals);
```

Provide a stack trace only on the four listed signals:

```
use sigtrap qw(BUS SEGV PIPE ABRT);
```

Die on an INT or a QUIT signal:

```
use sigtrap qw(die INT QUIT);
```

Die on any of HUP, INT, PIPE, or TERM:

```
use sigtrap qw(die normal-signals);
```

Die on HUP, INT, PIPE, or TERM—except don't change the behavior for signals that have already been trapped or ignored elsewhere in the program:

```
use sigtrap qw(die untrapped normal-signals);
```

Die on receipt of any currently untrapped normal-signals; additionally, provide a stack backtrace on receipt of any of the error-signals:

Pragmata

```
use sigtrap qw(die untrapped normal-signals
                stack-trace any error-signals);
```

Install the routine `my_handler` as the handler for the `normal-signals`:

```
use sigtrap 'handler' => \&my_handler, 'normal-signals';
```

Install `my_handler` as the handler for the `normal-signals`; provide a Perl stack backtrace on receipt of any of the `error-signals`:

```
use sigtrap qw(handler my_handler normal-signals
                stack-trace error-signals);
```

use strict

```
use strict;          # Install all three strictures.

use strict "vars";   # Variables must be predeclared.
use strict "refs";   # Can't use symbolic references.
use strict "subs";   # Bareword strings must be quoted.

use strict;          # Install all...
no strict "vars";    # ...then renege on one.
```

This lexically scoped pragma changes some basic rules about what Perl considers to be legal code. Sometimes these restrictions seem too strict for casual programming, such as when you're just trying to whip up a five-line filter program. The larger your program, the more you need to be strict about it.

Currently, there are three possible things to be strict about: subs, vars, and refs. If no import list is supplied, all three restrictions are assumed.

strict 'refs'

This generates a run-time error if you use symbolic references, intentionally or otherwise. See Chapter 8 for more about these.

```
use strict 'refs';

$ref = \$foo;        # Store "real" (hard) reference.
print $$ref;         # Dereferencing is ok.

$ref = "foo";        # Store name of global (package) variable.
print $$ref;         # WRONG, run-time error under strict refs.
```

Symbolic references are suspect for various reasons. It's surprisingly easy for even well-meaning programmers to invoke them accidentally; strict 'refs' guards against that. Unlike real references, symbolic references can only refer to global variables. They aren't reference-counted. And there's often a better way to do what you're doing: instead of referencing a symbol in a global symbol table, use a hash as its own little mini-symbol table. It's more efficient, more readable, and less error prone.

Nevertheless, some sorts of valid manipulation really do require direct access to the package's global symbol table of variables and function names. For example, you might want to examine the @EXPORT list or the @ISA superclass of a given package whose name you don't know in advance. Or you might want to install a whole slew of function calls that are all aliases to the same closure. This is just what symbolic references are best at, but to use them while use strict is in effect, you must first undo the "refs" stricture:

```
# make a bunch of attribute accessors
for my $methname (qw/name rank serno/) {
    no strict 'refs';
    *$methname = sub { $_[0]->{ __PACKAGE__ . $methname };
}
```

strict 'vars'

Under this stricture, a compile-time error is triggered if you attempt to access a variable that hasn't met at least one of the following criteria:

- Predefined by Perl itself, such as @ARGV, %ENV, and all the global punctuation variables such as $. or $_.

- Declared with our (for a global) or my (for a lexical).

- Imported from another package. (The use vars pragma fakes up an import, but use our instead.)

- Fully qualified using its package name and the double-colon package separator.

Just using a local operator isn't good enough to keep use strict 'vars' happy because, despite its name, that operator doesn't change whether the named variable is global or not. It just gives the variable a new, temporary value for the duration of block at run time. You still need to use our to declare a global variable, or my to declare a lexical variable. You can, however, localize an our:

```
local our $law = "martial";
```

Globals predefined by Perl are exempt from these requirements. This applies to program-wide globals (those forced into package main like @ARGV or $_) and to per-package variables like $a and $b, which are normally used by the sort function. Per-package variables used by modules like Exporter still need to be declared using our:

```
our @EXPORT_OK = qw(name rank serno);
```

strict 'subs'

This stricture makes Perl treat all barewords as syntax errors. A *bareword* ("bear-word" in some dialects) is any bare name or identifier that has no other interpretation forced by context. (Context is often forced by a nearby keyword or token, or by predeclaration of the word in question.) Historically, barewords were interpreted as unquoted strings. This stricture outlaws that interpretation. If you mean to use it as a string, quote it. If you mean to use it as a function call, predeclare it or use parentheses.

As a particular case of forced context, remember that a word that appears by itself in curly braces or on the lefthand side of the => operator counts as being quoted, and so is not subject to this restriction.

```
use strict 'subs';

$x = whatever;        # WRONG: bareword error!
$x = whatever();      # This always works, though.

sub whatever;         # Predeclare function.
$x = whatever;        # Now it's ok.

# These uses are permitted, because the => quotes:
%hash = (red => 1, blue => 2, green => 3);

$rednum = $hash{red};                # Ok, braces quote here.

# But not this one:
@coolnums = @hash{blue, green};      # WRONG: bareword error.
@coolnums = @hash{"blue", "green"};  # Ok, words now quoted.
@coolnums = @hash{qw/blue green/};   # Likewise.
```

use subs

```
use subs qw/winken blinken nod/;
@x = winken 3..10;
@x = nod blinken @x
```

This pragma predeclares as standard subroutines all the names in the argument list. The advantage here is that you may now use those functions without parentheses as list operators, just as if you'd declared them yourself. This is not necessarily as useful as full declarations, because it doesn't allow prototypes or attributes, such as:

```
sub winken(@);
sub blinken(\@) : locked;
sub nod($) : lvalue;
```

Because it is based on the standard import mechanism, the use subs pragma is not lexically scoped but package scoped. That is, the declarations are effective for the entire file in which they appear, but only in the current package. You may not rescind such declarations with no subs.

use vars

```
use vars qw($frobbed @munge %seen);
```

This pragma, once used to declare a global variable, is now somewhat deprecated in favor of the our modifier. The previous declaration is better accomplished using:

```
our($frobbed, @munge, %seen);
```

or even:

```
our $frobbed = "F";
our @munge = "A" .. $frobbed;
our %seen = ();
```

No matter which of these you use, remember that they're talking about package globals, not file-scoped lexicals.

use warnings

```
use warnings;    # same as importing "all"
no warnings;     # same as unimporting "all"

use warnings::register;
if (warnings::enabled()) {
    warnings::warn("some warning");
}

if (warnings::enabled("void")) {
    warnings::warn("void", "some warning");
}
```

This lexically scoped pragma permits flexible control over Perl's built-in warnings, both those emitted by the compiler as well as those from the run-time system.

Once upon a time, the only control you had in Perl over the treatment of warnings in your program was through either the **-w** command-line option or the $^W variable. Although useful, these tend to be all-or-nothing affairs. The **-w** option ends up enabling warnings in pieces of module code that you may not have written, which is occasionally problematic for you and embarrassing for the original author. Using $^W to either disable or enable blocks of code can be less than optimal

because it works only during execution time, not during compile time.* Another
issue is that this program-wide global variable is scoped dynamically, not lexically.
That means that if you enable it in a block and then from there call other code,
you again risk enabling warnings in code not developed with such exacting standards in mind.

The warnings pragma circumvents these limitations by being a lexically scoped,
compile-time mechanism that permits finer control over where warnings can or
can't be triggered. A hierarchy of warning categories (see Figure 31-1) has been
defined to allow groups of warnings to be enabled or disabled in isolation from
one another. (The exact categorization is experimental and subject to change.)
These categories can be combined by passing multiple arguments to use or no:

```
use warnings qw(void redefine);
no  warnings qw(io syntax untie);
```

If multiple instances of the warnings pragma are active for a given scope, their
effects are cumulative:

```
use warnings "void"; # Only "void" warnings enabled.
...
use warnings "io";   # Both "void" and "io" warnings now enabled.
...
no warnings "void";  # Only "io" warnings now enabled.
```

To make fatal errors of all warnings enabled by a particular warnings pragma, use
the word FATAL at the front of the import list. This is useful when you would prefer a certain condition that normally causes only a warning to abort your program.
Suppose, for example, that you considered it so improper to use an invalid string
as a number (which normally produces a value of 0) that you want this brazen act
to kill your program. While you're at it, you decide that using uninitialized values
in places where real string or numeric values are expected should also be cause
for immediate suicide:

```
{
    use warnings FATAL => qw(numeric uninitialized);
    $x = $y + $z;
}
```

Now if either $y or $z is uninitialized (that is, holds the special scalar value,
undef), or if they contain strings that don't cleanly convert into numeric values,
instead of going merrily on its way, or at most issuing a small complaint if you had
-w enabled, your program will now raise a exception. (Think of this as Perl running in Python mode.) If you aren't trapping exceptions, that makes it a fatal error.
The exception text is the same as would normally appear in the warning message.

---

* In the absence of BEGIN blocks, of course.

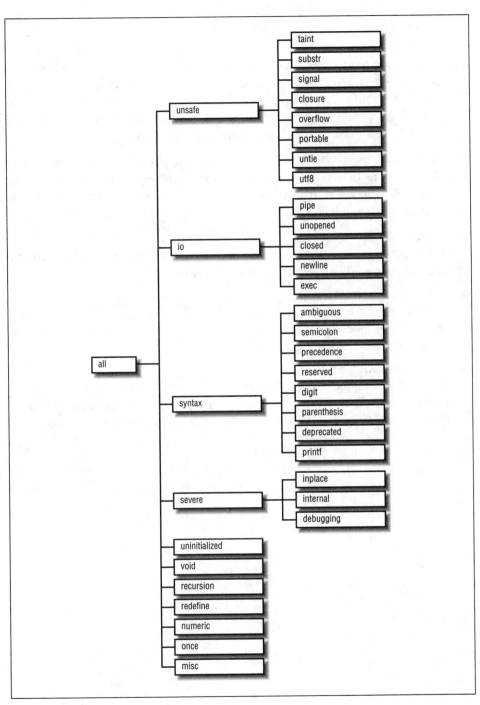

Figure 31-1. Perl's warning categories

The warnings pragma ignores the **-w** command-line switch and the value of the $^W variable; the pragma's settings take precedence. However, the **-W** command-line flag overrides the pragma, enabling full warnings in all code within your program, even code loaded with do, require, or use. In other words, with **-W**, Perl pretends that every block in your program has a use warnings 'all' pragma. Think of it as a *lint*(1) for Perl programs. (But see also the online documentation for the B::Lint module.) The **-X** command-line flag works the other way around. It pretends that every block has no warnings 'all' in effect.

Several functions are provided to assist module authors who want to make their module's functions behave like built-in functions with respect to the lexical scoping of the caller (that is, so that users of the module can lexically enable or disable warnings the module might issue):

warnings::register
> Registers the current module name as a new category of warnings, so that users of your module can turn off warnings from it.

warnings::enabled(*CATEGORY*)
> Returns true if the warnings category *CATEGORY* is enabled in the lexical scope of the calling module. Otherwise, it returns false. If *CATEGORY* is not supplied, the current package name is used.

warnings::warn(*CATEGORY, MESSAGE*)
> If the calling module has *not* set *CATEGORY* to "FATAL", prints *MESSAGE* to STDERR. If the calling module has set *CATEGORY* to "FATAL", prints *MESSAGE* to STDERR, then dies. If *CATEGORY* is not supplied, the current package name is used.

32

Standard Modules

The previous edition of this book included comprehensive, definitive coverage for all modules that were part of the standard Perl distribution. But if we did that again now, you'd pay twice what you're paying for this book, not to mention what you'd have to pay the chiropractor after trying to carry the book home. Over the last few years, more and more modules have come bundled standard; we're up to around two hundred of them right now. Some of these, such as CGI, have remarkably extensive documentation in their own right. And if you're using ActiveState's distribution of Perl, your standard library is even more luxed out.

So instead, we provide a complete listing of the standard modules, sorted by type, along with a brief description of what each module does. Then we cherry pick a few of our favorite modules by providing examples of typical uses, followed by a short description of how they work, just to give you a taste of using them. The descriptions are suggestive rather than comprehensive, and virtually all the modules have features beyond those shown. However, complete documentation for all standard modules is included with every Perl distribution, so you can just look up the details on your own system using the *perldoc* program, your system's *man*(1) command, or your favorite browser. See the section "Online Documentation" in the Preface. Ask your Local Expert if you can't find the docs, because they're almost certainly installed *somewhere* on your system. Even if they're not, you can always read the pod docs directly from the modules themselves, because all module docs come embedded in their corresponding module (*.pm*) files, and pod was designed to be somewhat readable. (Unlike, say, HTML.)

Modules

Listings by Type

Normal module names begin with an uppercase letter. Lowercase names indicate pragmas that you'll find documented in Chapter 31, *Pragmatic Modules*, rather than in this chapter.

Data Types

These modules extend Perl's type system (or lack thereof) in various ways.

Module	Description
Class::Struct	Create struct-like Perl object classes
constant	Declare constant scalars and lists
integer	Force Perl to do arithmetic with integers instead of floating point
Math::BigFloat	Calculate with arbitrary length floating-point math
Math::BigInt	Calculate with arbitrary length integer math
Math::Complex	Calculate with complex numbers and associated mathematical functions
Math::Trig	Load many trigonometric and related functions
overload	Overload Perl operators on objects
Symbol	Manipulate Perl symbol tables and generate anonymous typeglobs
Time::Local	Efficiently compute epoch time given localtime or gmtime

String Processing, Language Text Processing, Parsing, and Searching

These modules do things with (or to) text.

Module	Description
Search::Dict	Use a binary search for a string in a sorted text file
Text::Abbrev	Create an abbreviation table from a list
Text::ParseWords	Parse text into a list of tokens or an array of arrays
Text::Soundex	Use Knuth's Soundex algorithm
Text::Tabs	Expand or unexpand tabs like *expand*(1) and *unexpand*(1)
Text::Wrap	Wrap lines to form simple paragraphs

Option, Argument, Parameter, and Configuration File Processing

These modules process your command line.

Module	Description
Getopt::Long	
	Process extended command-line options in long form (–xxx)
Getopt::Std	Process single-character switches with switch clustering (-xyz)

Filenames, Filesystems, and File Locking

These modules provide cross-platform methods of file access.

Module	Description
Cwd	Get the pathname of the current working directory
File::Basename	Portably parse a pathname into directory, basename, and extension components
File::CheckTree	Run many file test checks on a set of directory trees
File::Compare	Portably compare contents of filenames or filehandles
File::Copy	Portably copy filenames or filehandles or move filenames
File::DosGlob	Do Microsoft-style fileglobbing
File::Find	Traverse a file tree like *find*(1)
File::Glob	Use Unix-style fileglobbing
File::Path	Portably create or remove a series of directories
File::Spec	Use portable filename operations (object-oriented interface)
File::Spec::Functions	Use portable filename operations (functional interface)
File::Spec::Mac	Use filename operations for Mac OS files
File::Spec::OS2	Use filename operations for OS/2 files
File::Spec::Unix	Use filename operations for Unix files
File::Spec::VMS	Use filename operations for VMS files
File::Spec::Win32	Use filename operations for Microsoft files
File::stat	Override built-in stat and lstat functions with a method interface

Modules

Filehandle, Directory Handle, and Stream I/O Utilities

These modules provide object-oriented file, directory, and IPC access.

Module	Description
DirHandle	Use object methods for directory handles
FileCache	Keep more files concurrently open for output than your system permits
FileHandle	Use object methods for filehandles
IO	Provide a frontend to load all of IO::Dir, IO::File, IO::Handle, IO::Pipe, IO::Seekable, and IO::Socket
IO::Dir	Use object methods for directory handles
IO::File	Use file-related object methods for filehandles
IO::Handle	Use generic object methods for filehandles
IO::Pipe	Use object methods for pipes
IO::Poll	Provide an object interface to *poll*(2) syscall
IO::Seekable	Use object methods for seekable I/O objects
IO::Select	Use a convenient OO interface to the *select*(2) syscall
SelectSaver	Save and restore selected filehandle

Internationalization and Locale

These modules help you perform Un-American Activities.

Module	Description
bytes	Enforce old byte-oriented semantics
charnames	Define character names used in \N{*name*} escapes in string literals
I18N::Collate	Compare 8-bit scalar data according to current locale (deprecated)
locale	Use or avoid POSIX locales for built-in operations
utf8	Turn on UTF-8 and Unicode support explicitly

Operating System Interfaces

These modules tweak your interface to the operating system.

Module	Description
Fcntl	Load the C library's *fcntl.h* definitions as Perl constants
filetest	Control the file test operators (-r, -w, etc.) for nontraditional filesystems
open	Set default disciplines for open function calls
POSIX	Use the Perl interface to POSIX 1003.1
Shell	Run shell commands transparently within Perl
sigtrap	Enable simple signal handling
Sys::Hostname	Portably try every conceivable way to determine the current hostname
Sys::Syslog	Use the C library's *syslog*(3) functions
Time::gmtime	Override the built-in gmtime function with a method interface
Time::localtime	Override the built-in localtime function with a method interface
Time::tm	Provide the internal object used by Time::gmtime and Time::localtime
User::grent	Override built-in getgr* functions with a method interface
User::pwent	Override built-in getpw* functions with a method interface

Networking and Interprocess Communication

These modules provide abstract interfaces around the basic interfaces we wrote about in Chapter 16, *Interprocess Communication*.

Module	Description
IO::Socket	Use a generic object interface to socket communications
IO::Socket::INET	Use an object interface for Internet-domain sockets
IO::Socket::UNIX	Use an object interface for Unix-domain (local) sockets
IPC::Msg	Use object methods for working with System V messages (SysV Msg IPC object class)
IPC::Open2	Open a process for simultaneous reading and writing
IPC::Open3	Open a process for reading, writing, and error handling
IPC::Semaphore	Use object methods for System V semaphores
IPC::SysV	Define constants for all System V IPC mechanisms
Net::hostent	Override built-in gethost* functions with a method interface
Net::netent	Override built-in getnet* functions with a method interface
Net::Ping	Check a remote host for reachability
Net::protoent	Override built-in getproto* functions with a method interface
Net::servent	Override built-in getserv* functions with a method interface
Socket	Load the C library *socket.h* definitions and structure manipulators

Modules

World Wide Web

These modules interface to the WWW. You may have heard of it.

Module	Description
CGI	Access CGI forms and powerful automated HTML generation
CGI::Apache	Make your CGI script work under the Perl-Apache API
CGI::Carp	Write to the *httpd*(8) (or other) CGI error log
CGI::Cookie	Set and get HTTP cookies
CGI::Fast	Use the Fast CGI protocol
CGI::Pretty	Produce nicely formatted HTML code
CGI::Push	Do server-push CGI scripting

DBM Interfaces

These modules load various database management libraries.

Module	Description
AnyDBM_File	Provide a framework for multiple DBM libraries
DB_File	Provide tied access to the *db*(3) library (version 1.x Berkeley DB)
GDBM_File	Provide tied access to the *gdbm*(3) library
NDBM_File	Provide tied access to the *ndbm*(3) library
SDBM_File	Provide tied access to SDBM (simple DBM) files

User Interfaces

These modules provide a decent OS CLI I/O API, ASAP.

Module	Description
Term::Cap	Use the *termcap*(3) library
Term::Complete	Do programmable command completion on word lists
Term::ReadLine	Use any of several readline packages

Authentication, Security, and Encryption

These modules work with sandboxes.

Module	Description
Opcode	Enable or disable named opcodes when compiling Perl code for use with the Safe module
ops	Restrict unsafe operations when compiling
Safe	Compile and execute code in restricted compartments

Perl Language Extensions and Internals

(Not to be confused with Intentions and Externals.)

Module	Description
attributes	Get or set subroutine or variable attributes
attrs	Get or set subroutine or variable attributes (obsolete)
base	Establish inheritance of base class at compile time
Data::Dumper	Serialize Perl data structures
DB	Access the Perl debugger's experimental API
Devel::DProf	Profile a Perl program's execution
Devel::Peek	Load data debugging tools for XS programmers
diagnostics	Force verbose warnings and suppress duplicates
Dumpvalue	Provide screen dump of data
English	Use longer variable names for built-in punctuation variables
Env	Access environment variables in %ENV as regular scalars
Errno	Load the C library's *errno.h* definitions and tie the %! variable
Fatal	Replace built-ins with versions that raise exceptions on failure
fields	Declare compile-time verified access to a class's data attributes
less	Request less of something from Perl (unimplemented)
re	Alter default regular expression behavior
strict	Restrict sloppy constructs
subs	Predeclare the subroutine names in current the package
vars	Predeclare global variables (obsolete—see our in Chapter 29, *Functions*)

Convenient Classes

These modules provide base classes and other conveniences.

Module	Description
Tie::Array	Provide a base class for tied arrays
Tie::Handle	Provide base class definitions for tied handles
Tie::Hash	Provide base class definitions for tied hashes
Tie::RefHash	Provide references as hash keys
Tie::Scalar	Provide base class definitions for tied scalars
Tie::SubstrHash	Hash a fixed-size table with a fixed-length key
UNIVERSAL	Provide a base class for *all* classes (blessed references)

Modules

Warnings and Exceptions

What to do when things go rwong.

Module	Description
Carp	Provide routines that `warn` and `die` from the perspective of the caller
warnings	Control warnings within the lexical scope

Documentation Support

And there's an awful lot of documentation to support.

Module	Description
Pod::Checker	Check pod documents for syntax errors (used by *podchecker*(1))
Pod::Functions	List built-in functions by type
Pod::Html	Convert pod files to HTML (used by *pod2html*(1))
Pod::InputObjects	Manage documentation support
Pod::Man	Convert pod to *troff*(1) format for the *man*(1) system (used by *pod2man*(1))
Pod::Parser	Provide a base class for creating pod filters and translators
Pod::Select	Extract selected sections of pod from input (used by *podselect*(1))
Pod::Text	Convert pod data to formatted ASCII text (used by *pod2text*(1))
Pod::Text::Color	Convert pod data to formatted ASCII text with ANSI color escapes
Pod::Text::Termcap	Convert pod data to ASCII text with terminal-specific escapes
Pod::Usage	Print a usage message derived from embedded pod documentation

Module Installation Support

These modules help other modules jump through various hoops.

Module	Description
AutoLoader	Load subroutines only on demand
AutoSplit	Split a package for autoloading
autouse	Postpone module loading until a function is used from that module
blib	Use the library from MakeMaker's uninstalled version of an extension
Config	Access Perl configuration information
CPAN	Query, download, and build Perl modules from CPAN sites
Devel::SelfStubber	Generate stubs for a module using SelfLoader
DynaLoader	Dynamically load C or C++ libraries as Perl extensions
Exporter	Implement default import method for traditional modules
ExtUtils::Command	Provide utilities to replace common external commands in *Makefile*
ExtUtils::Embed	Provide utilities for embedding Perl in C or C++ programs
ExtUtils::Install	Install files into the system's Perl library
ExtUtils::Installed	Manage inventory of installed modules
ExtUtils::Liblist	Determine which libraries to use and how to use them
ExtUtils::MakeMaker	Create a *Makefile* for a Perl extension
ExtUtils::Manifest	Load tools to write and check a *MANIFEST* file
ExtUtils::Miniperl	Write the C code for *perlmain.c*
ExtUtils::Mkbootstrap	Create a bootstrap file for use by DynaLoader
ExtUtils::Mksymlists	Write linker options files for dynamic extension
ExtUtils::MM_Cygwin	Override Unix behavior methods in ExtUtils::MakeMaker
ExtUtils::MM_OS2	Override Unix behavior methods in ExtUtils::MakeMaker
ExtUtils::MM_Unix	Provide methods used by ExtUtils::MakeMaker
ExtUtils::MM_VMS	Override Unix behavior methods in ExtUtils::MakeMaker
ExtUtils::MM_Win32	Override Unix behavior methods in ExtUtils::MakeMaker
ExtUtils::Packlist	Manage *.packlist* files
ExtUtils::testlib	Add *blib/** directories to @INC
FindBin	Locate installation directory of the Perl program that is running
lib	Manipulate @INC at compile time
SelfLoader	Load functions only on demand
XSLoader	Dynamically load C or C++ libraries as Perl extensions

Modules

Development Support

These modules are for timing and testing, to see how much faster and cleaner your code doesn't run anymore.

Module	Description
Benchmark	Compare running times of alternate code versions
Test	Use a simple framework for writing test scripts
Test::Harness	Run standard test scripts with statistics

Perl Compiler and Code Generator

These modules support various backend code generators for Perl.

Module	Description
B	Load Perl code generators (a.k.a. the "Perl compiler")
B::Asmdata	Provide autogenerated data about Perl ops to produce bytecode
B::Assembler	Assemble Perl bytecode
B::Bblock	Walk basic blocks in the syntax tree
B::Bytecode	Use the Perl compiler's bytecode backend
B::C	Use the Perl compiler's C translation backend
B::CC	Use the Perl compiler's optimized C translation backend
B::Debug	Walk the Perl syntax tree, printing debug info about ops
B::Deparse	Use the Perl compiler backend to reproduce Perl code
B::Disassembler	Disassemble Perl bytecode
B::Lint	Catch dubious constructs
B::Showlex	Show lexical variables used in functions or files
B::Stash	Show what stashes are loaded
B::Terse	Walk the Perl syntax tree, printing terse info about ops
B::Xref	Generate cross-reference reports for Perl programs
ByteLoader	Load byte-compiled Perl code
O	Provide a generic interface to Perl compiler backends

Microsoft-Related Modules

If you got the Perl distribution for Microsoft systems from ActiveState, you already have the following Microsoft-only modules included for you. If you just grabbed the standard source distribution (maybe you want to build it under the Cygwin Unix-emulation environment) but you're running on Wintel, you can get all of these modules from CPAN.

Module	Description
Win32::ChangeNotify	Monitor events related to files and directories
Win32::Console	Use Win32 console and character mode functions
Win32::Event	Use Win32 event objects from Perl
Win32::EventLog	Process Win32 event logs from Perl
Win32::File	Manage file attributes in Perl
Win32::FileSecurity	Manage FileSecurity Discretionary Access Control Lists in Perl
Win32::IPC	Load the base class for Win32 synchronization objects
Win32::Internet	Access *WININET.DLL* functions
Win32::Mutex	Use Win32 mutex objects from Perl
Win32::NetAdmin	Manage network groups and users in Perl
Win32::NetResource	Manage network resources in Perl
Win32::ODBC	Use ODBC Extension for Win32
Win32::OLE	Use OLE automation extensions
Win32::OLE::Const	Extract constant definitions from *TypeLib*
Win32::OLE::Enum	Use OLE Automation Collection Objects
Win32::OLE::NLS	Use OLE National Language Support
Win32::OLE::Variant	Create and modify OLE VARIANT variables
Win32::PerfLib	Access the Windows NT Performance Counter
Win32::Process	Create and manipulate processes
Win32::Semaphore	Use Win32 semaphore objects
Win32::Service	Manage system services
Win32::Sound	Play with Windows sounds
Win32::TieRegistry	Mung the registry
Win32API::File	Access low-level Win32 system API calls for files and directories
Win32API::Net	Manage Windows NT LanManager accounts
Win32API::Registry	Access low-level Win32 system API calls from *WINREG.H*

Benchmark

```
use Benchmark qw(timethese cmpthese timeit countit timestr);

# You can always pass in code as strings:
timethese $count, {
    'Name1' => '...code1...',
    'Name2' => '...code2...',
};
```

```
# Or as subroutines references:
timethese $count, {
    'Name1' => sub { ...code1... },
    'Name2' => sub { ...code2... },
};

cmpthese $count, {
    'Name1' => '...code1...',
    'Name2' => '...code2...',
};

$t = timeit $count, '...code...';
print "$count loops of code took:", timestr($t), "\n";

$t = countit $time, '...code...';
$count = $t->iters;
print "$count loops of code took:", timestr($t), "\n";
```

The Benchmark module can help you determine which of several possible choices executes the fastest. The timethese function runs the specified code segments the number of times requested and reports back how long each segment took. You can get a nicely sorted comparison chart if you call cmpthese the same way.

Code segments may be given as function references instead of strings (in fact, they must be if you use lexical variables from the calling scope), but call overhead can influence the timings. If you don't ask for enough iterations to get a good timing, the function emits a warning.

Lower-level interfaces are available that run just one piece of code either for some number of iterations (timeit) or for some number of seconds (countit). These functions return Benchmark objects (see the online documentation for a description). With countit, you know it will run in enough time to avoid warnings, because you specified a minimum run time.

To get the most out of the Benchmark module, you'll need a good bit of practice. It isn't usually enough to run a couple different algorithms on the same data set, because the timings only reflect how well those algorithms did on that particular data set. To get a better feel for the general case, you'll need to run several sets of benchmarks, varying the data sets used.

For example, suppose you wanted to know the best way to get a copy of a string without the last two characters. You think of four ways to do so (there are, of course, several others): chop twice, copy and substitute, or use substr on either the left- or righthand side of an assignment. You test these algorithms on strings of length 2, 200, and 20_000:

```
use Benchmark qw/countit cmpthese/;
sub run($) { countit(5, @_) }
for $size (2, 200, 20_000) {
```

```
        $s = "." x $len;
        print "\nDATASIZE = $size\n";
        cmpthese {
            chop2    => run q{
                $t = $s; chop $t; chop $t;
            },
            subs     => run q{
                ($t = $s) =~ s/..\Z//s;
            },
            lsubstr  => run q{
                $t = $s; substr($t, -2) = '';
            },
            rsubstr  => run q{
                $t = substr($s, 0, length($s)-2);
            },

        };
    }
```

which produces the following output:

```
DATASIZE = 2
                Rate    subs lsubstr   chop2 rsubstr
subs      181399/s      --    -15%    -46%    -53%
lsubstr   214655/s     18%      --    -37%    -44%
chop2     338477/s     87%     58%      --    -12%
rsubstr   384487/s    112%     79%     14%      --


DATASIZE = 200
                Rate    subs lsubstr rsubstr   chop2
subs      200967/s      --    -18%    -24%    -34%
lsubstr   246468/s     23%      --     -7%    -19%
rsubstr   264428/s     32%      7%      --    -13%
chop2     304818/s     52%     24%     15%      --


DATASIZE = 20000
              Rate rsubstr    subs lsubstr   chop2
rsubstr   5271/s       --    -42%    -43%    -45%
subs      9087/s      72%      --     -2%     -6%
lsubstr   9260/s      76%      2%      --     -4%
chop2     9660/s      83%      6%      4%      --
```

With small data sets, the "rsubstr" algorithm runs 14% faster than the "chop2" algorithm, but in large data sets, it runs 45% slower. On empty data sets (not shown here), the substitution mechanism is the fastest. So there is often no best solution for all possible cases, and even these timings don't tell the whole story, since you're still at the mercy of your operating system and the C library Perl was built with. What's good for you may be bad for someone else. It takes a while to develop decent benchmarking skills. In the meantime, it helps to be a good liar.

Modules

Carp

```
use Carp;
croak "We're outta here!";

use Carp qw(:DEFAULT cluck);
cluck "This is how we got here!";
```

The Carp module lets you write modules whose functions report errors the way built-in operators report errors—from the perspective of the users of your module. The Carp module supplies routines that you use much like the standard built-in functions warn and die, but that change the filename and line number so it looks like the error originated from the user's code instead of your code. In short, Carp is great way to misdirect blame.

There are actually four functions. The carp function works like the warn operator, but with caller-relative filename and line number information. The croak function works like die does—raising an exception—but again gives caller-relative information. If you prefer a longer lament, use cluck and confess instead of carp and croak respectively, and you'll get a full stack backtrace reporting who called whom and with what arguments (in the library with a lead pipe, no doubt). You have to import cluck explicitly, because it's not normally exported. People don't often want full stack traces on mere warnings, for some reason.

CGI

```
use CGI qw(:standard);
$who   = param("Name");
$phone = param("Number");
@picks = param("Choices");
```

The CGI module helps manage HTML forms, especially multistage forms where passing state from one stage to another is critical. The extremely simple example above expects to process a form with two parameters that take single values, such as text fields or radio buttons, and one that takes multiple values, like scrolling lists specified as "MULTIPLE". The module is several orders of magnitude fancier than this, supporting such features as convenient cookie processing, persistent values for multiscreen shopping carts, and dynamic generation of HTML lists and tables you might pull from a database—just to name a few. Support for turbocharged execution of precompiled Perl scripts through Apache's mod_perl facility is also provided. The O'Reilly book *Writing Apache Modules with Perl and C,* by Lincoln Stein and Doug MacEachern, can tell you all about this.

CGI::Carp

```
use CGI::Carp;
warn "This is a complaint";      # Stamp it with progname and date.
die "But this one is serious";   # But don't cause server 500 errors.

use CGI::Carp qw(carpout);       # Import this function.
open(LOG, ">>/var/tmp/mycgi-log")
    or die "Can't append to mycgi-log: $!\n";
carpout(*LOG);                   # Now uses program-specific errlog.

use CGI::Carp qw(fatalsToBrowser);
die "Fatal error messages are now sent to browser, too";
```

The `CGI::Carp` module provides versions of the `warn` and `die` Perl built-in functions, plus the `Carp` module's `carp`, `cluck`, `confess`, and `croak` functions which are more verbose and safer, too. They're more verbose because each message includes the date and time with the name of the program issuing the message, which helps when you're using a log file shared by a hundred different programs scribbling a thousand different messages on it at the same time.

The module is also kinder to web surfers, since premature death in a CGI script tends to cause inscrutable "Server 500" errors when the proper HTTP header doesn't get out to the server before your program pegs out, and this module makes sure that doesn't happen. The `carpout` function redirects all warnings and errors to the filehandle specified. The `fatalsToBrowser` directive sends a copy of such messages to the user's browser, too. These facilities ease debugging of problems in CGI scripts.

Class::Struct

```
use Class::Struct;

struct Manager => {            # Creates a Manager->new() constructor.
    name    => '$',            # Now name() method accesses a scalar value.
    salary  => '$',            # And so does salary().
    started => '$',            # And so does started().
};

struct Shoppe => {             # Creates a Shoppe->new() constructor.
    owner   => '$',            # Now owner() method accesses a scalar.
    addrs   => '@',            # And addrs() method accesses an array.
    stock   => '%',            # And stock() method accesses a hash.
    boss    => 'Manager',      # Initializes with Manager->new().
};

$store = Shoppe->new();
$store->owner('Abdul Alhazred');
$store->addrs(0, 'Miskatonic University');
$store->addrs(1, 'Innsmouth, Mass.');
```

```
$store->stock("books", 208);
$store->stock("charms", 3);
$store->stock("potions", "none");
$store->boss->name('Prof L. P. Haitch');
$store->boss->salary('madness');
$store->boss->started(scalar localtime);
```

The Class::Struct module provides a way to "declare" a class as having objects whose fields are of a specific type. The function that does this is called struct. Because structures or records are not base types in Perl, each time you want to create a class to provide a record-like data object, you have to define a constructor method along with accessor methods for each data field, sometimes called "wrapper" methods. The Class::Struct module's struct function alleviates this tedium by creating a class for you on the fly. You just tell it what data members should exist and their types. The function creates a constructor method named new in the package specified by the first argument, plus an attribute accessor method for each member, as specified by the second argument, which should be a hash reference.

Field types are specified as either a built-in type using the customary "$", "@", "%", and "&" symbols, or as another class using the class name. The type of each field will be enforced when you try to set the value.

Many standard modules use Class::Struct to create their objects and accessors, including Net::hostent and User::pwent, whose source you can look at as a model. See also the CPAN modules Tie::SecureHash and Class::Multimethods for more elaborate approaches to autogeneration of classes and accessor methods. See the section "Managing Instance Data" in Chapter 12, *Objects*.

Config

```
use Config;
if ($Config{cc} =~ /gcc/) {
    print "This perl was built by GNU C.\n";
}
use Config qw(myconfig config_sh config_vars);
print myconfig();    # like perl -V without a pattern
print config_sh();   # gives absolutely everything

config_vars qw/osname osvers archname/;
```

The configuration mechanism that builds and installs Perl assembles a wealth of information about your system. The Config module exports by default a tied hash variable named %Config, which provides access to over 900 different configuration values. (These values are also available through Perl's **-V**:*PATTERN* command-line switch.) Config also provides three functions that give more shell-like access to these values, as shown above. For instance, that last call might print out:

```
osname='openbsd';
osvers='2.6';
archname='OpenBSD.sparc-openbsd';
```

The module's online documentation describes the configuration variables and their possible values. Be aware that if you move your *perl* executable to a system other than the one on which it was built, these values may not reflect the current reality; for instance, if you're running a Linux or a Solaris binary on a BSD system.

CPAN

```
# Get interactive CPAN shell.
% perl -MCPAN -e shell

# Just ask for upgrade recommendations.
% perl -MCPAN -e 'CPAN::Shell->r'

# Install the named module in batch mode.
% perl -MCPAN -e "install Class::Multimethods"
```

The CPAN module is an automated, user-friendly interface to the Comprehensive Perl Archive Network described in Chapter 22, *CPAN*. Unlike most modules you encounter, it's intended to be called from the command line, just like a little program. The first time you call it, the module prompts for the default CPAN mirror site and other information it needs. After that, you can fire up its interactive shell to make queries and select modules to install, ask the module for recommendations on which modules need an upgrade, or just have it install one particular module.

Cwd

```
use Cwd;
$dir = getcwd();      # Where am I?

use Cwd 'chdir';
chdir "/tmp";         # Updates $ENV{PWD}.

use Cwd 'realpath';
print realpath("/usr////spool//mqueue/../");  # prints /var/spool
```

The Cwd module provides platform-independent functions to determine your process's current working directory. This is better than shelling out to *pwd*(1) because non-POSIX-conforming systems aren't guaranteed to have such a command, and Perl runs on more than just POSIX platforms. The getcwd function, which is exported by default, returns the current working directory using whatever mechanism is deemed safest on the current platform. If you import the chdir function, it overrides the built-in operator with the module's operator, which maintains the $ENV{PWD} environment variable; commands you might launch later that would care about that variable would then have a consistent view of their world. The realpath function resolves its pathname argument of any symbolic links and relative-path components to return a full path directory in canonical form, just like *realpath*(3).

Data::Dumper

```
use Data::Dumper;
print Dumper($store);
```

When used on the example from Class::Struct, this prints:

```
$VAR1 = bless( {
            'Shoppe::owner' => 'Abdul Alhazred',
            'Shoppe::stock' => {
                                 'charms' => 3,
                                 'books' => 208,
                                 'potions' => 'none'
                               },
            'Shoppe::boss' => bless( {
                                 'Manager::name' =>
                                     'Prof L. P. Haitch',
                                 'Manager::salary' =>
                                     'madness',
                                 'Manager::started' =>
                                     'Sat Apr  1 16:18:13 2000'
                               }, 'Manager' ),
            'Shoppe::addrs' => [
                                 'Miskatonic University',
                                 'Innsmouth, Mass.'
                               ]
          }, 'Shoppe' );
```

The Data::Dumper module's Dumper function takes a list of scalars (including references, which can even refer to objects) and returns a printable or evalable string that accurately reproduces an faithful copy of the original. You could use this to write out a saved version of a data structure to a regular disk file or into a DBM file, or to pass it to another process over a pipe or socket connection. This module can be used with MLDBM from CPAN and DB_File to implement a DBM file that can transparently store complex data values, not just flat strings. Other stringification (or *serialization,* or *marshalling*) modules include Storable and FreezeThaw, both available from CPAN.

DB_File

```
use DB_File;
```

Tie a hash to a DBM-style file:

```
tie(%hash, "DB_File", $filename)        # Open database.
    or die "Can't open $filename: $!";

$v = $hash{"key"};                      # Retrieve from database.
$hash{"key"} = "value";                 # Put value into database.
untie %hash;
```

Tie a hash to a B-tree file, but still access as a regular DBM hash:

```
tie(%hash, "DB_File", "mytree", O_RDWR|O_CREAT, 0666, $DB_BTREE)
    or die "Cannot open file 'mytree': $!";

while (($k, $v) = each %hash) {         # Do in-order traversal.
    print "$k => $v\n";
}
```

Tie an array to a plain text file:

```
tie(@lines, "DB_File", $textfile, O_RDWR|O_CREAT, 0666, $DB_RECNO)
    or die "Cannot open textfile $textfile: $!";

# Write a few lines to the file, overwriting any old contents.
$lines[0] = "first line";
$lines[1] = "second line";
$lines[2] = "third line";

push @lines, "penult", "last";  # Append two lines to the file.
$wc = scalar @lines;            # Count lines in file.
$last = pop @lines;             # Delete and retrieve last line.
```

The DB_File module provides tied access to Berkeley DB.* The default tie function gives you a standard DBM-style database with some features that no other DBM library provides: there are no size limits on either keys or values, and your data is stored in a byte-order independent format.

The second tie mechanism uses B-trees to give you a true ISAM (indexed sequential access method) file, that is, a hash whose keys are automatically ordered—alphabetically by default, but configurable by the user.

The third tie mechanism binds an array to a file of records (text lines by default) so that changes to the array are automatically reflected on disk. This simulates random access by line number on a regular text file. The standard interface conforms

---

* Providing you have that library installed on your system. If not, you can build and install it easily enough.

Modules

to version 1.x of Berkeley DB; if you want to make use of the new features available in Berkeley DB 2.x or 3.x, use the CPAN module `BerkeleyDB` instead.

Starting with version 2.x, Berkeley DB has internal support for locking; earlier versions did not. See the section "File Locking" in Chapter 16 for a description of how you can safely lock any kind of database file using `flock` on a semaphore file.

Dumpvalue

```
use Dumpvalue;

Dumpvalue->new->dumpValue($store);
```

When used on the example from `Class::Struct`, this prints:

```
'Shoppe::addrs' => ARRAY(0x9c1d4)
   0  'Miskatonic University'
   1  'Innsmouth, Mass.'
'Shoppe::boss' => Manager=HASH(0xa5754)
   'Manager::name' => 'Prof L. P. Haitch'
   'Manager::salary' => 'madness'
   'Manager::started' => 'Sat Apr  1 16:18:13 2000'
'Shoppe::owner' => 'Abdul Alhazred'
'Shoppe::stock' => HASH(0xfdbb4)
   'books' => 208
   'charms' => 3
   'potions' => 'none'
```

This is another module to help display complex data. It's not so much meant for marshalling as it is for pretty printing. It's used by the Perl debugger's **x** command. As such, it offers a dizzying wealth of options to control the output format. It also provides convenient access to Perl's package symbol tables to dump out the contents of an entire package.

English

```
use English;

# Use awk-style names.
$RS = '';                   # instead of $/
while (<>) {
    next if $NR < 10;       # instead of $.
    ...
}

# Same thing, but even more cobolaciously.
$INPUT_RECORD_SEPARATOR = '';
while (<>) {
    next if $INPUT_LINE_NUMBER < 10;
    ...
}
```

The English module provides cumbersome aliases for the built-in variables for prodigious typists with a visceral dislike for nonalphabetic identifiers (and a visceral *like* for the Caps Lock key). As with all imports, these aliases are only available in the current package. The variables are still available under their real names. For example, once you use this module, you can use $PID if $$ bothers you, or $PROGRAM_NAME if $0 makes you queasy. Some variables have more than one alias. See Chapter 28, *Special Names*, for a complete description of all built-in variables, along with their English aliases.

Errno

```
use Errno;
unless (open(FH, $pathname)) {
    if ($!{ENOENT}) {  # We don't need an import for this!
        warn "$pathname does not exist\n";
    }
    else {
        warn "open failed on '$pathname': $!";
    }
}

use Errno qw(EINTR EIO :POSIX);
if ($! == ENOENT) { .... }
```

The Errno module makes available the symbolic names for the error status values set when a syscall fails, but does not export them by default. The module has a single export tag, ":POSIX", which exports only those symbols defined by the POSIX 1003.1 standard. The module also makes the global %! variable magical using tie. You can subscript into the %! hash using any valid errno on your system, not just the POSIX ones, and its value is true only if that's the current error.

Exporter

Inside your *MyModule.pm* file:

```
package MyModule;

use strict;
use Exporter;

our $VERSION = 1.00;          # Or higher...
our @ISA = qw(Exporter);

our @EXPORT      = qw(f1 %h);  # Symbols imported by default.
our @EXPORT_OK   = qw(f2 f3);  # Symbols imported only by request.
our %EXPORT_TAGS = (           # Mappings for :shortcuts.
    a => [qw(f1 f2 f3)],
    b => [qw(f2 %h)],
);
```

```
# Your code here.

1;
```

From a program or another module that makes use of your module:

```
use MyModule;                  # Import everything in @EXPORT.
use MyModule ();               # Load module, no imports at all.
use MyModule "f1", "f2", "%h"; # Two subs and a variable.
use MyModule qw(:DEFAULT f3);  # All in @EXPORT + one sub.
use MyModule "f4";             # Fatal because f4 not exported.
```

Whenever anyone invokes a use declaration to load your module, it calls the import method from your module to fetch any symbols it needs into the package of the invoker. Your module (the one doing the exporting) can define the import method any way it pleases, but the standard way is to inherit the method from the Exporter class module. That is what the code above arranges.

The Exporter module serves as a base class for modules that wish to establish their own exports. Oddly, object-oriented modules typically don't use Exporter, since they don't normally export anything (method calls don't need to be exported). However, the Exporter module itself is accessed in an OO fashion because of the @ISA array you installed, as in our example. When another program or module uses your module, the import method is invoked as a class method in your module: MyModule->import(*LIST*). However, since you didn't define an import method in your module, you'll automatically make use of the Exporter::import method through inheritance.

The module's @EXPORT array contains a list of symbols (functions and even variables) that the calling code automatically imports with an unadorned use statement. The @EXPORT_OK array holds symbols that can be imported if specifically requested by name. The $VERSION number is consulted if the use statement requests that a particular version (or newer) of the module. Many, many other features are available. See Chapter 11, *Modules*, as well as the online manpage for the Exporter module.

Fatal

The Fatal module makes functions fail more spectacularly. It replaces functions that normally return false upon failure with wrappers that raise an exception if the real function returns false. That way you can safely use these functions without testing their return values explicitly on each call.

Both user-defined functions and built-in functions may be wrapped, except for those built-ins that cannot be expressed via prototypes. Attempting to override a nonoverridable built-in raises an exception. These include system, print, printf, exec, split, grep, and map—or more generally, any *FUNC* for which prototype "CORE::*FUNC*" returns false, including the prototype function itself.

If the symbol :void appears in the import list, functions named later in the list are limited to raising an exception when the function is called in void context—that is, when the return value is ignored. (Be careful about the last statement in a subroutine.) For example:

```
use Fatal qw(:void open close);

# open properly checked, so no exception is raised on failure.
if (open(FH, "< /nonesuch") { warn "no /nonesuch: $!"; }

# close not properly checked, so failure raises an exception.
close FH;
```

Fcntl

```
use Fcntl;              # Import standard fcntl.h constants.
use Fcntl ":flock";     # Import LOCK_* constants.
use Fcntl ":seek";      # Import SEEK_CUR, SEEK_SET, SEEK_END.
use Fcntl ":mode";      # Import S_* stat checking constants.
use Fcntl ":Fcompat";   # Import F* constants.
```

The Fcntl module provides constants for use with various Perl built-in functions. The default set of imports includes constants like F_GETFL and F_SETFL for fcntl, SEEK_SET and SEEK_END for seek and sysseek, and O_CREAT and O_EXCL for sysopen. Supported import tags include ":flock" to access the LOCK_EX, LOCK_NB, LOCK_SH, and LOCK_UN constants for flock; ":mode" to get at constants from *sys/stat.h* like S_IRUSR and S_ISFIFO; ":seek" to get at the three arguments for seek and sysseek; and ":Fcompat" to get the old-style symbols with a leading "F" but not "F_", like FAPPEND, FASYNC, and FNONBLOCK. See the online documentation for the Fcntl module and your operating system's documentation on the relevant syscalls, like *fcntl*(2), *lseek*(2), *open*(2), and *stat*(2).

File::Basename

```
use File::Basename;

$fullname = "/usr/local/src/perl-5.6.1.tar.gz";

$file = basename($fullname);
# file="perl-5.6.1.tar.gz"

$dir = dirname($fullname);
# dir="/usr/local/src"
```

Modules

```
($file,$dir,$ext) = fileparse($fullname, qr/\..*/);
# dir="/usr/local/src/" file="perl-5" ext=".6.1.tar.gz"

($file,$dir,$ext) = fileparse($fullname, qr/\.[^.]*/);
# dir="/usr/local/src/" file="perl-5.6.1.tar" ext=".gz"

($file,$dir,$ext) = fileparse($fullname, qr/\.\D.*/);
# dir="/usr/local/src/" file="perl-5.6.1" ext=".tar.gz"

($file,$dir,$bak) = fileparse("/tmp/file.bak",
                         qr/~+$/, qr/\.(bak|orig|save)/)
# dir="/tmp/" file="file" ext=".bak"

($file,$dir,$bak) = fileparse("/tmp/file~",
                         qr/~+$/, qr/\.(bak|orig|save)/)
# dir="/tmp/" file="file" ext="~"
```

The `File::Basename` module provides functions to parse pathnames into their individual components. The `dirname` function pulls out the directory portion and `basename` the nondirectory portion. The more elaborate `fileparse` function picks out the full pathname into the directory name, the filename, and the suffix; you must supply a list of regular expressions describing the suffixes that interest you. The examples above illustrate how choice of suffix patterns affects the result. By default, these functions parse pathnames according to the native conventions of your current platform. The `fileparse_set_fstype` function selects a different platform's parsing rules, such as `fileparse_set_fstype("VMS")` to parse names using VMS rules, even when running on non-VMS systems.

File::Compare

```
use File::Compare;

printf "fileA and fileB are %s.\n",
    compare("fileA","fileB") ? "different" : "identical";

use File::Compare 'cmp';
sub munge($) {
    my $line = $_[0];
    for ($line) {
        s/^\s+//;    # Trim leading whitespace.
        s/\s+$//;    # Trim trailing whitespace.
    }
    return uc($line);
}

if (not cmp("fileA", "fileB", sub {munge $_[0] eq munge $_[1]} ) ) {
    print "fileA and fileB are kinda the same.\n";
}
```

The `File::Compare` module provides one function, `compare`, which compares the contents of the two files passed to it. It returns 0 if the files contain the same data, 1 if they contain different data, and –1 if an error was encountered in accessing the named files. If you pass a subroutine reference as the third argument, that function is repeatedly called to determine whether any two lines are equivalent. For compatibility with the *cmp*(1) program, you may explicitly import the function as `cmp`. (This does not affect the binary `cmp` operator.)

File::Copy

```
use File::Copy;

copy("/tmp/fileA", "/tmp/fileA.orig")   or die "copy failed: $!";
copy("/etc/motd", *STDOUT)              or die "copy failed: $!";
move("/tmp/fileA", "/tmp/fileB")        or die "move failed: $!";

use File::Copy qw/cp mv/;               # Get normal Unix names.
cp "/tmp/fileA", "/tmp/fileA.orig"      or die "copy failed: $!";
mv "/tmp/fileA", "/tmp/fileB"           or die "move failed: $!";
```

The `File::Copy` module exports two functions, `copy` and `move`, that respectively copy or rename their first argument to their second argument, similar to calling the Unix *cp*(1) and *mv*(1) commands (names you may use if you import them explicitly). The `copy` function also accepts filehandles as arguments. These functions return true when they work and false when they fail, setting `$!` (`$OS_ERROR`) as appropriate. (Unfortunately, you can't tell whether something like "Permission denied" applies to the first file or to the second one.) These functions are something of a compromise between convenience and precision. They do not support the numerous options and optimizations found in *cp*(1) and *mv*(1), such as recursive copying, automatic backups, retention of original timestamps and ownership information, and interactive confirmation. If you need any of those features, it's probably best to call your platform's versions of those commands.* Just realize that not all systems support the same commands or use the same options for them.

```
system("cp -R -pi /tmp/dir1 /tmp/dir2") == 0
    or die "external cp command status was $?";
```

File::Find

```
use File::Find;

# Print out all directories below current one.
find sub { print "$File::Find::name\n" if -d }, ".";
```

---

* Or get the PPT versions if your platform is tool-challenged.

```
# Compute total space used by all files in listed directories.
@dirs = @ARGV ? @ARGV : ('.');
my $sum = 0;
find sub { $sum += -s }, @dirs;
print "@dirs contained $sum bytes\n";

# Alter default behavior to go through symlinks
# and visit subdirectories first.
find { wanted => \&myfunc, follow => 1, bydepth => 1 }, ".";
```

The `File::Find` module's `find` function recursively descends directories. Its first argument should be a reference to a function, and all following arguments should be directories. The function is called on each filename from the listed directories. Within that function, the `$_` variable is set to the basename of the current filename visited, and the process's current working directory is by default set to that directory. The package variable `$File::Find::name` is the full pathname of the visited filename. An alternative calling convention takes as its first argument a reference to a hash containing option specifications, including "wanted", "bydepth", "follow", "follow_fast", "follow_skip", "no_chdir", "untaint", "untaint_pattern", and "untaint_skip", as fully explained in the online documentation. This module is also used by the standard *find2perl*(1) translator program that comes with Perl.

File::Glob

```
use File::Glob ':glob';        # Override glob built-in.
@list = <*.[Cchy]>;            # Now uses POSIX glob, not csh glob.

use File::Glob qw(:glob csh_glob);
@sources = bsd_glob("*.{C,c,h,y,pm,xs}", GLOB_CSH);
@sources = csh_glob("*.{C,c,h,y,pm,xs}");   # (same thing)

use File::Glob ':glob';
# call glob with extra arguments
$homedir = bsd_glob('~jrhacker', GLOB_TILDE | GLOB_ERR);
if (GLOB_ERROR) {
    # An error occurred expanding the home directory.
}
```

The `File::Glob` module's `bsd_glob` function implements the *glob*(3) routine from the C library. An optional second argument contains flags governing additional matching properties. The `:glob` import tag imports both the function and the necessary flags.

The module also implements a `csh_glob` function. This is what the built-in Perl `glob` and *GLOBPAT* fileglobbing operators really call. Calling `csh_glob` is (mostly) like calling `bsd_glob` this way:

```
bsd_glob(@_ ? $_[0] : $_,
    GLOB_BRACE | GLOB_NOMAGIC | GLOB_QUOTE | GLOB_TILDE);
```

If you import the `:glob` tag, then all calls to the built-in fileglobbing operators in the current package will really call the module's `bsd_glob` function instead of its `csh_glob` function. One reason you might want to do this is that, although `bsd_glob` handles patterns with whitespace in them correctly, `csh_glob` handles them, um, in the historical fashion. Old scripts would write `<*.c *.h>` to glob both of those. Neither function is bothered by whitespace in the actual filenames, however.

The `bsd_glob` function takes an argument containing the fileglobbing pattern (not a regular expression pattern) plus an optional flags argument. Filenames with a leading dot are not matched unless specifically requested. The return value is influenced by the flags in the second argument, which should be bitwise ORed together:*

GLOB_BRACE

> Preprocess the string to expand `{pat,pat,...}` strings as *csh*(1) would. The pattern `{}` is left unexpanded for historical reasons, mostly to ease typing of *find*(1) patterns.

GLOB_CSH

> Synonym for GLOB_BRACE | GLOB_NOMAGIC | GLOB_QUOTE | GLOB_TILDE.

GLOB_ERR

> Return an error when `bsd_glob` encounters a directory it cannot open or read. Ordinarily, `bsd_glob` skips over the error, looking for more matches.

GLOB_MARK

> Return values that are directories with a slash appended.

GLOB_NOCASE

> By default, filenames are case sensitive; this flag makes `bsd_glob` treat case differences as insignificant. (But see below for exceptions on MS-DOSish systems).

GLOB_NOCHECK

> If the pattern does not match any pathname, then makes `bsd_glob` return a list consisting of only the pattern, as */bin/sh* does. If GLOB_QUOTE is set, its effect is present in the pattern returned.

---

* Due to restrictions in the syntax of the built-in `glob` operator, you may need to call the function as `bsd_glob` if you want to pass it the second argument.

GLOB_NOMAGIC

Same as GLOB_NOCHECK but it only returns the pattern if it does not contain any of the special characters *, ? or [. NOMAGIC is provided to simplify implementing the historic *csh*(1) globbing behavior and should probably not be used anywhere else.

GLOB_NOSORT

By default, the pathnames are sorted in ascending order (using normal character comparisons irrespective of locale setting). This flag prevents that sorting for a small increase in speed.

GLOB_QUOTE

Use the backslash character \ for quoting: every occurrence of a backslash followed by a character in the pattern is replaced by that character, avoiding any special interpretation of the character. (But see below for exceptions on MS-DOSish systems).

GLOB_TILDE

Allow patterns whose first path component is ~*USER*. If *USER* is omitted, the tilde by itself (or followed by a slash) represents the current user's home directory.

The bsd_glob function returns a (possibly empty) list of matching paths, which will be tainted if that matters to your program. On error, GLOB_ERROR will be true and $! ($OS_ERROR) will be set to the standard system error. GLOB_ERROR is guaranteed to be false if no error occurred, and to be either GLOB_ABEND or GLOB_NOSPACE otherwise. (GLOB_ABEND means that the bsd_glob was stopped due to some error, GLOB_NOSPACE because it ran out of memory.) If bsd_glob had already found some matching paths when the error occurred, it returns the list of filenames found so far, *and also sets* GLOB_ERROR. Note that this implementation of bsd_glob varies from most others by not considering ENOENT and ENOTDIR as terminating error conditions. Instead, it continues processing despite those errors, unless the GLOB_ERR flag is set.

If no flag argument is supplied, your system's defaults are followed, meaning that filenames differing only in case are indistinguishable from one another on VMS, OS/2, old Mac OS (but not Mac OS X), and Microsoft systems (but not when Perl was built with Cygwin). If you supply any flags at all and still want this behavior, then you must include GLOB_NOCASE in the flags. Whatever system you're on, you can change your defaults up front by importing the :case or :nocase flags.

On MS-DOSish systems, the backslash is a valid directory separator character.* In this case, use of backslash as a quoting character (via GLOB_QUOTE) interferes with

---

* Although technically, so is a slash—at least as far as those kernels and syscalls are concerned; command shells are remarkably less enlightened.

the use of backslash as a directory separator. The best (simplest, most portable) solution is to use slashes for directory separators, backslashes for quoting. However, this does not match some users' expectations, so backslashes (under GLOB_QUOTE) quote only the glob metacharacters [,], {, }, -, ˜, and \ itself. All other backslashes are passed through unchanged, if you can manage to get them by Perl's own backslash quoting in strings. It may take as many as four backslashes to finally match one in the filesystem. This is so completely insane that even MS-DOSish users should strongly consider using slashes. If you really want to use backslashes, look into the standard `File::DosGlob` module, as it might be more to your liking than Unix-flavored fileglobbing.

File::Spec

```
use File::Spec;       # OO style

$path = File::Spec->catfile("subdir", "filename");
    # 'subdir/filename' on Unix, OS2, or Mac OS X
    # 'subdir:filename' on (old) Apple Macs
    # 'subdir\filename' on Microsoft

$path = File::Spec->catfile("", "dir1", "dir2", "filename");
    # '/dir1/dir2/filename' on Unix, OS2, or Mac OS X
    # ':dir1:dir2:filename' on (old) Apple Macs
    # '\dir1\dir2\filename' on Microsoft

use File::Spec::Unix;
$path = File::Spec::Unix->catfile("subdir", "filename");
    # 'subdir/filename' (even when executed on non-Unix systems)

use File::Spec::Mac;
$path = File::Spec::Mac->catfile("subdir", "filename");
    # 'subdir:filename'

use File::Spec::Win32;
$path = File::Spec::Win32->catfile("subdir", "filename";)
    # 'subdir\filename'

# Use functional interface instead.
use File::Spec::Functions;
$path = catfile("subdir", "filename");
```

The `File::Spec` family of modules lets you construct paths using directories and filenames without hardcoding platform-specific directory separators. Supported systems include Unix, VMS, Mac, and Win32. These modules all offer a `catfile` class method that catenates together each path component using the specified platform's path separator. The `File::Spec` module returns different results depending on your current platform. The others return results specific to that platform. The `File::Spec::Functions` module provides a functional interface.

Modules

File::stat

```
use File::stat;
$st = stat($file)        or die "Can't stat $file: $!";
if ($st->mode & 0111 and $st->nlink > 1)) {
    print "$file is executable with many links\n";
}

use File::stat ":FIELDS";
stat($file)              or die "Can't stat $file: $!";
if ($st_mode & 0111 and $st_nlink > 1) ) {
    print "$file is executable with many links\n";
}

@statinfo = CORE::stat($file);    # Access overridden built-in.
```

The `File::stat` module provides a method interface to Perl's built-in `stat` and `lstat` functions by replacing them with versions that return a `File::stat` object (or `undef` on failure). This object has methods that return the like-named structure field name from the traditional *stat*(2) syscall; namely, `dev`, `ino`, `mode`, `nlink`, `uid`, `gid`, `rdev`, `size`, `atime`, `mtime`, `ctime`, `blksize`, and `blocks`. You may also import the structure fields into your own namespace as regular variables using the ":FIELDS" import tag. (This still overrides your `stat` and `lstat` built-ins.) These fields show up as scalar variables named with a "st_" in front of the field name. That is, the `$st_dev` variable corresponds to the `$st->dev` method.

File::Temp

```
use File::Temp qw(tempfile tempdir);

$dir = tempdir(CLEANUP => 1);
($fh, $filename) = tempfile(DIR => $dir);
($fh, $filename) = tempfile($template, DIR => $dir);
($fh, $filename) = tempfile($template, SUFFIX => ".data");
$fh = tempfile();

use File::Temp ':mktemp';

($fh, $filename) = mkstemp("tmpfileXXXXX");
($fh, $filename) = mkstemps("tmpfileXXXXXX", $suffix);
$tmpdir = mkdtemp($template);
$unopened_file = mktemp($template);
```

New to version 5.6.1 of Perl, the `File::Temp` module provides convenient functions for creating and opening temporary files securely. It's better to use this module than to try to pick a temporary file on your own. Otherwise, you'll just fall into all the same traps as everyone else before you. This module guards you against various subtle race conditions, as well as the dangers of using directories that others can write to; see Chapter 23, *Security*. The `tempfile` function returns both a filehandle and filename. It's safest to use the filehandle that's already open and ignore the filename entirely (except perhaps for error messages). Once the file is closed, it is automatically deleted. For compatibility with the C library, the :mktemp import tag provides access to functions with names familiar to C programmers, but please remember that filenames are always less secure than filehandles.

FileHandle

```
use FileHandle;

$fh = new FileHandle;
if ($fh->open("< file")) {
    print $line while defined($line = $fh->getline);
    $fh->close;
}

$pos = $fh->getpos;      # like tell()
$fh->setpos($pos);       # like seek()

($readfh, $writefh) = FileHandle::pipe();

autoflush STDOUT 1;
```

The FileHandle module mostly serves as a mechanism for cloaking Perl's punctuation variables in longer, more OO-looking calls. It is provided for compatibility with older releases, but is now really only a frontend for several more specific modules, like IO::Handle and IO::File.* Its best property is the low-level access it provides to certain rare functions from the C library (*clearerr*(3), *fgetpos*(3), *fsetpos*(3), and *setvbuf*(3)).

Variable	Method
$|	autoflush
$,	output_field_separator
$\	output_record_separator
$/	input_record_separator
$.	input_line_number
$%	format_page_number
$=	format_lines_per_page
$-	format_lines_left
$~	format_name
$^	format_top_name
$:	format_line_break_characters
$^L	format_formfeed

---

* Because it loads so much code, this module costs you a megabyte or so of memory.

Instead of saying:

```
$ofh = select(HANDLE);
$~ = 'SomeFormat';
$| = 1;
select($ofh);
```

you can just say:

```
use FileHandle;
HANDLE->format_name('SomeFormat');
HANDLE->autoflush(1);
```

Currently, three methods (`output_field_separator`, `output_record_separator`, and `input_record_separator`) only pretend to be per-handle methods: setting them on one handle actually affects all filehandles. They are therefore only supported as class methods, not as per-filehandle methods. This restriction may be lifted someday.

To get a lexically scoped filehandle, instead of using filehandle autovivification:

```
open my $fh, "< somefile"
    or die "can't open somefile: $!";
```

one could say:

```
use FileHandle;
my $fh = FileHandle->new("< somefile")
    or die "can't open somefile: $!";
```

FileHandle inherits from `IO::File`, which inherits from `IO::Handle` and `IO::Seekable`. Virtually all the module's functionality is available more efficiently through basic, unadorned Perl calls, except for the following, not all of which may be implemented on all non-Unix platforms:

HANDLE->blocking(*EXPR*)

> Called with an argument, enables nonblocking I/O if the argument is false, and disables nonblocking (that is, enables blocking) if the argument is true. The method returns the previously set value (which is still the current setting if no argument was given). On error, `blocking` sets `$!` and returns `undef`. This could be done using `fcntl` directly, but the `FileHandle` interface is much easier to use.

HANDLE->clearerr

> Calls the C library function *clearerr*(3) to clear the handle's internal end-of-file and error status indicators.

HANDLE->error

Calls the C library function *ferror*(3) to test the error indicator for the given handle, returning whether that internal indicator is set. The error indicator can be reset reliably only via the clearerr method. (Some systems also reset it on calls to the seek operator.)

HANDLE->formline(*PICTURE, LIST*)

This is the same as saving the old accumulator variable ($^A), calling the formline function with the given *PICTURE* and *LIST*, outputting the resulting contents of the accumulator to the given handle, and finally restoring the original accumulator. For example, here's how to output a long text variable, with automatic word-wrapping at column 72:

```
use FileHandle;
STDOUT->formline("^" . ("<" x 72) . "~~\n", $long_text);
```

HANDLE->getpos

Calls the C library function *fgetpos*(3), providing an alternative interface to tell. On some (non-UNIX) systems the return value may be a complex object, and getpos and setpos may be the only way to portably reposition a text stream.

FileHandle->new_tmpfile

Calls the C library function *tmpfile*(3) to create a new temporary file opened for read-write mode and returns a handle to this stream. On systems where this is possible, the temporary file is anonymous—that is, it is unlinked after creation, but held open. You should use this function, or POSIX::tmpnam as described under the POSIX module, to safely create a temporary file without exposing yourself to subtle but serious security problems through race conditions. As of the 5.6.1 release of Perl, the File::Temp module is now the preferred interface.

HANDLE->setbuf(*BUFFER*)

Calls the C library function *setbuf*(3) with the given *BUFFER* variable. It passes undef to indicate unbuffered output. A variable used as a buffer by setbuf or setvbuf *must not be modified in any way* until the handle is closed, or until setbuf or setvbuf is called again. Otherwise, memory corruption may result, and you will be sad.

HANDLE->setpos(*EXPR*)

Calls the C library function *fsetpos*(3), providing an alternative interface to seek. The argument should only be the return value from getpos, described earlier.

HANDLE->setvbuf(*BUFFER*, *TYPE*, *SIZE*)

Calls the C library function *setvbuf*(3) with the given *BUFFER*. The standard C library constants _IONBF (unbuffered), _IOLBF (line buffered), and _IOFBF (fully buffered) are available for the *TYPE* field if explicitly imported. See the warning under setbuf.

HANDLE->sync

Calls the C library function *fsync*(3) to synchronize a file's in-memory state with the physical medium. Note that sync operates not on the handle, but on the file descriptor, so any data held by buffers will not be synchronized unless flushed first.

HANDLE->untaint

Marks the filehandle or directory handle as providing untainted data. When running under taint mode (see Chapter 23), data read in from external files is considered untrustworthy. Do not invoke this method blindly: you're circumventing Perl's best attempts to protect you from yourself.

Getopt::Long

If your program says:

```
use Getopt::Long;
GetOptions("verbose"  => \$verbose,
           "debug"    => \$debug,
           "output=s" => \$output);
```

it can be called from the command line like this:

```
% prog --verbose more args here
% prog --debug more args here
% prog -v -d more args here
% prog --output=somefile more args here
% prog -o somefile more args here
```

The Getopt::Long module provides a GetOptions function to process command-line switches with long names. It includes support for things like abbreviating switches, typed arguments like Boolean or string or integer or float, array variables for repeating options, user-defined validation routines, POSIX-conforming versus FSF-style processing, case-insensitive options, and traditional bundling of short options—just to name a few out of its vast cornucopia of features. If this module is overkill, consider the more traditional Getopt::Std module described next. If this module is underkill, check out the CPAN module Getopt::Declare, which provides a more declarative syntax for option specification.

Getopt::Std

```
use Getopt::Std;
```

You can use getopt and getopts with globals:

```
our ($opt_o, $opt_i, $opt_f);
getopt('oif');              # -o, -i, and -f all take arguments.
                            # Sets global $opt_* variables.
getopts('oif:');            # Now -o & -i are boolean; -f takes an arg.
                            # Still sets global $opt_* as side effect.
```

Or you can use them with a private options hash:

```
my %opts;
getopt('oif', \%opts);      # We'll place results here.
getopts('oif:', \%opts);    # All three still take arguments.
                            # Now -o and -i are boolean flags
                            # and only -f takes an argument.
```

The Getopt::Std module provides two functions, getopt and getopts, to help you parse command-line arguments for single-character options. Of the two, getopts is the more useful because it lets you specify that some options take arguments and others don't, whereas getopt assumes all options take arguments. By specifying to getopts a letter with a colon after it, you indicate that that argument takes an argument; otherwise, a Boolean flag is expected. Standard option clustering is supported. Ordering doesn't matter, so options taking no arguments may be grouped together. Options that do take an argument must be the last in a group or by themselves, and their argument may either come immediately after the option in the same string, or else as the next program argument. Given the example getopts use above, these are equivalent calls:

```
% prog -o -i -f TMPFILE more args here
% prog -o -if TMPFILE more args here
% prog -io -fTMPFILE more args here
% prog -iofTMPFILE more args here
% prog -oifTMPFILE more args here
```

IO::Socket

```
use IO::Socket;
```

As a client:

```
$socket = new IO::Socket::INET (PeerAddr => $remote_host,
                                PeerPort => $remote_port,
                                Proto    => "tcp",
                                Type     => SOCK_STREAM)
    or die "Can't connect to $remote_host:$remote_port : $!\n";
```

Modules

```
    # Or use the simpler single-argument interface.
    $socket = IO::Socket::INET->new("$remote_host:$remote_port");
                                # "localhost:80", for example.

    print $socket "data\n";
    $line = <$socket>;
```

As a server:

```
    $server = IO::Socket::INET->new(LocalPort => $server_port,
                                Type       => SOCK_STREAM,
                                Reuse      => 1,
                                Listen     => 10 )  # or SOMAXCONN
        or die "Can't be a TCP server on port $server_port : $!\n";

    while ($client = $server->accept()) {
        # $client is the new connection
        $request = <$client>;
        print $client "answer\n";
        close $client;
    }

    # Make simple TCP connecting function that returns a filehandle
    # for use in simple client programs.
    sub tcp_connect {
        my ($host, $service) = @_;
        require IO::Socket;
        return IO::Socket::INET->new(join ":", $host, $service);
    }
    my $fh    = tcp_connect("localhost", "smtp");  # with scalar
    local *FH = tcp_connect("localhost", "smtp");  # with handle
```

The IO::Socket module provides a higher-level approach to socket handling than
the raw Socket module. You may use it in an object-oriented fashion, although this
isn't mandatory, because the return values are proper filehandles and may be used
as such, as shown in the tcp_connect function in the example. This module inherits methods from IO::Handle, and itself requires IO::Socket::INET and
IO::Socket::UNIX. See the description of the FileHandle module for other interesting features. See Chapter 16 for a description of using sockets.

IPC::Open2

```
    use IPC::Open2;

    local(*HIS_OUT, *HIS_IN);  # Create local handles if needed.

    $childpid = open2(*HIS_OUT, *HIS_IN, $program, @args)
        or die "can't open pipe to $program: $!";
    print HIS_IN "here's your input\n";
    $his_output = <HIS_IN>;
    close(HIS_OUT);
    close(README);
    waitpid($childpid, 0);
```

The `IPC::Open2` module's one exported function, `open2`, starts up another program and provides both read and write access to that command. The first two arguments should be valid filehandles (or else empty variables into which autogenerated filehandles can be placed). The remaining arguments are the program plus its arguments, which if passed in separately will not be subject to shell interpolation. This module does not reap the child process after it exits. Except for short programs where it's acceptable to let the operating system take care of this, you need to do this yourself. This is normally as simple as calling `waitpid $pid, 0` when you're done with that child process. Failure to do this can result in an accumulation of defunct ("zombie") processes.

In practice, this module doesn't work well with many programs because of the way buffering works in C's standard I/O library. If you control the source code to both programs, however, you can easily circumvent this restriction by flushing your output buffers more frequently than the default. If you don't, programs can be annoyingly miserly in their hoarding of output. Another potential pitfall is deadlock: if both processes are reading at the same time, and no one is writing, then your program will hang. See Chapter 16 for more discussion.

IPC::Open3

```
use IPC::Open3;

local(*HIS_IN, *HIS_OUT, *HIS_ERR);

$childpid = open3(*HIS_IN, *HIS_OUT, *HIS_ERR, $cmd, @args);
print HIS_IN "stuff\n";
close(HIS_IN);              # Give end of file to kid.
@outlines = <HIS_OUT>;     # Read till EOF.
@errlines = <HIS_ERR>;     # XXX: block potential if massive
print "STDOUT:\n", @outlines, "\n";
print "STDERR:\n", @errlines, "\n";
close HIS_OUT;
close HIS_ERR;
waitpid($childpid, 0);
if ($?) {
    print "That child exited with wait status of $?\n";
}
```

The `IPC::Open3` module works like `IPC::Open2` (the latter is implemented in terms of the former), except that `open3` provides access to the standard input, the standard output, *and* the standard error handles of the program you launch. The same caveats apply as with `open2` (see the previous entry), plus a few more. The order of arguments is different in `open3` than with `open2`. Instead of passing the handle to read from first and the handle to write to second, this time it's the other way around. Also, with `open3`, danger of deadlock is even greater than before. If you try to read through end-of-file on one of the child's two output handles, but meanwhile there's a great deal of output on the other handle, the peer process blocks and appears to hang. Use either the four-argument form of select or the standard IO::Select module to circumvent this. See Chapter 16 for more details.

Math::BigInt

```
use Math::BigInt;
$i = Math::BigInt->new($string);

use Math::BigInt ':constant';
print 2**200;
```

This prints:

```
+1606938044258990275541962092341162602522202993782792835301376
```

The Math::BigInt module provides objects that represent integers with arbitrary precision and overloaded arithmetical operators. Create these objects using the new constructor, or, within a lexical scope, by importing the special value ":constant", after which all numeric literals through the end of that lexical scope are treated as Math::BigInt objects. All standard integer operators are implemented, including (as of the 5.6 release of Perl) the bitwise logical operators. Under the current implementation, this module is not what you'd call blazingly fast, but this may be addressed in the future. (We'd like to see you how fast *you* are at calculating 2**200 in your head.)

Math::Complex

```
use Math::Complex;

$z = Math::Complex->make(5, 6);
$z = cplx(5, 6);            # same thing, but shorter
$t = 4 - 3*i + $z;         # do standard complex math
print "$t\n";              # prints 9+3i

print sqrt(-9), "\n";      # prints 3i
```

The Math::Complex module provides complex number objects with overloaded operators. These are numbers with both real and imaginary portions, like those satisfying even-numbered integral roots of negative numbers as shown above. Besides arithmetical operators, many built-in math functions are also overridden by versions that understand complex numbers, including abs, log, sqrt, sin, cos, and atan2. Other functions provided are Re and Im to provide the real and imaginary portions of their complex arguments, plus a full battery of extended trigonometric functions, such as tan, asin, acos, sinh, cosh, and tanh. The module also exports the constant i, which, as you might imagine, holds the value of *i*; that is, the square root of –1.

Math::Trig

```
use Math::Trig;

$x = tan(0.9);
$y = acos(3.7);
$z = asin(2.4);

$halfpi = pi/2;

$rad = deg2rad(120);
```

Perl itself defines only three trigonometric functions: sin, cos, and atan2. The Math::Trig module overrides these with fancier versions and supplies all the rest of the trig functions, including tan, csc, cosec, sec, cot, cotan, asin, acos, atan, sinh, cosh, tanh, and many others. Additionally, the constant pi is defined, as are conversion functions like deg2rad and grad2rad. Support is provided for Cartesian, spherical, and cylindrical coordinates systems. This module makes implicit use of Math::Complex as needed (and vice versa) for computations requiring imaginary numbers.

Net::hostent

```
use Socket;
use Net::hostent;

print inet_ntoa(gethost("www.perl.com")->addr);    # prints 208.201.239.50
printf "%vd", gethost("www.perl.com")->addr;        # same thing

print gethost("127.0.0.1")->name;                   # prints localhost

use Net::hostent ':FIELDS';
if (gethost($name_or_number)) {
    print "name is $h_name\n";
    print "aliases are $h_aliases\n";
    print "addrs are ",
        join ", " => map { inet_ntoa($_) } @h_addr_list;
}
```

This module's default exports override the core gethostbyname and gethostbyaddr functions, replacing them with versions that return a Net::hostent object (or undef on failure). This object has attribute accessor methods that return the like-named structure field name from the C library's struct hostent from *netdb.h*: name, aliases, addrtype, length, or addr_list. The aliases and addr_list methods return array references; the rest return scalars. The addr method is equivalent to the initial element in the addr_list array reference. The gethost function is a frontend that forwards a numeric argument to gethostbyaddr by way of the

Socket::inet_aton function and the rest to gethostbyname. As with the other semipragmatic modules that override list-returning built-ins, if you import the ":FIELDS" tag, you can access scalar or array package variables by the same names as the method calls by using a leading "h_". This still overrides your core functions, though.

POSIX

```
use POSIX;

# Round floats up or down to nearest integer.
$n = ceil($n);       # round up
$n = floor($n);      # round down

# Produces "2000-04-01" for today.
$datestr = strftime("%Y-%m-%d", localtime);

# Produces "Saturday 04/01/00" for same date.
$datestr = strftime("%A %D", localtime);

# Try new temporary filenames until we get one
# that didn't already exist; see also File::Temp
# on CPAN, or in v5.6.1.
do {
    $name = tmpnam();
} until sysopen(FH, $name, O_CREAT|O_EXCL|O_RDWR, 0666);

# Check for whether system has insecure chown giveaway.
if (sysconf(_PC_CHOWN_RESTRICTED)) {
    print "Hurray -- only the superuser may call chown\n";
}

# Find current system's uname info.
my($kernel, $hostname, $release, $version, $hardware) = uname();

use POSIX ":sys_wait_h";
while (($dead_pid = waitpid(-1, &WNOHANG)) > 0) {
    # Do something with $dead_pid if you want.
}

# Become new session/process-group leader (needed to create daemons
# unaffected by keyboard signals or exiting login shells).
setsid(0)            or die "setsid failed: $!";
```

Perl's POSIX module permits you to access all (or nearly all) the standard POSIX 1003.1 identifiers, plus a few more from ANSI C that we didn't know where else to put. This module provides more functions than any other. See its online documentation for the gory details or the *POSIX Programmer's Guide*, by Donald Lewine (O'Reilly, 1991).

Identifiers that are parameterless #defines in C, such as EINTR or O_NDELAY, are automatically exported into your namespace as constant functions. Functions that aren't normally available in Perl (like floor, ceil, strftime, uname, setsid, setlocale, and sysconf) are exported by default. Functions with the same name as a Perl built-in, like open, are not exported unless specifically requested, but most folks are likely to prefer fully qualified function names to distinguish POSIX::open from CORE::open.

A few functions are not implemented because they are C-specific. If you attempt to call these, they print a message telling you that they aren't implemented, and suggest using the Perl equivalent should one exist. For example, trying to access the setjmp function elicits the message "setjmp() is C-specific: use eval {} instead", and tmpfile tells you to "Use method IO::File::new_tmpfile()". (But as of 5.6.1 you should be using File::Temp instead.)

The POSIX module lets you get as close to the operating system (or those parts of the POSIX standard addresses, at least) as any C programmer could. This lets you do some phenomenally powerful and useful things, like blocking signals and controlling the terminal I/O settings. However, it also means that your code will end up looking quasi-C-like. By way of useful demonstration of how to get around input buffering, here's an example of a complete program for getting unbuffered, single-character input under any POSIX system:

```perl
#!/usr/bin/perl -w
use strict;
$| = 1;
for (1..4) {
    my $got;
    print "gimme: ";
    $got = getone();
    print "--> $got\n";
}
exit;

BEGIN {
    use POSIX qw(:termios_h);
    my ($term, $oterm, $echo, $noecho, $fd_stdin);
    $fd_stdin = fileno(STDIN);
    $term     = POSIX::Termios->new();
    $term->getattr($fd_stdin);
    $oterm    = $term->getlflag();
    $echo     = ECHO | ECHOK | ICANON;
    $noecho   = $oterm & ~$echo;
    sub cbreak {
        $term->setlflag($noecho);
        $term->setcc(VTIME, 1);
        $term->setattr($fd_stdin, TCSANOW);
    }
```

Modules

```
        sub cooked {
            $term->setlflag($oterm);
            $term->setcc(VTIME, 0);
            $term->setattr($fd_stdin, TCSANOW);
        }
        sub getone {
            my $key = "";
            cbreak();
            sysread(STDIN, $key, 1);
            cooked();
            return $key;
        }
    }
    END { cooked() }
```

The POSIX module's manpage provides a complete listing of which functions and constants it exports. It has so many that you'll often wind up importing only a subset of them, such as ":sys_wait_h", ":sys_stat_h", or ":termios_h". An example of blocking signals with the POSIX module is given in Chapter 16.

Safe

```
    use Safe;

    $sandbox = Safe->new();              # anonymous sandbox
    $sandbox = Safe->new("PackName");    # in that symbol table

    # Enable or disable opcodes by group or name.
    $sandbox->permit(qw(:base_core));
    $sandbox->permit_only(qw(:base_core :base_loop :base_mem));
    $sandbox->deny("die");

    # like do(), but in the sandbox
    $ok = $sandbox->rdo($filename);

    # like eval(), but in the sandbox
    $ok = $sandbox->reval($code);        # without 'use strict'
    $ok = $sandbox->reval($code, 1);     # with 'use strict'
```

The Safe module attempts to provide a restricted environment to protect the rest of the program from dangerous operations. It uses two different strategies to do this. Much as an anonymous FTP daemon's use of *chroot*(2) alters the view of the root of the filesystem, creating a compartment object with Safe->new("Pack-Name") alters that compartment's view of its own namespace. The compartment now sees as its root symbol table (main::) the symbol table that the rest of the program sees as PackName::. What looks like Frobnitz:: on the inside of the compartment is really PackName::Frobnitz:: on the outside. If you don't give an argument to the constructor, a random new package name is selected for you.

The second and more important facility that a `Safe` compartment provides is a way to limit code that is deemed legal within an `eval`. You can tweak the allowable opcode set (legal Perl operations) using method calls on your `Safe` object. Two methods are available to compile code in a `Safe` compartment: `rdo` ("restricted do") for files and `reval` ("restricted eval") for strings. These are like `do` on a filename and `eval` on a string but execute in a restricted namespace with limited opcodes. The first argument is the filename or string to compile, and the optional second argument is whether the code should be compiled under `use strict`.

This module is scheduled for a rewrite (we intend to isolate the sandbox into a different interpreter thread for additional safety), so be sure to check the `Safe` manpage for updates. See also Chapter 23.

Socket

```
use Socket;

$proto = getprotobyname('udp');
socket(SOCK, PF_INET, SOCK_DGRAM, $proto)
    or die "socket: $!";
$iaddr = gethostbyname('hishost.com');
$port  = getservbyname('time', 'udp');
$sin   = sockaddr_in($port, $iaddr);
send(SOCK, 0, 0, $sin)
    or die "send: $!";

$proto = getprotobyname('tcp');
socket(SOCK, PF_INET, SOCK_STREAM, $proto)
    or die "socket: $!";
$port = getservbyname('smtp', 'tcp');
$sin  = sockaddr_in($port,inet_aton("127.1"));
$sin  = sockaddr_in(7,inet_aton("localhost"));
$sin  = sockaddr_in(7,INADDR_LOOPBACK);
connect(SOCK,$sin)
    or die "connect: $!";

($port, $iaddr) = sockaddr_in(getpeername(SOCK));
$peer_host = gethostbyaddr($iaddr, AF_INET);
$peer_addr = inet_ntoa($iaddr);

$proto = getprotobyname('tcp');
socket(SOCK, PF_UNIX, SOCK_STREAM, $proto)
    or die "connect: $!";
unlink('/tmp/usock');   # XXX: intentionally ignore failure
$sun = sockaddr_un('/tmp/usock');
connect(SOCK,$sun)      or die "connect: $!";

use Socket qw(:DEFAULT :crlf);
# Now you can use CR(), LF(), and CRLF() or
# $CR, $LF, and $CRLF for line-endings.
```

The Socket module provides access to constants from the C library's *sys/socket.h* #include file to use with Perl's low-level socket functions. It also provides two functions, inet_aton and inet_ntoa, to convert between ASCII (like "127.0.0.1") and packed network representations of IP addresses, and two special packer/unpacker functions, sockaddr_in and sockaddr_un, which manipulate the binary socket addresses needed by those low-level calls. The :crlf import tag gives symbolic names for the various end-of-line conventions so you don't have to rely upon native interpretations of \r and \n, which vary. Most Internet protocols prefer CRLF but tolerate LF. The standard IO::Socket module provides a higher-level interface to TCP. See Chapter 16.

Symbol

```
use Symbol "delete_package";
delete_package("Foo::Bar");
print "deleted\n" unless exists $Foo::{"Bar::"};

use Symbol "gensym";
$sym1 = getsym();          # Returns new, anonymous typeglob.
$sym2 = getsym();          # Yet another new, anonymous typeglob.

package Demo;
use Symbol "qualify";
$sym = qualify("x");                # "Demo::x"
$sym = qualify("x", "Foo");         # "Foo::x"
$sym = qualify("Bar::x");           # "Bar::x"
$sym = qualify("Bar::x", "Foo");    # "Bar::x"

use Symbol "qualify_to_ref";
sub pass_handle(*) {
    my $fh = qualify_to_ref(shift, caller);
    ...
}
# Now you can call pass_handle with FH, "FH", *FH, or \*FH.
```

The Symbol module provides functions to help manipulate global names: type-globs, format names, filehandles, package symbol tables, and anything else you might want to name via a symbol table. The delete_package function completely clears out a package's namespace (effectively anonymizing any extra references to the symbol table's referents, including references from precompiled code). The gensym function returns an anonymous typeglob each time it is called. (This function isn't used so much these days, now that undefined scalars autovivify into proper filehandles when used as arguments to open, pipe, socket, and the like).

The qualify function takes a name that may or may not be completely package-qualified, and returns a name that is. If it needs to prepend the package name, it will use the name specified via the second argument (or if omitted, your current package name). The `qualify_to_ref` function works similarly, but produces a reference to the typeglob the symbol would represent. This is important in functions that accept filehandles, directory handles, or format names as arguments but don't require these to be passed by reference. For example, functions prototyped with a typeglob accept any of these forms, but don't automatically convert barewords to symbol table references. By converting that argument with `qualify_to_ref`, you can now use the supplied handle even with `strict` refs in effect. You may also `bless` it into objectdom, since it's a proper reference.

Sys::Hostname

```
use Sys::Hostname;
$hostname = hostname();
```

The `Sys::Hostname` module supplies just one function, `hostname`, which makes up for that fact by busting its behind to try to figure out what your current host calls itself. On those systems that support the standard *gethostname*(2) syscall, this is used, as it's the most efficient method.* On other systems, output from the standard *hostname*(1) is used. On still others, it calls the *uname*(3) function in your C library, which is also accessible as `POSIX::uname` from Perl. If these strategies all fail, more valiant attempts are made. Whatever your native system thinks makes sense, Perl tries its best to go along with it. On some systems, this hostname may not be fully qualified with the domain name; see the `Net::Domain` module from CPAN if you need that.

Another consideration is that `hostname` returns just one value, but your system could have multiple network interfaces configured, so you might not get back the name associated with the interface you're interested in if you're planning on using this module for certain sorts of socket programming. There are cases where you'll probably have to scrounge around in the output from the *ifconfig*(8) command, or your system's moral equivalent.

Sys::Syslog

```
use Sys::Syslog;                           # Misses setlogsock.
use Sys::Syslog qw(:DEFAULT setlogsock);   # Also gets setlogsock.

openlog($program, 'cons,pid', 'user');
syslog('info', 'this is another test');
syslog('mail|warning', 'this is a better test: %d', time());
closelog();
```

---

* Which is available directly as the unexported `Sys::Hostname::ghname` function, but don't tell anyone we told you.

```
    syslog('debug', 'this is the last test');

    setlogsock('unix');
    openlog("$program $$", 'ndelay', 'user');
    syslog('info', 'problem was %m'); # %m == $! in syslogese
    syslog('notice', 'fooprogram: this is really done');

    setlogsock("unix");              # "inet" or "unix"
    openlog("myprogname", $logopt, $facility);
    syslog($priority, $format, @args);
    $oldmask = setlogmask($mask_priority);
    closelog();
```

The `Sys::Syslog` module acts like your C library's *syslog*(3) function, sending messages to your system log daemon, *syslogd*(8). It is especially useful in daemons and other programs lacking a terminal to receive diagnostic output, or for security-minded programs that want to produce a more lasting record of their actions (or someone else's actions). Supported functions are:

openlog *IDENT, OPTLIST, FACILITY*
> Establishes a connection with your friendly syslog daemon. *IDENT* is the string to log messages under (like $0, your program name). *OPTLIST* is a string with comma-separated options such as "cons", "pid", and "ndelay". *FACILITY* is something like "auth", "daemon", "kern", "lpr", "mail", "news" or "user" for system programs, and one of "local0" .. "local7" for local ones. Further messages are logged using the given facility and identifying string.

syslog *PRIORITY, FORMAT, ARGS*
> Sends a message to the daemon using the given *PRIORITY*. The *FORMAT* is just like `printf`—filling in percent escapes using the following *ARGS*—except that following the conventions of the standard *syslog*(3) library function, the special escape "%m" interpolates `errno` (Perl's $! variable) at that point.

setlogsock *TYPE*
> *TYPE* must be either "inet" or "unix". Some systems' daemons do not by default pay attention to incoming Internet-domain syslog messages, so you might set this to "unix" instead, since it's not the default.

closelog
> Severs the connection with the daemon.

For this module to work prior to the 5.6.0 release of Perl, your sysadmin had to run *h2ph*(1) on your *sys/syslog.h* include file to create a *sys/syslog.ph* library file. However, this wasn't done by default at Perl installation time. Later releases now use an XS interface, so the *sys/syslog.ph* preparation is no longer needed.

Term::Cap

```
use Term::Cap;

$ospeed = eval {
    require POSIX;
    my $termios = POSIX::Termios->new();
    $termios->getattr;
    $termios->getospeed;
} || 9600;

$terminal = Term::Cap->Tgetent({ TERM => undef, OSPEED => $ospeed });
$terminal->Tputs('cl', 1, STDOUT);           # Clear screen.
$terminal->Tgoto('cm', $col, $row, STDOUT);  # Position cursor.
```

The Term::Cap module provides access to your system's *termcap*(3) library routines. See your system documentation for details. Systems that have only *terminfo*(5) and not *termcap*(5) will lose. (Many terminfo systems can emulate termcap.) However, on CPAN you can find a Term::Info module, as well as Term::ReadKey, Term::ANSIColor, and various Curses modules to help you with single-key input, colored output, or managing terminal screens, at a higher level than Term::Cap or Term::Info.

Text::Wrap

```
use Text::Wrap;  # Imports wrap().

@lines = (<<"EO_G&S" =~ /\S.*\S/g);

    This particularly rapid,
    unintelligible
    patter isn't generally
    heard,
    and if
    it is, it
    doesn't matter.

EO_G&S

$Text::Wrap::columns = 50;
print wrap(" " x 8, " " x 3, @lines), "\n";
```

This prints:

```
        This particularly rapid, unintelligible
   patter isn't generally heard, and if it is, it
   doesn't matter.
```

The Text::Wrap module implements a simple paragraph formatter. Its **wrap** function formats a single paragraph at a time by breaking lines at word boundaries. The first argument is the prefix prepended to the first line returned. The second argument is the prefix string used for all lines save the first. All remaining arguments are joined together using a newline as the separator and returned as one reformatted paragraph string. You'll have to figure out your terminal's width yourself, or at least specify what you want in `$Text::Wrap::columns`. Although one could use the `TIOCGWINSZ` `ioctl` call to figure out the number of columns, it would be easier for those not used to C programming to install the CPAN module `Term::ReadKey` and use that module's `GetTerminalSize` routine.

Time::Local

```
use Time::Local;
$time = timelocal($sec,$min,$hours,$mday,$mon,$year);
$time = timegm($sec,$min,$hours,$mday,$mon,$year);

$time = timelocal(50, 45, 3, 18, 0, 73);
print "Scalar localtime gives: ", scalar(localtime($time)), "\n";
$time += 28 * 365.2425 * 24 * 60 * 60;
print "Twenty-eight years of seconds later, it's now\n\t",
    scalar(localtime($time)), "\n";
```

This prints:

```
Scalar localtime gives: Thu Jan 18 03:45:50 1973
Twenty-eight years of seconds later, it's now
        Wed Jan 17 22:43:26 2001
```

The `Time::Local` module provides two functions, `timelocal` and `timegm`, that work like inverse functions for the standard `localtime` and `gmtime` functions, respectively. That is, they take a list of numeric values for the various components of what `localtime` returns in list context and figure out what input to `localtime` would produce those values. You might do this if you wanted to compare or run calculations on two different dates. Although these are not general-purpose functions for parsing dates and times, if you can arrange to have your input in the right format, they often suffice. As you can see from the example above, however, time has its oddities, and even simple calculations often fail to do the job intended due to leap years, leap seconds, and the phase of the moon. Two large but fully featured CPAN modules address these issues and more: `Date::Calc` and `Date::Manip`.

Time::localtime

```
use Time::localtime;
printf "Year is %d\n", localtime->year() + 1900;

$now = ctime();

use Time::localtime;
use File::stat;
$date_string = ctime(stat($file)->mtime);
```

This module's overrides the core `localtime` function, replacing it with a version that returns a `Time::tm` object (or `undef` on failure). The `Time::gmtime` module does the same thing, except it replaces the core `gmtime` function, instead. The returned object has methods that access the like-named structure field names from the C library's `struct tm` out of *time.h*; namely sec, min, hour, mday, mon, year, wday, yday, and isdst. The `ctime` function provides a way of getting at (the scalar sense of) the original `CORE::localtime` function. Note that the values returned are straight out of a `struct tm`, so they have the same ranges found there; see the example above for the correct way to produce a four-digit year. The `POSIX::strftime` function is even more useful for formatting dates and times in a variety of appealing styles.

User::grent

```
use User::grent;
$gr = getgrgid(0)            or die "No group zero";
if ($gr->name eq "wheel" && @{$gr->members} > 1) {
    print "gid zero name wheel, with other members";
}

$gr = getgr($whoever);  # Accepts both string or number.

use User::grent ':FIELDS';
getgrgid(0)                  or die "No group zero";
if ($gr_name eq "wheel" && @gr_members > 1) {
    print "gid zero name wheel, with other members";
}
```

This module's default exports override the core getgrent, getgruid, and getgrnam functions, replacing them with versions that return a `User::grent` object (or `undef` on failure). This object has methods that access the like-named structure fields from the C library's `struct group` out of *grp.h*; namely name, passwd, gid, and members (not mem as in C!). The first three return scalars, the last an array reference. You may also import the structure fields into your own namespace as regular variables using the ":FIELDS" import tag, although this still overrides your core functions. The variables (three scalars and an array) are named with a preceding "gr_". The getgr function is a simple frontend switch that forwards any numeric argument to getgrgid and any string argument to getgrnam.

User::pwent

```
use User::pwent;                # Default overrides built-ins only.
$pw = getpwnam("daemon")   or die "No daemon user";
if ($pw->uid == 1 && $pw->dir =~ m#^/(bin|tmp)?$# ) {
    print "gid 1 on root dir";
}
```

```
$pw = getpw($whoever);              # Accepts both string or number.
$real_shell = $pw->shell || '/bin/sh';
for (($fullname, $office, $workphone, $homephone) =
        split /\s*,\s*/, $pw->gecos)
{
    s/&/ucfirst(lc($pw->name))/ge;
}

use User::pwent qw(:FIELDS);        # Sets globals in current package.
getpwnam("daemon")          or die "No daemon user";
if ($pw_uid == 1 && $pw_dir =~ m#^/(bin|tmp)?$# ) {
    print "gid 1 on root dir";
}

use User::pwent qw/pw_has/;
if (pw_has(qw[gecos expire quota])) { .... }
if (pw_has("name uid gid passwd")) { .... }
printf "Your struct pwd supports [%s]\n", scalar pw_has();
```

By default, this module's exports override the core getpwent, getpwuid, and getpwnam functions, replacing them with versions that return a User::pwent object (or
undef on failure). It is often better to use the module than the core functions it
replaces, because the built-ins overload or even omit various slots in the return list
in the name of backward compatibility.

The returned object has methods that access the similarly named structure field
name from the C's passwd structure from *pwd.h*, stripped of their leading "pw_"
parts, namely name, passwd, uid, gid, change, age, quota, comment, class, gecos, dir,
shell, and expire. The passwd, gecos, and shell fields are tainted. You may also
import the structure fields into your own namespace as regular variables using the
":FIELDS" import tag, although this still overrides your core functions. Access these
fields as scalar variables named with a "pw_" prepended to the method name. The
getpw function is a simple frontend switch that forwards a numeric argument to
getpwuid and a string argument to getpwnam.

Perl believes that no machine ever has more than one of change, age, or quota
implemented, nor more than one of either comment or class. Some machines do
not support expire, gecos, or allegedly, even passwd. You may call these methods
no matter what machine you're on, but they'll return undef if unimplemented. See
passwd(5) and *getpwent*(3) for details.

You can determine whether these fields are implemented by asking the importable
pw_has function about them. It returns true if all parameters are supported fields
on the build platform or false if one or more were not, and it raises an exception if
you ask about a field whose name it doesn't recognize. If you pass no arguments,
it returns the list of fields your C library thinks are supported.

Interpretation of the gecos field varies between systems but often holds four comma-separated fields containing the user's full name, office location, work phone number, and home phone number. An & in the gecos field should be replaced by the user's properly capitalized login name. The shell field, if blank, must be assumed to be */bin/sh*, although Perl does not do this for you. The passwd is one-way hashed gobbledygook, not clear text, and may not be unhashed save by brute-force guessing. Secure systems often use a more secure hashing than DES. On systems supporting shadow password systems, Perl automatically returns the shadow password entry when called by a suitably empowered user, even if your underlying vendor-provided C library was too short-sighted to realize it should do this.

33

Diagnostic Messages

These messages are classified as follows (listed in increasing order of desperation):

Class	Meaning
(W)	A warning (optional)
(D)	A deprecation (optional)
(S)	A severe warning (mandatory)
(F)	A fatal error (trappable)
(P)	An internal error (panic) that you should never see (trappable)
(X)	A very fatal error (nontrappable)
(A)	An alien error message (not generated by Perl)

The majority of messages from the first three classifications above (W, D, and S) can be controlled using the warnings pragma or the **-w** and **-W** switches. If a message can be controlled by the warnings pragma, its warning category is given after the classification letter; for example, (W misc) indicates a miscellaneous warning. The warnings pragma is described in Chapter 31, *Pragmatic Modules*.

Warnings may be captured rather than printed by setting $SIG{__WARN__} to a reference to a routine that will be called on each warning. You can also capture control before a trappable error "dies" by setting $SIG{__DIE__} to a subroutine reference, but if you don't call die within the handler, the exception is still thrown when you return from it. In other words, you're not allowed to "de-fatalize" an exception that way. You must use eval for that.

Default warnings are always enabled unless they are explicitly disabled with the warnings pragma or the **-X** switch.

In the following messages, `%s` stands for an interpolated string that is determined only when the message is generated. (Similarly, `%d` stands for an interpolated number—think `printf` formats, but we use `%d` to mean a number in any base here.) Note that some messages *begin* with `%s`—which means that listing them alphabetically is problematical. You should search among these messages if the one you are looking for does not appear in the expected place. The symbols `"%-?@` sort before alphabetic characters, while `[` and `\` sort after.

If you decide a bug is a Perl bug and not your bug, you should try to reduce it to a minimal test case and then report it with the *perlbug* program that comes with Perl.

`"%s" variable %s masks earlier declaration in same %s`
> (W misc) A `my` or `our` variable has been redeclared in the current scope or statement, effectively eliminating all access to the previous instance. This is almost always a typographical error. Note that the earlier variable will still exist until the end of the scope or until all closure referents to it are destroyed.

`"my sub" not yet implemented`
> (F) Lexically scoped subroutines are not yet implemented. Don't try that yet.

`"my" variable %s can't be in a package`
> (F) Lexically scoped variables aren't in a package, so it doesn't make sense to try to declare one with a package qualifier in front. Use `local` if you want to localize a package variable.

`"no" not allowed in expression`
> (F) The `no` keyword is recognized and executed at compile time and returns no useful value.

`"our" variable %s redeclared`
> (W misc) You seem to have already declared the same global once before in the current lexical scope.

`"use" not allowed in expression`
> (F) The `use` keyword is recognized and executed at compile time and returns no useful value.

`'!' allowed only after types %s`
> (F) The `'!'` is allowed in `pack` and `unpack` only after certain types.

`'|' and '<' may not both be specified on command line`
> (F) This is an error peculiar to VMS. Perl does its own command-line redirection. It found that STDIN was a pipe and that you also tried to redirect STDIN using <. Only one STDIN stream to a customer, please.

'|' and '>' may not both be specified on command line

(F) This is an error peculiar to VMS. Perl does its own command-line redirection and thinks you tried to redirect STDOUT both to a file and into a pipe to another command. You need to choose one or the other, though nothing's stopping you from piping into a program or Perl script that splits the output into two streams, such as:

```
open(OUT,">$ARGV[0]") or die "Can't write to $ARGV[0]: $!";
while (<STDIN>) {
    print;
    print OUT;
}
close OUT;
```

/ cannot take a count

(F) You had an unpack template indicating a counted-length string, but you have also specified an explicit size for the string.

/ must be followed by a, A, or Z

(F) You had an unpack template indicating a counted-length string, which must be followed by one of the letters a, A or Z to indicate what sort of string is to be unpacked.

/ must be followed by a*, A*, or Z*

(F) You had a pack template indicating a counted-length string. Currently, the only things that can have their length counted are a*, A* or Z*.

/ must follow a numeric type

(F) You had an unpack template that contained a #, but this did not follow some numeric unpack specification.

% may only be used in unpack

(F) You can't pack a string by supplying a checksum, because the checksumming process loses information, and you can't go the other way.

Repeat count in pack overflows

(F) You can't specify a repeat count so large that it overflows your signed integers.

Repeat count in unpack overflows

(F) You can't specify a repeat count so large that it overflows your signed integers.

/%s/: Unrecognized escape \\%c passed through

(W regexp) You used a backslash-character combination that is not recognized by Perl. This combination appears in an interpolated variable or a '-delimited regular expression. The character was understood literally.

`/%s/: Unrecognized escape \\%c in character class passed through`

(W regexp) You used a backslash-character combination that is not recognized by Perl inside character classes. The character was understood literally.

`/%s/ should probably be written as "%s"`

(W syntax) You have used a pattern where Perl expected to find a string, as in the first argument to `join`. Perl will treat the true or false result of matching the pattern against `$_` as the string, which is probably not what you had in mind.

`%s (...) interpreted as function`

(W syntax) You've run afoul of the rule that says that any list operator followed by parentheses turns into a function, with all the list operators arguments found inside the parentheses.

`%s() called too early to check prototype`

(W prototype) You've called a function that has a prototype before the parser saw a definition or declaration for it, and Perl could not check that the call conforms to the prototype. You need to either add an early prototype declaration for the subroutine in question, or move the subroutine definition ahead of the call to get proper prototype checking. Alternatively, if you are certain that you're calling the function correctly, you may put an ampersand before the name to avoid the warning.

`%s argument is not a HASH or ARRAY element`

(F) The argument to `exists` must be a hash or array element, such as:

```
$foo{$bar}
$ref->{"susie"}[12]
```

`%s argument is not a HASH or ARRAY element or slice`

(F) The argument to `delete` must be either a hash or array element, such as:

```
$foo{$bar}
$ref->{"susie"}[12]
```

or a hash or array slice, such as:

```
@foo[$bar, $baz, $xyzzy]
@{$ref->[12]}{"susie", "queue"}
```

`%s argument is not a subroutine name`

(F) The argument to `exists` for `exists &sub` must be a subroutine name, and not a subroutine call. `exists &sub()` will generate this error.

`%s did not return a true value`

> (F) A required (or used) file must return a true value to indicate that it compiled correctly and ran its initialization code correctly. It's traditional to end such a file with a `1;`, though any true value would do.

`%s found where operator expected`

> (S) The Perl lexer knows whether to expect a term or an operator. If it sees what it knows to be a term when it was expecting to see an operator, it gives you this warning. Usually it indicates that an operator or delimiter was omitted, such as a semicolon.

`%s had compilation errors`

> (F) The final summary message when a *perl -c* fails.

`%s has too many errors`

> (F) The parser has given up trying to parse the program after 10 errors. Further error messages would likely be uninformative.

`%s matches null string many times`

> (W regexp) The pattern you've specified would be an infinite loop if the regular expression engine didn't specifically check for that.

`%s never introduced`

> (S internal) The symbol in question was declared but somehow went out of scope before it could possibly have been used.

`%s package attribute may clash with future reserved word: %s`

> (W reserved) A lowercase attribute name was used that had a package-specific handler. That name might have a meaning to Perl itself some day, even though it doesn't yet. Perhaps you should use a mixed-case attribute name, instead.

`%s syntax OK`

> (F) The final summary message when a *perl -c* succeeds.

`%s: Command not found`

> (A) You've accidentally run your script through *csh* instead of Perl. Check the `#!` line, or manually feed your script into Perl yourself with *perl scriptname*.

`%s: Expression syntax`

> (A) You've accidentally run your script through *csh* instead of Perl. Check the `#!` line, or manually feed your script into Perl yourself with *perl scriptname*.

`%s: Undefined variable`

> (A) You've accidentally run your script through *csh* instead of Perl. Check the `#!` line, or manually feed your script into Perl yourself with *perl scriptname*.

`%s: not found`

(A) You've accidentally run your script through the Bourne shell instead of Perl. Check the `#!` line, or manually feed your script Perl yourself with *perl scriptname.*

`(in cleanup) %s`

(W misc) This prefix usually indicates that a DESTROY method raised the indicated exception. Since destructors are usually called by the system at arbitrary points during execution, and often a vast number of times, the warning is issued only once for any number of failures that would otherwise result in the same message being repeated.

Failure of user callbacks dispatched using the G_KEEPERR flag could also result in this warning. See *perlcall*(1).

`(Missing semicolon on previous line?)`

(S) This is an educated guess made in conjunction with the message "`%s found where operator expected.`" Don't automatically put a semicolon on the previous line just because you saw this message.

`-P not allowed for setuid/setgid script`

(F) The script would have to be opened by the C preprocessor by name, which provides a race condition that breaks security.

`-T and -B not implemented on filehandles`

(F) Perl can't peek at the standard I/O buffer of filehandles when it doesn't know about your kind of standard I/O. You'll have to use a filename instead.

`-p destination: %s`

(F) An error occurred during the implicit output invoked by the **-p** command-line switch. (This output goes to STDOUT unless you've redirected it with `select`.)

`500 Server error`

See Server error.

`?+* follows nothing in regexp`

(F) You started a regular expression with a quantifier. Backslash it if you meant it literally.

`@ outside of string`

(F) You had a pack template that specified an absolute position outside the string being unpacked.

`<> should be quotes`

(F) You wrote `require <file>` when you should have written `require 'file'`.

`\1 better written as $1`

(W syntax) Outside of patterns, backreferences live on as variables. The use of backslashes is grandfathered on the righthand side of a substitution, but stylistically it's better to use the variable form because other Perl programmers will expect it, and it works better if there are more than nine backreferences.

`accept() on closed socket %s`

(W closed) You tried to do an accept on a closed socket. Did you forget to check the return value of your `socket` call?

`Allocation too large: %lx`

(X) You can't allocate more than 64K on an MS-DOS machine.

`Applying %s to %s will act on scalar(%s)`

(W misc) The pattern match (`//`), substitution (`s///`), and transliteration (`tr///`) operators work on scalar values. If you apply one of them to an array or a hash, it will convert the array or hash to a scalar value—the length of an array or the population info of a hash—and then work on that scalar value. This is probably not what you meant to do.

`Arg too short for msgsnd`

(F) `msgsnd` requires a string at least as long as `sizeof(long)`.

`Ambiguous use of %s resolved as %s`

(W ambiguous|S) You said something that may not be interpreted the way you thought. Normally it's pretty easy to disambiguate it by supplying a missing quote, operator, pair of parentheses, or declaration.

`Ambiguous call resolved as CORE::%s(), qualify as such or use &`

(W ambiguous) A subroutine you have declared has the same name as a Perl keyword, and you have used the name without qualification for calling one or the other. Perl decided to call the built-in because the subroutine is not imported.

To force interpretation as a subroutine call, either put an ampersand before the subroutine name or qualify the name with its package. Alternatively, you can import the subroutine (or pretend that it's imported with the `use subs` pragma).

To silently interpret it as the Perl operator, use the `CORE::` prefix on the operator (e.g., `CORE::log($x)`) or declare the subroutine to be an object method.

`Args must match #! line`

(F) The setuid emulator requires that the arguments Perl was invoked with match the arguments specified on the `#!` line. Since some systems impose a one-argument limit on the `#!` line, try combining switches; for example, turn `-w -U` into `-wU`.

Argument "%s" isn't numeric

> (W numeric) The indicated string was fed as an argument to an operator that expected a numeric value instead. If you're fortunate, the message will identify which operator was so unfortunate.

Array @%s missing the @ in argument %d of %s()

> (D deprecated) Really old Perls let you omit the @ on array names in some spots. This is now heavily deprecated.

assertion botched: %s

> (P) The malloc package that comes with Perl had an internal failure.

Assertion failed: file "%s"

> (P) A general assertion failed. The file in question must be examined.

Assignment to both a list and a scalar

> (F) If you assign to a conditional operator, the second and third arguments must either both be scalars or both be lists. Otherwise, Perl won't know which context to supply to the right side.

Attempt to free non-arena SV: 0x%lx

> (P internal) All SV objects are supposed to be allocated from arenas that will be garbage collected on exit. An SV was discovered to be outside any of those arenas.

Attempt to free nonexistent shared string

> (P internal) Perl maintains a reference-counted internal table of strings to optimize the storage and access of hash keys and other strings. This message indicates that someone tried to decrement the reference count of a string that can no longer be found in the table.

Attempt to free temp prematurely

> (W debugging) Mortalized values are supposed to be freed by the internal free_tmps routine. This message indicates that something else is freeing the SV before the free_tmps routine gets a chance, which means that the free_tmps routine will be freeing an unreferenced scalar when it does try to free it.

Attempt to free unreferenced glob pointers

> (P internal) The reference counts got screwed up on symbol aliases.

Attempt to free unreferenced scalar

> (W internal) Perl went to decrement the reference count of a scalar to see if it would go to 0, and discovered that it had already gone to 0 earlier and should have been freed and, in fact, probably was freed. This could indicate that SvREFCNT_dec was called too many times, or that SvREFCNT_inc was called too few times, or that the SV was mortalized when it shouldn't have been, or that memory has been corrupted.

`Attempt to join self`

(F) You tried to join a thread from within itself, which is an impossible task. You may be joining the wrong thread, or you may need to move the join to some other thread.

`Attempt to pack pointer to temporary value`

(W pack) You tried to pass a temporary value (like the result of a function, or a computed expression) to the p template of pack template. This means the result contains a pointer to a location that could become invalid anytime, even before the end of the current statement. Use literals or global values as arguments to the p template of pack to avoid this warning.

`Attempt to use reference as lvalue in substr`

(W substr) You supplied a reference as the first argument to substr used as an lvalue, which is pretty strange. Perhaps you forgot to dereference it first.

`Bad arg length for %s, is %d, should be %d`

(F) You passed a buffer of the wrong size to one of msgctl, semctl or shmctl. In C parlance, the correct sizes are, respectively, sizeof(struct msqid_ds *), sizeof(struct semid_ds *), and sizeof(struct shmid_ds *).

`Bad filehandle: %s`

(F) A symbol was passed to something wanting a filehandle, but the symbol has no filehandle associated with it. Perhaps you didn't do an open, or did it in another package.

`Bad free() ignored`

(S malloc) An internal routine called free on something that had never been malloced in the first place. Mandatory, but can be disabled by setting environment variable PERL_BADFREE to 1.

This message can be seen quite often with DB_File on systems with "hard" dynamic linking, like AIX and OS/2. It's a bug in Berkeley DB.

`Bad hash`

(P) One of the internal hash routines was passed a null HV pointer.

`Bad index while coercing array into hash`

(F) The index looked up in the hash found as the 0th element of a pseudo-hash is not legal. Index values must be 1 or greater.

`Bad name after %s::`

(F) You started to name a symbol by using a package prefix and then didn't finish the symbol. In particular, you can't interpolate outside of quotes, so:

```
$var = 'myvar';
$sym = mypack::$var;
```

is not the same as:

```
$var = 'myvar';
$sym = "mypack::$var";
```

Bad realloc() ignored

(S malloc) An internal routine called `realloc` on something that had never been `malloced` in the first place. Mandatory, but can be disabled by setting environment variable `PERL_BADFREE` to 1.

Bad symbol for array

(P) An internal request asked to add an array entry to something that wasn't a symbol table entry.

Bad symbol for filehandle

(P) An internal request asked to add a filehandle entry to something that wasn't a symbol table entry.

Bad symbol for hash

(P) An internal request asked to add a hash entry to something that wasn't a symbol table entry.

Badly placed ()'s

(A) You've accidentally run your script through *csh* instead of Perl. Check the `#!` line, or manually feed your script into Perl yourself with *perl scriptname*.

Bareword "%s" not allowed while "strict subs" in use

(F) With `strict subs` in use, a bareword is only allowed as a subroutine identifier, in curly brackets or to the left of the => symbol. Perhaps you need to predeclare a subroutine?

Bareword "%s" refers to nonexistent package

(W bareword) You used a qualified bareword of the form `Foo::`, but the compiler saw no other uses of that namespace before that point. Perhaps you need to predeclare a package?

Bareword found in conditional

(W bareword) The compiler found a bareword where it expected a conditional, which often indicates that an `||` or `&&` was parsed as part of the last argument of the previous construct, for example:

```
open FOO || die;
```

It may also indicate a misspelled constant that has been interpreted as a bareword:

```
use constant TYPO => 1;
if (TYOP) { print "foo" }
```

The `strict` pragma is useful in avoiding such errors.

`BEGIN failed--compilation aborted`

(F) An untrapped exception was raised while executing a `BEGIN` subroutine. Compilation stops immediately and the interpreter is exited.

`BEGIN not safe after errors--compilation aborted`

(F) Perl found a `BEGIN` subroutine (or a use directive, which implies a `BEGIN`) after one or more compilation errors had already occurred. Since the intended environment for the `BEGIN` could not be guaranteed (due to the errors), and since subsequent code likely depends on its correct operation, Perl just gave up.

`Binary number > 0b11111111111111111111111111111111 non-portable`

(W portable) The binary number you specified is larger than $2**32-1$ (4,294,967,295) and therefore nonportable between systems.

`bind() on closed socket %s`

(W closed) You tried to do a `bind` on a closed socket. Did you forget to check the return value of your `socket` call?

`Bit vector size > 32 non-portable`

(W portable) Using bit vector sizes larger than 32 is nonportable.

`Bizarre copy of %s in %s`

(P) Perl detected an attempt to copy an internal value that is not copiable.

`Buffer overflow in prime_env_iter: %s`

(W internal) A warning peculiar to VMS. While Perl was preparing to iterate over `%ENV`, it encountered a logical name or symbol definition which was too long, so it was truncated to the string shown.

`Callback called exit`

(F) A subroutine invoked from an external package via `call_sv` exited by calling `exit`.

`Can't "goto" out of a pseudo block`

(F) A `goto` statement was executed to jump out of what might look like a block, except that it isn't a proper block. This usually occurs if you tried to jump out of a sort block or subroutine, which is a no-no.

`Can't "goto" into the middle of a foreach loop`

(F) A `goto` statement was executed to jump into the middle of a foreach loop. You can't get there from here.

`Can't "last" outside a loop block`

(F) A `last` statement was executed to break out of the current block, except that there's this itty-bitty problem called there isn't a current block. Note that an `if` or `else` block doesn't count as a "loopish" block, nor does a block given to `sort`, `map`, or `grep`. You can usually double the curlies to get the same effect, though, because the inner curlies will be considered a block that loops once.

`Can't "next" outside a loop block`

    (F) A `next` statement was executed to reiterate the current block, but there isn't a current block. Note that an `if` or `else` block doesn't count as a "loopish" block, nor does a block given to `sort`, `map`, or `grep`. You can usually double the curlies to get the same effect though, because the inner curlies will be considered a block that loops once.

`Can't read CRTL environ`

    (S) This is a warning peculiar to VMS. Perl tried to read an element of `%ENV` from the CRTL's internal environment array and discovered the array was missing. You need to figure out where your CRTL misplaced its environ or define `PERL_ENV_TABLES` (see *perlvms*(1)) so that the environ array is not searched.

`Can't "redo" outside a loop block`

    (F) A `redo` statement was executed to restart the current block, but there isn't a current block. Note that an `if` or `else` block doesn't count as a "loopish" block, nor does a block given to `sort`, `map`, or `grep`. You can usually double the curlies to get the same effect though, because the inner curlies will be considered a block that loops once.

`Can't bless non-reference value`

    (F) Only hard references may be blessed. This is how Perl "enforces" encapsulation of objects.

`Can't break at that line`

    (S internal) This warning is intended to be printed only while running within the debugger, indicating the line number specified wasn't the location of a statement that could be stopped at.

`Can't call method "%s" in empty package "%s"`

    (F) You called a method correctly, and it correctly indicated a package functioning as a class, but that package doesn't have *anything* defined in it, let alone methods.

`Can't call method "%s" on unblessed reference`

    (F) A method call must know in what package it's supposed to run. It ordinarily finds this out from the object reference you supply, but you didn't supply an object reference in this case. A reference isn't an object reference until it has been blessed.

`Can't call method "%s" without a package or object reference`

    (F) You used the syntax of a method call, but the slot filled by the object reference or package name contains an expression that returns a defined value that is neither an object reference nor a package name. Something like this will reproduce the error:

```
$BADREF = 42;
process $BADREF 1,2,3;
$BADREF->process(1,2,3);
```

Can't call method "%s" on an undefined value

(F) You used the syntax of a method call, but the slot filled by the object reference or package name contains an undefined value. Something like this will reproduce the error:

```
$BADREF = undef;
process $BADREF 1,2,3;
$BADREF->process(1,2,3);
```

Can't chdir to %s

(F) You called *perl -x/foo/bar*, but */foo/bar* is not a directory that you can chdir to, possibly because it doesn't exist.

Can't check filesystem of script "%s" for nosuid

(P) For some reason you can't check the filesystem of the script for nosuid.

Can't coerce %s to integer in %s

(F) Certain types of SVs, in particular symbol table entries (typeglobs), can't be forced to stop being what they are. So you can't say things like:

```
*foo += 1;
```

You *can* say:

```
$foo = *foo;
$foo += 1;
```

but then $foo no longer contains a glob.

Can't coerce %s to number in %s

(F) Certain types of SVs, in particular symbol table entries (typeglobs), can't be forced to stop being what they are.

Can't coerce %s to string in %s

(F) Certain types of SVs, in particular symbol table entries (typeglobs), can't be forced to stop being what they are.

Can't coerce array into hash

(F) You used an array where a hash was expected, but the array has no information on how to map from keys to array indices. You can do that only with arrays that have a hash reference at index 0.

Can't create pipe mailbox

(P) This is an error peculiar to VMS. The process is suffering from exhausted quotas or other plumbing problems.

`Can't declare class for non-scalar %s in "%s"`

(S) Currently, only scalar variables can declared with a specific class qualifier in a `my` or `our` declaration. The semantics may be extended for other types of variables in future.

`Can't declare %s in "%s"`

(F) Only scalar, array, and hash variables may be declared as `my` or `our` variables. They must have ordinary identifiers as names.

`Can't do inplace edit on %s: %s`

(S inplace) The creation of the new file failed for the indicated reason.

`Can't do inplace edit without backup`

(F) You're on a system such as MS-DOS that gets confused if you try reading from a deleted (but still opened) file. You have to say *-i.bak*, or some such.

`Can't do inplace edit: %s would not be unique`

(S inplace) Your filesystem does not support filenames longer than 14 characters and Perl was unable to create a unique filename during inplace editing with the **-i** switch. The file was ignored.

`Can't do inplace edit: %s is not a regular file`

(S inplace) You tried to use the **-i** switch on a special file, such as a file in */dev*, or a FIFO. The file was ignored.

`Can't do setegid!`

(P) The `setegid` call failed for some reason in the setuid emulator of *suidperl*.

`Can't do seteuid!`

(P) The setuid emulator of *suidperl* failed for some reason.

`Can't do setuid`

(F) This typically means that ordinary *perl* tried to `exec` *suidperl* to do setuid emulation, but couldn't `exec` it. It looks for a name of the form *sperl5.000* in the same directory that the perl executable resides under the name *perl5.000*, typically */usr/local/bin* on Unix machines. If the file is there, check the execute permissions. If it isn't, ask your sysadmin why not.

`Can't do waitpid with flags`

(F) This machine doesn't have either `waitpid` or `wait4`, so only `waitpid` without flags is emulated.

`Can't do {n,m} with n > m`

(F) Minima must be less than or equal to maxima. If you really want your regexp to match something 0 times, just use {0}.

`Can't emulate -%s on #! line`

(F) The `#!` line specifies a switch that doesn't make sense at this point. For example, it would be kind of silly to put a **-x** on the `#!` line.

`Can't exec "%s": %s`

(W exec) A system, exec, or piped open call could not execute the named program for the indicated reason. Typical reasons include the permissions were wrong on the file, the file wasn't found in $ENV{PATH}, the executable in question was compiled for another architecture, or the `#!` line in a script points to an interpreter that can't be run for similar reasons. (Or maybe your system doesn't support `#!` at all.)

`Can't exec %s`

(F) Perl was trying to execute the indicated program for you because that's what the `#!` line said to do. If that's not what you wanted, you may need to mention perl on the `#!` line somewhere.

`Can't execute %s`

(F) You used the **-S** switch, but the copies of the script to execute found in the PATH did not have correct permissions.

`Can't find %s on PATH, '.' not in PATH`

(F) You used the **-S** switch, but the script to execute could not be found in the PATH, or at least not with the correct permissions. The script exists in the current directory, but PATH prohibits running it.

`Can't find %s on PATH`

(F) You used the **-S** switch, but the script to execute could not be found in the PATH.

`Can't find label %s`

(F) You said to goto a label that isn't mentioned anywhere that it's possible for us to go to.

`Can't find string terminator %s anywhere before EOF`

(F) Perl strings can stretch over multiple lines. This message means that the closing delimiter was omitted. Because bracketed quotes count nesting levels, the following is missing its final parenthesis:

```
print q(The character '(' starts a side comment.);
```

If you're getting this error from a here document, you may have included unseen whitespace before or after your closing tag. A good programmer's editor will have a way to help you find these characters.

`Can't fork`

(F) A fatal error occurred trying to fork.

`Can't get filespec - stale stat buffer?`

(S) This warning is peculiar to VMS. This arises because of the difference between access checks under VMS and under the Unix model Perl assumes. Under VMS, access checks are done by filename, rather than by bits in the stat buffer, so that ACLs and other protections can be taken into account. Unfortunately, Perl assumes that the stat buffer contains all the necessary information and passes it, instead of the filespec, to the access-checking routine. It will try to retrieve the filespec using the device name and FID present in the stat buffer, but if you have made a subsequent call to the CRTL stat routine, this won't work because the device name is overwritten with each call. If this warning appears, the name lookup failed and the access-checking routine gave up and returned false, just to be conservative. (Note: the access-checking routine knows about the Perl stat operator and file tests, so you shouldn't ever see this warning in response to a Perl command; it arises only if some internal code takes stat buffers lightly.)

`Can't get pipe mailbox device name`

(P) This error is peculiar to VMS. After creating a mailbox to act as a pipe, Perl can't retrieve its name for later use.

`Can't get SYSGEN parameter value for MAXBUF`

(P) This error is peculiar to VMS. Perl asked $GETSYI how big you want your mailbox buffers to be, and it didn't get an answer.

`Can't goto subroutine outside a subroutine`

(F) The deeply magical goto *SUBROUTINE* call can only replace one subroutine call for another. It can't manufacture one out of whole cloth. In general, you should be calling it out of only an AUTOLOAD routine anyway.

`Can't goto subroutine from an eval-string`

(F) The goto *SUBROUTINE* call can't be used to jump out of an eval string. (You can use it to jump out of an eval *BLOCK*, but you probably don't want to.)

`Can't ignore signal CHLD, forcing to default`

(W signal) Perl has detected that it is being run with the SIGCHLD signal (sometimes known as SIGCLD) disabled. Since disabling this signal will interfere with proper determination of exit status of child processes, Perl has reset the signal to its default value. This situation typically indicates that the parent program under which Perl may be running (e.g., *cron*) is being very careless.

Can't localize through a reference

(F) You said something like `local $$ref`, which Perl can't currently handle because when it goes to restore the old value of whatever `$ref` pointed to after the scope of the `local` is finished, it can't be sure that `$ref` will still be a reference.

Can't localize lexical variable %s

(F) You used `local` on a variable name that was previously declared as a lexical variable using `my`. This is not allowed. If you want to localize a package variable of the same name, qualify it with the package name.

Can't localize pseudohash element

(F) You said something like `local $ar->{'key'}`, where `$ar` is a reference to a pseudohash. That hasn't been implemented yet, but you can get a similar effect by localizing the corresponding array element directly—`local $ar->[$ar->[0]{'key'}]`.

Can't locate auto/%s.al in @INC

(F) A function (or method) was called in a package that allows autoloading, but there is no function to autoload. Most probable causes are a misprint in a function/method name or a failure to `AutoSplit` the file, say, by doing `make install`.

Can't locate %s

(F) You said to `do` (or `require`, or `use`) a file that couldn't be found. Perl looks for the file in all the locations mentioned in `@INC`, unless the filename included the full path to the file. Perhaps you need to set the `PERL5LIB` or `PERL5OPT` environment variable to say where the extra library is, or maybe the script needs to add the library name to `@INC`. Or maybe you just misspelled the name of the file.

Can't locate object method "%s" via package "%s"

(F) You called a method correctly, and it correctly indicated a package functioning as a class, but that package doesn't define that particular method, nor does any of its base classes.

Can't locate package %s for @%s::ISA

(W syntax) The `@ISA` array contained the name of another package that doesn't seem to exist.

Can't make list assignment to \%ENV on this system

(F) List assignment to `%ENV` is not supported on some systems, notably VMS.

Can't modify %s in %s

(F) You aren't allowed to assign to the item indicated or otherwise try to change it, such as with an autoincrement.

`Can't modify non-lvalue subroutine call`

(F) Subroutines meant to be used in lvalue context should be declared as such.

`Can't modify nonexistent substring`

(P) The internal routine that does assignment to a `substr` was handed a NULL.

`Can't msgrcv to read-only var`

(F) The target of a `msgrcv` must be modifiable to be used as a receive buffer.

`Can't open %s: %s`

(S inplace) The implicit opening of a file through use of the `<>` filehandle, either implicitly under the **-n** or **-p** command-line switches or explicitly, failed for the indicated reason. Usually this is because you don't have read permission for a file which you named on the command line.

`Can't open bidirectional pipe`

(W pipe) You tried to say `open(CMD, "|cmd|")`, which is not supported. You can try any of several modules in the Perl library to do this, such as `IPC::Open2`. Alternatively, direct the pipe's output to a file using >, and then read it in under a different filehandle.

`Can't open error file %s as stderr`

(F) This is an error peculiar to VMS. Perl does its own command-line redirection, and it couldn't open the file specified after 2> or 2>> on the command line for writing.

`Can't open input file %s as stdin`

(F) This is an error peculiar to VMS. Perl does its own command-line redirection, and it couldn't open the file specified after < on the command line for reading.

`Can't open output file %s as stdout`

(F) This is an error peculiar to VMS. Perl does its own command-line redirection, and it couldn't open the file specified after > or >> on the command line for writing.

`Can't open output pipe (name: %s)`

(P) This is an error peculiar to VMS. Perl does its own command-line redirection, and it couldn't open the pipe into which to send data destined for STD-OUT.

`Can't open perl script "%s": %s`

(F) The script you specified can't be opened for the indicated reason.

`Can't redefine active sort subroutine %s`

(F) Perl optimizes the internal handling of sort subroutines and keeps pointers into them. You tried to redefine one such sort subroutine when it was currently active, which is not allowed. If you really want to do this, you should write `sort { &func } @x` instead of `sort func @x`.

`Can't remove %s: %s, skipping file`

(S inplace) You requested an inplace edit without creating a backup file. Perl was unable to remove the original file to replace it with the modified file. The file was left unmodified.

`Can't rename %s to %s: %s, skipping file`

(S inplace) The rename done by the **-i** switch failed for some reason, probably because you don't have write permission to the directory.

`Can't reopen input pipe (name: %s) in binary mode`

(P) An error peculiar to VMS. Perl thought STDIN was a pipe, and tried to reopen it to accept binary data. Alas, it failed.

`Can't reswap uid and euid`

(P) The `setreuid` call failed for some reason in the setuid emulator of *suidperl*.

`Can't return outside a subroutine`

(F) The `return` statement was executed in mainline code, that is, where there was no subroutine call to return out of.

`Can't return %s from lvalue subroutine`

(F) Perl detected an attempt to return illegal lvalues (such as temporary or readonly values) from a subroutine used as an lvalue. This is not allowed.

`Can't stat script "%s"`

(P) For some reason, you can't `fstat` the script even though you have it open already. Bizarre.

`Can't swap uid and euid`

(P) The `setreuid` call failed for some reason in the setuid emulator of *suidperl*.

`Can't take log of %g`

(F) For ordinary real numbers, you can't take the logarithm of a negative number or zero. There's a `Math::Complex` package that comes standard with Perl, though, if you really want to do that for the negative numbers.

`Can't take sqrt of %g`

(F) For ordinary real numbers, you can't take the square root of a negative number. There's a `Math::Complex` package that comes standard with Perl, though, if you really want to do that.

`Can't undef active subroutine`

> (F) You can't undefine a routine that's currently running. You can, however, redefine it while it's running, and you can even `undef` the redefined subroutine while the old routine is running. Go figure.

`Can't unshift`

> (F) You tried to unshift an "unreal" array that can't be `unshifted`, such as the main Perl stack.

`Can't upgrade that kind of scalar`

> (P) The internal `sv_upgrade` routine adds "members" to an SV, making it into a more specialized kind of SV. The top several SV types are so specialized, however, that they cannot be interconverted. This message indicates that such a conversion was attempted.

`Can't upgrade to undef`

> (P) The undefined SV is the bottom of the totem pole, in the scheme of upgradability. Upgrading to `undef` indicates an error in the code calling `sv_upgrade`.

`Can't use %%! because Errno.pm is not available`

> (F) The first time the `%!` hash is used, Perl automatically loads the `Errno` module. The `Errno` module is expected to tie the `%!` hash to provide symbolic names for `$!` errno values.

`Can't use "my %s" in sort comparison`

> (F) The global variables `$a` and `$b` are reserved for sort comparisons. You mentioned `$a` or `$b` in the same line as the `<=>` or `cmp` operator, and the variable had earlier been declared as a lexical variable. Either qualify the sort variable with the package name, or rename the lexical variable.

`Bad evalled substitution pattern`

> (F) You've used the `/e` switch to evaluate the replacement for a substitution, but Perl found a syntax error in the code to evaluate, most likely an unexpected right brace }.

`Can't use %s for loop variable`

> (F) Only a simple scalar variable may be used as a loop variable on a `foreach`.

`Can't use %s ref as %s ref`

> (F) You've mixed up your reference types. You have to dereference a reference of the type needed. You can use the `ref` function to test the type of the reference, if need be.

`Can't use \%c to mean $%c in expression`

> (W syntax) In an ordinary expression, backslash is a unary operator that creates a reference to its argument. The use of backslash to indicate a backreference to a matched substring is valid only as part of a regular expression

pattern. Trying to do this in ordinary Perl code produces a value that prints out looking like SCALAR(0xdecaf). Use the $1 form instead.

Can't use bareword ("%s") as %s ref while "strict refs" in use

(F) Only hard references are allowed by strict refs. Symbolic references are disallowed.

Can't use string ("%s") as %s ref while "strict refs" in use

(F) Only hard references are allowed by strict refs. Symbolic references are disallowed.

Can't use an undefined value as %s reference

(F) A value used as either a hard reference or a symbolic reference must be a defined value. This helps to delurk some insidious errors.

Can't use global %s in "my"

(F) You tried to declare a magical variable as a lexical variable. This is not allowed because the magic can be tied to only one location (namely the global variable) and it would be incredibly confusing to have variables in your program that looked like magical variables but weren't.

Can't use subscript on %s

(F) The compiler tried to interpret a bracketed expression as a subscript. But to the left of the brackets was an expression that didn't look like an array reference, or anything else subscriptable.

Can't weaken a nonreference

(F) You attempted to weaken something that was not a reference. Only references can be weakened.

Can't x= to read-only value

(F) You tried to repeat a constant value (often the undefined value) with an assignment operator, which implies modifying the value itself. Perhaps you need to copy the value to a temporary variable, and repeat that.

Can't find an opnumber for "%s"

(F) A string of a form CORE::*word* was given to prototype, but there is no built-in with the name *word*.

Can't resolve method '%s' overloading '%s' in package '%s'

(F|P) An error occurred when resolving overloading specified by a method name (as opposed to a subroutine reference): no such method callable via the package. If the method name is ???, this is an internal error.

Character class [:%s:] unknown

(F) The class in the character class [: :] syntax is unknown.

Diagnostics

Character class syntax [%s] belongs inside character classes

(W unsafe) The character class constructs [: :], [= =], and [. .] go *inside* character classes, for example: /[012[:alpha:]345]/. Note that the [= =] and [. .] constructs are not currently implemented; they are simply placeholders for future extensions.

Character class syntax [. .] is reserved for future extensions

(W regexp) Within regular expression character classes ([]), the syntax beginning with [. and ending with .] is reserved for future extensions. If you need to represent those character sequences inside a regular expression character class, just quote the square brackets with the backslash: \[. and .\].

Character class syntax [= =] is reserved for future extensions

(W regexp) Within regular expression character classes ([]), the syntax beginning with [= and ending with =] is reserved for future extensions. If you need to represent those character sequences inside a regular expression character class, just quote the square brackets with the backslash: \[= and =\].

chmod() mode argument is missing initial 0

(W chmod) A novice will sometimes say:

```
chmod 777, $filename
```

not realizing that 777 will be interpreted as a decimal number, equivalent to 01411. Octal constants are introduced with a leading 0 in Perl, as in C.

Close on unopened file <%s>

(W unopened) You tried to close a filehandle that was never opened.

Compilation failed in require

(F) Perl could not compile a file specified in a require statement. Perl uses this generic message when none of the errors that it encountered were severe enough to halt compilation immediately.

Complex regular subexpression recursion limit (%d) exceeded

(W regexp) The regular expression engine uses recursion in complex situations where backtracking is required. Recursion depth is limited to 32,766, or perhaps less in architectures where the stack cannot grow arbitrarily. ("Simple" and "medium" situations are handled without recursion and are not subject to a limit.) Try shortening the string under examination; looping in Perl code (e.g., with while) rather than in the regular expression engine; or rewriting the regular expression so that it is simpler or backtracks less.

connect() on closed socket %s

(W closed) You tried to do a connect on a closed socket. Did you forget to check the return value of your socket call?

`Constant is not %s reference`

(F) A constant value (perhaps declared using the `use constant` pragma) is being dereferenced, but it amounts to the wrong type of reference. The message indicates the type of reference that was expected. This usually indicates a syntax error in dereferencing the constant value.

`Constant subroutine %s redefined`

(S | W redefine) You redefined a subroutine that had previously been eligible for inlining.

`Constant subroutine %s undefined`

(W misc) You undefined a subroutine that had previously been eligible for inlining.

`constant(%s): %s`

(F) The parser found inconsistencies either while attempting to define an overloaded constant or when trying to find the character name specified in the `\N{...}` escape. Perhaps you forgot to load the corresponding `overload` or `charnames` pragma?

`Copy method did not return a reference`

(F) The method that overloads = is buggy.

`CORE::%s is not a keyword`

(F) The `CORE::` namespace is reserved for Perl keywords.

`Corrupt malloc ptr 0x%lx at 0x%lx`

(P) The `malloc` package that comes with Perl had an internal failure.

`corrupted regexp pointers`

(P) The regular expression engine got confused by what the regular expression compiler gave it.

`corrupted regexp program`

(P) The regular expression engine got passed a regexp program without a valid magic number.

`Deep recursion on subroutine "%s"`

(W recursion) This subroutine has called itself (directly or indirectly) 100 times more than it has returned. This probably indicates an infinite recursion, unless you're writing strange benchmark programs, in which case it indicates something else.

`defined(@array) is deprecated`

(D deprecated) `defined` is not usually useful on arrays because it checks for an undefined *scalar* value. If you want to see if the array is empty, just use `if (@array) { # not empty }`.

`defined(%hash) is deprecated`

> (D deprecated) `defined` is not usually useful on hashes because it checks for an undefined *scalar* value. If you want to see if the hash is empty, just use `if (%hash) { # not empty }`.

`Delimiter for here document is too long`

> (F) In a here document construct like <<FOO, the label FOO is too long for Perl to handle. You have to be seriously twisted to write code that triggers this error.

`Did not produce a valid header`

> See `Server error`.

`(Did you mean &%s instead?)`

> (W) You probably referred to an imported subroutine &FOO as $FOO or some such.

`(Did you mean "local" instead of "our"?)`

> (W misc) Remember that `our` does not localize the declared global variable. You have declared it again in the same lexical scope, which seems superfluous.

`(Did you mean $ or @ instead of %?)`

> (W) You probably said %hash{$key} when you meant $hash{$key} or @hash{@keys}. On the other hand, maybe you just meant %hash and got carried away.

`Died`

> (F) You passed `die` an empty string (the equivalent of `die ""`) or you called it with no args and both $@ and $_ were empty.

`(Do you need to predeclare %s?)`

> (S) This is an educated guess made in conjunction with the message "%s found where operator expected". It often means a subroutine or module name is being referenced that hasn't been declared yet. This may be because of ordering problems in your file or because of a missing `sub`, `package`, `require`, or `use` statement. If you're referencing something that isn't defined yet, you don't actually have to define the subroutine or package before the current location. You can use an empty `sub foo;` or `package FOO;` to enter a "forward" declaration.

`Document contains no data`

> See `Server error`.

`Don't know how to handle magic of type '%s'`

> (P) The internal handling of magical variables has been cursed.

do_study: out of memory

(P) This should have been caught by safemalloc instead.

Duplicate free() ignored

(S malloc) An internal routine called free on something that had already been freed.

elseif should be elsif

(S) There is no keyword "elseif" in Perl because Larry thinks it's ugly. Your code will be interpreted as an attempt to call a method named elseif for the class returned by the following block. This is unlikely to be what you want.

%s failed--call queue aborted

(F) An untrapped exception was raised while executing a CHECK, INIT, or END subroutine. Processing of the remainder of the queue of such routines has been prematurely ended.

entering effective %s failed

(F) While under the use filetest pragma, switching the real and effective UIDs or GIDs failed.

Error converting file specification %s

(F) This is an error peculiar to VMS. Because Perl may have to deal with file specifications in either VMS or Unix syntax, it converts them to a single form when it must operate on them directly. Either you've passed an invalid file specification to Perl, or you've found a case the conversion routines don't handle. Drat.

%s: Eval-group in insecure regular expression

(F) Perl detected tainted data when trying to compile a regular expression that contains the (?{ ... }) zero-width assertion, which is unsafe.

%s: Eval-group not allowed, use re 'eval'

(F) A regular expression contained the (?{ ... }) zero-width assertion, but that construct is only allowed when the use re 'eval' pragma is in effect.

%s: Eval-group not allowed at run time

(F) Perl tried to compile a regular expression containing the (?{ ... }) zero-width assertion at run time, as it would when the pattern contains interpolated values. Since that is a security risk, it is not allowed. If you insist, you may still do this by explicitly building the pattern from an interpolated string at run time and using that in an eval.

Excessively long <> operator

(F) The contents of a <> operator may not exceed the maximum size of a Perl identifier. If you're just trying to glob a long list of filenames, try using the glob operator or putting the filenames into a variable and globbing that.

Diagnostics

`Execution of %s aborted due to compilation errors`

(F) The final summary message when a Perl compilation fails.

`Exiting eval via %s`

(W exiting) You are exiting an `eval` by unconventional means, such as a `goto` or a loop control statement.

`Exiting format via %s`

(W exiting) You are exiting a `format` by unconventional means, such as a `goto` or a loop control statement.

`Exiting pseudoblock via %s`

(W exiting) You are exiting a rather special block construct (like a sort block or subroutine) by unconventional means, such as a `goto` or a loop control statement.

`Exiting subroutine via %s`

(W exiting) You are exiting a subroutine by unconventional means, such as a `goto` or a loop control statement.

`Exiting substitution via %s`

(W exiting) You are exiting a substitution by unconventional means, such as a `return`, a `goto`, or a loop control statement.

`Explicit blessing to '' (assuming package main)`

(W misc) You are blessing a reference to a zero-length string. This has the effect of blessing the reference into the package `main`. This is usually not what you want. Consider providing a default target package, such as `bless($ref, $p || 'MyPackage');`

`false [] range "%s" in regexp`

(W regexp) A character class range must start and end at a literal character, not another character class like `\d` or `[:alpha:]`. The – in your false range is interpreted as a literal –. Consider quoting the – like this: `\-`.

`Fatal VMS error at %s, line %d`

(P) This is an error peculiar to VMS. Something untoward happened in a VMS system service or RTL routine; Perl's exit status should provide more details. The filename in `at %s` and the line number in `line %d` tell you which section of the Perl source code is distressed.

`fcntl is not implemented`

(F) Your machine apparently doesn't implement `fcntl`. What is this, a PDP-11 or something?

`Filehandle %s never opened`

(W unopened) An I/O operation was attempted on a filehandle that was never initialized. You need to do an `open` or a `socket` call, or call a constructor from the `FileHandle` module.

Filehandle %s opened only for input

> (W io) You tried to write on a read-only filehandle. If you intended it to be a read-write filehandle, you needed to open it with +< or +> or +>> instead of with < or nothing. If you intended only to write the file, use > or >>.

Filehandle %s opened only for output

> (W io) You tried to read from a filehandle opened only for writing. If you intended it to be a read/write filehandle, you needed to open it with +< or +> or +>> instead of with < or nothing. If you intended only to read from the file, use <.

Final $ should be \$ or $name

> (F) You must now decide whether the final $ in a string was meant to be a literal dollar sign or was meant to introduce a variable name that happens to be missing. So you have to add either the backslash or the name.

Final @ should be \@ or @name

> (F) You must now decide whether the final @ in a string was meant to be a literal "at" sign or was meant to introduce a variable name that happens to be missing. So you have to add either the backslash or the name.

flock() on closed filehandle %s

> (W closed) The filehandle you're attempting to flock got itself closed some time before now. Check your logic flow. flock operates on filehandles. Are you attempting to call flock on a dirhandle by the same name?

Format %s redefined

> (W redefine) You redefined a format. To suppress this warning, say:

```
{
    no warnings;
    eval "format NAME =...";
}
```

Format not terminated

> (F) A format must be terminated by a line with a solitary dot. Perl got to the end of your file without finding such a line.

Found = in conditional, should be ==

> (W syntax) You said:

```
if ($foo = 123)
```

> when you meant:

```
if ($foo == 123)
```

> (or something like that).

`gdbm store returned %d, errno %d, key "%s"`

> (S) A warning from the `GDBM_File` extension that a store failed.

`gethostent not implemented`

> (F) Your C library apparently doesn't implement `gethostent`, probably because if it did, it'd feel morally obligated to return every hostname on the Internet.

`get%sname() on closed socket %s`

> (W closed) You tried to get a socket or peer socket name on a closed socket. Did you forget to check the return value of your `socket` call?

`getpwnam returned invalid UIC %#o for user "%s"`

> (S) A warning peculiar to VMS. The call to `sys$getuai` underlying the `getpwnam` operator returned an invalid UIC.

`getsockopt() on closed socket %s`

> (W closed) You tried to get a socket option on a closed socket. Did you forget to check the return value of your `socket` call?

`glob failed (%s)`

> (W glob) Something went wrong with the external program(s) used for `glob` and `<*.c>`. Usually, this means that you supplied a `glob` pattern that caused the external program to fail and exit with a nonzero status. If the message indicates that the abnormal exit resulted in a core dump, this may also mean that your *csh* (C shell) is broken. If so, you should change all of the *csh*-related variables in *config.sh*: If you have *tcsh*, make the variables refer to it as if it were *csh* (e.g., `full_csh='/usr/bin/tcsh'`); otherwise, make them all empty (except that `d_csh` should be `'undef'`) so that Perl will think *csh* is missing. In either case, after editing *config.sh*, run *./Configure -S* and rebuild Perl.

`Glob not terminated`

> (F) The lexer saw a left angle bracket in a place where it was expecting a term, so it's looking for the corresponding right angle bracket and not finding it. Chances are you left some needed parentheses out earlier in the line, and you really meant a < symbol.

`Global symbol "%s" requires explicit package name`

> (F) You've said `use strict vars`, which indicates that all variables must either be lexically scoped (using `my`), declared beforehand using `our`, or explicitly qualified to say which package the global variable is in (using `::`).

`Got an error from DosAllocMem`

> (P) This is an error peculiar to OS/2. Most probably you're using an obsolete version of Perl, so this error should not happen anyway.

`goto must have label`

(F) Unlike with `next` or `last`, you're not allowed to `goto` an unspecified destination.

`Had to create %s unexpectedly`

(S internal) A routine asked for a symbol from a symbol table that ought to have existed already, but for some reason it didn't and had to be created on an emergency basis to prevent a core dump.

`Hash %%s missing the % in argument %d of %s()`

(D deprecated) Really old Perl let you omit the `%` on hash names in some spots. This is now heavily deprecated.

`Hexadecimal number > 0xffffffff non-portable`

(W portable) The hexadecimal number you specified is larger than 2**32-1 (4,294,967,295) and therefore nonportable between systems.

`Identifier too long`

(F) Perl limits identifiers (names for variables, functions, etc.) to about 250 characters for simple names, and somewhat more for compound names (like `$A::B`). You've exceeded Perl's limits. Future versions of Perl are likely to eliminate these arbitrary limitations.

`Ill-formed CRTL environ value "%s"`

(W internal) This is a warning peculiar to VMS. Perl tried to read the CRTL's internal environ array and encountered an element without the `=` delimiter used to separate keys from values. The element is ignored.

`Ill-formed message in prime_env_iter: |%s|`

(W internal) This is a warning peculiar to VMS. Perl tried to read a logical name or CLI symbol definition when preparing to iterate over `%ENV` and didn't see the expected delimiter between key and value, so the line was ignored.

`Illegal character %s (carriage return)`

(F) Perl normally treats carriage returns in the program text as it would any other whitespace, which means you should never see this error when Perl was built using standard options. For some reason, your version of Perl appears to have been built without this support. Talk to your Perl administrator.

`Illegal division by zero`

(F) You tried to divide a number by 0. Either something was wrong in your logic, or you need to put a conditional in to guard against meaningless input.

`Illegal modulus zero`

(F) You tried to divide a number by 0 to get the remainder. Most numbers don't take to this kindly.

`Illegal binary digit %s`

(F) You used a digit other than 0 or 1 in a binary number.

`Illegal octal digit %s`

(F) You used an 8 or 9 in a octal number.

`Illegal binary digit %s ignored`

(W digit) You may have tried to use a digit other than 0 or 1 in a binary number. Interpretation of the binary number stopped before the offending digit.

`Illegal octal digit %s ignored`

(W digit) You may have tried to use an 8 or 9 in a octal number. Interpretation of the octal number stopped before the 8 or 9.

`Illegal hexadecimal digit %s ignored`

(W digit) You may have tried to use a character other than 0 through 9, A through F, or a through f in a hexadecimal number. Interpretation of the hexadecimal number stopped before the illegal character.

`Illegal number of bits in vec`

(F) The number of bits in `vec` (the third argument) must be a power of two from 1 to 32 (or 64, if your platform supports that).

`Illegal switch in PERL5OPT: %s`

(X) The `PERL5OPT` environment variable may only be used to set the following switches: `-[DIMUdmw]`.

`In string, @%s now must be written as \@%s`

(F) It used to be that Perl would try to guess whether you wanted an array interpolated or a literal `@`. It did this when the string was first used at run time. Now strings are parsed at compile time, and ambiguous instances of `@` must be disambiguated, either by prepending a backslash to indicate a literal, or by declaring (or using) the array within the program before the string (lexically). (Someday it will simply assume that an unbackslashed `@` interpolates an array.)

`Insecure dependency in %s`

(F) You tried to do something that the tainting mechanism didn't like. The tainting mechanism is turned on when you're running setuid or setgid, or when you specify **-T** to turn it on explicitly. The tainting mechanism labels all data that's derived directly or indirectly from the user, who is considered to be unworthy of your trust. If any such data is used in a "dangerous" operation, you get this error.

`Insecure directory in %s`

(F) You can't use `system`, `exec`, or a piped open in a setuid or setgid script if `$ENV{PATH}` contains a directory that is writable by the world.

`Insecure $ENV{%s} while running %s`

(F) You can't use `system`, `exec`, or a piped open in a setuid or setgid script if any of $ENV{PATH}, $ENV{IFS}, $ENV{CDPATH}, $ENV{ENV}, or $ENV{BASH_ENV} are derived from data supplied (or potentially supplied) by the user. The script must set the path to a known value, using trustworthy data.

`Integer overflow in %s number`

(W overflow) The hexadecimal, octal, or binary number you have specified either as a literal or as an argument to `hex` or `oct` is too big for your architecture and has been converted to a floating-point number. On 32-bit machines, the largest hex, octal, or binary number representable without overflow is 0xFFFFFFFF, 037777777777, or 0b11111111111111111111111111111111 respectively. Note that Perl transparently promotes all numbers to a floating-point representation internally—subject to loss of precision errors in subsequent operations.

`Internal inconsistency in tracking vforks`

(S) This is a warning peculiar to VMS. Perl keeps track of the number of times you've called `fork` and `exec`, to determine whether the current call to `exec` should affect the current script or a subprocess (see "exec LIST" in *perlvms*(1)). Somehow, this count has become scrambled, so Perl is making a guess and treating this `exec` as a request to terminate the Perl script and execute the specified command.

`internal disaster in regexp`

(P) Something went badly wrong in the regular expression parser.

`internal urp in regexp at /%s/`

(P) Something went badly awry in the regular expression parser.

`Invalid %s attribute: %s`

(F) The indicated attribute for a subroutine or variable was not recognized by Perl or by a user-supplied handler.

`Invalid %s attributes: %s`

(F) The indicated attributes for a subroutine or variable were not recognized by Perl or by a user-supplied handler.

`invalid [] range "%s" in regexp`

(F) The range specified in a character class had a minimum character greater than the maximum character.

`Invalid conversion in %s: "%s"`

(W printf) Perl does not understand the given format conversion.

`Invalid separator character %s in attribute list`

(F) Something other than a colon or whitespace was seen between the elements of an attribute list. If the previous attribute had a parenthesized parameter list, perhaps that list was terminated too soon.

`Invalid type in pack: '%s'`

(F) The given character is not a valid pack type.

(W pack) The given character is not a valid pack type, but it used to be silently ignored.

`Invalid type in unpack: '%s'`

(F) The given character is not a valid unpack type.

(W unpack) The given character is not a valid unpack type, but it used to be silently ignored.

`ioctl is not implemented`

(F) Your machine apparently doesn't implement `ioctl`, which is pretty strange for a machine that supports C.

`junk on end of regexp`

(P) The regular expression parser is confused.

`Label not found for "last %s"`

(F) You named a loop to break out of, but you're not currently in a loop of that name, not even if you count where you were called from.

`Label not found for "next %s"`

(F) You named a loop to continue, but you're not currently in a loop of that name, not even if you count where you were called from.

`Label not found for "redo %s"`

(F) You named a loop to restart, but you're not currently in a loop of that name, not even if you count where you were called from.

`leaving effective %s failed`

(F) While under the `use filetest` pragma, switching the real and effective UIDs or GIDs failed.

`listen() on closed socket %s`

(W closed) You tried to do a listen on a closed socket. Did you forget to check the return value of your `socket` call?

`Lvalue subs returning %s not implemented yet`

(F) Due to limitations in the current implementation, array and hash values cannot be returned in subroutines used in lvalue context.

Malformed PERLLIB_PREFIX

(F) This is an error peculiar to OS/2. PERLLIB_PREFIX should be of the form:

> *prefix1;prefix2*

or:

> *prefix1 prefix2*

with nonempty *prefix1* and *prefix2*. If *prefix1* is indeed a prefix of a built-in library search path, *prefix2* is substituted. The error may appear if components are not found, or are too long. See PERLLIB_PREFIX in the *README.os2* file bundled with the Perl distribution.

Method for operation %s not found in package %s during blessing

(F) An attempt was made to specify an entry in an overloading table that doesn't resolve to a valid subroutine.

Method %s not permitted

See Server error.

Might be a runaway multi-line %s string starting on line %d

(S) An advisory indicating that the previous error may have been caused by a missing delimiter on a string or pattern, because the string eventually ended earlier on the current line.

Misplaced _ in number

(W syntax) An underline in a decimal constant wasn't at a 3-digit boundary.

Missing $ on loop variable

(F) Apparently, you've been programming in *csh* too much. Variables are always mentioned with the $ in Perl, unlike in the shells, where it can vary from one line to the next.

Missing %sbrace%s on \N{}

(F) You used the wrong syntax of character name literal \N{charname} within double-quotish context.

Missing comma after first argument to %s function

(F) While certain functions allow you to specify a filehandle or an "indirect object" before the argument list, this ain't one of them.

Missing command in piped open

(W pipe) You used the open(FH, "| command") or open(FH, "command |") construction, but the command was missing or blank.

(Missing operator before %s?)

(S) This is an educated guess made in conjunction with the message "%s found where operator expected". Often the missing operator is a comma.

Missing right curly or square bracket

(F) The lexer counted more opening curly or square brackets than closing ones. As a general rule, you'll find it's missing near the place you were last editing.

Modification of a read-only value attempted

(F) You tried, directly or indirectly, to change the value of a constant. You didn't, of course, try 2 = 1, because the compiler catches that. But an easy way to do the same thing is:

```
sub mod { $_[0] = 1 }
mod(2);
```

Another way is to assign to a substr that's off the end of the string.

Modification of non-creatable array value attempted, subscript %d

(F) You tried to make an array value spring into existence, and the subscript was probably negative, even counting from end of the array backward.

Modification of non-creatable hash value attempted, subscript "%s"

(P) You tried to make a hash value spring into existence, and it couldn't be created for some peculiar reason.

Module name must be constant

(F) Only a bare module name is allowed as the first argument to a use.

msg%s not implemented

(F) You don't have System V message IPC on your system.

Multidimensional syntax %s not supported

(W syntax) Multidimensional arrays aren't written like $foo[1,2,3]. They're written like $foo[1][2][3], as in C.

Missing name in "my sub"

(F) The reserved syntax for lexically scoped subroutines requires that they have a name with which they can be found.

Name "%s::%s" used only once: possible typo

(W once) Typographical errors often show up as unique variable names. If you had a good reason for having a unique name, then just mention it again somehow to suppress the message. The our declaration is provided for this purpose.

Negative length

(F) You tried to do a read/write/send/recv operation with a buffer length that is less than 0. This is difficult to imagine.

nested *?+ in regexp

(F) You can't quantify a quantifier without intervening parentheses. So things like ** or +* or ?* are illegal.

Note, however, that the minimal matching quantifiers, *?, +?, and ?? appear to be nested quantifiers, but aren't.

No #! line

(F) The setuid emulator requires that scripts have a well-formed #! line even on machines that don't support the #! construct.

No %s allowed while running setuid

(F) Certain operations are deemed to be too insecure for a setuid or setgid script to even attempt. Generally speaking, there will be another way to do what you want that is, if not secure, at least securable.

No -e allowed in setuid scripts

(F) A setuid script can't be specified by the user.

No %s specified for -%c

(F) The indicated command-line switch needs a mandatory argument, but you haven't specified one.

No comma allowed after %s

(F) A list operator that has a filehandle or "indirect object" is not allowed to have a comma between that and the following arguments. Otherwise, it would be interpreted as just another argument.

One obscure situation where this message occurs is when you expect a constant to be imported into your namespace with use or import, but no such importing took place (say, because your operating system doesn't support that particular constant). You should have used an explicit import list for the constants you expect to see. An explicit import list would probably have caught this error earlier. Or maybe there's just a typo in the name of the constant.

No command into which to pipe on command line

(F) This is an error peculiar to VMS. Perl handles its own command-line redirection and found a | at the end of the command line, so it doesn't know where you want to pipe the output from this command.

No DB::DB routine defined

(F) The currently executing code was compiled with the **-d** switch, but for some reason the *perl5db.pl* file (or some facsimile thereof) didn't define a routine to be called at the beginning of each statement. Which is odd, because the file should have been required automatically and should have blown up the require if it didn't parse right.

No dbm on this machine

(P) This is counted as an internal error; every machine should supply a DBM nowadays because Perl comes with SDBM.

No DBsub routine

(F) The currently executing code was compiled with the **-d** switch, but for some reason the *perl5db.pl* file (or some facsimile thereof) didn't define a DB::sub routine to be called at the beginning of each ordinary subroutine call.

No error file after 2> or 2>> on command line

(F) This is an error peculiar to VMS. Perl handles its own command-line redirection, and found a 2> or a 2>> on the command line, but it can't find the name of the file to which to write data destined for STDERR.

No input file after < on command line

(F) This is an error peculiar to VMS. Perl handles its own command-line redirection and found a < on the command line, but it can't find the name of the file from which to read data for STDIN.

No output file after > on command line

(F) This is an error peculiar to VMS. Perl handles its own command-line redirection and found a lone > at the end of the command line, but it doesn't know where you wanted to redirect STDOUT.

No output file after > or >> on command line

(F) This is an error peculiar to VMS. Perl handles its own command-line redirection and found a > or a >> on the command line, but it can't find the name of the file to which to write data destined for STDOUT.

No package name allowed for variable %s in "our"

(F) Fully qualified variable names are not allowed in our declarations, because they don't make much sense under existing semantics. Such syntax is reserved for future extensions.

No Perl script found in input

(F) You called *perl -x*, but no line was found in the file beginning with #! and containing the word "perl".

No setregid available

   (F) *Configure* didn't find anything resembling the `setregid` call for your system.

No setreuid available

   (F) *Configure* didn't find anything resembling the `setreuid` call for your system.

No space allowed after -%c

   (F) The argument to the indicated command-line switch must follow immediately after the switch, without intervening spaces.

No such pseudohash field "%s"

   (F) You tried to access an array as a hash, but the field name used is not defined. The hash at index 0 should map all valid field names to array indices for that to work.

No such pseudohash field "%s" in variable %s of type %s

   (F) You tried to access a field of a typed variable, but the type does not know about the field name. The field names are looked up in the `%FIELDS` hash in the type package at compile time. The `%FIELDS` hash is usually set up with the `fields` pragma.

No such pipe open

   (P) This is an error peculiar to VMS. The internal routine `my_pclose` tried to close a pipe that hadn't been opened. This should have been caught earlier as an attempt to close an unopened filehandle.

No such signal: SIG%s

   (W signal) The signal name you specified as a subscript to `%SIG` was not recognized. Say *kill -l* in your shell to see the valid signal names on your system.

no UTC offset information; assuming local time is UTC

   (S) This is a warning peculiar to VMS. Perl was unable to find the local time zone offset, so it assumes that the local system time and the UTC are equivalent. If they're not, define the logical name `SYS$TIMEZONE_DIFFERENTIAL` to translate to the number of seconds that need to be added to UTC to get local time.

Not a CODE reference

   (F) Perl was trying to evaluate a reference to a code value (that is, a subroutine) but found a reference to something else instead. You can use the `ref` function to find out what kind of ref it really was.

Not a format reference

(F) We're not sure how you managed to generate a reference to an anonymous format, but this message indicates that you did and that it didn't exist.

Not a GLOB reference

(F) Perl was trying to evaluate a reference to a "typeglob" (that is, a symbol table entry that looks like *foo) but found a reference to something else instead. You can use the ref function to find out what kind of ref it really was.

Not a HASH reference

(F) Perl was trying to evaluate a reference to a hash value but found a reference to something else instead. You can use the ref function to find out what kind of ref it really was.

Not a perl script

(F) The setuid emulator requires that scripts have a well-formed #! line even on machines that don't support the #! construct. The line must mention "perl".

Not a SCALAR reference

(F) Perl was trying to evaluate a reference to a scalar value but found a reference to something else instead. You can use the ref function to find out what kind of ref it really was.

Not a subroutine reference

(F) Perl was trying to evaluate a reference to a code value (that is, a subroutine) but found a reference to something else instead. You can use the ref function to find out what kind of ref it really was.

Not a subroutine reference in overload table

(F) An attempt was made to specify an entry in an overloading table that doesn't somehow point to a valid subroutine.

Not an ARRAY reference

(F) Perl was trying to evaluate a reference to an array value but found a reference to something else instead. You can use the ref function to find out what kind of ref it really was.

Not enough arguments for %s

(F) The function requires more arguments than you specified.

Not enough format arguments

(W syntax) A format specified more picture fields than the next line supplied.

Null filename used

(F) You can't require the null filename, especially because on many machines that means the current directory!

Null picture in formline

> (F) The first argument to `formline` must be a valid format picture specification. The argument was found to be empty, which probably means you supplied it an uninitialized value.

NULL OP IN RUN

> (P debugging) Some internal routine called `run` with a null opcode pointer.

Null realloc

> (P) An attempt was made to realloc NULL.

NULL regexp argument

> (P) The internal pattern-matching routines blew it big time.

NULL regexp parameter

> (P) The internal pattern-matching routines are out of their gourd.

Number too long

> (F) Perl limits the representation of decimal numbers in programs to about about 250 characters. You've exceeded that length. Future versions of Perl are likely to eliminate this arbitrary limitation. In the meantime, try using scientific notation (e.g., `1e6` instead of `1_000_000`).

Octal number > 037777777777 non-portable

> (W portable) The octal number you specified is larger than $2**32-1$ (4,294,967,295) and therefore nonportable between systems.

Octal number in vector unsupported

> (F) Numbers with a leading `0` are not currently allowed in vectors. The octal number interpretation of such numbers may be supported in a future version.

Odd number of elements in hash assignment

> (W misc) You specified an odd number of elements to initialize a hash, which is odd because hashes come in key/value pairs.

Offset outside string

> (F) You tried to do a `read/write/send/recv` operation with an offset pointing outside the buffer. This is difficult to imagine. The sole exception to this rule is that `sysreading` past the buffer will extend the buffer and zero-pad the new area.

oops: oopsAV

> (S internal) An internal warning indicating that the grammar is screwed up.

oops: oopsHV

> (S internal) An internal warning indicating that the grammar is screwed up.

Operation '%s': no method found, %s

(F) An attempt was made to perform an overloaded operation for which no handler was defined. While some handlers can be autogenerated in terms of other handlers, there is no default handler for any operation, unless the fall-back overloading key is specified to be true.

Operator or semicolon missing before %s

(S ambiguous) You used a variable or subroutine call when the parser was expecting an operator. The parser has assumed you really meant to use an operator, but this is highly likely to be incorrect. For example, if you accidentally say *foo *foo, it will be interpreted as if you'd said *foo * 'foo'.

Out of memory!

(X) Perl's internal malloc function returned 0, indicating that the remaining memory (or virtual memory) was insufficient to satisfy the request. Perl has no option but to exit immediately.

Out of memory for yacc stack

(F) The *yacc* parser wanted to grow its stack so it could continue parsing, but realloc wouldn't give it more memory, virtual or otherwise.

Out of memory during request for %s

(X|F) The malloc function returned 0, indicating that the remaining memory (or virtual memory) was insufficient to satisfy the request.

The request was judged to be small, so the possibility to trap it depends on the way Perl was compiled. By default, it is not trappable. However, if compiled for this purpose, Perl may use the contents of $^M as an emergency pool after dieing with this message. In this case, the error is trappable *once*.

Out of memory during "large" request for %s

(F) Perl's internal malloc function returned 0, indicating that the remaining memory (or virtual memory) was insufficient to satisfy the request. However, the request was judged large enough (compile-time default is 64K), so a possibility to shut down by trapping this error is granted.

Out of memory during ridiculously large request

(F) You can't allocate more than 2**31+"small amount" bytes. This error is most likely to be caused by a typo in the Perl program (e.g., $arr[time] instead of $arr[$time]).

page overflow

(W io) A single call to write produced more lines than can fit on a page.

panic: ck_grep

(P) The program failed an internal consistency check while trying to compile a grep.

panic: ck_split

(P) The program failed an internal consistency check while trying to compile a split.

panic: corrupt saved stack index

(P) The savestack was requested to restore more localized values than there are in the savestack.

panic: del_backref

(P) The program failed an internal consistency check while trying to reset a weak reference.

panic: die %s

(P) We popped the context stack to an eval context and then discovered it wasn't an eval context.

panic: do_match

(P) The internal pp_match routine was called with invalid operational data.

panic: do_split

(P) Something terrible went wrong in setting up for the split.

panic: do_subst

(P) The internal pp_subst routine was called with invalid operational data.

panic: do_trans

(P) The internal do_trans routine was called with invalid operational data.

panic: frexp

(P) The library function frexp failed, making printf("%f") impossible.

panic: goto

(P) We popped the context stack to a context with the specified label and then discovered it wasn't a context in which we know how to do a goto.

panic: INTERPCASEMOD

(P) The lexer got into a bad state at a case modifier.

panic: INTERPCONCAT

(P) The lexer got into a bad state parsing a string with brackets.

panic: kid popen errno read

(F) The forked child returned an incomprehensible message about its errno.

panic: last

(P) We popped the context stack to a block context and then discovered it wasn't a block context.

panic: leave_scope clearsv

(P) A writable lexical variable became read-only somehow within the scope.

`panic: leave_scope inconsistency`

(P) The savestack probably got out of sync. At least, there was an invalid `enum` on the top of it.

`panic: malloc`

(P) Something requested a negative number of bytes of `malloc`.

`panic: magic_killbackrefs`

(P) The program failed an internal consistency check while trying to reset all weak references to an object.

`panic: mapstart`

(P) The compiler is screwed up with respect to the `map` function.

`panic: null array`

(P) One of the internal array routines was passed a null AV pointer.

`panic: pad_alloc`

(P) The compiler got confused about which scratchpad it was allocating and freeing temporaries and lexicals from.

`panic: pad_free curpad`

(P) The compiler got confused about which scratchpad it was allocating and freeing temporaries and lexicals from.

`panic: pad_free po`

(P) An invalid scratchpad offset was detected internally.

`panic: pad_reset curpad`

(P) The compiler got confused about which scratchpad it was allocating and freeing temporaries and lexicals from.

`panic: pad_sv po`

(P) An invalid scratchpad offset was detected internally.

`panic: pad_swipe curpad`

(P) The compiler got confused about which scratchpad it was allocating and freeing temporaries and lexicals from.

`panic: pad_swipe po`

(P) An invalid scratchpad offset was detected internally.

`panic: pp_iter`

(P) The `foreach` iterator got called in a nonloop context frame.

`panic: realloc`

(P) Something requested a negative number of bytes of `realloc`.

`panic: restartop`

(P) Some internal routine requested a `goto` (or something like it) but didn't supply the destination.

`panic: return`

(P) We popped the context stack to a subroutine or `eval` context and then discovered it wasn't a subroutine or `eval` context.

`panic: scan_num`

(P) Perl's internal `scan_num` got called on something that wasn't a number.

`panic: sv_insert`

(P) The `sv_insert` routine was told to remove more string than there was string.

`panic: top_env`

(P) The compiler attempted to do a `goto`, or something weird like that.

`panic: yylex`

(P) The lexer got into a bad state while processing a case modifier.

`panic: %s`

(P) An internal error.

`Parentheses missing around "%s" list`

(W parenthesis) You said something like:

```
my $foo, $bar = @_;
```

when you meant:

```
my ($foo, $bar) = @_;
```

Remember that `my`, `our`, and `local` bind tighter than the comma.

`Perl %3.3f required--this is only version %s, stopped`

(F) The module in question uses features of a version of Perl more recent than the currently running version. How long has it been since you upgraded, anyway?

`PERL_SH_DIR too long`

(F) This is an error peculiar to OS/2. `PERL_SH_DIR` is the directory that contains the *sh* shell. See `PERL_SH_DIR` in the *README.os2* file bundled with the Perl distribution.

`Permission denied`

(F) The setuid emulator in *suidperl* decided you were up to no good.

`pid %x not a child`

(W exec) This is a warning peculiar to VMS; `waitpid` was asked to wait for a process that isn't a subprocess of the current process. While this is fine from VMS's perspective, it's probably not what you intended.

POSIX getpgrp can't take an argument

(F) Your system has POSIX `getpgrp`, which takes no argument, unlike the BSD version, which takes a PID.

Possible Y2K bug: %s

(W y2k) You are concatenating the number 19 with another number, which could be a potential year 2000 problem.

Possible attempt to put comments in qw() list

(W qw) `qw` lists contain items separated by whitespace; as with literal strings, comment characters are not ignored but are instead treated as literal data. (You may have used delimiters other than the parentheses shown here; braces are also frequently used.)

You probably wrote something like this:

```
@list = qw(
    a # a comment
    b # another comment
);
```

when you should have written this:

```
@list = qw(
    a
    b
);
```

If you really want comments, build your list the old-fashioned way, with quotes and commas:

```
@list = (
    'a',    # a comment
    'b',    # another comment
);
```

Possible attempt to separate words with commas

(W qw) `qw` lists contain items separated by whitespace; therefore, commas aren't needed to separate the items. (You may have used delimiters other than the parentheses shown here; braces are also frequently used.)

You probably wrote something like this:

```
qw( a, b, c );
```

which puts literal commas into some of the list items. Write it without commas if you don't want them to appear in your data:

```
qw( a b c );
```

`Possible memory corruption: %s overflowed 3rd argument`

(F) An `ioctl` or `fcntl` returned more than Perl was bargaining for. Perl guesses a reasonable buffer size but puts a sentinel byte at the end of the buffer just in case. This sentinel byte got clobbered, and Perl assumes that memory is now corrupted.

`pragma "attrs" is deprecated, use "sub NAME : ATTRS" instead`

(W deprecated) You have written something like this:

```
sub doit
{
    use attrs qw(locked);
}
```

You should use the new declaration syntax instead:

```
sub doit : locked
{
    ...
```

The `use attrs` pragma is now obsolete and is only provided for backward compatibility.

`Precedence problem: open %s should be open(%s)`

(S precedence) The old irregular construct:

```
open FOO || die;
```

is now misinterpreted as:

```
open(FOO || die);
```

because of the strict regularization of Perl 5's grammar into unary and list operators. (The old `open` was a little of both.) You must put parentheses around the filehandle or use the new `or` operator instead of `||`.

`Premature end of script headers`

See `Server error`.

`print() on closed filehandle %s`

(W closed) The filehandle you're printing on got itself closed sometime before now. Check your logic flow.

`printf() on closed filehandle %s`

(W closed) The filehandle you're writing to got itself closed sometime before now. Check your logic flow.

Process terminated by SIG%s

> (W) This is a standard message issued by OS/2 applications, while Unix applications die in silence. It is considered a feature of the OS/2 port. One can easily disable this warning by setting appropriate signal handlers. See also "Process terminated by SIGTERM/SIGINT" in the *README.os2* file bundled with the Perl distribution.

Prototype mismatch: %s vs %s

> (S unsafe) The subroutine being declared or defined had previously been declared or defined with a different function prototype.

Range iterator outside integer range

> (F) One (or both) of the numeric arguments of the range operator .. are outside the range that can be represented by integers internally. One possible workaround is to force Perl to use magical string increments by prepending 0 to your numbers.

readline() on closed filehandle %s

> (W closed) The filehandle you're reading from got itself closed sometime before now. Check your logic flow.

realloc() of freed memory ignored

> (S malloc) An internal routine called realloc on something that had already been freed.

Reallocation too large: %lx

> (F) You can't allocate more than 64K on an MS-DOS machine.

Recompile perl with -DDEBUGGING to use -D switch

> (F debugging) You can't use the **-D** option unless the code to produce the desired output is compiled into Perl, which entails some overhead, which is why it's currently left out of your copy.

Recursive inheritance detected in package '%s'

> (F) More than 100 levels of inheritance were used. This probably indicates an unintended loop in your inheritance hierarchy.

Recursive inheritance detected while looking for method '%s' in package '%s'

> (F) More than 100 levels of inheritance were encountered while a method was invoked. This probably indicates an unintended loop in your inheritance hierarchy.

Reference found where even-sized list expected

> (W misc) You gave a single reference when Perl was expecting a list with an even number of elements (for assignment to a hash). This usually means that you used the anonymous hash constructor when you meant to use parens. In any case, a hash requires key/value *pairs*:

```
%hash = { one => 1, two => 2, };     # WRONG
%hash = [ qw( an anon array /)];     # WRONG
%hash = ( one => 1, two => 2, );     # right
%hash = qw( one 1 two 2 );           # also fine
```

Reference is already weak

(W misc) You have attempted to weaken a reference that is already weak. Doing so has no effect.

Reference miscount in sv_replace()

(W internal) The internal sv_replace function was handed a new SV with a reference count of other than 1.

regexp *+ operand could be empty

(F) The part of the regexp subject to either the * or + quantifier could match an empty string.

regexp memory corruption

(P) The regular expression engine got confused by what the regular expression compiler gave it.

regexp out of space

(P) This is a "can't happen" error, because safemalloc should have caught it earlier.

Reversed %s= operator

(W syntax) You wrote your assignment operator backward. The = must always come last, to avoid ambiguity with subsequent unary operators.

Runaway format

(F) Your format contained the ~~ repeat-until-blank sequence, but it produced 200 lines at once, and the 200th line looked exactly like the 199th line. Apparently, you didn't arrange for the arguments to exhaust themselves either by using ^ instead of @ (for scalar variables) or by shifting or popping (for array variables).

Scalar value @%s[%s] better written as $%s[%s]

(W syntax) You've used an array slice (indicated by @) to select a single element of an array. Generally, it's better to ask for a scalar value (indicated by $). The difference is that $foo[&bar] always behaves like a scalar, both when assigning to it and when evaluating its argument, while @foo[&bar] behaves like a list when you assign to it and provides a list context to its subscript, which can do weird things if you're expecting only one subscript.

On the other hand, if you were actually hoping to treat the array element as a list, you need to look into how references work, because Perl will not magically convert between scalars and lists for you.

`Scalar value @%s{%s} better written as $%s{%s}`

(W syntax) You've used a hash slice (indicated by @) to select a single element of a hash. Generally, it's better to ask for a scalar value (indicated by $). The difference is that `$foo{&bar}` always behaves like a scalar, both when assigning to it and when evaluating its argument, while `@foo{&bar}` behaves like a list when you assign to it, and provides a list context to its subscript, which can do weird things if you're expecting only one subscript.

On the other hand, if you were actually hoping to treat the hash element as a list, you need to look into how references work, because Perl will not magically convert between scalars and lists for you.

`Script is not setuid/setgid in suidperl`

(F) Oddly, the *suidperl* program was invoked on a script without a setuid or setgid bit set. This doesn't make much sense.

`Search pattern not terminated`

(F) The lexer couldn't find the final delimiter of a `//` or `m{}` construct. Remember that bracketing delimiters count nesting levels. Omitting the leading $ from a variable `$m` may cause this error.

`%sseek() on unopened file`

(W unopened) You tried to use the `seek` or `sysseek` function on a filehandle that either was never opened or has since been closed.

`select not implemented`

(F) This machine doesn't implement the `select` system call.

`sem%s not implemented`

(F) You don't have System V semaphore IPC on your system.

`semi-panic: attempt to dup freed string`

(S internal) The internal `newSVsv` routine was called to duplicate a scalar that had previously been marked as free.

`Semicolon seems to be missing`

(W semicolon) A nearby syntax error was probably caused by a missing semicolon, or possibly some other missing operator, such as a comma.

`send() on closed socket %s`

(W closed) The socket you're sending to got itself closed sometime before now. Check your logic flow.

`Sequence (? incomplete`

(F) A regular expression ended with an incomplete extension (?.

`Sequence (?#... not terminated`

(F) A regular expression comment must be terminated by a closing parenthesis. Embedded parentheses aren't allowed.

`Sequence (?%s...) not implemented`

(F) A proposed regular expression extension has reserved the character but has not yet been written.

`Sequence (?%s...) not recognized`

(F) You used a regular expression extension that doesn't make sense.

`Server error`

This is the error message generally seen in a browser window when you try to run a CGI program (including SSI) over the web. The actual error text varies widely from server to server. The most frequently seen variants are "`500 Server error`", "`Method (something) not permitted`", "`Document contains no data`", "`Premature end of script headers`", and "`Did not produce a valid header`".

This is a CGI error, not a Perl error.

You need to make sure your script is executable, is accessible by the user CGI is running the script under (which is probably not the user account you tested it under), does not rely on any environment variables (like `PATH`) from the user it isn't running under, and isn't in a location where the CGI server can't find it, basically, more or less. Please see the following for more information:

http://www.perl.com/CPAN/doc/FAQs/cgi/idiots-guide.html
http://www.perl.com/CPAN/doc/FAQs/cgi/perl-cgi-faq.html
ftp://rtfm.mit.edu/pub/usenet/news.answers/www/cgi-faq
http://hoohoo.ncsa.uiuc.edu/cgi/interface.html
http://www-genome.wi.mit.edu/WWW/faqs/www-security-faq.html

You should also look at the Perl FAQ.

`setegid() not implemented`

(F) You tried to assign to $), but your operating system doesn't support the `setegid` system call (or equivalent), or at least *Configure* didn't think so.

`seteuid() not implemented`

(F) You tried to assign to $>, but your operating system doesn't support the `seteuid` system call (or equivalent), or at least *Configure* didn't think so.

`setpgrp can't take arguments`

(F) Your system has the `setpgrp` from BSD 4.2, which takes no arguments, unlike POSIX `setpgid`, which takes a process ID and process group ID.

`setrgid() not implemented`

> (F) You tried to assign to $(, but your operating system doesn't support the setrgid system call (or equivalent), or at least *Configure* didn't think so.

`setruid() not implemented`

> (F) You tried to assign to $<, but your operating system doesn't support the setruid system call (or equivalent), or at least *Configure* didn't think so.

`setsockopt() on closed socket %s`

> (W closed) You tried to set a socket option on a closed socket. Did you forget to check the return value of your socket call?

`Setuid/gid script is writable by world`

> (F) The setuid emulator won't run a script that is writable by the world, because the world might have written on it already.

`shm%s not implemented`

> (F) You don't have System V shared memory IPC on your system.

`shutdown() on closed socket %s`

> (W closed) You tried to do a shutdown on a closed socket. Seems a bit superfluous.

`SIG%s handler "%s" not defined`

> (W signal) The signal handler named in %SIG doesn't, in fact, exist. Perhaps you put it into the wrong package?

`sort is now a reserved word`

> (F) An ancient error message that almost nobody ever runs into anymore. But before sort was a keyword, people sometimes used it as a filehandle.

`Sort subroutine didn't return a numeric value`

> (F) A sort comparison routine must return a number. You probably blew it by not using <=> or cmp, or by not using them correctly.

`Sort subroutine didn't return single value`

> (F) A sort comparison subroutine cannot return a list value with more or less than one element.

`Split loop`

> (P) The split was looping infinitely. (Obviously, a split shouldn't iterate more times than there are characters of input, which is what happened.)

`Stat on unopened file <%s>`

> (W unopened) You tried to use the stat function (or an equivalent file test) on a filehandle that either was never opened or has since been closed.

`Statement unlikely to be reached`

(W exec) You did an `exec` with some statement after it other than a `die`. This is almost always an error, because `exec` never returns unless there was a failure. You probably wanted to use `system` instead, which does return. To suppress this warning, put the `exec` in a block by itself.

`Strange *+?{} on zero-length expression`

(W regexp) You applied a regular expression quantifier in a place where it makes no sense, such as on a zero-width assertion. Try putting the quantifier inside the assertion instead. For example, the way to match `abc` provided that it is followed by three repetitions of `xyz` is `/abc(?=(?:xyz){3})/`, not `/abc(?=xyz){3}/`.

`Stub found while resolving method '%s' overloading '%s' in package '%s'`

(P) Overloading resolution over `@ISA` tree may be broken by importation stubs. Stubs should never be implicitly created, but explicit calls to `can` may break this.

`Subroutine %s redefined`

(W redefine) You redefined a subroutine. To suppress this warning, say:

```
{
    no warnings;
    eval "sub name { ... }";
}
```

`Substitution loop`

(P) The substitution was looping infinitely. (Obviously, a substitution shouldn't iterate more times than there are characters of input, which is what happened.)

`Substitution pattern not terminated`

(F) The lexer couldn't find the interior delimiter of an `s///` or `s{}{}` construct. Remember that bracketing delimiters count nesting levels. Omitting the leading `$` from variable `$s` may cause this error.

`Substitution replacement not terminated`

(F) The lexer couldn't find the final delimiter of an `s///` or `s{}{}` construct. Remember that bracketing delimiters count nesting levels. Omitting the leading `$` from variable `$s` may cause this error.

`substr outside of string`

(W substr|F) You tried to reference a `substr` that pointed outside of a string. That is, the absolute value of the offset was larger than the length of the string. This warning is fatal if `substr` is used in an lvalue context (as the left-hand side of an assignment or as a subroutine argument, for example).

`suidperl is no longer needed since %s`

> (F) Your Perl was compiled with **-DSETUID_SCRIPTS_ARE_SECURE_NOW**, but a version of the setuid emulator somehow got run anyway.

`switching effective %s is not implemented`

> (F) While under the use `filetest` pragma, we cannot switch the real and effective UIDs or GIDs.

`syntax error`

> (F) This message probably means you had a syntax error. Common reasons include:

- A keyword is misspelled.

- A semicolon is missing.

- A comma is missing.

- An opening or closing parenthesis is missing.

- An opening or closing brace is missing.

- A closing quote is missing.

> Often another error message will be associated with the syntax error with more information. (Sometimes it helps to turn on **-w**.) The error message itself often tells you where in the line Perl decided to give up. Sometimes the actual error is several tokens before this, because Perl is good at understanding random input. Occasionally, the line number may be misleading, and once in a blue moon the only way to figure out what's triggering the error is to call *perl* -c repeatedly, chopping away half the program each time to see if the error goes away. Sort of the cybernetic version of 20 questions.

`syntax error at line %d: '%s' unexpected`

> (A) You've accidentally run your script through the Bourne shell instead of Perl. Check the `#!` line, or manually feed your script into Perl yourself.

`System V %s is not implemented on this machine`

> (F) You tried to do something with a function beginning with `sem`, `shm`, or `msg` but System V IPC is not implemented in your machine. (In some machines, the functionality can exist but may be unconfigured.)

`syswrite() on closed filehandle %s`

> (W closed) The filehandle you're writing to got itself closed sometime before now. Check your logic flow.

`Target of goto is too deeply nested`

> (F) You tried to use `goto` to reach a label that was too deeply nested for Perl to reach. Perl is doing you a favor by refusing.

`tell()` on unopened file

> (W unopened) You tried to use the `tell` function on a filehandle that either was never opened or has since been closed.

Test on unopened file *%s*

> (W unopened) You tried to invoke a file test operator on a filehandle that isn't open. Check your logic.

That use of `$[` is unsupported

> (F) Assignment to `$[` is now strictly circumscribed and interpreted as a compiler directive. You may say only one of:

```
$[ = 0;
$[ = 1;
...
local $[ = 0;
local $[ = 1;
...
```

> This is to prevent the problem of one module inadvertently changing the array base out from under another module.

The *%s* function is unimplemented

> The function indicated isn't implemented on this architecture, according to the probings of *Configure*.

The `crypt()` function is unimplemented due to excessive paranoia

> (F) *Configure* couldn't find the `crypt` function on your machine, probably because your vendor didn't supply it, probably because they think the U.S. government thinks it's a secret or at least will continue to pretend that it is.

The stat preceding `-l _` wasn't an lstat

> (F) It makes no sense to test the current stat buffer for symbolic linkhood if the last `stat` that wrote to the stat buffer already went past the symlink to get to the real file. Use an actual filename instead.

This Perl can't reset CRTL environ elements (*%s*)
This Perl can't set CRTL environ elements (*%s=%s*)

> (W internal) These are warnings peculiar to VMS. You tried to change or delete an element of the CRTL's internal environ array, but your copy of Perl wasn't built with a CRTL that contained the internal `setenv` function. You'll need to rebuild Perl with a CRTL that does, or redefine PERL_ENV_TABLES (see *perlvms*(1)) so that the environ array isn't the target of the change to %ENV that produced the warning.

times not implemented

> (F) Your version of the C library apparently doesn't do `times`. I suspect you're not running on Unix.

`Too few args to syscall`

> (F) There has to be at least one argument to `syscall` to specify the system call to call, silly dilly.

`Too late for "-T" option`

> (X) The `#!` line (or local equivalent) in a Perl script contains the **-T** option, but Perl was not invoked with **-T** in its command line. This is an error because by the time Perl discovers a **-T** in a script, it's too late to properly taint everything from the environment. So Perl gives up.

> If the Perl script is being executed as a command using the `#!` mechanism (or its local equivalent), this error can usually be fixed by editing the `#!` line so that the **-T** option is a part of Perl's first argument: e.g., change `perl -n -T` to `perl -T -n`.

> If the Perl script is being executed as *perl scriptname*, then the **-T** option must appear on the command line: *perl -T scriptname*.

`Too late for "-%s" option`

> (X) The `#!` line (or local equivalent) in a Perl script contains the **-M** or **-m** option. This is an error because **-M** and **-m** options are not intended for use inside scripts. Use a use declaration instead.

`Too late to run %s block`

> (W void) A `CHECK` or `INIT` block is being defined during run time proper, when the opportunity to run them has already passed. Perhaps you are loading a file with `require` or `do` when you should be using use instead. Or perhaps you should put the `require` or `do` inside a `BEGIN` block.

`Too many ('s`
`Too many )'s`

> (A) You've accidentally run your script through *csh* instead of Perl. Check the `#!` line, or manually feed your script into Perl yourself.

`Too many args to syscall`

> (F) Perl supports a maximum of only 14 arguments to `syscall`.

`Too many arguments for %s`

> (F) The function requires fewer arguments than you specified.

`trailing \ in regexp`

> (F) The regular expression ends with an unbackslashed backslash. Backslash it.

`Transliteration pattern not terminated`

> (F) The lexer couldn't find the interior delimiter of a `tr///` or `tr[][]` or `y///` or `y[][]` construct. Omitting the leading `$` from variables `$tr` or `$y` may cause this error.

Transliteration replacement not terminated

(F) The lexer couldn't find the final delimiter of a `tr///` or `tr[][]` construct.

truncate not implemented

(F) Your machine doesn't implement a file truncation mechanism that *Configure* knows about.

Type of arg %d to %s must be %s (not %s)

(F) This function requires the argument in that position to be of a certain type. Arrays must be *@NAME* or *@{EXPR}*. Hashes must be *%NAME* or *%{EXPR}*. No implicit dereferencing is allowed—use the *{EXPR}* form as an explicit dereference.

umask: argument is missing initial 0

(W umask) A umask of 222 is incorrect. It should be 0222 because octal literals always start with 0 in Perl, as in C.

umask not implemented

(F) Your machine doesn't implement the umask function, and you tried to use it to restrict permissions for yourself (*EXPR* & 0700).

Unable to create sub named "%s"

(F) You attempted to create or access a subroutine with an illegal name.

Unbalanced context: %d more PUSHes than POPs

(W internal) The exit code detected an internal inconsistency in how many execution contexts were entered and left.

Unbalanced saves: %d more saves than restores

(W internal) The exit code detected an internal inconsistency in how many values were temporarily localized.

Unbalanced scopes: %d more ENTERs than LEAVEs

(W internal) The exit code detected an internal inconsistency in how many blocks were entered and left.

Unbalanced tmps: %d more allocs than frees

(W internal) The exit code detected an internal inconsistency in how many mortal scalars were allocated and freed.

Undefined format "%s" called

(F) The format indicated doesn't seem to exist. Perhaps it's really in another package?

Undefined sort subroutine "%s" called

(F) The sort comparison routine specified doesn't seem to exist. Perhaps it's in a different package?

`Undefined subroutine &%s called`

(F) The subroutine indicated hasn't been defined, or if it was, it has since been undefined.

`Undefined subroutine called`

(F) The anonymous subroutine you're trying to call hasn't been defined, or if it was, it has since been undefined.

`Undefined subroutine in sort`

(F) The sort comparison routine specified is declared but doesn't seem to have been defined yet.

`Undefined top format "%s" called`

(F) The format indicated doesn't seem to exist. Perhaps it's really in another package?

`Undefined value assigned to typeglob`

(W misc) An undefined value was assigned to a typeglob, such as `*foo = undef`. This does nothing. It's possible that you really mean `undef *foo`.

`unexec of %s into %s failed!`

(F) The unexec routine failed for some reason. See your local FSF representative, who probably put it there in the first place.

`Unknown BYTEORDER`

(F) There are no byte-swapping functions for a machine with this byte order.

`Unknown open() mode '%s'`

(F) The second argument of three-argument `open` is not in the list of valid modes: `<, >, >>, +<, +>, +>>, -|, |-`.

`Unknown process %x sent message to prime_env_iter: %s`

(P) This is an error peculiar to VMS. Perl was reading values for `%ENV` before iterating over it, and someone else stuck a message in the stream of data Perl expected. Someone's very confused, or perhaps trying to subvert Perl's population of `%ENV` for nefarious purposes.

`unmatched () in regexp`

(F) Unbackslashed parentheses must always be balanced in regular expressions. If you're a *vi* user, the `%` key is valuable for finding the matching parenthesis.

`Unmatched right %s bracket`

(F) The lexer counted more closing curly or square brackets than opening ones, so you're probably missing a matching opening bracket. As a general rule, you'll find the missing one (so to speak) near the place you were last editing.

unmatched [] in regexp

   (F) The brackets around a character class must match. If you wish to include a closing bracket in a character class, backslash it or put it first.

Unquoted string "%s" may clash with future reserved word

   (W reserved) You used a bareword that might someday be claimed as a reserved word. It's best to put such a word in quotes, or capitalize it somehow, or insert an underbar into it. You might also declare it as a subroutine.

Unrecognized character %s

   (F) The Perl parser has no idea what to do with the specified character in your Perl script (or eval). Perhaps you tried to run a compressed script, a binary program, or a directory as a Perl program.

Unrecognized escape \\%c passed through

   (W misc) You used a backslash-character combination that is not recognized by Perl.

Unrecognized signal name "%s"

   (F) You specified a signal name to the kill function that was not recognized. Say *kill -l* in your shell to see the valid signal names on your system.

Unrecognized switch: -%s (-h will show valid options)

   (F) You specified an illegal option to Perl. Don't do that. (If you think you didn't do that, check the #! line to see if it's supplying the bad switch on your behalf.)

Unsuccessful %s on filename containing newline

   (W newline) A file operation was attempted on a filename, and that operation failed, probably because the filename contained a newline, probably because you forgot to chop or chomp it off.

Unsupported directory function "%s" called

   (F) Your machine doesn't support opendir and readdir.

Unsupported function fork

   (F) Your version of executable does not support forking.

   Note that under some systems, like OS/2, there may be different flavors of Perl executables, some of which may support fork, some not. Try changing the name you call Perl by to perl_, perl__, and so on.

Unsupported function %s

   (F) This machine doesn't implement the indicated function, apparently. At least, *Configure* doesn't think so.

`Unsupported socket function "%s" called`

(F) Your machine doesn't support the Berkeley socket mechanism, or at least that's what *Configure* thought.

`Unterminated <> operator`

(F) The lexer saw a left angle bracket in a place where it was expecting a term, so it's looking for the corresponding right angle bracket and not finding it. Chances are you left some needed parentheses out earlier in the line, and you really meant a < symbol.

`Unterminated attribute parameter in attribute list`

(F) The lexer saw an opening (left) parenthesis character while parsing an attribute list, but the matching closing (right) parenthesis character was not found. You may need to add (or remove) a backslash character to get your parentheses to balance.

`Unterminated attribute list`

(F) The lexer found something other than a simple identifier at the start of an attribute, and it wasn't a semicolon or the start of a block. Perhaps you terminated the parameter list of the previous attribute too soon.

`Use of $# is deprecated`

(D deprecated) This was an ill-advised attempt to emulate a poorly defined *awk* feature. Use an explicit `printf` or `sprintf` instead.

`Use of $* is deprecated`

(D deprecated) This variable magically activated multiline pattern matching, both for you and for any luckless subroutine that you happen to call. You should use the `//m` and `//s` modifiers now to do that without the dangerous action-at-a-distance effects of $*.

`Use of %s in printf format not supported`

(F) You attempted to use a feature of `printf` that is accessible from only C. This usually means there's a better way to do it in Perl.

`Use of bare << to mean <<"" is deprecated`

(D deprecated) You are now encouraged to use the explicitly quoted form if you wish to use an empty line as the terminator of the here document.

`Use of implicit split to @_ is deprecated`

(D deprecated) You make a lot of work for the compiler when you clobber a subroutine's argument list, so it's better to assign the results of a `split` explicitly to an array (or list).

Use of inherited AUTOLOAD for non-method %s() is deprecated

    (D deprecated) As an (ahem) accidental feature, AUTOLOAD subroutines were looked up as methods (using the @ISA hierarchy) even when the subroutines to be autoloaded were called as plain functions (e.g., Foo::bar()), not as methods (e.g., Foo->bar() or $obj->bar()).

    This bug was rectified in Perl 5.005, which used method lookup only for methods' AUTOLOADs. However, a significant base of existing code may be using the old behavior. So, as an interim step, Perl 5.004 issued this optional warning when nonmethods used inherited AUTOLOADs.

    The simple rule is this: inheritance will not work when autoloading nonmethods. The simple fix for old code is this: in any module that used to depend on inheriting AUTOLOAD for nonmethods from a base class named BaseClass, execute *AUTOLOAD = \&BaseClass::AUTOLOAD during startup.

    In code that currently says use AutoLoader; @ISA = qw(AutoLoader);, you should remove AutoLoader from @ISA and change use AutoLoader; to use AutoLoader 'AUTOLOAD';.

Use of reserved word "%s" is deprecated

    (D deprecated) The indicated bareword is a reserved word. Future versions of Perl may use it as a keyword, so you're better off either explicitly quoting the word in a manner appropriate for its context of use, or using a different name altogether. The warning can be suppressed for subroutine names by either adding an & prefix or using a package qualifier, e.g., &our() or Foo::our().

Use of %s is deprecated

    (D deprecated) The construct indicated is no longer recommended, generally because there's a better way to do it, and also because the old way has bad side effects.

Use of uninitialized value%s

    (W uninitialized) An undefined value was used as if it were already defined. It was interpreted as a "" or a 0, but maybe it was a mistake. To suppress this warning assign a defined value to your variables.

Useless use of "re" pragma

    (W) You did a use re without any arguments. That isn't very useful.

Useless use of %s in void context

    (W void) You did something without a side effect in a context that does nothing with the return value, such as a statement that doesn't return a value from a block or the left side of a scalar comma operator. For example, you'd get this if you mixed up your C precedence with Python precedence and said:

```
$one, $two = 1, 2;
```

when you meant to say:

```
($one, $two) = (1, 2);
```

Another common error is using ordinary parentheses to construct a list reference when you should be using square or curly brackets, for example, if you say:

```
$array = (1,2);
```

when you should have said:

```
$array = [1,2];
```

The square brackets explicitly turn a list value into a scalar value, while parentheses do not. So when a parenthesized list is evaluated in a scalar context, the comma is treated like C's comma operator, which throws away the left argument, which is not what you want.

untie attempted while %d inner references still exist
    (W untie) A copy of the object returned from tie (or tied) was still valid when untie was called.

Value of %s can be "0"; test with defined()
    (W misc) In a conditional expression, you used <HANDLE>, <*> (glob), each, or readdir as a Boolean value. Each of these constructs can return a value of "0"; that would make the conditional expression false, which is probably not what you intended. When using these constructs in conditional expressions, test their values with the defined operator.

Value of CLI symbol "%s" too long
    (W misc) This is a warning peculiar to VMS. Perl tried to read the value of an %ENV element from a CLI symbol table and found a resultant string longer than 1,024 characters. The return value has been truncated to 1,024 characters.

Variable "%s" is not imported%s
    (F) While use strict in effect, you referred to a global variable that you apparently thought was imported from another module, because something else of the same name (usually a subroutine) is exported by that module. It usually means you put the wrong funny character on the front of your variable.

Variable "%s" may be unavailable

(W closure) An inner (nested) *anonymous* subroutine is inside a *named* subroutine, and outside that is another subroutine; and the anonymous (innermost) subroutine is referencing a lexical variable defined in the outermost subroutine. For example:

```
sub outermost { my $a; sub middle { sub { $a } } }
```

If the anonymous subroutine is called or referenced (directly or indirectly) from the outermost subroutine, it will share the variable as you would expect. But if the anonymous subroutine is called or referenced when the outermost subroutine is not active, it will see the value of the shared variable as it was before and during the *first* call to the outermost subroutine, which is probably not what you want.

In these circumstances, it is usually best to make the middle subroutine anonymous, using the sub {} syntax. Perl has specific support for shared variables in nested anonymous subroutines; a named subroutine in between interferes with this feature.

Variable "%s" will not stay shared

(W closure) An inner (nested) *named* subroutine is referencing a lexical variable defined in an outer subroutine.

When the inner subroutine is called, it will probably see the value of the outer subroutine's variable as it was before and during the *first* call to the outer subroutine; in this case, after the first call to the outer subroutine is complete, the inner and outer subroutines will no longer share a common value for the variable. In other words, the variable will no longer be shared.

Furthermore, if the outer subroutine is anonymous and references a lexical variable outside itself, then the outer and inner subroutines will *never* share the given variable.

This problem can usually be solved by making the inner subroutine anonymous, using the sub {} syntax. When inner anonymous subs that reference variables in outer subroutines are called or referenced, they are automatically rebound to the current values of such variables.

Variable syntax

(A) You've accidentally run your script through *csh* instead of Perl. Check the #! line, or manually feed your script into Perl yourself.

`Version number must be a constant number`

(P) The attempt to translate a *use Module n.n LIST* statement into its equivalent `BEGIN` block found an internal inconsistency with the version number.

`perl: warning: Setting locale failed.`

(S) The whole warning message will look something like:

```
perl: warning: Setting locale failed.
    perl: warning: Please check that your locale settings:
        LC_ALL = "En_US",
        LANG = (unset)
    are supported and installed on your system.
    perl: warning: Falling back to the standard locale ("C").
```

(Which locale settings failed will vary.) This error means that Perl detected that you or your system administrator have set up the so-called variable system but Perl could not use those settings. This was not dead serious, fortunately: there is a "default locale" called "C" that Perl can and will use, so the script will be run. Before you really fix the problem, however, you will get the same error message each time you run Perl. How to really fix the problem can be found in *perllocale*(1), under the section "Locale Problems".

`Warning: something's wrong`

(W) You passed `warn` an empty string (the equivalent of `warn ""`), or you called it with no arguments and `$_` was empty.

`Warning: unable to close filehandle %s properly`

(S) The implicit `close` done by an `open` got an error indication on the `close`. This usually indicates your filesystem ran out of disk space.

`Warning: Use of "%s" without parentheses is ambiguous`

(S ambiguous) You wrote a unary operator followed by something that looks like a binary operator but could also be interpreted as a term or unary operator. For instance, if you know that the `rand` function has a default argument of 1.0, and you write:

```
rand + 5;
```

you may *think* you wrote the same thing as:

```
rand() + 5;
```

but in actual fact, you got:

```
rand(+5);
```

So use parentheses to say what you really mean.

`write() on closed filehandle %s`

(W closed) The filehandle you're writing to got itself closed sometime before now. Check your logic flow.

`X outside of string`

(F) You had a `pack` template that specified a relative position before the beginning of the string being unpacked.

`x outside of string`

(F) You had a `pack` template that specified a relative position after the end of the string being unpacked.

`Xsub "%s" called in sort`

(F) The use of an external subroutine as a sort comparison is not yet supported.

`Xsub called in sort`

(F) The use of an external subroutine as a sort comparison is not yet supported.

`You can't use -l on a filehandle`

(F) A filehandle represents an opened file, and when you opened the file, it already went past any symlink you are presumably trying to look for. Use a filename instead.

`YOU HAVEN'T DISABLED SET-ID SCRIPTS IN THE KERNEL YET!`

(F) And you probably never will, because you probably don't have the sources to your kernel, and your vendor probably doesn't give a rip about what you want. Your best bet is to put a setuid C wrapper around your script with the *wrapsuid* script in the `eg` directory of the Perl distribution.

`You need to quote "%s"`

(W syntax) You assigned a bareword as a signal handler name. Unfortunately, you already have a subroutine of that name declared, which means that Perl 5 will try to call the subroutine when the assignment is executed, which is probably not what you want. (If it *is* what you want, put an `&` in front.)

When we italicize a word or phrase in here, it usually means you can find it defined elsewhere in the glossary. Think of them as hyperlinks.

accessor method

A *method* used to indirectly inspect or update an *object*'s state (its *instance variables*).

actual arguments

The *scalar values* that you supply to a *function* or *subroutine* when you call it. For instance, when you call power("puff"), the string "puff" is the actual argument. See also *argument* and *formal arguments*.

address operator

Some languages work directly with the memory addresses of values, but this can be like playing with fire. Perl provides a set of asbestos gloves for handling all memory management. The closest to an address operator in Perl is the backslash operator, but it gives you a *hard reference*, which is much safer than a memory address.

algorithm

A well-defined sequence of steps, clearly enough explained that even a computer could do them.

alias

A nickname for something, which behaves in all ways as though you'd used the original name instead of the nickname. Temporary aliases are implicitly created in the loop variable for foreach loops, in the $_ variable for

map or grep operators, in $a and $b during sort's comparison function, and in each element of @_ for the *actual arguments* of a subroutine call. Permanent aliases are explicitly created in *packages* by *importing* symbols or by assignment to *typeglobs*. Lexically scoped aliases for package variables are explicitly created by the our declaration.

alternatives

A list of possible choices from which you may select only one, as in "Would you like door A, B, or C?" Alternatives in regular expressions are separated with a single vertical bar: |. Alternatives in normal Perl expressions are separated with a double vertical bar: ||. Logical alternatives in *Boolean* expressions are separated with either || or or.

anonymous

Used to describe a *referent* that is not directly accessible through a named *variable*. Such a referent must be indirectly accessible through at least one *hard reference*. When the last hard reference goes away, the anonymous referent is destroyed without pity.

architecture

The kind of compluter you're working on, where one "kind" of computer means all those computers sharing a compatible machine language. Since Perl programs are (typically) simple text files, not executable images, a Perl program is much less sensitive to the architecture it's running on than programs in other languages, such as C, that are compiled into machine code. See also *platform* and *operating system*.

argument

A piece of data supplied to a *program, subroutine, function,* or *method* to tell it what it's supposed to do. Also called a "parameter".

ARGV

The name of the array containing the *argument vector* from the command line. If you use the empty <> operator, ARGV is the name of both the *filehandle* used to traverse the arguments and the *scalar* containing the name of the current input file.

arithmetical operator

A *symbol* such as + or / that tells Perl to do the arithmetic you were supposed to learn in grade school.

array

An ordered sequence of *values,* stored such that you can easily access any of the values using an *integer subscript* that specifies the value's *offset* in the sequence.

array context

An archaic expression for what is more correctly referred to as *list context.*

ASCII

The American Standard Code for Information Interchange (a 7-bit character set adequate only for poorly representing English text). Often used loosely to describe the lowest 128 values of the various ISO-8859-X character sets, a bunch of mutually incompatible 8-bit codes best described as half ASCII. See also *Unicode.*

assertion

A component of a *regular expression* that must be true for the pattern to match but does not necessarily match any characters itself. Often used specifically to mean a *zero-width* assertion.

assignment

An *operator* whose assigned mission in life is to change the value of a *variable.*

assignment operator

Either a regular *assignment,* or a compound *operator* composed of an ordinary assignment and some other operator, that changes the value of a variable in place, that is, relative to its old value. For example, $a += 2 adds 2 to $a.

associative array

See *hash.* Please.

associativity

Determines whether you do the left *operator* first or the right *operator* first when you have "A *operator* B *operator* C" and the two operators are of the same precedence. Operators like + are left associative, while operators like ** are right associative. See Chapter 3, *Unary and Binary Operators,* for a list of operators and their associativity.

asynchronous

Said of events or activities whose relative temporal ordering is indeterminate because too many things are going on at once. Hence, an asynchronous event is one you didn't know when to expect.

atom

A *regular expression* component potentially matching a *substring* containing one or more characters and treated as an indivisible syntactic unit by any following *quantifier.* (Contrast with an *assertion* that matches something of *zero width* and may not be quantified.)

atomic operation

When Democritus gave the word "atom" to the indivisible bits of matter, he meant literally something that could not be cut: *a-* (not) + *tomos* (cuttable). An atomic operation is an action that can't be interrupted, not one forbidden in a nuclear-free zone.

attribute

A new feature that allows the declaration of *variables* and *subroutines* with modifiers as in sub foo : locked method. Also, another name for an *instance variable* of an *object.*

autogeneration

A feature of *operator overloading* of *objects,* whereby the behavior of certain *operators* can be reasonably deduced using more fundamental operators. This assumes that the overloaded operators will often have the same relationships as the regular operators. See Chapter 13, *Overloading.*

autoincrement

To add one to something automatically, hence the name of the the ++ operator. To instead subtract one from something automatically is known as an "autodecrement".

autoload

To load on demand. (Also called "lazy" loading.) Specifically, to call an AUTOLOAD subroutine on behalf of an undefined subroutine.

autosplit

To split a string automatically, as the **-a** *switch* does when running under **-p** or **-n** in order to emulate *awk*. (See also the AutoSplit module, which has nothing to do with the **-a** switch, but a lot to do with autoloading.)

autovivification

A Greco-Roman word meaning "to bring oneself to life". In Perl, storage locations (*lvalues*) spontaneously generate themselves as needed, including the creation of any *hard reference* values to point to the next level of storage. The assignment $a[5][5][5][5][5] = "quintet" potentially creates five scalar storage locations, plus four references (in the first four scalar locations) pointing to four new anonymous arrays (to hold the last four scalar locations). But the point of autovivification is that you don't have to worry about it.

AV

Short for "array value", which refers to one of Perl's internal data types that holds an *array*. The AV type is a subclass of *SV*.

awk

Descriptive editing term—short for "awkward". Also coincidentally refers to a venerable text-processing language from which Perl derived some of its high-level ideas.

backreference

A substring *captured* by a subpattern within unadorned parentheses in a *regex*. Backslashed decimal numbers (\1, \2, etc.) later in the same pattern refer back to the corresponding subpattern in the current match. Outside the pattern, the numbered variables ($1, $2, etc.) continue to refer to these same values, as long as the pattern was the last successful match of the current dynamic scope.

backtracking

The practice of saying, "If I had to do it all over, I'd do it differently," and then actually going back and doing it all over differently. Mathematically speaking, it's returning from an unsuccessful recursion on a tree of possibilities. Perl backtracks when it attempts to match patterns with a *regular expression*, and its earlier attempts don't pan out. See "The

Little Engine That /Could(n't)?/" in Chapter 5, *Pattern Matching*.

backward compatibility

Means you can still run your old program because we didn't break any of the features or bugs it was relying on.

bareword

A word sufficiently ambiguous to be deemed illegal under use strict 'subs'. In the absence of that stricture, a bareword is treated as if quotes were around it.

base class

A generic *object* type; that is, a *class* from which other, more specific classes are derived genetically by *inheritance*. Also called a "superclass" by people who respect their ancestors.

big-endian

From Swift: someone who eats eggs big end first. Also used of computers that store the most significant *byte* of a word at a lower byte address than the least significant byte. Often considered superior to little-endian machines. See also *little-endian*.

binary

Having to do with numbers represented in base 2. That means there's basically two numbers, 0 and 1. Also used to describe a "nontext file", presumably because such a file makes full use of all the binary bits in its bytes. With the advent of *Unicode*, this distinction, already suspect, loses even more of its meaning.

binary operator

An *operator* that takes two *operands*.

bind

To assign a specific *network address* to a *socket*.

bit

An integer in the range from 0 to 1, inclusive. The smallest possible unit of information storage. An eighth of a *byte* or of a dollar. (The term "Pieces of Eight" comes from being able to split the old Spanish dollar into 8 bits, each of which still counted for money. That's why a 25-cent piece today is still "two bits".)

bit shift

The movement of bits left or right in a computer word, which has the effect of multiplying or dividing by a power of 2.

bit string

A sequence of *bits* that is actually being thought of as a sequence of bits, for once.

bless

In corporate life, to grant official approval to a thing, as in, "The VP of Engineering has blessed our WebCruncher project." Similarly in Perl, to grant official approval to a *referent* so that it can function as an *object*, such as a WebCruncher object. See the `bless` function in Chapter 29, *Functions*.

block

What a *process* does when it has to wait for something: "My process blocked waiting for the disk." As an unrelated noun, it refers to a large chunk of data, of a size that the *operating system* likes to deal with (normally a power of two such as 512 or 8192). Typically refers to a chunk of data that's coming from or going to a disk file.

BLOCK

A syntactic construct consisting of a sequence of Perl *statements* that is delimited by braces. The `if` and `while` statements are defined in terms of *BLOCK*s, for instance. Sometimes we also say "block" to mean a lexical scope; that is, a sequence of statements that act like a *BLOCK*, such as within an `eval` or a file, even though the statements aren't delimited by braces.

block buffering

A method of making input and output efficient by passing one *block* at a time. By default, Perl does block buffering to disk files. See *buffer* and *command buffering*.

Boolean

A value that is either *true* or *false*.

Boolean context

A special kind of *scalar context* used in conditionals to decide whether the *scalar value* returned by an expression is *true* or *false*. Does not evaluate as either a string or a number. See *context*.

breakpoint

A spot in your program where you've told the debugger to stop *execution* so you can poke around and see whether anything is wrong yet.

broadcast

To send a *datagram* to multiple destinations simultaneously.

BSD

A psychoactive drug, popular in the 80s, probably developed at U. C. Berkeley or thereabouts. Similar in many ways to the prescription-only medication called "System V", but infinitely more useful. (Or, at least, more fun.) The full chemical name is "Berkeley Standard Distribution".

bucket

A location in a *hash table* containing (potentially) multiple entries whose keys "hash" to the same hash value according to its hash function. (As internal policy, you don't have to worry about it, unless you're into internals, or policy.)

buffer

A temporary holding location for data. *Block buffering* means that the data is passed on to its destination whenever the buffer is full. *Line buffering* means that it's passed on whenever a complete line is received. *Command buffering* means that it's passed every time you do a `print` command (or equivalent). If your output is unbuffered, the system processes it one byte at a time without the use of a holding area. This can be rather inefficient.

built-in

A *function* that is predefined in the language. Even when hidden by *overriding*, you can always get at a built-in function by *qualifying* its name with the `CORE::` pseudo-package.

bundle

A group of related modules on *CPAN*. (Also, sometimes refers to a group of command-line switches grouped into one *switch cluster*.)

byte

A piece of data worth eight *bits* in most places.

bytecode

A pidgin-like language spoken among 'droids when they don't wish to reveal their orientation (see *endian*). Named after some similar languages spoken (for similar reasons) between compilers and interpreters in the late 20th century. These languages are characterized by representing everything as a non-architecture-dependent sequence of bytes.

C

A language beloved by many for its inside-out *type* definitions, inscrutable *precedence* rules, and heavy *overloading* of the function-call mechanism. (Well, actually, people first switched to C because they found lowercase identifiers easier to read than upper.) Perl is written in C, so it's not surprising that Perl borrowed a few ideas from it.

C preprocessor

The typical C compiler's first pass, which processes lines beginning with # for conditional compilation and macro definition and does various manipulations of the program text based on the current definitions. Also known as *cpp*(1).

call by reference

An *argument*-passing mechanism in which the *formal arguments* refer directly to the *actual arguments*, and the *subroutine* can change the actual arguments by changing the formal arguments. That is, the formal argument is an *alias* for the actual argument. See also *call by value*.

call by value

An *argument*-passing mechanism in which the *formal arguments* refer to a copy of the *actual arguments*, and the *subroutine* cannot change the actual arguments by changing the formal arguments. See also *call by reference*.

callback

A *handler* that you register with some other part of your program in the hope that the other part of your program will *trigger* your handler when some event of interest transpires.

canonical

Reduced to a standard form to facilitate comparison.

capturing

The use of parentheses around a *subpattern* in a *regular expression* to store the matched *substring* as a *backreference*. (Captured strings are also returned as a list in *list context*.)

character

A small integer representative of a unit of orthography. Historically, characters were usually stored as fixed-width integers (typically in a byte, or maybe two, depending on the character set), but with the advent of UTF-8, characters are often stored in a variable number of bytes depending on the size of the integer that represents the character. Perl manages this transparently for you, for the most part.

character class

A square-bracketed list of characters used in a *regular expression* to indicate that any character of the set may occur at a given point. Loosely, any predefined set of characters so used.

character property

A predefined *character class* matchable by the \p *metasymbol*. Many standard properties are defined for *Unicode*.

circumfix operator

An *operator* that surrounds its *operand*, like the angle operator, or parentheses, or a hug.

class

A user-defined *type*, implemented in Perl via a *package* that provides (either directly or by inheritance) *methods* (that is, *subroutines*) to handle *instances* of the class (its *objects*). See also *inheritance*.

class method

A *method* whose *invocant* is a *package* name, not an *object* reference. A method associated with the class as a whole.

client

In networking, a *process* that initiates contact with a *server* process in order to exchange data and perhaps receive a service.

cloister

A *cluster* used to restrict the scope of a *regular expression modifier*.

closure

An *anonymous* subroutine that, when a reference to it is generated at run time, keeps track of the identities of externally visible *lexical variables* even after those lexical variables have supposedly gone out of *scope*. They're called "closures" because this sort of behavior gives mathematicians a sense of closure.

cluster

A parenthesized *subpattern* used to group parts of a *regular expression* into a single *atom*.

CODE

The word returned by the ref function when you apply it to a reference to a subroutine. See also *CV*.

code generator

A system that writes code for you in a low-level language, such as code to implement the backend of a compiler. See *program generator*.

code subpattern

A *regular expression* subpattern whose real purpose is to execute some Perl code, for example, the `(?{...})` and `(??{...})` subpatterns.

collating sequence

The order into which *characters* sort. This is used by *string* comparison routines to decide, for example, where in this glossary to put "collating sequence".

command

In *shell* programming, the syntactic combination of a program name and its arguments. More loosely, anything you type to a shell (a command interpreter) that starts it doing something. Even more loosely, a Perl *statement*, which might start with a *label* and typically ends with a semicolon.

command buffering

A mechanism in Perl that lets you store up the output of each Perl *command* and then flush it out as a single request to the *operating system*. It's enabled by setting the `$|` (`$AUTOFLUSH`) variable to a true value. It's used when you don't want data sitting around not going where it's supposed to, which may happen because the default on a *file* or *pipe* is to use *block buffering*.

command name

The name of the program currently executing, as typed on the command line. In C, the *command* name is passed to the program as the first command-line argument. In Perl, it comes in separately as `$0`.

command-line arguments

The *values* you supply along with a program name when you tell a *shell* to execute a *command*. These values are passed to a Perl program through `@ARGV`.

comment

A remark that doesn't affect the meaning of the program. In Perl, a comment is introduced by a `#` character and continues to the end of the line.

compilation unit

The *file* (or *string*, in the case of `eval`) that is currently being compiled.

compile phase

Any time before Perl starts running your main program. See also *run phase*. Compile phase is mostly spent in *compile time*, but may also be spent in *run time* when `BEGIN` blocks, `use` declarations, or constant subexpressions are being evaluated. The startup and import code of any `use` declaration is also run during compile phase.

compile time

The time when Perl is trying to make sense of your code, as opposed to when it thinks it knows what your code means and is merely trying to do what it thinks your code says to do, which is *run time*.

compiler

Strictly speaking, a program that munches up another program and spits out yet another file containing the program in a "more executable" form, typically containing native machine instructions. The *perl* program is not a compiler by this definition, but it does contain a kind of compiler that takes a program and turns it into a more executable form (*syntax trees*) within the *perl* process itself, which the *interpreter* then interprets. There are, however, extension *modules* to get Perl to act more like a "real" compiler. See Chapter 18, *Compiling*.

composer

A "constructor" for a *referent* that isn't really an *object*, like an anonymous array or a hash (or a sonata, for that matter). For example, a pair of braces acts as a composer for a hash, and a pair of brackets acts as a composer for an array. See the section "Creating References" in Chapter 8, *References*.

concatenation

The process of gluing one cat's nose to another cat's tail. Also, a similar operation on two *strings*.

conditional

Something "iffy". See *Boolean context*.

connection

In telephony, the temporary electrical circuit between the caller's and the callee's phone. In networking, the same kind of temporary circuit between a *client* and a *server*.

construct

As a noun, a piece of syntax made up of smaller pieces. As a transitive verb, to create an *object* using a *constructor*.

constructor

Any *class method*, *instance method*, or *subroutine* that composes, initializes, blesses, and returns an *object*. Sometimes we use the term loosely to mean a *composer*.

context

The surroundings, or environment. The context given by the surrounding code determines what kind of data a particular *expression* is expected to return. The three primary contexts are *list context*, *scalar context*, and *void context*. Scalar context is sometimes subdivided into *Boolean context*, *numeric context*, *string context*, and *void context*. There's also a "don't care" context (which is dealt with in Chapter 2, *Bits and Pieces*, if you care).

continuation

The treatment of more than one physical *line* as a single logical line. *Makefile* lines are continued by putting a backslash before the *newline*. Mail headers as defined by RFC 822 are continued by putting a space or tab *after* the newline. In general, lines in Perl do not need any form of continuation mark, because *whitespace* (including newlines) is gleefully ignored. Usually.

core dump

The corpse of a *process*, in the form of a file left in the *working directory* of the process, usually as a result of certain kinds of fatal error.

CPAN

The Comprehensive Perl Archive Network. (See the Preface and Chapter 22, *CPAN*, for details.)

cracker

Someone who breaks security on computer systems. A cracker may be a true *hacker* or only a *script kiddie*.

current package

The *package* in which the current statement is compiled. Scan backwards in the text of your program through the current *lexical scope* or any enclosing lexical scopes till you find a package declaration. That's your current package name.

current working directory

See *working directory*.

currently selected output channel

The last *filehandle* that was designated with `select(FILEHANDLE)`; STDOUT, if no filehandle has been selected.

CV

An internal "code value" typedef, holding a *subroutine*. The CV type is a subclass of *SV*.

dangling statement

A bare, single *statement*, without any braces, hanging off an `if` or `while` conditional. C allows them. Perl doesn't.

data structure

How your various pieces of data relate to each other and what shape they make when you put them all together, as in a rectangular table or a triangular-shaped tree.

data type

A set of possible values, together with all the operations that know how to deal with those values. For example, a numeric data type has a certain set of numbers that you can work with and various mathematical operations that you can do on the numbers but would make little sense on, say, a string such as `"Kilroy"`. Strings have their own operations, such as *concatenation*. Compound types made of a number of smaller pieces generally have operations to compose and decompose them, and perhaps to rearrange them. *Objects* that model things in the real world often have operations that correspond to real activities. For instance, if you model an elevator, your elevator object might have an `open_door()` *method*.

datagram

A packet of data, such as a *UDP* message, that (from the viewpoint of the programs involved) can be sent independently over the network. (In fact, all packets are sent independently at the *IP* level, but *stream* protocols such as *TCP* hide this from your program.)

DBM

Stands for "Data Base Management" routines, a set of routines that emulate an *associative array* using disk files. The routines use a dynamic hashing scheme to locate any entry with only two disk accesses. DBM files allow a Perl program to keep a persistent *hash* across multiple invocations. You can `tie` your hash variables to various DBM implementations—see *AnyDBM_File*(3) and the entry on DB_File in Chapter 32, *Standard Modules*.

declaration

An *assertion* that states something exists and perhaps describes what it's like, without giving any commitment as to how or where you'll use it. A declaration is like the part of your recipe that says, "two cups flour, one large egg, four or five tadpoles..." See *statement* for its opposite. Note that some declarations also function as statements. Subroutine declarations also act as definitions if a body is supplied.

decrement

To subtract a value from a variable, as in "decrement $x" (meaning to remove 1 from its value) or "decrement $x by 3".

default

A *value* chosen for you if you don't supply a value of your own.

defined

Having a meaning. Perl thinks that some of the things people try to do are devoid of meaning, in particular, making use of variables that have never been given a *value* and performing certain operations on data that isn't there. For example, if you try to read data past the end of a *file*, Perl will hand you back an undefined value. See also *false*, and the defined operator in Chapter 29.

delimiter

A *character* or *string* that sets bounds to an arbitrarily-sized textual object, not to be confused with a *separator* or *terminator*. "To delimit" really just means "to surround" or "to enclose" (like these parentheses are doing).

dereference

A fancy computer science term meaning "to follow a *reference* to what it points to". The "de" part of it refers to the fact that you're taking away one level of *indirection*.

derived class

A *class* that defines some of its *methods* in terms of a more generic class, called a *base class*. Note that classes aren't classified exclusively into base classes or derived classes: a class can function as both a derived class and a base class simultaneously, which is kind of classy.

descriptor

See *file descriptor*.

destroy

To deallocate the memory of a *referent* (first triggering its DESTROY method, if it has one).

destructor

A special *method* that is called when an *object* is thinking about *destroying* itself. A Perl program's DESTROY method doesn't do the actual destruction; Perl just *triggers* the method in case the *class* wants to do any associated cleanup.

device

A whiz-bang hardware gizmo (like a disk or tape drive or a modem or a joystick or a mouse) attached to your computer, that the *operating system* tries to make look like a *file* (or a bunch of files). Under Unix, these fake files tend to live in the */dev* directory.

directive

A *pod* directive. See Chapter 26, *Plain Old Documentation*.

directory

A special file that contains other files. Some *operating systems* call these "folders", "drawers", or "catalogs".

directory handle

A name that represents a particular instance of opening a directory to read it, until you close it. See the opendir function.

dispatch

To send something to its correct destination. Often used metaphorically to indicate a transfer of programmatic control to a destination selected algorithmically, often by lookup in a table of function *references* or, in the case of object *methods*, by traversing the inheritance tree looking for the most specific definition for the method.

distribution

A standard, bundled release of a system of software. The default usage implies source code is included. If that is not the case, it will be called a "binary-only" distribution.

dweomer

An enchantment, illusion, phantasm, or jugglery. Said when Perl's magical *dwimmer* effects don't do what you expect, but rather seem to be the product of arcane dweomercraft, sorcery, or wonder working. [From Old English]

dwimmer

DWIM is an acronym for "Do What I Mean", the principle that something should just do what you want it to do without an undue amount of fuss. A bit of code that does "dwimming" is a "dwimmer". Dwimming can require a great deal of behind-the-scenes magic, which (if it doesn't stay properly behind the scenes) is called a *dweomer* instead.

dynamic scoping

Dynamic scoping works over a dynamic scope, making variables visible throughout the rest of the *block* in which they are first used and in any *subroutines* that are called by the rest of the block. Dynamically scoped variables can have their values temporarily changed (and implicitly restored later) by a `local` operator. (Compare *lexical scoping*.) Used more loosely to mean how a subroutine that is in the middle of calling another subroutine "contains" that subroutine at *run time*.

eclectic

Derived from many sources. Some would say *too* many.

element

A basic building block. When you're talking about an *array*, it's one of the items that make up the array.

embedding

When something is contained in something else, particularly when that might be considered surprising: "I've embedded a complete Perl interpreter in my editor!"

empty subclass test

The notion that an empty *derived class* should behave exactly like its *base class*.

en passant

When you change a *value* as it is being copied. [From French, "in passing", as in the exotic pawn-capturing maneuver in chess.]

encapsulation

The veil of abstraction separating the *interface* from the *implementation* (whether enforced or not), which mandates that all access to an *object*'s state be through *methods* alone.

endian

See *little-endian* and *big-endian*.

environment

The collective set of *environment variables* your *process* inherits from its parent. Accessed via `%ENV`.

environment variable

A mechanism by which some high-level agent such as a user can pass its preferences down to its future offspring (child *processes*, grand-child processes, great-grandchild processes, and so on). Each environment variable is a *key/value* pair, like one entry in a *hash*.

EOF

End of File. Sometimes used metaphorically as the terminating string of a *here document*.

errno

The error number returned by a *syscall* when it fails. Perl refers to the error by the name `$!` (or `$OS_ERROR` if you use the English module).

error

See *exception* or *fatal error*.

escape sequence

See *metasymbol*.

exception

A fancy term for an error. See *fatal error*.

exception handling

The way a program responds to an error. The exception handling mechanism in Perl is the `eval` operator.

exec

To throw away the current *process*'s program and replace it with another without exiting the process or relinquishing any resources held (apart from the old memory image).

executable file

A *file* that is specially marked to tell the *operating system* that it's okay to run this file as a program. Usually shortened to "executable".

execute

To run a *program* or *subroutine*. (Has nothing to do with the `kill` built-in, unless you're trying to run a *signal handler*.)

execute bit

The special mark that tells the operating system it can run this program. There are actually three execute bits under Unix, and which bit gets used depends on whether you own the file singularly, collectively, or not at all.

exit status

See *status*.

export

To make symbols from a *module* available for *import* by other modules.

expression

Anything you can legally say in a spot where a *value* is required. Typically composed of *literals, variables, operators, functions,* and *subroutine* calls, not necessarily in that order.

extension

A Perl module that also pulls in compiled C or C++ code. More generally, any experimental option that can be compiled into Perl, such as multithreading.

false

In Perl, any value that would look like `""` or `"0"` if evaluated in a string context. Since undefined values evaluate to `""`, all undefined values are false, but not all false values are undefined.

FAQ

Frequently Asked Question (although not necessarily frequently answered, especially if the answer appears in the Perl FAQ shipped standard with Perl).

fatal error

An uncaught *exception*, which causes termination of the *process* after printing a message on your *standard error* stream. Errors that happen inside an `eval` are not fatal. Instead, the `eval` terminates after placing the exception message in the `$@` (`$EVAL_ERROR`) variable. You can try to provoke a fatal error with the `die` operator (known as throwing or raising an exception), but this may be caught by a dynamically enclosing `eval`. If not caught, the `die` becomes a fatal error.

field

A single piece of numeric or string data that is part of a longer *string, record,* or *line*. Variable-width fields are usually split up by *separators* (so use `split` to extract the fields), while fixed-width fields are usually at fixed positions (so use `unpack`). *Instance variables* are also known as "fields".

FIFO

First In, First Out. See also *LIFO*. Also, a nickname for a *named pipe*.

file

A named collection of data, usually stored on disk in a *directory* in a *filesystem*. Roughly like a document, if you're into office metaphors. In modern filesystems, you can actually give a file more than one name. Some files have special properties, like directories and devices.

file descriptor

The little number the *operating system* uses to keep track of which opened *file* you're talking about. Perl hides the file descriptor inside a *standard I/O* stream and then attaches the stream to a *filehandle*.

file test operator

A built-in unary operator that you use to determine whether something is *true* about a file, such as `-o $filename` to test whether you're the owner of the file.

fileglob

A "wildcard" match on *filenames*. See the `glob` function.

filehandle

An identifier (not necessarily related to the real name of a file) that represents a particular instance of opening a file until you close it. If you're going to open and close several different files in succession, it's fine to open each of them with the same filehandle, so you don't have to write out separate code to process each file.

filename

One name for a file. This name is listed in a *directory*, and you can use it in an `open` to tell the *operating system* exactly which file you want to open, and associate the file with a *filehandle* which will carry the subsequent identity of that file in your program, until you close it.

filesystem

A set of *directories* and *files* residing on a partition of the disk. Sometimes known as a "partition". You can change the file's name or even move a file around from directory to directory within a filesystem without actually moving the file itself, at least under Unix.

filter

A program designed to take a *stream* of input and transform it into a stream of output.

flag

We tend to avoid this term because it means so many things. It may mean a command-line *switch* that takes no argument itself (such as Perl's **-n** and **-p** flags) or, less frequently, a single-bit indicator (such as the O_CREAT and O_EXCL flags used in sysopen).

floating point

A method of storing numbers in "scientific notation", such that the precision of the number is independent of its magnitude (the decimal point "floats"). Perl does its numeric work with floating-point numbers (sometimes called "floats"), when it can't get away with using *integers*. Floating-point numbers are mere approximations of real numbers.

flush

The act of emptying a *buffer*, often before it's full.

FMTEYEWTK

Far More Than Everything You Ever Wanted To Know. An exhaustive treatise on one narrow topic, something of a super-*FAQ*. See Tom for far more.

fork

To create a child *process* identical to the parent process at its moment of conception, at least until it gets ideas of its own. A thread with protected memory.

formal arguments

The generic names by which a *subroutine* knows its *arguments*. In many languages, formal arguments are always given individual names, but in Perl, the formal arguments are just the elements of an array. The formal arguments to a Perl program are $ARGV[0], $ARGV[1], and so on. Similarly, the formal arguments to a Perl subroutine are $_[0], $_[1], and so on. You may give the arguments individual names by assigning the values to a my list. See also *actual arguments*.

format

A specification of how many spaces and digits and things to put somewhere so that whatever you're printing comes out nice and pretty.

freely available

Means you don't have to pay money to get it, but the copyright on it may still belong to someone else (like Larry).

freely redistributable

Means you're not in legal trouble if you give a bootleg copy of it to your friends and we find out about it. In fact, we'd rather you gave a copy to all your friends.

freeware

Historically, any software that you give away, particularly if you make the source code available as well. Now often called *open source software*. Recently there has been a trend to use the term in contradistinction to *open source software*, to refer only to free software released under the Free Software Foundation's GPL (General Public License), but this is difficult to justify etymologically.

function

Mathematically, a mapping of each of a set of input values to a particular output value. In computers, refers to a *subroutine* or *operator* that returns a *value*. It may or may not have input values (called *arguments*).

funny character

Someone like Larry, or one of his peculiar friends. Also refers to the strange prefixes that Perl requires as noun markers on its variables.

garbage collection

A misnamed feature—it should be called, "expecting your mother to pick up after you". Strictly speaking, Perl doesn't do this, but it relies on a reference-counting mechanism to keep things tidy. However, we rarely speak strictly and will often refer to the reference-counting scheme as a form of garbage collection. (If it's any comfort, when your interpreter exits, a "real" garbage collector runs to make sure everything is cleaned up if you've been messy with circular references and such.)

GID

Group ID—in Unix, the numeric group ID that the *operating system* uses to identify you and members of your *group*.

glob

Strictly, the shell's * character, which will match a "glob" of characters when you're trying to generate a list of filenames. Loosely, the act of using globs and similar symbols to do pattern matching. See also *fileglob* and *typeglob*.

global

Something you can see from anywhere, usually used of *variables* and *subroutines* that are visible everywhere in your program. In Perl, only certain special variables are truly global—most variables (and all subroutines) exist only in the current *package*. Global variables can be declared with our. See "Global Declarations" in Chapter 4, *Statements and Declarations*.

global destruction

The *garbage collection* of globals (and the running of any associated object destructors) that takes place when a Perl *interpreter* is being shut down. Global destruction should not be confused with the Apocalypse, except perhaps when it should.

glue language

A language such as Perl that is good at hooking things together that weren't intended to be hooked together.

granularity

The size of the pieces you're dealing with, mentally speaking.

greedy

A *subpattern* whose *quantifier* wants to match as many things as possible.

grep

Originally from the old Unix editor command for "Globally search for a Regular Expression and Print it", now used in the general sense of any kind of search, especially text searches. Perl has a built-in grep function that searches a list for elements matching any given criterion, whereas the *grep*(1) program searches for lines matching a *regular expression* in one or more files.

group

A set of users of which you are a member. In some operating systems (like Unix), you can give certain file access permissions to other members of your group.

GV

An internal "glob value" typedef, holding a *typeglob*. The GV type is a subclass of *SV*.

hacker

Someone who is brilliantly persistent in solving technical problems, whether these involve golfing, fighting orcs, or programming. Hacker

is a neutral term, morally speaking. Good hackers are not to be confused with evil *crackers* or clueless *script kiddies*. If you confuse them, we will presume that you are either evil or clueless.

handler

A *subroutine* or *method* that is called by Perl when your program needs to respond to some internal event, such as a *signal*, or an encounter with an operator subject to *operator overloading*. See also *callback*.

hard reference

A *scalar value* containing the actual address of a *referent*, such that the referent's *reference* count accounts for it. (Some hard references are held internally, such as the implicit reference from one of a *typeglob*'s variable slots to its corresponding referent.) A hard reference is different from a *symbolic reference*.

hash

An unordered association of *key/value* pairs, stored such that you can easily use a string *key* to look up its associated data *value*. This glossary is like a hash, where the word to be defined is the key, and the definition is the value. A hash is also sometimes septisyllabically called an "associative array", which is a pretty good reason for simply calling it a "hash" instead.

hash table

A data structure used internally by Perl for implementing associative arrays (hashes) efficiently. See also *bucket*.

header file

A file containing certain required definitions that you must include "ahead" of the rest of your program to do certain obscure operations. A C header file has a *.h* extension. Perl doesn't really have header files, though historically Perl has sometimes used translated *.h* files with a *.ph* extension. See require in Chapter 29. (Header files have been superseded by the *module* mechanism.)

here document

So called because of a similar construct in *shells* that pretends that the *lines* following the *command* are a separate *file* to be fed to the command, up to some terminating string. In Perl, however, it's just a fancy form of quoting.

hexadecimal

A number in base 16, "hex" for short. The digits for 10 through 16 are customarily represented by the letters a through f. Hexadecimal constants in Perl start with 0x. See also the hex function in Chapter 29.

home directory

The directory you are put into when you log in. On a Unix system, the name is often placed into $ENV{HOME} or $ENV{LOGDIR} by *login*, but you can also find it with (getpwuid($<))[7]. (Some platforms do not have a concept of a home directory.)

host

The computer on which a program or other data resides.

hubris

Excessive pride, the sort of thing Zeus zaps you for. Also the quality that makes you write (and maintain) programs that other people won't want to say bad things about. Hence, the third great virtue of a programmer. See also *laziness* and *impatience*.

HV

Short for a "hash value" typedef, which holds Perl's internal representation of a hash. The HV type is a subclass of *SV*.

identifier

A legally formed name for most anything in which a computer program might be interested. Many languages (including Perl) allow identifiers that start with a letter and contain letters and digits. Perl also counts the underscore character as a valid letter. (Perl also has more complicated names, such as *qualified* names.)

impatience

The anger you feel when the computer is being lazy. This makes you write programs that don't just react to your needs, but actually anticipate them. Or at least that pretend to. Hence, the second great virtue of a programmer. See also *laziness* and *hubris*.

implementation

How a piece of code actually goes about doing its job. Users of the code should not count on implementation details staying the same unless they are part of the published *interface*.

import

To gain access to symbols that are exported from another module. See use in Chapter 29.

increment

To increase the value of something by 1 (or by some other number, if so specified).

indexing

In olden days, the act of looking up a *key* in an actual index (such as a phone book), but now merely the act of using any kind of key or position to find the corresponding *value*, even if no index is involved. Things have degenerated to the point that Perl's index function merely locates the position (index) of one string in another.

indirect filehandle

An *expression* that evaluates to something that can be used as a *filehandle*: a *string* (filehandle name), a *typeglob*, a typeglob *reference*, or a low-level *IO* object.

indirect object

In English grammar, a short noun phrase between a verb and its direct object indicating the beneficiary or recipient of the action. In Perl, print STDOUT "$foo\n"; can be understood as "verb indirect-object object" where STDOUT is the recipient of the print action, and "$foo" is the object being printed. Similarly, when invoking a *method*, you might place the invocant between the method and its arguments:

```
$gollum = new Pathetic::Creature "Smeagol";
give $gollum "Fisssssh!";
give $gollum "Precious!";
```

indirect object slot

The syntactic position falling between a method call and its arguments when using the indirect object invocation syntax. (The slot is distinguished by the absence of a comma between it and the next argument.) STDERR is in the indirect object slot here:

```
print STDERR "Awake! Awake! Fear, Fire,
    Foes! Awake!\n";
```

indirection

If something in a program isn't the value you're looking for but indicates where the value is, that's indirection. This can be done with either *symbolic references* or *hard references*.

infix

An *operator* that comes in between its *operands*, such as multiplication in 24 * 7.

inheritance

What you get from your ancestors, genetically or otherwise. If you happen to be a *class*, your ancestors are called *base classes* and your descendants are called *derived classes*. See *single inheritance* and *multiple inheritance*.

instance

Short for "an instance of a class", meaning an *object* of that *class*.

instance variable

An *attribute* of an *object*; data stored with the particular object rather than with the class as a whole.

integer

A number with no fractional (decimal) part. A counting number, like 1, 2, 3, and so on, but including 0 and the negatives.

interface

The services a piece of code promises to provide forever, in contrast to its *implementation*, which it should feel free to change whenever it likes.

interpolation

The insertion of a scalar or list value somewhere in the middle of another value, such that it appears to have been there all along. In Perl, variable interpolation happens in double-quoted strings and patterns, and list interpolation occurs when constructing the list of values to pass to a list operator or other such construct that takes a *LIST*.

interpreter

Strictly speaking, a program that reads a second program and does what the second program says directly without turning the program into a different form first, which is what *compilers* do. Perl is not an interpreter by this definition, because it contains a kind of compiler that takes a program and turns it into a more executable form (*syntax trees*) within the *perl* process itself, which the Perl *run-time* system then interprets.

invocant

The agent on whose behalf a *method* is invoked. In a *class* method, the invocant is a package name. In an *instance* method, the invocant is an object reference.

invocation

The act of calling up a deity, daemon, program, method, subroutine, or function to get it do what you think it's supposed to do. We usually "call" subroutines but "invoke" methods, since it sounds cooler.

I/O

Input from, or output to, a *file* or *device*.

IO

An internal I/O object. Can also mean *indirect object*.

IP

Internet Protocol, or Intellectual Property.

IPC

Interprocess Communication.

is-a

A relationship between two *objects* in which one object is considered to be a more specific version of the other, generic object: "A camel is a mammal." Since the generic object really only exists in a Platonic sense, we usually add a little abstraction to the notion of objects and think of the relationship as being between a generic *base class* and a specific *derived class*. Oddly enough, Platonic classes don't always have Platonic relationships—see *inheritance*.

iteration

Doing something repeatedly.

iterator

A special programming gizmo that keeps track of where you are in something that you're trying to iterate over. The foreach loop in Perl contains an iterator; so does a hash, allowing you to each through it.

IV

The integer four, not to be confused with six, Tom's favorite editor. IV also means an internal Integer Value of the type a *scalar* can hold, not to be confused with an *NV*.

JAPH

"Just Another Perl Hacker," a clever but cryptic bit of Perl code that when executed, evaluates to that string. Often used to illustrate a particular Perl feature, and something of an ungoing Obfuscated Perl Contest seen in Usenix signatures.

key

The string index to a *hash*, used to look up the *value* associated with that key.

keyword

See *reserved words*.

label

A name you give to a *statement* so that you can talk about that statement elsewhere in the program.

laziness

The quality that makes you go to great effort to reduce overall energy expenditure. It makes you write labor-saving programs that other people will find useful, and document what you wrote so you don't have to answer so many questions about it. Hence, the first great virtue of a programmer. Also hence, this book. See also *impatience* and *hubris*.

left shift

A *bit shift* that multiplies the number by some power of 2.

leftmost longest

The preference of the *regular expression* engine to match the leftmost occurrence of a *pattern*, then given a position at which a match will occur, the preference for the longest match (presuming the use of a *greedy* quantifier). See Chapter 5 for *much* more on this subject.

lexeme

Fancy term for a *token*.

lexer

Fancy term for a *tokener*.

lexical analysis

Fancy term for *tokenizing*.

lexical scoping

Looking at your *Oxford English Dictionary* through a microscope. (Also known as *static scoping*, because dictionaries don't change very fast.) Similarly, looking at variables stored in a private dictionary (namespace) for each scope, which are visible only from their point of declaration down to the end of the lexical scope in which they are declared. —Syn. *static scoping*. —Ant. *dynamic scoping*.

lexical variable

A *variable* subject to *lexical scoping*, declared by my. Often just called a "lexical". (The our declaration declares a lexically scoped name for a global variable, which is not itself a lexical variable.)

library

Generally, a collection of procedures. In ancient days, referred to a collection of subroutines in a *.pl* file. In modern times, refers more often to the entire collection of Perl *modules* on your system.

LIFO

Last In, First Out. See also *FIFO*. A LIFO is usually called a *stack*.

line

In Unix, a sequence of zero or more nonnewline characters terminated with a *newline* character. On non-Unix machines, this is emulated by the C library even if the underlying *operating system* has different ideas.

line buffering

Used by a *standard I/O* output stream that flushes its *buffer* after every *newline*. Many standard I/O libraries automatically set up line buffering on output that is going to the terminal.

line number

The number of lines read previous to this one, plus 1. Perl keeps a separate line number for each source or input file it opens. The current source file's line number is represented by __LINE__. The current input line number (for the file that was most recently read via <FH>) is represented by $. ($INPUT_LINE_NUMBER) variable. Many error messages report both values, if available.

link

Used as a noun, a name in a *directory*, representing a *file*. A given file can have multiple links to it. It's like having the same phone number listed in the phone directory under different names. As a verb, to resolve a partially compiled file's unresolved symbols into a (nearly) executable image. Linking can generally be static or dynamic, which has nothing to do with static or dynamic scoping.

LIST

A syntactic construct representing a commaseparated list of expressions, evaluated to produce a *list value*. Each *expression* in a *LIST* is evaluated in *list context* and interpolated into the list value.

list

An ordered set of scalar values.

list context

The situation in which an *expression* is expected by its surroundings (the code calling it) to return a list of values rather than a single value. Functions that want a *LIST* of arguments tell those arguments that they should produce a list value. See also *context*.

list operator

An *operator* that does something with a list of values, such as join or grep. Usually used for named built-in operators (such as print, unlink, and system) that do not require parentheses around their *argument* list.

list value

An unnamed list of temporary scalar values that may be passed around within a program from any list-generating function to any function or construct that provides a *list context*.

literal

A token in a programming language such as a number or *string* that gives you an actual *value* instead of merely representing possible values as a *variable* does.

little-endian

From Swift: someone who eats eggs little end first. Also used of computers that store the least significant *byte* of a word at a lower byte address than the most significant byte. Often considered superior to big-endian machines. See also *big-endian*.

local

Not meaning the same thing everywhere. A global variable in Perl can be localized inside a *dynamic scope* via the local operator.

logical operator

Symbols representing the concepts "and", "or", "xor", and "not".

lookahead

An *assertion* that peeks at the string to the right of the current match location.

lookbehind

An *assertion* that peeks at the string to the left of the current match location.

loop

A construct that performs something repeatedly, like a roller coaster.

loop control statement

Any statement within the body of a loop that can make a loop prematurely stop looping or skip an *iteration*. Generally you shouldn't try this on roller coasters.

loop label

A kind of key or name attached to a loop (or roller coaster) so that loop control statements can talk about which loop they want to control.

lvaluable

Able to serve as an *lvalue*.

lvalue

Term used by language lawyers for a storage location you can assign a new *value* to, such as a *variable* or an element of an *array*. The "l" is short for "left", as in the left side of an assignment, a typical place for lvalues. An *lvaluable* function or expression is one to which a value may be assigned, as in pos($x) = 10.

lvalue modifier

An adjectival pseudofunction that warps the meaning of an *lvalue* in some declarative fashion. Currently there are three lvalue modifiers: my, our, and local.

magic

Technically speaking, any extra semantics attached to a variable such as $!, $0, %ENV, or %SIG, or to any tied variable. Magical things happen when you diddle those variables.

magical increment

An *increment* operator that knows how to bump up alphabetics as well as numbers.

magical variables

Special variables that have side effects when you access them or assign to them. For example, in Perl, changing elements of the %ENV array also changes the corresponding environment variables that subprocesses will use. Reading the $! variable gives you the current system error number or message.

Makefile

A file that controls the compilation of a program. Perl programs don't usually need a *Makefile* because the Perl compiler has plenty of self-control.

man

The Unix program that displays online documentation (manual pages) for you.

manpage

A "page" from the manuals, typically accessed via the *man*(1) command. A manpage contains a SYNOPSIS, a DESCRIPTION, a list of BUGS, and so on, and is typically longer than a page. There are manpages documenting *commands, syscalls, library functions, devices, protocols, files,* and such. In this book, we call any piece of standard Perl documentation (like *perlop* or *perldelta*) a manpage, no matter what format it's installed in on your system.

matching

See *pattern matching.*

member data

See *instance variable.*

memory

This always means your main memory, not your disk. Clouding the issue is the fact that your machine may implement *virtual* memory; that is, it will pretend that it has more memory than it really does, and it'll use disk space to hold inactive bits. This can make it seem like you have a little more memory than you really do, but it's not a substitute for real memory. The best thing that can be said about virtual memory is that it lets your performance degrade gradually rather than suddenly when you run out of real memory. But your program can die when you run out of virtual memory too, if you haven't thrashed your disk to death first.

metacharacter

A *character* that is *not* supposed to be treated normally. Which characters are to be treated specially as metacharacters varies greatly from context to context. Your *shell* will have certain metacharacters, double-quoted Perl *strings* have other metacharacters, and *regular expression* patterns have all the double-quote metacharacters plus some extra ones of their own.

metasymbol

Something we'd call a *metacharacter* except that it's a sequence of more than one character. Generally, the first character in the sequence must be a true metacharacter to get the other characters in the metasymbol to misbehave along with it.

method

A kind of action that an *object* can take if you tell it to. See Chapter 12, *Objects.*

minimalism

The belief that "small is beautiful." Paradoxically, if you say something in a small language, it turns out big, and if you say it in a big language, it turns out small. Go figure.

mode

In the context of the *stat*(2) syscall, refers to the field holding the *permission bits* and the type of the *file.*

modifier

See *statement modifier, regular expression modifier,* and *lvalue modifier,* not necessarily in that order.

module

A *file* that defines a *package* of (almost) the same name, which can either *export* symbols or function as an *object* class. (A module's main *.pm* file may also load in other files in support of the module.) See the *use* built-in.

modulus

An integer divisor when you're interested in the remainder instead of the quotient.

monger

Short for Perl Monger, a purveyor of Perl.

mortal

A temporary value scheduled to die when the current statement finishes.

multidimensional array

An array with multiple subscripts for finding a single element. Perl implements these using *references*—see Chapter 9, *Data Structures.*

multiple inheritance

The features you got from your mother and father, mixed together unpredictably. (See also *inheritance,* and *single inheritance.*) In computer languages (including Perl), the notion that a given class may have multiple direct ancestors or *base classes.*

named pipe

A *pipe* with a name embedded in the *filesystem* so that it can be accessed by two unrelated *processes.*

namespace

A domain of names. You needn't worry about whether the names in one such domain have been used in another. See *package.*

network address

The most important attribute of a socket, like your telephone's telephone number. Typically an IP address. See also *port*.

newline

A single character that represents the end of a line, with the ASCII value of 012 octal under Unix (but 015 on a Mac), and represented by \n in Perl strings. For Windows machines writing text files, and for certain physical devices like terminals, the single newline gets automatically translated by your C library into a line feed and a carriage return, but normally, no translation is done.

NFS

Network File System, which allows you to mount a remote filesystem as if it were local.

null character

A character with the ASCII value of zero. It's used by C to terminate strings, but Perl allows strings to contain a null.

null list

A *list value* with zero elements, represented in Perl by ().

null string

A *string* containing no characters, not to be confused with a string containing a *null character*, which has a positive length and is *true*.

numeric context

The situation in which an expression is expected by its surroundings (the code calling it) to return a number. See also *context* and *string context*.

NV

Short for Nevada, no part of which will ever be confused with civilization. NV also means an internal floating-point Numeric Value of the type a *scalar* can hold, not to be confused with an *IV*.

nybble

Half a *byte*, equivalent to one *hexadecimal* digit, and worth four *bits*.

object

An *instance* of a *class*. Something that "knows" what user-defined type (class) it is, and what it can do because of what class it is. Your program can request an object to do things, but the object gets to decide whether it wants to do them or not. Some objects are more accommodating than others.

octal

A number in base 8. Only the digits 0 through 7 are allowed. Octal constants in Perl start with 0, as in 013. See also the oct function.

offset

How many things you have to skip over when moving from the beginning of a string or array to a specific position within it. Thus, the minimum offset is zero, not one, because you don't skip anything to get to the first item.

one-liner

An entire computer program crammed into one line of text.

open source software

Programs for which the source code is freely available and freely redistributable, with no commercial strings attached. For a more detailed definition, see *http://www.open-source.org/osd.html*.

operand

An *expression* that yields a *value* that an *operator* operates on. See also *precedence*.

operating system

A special program that runs on the bare machine and hides the gory details of managing *processes* and *devices*. Usually used in a looser sense to indicate a particular culture of programming. The loose sense can be used at varying levels of specificity. At one extreme, you might say that all versions of Unix and Unix-lookalikes are the same operating system (upsetting many people, especially lawyers and other advocates). At the other extreme, you could say this particular version of this particular vendor's operating system is different from any other version of this or any other vendor's operating system. Perl is much more portable across operating systems than many other languages. See also *architecture* and *platform*.

operator

A gizmo that transforms some number of input values to some number of output values, often built into a language with a special syntax or symbol. A given operator may have specific expectations about what *types* of data you give as its arguments (*operands*) and what type of data you want back from it.

operator overloading

A kind of *overloading* that you can do on built-in *operators* to make them work on *objects* as if the objects were ordinary scalar values, but with the actual semantics supplied by the object class. This is set up with the overload *pragma*—see Chapter 13.

options
See either *switches* or *regular expression modifiers*.

overloading
Giving additional meanings to a symbol or construct. Actually, all languages do overloading to one extent or another, since people are good at figuring out things from *context*.

overriding
Hiding or invalidating some other definition of the same name. (Not to be confused with *overloading*, which adds definitions that must be disambiguated some other way.) To confuse the issue further, we use the word with two overloaded definitions: to describe how you can define your own *subroutine* to hide a built-in *function* of the same name (see "Overriding Built-in Functions" in Chapter 11, *Modules*) and to describe how you can define a replacement *method* in a *derived class* to hide a *base class*'s method of the same name (see Chapter 12).

owner
The one user (apart from the superuser) who has absolute control over a *file*. A file may also have a *group* of users who may exercise joint ownership if the real owner permits it. See *permission bits*.

package
A *namespace* for global *variables*, *subroutines*, and the like, such that they can be kept separate from like-named *symbols* in other namespaces. In a sense, only the package is global, since the symbols in the package's symbol table are only accessible from code compiled outside the package by naming the package. But in another sense, all package symbols are also globals—they're just well-organized globals.

pad
Short for *scratchpad*.

parameter
See *argument*.

parent class
See *base class*.

parse tree
See *syntax tree*.

parsing
The subtle but sometimes brutal art of attempting to turn your possibly malformed program into a valid *syntax tree*.

patch
To fix by applying one, as it were. In the realm of hackerdom, a listing of the differences between two versions of a program as might be applied by the *patch*(1) program when you want to fix a bug or upgrade your old version.

PATH
The list of *directories* the system searches to find a program you want to *execute*. The list is stored as one of your *environment variables*, accessible in Perl as $ENV{PATH}.

pathname
A fully qualified filename such as */usr/bin/perl*. Sometimes confused with PATH.

pattern
A template used in *pattern matching*.

pattern matching
Taking a pattern, usually a *regular expression*, and trying the pattern various ways on a string to see whether there's any way to make it fit. Often used to pick interesting tidbits out of a file.

permission bits
Bits that the *owner* of a file sets or unsets to allow or disallow access to other people. These flag bits are part of the *mode* word returned by the stat built-in when you ask about a file. On Unix systems, you can check the *ls*(1) manpage for more information.

Pern
What you get when you do Perl++ twice. Doing it only once will curl your hair. You have to increment it eight times to shampoo your hair. Lather, rinse, iterate.

pipe
A direct *connection* that carries the output of one *process* to the input of another without an intermediate temporary file. Once the pipe is set up, the two processes in question can read and write as if they were talking to a normal file, with some caveats.

Glossary

pipeline

A series of *processes* all in a row, linked by *pipes*, where each passes its output stream to the next.

platform

The entire hardware and software context in which a program runs. A program written in a platform-dependent language might break if you change any of: machine, operating system, libraries, compiler, or system configuration. The *perl* interpreter has to be compiled differently for each platform because it is implemented in C, but programs written in the Perl language are largely platform-independent.

pod

The markup used to embed documentation into your Perl code. See Chapter 26.

pointer

A *variable* in a language like C that contains the exact memory location of some other item. Perl handles pointers internally so you don't have to worry about them. Instead, you just use symbolic pointers in the form of *keys* and *variable* names, or *hard references*, which aren't pointers (but act like pointers and do in fact contain pointers).

polymorphism

The notion that you can tell an *object* to do something generic, and the object will interpret the command in different ways depending on its type. [<Gk many shapes]

port

The part of the address of a TCP or UDP socket that directs packets to the correct process after finding the right machine, something like the phone extension you give when you reach the company operator. Also, the result of converting code to run on a different platform than originally intended, or the verb denoting this conversion.

portable

Once upon a time, C code compilable under both BSD and SysV. In general, code that can be easily converted to run on another *platform*, where "easily" can be defined however you like, and usually is. Anything may be considered portable if you try hard enough. See *mobile home* or *London Bridge*.

porter

Someone who "carries" software from one *platform* to another. Porting programs written in platform-dependent languages such as C can be difficult work, but porting programs like Perl is very much worth the agony.

POSIX

The Portable Operating System Interface specification.

postfix

An *operator* that follows its *operand*, as in $x++.

pp

An internal shorthand for a "push-pop" code, that is, C code implementing Perl's stack machine.

pragma

A standard module whose practical hints and suggestions are received (and possibly ignored) at compile time. Pragmas are named in all lowercase.

precedence

The rules of conduct that, in the absence of other guidance, determine what should happen first. For example, in the absence of parentheses, you always do multiplication before addition.

prefix

An *operator* that precedes its *operand*, as in ++$x.

preprocessing

What some helper *process* did to transform the incoming data into a form more suitable for the current process. Often done with an incoming *pipe*. See also *C preprocessor*.

procedure

A *subroutine*.

process

An instance of a running program. Under multitasking systems like Unix, two or more separate processes could be running the same program independently at the same time—in fact, the fork function is designed to bring about this happy state of affairs. Under other operating systems, processes are sometimes called "threads", "tasks", or "jobs", often with slight nuances in meaning.

program generator

A system that algorithmically writes code for you in a high-level language. See also *code generator*.

progressive matching

Pattern matching that picks up where it left off before.

property

See either *instance variable* or *character property*.

protocol

In networking, an agreed-upon way of sending messages back and forth so that neither correspondent will get too confused.

prototype

An optional part of a *subroutine* declaration telling the Perl compiler how many and what flavor of arguments may be passed as *actual arguments*, so that you can write subroutine calls that parse much like built-in functions. (Or don't parse, as the case may be.)

pseudofunction

A construct that sometimes looks like a function but really isn't. Usually reserved for *lvalue* modifiers like my, for *context* modifiers like scalar, and for the pick-your-own-quotes constructs, q//, qq//, qx//, qw//, qr//, m//, s///, y///, and tr///.

pseudohash

A reference to an array whose initial element happens to hold a reference to a hash. You can treat a pseudohash reference as either an array reference or a hash reference.

pseudoliteral

An *operator* that looks something like a *literal*, such as the output-grabbing operator, `command`.

public domain

Something not owned by anybody. Perl is copyrighted and is thus *not* in the public domain—it's just *freely available* and *freely redistributable*.

pumpkin

A notional "baton" handed around the Perl community indicating who is the lead integrator in some arena of development.

pumpking

A *pumpkin* holder, the person in charge of pumping the pump, or at least priming it.

Must be willing to play the part of the Great Pumpkin now and then.

PV

A "pointer value", which is Perl Internals Talk for a char*.

qualified

Possessing a complete name. The symbol $Ent::moot is qualified; $moot is unqualified. A fully qualified filename is specified from the top-level directory.

quantifier

A component of a *regular expression* specifying how many times the foregoing *atom* may occur.

readable

With respect to files, one that has the proper permission bit set to let you access the file. With respect to computer programs, one that's written well enough that someone has a chance of figuring out what it's trying to do.

reaping

The last rites performed by a parent *process* on behalf of a deceased child process so that it doesn't remain a *zombie*. See the wait and waitpid function calls.

record

A set of related data values in a *file* or *stream*, often associated with a unique *key* field. In Unix, often commensurate with a *line*, or a blank-line-terminated set of lines (a "paragraph"). Each line of the */etc/passwd* file is a record, keyed on login name, containing information about that user.

recursion

The art of defining something (at least partly) in terms of itself, which is a naughty no-no in dictionaries but often works out okay in computer programs if you're careful not to recurse forever, which is like an infinite loop with more spectacular failure modes.

reference

Where you look to find a pointer to information somewhere else. (See *indirection*.) References come in two flavors, *symbolic references* and *hard references*.

referent

Whatever a reference refers to, which may or may not have a name. Common types of referents include scalars, arrays, hashes, and subroutines.

regex

See *regular expression.*

regular expression

A single entity with various interpretations, like an elephant. To a computer scientist, it's a grammar for a little language in which some strings are legal and others aren't. To normal people, it's a pattern you can use to find what you're looking for when it varies from case to case. Perl's regular expressions are far from regular in the theoretical sense, but in regular use they work quite well. Here's a regular expression: /Oh s.*t./. This will match strings like "Oh say can you see by the dawn's early light" and "Oh sit!". See Chapter 5.

regular expression modifier

An option on a pattern or substitution, such as /i to render the pattern case insensitive. See also *cloister.*

regular file

A *file* that's not a *directory,* a *device,* a named *pipe* or *socket,* or a *symbolic link.* Perl uses the -f file test operator to identify regular files. Sometimes called a "plain" file.

relational operator

An *operator* that says whether a particular ordering relationship is *true* about a pair of *operands.* Perl has both numeric and string relational operators. See *collating sequence.*

reserved words

A word with a specific, built-in meaning to a *compiler,* such as if or delete. In many languages (not Perl), it's illegal to use reserved words to name anything else. (Which is why they're reserved, after all.) In Perl, you just can't use them to name *labels* or *filehandles.* Also called "keywords".

return value

The *value* produced by a *subroutine* or *expression* when evaluated. In Perl, a return value may be either a *list* or a *scalar.*

RFC

Request For Comment, which despite the timid connotations is the name of a series of important standards documents.

right shift

A *bit shift* that divides a number by some power of 2.

root

The superuser (UID == 0). Also, the top-level directory of the filesystem.

RTFM

What you are told when someone thinks you should Read The Fine Manual.

run phase

Any time after Perl starts running your main program. See also *compile phase.* Run phase is mostly spent in *run time* but may also be spent in *compile time* when require, do FILE, or eval STRING operators are executed or when a substitution uses the /ee modifier.

run time

The time when Perl is actually doing what your code says to do, as opposed to the earlier period of time when it was trying to figure out whether what you said made any sense whatsoever, which is *compile time.*

run-time pattern

A pattern that contains one or more variables to be interpolated before parsing the pattern as a *regular expression,* and that therefore cannot be analyzed at compile time, but must be re-analyzed each time the pattern match operator is evaluated. Run-time patterns are useful but expensive.

RV

A recreational vehicle, not to be confused with vehicular recreation. RV also means an internal Reference Value of the type a *scalar* can hold. See also *IV* and *NV* if you're not confused yet.

rvalue

A *value* that you might find on the right side of an *assignment.* See also *lvalue.*

scalar

A simple, singular value; a number, *string,* or *reference.*

scalar context

The situation in which an *expression* is expected by its surroundings (the code calling it) to return a single *value* rather than a *list* of values. See also *context* and *list context.* A scalar context sometimes imposes additional constraints on the return value—see *string context* and *numeric context.* Sometimes we talk about a *Boolean context* inside conditionals, but this imposes no additional constraints, since any scalar value, whether numeric or *string*, is already true or false.

scalar literal

A number or quoted *string*—an actual *value* in the text of your program, as opposed to a *variable*.

scalar value

A value that happens to be a *scalar* as opposed to a *list*.

scalar variable

A *variable* prefixed with $ that holds a single value.

scope

How far away you can see a variable from, looking through one. Perl has two visibility mechanisms: it does *dynamic scoping* of `local` *variables*, meaning that the rest of the *block*, and any *subroutines* that are called by the rest of the block, can see the variables that are local to the block. Perl does *lexical scoping* of `my` variables, meaning that the rest of the block can see the variable, but other subroutines called by the block *cannot* see the variable.

scratchpad

The area in which a particular invocation of a particular file or subroutine keeps some of its temporary values, including any lexically scoped variables.

script

A text *file* that is a program intended to be *executed* directly rather than *compiled* to another form of file before execution. Also, in the context of *Unicode*, a writing system for a particular language or group of languages, such as Greek, Bengali, or Klingon.

script kiddie

A *cracker* who is not a *hacker*, but knows just enough to run canned scripts. A cargo-cult programmer.

sed

A venerable Stream EDitor from which Perl derives some of its ideas.

semaphore

A fancy kind of interlock that prevents multiple *threads* or *processes* from using up the same resources simultaneously.

separator

A *character* or *string* that keeps two surrounding strings from being confused with each other. The `split` function works on separators. Not to be confused with *delimiters* or *terminators*. The "or" in the previous sentence separated the two alternatives.

serialization

Putting a fancy *data structure* into linear order so that it can be stored as a *string* in a disk file or database or sent through a *pipe*. Also called marshalling.

server

In networking, a *process* that either advertises a *service* or just hangs around at a known location and waits for *clients* who need service to get in touch with it.

service

Something you do for someone else to make them happy, like giving them the time of day (or of their life). On some machines, well-known services are listed by the `getservent` function.

setgid

Same as *setuid*, only having to do with giving away *group* privileges.

setuid

Said of a program that runs with the privileges of its *owner* rather than (as is usually the case) the privileges of whoever is running it. Also describes the bit in the mode word (*permission bits*) that controls the feature. This bit must be explicitly set by the owner to enable this feature, and the program must be carefully written not to give away more privileges than it ought to.

shared memory

A piece of *memory* accessible by two different *processes* who otherwise would not see each other's memory.

shebang

Irish for the whole McGillicuddy. In Perl culture, a portmanteau of "sharp" and "bang", meaning the #! sequence that tells the system where to find the interpreter.

shell

A *command*-line *interpreter*. The program that interactively gives you a prompt, accepts one or more *lines* of input, and executes the programs you mentioned, feeding each of them their proper *arguments* and input data. Shells can also execute scripts containing such commands. Under Unix, typical shells include the Bourne shell (*/bin/sh*), the C shell (*/bin/csh*), and the Korn shell (*/bin/ksh*). Perl is not strictly a shell because it's not interactive (although Perl programs can be interactive).

side effects

Something extra that happens when you evaluate an *expression*. Nowadays it can refer to almost anything. For example, evaluating a simple assignment statement typically has the "side effect" of assigning a value to a variable. (And you thought assigning the value was your primary intent in the first place!) Likewise, assigning a value to the special variable $| ($AUTOFLUSH) has the side effect of forcing a flush after every `write` or `print` on the currently selected filehandle.

signal

A bolt out of the blue; that is, an event triggered by the *operating system*, probably when you're least expecting it.

signal handler

A *subroutine* that, instead of being content to be called in the normal fashion, sits around waiting for a bolt out of the blue before it will deign to *execute*. Under Perl, bolts out of the blue are called signals, and you send them with the `kill` built-in. See the `%SIG` hash in Chapter 28, *Special Names*, and the section "Signals" in Chapter 16, *Interprocess Communication.*

single inheritance

The features you got from your mother, if she told you that you don't have a father. (See also *inheritance* and *multiple inheritance*.) In computer languages, the notion that *classes* reproduce asexually so that a given class can only have one direct ancestor or *base class*. Perl supplies no such restriction, though you may certainly program Perl that way if you like.

slice

A selection of any number of *elements* from a *list*, *array*, or *hash*.

slurp

To read an entire *file* into a *string* in one operation.

socket

An endpoint for network communication among multiple *processes* that works much like a telephone or a post office box. The most important thing about a socket is its *network address* (like a phone number). Different kinds of sockets have different kinds of addresses—some look like filenames, and some don't.

soft reference

See *symbolic reference.*

source filter

A special kind of *module* that does *preprocessing* on your script just before it gets to the *tokener.*

stack

A device you can put things on the top of, and later take them back off in the opposite order in which you put them on. See *LIFO.*

standard

Included in the official Perl distribution, as in a standard module, a standard tool, or a standard Perl *manpage.*

standard error

The default output *stream* for nasty remarks that don't belong in *standard output*. Represented within a Perl program by the *filehandle* STDERR. You can use this stream explicitly, but the `die` and `warn` built-ins write to your standard error stream automatically.

standard I/O

A standard C library for doing *buffered* input and output to the *operating system*. (The "standard" of standard I/O is only marginally related to the "standard" of standard input and output.) In general, Perl relies on whatever implementation of standard I/O a given operating system supplies, so the buffering characteristics of a Perl program on one machine may not exactly match those on another machine. Normally this only influences efficiency, not semantics. If your standard I/O package is doing block buffering and you want it to *flush* the buffer more often, just set the $| variable to a true value.

standard input

The default input *stream* for your program, which if possible shouldn't care where its data is coming from. Represented within a Perl program by the *filehandle* STDIN.

standard output

The default output *stream* for your program, which if possible shouldn't care where its data is going. Represented within a Perl program by the *filehandle* STDOUT.

stat structure

A special internal spot in which Perl keeps the information about the last *file* on which you requested information.

statement

A *command* to the computer about what to do next, like a step in a recipe: "Add marmalade to batter and mix until mixed." A statement is distinguished from a *declaration*, which doesn't tell the computer to do anything, but just to learn something.

statement modifier

A *conditional* or *loop* that you put after the *statement* instead of before, if you know what we mean.

static

Varying slowly compared to something else. (Unfortunately, everything is relatively stable compared to something else, except for certain elementary particles, and we're not so sure about them.) In computers, where things are supposed to vary rapidly, "static" has a derogatory connotation, indicating a slightly dysfunctional *variable, subroutine,* or *method.* In Perl culture, the word is politely avoided.

static method

No such thing. See *class method.*

static scoping

No such thing. See *lexical scoping.*

static variable

No such thing. Just use a *lexical variable* in a scope larger than your *subroutine.*

status

The *value* returned to the parent *process* when one of its child processes dies. This value is placed in the special variable $?. Its upper eight *bits* are the exit status of the defunct process, and its lower eight bits identify the signal (if any) that the process died from. On Unix systems, this status value is the same as the status word returned by *wait*(2). See system in Chapter 29.

STDERR

See *standard error.*

STDIN

See *standard input.*

STDIO

See *standard I/O.*

STDOUT

See *standard output.*

stream

A flow of data into or out of a process as a steady sequence of bytes or characters, without the appearance of being broken up into packets. This is a kind of *interface*—the underlying *implementation* may well break your data up into separate packets for delivery, but this is hidden from you.

string

A sequence of characters such as "He said !@#*&%@*?!". A string does not have to be entirely printable.

string context

The situation in which an expression is expected by its surroundings (the code calling it) to return a *string.* See also *context* and *numeric context.*

stringification

The process of producing a *string* representation of an abstract object.

struct

C keyword introducing a structure definition or name.

structure

See *data structure.*

subclass

See *derived class.*

subpattern

A component of a *regular expression* pattern.

subroutine

A named or otherwise accessible piece of program that can be invoked from elsewhere in the program in order to accomplish some subgoal of the program. A subroutine is often parameterized to accomplish different but related things depending on its input *arguments.* If the subroutine returns a meaningful *value*, it is also called a *function.*

subscript

A *value* that indicates the position of a particular *array element* in an array.

substitution

Changing parts of a string via the s/// operator. (We avoid use of this term to mean *variable interpolation*.)

substring

A portion of a *string*, starting at a certain *character* position (*offset*) and proceeding for a certain number of characters.

superclass

See *base class*.

superuser

The person whom the *operating system* will let do almost anything. Typically your system administrator or someone pretending to be your system administrator. On Unix systems, the *root* user. On Windows systems, usually the Administrator user.

SV

Short for "scalar value". But within the Perl interpreter every *referent* is treated as a member of a class derived from SV, in an object-oriented sort of way. Every *value* inside Perl is passed around as a C language SV* pointer. The SV *struct* knows its own "referent type", and the code is smart enough (we hope) not to try to call a *hash* function on a *subroutine*.

switch

An option you give on a command line to influence the way your program works, usually introduced with a minus sign. The word is also used as a nickname for a *switch statement*.

switch cluster

The combination of multiple command-line switches (e.g., **-a -b -c**) into one switch (e.g., **-abc**). Any switch with an additional *argument* must be the last switch in a cluster.

switch statement

A program technique that lets you evaluate an *expression* and then, based on the value of the expression, do a multiway branch to the appropriate piece of code for that value. Also called a "case structure", named after the similar Pascal construct. Most switch statements in Perl are spelled for. See "Case Structures" in Chapter 4.

symbol

Generally, any *token* or *metasymbol*. Often used more specifically to mean the sort of name you might find in a *symbol table*.

symbol table

Where a *compiler* remembers symbols. A program like Perl must somehow remember all the names of all the *variables*, *filehandles*, and *subroutines* you've used. It does this by placing the names in a symbol table, which is implemented in Perl using a *hash table*. There is a separate symbol table for each *package* to give each package its own *namespace*.

symbolic debugger

A program that lets you step through the *execution* of your program, stopping or printing things out here and there to see whether anything has gone wrong, and if so, what. The "symbolic" part just means that you can talk to the debugger using the same symbols with which your program is written.

symbolic link

An alternate filename that points to the real *filename*, which in turn points to the real *file*. Whenever the *operating system* is trying to parse a *pathname* containing a symbolic link, it merely substitutes the new name and continues parsing.

symbolic reference

A variable whose value is the name of another variable or subroutine. By *dereferencing* the first variable, you can get at the second one. Symbolic references are illegal under use strict 'refs'.

synchronous

Programming in which the orderly sequence of events can be determined; that is, when things happen one after the other, not at the same time.

syntactic sugar

An alternative way of writing something more easily; a shortcut.

syntax

From Greek, "with-arrangement". How things (particularly symbols) are put together with each other.

syntax tree

An internal representation of your program wherein lower-level *constructs* dangle off the higher-level constructs enclosing them.

syscall

A *function* call directly to the *operating system*. Many of the important subroutines and functions you use aren't direct system calls, but are built up in one or more layers above the system call level. In general, Perl programmers don't need to worry about the distinction. However, if you do happen to know which Perl functions are really syscalls, you can predict which of these will set the $! ($ERRNO) variable on failure. Unfortunately, beginning programmers often confusingly employ the term "system call" to mean what happens when you call the Perl system function, which actually involves many syscalls. To avoid any confusion, we nearly always use say "syscall" for something you could call indirectly via Perl's syscall function, and never for something you would call with Perl's system function.

tainted

Said of data derived from the grubby hands of a user and thus unsafe for a secure program to rely on. Perl does taint checks if you run a *setuid* (or *setgid*) program, or if you use the **-T** switch.

TCP

Short for Transmission Control Protocol. A protocol wrapped around the Internet Protocol to make an unreliable packet transmission mechanism appear to the application program to be a reliable *stream* of bytes. (Usually.)

term

Short for a "terminal", that is, a leaf node of a *syntax tree*. A thing that functions grammatically as an *operand* for the operators in an expression.

terminator

A *character* or *string* that marks the end of another string. The $/ variable contains the string that terminates a readline operation, which chomp deletes from the end. Not to be confused with *delimiters* or *separators*. The period at the end of this sentence is a terminator.

ternary

An *operator* taking three *operands*. Sometimes pronounced *trinary*.

text

A *string* or *file* containing primarily printable characters.

thread

Like a forked process, but without *fork*'s inherent memory protection. A thread is lighter weight than a full process, in that a process could have multiple threads running around in it, all fighting over the same process's memory space unless steps are taken to protect threads from each other. See Chapter 17, *Threads*.

tie

The bond between a magical variable and its implementation class. See the tie function in Chapter 29 and Chapter 14, *Tied Variables*.

TMTOWTDI

There's More Than One Way To Do It, the Perl Motto. The notion that there can be more than one valid path to solving a programming problem in context. (This doesn't mean that more ways are always better or that all possible paths are equally desirable—just that there need not be One True Way.)

token

A morpheme in a programming language, the smallest unit of text with semantic significance.

tokener

A module that breaks a program text into a sequence of *tokens* for later analysis by a parser.

tokenizing

Splitting up a program text into *tokens*. Also known as "lexing", in which case you get "lexemes" instead of tokens.

toolbox approach

The notion that, with a complete set of simple tools that work well together, you can build almost anything you want. Which is fine if you're assembling a tricycle, but if you're building a defranishizing comboflux regurgalator, you really want your own machine shop in which to build special tools. Perl is sort of a machine shop.

transliterate

To turn one string representation into another by mapping each character of the source string to its corresponding character in the result string. See the tr/// operator in Chapter 5.

trigger

An event that causes a *handler* to be run.

trinary

Not a stellar system with three stars, but an *operator* taking three *operands*. Sometimes pronounced *ternary*.

troff

A venerable typesetting language from which Perl derives the name of its $% variable and which is secretly used in the production of Camel books.

true

Any scalar value that doesn't evaluate to 0 or "".

truncating

Emptying a file of existing contents, either automatically when opening a file for writing or explicitly via the truncate function.

type

See *data type* and *class*.

type casting

Converting data from one type to another. C permits this. Perl does not need it. Nor want it.

typed lexical

A *lexical variable* that is declared with a *class* type: my Pony $bill.

typedef

A type definition in the C language.

typeglob

Use of a single identifier, prefixed with *. For example, *name stands for any or all of $name, @name, %name, &name, or just name. How you use it determines whether it is interpreted as all or only one of them. See "Typeglobs and File-handles" in Chapter 2.

typemap

A description of how C types may be transformed to and from Perl types within an *extension* module written in *XS*.

UDP

User Datagram Protocol, the typical way to send *datagrams* over the Internet.

UID

A user ID. Often used in the context of *file* or *process* ownership.

umask

A mask of those *permission bits* that should be forced off when creating files or directories, in order to establish a policy of whom you'll ordinarily deny access to. See the umask function.

unary operator

An operator with only one *operand*, like ! or chdir. Unary operators are usually prefix operators; that is, they precede their operand. The ++ and -- operators can be either prefix or postfix. (Their position *does* change their meanings.)

Unicode

A character set comprising all the major character sets of the world, more or less. See *http://www.unicode.org*.

Unix

A very large and constantly evolving language with several alternative and largely incompatible syntaxes, in which anyone can define anything any way they choose, and usually do. Speakers of this language think it's easy to learn because it's so easily twisted to one's own ends, but dialectical differences make tribal intercommunication nearly impossible, and travelers are often reduced to a pidgin-like subset of the language. To be universally understood, a Unix shell programmer must spend years of study in the art. Many have abandoned this discipline and now communicate via an Esperanto-like language called Perl. In ancient times, Unix was also used to refer to some code that a couple of people at Bell Labs wrote to make use of a PDP-7 computer that wasn't doing much of anything else at the time.

value

An actual piece of data, in contrast to all the variables, references, keys, indexes, operators, and whatnot that you need to access the value.

variable

A named storage location that can hold any of various kinds of *value*, as your program sees fit.

variable interpolation

The *interpolation* of a scalar or array variable into a string.

variadic

Said of a *function* that happily receives an indeterminate number of *actual arguments*.

vector

Mathematical jargon for a list of *scalar values*.

virtual

Providing the appearance of something without the reality, as in: virtual memory is not real memory. (See also *memory*.) The opposite of "virtual" is "transparent", which means providing the reality of something without the appearance, as in: Perl handles the variable-length UTF-8 character encoding transparently.

void context

A form of *scalar context* in which an *expression* is not expected to return any *value* at all and is evaluated for its *side effects* alone.

v-string

A "version" or "vector" *string* specified with a v followed by a series of decimal integers in dot notation, for instance, v1.20.300.4000. Each number turns into a *character* with the specified ordinal value. (The v is optional when there are at least three integers.)

warning

A message printed to the STDERR stream to the effect that something might be wrong but isn't worth blowing up over. See warn in Chapter 29 and the use warnings pragma in Chapter 31, *Pragmatic Modules*.

watch expression

An expression which, when its value changes, causes a breakpoint in the Perl debugger.

whitespace

A *character* that moves your cursor but doesn't otherwise put anything on your screen. Typically refers to any of: space, tab, line feed, carriage return, or form feed.

word

In normal "computerese", the piece of data of the size most efficiently handled by your computer, typically 32 bits or so, give or take a few powers of 2. In Perl culture, it more often refers to an alphanumeric *identifier* (including underscores), or to a string of nonwhitespace *characters* bounded by whitespace or string boundaries.

working directory

Your current *directory*, from which relative pathnames are interpreted by the *operating system*. The operating system knows your current directory because you told it with a chdir or because you started out in the place where your parent *process* was when you were born.

wrapper

A program or subroutine that runs some other program or subroutine for you, modifying some of its input or output to better suit your purposes.

WYSIWYG

What You See Is What You Get. Usually used when something that appears on the screen matches how it will eventually look, like Perl's format declarations. Also used to mean the opposite of magic because everything works exactly as it appears, as in the three-argument form of open.

XS

An extraordinarily exported, expeditiously excellent, expressly eXternal Subroutine, executed in existing C or C++ or in an exciting new extension language called (exasperatingly) XS. Examine Chapter 21, *Internals and Externals*, for the exact explanation.

XSUB

An external *subroutine* defined in *XS*.

yacc

Yet Another Compiler Compiler. A parser generator without which Perl probably would not have existed. See the file *perly.y* in the Perl source distribution.

zero width

A subpattern *assertion* matching the *null string* between *characters*.

zombie

A process that has died (exited) but whose parent has not yet received proper notification of its demise by virtue of having called wait or waitpid. If you fork, you must clean up after your child processes when they exit, or else the process table will fill up and your system administrator will Not Be Happy with you.

Glossary

Index

About the Authors

Larry Wall is the inventor of Perl. He has also authored some other popular free programs available for Unix, including the *rn* news reader and the ubiquitous *patch* program. By training Larry is actually a linguist, having wandered about both U.C. Berkeley and U.C.L.A. as a grad student. Over the course of years, he has spent time at Unisys, JPL, NetLabs, and Seagate, playing with everything from discrete event simulators to network-management systems, with the occasional spacecraft thrown in. It was at Unisys, while trying to glue together a bicoastal configuration management system over a 1200 baud encrypted link using a hacked-over version of Netnews, that Perl was born. Larry currently works for O'Reilly & Associates.

Tom Christiansen is a freelance consultant specializing in Perl training and writing. Tom has been involved with Perl since day zero of its initial public release in 1987. Lead author of *Perl Cookbook* and co-author of *Learning Perl* and *Learning Perl on Win32 Systems*, Tom is also the major caretaker of Perl's online documentation. He holds undergraduate degrees in computer science and Spanish and a Master's in computer science. He now lives in Boulder, Colorado.

Dr. Jon Orwant is the CTO of O'Reilly & Associates and Editor in Chief of *The Perl Journal*. He is the co-author of *Mastering Algorithms with Perl* (O'Reilly) and author of the *Perl 5 Interactive Course* (Macmillan). Before joining O'Reilly, he was a member of the Electronic Publishing Group at the MIT Media Lab, where he received his Ph.D. for research involving the prediction of user behavior, the automation of game programming, and computer-generated personalized news and entertainment. Jon also serves on the advisory boards of VerticalSearch.com, Focalex, Inc., and YourCompass, Inc.

Jon is a frequent speaker at conferences, speaking to such diverse gatherings as (most recently) programmers, journalists, and lottery executives. He enjoys writing both code and prose, and his three biggest vices are gambling, wine, and mathematics. He also created the world's first Internet stock-picking game in 1994 (a Perl TCP/IP server written in one night to settle a bet) but never thought of making money from it. He is embarrassed to be related, however distantly, to both Billy Crystal and Milton Berle.

Colophon

Our look is the result of reader comments, our own experimentation, and feedback from distribution channels. Distinctive covers complement our distinctive approach to technical topics, breathing personality and life into potentially dry subjects.

The animal on the cover of *Programming Perl, Third Edition* is a dromedary (one-hump camel). Camels are large ruminant mammals, weighing between 1,000 and 1,600 pounds and standing six to seven feet tall at the shoulders. They are well known for their use as draft and saddle animals in the desert regions, especially of Africa and Asia. Camels can go for days without water. If food is scarce, they will eat anything, even their owner's tent. Camels live up to 50 years.

Melanie Wang was the production editor and copyeditor for *Programming Perl, Third Edition*. Colleen Gorman and Maureen Dempsey provided quality control. Maeve O'Meara, Mary Sheehan, Emily Quill, Jeffrey Holcomb, Ann Schirmer, Colleen Gorman, Darren Kelly, Madeleine Newell, and Betty Hugh provided production support. Ellen Troutman Zaig wrote the index.

Edie Freedman designed the cover of this book using a 19th-century engraving from the Dover Pictorial Archive. Emma Colby produced the cover layout with QuarkXPress 4.1 using Adobe's ITC Garamond font.

Alicia Cech and David Futato designed the interior layout based on a series design by Nancy Priest. The authors' text in POD was converted by Lenny Muellner into DocBook 3.1 SGML. The print version of this book was created by translating the SGML source into a set of *gtroff* macros using a Perl filter developed at O'Reilly & Associates by Norman Walsh. Steve Talbott designed and wrote the underlying macro set on the basis of the GNU *gtroff -ms* macros; Lenny Muellner adapted them to SGML and implemented the book design. The GNU groff text formatter version 1.11 was used to generate PostScript output. Mike Sierra provided crucial help with the Chinese and Japanese Unicode characters in Chapter 15. The text and heading fonts are ITC Garamond Light and Garamond Book. The illustrations that appear in the book were produced by Robert Romano and Rhon Porter using Macromedia FreeHand 8 and Adobe Photoshop 5.

Whenever possible, our books use a durable and flexible lay-flat binding. If the page count exceeds the lay-flat binding's page limit, perfect binding is used.